EXPLORE
AUSTRALIA

EXPLORE AUSTRALIA

ARAFU

TIMOR

SEA

DARWIN

○ J

Litchfield ★
National Park

★ Ka
Na

KAT

Wyndham ○ Kununurra

DALY WATER

VICTORIA

Gibb RIVER Rd

Derby ○ ★
The Kimberley

★ Bungle Bungles

Broome ○ *NORTHERN*

Fitzroy
Crossing ○ ○ HALLS
CREEK

TENNANT

HWY

INDIAN

OCEAN

Port Hedland ○ *GREAT*

HWY

GREAT SANDY DESERT

N O R T H E R N

TANAMI

Newman ○ *TROPIC* *OF* *CAPRICORN*

GIBSON DESERT

★ Kings
Canyon

Hwy Yulara

★ Uluru
(Ayers Rock)

W E S T E R N   A U S T R A L I A

WEST

COASTAL

Carnarvon ○

Monkey Mia ★

Meekatharra ○

Outback

NORTHERN

GREAT

Mount Magnet ○

Laverton ○

○ Leonora

S O U T H

Co

M

Geraldton ○ *BRAND*

NULLARBOR *PLAIN*

Coolgardie ○ Kalgoorlie-Boulder ○

Pinnacles ★ *HWY*

Southern Cross ○

Eucla ○ *HWY*

Caiguna ○ *EYRE*

Northam ○

PERTH

Rottnest Island ★

GREAT *EASTERN*

★ Wave Rock

HWY

Norseman ○

GREAT AUSTRALIAN BIGH

Bunbury ○ *SOUTH*

COAST *HWY*

Esperance ○

Margaret River
Wine Region ★
CAPE LEEUWIN

SOUTH *WESTERN* *HWY*

Albany ○

SOUTHERN

OCEAN

0   100

Road map symbols

————	Freeway
-------------	Freeway under construction
M31 — 31	Highway, sealed, with National Highway Route Marker
A1 — 1	Highway, sealed, with National Route Marker
5	Highway, sealed, with Metroad Route Marker
▪▪▪▪▪▪▪▪▪	Highway, unsealed
- - - - - - -	Highway under construction
C141 — 26	Main road, sealed, with State Route Marker
▪▪▪▪▪▪	Main road, unsealed, with Tourist Route
- - - - - - -	Main road under construction
————	Secondary road, sealed, (suburbs maps only)
- - - - - - -	Secondary road, unsealed, (suburbs maps only)
→	Other road, sealed, with traffic direction arrow
- - - - - - -	Other road, unsealed
═══════	Mall
▪ ▪ ▪ ▪	Vehicle track
· · · · · · ·	Walking track
—┼—┼— Paratoo	Railway, with station
—┼— Flagstaff	Underground railway, with station
▽ 114 ▽	Total kilometres between two points
▽ 45 ▽	Intermediate kilometres
- · - · - · -	State border
▬ ▬ ▬ ▬	Fruit fly exclusion zone boundary
SYDNEY ⊙	State capital city
GEELONG ○	Town, over 50 000 inhabitants
Bundaberg ○	Town, 10 000 – 50 000 inhabitants
Katherine ○	Town, 5 000 – 10 000 inhabitants
Narrogin ○	Town, 1 000 – 5 000 inhabitants
Robe ○	Town, 200 – 1 000 inhabitants
Miena ○	Town, under 200 inhabitants
BELCONNEN ○	Suburb, on state and region maps
Belconnen	Suburb, on suburban maps
Williamsford	Locality
Alroy Downs □	Pastoral station homestead
Borroloola ○	Major Aboriginal community
Murgenella ○	Aboriginal community
Fortesque Roadhouse ▣	Roadhouse
✈	Commercial airport
•▪	Place of interest
•	Landmark feature
▪	General interest feature
▪	Accommodation
+	Hill, mountain
⚒	Mine site
★	Lighthouse
	River, waterfall
	Lake
	Intermittent lake
TO GOULBURN	Route destination
237	Adjoining page number
	National park
	Other reserve
	Other named area
	Aboriginal / Torres Strait Islander land
	Prohibited area
❶	Text entry in A–Z listing

Wildlife-watching symbols

Wildlife symbols indicate fauna found in particular areas which may be of interest to visitors. The symbols are used on the wildlife-watching maps that appear on the following pages: 48 (NSW), 167 (Vic.), 269 (SA), 341 (WA), 412 (NT), 464 (Qld), 558 (Tas.).

🦔	bandicoots/quolls	🦘	kangaroos/wallabies
🦇	bats	🐨	koalas
🐦	birds	🦎	lizards
🦋	Bogong moths	🐧	penguins
🦋	butterflies		platypuses
🐊	crocodiles		possums
🐕	dingoes		quokkas
🐬	dolphins		seals/sea lions
	dugongs	🐌	snakes
	echidnas		Tasmanian devils
🐟	fish		tree kangaroos
	flying foxes	🐢	turtles
🐸	frogs		whales
	gliders		wombats
	glow-worms		

Road distances in kilometres

	ADELAIDE	BRISBANE	CANBERRA	DARWIN	MELBOURNE	PERTH	SYDNEY
Adelaide		2055	1198	3051	732	2716	1415
Albury	925	1440	352	3937	308	3583	565
Alice Springs	1544	2998	2658	1503	2255	3549	2931
Ballarat	618	1743	777	3645	112	3309	973
Bendigo	639	1619	653	3671	147	3335	849
Birdsville	1223	1463	2153	2246	2470	3293	2129
Brisbane	2055		1246	3429	1671	4289	984
Broken Hill	515	1545	1108	3128	825	2824	1154
Broome	4269	4646	4975	1880	4996	2233	5112
Cairns	3384	1699	2954	2885	3055	6050	2685
Canberra	1198	1246		4003	656	3741	292
Darwin	3051	3429	4003		3189	4049	4301
Geelong	832	1705	734	3842	72	3410	930
Geraldton	3135	4787	4329	3743	3853	419	4529
Kalgoorlie	2195	3634	3381	4021	2935	593	3451
Katherine	2731	3109	3683	320	3469	3756	3670
Mackay	2822	975	2216	2913	2318	5275	1948
Melbourne	732	1671	656	3789		3456	873
Mildura	395	1662	801	3444	549	3108	1023
Mount Gambier	452	2071	1114	3509	452	3161	1298
Newcastle	1580	850	423	3818	1036	4282	155
Perth	2716	4363	3741	4049	3456		3972
Port Augusta	318	1754	1343	2731	1058	2398	1574
Port Hedland	4348	5178	5542	2413	5066	1632	5742
Rockhampton	2488	641	1882	2954	1984	5199	1614
Sydney	1415	984	292	4301	873	3972	
Tennant Creek	2054	2457	3063	997	2792	4622	3050
Townsville	3214	1367	2608	2541	2710	5911	2340
Wagga Wagga	949	1342	253	3672	447	3668	472

Hobart to Launceston 200 kilometres

EXPLORE AUSTRALIA

THE COMPLETE TOURING COMPANION

VIKING

Contents

Colours of Australia

The Australian landscape is as varied as it is vast, as splendid in detail as in panorama. Those who take time to explore this continent will encounter remarkable diversity, reflected in images of stunning colour and texture.

Nature reigns supreme in broad tracts of wilderness. From mossy southern glades to the tangled canopies of the tropical north, Australia's forests provide sanctuary for some of nature's most intriguing creatures.

Expansive wetlands teem with wildlife –
from the dense mangrove waterways of
northern Queensland, to the lily-filled
lagoons of Kakadu and the ti-tree
swamps of southern Australia.

Australia boasts a magnificent 37000 kilometres of coastline, with white sandy beaches and turquoise waters. The continent is encircled by a swirling pattern of currents – warm tropical waters in the north and cool waters in the south. Every year whales migrate north from the icy Antarctic waters to breed where cool and warm waters meet.

The Great Barrier Reef is one of the natural wonders of the world. This maze of coral reefs and cays, extending thousands of kilometres along the Queensland coast, supports an extraordinary collection of marine life. The myriad colours of the reef are incomparable.

Australia's unique animals are the legacy of millions of years of isolation. This island continent is home to many wonderfully strange creatures such as the kangaroo and the koala, and an astonishing range of reptiles and birds.

At the centre of the continent is Ulu_ru,
a timeless monolith so compelling that
it draws millions of visitors each year.
Those who explore the surrounding
landscape will discover a desert rich
in colour and life.

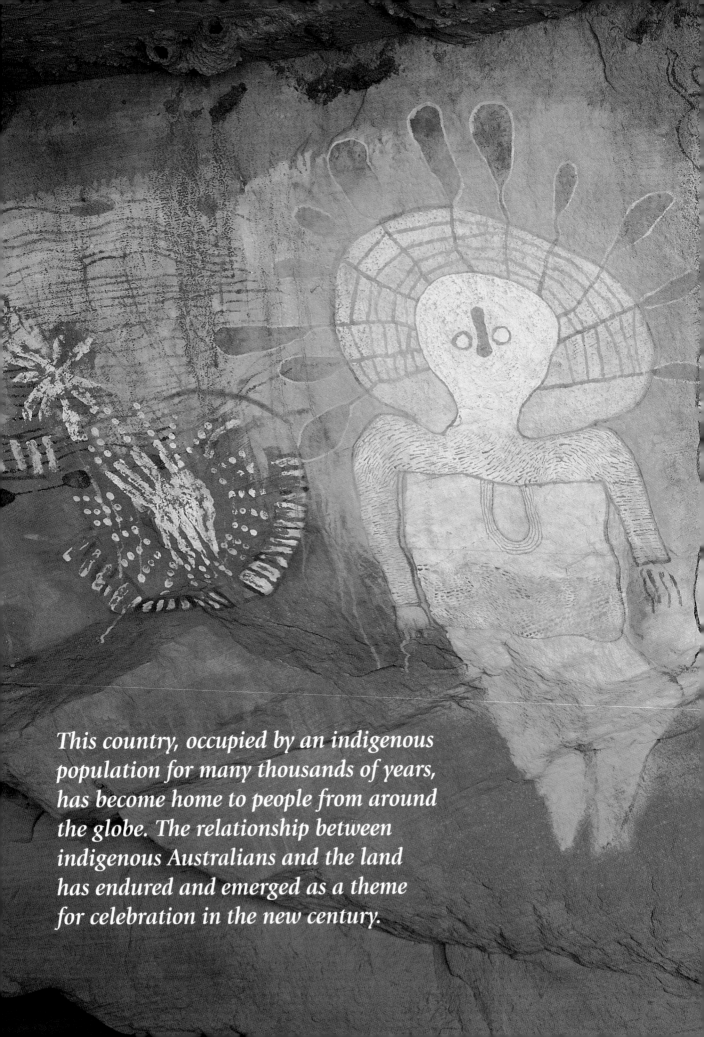

This country, occupied by an indigenous population for many thousands of years, has become home to people from around the globe. The relationship between indigenous Australians and the land has endured and emerged as a theme for celebration in the new century.

NEW SOUTH WALES

Cape Byron Lighthouse, northern New South Wales

N ew South Wales is a State of contrasts. Within an area of 801 428 square kilometres, there are extremes of country ranging from pristine beaches and tracts of subtropical rainforest, to snow-covered alpine vistas.

In 1770 Captain Cook took possession for the British of all Australian territories east of the 135th meridian of east longitude and named them New South Wales. Today the founding State has shrunk somewhat and occupies just 10 per cent of the continent.

Sydney Cove was established as the site of a penal colony in 1788. In 1813 Blaxland, Lawson and Wentworth made the first officially recognised crossing of the Blue Mountains. Further exploration quickly followed and settlement fanned out from Sydney. Sydney itself thrived and its citizens agitated against the stigma of the penal presence, with the result that transportation of convicts ended in 1840.

The gold rush of the 1850s swelled the population and led to much development throughout the State. In 1856, with the granting of responsible government, the State was well on its way.

Today New South Wales is the most populous State. It produces two-thirds of the nation's black coal, while the lead-zinc mines of Broken Hill and the gold-copper mines near Orange are major sources of mineral wealth. New South Wales is the nation's main wheat producer and has more than one-third of the nation's sheep population; diversification has been impressive in recent years, with the development of crops such as cotton, rice and canola.

The State is divided naturally into four regions: the sparsely-populated western plains; the high tablelands and peaks of the Great Dividing Range; the pastoral country of the Range's western slopes; and the fertile coastal region.

The climate varies with the landscape: subtropical along the north coast, temperate on the south coast. The north-west has dry summers, and the high country has brisk winters with extremes of cold in the highest alpine areas. Sydney has a midsummer average of 26°C and a midwinter average of 17°C.

Sydney offers the shopping, restaurants and nightlife expected of a great cosmopolitan city, yet within a 200-kilometre radius is much of the best country in New South Wales: superb beaches, the myriad of intricate bays and inlets of Pittwater, the Hawkesbury River, the beautiful Shoalhaven River and the Illawarra coastline. The scenic Blue Mountains and the Jenolan Caves can be reached in a day trip. From Sydney, the Pacific Highway runs north via Newcastle and the popular resort

NOT TO BE MISSED

IN NEW SOUTH WALES	Map Ref.
BERRIMA Historic village in the beautiful Southern Highlands	110 B6
FOSSICKER'S WAY Scenic drive from Nundle through the New England region	117 K12
HILL END Once a boom town, now a fascinating ghost town	98 A1
HUNTER VALLEY Good food and wine in delightful country surroundings	107
JENOLAN CAVES Magnificent limestone caves within a flora and fauna reserve	98 F8
KATOOMBA SCENIC SKYWAY AND RAILWAY Hair-raising ride down cliff-face into Jamison Valley	98 H7
RIVERBOAT POSTMAN An unusual way to cruise the Hawkesbury River	102 E11
SKITUBE An exciting train ride through Thredbo Valley in the Snowy Mountains	112 D11
WARRUMBUNGLE NATIONAL PARK Spectacular scenery with gorges, rocky outcrops and freshwater springs	116 E11
WESTERN PLAINS ZOO (DUBBO) Where landscaped parklands provide natural habitats for the animals and walking trails for visitors	114 E2

Mungo National Park, in the south-west

town of Port Macquarie on the Central Coast. Inland are the rich Hunter Valley vineyards, source of some of Australia's finest wines. Further north, the highway passes through country that is hilly and subtropical, with beaches to the east and the New England tablelands to the west.

The State's extreme north-west is still frontier territory and has limited tourist facilities. If you enjoy getting off the beaten track, and if you and your car are well prepared, the region can be very rewarding. Highlights include the mining towns of Lightning Ridge and Broken Hill. The lunar landscape of Mungo National Park, in the south-west of the State, is another great outback destination. The best time for touring is between March and November when the temperature is relatively cool and the days are clear and dry.

Many relics of the goldmining and agricultural history of the State can be seen in and around such inland towns as Bathurst, Dubbo, Griffith and Wagga Wagga. Towards the Victorian border, where the Murray River forms a natural boundary, irrigation supports vineyards and citrus groves. The Murray River towns

CLIMATE GUIDE

SYDNEY

	J	F	M	A	M	J	J	A	S	O	N	D
Maximum °C	26	26	25	22	19	17	16	18	20	22	24	25
Minimum °C	19	19	17	15	11	9	8	9	11	13	16	17
Rainfall mm	104	113	134	126	121	131	101	80	69	79	83	78
Raindays	12	12	13	12	12	12	10	10	11	12	11	12

COFFS HARBOUR REGION

	J	F	M	A	M	J	J	A	S	O	N	D
Maximum °C	27	27	26	24	21	19	19	20	22	23	25	26
Minimum °C	19	19	18	15	11	9	7	8	11	14	16	18
Rainfall mm	197	221	241	180	161	119	73	90	67	97	125	150
Raindays	16	15	17	13	11	10	8	8	9	12	11	14

ALPINE REGION

	J	F	M	A	M	J	J	A	S	O	N	D
Maximum °C	21	21	18	14	10	6	5	6	9	13	16	19
Minimum °C	7	7	6	2	0	-3	-4	-2	-1	2	3	5
Rainfall mm	110	90	122	131	183	146	144	184	200	220	161	113
Raindays	11	10	11	13	15	16	16	17	17	17	15	12

MERIMBULA REGION

	J	F	M	A	M	J	J	A	S	O	N	D
Maximum °C	24	25	23	21	19	16	16	17	18	20	21	23
Minimum °C	15	15	14	11	8	6	4	5	7	9	12	14
Rainfall mm	80	71	95	71	70	64	37	45	52	77	85	65
Raindays	10	9	10	9	10	9	7	9	10	11	12	11

CALENDAR OF EVENTS

JANUARY

Public holidays: New Year's Day; Australia Day. *Sydney:* Sydney Festival (incl. Opera in the Park; Ferryathon). *Barraba:* Australia's Smallest Country Music Festival. *Bermagui:* Blue Water Fishing Classic. *Bombala:* Wool and Wood Festival. *Brunswick Heads:* Fish and Chips (wood chop) Festival. *Cooma:* Rodeo. *Corowa:* Federation Festival. *Culburra:* Open Fishing Carnival. *Deniliquin:* Sun Festival; Twilight Race Meeting; Rodeo. *Finley:* Country Music Festival; Rodeo. *Forbes:* Jazz Festival; Flatlands Hang-Gliding Championships. *Frederickton:* Blues Festival. *Goulburn:* Australian Blues Music Festival (sometimes Feb.). *Gulgong:* Folk Festival. *Gunnedah:* National Tomato Competition. *Guyra:* Lamb and Potato Festival (inc. Hydrangea Festival). *Inverell:* Great Inland Fishing Festival. *Nelligen:* Country Music Festival. *Newcastle:* National Maritime Regatta. *Parkes:* Elvis Revival. *Picton:* Rodeo. *Port Macquarie:* Golden Lure Tournament. *Shellharbour:* Australia Day Breakfast by the Lake. *Tamworth:* Country Music Festival; National Pro Rodeo. *Taree:* Craftathon. *The Entrance:* Entertainment on Waterfront Stage. *Thredbo:* Blues Festival. *Tocumwal:* Classic Fishing Competition. *Tumbarumba:* New Year's Day Rodeo. *Tweed Heads:* Jet Sprint Racing. *Wingham:* Summer Rodeo.

FEBRUARY

Sydney: Gay and Lesbian Mardi Gras. *Albury:* Festival of Sport. *Barham:* Country Music Stampede; Flywheelers Rally. *Bega:* Far South Coast National Show. *Bermagui:* International Dog Show. *Berry:* Agricultural Show. *Bingara:* National Servicemens Reunion. *Bungendore:* Country Muster. *Camden:* Heritage Wine and Food Fair. *Cessnock:* Vintage Festival. *Cobargo:* Agricultural Show. *Glen Innes:* Agricultural Show. *Gunning:* Agricultural Show. *Guyra:* Agricultural Show. *Katoomba:* Blue Mountains Folk Festival. *Kiama:* Jazz Festival; Seven-a-Side Rugby Competition. *Maitland:* Agricultural Show. *Nelson Bay:* NSW Game-Fishing Association Inter-Club Tournament. *Orange:* Banjo Paterson Festival. *Rylstone:* Rylstone-Kandos Agricultural Show. *Temora:* Golden Gift (foot race and festival); Jazz in the Park. *Tumbarumba:* Tumbafest (food and wine festival). *Wentworth Falls:* Regatta Day.

MARCH

Sydney: Archibald, Sulman and Wynne Prize exhibitions. *Albury:* Festival of Sport (contd). *Armidale:* Autumn Festival. *Barham:* Business Expo. *Bega:* Cheese Pro-Am. *Bermagui:* Seaside Fair; Tag and Release Game-Fishing Tournament. *Blackheath:* Mountains Herb Fest. *Blayney:* Agricultural Show. *Cooma:* Agricultural Show. *Crookwell:* Country Weekend. *Cowra:* Festival of International Understanding. *Deniliquin:* Merino Field Days. *Eden:* Amateur Fish Club Competition. *Forbes:* Ben Hall Bike Show. *Glen Innes:* Minerama Gem Festival. *Goulburn:* Rose Show; Weekend of Heritage. *Grenfell:* Rugby Sevens. *Gunnedah:* Week of Speed. *Hay:* Riverina Stud Merino Field Day. *Inverell:* Art Exhibition. *Jamberoo:* Illawarra Folk Festival. *Jindabyne:* Strzelecki Polish Festival.

Lismore: Square Dance Festival. *Lockhart:* Verandah Town Music Festival. *Maitland:* Craft-a-Fair. *Manilla:* NSW Hang-Gliding Championships. *Medlow Bath:* Blue Mountains Herb Fest. *Moss Vale:* Agricultural Show. *Muswellbrook:* Agricultural Show. *Narrandera:* John O'Brien Bush Festival. *Nelson Bay:* NSW Game-Fishing Association Inter-Club Tournament (contd); Billfish Shootout. *Newcastle:* Surfest; Beaumont Street Jazz and Arts Festival. *Orange:* Banjo Paterson Festival (contd). *Picton:* Festival of Steam. *Queanbeyan:* Psychic Fair. *Robertson:* Agricultural Show. *Temora:* Rural Museum Exhibition Day. *Thirlmere (near Picton):* Festival of Steam. *Tocumwal:* Pioneer Skills Day. *Wagga Wagga:* Australian Veterans Games (even-numbered years). *Walcha:* Agricultural Show. *Wauchope:* Lasiandra Festival. *Wellington:* The Wellington Boot (horseraces); Vintage Fair. *Wiangaree:* Rodeo. *Wyong:* Shire Festival of Arts. *Yass:* Picnic Races.

EASTER

Public holidays: Good Friday; Easter Monday. *Sydney:* Royal Easter Show. *Balranald:* Homebush Gymkhana. *Bermagui:* Four Winds Easter Concerts; Victorian Game-Fishing Tournament. *Berridale:* Fair. *Bingara:* Gold Rush Festival; Easterfish. *Bourke:* Fishing Competition. *Brunswick Heads:* Blessing of the Fleet; Fishing Competition. *Byron Bay:* East Coast Blues Festival. *Canowindra:* Model Aircraft Championships. *Central Tilba:* Tilba Festival. *Coonabarabran:* Carnival. *Corowa:* Billy Cart Races. *Deniliquin:* Jazz Festival. *Dorrigo:* Arts and Crafts Exhibition. *Dubbo:* Orana Country Music Easter Festival. *Gilgandra:* Vintage Farm and Steam Rally. *Grenfell:* Guinea Pig Races. *Griffith:* Festival. *Huskisson:* White Sands Carnival. *Khancoban:* Festival and Fireworks. *Lake Windamere (near Rylstone):* Fishing Festival. *Leeton:* Sunrice Festival (even-numbered years). *Lightning Ridge:* Great Goat Race; Rodeo. *Macksville:* Patchwork and Quilt Display. *Maclean:* Highland Gathering. *Moree:* Carnival of Sport. *Moulamein:* Yabby Races. *Nambucca Heads:* Country Music Festival. *Parkes:* Sports Festival. *Taree:* Aquatic Festival. *Tenterfield:* Oracles of the Bush (culture and poetry). *Terrigal Beach:* Food, Wine and Chocolate Festivals. *Tocumwal:* Easter Eggs-Travaganza. *Ulladulla:* Blessing of the Fleet.

APRIL

Public holiday: Anzac Day. *Sydney:* AJC Autumn Racing Carnival (incl. Sydney Cup Week); Archibald, Sulman and Wynne Prize exhibitions (contd). *Batlow:* Apple Harvest Festival. *Bookham:* Sheep Show and Country Fair. *Bowraville:* Blues Festival. *Braidwood:* Heritage Festival. *Brewarrina:* Agricultural Show. *Bundanoon:* Bundanoon is Brigadoon Annual Highland Gathering. *Campbelltown:* Agricultural Show. *Canowindra:* Marti's Balloon Fiesta. *Cessnock:* Harvest Festival; Mt View Autumn Festival. *Condobolin:* Centre Trek (car rally). *Dungog:* Rodeo. *Forster:* Australian Ironman Triathlon. *Gladstone:* Pumpkin Festival. *Gunnedah:* Grey Mardi Gras. *Guyra:* Rugby Seven Carnival. *Holbrook:* Beef Fest (even-numbered

Swampy Plains River in Kosciuszko National Park

Ben Boyd National Park on the southern coastline

CALENDAR OF EVENTS (contd)

years). *Macksville:* Nambucca River Show. *Maitland:* Heritage Month; Hunter Valley Steamfest. *Milton:* Scarecrow Festival. *Murrurundi:* Sheepdog Trials. *Narrabri:* Agricultural Show. *Nyngan:* Anzac Day Race Meeting; Agricultural Show. *Orange:* Food of Orange District Week. *Sandy Hollow:* Bush Ride. *Taree:* Taree and District Eisteddfod. *Tenterfield:* Oracles of the Bush. *Tumut:* Festival of the Falling Leaf. *Uralla:* New England Grand Parade (classic car race). *Wauchope:* Demolition Derby; Rusty Iron Rally. *Wee Waa:* Agricultural Show. *Wentworth:* Henley on Darling (rowing regatta); Heritage Week. *Wentworth Falls:* Autumn Festival. *Yass:* Agricultural Show and Rodeo.

MAY

Sydney: Australian Fashion Week. *Armidale:* Saumarez Fair; Wool Expo. *Barham:* Tentpegging Championships. *Casino:* Beef Week Festival. *Cessnock:* Mt View Autumn Festival (contd). *Cobar:* Agricultural Show. *Dubbo:* Agricultural Show. *Gilgandra:* Agricultural Show. *Glen Innes:* Celtic Festival. *Gloucester:* Shakespeare Festival. *Hay:* Sheep Show. *Kempsey:* Agricultural Show; South-West Rocks Fishing Classic. *Lismore:* Trinity Arts Festival. *Macksville:* Egg-Throwing Championships; Trek to 'the pub with no beer'. *Maitland:* Tocal Field Days. *Menindee:* Island Speedboat Championships. *Merriwa:* Polocrosse Carnival. *Morpeth:* Jazz Festival. *Murwillumbah:* Fish 'n' Nana Festival. *Nimbin:* Mardi Gras Festival. *Scone:* Horse Festival. *Sussex Inlet:* Fishing Carnival. *Tamworth:* Gold Cup Race Meeting. *Taree:* Taree and District Eisteddfod (contd). *Thredbo:* Jazz Festival. *Tumut:* Festival of the Falling Leaf (contd). *Walgett:* Agricultural Show. *Warren:* Golden Fleece Race Day. *Wauchope:* Timbertown Empire Day Celebrations. *White Cliffs:* Gymkhana and Rodeo. *Windsor:* Bridge to Bridge Power Boat Classic. *Wingham:* Manning Valley Beef Week. *Yanco:* Murrumbidgee Farm Fair.

JUNE

Public holiday: Queen's Birthday. *Sydney:* Film Festival; Feast of Sydney: Food and Wine Festival (at Manly). *Barham:* Jazz Festival; Doll and Teddy Show. *Bingara:* Open Tennis Tournament. *Casino:* Primex (Primary Industry Exhibition). *Cessnock:* Artscrawl. *Coonamble:* Rodeo and Campdraft. *Dubbo:* Eisteddfod. *Grenfell:* Henry Lawson Festival of Arts; Guinea Pig Races. *Gulgong:* Henry Lawson Festival. *Katoomba:* Winter Magic Festival; Yulefest. *Kiama:* Folk Music Festival. *Lake Cargelligo:* Blue Water Art and Craft Festival. *Lightning Ridge:* Opal Open Pistol Shoot. *Lismore:* Lantern Parade. *Manilla:* Lake Keepit Kool Sailing Regatta. *Merimbula:* Jazz Festival. *Merriwa:* Festival of Fleeces. *Nambucca Heads:* Ken Howard Memorial Bowls Competition. *Narrabri:* Farmcraft. *Parkes:* Picnic Races. *Shoal Bay:* Jazz, Wine and Food Fair. *Snowy Mountains Region:* Opening of ski season (long weekend). *Southern Highlands Region:* Christmas in June. *Tamworth:* Fireside Bush Poetry Festival. *Taree:* Non Conventional Homes Eco Tour and Envirofair. *Tibooburra:* Festival (sometimes held in July). *Tocumwal:* Country Craft Fiesta. *Tweed Heads:* Wintersun Carnival; Greenback Fishing Competition. *Wentworth:* Tri-State Rowing Regatta.

JULY

Barraba: Frost over Barraba Art Festival. *Byron Bay:* A Taste of Byron Food Festival. *Cobargo:* Annual Craft Day. *Corowa:* Breakaway Festival. *Cowra:* Picnic Races. *Evans Head:* Fishing Classic. *Grafton:* Racing Carnival. *Iluka:* Amateur Fishing Classic. *Katoomba:* Yulefest (contd). *Kempsey:* Off-Road Race. *Kyogle:* Fairymount Festival. *Lightning Ridge:* Opal and Gem Festival. *Morpeth:* Craft Carnival. *Stroud:* International Brick and Rolling-Pin Throwing. *Tweed Heads:* Jet Sprint Racing. *Urunga:* Bowling Club Carnival.

AUGUST

Sydney: Sun City to Surf (fun run to Bondi Beach). *Barham:* Country Music Stampede. *Bingara:* Orange Festival. *Bellingen:* Jazz Festival. *Casino:* Gold Cup (horserace). *Cobar:* Festival of the Miner's Ghost. *Coffs Harbour:* Winter Fair (antiques). *Condobolin:* Agricultural Show. *Cootamundra:* Wattle Festival. *Dubbo:* Jazz Festival. *Evans Head:* Bowling Carnival. *Gosford:* Australian Orchid Spectacular. *Gunnedah:* Ag Quip (Agricultural Field Days). *Katoomba:* Yulefest (contd). *Maclean:* Aquatic Powerboat Regatta. *Menindee:* Burke and Wills Fishing Challenge. *Morpeth:* Wierd and Wonderful Novelty Teapot Exhibition. *Murwillumbah:* Tweed Valley Banana Festival. *Nambucca Heads:* VW Spectacular (odd-numbered years). *Narrandera:* Camellia Show. *Newcastle:* Jazz Festival; Conservatorium Keyboard Festival; Cathedral Flower Festival. *Nundle:* Camp Drafting and Dog Trials. *Nyngan:* Dog Trials. *Temora:* Wheels and Wings (vintage cars and planes). *The Channon (near Nimbin):* Opera at the Channon. *Tweed Heads:* Bowls Tournament. *Ulladulla:* Festival of Food and Wine by the Sea. *Wellington:* Eisteddfod.

SEPTEMBER

Sydney: National Rugby League Grand Final; Festival of the Winds (kite-flying, held at Bondi); Sunscreen: A Sydney Celebration of Cinema. *Barham:* Pro-Am Golf Tournament. *Batlow:* Daffodil Show. *Bourke:* Mateship Festival; Police and Community Outback Trek. *Bowral:* Tulip Time Festival; District Art Society Exhibition. *Broke:* Village Fair. *Broken Hill:* Silver City Show. *Byron Bay:* Rainforest Festival. *Camden:* Camden Park House Open Weekend. *Canowindra:* Agricultural Show. *Cessnock:* Budburst Festival. *Coffs Harbour:* Spring Orchid Show; Garden Competition. *Come-by-Chance:* Picnic Races. *Dungog:* Spring Festival. *Finley:* Agricultural Show. *Forbes:* Agricultural Show. *Glenbrook:* Legacy Gardens Festival. *Gloucester:* Mountain Man Triathlon. *Gosford:* Springtime Flora Festival. *Gunnedah:* Vintage Car Swap Meet. *Hawkesbury (Richmond, Windsor):* District Orchid Spring Show; Waratah Festival. *Hay:* Agricultural Show. *Henty:* Machinery Field Days. *Kempsey:* Country Music Festival. *Lake Cargelligo:* Lake Show. *Leura:* Legacy Gardens Festival. *Lismore:* Cup Day. *Maclean:* Cane Harvest Festival. *Maitland:* Garden Ramble. *Mudgee:* Wine Festival. *Mullumbimby:* Chincogan Fiesta. *Newcastle:* Hamilton Fiesta; Cathedral Music Festival. *Nimbin:* Agricultural Show; Spring Arts Festival. *Nundle:* Camp Drafting and Dog Trials (contd). *Nyngan:* Spring Into Nyngan (festival). *Scone:* Hunter Valley Horse Expo. *Shellharbour:* Festival of the Forest. *Stroud:* Rodeo. *Temora:* NSW Drag

retain evidence of the riverboat era when the Murray was a major transport route.

The Princes Highway leads south from Sydney down the Illawarra Coast, famous for its panoramic views and excellent beaches. Inland is the Southern Highlands, a favourite destination for bushwalkers, garden-lovers and those with an interest in antiques and craft.

The southern section of the New South Wales coast is dotted with peaceful fishing villages and popular holiday towns. Heading inland from Bega, it is only a two-hour drive to the Snowy Mountains, an area which features well-equipped snow resorts and the grandeur of Kosciuszko National Park.

> **VISITOR INFORMATION**
> *New South Wales Visitor Information Line*
> *13 2007*
> *www.tourism.nsw.gov.au*

Clyde Mountain, southern New South Wales

CALENDAR OF EVENTS (contd)

Boat Championships. *Toukley:* Gathering of the Clans. *Tweed Heads:* Rainforest Week. *Tyalgum:* Music Festival. *Walcha:* Timber Expo (even-numbered years). *Wollombi:* Folk Festival.

OCTOBER
Public Holiday: Labour Day. *Sydney:* Sculpture by the Sea. *Albury:* Food and Wine Festival. *Bathurst:* Bathurst Supertourers Car Races. *Bega:* Bega Valley Art Awards. *Bellingen:* World Music, Dance and Arts Festival. *Bingara:* Fossickers Way Veterans Week of Golf. *Borenore:* Australian National Field Days. *Bowral:* Tulip Time Festival; District Art Society Exhibition (contd). *Bowraville:* Back to Bowra Festival. *Brewarrina:* Darling River Outback Surfboat Classic. *Broken Hill:* Country Music Festival. *Bundanoon:* Village Garden Ramble. *Bungendore:* Rodeo. *Byron Bay:* Rainforest Festival (contd). *Casino:* Agricultural Show. *Cessnock:* Jazz in the Vines; Opera in the Vineyards. *Condobolin:* Art Exhibition. *Cooma:* Cooma Fest. *Coonabarabran:* Festival of the Stars; Coona Cup Racing Carnival. *Coonamble:* Gold Cup Race Meeting. *Cootamundra:* Agricultural Show. *Cowra:* Sakura Matsuri (Cherry Blossom Festival). *Deniliquin:* Play on the Plains Festival. *Eden:* Whale Festival. *Forbes:* Carnivale Balloon Spectacular. *Forster:* Oyster Festival. *Gilgandra:* Coo-ee Festival. *Glenbrook:* Gardens Festival (contd). *Gosford:* Mangrove Mountain District Country Fair; City Arts Festival; Gosford to Lord Howe Island Yacht Race. *Goulburn:* Lilac City Festival. *Grafton:* Bridge to Bridge Ski Race; Jacaranda Festival. *Grenfell:* Iris Festival. *Griffith:* Festival of Gardens. *Gulgong:* Heritage Weekend. *Gundagai:* Spring Flower Show. *Gunnedah:* Two Rivers Cultural Festival. *Gunning:* Festival. *Hawkesbury (Richmond, Windsor):* Fruits of the Hawkesbury Festival (contd). *Inverell:* Sapphire City Floral Festival. *Khancoban:* Spring Festival. *Kiama:* Seaside Festival. *Kundabung (near Kempsey):* Australasian Bull-Riding titles. *Kyogle:* Agricultural Show. *Lake Cargelligo:* Rodeo. *Leura:* Garden Festival; Village Fair; Greystanes Spring Gardens. *Lismore:* River City Music Festival; North Coast National Show. *Lithgow:* National Go-Kart Championships. *Lockhart:* Picnic Races. *Macksville:* Pro-Ag Field Day. *Manilla:* Festival of Spring Flowers. *Merimbula:* Country Music Festival. *Milton:* Settlers Fair. *Moonan Flat (near Scone):* Jazz by the River. *Moruya:* Jazz Festival. *Murrurundi:* Bushman's Carnival. *Muswellbrook:* Spring Carnival. *Nambucca Heads:* Show'n'Shine Hot Rod Exhibition. *Narooma:* International Blues Festival. *Narrabri:* Spring Festival. *Narrandera:* Tree-mendous Festival. *Newcastle:* Mattara Festival. *Nowra:* Spring Festival. *Parkes:* Country Music Spectacular. *Picton:* Agricultural Show; Music Festival; White Waratah Festival. *Port Macquarie:* Discovery Concert. *Scone:* Hunter Valley Horse Expo (contd). *Singleton:* Festival of Wine and Roses. *Stroud:* Rodeo (contd). *Tathra:* Amateur Fishing Competition. *Temora:* Antique Engine Field Day and Swap Meet. *Tenterfield:* Federation Festival; Spring Wine Festival; Highland Gathering. *Tibooburra:* Gymkhana and Rodeo. *Tocumwell:* Race and Open Garden. *Toukley:* Cycle Classic. *Walcha:* Ride the Rim (mountain-bike ride). *Warialda:* Flower Show. *Wauchope:* Colonial Carnival. *Wellington:* Festivale. *Windsor:* Bridge to Bridge Canoe Classic; Bridge to Bridge Water Ski Classic; Fruits of the Hawkesbury Festival. *Wyong:* Cycle Classic. *Yamba:* Family Fishing Festival; Seafood Expo. *Yass:* Days of Wine and Roses. *Yerong Creek:* Vintage Day.

NOVEMBER
Sydney: International Motor Show; Sculpture by the Sea (contd); Cycle Classic. *Adaminaby:* Trout Festival; Race Meeting. *Albury:* Festival of the Bogong Moth. *Armidale:* St Peters Town and Country Garden Tours. *Appin:* Highland Gathering and Pioneer Festival. *Barraba:* Barrabor Cultural Festival. *Bathurst:* FAI 1000 Car Race (V8 Supercars). *Blackheath:* Rhododendron Festival. *Bombala:* Riverside Festival. *Borenore:* Australian National Field Days (contd). *Braidwood:* Music at the Creek; The Quilt Event. *Bulahdelah:* Show and Rodeo. *Burrinjuck:* Ski Classic. *Byron Bay:* Buzz Film Festival. *Campbelltown:* Festival of Fisher's Ghost. *Cessnock:* Brockenback Trail Wine Affair Weekend. *Coonamble:* Country Music Festival. *Cowra:* Chardonnay Festival. *Dungog:* Agricultural Show. *Exeter:* Old English Fayre. *Finley:* Craft Fair. *Forster:* Half Ironman Triathlon. *Glen Innes:* Land of the Beardies Bush Festival. *Glenbrook:* Spring Festival. *Grafton:* Jacaranda Festival (contd); Bridge to Bridge Sailing Classic. *Grenfell:* Grenfell Guineas (horserace). *Gundagai:* Dog on the Tucker Box Festival. *Guyra:* Rodeo. *Hawkesbury (Richmond, Windsor):* Fruits of the Hawkesbury Festival (contd). *Jindabyne:* Snowy Mountains Trout Festival. *Kyogle:* Charity Golf Tournament. *Macksville:* Macksville Gift. *Moree:* Golden Grain and Cotton Festival. *Murrumburrah:* Picnic Races. *Muswellbrook:* Spring Carnival (contd). *Narromine:* Festival of Flight. *Nelson Bay:* Regional Boat Show. *Ourimbah:* Firefly Festival. *Queanbeyan:* Agricultural Show. *Scone:* Rodeo. *Stroud:* Branch Picnic Races. *Temora:* Battle of the Bands (youth band competition). *Tenterfield:* Campdraft. *The Channon (near Nimbin):* Music Bowl Live Band Concert. *Tumbarumba:* Heritage Week. *Uralla:* Thunderbolt Country Fair. *Warren:* Cotton Cup Racing Carnival. *Wentworth:* Wentworth Cup. *Windsor:* Bridge to Bridge Water Ski Classic (contd). *Wingham:* Show and Rodeo. *Woy Woy:* Oyster and Wine Festival. *Yass:* Rodeo. *Young:* National Cherry Festival.

DECEMBER
Public holidays: Christmas Day; Boxing Day. *Sydney:* World Series Cricket; Carols by Candlelight (in the Domain); Sydney–Hobart Yacht Race. *Adelong:* Home, Craft and Garden Fair. *Balranald:* Christmas Festival. *Barraba:* Horton Valley Rodeo. *Abercrombie Caves (near Bathurst):* Carols in the Caves. *Bega:* Showjumping Cup. *Bingara:* Country Christmas Carnival. *Conargo:* Twilight Race Meeting and Rodeo. *Coffs Harbour:* Pittwater to Coffs Harbour Yacht Classic. *Conargo:* Twilight Race Meeting and Rodeo. *Condobolin:* Rodeo. *Jindabyne:* Lake Jindabyne Sailing Club Hobie Cat Races. *Lake Cargelligo:* Lake Festivale. *Moulamein:* Horseracing Cup. *Nundle:* Camp Drafting and Dog Trials. *Ourimbah:* Firefly Festival (contd). *The Entrance:* Tuggerah Lakes Mardi Gras Festival. *Tibooburra:* Night Rodeo. *Yass:* Cup (horserace). *Young:* National Cherry Festival (contd).

Note: The information given here was accurate at the time of printing. However, as the timing of events held annually is subject to change and some events may extend into the following month, it is best to check with the local tourism authority or event organisers to confirm the details. The calendar is not exhaustive. Most towns and regions hold sporting competitions, arts and craft exhibitions, agricultural and flower shows, music festivals and other such events annually. Details of these events are available from local tourism outlets.

Sydney

Sydney is Australia's largest city (population 4 million) and has the features you would expect of a big metropolis: great restaurants, theatre, extensive shopping, superb architecture, cultural diversity, and interesting historic sites. All this, set within an unspoiled landscape of sweeping surf beaches, bushland, soaring cliffs and the glittering waters of Sydney Harbour, makes this city an irresistible destination.

EXPLORING SYDNEY

Sydney is not a difficult city to negotiate despite the fact that many of its roads developed from the bullock tracks of the early colony. The transport system is large and well integrated, and a transport information phone number provides callers with tips on tickets, connections and timetables. Buy composite tickets and avoid the high costs of single fares. All the major attractions within the city can be reached easily on foot; to get to Darling Harbour take the monorail, light rail or ferry. For the many outlying attractions such as Manly, Taronga Zoo and the harbourside eastern suburbs, take a ferry ride and enjoy the harbour experience. If you are driving, an up-to-date road map is essential, given the number of changes to the network of late. Beware of having to use parking meters – they are very expensive. Inquire about the Explorer Buses that do circuits of the city attractions (red buses), the bay and beach attractions (blue), and the shuttle to the airport (yellow).

SYDNEY'S ICONS

The elegant soaring sails of the **Sydney Opera House** and the great arch of the **Sydney Harbour Bridge** dominate the harbour foreshore. Standing sentinel at the eastern end of Circular Quay, the Opera House is a breathtaking spectacle with its million white tiles glinting in the sun and surrounded by the blue of the harbour. Its beauty belies its rather traumatic gestation period. The building was completed in 1973, but only after its Danish architect Jørn Utzon resigned in protest because of economically driven changes to his plans for the building's interior. Nevertheless, the Opera House is regarded as a stunning masterpiece and

Sydney Harbour Bridge

CITY CENTRE

To explore the city centre, start at **Circular Quay** on Sydney Cove, symbolic point of arrival for the city. Directly in front of the Quay is **Customs House**, an 1885 Classical Revival building, now home to a display of contemporary and indigenous art and culture, and interactive displays on Sydney's urban development.

Head east along Alfred Street, then take Phillip Street south towards the city. Along here you will find the **Justice and Police Museum**, which documents and displays the history of crime and punishment in Sydney – a limitless charter in this city of convict beginnings. On the intersection of Phillip and Bridge streets is the **Museum of Sydney**, built on the site of the first Government House. The amalgam of the old and the new is a theme of the innovative museum building – inside, the exhibitions chart the environmental, Aboriginal and European history of Sydney. Further down Bridge Street is the magnificent sandstone **Department of Lands** building (1887–90), with the niches in its facade filled with statues of prominent colonists. The length of Bridge Street, and the other small and irregular streets in the immediate area, offer some superb examples of ornate 19th-century architecture, with many of the buildings made from the distinctive Hawkesbury sandstone.

From Bridge Street, turn into Pitt Street to reach **Martin Place**, a sweeping pedestrian mall lined with some beautiful Victorian and Art Deco buildings. In the block between Pitt and George streets is the former General Post Office, which took 25 years to build and has now been transformed into **The Westin Sydney** hotel, with stunning interiors. Follow Pitt Street along to the main retail precinct of Sydney, which radiates out from the **Pitt Street Mall**. The magnificent arcade **The Strand**, opened in 1892, is a remnant of an era of grand jewel-like shopping arcades crammed with tiny boutiques and specialty shops. Access to the **AMP Tower Centrepoint** is around the corner on Market Street; here you

one of the great buildings of the 20th century. A guided tour of the building and its theatres is highly recommended.

The harbour bridge, opened in 1932, was designed by the engineer John Bradfield and is the second longest single span bridge in the world. (New York's Bayonne Bridge wins by a matter of centimetres.) Its broad deck is 134 metres above the water and carries 8 lanes for traffic, a double-track railway, a cycle lane and a pedestrian walkway offering stunning views. Pedestrian access is via Cumberland Street in The Rocks. The south-eastern Pylon Lookout contains a museum featuring old photographs of this grand Sydney icon. It also offers magnificent harbour views from its viewing platform. The more adventurous can join a guided three-hour climb to the very top of the bridge. A headset links you to your guide and you wear a safety harness.

GETTING AROUND
Airport shuttle bus
Airport Express 13 1500
Motoring organisation
National Roads & Motorists Association (NRMA) 13 2132
Car rental
Avis 1800 225 533; Bayswater Car Rental (02) 9360 3622; Budget 13 2727; Hertz 13 3039; Thrifty 1300 367 227
Public transport
Bus, Train and Ferry Information Line 13 1500
Bus tours and specialty trips
Explorer Buses: red (city sights); blue (Bondi and eastern suburbs); yellow (airport) 13 1500
Metro Monorail
(02) 8584 5288
Metro Light Rail
(02) 8584 5288
Taxis
ABC Cabs (02) 9906 7211; Legion Cabs 13 1451; Manly Cabs 13 1668; Premier Taxis 13 1017
Water Taxis
Harbour Shuttle (02) 9810 5010; Water Taxis Australia (02) 9955 3222
Cruises
Bounty Cruises (02) 9247 1789; Captain Cook Cruises (02) 9206 1111; Matilda & Sail Venture Cruises (02) 9264 7377; Sydney Showboats (02) 9552 2722

NOT TO BE MISSED

IN SYDNEY	Map Ref.
AMP TOWER CENTREPOINT For a bird's eye view of the city	90 E8
ART GALLERY OF NEW SOUTH WALES One of the most comprehensive collections in the country	90 H7
FERRY TRIP TO WATSONS BAY The foreshore of the eastern suburbs on display	93 Q8
HOMEBUSH BAY Focus of the Sydney 2000 Olympic Games	92 F8
MUSEUM OF SYDNEY A thought-provoking survey of what has made Sydney the place it is	90 F5
NATIONAL MARITIME MUSEUM The maritime adventures of an island continent	90 B8
NORTH HEAD The best coastal views in Sydney	93 R7
SYDNEY OPERA HOUSE An architectural giant of the 20th century	90 G3
OXFORD STREET Heartland of gay Sydney	90 F10
SYDNEY FISH MARKET Sydney seafood at its tastiest	93 L10

TOP EVENTS

Sydney Festival (Jan.)
Arts, culture and summer fun

Gay and Lesbian Mardi Gras (Feb.)
Sydney's biggest party

Archibald Prize Exhibition (Mar.–Apr.)
National portrait prize – and the best gossip in Sydney

Australian Fashion Week (May)
The latest in Australian and international designs

Sydney Film Festival (June)
A winter retreat for filmophiles

Feast of Sydney (June–July)
Food and wine festival

Australian International Motor Show (Nov.)
Latest and futuristic models in a 10-day showcasing

can shop or take Sydney Sky-ride (a theme-park ride). An observation deck at 250 metres, the highest in the Southern Hemisphere, offers views to 85 kilometres on a clear day. Sculptures of athletes around the top of the tower add an Olympic touch to this Sydney landmark.

Continue west along Market Street, past the Pitt Street Mall to George Street and head south. Stop in at the **Sydney Hilton** to visit the Marble Bar, an 1893 bar designed in the Italian Renaissance style and rebuilt within the Hilton in the 1970s. Further along, more Italian opulence is to be found in the **Queen Victoria Building**, dubbed 'the most beautiful shopping centre in the world' by designer Pierre Cardin. The massive multiple-domed structure was built in 1898 as a produce market. Just across Druitt Street is the **Sydney Town Hall**, constructed in

the 1860s, on the site of a cemetery, to the designs of six different architects, which may explain its eclecticism. It houses a 19th-century organ with 8500 pipes and hosts regular concerts. Next door is **St Andrew's Cathedral**, Australia's oldest cathedral site, the foundation of which was laid in 1819; it contains memorials to Sydney's pioneers.

MACQUARIE STREET AND AROUND HYDE PARK

While The Rocks preserves much of the history of Sydney's early domestic, industrial and maritime history, it is **Macquarie Street** that holds the memory of the grand public endeavours of the Colonial Georgian and Victorian periods. At the harbour end of Macquarie Street is **Government House** (1837–45), set within the lush surroundings of the Royal Botanic Gardens. The magnificent state rooms, resplendent with 19th- and early 20th-century furnishings, may be seen on guided tours.

Further along, the **State Library of NSW** is the State's main reference library. In the old section of the building (1906) is the Mitchell Library, with its priceless collection of Australiana. Next door are three buildings, once all part of the original Sydney Hospital (dating from 1811), or the Rum Hospital as it was called, having being built by rum traders who performed the community service in exchange for the right to import that most valuable currency. **Parliament of NSW** was the northern wing of the hospital, but became the seat of Government in the 1820s. Visitors can take a tour or view proceedings from the public galleries. The **Mint Museum**, now closed to the public, was the southern wing, but was appropriated in the 1850s when a building was needed to mint the gold from the NSW goldfields. Lying between the two is the present **Sydney Hospital**, built in 1894 after the original central building nearly collapsed as a result of the shoddy work of the rum builders. It is interesting to compare the elegance and restraint of the Georgian 'wings', with the high campery of the Victorian building.

Next stop is **Hyde Park Barracks Museum**, considered by many to be the finest example of Georgian Colonial

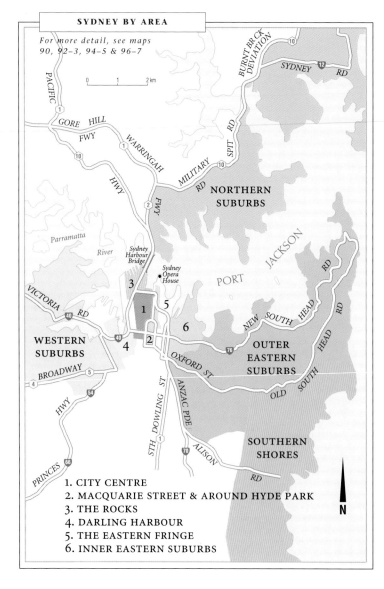

SYDNEY BY AREA

1. CITY CENTRE
2. MACQUARIE STREET & AROUND HYDE PARK
3. THE ROCKS
4. DARLING HARBOUR
5. THE EASTERN FRINGE
6. INNER EASTERN SUBURBS

architecture in the city. It was designed by Francis Greenway, completed in 1819, and used initially to house convicts. It now houses a fascinating museum of social and architectural history. Another Greenway building, **St James Church**, is to be found diagonally opposite in Queens Square. It was consecrated in 1824, making it Sydney's oldest church.

Macquarie Street veers east into College Street, where the soaring spires of **St Mary's Cathedral** are a sight impossible to miss. The cathedral was built in 1882 by one of the world's chief proponents of the Gothic Revival style, William Wardell. Opposite, **Hyde Park** forms a small but important green corridor for the city centre. It was decreed and named in 1810 by Governor Macquarie and is now home to some interesting civic memorials, including the Art Deco **Anzac Memorial** at its southern end. In Elizabeth Street, on the opposite side of Hyde Park, is **The Great Synagogue**, consecrated in 1878. Sydney's Jewish population was first established with the arrival of 16 Jewish convicts on the First Fleet.

Return to College Street and head south to the **Australian Museum**, Australia's oldest and most traditional museum, housing natural history displays, including one of the world's best indigenous Australian exhibitions, and the fascinating gallery Biodiversity – life supporting life.

THE ROCKS

The Rocks, with its winding streets and sandstone buildings, provides an intact and almost complete chronological overview of Sydney in the 19th century. Once the poorest area of Sydney, it now features the very popular weekend market, street entertainment, galleries, craft shops, traditional pubs and outdoor cafes. And of course there are the many historic sites of interest, best explored by picking up a copy of the excellent self-guide walking tour from the **Sydney Visitor Centre** in the old Sailors' Home in George Street.

Down on the waterfront, **Campbell's Storehouse** has been a Sydney landmark since building began in 1839. A little further along the waterfront towards the city is **Cadmans Cottage**, built in 1816

AMP Tower Centrepoint

THEATRES AND CINEMAS

Map Ref.

BELVOIR STREET THEATRE
An old tomato sauce factory in Surry Hills, now staging Sydney's most innovative theatre — 93 M11

CAPITOL THEATRE
1920s cinema designed as an Italian palace, hosts blockbuster musicals — 90 D11

CONCERT HALL
One of the best concert halls in the world, located at the Opera House — 90 G3

PANASONIC IMAX THEATRE
A giant screen and a crystal clear format — 90 C9

STATE THEATRE
A 1929 temple to cinema-going, complete with golden baroque interiors — 90 E8

WHARF THEATRE COMPLEX
Spectacular old wharf at Walsh Bay with breathtaking views; home to Sydney Theatre and Sydney Dance Companies — 90 D2

For a complete guide of what's on around Sydney, buy the *Sydney Morning Herald* on Friday for its lift-out 'Metro' section.

HISTORY

The first inhabitants of the Sydney area were the Eora Aboriginal people, who had hunted and fished these shores for some 20 000 years before Captain Cook arrived in Botany Bay in 1770. Seventeen years later Captain Arthur Phillip was entrusted with the command of the First Fleet to claim the vast southern land for the British Empire. The fleet arrived in the dry month of January, 1788, and were disappointed by the parched landscape of Botany Bay: the site was relatively unprotected, lacked good water and fertile land. They sailed north on 26 January to claim the shores of Sydney Cove. The first settlement, which consisted of tents, then wooden huts and buildings of brick and sandstone, was centred around the area now known as Circular Quay. When Lachlan Macquarie became the Governor in 1810, he found a city that did not meet his expectations for a seat of government. With the help of convict architect Francis Greenway, he immediately set about transforming Sydney into a proud city with fine streets and public buildings. As the city developed, it became both 'mean and princely', a mixture of broad, tree-lined avenues and narrow streets and alleys, grand Georgian-style buildings and tiny cottages and terraces.

and the oldest existing residence in Australia. It now houses an information centre for Sydney Harbour National Park. Nearby, lodged in an Art Deco building on the western flank of Circular Quay, is the **Museum of Contemporary Art**, the first institution in Australia dedicated to the contemporary visual arts. Behind the museum, up the hill in Gloucester Street, is **Susannah Place**, a block of terraces boasting continuous domestic occupancy from 1844–1990. Now a museum (open weekends), its displays evoke the domestic, working-class culture of the old Rocks. Nearby is Argyle Street, site of the **Argyle Stores** built in stages between 1826 and the 1880s, now a retail centre, and the **Argyle Cut**, a tunnel hewn from the rock by convicts.

From Argyle Street you can take the pedestrian footpath north along Cumberland Street, which crosses the Sydney Harbour Bridge. The quiet streets of **Millers Point**, to the west of the bridge, are where you will find some magnificent Georgian terraces, particularly in Lower Fort Street, and one of Sydney's oldest pubs, **The Hero of**

Waterloo Hotel. Another historic pub is nearby, the **Lord Nelson Hotel** in Kent Street. Also in this area – on a more heavenly plane – is **The Garrison Church (Holy Trinity)**, and **Sydney Observatory** (1858), in Observatory Park, featuring night viewing and an astronomy museum. Nearby, housed in an old military hospital dating from 1815, are the offices of the **National Trust Centre** and the **S. H. Ervin Gallery** with its regular historical and contemporary cultural exhibitions.

DARLING HARBOUR

Darling Harbour is a major leisure precinct, with wonderful landscaped plazas and walkways and a whole series of stark structuralist buildings housing some of the city's major cultural and entertainment institutions. Ferries, the Monorail and the Light Rail provide the links from the city. Visitors to the area should inquire about composite tickets available for many of the attractions. At Darling Harbour, a fleet of People Movers, trucks styled to look like mini-trains, pick up and drop off at key points.

The National Trust-classified **Pyrmont Bridge** crosses Darling Harbour. Near the bridge's eastern end is the **Sydney Aquarium**. Here you will find underwater tunnels from which you can view an amazing array of sea life, including giant sharks and stingrays, and a host of other displays – from a tank of Australian fur seals to a living replica of the Great Barrier Reef. From the aquarium, walk south along the foreshore to **Cockle Bay Wharf**, a food and dining precinct with three levels of terraces, waterfront promenades, a food court, al fresco cafes and five-star restaurants. Nearby is the **Panasonic IMAX Theatre**, featuring an 8-storey-high screen, and just beyond is **Sega World Sydney**, an $80 million dollar high-tech fun parlour and theme park.

A short distance away (follow the signs) is one of Sydney's most tranquil little corners, the **Chinese Garden**. A gift from Guangdong Province in China, the garden incorporates a traditional design of lakes, waterfalls, pavilions and rare exotic species. From here, walk along Pier Street to reach **Chinatown**,

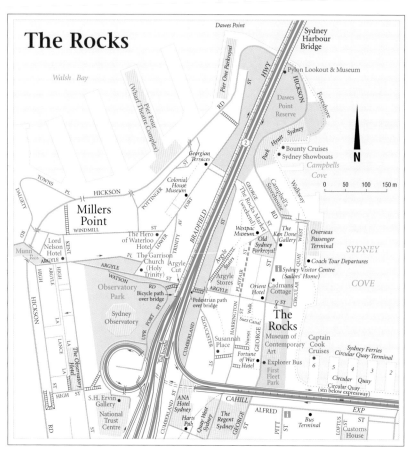

The Rocks

the cultural and commercial heartland for Sydney's large Chinese population. The many Chinese restaurants and shops of the district cluster around the pedestrian mall of Dixon Street and spill over into the connecting streets. At the south end is **Paddy's Markets**, a rather suburbanised version of the magnificently rowdy fresh food markets that were once here.

Catch the Monorail or Light Rail or walk across to the **Powerhouse Museum**, off Harris Street. The museum is in a dramatically renovated and extended old power station. The collection, housed here since 1988, provides a user-friendly, imaginative overview of the cultural, social, technological and scientific efforts and achievements of Australia and, in some instances, other parts of the world. Further north along Harris St you can visit **The Sydney Art Gallery**, a large commercial gallery featuring Australian art, including sculpture. Adjacent is the **Sydney Motor Museum**, where displays cover over a century of automotive history.

At the north-western corner of Darling Harbour is the **National Maritime Museum**. This world-class institution houses a series of imaginative displays that chart what must be the single most important theme in the history of this island continent: all maritime traditions are covered, from the seagoing ways of the Aboriginal people to European exploration, transportation, war, trade, immigration and of course beach culture. From here take the People Mover or Monorail to **Harbourside**, a shopping centre with restaurants, inexpensive eateries and an exciting sound and visual experience – Cinimagic.

Nearby, on the western edge of Darling Harbour, **Star City**, Sydney's first and only legal casino, features interiors inspired by the Australian landscape, and bars, restaurants, shops, theatres and a hotel. Use the Light Rail to get there.

The Light Rail can be taken from Star City to the **Sydney Fish Market**, a short distance away in Pyrmont. This large, vibrant complex, with its many stalls selling an outstanding array of seafood, is a mecca for those pilgrims on the trail of Sydney's best gourmet experiences.

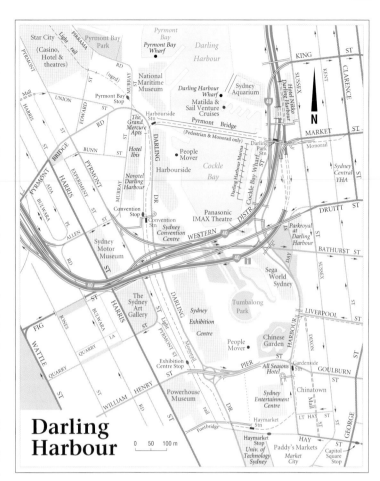

Darling Harbour

0   50   100 m

THE EASTERN FRINGE

The eastern fringe of the city centre includes the parklands of The Domain and the Royal Botanic Gardens, and is one of the most beautiful parts of Sydney. It is also an area that, in its essential character, has hardly changed since the early years of the colony, thanks to Governor Lachlan Macquarie who had the wit to claim the beautiful foreshore as parkland, thereby thwarting two centuries of potential development.

Start at the **Art Gallery of New South Wales** on Art Gallery Road in The Domain. The gallery is housed in a magnificent late-19th-century structure with the classical features so favoured for public buildings at the time. It houses major national and international collections, including the largest permanent collection of Aboriginal art in the world. Opposite is one of the two parts of **The Domain** where, during the Sydney Festival, huge opera, jazz and classical music concerts are held (they are free). The other part of The

Sega World Sydney at Darling Harbour

Sydney Opera House, the city's favourite icon

SHOPPING

*In the city, **David Jones** is the most beautiful department store, **Gowings** offers the best value and the **Queen Victoria Building** is splendid with its historic Byzantine-influenced architecture. **Chifley Plaza** and **Castlereagh Street** get the stripes for exclusivity. Further out, **Oxford Street, Surry Hills** is for the brave and the stylish; **Oxford Street, Paddington** is for the wickedly extravagant and the antique stores of **Queen Street, Woollahra** are for the envious. The best shopping neighbourhoods are **Double Bay** and **Mosman**. The best markets are held at **The Rocks** (all weekend), Sydney Opera House (Sundays), and Paddington, **Glebe** and **Balmain**, all of which are held on Saturdays. The best food market is the **Sydney Fish Market**.*

Domain runs north towards the harbour along Mrs Macquaries Road, past **Mrs Macquaries Chair**, which the Governor ordered to be carved out of the sandstone ledge for his wife, so that she could sit before her favourite harbour view. The road loops around the point, offering extraordinary glimpses of the inner city foreshore.

The **Royal Botanic Gardens** occupy a prime position on the shores of Farm Cove. The site of Sydney's first farm, they were declared in 1816, and have since then been developed into a magnificent sweep of landscaped grounds, with some 17 000 native and exotic species and a series of fascinating botanic and historic attractions. The gardens' visitor facilities include an excellent cafe/restaurant, a garden shop, a People Mover for tired legs and an impressive self-guide audio trail. Follow the foreshore or catch a People Mover around to Bennelong Point, the site of the Sydney Opera House.

INNER EASTERN SUBURBS

The fascinating **Kings Cross** district marks the eastern border of the city. The 19th- and 20th-century houses and apartment blocks, set along European-style tree-lined avenues, have over many years been home to an incongruous mix of migrants, artists, intellectuals, the wealthy and the seriously disadvantaged. The area – something of an Australian Soho – is still one of the most culturally diverse sections of the city, and certainly one of its liveliest. Catch a train to Kings Cross Station or walk through **Woolloomooloo**, a small suburb with a maritime history evidenced today by its tiny cottages, once the homes of the wharf labourers, and the 1914 **Woolloomooloo Finger Wharf** on Cowper Wharf Road. Further along the same road is **Garden Island**, Sydney's naval base, usually closed to the public, but rows of navy ships can be seen berthed at the docks.

Take the **McElhone Stairs** to **Potts Point**, the 'upper class end of a lower class district', as used to be the case. The leafy avenue of Victoria Street has some spectacular examples of multi-storey Georgian and Victorian terraces, while Macleay Street is the site for a series of beautiful apartment blocks built in the first few decades of the 20th century, many of them boasting exquisite Art Deco features.

In Elizabeth Bay on Onslow Avenue is one of the district's few remaining mansions – **Elizabeth Bay House**, built in 1839 for the Colonial Secretary, to a design by prominent colonial architect, John Verde. This spectacular property, praised particularly for its vestibule with a domed ceiling and sweeping staircase, is fully furnished as a museum charting the life of the well-to-do classes in 19th-century Sydney.

Elizabeth Bay leads to the Darlinghurst Road end of Kings Cross, the district's strip of sleaze. Past the intersection of William Street is the lively cafe precinct of Victoria Street, and the **Sydney Jewish Museum** on Darlinghurst Road towards Oxford Street. The museum is a moving and impressive centre, which explores the history of Judaism, the Australian Jewish heritage and the terrible legacy of the Holocaust. Opposite, on the corner of Burton Street, behind massive stone walls, is the old **Darlinghurst Gaol**, built in the early 1800s, and an art college since 1921.

OUTER EASTERN SUBURBS

The eastern suburbs run along the South Head peninsula. Flanked by the harbour on one side and ocean on the other, and possessed of beautiful views and leafy surrounds, they represent Sydney's expensive strip of real estate. **Surry Hills** and **Paddington**, both slums just 30 years ago, have been revamped with the dollar of the young professional classes. Both feature an extraordinary range of 19th-century terrace housing, and streets that are in many instances completely intact from that era. Surry Hills has always veered on the side of the working class and its terraces are at the cramped end of the scale. One of its main attractions is the **Brett Whiteley Studio** in Raper Street, which houses many of the paintings of this famous Australian artist who died prematurely in 1992.

Among the galleries, shops and restaurants of Paddington, there are very interesting historic sites, including the massive **Victoria Barracks** in Oxford Street, built in the 1840s and considered one of the best examples of Imperial military architecture in the world. Pick up a copy of the National Trust's self-guide brochure *Paddington Walk*, and stroll along the north-facing hills of this expensive little pocket. Just beyond Paddington, off Oxford Street, is **Centennial Park**, 220 hectares of woodlands, lakes, trails and cultivated gardens.

The habourside suburbs are best seen from a Rose Bay–Watsons Bay ferry, which skirts along the foreshores of Darling Point, Potts Point and Vaucluse, providing views of the exclusive houses and gardens en route. **Vaucluse House**, located in Olola Avenue, Vaucluse, Australia's most expensive suburb, is one of the city's most important historic sites. The house belonged to W. C. Wentworth, one of three explorers to first cross the Blue Mountains, and a major public figure in the colony. He and his wife Sarah, both with solid convict connections, moved into the house in 1829, and over the years made a series of eccentric additions to the property to house their growing family. Set within a spectacular 19th-century landscaped garden, it is fully furnished and open to the public.

The last suburb on the peninsula is **Watsons Bay**, a maritime village, virtually unchanged this century except for the expensive makeovers to the tiny weatherboard cottages that line the impossibly narrow streets. This suburb of great charm has been one of Sydney's most popular places for a picnic and a walk for many years. To get here, you can catch the ferry from Circular Quay, then relax on the foreshore with fish and chips or take a stroll to the swimming beach of **Camp Cove**. Follow the path through

---

SYDNEY ON FOOT
There are numerous walks around Sydney; many have self-guide brochures.

A Walk Around Sydney Harbour Bridge
See all the main attractions in the area

Balmain without Bugs
Historic walk around Balmain

Bondi to Clovelly
A clifftop walk taking in the best urban beaches in the world

Bondi Walkabout
A self-guide walk through this famous beach area

Go Walkabout on Sydney Ferries
Take a ferry to points along the harbour foreshore, and walk from there

Hermitage Foreshore Walk
Bushland, historic properties and views from Nielsen Park to Rose Bay

Kings Cross Walking Tour
Guided walks through Kings Cross and city

Manly Scenic Walk
Hike across cliffs, through bush and past historic fortifications; superb views

Paddington Walk
A tour of the historic highs and lows of this famous suburb

The Rocks
A stroll through Sydney's most historic district

South Head and Watsons Bay
A stroll for maritime buffs and lovers of wild coastal scenery

For further information and bookings, contact the **Sydney Visitor Centre**

Mosman Bay, view from Cremorne Point

Manly Cove, Manly's harbourside beach

the national park at the east end of the beach, out to the point of South Head; wander back along the ocean side of the peninsula. Along the clifftops you will pass **The Gap**, a notorious suicide spot, and **Macquarie Lighthouse**, which has been guiding ships through the heads since 1883.

SOUTHERN SHORES

Sydney's southern suburbs, best known for their spectacular beaches, also boast some of Australia's most important historic sites. The sweeping crescent of **Bondi Beach** marks the start of the southern beaches. With its excellent swimming, strolling and picnicking spots, it offers a summer haven for the city only 7 kilometres away. The surrounding suburb is full of life, with many cafes, restaurants, interesting shops and Sunday markets. Further south, **Tamarama** is known for its in-crowd, while **Bronte** is more of a family affair, with spacious foreshore parklands. The magnificent 19th-century **Waverley Cemetery** sits on the hill past the southern end of the beach.

Further south is **Botany Bay**, the site of the first recorded European landing on the east coast of Australia. On its northern peninsula is **La Perouse**, reached from the city via Anzac Parade or Bunnerong Road. It is named for the French navigator who set up camp here in 1778, having being pipped to the colonisation post by the First Fleet, which had set down a few days earlier. Preserved by the Botany Bay National Park, the area contains the **La Perouse Monument**, **La Perouse Museum** and **Bare Island**, the last a curious 19th-century fortification built to protect the southern coastline from what the colonists were sure was an imminent Russian invasion. **Kurnell** lies across the bay on the southern peninsula and is where Captain Cook and the crew of the *Endeavour* stepped ashore in 1770. The event is commemorated and explained with displays in **The Discovery Centre**, which also has excellent exhibits on the Aboriginal culture and natural environment of the area.

The sunsoaked beachside suburb of **Cronulla** forms the southern border of Sydney. Catch a train from the city to Cronulla, then hop aboard a ferry to explore **Port Hacking**, or to take a ride to the **Royal National Park** across the water. The **Sydney Tramway Museum** is located inland at Loftus and reached via the Princes Highway. The museum has the largest collection of trams in the Southern Hemisphere and runs novelty tram trips.

WESTERN SUBURBS

Immediately to the west of the city are the suburbs of **Balmain** and **Glebe**. Both are essentially working-class districts that have found themselves elevated to 'desirable' by the increasing number of Sydneysiders who want to live where the action is. Glebe can be reached by one of the bus routes along Parramatta Road, whereas Balmain is best reached by ferry. They are wonderful places to explore on foot, full of aged sandstone churches, weatherboard cottages, Victorian terraces, the odd imposing mansion and networks of tiny streets, which every so often reveal glittering harbour views framed by rooftops and trees. Darling Street in Balmain is particularly interesting for its many 19th-century public buildings. The shops, restaurants and cafes that fill the village-like centres of these suburbs are terrific, as are the lively weekend markets. Across Parramatta Road from Glebe is the **University of Sydney**, Australia's oldest university, famed for its ivy-covered 19th-century buildings and beautiful landscaping.

Homebush Bay on the southern shores of the Parramatta River is where you will find **Sydney Olympic Park**, one of Sydney's major tourist attractions. Also of interest is the magnificent **Bicentennial Park**, with its 60 hectares of dryland and 40 hectares of conservation wetlands replicating the complex ecology of one Australia's most sensitive natural environments.

Parramatta, 22 kilometres west of the city centre, is a city within Sydney, yet retains its individuality and is the location of some of the nation's most historic sites. (See Day Tours from Sydney p. 34).

NORTHERN SUBURBS

The northern suburbs of Sydney have for a long time represented the best of the good life, the place where a big cosmopolitan city meets a superb natural landscape of native bush, stunning surf beaches and tiny shell-like harbour coves.

The North Shore is reached via the Harbour Bridge or the Harbour Tunnel (both off the Cahill Expressway), with many areas accessible by ferry from Circular Quay. **Taronga Zoo** is best reached by ferry. From the wharf, visitors are whisked to the top of the hill via cable car, with knockout harbour views part of the experience. The zoo, set within 30 hectares of harbourside bushland, was first opened in 1916. Its thousands of animals are housed within enclosures that are designed to be kind to animals and spectators alike. Of particular interest is the Free Flight Birdshow, an extraordinary display staged in an open amphitheatre, and the Friendship Farm, where children can meet tame animals.

Balmoral Beach, several suburbs north along Spit Road, is one of Sydney's loveliest harbourside beaches. Further north is Manly, Sydney's version of an old-fashioned, seaside, holiday village. Although well and truly a suburb, it has always had the laid-back festive atmosphere of a place 'a thousand miles from care' as the slogan goes. Catch the **Manly Ferry**, visit the old-fashioned fun park and take a stroll along **The Corso**, which crosses the narrow strip of land separating harbour and ocean. Swim at **Manly Beach**, one of Sydney's best, or walk south to the pretty rock pools of Fairy Bower Beach, and the protected waters of Shelly Beach. Visit **Oceanworld**, a top-class aquarium, or take a bus to North Head for a trip around Sydney's **Old Quarantine Station**.

A drive north along Pittwater Road reveals many of Sydney's picturesque northern beaches and it is tempting to stop at every one. (See Day Tours from Sydney p. 34).

It is not surprising that Sydney, the 2000 Olympic Games host and Australia's premier city, with its stunning harbour, cosmopolitan lifestyle, mild climate and diverse range of attractions and experiences, is a popular destination for both interstate and international visitors.

The Sydney 2000 Olympic Games

In September 1993, after an exhaustive bidding process, Sydney won the right to host the Olympic Games in the year 2000. Almost immediately, preparations were under way for what will be the biggest event ever staged in Australia, and the first major international event of the new millennium.

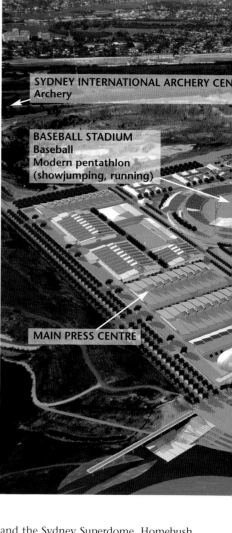

SYDNEY INTERNATIONAL ARCHERY CEN
Archery

BASEBALL STADIUM
Baseball
Modern pentathlon
(showjumping, running)

MAIN PRESS CENTRE

The Olympic Games will be held from 15 September to 1 October 2000. More than 10 000 athletes from 200 countries will participate in 28 sports. Five thousand support staff will be on hand, and some 15 000 members of the media will be there recording every athletic feat. Following on, the largest Paralympic Games ever will be held from 18 to 29 October 2000, when 4000 athletes from 125 countries will participate in 18 sports.

Some $3.2 billion dollars has been set aside for the sporting venues, and billions more for civic projects, with roads, public transport and urban beautification the priorities. The main focus of Olympic activity is Homebush Bay, site of Sydney Olympic Park and the major sporting facilities, but events will be staged in venues across Sydney.

HOMEBUSH BAY

The work undertaken at Homebush Bay represents the largest remediation project in the history of Australia. Previously something of an industrial wasteland, the site has become a huge riverside recreational area, complete with swathes of parkland and a residential suburb – the pride and joy of a city where there is considerable competition for attention.

For the first time in the history of the Olympic Games, all athletes will be housed at the one site. The Athletes Village situated on the western flank of Homebush Bay covers some 94 hectares, and will be comprised of 650 permanent homes and 500 modular homes. Beyond

the Olympic Games the village will become a suburb of around 2000 homes.

A major attraction at Homebush Bay, and perhaps the greatest legacy of the Olympic Games, will be Millennium Parklands, spreading east and west across the shores of the bay, and representing a major re-greening of a denuded urban landscape. It incorporates Bicentennial Park, already complete, which includes some 40 hectares of native wetlands.

SYDNEY OLYMPIC PARK

The sporting venues of Sydney Olympic Park will host 15 of the 28 sports. Head of the field is the Olympic Stadium, which, with its massive steel 'wings' and seating capacity of 110 000, is the biggest stadium in Olympic history. Here the opening and closing ceremonies will be staged, along with the major athletic events.

The Sydney International Aquatic Centre, the best in the world according to IOC head, Juan Samaranch, is already a popular leisure centre with its two full-length pools, diving pool and its kiddies' pool that simulates raging rapids. Its normal spectator capacity is 4000, but come the Olympic Games, this will treble, thanks to a unique design by prominent architect Philip Cox. The competition pool has 10 lanes, an anti-wave device and special heating to maintain temperatures at an optimum level for performance.

Other venues include the State Hockey Centre, State Sports Centre, Tennis Centre

and the Sydney Superdome. Homebush Bay will also house the press centre for the massive media contingent.

The Homebush Bay Information Centre will not operate during the Olympic Games. Presently it offers displays on all the venues and runs tours of the Sydney Olympic Park facilities.

OTHER VENUES

Numerous sites around Sydney have been brought into use for the Olympic Games. Some facilities have been purpose built, such as the Sydney International Regatta Centre at Penrith Lakes, while in other cases, full use is being made of existing features both natural and man-made. Many of the city's favourite places have enlisted for Olympic service. Bondi is down as the venue for beach volleyball. The Centennial Parklands are included in the routes for two of the big free events, the marathon and the road cycling event, while the Sydney Opera House will oversee the start of the first ever

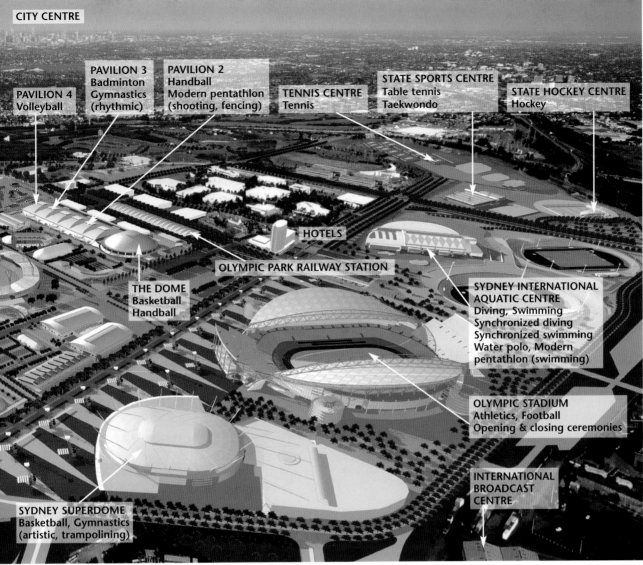

CITY CENTRE

PAVILION 4
Volleyball

PAVILION 3
Badminton
Gymnastics
(rhythmic)

PAVILION 2
Handball
Modern pentathlon
(shooting, fencing)

TENNIS CENTRE
Tennis

STATE SPORTS CENTRE
Table tennis
Taekwondo

STATE HOCKEY CENTRE
Hockey

HOTELS

OLYMPIC PARK RAILWAY STATION

THE DOME
Basketball
Handball

**SYDNEY INTERNATIONAL
AQUATIC CENTRE**
Diving, Swimming
Synchronized diving
Synchronized swimming
Water polo, Modern
pentathlon (swimming)

OLYMPIC STADIUM
Athletics, Football
Opening & closing ceremonies

**INTERNATIONAL
BROADCAST
CENTRE**

SYDNEY SUPERDOME
Basketball, Gymnastics
(artistic, trampolining)

Homebush Bay, the main focus of Olympic activity

Olympic Games triathlon. As well, the Sydney Exhibition, Entertainment and Convention centres at Darling Harbour have been requisitioned for a variety of indoor sports.

TRANSPORT

Transport was always going to be the challenge for Sydney, as any peak-hour commuter would attest to. In anticipation of the worst, the transport system has been treated to a major overhaul, and in the afterglow of the games, Sydney will find itself with some fairly decent improvements to what is already an extensive public transport system. A rail link with the Western Line has been created, as well as the Olympic Park Railway Station, capable of serving 30 trains carrying 50 000 people an hour. A ferry wharf has been built to service the RiverCats ferrying visitors up Parramatta River from Circular Quay (its use will be limited to athletes and officials during the Olympic Games).

Fleets of buses will come from all around Sydney, during the Olympic Games, delivering 28 000 visitors an hour to Sydney Olympic Park. Upgrading of transport facilities is taking place at most of the other sites hosting events around Sydney. Cars will be banned from Homebush Bay during the Olympic Games, but even in the lead-up period, visitors are being encouraged to take a relaxing river trip or train ride.

FESTIVALS

Celebrating culture and community, as well as great sporting feats, has been an integral part of the modern Olympic movement. Sydney has decided to meet its cultural obligations by staging four arts festivals between 1997 and the year 2000. The Festival of the Dreaming and A Sea Change took place in 1997 and 1998 respectively; the 1999 festival, Reaching the World, saw many of Australia's top artists travel overseas to display the best of Australian culture; and ushering

in the Sydney 2000 Olympic Games, the Harbour of Life festival, promises to be a magnificent finale, encapsulating all the energy and beauty of Sydney, and of the Games of the new Millennium.

For Sydney and the rest of Australia, the Sydney 2000 Olympic Torch Relay will be the major community event of the games. The torch will arrive in Uluru from Greece and be carried 27 000 kilometres around the country (the longest route ever) by 10 000 torchbearers. It will pass through 1000 towns and suburbs, within an hour's reach of 85 per cent of the Australian population, igniting a series of local celebrations as it goes, before arriving in Sydney for the opening ceremony.

USEFUL INFORMATION
*Inquiries should be directed to the Sydney 2000 Games Information Service; 13 6363, or visit the official web site www.olympics.com
For tours of Sydney Olympic Park, contact the Homebush Bay Information Centre; (02) 9714 7888.*

DAY TOURS
from Sydney

The range of day tours available from Sydney is almost unrivalled for the variety of scenic and recreational attractions on offer. East of the city are the blue waters of the Pacific Ocean and to the west lie the beautiful peaks and valleys of the Blue Mountains. The northern edge is fringed by Ku-ring-gai Chase National Park and the Hawkesbury River; the southern edge, by the Royal National Park. Beyond the northern fringe lies the famous Hunter Valley, Australia's first commercial wine-producing area. To the south is the gentle rural landscape of the Southern Highlands, while stretching along the coast both north and south of the city are numerous fine surfing beaches.

DAY TOURS FROM SYDNEY
For more detail, see maps 92–3, 94–5, 96–7, 99, 100–1 & 110

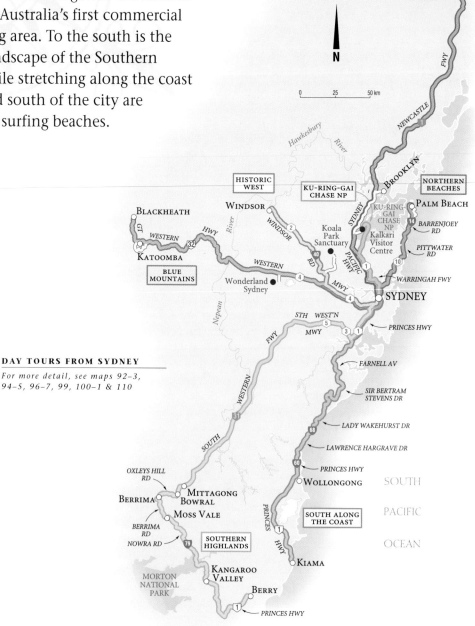

One of the many scenic beaches north of Manly

BLUE MOUNTAINS

124 km to Blackheath via Parramatta Road ④, Western Motorway ④ and Great Western Highway ㉜

Just over 50 kilometres west of Sydney are the Blue Mountains, incorporating the massive spread of the **Blue Mountains National Park**. Cliffs, woodlands and misty valleys, and prolific wildlife, offer a retreat for city dwellers. Visitors with only a day to spare should confine themselves to the towns and nearby attractions on the main route of the Great Western Highway, including Leura (boutique village, restaurants and mountain gardens); **Katoomba** (home of the Three Sisters); and **Blackheath** (starting point for terrific bushwalks).

Leave Sydney via Parramatta Road (continuation of Broadway from Central Station) turning onto the Western Motorway, which becomes the Great Western Highway. This takes you to Leura, then take Tourist Drive ⑤, which follows the clifftop route between Leura and Katoomba and provides a short but spectacular scenic drive off the main highway. See the Blue Mountains Experience p. 38 for a more extensive journey through this superb landscape.

For families, Wonderland Sydney, incorporating the Australian Wildlife Park, is a whole day out in itself. Turn left off the Western Motorway, approximately 42 kilometres from the city centre, into Wallace Road. **See also:** National Parks p. 42 and individual entries in A–Z listing for parks and towns in bold type.

SOUTH ALONG THE COAST

133 km to Kiama via Princes Highway ①, Farnell Avenue, Sir Bertram Stevens Drive, Lady Wakehurst Drive and Lawrence Hargrave Drive (all route ㊽) and Princes Highway ㊾ ①

The **Royal National Park** protects 15 000 hectares of land on Sydney's southern border. A day tour can include highlights of the park and the magnificent coastal landscape beyond, as well as the large provincial city of **Wollongong** and the seaside holiday town of **Kiama**.

Take the Princes Highway out of Sydney and turn left at Loftus into Royal National Park along Farnell Avenue. At Audley, visit the park information centre, where you will also find picnic grounds nearby and 19th-century buildings. Established in 1879, the Royal is the second oldest national park in the world and preserves a beautiful native landscape of heathland, woodland, swampland and rainforest, and a coastline of sandy coves and soaring cliffs – some of it easily seen by car, or for walkers via the 150-kilometre network of trails.

From Audley, follow Sir Bertram Stevens Drive south, taking a detour off to Wattamolla and Garie Beach, for their ocean views, swimming and picnic spots. Pick up Lady Wakehurst Drive, and turn south on to Lawrence Hargrave Drive just below the southern border of the park. From here you will encounter some of the most spectacular coastal scenery in Australia. The road leads down from the clifftop, and winds in and out of small inlets and past old coalmining towns, including Coalcliff,

Scarborough, Wombarra and Coledale. Further south, between the surf coast and the massive rainforest-covered escarpment of Morton National Park, is the sprawling city of Wollongong.

Follow the signs along the Princes Highway to Kiama, a pretty village with wooden houses and huge pines, and the site of the famous blowhole. East of Kiama, just out of **Jamberoo**, visit the Minnamurra Rainforest Centre in Budderoo National Park, and take the elevated boardwalk to the waterfalls. The most direct return route to Sydney is via the Princes Highway. **See also:** National Parks p. 42 and individual entries in A–Z listing for parks and towns in bold type.

HISTORIC WEST

62 km to Windsor via Parramatta Road ④, Western Motorway ④, James Ruse Drive ㊺ and Windsor Road ㊵ ②

To the west of Sydney, in Parramatta and around **Windsor**, are some of Australia's most historic sites, dating back to the first years of the colony, when settlers found fertile land along the flats of the Parramatta and Hawkesbury rivers.

Take Parramatta Road (continuation of Broadway from Central Station) out of the city centre. Turn onto the Western Motorway and continue past Sydney Olympic Park before turning off onto James Ruse Drive. Stop at the information centre, 346 Church Street, for the self-guide brochure to the historic sites of the area. Elizabeth Farm (1793) at 70 Alice Street is one of the main attractions. Once home of John and Elizabeth Macarthur, pioneers of the Australian wool industry, it contains part of the oldest surviving European building in Australia. Another highlight is Old Government House (1799) in Parramatta Park, Australia's oldest public building, housing the best collection of colonial furniture in the country.

Those with children might take a right-hand turn off James Ruse Drive onto Pennant Hills Road to reach Koala Park Sanctuary in West Pennant Hills. Travellers who want to stay on the heritage trail should continue on James Ruse Drive a little further, before turning off onto Windsor Road. On the way to Windsor, stop at Rouse Hill Estate (1813), a two-storey Georgian Colonial farmhouse set within a large property. The house, partly furnished, has guided tours Thursday and Sunday; bookings essential, (02) 9627 5108.

Continue to Windsor, one of the oldest towns in Australia; it was established in 1794 and named in 1810 by Governor Lachlan Macquarie (there were five townships in all named by Macquarie, including the nearby township of **Richmond**). The entire district, with its villages of Georgian Colonial houses, churches and hotels, and its pocket-sized farms stretching along the river flats, provides a taste of what country life was like in colonial Australia. For ideas on what to see and do, call Tourism Hawkesbury, Clarendon, (02) 4588 5895 or visit the Hawkesbury Museum in Thompson Square, Windsor. **See also:** individual entries in A–Z listing for towns in bold type.

NORTHERN BEACHES

42 km to Palm Beach via Military Road ⑩ *, Pittwater Road* ⑩ *and Barrenjoey Road* ⑭

Sydney's most scenic beaches stretch north of Manly, running to the tip of the sun-soaked Palm Beach peninsula. The peninsula is flanked on its eastern side by the Pacific Ocean, on its western side by Pittwater, and capped at its head by the sparkling waters of Broken Bay, the mouth of the Hawkesbury River.

Take Military Road from the northern side of Sydney Harbour Bridge, cross The Spit Bridge and then follow Pittwater Road to Barrenjoey Road, which runs the length of the Palm Beach peninsula.

Look to your left for views of the calm stretch of Pittwater. Alternatively, turn off onto Whale Beach Road, just past Avalon, for a short scenic drive dipping in and out towards the coastline, and offering superb views of the cliff-encased Whale Beach and some of Sydney's most spectacular homes.

At Palm Beach you can swim at the ocean beach or at the protected beaches of Pittwater; have lunch at one of the waterfront restaurants; take a stroll around the streets for a look at the holiday homes of Australia's wealthiest; or take an hour-long walk to Barrenjoey Lighthouse, at the very tip of the peninsula. To see something of **Ku-ring-gai Chase National Park**, pick up a ferry from the wharf off Barrenjoey Road (contact Palm Beach Ferries, (02) 9974 5235), and take a tour of the shoreline, going ashore at The Basin to see the Aboriginal Engraving Site, about an hour's walk inland. **See also:** National Parks p. 42 for parks in bold type.

KU-RING-GAI CHASE NATIONAL PARK

31 km to Kalkari Visitor Centre via Warringah Freeway ① *, Pacific Highway* ① *and Bobbin Head Road*

The southern shores of Broken Bay – a maze of bush-clad cliffs and tiny coves – are enclosed by the magnificent **Ku-ring-gai Chase National Park**, one of the State's most popular parks. The Palm Beach peninsula and the park are virtually adjacent, but the district's complex geography means that zipping from one to another puts kilometres on the clock.

Take the Warringah Freeway from the northern side of Sydney Harbour Bridge, then the Pacific Highway through the northern suburbs, before turning right into Bobbin Head Road, which leads into the park. Continue on to Bobbin Head, a peaceful waterside settlement, set against the narrow finger of Cowan Creek, and then follow the road as it turns into Ku-ring-gai Chase Road. At the Kalkari Visitor Centre you can pick up a variety of walking brochures, including one on the Discovery Walk which starts just near the centre and provides a geological and ecological summary of the area. To return to the city, turn left onto the

Sydney–Newcastle Freeway at the end of Ku-ring-gai Chase Road.

For a cruise with Australia's last riverboat postman, take the Sydney–Newcastle Freeway further north, turning off at Brooklyn. Afternoon cruises along the Hawkesbury are offered, but to join the mail run that visits the tiny river settlements, you will have to front at 9.30 a.m. on a weekday. For further information, contact the Hawkesbury River Visitor Information Centre, 1/5 Bridge Street, Brooklyn; (02) 9985 7947. **See also:** National Parks p. 42 for parks in bold type.

SOUTHERN HIGHLANDS

120 km to Mittagong via Princes Highway ① *, King Georges Road* ③ *, South Western Motorway* ⑤ *and South Western Freeway* ㉛

The Southern Highlands region, set south-west of Sydney, offers superb scenic driving along country roads past historic villages, with the spectacular Australian landscape providing a backdrop to a countryside otherwise very northern European in character.

Take the Princes Highway out of the city, turning right onto King Georges Road at Carss Park and then onto the South Western Motorway, which becomes the South Western Freeway. Take the turn-off for **Mittagong**, one of the main towns of the district, also the site of the Southern Highlands Visitor Information Centre where you can pick up brochures on the many attractions in the area.

Follow the signs to **Bowral**, a beautiful old town with cafes and restaurants, European trees and many historic buildings. Turn onto Oxley Drive for a quick trip up Mount Gibraltar and some exceptional views of the district. From Bowral, cross the railway bridge on the western side of town, turn left to get to Oxley Hill Road and the Hume Highway to reach the next stop, **Berrima**, an exceptionally well-preserved Georgian settlement with buildings dating back to the 1830s.

Follow Berrima Road to **Moss Vale**, then take the Illawarra Highway on the northern side of town, before turning onto Nowra Road. This route leads away from the main Southern Highlands district to the escarpment that marks the

Fitzroy Falls in Morton National Park

drop towards the coast. The Fitzroy Falls, part of **Morton National Park**, are reached via this road. Visit the National Parks and Wildlife Service Visitor Centre at the town of Fitzroy Falls for information on the boardwalk to the spectacular falls and the 3-kilometre walk along the edge of the escarpment.

Continue down the escarpment to the small hillside village of Kangaroo Valley. The rural scenery around here is some of the best in the State. Pull in at the Cambewarra Lookout for views of the rugged escarpment country alongside a picturesque spread of small farms stretching out to the coastal plain. When you reach the Princes Highway, turn left to reach the small historic town of **Berry**, then follow the highway north along the coast to return to Sydney. **See also:** National Parks p. 42 and individual entries in A–Z listing for parks and towns in bold type.

HUNTER VALLEY

157 km to Cessnock via Warringah Freeway ①, Pacific Highway ① and Sydney–Newcastle Freeway ①

The Hunter Valley dates back to the 1830s, making it Australia's oldest 0wine district. There are two distinct wine-growing areas, the Upper Hunter and the Lower Hunter. The Lower Hunter, located near **Cessnock**, is closer to Sydney and probably more interesting as a day tour. The best time to see vineyards in full swing is usually around February.

At the northern end of the Sydney Harbour Bridge, pick up the Warringah Freeway and then the Pacific Highway, before taking the Sydney–Newcastle Freeway to the Cessnock turn-off.

The visitor information centre at Turner Park, Aberdare Rd in Cessnock is the best place to plan your day in the Hunter Valley. The wineries, of which there are more than 70, are generally located on the western flank of the town, some 15 kilometres out. Start on Mount View Road for a scenic introduction to the district, and work your way north-west along the network of country roads and lanes that link the wineries; most are open daily for tastings and cellar door sales. Rothbury Estate is a great place to drop in for lunch and probably marks the northern limit of what you could reasonably cover in a day. Other wineries of note include the historic Tyrrell's (established 1858), the boutique-style family owned Petersons Wines, and a couple of giants on the Australian wine-making landscape, Lindemans Ben Ean and McWilliam's Mount Pleasant Estate. Expect to travel about 60 kilometres on your winery circuit, and remember to make sure that there is a driver on board not partaking of the pleasures. **See also:** Vineyards and Wineries p. 53 and individual entries in A–Z listing for towns in bold type.

CLASSIC TOUR

Blue Mountains Experience

Glenbrook to Mount Tomah (194 km)

You will find drama and interest around every bend on this Blue Mountains tour. Take a day or three to experience the natural beauty of the mountains – from the grandeur of the escarpment and its thundering waterfalls, to the detail of gorgeous red waratahs and delicate orchids. Perceived by early European settlers as a barrier to valuable western pastures, the towering sandstone cliffs and deep valleys were finally traversed by explorers Blaxland, Wentworth and Lawson in 1813. Within two years, a ridge-top track had been completed using convict labour. Today, the Great Western Highway follows a similar route.

❶ Red Hands

The Blue Mountains Experience begins at the Blue Mountains Visitor Information Centre on the Great Western Highway in Glenbrook, 66 km west of Sydney. Your first stop is the **Red Hands Cave**, one of the best-preserved examples of Aboriginal hand stencils and prints in the Sydney region. The images on the cave wall – believed to be between 500 and 1600 years old – were made using the hand as a stencil and blowing a spray of ochre from the mouth. It is estimated that the Daruk Aboriginal people occupied this area for over 14 000 years.

To reach the cave, turn left into Ross Street just after the information centre and follow the signs through Glenbrook to the Blue Mountains National Park. From the entrance, continue to the Oaks Picnic Area (the road is unsealed after 2.5 kilometres); turn right for the Red Hands Picnic Area. A 300-metre walking track leads to the cave.

If you wish to incorporate some wildlife-watching into your Blue Mountains tour, turn right just after the Iron Barks Picnic Area on your way back to the park entrance. Keep right at the fork in the road. The road descends into the natural amphitheatre of Euroka Clearing. Eastern grey kangaroos are commonly seen grazing on the pastures, and the birdlife is prolific.

❷ Historic link

After rejoining the highway, watch for the turn-off to **Lennox Bridge** coming up soon on your right. This solid arched bridge, the oldest on the Australian mainland, was hewn by convicts from local sandstone in 1833, forming an essential link on the road across the mountains.

❸ Artist's hideaway

Back on the highway, continue through the villages of Blaxland, Warrimoo, Valley Heights and Springwood. On the outskirts of Faulconbridge, take the signposted turn-off to the

Norman Lindsay Gallery and Museum

Norman Lindsay Gallery and Museum. Norman Lindsay (1879–1969) lived and worked in this stone cottage for most of his long, creative life. You might recognise the house as the setting for the film *Sirens* (1993). Today, it displays a collection of Lindsay's work, including his famous depictions of female nudes, as well as puppets representing characters from his classic children's book, *The Magic Pudding* (1918). The studio remains much as the artist left it – an unfinished painting is surrounded with favourite brushes and half-squeezed tubes of paint.

Norman Lindsay Gallery and Museum
14 Norman Lindsay Cres.
Faulconbridge
Phone: (02) 4751 1067
Open: 10 a.m.–4 p.m. daily

❹ Scenic overview

The highway then follows a narrow ridgeline through the mountain hamlets of Linden, Woodford, Hazelbrook, Lawson and Bullaburra. At certain points,

Valley of the Waters

there are sweeping views across the Blue Mountains National Park. From the town of Wentworth Falls, take Falls Road to **Wentworth Falls Picnic Area**. A 500-metre track leads to Princes Rock Lookout for superb views of Wentworth Falls, Jamison Valley and King's Tableland. You might also like to take the 1-kilometre circuit trail, which extends down into the valley to Weeping Rock, past patterned rocks with mysterious face-like features.

❺ Valley of the Waters

Return along Falls Road as far as Fletcher Street and turn left to the Conservation Hut Cafe and **Valley of the Waters Picnic Area**. Follow the 500-metre walking track to Queen Victoria and Empress lookouts for panoramic views over distant mountains and valleys. To join the more challenging Valley of the Waters Nature Track, continue until you reach a small creek and track junction. This 4-kilometre circuit takes in fern-fringed Asmodeus Pool and the windswept heights of Edinburgh Castle Rock.

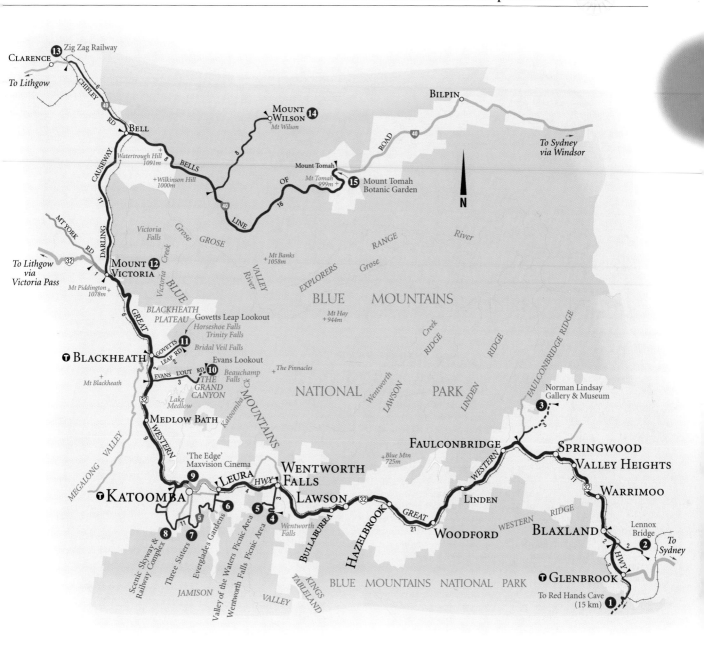

6 Ornamental windows

After returning to the highway, you will soon reach the turn-off to Leura Mall, starting point of Tourist Drive 🔟. This picture-postcard street is lined with antique stores, galleries, gift shops and cafes. To visit **Everglades Gardens**, turn left from the mall into Craigend Street and right at Everglades Avenue. This splendid example of 1930s garden design is a testimony to its creator, Danish master gardener, Paul Sorensen. Rest by the grotto pool or view Jamison Valley through ornamental garden windows. The Art Deco interior of Van de Velde House is also open to the public and now houses a tearoom.

Everglades Gardens
37 Everglades Ave
Leura
Phone: (02) 4784 1938
Open: 10 a.m.–5 p.m. daily
(spring/summer);
10 a.m.–4 p.m. daily (autumn/winter)

7 Three Sisters

Join Tourist Drive 🔟, which leads past pretty Leura Falls and along the cliff tops to Echo Point, viewing area for the famous **Three Sisters** rock formation. This 'not-to-be-missed' scenic highlight is a busy stopping point for visitors. King parrots, galahs, gang gangs and crimson rosellas gather around the Echo Point Visitor Information Centre, adding

to the colour and sense of activity. If quiet contemplation is more your style, take time to explore the network of marked trails around the escarpment.

8 In suspense

Continue along Tourist Drive 🔟 to **Katoomba Scenic Railway**. The railway was built in the 1880s to haul coal from tunnel mouth to cliff top. In 1945 the colliery closed, and the steepest incline railway in the world became a popular tourist attraction. The **Scenic Skyway** departs from the same point, transporting passengers a distance of 350 metres in a cable-car suspended almost 300 metres above the Jamison Valley floor.

Katoomba Scenic Skyway and Railway
Cnr Violet St and Cliff Dr.
Katoomba
Phone: (02) 4782 2699
Open: 9 a.m.–5 p.m. daily

9 Take the plunge

Tourist Drive 🔟 rejoins the highway on the western edge of Katoomba. Take care as you turn right along the highway back towards Leura. After about 1 kilometre, turn left and follow the signs to **'The Edge' Maxvision Cinema**, where fast-moving images are projected onto a larger-than-life screen (18 metres x 24 metres). Here you can soar over mist-filled valleys, scale vertical cliffs and plunge over waterfalls … all without leaving your seat.

Three Sisters

'The Edge' Maxvision Cinema
225–237 Great Western Hwy
(access through Civic Pl.)
Katoomba
Phone: (02) 4782 8900
Open: 6 screenings daily

⑩ Through the canyon

Follow the highway through Medlow Bath and turn right onto Evans Lookout Road, just before Blackheath. Continue 3 kilometres for superb views of the Grose Valley from **Evans Lookout**. Alternatively, park your car at Neates Glen (2 kilometres along the road) and take the Grand Canyon Walk, an adventurous 5-kilometre track that leads past moss-covered rocks, through a tunnel and under rocky overhangs. The enclosed canyon atmosphere provides a wonderful contrast to the vistas that unfold at Evans Lookout up ahead. Sturdy shoes and steady footing are essential for this walk; after heavy rains, contact the Heritage Centre (see below) to check track conditions.

⑪ The leap

From Blackheath, take a right-hand turn off the highway onto Govetts Leap Road and head towards the the National Parks and Wildlife Service Heritage Centre and **Govetts Leap Lookout**. The Heritage Centre, managed by the National Parks and Wildlife Service, has an interactive display on the geology, wildlife, and Aboriginal and European history of the mountains. Inquire here about ranger-guided bushwalks and special holiday programmes.

The 1.8-kilometre Fairfax Heritage Track, specially designed to

suit wheelchairs and prams, extends from the Heritage Centre to Govetts Leap Lookout. This view of the Grose Valley and Bridal Veil Waterfall is one of the Blue Mountains' greatest sights. In 1836, Charles Darwin described the vista as 'perhaps even more stupendous' than that obtained from Wentworth Falls. Darwin noted that 'the gulf was filled with a thin blue haze which ... added to the apparent depth at which the forest was stretched out beneath our feet.'

National Parks and Wildlife
Service Heritage Centre
Govetts Leap Rd
Blackheath
Phone: (02) 4787 8877
Open: 9 a.m.–4.30 p.m. daily

⑫ Above the pass

After Blackheath, continue along the highway to historic **Mount Victoria**, perched above the western escarpment. The 19th-century Refreshment Rooms at the Railway Station, once the rest-stop on a busy passenger line, now house a treasure trove of historic artifacts.

Between 1814 and 1920, several attempts were made to find the best route down into the valley. These old roads now form a network of walking tracks which can be accessed via Mt York Road, on the right side of the highway just before it descends through Victoria Pass. The track head is about 2 kilometres from the highway.

Mt Victoria and District Museum
Refreshment Rooms, Railway Station
Station St
Mount Victoria

Phone: (02) 4787 1190
Open: 2 p.m.–5 p.m. Sat., Sun.,
public and school holidays

⑬ Zig Zag

Depart the Great Western Highway at Mount Victoria. Follow the Darling Causeway to Bell and turn left along Chifley Road to Zig Zag Railway. Another longer but more interesting option is to continue along the Great Western Highway from Mount Victoria, and approach the Zig Zag Railway via Hartley and Lithgow (40 kilometres). The historic site of Hartley, which features a Greek Revival sandstone courthouse (1837), is a fascinating attraction in its own right.

The Zig Zag Railway, built between 1866 and 1869, has been described as one of the engineering wonders of the 19th century. Built to bring the Great Western Railway Line from the top of the Blue Mountains down the steep mountainside into the Lithgow Valley, it comprises a series of gently sloping ramps in Z-formation. The Zig Zag was replaced by a deviation through the escarpment in 1910. Today, visitors can ride the steam train through tunnels and cliff-cuttings and over sandstone viaducts.

Zig Zag Railway
Bells Line of Road
Clarence
Phone: (02) 6353 1795
Open: steam train operates weekends,
public and most school holidays (departs
10.30 a.m., 12.15 p.m., 2 p.m. and
3.45 p.m.); vintage rail motor trip and
depot tour operates during the week
(departs 11 a.m., 1 p.m. and 3 p.m.)

Why are the Blue Mountains so blue?
The blue haze comes from the many fine droplets of oil constantly dispersed by the dense eucalyptus forest. These droplets cause the blue light rays of the sun to be scattered more effectively, thus intensifying the usual light refraction phenomenon (Rayleigh Scattering) which causes distant objects to appear blue.

⑭ Glorious gardens

From Bell, take the Bells Line of Road towards Bilpin. Those with an interest in gardens would be well-advised to take a short diversion to **Mount Wilson**, famous for its English-style private gardens. Many of these gardens, established by Sydney's leisured elite in the 19th century, are now open to the public on a regular basis. For open hours, visit the Blue Mountains Visitor Information Centre in Glenbrook or call 1300 653 408.

⑮ Seasonal colours

Located further along the Bells Line of Road, **Mount Tomah Botanic Garden** features 28 hectares of magnificent colour: protea and heath in winter, cherry blossoms, bulbs, rhododendrons and azaleas in spring, alpine flowers in summer and shades of russet foliage in autumn. At 1000 metres above sea level, Mount Tomah specialises in cool-climate plants from around the world. On a clear day, views extend 180 kilometres across the canyon country towards the Hunter Valley.

Mount Tomah Botanic Garden
Bells Line of Road
Mount Tomah
Phone: (02) 4567 2154
Open: 10 a.m.–4 p.m. daily, Mar.–Sept.;
10 a.m.–5 p.m. daily, Oct.–Feb.

Returning to Sydney...

From Mount Tomah, the road descends past the orchards and roadside fruit stalls of Bilpin, through the foothills and onto the plains of the Hawkesbury River. To return to Sydney, continue through Richmond and Windsor and along Route ㊵ (111 kilometres).

NEW SOUTH WALES from A to Z

Snow gums near Adaminaby

Adaminaby
Pop. 366

MAP REF. 112 H5, 113 D8, 138 E9, 241 L1
This small town was moved in the 1950s to its present site; the old town site was flooded to form Lake Eucumbene as part of the Snowy Mountains Scheme. Located on the Snowy Mountains Hwy, the town is a good base for skiers and anglers. The ski area of Mt Selwyn (cross-country and downhill) is nearby. Also nearby is Lake Eucumbene, with a range of holiday resorts and excellent fishing. **In town:** World's largest trout, Baker St. Nov.: Trout Festival (fishing competition); Race Meeting. **In the area:** Power stations: tours and interactive displays; details from information centre. Fishing boat hire at: Old Adaminaby (8 km SW); Anglers Reach (16 km W); Buckenderra (39 km S). Horse-riding, mountain-bike hire and fly-fishing tours available. Historic goldmining site at Kiandra, 38 km NW. Yarrangobilly Caves and thermal pool, 59 km NW off Snowy Mountains Hwy in Kosciuszko National Park. **Visitor information:** The Pantry, 11 Denison St; (02) 6454 2453.

Adelong
Pop. 782

MAP REF. 113 B5, 114 D13
This picturesque tablelands town on the Snowy Mountains Hwy became a thriving community following the discovery of reef gold in 1857. **In town:** National Trust-classified Tumut St: old Bank of NSW (1882), now a B&B; Beaufort House (1915), originally established as a hotel, now has hotel accommodation and gallery; Gold Fields Galleries, for art and craft; restored Old Pharmacy, now a guest house and restaurant. Village Walk: includes police station (1861) in Campbell St, St James Catholic Church (1868) in Gundagai St, and ends at Adelong Falls Reserve; brochures available. Dec.: Home, Craft and Garden Fair. **In the area:** Adelong Falls Reserve, 1 km N on Tumblong–Gundagai Rd, where Reefer Battery operated until 1910, driven by water from falls (ruins still visible); picnic area, three marked walking trails, gold fossicking. **Visitor information:** York's Newsagency, Tumut St; (02) 6946 2051.

Albury
Pop. 41 491

MAP REF. 121 Q13, 239 P4, 240 C1
Albury-Wodonga is situated beside the Murray River, 572 km SW of Sydney. Once the meeting-place for local Aboriginal groups, today the Albury region makes a convenient stopover for motorists driving via the Hume Hwy between Sydney and Melbourne. The building of the Hume Weir in 1936 created Lake Hume, one of the most extensive artificial lakes in Australia. **In town:** Albury Regional Museum, in former Turk's Head Inn, Wodonga Pl., features display on Australia's largest post-war migrant centre at Bonegilla (Vic.). Botanical Gardens (1871), cnr Wodonga Pl. and Dean St. The Parklands (comprising Hovell Tree Reserve, Noreuil and Australia parks), on western side of Wodonga Pl. at town entrance; river-side walks, river swimming, kiosk and picnic areas. Noreuil Park is departure point for Murray River cruises on the PS *Cumberoona*. Albury Regional Art Centre, Dean St, has extensive Sir Russell Drysdale collection. 360° views from Albury Monument Hill at end of Dean St. Performing Arts Centre, Civic Centre, Swift St. Kids Play World, Young St, indoor play centre and cafe. Local dairy products at Haberfield's Milk Dairy Shop, Hovell St (tours during business hours). Rotary Community Market, Sun., Tax Office car park, Townsend St. Feb.–Mar.: Festival of Sport. Oct.: Food and Wine Festival. Nov.: Festival of the Bogong Moth. **In the area:** Ettamogah Wildlife Sanctuary, 12 km NE on Hume Hwy. Nearby, cartoonist Ken Maynard's Ettamogah Pub. Cooper's Ettamogah Winery, 3 km further along hwy. Australian Newsprint Mill, 15 km N (tours by appt). Linbrae Camel Farm, 16 km N off Urana Rd: winery and river treks. Jindera Pioneer Museum, 14 km NW, featuring traditional general store. Hume and Hovell Walking Track from Albury to Gunning, 440 km, 23-day trek for long-distance walkers, caters for half-day, one-day and weekend walks; contact Department of Lands, Sydney; (02) 9228 6111. A section of this track and other trails are part of the Albury–Wodonga Trail System; for further information contact Albury-Wodonga Regional Parklands. Hot-air ballooning, skydiving, trail-riding, fishing tours, canoe hire, and tours to wineries and Mad Dan Morgan (the infamous bushranger) country. Bogong Mountains, gateway to Victorian snow-fields and high country, 130 km S. Lake Hume, 14 km E, a paradise for all water sport enthusiasts. Hume Weir Trout Farm, nearby, offers trout feeding and fishing. Upstream of weir, Wymah Ferry, still in operation. **Visitor information:** Lincoln Causeway, Wodonga; (02) 6041 3875, freecall 1800 800 743. Web site albury. wodonga.com/tourism **See also:** The Mighty Murray (Vic.) p. 201.

National Parks

The national parks of New South Wales encompass areas ranging from World Heritage-listed rainforests to unspoiled beaches. Tourists return time and time again to these popular scenic retreats, which offer a wide range of activities for holiday-makers. Many of the State's parks are found along the coast, their rugged headlands, quiet inlets and sweeping beaches pounded by the crashing surf. The easy accessibility of these coastal parks accounts for their popularity.

AROUND SYDNEY

Sydney Harbour National Park is made up of pockets of bushland and other open space encircling Sydney Harbour and is the closest national park to the city. One way to explore the park is to follow the Manly-to-Spit walk, which meanders through bushland on the northern edges of the harbour. Harbour islands offer secluded picnic destinations and there are daily visits to Fort Denison from Circular Quay.

On the southern edge of Sydney is **Botany Bay National Park**. The northern section contains the sandy beaches of La Perouse, the historic fort on Bare Island (guided tours) and a maritime museum. The southern section at Kurnell protects the site of Captain Cook's first Australian landing in 1770; the Discovery Centre provides an insight into the history of the area.

The **Royal National Park**, just 32 kilometres south of Sydney, was the first national park to be proclaimed in Australia. It was established in 1879 and has over 15 000 hectares of sandstone plateau country, broken along the coastline by fine surf beaches. The Hacking River runs almost the entire length of the park. Boats may be hired at Audley and visitors can row in leisurely fashion along the river.

Lane Cove National Park, located within the northern urban area of Sydney, offers good walks and is extremely popular with families. There are many picnic areas next to the river, some of which can be reserved. The river is good for boating (non-powered only), and visitors can enjoy a ride on a paddle-wheeler. A wildlife shelter and wildlife shop are popular features of the park.

Further inland, to the west of Sydney, are splendid parks nestling in the mountains that overawed the early explorers. Year after year, innumerable visitors return to the **Blue Mountains National Park**, where mysterious blue mists shroud the immense valleys of the Grose and Coxs rivers, creating ever-changing patterns of green, blue and purple. At Katoomba, pillars of weathered sandstone rise abruptly like isolated church spires: these are the Three Sisters, the most popular tourist attraction in the Blue Mountains. The Grose and Jamison valleys offer many walks with spectacular views.

Just north of Sydney are two prominent national parks, on the southern and northern shores of the Hawkesbury River: **Ku-ring-gai Chase** and **Brisbane Water national parks**. These parks have sheltered creeks and inlets, ideal for boating, and bushland walking tracks through colourful wildflowers.

Ku-ring-gai Chase, established in 1894 and only 24 kilometres from Sydney, hugs the shores of Cowan Creek, Broken Bay and Pittwater. The eucalypt forest, scrub and heath are home to a wide range of animal life, including the shy swamp wallaby, the elusive lyrebird, honeyeaters, waterbirds, colourful parrots and lorikeets. Walking tracks lead to Aboriginal hand stencils and rock engravings.

Brisbane Water also has sandstone landscapes rich in Aboriginal art. There are scenic views from Warrah Trig and Staples Lookout, while Somersby Falls and Girrakool picnic areas mark the beginning of rainforest walks.

Nearby on the coast is **Bouddi National Park** which protects the coast and bush at the eastern entrance to Broken Bay and the coastal foreshore from Killcare Heights to McMasters Beach; it also covers a large offshore area near the beautiful Maitland Bay. Walking tracks lead to secluded, unspoiled beaches and pockets of rainforest.

Upstream along the Hawkesbury River is **Dharug National Park**, its sandstone cliffs rising high above the meandering river. A network of walking tracks includes a section of the convict-built Old Great North Road.

IN THE NORTH-EAST OF THE STATE

The largest coastal lake system in New South Wales is protected by the **Myall Lakes National Park**, an important waterbird habitat. Water is the focus of tourist activities: you can

World Heritage-listed rainforest in Mount Warning National Park

enjoy sailing and canoeing on the quiet lake waters, or surfing and beach fishing off the shores of the Pacific Ocean.

Barrington Tops, one of the State's most popular national parks, is a World Heritage-listed Area with a section set aside as wilderness. It has a mountainous plateau (1600 metres), providing spectacular views of the surrounding Hunter Valley and, in the distance, the Pacific Ocean, but visitors should be prepared for sudden bad weather. The stands of snow gums here give way, at about 1000 metres, to forests of Antarctic beech, with lichens, mosses and tree ferns. The lowest areas of the park feature subtropical rainforests, rivers, waterfalls and rapids. Many of the walking tracks in the park are suitable for families. Longer walks, ranging from 4–5 hours to overnight, are suitable for more experienced bushwalkers.

The World Heritage-listed **New England National Park**, which preserves one of the largest remaining areas of rainforest in New South Wales, is 576 kilometres north-east of Sydney. The park covers three distinct zones: subalpine with tall snow gums; temperate forests of ancient moss-covered Antarctic beeches; and true subtropical rainforests, rich in ferns, vines and orchids. The park has a diverse range of flora and fauna, including the rare rufous scrub-bird. Some 20 kilometres of walking tracks reveal to visitors the charm of the rainforest, while the trackless wilderness attracts more experienced bushwalkers. Nearby, the World Heritage-listed **Dorrigo National Park** protects some of the rainforests of northern New South Wales. At the Dorrigo Rainforest

Centre, visitors can experience the sights, sounds and smells of rainforests. The Skywalk provides magnificent views over the rainforest canopy to the Bellinger Valley and Pacific Ocean beyond.

Yuraygir and **Bundjalung national parks**, to the south and north respectively of the Clarence River on the far north coast, are a water wonderland with isolated beaches, quiet lakes and striking scenery. The parks deserve their reputation as prime areas for fishing. Surfing is also popular; waterways invite exploration by canoe; and the estuaries offer safe swimming. Heathwalking offers opportunities for birdwatching and nature photography, particularly in spring when both parks explode in a spectacle of colour.

In the far north of the State, **Border Ranges**, **Mount Warning** and **Nightcap national parks** offer the visitor vistas of World Heritage-listed rainforest. Border Ranges National Park includes the rim of the ancient volcano once centred on Mount Warning to the east. The best access is via the spectacular Tweed Range Scenic Drive. Stunning escarpments, waterfalls, and walking tracks from picnic areas abound in the eastern part.

Known to the Aborigines as 'Wollumbin', the cloud-catcher, Mount Warning (1157 metres) dominates the landscape and catches the first rays of the rising sun on the continent. A walk through Breakfast Creek rainforest leads to a steep climb to the summit. Nightcap National Park is part of the volcanic remnants of Mount Warning and includes Protesters Falls, named after the 1979 anti-logging protest.

Further inland are two well-known national parks: Warrumbungle and Mount Kaputar. **Warrumbungle National Park**, on the western side of the Great Divide, is 491 kilometres north-west of Sydney. Here is some of the most spectacular scenery in the nation: sheltered gorges, rocky spires and volcanic peaks. At Warrumbungle, east meets west: the dry western plains and moist eastern coast combine to give high peaks covered with gums and lower forests filled with fragrant native trees and shrubs. In the spring and summer months the colourful displays of wildflowers and the calls of brightly plumaged birds lure many visitors. There are also easy access tracks for families and the disabled.

Mount Kaputar National Park, near Narrabri, is one of Australia's most accessible wilderness areas. Several lookouts can be reached by car or are only a short walk from your car. The park's vegetation ranges from dry sclerophyll forest to subalpine, and the park is rich in flora and fauna. One of the highlights is Sawn Rocks, a 40-metre-high rock formation resembling a series of organ pipes.

The stark beauty of Mungo National Park

IN THE SOUTH-EAST OF THE STATE

There are a number of national parks in the southern part of the State, including **Morton National Park**, particularly known for the Fitzroy and Belmore falls, and **Budderoo National Park**, which includes the award-winning Minnamurra Rainforest Centre, where an elevated boardwalk takes you into the rainforest canopy.

Over 9000 hectares of rocky but beautiful coastline flanking Twofold Bay make up **Ben Boyd National Park**. Flowering heaths and colourful banksias add to the area's attraction. Boyd's Tower, constructed in the 1840s, is a prominent feature of the park.

Booderee National Park on the South Coast falls within a section of the ACT. It is owned by the Wreck Bay Aboriginal Community, who have joint management with Parks Australia; for all inquiries contact the on-site information centre; (02) 4443 0977. The park falls across a beautiful bush-clad landscape, which encircles the clear waters and white beaches of Jervis Bay. Highlights include Aboriginal heritage sites, wildlife and some of the most dramatic underwater landcape in NSW (scuba and snorkelling available).

The largest national park in New South Wales is **Kosciuszko**. It includes mainland Australia's only glacial lakes, as well as limestone caves, grasslands, heaths and woodlands. Situated 450 kilometres south-west of Sydney, this park is of particular significance because it embraces a large area of the continent's largest alpine region and contains Australia's highest mountains as well as the sources of the important Murray, Snowy and Murrumbidgee rivers. The most extensive snow fields of the nation are here, centred around Thredbo, Perisher, Smiggin Holes, Mount Blue Cow, Mount Selwyn and Charlotte Pass. There are easy grades for beginners and slopes for expert skiers. Although Kosciuszko is associated with winter sports, it is also a superb summer retreat with its crisp, clean air, crystal-clear lakes and a wonderful display of alpine wildflowers. It is a popular venue for those who enjoy camping, fishing, boating and bushwalking. Yarrangobilly Caves are a feature of the park and are open year-round, subject to winter road conditions. Yarrangobilly boasts five tourist caves – one with wheelchair access – a naturally heated thermal pool, nature trails and picnic facilities.

IN THE WEST OF THE STATE

In the far west of New South Wales are four outstanding national parks. **Kinchega**, 110 kilometres south-east of Broken Hill, contains the beautiful saucer-shaped overflow lakes of the Darling River. The lakes provide an important breeding ground for a wide variety of waterbirds, including herons, ibises, spoonbills and black swans. Walking tracks pass through forests of river red gums, and scenic drives follow the course of the river and the lake shores.

North-east of Wentworth is the World Heritage-listed **Mungo National Park**, part of the Willandra Lakes World Heritage Area. The shores of the now dry lake hold a continuous record of Aboriginal life dating back more than 40 000 years. The remarkable Walls of China, a great crescent of dunes, stretches along the eastern shore of the lake bed. Visitors can enjoy the park on a day trip or take advantage of the shearers' quarters accommodation or camping facilities. Self-guide walking tracks and a 60-kilometre self-guide drive tour give visitors the opportunity to see and learn about the many attractions of the park.

Mutawintji National Park, 130 kilometres north-east of Broken Hill, offers breathtaking gorge and desert-plain scenery, and a rich heritage of Aboriginal art accessible by tour from Broken Hill.

The most remote national park in the State is **Sturt**, 1400 kilometres from Sydney and 330 kilometres north of Broken Hill. This is an ideal place for those who want to get away from it all and experience the real Australian outback. The park comprises scenic red sand dunes, rocky ridges, ephemeral lakes and Mitchell grass plains. Visitors must come well prepared but may camp in the park and enjoy bushwalking over the sandplains. Wildflowers, which include the scarlet and black Sturt's desert pea, are abundant in good seasons. Fort Grey, where Sturt and his party built a stockade to protect their supplies, is worth a visit, even though there is little evidence of his occupation today.

For further information about the national parks of New South Wales, contact the National Parks and Wildlife Service, 43 Bridge St (PO Box 1967), Hurstville NSW 2220; (02) 9585 6333. The National Parks and Wildlife Service has produced an excellent brochure *Visitor Guide to National Parks in NSW,* which can be obtained free from its visitor centres and offices, or by mail. Web site www.npws.nsw.gov.au

Alstonville Pop. 4725

MAP REF. 117 Q3, 525 Q12

Alstonville nestles in lush surroundings at the top of the Ballina Cutting between Ballina and Lismore. The village is known for its immaculately maintained gardens and its beautiful purple tibouchina trees, which blossom in Mar. Surrounding properties produce potatoes, sugarcane, coffee, tropical fruits, macadamia nuts and avocados. **In town:** Lumley Park, Bruxner Hwy, features open-air pioneer transport museum. In Budgen Ave: Kolinda Gallery and Ward's Antiques for local art and craft. Elizabeth Ann Brown Park, Main St, a rainforest park with picnic facilities. **In the area:** Summerland House With No Steps, 3 km S, a unique enterprise with nursery, gardens, craft cottage, tropical fruit processing and packaging factory, fruit sales and tearooms, all run by disabled people. Nearby, Victoria Park, boardwalk and picnic area. **Visitor information:** Ballina Visitor Information Centre, cnr Las Balsas Plaza and River St, Ballina; (02) 6686 3484.

Armidale Pop. 21 330

MAP REF. 117 L9

Situated midway between Sydney and Brisbane in the New England Ranges (altitude 980 m), this university city is the centre of the New England district and has more than 30 National Trust-classified buildings. **In town:** Armidale Heritage Trolley Tours: 2-hr tour includes Railway Museum and University of New England; departs from information centre daily. In Kentucky St: New England Regional Art Museum, contains Hinton Collection, Australia's most valuable provincial art collection; Aboriginal Cultural Centre and Keeping Place: museum, education centre, Aboriginal craft displays. Newling Gallery in Old Teachers College, Faulkner St, exhibitions by local artists. Folk Museum in National Trust-classified building, cnr Faulkner and Rusden sts, displays pioneer relics. Railway Museum, adjacent to station in Brown St (open by appt or as part of trolley tour). In Dangar St: Gothic Revival-style St Mary's Roman Catholic Cathedral (1912); St Peter's Anglican Cathedral (1875), built of 'Armidale blues' bricks. The Stables (1872), Moore St, now craft shop. Courthouse (1860) and Imperial Hotel (1890) in Beardy St. Central Park, Dangar St, has useful relief map of area. Self-guide heritage walk (3 km) and heritage drive (25 km) of city; brochures available. Markets in Mall, last Sun. each month. Mar.: Autumn Festival. **In the area:** Excellent trout fishing. University of New England, 5 km NW: features historic Booloominbah homestead, now administration building (guided tours Mon., bookings essential); Antiquities Museum; Zoology Museum, and kangaroo and deer park. Dumaresq Dam, 15 km NE, features walking tracks, non-power boating, swimming and trout fishing (Oct.–June). At former mining town of Hillgrove, 31 km E: Rural Life and History Museum with goldmining equipment (check opening times); self-guide town walk through old town site (brochure available). Oxley Wild Rivers National Park: Wollomombi Falls (40 km E), one of the highest falls in the State, plunging 220 m; Dangars Falls (21 km SE), 120 m waterfall in spectacular gorge setting. National Trust-owned Saumarez homestead (1888), 5 km S, guided tours of house and self-guide farm and garden tours (homestead closed mid-June–end-Aug.). Mount Yarrowyck Nature Reserve, 27 km W, 3-km walk to Aboriginal heritage sites. Numerous self-guide scenic drives; brochures available. **Visitor information:** 82 Marsh St; (02) 6772 4655, freecall 1800 627 736. **See also:** New England p. 49. Web site www.newengland.org/armidale

Ballina Pop. 16 056

MAP REF. 117 Q3, 525 R12

Ballina is a fishing town at the mouth of the Richmond River in northern NSW. Ideal year-round temperatures, golden beaches, and picturesque farmlands make the area a popular family holiday destination. Cedar-cutters were among the first European settlers, attracted by the red cedar trees along the shores of the river. Farmers followed and by 1900 a dairy-farming industry was established alongside sugarcane plantations. **In town:** Naval and Maritime Museum, Regatta Ave, behind information centre, features a restored Las Balsas Expedition raft that sailed from South America in 1973. Kerry Saxby Walkway, begins behind information centre and follows river to its mouth; brochure available. The Big Prawn Complex, Pacific Hwy, features fresh seafood, opal and gem museum, and art and craft. Summerland Antiques, Pacific Hwy, and Heath's Collectables, Southern Cross Dr., for antiques and bric-a-brac. *Richmond Princess* and *Bennelong* river cruises. Shaws Bay, off Compton Dr., swimming and picnic spot ideal for families. Shelly Beach, off Shelly Beach Rd: rock pools, wading pool for toddlers; beachside cafe; dolphin-watching year-round; humpback whales sighted June–July and Sept.–Oct. Markets at Outdoor Entertainment Reserve, Canal Rd, 3rd Sun. each month. **In the area:** Self-guide driving tours, including River Drive; leaflets available. Deep-sea fishing, whale-watching and 4WD eco tours. Thursday Plantation Tea Tree Oil, 3 km W; guided tours. **Visitor information:** cnr Las Balsas Plaza and River St; (02) 6686 3484. Web site www.ballina.tropicalnsw.com.au

Balranald Pop. 1419

MAP REF. 120 H8, 237 N6

Balranald is set in wool, cattle, wheat, fruit and timber country on the Murrumbidgee River, 438 km NW of Melbourne. **In town:** Historical Museum in Heritage Park, Market St, includes gaol, Murray pine school house, museum with local history displays (open Wed. 2–4 p.m.), picnic/barbecue facilities and information centre. Picturesque Memorial Drive. Self-guide town walk; brochure available. Easter: Homebush Gymkhana. Dec.: Christmas Festival (on Christmas Eve). **In the area:** Balranald Weir (when water is low-level) for picnics, barbecues and fishing. Yanga Lake, 7 km SE, offers good fishing and water sports. Historic Homebush Hotel (1878), 25 km N. Redbank Weir, 58 km NE on Homebush–Oxley Rd for barbecues and picnics. World Heritage-listed Mungo National Park, 150 km NW, features The Walls of China (sand dunes); record of 40 000 years of Aboriginal life; maps available. **Visitor information:** Historical Museum, Market St; (03) 5020 1599. **See also:** National Parks p. 42.

Barham Pop. 1167

MAP REF. 120 I12, 235 Q2, 237 Q13, 238 B1

Barham and its twin town Koondrook (in Vic. on the other side of the Murray River) are centres for the timber, cattle, fat-lamb, dairying and tourism industries. **In town:** Self-guide historic walks, brochure available. Barham Lakes Complex, Murray St, includes artificial lakes, walking track and picnic/barbecue facilities. Sept.: Pro-Am Golf Tournament. **In the area:** Around Koondrook, historic sawmilling town and river port: self-guide historic Koondrook Walk, brochure available; Redgum Forest to Furniture, 4 manufacturers in Grigg and Punt rds; Gannawarra

Wetlander Cruises, 15 km S; Kerang Ibis Rookery, 28 km SW on Murray Valley Hwy; State Forest, East Barham Rd. At Murrabit, 20 km NW, market, 1st Sat. each month. Feb.: Flywheelers Rally (restored machinery show). May: Tentpegging Championships. **Visitor information:** Golden Rivers Tourism, 25 Murray St; (03) 5453 3100, freecall 1800 621 8820. Web site www.goldenrivers.com

Barooga   Pop. 999

MAP REF. 121 M13, 239 J3

A small but rapidly growing town near the Victorian town of Cobram, Barooga's beautiful setting and abundant wildlife make it a popular holiday town. **In town:** Sandy beaches along Murray River. In Vermont St: Dalveile Gallery, features antique oil lamp collection; Botanical Gardens. Binghi Boomerang Factory, Tocumwal Rd. Lions Market, Vermont St, 3rd Sat. each month. Jan., Easter, June, Aug.: major golf events. **In the area:** Citrus- and grape-growing. Brentwood Fruit Juices, 6 km E, tours. **Visitor information:** The Old Grain Store, cnr Station St and Punt Rd, Cobram; (03) 5872 2132, freecall 1800 607 607. **See also:** The Mighty Murray (Vic.) p. 201.

Barraba   Pop. 1267

MAP REF. 116 I8

Surrounded by magnificent mountain scenery on the Manilla River in the Nandewar Range, Barraba is an agricultural and pastoral centre, and an ideal base for exploring the eastern section of the Nandewar Mountains. **In town:** Nandewar Historical Museum, Queen St (open by appt). Clay Pan and Fuller Gallery, Queen St, for art, craft and pottery. Heritage-listed Thomas Jones and Son pipe organ in Anglican church, Fitzroy St. Jan.: Australia's Smallest Country Music Festival (quite large). Nov.: Barrarbor Cultural Festival (celebrating music and trees). Dec.: Horton Valley Rodeo. **In the area:** Birdwatching trails, 171 species including the rare regent honeyeater; leaflet available. Adam's Lookout, 4 km N, for views of town. Horton River Falls, 38 km W, for scenery, swimming and bushwalking. Barraba Track and Mt Kaputar National Park, 48 km W, for scenery, swimming and bushwalking (4WD and walking-track access only). Split Rock Dam and The Glen Riddle Recreation Reserve, 15 km SE: boating, fishing, water-skiing and picnicking. Ironbark Creek,

18 km E, for gold fossicking. **Visitor information:** 116 Queen St; (02) 6782 1255. **See also:** New England p. 61.

Batemans Bay   Pop. 9568

MAP REF. 113 H7, 139 N7

Crayfish and oysters are the specialty of this holiday town on the Princes Hwy 285 km S of Sydney. Located at the estuary of the Clyde River, Batemans Bay provides convenient access to both the river and the Pacific Ocean. **In town:** *Clyde Princess* and MV *Merinda* river cruises (depart Ferry Wharf). On Beach Rd: 27-hole golf course; Birdland Animal Park with rainforest trail. Houseboats for hire. Fishing charters available. Market at High School, Glenella Rd, 3rd Sun. each month. **In the area:** Murramarang National Park, 10 km NE, a coastal park noted for its mostly undisturbed coastline and kangaroos on beach. Durras Lake, 8 km NE, for fishing and swimming. Historic Nelligen, 10 km NW, on Clyde River; Country Music Festival here each Jan. At Mogo, 8 km S: art and craft outlets; Mogo Goldfields Park with working goldmine; Old Mogo Town, 19th-century re-created goldmining town; Mogo Zoo. Calligraphy Gallery, 12 km SE, for local art. Surfing at Malua Bay, 14 km SE. **Visitor information:** Eurobodalla Coast Visitors Centre, cnr Princes Hwy and Beach Rd; (02) 4472 6900, freecall 1800 802 528. Web site www.naturecoast-tourism.com.au **See also:** The South Coast p. 59.

Bathurst   Pop. 26 029

MAP REF. 98 B4, 114 H6

Bathurst, 211 km W of Sydney on the Macquarie River, is the centre of a pastoral and fruit- and grain-growing district. The birthplace of former Prime Minister J. B. Chifley, it is better known today for its motor-racing circuit, Mount Panorama. The townscape has an abundance of Georgian and Victorian architecture; the main street is lined with elegant lampposts. **In town:** Self-guide historic walking tour and fossicker's self-drive tour (leaflets available). Ben Chifley Cottage, Busby St. In Russell St: Historical Society Museum in East Wing of courthouse; Miss Traill's House (c. 1845), containing items collected by one family over 100 years, which record history of town and reflect family's passion for horse-breeding and racing. Bathurst Regional Art Gallery, Keppel St. Machattie

Park, bounded by Keppel, William and George sts, Victorian-era gardens with sculptures and glasshouses. Oct.: Bathurst (Supertourers) Car Races. Nov.: FAI 1000 (V8 Supercar Race). **In the area:** Southwest of city centre at Mt Panorama on Panorama Ave: Bathurst Goldfields, a reconstruction of historic goldmining area; National Motor Racing Museum at Mt Panorama Motor Racing Circuit; views from summit of Mt Panorama; nearby, McPhillamy Park features Sir Joseph Banks Nature Reserve. Abercrombie Caves, 72 km S on Bathurst–Goulburn Rd: limestone cave system featuring largest natural limestone bridge in Southern Hemisphere; guided and self-guide tours; Carols in the Caves held here in Dec. Abercrombie House (1870s), 6 km W on Ophir Rd, baronial-style Gothic mansion. Wallaby Rocks, 40 km N, sheer wall of rock rising from Turon River, ideal swimming and picnic spot. Sofala, historic gold town, 42 km N, setting for scenes from *The Cars That Ate Paris* (1974) and *Sirens* (1994). Hill End Historic Site, 86 km NW, former goldfield with many original buildings; area has inspired paintings by Russell Drysdale, Donald Friend, John Olsen and Brett Whiteley; National Parks and Wildlife Service Visitor Centre in old Hill End Hospital, includes historical display and information on panning and fossicking (equipment for hire). Old gold towns nearby include Peel, Wattle Flat, Rockley, O'Connell and Trunkey. Bathurst Sheep and Cattle Drome at Rossmore Park, 6 km NE on Limekilns Rd, features performing sheep and cattle, and milking, shearing and sheepdog demonstrations. **Visitor information:** 28 William St; (02) 6332 1444. Web site www. bathurstcity.com

Batlow   Pop. 1069

MAP REF. 113 B6, 114 D13, 138 A4

This timber-milling and former goldmining town is situated in the Great Dividing Range 28 km S of Tumut, in a district known for its apples, pears and berry fruits. **In town:** Historical Society Museum, Mayday Rd. Fruits of Batlow Packing Complex, Old Tumbarumba Rd (tours by appt). Cascade Fuchsia Nursery, Fosters Rd (open Oct.–Apr.). Superb views of town and peaks of Snowy Mountains from Weemala Lookout, H. V. Smith Dr. Apr.: Apple Harvest Festival. Sept.: Daffodil Show. **In the area:** Hume and Hovell Lookout, 6 km E, for views over Blowering Reservoir; picnic area at site where explorers paused in 1824. Blowering Reservoir, 20 km E. Springfield Orchard, 6 km N on Tumut Rd, grows 16 apple varieties; picnic/barbecue facilities. Pick-your-own berry fruits and cherries at farms on Tumut Rd. Access points for short-section walks on 440-km Hume and Hovell Walking Track, which runs from Gunning to Albury. Batlow District Drive, south of town, links various walks and forest parks in Bago State Forest; brochure available. Spectacular Buddong Falls, 25 km S; accessible during fine weather only. **Visitor information:** Old Butter Factory, Adelong Rd, Tumut; (02) 6947 1849. Web site www.tumut.nsw.gov.au/trrc

Bega

Pop. 4190

MAP REF. 111 F7, 113 G10, 241 Q6

It is possible to surf and ski on the same day from Bega, set as it is between the beach and the Kosciuszko snow resorts. The town is near the junction of the Princes and Snowy Mountains hwys, which link Sydney, Melbourne and Canberra. **In town:** Bega Family Museum, cnr Bega and Auckland sts. Feb.: Far South Coast National Show. Mar.: Cheese Pro-Am. Oct.: Bega Valley Art Awards. Dec.: Showjumping Cup. **In the area:** Fine views from Dr George Lookout (8 km NE) and Bega Valley Lookout (3 km N). Bega Cheese Heritage Centre, 3 km N, faithful reproduction of original cheese factory building with displays of old cheese-making techniques. See cows being milked at Brogo Valley Rotolactor, 18 km N (by appt only; fee applies). Mumbulla Falls, 19 km NE, tranquil rock pools, natural waterslides, boardwalks, viewing platforms, picnic area. Grevillea Estate Winery, 5 km W on Buckajo Rd, see cows being milked in dairy, 3 p.m. daily. Historic village of Candelo, 24 km SW, with its old-world charm untouched by time; market (largest on south coast) held 1st Sun. each month. Brogo Dam, 30 km NW, wildlife, bass-fishing, swimming, picnic area, boat-ramp, canoe-hire. **Visitor information:** Gipps St; (02) 6492 2045. Web site www.sapphirecoast.com.au **See also:** The South Coast p. 59.

Bellingen

Pop. 2690

MAP REF. 117 P8

Bellingen is an attractive tree-lined town on the banks of the Bellinger River in the rich dairylands of the Bellinger Valley. In pioneer days it was a timber-getting and ship-building centre. More recently, it has become a haven for alternative-lifestylers, including farmers and artisans. The area is also known as the setting for Peter Carey's *Oscar and Lucinda*. **In town:** Much of town classified by Heritage Commission. In Hyde St: Bellingen Museum, has pioneer memorabilia (check opening times); restored Hammond and Wheatley Emporium; Sweetwater Gallery. Local art and craft at The Yellow Shed, cnr Hyde and Prince sts, and at The Old Butter Factory (1906), Doepel La. Canoe hire. Markets at Bellingen Park, Church St, 3rd Sat. each month. Aug.: Jazz Festival. Oct.: World Music, Dance and Arts Festival. **In the area:** Riverside walks and canoeing on Bellinger River. Bike tours into forest areas, maps available; state forests for bush-walking and horseriding. Scenic Bellingen Bat Island in river, with flying fox colony. Raleigh Vineyard and Winery, 11 km E. Picnicking at Thora, 14 km NW, at foot of Dorrigo Plateau. Trout fishing and fly-fishing in streams on Dorrigo Plateau (area between Dorrigo and Urunga). Scenic drive north-east through farmlands and wooded valleys, across Never Never Creek to the Promised Land (brochure available); swimming holes and picnic areas; road continues to Dorrigo National Park. Gambaarri Aboriginal Cultural Tours to same area. **Visitor information:** Pacific Hwy, Urunga; (02) 6655 5711. Web site www.bellingen.nsw.gov.au/tourism/bellinger.html

Bermagui

Pop. 1196

MAP REF. 111 H4, 113 H9, 139 M13, 241 R4

Fishing in all forms – lake, estuary, deep-sea and big-game – is excellent in this delightful small port, 13 km from the Princes Hwy. It was much publicised for its fishing by American novelist/sportsman Zane Grey in the 1930s. Because of its close proximity to the Continental Shelf, the town plays host to numerous game-fishing tournaments Nov.–June. The town's harbour is the safest on the south coast. **In town:** Diving, deep-sea and game-fishing charters. Fresh fish and prawns for sale at Fish Co-op at harbourside. Humpback whale-, southern right whale- and dolphin-watching cruises depart from harbour Sept.–Nov. Craft market, last Sun. each month. Jan.: Blue Water Fishing Classic. Feb.: International Dog Show. Mar.: Seaside Fair; Tag and Release Game-Fishing Tournament. Easter: Four Winds Easter Concerts; Victorian Game-Fishing Tournament. **In the area:** Beautiful rock pools, particularly Blue Pool; rugged coastline and unspoiled countryside. Safe swimming at Horseshoe Bay Beach. Good surfing at Beares, Mooreheads, Cuttagee and Haywards beaches. Coastal walk (8 km) to Wallaga Lake, passing through wetland reserves, and remnants of Montreal Goldfields. At Wallaga Lake, 8 km N: Camel Rock, unusual rock formation on shoreline; Umbarra Cultural Centre, offering Aboriginal cultural tours; Wallaga Lake National Park, for boating, fishing, swimming, bushwalking and picnicking, and walking trail to summit of Mt Dromedary. Cobargo, 20 km W on Princes Hwy, an unspoiled historic working village with several art galleries, wood and leather crafts, iron forge, pottery and tearooms; country market, 4th Sat. each month in RSL Hall grounds. **Visitor information:** Lamont St; (02) 6493 3054, freecall 1800 645 808. **See also:** The South Coast p. 59.

Berridale

Pop. 1295

MAP REF. 112 I10, 113 D9, 138 E12, 241 L4

This small town is located near Lake Eucumbene, Lake Jindabyne and the ski fields of southern NSW. **In town:** St Marys Church (1860), Mary St, off Kosciuszko Rd. Berridale School (1883), Oliver St. In Exchange Sq.: Berridale Inn (1863) and Berridale Store (1863). Easter: Fair. **In the area:** On Old Dalgety Rd: Snowy River Winery, 12 km S, has tastings and restaurant. At Dalgety, 18 km S, historic Buckley's Crossing Hotel (1889) marks spot where cattle used to cross the Snowy River. Snowy River Ag Barn and Fibre Centre, 21 km S. Eucumbene Trout Farm, 19 km N, has sales, horseriding and tours. **Visitor information:** Berridale Store, 64 Jindabyne Rd; (02) 6456 3206.

Berrima

Pop. 815

MAP REF. 110 B6, 113 H3, 115 J10

A superbly preserved 1830s village, Berrima is on the Old Hume Hwy in the Southern Highlands. **In town:** Self-guide historical walking tour, brochure available. Many old buildings restored as craft and antique shops, restaurants and galleries. In Market Pl.: White Horse Inn (1832), now a restaurant; historical museum; Australian Alpaca Centre, selling knitwear. The Surveyor General (1835), Old Hume Hwy, Australia's oldest continually licensed hotel. Gaol (1839), Argyle St, still in use. Courthouse (1838), Wilshire St, finest building in town, first trial by jury in Australia held here in 1841, now a museum

Wildlife-Watching

The rich variety of wildlife in New South Wales includes eastern grey kangaroos and lyrebirds, along with inquisitive dolphins, basking sea lions, and huge humpback whales which navigate the State's coast each year.

IN SYDNEY

Australia's largest city is not the perfect environment for native animals, though several species have found a niche. For a colourful and noisy spectacle visit the seaside suburb of **Manly**, where thousands of raucous rainbow lorikeets arrive each evening to roost in the Norfolk pines along the ocean-beach foreshore.

Sydney's other winged residents are somewhat quieter. A large colony of flying foxes – up to 50 000 in summer months – lives in Ku-ring-gai Flying Fox Reserve in Sydney's northern suburbs. The reserve itself is not open to the public, although the bats can still be seen from Rosedale Road bridge in **Gordon**. After spending the day hanging in trees, they take to the air at dusk along particular 'flight paths' to feed on flowering trees.

AROUND SYDNEY

Royal National Park south of Sydney provides a green buffer against the city's southern suburbs, and many birds thrive here. Sulphur-crested cockatoos are happy to make their presence known, though it is worth keeping an eye out for quieter birds, such as heath wrens, satin bowerbirds, lyrebirds and top-knot pigeons. Diamond pythons, eastern water dragons and lace monitors can be seen by observant reptile-watchers.

The famous **Blue Mountains National Park** is a prime location for eastern grey kangaroos. A large mob lives around Euroka Clearing at the eastern end of the park near Glenbrook. While they are most active at dawn and dusk, there are usually eastern greys about at any time of day.

Bottlenose dolphins at play near Port Stephens

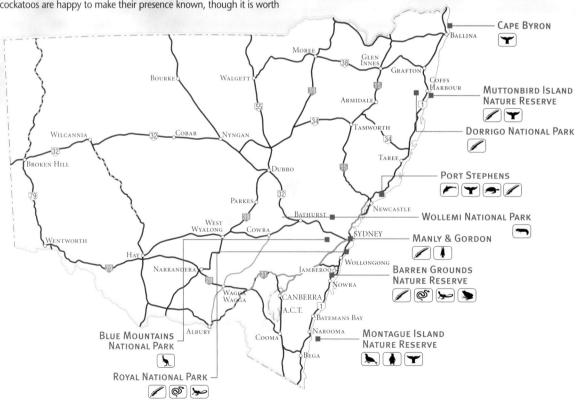

North of Blue Mountains National Park, in the adjoining **Wollemi National Park**, is the Glow Worm Tunnel, home to the iridescent larvae of the fungus gnat. A kilometre-long walk will take you to the tunnel entrance, after which you will need a torch to negotiate the uneven and sometimes slippery ground inside. To see the glow-worms, turn off your torch and wait quietly for a few minutes. Tiny blue spots of light will gradually become visible on the damp walls of the tunnel.

IN THE NORTH-EAST OF THE STATE

Humpback whales are regular visitors to the waters off **Cape Byron**, near Byron Bay township, following the demise of the east-coast whaling industry in 1963. Between two and three thousand now migrate from Antarctica to their northern breeding grounds, passing the cape in June and July. They return either pregnant or with newborn calves between September and October. A calm ocean and a pair of binoculars will increase your chances of witnessing humpback whale acrobatics.

Further south is **Muttonbird Island Nature Reserve**. The island, linked to the city of Coffs Harbour by bridge, has a sizeable population of short-tailed shearwaters (muttonbirds), between August and April each year. Dawn and dusk are the best times to look skywards as the shearwaters fly out and return from fishing excursions. Also keep an eye on the ocean for passing humpback whales in season.

Just inland from Coffs Harbour is the rainforest of **Dorrigo National Park**. Brush turkeys are a common sight around the park's picnic areas; these bald-headed ground dwellers are brash characters, very much at home among human visitors. The Walk with the Birds Boardwalk is a good way to see other forest birds, including yellow robins, thornbills and riflebirds. The Lyrebird Link Track provides an opportunity to see one of Dorrigo's numerous lyrebirds. Another park resident is the regent bowerbird; the male is well known for its habit of collecting blue objects to decorate its bower in the hope of attracting a mate.

ON THE CENTRAL COAST

The deep, clean waters around **Port Stephens** are a great place to see bottlenose dolphins at play. Fortunately the 60 or so resident dolphins seem to enjoy some 'people-watching' themselves. They will often ride on bow waves of dolphin-viewing boats, turning on their sides to glance at the excited humans aboard. If they are in a playful mood, they will also barrel-roll and swim upside down. And with the right combination of tide and swell, they can be seen surfing the breakers at Port Stephens.

A sail-powered catamaran operates out of Nelson Bay, within Port Stephens, to view migrating humpback whales in season (June, July, September and October). Watching these marine entertainers as they tail-slap, pectoral fin-wave and launch their 30-tonne bodies clear of the water is a memorable experience. Turtles, sea eagles and short-tailed shearwaters (muttonbirds) are also likely to make an appearance. Later in the season minke whales follow shoals of pilchards along the coast.

ON THE SOUTH COAST

Thirty minutes by boat from the coastal town of Narooma is **Montague Island Nature Reserve**, home to hundreds of Australian fur seals. August to December are the best times to view and

Regent bowerbirds can be spotted in Dorrigo National Park

photograph large numbers of these protected sea mammals as they sun themselves on the rocks. Montague Island is one of the few 'haul-out' sites for these seals on the Australian coastline; boat tours operate to the colony on a daily basis.

A second boat tour heads for the nightly penguin parade. Each evening at dusk the island's penguins return from their daily fishing excursion at sea. June to March are the best times to see the birds emerge from the waves and waddle up the beach to their burrows. Between mid-September and mid-November the tour-boat skippers watch for migrating whales as there is a good chance of spotting a humpback at this time of year.

IN THE SOUTHERN HIGHLANDS

Within **Barren Grounds Nature Reserve** near Jamberoo is a bird observatory that offers some unique wildlife-watching experiences. This non-profit environmental education venture, set up by Birds Australia, hosts regular nature-based weekend activities.

Popular workshops include a lyrebird-watching weekend in winter, when the birds' courtship displays and songs are at their finest. The Birds for Beginners weekends combine birdwatching with useful information, while the Slither and Croaker weekend concentrates on searching for reptiles and frogs. There is also a bird-banding workshop where visitors can watch birds being trapped, banded, measured and released. Phone (02) 4236 0195 for bookings. The observatory has several good walking tracks for birdwatchers to view yellow-tailed black cockatoos, beautiful firetails, yellow robins and the endangered ground parrot.

WILDLIFE-WATCHING ETHICS

Do not disturb wildlife or wildlife habitats. Keep the impact of your presence to a minimum. Use available cover or hides wherever possible.

Do not feed wildlife, even in urban areas.
(Note: supervised feeding is allowed at some locations.)

Be careful not to introduce exotic plants and animals – definitely no pets.

Stay on defined trails.

For more information on wildlife-watching in national parks contact the National Parks and Wildlife Service, 43 Bridge St (PO Box 1967), Hurstville NSW 2220; (02) 9585 6444. Web site www.npws.nsw.gov.au

with displays and video of early Berrima. **In the area:** Joadja Winery, 8 km NW. Amber Park Emu and Ostrich Farm, 11 km NW. **Visitor information:** Southern Highlands Visitor Information Centre, 62–70 Main St, Mittagong; (02) 4871 2888 or 1300 657 559. **See also:** Day Tours from Sydney p. 34.

Berry
Pop. 1604

MAP REF. 110 F11, 113 I4, 115 K11
Old English trees add to the charm of this town on the Princes Hwy, 18 km NE of Nowra. Situated in rich dairy country, it was founded by David Berry, whose brother Alexander was the first European settler in the Shoalhaven area. **In town:** Many National Trust-classified buildings including Historical Museum, Queen St. Variety of antique shops and galleries. Markets: 1st Sun. each month at Showgrounds; 3rd Sun. each month at the Great Southern Hotel, Queen St. Feb.: Agricultural Show. **In the area:** Coolangatta, 11 km SE, a group of convict-built cottages, winery and accommodation on site of first European settlement in area in 1822. Wineries open for tastings and sales: Jasper Valley Wines, 4 km S; The Silos Winery, 6 km S; Coolangatta Estate, 11 km SE. **Visitor information:** Shoalhaven Visitors Centre, cnr Princes Hwy and Pleasant Way, Nowra; (02) 4421 0778. Web site www.shoalhaven.nsw.gov.au

Bingara
Pop. 1236

MAP REF. 116 I6
Around this fascinating town, garnets, rhodonite, jasper, tourmaline and gold may be found in the creeks and rivers (maps available). **In town:** Self-guide historical/scenic town drive and town walks, brochures available. Stamper battery at site of former All Nations Gold Mine, top of Hill St. National Trust-classified Museum (1860) in slab building thought to be town's first hotel, displays gems and minerals, 19th-century furniture and photographs, and working smithy. Murray Cod Hatchery, Bandalong St (open by appt). Gwydir River Rides (trail rides), Maitland St. Walking track along Gwydir River. Easter: Gold Rush Festival; Easterfish. Aug.: Orange Festival (includes street markets). Dec.: Country Christmas Carnival. **In the area:** Birdwatching, details from information centre. Rocky Creek glacial area, 37 km SW, unusual conglomerate rock formations. Sawn Rocks, 70 km SW, pipe-shaped volcanic rock formations.

At Upper Bingara, 24 km S: remains of old gold and copper mines; Three Creeks Tourist Goldmine, a working mine where visitors can pan for gold. **Visitor information:** 64 Maitland St; (02) 6724 0066. **See also:** New England p. 61.

Blackheath
Pop. 4119

MAP REF. 98 H6, 100 C5, 115 J7
This pretty resort town, the highest in the Blue Mountains, has some of the most breathtaking views in the area. Known for its comfortable guesthouses and annual Rhododendron Festival, it is a popular retreat for Sydneysiders. **In town:** Statue commemorating the popular myth of Govett (a 'daring bushranger'), centre of town. Market at Community Centre, Great Western Hwy, 3rd Sun. each month. Nov.: Rhododendron Festival. **In the area:** Rhododendrons and azaleas at Bacchante Gardens, 1.5 km N. Pulpit Rock Reserve and Lookout, 6 km NE off Hat Hill Rd. On Govetts Leap Rd: at National Parks and Wildlife Heritage Centre (2.4 km E), interpretive display on geology, wildlife and Aboriginal European history of the mountains; starting point for Fairfax Heritage Track walk (1 hr return); Govetts Leap Lookout (3 km E). Evans Lookout, 6 km E, offers views of the Grose Valley and 190-m Bridal Veil Falls, the longest single-drop falls in the mountains. Mermaid Cave, 4 km S on Megalong Rd. Shipley Tea Rooms, 4.6 km S on Shipley Rd, for art exhibitions (open weekends). Hargraves Lookout on Panorama Point Rd, 2.8 km SW of Shipley Tea Rooms; Mt Blackheath Lookout on Mt Blackheath Rd, 3.6 km N of tearooms. Horseriding at Werriberri Trail Rides in Megalong Valley, 9 km S; at nearby Megalong Australian Heritage Centre, horseriding and tourist farm. Mount Victoria, 6 km NW, an historic village with craft shops, museum and Mt Vic Flicks historic cinema (open Thurs.–Sun. and school holidays). At Medlow Bath, 5 km S: Hydro Majestic Hotel, once a health resort; Blue Mountains Herb Fest held here in Mar. **Visitor information:** Great Western Hwy, Glenbrook; 1300 653 408. **See also:** Blue Mountains Experience p. 38; National Parks p. 42; Wildlife-Watching p. 48.

Blayney
Pop. 2672

MAP REF. 114 G6
A major regional centre on the Mid Western Hwy between Cowra and Bathurst. **In town:** Buildings classified

by National Trust. Avenues of deciduous trees, particularly beautiful in autumn. In Adelaide St: On Adelaide, for local craft; The Cottage, for local craft and visitor information; Heritage Park, with small wetland area. Mar.: Agricultural Show. **In the area:** Carcoar Dam, 12 km SW, for water sports; camping and picnic/barbecue facilities nearby. National Trust-classified village of Carcoar, 14 km SW, scene of NSW's first bank hold-up in 1863. At Newbridge, 20 km E, historic buildings and craft outlets. Abercrombie Caves, 50 km SE: set in a 220-hectare reserve featuring the largest natural arch in the Southern Hemisphere, tours available; Carols in the Caves held in Dec. Local art and craft at Taroona Wool Park (5 km NE) and Cottesbrook Gallery (15 km NE), both on Mid Western Hwy. At Millthorpe, National Trust-classified village, 11 km NW: quaint shop fronts; art and craft shops; historic churches; Golden Memories Museum, a huge complex with blacksmith's shop and old-style kitchen. **Visitor information:** Shire Council, 91 Adelaide St; (02) 6368 2104.

Bombala
Pop. 1380

MAP REF. 111 A9, 113 E11, 241 N7
This small town on the Monaro Hwy, 83 km S of Cooma, is the centre for the surrounding wool, beef cattle, fat lamb, vegetable and softwood timber-producing area. The Bombala River is also known for an abundance of platypuses and good trout fishing. **In town:** Self-guide historical walk (1 hr) includes courthouse (1882), cnr High and Dickinson sts; School of Art (1871), Caveat St (leaflet available). Toorallie Woollen Mill, Maybe St (check opening times). Endeavour Reserve, Caveat St, has 2-km return walking track. Bicentennial Park, Mahratta St, with pleasant river walk. In Railway Park, Monaro Hwy: historic engine shed (open by appt.); Lavender House, local lavender produce, museum of local artifacts and farm implements. Jan.: Wool and Wood Festival. Nov.: Riverside Festival. **In the area:** Fly-fishing and trout fishing, maps available. Platypus Sanctuary, 3 km S, just off Monaro Hwy on road to Delegate. On Monaro Hwy, Burnima Homestead (1880s), 6 km N (open by appt). Early Settlers Hut at Delegate, 36 km SW. Scenic drives (gold-fossicking along route) to Bendoc Mines in Vic., 57 km SW. Coolumbooka Nature Reserve, 15 km NE. **Visitor information:** Mobil Service Station, 125 Maybe St; (02) 6458 3047.

Bourke
Pop. 2775

MAP REF. 119 N5

Anything 'Back o' Bourke' is the real outback. Bourke itself is claimed to be the largest centre for wool shipment in the world, servicing a vast area of sheep country that produces up to 25 000 bales of wool a year. In recent times, crops such as citrus fruits, table grapes and cotton have been successful because of irrigation from the Darling River. **In town:** Many colonial buildings; self-drive historical mud-map tours, leaflet available. Old Railway Station, Anson St, has displays of Aboriginal artifacts, and local history and products. In Cobar Rd: Fred Hollows' grave and memorial in cemetery; Cotton Gin, tours in season. Bridge (1883) over Darling River, first lift-up bridge in NSW. Lock and weir, only such structure on Darling. Replica of historic wharf, Sturt St, a reminder of days when Bourke was a busy paddle-steamer port. Minibus tours of historic Bourke and of fruit and cotton farms; bookings essential, details from information centre. Easter: Fishing Competition. Sept.: Mateship Festival; Police and Community Outback Trek. Oct.: Rodeo. **In the area:** At airport, 5 km N, ultralight scenic flights, details from information centre. Replica of Fort Bourke Stockade, 20 km SW, memorial to early explorer Major Thomas Mitchell. Mt Gundabooka, 74 km S, wildlife sanctuary featuring caves with Aboriginal art (tours, contact National Parks and Wildlife Service; (08) 8088 5933). Mt Oxley, 40 km SE, views of plains from summit. **Visitor information:** Old Railway Station, Anson Street; (02) 6872 1222. Web site www.outbacknsw.org.au/bourke

Bowral
Pop. 8705

MAP REF. 110 C6, 113 I3, 115 J10

The township of Bowral nestles below Mount Gibraltar, 107 km S of Sydney. Originally a popular summer retreat for wealthy Sydney residents who left a legacy of stately mansions and beautiful gardens, Bowral is now the commercial centre of the Southern Highlands. **In town:** Corbett Gardens, Merrigang St, showpiece of Tulip Time Festival. Bradman Oval, near house where cricketer Sir Donald Bradman spent his youth, and Bradman Museum, St Jude St. Historic buildings, mostly in Wingecarribee and Bendooley sts. Specialty shopping and antiques, especially in Bong Bong St. Market, 3rd Sun. each month at Rudolf Steiner School, Lyell Ave.

Historic buildings at Silverton, near Broken Hill

Sept.–Oct.: Tulip Time Festival; District Art Society Exhibition. **In the area:** Lookout on Mt Gibraltar, 2 km N; also bushwalking trails. **Visitor information:** Southern Highlands Visitor Information Centre, 62–70 Main St, Mittagong; (02) 4871 2888 or 1300 657 559.

Braidwood
Pop. 940

MAP REF. 113 G6, 114 H13, 139 L4

This old town, 86 km S of Goulburn, has been declared a historic town by the National Trust. Gazetted in 1839, Braidwood was a pastoral centre before the discovery of gold in the area in 1851, after which it developed as the principal town of the southern goldfields. Much of the architecture from this period has survived. *Ned Kelly* (1969), *The Year My Voice Broke* (1986) and *On Our Selection* (1994) were all filmed here. **In town:** Museum, Wallace St, displays of local Aboriginal history, Chinese settlement and goldmining artifacts (open Fri.–Mon., daily during school holidays). Historic buildings include: St Andrews Church, Elrington St; St Bedes, and Royal Mail Hotel with its beautiful iron lacework, both in Wallace St. Self-guide tour of historic buildings, leaflets available. Galleries; craft and antique shops. Apr.: Heritage Festival. Nov.: Music at the Creek; The Quilt Event. **In the area:** Scenic drives, brochure available. Rainbow Valley Trout Farm at Mongarlowe, 14 km E, opportunity to catch and purchase. The Big Hole, a large sink hole, and the Marble Arch rock formation, 45 km S near Gundillion. **Visitor information:** National Theatre, Wallace St; (02) 4842 1144.

Brewarrina
Pop. 1113

MAP REF. 119 Q5

Located 97 km E of Bourke, the town of Brewarrina developed in the 1860s as a river-crossing for stock, later becoming an important river port. Today, the main industries include wool and wheat production. **In town:** Aboriginal stone fish-traps in Barwon River, once a significant food source for local Aborigines. In Bathurst St: Aboriginal Cultural Museum, displays aspects of Aboriginal life from Dreamtime to present (open Mon.–Fri.); Settlers Museum, shows local river and town life in the 1800s (open by appt). Many 19th-century buildings, built when town was a thriving river port. Self-guide drive, brochure available. Wildlife park, Doyle St. Apr.: Agricultural Show. Oct.: Darling River Outback Surfboat Classic. **In the area:** Fishing in the Barwon River. Start of Darling River Run (self-drive tour), brochure available. Narran Lake, 40 km NE, features native birdlife and other fauna. **Visitor information:** Shire Offices, Bathurst St; (02) 6839 2106. Web site www.outbacknsw.org.au

Broken Hill
Pop. 20 963

MAP REF. 118 B12

This artificial oasis in the vast arid lands of far western NSW was created to serve the miners working in the rich silver-lead-zinc mines of the Barrier Range. The mines produce around 2 million tonnes of ore annually. The green parks and colourful gardens, 1170 km NW of Sydney, seem unreal in the semi-desert setting. The city's water supply comes from local storage schemes and the Menindee Lakes on the Darling River. Note that Broken Hill operates on Central Standard Time, half an hour behind the rest of NSW. **In town:** Silver Trail self-guide historical town drive, booklet available. National Trust-classified historic streetscape, Argent St. Railway, Mineral and Train Museum, cnr Blende and Bromide sts. Albert Kersten Geocentre, cnr Crystal and Bromide sts. White's Mineral Art and Mining Museum, Allendale St. Joe Keenan's Lookout, Marks St, for view of town and mine dumps. Many art galleries, including Broken Hill City Art Gallery, cnr Blende and Chloride sts. Broken Hill is home of Brushmen of the Bush, a group of artists that includes Pro Hart and Jack Absalom. Thankakali Aboriginal Arts and Crafts, cnr Buck and Beryl sts: works created on premises; artists will explain works and symbols; sales. School of the Air, cnr McCulloch and Lane sts (open by appt, book at information centre). Delprat's Underground Tourist Mine, access via Iodide St, daily 2-hr tours (check times). Moslem mosque, Buck St, built by Afghan community in 1891. Zinc Twin Lakes, off Wentworth Rd, South Broken Hill. Sept.: Silver City Show. Oct.: Country Music Festival. **In the area:** Royal Flying Doctor Service, 10 km S (book visits at information centre). Mutawintji National Park, 130 km NE, features magnificent scenery and Aboriginal historic site, rich in rock engravings and paintings; access to site on 2-hr tour, twice weekly Apr.–Nov.; contact National Parks and Wildlife Service on (08) 8088 5933 to check road conditions and book tour. Collection of stone sculptures on hillside in Living Desert, 5 km N on Nine Mile Rd, outcome of 1993 international sculpture symposium; leaflet available. Excellent viewing of wildlife on Sundown Nature Trail (2.8 km return), begins 9 km N on Tibooburra Rd (take water); leaflet available. National Trust-classified Silverton, 27 km NW, where silver chlorides were discovered 1883; Silverton Hotel (1880), regularly features in films, documentaries and advertisements (film set photographs displayed on walls); Silverton Heritage Walking Trail (self-guide leaflet available); Silverton Gaol (1889); Nelson's Pioneer Museum; Silverton Camel Farm offers 15-min ride around outskirts of town. Mundi Mundi Plain Lookout, further 10 km N, desolate landscape was setting for *Mad Max II* (1981), *Young Einstein* (1988) and *The Adventures of Priscilla,*

Queen of the Desert (1994). Daydream Mine, 13 km NE of Silverton, operated in 1880s, 45-min guided tours weekdays (10 a.m.–3.30 p.m.). **Visitor information:** cnr Blende and Bromide sts; (08) 8087 6077. Web site www.murrayoutback.org.au

Brunswick Heads Pop. 1835

MAP REF. 117 Q2, 525 Q12

This town at the mouth of the Brunswick River is well known for its outstanding fishing, and is the base for a large commercial fishing fleet. **In town:** Canoe and paddleboat hire at The Pirate Ship on river, off Mullumbimby St. Surfing and swimming. Market at Banner Park, Fawcett St, 1st Sat. each month. Jan.: Fish and Chips (wood chop) Festival. Easter: Blessing of the Fleet; Fishing Competition. **In the area:** New Brighton Hotel, an old pub with character, 7 km NW at Billinudgel. **Visitor information:** 80 Jonson St, Byron Bay; (02) 6685 8050.

Bulahdelah Pop. 1113

MAP REF. 115 O3

Situated on the Pacific Hwy at the foot of Alum Mountain, Bulahdelah is a good base for bushwalking and houseboating. The town is surrounded by State forests and the beautiful Myall Lakes. Nov.: Show and Rodeo. **In the area:** Bulahdelah Mountain Park, a lovely park with picnic/barbecue facilities, remains of machinery used for alunite mining, rare orchids and walking track. In Bulahdelah State Forest, 14 km N off the Lakes Way, is State's tallest known tree, a flooded gum (*Eucalyptus grandis*). At Wootton, 15 km N, walking trail along a reconstructed timber railway to historic trestle bridge with picnic/barbecue facilities nearby. Myall Lakes National Park, 12 km E: contains large network (10 000 ha) of coastal lakes; ideal for water sports; houseboats for hire; bushwalking and camping in surrounding rainforest. Near fishing village of Seal Rocks, 40 km E: beaches; camping areas; Sugarloaf Point Lighthouse (1875), grounds open to public (check times), whale-spotting near base of lighthouse June–Aug. Whoota Whoota Lookout, 43 km NE in Wallingat State Forest, for magnificent views of coast and lake system. **Visitor information:** Great Lakes Tourism, Little St, Forster; (02) 6554 8799. Web site www.greatlakes.org.au

Bundanoon Pop. 1763

MAP REF. 110 A9, 113 H3, 115 J10

This town is 30 km SW of Mittagong. The area is famous for its deep gullies and views over the rugged mountains and gorges of Morton National Park. Drive and walk to several lookouts. Bundanoon was once a honeymoon resort; today it boasts an English-style pub, delightful guesthouses, a health resort, and a train stop in the heart of town. Market at Memorial Hall, Railway Ave, 1st Sun. each month. Apr.: Bundanoon is Brigadoon Annual Highland Gathering. Oct.: Village Garden Ramble. **In the area:** Bundanoon section of Morton National Park has spectacular lookouts, walking tracks and glow worms visible at night in Glow Worm Glen (access is from the end of William St, a 25-min. walk, or Riverview Rd, a 40-min. walk). Exeter, a small village 7 km N; Old English Fayre held in Nov.; fine horse studs in the area. **Visitor information:** Southern Highlands Visitor Information Centre, 62–70 Main St, Mittagong; (02) 4871 2888 or 1300 657 559. **See also:** National Parks p. 42.

Byron Bay Pop. 6130

MAP REF. 117 R2, 525 R12

Before European settlement, Byron Bay was the meeting place for local Aborigines celebrating the abundance of seafood and game in the coastal strip. Today the township of Byron Bay has become a mecca for surfing enthusiasts, backpackers and family holiday-makers. Nearby Watego Beach is the only beach on the eastern seaboard that is north-facing, making it immensely popular with surfers. Cape Byron itself is the most easterly point on the Australian mainland, its working lighthouse a majestic landmark atop 100-m-high cliffs. **In town:** Country town-like atmosphere with mixture of trendy cafes and boutiques selling everything from hemp clothing to lentil burgers. Also popular for discount surfboards, jewellery, clothing, handmade glassware and timber furniture. Dairy products, coffee, macadamia nuts and tropical fruits are produced locally. Market in Butler St, 1st Sun. each month. Easter: East Coast Blues Festival. July: A Taste of Byron Food Festival. Nov.: Buzz Film Festival. **In the area:** Bushwalking, horseriding, fishing, swimming, diving, kite-flying, skydiving. On Cape Byron, 3 km SE: Cape Byron Lighthouse, visitor centre with cultural and natural history of area;

Vineyards and Wineries

A vineyard holiday takes you through peaceful, ordered countryside and gives you the chance to learn more about wine and its making at first hand. It also gives you a perfect excuse for wine-tasting and sampling the local wines with a meal in a first-class restaurant in the area. The obvious place to head for in New South Wales is the famous Hunter Valley: the Lower Hunter Valley (around **Cessnock**) and the Upper Hunter Valley (around Denman). The region is not far from Sydney (2 hours' drive each way) and, with over 70 wineries, is one of the most important wine-growing districts in Australia. Although it can be a pleasant day trip from Sydney to the Hunter, it is well worth booking accommodation for at least one night, to do it justice.

The Hunter is Australia's oldest commercial wine-producing area, wine having first been made there in the 1830s. The Hunter's table wines, both red and white, still rank among the best in Australia.

Most of the early colonial vineyards in the region have vanished. Some family concerns have been taken over by the larger companies such as Southcorp (Lindemans) and Penfolds (McWilliams).

The high reputation of the district is maintained by such well-known properties as McWilliam's Mount Pleasant Estate, Oakvale Winery, Tulloch's Wines, Wyndham Estate and Rothbury Estate.

Most wineries welcome visitors and are open for inspection and wine-tastings daily. Several have picnic grounds, barbecue facilities and excellent restaurants which make for a pleasant day's outing.

The Cellar at McGuigan Cellars, Blaxland's at Pokolbin and the Casuarina at Pokolbin are among the restaurants in the area.

The McGuigan Cellars at Pokolbin has wine-tastings, wine sales, a gallery, accommodation at the Hunter Valley Gardens Lodge, specialty shops, a cheese factory, a restaurant, kiosk, picnic facilities and an aquagolf driving range.

It is best to go at vintage time – usually around February in the Hunter – if you want to see a vineyard in full swing. However, this is the most hectic time of year for vignerons, so do not expect their undivided attention. For an idea of the range of wineries in the district, try Tyrrell's and Drayton's wineries for a glimpse of the more traditional family approach, and Lindemans Ben Ean or Hermitage Road Cellars and Winery for the modern 'big company' style.

South of Sydney at **Camden** is Gledswood, birthplace of Australia's wine industry. The first vines were planted here in 1827; the winery was re-established as Gledswood Cellars in 1970. The winery also offers a restaurant, shearing demonstrations, horserides and picnic facilities.

You could also have an enjoyable wine-tasting holiday in the Riverina towns of **Griffith** and **Leeton**, in the other main winegrowing area of the State. Griffith, Leeton and **Narrandera** are the main towns in the Murrumbidgee Irrigation Area, which grows 70 per cent of the State's wine-producing grapes. Well-known wineries such as McWilliam's, De Bortoli Wines and Rossetto and Sons are open to visitors who wish to taste the wines of the Riverina. In Leeton, visitors are welcome to sample the vintages at Toorak Winery and Lillypilly Estate.

Around **Mudgee**, 261 kilometres north-west of Sydney, fine wines are produced from some dozen wineries. Other smaller vineyards are scattered throughout the State – some of them quite close to Sydney.

For further information on the Lower Hunter area, contact the Hunter Valley Wine Country Information Centre, Turner Park, Aberdare Rd, Cessnock; (02) 4990 4477. For information on the other wine areas, contact the local visitor information centres. Web site www.winecountry. com.au **See also:** individual entries in A–Z town listing for details on towns in bold type. **Map reference:** 107 (for Hunter Valley).

One of the many views when travelling through the vineyards of the Hunter Valley

humpback whales pass June–July and Sept.–Oct.; dolphin-watching year-round. Broken Head Nature Reserve, 9 km S, for rainforest, secluded beaches and dolphin-watching. Bangalow, 10 km SW: rustic village in magnificent scenery; art, craft and antique shops; walking tracks; market 4th Sun. each month. **Visitor information:** 80 Jonson St; (02) 6685 8050. **See also:** Wildlife-Watching p. 48.

Camden   Pop. 10 896

MAP REF. 99 K10, 110 F1, 113 I1, 115 J8

In 1805 John Macarthur was granted 5000 acres (2023 ha) at what was known as the Cowpastures; he named the area Camden Park. It was here his wife Elizabeth conducted her famous sheep-breeding experiments. The town of Camden dates from 1840, and is 60 km SW of Sydney on Camden Valley Way. **In town:** Self-guide walk and scenic drive, brochures available. Historic buildings, including: Belgenny Farm (1819) and Camden Park House (1834), open one weekend in Sept. only, both part of Macarthur's Camden Estate, Elizabeth Macarthur Ave; Church of St John the Evangelist (1840–49), John St; Camelot, designed by J. Horbury Hunt, and Kirkham Stables (1816), both in Kirkham La. Camden History Museum, John St. Market, 3rd Sat. each month at Onslow Park, 1 km S on Cawdor Rd. Feb.: Heritage Wine and Food Fair. Sept.: Camden Park House Open Weekend. **In the area:** At Narellan, 3 km NE, Museum of Aviation. Oran Park Raceway, 4 km NE, venue for bike, car and truck racing. Kirkham Estate Winery, 1 km N on Camden Valley Way, has regular jazz evenings. Struggletown Fine Arts Complex, 3 km N. Historic Gledswood homestead and winery, 10 km N; unique opportunity to experience a working colonial farm. Vicarys Winery, 25 km N (open daily). Camden Aerodrome, 3 km NW, for ballooning and gliding; vintage aircraft on display. Global Ballooning, 1-hr hot-air balloon flights over Camden Valley, bookings essential; 1800 627 661. Markets held at Cobbitty, 11 km NW, 1st Sat. each month. Wollondilly Heritage Centre and slab-built St Matthew's Church (1838) at The Oaks, 16 km W. Burragorang Lookout, 24 km W, for views over Lake Burragorang. Further west, Yerranderie, fascinating old silver-mining town; reached by 6-hr 4WD journey from Camden or 30-min. plane flight. **Visitor information:** Oxley Cottage, Camden Valley Way; (02) 4658 1370. **See also:** Vineyards and Wineries p. 53.

Campbelltown   Pop. 11 409

MAP REF. 99 L10, 110 G1, 115 K8

Founded and named by Governor Macquarie in 1820 after his wife's maiden name, Campbelltown is now a rapidly growing city 50 km SW of Sydney. It is also the location for the legend of Fisher's ghost. In 1826, an ex-convict, Frederick Fisher, disappeared. A local farmer claimed to have seen the ghost of Fisher pointing at the creek bank where his body was subsequently found. **In town:** Self-guide heritage walks, leaflet available. Campbelltown City Bicentennial Art Gallery and Japanese Gardens, Art Gallery Rd, cnr Camden and Appin rds. Historic buildings: Glenalvon (1840) and Richmond Villa (1830–40), Lithgow St; colonial houses, 284–298 Queen St; St Peter's Church (1823), Cordeaux St; Old St John's Church, cnr Broughton and George sts, with grave of James Ruse; Emily Cottage (1840), cnr Menangle and Camden rds; and Campbelltown Art and Craft Society (licensed as Farrier's Arms Inn in 1843), Courthouse (1888) and Fisher's Ghost Restaurant, formerly Kendall's Millhouse (1844), all in Queen St. Stables Museum, Lithgow St, has display of historic farm machinery and household goods. Apr.: Agricultural Show. Nov.: Festival of Fisher's Ghost. **In the area:** Winery tours, horseriding and go-kart racing; details from information centre. Eschol Park House (1820), 15 km N. Steam and Machinery Museum, 5 km SW on Menangle Rd. At Menangle, 9 km SW: The Store (1904), old-style country store selling everything from antiques to ice-creams; St James' Church (1876). Mount Annan Botanic Gardens, 3 km W, magnificent display of Australian native plants. At Appin, coal-mining town, 16 km S: monument to explorers Hume and Hovell who began their 1824 expedition to Port Phillip from this district; weekend markets in 10 locations, leaflet available; celebration of Scottish links through Highland Gathering and Pioneer Festival each Nov. **Visitor information:** Art Gallery Rd; (02) 4645 8921. Web site www.mycommunity.com.au/campbelltown

Canowindra   Pop. 1656

MAP REF. 114 E7

Bushranger Ben Hall and his gang commandeered this township in 1863. Canowindra today is known as the 'Balloon Capital of Australia' as more balloon flights take place here than anywhere else in Australia. In 1956, fish fossils of world significance, 360 million years old, were discovered 9 km SW; another major dig took place in 1993. Situated on the Belubula River, Canowindra is noted for its curving main street and fine buildings; the entire commercial section in Gaskill St has been classified by the National Trust as a Heritage Conservation Area. **In town:** In Gaskill St: Age of Fishes Museum, display includes fossils from area; local memorabilia museum (open Sun. p.m.); antique shops. Gondwana Dreaming Fossil Historical Digs; digs at 3 sites can be arranged. Hot-air balloon rides, Mar.–Nov. (weather permitting). Historical tourist drive and riverbank self-guide walks, brochures available. Apr.: Marti's Balloon Fiesta. Easter: Model Aircraft Championships. Sept.: Agricultural Show. **In the area:** Numerous wineries and vineyards, including Hamiltons Bluff, 1 km N and Wallington Wines and Swinging Bridge, 10 km NW. **Visitor information:** Age of Fishes Museum, Gaskill St; (02) 6344 1008.

Casino   Pop. 9990

MAP REF. 117 P3, 525 P12

Situated beside the Richmond River, this typical country town with its wide streets and verandahed hotels is an important commercial centre for the surrounding beef-cattle region. **In town:** Self-guide heritage and scenic walks and drives, brochures available. In Walker St: Bicentennial Mural; Casino Folk Museum (open Wed. p.m. and Sun. a.m.). Many fine buildings including public school and court-house, both in Walker St; St Mark's Church of England, West St; and Cecil Hotel, post office and Tattersall's Hotel, all in Barker St. Mini railway, West St, operates each Sun. Adjacent, Jabiru–Geneebeinga Wetlands. Eight parks in town and attractive picnic spots beside Richmond River. Tours of meat works, by appt only. May: Beef Week Festival. June: Primex (primary industry exhibition). Aug.: Gold Cup (horseracing). Oct.: Agricultural Show. **In the area:** Fossicking for gold, labradorite and smoky and clear quartz. Freshwater fishing on Cooke's Weir and Richmond River. **Visitor information:** Centre St; (02) 6662 3566. Web site www.richmondnet.com.au/casino

Cessnock
Pop. 14 860

MAP REF. 106 B10, 107 E12, 115 M4

Many excellent Hunter River table wines are produced in the Cessnock district. The economy of the city, formerly based on coal mining, is now centred on wine and tourism. **In town:** Galleries, and antique and craft shops. Feb.: Vintage Festival. Apr.: Harvest Festival. Sept.: Budburst Festival (food, wine, street parade). Oct.: Jazz in the Vines; Opera in the Vineyards. **In the area:** More than 70 quality wineries in Pokolbin area, most open for tastings and sales (see Hunter Valley map p. 107). Hot-air ballooning at Rothbury, 11 km N. Local art at Branxton Inn and Gallery, 22 km N at Branxton. Rusa Park Zoo, an exotic wildlife park at Nulkaba, 7 km NW. At Pokolbin, 13 km NW: Hunter Valley Aqua Golf, Broke Rd; Hunter Valley Cheese Factory at McGuigan Cellars complex, McDonalds Rd, for tastings, sales and viewing of processes. Picturesque village of Wollombi, 29 km SW, once Aboriginal meeting-place, has wealth of historic buildings, including beautiful St John's Anglican Church (1846); courthouse (1866), now Endeavour Museum (open Sun.); old-style combined general store and post office; tours of Aboriginal cave paintings (inquire at general store); Undercliff Winery and Studio (for etchings); Folk Festival (music, theatre, Aboriginal culture) in Sept. Watagan Mountains and State Forest, 33 km SE: splendid views and picnic/barbecue facilities at Heaton, Hunter's and McLean's lookouts. Bimbadeen Lookout over Hunter Valley, 10 km E. German Tourist and Holiday Estate, 10 km NE, has pottery, art gallery, Windarra Winery and restaurant. Charlicia Alpacas, Talga Rd, Rothbury: pat the animals; rugs and garments for sale; picnic/barbecue facilities. Richmond Vale Railway Museum, 17 km NE, offers steam-train rides (open 1st, 2nd and 3rd Sun. each month). Local art at Butterflies Gallery, 17 km NE (open Fri.–Tues.). **Visitor information:** Turner Park, Aberdare Rd; (02) 4990 4477.

Cobar
Pop. 4524

MAP REF. 119 N10

A mining town with wide tree-lined streets, Cobar is 723 km NW of Sydney. The town is at the junction of Kidman Way and the Barrier Hwy, the main road into the NSW, Qld and NT outback. Since the opening of the CSA copper mine in the mid-1960s, and the introduction of a channel water supply, the town has been transformed from an arid landscape into a green oasis. There is an abundance of native flora and fauna in the area. The Elura silver-lead-zinc mine opened in 1983, and the Peak goldmine in 1992 (Golden Walk tour of Peak mine, brochure available). Wool is the other primary industry. **In town:** Self-guide heritage walks (brochure available) and heritage bus tours of town and surroundings. Great Cobar Outback Heritage Centre, Barrier Hwy, features pastoral and mining displays. Fine early architecture, including courthouse and police station, Barton St; St Laurence O'Toole Catholic Church, Prince St; Great Western Hotel, Marshall St, with longest iron-lace verandah in NSW. Commonwealth Meteorological Station, Louth Rd (open by appt). Market, last Sat. each month at railway station. May: Agricultural Show. Aug.: Festival of the Miner's Ghost. **In the area:** Aboriginal cave paintings at Mount Grenfell Historic Site, turn-off 40 km W on Barrier Hwy, near Mount Grenfell homestead; picnic area nearby. Historic, deserted mining town of Mount Drysdale, 34 km N; tours available. **Visitor information:** Great Cobar Outback Heritage Centre, Barrier Hwy; (02) 6836 1452. Web site www.outbacknsw.org.au

Coffs Harbour
Pop. 22 177

MAP REF. 117 P8

One of the larger centres on the Holiday Coast, this subtropical holiday town is 555 km N of Sydney on the Pacific Hwy. The surrounding district produces timber, bananas, vegetables, dairy products and fish. Coffs Harbour is really two towns – one on the highway and the other near the harbour and railway station. **In town:** Coffs Harbour Explorer offers bus tours of town and surroundings. Self-guide walks, including Jetty Walk and Coffs Creek Walk, brochures available. In High St: Historic Pier Hotel (1908, rebuilt 1920s); jetty (1892, rebuilt 1997); Coffs Harbour Museum. The Marina: departure point for fishing charters and scuba-diving; whale-watching trips to the Solitary Islands (June–Nov.). A walk along northern sea wall of harbour leads to Muttonbird Island Nature Reserve, a vantage point to see migration of humpback whales June–Nov., and to see short-tailed shearwaters (muttonbirds) Aug.–Apr. North of jetty, Pet Porpoise Pool, Orlando St: performing porpoises and seals; research and nursery facilities. Aquajet Waterslide, Park Beach Rd. North Coast Regional Botanical Gardens complex, Hardacre St, has splendid rainforest and prolific birdlife. Sun. markets at jetty. Aug.: Winter Fair (antiques). Sept.: Spring Orchid Show; Garden Competition. Dec.: Pittwater to Coffs Harbour Yacht Classic. **In the area:** Whitewater rafting (on Nymboida River and Goolang Creek), canoeing, reef fishing, diving, horseriding through rainforest, Harley rides and 4WD tours; Gambaari Aboriginal Cultural Tour of coastal area; self-guide tours through Wedding Bells State Forest and the Dorrigo region (4WD only), brochures available. Clog-making and Dutch village at Clog Barn on Pacific Hwy, 2 km N. The Big Banana, 4 km N along Pacific Hwy, an unusual concrete landmark in form of huge banana with displays illustrating banana industry; skywalk through banana plantation alongside. Big Banana Theme Park features Aboriginal Dreamtime Cave experience, 'realistic' bunyip, and ice-skating rink. World of Horticulture, with monorail, is nearby. Coffs Harbour Zoo, 14 km N. Bruxner Park Flora Reserve, Korora, 9 km NW, a dense tropical jungle area of vines, ferns and orchids; bushwalking tracks and picnic area at Park Creek. Georges Gold Mine tours, 38 km W. **Visitor information:** Pacific Hwy; (02) 6652 1522. **See also:** Wildlife-Watching p. 48.

Condobolin
Pop. 3100

MAP REF. 114 A5, 121 Q3

On the Lachlan River, 475 km W of Sydney, Condobolin is the centre of a red-soil plains district producing wheat, wool, beef cattle, fat lambs, fruit and mixed farm products. Apr.: Centre Trek (car rally). Aug.: Agricultural Show. Oct.: Art Exhibition. Dec.: Rodeo. **In the area:** Aboriginal relics, 40 km W, including monument marking burial place of one of the last Lachlan group elders. Gum Bend Lake, 5 km W, good for fishing and water sports. Agricultural research station, 10 km E (open weekdays). Mt Tilga, 8 km N, said to be geographic centre of NSW; steep climb (approx. 2 km) to summit, but view is worth it. **Visitor information:** Shire Offices, 58–64 Molong St; (02) 6895 4444.

Siding Spring Observatory, near Coonabarabran, has Australia's largest optical telescope

Cooma   Pop. 7150

MAP REF. 111 A2, 113 E9, 138 G11, 241 M3
This modern tourist centre at the junction of the Monaro and Snowy Mountains hwys, on the Southern Tablelands of NSW, was once dubbed Australia's most cosmopolitan town. Thousands of migrants from many different countries worked in the region on the Snowy Mountains Scheme. It is a busy tourist centre year-round, and the jumping-off point for the Snowies. Motorists are advised to check their tyres and stock up on petrol and provisions before setting off for the alpine country. **In town:** Self-guide Lambie Town Walk includes National Trust-classified buildings in Lambie St, a street lined with huge oaks, pines and elms (brochure available). In Vale St: Old Gaol (tours, check times); courthouse (1887), designed by noted colonial architect James Barnet. Cooma Hospital (1867), Bombala St. St Paul's Church, Commissioner St, constructed with local alpine ash and granite with beautiful stained-glass windows; first service held here 1869. In Centennial Park, Sharp St: International Avenue of Flags, with flags of 27 countries unfurled in 1959 to commemorate 10th anniversary of Snowy Mountains Hydro-electric Authority and in recognition of workers' nationalities; The Time Walk, district history depicted in 40 ceramic mosaics. Also in Sharp St, Southern Cloud Park, features Southern Cloud Memorial, a display of remains of *Southern Cloud* aircraft, which crashed here in 1931 and was found in 1958. Snowy Mountains Authority Information Centre, Monaro Hwy, has displays and films on

Snowy Mountains Scheme. Alongside, Snowy Memorial, commemorating 121 people who lost their lives working on the scheme. Nanny Goat Hill Lookout, Massie St, offers views of town. Local art and craft at Loegoss Gallery and The Little Gallery, both in Sharp St. Raglan Gallery and Cultural Centre, Lambie St, originally an inn built 1854: works by local artists; permanent local history display. Bike track between Lambie St and Rotary Oval follows Cooma Creek. Weekend historic railcar trips from Cooma to Bunyan (departure details from information centre). Market, 3rd Sun. each month in Centennial Park. Jan.: Rodeo. Mar.: Agricultural Show. Oct.: Cooma Fest. **In the area:** Mt Gladstone Lookout, 6.5 km W: spectacular views; mountain-bike trails; Austrian Teahouse. Lama World, 19 km W on Snowy Mountains Hwy, cafe and shop open daily; tours and llama 'bushwalks' (bookings essential, (02) 6452 4593). Kosciuszko Memorial, 2.5 km N, donated in 1988 by the Polish Government, commemorating Tadeuz Kosciuszko (champion of the underprivileged) after whom Australia's highest mountain was named. Transylvania Winery, 14 km N on Monaro Hwy. Tuross Falls, in Wadbilliga National Park, 30 km E; 4WD access only to falls. **Visitor information:** 119 Sharp St; (02) 6450 1742, freecall 1800 636 525.

Coonabarabran   Pop. 3012

MAP REF. 116 F11
A tourist-conscious town in the Warrumbungle Mountains on the Castlereagh River, 465 km NW of Sydney, near

Warrumbungle National Park. **In town:** Crystal Kingdom, Newell Hwy, exhibits unique collection of minerals from Warrumbungle Range. At information centre, Australian Museum Diprotodon Display, featuring pre-historic animal remains from local area including a massive diprotodon skeleton. Easter: Carnival (includes market on Easter Sat.). Oct.: Festival of the Stars (includes Coona Cup Racing Carnival). **In the area:** Aboriginal cultural and ecological tours. Signposted scenic drives, self-guide brochures available. On National Park Rd: Skywatch Night and Day Observatory, 2 km NW, has interactive display, planetarium, opportunity to view night sky through telescopes, and 18-hole Astro Mini Golf (with space themes); Siding Spring Observatory, 28 km W, has Australia's largest optical telescope (3.9 m) (open day in Oct.), permanent hands-on exhibition 'Exploring the Universe', science shop and cafe. Warrumbungle National Park, 35 km W, features the Breadknife volcanic plug (a 90-m-high rock wall), bushwalking, rock-climbing, colourful wildflowers, nature study and camping facilities (guided walks in school holidays or by appt). Pilliga Pottery and Bush Cafe, 34 km NW, off Newell Hwy, terracotta pottery, showrooms and tea-rooms in bushland setting. Pilliga Scrub, 'A million wild acres', near Baradine, 44 km NW: 450 000-ha forest (biggest in NSW) of white cypress and ironbark with plains of dense heath and scrub; koala habitat; picnic areas (good koala-spotting at The Alloes); forest drives and walking tracks, maps available. Impressive sandstone caves, 35 km NE (not signposted; directions from information centre). **Visitor information:** Newell Hwy; (02) 6842 1441. Web site www.lisp.com.au/coonabarabran

Coonamble   Pop. 2754

MAP REF. 116 C10
This town on the Castlereagh Hwy is situated on the Western Plains, 518 km NW of Sydney. The district produces wheat, wool, fat lamb, beef, cypress pine and hardwood timber. **In town:** Historical Museum, in former police station and stables, Aberford St (open weekdays 10 a.m.–4 p.m.). Historical town walk, self-guide brochure available. May: Agricultural Show. June: Rodeo and Campdraft. Oct.: Gold Cup Race Meeting. Nov.: Country Music Festival. **In the area:** Hot bore baths, maps available. Warrana

Creek Weir, on southern outskirts of town, for boating, swimming and fishing. Macquarie Marshes, 80 km W, a breeding ground and sanctuary for waterbirds. At Gulargambone, 45 km S: restored steam train in Memorial Park; Gular Crays, Armitree St, large yabby hatchery, tours, cooking ideas. Swimming at Hollywood Bore, 45 km NE. **Visitor information:** Shire Council, Castlereagh St; (02) 6822 1333.

Cootamundra　Pop. 5879

MAP REF. 113 B3, 114 D10

This town on the Olympic Way, 427 km SW of Sydney, is less than 2 hours' drive from Canberra, and is well known for the Cootamundra wattle (*Acacia baileyana*). The town has a strong retail sector and is a large stock-selling centre for the surrounding pastoral and agricultural rural holdings. **In town:** Self-guide 'Two Foot Tour' around town, brochure available. Local crafts at information centre and at the Art and Craft Centre, Hovell St. Birthplace of Sir Donald Bradman, town's most famous son, at 89 Adams St. Memorabilia Cottage, next to Bradman's birthplace, displays local historical material. Captains Walk, Jubilee Park, Wallendoon St, bronze sculptures of past cricket captains. Cootamundra Public School Museum, Cooper St (check opening times). Pioneer Park, natural bushland with 1.3-km walking trail, on northern outskirts of town. Rotary markets at Albert Park, Bourke St, last Sun. each month. Aug.: Wattle Festival. Oct.: Agricultural Show. **In the area:** At Murrumburrah, 15 km NE: Harden-Murrumburrah Historical Museum (open weekends); local craft; picnic areas; Picnic Races held here in Nov. The Milestones, a series of sculptures representing the significance of wheat to this district, located between Cootamundra and Wallendbeen, 19 km NE. Wineries in the Harden area, 37 km NE; cellar-door sales. Kamilaroi Cottage Violets, 25 km N, violet farm (tours by appt). Yandilla Mustard Seed Oil, 26 km N (tours by appt). **Visitor information:** Railway station, Hovell St; (02) 6942 4212, freecall 1800 350 203.

Corowa　Pop. 5161

MAP REF. 121 O13, 239 M3

Birthplace of Australia's Federation, Corowa took its name from *currawa*, an Aboriginal word describing the pine trees that once grew there in profusion. A typical Australian country town, Corowa's wide main street, Sanger St, lined with turn-of-

the-century verandahed buildings, runs down to the banks of the Murray River. Tom Roberts' painting *Shearing of the Rams*, displayed in the National Gallery of Victoria, was completed 1889 at Brocklesby Station, just out of town. **In town:** Federation Museum, Queen St. Self-guide historical walk (guide on request for groups). Gliding joyflights and skydiving at aerodrome off Redlands Rd (weekends, weather permitting). Market in Sanger St, 1st Sun. each month. Jan.: Federation Festival. Easter: Billy Cart Races. July: Breakaway Festival. **In the area:** All Saints Estate, 5 km SE at Wahgunyah, one of the most historic and fascinating wineries in Victoria's Rutherglen district, features red-brick castle (1878) and Winemakers Hall of Fame. **Visitor information:** 88 Sanger St; (02) 6033 3221.

Cowra　Pop. 8544

MAP REF. 114 F8

The peaceful air of this busy country town on the Lachlan River belies its dramatic history. On 5 August 1944, over 1000 Japanese prisoners attempted to escape from a nearby POW camp. Four Australian soldiers and 231 Japanese prisoners died in the ensuing struggle. Blessed with rich soil and irrigated by the nearby river, Cowra is now being promoted as a destination for lovers of food and wine – asparagus, trout, beef, lamb and smallgoods are some of the quality local produce. **In town:** Australia's World Peace Bell, Darling St. Information centre has fascinating POW interpretive display; adjacent, Cowra Rose Garden. Italian POW monument, Kendal St, built in recognition of Italians who lost their lives in WW II; Italian POWs interned at Cowra forming a strong Cowra-Italy friendship (another Italian monument located at POW camp outside town). Lachlan Valley Railway and Steam Museum, Campbell St, has displays and train rides (check times). Colemane's Country Corner, cnr Mulyan and Cooyal sts, a country music museum. Cowra Mill Winery, Vaux St, winery in former flour mill (1861). Aboriginal murals on pylons of bridge over Lachlan River, by local artist Kym Freeman. Cowra Heritage Walk, self-guide brochure available. Mar.: Festival of International Understanding (including ringing of World Peace Bell). July: Picnic Races. Oct.: Sakura Matsuri (Cherry Blossom Festival). Nov.: Chardonnay Festival. **In the area:** Australian and Japanese War Cemeteries, 5 km N, beside

Cowra–Canowindra Rd (Australian soldiers who died are buried in Australian War Cemetery; Japanese soldiers who died during escape, and Japanese internees who died in Australia during World War II, are buried in Japanese War Cemetery). Sakura Ave, 5 km of flowering cherry trees, links cemeteries with POW camp and Japanese Garden which is setting for the Cultural Centre, traditional tea house, bonsai house, pottery and display of Japanese artifacts. Historic Croote Cottage, 25 km NW at Gooloogong, built by convicts and raided by bushrangers (open by appt). Conimbla National Park, 27 km W. Darby Falls Observatory, 25 km SE, where amateur astronomer has telescopes available nightly. Lake Wyangala and Grabine Lakeside State Park, 40 km SE, a mecca for water sports and fishing enthusiasts. Cowra museums (war, rail and rural museums in one complex), 5 km E on Sydney Rd. Self-guide drives, including a wine-lovers' drive, through surrounding countryside; brochure available. Numerous wineries open for tastings; details from information centre. **Visitor information:** Olympic Park, junction Boorowa, Grenfell and Young rds; (02) 6342 4333. Web site www.cowra.org

Crookwell　Pop. 2016

MAP REF. 113 F2, 114 H10

Located 46 km NW of Goulburn, Crookwell is the centre of a rich agricultural and pastoral district, producing wool, beef, fat lambs, apples and pears, and is the State's major supplier of certified seed potatoes. **In town:** Weaving Mill and Gallery, Denison La. (open Wed.–Sun.). Self-drive bushranger trails, brochure available. Market at Uniting Church, Goulburn St, 1st Sat. each month. Mar.: Crookwell Country Weekend. Spring and autumn: Open Gardens Weekend (dates from information centre). **In the area:** Quaint historic villages associated with gold, coppermining and bushranging, including Tuena, Peelwood, Laggan, Bigga, Binda (all north of town) and Roslyn (south, and birthplace of poet Dame Mary Gilmore). Redground Lookout, 8 km NW. Willow Vale Mill, 9 km NE at Laggan, restored flour mill with restaurant and accommodation. Wombeyan Caves, 60 km NE, has five caves open to public. Snowy Mountain Lookout, 42 km NW. Upper reaches of Lake Wyangala and Grabine Lakeside State Park, 65 km NW, for water-skiing, picnicking, fishing, bushwalking and camping. **Visitor information:** 44 Goulburn St; (02) 4832 1988.

Culcairn   Pop. 1164

MAP REF. 121 Q12, 239 Q1

Dating back to 1880 and planned to service the railway between Sydney and Melbourne, Culcairn today reflects the district's rural prosperity. Bushranger Dan Morgan began his life of crime at Round Hill Station, with a hold-up on 19 June 1864. The town owes its picturesque tree-lined streets and parks to its unlimited underground water supply (discovered 1926). **In town:** Historic Culcairn Hotel (1891), Railway Pde. Many National Trust-classified buildings on Railway Pde and Olympic Way. Also in Railway Pde, French's Furniture, for rustic Australian-style furniture. Local crafts at N & H Crafts, Balfour St. Centenary Mural, Main St. Artesian pumping station, Gordon St. **In the area:** John McLean's Grave, 3 km E; a price was put on Morgan's head after he shot McLean. Round Hill Station, Holbrook Rd. At Walla Walla, 18 km SW: Old Schoolhouse (1875), museum and largest Lutheran church (1924) in NSW. Morgan's Lookout, 18 km NW. Premier Yabbies, 7 km S, hatchery and catch-your-own (closed Tues.). Pioneer Museum at Jindera, 42 km S. **Visitor information:** Post Office, 33a Balfour St; (02) 6029 8521.

Deniliquin   Pop. 7816

MAP REF. 121 L11

At the centre of the most extensive irrigation area in Australia, Deniliquin has the largest rice export mill in the world. The town is located beside the Edward River, 750 km SW of Sydney. The northern part of the district is famed for its merino sheep studs, including Wanganella and Boonoke. **In town:** Historical and nature walk, self-guide brochure available. National Trust-classified Old George Street Public School (1879), George St, now houses Peppin Heritage Centre, a museum dedicated to the development of merino sheep industry by the Peppin family last century; also houses the information centre and presents history of local rice and irrigation industry. Other National Trust-classified buildings: Courthouse (1883), Poictiers St; former Anglican church (1887), now Multi Arts Centre, Cressy St, surrounded by Waring Gardens; former Police Inspectors Residence (1880s), MacCauley St, now home to Deniliquin Historical Society (check opening times). Sun Rice Centre, Rice Mill Rd, has visitors centre and presentations (weekdays). Blake Botanic Reserve, cnr Harfleur and Fowler sts, community project to present local flora in their natural environments. Island Sanctuary, off Cressy St footbridge, features free-ranging kangaroos and prolific birdlife. River beaches, including McLean and Willoughby's beaches. Market, 4th Sat. each month. Soroptomist Market, in McFaulls Park, Civic Centre, 2nd Sun. in Mar. and Oct. Jan.: Sun Festival. Easter: Jazz Festival. Oct.: 'Play on the Plains' Festival. **In the area:** Pioneer Tourist Park, 2 km N: art and craft gallery; nursery; blacksmith shop; antique steam and pump display; mini rural museum. Bird Observatory Tower at Mathoura, 34 km S. Irrigation works at Lawsons Syphon, 7 km E and Stevens Weir, 25 km W. Conargo Pub, 25 km NE, authentic bush pub with gallery of photographs depicting history of merino wool in the area. **Visitor information:** Peppin Heritage Centre, George St; (03) 5881 2878, freecall 1800 650 712.

Dorrigo   Pop. 1013

MAP REF. 117 O8

This important timber town, located on the eastern edge of the Dorrigo Plateau, is surrounded by magnificent river, mountain and forest scenery. Today, Dorrigo is increasingly recognised as a place to enjoy country cooking and browse through art and craft shops. **In town:** Historical Museum, Cudgery St (check opening times). For local crafts: Calico Cottage, Hickory St, and The Art Place and Country Crafts, Cudgery St. Wood Fired Bakery, Hickory St. Market at Showground, Armidale Rd, 1st Sat. each month. Easter: Arts and Crafts Exhibition. Oct.: Spring Festival. **In the area:** Trout fishing and white-water rafting. Scenic drives, brochures available. Dangar Falls, 2 km N, viewing platform over wall of water 30 m high. Ebor Falls, 46 km W, in Guy Fawkes River National Park, where river plunges off the tablelands; cliff-top viewing platforms above. Cathedral Rock National Park, 56 km SW, picnicking and many walks (including 2-hr loop walk to the summit of Cathedral Rock for 360° views of tableland). L. P. Dutton Trout Hatchery near Ebor, 63 km SW. Point Lookout, 74 km SW, in New England National Park, for stunning views over head of Bellinger Valley, across to ocean. Dorrigo National Park, 3 km E, features luxuriant rainforest waterfalls; wide variety of birds including bowerbirds and lyrebirds; Rainforest Centre, with picnic facilities, cafe, video theatre and exhibitions; Skywalk, board-walk offering views over canopy of World Heritage-listed rainforest; Walk with the Birds Birdwalk. Griffiths Lookout, 6 km S, for sweeping views of ranges. **Visitor information:** Hickory St; (02) 6657 2486. **See also:** Wildlife-Watching p. 48.

Dubbo   Pop. 30 102

MAP REF. 114 E2

This pleasant city on the banks of the Macquarie River, 420 km NW of Sydney, is recognised as the regional capital of western NSW, and supports many agricultural and secondary industries. **In town:** In Macquarie St: Old Dubbo Gaol, featuring original gallows and solitary confinement cells, and animatronic robots telling story of convicts; Dubbo Museum; Indiginart, Aboriginal art and craft from central/western New South Wales. Dubbo Art Gallery, Darling St, constantly developing collection of 'Animals in Art', generally on display during school holidays (open Wed.–Mon.). Market at Dubbo Showgrounds, 2nd Sun. each month. Easter: Orana Country Music Easter Festival. May: Agricultural Show. June: Eisteddfod. Aug.: Jazz Festival. **In the area:** Western Plains Zoo, 5 km S, Australia's first open-range zoo: over 1000 animals from five continents, set in more than 300 ha of natural bushland; program of keeper talks and early morning walks; accommodation. Tracker Riley Cycleway from Dubbo to zoo (5 km); inquire at information centre for directions and bicycle hire. Heritage drives, self-guide brochures available. Macquarie River cruises. Military Museum, 8 km S, with open-air exhibits. Dundullimal homestead (1840s), 7 km SE on Obley Rd, restored squatter's slab-style homestead, with working saddler and blacksmith, animals and Woolshed Cafe. Wellington Caves and phosphate mine, 58 km SE: huge stalagmite; unique limestone coral; fossils; guided tours. Opposite caves, Japanese gardens, a gift from sister city of Osawano. Burrendong Arboretum, 80 km SE: 160 ha preserving endangered plants; constructed rainforest with water features, paths and bridges. Lake Burrendong for water sports; picnic/barbecue and camping facilities. Golfworld, 3 km N in Fitzroy St, has driving range and mini-golf course. Jinchilla Gardens and Gallery, 12 km N, off Gilgandra Rd. **Visitor information:** cnr Erskine and Macquarie sts; (02) 6884 1422. Web site www.dubbo.com.au

Dungog   Pop. 2181

MAP REF. 106 A1, 115 N3

Dungog was established in 1838 as a military post to prevent bushranging in the area. Situated on the upper reaches of the Williams River, the town is on a main access route to Barrington Tops National Park, making it an ideal base for bushwalkers. Apr.: Rodeo. Sept.: Spring Festival. Nov.: Agricultural Show. **In the area:** Chichester Dam, 23 km N, in picturesque mountain setting; nearby Duncan Park is ideal for picnicking. Telegherry Forest Park, 30 km N, with walking trails along Telegherry River and picnic, swimming and camping spots. Good walking trails in surrounding State forest. World Heritage-listed Barrington Tops National Park, 40 km N, has unusual native flora and rich variety of wildlife; good bushwalking, including Jerusalem Creek Trail to waterfalls; forest drives. Superb views from Mt Allyn (1100 m), 40 km NW. Clarence Town historic village, 24 km SE, one of the first European settlements in Australia. **Visitor information:** cnr Brown and Dowling sts; (02) 4992 2212. Web site www.dungong.nsw.gov.au **See also:** National Parks p. 42.

Eden   Pop. 3106

MAP REF. 111 F11, 113 G11, 241 Q8

Eden is a quiet former whaling town on Twofold Bay, 512 km S of Sydney, with an outstanding natural harbour. Fishing and timber-getting are the main industries. **In town:** Eden Killer Whale Museum, Imlay St, features skeleton of 'Tom the killer whale', who assisted early whalers in locating their prey. Whale-watching (particularly humpbacks) Oct.–Nov., from platforms on Showground Rd along Aslings Beach. Mar.: Amateur Fish Club Competition. Oct.: Eden Whale Festival. **In the area:** Whale-watching and other bay cruises available. At Jiggamy Farm, near Pambula Lake, 9 km N, Aboriginal cultural experience and introduction to bush tucker at Monarroo Bubbaroo Guddoo Keeping Place. Ben Boyd National Park, extending north and south of Eden, has outstanding scenery and fishing, swimming, wreck-diving, bushwalking

The South Coast

The southern coast of New South Wales, from Batemans Bay to the Victorian border, is one of the finest areas for fishing in southern Australia. It is also a haven for anyone who enjoys swimming, surfing or bushwalking in an unspoiled setting.

One of the attractions of this stretch of coast is the variety of country: superb white surf beaches and crystal-clear blue sea against a backdrop of mountains, gentle hills, lakes and inlets. The coast is dotted with quaint little fishing and holiday towns, offering a wide range of accommodation, including caravan parks. These towns are not highly commercialised, although many of them triple their population in the peak summer months.

Peaceful **Batemans Bay**, at the estuary of the Clyde River, is very popular with the landlocked residents of Canberra, the national capital. **Narooma**, Montague Island and **Bermagui** are well known for their game-fishing; black marlin, blue fin and hammerhead sharks are the main catch. Narooma also boasts a superb 18-hole cliff-side golf course.

Bega, to the south, is the unofficial capital of the area and is an important dairying and cheese-making centre. As Bega is about 10 minutes inland from the coast and 2 hours from the snow fields, the town's proud boast is that you can ski in the Snowies and surf in the Pacific on the same day. South-east of Bega is the seaside town of Tathra with its National Trust-classified historic wharf. Further south is the popular holiday resort of **Merimbula** and its sister village of Pambula.

The southernmost town of the region is the quaint old fishing town of **Eden** and its former rival settlement Boydtown, both reminders of the colourful whaling days of the last century. Whale-watching is popular in Eden in the months of October and November.

Rugged coastline east of Boydtown

Fishing is excellent all along the coast. You can catch a variety of fish, including rock cod, bream and jewfish, from the beach or net crayfish off the rockier parts of the coast. Prawning is good in the scattered inlets, and trout and perch can be caught in the many rivers draining from the mountains.

The region's year-round mild climate has made it a favourite with visitors, but you must book well ahead in the peak holiday period.

For further information, contact Sapphire Coast Tourism, 2/163 Auckland St, Bega; (02) 6492 3313, freecall 1800 633 012. Web site address www.sapphirecoast.com.au **See also:** Wildlife-Watching p. 48 and individual entries in A–Z town listing for towns in bold type. **Map references:** 111, 113 H11, 127.

and camping; in park are Boyd's Tower (1840s) at Red Point (32 km SE), and the Pinnacles, red and white earth formations (8 km N). On perimeter of park, 9 km S, on shores of Twofold Bay, former rival settlement of Boydtown has convict-built Seahorse Inn (still licensed), safe beach and excellent fishing. Davidson Whaling Station Historic Site on Kiah Inlet, 30 km SE. Harris Daishowa Chipmill Visitors Centre, Jews Head, 34 km SE, has displays on logging and milling (open daily, tours Thurs. 10.30 a.m.). Scenic drive and easy rainforest walk at Nadgee State Forest, 35 km SE. Green Cape Lighthouse, 45 km SE, tours. Good fishing and 4WD tracks at Wonboyn Lake, 40 km S; scenic area between Ben Boyd National Park and Nadgee Nature Reserve. **Visitor information:** Princes Hwy; (02) 6496 1953. Web site www.sapphirecoast.com.au **See also:** The South Coast p. 59.

Eugowra   Pop. 612

MAP REF. 114 E6

Eugowra is situated in the rich basin of the Lachlan River. It was near this small town on the Orange–Forbes Road that 'the great gold-escort robbery' occurred in 1862. Today, Eugowra is known for its craft cottages and hand-crafted jewellery. **In town:** Eugowra Museum, displaying Aboriginal artifacts, gemstones, early farm equipment and wagons. Nangar Gems, Norton St, for sapphires, opals, emeralds and garnets. **In the area:** Escort Rock, 3 km E, where bushranger Frank Gardiner and gang (which included Ben Hall) hid before ambush of Forbes gold escort; plaque on road gives details, unlocked gate allows entry. Nanami Lane Lavender Farm, 19 km SE. **Visitor information:** Orange Information Centre, Civic Gardens, Byng St, Orange; (02) 6361 5226.

Evans Head   Pop. 2613

MAP REF. 117 Q4, 525 Q13

Situated off the Pacific Hwy via Woodburn, this holiday and fishing town is the centre of the NSW prawning industry. It has extensive surf beaches and sandy river flats. Rock, beach, river and ocean fishing, boating and windsurfing are popular activities. Markets, cnr Oak and Park sts, 4th Sat. each month. July: Fishing Classic. Aug.: Bowling Carnival. **In the area:** At Bundjalung National Park, just south: Aboriginal relics, fishing, swimming and bushwalking. Broadwater National Park, 5 km N, for bushwalking,

birdwatching, fishing and swimming. At Woodburn, 11 km NW, Riverside Park beside Richmond River; further 14 km S at New Italy, monument and remains of settlement, result of the ill-fated Marquis de Ray expedition in 1880. In New Italy Complex, Guuragai Aboriginal Arts and Crafts offers quality works and information about Aboriginal culture. **Visitor information:** The Professionals Real Estate, 9 Oak St; (02) 6682 4611.

Finley   Pop. 2137

MAP REF. 121 M12, 238 I1

This town on the Newell Hwy, 21 km from the Victorian border, is the centre of the Berriquin irrigation scheme. **In town:** Mary Lawson Wayside Rest, Log Cabin (replica) and museum, Murray St (Newell Hwy), has display of rural heritage and information centre. Finley Lake, north of town on Newell Hwy, for boating and sailboarding; picnic areas on lake banks. Jan.: Rodeo and Country Music Festival. Sept.: Agricultural Show. **In the area:** Historic town of Berrigan, 22 km E, best known for its connections with horseracing. Near Berrigan, Sojourn Station Art Studio (3 km SE) and Grassleigh Woodturning (15 km NE). **Visitor information:** Mary Lawson Wayside Rest, Murray St; (03) 5883 2195.

Forbes   Pop. 7467

MAP REF. 114 D6

Bushranger Ben Hall was shot by police in 1865 just outside this former gold-mining town, located 386 km W of Sydney beside the Lachlan River. Today the town's industries include an abattoir, feed lots, pet food manufacture, and export of beef and hay. **In town:** Many historic buildings, especially in Camp and Lachlan sts. Bushranger Hall of Fame in Albion Hotel, Lachlan St. Historic town walk, brochure available. Historical museum, Cross St, featuring relics associated with colonial life and with Ben Hall. Cemetery, Bogan Gate Rd, has graves of Ben Hall, Kate Foster (Ned Kelly's sister), and Rebecca Shields (Captain Cook's niece). Memorial in King George V Park, Lawler St, where 'German Harry' discovered gold in 1861. In small park in Dowling St, memorial marks spot where explorer John Oxley first passed through Forbes. Fossil sites on town outskirts, details from information centre. Markets in Lawler St, last Sat. each month. Jan.: Jazz Festival; Flatlands Hang-Gliding

Championships. Mar.: Ben Hall Bike Show. Sept.: Agricultural Show. Oct.: Carnivale (balloon spectacular). **In the area:** Sandhills Vineyard, 5 km E off Orange Rd. Lachlan Vintage Village, 1 km S, historic buildings re-create district life 1860–1900, including gold rush era. Gum Swamp Sanctuary for varied birdlife and other fauna, 4 km S. **Visitor information:** Old Railway Station, Union St; (02) 6852 4155. Web site www.forbes.nsw.gov.au/fbsinfo

Forster   Pop. 10 443

MAP REF. 115 P2

Forster is connected by a bridge to its twin town Tuncurry on the opposite side of Wallis Lake, a holiday area in the Great Lakes district. The area is well known for its fishing and is a major producer of oysters. Launches and boats may be hired for lake and deep-sea fishing. **In town:** Forster Arts and Craft Centre, Breese Pde. Tobwabba Art Studio, cnr Breckenridge and Little sts, specialises in urban coastal Aboriginal art, from paintings on canvas to decorative tiles. Wallis Lake Fishermen's Co-op, Wharf St (Tuncurry), for fresh and cooked oysters and ocean fish. Dolphin-spotting cruises and lake cruises available. Dolphins can also be seen from Tuncurry Breakwall and Bennetts Head. Pebbly Beach Bicentennial Walk, gentle 2-km walk to Bennetts Head, commences at baths off North St. Apr.: Australian Ironman Triathlon. Oct.: Oyster Festival. Nov.: Half Ironman Triathlon. **In the area:** 4WD nature and eco tours of Great Lakes area, includes bushwalks. Curtis Collection Museum of vintage cars, 3 km S. Cape Hawke, 8 km S, take steep 400-m track to summit for views of Wallis Lake, Seal Rocks and inland to Great Dividing Range. The Green Cathedral, at Tiona on shores of Wallis Lake, 13 km S, open-air church, complete with pews and altar, sheltered by a natural cabbage tree palm canopy. Booti Booti National Park, 17 km S (access from The Lakes Way), includes Elizabeth, Boomerang and Blueys beaches, for surfing, swimming and fishing. Smiths Lake, 30 km S, sheltered lake for safe swimming. Sugar Creek Toymakers, 38 km S at Bungwahl. **Visitor information:** Great Lakes Tourism, Little St; (02) 6554 8799. Web site www.greatlakes.org.au

Gerringong   Pop. 2891

MAP REF. 110 G10, 115 K11

Spectacular views of white sand and rolling breakers can be seen from this town, 10 km S of Kiama on the Illawarra Coast. **In town:** Heritage museum, Blackwood St (check opening times). **In the area:** Surfing, fishing and swimming at local beaches. Gerroa and Seven Mile beaches, 3 km S, world-famous as windsurfing locations. Memorial to pioneer aviator Sir Charles Kingsford Smith and lookout at northern end of Seven Mile Beach, site of his take-off to New Zealand in the *Southern Cross* in 1933. Bushwalks through Seven Mile Beach National Park, 13 km S, brochures available; camping and picnic areas. **Visitor information:** Blowhole Pt Rd, Kiama; (02) 4232 3322. Web site www.kiama.com.au

Gilgandra   Pop. 2822

MAP REF. 116 D13

A historic town at the junction of three highways, Gilgandra is the centre for the surrounding wool and farming country. It was the home of the famous 'Coo-ee March', which left from Gilgandra for Sydney in 1915 to recruit more soldiers for World War I. The area is also known for its windmills, which once provided sub-artesian water. **In town:** Heritage Museum at information centre, Newell Hwy, displays memorabilia from 'Coo-ee March'. Film *The Chant of Jimmy Blacksmith* was based on Breelong Massacre, which took place near Gilgandra; related items in museum. Also on Newell Hwy: Orana Cactus World; Rural Museum, featuring antique farm machinery (check opening times). Hitchen House Museum, Miller St, has memorabilia from world wars I and II, and Vietnam. At Gil Nursery, Eiraben St, model railway exhibition. The Observatory and Display Centre, cnr Wamboin and Willie sts. Tourist drives around town and to Flora Reserve, brochures available. Easter: Vintage Farm and Steam Rally. May: Agricultural Show. Oct.: Coo-ee Festival. **In the area:** Gilgandra Flora Reserve, 14 km NE, has wildflowers in spring. **Visitor information:** Coo-ee March Memorial Park, Newell Hwy; (02) 6847 2045.

Glen Innes   Pop. 6101

MAP REF. 117 L6

Gazetted in 1852, this highland town was the scene of many bushranging exploits. In a beautiful setting, at an elevation of 1073 m, it is now the centre of a rich farming district where sapphire mining is important. **In town:** Many historic public buildings, particularly in Grey St; self-guide walks, brochures available. Centennial Parklands with Martin's Lookout, Meade St, now site of Celtic monument 'Australian Standing Stones'; Crofters Cottage, adjacent, provides explanation of monument. Cooramah Aboriginal Cultural Centre, cnr McKenzie St and New England Hwy, for Aboriginal art and craft, historic artifacts, restaurant with bush tucker. Land of the Beardies History House, cnr Ferguson St and West Ave, a folk museum in town's first hospital and set in extensive grounds, with reconstructed slab hut, period room settings and pioneer relics. Market in Grey St, 2nd Sun. each month. Feb.: Show. Mar.: Minerama Gem Festival.

New England

Despite the scenery, it is worth keeping your eyes on the ground if you pull over for a rest in the New England area. Some of the best fossicking specimens in the district have been found by the roadside. All kinds of quartz, jaspers, serpentine, crystal and chalcedony are found in this area – not to mention sapphires, diamonds and gold, though these are harder to find.

The round trip from **Nundle**, through **Tamworth**, **Manilla**, **Barraba**, **Bingara**, **Warialda**, then on to the New England towns of **Inverell** and **Glen Innes** and back, is known as 'The Fossickers' Way' and tourist signs have been placed at intervals to guide the motorist. Nearby is the Copeton Dam, which holds two-and-a-half times as much water as Sydney Harbour, with part of its foreshores forming Copeton State Recreational Area.

Glen Innes and Inverell have nearby sapphire reserves where fossickers may hire tools and try their luck. One of the largest finds to date in the Nullamanna Fossicking Reserve, near Inverell, is a 70-carat blue, valued at $3000.

The New England district is the largest area of highlands in Australia, and has plenty to offer besides gemstones. The countryside is varied and lovely, with magnificent mountains, and streams cascading into spectacular gorges, contrasting with the rich blacksoil plains

Rural scene near Glen Innes

of wheat and cotton to the west. Some of the State's most outstanding national parks and World Heritage features are found in New England, and the Southern Hemisphere's largest granite monolith, Bald Rock, is located near **Tenterfield**.

Fishing is excellent, with trout in the streams of the tablelands, and cod and yellow-belly in the lower New England rivers to the west. You can also fish, picnic, swim, sail or water-ski at Pindari and Copeton dams.

Other towns in the New England area – Ashford, Delungra, **Guyra**, Tingha, **Walcha**, **Uralla** and Deepwater, and the university city of **Armidale** – also have much to offer.

For further information, contact the Visitors Centre and Coach Station, 82 Marsh St, Armidale; (02) 6772 4655, freecall 1800 627 736. Web site www.new-england.org/armidale **See also:** individual entries in A–Z town listing for towns in bold type. **Map reference:** 117 M7.

Goulburn Courthouse features an interesting dome

May: Celtic Festival. Nov.: Land of the Beardies Bush Festival. **In the area:** Scenic mountain and riverside country. Good fishing for trout, perch and cod; fishing safaris at Deepwater, 40 km N. Fossicking for sapphire, topaz and quartz; includes Emmaville, old mining town 39 km NW, and Torrington 66 km NW (also has unique rock formations). Horse treks, with accommodation at historic bush pubs available. Convict-carved tunnel, halfway between Glen Innes and Grafton, on Old Grafton Rd. Gibraltar Range National Park, 70 km NE, has impressive falls, and The Needles and Anvil Rock granite formations. World Heritage-listed Washpool National Park, 75 km NE, a rainforest wilderness area. At The Willows, 45 km NW: farm and Aboriginal tourism centre with activities reflecting traditional lifestyle (permit from Cooramah Centre in town); fishing, bushwalking, camping, 4WD tracks. Unusual balancing rock formations at Stonehenge, 18 km S. Guy Fawkes River National Park, 77 km SE, wild river area ideal for bushwalking, canoeing and fishing. **Visitor information:** Church St; (02) 6732 2397. **See also:** New England p. 61.

Glenbrook   Pop. 5059

MAP REF. 99 J7, 101 Q8
As with many other towns in the lower Blue Mountains, Glenbrook began as a water-stop for the steam engines that came up the Lapstone Zig Zag Railway line. **In town:** Lapstone Zig Zag Walking Track (3 km return), northern outskirts of town, follows cutting for original Lapstone Zig Zag Railway; features Lennox Bridge, Knapsack Bridge and numerous lookouts.

Nearby monument to John Whitton, who had a key role in the development of the railway. Market at Community Hall, Great Western Hwy, 1st Sun. each month (not Jan.). Sept.– Oct.: Legacy Gardens Festival. Nov.: Spring Festival. **In the area:** Convict-built Lennox Bridge, 5km NW on Mitchells Pass Rd, oldest surviving bridge on the mainland. Wascoe Siding Miniature Railway (operates 1st Sun. each month), 2.5 km W off Great Western Hwy. Euroka Clearing, 4 km S, popular for camping and eastern grey kangaroos; Red Hands Cave, 15 km S, historic Aboriginal stencils and handprints; details at information centre. At Linden, 20 km W: Kings Cave; nearby, Caleys Repulse Cairn, commemorating early surveyor George Caley. Faulconbridge, 16 km NW: Corridor of Oaks, trees planted by recent Australian Prime Ministers; grave of Sir Henry Parkes, 'father' of Federation; Norman Lindsay Gallery and Museum (open daily). At Springwood, 12 km NW: Ivy Markets at Civic Centre, Macquarie Rd, 2nd Sat. each month (not Jan.); Blue Gum Market at school in Macquarie Rd, 4th Sat. each month; Hawkesbury Lookout, further 10 km NE on Hawkesbury Rd, offers views across plains to Penrith. **Visitor information:** Great Western Hwy, Glenbrook; freecall 1300 653 408. **See also:** Blue Mountains Experience p. 38; National Parks p. 42; Wildlife-Watching p. 48.

Gloucester   Pop. 2634

MAP REF. 115 N1
This town lies at the foot of a range of monolithic hills, The Bucketts, at the junction of three tributaries of the

Manning River. Set in dairy, timber and beef-cattle country, Gloucester is known for its gourmet-quality Barrington beef and perch. **In town:** Heritage walk, brochure available. Belbouri Aboriginal Art Centre, Hume St. Market at Billabong Park, Denison St, Sat. of each long weekend. May: Shakespeare Festival. Sept.: Mountain Man Triathlon (kayaking, mountain-biking and running). **In the area:** Excellent fishing for trout and perch. The Bucketts Walk (1 hr 30 min. return), just west of town, leads up Bucketts Mountain Range offering good views. Scenic flights from aerodrome, 4 km S. Views from Mograni Lookout (5 km E), Kia-ora Lookout (4 km N) and Berrico Trig Station (14 km W). Goldtown, at Copeland, 16 km W, former site of Mountain Maid Goldmine (1876), now largely covered with rainforest: underground mine tours; gold-panning; historical museum (check opening times). Barrington Tops Forest Drive from Gloucester to Scone (sections of road may be covered with ice and snow in winter), features rainforest walks, picnic spots and views of rugged eastern escarpment; self-guide drive and walk brochures available. Variety of farm tours by appt. **Visitor information:** 27 Denison St; (02) 6558 1408. Web site www.gloucester.org.au

Gosford   Pop. 25 690

MAP REF. 99 P4, 102 F6, 115 M6
Gosford, part of the scenic Central Coast, is 85 km N of Sydney on the beautiful Brisbane Water. Sept.: Springtime Flora Festival; Gosford to Lord Howe Island Yacht Race. Oct.: Mangrove Mountain District Country Fair; Gosford City Arts Festival. **In the area:** Gosford City Arts Centre, Webb St, 3 km E, has local art and craft and Japanese Garden. Henry Kendall Cottage (1838), 3 km SW in Henry Kendall St, where poet lived 1874–5; picnic/barbecue facilities in pleasant grounds. Australian Reptile Park and Wildlife Sanctuary, at Somersby, 15 km SW, features a snake house with taipans and pythons, goannas and a platypus. Adjacent is Old Sydney Town, a reconstruction of early pioneer settlement. Somersby Falls, near Old Sydney Town, ideal picnic spot. Aboriginal engraving site at Bulgandry, 10 km SW in Brisbane Water National Park; also spectacular waratahs here in spring. Bouddi National Park, 17 km SE, for bushwalking, camping, fishing and swimming. Central Coast Winery, 11 km NE. Forest of Tranquillity at Ourimbah, 14 km NW,

walking trails through rainforest; Firefly Festival held here mid-Nov.–mid-Dec. **Visitor information:** 200 Mann St; (02) 4385 4430, freecall 1800 806 258. **See also:** National Parks p. 42.

Goulburn   Pop. 21 293

MAP REF. 113 G3, 114 H11

This provincial city, steeped in history, can be approched from the Hume Hwy bypass some 202 km SW of Sydney. It is the centre of a wealthy farming district at the junction of the Wollondilly and Mulwaree rivers beyond the Southern Highlands. **In town:** National Trust-classified coach-house Riversdale (1840), Maud St. St Clair History House (c.1843), Sloane St, a 20-room mansion restored by local historical society. Garroorigang, Braidwood Rd, South Goulburn (1857), private home in almost original condition. Old Goulburn Brewery Hotel, Bungonia Rd. Goulburn Courthouse, Montague St, has interesting dome. In Bourke St: Regional Art Gallery; St Saviour's Cathedral. Cathedral of St Peter and St Paul, cnr Bourke and Verner sts. Two-foot Walking Tour (2 hours) of historic town buildings, brochure available. Fibre Design gallery, Montague St. The Big Merino, a 15-m sculptured relief, Hume Hwy, has displays of wool products and Australiana for sale. South Hill, Garoorigang Rd, features woollen art. Excellent picnic/barbecue facilities on Wollondilly River at Marsden Weir. Rocky Hill War Memorial, Memorial Dr., city's best-known landmark, built in memory of local World War I soldiers. East Goulburn Markets, 3rd Sat. each month. Jan./Feb.: Australian Blues Music Festival. Mar.: Rose Show; Weekend of Heritage. Oct.: Lilac City Festival. **In the area:** Shearing and sheepdog demonstrations (by appt) at Pelican Sheep Station, 10 km S. Geologically interesting Bungonia State Recreation Area, 35 km E; range of walks, including one through the spectacular Bungonia Gorge, brochures available. **Visitor information:** Sloane St; (02) 4823 4492.

Grafton   Pop. 16 562

MAP REF. 117 P6

A garden city, noted for its riverbank parks and the jacaranda, wheel and flame trees lining its wide streets, Grafton is at the junction of the Pacific and Gwydir hwys, 665 km N of Sydney. **In town:** Numerous National Trust-classified buildings. Schaeffer House (1900), Fitzroy St, now district historical museum. Stately Prentice House, Fitzroy St, houses a fine regional art gallery. Susan Island in Clarence River, a rainforest recreation reserve and home to large fruit bat colony. Rivercat for self-drive hire or skippered cruises. Alumy Greek Markets, Southgate Rd, last Sat. each month; Southside Markets, cnr Spring and New sts, South Grafton, 3rd Sat. each month. July: Racing Carnival (horse-racing). Oct.: Bridge to Bridge Ski Race. Oct.–Nov.: Jacaranda Festival. Nov.: Bridge to Bridge Sailing Classic. **In the area:** Four major national parks within hour's drive: Yuraygir (50 km E), Bundjalung (70 km N), Washpool (88 km NW) and Gibraltar Range (92 km NW). National Trust-classified Ulmarra village, 12 km NE, a turn-of-the-century river port. Houseboat hire at Brushgrove, 20 km NE. Weekend gliding at Eatonsville, 18 km NW. Four scenic drives, self-guide brochures available. Canoeing and rafting on wild rivers in surrounding area. **Visitor information:** cnr Spring St and Pacific Hwy, South Grafton; (02) 6642 4677.

Grenfell   Pop. 1956

MAP REF. 113 B1, 114 D8

The birthplace of poet and short-story writer Henry Lawson, this small town is 377 km W of Sydney, on the Mid Western Hwy. **In town:** Henry Lawson Obelisk, next to Lawson Park on road south to Young, on site of house where poet is believed to have been born in 1867. Bust of Henry Lawson, Main St. Historic George St has many buildings dating back to 1860s. Guide to Historic Buildings of Grenfell (walk) and Tour of Grenfell Town (drive); brochures available. Museum, Camp St (open weekends). Off Mid Western Hwy, O'Brien's Reef Lookout, where gold was discovered, has walkway and picnic facilities; endemic garden and iris garden adjacent to lookout (access from O'Brien St). Grenfell House (1907), Weddin St, former convent, now tearooms and B&B. Easter: Guinea Pig Races. June: Henry Lawson Festival of Arts; Guinea Pig Races. Oct.: Iris Festival. Nov.: Grenfell Guineas (horseracing). **In the area:** Weddin Mountains National Park, 18 km SW, for bushwalking, camping and picnicking; area used as hideout by bushrangers Ben Hall, Frank Gardiner, Johnnie Gilbert and others; easy walk to Ben Hall's Cave and to Seaton's Farm, a historic homestead within park; self-guide drive/walk, brochure available. Site of Ben Hall's farmhouse and stockyards, 25 km W, on Sandy Creek Rd, off Mid Western Hwy. Lirambenda Riding School and Animal Farm, 20 km S. Adelargo Drive, features Cypress Valley Ostrich Facility, 30 km NE on Peaks Creek Rd; self-guide brochure available. Company Dam Nature Reserve, 1 km NW, for bushwalking. Old Richmond Cottage, 30 km W at Quandialla, for tours of cottage gardens, bush stories, poetry readings and devonshire teas (by appt only). **Visitor information:** CWA Craft Centre, 68 Main St; (02) 6343 1612.

Griffith   Pop. 14 209

MAP REF. 121 N7

A thriving city developed as a result of the introduction of irrigation, Griffith was designed by Walter Burley Griffin, architect of Canberra, and named after Sir Arthur Griffith, the first Minister for Public Works in the NSW government. Of a diversity of industries, rice is the most profitable, followed by citrus fruits, grapes, vegetables, eggs and poultry. Griffith is also well known as a wine-producing area; there are over a dozen wineries in the district, while the Murrumbidgee Irrigation Area produces more than 70 percent of the State's wines. **In town:** Two Foot Tour and self-drive tour, brochures available. Riverina Grove, Whybrow St, local jar produce (tastings). In Banna Ave: Regional Theatre has stage curtain designed and created by 300 residents, to reflect city, surrounding villages and industries; Regional Art Gallery, has monthly exhibitions. Griffith Cottage Gallery, Bridge Rd. Crafty Spot, Benerembah St. Market, each Sun. in Wakaden St. Easter: Festival of Griffith. Oct.: Festival of Gardens. **In the area:** Pioneer Park Museum, set in 18 ha of bushland 2 km N, features drop-log buildings, memorabilia from early 20th century and Bagtown Village, re-created to give insight into development of area. Belle Amour (5 km N) and Casuarina (11 km N), private gardens open Sept.–May (check opening times). Lake Wyangan, 10 km NW, for water sports. Bagtown Cemetery, 5 km S, a reminder of pioneering days. Catania Fruit Salad Farm, 8 km S on Cox Rd at Hanwood, horticultural farm offering demonstrations of processes (guided tours daily, 1.30 p.m.). Cocoparra National Park, 25 km NE, for wildflowers and birdlife. Many wineries in area, most open for tastings and cellar-door sales. **Visitor information:** cnr Banna and Jondaryan aves; (02) 6962 4145. **See also:** Vineyards and Wineries p. 53.

Gulgong   Pop. 2018

MAP REF. 114 H2

This old goldmining town, 29 km NW of Mudgee, is known as 'the town on the (original) $10 note'. In the 1870s it was packed with fortune hunters from all over the world. Some of its glory remains in the many restored buildings; the town's narrow streets are lined with clapboard and iron buildings, decorated with their original iron lace. **In town:** Henry Lawson Centre, Mayne St, boasts largest collection of Lawson memorabilia outside Sydney's Mitchell Library. Historic buildings on Two Foot Tour (brochures available) include: Prince of Wales Opera House, Mayne St; Ten Dollar Town Motel (formerly Royal Hotel), cnr Mayne and Medley sts; American Tobacco Warehouse and Fancy Goods Emporium, Mayne St; Pioneers Museum, cnr Herbert and Bayly sts. Red Hill, off White St, site of original gold strike, features restored stamper mill, poppet head, memorial and statue of Henry Lawson. Jan.: Folk Festival. June: Henry Lawson Festival. Oct.: Heritage Weekend (at Pioneer Museum). **In the area:** At Ulan, 22 km NE: Ulan Coal Mine, viewing areas overlook this large open-cut mine; Hands on the Rock, rock paintings. In Goulburn River National Park, The Drip, 50-m curtains of water dripping through rocks alongside Goulburn River. Talbragar Fossil Fish Beds, 35 km NE, one of few Jurassic Period fossil deposits in Australia. **Visitor information:** 109 Herbert St; (02) 6374 1202.

Gundagai   Pop. 2064

MAP REF. 113 B5, 114 D12

Much celebrated in song and verse, this town on the Murrumbidgee River at the foot of Mt Parnassus, 398 km SW of Sydney, has become part of Australian folklore. Its history includes Australia's worst flood disaster in 1852 when 89 people drowned; nearby gold rushes; and many bushranging attacks. Today it is the centre of a rich pastoral and agricultural district that produces wool, wheat, fruit and vegetables. **In town:** Marble carving of cathedral, comprising over 20 000 pieces, by Frank Rusconi (sculptor of tucker box dog) on display in information centre, Sheridan St. Also in Sheridan St: Gabriel Gallery, with its outstanding collection of early photographs, letters and possessions of poet Henry Lawson; National Trust-classified courthouse (1859), scene of historic trials, including that of notorious bushranger

Captain Moonlite; National Trust-classified Prince Alfred Bridge (1866), longest timber viaduct in Australia. Historical museum, Homer St. National Trust-classified St John's Anglican Church (1861), cnr Otway and Punch sts. Excellent views from Mt Parnassus Lookout, Hanley St, and Rotary Lookout, Luke St, South Gundagai. Oct.: Spring Flower Show. Nov.: Dog on the Tucker Box Festival. **In the area:** The Dog on the Tucker Box, 'five miles from Gundagai' (8 km N), monument to pioneer teamsters and their dogs, celebrated in song by Jack O'Hagan; nearby larger-than-life copper statues of Dad and Dave characters from writings of Steele Rudd; kiosk; fernery; ruins of Five Mile Pub. Asparagus plantation at Jugiong, 41 km NE (sales daily Oct.–Dec.). **Visitor information:** Sheridan St; (02) 6944 1341.

Gunnedah   Pop. 8315

MAP REF. 116 H10

A prosperous town on the banks of the Namoi River, Gunnedah is in rich pastoral and agricultural country, and is one of the largest stock-marketing centres in NSW. Other industries include a brickworks, a tannery, flour mills and open-cut and underground coal mines. **In town:** Self-drive town tour and Bindea Town Walk; brochures available. In Anzac Park, South St: Water Tower Museum; Dorothea MacKellar Memorial statue (MacKellar was an Australian poet and author of 'My Country'). Opposite at information centre, collection of Dorothea MacKellar's memorabilia. Rural Museum, Mullaley Rd. Red Chief Memorial to an Aboriginal warrior of Gunn-e-dar group, State Office building in Abbott St. Old Bank Gallery, Conadilly St. Creative Arts Centre, Chandos St. Eighth Division Memorial Avenue of flowering gums. Market, 3rd Sat. each month in Wolsely Park, Conadilly St. Sheep and cattle sales at Saleyards, Boggabri Rd, each Tues. Jan.: National Tomato Competition. Apr.: Grey Mardi Gras (celebration for senior citizens). Aug.: Ag Quip (Agricultural Field Days). Sept.: Vintage Car Swap Meet. **In the area:** Porcupine Lookout, 3 km SE, offers views over town and surrounding agricultural area. Lake Keepit Dam and State Recreation Centre, 34 km NE, for water sports, bushwalking, gliding club, picnicking, camping, caravan park. Waterways Wildlife Park, 7 km W on Mullaley Rd. 150° East Time Meridian, 28 km W. **Visitor information:** Anzac Park, South St; (02) 6740 2230. Web site www.infogunnedah.com.au

Gunning   Pop. 486

MAP REF. 113 E4, 114 G11

This town, on the Old Hume Hwy between Goulburn and Yass, is in the centre of pastoral country. **In town:** In Yass St: Pye Cottage, a slab-style pioneer cottage; historic post office; Telegraph Hotel; old courthouse; Do Duck Inn (now B&B). Feb.: Agricultural Show. Oct.: Festival. **In the area:** Greendale Pioneer Cemetery, Gunning–Boorowa Rd. Hume and Hovell Walking Track extends from Gunning to Albury, a distance of 440 km and a 23-day trek for long distance walkers; half-day, one-day and weekend walks at various points along route (contact Department of Land and Water Conservation, Wagga Wagga; (02) 6921 2503). **Visitor information:** Gunning Motel, Yass St; (02) 4845 1191.

Guyra   Pop. 1801

MAP REF. 117 L8

Guyra is Aboriginal for 'fish may be caught', and the local streams are excellent for fishing. At 1320 m, this small town in the Great Dividing Range is one of the highest in NSW. The area has a rich mining history, but today it is known for its fat lambs, beef, wool and potatoes. **In town:** In Bradley St: Historical Society Museum (open by appt); Railway Station, with large display of antique machinery. Waterbirds at Mother of Ducks Lagoon, McKie Pde. Jan.: Lamb and Potato Festival (includes Hydrangea Festival). Feb.: Agricultural Show. Apr.: Rugby Seven Carnival. Nov.: Rodeo. **In the area:** Chandler's Peak, 20 km E, for spectacular views. Llangothlin Handcraft Hall on Hwy, 10 km N. Thunderbolt's Cave, 10 km S. **Visitor information:** Crystal Trout Caravan Park, New England Hwy; (02) 6779 1241. **See also:** New England p. 61.

Hay   Pop. 2896

MAP REF. 121 K8

Hay, established 1859, was named after the politician and pastoralist Sir John Hay. The commercial centre for a huge area of semi-arid grazing country, Hay is on the banks of the Murrumbidgee River at the junction of the Cobb, Mid Western and Sturt hwys. Increasing irrigation from the Murrumbidgee has led to an expansion in rice- vegetable- and fruit-growing. The area supports a strong beef industry and many world-famous sheep studs, including Mungadal, Uardry and Cedar Grove.

In town: Self-guide historical town walk and scenic drive, brochures available. In Lachlan St: historical buildings, including post office (1881), Shire office (1877), and Lands office (1896), an early example of a government building designed specifically for the harsh outback environment; Witcombe Fountain (1883) and plaque, commemorating journey of explorer Charles Sturt along Murrumbidgee and Murray rivers 1829–30; coach-house in main shopping area, featuring original Cobb & Co. coach that plied the Deniliquin–Hay–Wilcannia run until 1901. Hay Gaol Museum, Church St, has pioneer relics. Restored courthouse (1892), Moppett St. Restored railway station (1882), Murray St, houses POW Internment Camp Interpretive Centre: documents WWII internment of over 3000 prisoners of war in Hay. Hay Park, cnr Moppett and Pine sts. Nature walk along banks of river, southern end of town off Brunker St. Sandy river beaches along Murrumbidgee for swimming, boating and fishing. Hay Wetlands, north-western edge of town; breeding ground for many inland bird species; directions from information centre. Bishop's Lodge, South Hay (1888), restored as museum, exhibition gallery and conference centre; Spring Market held here 3rd Sun. in Oct. Mar.: Riverina Stud Merino Field Day. May: Sheep Show. Sept.: Agricultural Show **In the area:** Ruberto's Winery, Sturt Hwy, South Hay. Sunset viewing area, 16 km N on Booligal Rd. John Oxley Memorial at Booligal, 78 km N on Lachlan River; town mentioned in Banjo Paterson's poem 'Hay and Hell and Booligal'. Weir on Murrumbidgee River, 12 km W. Villages of Maude (53 km W), with attractive picnic areas near weir, and Oxley (87 km NW), with its river red gums along river and prolific wildlife (best seen at dusk). **Visitor information:** 407 Moppett St; (02) 6993 4045.

Henty   Pop. 878

MAP REF. 114 A13, 121 Q11
The historic pastoral township of Henty is in the heart of Morgan Country, so called because of the infamous but ill-fated bushranger Dan Morgan. Almost midway between Albury-Wodonga and Wagga Wagga, Henty can be reached by the Olympic Way or by the Hume Hwy and Boomerang Way. **In town:** Headlie Taylor Header Memorial, Henty Park, off Allen St, a tribute to mechanical header-harvester (invented 1914) that revolutionised the grain industry. Mini Museum under

Fishing boats at Iluka

supermarket in Sladen St, has town and commercial memorabilia. Sept.: Machinery Field Days. **In the area:** Sergeant Smith Memorial Stone, 2 km W on Pleasant Hills Rd, marks site where Dan Morgan fatally wounded a policeman. Doodle Cooma Swamp (2000 ha), breeding area for waterbirds, is visible from memorial stone. At Pleasant Hills, 27 km W, unique headstones on graves of German descendants in area. Buckargingah Woolshed, built of chocks and logs (no nails), 11 km E on Cookardinia Rd. Vintage Day held in Yerong Creek, 17 km N, each Oct. **Visitor information:** Dales Everyday Supermarket, Sladen St; (02) 6929 3302.

Holbrook   Pop. 1331

MAP REF. 121 R12, 239 R1
This small town is a well-known stock-breeding centre, 521 km SW of Sydney, on the Hume Hwy. **In town:** Bronze statue of Commander Holbrook, as well as his submarine, in Holbrook Park, Hume Hwy; submarine is a scale model of one in which Commander N. D. Holbrook won the VC in WW I; town (formerly Germanton) was renamed in his honour. Adjacent to park, 30 m submarine formerly called the Otway, decommissioned in 1995. Woolpack Inn Museum, in former hotel (1860), Albury St, features 20 rooms furnished in turn-of-the-century style, bakery, horse-drawn vehicles and farm equipment. Ten Mile Creek, behind museum, attractive area for picnics. Apr.: Beef Fest (even-numbered years). Nov.: Agricultural Show. **In the area:** Ultralight Centre, 3 km N at Holbrook Airport; flights and instruction available. Hume and Hovell Walking Track, access from Woomargama, 15 km S; brochure available. **Visitor information:** Woolpack Inn Museum, 83 Albury St (Hume Hwy); (02) 6036 2131.

Huskisson   Pop. 3350

MAP REF. 113 I4, 115 K12, 139 R1
A thriving town, Huskisson is 24 km SE of Nowra, on the shores of Jervis Bay. Jervis Bay is renowned for its clear water and is frequently used as a location for underwater film sequences. **In town:** Lady Denman Heritage Complex, Woollamia Rd, provides history of wooden shipbuilding at Huskisson; also in Complex, Laddie Timbery's Aboriginal Art and Craft Centre, bushtucker demonstrations and talks on request; Museum of Jervis Bay Science and the Sea has fine maritime and surveying collections. Antique and craft shops. Diving and dolphin-watching cruises. Market, 2nd Sun. each month at White Sands Park. Easter: White Sands Carnival. **In the area:** Water sports, particularly diving. Excellent fishing. Barry's Bush Tucker Tours, guided native walks, Aboriginal history, bush tucker. NSW Jervis Bay National Park, locations north and south of town: walking tracks; mangrove boardwalk. Booderee National Park, locations south of town: Cape St George Lighthouse; Booderee Botanic Gardens; boat-launching facilities; magnificent beaches. **Visitor information:** Shoalhaven Visitors Centre, cnr Princes Hwy and Pleasant Way, Nowra; (02) 4421 0778. Web site www.shoalhaven.nsw.gov.au **See also:** National Parks p. 42.

Iluka   Pop. 1863

MAP REF. 117 Q5
A coastal resort alongside the mouth of the Clarence River, Iluka is well known for its fishing. A deep-sea fishing fleet operates from the harbour. **In town:** Daily passenger ferry services to Yamba. River cruises from Boatshed, Wed. and Fri. July: Amateur Fishing Classic.

In the area: World Heritage-listed Iluka Rainforest, in Bundjalung National Park, at northern edge of town; park has a variety of birdlife, and offers excellent fishing, swimming, surfing, canoeing, walking and camping. Woombah Coffee Plantation, 14 km W, world's southern-most coffee plantation (tours by appt). **Visitor information:** Lower Clarence Visitors Centre, Ferry Park, Pacific Hwy, Maclean; (02) 6645 4121.

Inverell   Pop. 9378

MAP REF. 117 K6
Known as 'Sapphire City', this town, 67 km W of Glen Innes, is surrounded by fertile farming land and rich mineral deposits. Zircons, sapphires, industrial diamonds and tin are mined in the area. **In town:** National Trust-classified courthouse, Otho St. Pioneer Village, Tingha Rd, has buildings dating from 1840, moved from their original sites, including Grove homestead, Paddy's Pub and Mt Drummond Woolshed. Visitor Centre and Mining Museum in Water Towers Complex, Campbell St. Art Society Gallery, Evans St. Gem Centre, Byron St. Transport Museum, Taylor Ave, displays beautiful and rare vehicles. Town Stroll (self-guide), and Town and Country Drive; leaflets available. Hobby Market, 1st Sun. each month; Sapphire City market, 3rd Sun. each month. Jan.: Great Inland Fishing Festival. Mar.: Art Exhibition. Oct.: Sapphire City Floral Festival. **In the area:** Gem-fossicking areas. Lake Inverell Reserve, 3 km E. Draught Horse Centre, Fishers Rd, 4 km E, with six breeds, has display of harness and memorabilia. See working sapphire mine at DeJon Sapphire Centre, 19 km E on Glen Innes Rd. Smith's Mining and Natural History Museum, 36 km SE at Green Valley Farm. Lookout, 2 km W, excellent views of township and surrounds. Goonoowigall Bushland Reserve, 5 km S. Gilgai Winery, 12 km S. Copeton Dam State Recreation Area, northern foreshore 17 km S, for boating, water-skiing, swimming, fishing, bushwalking, rock-climbing, adventure playgrounds, water slides and picnic/barbecue facilities; on western shore of dam, golf course where kangaroos graze at dusk. Honey Farm and Bottle Museum, 8 km SW, opportunity to view bees working under glass. Gwydir Ranch 4WD Park, 28 km W. Pindari Dam, 58 km N, offers fishing, swimming, camping and picnic/barbecue facilities.

Kwiambal National Park, 90 km N: Macintyre Falls; Ashford Caves (bat nurseries, view with torch); swimming, bushwalking, camping; kangaroos, emus, koalas and other native animals. **Visitor information:** Water Towers Complex, Campbell St; (02) 6728 8161. Web site www.northnet.com.au/~inverell **See also:** New England p. 61.

Jamberoo   Pop. 883

MAP REF. 110 G9, 115 K10
Jamberoo, 10 km W of Kiama, is in one of the most picturesque areas of the NSW coast, with lush pastures surrounded by towering escarpments. The district has been well known for the quality of its dairy products since early European settlement days. **In town:** Jamberoo Hotel, Allowrie St, features bush bands Sun. p.m. Market, Kevin Walsh Oval, last Sun. each month. Mar.: Illawarra Folk Festival. **In the area:** Jamberoo Recreation Park, 3 km N, family fun park. Saddleback Lookout, 7 km S, for 180° views of coast; starting point for Hoddles Trail, a one-hour walk to Barren Grounds escarpment, excellent views. Walking trails and birdwatching in Barren Grounds Bird Observatory and Nature Reserve, 10 km SW on Drualla Rd; various wildlife-watching activities and workshops available (bookings essential). Minnamurra Rainforest Centre, 4 km W: elevated timber boardwalk through rainforest; paved walkway to Minnamurra Falls. **Visitor information:** Kiama Visitors Centre, Blowhole Point Rd, Kiama; (02) 4232 3322. Web site www.kiama.com.au **See also:** Wildlife-Watching p. 48.

Jerilderie   Pop. 871

MAP REF. 121 M11
This town on the Newell Hwy was held by the Kelly gang for two days in 1879 when they captured the police station, cut the telegraph wires and robbed the bank. Today it is the centre of the largest merino stud area in NSW and supports an expanding vegetable industry. **In town:** Telegraph Office Museum, Powell St; next door, The Willows historic home (1878), has craft and tearoom. Original courthouse (1874), now library, Newell Hwy. Doll World, Bolton St, displays large collection from around the world. Lake Jerilderie for water sports; adjacent, Luke Park features Steel Wings, one of the largest windmills in Southern Hemisphere. Opposite park, Mini Heritage

Steam Rail, operates 2nd and 5th Sun. each month. **In the area:** Coleambally, 62 km N, centre of Coleambally Irrigation Area, features Wineglass Water Tower, Brolga Pl. **Visitor information:** The Willows, Powell St; (03) 5886 1666.

Jindabyne   Pop. 1670

MAP REF. 112 G11, 113 D9, 138 C12, 241 K4
Now on the shores of Lake Jindabyne at the foothills of the Snowy Mountains, the original township was beside the Snowy River. From 1962, residents moved to the new site chosen by the Snowy Mountains Hydro-Electric Authority. The River was then dammed to form a water storage area as part of the Snowy Mountains Scheme. At an altitude of 930 m and in the heart of the Snowy Mountains, Jindabyne attracts skiers in winter and anglers, water-sports enthusiasts and bushwalkers in summer. **In town:** Snowy Region Visitor Centre, Kosciuszko Rd. Walkway and cycleway around lake's foreshore, from Banjo Paterson Park on Kosciuszko Rd to Snowline Caravan Park. Mar.: Strzelecki Polish Festival. Nov.: Snowy Mountains Trout Festival. Dec.: Lake Jindabyne Sailing Club Hobie Cat Races. **In the area:** Scenic walks of varying lengths, brochure and map available. Lake Jindabyne, well stocked with trout, also ideal for boating, water-skiing and other water sports; lake cruises in summer. Crackenback Cottage, 12 km SW, has craft shop, timber maze and restaurant. Winter shuttle-bus service to Bullocks Flat and Thredbo. At Bullocks Flat, 20 km SW, terminal for Skitube, a European-style alpine train to Perisher and Mt Blue Cow (operates daily year-round). After snow has melted, 50-min. drive south-west from Jindabyne leads to Charlotte Pass and 300-m boardwalk to view main range; 16-km return walk to summit of Mt Kosciuszko. Wallace Craigie Lookout, 40 km SW, for excellent views of Snowy River Valley. Gaden Trout Hatchery, 10 km NW (tours daily; barbecues alongside Thredbo River). At Sawpit Creek, 14 km NW: Kosciuszko Education Centre has interactive displays and children's environment programs; at picnic area, start of Palliabo (walking) Track. Snowy Valley Lookout, 8 km N, view of Lake Jindabyne. Kunama Galleries, 7 km NE. **Visitor information:** Snowy Region Visitor Centre, Kosciuszko Rd; (02) 6450 5600. **See also:** National Parks p. 42.

Junee   Pop. 3681

MAP REF. 113 A4, 114 C11, 121 R9

Junee is an important railhead town and commercial centre, 482 km SW of Sydney on the Olympic Way. **In town:** Monte Cristo homestead, overlooking town, a restored Colonial mansion with carriage collection. 19th-century railway refreshment rooms, Railway Sq., now cafe and information centre. Roundhouse Museum, Harold St, features 32-m turntable, 42 repair bays, original workshop, locomotives and memorabilia (check opening times). Historical Museum, Lorne St (check opening times). **In the area:** Clock Museum, 17 km NE at Illabo. Turn-off at Bethungra for Bethungra Dam, ideal for canoeing and sailing. Bethungra Rail Spiral, unique engineering feat, 33 km NE. **Visitor information:** Historic Railway Cafe and Information Centre, Railway Sq.; (02) 6924 4200.

Katoomba   Pop. 11 795

MAP REF. 98 H7, 100 E9, 115 J7

Katoomba of the main residential and tourist centre of the Blue Mountains. Nearby, the smaller towns of Leura and Wentworth Falls have many interesting features and superb mountain scenery. Developed as a coal mine last century, Katoomba was soon attracting wealthy Sydney holiday-makers. The coal mine foundered, but Katoomba continued to develop as a tourist destination. **In town:** Maxvision Cinema, Great Western Hwy (access through Civic Pl.), daily screenings of *The Edge* (images of the Blue Mountains) on a six-storey-high screen. Markets at Civic Centre, Katoomba St, 1st and 3rd Sat. each month. Feb.: Blue Mountains Folk Festival. June: Winter Magic Festival. Yulefest held during June, July and Aug. throughout the region. **In the area:** Excellent bushwalking, cycling, abseiling and 4WD tracks. West of town off highway, Explorers Tree (with carved initials). *South of town:* Echo Point, best place to view the famous Three Sisters rock formation (floodlit at night); Orphan Rock and Katoomba Falls, also floodlit; Giant Stairway bushwalk. Scenic Skyway and Railway Complex, cnr Violet St and Cliff Dr.: Skyway, first horizontal passenger-carrying ropeway in Australia, travels 350 m across mountain gorge; Scenic Railway, built late 1800s to transport coal and miners, is reputed to be world's steepest railway. *At and around Leura, 3 km E:* Leura Mall, beautiful tree-lined main

Cascades near Katoomba, in the Blue Mountains

street and gardens with many specialty shops, galleries and restaurants. Everglades Gardens, Everglades Ave, celebrated 1930s garden, includes gallery devoted to its creator, Danish master gardener Paul Sorensen. Leuralla, Olympian Pde, a historic Art Deco mansion with major collection of toys, dolls, trains and railway memorabilia. Cascades, just south of town, where Leura Creek cascades into the valley. Dramatic views from Sublime Point; Cliff Drive offers spectacular views at lookouts and picnic spots. Walking tracks along cliff tops and descending into Jamison Valley. market at public school, Great Western Highway, 1st Sun. each month. Sept.–Oct.: Legacy Gardens Festival. Oct.: Leura Garden Festival; Leura Village Fair; Greystanes Spring Gardens. *At Wentworth Falls, 7 km E:* Conservation Hut Cafe, an eco-designed cafe with splendid views; Valley of the Waters Picnic Area. Kings Tableland Observatory (open evenings Fri.–Sun.). At Hazelbrook, a further 10 km E, Selwood Science and Puzzles has puzzle room, science kits, bookshop and local artwork. Feb.: Regatta Day (on Wentworth Falls Lake). Apr.: Autumn Festival. *At Jenolan Caves, 75 km SW:* Some of the most splendid underground caves and above-ground arches in Australia, in flora and fauna reserve. *At Yerranderie, 200 km S via Oberon:* Silver-mining ghost town surrounded by 2430-ha wildlife reserve (4WD access only); several historic buildings including museum and quaint hostel-style accommodation. **Visitor information:** Great Western Hwy, Glenbrook; 1300 653 408. **See also:** Blue Mountains Experience p. 38; National Parks p. 42; Wildlife-Watching p. 48.

Kempsey   Pop. 8630

MAP REF. 103 G3, 117 O11

Kempsey, situated in the Macleay River Valley, 428 km N of Sydney, is the commercial centre of a growing district of dairying, horticulture, tourism and light industry, including the Akubra hat factory. **In town:** Historical walks through Kempsey, as well as West and East Kempsey; brochures available. Wigay Aboriginal Cultural Park, Sea Street, Aboriginal cultural experience, including introduction to bush tucker. Macleay River Historical Society Museum and Settlers Cottage, Pacific Hwy, South Kempsey. Video of the Akubra hat-making process can be seen at information centre. Markets at racecourse, North St, 1st Sat. each month. May: Agricultural Show; South West Rocks Fishing Classic. July: Off-road Race. Sept.: Country Music Festival. **In the area:** Walks in nature reserves, and self-guide scenic and historical drives, brochures available. At Frederickton, 8 km NE, Blues Festival in Jan. At Gladstone, 15 km NE, Pumpkin Festival in Apr. At South West Rocks, 37 km NE: good beach; maritime history display at restored Boatmans Cottage (1902); handfeeding of fish at Everglades Aquarium; water sports, camping, boat hire. Nearby, Trial Bay Gaol (1886), public works prison until 1903, reopened to hold 'enemy aliens' in WW II; Smoky Cape Lighthouse (1889), not open to public, but excellent views from headland; Gaol Break Festival held at Easter. Barnett's Rainbow Beach Oyster Barn, 31 km NE, direct purchases; watch oysters being processed. Hat Head National Park, 32 km E, a coastal park with magnificent sand dunes and unspoiled beaches;

birdwatching, snorkelling, swimming and walking tracks (brochures available); whale-watching from Korogoro Point (May–July and Sept.–Oct.). Crescent Head, 20 km SE, popular seaside holiday town; Aboriginal bora ring, old ceremonial ground, 23 km SE. Fish Rock Cave, noted for diving, just off Smoky Cape. At Kundabung, 12 km S, Australasian bull-riding titles held each Oct. Brandybrook Lavender Farm, at Clybucca, 23 km N. At Turners Flat, 15 km NW, M. A. J. Artworks has porcelain tableware. Bellbrook, 47 km NW, a National Trust-classified village. **Visitor information:** Pacific Hwy, South Kempsey; (02) 6563 1555, freecall 1800 642 480. Web site www.slnsw.gov.au.kempsey

Khancoban   Pop. 379

MAP REF. 112 A9, 113 B9, 240 I3
Set in the lush green Upper Murray Valley at the western end of the Alpine Way, 108 km NW of Jindabyne, this small modern town was built by the Snowy Mountains Authority. **In town:** Lady Hudson Rose Garden, Mitchell Ave. National Parks and Wildlife Service, Scott St, have displays and videos of Snowy Mountains Scheme and Kosciuszko National Park. Easter: Festival and Fireworks. Oct.: Spring Festival. **In the area:** Trout fishing, bushwalking, water sports, whitewater rafting; fishing tours. Permit required for vehicles entering national park. On Alpine Way: Murray 1 Power Station and Visitor Centre, 10 km SE, has interactive display, and tours for booked groups; further 1 km SE, power station viewing area; spectacular mountain views from Scammell's Spur Lookout, 20 km SE; Olsen's Lookout, turn-off 29 km SE, magnificent views of main range; Geehi Rest Area, 32 km SE, wheelchair access walking track and toilets, brilliant spring and autumn wildflowers; Tom Groggin Rest Area, 50 km SE, close to the source of the Murray River. **Visitor information:** National Parks and Wildlife Service, Scott St; (02) 6076 9373.

Kiama   Pop. 11 711

MAP REF. 110 H9, 115 K10
The spectacular blowhole is the best-known attraction of this holiday town. Discovered by explorer George Bass in 1797, it sprays water up to heights of 60 m and is floodlit each evening. Kiama is the centre of a prosperous dairying and mixed farming district. **In town:** Terrace

houses, specialty and craft shops in Collins St. Family History Centre, Railway Pde, contains world-wide collection of records for tracing family history. Heritage walk, leaflet available. At Blowhole Point: Blowhole; Pilots Cottage Historical Museum; constructed rock pool; pelicans; cafe. Beaches for surfing, swimming and fishing. Market, 3rd Sun. each month. Feb.: Jazz Festival; Seven-a-Side Rugby Competition. June: Folk Music Festival. Oct.: Seaside Festival. **In the area:** Several scenic drives along coast and into hinterland, brochures available. Little Blowhole, 2 km S, off Tingira Cres. Cathedral Rocks, 3 km N at Jones Beach, a scenic rocky outcrop, best at dawn. **Visitor information:** Blowhole Point Rd; (02) 4232 3322.

Kyogle   Pop. 2866

MAP REF. 117 P2, 525 P12
Kyogle makes a good base for exploring the mountains nearby. It is also the centre of a lush dairy and mixed-farming area on the upper reaches of the Richmond River near the Qld border. **In town:** Captain Cook Memorial Lookout, Fairy St. July: Fairymount Festival. Oct.: Show. Nov.: Charity Golf Tournament. **In the area:** World Heritage-listed Border Ranges National Park, 27 km N, with forestry road access, walking tracks, camping facilities and views of Mt Warning and Tweed Valley; in eastern section, Tweed Range Scenic Drive (64 km) through pristine rainforest with deep gorges, creeks and waterfalls, brochure available. Rodeo in Mar. at Wiangaree, 15 km N. Scenic forest drive via Mt Lindesay, 45 km NW on NSW–Qld border, offers magnificent views, brochure available. Toonumbar Dam, 31 km W, with bushwalking and picnic/barbecue facilities nearby; at Bell's Bay, 2 km from dam, excellent bass-fishing and camping. Picnic spots include Roseberry Forest Park, 23 km N; Sheepstation Creek, in Border Ranges National Park. **Visitor information:** Kyogle Council, Stratheden St; (02) 6632 1611. **See also:** National Parks p. 42.

Lake Cargelligo   Pop. 1218

MAP REF. 121 O4
A small township, 586 km W of Sydney, with the same name as the lake alongside, Lake Cargelligo serves the surrounding agricultural and pastoral district. **In town:** The lake, 8 km long and 3.5 km wide, is ideal for fishing (silver perch, golden perch and redfin), boating, sailing, water-skiing

and swimming. The lake is also home to many bird species, including at times the rare black cockatoo. The information centre, Foster St, has a large gem collection. June: Blue Water Art and Craft Festival. Sept.: Lake Show. Oct.: Rodeo. Dec.: Lake Festivale. **In the area:** Lake Brewster, 41 km W: 1500 ha; bird-watchers' paradise; fishing and picnic area; no guns, dogs or boats. Nombinnie Nature Reserve, 45 km N, birdwatching, bushwalks, abundant spring wildflowers (Sept.–Dec.). **Visitor information:** Foster St; (02) 6898 1501.

Laurieton   Pop. 5823

MAP REF. 103 F10, 117 O12
The villages of Laurieton, North Haven and Dunbogan are scattered around a large inlet formed by the Camden Haven River mouth, 34 km S of Port Macquarie. This tidal inlet is ideal for estuary fishing. **In town:** Historical Museum, in old post office, Laurie St (open by appt). **In the area:** Oysters, lobsters, crabs, bream and flathead in local rivers and lakes. Seafront is a well-known fishing spot. Delightful bushwalks along seafront and around lakes. Markets at North Haven, 2 km NE, 5th Sun. of month. Kattang Nature Reserve, 5 km E, for spectacular coastal views and wildflowers. Crowdy Bay National Park, 5 km S: prolific birdlife and magnificent ocean beach; at Diamond Head, hut in which Kylie Tennant wrote *The Man and the Headland*; walking tracks offer stunning ocean views, brochures available. Magnificent views from viewing platforms on North Brother Mountain, in Dooragan National Park, 6 km W. Big Fella Gum Tree, 18 km SW, one of three exceptionally large trees in Middle Brother State Forest. At Kendall, 10 km W, several art and craft galleries including Craft Co-op in railway station; markets in Logans Crossing Rd, 1st and 3rd Sun. each month. Norfolk Punch Factory, 20 km W, see traditional English punch being made, tastings; small museum of historic kitchen appliances. Taramac Macadamia Farm, 23 km W (closed Mon. and Fri.). **Visitor information:** Pacific Hwy, Kew; (02) 6559 4400.

Leeton   Pop. 6615

MAP REF. 121 O8
Located 560 km SW of Sydney, Leeton is the first of the planned towns in the Murrumbidgee Irrigation Area and was designed by American architect Walter

Burley Griffin. The town is an important administrative and processing centre for the surrounding fruit, rice and wine grape industries. **In town:** Information centre (1913), Yanco Ave, a beautifully restored building with photographic displays, local artwork and heritage garden. Art Deco streetscape including Roxy Theatre and historic Hydro Hotel (1919) at Chelmsford Pl. Presentation on weekdays at SunRice Country Visitors Centre at rice mill, Calrose St (check times). Tours weekdays at National Foods Juice Factory, Brady Way. Riverina Cheese Factory, Massey Ave, has sales outlet at Fresh Fruit Market, Kurrajong Ave. Easter: SunRice Festival (even-numbered years, 10-day festival culminates Easter Mon). **In the area:** Tastings and tours at Toorak and Lillypilly Estate wineries, both near town. Fivebough Swamp, 2 km N, a waterbird sanctuary. Gliding and hot-air ballooning at Brobenah airfield, 9 km N. Whitton Courthouse and Historical Museum, 23 km W. Gogeldrie Weir, 23 km SW, for fishing. Murrumbidgee State Forest, 12 km S, scenic drives; self-guide brochure available. **Visitor information:** 10 Yanco Ave; (02) 6953 6481. Web site www.leeton.nsw.gov.au **See also:** Vineyards and Wineries p. 53.

Lennox Head   Pop. 4511

MAP REF. 117 R3, 525 R12

Just north of Ballina, Lennox Head has a charming seaside village atmosphere. The area is well known for beautiful Seven Mile Beach. **In town:** Freshwater Lake Ainsworth, 50 m from surfing beach, popular with windsurfers. Market on shores of lake, 2nd and 5th Sun. of month. **In the area:** Swimming, surfing, windsurfing, catamaraning, sailboarding and snorkelling. Many scenic walks and rainforests. Pat Morton Lookout, 1 km S: whale-watching June–July and Sept.–Oct.; below is world-renowned surfing spot known as 'The Point'. **Visitor information:** Ballina Visitor Information Centre, cnr Las Balsas Plaza and River St, Ballina; (02) 6686 3484.

Lightning Ridge   Pop. 1814

MAP REF. 116 B5

Lightning Ridge is a small opal-mining town in the world-renowned black opal fields, 74 km N of Walgett, via the Castlereagh Hwy. **In town:** Many displays of art and craft, including opal jewellery and gem opals. Underground mine tours. In Opal St: Bottle House Museum, has collection of bottles, minerals and mining relics; John Murray Art has paintings and photographs. In Pandora St: Gemopal Pottery; Goondee Aboriginal Keeping Place, featuring Aboriginal artifacts and educational tours of premises. Local craft market in Morilla St, each Fri. Easter: Great Goat Race; Rodeo. June: Opal Open Pistol Shoot. July: Opal and Gem Festival. **In the area:** Self-guide drives, maps available. Designated fossicking areas, inquire at information centre. Opal-cutting demonstrations and daily underground working-mine tours at the Big Opal on Three Mile Rd, southern outskirts of town. Walk-In-Mine, 2 km N, off Bald Hill Rd; Cactus Nursery nearby. Hot Artesian Bore Baths, 2 km NE. Fauna Orphanage, Opal St, 3 km S. Opal fields: Grawin, 65 km W and Sheepyards, 76 km W; details from information centre. **Visitor information:** Morilla St; (02) 6829 1466, freecall 1800 639 545.

Lismore   Pop. 28 380

MAP REF. 117 Q3, 525 Q12

Regional centre of the Northern Rivers district of NSW, a closely settled and intensively cultivated rural area, Lismore is situated beside Wilsons River (formerly the north arm of Richmond River), 821 km N of Sydney. **In town:** Rotary Rainforest Reserve, Rotary Dr., 6-ha tropical rainforest with boardwalk, in residental area. Indoor rainforest walk, and displays of local art and craft at information centre. Picnic areas and mini steam-train rides in surrounding Heritage Park, cnr Ballina and Molesworth sts. Cedar Log Memorial, Ballina St. In Molesworth St: Richmond River Historical Museum; Lismore Regional Art Gallery. Robinson's Lookout, Robinson Ave. Claude Riley Memorial Lookout, New Ballina Rd. Wilsons Park, Wyrallah St, East Lismore. River cruises on MV *Bennelong*, The Wharf, Magellan St. Heritage Walk, self-guide brochure available. Heritage Park market, 5th Sun. of month; Car Boot Markets, Shopping Square, Uralba St, 1st and 3rd Sun. each month. Mar.: Square Dance Festival. May: Trinity Arts Festival. June: Lantern Parade. Sept.: Cup Day. Oct.: River City Music Festival; North Coast National Show. **In the area:** At Alphadale, 11 km E: Macadamia Magic, a macadamia processing plant and tourist complex; Stephen Morris Glassware. Boatharbour Reserve, 5 km N on Bangalow Rd, has 17 ha of remnant rainforest, wildlife sanctuary, picnic area and walking tracks (maps available). Rocky Creek Dam, 25 km N, has platypus-viewing platform. Minyon Falls and Peates Mountain Lookout in Whian Whian State Forest, 25 km N. Three World Heritage-listed areas: Border Ranges National Park, 40 km N of Kyogle, Nightcap National Park, 27 km N, with spectacular Protesters Falls, and Mt Warning National Park near Murwillumbah, 105 km NE; check road conditions at information centre. Lismore Lake, 3 km S: good lagoon for swimming; picnic/barbecue facilities; adventure park. Tucki Tucki Koala Reserve, 15 km S, adjacent to Lismore–Woodburn Rd; Aboriginal ceremonial ground nearby. **Visitor information:** cnr Ballina and Molesworth sts; (02) 6622 0122. Web site www.liscity.nsw.gov.au **See also:** National Parks p. 42.

Lithgow   Pop. 11 441

MAP REF. 98 G5, 114 I6

This coal-mining city on the north-west fringes of the Blue Mountains is a must for railway enthusiasts. The city is highly industrialised with two power stations and several large factories; the surrounding countryside is beautiful. **In town:** Museum in Eskbank House, Bennett St: built 1841 by Thomas Brown, who discovered Lithgow coal seam; 19th-century furniture and vehicles; displays on industrial history of area; open Thurs.–Sun. Blast Furnace Park, a wetland restoration area off Inch St, with ruins of Australia's first blast furnace complex. State Mine Railway Heritage Park, State Mine Gully Rd, features mining and railway equipment, and historic mining buildings (check opening times). Small Arms Museum, Methven St (check opening times). Lithgow Art and Craft, Great Western Hwy, features local work. Art and Craft in the Park, at Queen Elizabeth Park, one Sat. each month, Aug.–May (contact information centre for dates). Oct.: National Go-Kart Championships. **In the area:** Zig Zag Railway, 10 km E via Bells Line of Road, a breathtaking stretch of railway built 1869 and later restored, offers train trips, 1 hr 40 min return. Magnificent Mt Tomah Botanic Garden, 35 km E. Glow Worm Tunnel, 37 km N in Wollemi National Park; 1-km

Menindee Lake guarantees Broken Hill's water supply

walk to glow-worms in disused rail tunnel (take a torch). Lake Wallace at Wallerawang, 11 km NW, for sailing and trout fishing. Mt Piper Power Station, 21 km NW (guided tours weekdays). Archvale Rainbow Trout Farm, 7 km W, for fishing and trout sales. Lake Lyell, 9 km W, for power boating, water-skiing and trout fishing. Hassans Walls Lookout, 5 km S via Hassans Walls Rd. At Hartley, 14 km SE: many historic buildings; village is administered by National Parks and Wildlife Service. In Kanangra–Boyd National Park, 92 km S: Jenolan Caves; Kanangra Walls, series of cliffs and valleys (check road conditions). **Visitor information:** 285 Main St; (02) 6351 2307. **See also:** Blue Mountains Experience p. 38; Wildlife-Watching p. 48.

Lockhart

Pop. 882

MAP REF. 121 P10

This pleasant historic town, situated 65 km SW of Wagga Wagga, was originally known as Green's Gunyah and renamed Lockhart in 1897. **In town:** National Trust-listed: Green St, a fine turn-of-the-century streetscape with wide, shady, shopfront verandahs; Showground grandstand (1906). Greens Gunyah Museum, cnr Green and Urana sts, historical museum and craft shop. Mar.: Verandah Town Music Festival. Oct.: Picnic Races. **In the area:** Galore Hill, 16 km N: caves where bushranger Mad Dog Morgan hid; walking tracks (brochures available) and lookouts; picnic/barbecue facilities. **Visitor information:** Lockhart Roadhouse, Urana St; (02) 6920 5531.

Macksville

Pop. 2712

MAP REF. 117 P9

Macksville is an attractive town beside the Nambucca River, south of Nambucca Heads. **In town:** In River St: Mary Boulton Pioneer Cottage, replica of pioneer home with furniture, costumes and horse-drawn vehicles; Star Hotel (1885). Craft markets on riverbank, 4th Sat. each month. Easter: Patchwork and Quilt Display. Apr.: Nambucca River Show. May: Egg-Throwing Championships; Trek to 'the pub with no beer'. Oct.: Pro-Ag Field Day. Nov.: Macksville Gift (Australia's second oldest footrace). **In the area:** Forest drives, brochures available. Holiday Coast Country Crafts, 4 km N on Pacific Hwy. Ngurrala Arts and Crafts Gallery, 8 km N on Wirrimbi Rd, authentic Aboriginal works, brochure available (open Mon.–Wed.). At Bowraville ('the verandah-post town'), 16 km NW: National Trust-classified main street; Joseph and Eliza Newman Folk Museum; Red Cedars Gallery; Bawrrung Cultural Centre (closed Sat.); Sat. markets; regular racedays at picturesque racecourse; Back to Bowra Festival each Oct. Bakers Creek Station, 30 km W, for horseriding, fishing, rainforest walking, canoeing and picnicking; accommodation available. Cosmopolitan Hotel (1903), 'the pub with no beer', made famous by song, at Taylors Arm, 26 km SW. Yarahappini Mt Lookout, 10 km S, for 360° views. Quantum Creations, 15 km S at Eungai Creek, for pottery and sculpture. Horseriding in Ingalba State Forest, 10 km SE. Scotts Head, 18 km SE, has excellent surfing, swimming and fishing; dolphins often seen offshore. **Visitor information:** 4 Pacific Hwy, Nambucca Heads; (02) 6568 6954.

Maclean

Pop. 3157

MAP REF. 117 P5

Maclean, on the Clarence River, about 740 km N of Sydney, is often referred to as 'the Scottish town in Australia'. Fishing fleets from this pretty town and from the nearby towns of Yamba and Iluka catch about 20 percent of the State's seafood. It is also a major base for river-prawning. Sugarcane and mixed-farm crops are grown in the surrounding area. **In town:** Self-guide historic buildings walk, brochure available. In River St: Scottish Corner; Civic Hall (1903). Free Presbyterian Church (1864), cnr Wharf and River sts. Bicentennial Museum and adjacent Stone Cottage (1879), Wharf St, on road to Maclean Lookout and Pinnacle Rocks. Arts and crafts at Ferry Park. Market, 2nd Sat. each month. Easter: Highland Gathering. Aug.: Aquatic Powerboat Regatta. Sept.: Cane Harvest Festival. **In the area:** 24-hr ferry service, 10 km SW, crosses river to Lawrence. Houseboat hire at Brushgrove, 21 km SW. Yuraygir National Park, 24 km SE, features clay and heavy soil formations, rock formations and sand dunes. **Visitor information:** Lower Clarence Visitors Centre, Ferry Park, Pacific Hwy; (02) 6645 4121.

Maitland

Pop. 50 108

MAP REF. 106 C7, 115 M4

On the Hunter River, 32 km NW of Newcastle, Maitland dates back to early colonial days. The city's winding High St has been recorded by the National Trust as a Conservation Area and most of the buildings date back to the 1800s. Settled by Europeans in 1818, when convicts were cedar-cutters, it was a flourishing township by the 1840s. **In town:** Self-guide heritage walks: East Maitland, Maitland Central Precinct and one designed for children; brochures available. National Trust properties in Church St: Georgian-style Grossmann House (1862), now a folk museum, and Brough House (1870), housing city's art collection, are mirror images. Cintra, Regent St, a Victorian mansion offering weekend B&B. Aberglasslyn House (1840), Aberglasslyn La., now a B&B, tours for booked groups or by appt. Former Maitland Gaol, John St, East Maitland, significant historic site, tours daily. Market, 1st Sun. each month at Showground. Feb.: Show. Mar.: Craft-a-Fair. Apr.: Heritage Month; Hunter Valley Steamfest.

Sept.: Garden Ramble. **In the area:** At National Trust-classified Morpeth, 5 km NE: historic buildings with superb iron lace, including St James Church (1830s); craft shops open Thurs.–Sun.; heritage walk, self-guide brochure available; Jazz Festival held in May; Craft Crawl in July; Weird and Wonderful Novelty Teapot Exhibition in Aug. Scenic drive to Walka Waterworks, 3 km N, former pumping station, now excellent recreation area. Signposted scenic drive to historic settlement of Paterson, 16 km N. Tocal Agricultural College, 14 km N, set in historic Georgian-style homestead (1820s), open by appt and on Tocal Field Days (1st weekend in May). At Lochinvar, 13 km W, Windermere Colonial homestead, a private sandstone residence built by convicts 1820s; open by appt. **Visitor information:** cnr New England Hwy and High St; (02) 4933 2611. Web site www.maitlandtourism. nsw.gov.au

Manilla   Pop. 2073

MAP REF. 117 J9
This small town, 42 km NW of Tamworth, is known for its meadery, one of only two in the State. **In town:** Dutton's Meadery, Barraba St, has tastings and sales of fresh honey and mead. In picturesque Manilla St: antique and coffee shops; Royce Cottage Historical Museum. Mar.: NSW Hang-Gliding Championships. June: Lake Keepit Kool Sailing Regatta. Oct.: Festival of Spring Flowers. **In the area:** Manilla Ski Gardens on Lake Keepit, 20 km SW. Warrabah National Park, 40 km NE, a peaceful riverside retreat. Swimming, fishing and canoeing on Namoi and Manilla rivers. **Visitor information:** cnr Murray and Peel sts, Tamworth; (02) 6755 4300. **See also:** New England p. 61.

Menindee   Pop. 385

MAP REF. 118 E13, 120 E1
It was at this small town, 111 km SE of Broken Hill, that the ill-fated Burke and Wills stayed in 1860 on their journey north. The nearby lake system is in contrast with the surrounding semi-arid countryside. **In town:** Maiden's Hotel, Yartla St, where Burke and Wills lodged. Ah Chung's Bakehouse Gallery, Menindee St. May: Inland Speedboat Championships. Aug.: Burke and Wills Fishing Challenge. **In the area:** Yachting, fishing, swimming; water sports and camping on lakes in area. Menindee

Lake, 1 km NW, part of water-storage scheme that guarantees water to Broken Hill. Menindee Lake Lookout, 10 km N. Copi Hollow, 18 km N, attracts water-skiers and power-boat enthusiasts. Kinchega National Park, 1 km W, has prolific wildlife, visitors centre (15 km W), wreck of paddlesteamer *Providence* on Darling River (10 km W), and restored shearers' quarters. **Visitor information:** Yartla St; (08) 8091 4274. Web site www.outbacknsw.org.au

Merimbula   Pop. 4383

MAP REF. 111 F9, 113 G11, 241 Q7
Excellent surfing, fishing and prawning at this small sea and lake town. Its sister village of Pambula also offers fine fishing and surfing. **In town:** Aquarium at Merimbula Wharf, Lake St. Old School Museum, Main St. June: Jazz Festival. Oct.: Country Music Festival. **In the area:** Scenic flights, lake cruises, whale-watching Oct.–Nov. and boat hire. Magic Mountain Family Recreation Park, 5 km N on Sapphire Coast Dr. Tura Beach, 5 km NE. Yellow Pinch Wildlife Park, 5 km E. Pambula, 7 km SW, historic village; market held 2nd Sun. each month. Walking track and lookout at nearby Pambula Beach, 10 km S; kangaroos and wallabies on foreshore early morning and late afternoon. **Visitor information:** Beach St; (02) 6495 1129. Web site www.sapphirecoast.com.au **See also:** The South Coast p. 59.

Merriwa   Pop. 937

MAP REF. 115 J2
This small town in the western Hunter region is noted for its early colonial buildings. **In town:** Self-guide historical walk, brochure available. Historical Museum in stone cottage (1857), Bettington St (check opening times). Bottle Museum, Vennacher St. May: Polocrosse Carnival. June: Festival of Fleeces (includes fireworks). **In the area:** Goulburn River National Park, 35 km S. Convict-built Flags Rd, runs from town to Gungal, 25 km SE. Cassilis, 45 km NW, has historic sandstone buildings. Coolah Tops National Park, 107 km NW: lookouts, waterfalls, glider possums, large snowgums; access by 4WD (alternative sealed-road access via Coolah). Official gem-fossicking area, 27 km SW. **Visitor information:** Shire Council, Vennacher St; (02) 6548 2109. Web site www.infohunt.nsw.gov.au/merriwa

Mittagong   Pop. 6088

MAP REF. 110 C6, 113 I2, 115 J10
The gateway to the Southern Highlands, Mittagong is 110 km S of Sydney. **In town:** Historic cemeteries and buildings. Lake Alexandra, Queen St. Market, 3rd Sat. each month at Uniting Church Hall, cnr Albert and Alice sts. **In the area:** Box Vale walking track commences at northern end of Welby, 4 km NW. Wombeyan Caves, 60 km NW; reached by scenic but narrow road (not suitable for caravans); tours daily. **Visitor information:** Southern Highlands Visitor Information Centre, 62–70 Main St; (02) 4871 2888 or 1300 657 559.

Molong   Pop. 1604

MAP REF. 114 F5
Molong is a charming rural town on the Mitchell Hwy, 35 km NW of Orange. **In town:** Second-hand furniture outlets and cafes. Yarn Market, Craft Cottage and Coach House Gallery, Bank St. **In the area:** Grave of Yuranigh, Aboriginal guide of explorer Sir Thomas Mitchell, 2 km E. Mitchell's Monument, 21 km S, marks site of explorer's base camp. **Visitor information:** Orange Visitor Information Centre, Civic Gardens, Byng St, Orange; (02) 6361 5226 or Railway Station Complex, Mitchell Hwy, Molong.

Moree   Pop. 9270

MAP REF. 116 G5
Situated on the junction of Mehi and Gwydir rivers, 640 km NW of Sydney, this town is the centre of a rich cotton-, wheat- and olive-growing region. It is best known for its artesian spa baths, said to relieve arthritis and rheumatism. **In town:** Spa complex, cnr Anne and Gosport sts. National Trust-classified Moree Lands Office (1894), cnr Frome and Heber sts; opposite, Moree Plains Regional Gallery. Barry Roberts historic walk, self-guide brochure available. Yurundiali Aboriginal Corporation, Endeavour La., operates a screen-print clothing factory (tours by appt). The Big Plane, Amaroo Dr., a DC3 transport plane at Amaroo Tavern. Market, 1st Sun. each month at Jellicoe Park. Easter: Carnival of Sport. Nov.: Golden Grain and Cotton Festival. **In the area:** At Trawalla, 35 km E, large pecan nut farm; tours. Inspection of cotton gins during harvesting season (Apr.–July). **Visitor information:** Lyle Houlihan Park, cnr Newell and Gwydir hwys; (02) 6757 3350. Web site www.moreeonline.net.au

Moruya   Pop. 2602

MAP REF. 113 H7, 139 M8

Many well-known old dairying estates were founded near this town, which was once a gateway to the Araluen and Braidwood goldfields. Situated on the Moruya River, 322 km S of Sydney, it is now a dairying and oyster-farming centre. Granite used in the pylons of the Sydney Harbour Bridge was quarried in the district. **In town:** Eurobodalla Historic Museum, in town centre, depicts discovery of gold at Mogo and general history of district. Courthouse (1880), Princes Hwy. St Marys Catholic Church (1889), Queen St. Markets in Main St, each Sat. Oct.: Jazz Festival. **In the area:** Good fishing, surfing and water sports. Black swan and sea-eagle colonies up-river at Yarragee. Deua National Park, 20 km W, for flora and fauna; Hanging Mountain and lookout in park. Nerrigundah, 44 km SW, former goldmining town. At Bodalla, 24 km S: Coomerang House, home of 19th-century industrialist and dairy farmer Thomas Sutcliffe Mort; Mort Memorial Church and historic cemetery. **Visitor information:** cnr Princes Hwy and Beach Rd, Batemans Bay; (02) 4472 6900, freecall 1800 802 528 or Narooma; (02) 4476 2881, freecall 1800 240 003.

Moss Vale   Pop. 6108

MAP REF. 110 B7, 113 I3, 115 J10

The industrial and agricultural centre of the Southern Highlands, this town stands on part of the 1000-acre parcel of land granted to Charles Throsby in 1819. **In town:** Leighton Gardens, Main St. Historic walk, brochure available. Southern High-lands Country Fair, 4th Sun. each month, at showground. Mar.: Agricultural Show. **In the area:** Cecil Hoskins Nature Reserve, 3 km NE, has abundance of birdlife. At Sutton Forest, 6 km SW, A Little Piece of Scotland, for all things Scottish; Sutton Forest Village Market, 3rd Sun. each month at Village Hall. Horse studs in surrounding countryside. **Visitor information:** Southern Highlands Visitor Information Centre, 62–70 Main St, Mittagong; (02) 4871 2888, or 1300 657 559.

Moulamein   Pop. 459

MAP REF. 120 I10, 237 P9

This town on the Edward River is the oldest in the Riverina. It was an early river crossing for cattle drovers and a busy inland port. Today, Moulamein is a service centre for the surrounding wheat district and a popular spot for river fishing. **In town:** Old Wharf (1850s), Morago St. Restored courthouse (1845), Nyang St (obtain key from Shire Offices). Riverside picnic areas. Lake Moulamein, Brougham St. Easter: Yabby Races. Dec.: Horseracing Cup. **Visitor information:** The Business Centre, Morago St, Moulamein; (03) 5887 5354 (weekdays) or 25 Murray St, Barham; (03) 5453 3100 (weekends).

Mudgee   Pop. 8195

MAP REF. 114 H3

This attractive town, with wide streets and gracious Victorian buildings, is the centre of one of the largest premium wine-producing regions in Australia. Located on the Cudgegong River, 264 km NW of Sydney, its local produce includes wine grapes (shiraz), fine wool, livestock and gourmet foods. The pleasantly undulating landscape has drawn many artists to the region. **In town:** Self-guide historical town walks, brochure available. Many National Trust-classified buildings. In Market St: St John's Church of England (1860); St Mary's Roman Catholic Church; railway station; town hall; Colonial Inn Museum. Honey Haven, cnr Hill End and Gulgong rds. Market, 1st and 2nd Sat. each month. Sept.: Wine Festival. **In the area:** Site of 'Old Bark School' attended by Henry Lawson, 6 km N; adjacent, Eurunderee Provisional School with displays of school life in 1876, 1900 and 1970 (check opening times). Munghorn Gap Nature Reserve, 34 km NE, features sandstone outcrops, 160 bird species, walking tracks and picnic areas. Water sports and trout fishing at Windamere Dam, 24 km SE; camping facilities. Pick-Your-Own Farm, 12 km S, has variety of fruit and vegetables (open Oct.–May). Mt Vincent Mead, Common Rd, 4 km SW, produces alcholic mead from honey (tastings and sales). Fragrant Farm, garden and craft shop, 8 km SW. Hargraves, 39 km SW, old goldmining town; gold-panning tours (inquire at Hargraves General Store at Bushlands Caravan Park). Eighteen local wineries, including Poets Corner Wines, Huntington Estate, Botobolar; signposted self-guide drives. **Visitor information:** 84 Market St; (02) 6372 1020. **See also:** Vineyards and Wineries p. 53.

Mullumbimby   Pop. 2870

MAP REF. 117 Q2, 525 Q12

Situated in lush subtropical country, Mullumbimby is some 850 km NE of Sydney. **In town:** Art Gallery, cnr Burringbar and Stuart sts. Antiques gallery in National Trust-classified Cedar House (1908), Dalley St. Brunswick Valley Historical Museum, in old post office (1907), Stuart St. Brunswick Valley Heritage Park, Tyagarah St, features rainforest plants. Market, 3rd Sat. each month at museum. Sept.: Chincogan Fiesta. **In the area:** Wanganui Gorge, 20 km W, 4-km bushwalk through gorge. Crystal Castle, 7 km SW, large display of natural quartz. Skydiving and paragliding at airstrip at Tyagarah, 13 km SE on Pacific Hwy. **Visitor information:** 80 Jonson St, Byron Bay; (02) 6685 8050.

Mulwala   Pop. 1593

MAP REF. 121 N13, 239 L3

On the foreshores of Lake Mulwala, this town is a major aquatic centre. Lake Mulwala is an artificial lake of over 6000 ha, formed by the damming of the Murray River at Yarrawonga Weir in 1939 to provide water for irrigation. **In town:** Yachting, water-skiing, sailboarding, swimming, canoeing and fishing. Everglade and Swamp Tours to waterbird rookeries and native animal habitats, bookings essential. Linley Park Animal Farm, Corowa Rd, has native and exotic animals, and horse and ponyrides (open long weekends and school holidays). Pioneer Museum, Melbourne St, featuring historic farming exhibits (open Wed.–Sun.). Tunzafun Amusement Park, Melbourne St, for mini-golf, mini-train and dodgem cars. Cruises on Lake Mulwala. **Visitor information:** Irvine Pde, Yarrawonga; (03) 5744 1989.

Murrurundi   Pop. 902

MAP REF. 117 J13

This picturesque town on the New England Hwy, set in a lush valley on the Pages River, is overshadowed by the Liverpool Ranges. **In town:** St Joseph's Catholic Church, Polding St, contains altar made of 1000 pieces of Italian marble. Self-guide historical town walk, brochure from Murrurundi Museum, Mayne St (check opening times). Paradise Park, Paradise Rd, is horseshoe-shaped and surrounded by mountains; kangaroos visit in evening. Just behind park, difficult walk called 'Through the

Eye of the Needle', referring to small gap in rocks to squeeze through; excellent view from top of rock formation. Apr.: Sheepdog Trials. Sept.: Billycart Competition. Oct.: Bushman's Carnival. **In the area:** Chilcott's Creek, 15 km N, where huge diprotodon remains were found; now held in the Australian Museum (Sydney). Wallabadah Rocks, 26 km NE, a large plug of an extinct volcano (959 m high); flowering orchids seen here in Oct. Burning Mountain, 20 km S at Wingen, a deep coal seam that has been smouldering at least 5000 years. **Visitor information:** Council Offices, 47 Mayne St; (02) 6546 6205.

Murwillumbah   Pop. 7657

MAP REF. 117 Q1, 525 Q11
Situated on the banks of the Tweed River, 31 km S of the Qld border in the beautiful Tweed Valley, Murwillumbah's local industries include cattle-raising and the growing of sugarcane, tropical fruits, tea and coffee. **In town:** World Heritage Rainforest Centre, cnr Pacific Hwy and Alma St, has educational displays on local vegetation and wildlife. Tweed River Regional Art Gallery, Tumbulgum Rd, home to Doug Moran National Portrait Prize. Tweed River Historical Society Museum, cnr Queensland Rd and Bent St, has displays of local history (check times). Market in Main St, 1st Sat. each month. Market in Showgrounds, 4th Sun. each month. May: Fish 'n' Nana Festival. Aug.: Tweed Valley Banana Festival. **In the area:** Tweed River houseboat hire, on Pacific Hwy, 1 km N of information centre. Lisnager Homestead (1902), just past Showgrounds on northern edge of town (open Sun. 10 a.m. –3 p.m.). Condong Sugar Mill, 5 km N (open July–Dec.). Tropical Fruitworld, 15 km N. Treetops Environment Centre, 8 km NE, features furniture crafted from salvaged timber. Madura Tea Estates, 12 km NE. At Tyalgum, 16 km E, Music Festival held in Sept. Hare Krishna Community Farm at Eungella, 10 km W; visitors welcome. Pioneer Plantation, Pottsville Rd, Mooball, 19 km SE, a working banana plantation with farm animals, native gardens and nectar-feeding birds (tours including 6WD trip to top of Banana Mountain). World Heritage-listed national parks within radius of 50 km W include Nightcap National Park (road access to Mt Nardi, one of highest peaks in park), Border Ranges National Park (featuring walking

Fishing boats at Wagonga Inlet, Narooma

tracks to Pinnacle Lookout with views of Mt Warning and Tweed Valley, Tweed Valley Lookout and Antarctic Beech Picnic Area) and Mt Warning National Park. Scenic drives, self-guide brochures available. **Visitor information:** World Heritage Rainforest Centre, cnr Pacific Hwy and Alma St; (02) 6672 1340. **See also:** National Parks p. 42.

Muswellbrook   Pop. 10 541

MAP REF. 115 K2
In the Upper Hunter Valley, Muswellbrook is the service centre for the surrounding agricultural area. There is also a large open-cut coal-mining industry. **In town:** Art Gallery in old town hall, Bridge St. Upper Hunter Wine Centre, Loxton House, Bridge St. Historical town walk, self-guide brochure available. Mar.: Agricultural Show. Oct.–Nov.: Spring Carnival. **In the area:** Seven local wineries open for tastings and sales, including Rosemount Estate (35 km SW) and Arrowfield Wines (28 km S). Wollemi National Park, 30 km SW, features Aboriginal carvings and paintings. Sandy Hollow, 36 km SW, Bush Ride held in Apr. Bayswater Power Station, 16 km S (tours Tues. and Fri., departing 1 p.m.). **Visitor information:** 87 Hill St; (02) 6541 4050, freecall 1800 065 773. Web site www.infohunt.nsw.gov.au/muswell

Nambucca Heads Pop. 6253

MAP REF. 117 P9
At the mouth of the Nambucca River, 552 km N of Sydney, this beautifully-sited town is ideal for boating, fishing, surfing,

water-skiing and swimming. **In town:** Copenhagen Mill and Shipyard Foreshore Walk, self-guide signposted historical walk. Headland Historical Museum, Headland Reserve. Model Train Museum, Pelican Cres. Stringer Art Gallery, Ridge St, for local art. Crafters Cottage, Ridge St. Mosaic sculpture, Bowra St. V-Wall Breakwater, Wellington Dr., where you can add your own graffiti to the rocks. Stuart Island Golf Club, in middle of river, Australia's only island set aside for a golf course. Gordon Park Rainforest, between town centre and Inner Harbour. Market, 2nd Sun. each month at Nambucca Plaza. Easter: Country Music Festival. June: Ken Howard Memorial Bowls Competition. Aug.: VW Spectacular (odd-numbered years). Oct.: Show 'n' Shine Hot Rod Exhibition. **In the area:** Breathtaking views from several lookouts. Scuba-diving training and charters. Wooden toys at Swiss Toymaker, 5 km N on Pacific Hwy (closed Sun.). At Valla Beach, 10 km N: Valla Art and Craft Gallery; Valla Smokehouse, gourmet smoked products; Australiana Workshop; Gallery of Hidden Treasures. **Visitor information:** 4 Pacific Hwy; (02) 6568 6954. Web site www.midcoast.com.au/~nambuct

Narooma   Pop. 3389

MAP REF. 111 I2, 113 H9, 139 N11, 241 R2
This popular fishing resort at the mouth of the Wagonga Inlet on the Princes Hwy, 360 km S of Sydney, is well known for its natural beauty. **In town:** Scenic cruises on *Wagonga Princess*; whale-watching cruises (mid-Sept.–mid-Nov.); Montague Island trips with National Parks guide to

see little (fairy) penguin colony and Australian and New Zealand fur seals (year-round, bookings essential); scuba-diving to shipwrecks. Oct.: International Blues Festival. **In the area:** Scenic golf course on cliff-top, Ballingalla St. Mystery Bay near Lake Corunna, 17 km s, haunt of lapidary collectors with its strange rock formations. Other inlets and lakes north and south of town. Central Tilba (founded 1895), 17 km sw just off Princes Hwy: a heritage area classified as 'unusual mountain village' by National Trust; old buildings, including ABC Cheese Factory in original 19th-century condition; new buildings to National Trust specifications; high quality arts and crafts; Tilba Festival each Easter. Nearby, Tilba Valley Vineyard. At Tilba Tilba, further 2 km s, Foxglove Spires, historic cottage surrounded by a 3.5-ha garden. At Wallaga Lake, 22 km sw, Umbarra Aboriginal Cultural Centre: locally made artifacts; hands-on cultural activities; tours to Aboriginal sites. **Visitor information:** Princes Hwy; (02) 4476 2881, freecall 1800 240 003. Web site www.naturecoast-tourism.com.au **See also:** Wildlife-Watching p. 48; The South Coast p. 59.

Narrabri   Pop. 6419

MAP REF. 116 G8

Situated between the Nandewar Range, including Mt Kaputar National Park and the extensive Pilliga scrub country, Narrabri is a major cotton-producing centre. **In town:** Historic buildings, including courthouse (1886), Maitland St. Self-guide town walk/drive, leaflets available. Riverside picnic area, Tibbereena St. Apr.: Agricultural Show. June: Farm-craft. Oct.: Spring Festival. **In the area:** Tours of cotton fields and gin processing plants (Apr.–June). CSIRO Australia Telescope, 25 km w: six giant radio telescopes; visitors centre (open Mon.–Fri.). Yarrie Lake, 32 km w, for birdwatching, water-skiing and windsurfing. Mt Kaputar National Park, 53 km e in dramatic volcanic mountain country; 360° views from peak take in one-tenth of NSW (drive to summit, or 3.5-km walk from main carpark); Sawn Rocks, wilderness area in northern section (via Bingara Rd), has spectacular basaltic formation; bright pink slug endemic to Nandewar Range, found nowhere else. **Visitor information:** Newell Hwy; (02) 6799 6760. Web site www.tournarrabri.nsw.gov.au

Narrandera   Pop. 4678

MAP REF. 121 P9

This historic town on the Murrumbidgee River, at the junction of the Newell and Sturt hwys, is an urban conservation area with several National Trust-classified buildings. Located 570 km sw of Sydney, it is the gateway to the Murrumbidgee Irrigation Area. **In town:** Lake Talbot Aquatic Playground, Lake Dr. Antiques in Larmer St. NSW Forestry Tree Nursery, Broad St (closed weekends). On Newell Hwy: Tiger Moth Memorial; Parkside Cottage Museum; information centre with 5.8-m playable guitar at Narrandera Park. My Dolls, Dangar Dr., doll and teddy-bear collection. Two Foot town heritage tour, Bundidgerry Walking Track through Nature Reserve (koalas in the wild), and Blue Arrow scenic drive; pamphlets available. Mar.: John O'Brien Bush Festival. Aug.: Camellia Show. Oct.: Tree-mendous Festival. **In the area:** Inland Fisheries Research Station, 6 km se, has visitors centre (open Mon.–Fri.). Berembed Weir, 40 km se, for picnicking, fishing and boating. Craig Top Deer Farm, 8 km nw (tours daily). **Visitor information:** Narrandera Park, Newell Hwy; (02) 6959 1766, freecall 1800 672 392. **See also:** Vineyards and Wineries p. 53.

Narromine   Pop. 3486

MAP REF. 114 D2

This town on the Macquarie River, 457 km nw of Sydney, is the centre of an area well known for quality agricultural products, including citrus fruit, tomatoes, corn, lamb, beef and cotton. It is also regarded as an outstanding gliding area. **In town:** At information centre, photographic history of area, from early 1900s. On Mitchell Hwy: Waterslide at Rose Gardens Caravan Park, eastern edge of town; at airport, western side of town, gliding and ultralight flying and Aviation Museum, with vintage aircraft and memorabilia. Market at Tom Perry Park, 1st Sun. every 2nd month. Nov.: Festival of Flight. **In the area:** Water-skiing along the Macquarie River. Tours of Highland View, large commercial lime orchard, 3 km nw on Mitchell Hwy. Tours of cotton gins, details from information centre. Swane's Rose Nursery, 5 km w. Narromine Iris Farm, 3 km s on Torringley Rd; over 600 varieties. Gui Gui Weir, 44 km n, for swimming, fishing and picnics. **Visitor information:** 37 Burraway St; (02) 6889 4596. Web site www.narromine.nsw.gov.au

Nelson Bay   Pop. 7001

MAP REF. 106 H2, 115 O4

The beautiful bay on which this town is situated is the main anchorage of Port Stephens, about 60 km n of Newcastle. **In town:** Restored Inner Lighthouse, Nelson Head, includes museum highlighting early history of area. Self-guide heritage walk from Dutchmans Bay to Little Beach (brochure available); dolphin-watching cruises; whale-watching cruises (June–July, Oct.–Nov., check with information centre); cruises on harbour, Myall River and to Broughton Island; dive charters; 4WD tours along coastal dunes; canoe, aquabike and boat hire. Shell Museum, Sandy Point Rd, Corlette. Craft market in Neil Carroll Park, Victoria Pde, 1st and 3rd Sun. each month (every Sun. in school holidays); markets in Lutheran Church grounds, 1st Sat. each month. Game-fishing tournaments (details from information centre). Nov.: Regional Boat Show. **In the area:** Native Flora Reserve at Little Beach, 1 km e. Gan Gan Lookout, 2 km sw on Nelson Bay Rd. Toboggan Hill Park, 5 km sw, has toboggan runs, mini-golf course, indoor wall-climbing and fun shed. On Nelson Bay Rd: Port Stephens Winery, 10 km sw (Jazz at the Winery held in Mar.); Oakvale Farm and Fauna World, 16 km sw at Salt Ash. Tomago House (1843), 30 km sw on Tomago Rd (open Sun.). Stockton Sand Dunes, accessible by 4WD (or safari) from Anna Bay or Williamtown, 38 km sw, huge dune area popular for sandboarding. At Shoal Bay, 2 km ne, Jazz, Wine and Food Fair held in June. Tomaree National Park, stretches along coast from Shoal Bay (3 km ne) to Anna Bay (10 km sw); signposted walk around headland; Fort Tomaree Lookout for 360° views (signposted walkway to top). Across bay (70 km by road), Yacaaba Lookout also offers 360° views. **Visitor information:** Port Stephens Visitor Information Centre, Victoria Pde; (02) 4981 1579. Web site www.portstephens.org.au **See also:** Wildlife-Watching p. 48; Port Stephens p. 75.

Newcastle   Pop. 270 324

MAP REF. 104, 106 G7, 115 N4

This large and vibrant city, 158 km n of Sydney, overlooks a spectacular harbour and is bordered by some of the finest surfing beaches in the world. After a significant earthquake in 1989, some rebuilding was necessary. Newcastle is a popular centre for visitors attracted to the magnificent coastline and the picturesque villages and vineyards of the nearby Hunter Valley region. **In town:** Queens Wharf, on Wharf Rd, centrepoint of foreshore redevelopment, has indoor and outdoor restaurants; 'boutique' brewery; observation tower linked by walkway to the City Mall, a part of Hunter St. Victorian-era terrace houses along nearby city streets. Regional Museum, Hunter St, includes interactive 'Supernova' museum for children. Regional Art Gallery, Laman St. Historic customs house (1877) in Watt St, now a bar and restaurant. City Hall (1929), King St. In King Edward Park, situated on waterfront: sunken gardens; panoramic ocean views; band rotunda

(1898); obelisk (1850), marks site of Newcastle's first windmill; Soldiers Baths (1880s), off Shortland Espl., now a public pool; Bogey Hole, hole cut in rocks by convict labour, also now a public pool. Merewether Baths, off Scenic Dr., largest ocean baths in Southern Hemisphere. River and harbour cruises. Fort Scratchley, Nobbys Rd, perched high above Newcastle Harbour, features network of tunnels, relics of gun emplacements and fascinating Military and Maritime museums. Blackbutt Reserve, off Carnley Ave in suburb of New Lambton, 182 ha of bushland with duck ponds, native animal enclosures, walking trails and picnic/barbecue facilities. Self-guide walks, including Town Walk, and Shipwreck

Walk along foreshore; maps available. Jan.: National Maritime Regatta. Mar.: Surfest; Beaumont Street Jazz and Arts Festival. Aug.: Conservatorium Keyboard Festival; Cathedral Flower Festival (music, flower displays). Sept.: Hamilton Fiesta; Cathedral Music Festival. Oct.: Mattara Festival. **In the area:** Many fine surf beaches. On and around Lake Macquarie, 20 km S, a huge aquatic playground with well-maintained parks lining foreshore: lake cruises from Toronto Wharf and Belmont Public Wharf; Dobell House, Dobell Dr., Wangi Wangi, home of artist Sir William Dobell, has collection of his work and memorabilia (check opening times); tours of power station at Eraring (bookings essential); Lake Macquarie

Port Stephens

The white volcanic sand and aquamarine waters of Port Stephens have a distinctly tropical look, and the annual average temperature is within about 2°C of that of the Gold Coast. This large deep-water port, less than an hour's drive from Newcastle, is one of the most unspoiled and attractive seaside holiday areas on the New South Wales coast. Two-and-a-half times the size of Sydney Harbour, and almost enclosed by two volcanic headlands, the harbour is fringed by sheltered white sandy beaches backed by stretches of natural bushland. In spring, wildflowers grow in profusion.

The deep, calm waters of the harbour are ideal for boating and there is excellent beach and estuary fishing for the keen angler. You can hire a range of boats, from aquascooters and catamarans to sailing and power boats. Various cruises are available, including cruises to watch bottlenose dolphins, Myall River cruises, lake cruises and whale-watching cruises (June–July to see humpbacks; end Sept.–Oct. to see humpbacks and minke whales). Excellent game-fishing waters are within reach outside the harbour, but local fishing clubs warn against going outside the heads unless you are an experienced sailor with a two-motor boat. The best way to reach these waters is aboard one of the many professional charter boats licensed to take anglers and sightseers outside the heads. Early in the afternoon you can watch the local fishing fleet coming into **Nelson Bay**, the main anchorage of the port.

Restaurants in the area offer seafood as a speciality. Sample a lobster supreme with a fine local wine. For dedicated oyster lovers, a trip to Moffat's Oyster Barn, set on Big Swan Bay, is a must. As well as viewing oyster cultivation and learning about their 4-year life cycle, you can enjoy a delicious meal of oysters. If you go by boat, keep within the well-marked channel to avoid oyster leases. The Barn is open weekends only, and bookings are essential.

For surfing, you can visit the spectacular ocean beaches outside the harbour. Within about 6 kilometres of Nelson Bay are Zenith,

An idyllic beach at Port Stephens

Wreck and Box beaches, Fingal Bay and One Mile Beach. Always popular are the 4WD tours along Stockton Beach, a huge sand-dune expanse – you can view Aboriginal shell middens, the *Sygna* wreck and World War II lines of defence. There are also camel and horse rides along Stockton Beach.

Other local attractions include: art galleries; craft markets; the toboggan run at Toboggan Hill Park, Nelson Bay; Oakvale Farm and Fauna World, Salt Ash; and Fighter World, RAAF Base Williamtown. There is a wide variety of accommodation in the area, including caravan and camping parks. The main towns, apart from Nelson Bay, are Shoal Bay, Fingal Bay, Anna Bay, Tanilba Bay, Lemon Tree Passage and Soldiers Point.

For further information about the area, contact the Port Stephens Visitor Information Centre, Victoria Pde, Nelson Bay; (02) 4981 1579. Web site www.portstephens.org.au **See also:** Wildlife-Watching p. 48 and individual entries in A–Z town listing for towns in bold type. **Map references:** 106 H2, 115 N4.

Heritage Afloat Fest held Apr. Munmorah State Recreation Area, a coastal recreation area south of Swansea. Shortland Wetlands, 15 km W, a bird and reptile habitat, with walking, cycling and canoeing trails. About 50 km NW is Australia's famous wine region, the Hunter Valley. Fighter World, museum and high-tech exhibition at Williamtown RAAF base, 20 km N. Yuelarbah Track, part of Great North Walk from Sydney to Newcastle, 25 km from Lake Macquarie to Newcastle harbour; pamphlet available. **Visitor information:** Wheeler Place, 363 Hunter St; (02) 4974 2999. Web site www.ncc.nsw.gov.au

Nimbin   Pop. 319

MAP REF. 117 Q2, 525 Q12

The Aquarius festival in 1973 established Nimbin as the alternative culture capital of Australia. Today Nimbin's peaceful, friendly atmosphere, and the buildings designed and decorated to reflect the community's ideas and beliefs, attract visitors wishing to experience an alternative lifestyle. **In town:** In Cullen St: shops, painted in psychedelic colours, featuring homemade products and local art and craft; Triple Blah Theatrette, showing variety of short films; Choices Cafe, offering great views over the valley; Nimbin Museum, dedicated to hippy culture and history of St Aquarius; town hall mural featuring Aboriginal art; Rainbow Power Company, Alternative Way, alternative power supplier, now exporting (tours). Market, Sat. at Alternative Way; Aquarius Fair, 3rd Sun. each month at Nimbin Community Centre, Cullen St, outlet for local craftspeople. May: Mardi Grass Festival, organised by the Nimbin HEMP (Help End Marijuana Prohibition) Embassy. Sept.: Agricultural Show; Spring Arts Festival. **In the area:** Eco-tours of area; spectacular volcanic Nimbin Rocks, 3 km S, on Lismore Rd. At The Channon, 15 km SE: 'alternative' craft market in Coronation Park, 2nd Sun. each month; Opera at The Channon in Aug.; Music Bowl Live Band Concert each Nov. World Heritage-listed Nightcap National Park, 5 km NE, features Protesters Falls (9.5 km NE), named after the landmark 1979 anti-logging protest, which led to the area being gazetted a national park. **Visitor information:** Lismore Visitor Information Centre, cnr Ballina and Molesworth sts, Lismore; (02) 6622 0122. Web site www.liscity.nsw.gov.au

Nowra   Pop. 17 614

MAP REF. 110 E12, 113 I4, 115 K11

Nowra is the principal town of the Shoalhaven district, a popular tourist area on the south coast. Bomaderry is on the northern side of the river. **In town:** Historic Houses Trust property Meroogal (1885), cnr Worrigee and West sts (open Sat. p.m. and Sun.). Shoalhaven Historical Museum, cnr Plunkett and Kinghorne sts, in old police station. On Shoalhaven River: fishing, water-skiing, canoeing, sailing, and cruises on MV *Christine* (depart from Nowra Wharf, Riverview Rd, check times). Hanging Rock, via Junction St, has fine views. Nowra Animal Park, Rockhill Rd. Bens Walk, alongside river; Bomaderry Creek Walk from Bomaderry, self-guide pamphlets available. Market, 3rd Sun. each month. Oct.: Spring Festival. **In the area:** Many beautiful beaches within 30-km radius of town. Cambewarra Estate winery (open weekends and public holidays), 5 km N on Illaroo Rd. Australian Naval Aviation Museum, 7 km SW at HMAS *Albatross*. Cambewarra Lookout, 12 km NW, for spectacular views of Shoalhaven River. At Kangaroo Valley, 23 km NW: historic buildings including Friendly Inn (National Trust-classified); Pioneer Settlement Reserve, reconstruction of dairy farm of 1880s; Hampden Bridge (1898), oldest suspension bridge in Australia; Kangaroo Valley Fruit World, a working fruit farm; canoeing and kayaking safaris to Kangaroo River and Shoalhaven Gorge. Fitzroy Falls in Morton National Park, 38 km NW; also in park (turn-off at Kangaroo Valley), Tallowa Dam water catchment area, 42 km NW, ideal for picnicking. Bundanon, National Estate-listed historic homestead, 21 km W, given to the nation by artist Arthur Boyd and his wife Yvonne; Bundanon collection and Arthur Boyd's studio, open 1st Sun. each month (obtain tickets from information centre, advance bookings essential). Marayong Emu Farm, Falls Creek, 11 km S. At Culburra, 21 km SE: nearby Lake Wollumboola and coastal beaches for surfing, swimming, prawning and fishing; beach patrolled in summer; Open Fishing Carnival held Jan. Fresh fish and oyster sales at Greenwell Point, 14 km E. **Visitor information:** Shoalhaven Visitors Centre, cnr Princes Hwy and Pleasant Way, Nowra; (02) 4421 0778. Web site www. shoalhaven.nsw.gov.au

Nundle   Pop. 270

MAP REF. 117 K12

The history of this small town began in the early gold-rush era of the 1850s. Well known for its fishing, Nundle is situated 56 km SE of Tamworth, at the foot of the Great Dividing Range in a sheep, cattle, wheat and timber district. The western edge of town is skirted by the Peel River. **In town:** In Jenkins St: Courthouse (1880); antique shop; historic Peel Inn (1860s). Goldmining display in restored coffin factory, Gill St. Aug.–Sept. and Dec.: Camp Drafting and Dog Trials. **In the area:** Hanging Rock and Sheba Dams Reserve, 11 km W, for picnicking, bushwalking and camping. Mineral fossicking at Hanging Rock (good samples of scheelite can be found); gold-panning on Peel River. Chaffey Reservoir, 11 km N, for fishing, sailing and picnicking; Dulegal Arboretum on foreshore. Fossickers Way tour through scenic New England countryside, brochure available. **Visitor information:** cnr Peel and Murray sts, Tamworth; (02) 6755 4300. **See also:** New England p. 61.

Nyngan   Pop. 2240

MAP REF. 119 R10

The centre of a sheep, wheat and wool district, Nyngan is 603 km NW of Sydney beside the Bogan River. **In town:** Historical town drive and Levee Tour (levee built after 1990 floods), brochures available. Historic buildings, especially in Cobar and Pangee sts. In Pangee St: Bicentennial Mural Wall; Flood Museum at railway station, has local memorabilia (open Mon.–Sat.). Railway Overbridge, heritage-classified footbridge, lookout over town. Cobb & Co Coach Yard, cnr Nymagee St and Monagee Rd, has old coaches, working forge, museum. Apr.: Anzac Day Race Meeting; Agricultural Show. Aug.: Dog Trials. Sept: Spring into Nyngan (festival). **In the area:** Cairn on private property, 65 km S, marking geographic centre of NSW. Grave of Richard Cunningham, 70 km S, botanist with explorer Major Mitchell's party, speared by Aborigines in 1835. Waterbird sanctuary and breeding ground in Macquarie Marshes, 64 km N. **Visitor information:** Nyngan Video Parlour, Pangee St; (02) 6832 1155. Web site www.slnsw.gov.au/nyngan

Orange
Pop. 30 705

MAP REF. 114 G6

This prosperous city is set in rich red volcanic soil on the slopes of Mt Canobolas, 264 km NW of Sydney. Orange is known for its food and wines, parks and gardens, and goldmining history. An obelisk marks the birthplace of the city's most famous citizen, poet A. B. (Banjo) Paterson; his birthday is celebrated with the Banjo Paterson Festival. **In town:** Historic Cook Park, Summer St, has begonia house (flowers Feb.–May), duck pond, fernery and picnic area; self-guide walk through park (brochure available). Botanic Gardens, Kearneys Drive. Museum, McNamara St. Civic Gardens, Byng St, comprises Regional Art Gallery, City Library, information centre and Civic Theatre. Self-guide historical walk, brochure available. Sun. market, Kmart carpark. Feb.–Mar.: Banjo Paterson Festival. Apr.: Food of Orange District Week. **In the area:** Campbell's Corner, 8 km S on Pinnacle Rd, a roadside picnic/barbecue spot. Lucknow, 10 km SE, old goldmining town. Ophir goldfields, 27 km N, site of first discovery of payable gold in Australia in 1851, features fossicking centre, picnic area, walking trails to historic gold tunnels (brochures available), and tours of working goldmine. At Borenore, 15 km W, National Field Days held Oct.–Nov. Borenore Caves, 17 km W, have picnic/barbecue facilities. Lake Canobolas Park, 8 km SW via Cargo Rd, has recreation and camping area, deer park, children's playground, picnic/barbecue facilities; trout fishing in Lake Canobolas. Mt Canobolas Park, a 1500-ha bird and animal sanctuary, 14 km SW. Cadia Mines, 25 km SE, largest gold and copper mine in the State; check annual open day. Several wineries open for tastings and sales (check times). **Visitor information:** Civic Gardens, Byng St; (02) 6361 5226.

Parkes
Pop. 10 094

MAP REF. 114 D5

The settlement of Bushmans was renamed Parkes following the visit of Sir Henry Parkes (1815–96) who was a major player in the lead-up to Australian Federation. Situated 364 km W of Sydney on the Newell Hwy, Parkes is today the commercial and industrial centre of an important agricultural area. **In town:** Tourist drive (90 min.), self-guide tour following arrows. Self-guide historical walks around Parkes

Picturesque Lake Canobolas, near Orange

include one of town's oldest houses, Balmoral, noted for its iron lacework; brochures available. Motor Museum, cnr Bogan and Dalton sts, displays vintage and veteran vehicles, and local art and craft. Henry Parkes Historical Museum, Clarinda St, has memorabilia and 1000-volume personal library of Sir Henry Parkes. In north Parkes: imposing views of town from Memorial Hill, at eastern end of Bushman St; Pioneer Park Museum, Pioneer St, in historic school and church, has displays of early farm machinery and transport; Kelly Reserve (Newell Hwy), playground and picnic/barbecue facilities in bush setting; Bushmans Hill Reserve (Newell Hwy), at site of old goldmine. Jan.: Elvis Revival. Easter: Sports Festival. June: Picnic Races. Oct.: Country Music Spectacular. **In the area:** Australia Telescope Visitors Centre, 23 km N, has excellent educational aids that explain use of giant saucer-shaped telescope. At Peak Hill, 48 km N: Peak Hill working goldmine; lookout offering views of goldmine. **Visitor information:** Kelly Reserve, Newell Hwy; (02) 6862 4365.

Picton
Pop. 2668

MAP REF. 99 J11, 110 E2, 113 I2, 115 K9

Picton, named after Sir Thomas Picton, hero of Waterloo, is 80 km SW of Sydney on Remembrance Dr. (former Hume Hwy). The old buildings and quiet hills of this small town are evocative of an earlier era. Picton's railway heritage is symbolised by a splendid railway viaduct. **In town:** Historic buildings: old railway viaduct (1862) over Stonequarry Creek, Webster St; St Mark's Church (1848), Menangle St; George IV Inn, Argyle St, incorporating Scharer's

Little Brewery. Self-guide historical walk, brochure available. Ghost tours around Picton, Fri. and Sat. nights. Country markets in Menangle Rd, 4th Sat. each month. Jan.: Rodeo. Oct.: Music Festival; Agricultural Show; White Waratah Festival. **In the area:** Sydney Skydiving Centre, 5 km E. On Remembrance Dr.: Jarvisfield (1865), 2 km N, home of pioneer landholders, now clubhouse of Antill Park Golf Club; Wool Away! Woolshed, 3 km N, has bush dances Fri. and Sat. nights. At Thirlmere, 5 km SW: NSW Rail Transport Museum; steam-train rides to Buxton each Sun. (Buxton Rail Craft Markets, 3rd Sun. each month); Festival of Steam held 1st Sun. in Mar. Further 3 km SW, Thirlmere Lakes National Park protects five linked freshwater lakes; scenic drive around lakes. Wirrimbirra Sanctuary, 13 km SW, native flora and fauna; overnight cabins available. Dingo Sanctuary, 15 km S (open Sat. and Sun.). Bridge-swinging (bungee jumping) at Maldon Suspension Bridge, 5 km SE. **Visitor information:** Old Post Office, cnr Argyle and Menangle sts; (02) 4677 3962.

Port Macquarie
Pop. 33 709

MAP REF. 103 G7, 117 P12

Founded as a convict settlement in 1821, and one of the oldest towns in the State, Port Macquarie is now a major holiday resort, situated at the mouth of the Hastings River, 423 km N of Sydney. **In town:** Award-winning Hastings Historical Museum, Clarence St, displays of convict and pioneer relics in 15 rooms of building (1835–40). Convict-built St Thomas' Church (1824–8), Hay St, designed by convict architect Thomas Owen, 3rd oldest surviving church in Australia.

Port Macquarie Historic Courthouse (1869), cnr Hay and Clarence sts (closed Sun.). Mid-North Coast Maritime Museum, William St, features relics from shipwrecks, model ships and photographs of early cargo and passenger ships. At end of Horton St: historic cemetery dating from 1842; Kooloonbung Creek Nature Reserve, 50 ha of natural bushland with board-walks. Roto House and Macquarie Nature Reserve, Lord St, a koala hospital and study centre. Port Macquarie Observatory, William St. Maritime museum, William St. Fantasy Glades, Pacific Dr., with rainforest gardens and picnic/barbecue facilities. Billabong Koala and Aussie Wildlife Park (Billabong Dr.) and Kingfisher Park (Kingfisher Rd), for close-up look at Australian animals. Town Beach, has surf at one end, sheltered coves at other. Peppermint Park has slides and roller-blading. River cruises daily. Walk following coastal headlands from breakwall to lighthouse (8 km). Hydro-golf, Boundary St, a golf course incorporating water targets. Market in Findlay Ave, 2nd and 4th Sun. each month. Jan.: Golden Lure Tournament (deep-sea fishing). **In the area:** Sea Acres Rainforest Centre, 4 km S, includes elevated 1.3 km boardwalk through canopy and guided tours of rainforest. At Lighthouse Beach, 10 km S: 16-km expanse of white sand; camel rides; dolphin-watching from shore; breathtaking views from grounds of Tacking Point Lighthouse at northern end of beach (lighthouse not open to public). Lake Cathie, 16 km S, holiday town between surf beach and tidal lake, for swimming and fishing. Scenic drives to Ellenborough Falls, 85 km SW and to Wauchope and Timbertown, 20 km W; 4WD tours into hinterland; bus tours of surrounding area (brochures available). Exceptionally good fishing and all water sports. Charter fishing; Harley Davidson motor-bike tours; horseriding; abseiling; skirmish (paintball game); skydiving. Cassegrain Winery, 13 km W; Discovery Concert held here under the stars each Oct. **Visitor information:** cnr Clarence and Hay sts; (02) 6581 8000, freecall 1800 025 935. Web site www.portmacquarieinfo.com.au

Queanbeyan Pop. 25 689

MAP REF. 113 E5, 114 G13, 135 G4, 138 H3

Adjoining Canberra, Queanbeyan has a special relationship with the Australian capital. The town, proclaimed in 1838, is named from a squattage held by an ex-convict innkeeper, Timothy Beard, on the Molonglo River and called 'Quinbean' ('clear waters'). **In town:** Self-guide walks through town, brochure available. History Museum, Farrer Pl. Byrne's Mill (1883), now a restaurant, Collett St. Byrne's Mill House, cnr Collett and Morisset sts, now Queanbeyan Books and Prints. Queanbeyan Art Society Inc., Trinculo Pl., exhibits local art and craft. Railway Historical Society Steam Train rides, depart station in Henderson St, check times and destinations. Cottage markets, 2nd Sun. each month (except Jan.). Mar.: Festival of Traditions; Psychic Fair (meetings of psychics, palmists and tarot-card readers). Oct.: Sporting Weekend Spectacular. Nov.: Agricultural Show. **In the area:** Molonglo Gorge, 2 km N, for bushwalking. At Bungendore, 26 km NE: historic village square con-tains Colonial-style shops; Bungendore Woodworks Gallery sells local art and craft; Country Muster held here in Feb. Lark Hill Winery, 7 km N of Bungendore, tastings and sales. Historic Bywong Goldmining Town, 31 km NE, a re-creation of early mining settlement. Googong Dam, 10 km S, for fishing; bushwalking and wildlife refuge on shore. London Bridge Woolshed and Shearers' Quarters, 24 km S; walk 1 km to limestone forma-tion. **Visitor information:** cnr Farrer Pl. and Lowe St; (02) 6298 0241.

Raymond Terrace Pop. 12 332

MAP REF. 106 E6, 115 N4

This town, set on the banks of the Hunter and William rivers, was an important wool-shipping centre in the 1840s. Several historic buildings remain. **In town:** Significant buildings: courthouse (1838, cnr William St and Pacific Hwy), still in use; Church of England and rectory (1830s, Glenelg St), built of hand-hewn sandstone; numerous buildings in historic King St, along waterfront. Sketchley Cottage, on Pacific Hwy, a museum of memorabilia (open Sun.). **In the area:** Hunter Region Botanic Gardens, 3 km S on Pacific Hwy at Motto Farm, has over 2000 native plants and several theme gardens. Fighter World, RAAF Base Williamtown, 16 km NE. Tiligerry Habitat, 34 km N, ecotourism centre with Aboriginal culture and guided walks to see koalas. Convict-built Tanilba House (1831), 36 km N (check times). **Visitor information:** Council Offices, 116 Pacific Hwy; (02) 4980 0255. Web site www.portstephens.org.au

Richmond Pop. 7972

MAP REF. 99 K6, 115 K7

One of the five Macquarie towns and sister town to Windsor, 6 km E, Richmond was proclaimed a town in 1810. **In town:** Historic buildings: Hobartville (privately owned), Castlereagh Rd; Toxana (1841), Windsor St, now an art gallery (open Thurs. and Sat.); St Peter's Church (1841), also in Windsor St, and adjacent graveyard where several notable pioneers, including William Cox and Australia's convict chronicler Margaret Catchpole, are buried. Lions Club Markets, Richmond Park, Windsor St, Sat. every 6 weeks; Bellbird Craft Markets, March St, 1st Sat. each month. Sept.: Hawkesbury District Orchid Spring Show; Hawkesbury Waratah Festival. Sept.–Nov.: Fruits of the Hawkesbury Festival. **In the area:** RAAF base, 3 km E on Windsor–Richmond Rd, oldest Air Force establishment in Australia; used for civilian flying from 1915. University of Western Sydney, 3 km S; foundation stone laid in 1895. Vale of Avoca Lookout, 20 km W, for stunning views over Grose Valley. Bellbird Hill Lookout at Kurrajong Heights, 13 km NW, for views across to Sydney skyline. Markets each Sat. at Bilpin, 31 km NW. Mountain Lagoon, 40 km NW, bushwalking, cabins; brochures available. Hawkesbury Lookout, 15 km SW. **Visitor information:** Tourism Hawkesbury, Ham Common Bicentenary Park, Clarendon; (02) 4588 5895. Web site www.hawkesburyvalley.com

Robertson Pop. 922

MAP REF. 110 E8, 113 I3, 115 K10

The link between the Southern High-lands and the coast, Robertson sits at the top of the Macquarie Pass. Vantage points in the area offer spectacular views of the coast. Robertson is also the centre of the largest potato-growing district in NSW. The idyllic countryside featured in the film *Babe* (1996). **In town:** The Cockatoo Run heritage railway (Port Kembla to Robertson, Tues., Thurs., Sat., Sun. Mar.–Nov.). Market, 2nd Sun. each month, at Robertson School of Arts. Mar.: Agricultural Show. **In the area:** In Morton National Park: Belmore Falls, 10 km SW; Fitzroy Falls, 15 km SW; NPWS Visitor Centre at the town of Fitzroy Falls. Manning Lookout over Kangaroo Valley, 16 km SW. Robertson Rainforest, 2 km S. Carrington Falls, in Budderoo National Park, 10 km SE. **Visitor information:** Southern Highlands Visitor Information

Centre, 62–70 Main St, Mittagong; (02) 4871 2888 or 1300 657 559. **See also:** National Parks p. 42.

Rylstone Pop. 723

MAP REF. 114 I4
This historic town is situated west of the Great Dividing Range on the Cudgegong River, 275 km NW of Sydney. **In town:** Historic buildings, especially in Louee St, including Bridge View Inn information centre and restaurant (formerly bank), and the post office. Self-guide historical town walk, brochure available. Feb.: Rylstone-Kandos Agricultural Show. **In the area:** Many camping spots and fishing areas on Capertee, Cudgegong and Turon rivers. Signposted scenic drives, self-guide brochure available. Bicentennial Museum (open weekends) at Kandos, 3 km S. Lake Windamere, 19 km W, for water sports and fishing; Fishing Festival held here at Easter; camping and picnic/barbecue facilities on shore. Fern Tree Gully, 16 km N, tree ferns in subtropical forest. Military Vehicle Museum, 20 km N. Dunn's Swamp, 18 km E, for camping, fishing and bushwalking. Glen Davis, 56 km SE on Capertee River, surrounded by sheer cliff faces; nearby, Wollemi National Park, for wilderness bushwalking and excellent canoeing. **Visitor information:** Bridge View Inn, Louee St; (02) 6379 1132. Web site www.rylstone.com

Scone Pop. 3468

MAP REF. 115 K1
This town, set in beautiful country on the New England Hwy, 280 km N of Sydney, is the world's second largest thoroughbred and horse-breeding centre. **In town:** In Kelly St: *Mare and Foal*, Elizabeth Park, life-size bronze sculpture by Gabriel Sterk; Australian Stock Horse Museum. Historical Society Museum, Kingdon St (open Wed. and Sun.). Market at information centre, last Sun. each month. May: Horse Festival. Sept.–Oct.: Hunter Valley Horse Expo. Nov.: Rodeo. **In the area:** Several wineries open for tastings. Tours of thoroughbred studs and sheep station. Lake Glenbawn, 15 km E, for water sports, good bass-fishing, lakeside horserides (summer), picnic/barbecue facilities and camping. At Moonan Flat, 50 km NE: Victoria Hotel (1865), Cobb & Co. coach stop during gold-rush era, reputedly patronised by bushranger Captain Thunderbolt; Jazz by the River each Oct. Burning Mountain at Wingen, 20 km N, a deep coal

The Golden Guitar near Tamworth

seam that has been smouldering for at least 5000 years. **Visitor information:** cnr Susan and Kelly sts; (02) 6545 1526. Web site www.infohunt.nsw.gov.au/scone

Shellharbour Pop. 3697

MAP REF. 110 H8, 115 K10
This attractive holiday resort, 7 km S of Lake Illawarra, is one of the oldest settlements on the South Coast. A thriving port in the 1830s, its importance declined once the South Coast railway opened. **In town:** Illawarra Light Railway Museum, Russell St, has train and tram rides, stationary engines and other artifacts. Jan.: Australia Day Breakfast by the Lake. Sept.: Festival of the Forest. **In the area:** Bike paths (also on route of Tourist Drive 10). Killalea Recreation Park, 3 km S, foreshore picnic area; beach here is ideal for surfing, diving, snorkelling and fishing. Blackbutt Forest Reserve, 2 km W, remnant of coastal plain forest in urban area, has walking trails with views of Lake Illawarra and Illawarra Escarpment. BMX circuit at Croom Regional Sporting Complex, 8 km W. Bass Point Aquatic and Marine Reserve, 5 km SE, has picnic area with views; good scuba-diving, snorkelling, fishing and surfing offshore. Lake Illawarra, 7 km N, boat hire. **Visitor information:** Shellharbour Square, Blackbutt; (02) 4221 6169.

Singleton Pop. 12 519

MAP REF. 115 L3
Set on the Hunter River in rich grazing land, Singleton is the geographical heart of the Hunter Valley. New wealth in the form

of huge open-cut coal mines has transformed Singleton into one of the most progressive country centres in the State. **In town:** Town walk, brochure available. Monolithic sundial on riverbank in James Cook Park, Ryan Ave. Sales of herbs at Dullwide Herbs, Falbrook Rd. Markets in Burdekin Park, New England Hwy, 4th Sun. each month. Oct.: Festival of Wine and Roses. **In the area:** Industry and wine tours, details from information centre. Royal Australian Infantry Corps Museum, 5 km S, traces development of the infantry corp from 15th century. Village Fair held in Sept. at Broke, 26 km S. Broke–Fordwich winery area of Hunter Valley, brochure available. Yengo National Park, 15 km S, features extensive Aboriginal carvings and paintings; tours. Wollemi National Park, 15 km SW, a large wilderness park. Pick your own oranges at Hillside Orange Orchard, 25 km SW on Windsor–Putty Rd. Lake St Clair, 25 km N, has extensive recreational and waterway facilities, camping on shore; nearby, magnificent views of Mt Royal Range. **Visitor information:** Shire Offices, Queen St; (02) 6578 7267. Web site www. singleton.nsw.gov.au

Stroud Pop. 598

MAP REF. 115 N3
There are many historic buildings in this delightful town, 75 km N of Newcastle. **In town:** Self-guide town walk covers 32 historic sites, brochure available. In Cowper St: Convict-built St John's Anglican Church, built of local clay bricks (1833), has beautiful stained glass windows and cedar furnishings; Rectory of St John's (1836); Stroud House (1832); Parish House (1837); courthouse, post office and Quambi House. Underground silo (one of 8 built 1841) at Silo Hill Reserve, off Broadway St. July: International Brick and Rolling-pin Throwing. Sept.–Oct.: Rodeo. Nov.: Branch Picnic Races. **Visitor information:** Great Lakes Tourism Board, Little St, Forster; (02) 6554 8799. Web site www.greatlakes.org.au

Tamworth Pop. 31 865

MAP REF. 117 J11
This prosperous city at the junction of the New England and Oxley hwys is the country music capital of Australia, as well as being the heart of many other cultural and musical activities. Thousands of fans flock here for the long-established 10-day Tamworth Country Music Festival. With its attractive public buildings and parks

and gardens, Tamworth is also the commercial capital of northern NSW. **In town:** Country Music Hands of Fame cornerstone at Hands of Fame Park, Kable Ave, has hand imprints of well-known country music stars. National Trust-classified Calala Cottage, Denison St, home of Tamworth's first mayor. City Gallery, Marius St, exhibits works by Turner, Hans Heysen and Will Ashton; also home of National Fibre Collection. Oxley Park Wildlife Sanctuary, north off Brisbane St. Oxley Lookout for views of city and rich Peel Valley, at top of White St; lookout is starting point for Kamilaroi walking track (6.2 km), brochure available. Powerstation Museum, cnr Peel and Darling sts, traces Tamworth's history as first city in Southern Hemisphere to have electric street lighting. At Tamworth RSL Club, Kable St: Tamworth Country Theatre, all-star live radio broadcasts, 3rd Sat. each month (bookings at information centre); Country Music Jamboree (Thurs., from 7.30 p.m.). Various line-dancing venues. Stamp and Coin Market, 1st Sat. each month at St Paul's Church, Church St. Market, 2nd Sun. each month at Showground Pavilion. Main St Markets, 3rd Sun. each month at Peel St Blvd. Jan.: Country Music Festival; National Pro Rodeo. May: Gold Cup Race Meeting. June: Fireside Bush Poetry Festival. **In the area:** Golden Guitar Complex, 6 km S on New England Hwy: fascinating gemstone collection; 12-metre Golden Guitar; Gallery of Stars Wax Museum; Great Australian Ice-creamery; famous Longyard Hotel. Opposite is Country Music Roll of Renown at Radio Centre, dedicated to country music artists who have contributed to Australia's heritage. Lake Keepit State Recreation Area, 57 km NW, for water sports; good visitor facilities. Fossickers Way tour through scenic New England countryside begins at historic goldmining town of Nundle, 63 km SE; brochures available. **Visitor information:** cnr Murray and Peel sts; (02) 6755 4300. Web site www.nnsw.com.au/tamworth **See also:** New England p. 61.

Taree   Pop. 16 702

MAP REF. 103 C13, 115 P1, 117 N13
Taree on the Pacific Hwy, 310 km N of Sydney, serves as the commercial hub of the Manning River district. **In town:** Self-guide historical walks through eastern and western sections of town, brochures available. Houseboat and dinghy hire, Crescent Ave. Taree Craft Centre, next to

information centre, Old Pacific Hwy, Taree North. Manning Regional Art Gallery, MacQuarie St (check opening times). Jan.: Craftathon. Easter: Aquatic Festival. Apr.–May: Eisteddfod. June: Conventional Homes Eco Tour and Envirofair. **In the area:** Weekly markets, details from information centre or web site; many art and craft galleries. 4 national parks and 11 nature reserves; horseriding, and 4WD and mountain-bike tours. Forest drives and walking trails in Manning Valley, brochures available. Joyflights over Manning Valley depart from airport, northern outskirts of town on Lansdowne Rd. Deep Water Shark Gallery, Peverill St, Tinonee, 8 km SW, for Aboriginal art and craft. Good surfing beaches on coast 16 km E. Manning River, a 150-km navigable waterway, with beaches, good fishing and holiday spots. The Big Buzz Funpark, 15 km S on Lakes Way, Rainbow Flat. Rainforest Nature Walk at Hallidays Point, 25 km SE, self-guide leaflet available. Crowdy Bay National Park, 40 km NE, offers wildflowers in spring, fishing, swimming, bushwalking and camping. Coorabakh National Park, 20 km NE on the Pacific Hwy, features scenic drive to Vincent's Lookout, Waitui Falls and Big Nellie Mountain (volcanic plug). High Adventure Air Park, 38 km NE on Pacific Hwy, a light airsports training and recreational centre. **Visitor information:** Manning Valley Visitor Information Centre, Old Pacific Hwy, Taree North; (02) 6552 1900, freecall 1800 801 522. Web site www.gtcc.nsw.gov.au/tourism

Tathra   Pop. 1684

MAP REF. 111 G8, 113 G10, 241 R6
Tathra is a relaxed seaside town, centrally located 18 km SE of Bega on the south coast of NSW, midway between Merimbula and Bermagui. Tathra is ideal for a family holiday, with its patrolled 3-km-long surf beach, safe swimming for small children at Mogareeka Inlet (the sandy mouth of the Bega River), and good fishing spots. Diving and deep-sea fishing charters at Kianinny Bay. **In town:** National Trust-classified historic wharf (1860s), Wharf Rd, has fishing platform and seafood cafe. Above wharf, Maritime Museum traces history of wharf and has replicas of early vessels. Oct.: Amateur Fishing Competition. **In the area:** Bournda National Park, 11 km S, for camping and bushwalking; at Lake Wallagoot in park, wetland area, birdwatching, fishing, prawning, swimming, water sports,

boat hire. Mimosa Rocks National Park, 17 km N, a picturesque coastal park named after the steamship *Mimosa*, wrecked on the massive blocks of volcanic rock in 1863. **Visitor information:** Tathra Wharf, Wharf Rd; (02) 6494 4062.

Temora   Pop. 4125

MAP REF. 113 A2, 114 C10, 121 R8
Temora is the commercial centre for the rich agricultural district of northern and western Riverina, which produces wheat, oats, canola, triticale, wool and meat stocks. The 1880s gold rush left a legacy of fine buildings throughout the town. **In town:** Heritage walk and drives, brochures available. Temora Rural Museum, Wagga Rd, has working displays, and rock and mineral collection (open p.m.). Skydive Centre, Aerodrome Rd, instruction and adventure jumps (open weekends). Quota Markets, Pale Face Park, last Sat. each month. Feb.: Golden Gift (foot race). Mar.: Temora Rural Museum Exhibition Day. Oct.: Antique Engine Field Day and Swap Meet. Nov.: Battle of the Bands (youth band competition). **In the area:** Lake Centenary, 3 km N, for boating, swimming and picnics. Paragon Gold Mine at Gidginbung, 15 km N (open by appt). **Visitor information:** Temora Community Centre, Hoskins St; (02) 6978 0500. Web site www.temora.nsw.gov.au

Tenterfield   Pop. 3205

MAP REF. 117 M4, 525 N13
The countryside around Tenterfield, at the northern end of the New England highlands in northern NSW, offers a contrast of rugged mountains and serene rural landscapes. Primarily a sheep- and cattle-grazing area, other industries include logging and sawmilling, and tourism. Autumn in Tenterfield is spectacular. **In town:** Centenary Cottage (1871), Logan St, has local history collection. Early residential buildings in Logan St. Self-guide historical town walk, leaflet available. Sir Henry Parkes Library and Museum in School of Arts (1876), Rouse St, features relics relating to Sir Henry Parkes, who made his famous Federation speech there in 1889. Handmade saddles at Tenterfield Saddler (1860s), High St. Cobb & Co. coach tours. Railway Markets at Railway Station, Railway Pde, 1st Sat. every 2nd month (beginning Feb.). Apr.: Oracles of the Bush (Australian culture and bush poetry festival). Oct.: Federation Festival; Spring Wine Festival; Highland Gathering.

The Snowy Mountains

The Snowy Mountains are a magnet to tourists all year round. The combination of easily accessible mountains, alpine heathlands, forests, lakes, streams and dams is hard to beat. In winter, skiers flock to the snug, well-equipped snow resorts in the area. When the snow melts it is time for fishing, bushwalking, cycling, horse-riding, water-skiing and boating.

The creation of the Snowy Mountains Hydro-electric Scheme was indirectly responsible for boosting tourism. The roads built for the scheme through the previously difficult and sometimes inaccessible mountain country helped to open up the area, which is now used for a range of recreational activities.

All the ski resorts of the Snowy Mountains are within Kosciuszko National Park, which is the largest national park in the State and includes the highest plateau in the Australian continent. Mount Kosciuszko (2228 m) is its highest peak. The major ski areas are: Thredbo, Perisher, Smiggin Holes, Mount Blue Cow, Guthega and Charlotte Pass in the southern part of Kosciuszko National Park; and Mount Selwyn in the northern part of the park. A park-use fee applies throughout the year on the Alpine Way and Kosciuszko Road; and during winter only on the road to Mount Selwyn.

Skiers enjoying the slopes at Mount Blue Cow

The resorts are easily accessible and the major centres have first-class amenities such as motels, hotels, restaurants, lodges, apres-ski entertainment, chairlifts, ski tows and expert instruction. The snow sports season officially begins on the long weekend in June and continues until the October long weekend.

Thredbo, 98 kilometres from Cooma at the foot of the Crackenback Range, hosted the World Cup ski race in 1989 and has facilities for skiers at all levels, including ski hire and instruction. The Crackenback Chairlift to the top of the range operates throughout the year. The village has a wide range of amenities, restaurants, cultural entertainment and outdoor recreation for every season.

Charlotte Pass, 104 kilometres from Cooma and 8 kilometres from the summit of Mount Kosciuszko, is a convenient base for ski tours to some of Australia's highest peaks and most spectacular ski runs.

Perisher, 94 kilometres from Cooma, is one of the highest ski resorts in the area and has all the facilities of a small town. It caters for both downhill and cross-country skiers; the Nordic Centre caters especially for cross-country. Ski hire and instruction are available.

Smiggin Holes, 92 kilometres from Cooma and linked to Perisher by ski lifts and a free shuttle bus service, is essentially for beginners and intermediate skiers. Ski hire and instruction are available.

Mount Blue Cow can be reached all year by Skitube underground railway, which runs from Bullocks Flat (20 kilometres from Jindabyne) up to Perisher and on to Mount Blue Cow, or from Perisher by the 'Interceptor' quad chairlift (winter only). There is limited overnight accommodation at Guthega and no overnight accommodation at Mount Blue Cow. Ski hire and instruction are available at Mount Blue Cow and Guthega.

A wide variety of accommodation is available at Perisher and Smiggin Holes. However, overnight parking is limited; overnight visitors are advised to use Skitube from Bullocks Flat on the Alpine Way. Perisher, Smiggin Holes, Mount Blue Cow and Guthega resorts have merged to become Perisher Blue Ski Resort.

Mount Selwyn, at the northern end of Kosciuszko National Park, is suitable for beginners, families and school groups. It is one of the main centres for cross-country skiing. There is no overnight accommodation; accommodation is available in nearby towns including Adaminaby. Ski hire and instruction are available.

For further information on the Snowy Mountains, contact the Snowy Region Visitor Centre, Kosciuszko Rd, Jindabyne; (02) 6450 5600. Web site www.npws.nsw.gov.au **See also:** Safe Skiing p. 611. **Map reference:** 112.

Nov.: Campdraft. **In the area:** Mt McKenzie Granite Drive, 30-km circular route beginning and ending at Molesworth St (in town), includes Ghost Gully. Bluff Rock, 10 km S on New England Hwy, unusual granite outcrop. Thunderbolt's Hideout, 11 km NE, reputed haunt of bushranger Captain Thunderbolt. Gold mine at Drake, 31 km NE. Boonoo Boonoo Falls (210-m drop), in Boonoo Boonoo National Park, 32 km NE. Good views from summit of Bald Rock, largest granite monolith in Australia, 35 km N in Bald Rock National Park; Woollool Woollool Aboriginal Culture Tours to Bald Rock (daily). Girraween National Park (in Qld) renowned for its wildflowers and massive granite outcrops. **Visitor information:** 157 Rouse St; (02) 6736 1082. Web site www.tenterfield.com **See also:** New England p. 61.

Terrigal   Pop. 8894

MAP REF. 99 Q4, 102 H5, 115 M6
Excellent surfing, boutiques and restaurants are some of the attractions of this popular holiday town on the Central Coast. Mar.: Terrigal Beach Food, Wine and Chocolate Festivals. **In the area:** The Skillion, 3 km SE, a headland offering coastal views. Several good surfing beaches: Wamberal Beach (3 km N); Shelly Beach (13 km N); Avoca Beach (7.5 km S). Central Park Family Fun Centre, 6 km N at Forresters Beach, has waterslide, fun cars and barbecues. Ken Duncan Gallery, Oak Rd, Matcham, 8 km NW, has largest privately owned photographic collection in Australia. Fragrant Garden, Portsmouth Rd, Erina, 4 km W, has display garden, gift shop and cafe; Central Coast Chilli Festival held here in Mar. Secluded beaches and pockets of rainforest at Bouddi National Park, 17 km S. Sea kayaking tours available. **Visitor information:** Central Coast Tourism, Rotary Park, Terrigal Dr.; (02) 4385 4430, freecall 1800 806 258.

The Entrance   Pop. 5348

MAP REF. 99 Q3, 102 H2, 115 M6
Blessed with clean beaches, this beautiful lakeside and ocean town between Sydney and Newcastle is the aquatic playground of these two cities. **In town:** Pelican feeding at 3.30 p.m. in Memorial Park, Marine Pde. Town Mall: 180 shops, pavement restaurants, playground for children and Sat. craft market. Art and craft market, each Sun. in Bayview Ave. Jan.: Entertainment on Waterfront Stage.

Dec.: Tuggerah Lakes Mardi Gras Festival. **In the area:** Bike tracks and horseriding. Fishing on lakes (Tuggerah, Budgewoi and Munmorah) and ocean beach; prawning on lakes in summer. Water sports on Lake Tuggerah. Extensive shell collection at Shell Museum, 1 km N at Dunleith Caravan Park. Bushwalking trails in Wyrrabalong National Park, 6 km N. Crackneck Point Lookout, 6 km S, for coastal views. **Visitor information:** Memorial Park, Marine Pde; (02) 4385 4430, freecall 1800 806 258.

Thredbo   Pop. 224

MAP REF. 112 C13, 113 C10
This popular mountain village lies in the heart of Kosciuszko National Park between Jindabyne and Khancoban. Its short history began in 1962 with a lease granted by the State government for resort development. In summer Thredbo attracts anglers, mountain-bikers and bushwalkers; a chairlift from the village places visitors within walking distance of Australia's highest summit, Mt Kosciuszko (2228 m). Winter snows transform Thredbo into one of the State's premier ski resorts; the ski season runs from the June long weekend to the October long weekend. **In town:** Chairlifts (including quad lifts) for access to marked downhill ski trails for beginners to advanced; also cross-country skiing, ski school and ski hire. In summer and early autumn: inline skate hire for use at the resort; Thredbo Bobsled rides; canoe hire for use in the resort ponds; walks around the village, including Meadows Nature Walk through ti-trees, and Thredbo Village Walk for the diversity of alpine architecture; mountain-bike riding on the Village Bike Track and various other tracks around Thredbo (bike hire available); Australian Institute of Sport Alpine Training Centre, used by athletes for high-altitude training, has a range of quality sporting facilities. Jan.: Blues Festival. May: Jazz Festival. **In the area:** Skiers can access Perisher and Mt Blue Cow ski fields via the Skitube from Bullocks Flat, 15 km NE. Crackenback chairlift operates year-round from the resort to Eagles Nest Mountain Hut; from here, in summer, a 12-km return walk among wildflowers along an alpine walkway leads to Mt Kosciuszko via Kosciuszko Lookout. Alternatively, return from Eagles Nest to Thredbo on Merritts Nature Walk. Guided alpine walks also available. Trout fishing on Thredbo River and at Lake Jindabyne, 34 km NE. Pilot Lookout, 10 km SE, magnificent view

dominated by The Pilot (1828 m) and on the Victorian side of the border, The Cobberas (1883 m). Horseriding and station accommodation at historic Tom Groggin, 24 km SW. **Visitor information:** Friday Dr.; (02) 6459 4198 or Snowy Region Visitor Centre, Kosciuszko Rd, Jindabyne; (02) 6450 5600. **See also:** The Snowy Mountains p. 81.

Tibooburra   Pop. 214

MAP REF. 118 D3
The name of this former gold town, 333 km N of Broken Hill, comes from an Aboriginal word meaning 'heaps of rocks'. The town is surrounded by granite outcrops and was previously known as The Granites. **In town:** In Briscoe St: courthouse (1887), houses National Parks and Wildlife Service Pastoralist Museum; Family Hotel (1882); Tibooburra Hotel (1883); Tibooburra Aboriginal Land Council 'Keeping Place', display includes tribal headdress; School of the Air (tours during term time). June (or July): Tibooburra Festival. Oct.: Gymkhana and Rodeo (long weekend). Dec.: Night Rodeo. **In the area:** Check road conditions before travelling; read section on Outback Motoring p. 603. Self-guide historical Goldmining Walk and Granite Scenic Walk in Sturt National Park, adjacent to town; park has 4 camping grounds and is a semi-desert area noted for its wildlife and geological features; Explorers Tree, at western end of park, tree faintly blazed by explorer Charles Sturt; outdoor pastoralist museum at Mt Wood (27 km E). Cameron Corner, 133 km NW, where three States meet. At former gold township of Milparinka, 40 km S: restored courthouse, remains of old police station, bank, general store and post office; Albert Hotel is town's only active concern. Depot Glen Billabong, 14 km NW of Milparinka, where Sturt was marooned for 6 months in 1845; 1 km further east, grave of James Poole, a member of Sturt's 1845 expedition. Further 7 km N of Depot Glen is Mt Poole, where Poole's Cairn commemorates Charles Sturt's expedition. **Visitor information:** National Parks and Wildlife Service, Briscoe St; (08) 8091 3308. Web site www.outbacknsw.org.au

Tocumwal   Pop. 1453

MAP REF. 121 M12, 238 I2
This Murray River town on the Newell Hwy is ideal for golf, boating, fishing, swimming, water-skiing and camping.

In town: In Foreshore Park, Deniliquin Rd: large fibreglass Murray cod; Foreshore Markets (dates from information centre). Miniature World of Trains, cnr Deniliquin Rd and Bridge St, has model-train display. Picnic area with lawns and sandy river beaches, 300 m from Newell Hwy, in town centre; river cruises. Walks, drives and bike tracks; self-guide brochures available. Mar.: Pioneer Skills Day. Easter: Easter Eggs-Travaganza. June: Country Craft Fiesta. Oct.: Open Garden Weekend. **In the area:** Two golf courses. Aerodrome, 5 km NE, largest RAAF base in Australia during World War II, now home to international Sportavia Soaring Centre (glider joy-flights and learn-to-glide packages). The Rocks and Blowhole, 8.5 km NE on Rocks Rd, have associations with local Aboriginal legend (details on information board); adjacent to working granite quarry. **Visitor information:** Foreshore Park, Deniliquin Rd; (03) 5874 2131, freecall 1800 677 271. Web site www.tocumwalgolf.com.au **See also:** The Mighty Murray (Vic.) p. 210.

Toukley
Pop. 4983

MAP REF. 99 Q2, 106 H13, 115 M6
Situated on the peninsula between Tuggerah and Budgewoi lakes, this coastal hamlet offers unspoilt beaches and breathtaking scenery. **In town:** Local art and visitor information, Art Centre, Wallarah Rd. Open-air markets, each Sun. at Shopping Centre car park, Yarralla Rd. Sept.: Gathering of the Clans (Scottish festival). Oct.: Cycle Classic. **In the area:** Lakes, venue for all water sports. In summer, prawning from lake foreshores. Rock pool at Cabbage Tree Bay, 5 km E. Norah Head Lighthouse, 5 km E. Many bushwalking trails in magnificent Munmorah State Recreation Area, 10 km N, and in Red Gum Forest in Wyrrabalong National Park, 4 km S. **Visitor information:** Central Coast Tourism, Rotary Park, Terrigal Dr., Terrigal; (02) 4385 4430, freecall 1800 806 258.

Tumbarumba
Pop. 1502

MAP REF. 113 B7
A former goldmining town in the western foothills of the Snowy Mountains, 504 km SW of Sydney, Tumbarumba has much to offer the visitor who prefers to get off the beaten track. It is an ideal base for day trips into the Snowy Mountains. **In town:** Bicentennial Botanic Gardens, Prince St. Wool and Craft Centre, Bridge St, includes

Far north coast view near Tweed Heads

Historical Society Museum, which features a working model of water-powered timber mill. Jan.: New Year's Day Rodeo. Feb.: Tumbafest (food and wine festival). Nov.: Heritage Week. **In the area:** Whitewater rafting, trout fishing, paragliding, gem-fossicking, mountain-bike trails, horse trail-rides. Site of old Union Jack Mining Area, 3 km N. Pioneer Women's Hut, 8 km NW on Wagga Rd, a fascinating domestic, rural history museum (open Wed., Sat. and Sun.). Paddy's River Falls, 16 km S, cascades drop 60 m; nearby, walking track and picnic area. Henry Angel Trackhead, 7 km SE on Tooma Rd, starting point for section of Hume and Hovell Walking Track; facilities for campers and picnickers. At Tooma, 34 km SE: historic hotel, tearooms and store. **Visitor information:** This 'n' That, 31 The Parade; (02) 6948 3444.

Tumut
Pop. 5915

MAP REF. 113 C5, 114 D12, 138 A2
Situated on the Snowy Mountains Hwy, 424 km SW of Sydney, Tumut attracts visitors all year. Close to ski resorts and the great dams of the Snowy Mountains Hydro-electric Scheme, it is also well known for spectacular mountain scenery. **In town:** Historical and tree-identifying walks, brochures available. Old Butter Factory Tourist Complex, Adelong Rd, for local art and craft and information centre. Fishing at Tumut-U-Fish, Fitzroy St. Millet broom factory, Snowy Mountains Hwy. Bakehouse Gallery, Wynyard St. Powered hang-gliding at airport, 6 km E off Snowy Mts Hwy. River walk along Tumut River,

from Elm Dr. Tours to power stations: Tumut 3 (45 km S) and Tumut 2 (115 km S); brochure available. Apr.–May: Festival of the Falling Leaf. **In the area:** Excellent fishing in Tumut and Goobragandra rivers. Whitewater rafting, canoeing, horseriding, abseiling, hang-gliding and scenic flights. Two access points for Hume and Hovell Walking Track (access points allow for shorter walks). Triton Trout Farm, 19 km E, fish sold at gate (open Wed.–Mon.). Largest African violet farm in Australia, 7 km S on Tumut Plains Rd (open Tues.–Sun.). Blowering Reservoir, 10 km S, major centre for water sports, fishing for rainbow trout, brown trout and perch; lookout over dam wall. Blowering Cliffs walk (5 km) in Kosciuszko National Park, 19 km S; set of outstanding granite cliffs overlooking reservoir. Talbingo Dam and Reservoir, 40 km S, tall rock-filled dam set in steep wooded country. Historic goldmining site at Kiandra, 95 km S. **Visitor information:** Old Butter Factory Tourist Complex, Adelong Rd (Snowy Mountains Hwy); (02) 6947 1849.

Tweed Heads
Pop. 37 775

MAP REF. 117 Q1, 519 I11, 525 Q11
Tweed Heads, the State's most northern town, and its twin town Coolangatta, across the border, are popular holiday destinations at the southern end of the Gold Coast. **In town:** World's first laser-beam lighthouse sits atop Point Danger, one half in NSW and the other in Qld; nearby, cliff-edge walk (dolphins may be seen offshore) and picnic spots. Tweed cruise boats, operating from River Tce, visit

locations along Tweed River. Fishing and diving charters, and houseboats for hire. Sun. craft market, Florence St. Jan.: Jet Sprint Racing. June: Wintersun Carnival; Greenback Fishing Competition. Sept.: Rainforest Week (promotes ecosystem awareness). Nov.: Agricultural Show. **In the area:** Idyllic beaches, reserves and coastal towns on Tweed Coast, particularly Kingscliff, 14 km S. Minjungbal Aboriginal Cultural Centre, just over Boyds Bay Bridge, features Aboriginal ceremonial bora ring, museum, and mangrove and rainforest walk. Melaleuca Station, 9 km S on Pacific Hwy at Chinderah, a re-created 1930s railway station in tea-tree plantation, has train rides, tea-tree oil distillation plant and animal nursery. Tropical Fruitworld, 15 km S on Pacific Hwy (tours of plantation). **Visitor information:** Wharf St; (07) 5536 4244. Web site www.tactic.nsw. gov.au

Ulladulla   Pop. 8384

MAP REF. 113 I6, 115 J13, 139 P4

The fishing town of Ulladulla is the main centre along this section of the South Coast: a stretch of beautiful coast, coastal lakes and lagoons with white sandy beaches. **In town:** Old building in town (c. 1868) houses Millard's Cottage Restaurant, Princes Hwy. Funland, Princes Hwy, large indoor family fun park. At Warden Head, lighthouse, views and walking tracks. Coomie Nulunga Cultural Trail (30 min.), starts Deering St, opposite Lighthouse Oval carpark. Native plants, birdlife and walks at South Pacific Heathland Reserve, Dowling St. Ulladulla Wildflower Reserve, Warden St. Coastal Patrol Markets, 2nd Sun. each month at harbour wharf. Easter: Blessing of the Fleet. Aug.: Festival of Food and Wine by the Sea. **In the area:** At historic Milton, 7 km NW on Princes Hwy: art galleries and outdoor cafes; Village Markets on hwy, 1st Sat. each month; Scarecrow Festival held Apr.; Settlers Fair held Oct. Pointer Gap Lookout, 20 km NW, for coastal views. Mollymook, 2 km N, for surfing and excellent fishing. Narrawallee Beach, 4 km N. Nearby Narrawallee Inlet has calm, shallow water ideal for children. Sussex Inlet, 47 km N, holds fishing carnival in May. Lakes Conjola (23 km NW) and Burrill (5 km SW), ideal for swimming, fishing and water-skiing. Pigeon House in beautiful Morton National Park, 25 km NW, walk to summit for breathtaking views (3-hr return). **Visitor information:** Princes Hwy; (02) 4455 1269.

Uralla   Pop. 2460

MAP REF. 117 L9

Rich gold discoveries were made in the vicinity of this charming New England town in the 1850s. **In town:** Self-guide Heritage Walking Tour, brochure available. In Bridge St: Hassett's Military Museum, displays local and national military history and memorabilia; statue of Thunderbolt, 'gentleman' bushranger who was shot dead by a local policeman in 1870 at nearby Kentucky Creek (his grave is in old Uralla Cemetery, John St); craft, antique and bric-a-brac shops. McCrossin's Mill (1870), Salisbury St, now a museum: goldfields history displays; re-created joss house honouring the Chinese who came to the diggings; Thunderbolt exhibits; collection of Thunderbolt paintings. Old Uralla courthouse, Hill St, now library. New England Brass and Iron Lace Foundry, operating since 1872 (check times). Market, 2nd Sat. each month. Apr.: New England Grand Parade (racing of classic cars). Nov.: Thunderbolt Country Fair. **In the area:** Dangars Lagoon, 5 km SE on Walcha Rd, a bird sanctuary and hide. Mt Yarrowyck Aboriginal rock-art site, 23 km NW off Bundarra Rd. Gold-fossicking, 5 km SW. Thunderbolt's Rock, 6 km S, used by the bushranger as lookout; climb with care. Tourist Drive 19 (signposted) includes historic Gostwyck Church (11 km SE) and Dangars Falls and Gorge (40 km S); self-guide drive brochure available. **Visitor information:** Bridge St; (02) 6778 4496. Web site www.new-england.org/uralla **See also:** New England p. 61.

Urunga   Pop. 2716

MAP REF. 117 P9

Located at the junction of the Bellinger and Kalang rivers, 28 km S of Coffs Harbour, Urunga is one of the best fishing spots on the north coast. **In town:** Water sports and fishing. In Morgo St: Oceanview Hotel (1927), original furniture; Urunga Museum (check times); safe lagoon swimming for children, with picnic reserve. On Anchor's Wharf, riverside restaurant and boat hire. Water Rat River Cruises. The Honey Place, Pacific Hwy, a huge concrete replica of an old-style European straw beehive, has a glass beehive display, honey-tasting, gallery and gardens. July: Bowling Club Carnival. **In the area:** Beautiful beach for surfing and swimming at Hungry Head, 3 km S. At Raleigh, 4 km N: Prince of Peace Anglican Church (1900); winery, horse-riding and go-kart complex. Bongil Bongil

National Park at Myleston, 15 km N, 10 km of coastal beaches with good fishing and swimming. **Visitor information:** Pacific Hwy; (02) 6655 5711. Web site www. bellingen.nsw.gov.au/tourism/bellinger.html

Wagga Wagga   Pop. 42 848

MAP REF. 114 B12, 121 R10

This prosperous city – the largest inland city in NSW – is 478 km SW of Sydney, just off the Hume Hwy. Wagga Wagga is a major centre for industry, commerce, education, and agriculture and is the home of two military bases. The town is known for its cultural pursuits and performing arts. **In town:** Botanic Gardens and mini-zoo on Willans Hill; a miniature railway runs through gardens (check times). Regional Art Gallery, cnr Baylis and Morrow sts, features National Art Glass Collection and incorporates Museum of the Riverina. Mar.: Australian Veterans Games (even-numbered years); contact information centre for other events. **In the area:** River cruises and walking tracks, details from information centre. Lake Albert, 7 km S, for water sports. RAAF Museum, 10 km E. Wagga Wagga Winery, 15 km NE; tasting area and restaurant have early Australiana theme. Charles Sturt Winery at Charles Sturt University (Riverina Campus), 6 km NW. Aurora Clydesdale Stud and Pioneer Farm, 9 km W of Collingullie on Sturt Hwy. Self-drive tours of military base at Kapooka, 9 km SW, brochures available. The Rock, 32 km SW, a small town noted for its unusual scenery; walking trails through a flora and fauna reserve lead to summit of The Rock (365 m approx.). **Visitor information:** Tarcutta St; (02) 6926 9621.

Walcha   Pop. 1623

MAP REF. 117 L10

This town on the eastern slopes of the Great Dividing Range was settled by Europeans in 1832. **In town:** Walking tour, includes sculptures and 'Lamington Capital of the World', brochures available. Pioneer Cottage and Museum, Derby St, features first Tiger Moth plane used for crop-dusting in Australia, and a replica of blacksmith's shop. Courthouse (1878), cnr Derby and Apsley sts. In South St: Anglican Church (1862); St Patricks Church (1881). Amaroo Museum and Cultural Centre, Derby St: Aboriginal art and craft; artists working on site; cultural information; visitors welcome to tour centre. Old School Gallery in Fitzroy St.

Mar.: Agricultural Show. Sept.: Timber Expo (even-numbered years). Oct.: Ride the Rim (mountain-bike ride). **In the area:** Trout fishing. Oxley Wild Rivers National Park, encompasses a high plateau, deep gorges and numerous waterfalls, including Apsley (20 km E) where 7 platforms and a bridge over the Apsley River provide access to both sides of gorge and waterfall; the Tia Falls area (35 km E) is also developed for visitors; 4WD access to Riverside and Youdales Hut, where there are unique campsites. **Visitor information:** 106E Fitzroy St; (02) 6777 1075. Web site www.northnet.com.au/~walchatc/index **See also:** New England p. 61.

Walgett
Pop. 1970

MAP REF. 116 C7
Walgett is at the junction of the Barwon and Namoi rivers, 272 km NW of Dubbo. With its airport and railhead, it is also the gateway to the opal fields around Lightning Ridge. **In town:** First European settler's grave on banks of Namoi River, northern end of town. Tracker Walford Track, signposted 1.5-km scenic walk from levee bank at end of Warrena St. Hot artesian springs pool at swimming pool, Montkeila St (open in summer; key from information centre in winter). May: Agricultural Show. **In the area:** Good fishing year-round; contact information centre for details of reserved conservation land and permits to fish. At Come-by-Chance, 65 km SE, Picnic Races held in Sept. Grawin, Glengarry and Sheepyard opal fields, 70 km W, brochures available. (Motorists are warned water is scarce; adequate supply should be carried.) One of largest inland lakes in Australia, Narran Lake, 96 km W via Cumborah Rd, is a wildlife sanctuary (no facilities for private visits). **Visitor information:** Shire Offices, 77 Fox St; (02) 6828 1399.

Warialda
Pop. 1287

MAP REF. 116 I5
The first administrative centre in the north-west of the State, this town on Gwydir Hwy, 61 km NW of Inverell, is in a rich farming and grazing district. **In town:** Historic buildings, especially on Stephen and Hope sts. Self-guide historical walk around town. Historic Carinda House, Stephen St, now a craft shop. Historic graves (from 1850s) in bushland setting at Pioneer Cemetery, Queen and Stephen sts. Well's Family Gem and Mineral Collection in Heritage Centre, Hope St. Koorilgur Nature Walk (3.6 km), features wildflowers and abundant birdlife, self-guide brochure available. May: Agricultural Show. Oct.: Flower Show. **In the area:** Good picnic spots, camping, fossicking, wildflowers and wildlife at Cranky Rock Nature Reserve, 8 km E. **Visitor information:** Yallaroi Shire Offices, Hope St; (02) 6729 1016 or Heritage Centre, Hope St; (02) 6729 0046. **See also:** New England p. 61.

Warren
Pop. 1909

MAP REF. 116 B13
The centre for the surrounding wool and cotton district, Warren is on the Oxley Hwy, 126 km NW of Dubbo. Located beside the Macquarie River, it is a popular spot for anglers. **In town:** Historical and nature walks and short driving tours, brochures available. In Burton St: Macquarie Park, on banks of river; The Craft Shop for local craft. Tiger Bay Wildlife Reserve, a wetlands reserve at northern outskirts of town on Oxley Hwy. May: Golden Fleece Race Day. Sept.: Macquarie Merino Field Days. Nov.: Cotton Cup Racing Carnival. **In the area:** Excellent racecourse ('Randwick of the West'), 3 km W, location for race days. **Visitor information:** The Craft Shop, Burton St; (02) 6847 3181. Web site www.slnsw.gov.au/warren

Wauchope
Pop. 4693

MAP REF. 103 E8, 117 O12
A major re-creation of a typical timber town of the 1880s at nearby Timbertown has put Wauchope on the tourist map. The town is the centre of a timber-getting, dairying, beef-cattle and mixed-farming area on the Oxley Hwy, 19 km W of Port Macquarie. Mar.: Lasiandra Festival. Apr.: Show; Demolition Derby; Rusty Iron Rally. May: Timbertown Empire Day Celebrations. Oct.: Colonial Carnival. **In the area:** Timbertown, re-created village, 3 km W on edge of Broken Bago State Forest, features shops, including craft gallery and leather goods outlet, working bullock team, horse-drawn wagons, smithy, woodturner, steam-powered train and sleeper-cutting demonstrations. Adjacent, small church houses Historical Society Museum. Broken Bago Winery, 8 km SW. Old Bottlebutt, 6 km S, largest known bloodwood tree in State. The Big Bull, 2 km E off Oxley Hwy, has dairy-farming display, hay rides and animal nursery.

Billabong Animal Park, 10 km E. **Visitor information:** cnr Hay and Clarence sts, Port Macquarie; (02) 6581 8000, freecall 1800 025 935. Web site www.portmacquarieinfo.com.au

Wee Waa
Pop. 1860

MAP REF. 116 F8
This small town near the Namoi River is the centre of a major cotton-growing district. **In town:** Guided tours (Apr.–Aug.) to Merah North Cotton Gin (9 km) and cotton farms. Apr.: Agricultural Show. **In the area:** Cuttabri Wine Shanty, 25 km SW, an original Cobb & Co. coach stop between Wee Waa and Pilliga. Cubbaroo Winery, 48 km W. Yarrie Lake, 24 km S, for boating and birdwatching. **Visitor information:** Newell Hwy, Narrabri; (02) 6799 6760. Web site www.tournarrabri.nsw.gov.au

Wellington
Pop. 4920

MAP REF. 114 F3
Limestone caves are one of the interesting features of this town at the junction of the Macquarie and Bell rivers, 362 km NW of Sydney. **In town:** Town walk and driving tours of surrounding countryside, self-guide brochures available. Historical Museum in old bank (1883), cnr Percy and Warne sts. Orana Aboriginal Corporation, Swift St, authentic Aboriginal ceramics, paintings, clothing and artifacts. Mar.: The Wellington Boot (horseraces); Vintage Fair. Aug.: Eisteddfod. Oct.: Festivale. **In the area:** Wellington Caves, 9 km S, features Cathedral Cave and smaller Gaden Cave with rare cave coral and phosphate mine (guided tours available). Nearby, aviary, opal shop, Japanese Gardens, picnic/barbecue facilities and kiosk. Markeita Cellars, 16 km S in village of Neurea. Rabbit Farm, 20 km SW, has shearing demonstrations of angora rabbits; also alpacas. At Burrendong and Mookerawa State parks, 32 km SE: Lake Burrendong, for water sports, fishing, camping, cabins, spectacular lake views from main wall; Burrendong Arboretum for birdwatching and walking tracks. Bakers Swamp Art Gallery, 22 km S on Mitchell Hwy, local artists. Further 6 km S, Eris Fleming Gallery. Glenfinlass Wines, 8 km SW on Parkes Rd. Nangara Gallery, 26 km SW, Aboriginal art and craft. From Mt Arthur Reserve, 3 km W of town, walking trails to lookout at summit of Mt Binjang; maps available. **Visitor information:** Cameron Park, Nanima Cr.; (02) 6845 1733.

Wentworth   Pop. 1504

MAP REF. 120 C6, 236 F2

This historic town at the junction of the Murray and Darling rivers was once a busy riverboat and customs port; today it is a quiet holiday town. **In town:** In Beverley St: Grandma's Place (museum); Old Wentworth Gaol (1881). Courthouse (1870s), Darling St. Historic convent (1912), Cadell St. Historic PS *Ruby*, in Fotherby Park, Wentworth St. River cruises on MV *Loyalty*, depart from end Darling St. Lock 10, weir and park for picnics. Easter: Henley on the Darling (rowing regatta). Nov.: Wentworth Cup (on Melbourne Cup Day). **In the area:** Heritage and nature driving trails. Houseboat hire. Harry Nana Aboriginal Cultural Tours to sites in area, details from information centre. Perry Sandhills, 5 km NW off Silver City Hwy. Model aircraft display at Yelta, 12 km SE. At Dareton, 12 km E, Tulklana Kumbi, Aboriginal art gallery. At Buronga, 26 km E: Australian Inland Botanical Gardens, River Rd; Orange World and Stanley Wine Co. both on Silver City Hwy. World Heritage-listed Mungo National Park, 157 km NE, features The Walls of China (sand dunes); record of 40 000 years of Aboriginal life; maps available. **Visitor information:** 28 Darling St; (03) 5027 3624. Web site www.outbacknsw.org.au/wentworth **See also:** National Parks p. 42; The Mighty Murray (Vic.) p. 210.

West Wyalong   Pop. 3419

MAP REF. 114 B8, 121 Q6

This former goldmining town, at the junction of the Mid Western and Newell hwys, celebrated its centenary in 1994. It is the business centre of a prosperous wheat, wool and mixed-farming area, and gateway to the Riverina and central west regions of the State. **In town:** On Newell Hwy: Aboriginal Artifacts Gallery (open Mon.–Fri.); Bland District Historical Museum, with scale model of a goldmine. Sept.: Agricultural Show. **In the area:** Bird sanctuary and fishing at Lake Cowal, 48 km NE via Clear Ridge, largest natural lake in NSW. Weethalle Whistlestop, 65 km W on Hay Rd, for Devonshire teas, art and craft. At Barmedman, 32 km SE, Mineral Water Pool, believed to provide relief from arthritis and rheumatism. **Visitor information:** McCann Park, Newell Hwy; (02) 6972 3645.

White Cliffs   Pop. 207

MAP REF. 118 F8

In White Cliffs, 93 km NW of Wilcannia, pioneering is a way of life. The opal fields were the first commercial fields in NSW; the first lease was granted in 1890, and in the turn-of-the-century boom years the fields supported 4500 people. Precious opal is still mined today. Jewelled opal 'pineapples' are found only in this area. Road access to the town is via a graded gravel road (sealed in parts), suitable for conventional cars and caravans when driven with care in dry weather. **In town:** Guided tours of town, including local historic features and opportunity to fossick for opal. Self-guide Heritage Trail, map available. *In town centre:* Historic buildings including old police station (1897), public school (1900) and post office (1900); camping, barbecue facilities and swimming-pool in Reserve; pioneer cemetery. *Just south of town centre:* Solar power station (tours); rugged outback golf course. *On the southern outskirts (Smith's Hill):* Top Level Opals; Outback Treasures (opal jewellery and Aboriginal art); Underground Dugout Motel. *On the eastern outskirts (Turley's Hill):* Eagles Gallery, underground complex with local art and craft (open on request); Jock's Place, dugout home and museum; P. J.'s Underground B&B. *On the northern outskirts:* Wellington's Underground Art Gallery; Brian Moore's Opal Showroom. May: Gymkhana and Rodeo. **In the area:** Mutawintji National Park, 90 km SW, guided tours of Aboriginal rock-art sites in cooler months (extremely hot in summer). **Visitor information:** General Store; (08) 8091 6611. Web site www.outbacknsw.org.au

Wilcannia   Pop. 688

MAP REF. 118 G10

Once 'the queen city of the west', this township, 196 km NE of Broken Hill, still has many impressive sandstone buildings. Proclaimed a town in 1864, Wilcannia was a key inland port in the days of paddle-steamers. Today it is the service centre for a far-flung rural population. **In town:** Self-guide historical tour (brochure available) introduces several fine stone buildings, including post office (1877), prison and courthouse (1880), and Athenaeum Chambers (1890), all in Reid St. Opening bridge (1895) across Darling River; paddle-steamer wharf upstream. **In the area:** At Tilpa, 140 km NE, historic hotel (continuous licence since 1894) on banks of Darling River. **Visitor information:** Shire Offices, Reid St; (08) 8091 5909. Web site www.outbacknsw.org.au

Windsor   Pop. 13 345

MAP REF. 99 L6, 115 K7

A town for lovers of history and early architecture, Windsor is one of the oldest towns in Australia, situated 56 km NW of Sydney. **In town:** Self-guide tourist walk/drive, brochures available. St Matthew's Church, Moses St, oldest Anglican Church in Australia, designed by Francis Greenway and convict-built in 1817. Nearby graveyard is even older. Courthouse, Court St, another Greenway building. In Thompson Sq.: The Doctor's House (1844), privately owned; Hawkesbury Museum, formerly Daniel O'Connell Inn (1843). Other fine buildings in historic George St and Thompson Sq. Markets, each Sun. in Windsor Mall. May: Bridge to Bridge Power Boat Classic. Oct.: Bridge to Bridge Canoe Classic; Fruits of the Hawkesbury Festival. Nov.: Bridge to Bridge Water Ski Classic. **In the area:** Self-guide tourist drives, including Grand Circular Tourist Drive; brochures available. Rouse Hill Estate (1813), 15 km E on Windsor Rd: historic rural property; guided tours Thurs. and Sun., bookings essential. Cattai National Park, 14 km NE, has historic homestead, picnic/barbecue facilities and camping area. Hawkesbury Heritage Farm, 6 km N: Rose Cottage, considered oldest timber dwelling in Australia; wagon and buggy collection; good picnic/barbecue facilities; open Thurs.–Sun. At Ebenezer, 11 km N: Tizzana Winery; Uniting Church (1809), claimed to be oldest Presbyterian church in Australia holding regular services; nearby, old cemetery and schoolhouse (1817). Wollemi National Park, 26 km N via Colo: spectacular Colo River; abseiling and canoeing; 4WD touring. **Visitor information:** Tourism Hawkesbury, Ham Common Bicentenary Park, Clarendon; (02) 4588 5895. Web site www.hawkesburyvalley.com **See also:** Wildlife-Watching p. 48.

Wingham   Pop. 4446

MAP REF. 103 B13, 115 O1, 117 N13

Established 1836, Heritage-listed Wingham is the oldest town along the Manning River. Timber-milling was once the main district activity, but has been overtaken by beef cattle and dairy farming. **In town:** Manning Valley Historical Museum, part of attractive village square with several prominent historic buildings, bounded by Isabella, Bent, Farquhar and Wynter sts. Historical walk through town, self-guide brochure from museum. Market, 2nd Sat. each month in Wynter St (a.m.). Jan.: Summer Rodeo. Mar.: Agricultural Show. May: Manning Valley Beef Week. Nov.: Show and Rodeo. **In the area:** Wingham Brush, Farquhar St, close to town centre, part of last 10 ha of subtropical flood-plain rainforest in NSW: orchids, ferns, Moreton Bay fig trees, grey-headed flying foxes and 100 bird species. On Tourist Drive 8, Ellenborough Falls, 40 km N, one of the highest single-drop falls in the Southern Hemisphere at 160 m. **Visitor information:** Manning Valley Visitor Information Centre, Old Pacific Hwy, Taree North; (02) 6552 1900, freecall 1800 801 522. Web site www.gtcc.nsw.gov.au/tourism

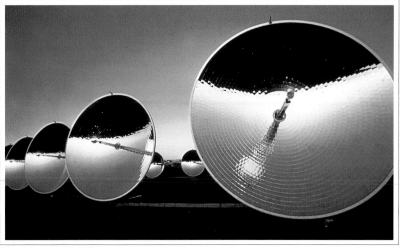
Solar power station, White Cliffs

Wisemans Ferry   Pop. 150

MAP REF. 99 M3, 115 L6
Situated beside the Hawkesbury River, 66 km NW of Sydney, Wisemans Ferry is an important area for water sports. Two vehicular ferries provide transport across the river. **In town:** Wisemans Ferry Inn, Old Northern Rd, was named after innkeeper and founder of original ferry service, and is said to be haunted by his wife, whom he allegedly pushed down the front steps of the inn to her death. **In the area:** Dharug National Park, on northern side of river: Aboriginal rock engravings; convict-built Old Great North Rd, great engineering feat of early colony; walking and cycling tracks along lower section (closed to vehicles) from ferry. **Visitor information:** Ham Common Bicentenary Park, Richmond Rd, Clarendon; (02) 4588 5895. Web site www.hawkesburyvalley.com **See also:** Day Tours from Sydney p. 34.

Wollongong   Pop. 219 761

MAP REF. 108, 110 H6, 115 K10
The area surrounding Wollongong, the third largest city in NSW, contains some of the South Coast's most spectacular scenery. **In town:** Guided walk and guided 4WD tour, details from information centre. Illawarra Historical Society Museum, Market St, includes a handicraft room and a Victorian parlour (check times). Wollongong City Gallery, cnr Burelli and Kembla sts. Mall in Crown St, with soaring steel arches and water displays. Wollongong Botanic Gardens in Northfields Ave, Keiraville. Rhododendron Park, Parrish Ave, Mt Pleasant. Surfing

beaches and rock pools, to north and south. Foreshore parks for picnicking. Wollongong Harbour, home to fishing fleet. On Endeavour Dr.: fish market; historic lighthouse (1872). On Port Kembla Harbour foreshore, at the southern end of the city, is highly automated steel mill operated by BHP, an export coal loader and largest grain-handling facility in NSW. Market, each Thurs. and Sat. at southern end of Harbour St. **In the area:** Nan Tien Temple, 5 km SW, Berkeley Rd, Berkeley, largest Buddhist temple in Southern Hemisphere with range of programs (closed Mon.). Lake Illawarra, 5 km S, stretching from South Pacific Ocean to foothills of Illawarra Range, has good prawning, fishing and sailing; boat hire. Australia's Industry World, 10 km S at Port Kembla, tours (check times) and visitor centre. Seaside village of Shellharbour, 23 km S; walking trails in nearby Blackbutt Reserve. Illawarra Escarpment, forming western backdrop to city, provides vantage points for lookouts at Stanwell Tops, Sublime Point, Mount Keira and Mount Kembla. Bulli Lookout, at top of escarpment in Bulli Pass Scenic Reserve, a steep, scenic drive with stunning coastal views. At University of Wollongong Campus East, Squires Way, Fairy Meadows, 2 km N: Science Centre, activities for all ages. Lawrence Hargrave Memorial and Lookout at Bald Hill, 36 km N, site of aviator Hargrave's first attempt at flight in early 1900s; now popular for hang-gliding. Symbio Wildlife Gardens, 32 km N at Stanwell Tops, features koalas, eagle-flying, wombats, reptiles, cow- and goat-milking. Mount Kembla, 10 km W, scene of tragic mining disaster in 1902: monument in church; original miners' huts; several historic buildings including former post office, now Historical Museum featuring

pioneer kitchen, blacksmith's shop and reconstruction of Mt Kembla disaster. **Visitor information:** 93 Crown St; (02) 4227 5545, freecall 1800 240 737.

Woolgoolga   Pop. 3772

MAP REF. 117 P7
This charming seaside town on the Pacific Hwy, 25 km N of Coffs Harbour, is popular with beach and offshore anglers. The banana industry became established in the district in the 1930s, attracting a sizeable population of Indian migrants. **In town:** Guru Nanak Sikh Temple, River St, place of worship for town's Indian population. Art Gallery, Turon Pde, exhibits local works. Market, Beach St, 2nd Sat. each month. **In the area:** Clean, sandy beaches. Yuraygir National Park, 10 km N, for bushwalking, canoeing, fishing, surfing, swimming, picnicking and camping on unspoiled coastline. Yarrawarra Aboriginal Cultural Centre and Tours, Red Rock Rd, Corindi Beach, 10 km N: locally produced art, craft, books and CDs; Bush Tucker Cafe; tours. Wedding Bells State Forest, 14 km NW. **Visitor information:** Pacific Hwy, Coffs Harbour; (02) 6652 1522.

Woy Woy   Pop. 11 038

MAP REF. 99 P4, 102 F8, 115 L6
Woy Woy, 90 km N of Sydney and 6 km S of Gosford, is the commercial centre for the holiday villages and national parks near the magnificent Brisbane Water and Broken Bay. Markets at Ettalong Beach, 3 km S on Ocean View Rd, each Sat. and Sun., and Mon. of long weekends. Nov.: Oyster and Wine Festival. **In the area:** Boating, fishing and swimming on Brisbane Water, Broken Bay and Hawkesbury River.

Mt Ettalong Lookout, 6 km S, for spectacular coastal views. Pearl Beach (12 km S), ideal for a stroll at sunset. Brisbane Water National Park, 3 km SW: noted for spring wildflowers, bushwalks and birdlife; Staples Lookout (7 km W), for magnificent coastal views; Bulgandry Aboriginal engravings (9 km W); Warrah Lookout, for views and wildflowers. Bouddi National Park, 12 km E, has good fishing, bushwalks and swimming areas; wreck of PS *Maitland* at Maitland Bay, a beautiful unspoiled coastal environment. Near entrance to park, Marie Byles Lookout offers good views of Sydney. Wreck of WW I ship *Parramatta*, Hawkesbury River near Milson Island; accessible only by boat. **Visitor information:** 18–22 The Boulevarde; (02) 4385 4430, freecall 1800 806 258.

Wyong
Pop. 6216

MAP REF. 99 P2, 102 F1, 115 M6

Wyong is on the Pacific Hwy between Tuggerah Lakes and the State Forests of Watagan, Olney and Ourimbah. The town developed after the construction of the Sydney to Newcastle railway, completed 1889. **In town:** District Museum, Cape Rd, has displays relating to early ferry services across lakes, and forest logging. Country Fair, 3rd Sun. each month, at racecourse on Racecourse Rd. Mar.: Wyong Shire Festival of the Arts. Oct.: Cycle Classic. **In the area:** Hinterland popular for bushwalking and camping. Burbank Nursery, 3 km S at Tuggerah, features 20 ha of azaleas (flowering Sept.). Fowlers Lookout over forest, 10 km SW. Macadamia Nut Plantation, 18 km W in beautiful Yarramalong Valley. The Durren Pottery, 20 km NW, uses local clay (open by appt). Bumble Hill Studio, 30 km NW at Kulnura, for ceramics, glasswork and paintings (open Fri.–Sun.). Frazer Park, 28 km NE, a recreational park in a natural bush setting. Within the State forests to the north: Mandalong Lookout, Muirs Lookout and picnic area in Olney State Forest; Wishing Well, destination for Watagan Mountains Walking Trail in Watagan State Forest; Flat Rock Lookout and picnic area in Corrabare State Forest. **Visitor information:** Central Coast Tourism, Rotary Park, Terrigal Dr., Terrigal; (02) 4385 4430, freecall 1800 806 258.

Yamba
Pop. 4721

MAP REF. 117 Q5

This prawning and fishing town at the mouth of the Clarence River offers sea, lake and river fishing. It is the largest coastal resort in the Clarence Valley. **In town:** Story House Museum, River St, displays records of early Yamba. Views from base of lighthouse, reached via steep Pilot St. Yamba Boatharbour Marina, off Yamba Rd; departure point for daily passenger ferry services to Iluka, river cruises (Thurs. and Sun.), deep-sea fishing charters and whale-watching trips. Houseboat hire and cruises at marina. Market, 4th Sun. each month, at oval on River St. Oct.: Family Fishing Festival; Seafood Expo. **In the area:** Lake Wooloweyah, 4 km S, for fishing and prawning. Yuraygir National Park, 5 km S, for swimming, fishing and bushwalking in area dominated by sand ridges and banksia heath. The Blue Pool, 5 km S at Angourie, a freshwater pool, 50 m from ocean, depth and origin unknown; popular swimming and picnic spot. **Visitor information:** Lower Clarence Visitors Centre, Ferry Park, Pacific Hwy, Maclean; (02) 6645 4121.

Yanco
Pop. 576

MAP REF. 121 O8

Located 8 km S of Leeton, this town is where Sir Samuel McCaughey developed his own irrigation scheme, which led to the establishment of the Murrumbidgee Irrigation Area. **In town:** In Binya St: Powerhouse Museum (last Sun. each month or by appt.); McCaughey Aquatic Park. Village Markets, Yanco Hall, Main Ave, last Sun. each month (a.m.). May: Murrumbidgee Farm Fair. **In the area:** Yanco Weir, 1 km N, for fishing. McCaughey's mansion, 3 km S, now an agricultural high school; nearby Yanco Agricultural Institute, open to public. Extensive red gum forests along the Murrumbidgee River; well-marked forest drives lead to sandy beaches and many pleasant fishing spots. **Visitor information:** 10 Yanco Ave, Leeton; (02) 6953 6481. Web site www.leeton.nsw.gov.au

Yass
Pop. 4840

MAP REF. 113 D4, 114 F11

Near the junction of two major highways (the Hume and the Barton), this interesting old town is on the Yass River, surrounded by rolling country-side, 280 km SW of Sydney and 55 km from Canberra. **In town:** Self-guide town walk and drive, maps available. Grave of Hamilton Hume, who discovered Yass Plains in 1824, in Yass Cemetery (signposted from Rossi St). National Trust-owned Cooma Cottage (1834), 3 km E, where Hume lived for almost 40 years (closed Tues.). Hamilton Hume Museum, Comur St. Railway Museum, Lead St, history of Yass Tramway (open Sun.). Market, 2nd Sat. each month. Mar.: Picnic Races. Apr.: Agricultural Show and Rodeo. Nov.: Rodeo. Dec.: Cup Raceday. **In the area:** Crisp Art Glass and Crisp-Gro Lavender Nursery, 19 km NW on Hume Hwy. Binalong Motor Museum and Southern Cross Glass, 37 km NW. At Bookham, 30 km W: Markets, 2nd Sun. each month; Sheep Show and Country Fair in Apr. At Wee Jasper, 50 km SW: Goodradigbee River for trout fishing; Micalong Creek; Carey's Caves, with superb limestone formations (guided tours); access point for Hume and Hovell Walking Track. Burrinjuck Waters State Park, 54 km SW off Hume Hwy, for bushwalking, cruises, water sports and fishing; Burrinjuck Ski Classic held in area each Nov., water level permitting. Numerous wineries in Murrumbateman area, 20 km S, on Barton Hwy. **Visitor information:** Coronation Park, Comur St; (02) 6226 2557.

Young
Pop. 6798

MAP REF. 113 C2, 114 D9

Attractive former goldmining town in the western foothills of the Great Dividing Range, 395 km SW of Sydney. Today, cherries, prunes and other stone fruit products are the area's best-known exports, as well as flour and fabricated steel. **In town:** Lambing Flat Folk Museum, Campbell St, for town history, including 'roll-up' flag carried by miners during infamous anti-Chinese Lambing Flat riots of 1861. Burrangong Art Gallery, Olympic Hwy. Blackguard Gully with historic pug-mill, on Boorowa Rd, a reconstruction showing early goldmining methods; gold-fossicking alongside gully (hire equipment from museum). The Price of Peace Garden and Cafe, Willawong St, overlooking town. Nov.–Dec.: National Cherry Festival. **In the area:** Stone fruit orchards open in season (pick your own cherries); list from information centre. Several wineries open for tastings and sales. J. D.'s Jam Factory, north-western outskirts of town on Grenfell Rd, open for tours, tastings and Devonshire teas. Chinaman's Dam recreation area, 4 km SE, has picnic/barbecue facilities, children's playground and scenic walks. Nearby, Pat's Doll and Memorabilia Hut. At Murringo, 21 km E: several historic buildings; glassblower and engraver. Yandilla Mustard Seed Oil, 20 km S. **Visitor information:** 2 Short St; (02) 6382 3394 or in NSW freecall 1800 628 233.

New South Wales

LOCATION MAP

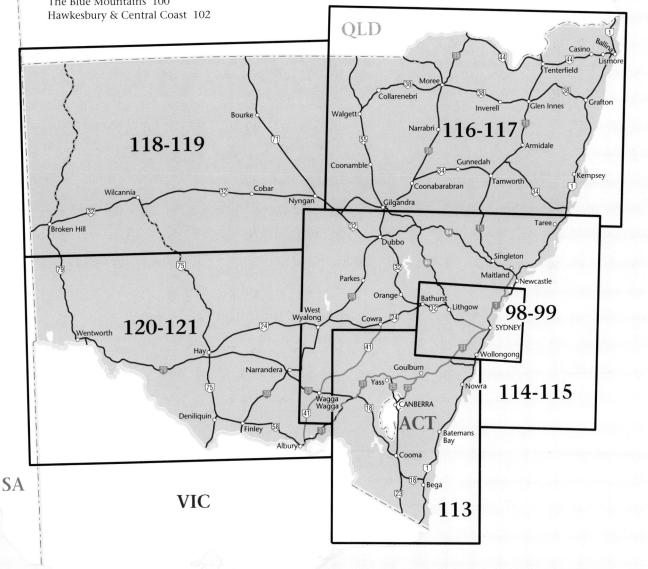

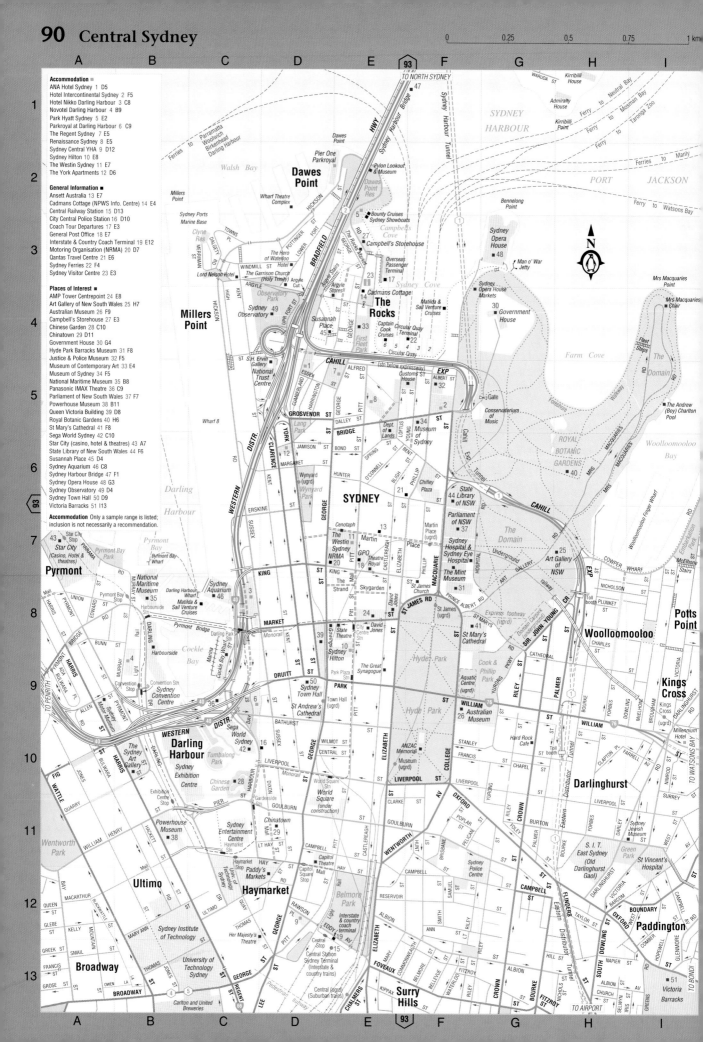

Accommodation ■
ANA Hotel Sydney 1 D5
Hotel Intercontinental Sydney 2 F5
Hotel Nikko Darling Harbour 3 C8
Novotel Darling Harbour 4 B9
Park Hyatt Sydney 5 E2
Parkroyal at Darling Harbour 6 C9
The Regent Sydney 7 E5
Renaissance Sydney 8 E5
Sydney Central YHA 9 D12
Sydney Hilton 10 E8
The Westin Sydney 11 E7
The York Apartments 12 D6

General Information ■
Ansett Australia 13 E7
Cadmans Cottage (NPWS Info. Centre) 14 E4
Central Railway Station 15 D13
City Central Police Station 16 D10
Coach Tour Departures 17 E3
General Post Office 18 E7
Interstate & Country Coach Terminal 19 E12
Motoring Organisation (NRMA) 20 D7
Qantas Travel Centre 21 E6
Sydney Ferries 22 F4
Sydney Visitor Centre 23 E3

Places of Interest ■
AMP Tower Centrepoint 24 E8
Art Gallery of New South Wales 25 H7
Australian Museum 26 F9
Campbell's Storehouse 27 E3
Chinese Garden 28 C10
Chinatown 29 D11
Government House 30 G4
Hyde Park Barracks Museum 31 F8
Justice & Police Museum 32 F5
Museum of Contemporary Art 33 E4
Museum of Sydney 34 F5
National Maritime Museum 35 B8
Panasonic IMAX Theatre 36 C9
Parliament of New South Wales 37 F7
Powerhouse Museum 38 B11
Queen Victoria Building 39 D8
Royal Botanic Gardens 40 H6
St Mary's Cathedral 41 F8
Sega World Sydney 42 C10
Star City (casino, hotel & theatres) 43 A7
State Library of New South Wales 44 F6
Susannah Place 45 D4
Sydney Aquarium 46 C8
Sydney Harbour Bridge 47 F1
Sydney Opera House 48 G3
Sydney Observatory 49 D4
Sydney Town Hall 50 D9
Victoria Barracks 51 I13

Accommodation Only a sample range is listed; inclusion is not necessarily a recommendation.

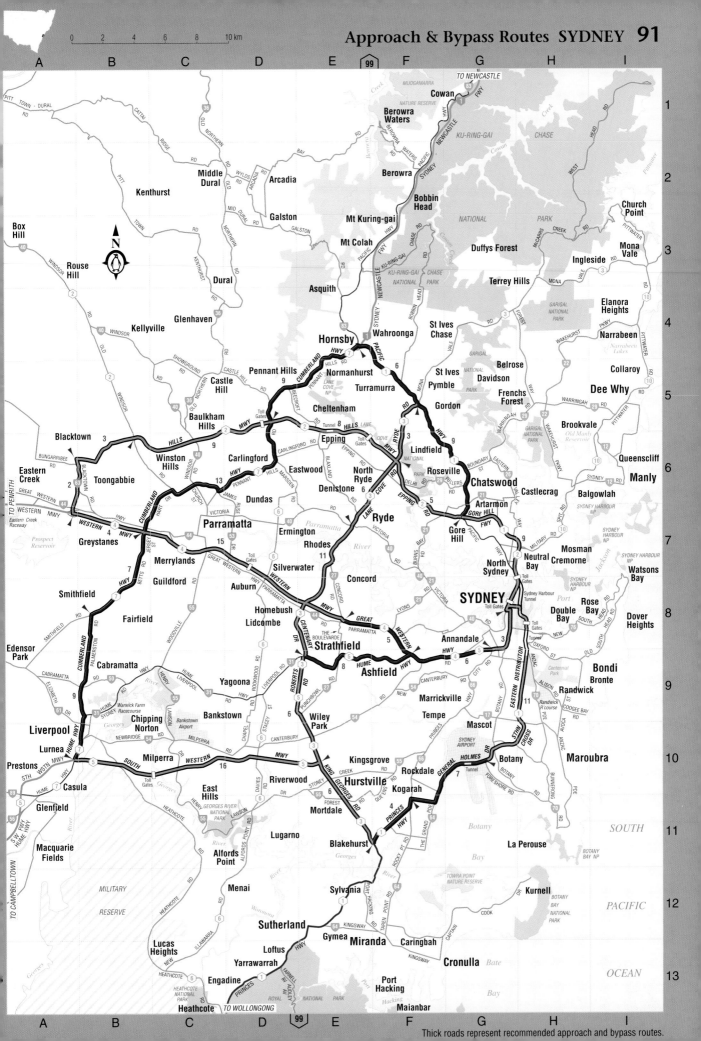

A B C D 94 E F G H I

Grid rows: 1 2 3 4 5 6 7 8 9 10 11 12 13

Castle Hill Country Club · Showground · Castle Hill · West Pennant Hills · Thornleigh · Normanhurst · Comenarra · Sydney Adventist Hospital · Turramurra

Baulkham Hills · Cumberland State Forest · Koala Park Sanctuary · Pennant Hills · South Turramurra · Twin Creek Reserve · West Pymble · Mac P

Darling Mills State Forest · Beecroft · Beecroft Golf Course · Cheltenham · Lane Cove NP · Macquarie University

Winston Hills · North Rocks · Carlingford · Epping · North Ryde

Old Toongabbie · Northmead · Telopea · Dundas Valley · Eastwood · Denistone

Pendle Hill · Wentworthville · Westmead Hospital · Cumberland Hospital · Dundas · Kissing Point · West Ryde · Ryde · Macquarie Hospital

Wentworthville · Westmead · Old Government House · Parramatta · Rydalmere · Melrose Park · Meadowbank · Ryde

Mays Hill · Harris Park · Camellia · Ermington · Rhodes · Putney · Glade Tennyson

Merrylands · Granville · Rosehill · Rosehill Gardens Racecourse · Silverwater · Silverwater Corrective Service Complex · Olympic Village · Homebush Bay · Sydney Olympic Park · Concord · Mortlake · Abbot · Cabarita

Guildford · Sydney Wool Centre · Auburn · Sydney Showgrounds · Olympic Park · Bicentennial Park · Concord Golf Course

Fairfield · Yennora · Auburn Golf Course · Lidcombe · Homebush West · State Sports Centre · North Strathfield · Canada Bay · Burwood

Villawood · Chester Hill · Berala · Rookwood · Rookwood Cemetery · Hudson Park Golf Course · Homebush · Strathfield · Croydon

Carramar · Sefton · Regents Park · Chullora · Strathfield Golf Course · Enfield · Croydon Park · Ashfi

Lansvale · Lansdowne · Bass Hill · Birrong · Greenacre · Belfield · Ashbury

Chipping Norton · Georges Hall · Condell Park · Bankstown · Yagoona · Mt Lewis · Punchbowl · Lakemba · Belmore · Clemton Park · Campsie

Warwick Farm Racecourse · Bankstown Airport · Riverwood Golf Course · Liverpool Golf Course · Mirambeena Regional Park · Canterbury · Canterbury Park Racecourse · Earlw · Hurls Pa

Georges River · Hume Hwy · Henry Lawson Dr · Cumberland Hwy · Great Western Hwy · Parramatta Rd · Liverpool Rd · Hume Hwy

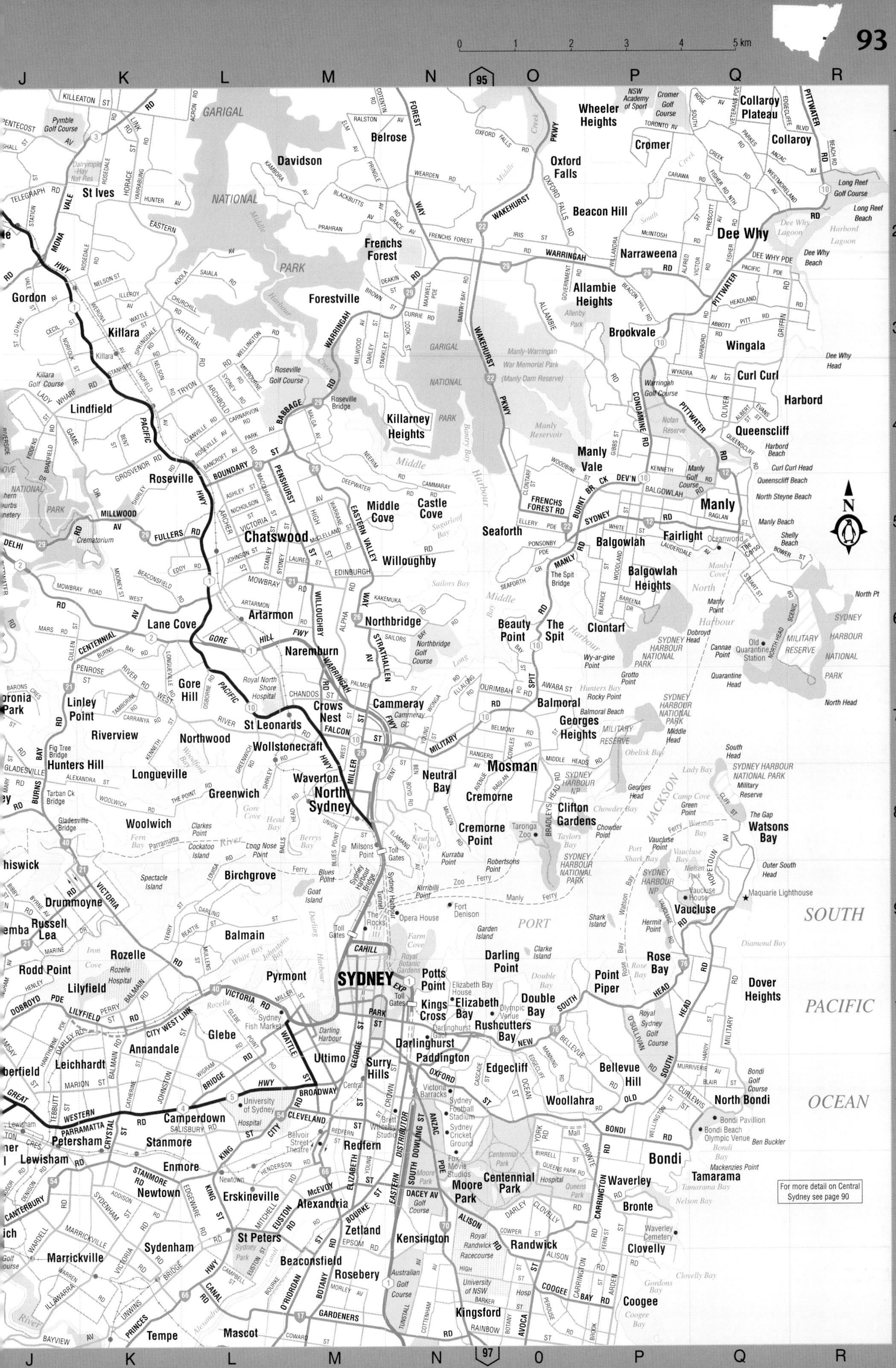

Grid references: J K L M N O P Q R across top and bottom; 1–13 down the right side.

Scale: 0 1 2 3 4 5 km

Suburbs and localities:

Wheeler Heights, NSW Academy of Sport, Cromer Golf Course, Collaroy Plateau, Collaroy, Belrose, Cromer, Davidson, Oxford Falls, Beacon Hill, Killeaton St, Pymble Golf Course, St Ives, Dairymple-Hay Nat Res, Garigal National Park, Gordon, Killara, Frenchs Forest, Forestville, Dee Why, Long Reef Golf Course, Long Reef Beach, Harbord Lagoon, Dee Why Lagoon, Dee Why Beach, Narraweena, Allambie Heights, Brookvale, Wingala, Curl Curl, Harbord, Killara Golf Course, Lindfield, Roseville, Roseville Golf Course, Roseville Bridge, Killarney Heights, Queenscliff, Harbord Beach, Curl Curl Head, Queenscliff Beach, North Steyne Beach, Manly Vale, Manly Golf Course, Chatswood, Middle Cove, Castle Cove, Willoughby, Seaforth, Balgowlah, Fairlight, Manly, Manly Beach, Lane Cove, Artarmon, Northbridge, Naremburn, Balgowlah Heights, Shelly Beach, North Head, Sydney Harbour National Park, Beauty Point, The Spit, Clontarf, Middle Head, North Point, Sydney Harbour, Linley Point, Gore Hill, Crows Nest, St Leonards, Cammeray, Royal North Shore Hospital, Balmoral, Georges Heights, Military Reserve, Obelisk Bay, Riverview, Northwood, Wollstonecraft, Waverton, North Sydney, Neutral Bay, Mosman, South Head, Hunters Hill, Longueville, Greenwich, Cremorne, Cremorne Point, Clifton Gardens, Taronga Zoo, Chowder Bay, Vaucluse, Watsons Bay, The Gap, Drummoyne, Russell Lea, Birchgrove, Balmain, Milsons Point, Sydney Harbour Bridge, Kirribilli, Fort Denison, Rodd Point, Lilyfield, Rozelle, Pyrmont, SYDNEY, The Rocks, Opera House, Royal Botanic Gardens, Farm Cove, Darling Point, Rose Bay, Dover Heights, Point Piper, Double Bay, Glebe, Annandale, Leichhardt, Ultimo, Darling Harbour, Kings Cross, Elizabeth Bay, Rushcutters Bay, Edgecliff, Bellevue Hill, Bondi, Camperdown, University of Sydney, Broadway, Surry Hills, Paddington, Woollahra, North Bondi, Bondi Beach, Petersham, Stanmore, Redfern, Moore Park, Centennial Park, Waverley, Bronte, Bondi, Tamarama, Newtown, Enmore, Erskineville, Alexandria, Zetland, Kensington, Randwick, Clovelly, Marrickville, Sydenham, St Peters, Beaconsfield, Rosebery, Tempe, Mascot, Kingsford, Coogee

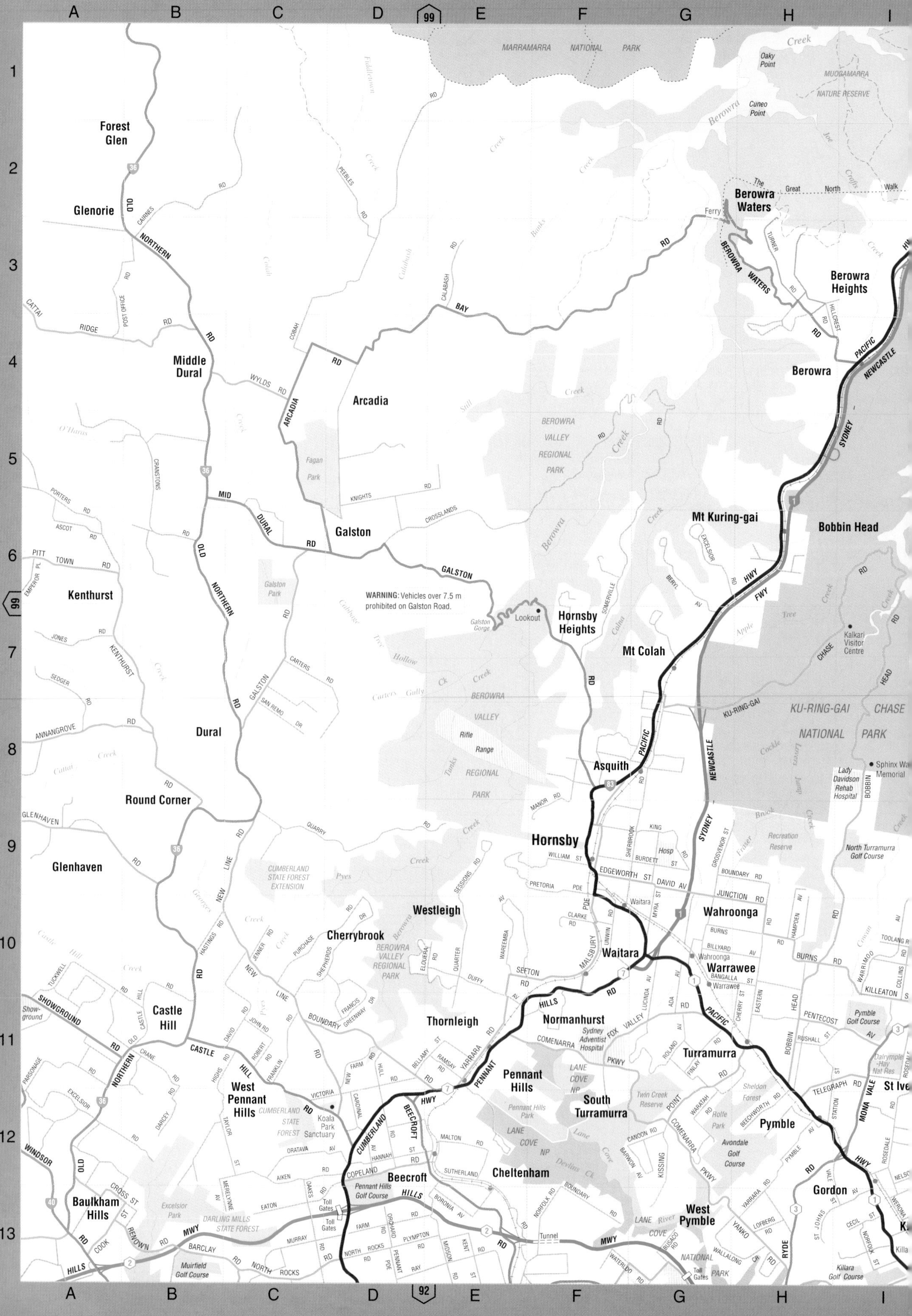

A B C D 99 E F G H I

1

MARRAMARRA NATIONAL PARK

Oaky Point

MUOGAMARRA NATURE RESERVE

Forest Glen

2

Berowra Waters

The

Berowra Heights

Glenorie

Ferry

Berowra

3

Berowra Waters

Middle Dural

Arcadia

Berowra

4

Wylds Rd

BEROWRA VALLEY REGIONAL PARK

Kenthurst

Galston Park

Galston

WARNING: Vehicles over 7.5 m prohibited on Galston Road.

Mt Kuring-gai

Bobbin Head

5

6

Galston Gorge

Lookout

Hornsby Heights

Mt Colah

Kalkari Visitor Centre

7

Dural

Carters Gully

BEROWRA VALLEY REGIONAL PARK

KU-RING-GAI CHASE NATIONAL PARK

8

Round Corner

Rifle Range

Asquith

Lady Davidson Rehab Hospital

Sphinx War Memorial

Glenhaven

Annangrove

Hornsby

9

CUMBERLAND STATE FOREST EXTENSION

Pyes Creek

North Turramurra Golf Course

10

Westleigh

Cherrybrook

BEROWRA VALLEY REGIONAL PARK

Waitara

Wahroonga

Warrawee

Pymble Golf Course

Killeaton

11

Castle Hill

Thornleigh

Normanhurst

Sydney Adventist Hospital

Pennant Hills

South Turramurra

Turramurra

St Ive

12

West Pennant Hills

Cumberland State Forest

Koala Park Sanctuary

Beecroft

Cheltenham

LANE COVE NP

Pennant Hills Park

Avondale Golf Course

Pymble

13

Baulkham Hills

Darling Mills State Forest

Toll Gates

Beecroft Golf Course

Tunnel

West Pymble

Gordon

Killara Golf Course

Muirfield Golf Course

Toll Gates

LANE COVE NATIONAL PARK

A B C D 92 E F G H I

J K L M N O P Q R

0 1 2 3 4 5 km

KU-RING-GAI CHASE NP

FWY

Porto Bay
Hawkesbury River
Gunyah Point
Juno Point
West Head
Barrenjoey Head
Barrenjoey Lighthouse
Lookout
Shark Rock

Challenger Head
Hungry Beach
LAMBERT
PENINSULA
Aboriginal Engraving Site
Great Mackerel Beach
Sandy Beach
Palm Beach
Barrenjoey Beach
Palm Beach Golf Course

Jerusalem Bay
VIZE SPUR
CENT SPUR
Little Pittwater Bay

Cowan Point
Hallets Beach
Refuge Bay
The Basin
BARRENJOEY
Whale Beach
Little Head

KU-RING-GAI CHASE
Cowan Water
PINTA RIDGE
FOLLY SPUR
Creek

Cowan
NATIONAL PARK
Yeomans Bay
WEST HEAD RD
Careel Bay
Longnose Point
Careel Bay
Bangalley Head

Cottage Point
COTTAGE POINT RD
Creek
Candle
Smiths Creek
Towlers Bay
NATIONAL PARK
Riviera
Patrick
GEORGE ST
St Michael's Cave
Hole in the Wall

LIBERATOR GENERAL
SAN MARTIN DR
Lovett Bay
PITTWATER
RIVERVIEW
CENTRAL RD
AVALON PDE
Avalon
Avalon Beach
TASMAN RD

KU-RING-GAI CHASE
NATIONAL PARK
Taylors Point
Long Beach
Avalon Golf Course
HUDSON
PLATEAU RD
Bilgola Head

Scotland Island
Refuge Cove
Scotland Island
Bilgola
RD

Church Point
Newport
IRRUBEL
MYOLA RD
Newport Beach
GLADSTONE RD
Bungan Head

Duffys Forest
Terrey Hills Country Club (Golf Course)
McCARRS
MINKARA
NARLA
LENTARA
CABBAGE TREE
PITTWATER RD
Bayview
Bayview GC
MONA
BASSETT
CRESCENT
Bungan Beach
BARRENJOEY ST
ST

NAMBA
BOORALIE
TOORONGA
COOYONG
CICADA GLEN RD
WALTER RD
SAMUEL ST
MAXWELL ST
PARK ST
DARLEY ST
EMMA ST

CHILTERN
LANE COVE RD
Ingleside
VINEYARD
WARRIEWOOD
MACPHERSON
Mona Vale
Mona Vale Golf Course
Mona Vale Hospital

Terrey Hills
MYOORA RD
MONA VALE RD
Baha'i Temple
POWDER
Monash Golf Course
INGLESIDE RD
GARDEN
Warriewood
WORKS
JACKSONS
North Narrabeen Reserve
Turimetta Head

FOREST
GARIGAL NATIONAL PARK
Deep Creek
Elanora Golf Course
ANANA
RICHARD RD
Elanora Heights
PITTWATER
OCEAN ST
Narrabeen Head
SOUTH

Ku-ring-gai Wildflower Garden
St Ives Showground
MONA VALE
PKWY
Narrabeen Lakes
WAKEHURST
Jamieson Park
Narrabeen
Beach
PACIFIC

GARIGAL NATIONAL PARK
Middle Harbour Creek
MORGAN
PKWY
NSW Academy of Sport
Wheeler Heights
Cromer Golf Course
EDGECLIFFE
Collaroy Plateau
PITTWATER
Collaroy
OCEAN

ACTION RD
RALSTON
COTENTIN RD
ELM AV
PRINGLE
OXFORD FALLS RD
TORONTO AV
ROSE
VETERANS
RAPKES
WESTMORELAND
ANZAC
BEACH RD
Long Reef Golf Course
Long Reef Point

KAMBORA
Belrose
WEARDEN RD
Oxford Falls
Cromer
CARAWA
FISHER RD NTH
Long Reef Beach

Davidson
BLACKBUTTS
WAKEHURST PKWY
OXFORD FALLS RD
Beacon Hill
McINTOSH
PRESCOTT
FISHER
Dee Why
Harbord
Dee Why Lagoon

PRAHRAN
Frenchs Forest
FRENCHS FOREST RD
IRIS ST
WARRINGAH RD
WILLANDRA
VICTOR RD
ALFRED
DEE WHY PDE
PACIFIC PDE
Dee Why Beach

KOALA
SAIALA
DEAKIN
MAXWELL PDE
Narraweena
BEACON HILL RD
Dee Why Head

Forestville
BROWN
ST
COOK
ALLAMBIE RD
Allambie Heights
Allenby Park
GOVERNMENT RD
HARBORD
PITT
ABBOTT
GRIFFIN RD
Wingala

WARRINGAH
WAKEHURST PKWY
GARIGAL NATIONAL PARK
Manly-Warringah War Memorial Park (Manly Dam Reserve)
Brookvale
Warringah GC
WYADRA AV
Curl Curl

CHURCHILL
WELLINGTON
ARTERIAL
TRYON
SYDNEY
MELBOURNE
Roseville Golf Course
Middle Harbour

PENGUIN
N

PACIFIC OCEAN

St Johns Park
Canley Heights
Canley Vale
Cabramatta
Carramar
Lansvale
Villawood
Chester Hill
Sefton
Berala
Rookwood
Strathfield
Regents Park
Chullora
Birrong
Mount Pritchard
Ashcroft
Hargrave Park
Warwick Farm
Lansdowne
Bass Hill
Georges Hall
Yagoona
Greenacre
Boronia
Mt Lewis
Punchbowl
Wiley Park
Lakemba
Liverpool
Chipping Norton
Condell Park
Bankstown
Bankstown Airport
Lurnea
Moorebank
Newbridge
Milperra
Milperra
Bankstown Golf Course
Bankstown Hospital
Roselands
Casula
Chatham Village
Wattle Grove
Hammondville
Western
Beaconsfield
Narwee
South
Revesby
Padstow
Riverwood
Beverly Hills
Panania
Peakhurst
Holsworthy
Holsworthy Barracks
Pleasure Point
East Hills
Picnic Point
Sandy Point
Georges River NP
Lugarno
Alfords Point
Illawong
Como
Oyster Bay
MILITARY RESERVE
Menai
Bangor
Bonnet Bay
Jannali
Woronora
Woronora Heights
Sutherland
Kirrawee
Loftus
Lucas Heights
Australian Nuclear Science and Technology Organisation
Yarrawarrah
Engadine
Heathcote
HEATHCOTE NATIONAL PARK
ROYAL NATIONAL PARK
Audley

0 1 2 3 4 5 km

J K L M N O P Q R

1
Croydon · Haberfield · Leichhardt · Annandale · Ultimo · Surry Hills · Paddington · Edgecliff · Bellevue Hill · Woollahra · Enfield · Ashfield · Broadway · University of Sydney · Victoria Barracks · Sydney Football Stadium · Bondi · Bondi Junction

2
Croydon Park · Ashbury · Summer Hill · Petersham · Camperdown · Stanmore · Enmore · Newtown · Redfern · Belvoir Street Theatre · Fox Movie Studios · Moore Park · Centennial Park · Waverley · Bronte · Clovelly
Canterbury · Dulwich Hill · Lewisham · Erskineville · Alexandria · Zetland · Kensington · Randwick · Coogee
Sydney Cricket Ground · Centennial Park · Queens Park · Randwick Racecourse · University of NSW

3
Campsie · Hurlstone Park · Marrickville · Sydenham · St Peters · Beaconsfield · Rosebery · Kingsford · Coogee
Clemton Park · Bexley · Earlwood · Tempe · Mascot · Eastlakes

4
Undercliffe · Turrella · Arncliffe · Qantas · Mascot · Eastlakes · Daceyville · Pagewood · Maroubra
Bexley North · Bardwell Park · Banksia · SYDNEY AIRPORT · Botany · The Lakes Golf Course · Bonnie Doon Golf Course

5
Kingsgrove · Bexley · Rockdale · Kyeemagh · Botany · Banksmeadow · Hillsdale · Matraville · Malabar
Hurstville · Kogarah · Brighton Le Sands · BOTANY BAY · Chifley

6
Carlton · Monterey · Container Terminal · Port Botany · Container Terminal · Long Bay · Malabar
Allawah · Beverley Park · Ramsgate · Phillip Bay · Prince Henry Hospital

7
Connells Point · Carss Park · Blakehurst · Sans Souci · Dolls Point · Little Bay · La Perouse

8
Sylvania · Sylvania Waters · Sandringham · BOTANY BAY · La Perouse Monument & Museum · Bare Island · Captain Cook's Landing Place · Kurnell · Cape Banks

9
Sylvania Heights · Taren Point · Towra Point Nature Reserve · Quibray Bay · Kurnell · Cape Solander

10
Miranda · Caringbah · Woolooware Bay · Weeney Bay · BOTANY BAY NATIONAL PARK · SOUTH

11
Yowie Bay · Woolooware · Recreation Reserve · Potter Point · PACIFIC

12
Dolans Bay · Cronulla · BATE BAY · OCEAN · North Cronulla Beach · South Cronulla Beach · Cronulla Point

13
Lilli Pilli · Port Hacking · Burraneer · ROYAL NATIONAL PARK · Maianbar · Port Hacking Point

A B C D E F G H I

1

Hill End
Historic Site
Turondale
Sofala
Historic Town
Wattle Flat
Glen Davis
Newnes
GARDENS OF STONE
NATIONAL

2

Palmers Oakey
Mt Wiagdon
1015m
Ben Bullen
PARK
Mt Davidson
1081m
Glow Worm Tunnel
Limekilns
WINBURNDALE
NATURE
RESERVE
Peel
Dark Corner
Cullen Bullen
Angus Place
WOLLEMI

3

Portland
Pipers Flat
Lidsdale
TURON
STATE FOREST
WINBURNDALE
NATURE
RESERVE
Sunny Corner
Wallerawang
Marrangaroo
NATIONAL
PARK

4

Dunkeld
Bathurst
Raglan
Glanmire
Mt Ovens
1272m
Meadow Flat
Bowenfels
Clarence
Newnes Junction
Evans Plains
Kelso
MITCHELL HWY
Walang
Yetholme
57
GREAT
Mount Lambie
Zig Zag Railway
Bell
Mount Wilson

5

Motor Racing Circuit
Orton Park
White Rock
Brewongle
Tarana Quarry
Rydal
Old Bowenfels
Lithgow
Hartley Vale
Hartley
77
Mt Tom
Mt Tomah
Botanic Ga
Perthville
WIMBOOL
NATURE RESERVE
Sodwalls
Glenroy
Little Hartley
WESTERN
Mt York
Georges Plains
Locksley
Tarana
EVANS
CROWN
NATURE
RESERVE
Mount Victoria
BLUE
43

6

The Lagoon
O'Connell
Carlwood
Lowther
Mt Piddington
1078m
Pulpit Rock
Reserve & Lookout
Govetts Leap Lookout
Evans Lookout
BLUE MOUN
Newbridge
Cow Flat
Wisemans Creek
47
LOWES
MOUNT
STATE
FOREST
Lowes Mount
Hampton
Bonfire Hill
1286m
Mount Blackheath
Lookout
Blackheath
Shipley
NATIONAL

7

Moorilda
Rockley
Historic Town
Hazelgrove
Medlow Bath
Hargraves
Lookout
Mini-Ha-Ha
Wentworth
Falls
Lawson
Hobbys Yards
Essington
Oberon
Duckmaloi
JENOLAN
STATE
FOREST
Gibraltar Rocks
1057m
Megalong
Explorers Tree
Scenic Skyway &
Railway Complex
Katoomba
Leura
Bullaburra
The Three Sisters
Echo Point

8

Trunkey
Mount David
Black Springs
Edith
BLACK RANGE
Jenolan Caves
Jenolan Caves
BLUE MOUNTAINS
NATIONAL

9

Abercrombie
Caves
Campbells
River
Shooters Hill
KANANGRA -
BOYD
Mt Cloudmaker
1164m
GANGERANG
McMahons
Lookout
Burraga
Isabella
93
RANGE
NATIONAL
Mt Guouogang
1290m
Kanangra Walls
Lake
Yerranderie
Historic Town
Nattai

10

Tuena
Abercrombie
Porters
Retreat
Mt Paalin
1210m
ENTRY
PROHIBIT
BURRAG
STA

11

Peelwood
ABERCROMBIE
RIVER
NATIONAL
PARK
BLUE
Mt Wrong
1214m
Mt Colong
1047m
Yerranderie
Historic Town
YERRANDERIE
STATE
RECREATION
AREA

12

Fullerton
Thalaba
MOUNTAINS
NATIONAL
Mt Armstrong
1091m
DIVIDING
BLUE

13

Binda
Golspie
Yalbraith
Richlands
GREAT
Broughtons
Lookout
Wombeyan
Caves
Lords Mountain
845m
Goodmans
Ford
Wombeyan Caves
Bullio
High
Range
NATIONAL

A B C D E F G H I

0 5 10 15 20 25 30 km

J K L 115 M N O 106 P Q R

1
Bucketty
Morisset Brightwaters Sunshine
Gwandalan Nords Wharf
HOWES RANGE
YENGO
Mandalong Mannering Catherine
Wyee Park Hill Bay
NATIONAL
Muirs Lookout MUNMORAH
OLNEY STATE FOREST Doyalson STATE
RECREATION
Higher Macdonald Lake AREA
BALA Cedar Brush Munmorah
PARK Cedar Brush Ridge BUDGEWOI

2
RANGE
Mangrove Reservoir
St Albans Kulnura Yarramalong Little Jilliby GOROKAN
WOMERAH Ravensdale TOUKLEY
Dooralong Jilliby NORAVILLE
PARR Upper Macdonald Cedar Brush NORAH HEAD
STATE Mangrove McPherson Wyong Creek
RECREATION Mountain STATE WYONG Tuggerah
AREA Upper Central FOREST OURIMBAH WYRRABALONG
Mangrove Creek Mangrove Fowlers Lookout 31 NATIONAL
RANGE Somersby TUGGERAH PARK

3
Colo Heights Ten Mile Peats Palm Palmdale THE ENTRANCE NORTH
Hollow Ridge Grove THE ENTRANCE
PUTTY Webbs Creek OURIMBAH TOOWOON BAY
DHARUG Mangrove Creek NARARA TUMBI LONG JETTY
RD Central Colo Wisemans Ferry NATIONAL LISAROW UMBI BATEAU BAY
Upper Colo Colo Laughtondale POINT MATCHAM FORRESTERS BEACH
Colo PARK CLARE GOSFORD WYRRABALONG
Heights Gunderman Glenworth NATIONAL PARK

4
Blaxlands Valley Mount KINCUMBER WAMBERAL
Ridge East Sackville Spencer White SYDNEY ERINA TERRIGAL
Kurrajong North The Skillion
Comleroy Glossodia MARRAMARRA Brisbane AVOCA BEACH
Road Kurmond Cattai NATIONAL Water MACMASTERS
Bellbird Hill Cattai PARK BEACH
Kurrajong Freemans Wilberforce MOONEY BOUDDI
Bowen Reach Glenorie MOONEY WOY NATIONAL
Mountain North Pitt Mooney WOY PARK
Richmond Richmond Town Maraylya Brooklyn ETTALONG
Clarendon SCHEYVILLE Patonga UMINA KILLCARE HEIGHTS
Windsor Londonderry NP Warrah WAGSTAFFE
Hawkesbury Museum Vineyard Nelson KU-RING-GAI CHASE Lookout BOUDDI NP

5
Vale of Avoca Lookout Kenthurst Cowan NATIONAL Broken Bay
Springwood Windsor RIVERSTONE Annangrove BEROWRA PARK PALM BEACH
Winmalee Downs Rouse Hill SOUTH
Valley Heights Marsden SCHOFIELDS Glenhaven PACIFIC WHALE BEACH
Warrimoo Park HORNSBY AVALON

6
Blaxland Penrith QUAKERS Galston NEWPORT
Glenbrook Kingswood ST MARYS HILL CASTLE Pymble MONA VALE
Erskine Park HILL HILLS PACIFIC FRENCHS ELANORA HEIGHTS
WESTERN MOUNT LANE FOREST NARRABEEN
Mulgoa Wonderland DRUITT BLACKTOWN COVE TERREY COLLAROY
Wallacia Sydney EASTERN MWY HILLS DEE WHY
HORSLEY CREEK PARRAMATTA PYMBLE OCEAN
Luddenham PARK RYDE CHATSWOOD MANLY
Radio CECIL GLADESVILLE LANE BALGOWLAH
Astronomy PARK MERRYLANDS COVE MOSMAN SYDNEY HARBOUR NP
Badgerys Centre HOMEBUSH BAY NORTH WATSONS BAY
Creek CABRAMATTA BALMAIN SYDNEY
Austral LIVERPOOL STRATHFIELD SYDNEY DOVER HEIGHTS
Rossmore MILPERRA BELFIELD PADDINGTON BONDI

9
LEPPINGTON REVESBY BANKSTOWN MARRICKVILLE COOGEE
Catherine Field BEXLEY SYDNEY KINGSFORD
Bringelly MACQUARIE PEAKHURST HURSTVILLE AIRPORT BOTANY MAROUBRA
Theresa Park FIELDS BLAKEHURST BRIGHTON LA PEROUSE
Cobbitty MINTO BRIGHTON LE SANDS
Oran Park MILITARY SUTHERLAND KURNELL
Brownlow Hill Raceway RESERVE SYLVANIA
NARELLAN LEUMEAH MIRANDA BOTANY BAY
CAMDEN CRONULLA NATIONAL PARK

10
GRASMERE CAMPBELLTOWN HEATHCOTE OCEAN
Mount The Oaks Wedderburn Audley Bundeena
Hunter Menangle Park HEATHCOTE Maianbar ROYAL
Menangle Waterfall NATIONAL
Mowbray Park HEATHCOTE PARK Garie Beach
Picton NATIONAL Helensburgh Wattamolla
Douglas Park PARK Otford
Appin DHARAWAL Stanwell Tops Lawrence Hargrave
Tahmoor Wilton STATE Stanwell Park Memorial & Lookout
RECREATION Coalcliff
AREA DHARAWAL Clifton
Bargo NATURE Scarborough
Yanderra RESERVE Wombarra

13
Picton Coledale
Yerrinbool Sublime Point Lookout
Austinmer
Thirroul
TO SHELLHARBOUR GORRIMAL

For more detail on Hawkesbury & Central Coast see page 102

For more detail on Sydney Suburbs see pages 92 - 97

For more detail on the Southern Highlands see page 110

N

J K 110 L M N O P Q R

A B C D E F G H I

98
40
98
98

BELLS LINE OF RD

DARLING

CAUSEWAY

TO LITHGOW

TO LITHGOW

• Walls Lookout

Rigby Hill 924m

• Mt Banks 1058m

VICTORIA FALLS RD

Victoria Falls

Grose

• Victoria Falls Lookout

Creek

• Baltzer Lookout

King

George

Brook

Explorers

EXPLORERS

River

• Bennett Lookout

Anvil Rock

• Mt Victoria 1044m

Sunset Rock

Mt Victoria 1044m

MOUNT VICTORIA: A blend of weatherboard and sandstone colonial buildings, Mount Victoria is an historic village with craft shops, an historical museum and a quaint cinema, Mt Vic Flicks.

Mount Victoria

Mt Paddington 1078m

BLUE

BLACKHEATH

PLATEAU

GREAT

32

Hat Hill 1033m

Grose

Edgeworth David Hill 864m

BUSHWALKS:
There are a number of scenic walks throughout the Blue Mou. These include:

1. The Fairfax Heritage Track (2 km, approx. 1 hour return): starts at Heritage Centre, finishes at Govetts Leap; several res wheelchair access.

2. Three Sisters Walk (approx. half hour return): Easy walk; the Information Centre at Echo Point, view of the Three Sister

3. Govett's Leap to Evan's Lookout (approx. 4 hours return): difficulty; a clifftop walk with spectacular views across the Gr

4. Valley of the Waters Nature Track (approx. 3 hours return) difficulty; waterfall circuit from the Conservation Hut Cafe at Falls.

5. National Pass Circuit (approx. 4 hours return): Difficult; sp clifftop and waterfall circuit from the Conservation Hut Cafe a Wentworth Falls.

Mt Hay 944m

BLUE MOUNTAINS

RANGE

only

• Pulpit Rock Reserve & Lookout

HAT HILL RD

• Cripps Lookout

Horseshoe Falls   Trinity Falls

Govetts Leap Lookout

Bacchante Gardens

NPWS Heritage Centre

Bridal Veil Falls

• Luchetti Lookout

Lockley Pylon

LYCON PLATEAU

MOUNT

NATIONAL PARK

Urella

Wirralie

Brook

GOVETTS LEAP RD

Fortress Hill 950m

• The Pinnacles

4WD

only

Govetts Statue

Blackheath ⊤

Evans Lookout

Beauchamp Falls

Flat Top 928m

Flat Top

Brook

Mount Blackheath Lookout

Mermaid Cave

EVANS LOOKOUT RD

Lake Greaves

THE GRAND

Arethusa Falls

4WD

• Mt Blackheath

Creek

Lake Medlow

5

• Walls Cave

CANYON

Mountains

Creek

RD

SHIPLEY RD

18

WESTERN

5

GRAND

CANYON

Katoomba Falls

GARDENS: The Blue Mountains region is justly famous for its beautiful gardens. One of the most famous is the Evergl Gardens, created by the Danish landscaper Paul Sorensen; daily. The Bacchante Gardens, at Blackheath, lovely all-yea round, are at their peak in late spring; open daily.

Sugarloaf Peak

Shipley Tea Rooms

Shipley

Medlow Bath
Hydro Majestic Hotel

MEGALONG VALLEY RD

11

Minni-Ha-Ha Falls

4WD only

DIVIDING

• Hargraves Lookout

Cascade Creek Dams

LEURA: Home to some of Australia's most beautiful gardens. The village with its unhurried atmosphere also offers beautifully restored historic buildings, charming tea houses, craft shops and galleries displaying the work of local artists.

Wentworth Falls Lake

RD

Wentworth Falls Lake

Wentworth Falls

Lawson

KANIMBLA VALLEY

Chaplowe

• Explorers Tree

The Edge Maxvision Cinema

BARTON ST

3

MEGALONG ST

Leura

HWY

Wentworth

BLAXLAND

4

RD

FALLS RD

14

RAILWAY

32

Bullabu

2

GENEVIEVE RD

• Werriberri Trail Rides

Megalong Australian Heritage Centre

Katoomba ⊤

KATOOMBA ST

Leura Mall

Conservation Hut Cafe

Valley of the Falls Picnic Area

Wentworth Fall Picnic Area

5

Wentworth Falls

• Megalong Head

Megalong

NARROW NECK RD

CLIFF DR

Scenic Skyway & Railway Complex

Katoomba Falls

Visitor Information

• Everglades Gardens

Cascades

Gordon Falls

• Cascades

Kings Table

QUEEN RD

SCENIC SKYWAY AND RAILWAY COMPLEX: The Scenic Skyway cnr Violet St & Cliff Dr., Katoomba is the first horizontal passenger-carrying ropeway in Australia. It travels about 350 m across the mountain gorge above Cooks Crossing and provides stunning views of Katoomba Falls, Orphan Rock and Jamison Valley. The Scenic Railway was built in the 1880s by the founder of the Katoomba coalmine to bring out the coal and transport the miners. Reputed to be the steepest railway in the world, it descends into the Jamison Valley at an average incline of 45 degrees through a sunlit, tree-clad gorge approximately 445 m in length.

Echo Point

Giant Stairway

• The Three Sisters

Sublime Point

ELIZABETH

THE THREE SISTERS: A major attraction of the Blue Mountains and one of Australia's best known rock formations. This trio of rocky pinnacles is floodlit at night.

Queen Victoria Hospital

KINGS RD

KEDUMBA RD

KINGS

TABLELAND

4WD only

Billy Healy Hill 637m

Megalong Ck

FIRE TRAIL

Castle Head 989m

GREAT

Katoomba

River

KEDUMBA

4WD

• Pinnacle Hill

NARROW NECK RD

JAMISON

VALLEY

Castle Track

VALLEY

TABLELAND

Euroka

BLUE

MOUNTAINS

Mt Solitary 965m

ERSKINE

Greenfields Lookover

• Melvilles Lookdown

VALLEY

NATIONAL

PARK

CEDAR

VALLEY

River

RANGE

KEDUMBA   VALLEY

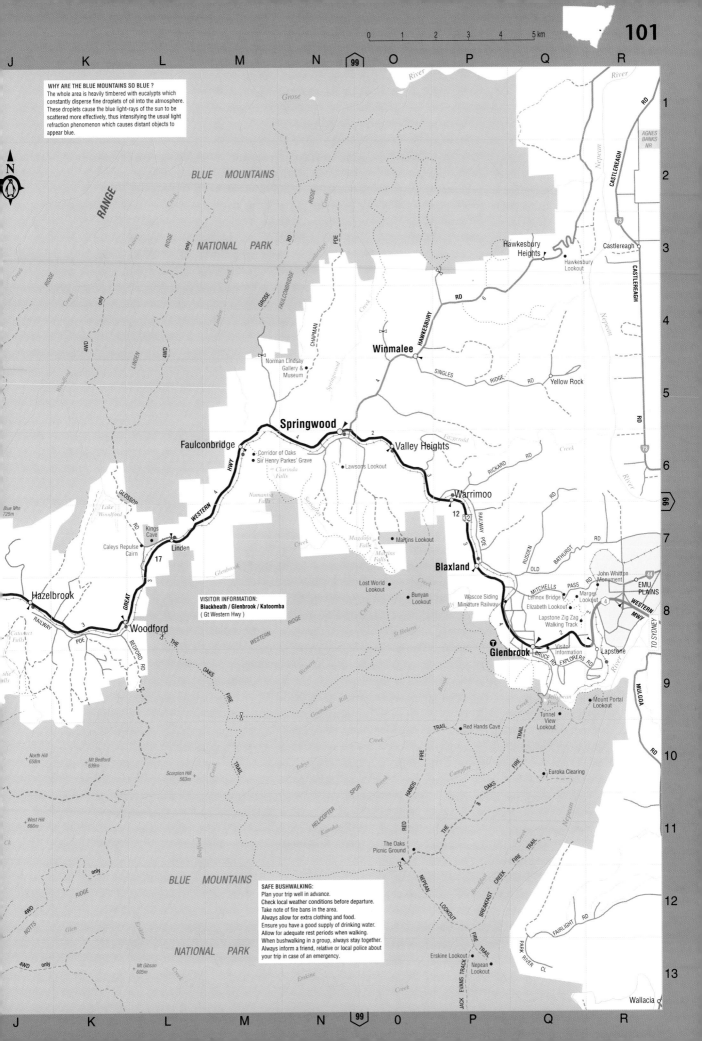

0   2   4   6   8   10 km

VISITOR INFORMATION:
The Entrance (Memorial Park, Marine Pde)
Wyong (Wallarah Point Park, Wallarah Rd, Gorokan)
Gosford (200 Mann St)
Terrigal (Rotary Park, Terrigal Dr)

NATIONAL PARKS: At **Wyrrabalong** swimming is possible at either Bateau Bay or Tuggerah Beach; waterbirds are a feature. **Bouddi** is renowned for its established walking trails; at Maitland Bay there is a shipwreck half-submerged on the beach. **Brisbane Water** offers spectacular water views and has many fine Aboriginal art sites. Further west, **Dharug** lines the river and has a popular family walking trail.

GREAT NORTH WALK: A section of this 250-km walking track, which runs between Sydney and Newcastle, passes through the Hawkesbury region. There are numerous access points, facilities and connections to public transport enabling families, campers and day trippers to enjoy day and weekend walks.

HAWKESBURY RIVER: A magnificent waterway navigable as far as Windsor and further for small craft. There are few settlements along the widest section of the river as most of the shore is protected as part of Brisbane Water and Ku-ring-gai Chase national parks.

RIVERBOAT POSTMAN: Visitors can join the river mail-boat run which leaves the ferry wharf at Dangar Rd, Brooklyn on weekdays. It takes three hours, ferrying mail, groceries and other necessities to residents with no road access.

SAFE BOATING:
Tell someone where you are going.
Carry adequate equipment.
Carry effective life jackets.
Carry enough fuel and water.
Ensure engine reliability.
Guard against fire.
Do not overload the craft.
Know the boating rules and local regulations; also distress signals.
Watch the weather.
Do not drink alcohol while boating.

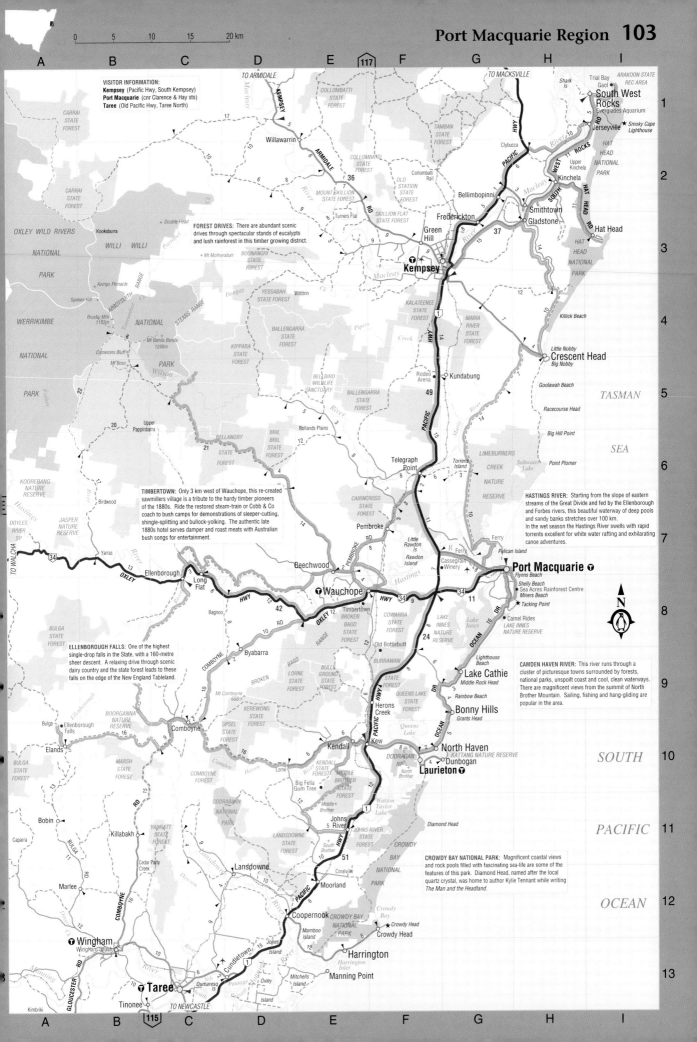

VISITOR INFORMATION:
Kempsey (Pacific Hwy, South Kempsey)
Port Macquarie (cnr Clarence & Hay sts)
Taree (Old Pacific Hwy, Taree North)

FOREST DRIVES: There are abundant scenic drives through spectacular stands of eucalypts and lush rainforest in this timber growing district.

TIMBERTOWN: Only 3 km west of Wauchope, this re-created sawmillers village is a tribute to the hardy timber pioneers of the 1880s. Ride the restored steam-train or Cobb & Co coach to bush camps for demonstrations of sleeper-cutting, shingle-splitting and bullock-yolking. The authentic late 1880s hotel serves damper and roast meats with Australian bush songs for entertainment.

ELLENBOROUGH FALLS: One of the highest single-drop falls in the State, with a 160-metre sheer descent. A relaxing drive through scenic dairy country and the state forest leads to these falls on the edge of the New England Tableland.

HASTINGS RIVER: Starting from the slope of eastern streams of the Great Divide and fed by the Ellenborough and Forbes rivers, this beautiful waterway of deep pools and sandy banks stretches over 100 km.
In the wet season the Hastings River swells with rapid torrents excellent for white water rafting and exhilarating canoe adventures.

CAMDEN HAVEN RIVER: This river runs through a cluster of picturesque towns surrounded by forests, national parks, unspoilt coast and cool, clean waterways. There are magnificent views from the summit of North Brother Mountain. Sailing, fishing and hang-gliding are popular in the area.

CROWDY BAY NATIONAL PARK: Magnificent coastal views and rock pools filled with fascinating sea-life are some of the features of this park. Diamond Head, named after the local quartz crystal, was home to author Kylie Tennant while writing *The Man and the Headland*.

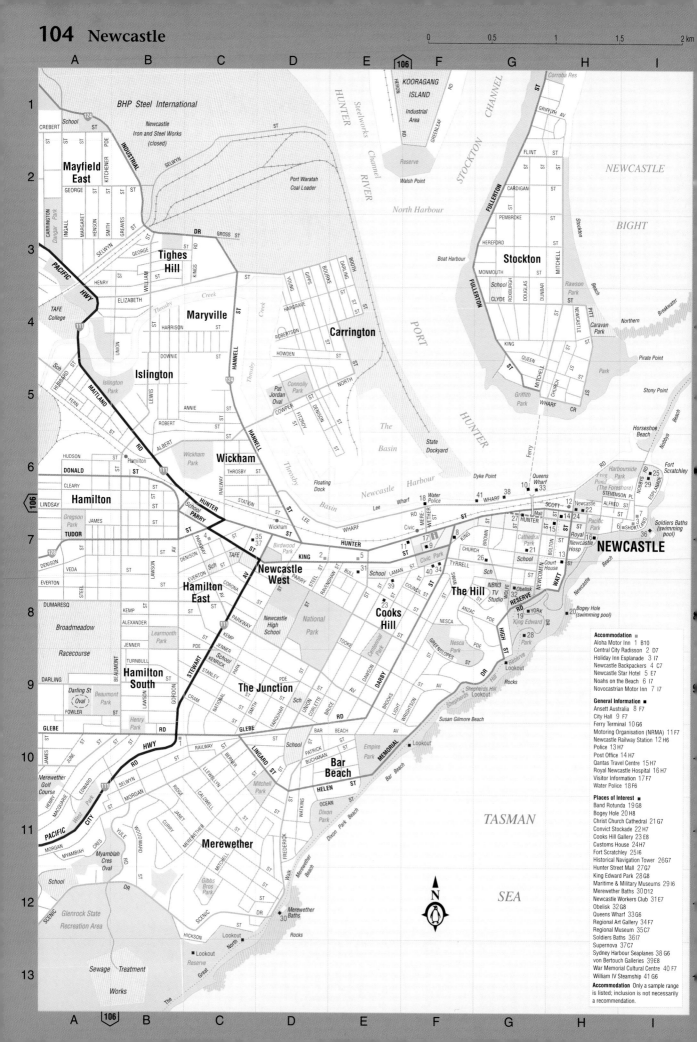

Mayfield East

Tighes Hill

Maryville

Islington

Carrington

Wickham

Hamilton

Stockton

KOORAGANG ISLAND
Industrial Area

BHP Steel International

Newcastle Iron and Steel Works (closed)

Port Waratah Coal Loader

North Harbour

HUNTER RIVER

Steelworks Channel

STOCKTON CHANNEL

NEWCASTLE BIGHT

Reserve

Walsh Point

PORT

HUNTER

Newcastle Harbour

The Basin

State Dockyard

Floating Dock

Throsby Basin

Boat Harbour

Stony Point

Horseshoe Beach

Fort Scratchley

Nobbys Beach

Pirate Point

Soldiers Baths (swimming pool)

Hamilton East

Newcastle West

Cooks Hill

The Hill

NEWCASTLE

Hamilton South

The Junction

Bar Beach

Merewether

Broadmeadow

Racecourse

Darling St Oval

Beaumont Park

Henry Park

National Park

Centennial Park

Newcastle High School

King Edward Park

Shepherds Hill Lookout

Susan Gilmore Beach

Empire Park

Bar Beach

Dixon Park Beach

Merewether Beach

Gibbs Bros Park

Glenrock State Recreation Area

Merewether Golf Course

Myamblah Cres Oval

Merewether Baths

TASMAN SEA

Sewage Treatment Works

N (penguin)

Accommodation ■
Aloha Motor Inn 1 B10
Central City Radisson 2 D7
Holiday Inn Esplanade 3 I7
Newcastle Backpackers 4 C7
Newcastle Star Hotel 5 E7
Noahs on the Beach 6 I7
Novocastrian Motor Inn 7 I7

General Information ■
Ansett Australia 8 F7
City Hall 9 F7
Ferry Terminal 10 G6
Motoring Organisation (NRMA) 11 F7
Newcastle Railway Station 12 H6
Police 13 H7
Post Office 14 H7
Qantas Travel Centre 15 H7
Royal Newcastle Hospital 16 H7
Visitor Information 17 F7
Water Police 18 F6

Places of Interest ■
Band Rotunda 19 G8
Bogey Hole 20 H8
Christ Church Cathedral 21 G7
Convict Stockade 22 H7
Cooks Hill Gallery 23 E8
Customs House 24 H7
Fort Scratchley 25 I6
Historical Navigation Tower 26 G7
Hunter Street Mall 27 G7
King Edward Park 28 G8
Maritime & Military Museums 29 I6
Merewether Baths 30 D12
Newcastle Workers Club 31 E7
Obelisk 32 G8
Queens Wharf 33 G6
Regional Art Gallery 34 F7
Regional Museum 35 C7
Soldiers Baths 36 I7
Supernova 37 C7
Sydney Harbour Seaplanes 38 G6
von Bertouch Galleries 39 E8
War Memorial Cultural Centre 40 F7
William IV Steamship 41 G6

Accommodation Only a sample range is listed; inclusion is not necessarily a recommendation.

Scale: 0 0.5 1 1.5 2 km

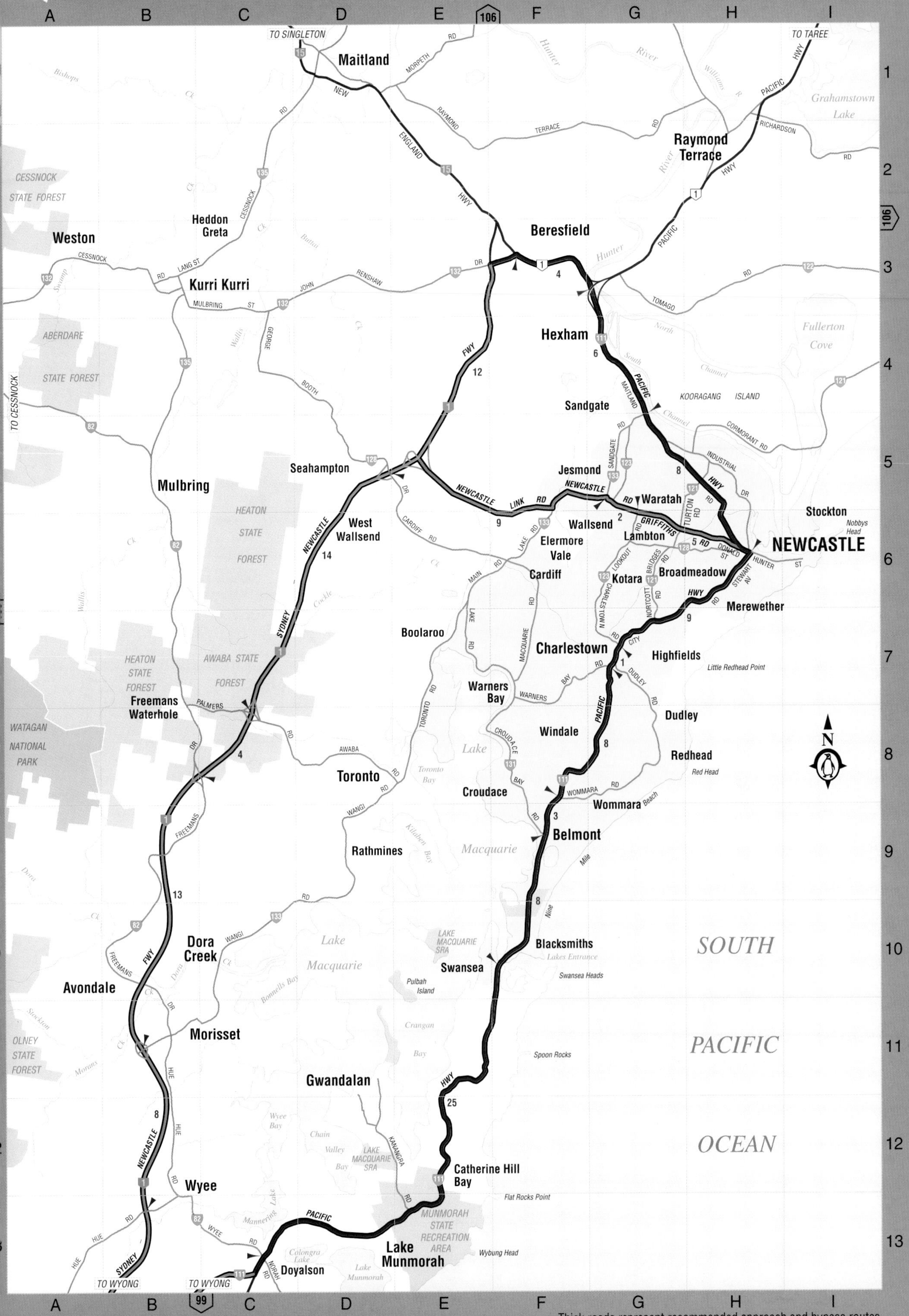

0 1 2 3 4 5km

A B C D E F G H I

TO SINGLETON

Maitland

TO TAREE

Raymond Terrace

Weston

Heddon Greta

CESSNOCK STATE FOREST

Kurri Kurri

Beresfield

Hexham

Sandgate

ABERDARE STATE FOREST

Mulbring

Seahampton

Jesmond

Waratah

Stockton

Nobbys Head

West Wallsend

Wallsend

Elermore Vale

Lambton

NEWCASTLE

Cardiff

Kotara

Broadmeadow

HEATON STATE FOREST

Boolaroo

Charlestown

Merewether

Warners Bay

Highfields

Little Redhead Point

AWABA STATE FOREST

Dudley

Freemans Waterhole

Windale

Redhead

Red Head

Toronto

Croudace

Wommara

Wommara Beach

WATAGAN NATIONAL PARK

Rathmines

Belmont

Macquarie

Dora Creek

SOUTH

Blacksmiths

Lakes Entrance

Avondale

Swansea

Swansea Heads

PACIFIC

OLNEY STATE FOREST

Morisset

Pulbah Island

Spoon Rocks

Gwandalan

OCEAN

Lake Macquarie SRA

Wyee

Catherine Hill Bay

Flat Rocks Point

MUNMORAH STATE RECREATION AREA

Wybung Head

Lake Munmorah

Doyalson

TO WYONG

TO WYONG

Thick roads represent recommended approach and bypass routes.

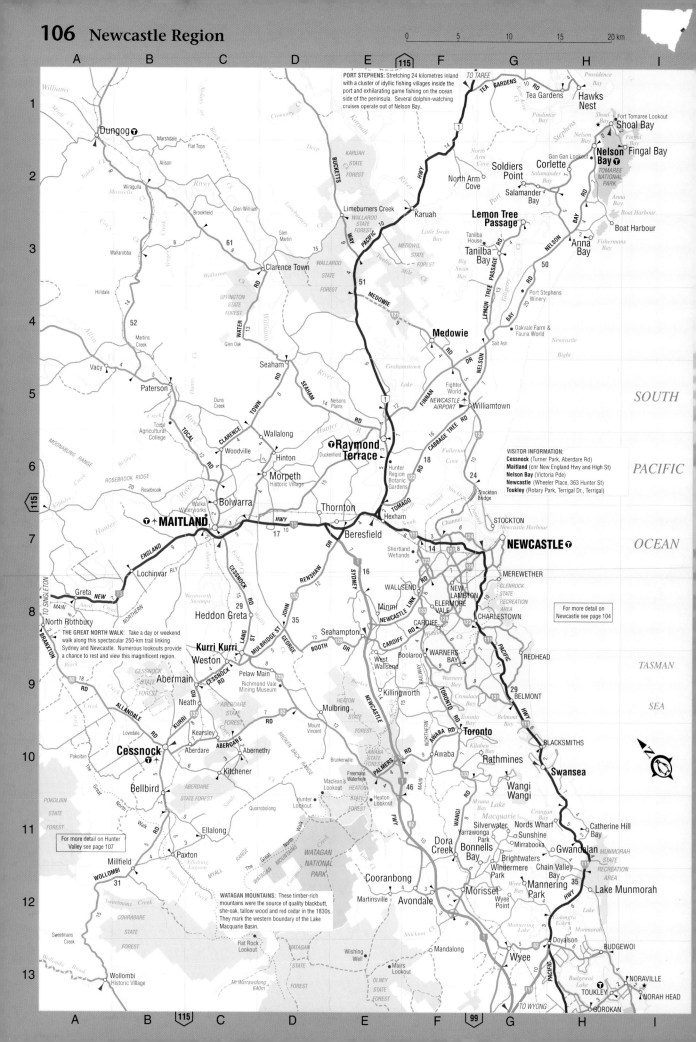

PORT STEPHENS: Stretching 24 kilometres inland with a cluster of idyllic fishing villages inside the port and exhilarating game fishing on the ocean side of the peninsula. Several dolphin-watching cruises operate out of Nelson Bay.

VISITOR INFORMATION:
Cessnock (Turner Park, Aberdare Rd)
Maitland (cnr New England Hwy and High St)
Nelson Bay (Victoria Pde)
Newcastle (Wheeler Place, 363 Hunter St)
Toukley (Rotary Park, Terrigal Dr., Terrigal)

For more detail on Newcastle see page 104

THE GREAT NORTH WALK: Take a day or weekend walk along this spectacular 250-km trail linking Sydney and Newcastle. Numerous lookouts provide a chance to rest and view this magnificent region.

For more detail on Hunter Valley see page 107

WATAGAN MOUNTAINS: These timber-rich mountains were the source of quality blackbutt, she-oak, tallow wood and red cedar in the 1830s. They mark the western boundary of the Lake Macquarie Basin.

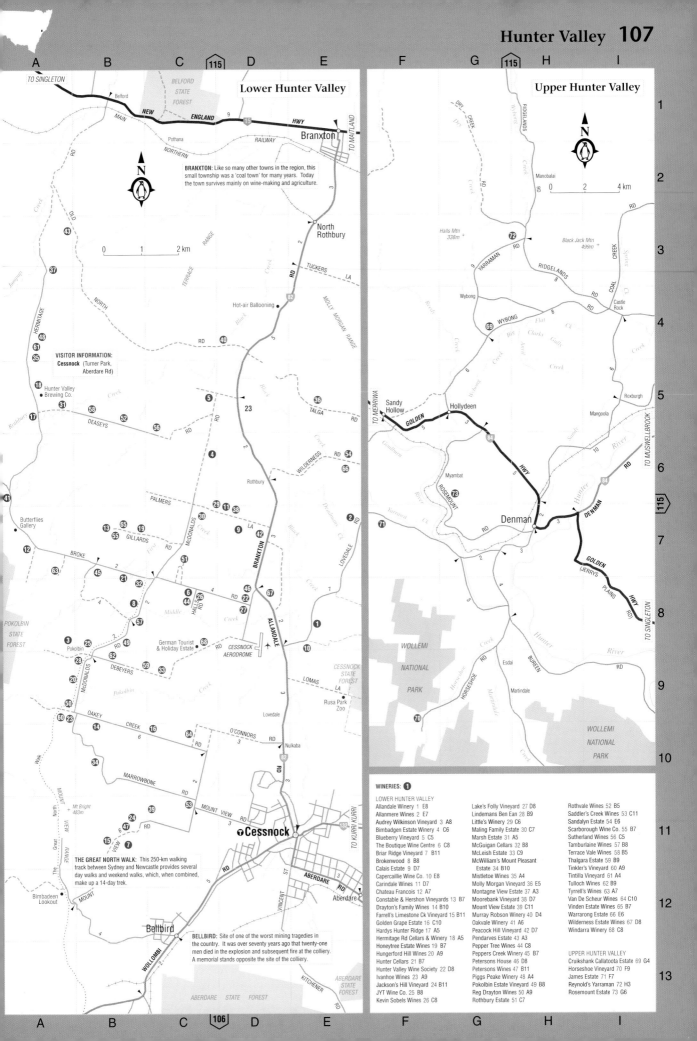

Lower Hunter Valley

Upper Hunter Valley

BRANXTON: Like so many other towns in the region, this small township was a 'coal town' for many years. Today the town survives mainly on wine-making and agriculture.

VISITOR INFORMATION:
Cessnock (Turner Park, Aberdare Rd)

THE GREAT NORTH WALK: This 250-km walking track between Sydney and Newcastle provides several day walks and weekend walks, which, when combined, make up a 14-day trek.

BELLBIRD: Site of one of the worst mining tragedies in the country. It was over seventy years ago that twenty-one men died in the explosion and subsequent fire at the colliery. A memorial stands opposite the site of the colliery.

WINERIES: ❶

LOWER HUNTER VALLEY
Allandale Winery 1 E8
Allanmere Wines 2 E7
Audrey Wilkinson Vineyard 3 A8
Bimbadgen Estate Winery 4 C6
Blueberry Vineyard 5 C5
The Boutique Wine Centre 6 C8
Briar Ridge Vineyard 7 B11
Brokenwood 8 B8
Calais Estate 9 D7
Capercaillie Wine Co. 10 E8
Carindale Wines 11 D7
Chateau Francois 12 A7
Constable & Hershon Vineyards 13 B7
Drayton's Family Wines 14 B10
Farrell's Limestone Ck Vineyard 15 B11
Golden Grape Estate 16 C10
Hardys Hunter Ridge 17 A5
Hermitage Rd Cellars & Winery 18 A5
Honeytree Estate Wines 19 B7
Hungerford Hill Wines 20 A9
Hunter Cellars 21 B7
Hunter Valley Wine Society 22 D8
Ivanhoe Wines 23 A9
Jackson's Hill Vineyard 24 B11
JYT Wine Co. 25 B8
Kevin Sobels Wines 26 C8

Lake's Folly Vineyard 27 D8
Lindemans Ben Ean 28 B9
Little's Winery 29 C6
Maling Family Estate 30 C7
Marsh Estate 31 A5
McGuigan Cellars 32 B8
McLeish Estate 33 C9
McWilliam's Mount Pleasant
  Estate 34 B10
Mistletoe Wines 35 A4
Molly Morgan Vineyard 36 E5
Montague View Estate 37 A3
Moorebank Vineyard 38 D7
Mount View Estate 39 C11
Murray Robson Winery 40 D4
Oakvale Winery 41 A6
Peacock Hill Vineyard 42 D7
Pendarves Estate 43 A3
Pepper Tree Wines 44 C8
Peppers Creek Winery 45 C8
Petersons House 46 D8
Petersons Wines 47 B11
Piggs Creek Winery 48 A4
Pokolbin Estate Vineyard 49 B8
Reg Drayton Wines 50 A9
Rothbury Estate 51 C7

Rothvale Wines 52 B5
Saddler's Creek Wines 53 C11
Sandalyn Estate 54 E6
Scarborough Wine Co. 55 B7
Sutherland Wines 56 C5
Tamburlaine Wines 57 B8
Terrace Vale Wines 58 B5
Thalgara Estate 59 B9
Tinkler's Vineyard 60 A9
Tintilla Vineyard 61 A4
Tulloch Wines 62 B9
Tyrrell's Wines 63 A7
Van De Scheur Wines 64 C10
Vinden Estate Wines 65 B7
Warrarong Estate 66 E6
Wilderness Estate Wines 67 D8
Windarra Winery 68 C8

UPPER HUNTER VALLEY
Cruikshank Callatoota Estate 69 G4
Horseshoe Vineyard 70 F9
James Estate 71 F7
Reynold's Yarraman 72 H3
Rosemount Estate 73 G6

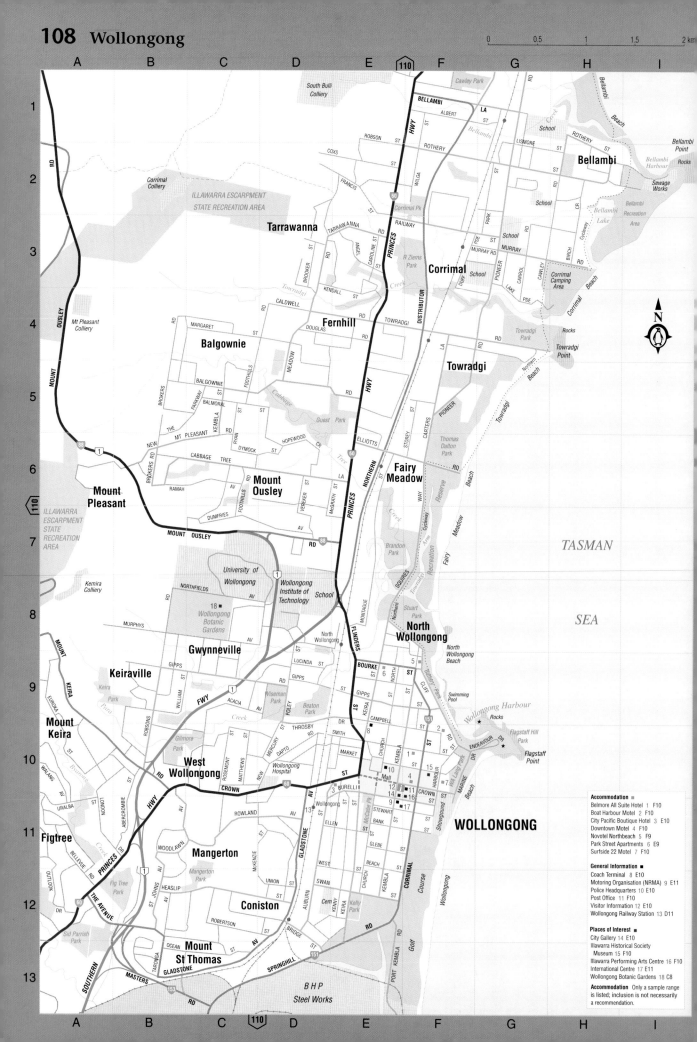

0   0.5   1   1.5   2 km

A   B   C   D   E   F   G   H   I

1

2

South Bulli
Colliery

Cawley Park

Bellambi
Beach

BELLAMBI

ALBERT

ROBSON

COXS

FRANCIS

Corrimal
Colliery

ILLAWARRA ESCARPMENT
STATE RECREATION AREA

Tarrawanna

TARRAWANNA

CAROLINE ST

Corrimal Pk

RAILWAY

ROTHERY

WILGA

LISMORE

School

ROTHERY

Creek

Bellambi

Bellambi

Bellambi
Point

Rocks

Bellambi
Harbour

Sewage
Works

3

ANGEL

BROKER

KENDALL

ST

Towradgi

Creek

R Ziems
Park

Corrimal

DISTRIBUTOR

DUFF

MURRAY RD

PARK

PDE

MURRAY

School

School

PIONEER

CARROL

BIRCH

CAWLEY

LAKE

RD

Corrimal
Camping
Area

Corrimal
Beach

Corrimal

4

CALDWELL

MARGARET

ST

Balgownie

DOUGLAS

Fernhill

TOWRADGI

TOWRADGI

RD

LA

RD

Towradgi

Towradgi
Park

Rocks

Towradgi
Point

5

BROKERS RD

FOOTHILLS

BALGOWNIE

BALMORAL

KEMBLA

THE

MT PLEASANT

RYAN

DYMOCK

HOPEWOOD

MEADOW

Cabbage

Guest Park

RD

HWY

ST

CARTERS

PIONEER

STOREY

Thomas
Dalton
Park

Northern

Beach

Towradgi

6

**Mount
Pleasant**

ILLAWARRA
ESCARPMENT
STATE
RECREATION
AREA

BROKERS RD

NEW

CABBAGE TREE

RAMAH

AV

FOOTHILLS

**Mount
Ousley**

VENEKER

McGRATH

LA

ELLIOTTS

NORTHERN

PRINCES

**Fairy
Meadow**

RD

WAY

Reserve

Fairy

Meadow

Beach

7

MOUNT OUSLEY

RD

DUMFRIES

AV

HWY

Creek

Brandon
Park

Fairy

Meadow

Cycleway

Recreation

TASMAN

8

Kemira
Colliery

University of
Wollongong

Northfields

AV

**Wollongong
Botanic
Gardens**

18

MURPHYS

Wollongong
Institute of
Technology

School

FLINDERS

MONTAGUE

North
Wollongong

SQUIRES

Stuart
Park

Northern

**North
Wollongong**

North Wollongong
Beach

SEA

9

Gwynneville

Keiraville

Keira
Park

GIPPS

WILLIAM

ACACIA

AV

RD

LUCINDA ST

GIPPS

Wiseman
Park

Foley

Beaton
Park

BOURKE

NORTH

ST

GIPPS

KEIRA

CLIFF

5

6

ST

Tarrawa Park

Swimming
Pool

2

Rocks

Wollongong Harbour

Flagstaff Hill
Park

10

**Mount
Keira**

EUREKA

WALANG

LONDON

ST

MOUNT

KEIRA

ROBSONS

Gilmore
Park

**West
Wollongong**

RD

FWY

ROSEMONT

MATHEWS

NEW

MERCURY

DAPTO

THROSBY

SMITH

Wollongong
Hospital

MARKET

ST

Mall

CROWN

Creek

DR

CAMPBELL

CHURCH

KEMBLA

8

10

4

1

12

15

HARBOUR

CROWN

11

MARINE

ENDEAVOUR   DR

Beach

Flagstaff
Point

11

Figtree

OUTLOOK

URALBA

ABERCROMBIE

PRINCES

HWY

WOODLAWN

Mangerton

Mangerton
Park

McKENZIE

ROWLAND

ROWLAND

ELLEN

GLEBE

Wollongong

BURELLI

STEWART

BANK

WEST

SWAN

CHURCH

BEACH

KEMBLA

3

9

14

16

17

CROWN

13

CORRIMAL

Showground

WA Lang Park

WOLLONGONG

Wollongong

12

Sid Parrish
Park

THE AVENUE

ST JOHNS

HEASLIP

AV

UNION

Coniston

ROBERTSON

AUBURN

GLADSTONE

KENNY   KEIRA

Cemy

McCabe Pk

Kelly
Park

RD

Golf   Course

Wollongong

13

Fig Tree
Park

TARONGA

OCEAN

**Mount
St Thomas**

GLADSTONE

MASTERS

ST

AV

BRIDGE

SPRINGHILL

*B H P
Steel Works*

PORT KEMBLA

RD

A   B   C   D   E   F   G   H   I

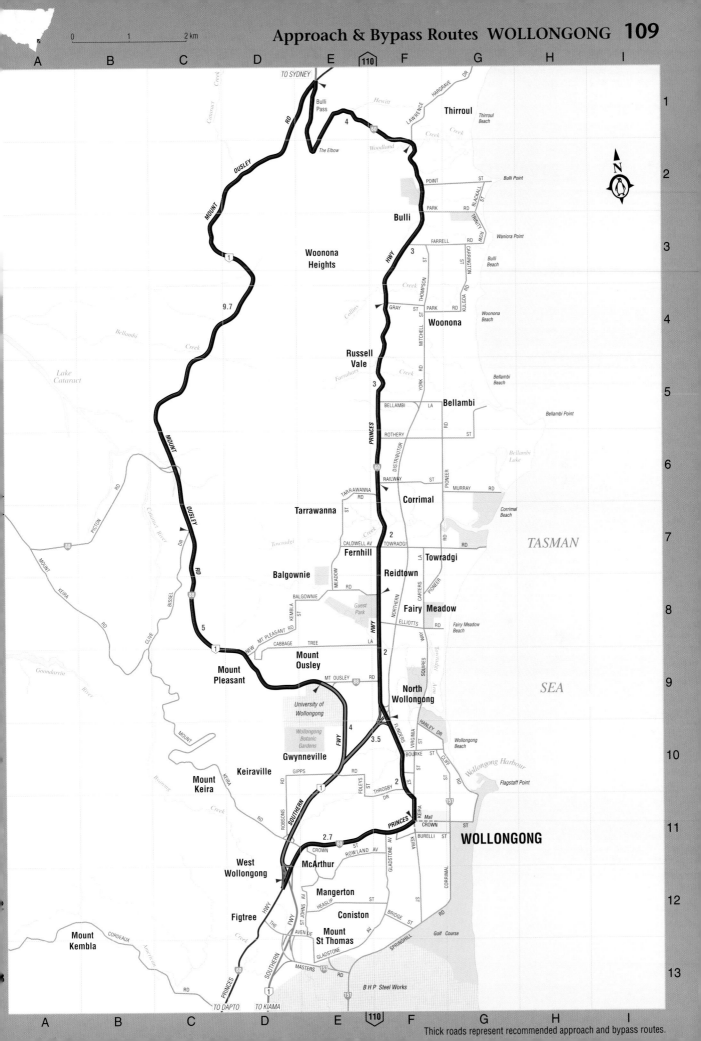

Thick roads represent recommended approach and bypass routes.

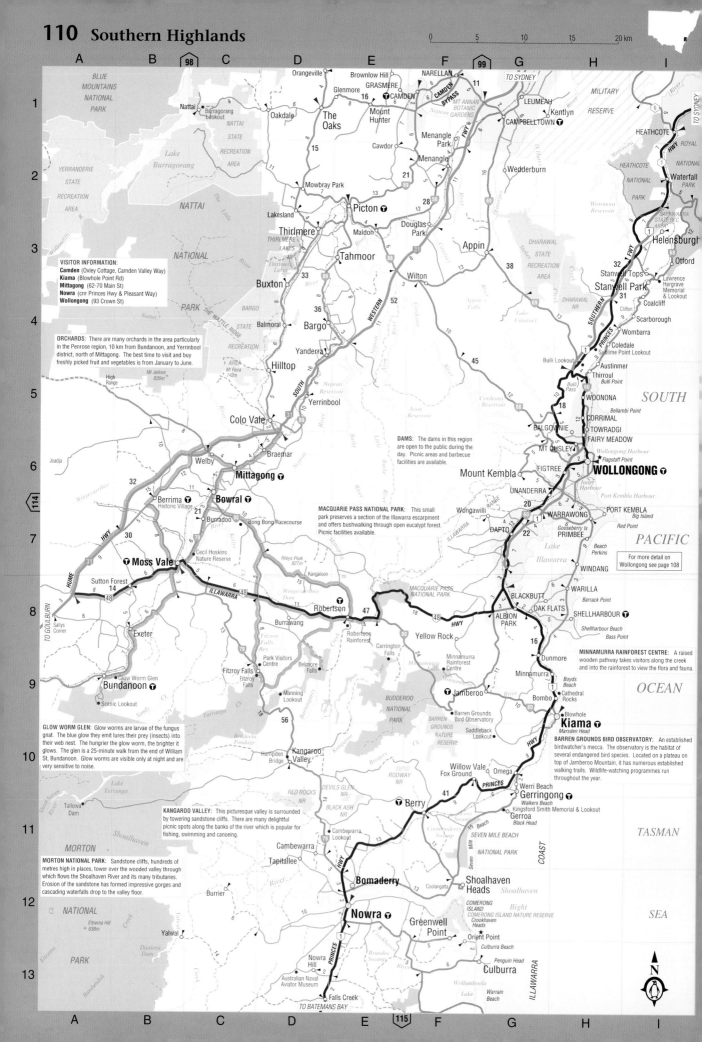

0 5 10 15 20 km

VISITOR INFORMATION:
Camden (Oxley Cottage, Camden Valley Way)
Kiama (Blowhole Point Rd)
Mittagong (62-70 Main St)
Nowra (cnr Princes Hwy & Pleasant Way)
Wollongong (93 Crown St)

ORCHARDS: There are many orchards in the area particularly in the Penrose region, 10 km from Bundanoon, and Yerrinbool district, north of Mittagong. The best time to visit and buy freshly picked fruit and vegetables is from January to June.

DAMS: The dams in this region are open to the public during the day. Picnic areas and barbecue facilities are available.

MACQUARIE PASS NATIONAL PARK: This small park preserves a section of the Illawarra escarpment and offers bushwalking through open eucalypt forest. Picnic facilities available.

MINNAMURRA RAINFOREST CENTRE: A raised wooden pathway takes visitors along the creek and into the rainforest to view the flora and fauna.

BARREN GROUNDS BIRD OBSERVATORY: An established birdwatcher's mecca. The observatory is the habitat of several endangered bird species. Located on a plateau on top of Jamberoo Mountain, it has numerous established walking trails. Wildlife-watching programmes run throughout the year.

GLOW WORM GLEN: Glow worms are larvae of the fungus gnat. The blue glow they emit lures their prey (insects) into their web nest. The hungrier the glow worm, the brighter it glows. The glen is a 25-minute walk from the end of William St, Bundanoon. Glow worms are visible only at night and are very sensitive to noise.

KANGAROO VALLEY: This picturesque valley is surrounded by towering sandstone cliffs. There are many delightful picnic spots along the banks of the river which is popular for fishing, swimming and canoeing.

MORTON NATIONAL PARK: Sandstone cliffs, hundreds of metres high in places, tower over the wooded valley through which flows the Shoalhaven River and its many tributaries. Erosion of the sandstone has formed impressive gorges and cascading waterfalls drop to the valley floor.

For more detail on Wollongong see page 108

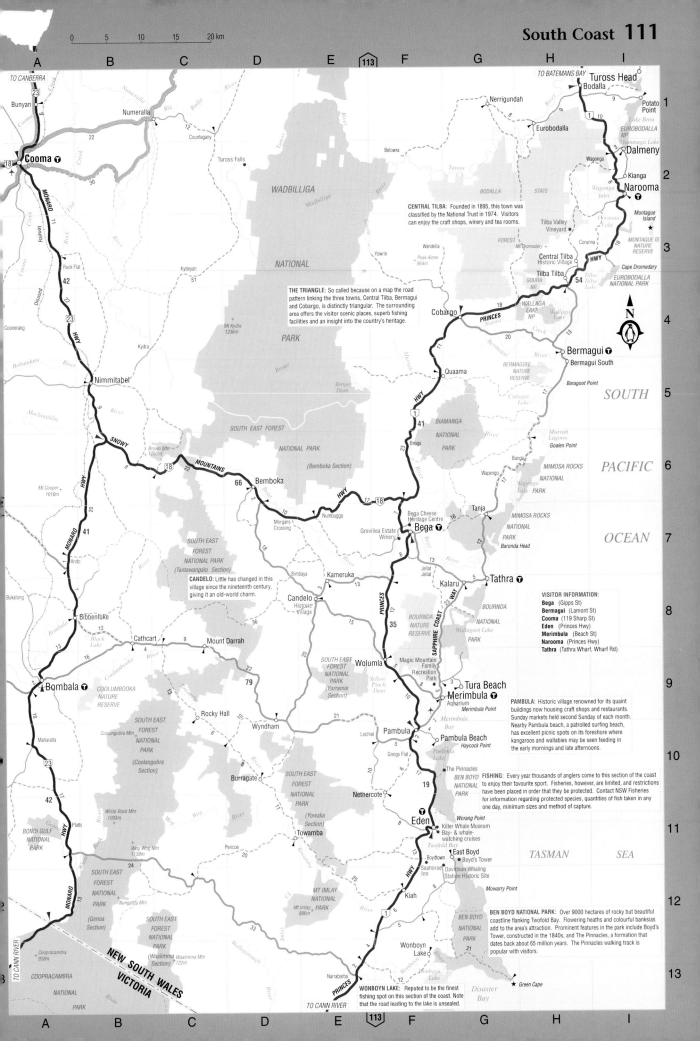

0   5   10   15   20 km

A   B   C   D   E   113   F   G   H   I

TO CANBERRA

Bunyan

23

Numeralla

Cooma

MONARO

HWY

23

Rock Flat

42

Nimmitabel

SNOWY

18   66   Bemboka

MOUNTAINS   HWY

Bibbenluke

Cathcart

Bombala

23

42

MONARO   HWY

BONDI GULF
NATIONAL
PARK

TO CANN RIVER

COOPRACAMBRA
NATIONAL
PARK

NEW SOUTH WALES
VICTORIA

Narrabarba

Princes

TO CANN RIVER

WADBILLIGA

NATIONAL

PARK

Countegany

Tuross Falls

Kybeyan

Mt Kydra
1236m

Kydra

Brown Mtn
1260m

Brogo
Dam

SOUTH EAST FOREST

NATIONAL PARK

(Bemboka Section)

Morgans
Crossing

Numbugga

SOUTH EAST
FOREST
NATIONAL PARK
(Tantawangalo Section)

Bimbaya

Kameruka

CANDELO: Little has changed in this
village since the nineteenth century,
giving it an old-world charm.

Candelo
Historic
Village

Mount Darrah

Rocky Hall

Wyndham

SOUTH EAST
FOREST
NATIONAL
PARK
(Yurammie
Section)

Wolumla

Burragate

SOUTH EAST
FOREST
NATIONAL
PARK
(Coolangubra
Section)

Nethercote

Towamba

SOUTH EAST
FOREST
NATIONAL
PARK
(Yowaka
Section)

MT IMLAY
NATIONAL
PARK

Mt Imlay
886m

SOUTH EAST
FOREST
NATIONAL
PARK
(Genoa
Section)

SOUTH EAST
FOREST
NATIONAL
PARK
(Waalimma
Section)

Waalimma Mtn
722m

TO BATEMANS BAY   Tuross Head

Bodalla

Nerrigundah

1   10

Eurobodalla

EUROBODALLA
NP

Mummuga Lake

Wagonga

Dalmeny

Kianga

Wagonga
Inlet   Narooma

CENTRAL TILBA: Founded in 1895, this town was
classified by the National Trust in 1974. Visitors
can enjoy the craft shops, winery and tea rooms.

Montague
Island

MONTAGUE IS
NATURE
RESERVE

Tilba Valley
Vineyard

Mt Dromedary

Central Tilba
Historic Village

Corunna   Cape Dromedary

Tilba Tilba

GOURA
NR   54

Tilba
Tilba
Lake

EUROBODALLA
NATIONAL PARK

THE TRIANGLE: So called because on a map the road
pattern linking the three towns, Central Tilba, Bermagui
and Cobargo, is distinctly triangular. The surrounding
area offers the visitor scenic places, superb fishing
facilities and an insight into the country's heritage.

Cobargo

18   WALLAGA
LAKE NP

PRINCES   Wallaga

Nutra   13

Bermagui

Bermagui South

BERMAGUEE
NATURE
RESERVE

Baragoot Point

Quaama

SOUTH

HWY   1

41   BIAMANGA

Brogo   NATIONAL

PARK

17   18

Bunga

Wapengo

MIMOSA ROCKS

NATIONAL

PARK

Murrah
Lagoon
Goalen Point

PACIFIC

Bega Cheese
Heritage Centre

Bega

Grevillea Estate
Winery

16   Tanja

MIMOSA ROCKS

NATIONAL

PARK

Baronda Head

OCEAN

Jellat
Jellat

Kalaru

Tathra

BOURNDA

NATIONAL

PARK

Wallagoot Lake

PRINCES

35

Magic Mountain
Family
Recreation Park

SAPPHIRE COAST WAY

23

Wolumla

Yellow
Pinch
Dam

Tura Beach

Merimbula

Aquarium   Merimbula Point

Merimbula
Bay

Lochiel

Pambula

Pambula Beach   Haycock Point

Greigs Flat

Pambula
Lake

The Pinnacles

BEN BOYD
NATIONAL
PARK

19

Eden

Killer Whale Museum
Bay- & whale-
watching cruises

Twofold Bay

East Boyd   Boyd's Tower

Boydtown   Davidson Whaling
Station Historic Site

Seahorse
Inn

Mowarry Point

Kiah

BEN BOYD
NATIONAL
PARK

Wonboyn
Lake

Green Cape

Disaster
Bay

TASMAN   SEA

VISITOR INFORMATION:
Bega (Gipps St)
Bermagui (Lamont St)
Cooma (119 Sharp St)
Eden (Princes Hwy)
Merimbula (Beach St)
Narooma (Princes Hwy)
Tathra (Tathra Wharf, Wharf Rd)

PAMBULA: Historic village renowned for its quaint
buildings now housing craft shops and restaurants.
Sunday markets held second Sunday of each month.
Nearby Pambula beach, a patrolled surfing beach,
has excellent picnic spots on its foreshore where
kangaroos and wallabies may be seen feeding in
the early mornings and late afternoons.

FISHING: Every year thousands of anglers come to this section of the coast
to enjoy their favourite sport. Fisheries, however, are limited, and restrictions
have been placed in order that they be protected. Contact NSW Fisheries
for information regarding protected species, quantities of fish taken in any
one day, minimum sizes and method of capture.

BEN BOYD NATIONAL PARK: Over 9000 hectares of rocky but beautiful
coastline flanking Twofold Bay. Flowering heaths and colourful banksias
add to the area's attraction. Prominent features in the park include Boyd's
Tower, constructed in the 1840s, and The Pinnacles, a formation that
dates back about 65 million years. The Pinnacles walking track is
popular with visitors.

WONBOYN LAKE: Reputed to be the finest
fishing spot on this section of the coast. Note
that the road leading to the lake is unsealed.

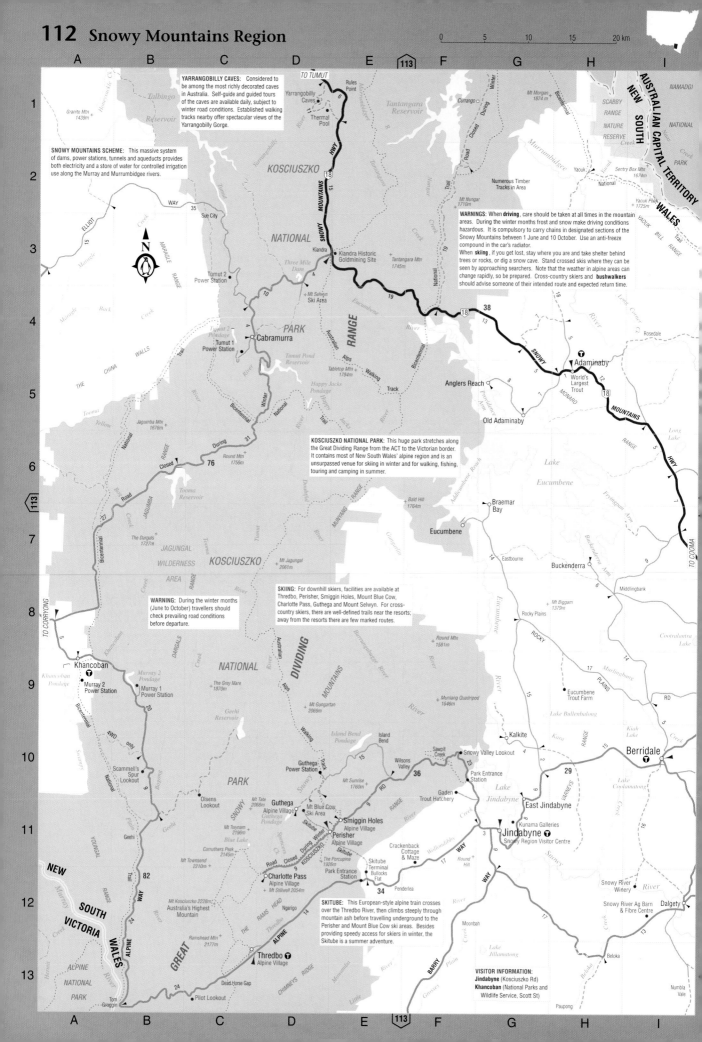

0   5   10   15   20 km

A   B   C   D   E   [113]   F   G   H   I

YARRANGOBILLY CAVES: Considered to be among the most richly decorated caves in Australia. Self-guide and guided tours of the caves are available daily, subject to winter road conditions. Established walking tracks nearby offer spectacular views of the Yarrangobilly Gorge.

TO TUMUT

SNOWY MOUNTAINS SCHEME: This massive system of dams, power stations, tunnels and aqueducts provides both electricity and a store of water for controlled irrigation use along the Murray and Murrumbidgee rivers.

Yarrangobilly Caves

Thermal Pool

Rules Point

Tantangara Reservoir

AUSTRALIAN CAPITAL TERRITORY

NEW SOUTH WALES

NAMADGI NATIONAL PARK

Granite Mtn 1439m

Talbingo Reservoir

KOSCIUSZKO

NATIONAL

Sue City

Tumut 2 Power Station

Kiandra

Kiandra Historic Goldmining Site

Three Mile Dam

Mt Selwyn Ski Area

Mt Morgan 1874m

Currango

SCABBY RANGE NATURE RESERVE

Yaouk

Sentry Box Mtn 1674m

Numerous Timber Tracks in Area

Mt Nungar 1710m

Yaouk Peak 1725m

WARNINGS: When **driving**, care should be taken at all times in the mountain areas. During the winter months frost and snow make driving conditions hazardous. It is compulsory to carry chains in designated sections of the Snowy Mountains between 1 June and 10 October. Use an anti-freeze compound in the car's radiator.
When **skiing**, if you get lost, stay where you are and take shelter behind trees or rocks, or dig a snow cave. Stand crossed skis where they can be seen by approaching searchers. Note that the weather in alpine areas can change rapidly, so be prepared. Cross-country skiers and **bushwalkers** should advise someone of their intended route and expected return time.

PARK

Tumut 2 - Pondage

Tumut 1 Power Station

Cabramurra

Tabletop Mtn 1784m

Tantangara Mtn 1745m

38

Adaminaby

World's Largest Trout

Anglers Reach

Old Adaminaby

SNOWY

MONARO

Tumut Pond Reservoir

Happy Jacks Pondage

Jagumba Mtn 1676m

Round Mtn 1756m

76

27

Toorna Reservoir

The Dargals 1727m

KOSCIUSZKO NATIONAL PARK: This huge park stretches along the Great Dividing Range from the ACT to the Victorian border. It contains most of New South Wales' alpine region and is an unsurpassed venue for skiing in winter and for walking, fishing, touring and camping in summer.

Bald Hill 1764m

Braemar Bay

Lake Eucumbene

Eucumbene

MOUNTAINS

RANGE

Long Lake

KOSCIUSZKO

WILDERNESS

AREA

JAGUNGAL

Mt Jagungal 2061m

Round Mtn 1581m

Eastbourne

Buckenderra

Middlingbank

Mt Biggam 1379m

Rocky Plains

Cootralantra Lake

WARNING: During the winter months (June to October) travellers should check prevailing road conditions before departure.

SKIING: For downhill skiers, facilities are available at Thredbo, Perisher, Smiggin Holes, Mount Blue Cow, Charlotte Pass, Guthega and Mount Selwyn. For cross-country skiers, there are well-defined trails near the resorts; away from the resorts there are few marked routes.

TO CORRYONG

Khancoban

Khancoban Pondage

Murray 2 Power Station

Murray 1 Power Station

The Grey Mare 1870m

NATIONAL

DIVIDING

MOUNTAINS

Mt Gungartan 2069m

Muniang Quadripod 1646m

Eucumbene Trout Farm

Lake Bullenbalong

PLAINS

Kiah Lake

Berridale

Scammell's Spur Lookout

Olsens Lookout

PARK

Geehi Reservoir

Island Bend Pondage

Island Bend

Guthega Power Station

Wilsons Valley

36

Sawpit Creek

Snowy Valley Lookout

Park Entrance Station

Kalkite

Lake Jindabyne

East Jindabyne

Lake Crackenback

Mt Tate 2068m

Guthega

Guthega Pondage

Mt Teynum 2196m

Carruthers Peak 2145m

Mt Townsend 2210m

Blue Lake

Mt Sunrise 1760m

Mt Blue Cow Ski Area

Smiggin Holes

Perisher

Gaden Trout Hatchery

Kunama Galleries

Jindabyne

Snowy Region Visitor Centre

NEW SOUTH WALES

VICTORIA

82

Mt Kosciuszko 2228m Australia's Highest Mountain

Mt Stilwell 2054m

Charlotte Pass Alpine Village

The Porcupine 1926m

Park Entrance Station

Skitube Terminal Bullocks Flat

Crackenback Cottage & Maze

Penderlea

34

Round Hill

Snowy River Winery

Dalgety

Snowy River Ag Barn & Fibre Centre

ALPINE NATIONAL PARK

Ramshead Mtn 2177m

Mt Kosciuszko

Pilot Lookout

Dead-Horse Gap

Thredbo Alpine Village

SKITUBE: This European-style alpine train crosses over the Thredbo River, then climbs steeply through mountain ash before travelling underground to the Perisher and Mount Blue Cow ski areas. Besides providing speedy access for skiers in winter, the Skitube is a summer adventure.

Moonbah

Lake Jillamatong

Beloka

Numbla Vale

Paupong

VISITOR INFORMATION:
Jindabyne (Kosciuszko Rd)
Khancoban (National Parks and Wildlife Service, Scott St)

A   B   C   D   E   [113]   F   G   H   I

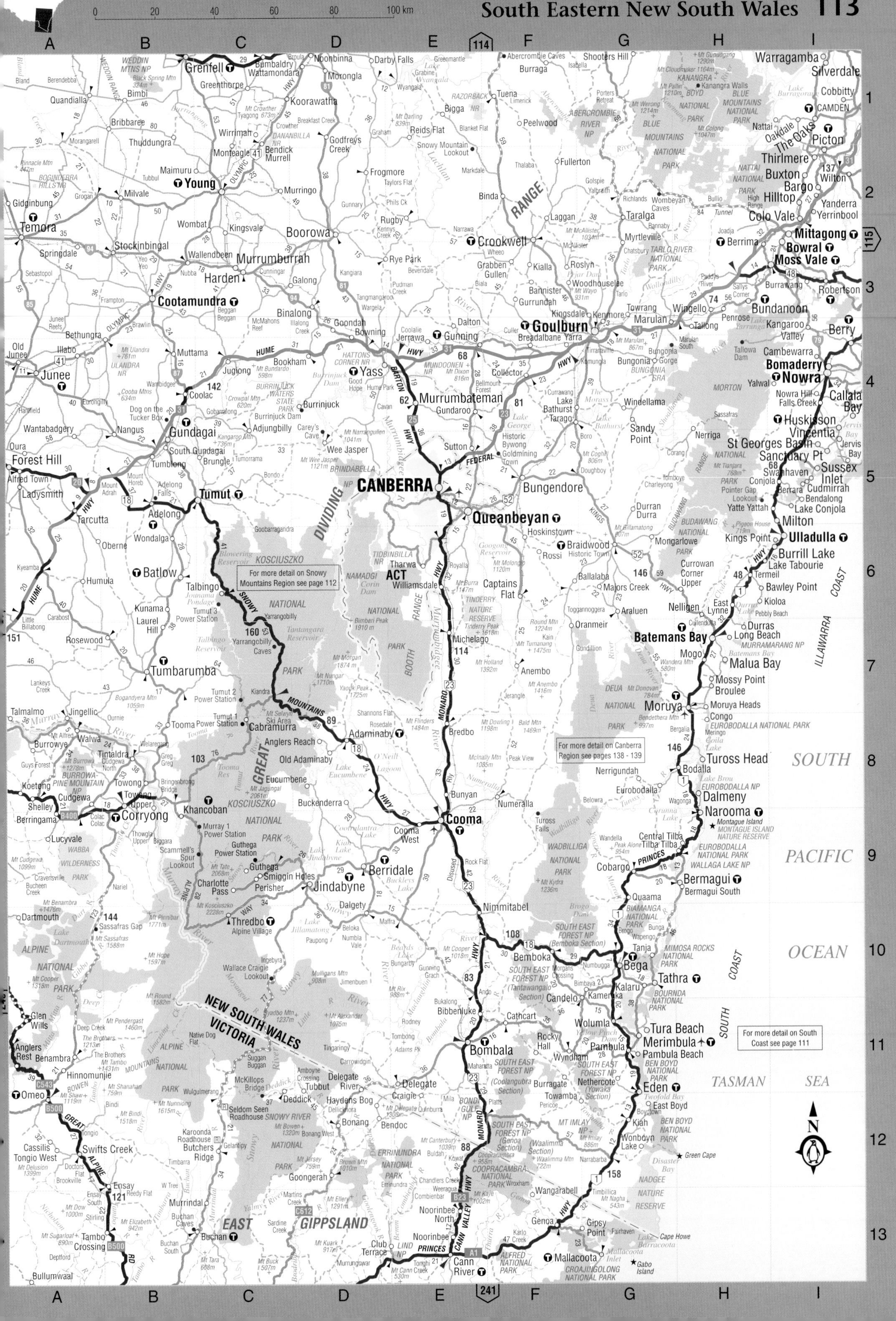
0 20 40 60 80 100 km
A B C D E F G H I
1 2 3 4 5 6 7 8 9 10 11 12 13
CANBERRA
ACT
Queanbeyan
Goulburn
Young
Temora
Cootamundra
Junee
Gundagai
Tumut
Batlow
Tumbarumba
Yass
Murrumbateman
Crookwell
Boorowa
Harden
Murrumburrah
Grenfell
Mittagong
Bowral
Moss Vale
Picton
Camden
Bundanoon
Nowra
Bomaderry
Ulladulla
Milton
Batemans Bay
Moruya
Narooma
Bermagui
Bega
Tathra
Merimbula
Eden
Braidwood
Bungendore
Captains Flat
Cooma
Jindabyne
Berridale
Thredbo
Adaminaby
Bombala
Delegate
Corryong
Khancoban
Cabramurra
Mallacoota
Cann River
Genoa
Omeo
Buchan
DIVIDING RANGE
KOSCIUSZKO NATIONAL PARK
SNOWY MOUNTAINS
NAMADGI NATIONAL PARK
BLUE MOUNTAINS NATIONAL PARK
MORTON NATIONAL PARK
DEUA NATIONAL PARK
WADBILLIGA NATIONAL PARK
ALPINE NATIONAL PARK
SNOWY RIVER NATIONAL PARK
ERRINUNDRA NATIONAL PARK
CROAJINGOLONG NATIONAL PARK
NEW SOUTH WALES
VICTORIA
EAST GIPPSLAND
SOUTH PACIFIC OCEAN
TASMAN SEA
HUME HWY
FEDERAL HWY
MONARO HWY
PRINCES HWY
For more detail on Snowy Mountains Region see page 112
For more detail on Canberra Region see pages 138 - 139
For more detail on South Coast see page 111
114
115
241

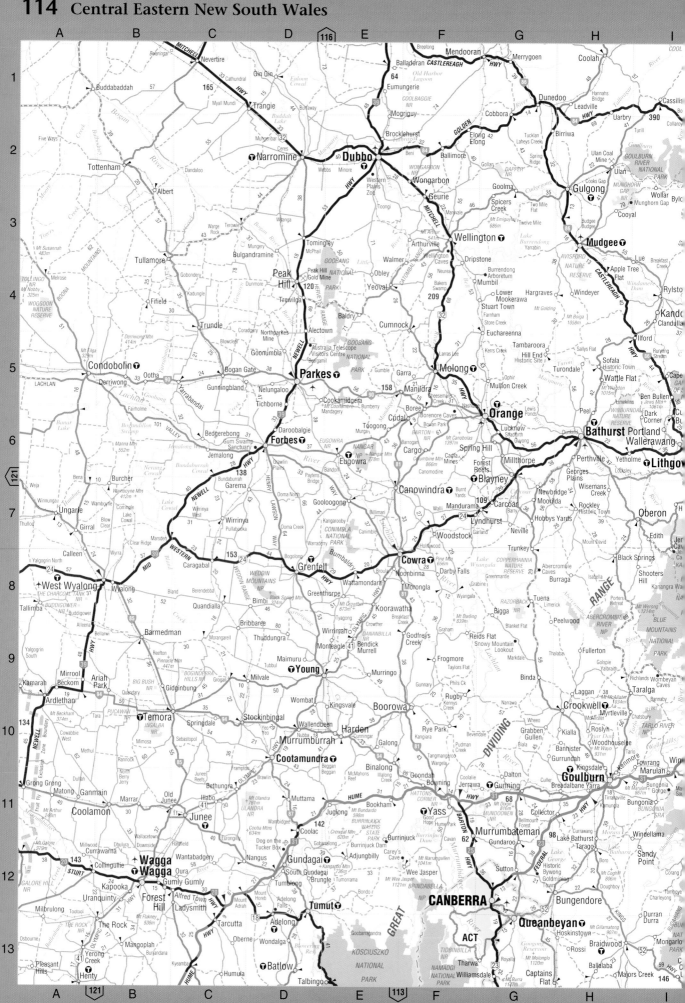

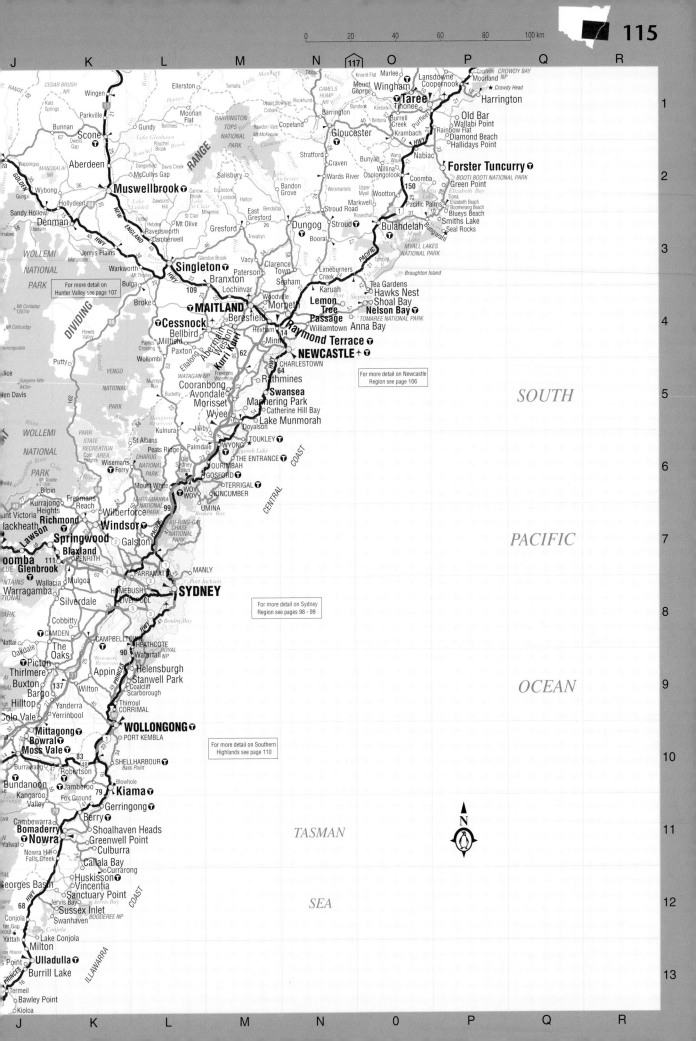

A B 524 C D E F G 525 H I

1

CARNARVON HWY
BARWON
Nindigully
55
Bungunya
Toobeah
16
65
Talwood 200
22
21
HWY
39
CUNNINGHAM
39
85

118
32
Gradule
48
50

2
Dirranbandi
Noondoo
20
44
Daymar
River
Machntyre
Goondiwindi
Boggabilla
Thallon
76
BOOMI
NR
Kurumbul
17

162
73
55
Boomi
37
153
BORONGA
NR
49
79
BRUXNER

QUEENSLAND
Hebel
Castlereagh
Lake Bokhara
55
Mungindi
Caloona
BOOMI WEST
NATURE
RESERVE
42
118
North Sta

3
NEW SOUTH WALES
19
26
CARNARVON
Weemelah
125
Garah
CAREUNGA
NR
127
Yallaro
Croppa
Creek

Goodooga
New Angledool
38
Neeworra
30
18
42
35
Moppin
Ashley
Camurra
MIDKIN
NR
Crooble
Milguy

4
47
132
21
23
Angledool Lake
Gundabloui
34
18
26
NEWELL HWY
Mosquito
Creek

Lightning Ridge Opal Mines
55
Mogil Mogil
210
38
Bullarah
GWYDIR
Moree
70
31
Pallamallawa
Biniguy
29
Wariald

5
Collarenebri
GWYDIR HWY
65
River
Gravesend
WARIALDA
HWY
Warialda Rail

Grawin Opal Mines
Cumborah
61
Pokataroo
42
Merrywinbone
Gurley
Tycannah
64
Terry Hie Hie
Elcombe
Binga

6
NARRAN LAKE NATURE RESERVE
58
Rowena
Millie
84
97
SAMILAROI NR

37
70
CASTLEREAGH
River
Waminda
Cryon
183
Bugilbone
Nowley
Doreen
Bellata
36
Caroda

7
Walgett
52
KAMILAROI
39
Edgeroi
Courada
Grattai Mtn
1310m
Rocky Creek
Uppe
Horto

Goangra
Burren Junction
37
50
Wee Waa
42
23
Narrabri
MOUNT KAPUTAR NP
Mt Kaputar
1508m
Cobbad

8
55
Coombogolong
Gidginbilla Dam
Cubbaroo
Merah North
HWY
Narrabri West
Narrabri
Deriah Mtn
855m
RANGE
Barr

Carinda
18
Come-by-Chance
Milchomi
Pilliga
Cuttabri
Yarrie Lake
CSIRO Australia Telescope
Turrawan
KAMILAROI
37

9
MACQUARIE MARSHES NATURE RESERVE
57
Gwabegar
Merebene
36
Baan Baa
Upper

Kenebri
118
Boggabri
99
Kelvin
Lake Keepit
40

10
Quambone
40
208
Baradine
71
Teridgerie
PILLIGA SCRUB
PILLIGA NATURE RESERVE
39
Emerald Hill
Rocky Glen
OXLEY
Gunnedah
Carroll
Carroll Gap

119
13
56
Coonamble
55
WARRUMBUNGLE
Wittenbri
NEWELL
106
Mullaley
34
43
Curlewis
Piallaway

11
14
43
Combara
Beladetle Dam
28
Bugaldie
Yearinan
RANGE
WARRUMBUNGLE NATIONAL PARK Siding Springs Observatory
Garrawilla
Coonabarabran
Ulamambri
Spring Ridge
Breeza
W C

31
Gradgery
16
Gular
42
Mt Exmouth 1206m
Skywatch Night and Day Observatory
Premer
Caroona
37

12
Canonba
Inglegar
77
Gulargambone
21
The Breadknife
Mt Genn +Cuanch
Mt Spire 1071m
Tooraweenah
Purlewaugh
Deringulla
Tambar Springs
Bomera
Colly Blue
Pine Ridge

Reedy Corner
Armatree
Dragon Cowal
94
34
Murrawal
BINNAWAY NR
Tamarang
Bundella

13
MITCHELL
164
Collie
55
Curban
Windurong
39 HWY
Bliddon
Bearbung
New Mollyann
Binnaway
Ulinda
Weetaliba
Connemarra
46
Blackville
Old

Miowera
34
OXLEY
36
Gilgandra
GILGANDRA FLORA RESERVE
WEETALIBAH NR
COOLAH TOPS NATIONAL PARK

Mullenguddery
59
Warren
Gigerline
Euloon Cowal
Cathundral
16
Balladoran
CASTLEREAGH
Breelong
Mendooran
Merrygoen
Neilrex
Coolah

A B 524 C D 114 E F 86 G H

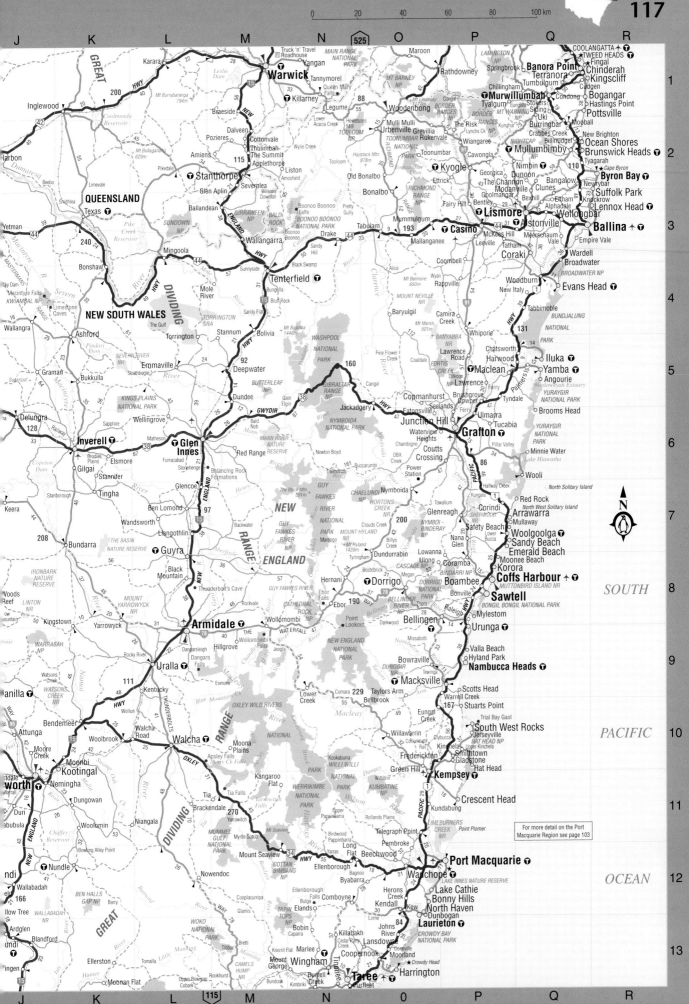

A · B · C · D · E · F · G · H · I

1 2 3 4 5 6 7 8 9 10 11 12 13

QUEENSLAND
NEW SOUTH WALES

Corner Store
Cameron Corner
STURT
Explorers Tree
NATIONAL
PARK
Frome
Waka
133
Binerah Downs
Dog
Onepah
Fence
Adelaide Gate
Teurika
Lake Callamulcha
Moombidary
Berrawinnia Downs
Ourimbah
Hamilton Gate
Waverley Gate
Warri Warri Gate
33
Creek
22
Tibooburra
Gun Vale
Pindera Downs
53
Clifton Downs
Whyjonta
Barrajong
Owen Downs
Koridina
Colane
Wanaa

Tilcha
Hewart Downs
Depot Glen
Poole's Cairn
Billabong
Poole's Grave
Milparinka
40
51
102
272
79
Baronna Downs
NOCOLECHE
NA

Winnathee
Hawker Gate House
Mt Shannon 332m
MT BROWN RANGE
Yandama
72
Yantara
Yantara Lake
Salt Lake
Lake Ulenia
Lake Altibouka
Petita
Bundarra
The Range
Nantilla

Smithville House
Creek
Lake Wallace
Pincally
Lake Bullea
Gumpopla
138
Glendara
Tongo Lake
163
Mid...
Basin

Big Salt Lake
Dalmuir
Cobham
Pulgamurtie
Mundai
Allandy
McCallum Park
Questa Park
Purnanga
Cawnalmurtee
McGurty Hill
254
Lake Yantabangee
Poloko Lake
Gilpoko Lake

Starvation Lake
Turleys Gate
Packsaddle
Pimpara Lake
Pine Ridge
47
333
Kooninberry Mtn
70
Pulchra
Caradoc
Goodwood
Peery Lake
Pa Ove...

Boughams Gate
Pine View
Westwood Downs
14
Nundora
Lake Bancannia
65
Nantherungie
MOONTHGORANGE RANGE
17
24
19
Oak Vale
44
White Cliffs Opal Mines
Mandalay
Peery
32
Talalara
Be...

Teilta
The Selection
16
CITY
Koonawarra
Wertago
73
MUTAWINTJI
COTURAUNDEE NATURE RESERVE
Cootawundi
Tarella
Coona Coona
Momba
Nine Mile Lakes
MacPhee... 275m

McDougalls Well
Floods Creek
46
BENGORO RANGE
BYNGNANO RANGE
NATIONAL
93
Mt Daubeny
Wild Duck
Ulalie
Lakes Dick
Marra...

NEW SOUTH WALES
SOUTH AUSTRALIA
Morphetts Creek
45
SILVER
PARK Aboriginal Historic Site
Jones Lake
Coora Lake
RANGE
Comarto
Mt Murchison 203m
Hamilton (ruin)
61
Onlilla Lake
River

Dog Fence
BARRIER RANGE
102
Wilangee
22
61
Glenora
119
Cawkers Well
HWY
Wilcannia
19
BARRIER
32 RANGE HWY
MACCULLOCHS
Poopelloe Lake
Wi...

MUNDI MUNDI PLAIN
Purnamoota
Daydream Mine
Stephens Creek
31
Little Topar Roadhouse
Hazel Vale
32
Churinga
Lake Woytchugga
Mena Murtee
COBB

Umberumberka Reservoir
Silverton Historic Town
27
HWY
77
BARRIER
196
Glen Lyon
SCOPES RANGE
154
Malta Lake
Tuttawaodka
75
Cowary

Broken Hill
49
32
79
51
Kinalung
Fruit Fly Exclusion Zone Boundary
Four Mile Lake
Teryawynia
Cowary
...165

BARRIER
Cockburn
47
SILVER
Quandong Roadhouse
Horse Lake
60
Box Tank
Copi Hollow
Pamamaroo Lake
Hamibre Lake
Dry Lake
Nyngynderry
185
Glen Albyn

Mutooroo
Burta
Ascot Vale
Pine Point
CITY HWY
Menindee
KINCHEGA NATIONAL PARK
Cawndilla Lake
392
Amphitheatre Lake
Wallace Lake
Big Ampi
Dead Horse Lake
Teryaweyna Lake
Glen Ora
Albemarle
Victoria Lake
MANARA HILLS

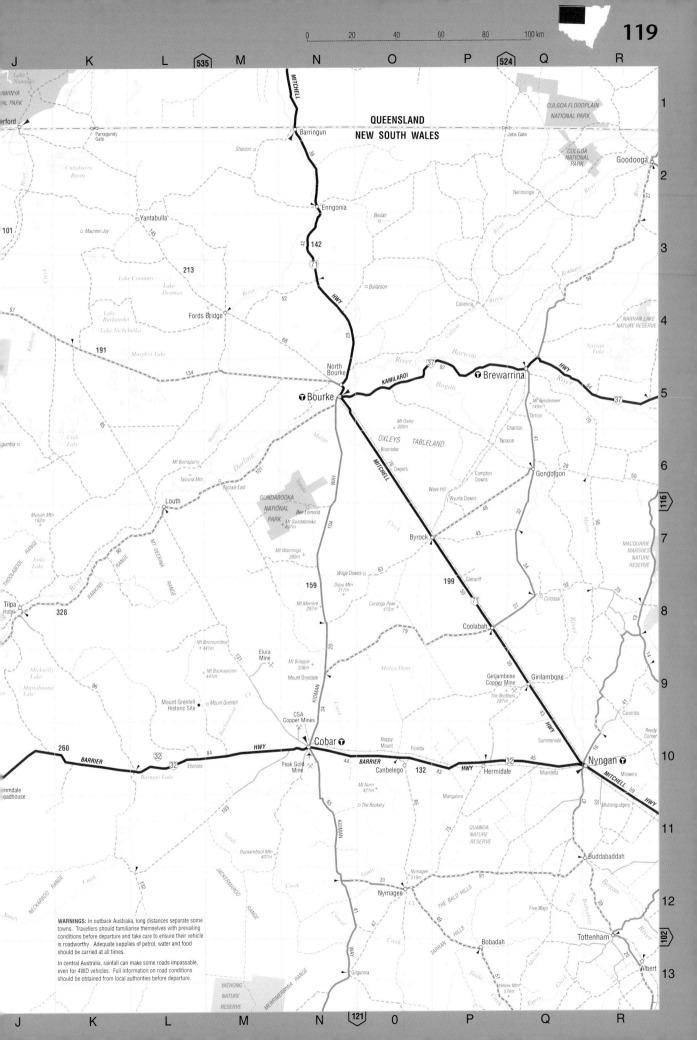

J K 535 L M N O P 524 Q R

0 20 40 60 80 100 km

1

QUEENSLAND
NEW SOUTH WALES

Lake Numala

AWINYA
AL PARK

erford

Parragundy Gate

Barringun

Sharoon

Jobs Gate

CULGOA FLOODPLAIN
NATIONAL PARK

Goodooga

CULGOA NATIONAL PARK

2

Cattabura Basin

Yantabulla

Maureen Joy

Enngonia

Beulah

Neilmongle

27

101

145

142

42

213

71

Bullaroon

Collerina

Birrie

Narran River

NARRAN LAKE NATURE RESERVE

94

3

Lake Coomany

Lake Deanan

52

HWY

62

Collerina

Bokhara River

4

57

Lake Burkanoko

Lake Nichebulka

191

Murphys Lake

68

Fords Bridge

134

Barwon River

Narran Lake

MITCHELL

KAMILAROI

North Bourke

River

37

97

Brewarrina

37

64

37

5

85

Utah Lake

Bourke

Mt Oxley
+ 309m

OXLEYS   TABLELAND

Booindal

Mt Bendemeer
149m
Tarrion

Chariton

Tarcoon

41

Gongolgon

28

50

6

jumbla

Darling River

Mt Burragurry

Talowla Mtn

Toorale East

GUNDABOOKA NATIONAL PARK

Ben Lomond

Mt Gundabooka
497m

Dwyers

76

Wave Hill

Wyurta Downs

Compton Downs

48

32

43

Colossal

56

MACQUARIE MARSHES NATURE RESERVE

116

7

Mulyah Mtn
162m+

Louth

MT OXLEY

104

Mt Wammiga
380m+

Byrock

199

Glenariff

34

32

25

13

RANGE

RANKINS RANGE

90

101

WAY

63

50

27

8

Tilpa
Hotel

328

Jinki Lake

Mt Merrera
297m

Dijou Mtn
317m

Coronga Peak
415m

71

Coolabah

79

14

9

Mickwilly Lake

Murtabunna Lake

96

131

Elura Mine

Mt Billagoe
336m

Mt Booroondara
+ 441m

Mt Buckwaroon
441m

20

34

Mount Drysdale

Girilambone Copper Mine

Girilambone

30

The Brothers
287m

HWY

41

Canonba

Rendy Corner

10

Mount Grenfell
Historic Site

Mount Grenfell

CSA Copper Mines

Boppy Mount

Florida

Summervale

16

260

BARRIER

32

84

HWY

Cobar

44

BARRIER

132

43

Hermidale

32

45

Miandetta

Nyngan

MITCHELL

59

HWY

mmdale
oadhouse

Elsinore

Barnato Lake

Peak Gold Mine

Canbelego

Mt Nurri
421m+

Mangalore

47

52

Mullengudgery

11

103

65

The Rookery

65

75

QUANDA NATURE RESERVE

91

Buddabaddah

Bogan River

12

132

Buckambool Mtn
407m

31

Nymagee

Nymagee
519m

THE BALD HILLS

Five Ways

38

Tottenham

102

13

KIDMAN

41

47

Bobadah

49

TARRAN HILLS

51

Yellow Mtn
574m

20

Albert

J K 121 L M N O P Q R

WARNINGS: In outback Australia, long distances separate some towns. Travellers should familiarise themselves with prevailing conditions before departure and take care to ensure their vehicle is roadworthy. Adequate supplies of petrol, water and food should be carried at all times.

In central Australia, rainfall can make some roads impassable, even for 4WD vehicles. Full information on road conditions should be obtained from local authorities before departure.

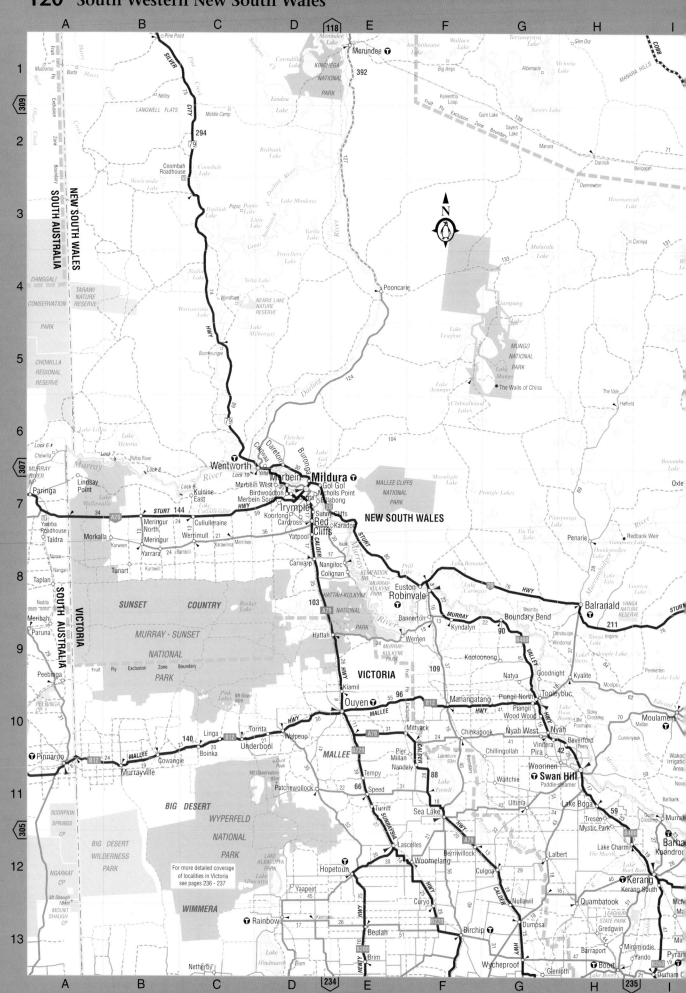

0 20 40 60 80 100 km

J K L M N 119 O P Q R

1

Albert
Tullamore
Fifield

2
Mount Hope
Melrose

KAJULIGAN NATURE RESERVE
YATHONG NATURE RESERVE

3
Ivanhoe
COBB 208
Mossgiel
Trida
Wee Elwah
Roto
Matakana
Euabalong West
Euabalong
Condobolin
Derriwong
Ootha

WILLANDRA NATIONAL PARK
NOMBINNIE NATURE RESERVE
LACHLAN VALLEY
Gunebang
Fairholme

4
Booligal
Lowlands
Wallanthery
Lake Cargelligo
Burgooney
Tullibigeal
Weja
Burcher
Manna Mtn

5
Hillston
Langtree
Gooravrie
Naradhan
Hannan
Gubbata
Kikoira
Gibsonvale
Ungarie
Girral
Calleen
Wyrra
Marsden
Clear Ridge

GOONAWARRA NATURE RESERVE
LOUGHNAN NR

6
Merriwagga
Allawah
Rankins Springs
Erigolia
Euatha
Weethalle
West Wyalong
Wyalong
Bland

WESTERN 254
COCOPARRA NR
HWY 24

7
Goolgowi
Gunbar
Gunbar South
Tabbita
Yenda
Binya
Moombooldool
Beckom
Mirrool
Ariah Park
Gidginbung
Barmedman

Tharbogang
Griffith
Bilbul
Yoogali
Hanwood
Barellan
Kamarah
Ardlethan
Quandary

8
One Tree
Hay
Carrathool
Bringagee
Murrami
Whitton
Wamoon
Leeton
Yanco
Colinroobie
Temora
Mimosa

STURT 168
MID HWY
NEWELL 134

9
Booroorban
Coleambally
Morundah
Grong Grong
Narrandera
Matong
Ganmain
Coolamon
Marrar
Old Junee
Junee

COBB 123
Cuddell
Gillenbah
Birrego
Kywong
Currawarna
Downside
Harefield

10
Wanganella
Bundure
Boree Creek
Wagga Wagga
Collingullie
Kapooka
Uranquinty
Forest Hill
Alfred Town
Ladysmith

HWY 182
Coonong
Lockhart
Milbrulong
The Rock

11
Conargo
Coree South
Logie Brae
Jerilderie
Urana
Osborne
Pleasant Hills
Yerong Creek
Henty
Mangoplah
Kyeamba

RIVERINA
Blighty
Mayrung
Myall Plains
Urangeline East
Rand
Cookardinia

12
Deniliquin
Finley
Berrigan
Oaklands
Daysdale
Walbundrie
Walla Walla
Culcairn
Morven
Holbrook

RIVERINA HWY 217
Savernake
Rennie
Coreen
Brocklesby
Gerogery
Woomargama

13
Moama
Echuca
Mathoura
Womboota
Tocumwal
Ulupna
Cobram
Yarrawonga
Numurkah
Mulwala
Corowa
Wahgunyah
Rutherglen
Howlong
Jindera
Albury
Wodonga
Bellbridge

NEW SOUTH WALES
VICTORIA
MURRAY VALLEY
BARMAH STATE PARK
Nathalia
Katamatite
Chiltern
Barnawartha
Bandiana
Granya

J K 238 L M N O P Q 239 R

AUSTRALIAN CAPITAL TERRITORY

Canberra in autumn

The nation's capital territory is a 2400 square-kilometre area with an air of spaciousness typical of eastern rural Australia. It is set in the valley of the Molonglo River, in the foothills of the Great Dividing Range. The capital city, Canberra, is remarkable for its extensive parklands and pockets of natural bush.

The Australian Capital Territory is surrounded by New South Wales and lies roughly halfway between Sydney and Melbourne. It was created by the Commonwealth Constitution Act of 1901 when the Commonwealth of Australia was inaugurated and a nation was formed from the six colonies.

One of the provisions of the Act was that the seat of government should be on land vested in the Commonwealth. Nine years of prolonged wrangling followed, as two Royal Commissions and parliamentary committees considered the various claims of established towns and cities to be the federal capital, before the location of the new territory and the site for the new city was decided. The area of Jervis Bay on the south coast of New South Wales was ceded to the Commonwealth to provide a seaport for the nation's capital.

Melbourne was the provisional seat of government until 1927 when a temporary building was erected in Canberra. This building was used until 1988 when the new House of Parliament was completed.

Canberra was built on an undulating plain in an amphitheatre of the Australian Alps. The Molonglo River, a tributary of the Murrumbidgee River, runs through the city and was dammed in 1964 to create Lake Burley Griffin, around which Canberra has been developed.

The land on which the city is sited was first seen by Europeans in 1820 when Charles Throsby Smith and his party of explorers arrived in the area. The first European settler, Joshua Moore, took up 1000 acres (2500 hectares) of land on the banks of the Murrumbidgee River in 1824. Moore named his property Canberry, which is an Aboriginal word meaning 'meeting place'.

There are four distinct seasons in the ACT: a warm spring, a hot dry summer, a brilliant cool autumn, and a cold winter with occasional snow.

CALENDAR OF EVENTS

JANUARY
Public holidays: New Year's Day; Australia Day.
Canberra: Australia Day Celebrations; Street Machine Summernats.

FEBRUARY
Canberra: Royal Canberra Show; National Poker Championships; Jazz Festival.

MARCH
Public holiday: Canberra Day. *Canberra:* Black Opal Stakes; Canberra National Multicultural Festival; Canberra District Vintage Festival; Autumn Fest; The Tour Championship PGA Golf; National Mountain Bike Championships.

EASTER
Public holidays: Good Friday; Easter Monday.

APRIL
Public holiday: Anzac Day. *Canberra:* Anzac Day Parade and Service at Australian War Memorial; Australian Science Festival; National Folk Festival; International Chamber Music Festival; Canberra District Vintage Festival (contd).

MAY
Canberra: Australian Science Festival (contd); International Chamber Music Festival (contd); Rally of Canberra.

JUNE
Public holiday: Queen's Birthday. *Canberra:* National Capital Dancesport Championships; National Capital 100 V8 Supercar Race.

JULY
Canberra: ANU Chess Festival; Kanga Cup Soccer.

SEPTEMBER
Canberra: Floriade.

OCTOBER
Public holiday: Labour Day. *Canberra:* Canberra Cup; Floriade (contd); Oktoberfest; Days of Wine and Roses; Embassy Open Day.

NOVEMBER
Canberra: Cycle Classic.

DECEMBER
Public holidays: Christmas Day; Boxing Day.

Note: The information given here was accurate at the time of printing. However, as the timing of events held annually is subject to change and some events may extend into the following month, it is best to check with the local tourism authority or event organisers to confirm the details.

Canberra

Canberra, capital of Australia and seat of Federal Government, is a model metropolis. One of the few completely planned cities in the world, its unique concentric circular streets are set graciously on the shores of Lake Burley Griffin and surrounded by rolling hills.

VISITOR INFORMATION
Canberra Visitors Centre
Northbourne Avenue, Dickson
(02) 6205 0044
www.canberratourism.com.au
Jolimont Centre
Northbourne Avenue, City
(for brochures)
Canberra Getaways
1800 100 660
(for accommodation and activities bookings)

HISTORY

When the land for the national capital was acquired by the Commonwealth Government in 1911, it contained only two small villages. Construction of the first public buildings started in 1913. The Depression and World War II slowed construction, but the rate of development has been spectacular since the mid-1950s; Canberra's population is now over 308 000. The city's fine public buildings, areas of parkland and bush reserves, leafy suburbs and broad tree-lined streets have resulted from the brilliant planning of its architect, Walter Burley Griffin, and from care taken in its development over the years.

The cultural, as well as the political, life of the country is preserved and on show in Canberra; this small city lays claim to some of the nation's most significant institutions, including a magnificent art gallery and one of the best war museums in the world. Grand public buildings and monuments, many architecturally renowned, complement the order and beauty of the city's original design.

Many visitors come to view the national collections or to see Federal politics in action, but Canberra has much more to offer. It has superb parklands and thousands of hectares of natural bushland to explore, cool-climate wineries and top class restaurants, a full calendar of cultural and sporting events, and excellent attractions for children.

EXPLORING THE CITY

Canberra is a city with a very high rate of car usage and it is not hard to see why: wide, traffic-free roads serve single-system public transport (bus only) that can be variable at off-peak times. However, most places can be reached by bus, and there are two routes that cover the major tourist attractions. The road infrastructure in Canberra is probably the best in Australia and visitors will find that they can cover long distances in an amazingly short time. Clean air, wide streets and plenty of parkland make Canberra a great place to explore by foot or bicycle. A boat cruise of Lake Burley Griffin is an essential visitor experience; tours depart from the Acton Ferry Terminal.

CANBERRA BY AREA

PARLIAMENTARY TRIANGLE AND BEYOND

The Parliamentary Triangle incorporates Canberra's important buildings, dotted around Lake Burley Griffin. The triangle's apex is Capital Hill, with

Canberra is awash with colour during Floriade

Commonwealth and Kings avenues as the side perimeters, and Constitution Avenue as the base. The grandest boulevard in Australia, Anzac Parade, crosses Constitution Avenue at right angles.

A good starting point for exploring Canberra is the **National Capital Exhibition**, on Barrine Drive at Regatta Point on the north side of the lake. Here you can see exhibits on the history and development of the city, and look out across the lake at the parliamentary precinct. From here, cross Commonwealth Avenue Bridge and on the left is the **Captain Cook Memorial Water Jet**.

Directly ahead lies **Parliament House**, Australia's most expensive building and Canberra's centrepiece. The building was completed in 1988, at a cost of $1.1 billion, to a design by the American-based company Mitchell, Giurgola and Thorpe (who won an international competition from 329 entries). It has 4500

rooms including a series of public places that reflect the major themes of Australian life. There are more than 3000 artworks, from which selections are displayed in the public spaces. Take a free tour of the building or schedule your visit to coincide with a sitting of either of the two Houses of Parliament, the Senate or the House of Representatives, and watch from the public galleries.

Directly in front of the new Parliament House lies **Old Parliament House** (a couple of minutes drive along King George Terrace or a quick walk along Federation Mall). Designed in 1927 by John Smith Murdoch, it was only ever intended as the provisional home for the parliament, but served this purpose for some 60 years. Now it offers a fascinating recollection of the events and intrigues of Australian political life. Tours are available and a special feature is the sound and light show, *Order! Order!* in the old House of Representatives chamber. In addition, its restored public spaces with their superb Art Deco detail now house the National Portrait Gallery, where changing exhibitions and programs acquaint visitors with the people of Australia's history. Around the building are the beautiful gardens of Old Parliament House, and adjacent in Queen Victoria Terrace is the National Archives, housed in one of Canberra's original buildings.

Travel north along Parks Place West to reach the **National Library of Australia**, established in 1901. The present building – a grand neo-classical structure built in 1968 – contains some 6 million books, as well as newspapers, periodicals, films, historical documents and photographs. There is an extensive collection of Australiana, including the diaries of Captain Cook's *Endeavour* voyages, and beautiful artworks, most notably the stained-glass windows by Leonard French. A short distance south-east along King Edward Terrace is **Questacon – National Science and Technology Centre**. This futuristic building features hands-on displays and experiments (everything from earthquakes to lightening strikes) within five galleries that wind around a circular rampway.

Further along, just off King Edward Terrace on Parkes Place East, is the

GETTING AROUND
Motoring organisation
National Roads and Motoring Association (NRMA) 13 2132

Car rental
Avis 1800 225 533; Budget 1300 362 848; Capital Car Rentals (02) 6282 7272; Hertz 13 3039; Thrifty 1300 367 227 Rumbles (02) 6280 7444

Public transport
ACTION Buses 13 1710

Lake cruises
Australian Capital Cruises (02) 6284 7160; Canberra Steam Boats 0419 418 846; Lakeside Ferry Services 017 828 355; Southern Cross Cruises (02) 6273 1784

Bicycle hire
Mr Spokes Bike Hire (02) 6257 1188 (near Acton Ferry Terminal)

Taxis
Canberra Cabs 13 2227

Calthorpes' House

High Court of Australia, Australia's final court of appeal and interpreter of the Constitution. The court was established in 1903 and moved to its present site in 1980. The building is notable for its glass-encased public gallery and timber courtrooms; murals by artist Jan Senberg reflect the history, functions and operations of the court. From Monday to Friday, visitors can look around the building, drop in on a case, and pick up information from the knowledgeable attendants. Across the road is the **National Gallery of Australia**, established in 1911 and housed here since 1982. Fittingly, the national collection provides a brilliant overview of Australian art, incorporating an extensive Aboriginal collection and works from all the major Australian artists since European settlement. The overseas collection is equally impressive and includes one of the most controversial works ever bought for Australia, Jackson Pollock's *Blue Poles*. One of the best gallery features is the Sculpture Garden, a series of native garden 'rooms' housing some 50 sculptures.

Cross Kings Avenue Bridge and turn left along Russell Drive (which becomes Constitution Avenue); just before Anzac Parade there is a left-hand turn into Wendouree Drive. Here you will find **Blundell's Cottage**, which was built in 1858 for the Campbell's ploughman. Robert Campbell was an early grazier in the district and his family became the district's most prominent clan in the years before the site was chosen as the national capital. The cottage re-creates the toil and struggle of the labouring classes in those early farming years. Retrace your steps, continuing along Constitution Avenue. After crossing Anzac Parade you will encounter more of the district's early history at **St John the Baptist Church and Schoolhouse Museum**. Both buildings date back to the 1840s; the schoolhouse serves as a museum re-creating an original classroom.

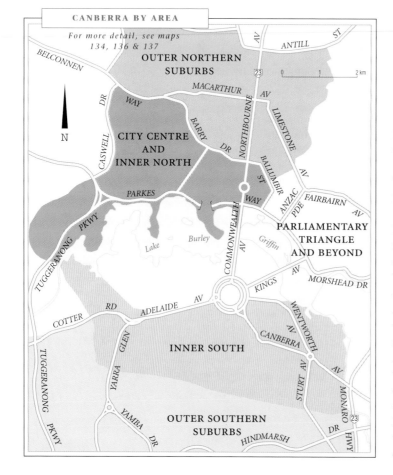

CANBERRA BY AREA

For more detail, see maps 134, 136 & 137

Return to Anzac Parade; at its northern end lies the **Australian War Memorial**. Opened in 1941, the War Memorial honours war victims through the Roll of Honour, with 100 000 names of Australians killed in war; the Pool of Reflection; the Hall of Memory; and the Tomb of the Unknown Soldier. It is probably the world's largest war museum, with its collection of an estimated four million items including weapons, planes, documents and paintings by some of Australia's well-known artists. It also offers the Sculpture Garden; the Bamber Command Experience, with audio-visual effects; and the Research Centre, which has on-line access for visitors to look up family history (appointments not necessary).

From here turn into Fairbairn Drive and a couple of kilometres along on the left is Mount Ainslie Drive, which leads to **Mount Ainslie Lookout** with its superb views over the Parliamentary Triangle and beyond. Further along Fairbairn Drive on the right is Northcott Drive, the location of **Duntroon House**, built by Robert Campbell in 1833, with later additions in 1856. This was the first substantial house in the area and has a lovely garden with plantings dating back to the 19th century. There are regular tours.

CITY CENTRE AND INNER NORTH

Compared with the stately splendour of the Parliamentary Triangle, the centre of Canberra looks modest. Nevertheless, there are some better-than-average attractions around the city centre and nearby district immediately to the north of the lake. Start at **Civic Square**, site of the **Legislative Assembly of the ACT**, the seat of governance for Canberra as opposed to that of the nation. The **Canberra Theatre Centre** and many of the city's private enterprise offices and legal offices are also here. Nearby is the **Canberra Centre**, the main shopping precinct for the city and site of the magnificent old St Kilda merry-go-round, and **Garema Place**, with its cafes frequented by local residents and workers.

The 145-hectare native landscaped grounds of the **Australian National University** hug the eastern edge of the inner city. A major attraction nearby on McCoy Circuit is **ScreenSound Australia**,

The Carillon at Lake Burley Griffin

ENTERTAINMENT
Pick up a copy of the Canberra Times *on Thursday for its lift-out entertainment guide 'Good Times'. There is usually a good selection of live music around town, ranging from rock concerts at the* **ANU Union** *to a spot of mellow jazz or soul at* **Tilley's Devine** *in Lyneham. The main theatre venue is the* **Canberra Theatre Centre** *in the city with a couple of smaller venues around town such as* **Gorman House Arts and Craft Market**, *catering to more eclectic tastes. For a quiet drink try the large hotels including the* **Hyatt**, *housed in magnificent 1920s Art Deco surrounds. The* **Casino Canberra** *in Binara Street is a boutique-style casino, its elegance enhanced by the absence of poker machines. At the casino is the* **Starz Supper Club**, *where you can watch a cabaret performance while you dine.*

LAKESIDE AND RIVERSIDE RETREATS

	Map Ref.
CASUARINA SANDS Where the Cotter and Murrumbidgee rivers meet	135 C4
COMMONWEALTH PARK Formal gardens and parkland on the lake	134 D5
COTTER DAM & RESERVE A riverside picnic, camping and swimming spot	135 C4
JERRABOMBERRA WETLANDS A nesting ground for waterbirds on the lake's southern shores	136 I11
KAMBAH POOL A beach and bushland retreat on the Murrumbidgee	135 D5
WESTON PARK A peaceful woodland and lakeside recreation area	136 E10

Questacon – National Science and Technology Centre

dedicated to the preservation of Australia's film and sound archive – everything from *Dad and Dave* to *Dame Edna*. Housed in an Art Deco building, formerly the Institute of Anatomy, the museum and archive has regularly updated displays and a 1930s cinema running old film footage.

From here turn south down Edinburgh Avenue, right into Parkes Way and right again into Clunies Ross Street for **CSIRO Discovery** (enter at Julius Road), which showcases Australian research with exhibitions and working displays. Then travel south-west along Clunies Ross Drive and turn right onto Black Mountain Drive for access to **Black Mountain**. The **Australian National Botanic Gardens** lie on the mountain's lower slopes. Envisaged by Walter Burley Griffin as a retreat for the city, they boast the largest collection of native plant species in the country. The species are organised into groupings re-creating Australia's major ecosystems. Highlights are the Rainforest Gully, representing the major rainforest types of Australia's entire east coast, and for young children an interpretive walk inspired by the sculptures of David Miller. Continue along Black Mountain Drive to reach the **Telstra Tower Lookout**, a 195-metre communications tower with

a viewing platform, an exhibition hall and a restaurant.

Return to Clunies Ross Street, which becomes Lady Denman Drive under the Parkes Way Bridge. Continue along Lady Denman Drive to the **National Aquarium and Wildlife Park**. The aquarium features an underwater tunnel that allows you to see an amazing collection of freshwater fish species through walls and ceiling of glass, while the wildlife sanctuary has native bushland where all the Australian favourites are on display.

INNER SOUTH

Beyond the Parliamentary Triangle lie Canberra's most desirable suburbs – the quiet, leafy streets of the inner south, containing official residences, Art Deco bungalows, the diplomatic precinct, the mint and a couple of charming urban villages.

The Lodge, on Adelaide Avenue immediately south-west of Parliament House, was built in 1926 as the official residence of the prime minister. Public access is only possible occasionally. Likewise at **Yarralumla Government House** on Dunrossil Drive, accessed by continuing along Adelaide Avenue, which becomes Cotter Road, and turning right. This 1820s building, now the official residence of the Governor-General, was part of a sheep station; there are views of the grounds from a lookout on Lady Denman Drive.

The **Royal Australian Mint** can be found on Denison Street in nearby Deakin: return to Adelaide Avenue and turn right into Kent Street. The mint, opened in 1965, produces around two million coins a day. Visitors can view the production process from the visitors' gallery, or look at the exhibits that detail the history of money minting.

Return to Adelaide Avenue and head towards the city, turning right along Hopetoun Crescent for a tour of the diplomatic precinct. Here, as well as throughout the nearby suburbs of Forrest and Red Hill (follow the signs for Tourist Drive 6), you will find most of Australia's diplomatic missions. Many of these have been built to represent the culture of their country of origin, and together provide a concentrated overview of worldwide architectural practice, with everything from American Colonialism to Eastern mysticism.

Hopetoun Crescent leads into Mugga Way, Red Hill and **Calthorpes' House**, a 1927 Spanish Mission-style house containing original furnishings and providing a fascinating glimpse of middle-class domestic life in the fledgling capital. Turn left into Flinders Way for the old-style inner-city shopping areas of **Manuka** and **Kingston**, both offering interesting shopping and an impressive range of cafes and restaurants. The **Canberra Railway Museum** is near the Kingston shops on Cunningham Avenue, off Wentworth Avenue. It houses Australia's oldest steam locomotive (1878), as well as other engines and some 40 carriages (open weekends and public holidays).

OUTER SOUTHERN SUBURBS

The long corridor of new suburbs south of the city are set against the superb Brindabella Range, merging harmoniously with the surrounding native bushland and pine forests. Follow Adelaide Avenue onto Cotter Road, travelling south out of the city. To visit the numerous attractions, follow the signs for Tourist Drive 5 around the outer edges of the southern suburbs. First stop is Mount Stromlo Observatory, which was established in 1942 and houses a huge telescope that charts the night skies; visitors can learn about the wonders of the galaxy at the hands-on **Stromlo Exploratory**. Next, look out for the right-hand turn-off to **Cotter Dam and Reserve**, a popular recreation area with swimming, camping and picnic facilities.

Continue along Tourist Drive 5 and take the left-hand turn-off to the **Canberra Deep Space Communications Complex** at Tidbinbilla. Look out for the aluminum communications dishes along the way. Opened in 1965, it is one of only three facilities forming NASA's deep space network, and it assists, by way of deep space tracking, some of the world's most significant space operations, such as the Mars Pathfinder mission. There is an excellent museum and display area on site with films, astronaut suits and space food among a plethora of hard facts on space exploration and technology.

Nearby is the **Tidbinbilla Nature Reserve** (look out for the native-animal carving at the entrance), 5500 hectares of bushland offering refuge for many species of native wildlife. There are 12 well-signed walking tracks, some beautiful picnic spots with free wood barbecues

MONUMENTS	
	Map Ref.
AUSTRALIAN–AMERICAN MEMORIAL Celebrates America's WW II contribution to Australia's defence	134 H8
ANZAC PARADE MEMORIALS Dramatic monuments commemorating the war efforts of 11 different groups	134 G5
CAPTAIN COOK MEMORIAL WATER JET A 150-metre water jet and terrestrial globe	134 D7
CARILLON Three-column belltower – a gift from the British Government to mark Canberra's Jubilee	134 F8
NATIONAL JEWISH MEMORIAL CENTRE Synagogue and memorial to World War II veterans	134 D12

SPORT
*The national basketball team, the Canberra Cannons, plays home games at the **Australian Institute of Sport** (AIS) Arena; the Rugby League side, the Raiders, can be seen at the AIS Bruce Stadium; as can the Rugby Union side, the ACT Brumbies. Canberra has nine golf courses offering very cheap rates; the private, as well as public, courses generally welcome visitors. Swimming pools are to be found at the AIS, **Phillip**, the **city** and **Manuka** (among others). There are around 900 kilometres of cycling tracks throughout the city and suburbs with the most popular being around the lake.*

CLIMATE GUIDE

CANBERRA

	J	F	M	A	M	J	J	A	S	O	N	D
Maximum °C	28	27	24	20	15	12	11	13	16	19	23	26
Minimum °C	13	13	11	7	3	1	0	1	3	6	9	11
Rainfall mm	58	56	53	49	49	37	40	48	52	68	62	53
Raindays	8	7	7	8	9	9	10	11	10	11	10	8

Old Parliament House

Parliament House

and an excellent information centre and cafe. Just past the reserve on the right is the turn-off to **Corin Forest Mountain Recreation**, wonderful for children with its 800-metre alpine slide, flying foxes, supervised winter snowplay, and picnic spots. Continue to tiny historic **Tharwa**; just south of the town is the **Cuppacumbalong Craft Centre**. In a beautiful 19th-century garden on the Murrumbidgee riverbank, this old homestead has become the showroom for quality works by Canberra's craftspeople.

You can follow the tourist route to **Namadgi National Park** (see Day Tours from Canberra p. 131) or head back towards the city via **Lanyon Homestead** and the satellite centre of Tuggeranong. Lanyon is one of Australia's most beautiful surviving homesteads from the 19th century. Set in a peaceful hollow along the banks of the Murrumbidgee and just shielded from the suburban sprawl, the homestead and its glorious gardens provide a glimpse of the 1850s when sheep-farming was to the district what politics is today. Part of the homestead has been restored and re-furnished in the style of the period, while another section houses the **Nolan Gallery**, which features important works by the prominent Australian artist Sidney Nolan.

Return to the city along Tharwa Drive, which leads onto the Monaro Highway for a quick trip through the bushland on the eastern edge of the suburban corridor.

OUTER NORTHERN SUBURBS

The edge of the northern suburbs is no more than 15 minutes away from the centre of the city, which means that the excellent attractions in the area, many with appeal for children, can be covered in a day.

The **Australian Institute of Sport** is to be found on Leverrier Street in Bruce (follow the signs from Northbourne Avenue for Belconnen). The institute opened in 1981 with a charter to provide top-class facilities for Australia's elite athletes. Members of the institute, some of them well-known, lead the tours. Highlights include the interactive museum **Sportex** – where you can pit your fitness levels against those recorded by our Olympians – and access to the venues where athletes on six-day-a-week training programs demonstrate the less glamorous side of sporting fame.

Near the northern end of Northbourne Avenue in Hawdon Place (right-hand turn into Antill Street just past the **Canberra Visitors Centre**),

is the **Canberra Planetarium and Observatory**, featuring research-grade telescopes for night-time viewing. Back on Northbourne Avenue, turn left onto the Barton Highway. First stop along the highway is the **National Dinosaur Museum** at Nicholls, which boasts a 300-exhibit display, including ten full-size replica skeletons. Close by, on the perimeter of the Gold Creek Country Club, is **Cockington Green**. Just off Gold Creek Road, it offers a detailed miniature re-creation of an English rural village, complete with tiny folk going about their business. In addition, there is an interesting collection of re-creations (also knee-high) of Australian and overseas buildings of architectural and historical merit.

Forming part of the Gold Creek complex is **Federation Square**, which boasts an excellent range of specialty shops, and the historic settlement of **Ginninderra Village**, its craft studios and art galleries set among historic buildings dating from the late 19th century.

Canberra, Australia's capital city, with its splendid public buildings, extensive parkland and leafy boulevards, is an impressive place to visit.

DAY TOURS
from Canberra

Canberra offers some phenomenal choices when it comes to day tours. There are the surf beaches of the south coast of New South Wales, the drama of the Australian Alps, the quiet beauty of the rural countryside, tiny historic villages, cool-climate wineries and grand swathes of native bushland perfect for a spot of trekking or trout angling. A couple of these places are a fair distance in terms of a round day trip, but compensation rests with the facts that it never takes more than 10 minutes to escape the city and that the roads servicing the capital are generally excellent.

DAY TOURS FROM CANBERRA

For more detail, see maps 112, 135, 136 & 138–9

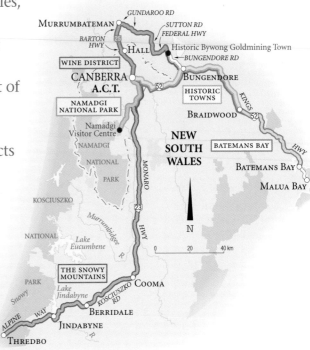

WINE DISTRICT

98 km to Bungendore via Barton Highway , Gundaroo Road, Murrumbateman Road, Sutton Road, Federal Highway and Bungendore Road

Canberra's cool, dry climate is proving a bonus for the winegrowers on the city's doorstep. The wineries are concentrated in the areas north and north-east of Canberra. The district is small compared to its counterparts elsewhere and the wineries are definitely in the boutique category, which means a friendly chat about vintages is never out of the question.

Take Northbourne Avenue out of the city. On your way stop at the Canberra Visitors Centre for a map and brochure detailing opening times for the wineries. Turn left onto the Barton Highway. The wineries start around the small town of Hall, where Canberra's northern suburbs give way to a gentle landscape of bush and undulating plains. There are several wineries in the immediate vicinity, including the Brindabella Hills Winery, built high on a ridge with beautiful views over the Brindabella Range and the Murrumbidgee River. Continue to

Murrumbateman, which serves as another centre for a cluster of wineries to be found just off the highway in the small network of roads around the town. Take a right turn out of Murrumbateman onto the Gundaroo Road, which becomes Murrumbateman Road, and look out for the turn-offs to the various wineries. Turn right at Sutton Road, and then left onto the Federal Highway. After about 7 kilometres, take the turn-off right to Bungendore; you'll find a handful of wineries in the Bungendore–Lake George Area, and from Lark Hill Winery there is an excellent view of Lake George. Return to Canberra via Bungendore and Kings Highway.

HISTORIC TOWNS

87 km to Braidwood via Kings Highway
These settlements beyond the capital are small, picturesque repositories for the district's 19th-century rural history. From the city, head towards Canberra

Airport along Pialligo Avenue, then turn right into Sutton Road and left onto Kings Highway. Bungendore, the first stop, is on the highway. This sleepy hollow comes alive on weekends with day trippers from the city dropping in to explore the antique shops, cafes and craft outlets. Of particular interest is the award-winning Bungendore Wood Works, a superb timber building that displays a broad selection of hand-crafted woodwork. A detour from Bungendore can be made to Historic Bywong Goldmining Town, a fascinating recreation of a 19th-century mining settlement, located off Bungendore Road, about 15 kilometres north-west of Bungendore.

Further along Kings Highway is **Braidwood**, a town classified in its entirety by the National Trust. Gazetted in 1838, it served as the centre for the southern goldfields in the 1850s and its elegant sandstone buildings are testament to that period of prosperity.

Curiosity Rocks, Lake Jindabyne

Today arts, crafts and antiques are the town's main commercial enterprise. Pick up a self-guide historic walk brochure from the information centre housed in the old theatre in Wallace Street. Return to Canberra via Kings Highway. **See also:** individual entries in New South Wales A–Z listing for towns in bold type.

BATEMANS BAY

146 km to Batemans Bay via Kings Highway 52

Batemans Bay is the centre of the Eurobodella ('Land of Many Waters') section of the South Coast holiday district of New South Wales, stretching from **Nowra** to the Victorian border. Take the Kings Highway out of Canberra, which cuts across the Monaro landscape of ancient hills before coming to the rugged edges of the Great Dividing Range. Here, the steep descent down the heavily forested slopes of Clyde Mountain is one of the highlights of the tour. The town of Batemans Bay straddles the mouth of the Clyde River, offering a peaceful haven for houseboats, oyster leases and swimming, fishing and other water sports. The best lunch on offer is one of freshly opened Clyde River oysters off the end of a jetty overlooking the river. For some surfing action continue to the beautiful beach at Malua Bay, on the southern side of the township. Just north of the town via the Princes Highway is Murramarang National Park, which features an undisturbed coastline complete with beach-going

kangaroos. **See also:** individual entries in New South Wales A–Z listing for towns in bold type.

THE SNOWY MOUNTAINS

210 km to Thredbo via Monaro 🛡 *and Snowy Mountains* 18 *highways, Kosciuszko Road and Alpine Way*

Winter in the Snowies means skiing, while the temperate months see an influx of bushwalkers, trout anglers and nature lovers. The district is enormous, but a day trip will allow for a quick sampling of a few highlights. Escape Canberra via the Monaro Highway (right turn off Canberra Avenue). First stop is **Cooma**, once the centre of the massive Snowy Mountains Hydro Electric Scheme. Take the Snowy Mountains Highway west out of town and pick up the Kosciuszko Road about 7 kilometres on. Pass through **Berridale** to **Jindabyne**, a major resort town where you will find the Snowy Region Visitor Centre. The town is built alongside Lake Jindabyne, which, along with Lake Eucumbene further north, presents some of the best trout angling opportunities in New South Wales. Continue on to **Thredbo** along the Alpine Way, taking the opportunity to enjoy the superb alpine scenery en route. Thredbo, nestled into the surrounds of the **Kosciuszko National Park**, marks the conclusion of the tour. This is one of Australia's premier ski-resorts and the starting point for many walks and other nature activities. The Crackenback Chairlift travels from Thredbo to Eagles Nest Mountain where a 6-kilometre

walkway leads to Australia's highest point – Mount Kosciuszko. **See also:** The Snowy Mountains in NSW section p. 83; National Parks in NSW section p. 42 and individual entries in New South Wales A–Z listing for parks and towns in bold type.

NAMADGI NATIONAL PARK

31 km to Namadgi Visitor Centre via Monaro Highway 🛡 *, Tharwa Drive and Naas Road*

This vast national park covers more than 40 per cent of the Australian Capital Territory and is the most northerly Alpine environment in Australia. It takes in a good section of the beautiful Brindabella Range, which dominates the Territory's south-western border, and is something of a mecca for trout fishers and bushwalkers. To reach Namadgi National Park, follow the Monaro Highway out of the city, and take the Tharwa Drive turn-off through Tuggeranong. This road leads to the village of Tharwa, before becoming Naas Road. From here it's only a matter of minutes to the Namadgi Visitor Centre, where you will find plenty of information about recreation areas and walking tracks. For a quick taste of the park's rainforest surroundings, take the 14-kilometre drive over Honeysuckle Creek to the Former Space Tracking Station. For a longer, more scenic drive, follow the Boboyan Road, which turns off towards the Old Orroral Homestead or continues further south. Make sure you inform park staff if you are planning to walk one of the longer routes – sections of Namadgi are extremely remote.

Australian Capital Territory

LOCATION MAP

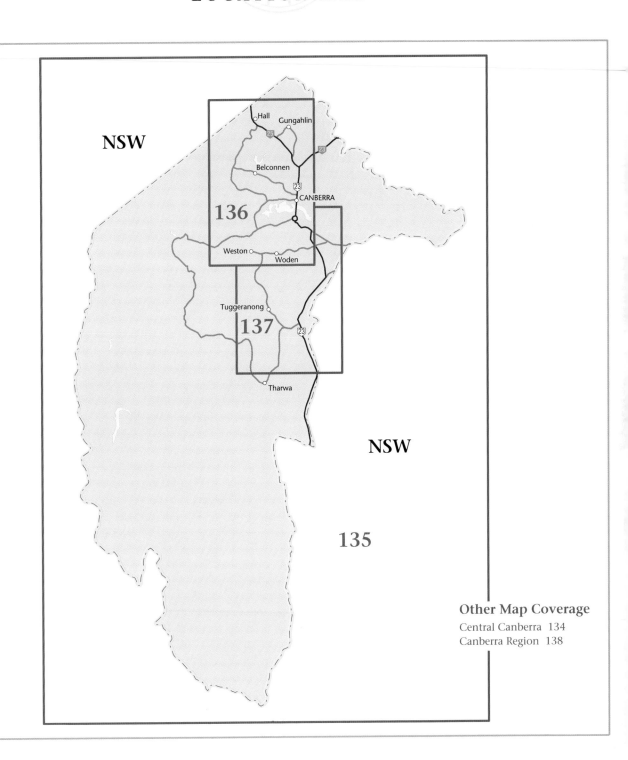

NSW

Hall
Gungahlin

Belconnen

CANBERRA

136

Weston
Woden

Tuggeranong

137

Tharwa

NSW

135

Other Map Coverage
Central Canberra 134
Canberra Region 138

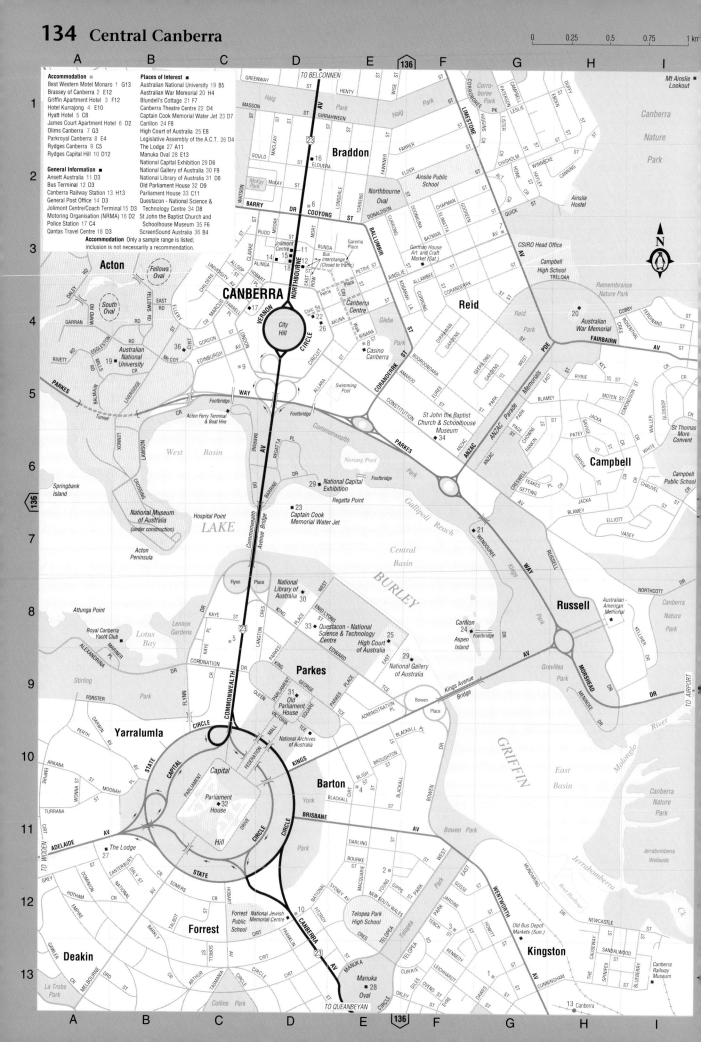

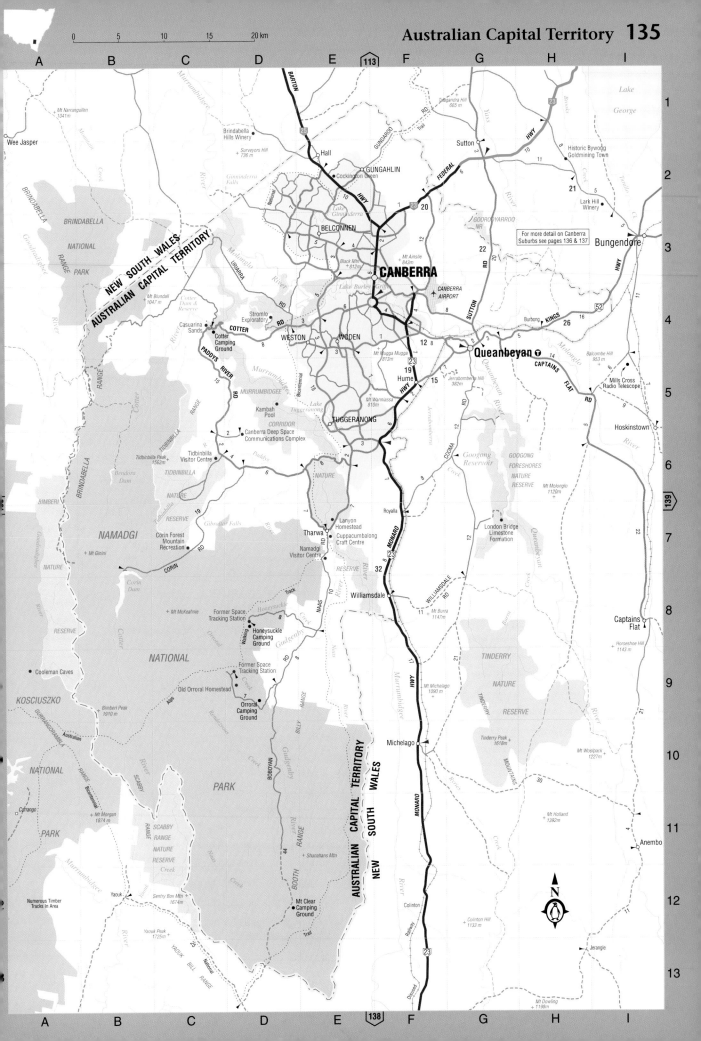

0   5   10   15   20 km

A   B   C   D   E   F   G   H   I

Wee Jasper

BRINDABELLA

BRINDABELLA
NATIONAL

RANGE
PARK

+ Mt Narrangullen
1041m

+ Mt Blundall
1047 m

NEW SOUTH WALES
AUSTRALIAN CAPITAL TERRITORY

Brindabella
Hills Winery

Surveyors Hill
+ 736 m

Hall

GUNGAHLIN

Cockington Green

BELCONNEN

Lake
Ginninderra

Black Mtn
+ 812m

CANBERRA

Mt Ainslie
843m

Lake Burley Griffin

CANBERRA
AIRPORT

Sutton

Historic Bywong
Goldmining Town

Lark Hill
Winery

For more detail on Canberra
Suburbs see pages 136 & 137

Bungendore

GOODROOYARROO
NR

21

22

26

Burbong

Stromlo
Exploratory

COTTER

Casuarina
Sands

Cotter
Dam &
Reserve

Cotter
Camping
Ground

PADDY'S

RIVER

WESTON

WODEN

Mt Mugga Mugga
813m

Queanbeyan

Jerrabomberra Hill
382m

Hume

19

Mills Cross
Radio Telescope

Balcombe Hill
953 m

CAPTAINS

FLAT

Hoskinstown

MURRUMBIDGEE

Kambah
Pool

Canberra Deep Space
Communications Complex

CORRIDOR

TUGGERANONG

Mt Wanniassa
810m

NATURE

Tidbinbilla Peak
1562m

Tidbinbilla
Visitor Centre

TIDBINBILLA

NATURE

RESERVE

Gibraltar Falls

Corin Forest
Mountain
Recreation

+ Mt Ginini

NAMADGI

NATURE

RESERVE

Corin
Dam

BIMBERI

Lanyon
Homestead

Tharwa

Cuppacumbalong
Craft Centre

Namadgi
Visitor Centre

RESERVE

CORIN

Googong
Reservoir

GOOGONG
FORESHORES
NATURE
RESERVE

Mt Molonglo
1120m
+

London Bridge
Limestone
Formation

Royalla

32

Cooleman Caves

KOSCIUSZKO

NATIONAL

PARK

+ Mt McKeahnie

+ Mt Ginini

Former Space
Tracking Station

Honeysuckle
Camping
Ground

Former Space
Tracking Station

Old Orroral Homestead

Orroral
Camping
Ground

NATIONAL

Bimberi Peak
1910m

Williamsdale

WILLIAMSDALE   RD

+ Mt Burra
1147m

TINDERRY

NATURE

RESERVE

Captains
Flat

Horseshoe Hill
1143 m

Codrango

+ Mt Morgan
1874m

SCABBY

RANGE

NATURE

RESERVE

PARK

BOBOYAN

GUDGENBY

RANGE

BILLY

RANGE

BOOTH   RANGE

AUSTRALIAN CAPITAL TERRITORY

NEW SOUTH WALES

Michelago

Mt Michelago
1090 m

TINDERRY

MOUNTAINS

Mt Woolpack
1227m

Mt Holland
1392m

Anembo

Numerous Timber
Tracks in Area

Yaouk

Sentry Box Mtn
1674m

Mt Clear
Camping
Ground

+ Shanahans Mtn

Colinton

MONARO   HWY

Colinton Hill
1133m

Mt Dowling
+ 1198m

Jerangle

Yaouk Peak
1725m +

YAOUK   BILL   RANGE

N

A   B   C   D   E   F   G   H   I

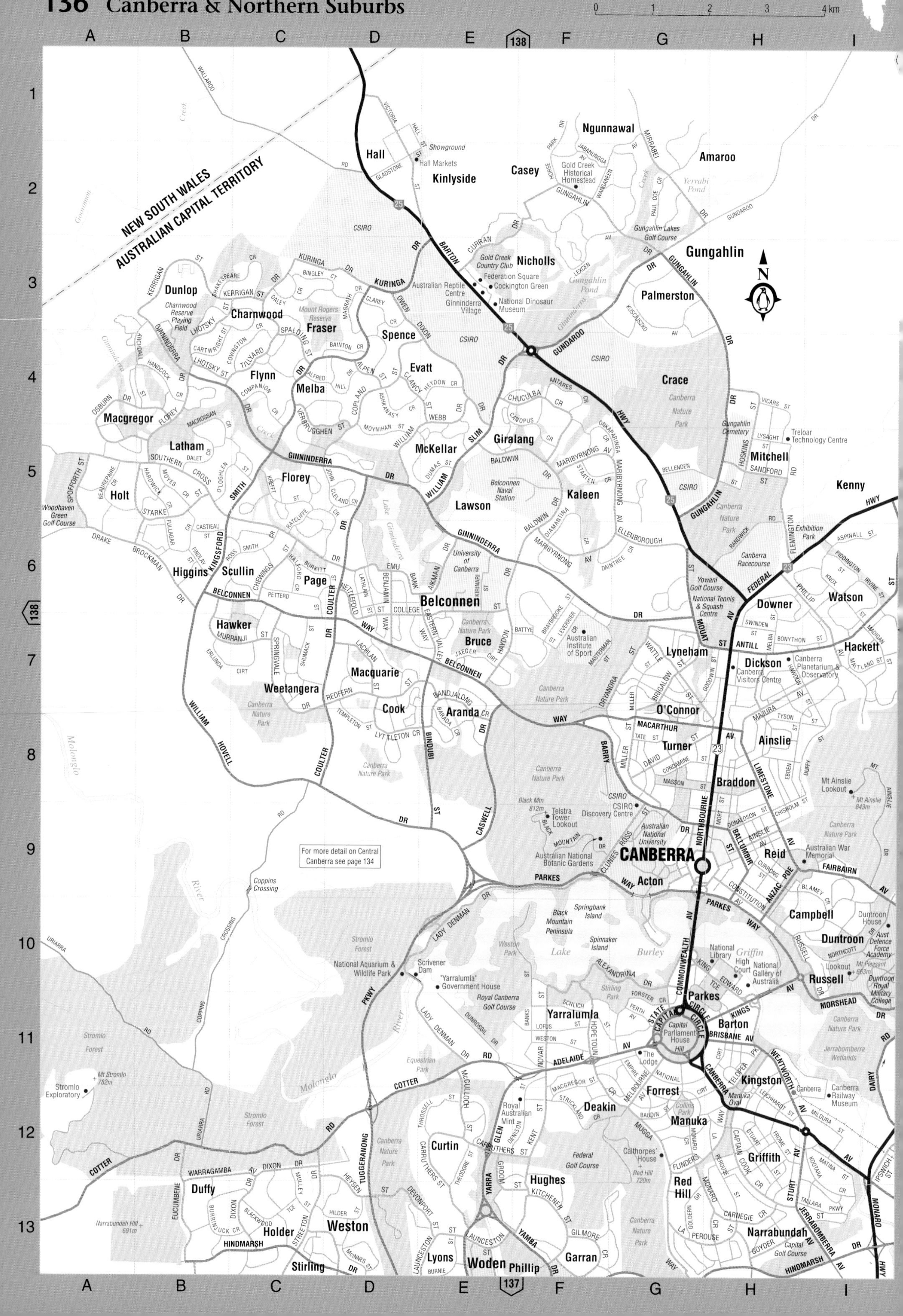

0   1   2   3   4 km

A   B   C   D   E   138   F   G   H   I

NEW SOUTH WALES
AUSTRALIAN CAPITAL TERRITORY

Hall
Showground
Hall Markets
Kinlyside
Casey
Ngunnawal
Amaroo

Gold Creek Historical Homestead
Yerrabi Pond

Gungahlin Lakes Golf Course

Dunlop
Charnwood Reserve Playing Field
Charnwood
Fraser
Spence
Nicholls
Gold Creek Country Club
Federation Square
Cockington Green
Australian Reptile Centre
Ginninderra Village
National Dinosaur Museum

Gungahlin
Palmerston

Mount Rogers Reserve

Kuringa

Flynn
Melba
Evatt
Crace

Macgregor
Latham
Chuculba
Canberra Nature Park

Gungahlin Cemetery
Treloar Technology Centre

Holt
Florey
McKellar
Giralang
Mitchell
Sandford

Baldwin

Lawson
Belconnen Naval Station
Kaleen
Kenny

Woodhaven Green Golf Course

Higgins
Scullin
Page
Belconnen
University of Canberra

Canberra Nature Park

Downer
Watson
Hackett

Hawker
Murranji
Bruce
Australian Institute of Sport
Lyneham
Canberra Racecourse
Yowani Golf Course
National Tennis & Squash Centre
Federal

Weetangera
Macquarie
Cook
Aranda

Canberra Nature Park

Dickson
Canberra Visitors Centre
Canberra Planetarium & Observatory

O'Connor
Turner
Ainslie
Mt Ainslie Lookout
Mt Ainslie 843m

Black Mtn 812m
Telstra Tower Lookout
CSIRO Discovery Centre
Australian National University
Braddon

Reid
Australian War Memorial

Canberra Nature Park

CANBERRA
Acton
Australian National Botanic Gardens

Campbell
Duntroon
Duntroon House
Aust Defence Force Academy
Mt Pleasant 663m
Duntroon Royal Military College

Russell
Morshead

For more detail on Central Canberra see page 134

Coppins Crossing

Stromlo Forest

National Aquarium & Wildlife Park
Scrivener Dam
Government House
"Yarralumla"

Black Mountain Peninsula
Springbank Island
Spinnaker Island
Lake
Burley
Griffin

National Library
High Court
National Gallery of Australia

Royal Canberra Golf Course

Yarralumla

Stirling Park
Alexandrina

Parkes
Commonwealth

Stromlo Forest
Mt Stromlo 782m
Stromlo Exploratory

Equestrian Park

The Lodge
Capital Parliament House Hill

Barton
Brisbane Av
Kingston
Canberra Railway Museum

Royal Australian Mint
Deakin
Forrest
Manuka
Manuka Oval

Jerrabomberra Wetlands

Curtin
Hughes
Federal Golf Course
Red Hill 720m

Griffith

Canberra Nature Park

Duffy
Narrabundah Hill 691m

Holder
Weston
Hindmarsh
Lyons
Stirling

Woden
Phillip
Garran
Red Hill
Narrabundah
Capital Golf Course

A   B   C   D   E   137   F   G   H   I

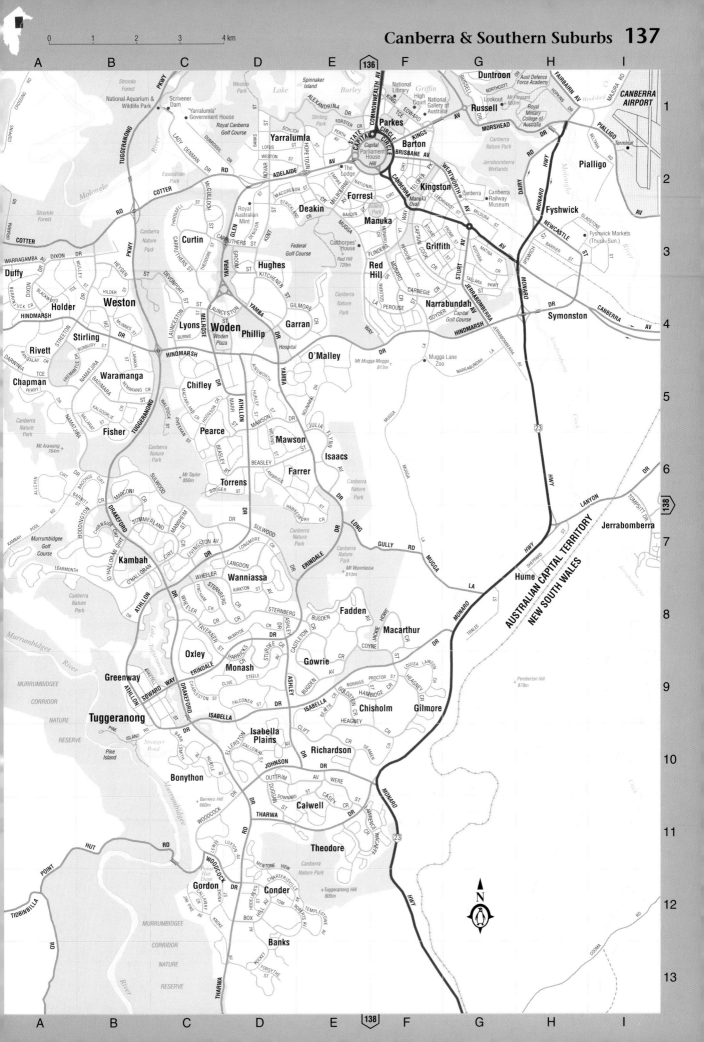

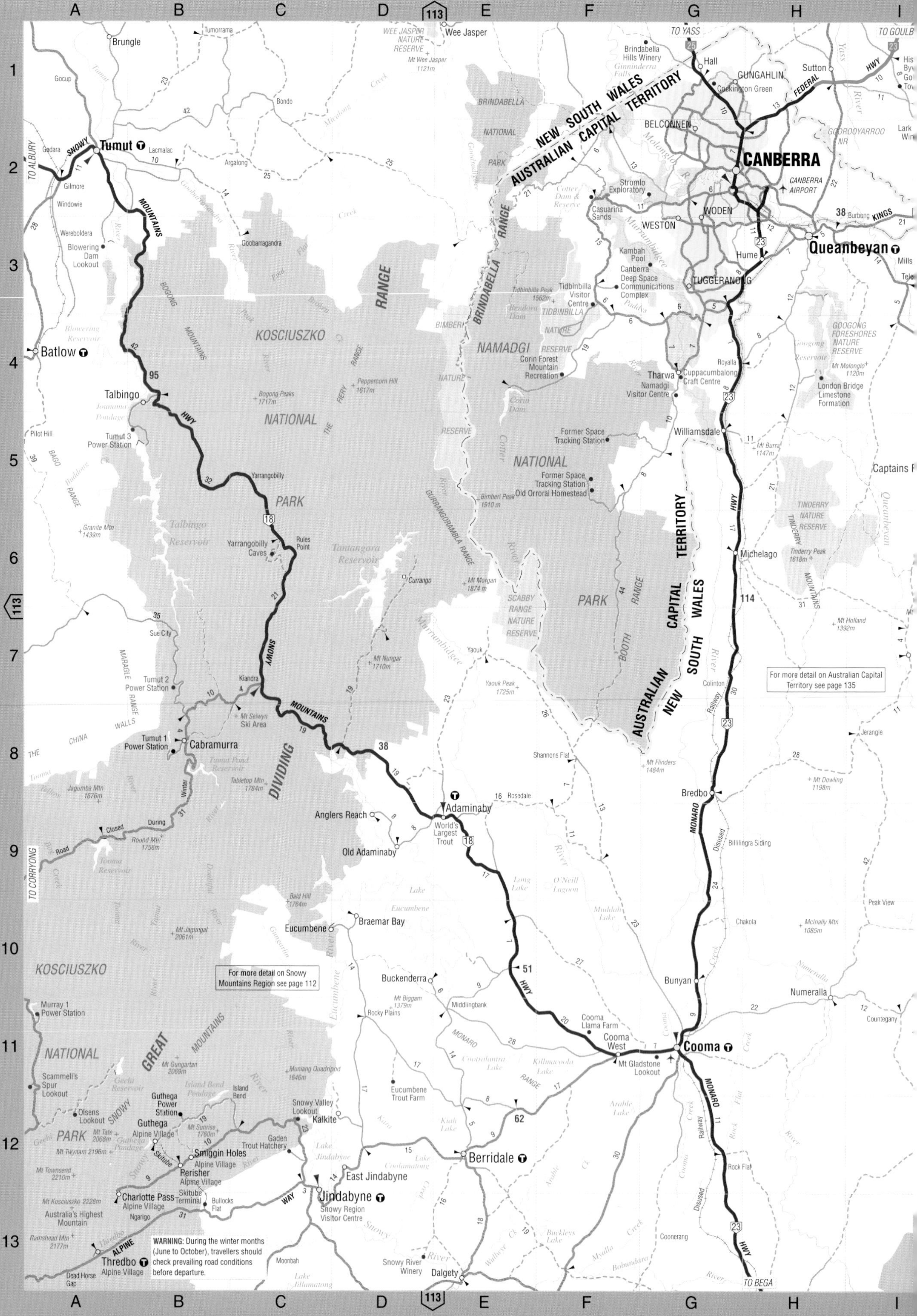

CANBERRA

NEW SOUTH WALES
AUSTRALIAN CAPITAL TERRITORY

KOSCIUSZKO NATIONAL PARK

BRINDABELLA RANGE

NAMADGI NATIONAL PARK

SNOWY MOUNTAINS

GREAT DIVIDING RANGE

Brungle
Gocup
Tumorrama
Wee Jasper
Mt Wee Jasper 1121m
WEE JASPER NATURE RESERVE
Hall
TO YASS
GUNGAHLIN
Sutton
Yass River
TO GOULB
Brindabella Hills Winery
Ginninderra Falls
Cockington Green
BELCONNEN
Gedara
Tumut
Lacmalac
Argalong
Bondo
GOOROOYARROO NR
Lark Win
CANBERRA AIRPORT
WESTON
WODEN
Stromlo Exploratory
Casuarina Sands
Cotter Dam & Reserve
Murrumbidgee R
Gilmore
Windowie
Goobarragandra
Weston
Kambah Pool
Canberra Deep Space Communications Complex
Tidbinbilla Visitor Centre
Tidbinbilla Peak 1562m
Bendora Dam
TIDBINBILLA
Hume
Burbong
KINGS
Queanbeyan
Mills Tele
Batlow
Wereboldera
Blowering Dam Lookout
Blowering Reservoir
Pilot Hill
Peppercorn Hill 1617m
Corin Forest Mountain Recreation
Corin Dam
Tharwa
Cuppacumbalong Craft Centre
Namadgi Visitor Centre
Royalla
GOOGONG FORESHORES NATURE RESERVE
Mt Molonglo 1120m
London Bridge Limestone Formation
Talbingo
Jounama Pondage
Tumut 3 Power Station
Yarrangobilly
Bogong Peaks 1717m
Former Space Tracking Station
Williamsdale
Mt Burra 1147m
Captains F
Granite Mtn 1439m
Yarrangobilly Caves
Rules Point
Tantangara Reservoir
Former Space Tracking Station
Old Orroral Homestead
Bimberi Peak 1910m
Michelago
Tinderry Peak 1618m
TINDERRY NATURE RESERVE
Talbingo Reservoir
Currango
Mt Morgan 1874m
SCABBY RANGE NATURE RESERVE
BOOTH RANGE
Mt Holland 1392m
Sue City
Yaouk
Yaouk Peak 1725m
Colinton
Tumut 2 Power Station
Kiandra
Mt Nungar 1710m
Jerangle
Mt Selwyn Ski Area
Cabramurra
Tumut 1 Power Station
Tumut Pond Reservoir
Tabletop Mtn 1784m
Shannons Flat
Mt Flinders 1484m
Bredbo
Mt Dowling 1198m
Jagumba Mtn 1676m
Anglers Reach
Adaminaby
World's Largest Trout
Rosedale
Billilingra Siding
Round Mtn 1756m
Tooma Reservoir
Old Adaminaby
Long Lake
O'Neill Lagoon
Muddah Lake
Chakola
McInally Mtn 1085m
Peak View
Murray 1 Power Station
Mt Jagungal 2061m
Eucumbene
Braemar Bay
Lake Eucumbene
Bunyan
Numeralla
KOSCIUSZKO NATIONAL PARK
Scammell's Spur Lookout
Mt Gungartan 2069m
Buckenderra
Mt Biggam 1379m
Rocky Plains
Middlingbank
Cooma Llama Farm
Cooma West
Countegany
Olsens Lookout
Geehi Reservoir
Guthega Power Station
Island Bend Pondage
Murrang Quadpod 1646m
MONARO RANGE
Cootralantra Lake
Killimicooola Lake
Cooma
Guthega
Guthega Alpine Village
Island Bend
Mt Sunrise 1780m
Eucumbene Trout Farm
Mt Gladstone Lookout
Rock Flat
Mt Tate 2068m
Smiggin Holes
Snowy Valley Lookout
Kalkite
Gaden Trout Hatchery
Kiah Lake
Arable Lake
Mt Twynam 2196m
Perisher Alpine Village
Lake Jindabyne
Berridale
Mt Townsend 2210m
Skitube Terminal
East Jindabyne
Mt Kosciuszko 2228m
Australia's Highest Mountain
Charlotte Pass Alpine Village
Bullocks Flat
Jindabyne
Snowy Region Visitor Centre
Ngarigo
Ramshead Mtn 2177m
Thredbo Alpine Village
Dead Horse Gap
Moonbah
Snowy River Winery
Dalgety
TO ALBURY
TO CORRYONG
TO BEGA

For more detail on Australian Capital Territory see page 135

For more detail on Snowy Mountains Region see page 112

WARNING: During the winter months (June to October), travellers should check prevailing road conditions before departure.

0 5 10 15 20 km

J K L M N O P Q R

1
Sandy Point
Nerriga
MORTON
Sassafras
Bulee Brook
Mt Sassafras 823m
TO NOWRA
NSW JERVIS BAY NP
Callala Bay
Huskisson
NSW JERVIS BAY NP
Boro
Mt Coghill 806m
Lower Boro
Corang
NATIONAL
Tomerong
St Georges Basin
Vincentia

2
Butmaroo
Mt Fairy
Doughboy
HWY
KINGS
49
Charleyong
Tomboye
PARK
Mt Tianjara 768m
Wandandian
Basin View
Sussex Inlet
Erowal Bay
Hyams Beach
Jervis Bay
Green Patch
Sanctuary Point
Swan Lake
JERVIS BAY TERRITORY
BOODEREE NATIONAL PARK
endore 22
Corang River
Mt Corang 883m

3
Rossi
Durran Durra
Mongarlowe
BUDAWANG
Currockbilly Mtn 823m
Pigeon House Mtn 719m
Pointer Gap Lookout
Yatte Yattah
Conjola
Berrara
Cudmirrah
Swanhaven
Fishermans Paradise
CONJOLA NATIONAL PARK
Bendalong
Manyana
Cunjurong
Lake Conjola
Narrawallee
NARRAWALLEE CREEK NR
stown
Mt Gillamatong 907m

4
Braidwood Historic Town
NATIONAL
52
59
Mt Mogood 391m
Milton
Kings Point
Mollymook
Ulladulla
Burrill Lake
Tabourie Lake
Burrill Lake
Ballalaba
Majors Creek
Reidsdale
Clyde Mtn 850m
Monga
Currowan Corner Upper

5
Round Mtn 1224m
Oranmeir
Araluen North
Araluen
Shallow Crossing
HWY
Nelligen
50
East Lynne
Benandarah
Termeil
Lake Tabourie
Bawley Point
MURRAMARANG ABORIGINAL RESERVE
Kioloa
ILLAWARRA
COAST

6
Kain
The Big Hole and Marble Arch
Gundillion
PRINCES
Runnyford
Cullendulla
Durras
Depot Beach
Pebbly Beach
Long Beach

7
19m
Wandera Mtn 580m
DEUA
NATIONAL
Mt Donovan 784m
Mogo
Batemans Bay
Batehaven
Shell Museum
Surf Beach
Malua Bay
MURRAMARANG NATIONAL PARK
Batemans Bay

8
PARK
27
Bimbimbie
Rosedale
Tomakin
Mossy Point
Broulee
Mogendoura
Yarragee
Gundary
Mullenderee
SOUTH

9
nembo
m
Jinden
Bendethera Mtn 997m
Moruya
Kiora
Moruya Heads
The Anchorage
Congo
EUROBODALLA NATIONAL PARK
Bergalia
Meringo
PACIFIC

10
DJA SWAMPS TURE RESERVE
a Mill
Nerrigundah
42
Turlinjah
Tuross Lake
Bodalla
Tuross Head
Potato Point
TASMAN
OCEAN

11
Belowra
Eurobodalla
EUROBODALLA NP
Mummuga Lake
Lake Brou
Wagonga
Dalmeny
Kianga
Narooma
BODALLA STATE
Billa Brilla Ck
COAST
SEA
DBILLIGA

12
Yowrie
Wandella
Peak Alone 954m
Mt Dromedary
Tilba Valley Vineyard
Corunna
Central Tilba Historic Village
Tilba Tilba
Corunna Lake
HWY
Montague Island
MONTAGUE ISLAND NATURE RESERVE
EUROBODALLA NATIONAL PARK
FOREST
GOURA NR
Tilba Tilba Lake
N

13
PARK
Cobargo
PRINCES
TO BEGA
Quaama
WALLAGA LAKE NP
Wallaga Lake
Narira Creek
Bermagui
Bermagui South
BERMAGUEE NATURE RESERVE
SOUTH

J K L M N O P Q R
113

VICTORIA

Port of Echuca on the Murray River

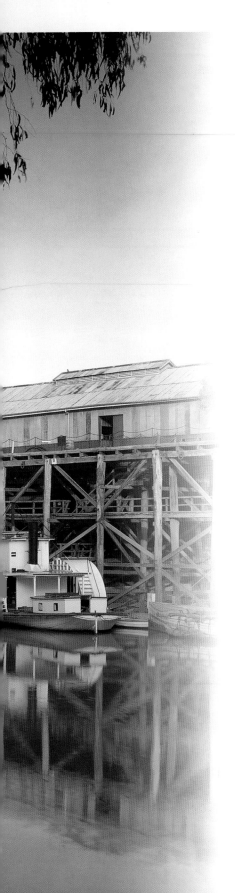

Victoria is an ideal State for the motoring tourist. In one day's drive, you can explore mountain country, pastoral landscapes and spectacular coastline, yet still arrive at your destination in time to watch the sunset.

A good network of sealed roads means Victoria's wonderful diversity of attractions, both natural and constructed, are easily accessible to the motoring tourist.

European occupation of Victoria began with an unsuccessful attempt at settlement in the Port Phillip area in 1803. It was not until 1834 that expeditions from Van Diemen's Land, searching for more arable land, settled along the south-west coast of Victoria. Their glowing reports prompted John Batman and John Fawkner to investigate the Port Phillip area and then purchase land on opposite sides of the Yarra from the local Aborigines. The Colonial Office in London expressed disapproval of these transactions, but in those times possession was nine-tenths of the law.

A squatting colony grew rapidly in the district and the new town was named Melbourne after the British Prime Minister of the day. Nervous of inheriting the penal system of settlement, Victoria sought separation from New South Wales; it was granted in 1851. At about that time, gold was discovered near Ballarat and the State's population more than doubled within a year.

Apart from a serious but short-lived setback caused by land speculation in the early 1890s, Victoria has gone from strength to strength ever since. Today Victoria is the most closely settled and industrialised part of the nation.

Melbourne's inner areas are graced by spacious parks and street upon street of elegant and well-preserved Victorian and Edwardian architecture, contrasting strongly with modern tower blocks. It is renowned also for its retail shopping, theatres, restaurants, cultural festivals and Australian Rules Football.

Beyond the city, the Dandenong Ranges, fifty kilometres to the east, are noted for their eucalypt forests and graceful tree ferns, their many established gardens and an increasing number of restaurants and galleries that are popular with visitors. Phillip Island, less than two hours' drive from Melbourne, is famed for its unique little (fairy) penguin parade and its large colony of fur seals. To the south and south-west, the Mornington and Bellarine peninsulas are Melbourne's favourite seaside playgrounds.

Despite its rather volatile weather, the State enjoys a generally temperate climate. Spring, late summer and autumn provide the most settled and pleasant touring weather.

NOT TO BE MISSED

IN VICTORIA
Map Ref.

ALPINE NATIONAL PARK
Bushwalking in summer and skiing in winter — 231 L1

BEECHWORTH
Old goldmining town with museums,
numerous relics and local gourmet produce — 239 O6

GIPPSLAND LAKES
One of the State's most outstanding
holiday areas — 231 Q5

THE GRAMPIANS
Beautiful scenery and wildflowers, particularly
in spring — 232 H2

PADDLESTEAMER RIDE AT ECHUCA
Experience the magnificent Murray — 238 E4

PENGUIN PARADE AT PHILLIP ISLAND
A delightful spectacle each evening at sunset — 219 M13

SOVEREIGN HILL
Fascinating re-creation of a goldmining township — 227 K11

**SPA TOWNS OF DAYLESFORD &
HEPBURN SPRINGS**
Mineral springs, great scenery — 216 E2

GREAT OCEAN ROAD
250 kilometres of breathtaking coastal scenery — 233 K11

WILSONS PROMONTORY
An impressive coastal national park — 231 J11

YARRA VALLEY
Good scenery and excellent wineries — 220

Each of Victoria's five main geographical regions has its own special attraction. The central and western districts, due north and west of Melbourne, offer highlights including the historic goldfield areas, with well-preserved, attractive towns such as Bendigo, Castlemaine and Ballarat, the popular spa towns of Daylesford and Hepburn Springs, and the Grampians National Park, particularly noted for its spring wildflowers and native fauna. Travelling south from these impressive ranges brings you into the western district, where rich grazing land is dotted with many splendid old properties. No exploration of this region would be complete without a drive along the Great Ocean Road. The rock formations in Port Campbell National Park are without doubt its most imposing sight. Further west is the whale-watching centre of Warrnambool, and the historic seaside township of Port Fairy.

The north-east high-country region has equally magnificent scenery, historic towns including Beechworth and Chiltern, and a number of winter ski resorts. In spring and summer, the wildflowers, sweeping views and clear air can be enjoyed with a fair degree of solitude. Down in the foothills, Lake Eildon is ideal for water sports and houseboats.

Gippsland stretches to the south-east; it contains some of the State's most beautiful and varied country. Rolling pastures lead to densely wooded hill country, still relatively unpopulated. National parks such as Tarra–Bulga and Wilsons Promontory are well worth visiting. The coastal region includes the Ninety Mile Beach which borders the Gippsland Lakes system – Australia's largest inland waterway – and the beautiful Croajingolong National Park wilderness.

Following the course of the Murray can be an interesting way of exploring Victoria's north. The river begins as a narrow alpine stream near Native Dog Flat and changes to a broad expanse near Lakes Hume and Mulwala. The river is lined with waterbird and wildlife reserves, flourishing citrus and wine-growing areas, and sandy river beaches, while the old riverboat towns, such as Echuca, Swan Hill and Mildura, powerfully evoke the region's history.

CLIMATE GUIDE

MELBOURNE

	J	F	M	A	M	J	J	A	S	O	N	D
Maximum °C	26	26	24	20	17	14	13	15	17	20	22	24
Minimum °C	14	14	13	11	8	7	6	7	8	9	11	13
Rainfall mm	48	47	52	57	58	49	49	50	59	67	60	59
Raindays	8	7	9	12	14	14	15	16	15	14	12	11

LAKES ENTRANCE REGION

	J	F	M	A	M	J	J	A	S	O	N	D
Maximum °C	24	24	22	20	17	15	15	16	17	19	20	22
Minimum °C	14	15	13	11	8	6	5	6	7	9	11	13
Rainfall mm	57	35	55	61	79	65	55	57	57	61	73	74
Raindays	8	7	10	10	12	13	12	14	13	13	13	11

BENDIGO REGION

	J	F	M	A	M	J	J	A	S	O	N	D
Maximum °C	29	29	25	21	16	13	12	14	16	20	24	26
Minimum °C	14	15	13	9	7	4	3	5	6	8	11	13
Rainfall mm	34	32	36	41	55	60	56	58	54	53	38	33
Raindays	5	4	5	7	10	12	13	13	11	10	7	6

ALPINE REGION

	J	F	M	A	M	J	J	A	S	O	N	D
Maximum °C	18	19	15	10	6	3	1	3	5	9	13	15
Minimum °C	8	9	7	4	1	-2	-4	-2	-1	1	4	5
Rainfall mm	88	59	121	154	195	175	266	256	210	179	168	172
Raindays	10	7	12	12	15	16	19	19	17	15	15	14

Wilsons Promontory National Park

VISITOR INFORMATION
Melbourne Visitor Information Service
Melbourne Town Hall
cnr Swanston and Little Collins sts, Melbourne
13 2842
www.tourism.vic.gov.au

CALENDAR OF EVENTS

JANUARY

Public holidays: New Year's Day; Australia Day. *Melbourne:* Australian Open (Grand Slam tennis championships); Summer Live (at the Arts Centre); Marvellous Melbourne Jazz Festival; Midsumma (Gay and Lesbian Festival). *Apollo Bay:* Beach Horse Races. *Ballarat:* Organs of the Ballarat Goldfields. *Cobram:* Peaches and Cream Festival (odd-numbered years). *Daylesford:* Daylesford Gift (horse race). *Erica (near Walhalla):* King of the Mountain Woodchop. *Geelong:* Waterfront Festival. *Hanging Rock (near Woodend):* Picnic Races. *Harrietville:* Classical Music Competition; Ride-On Mower Grand Prix. *Hoddles Creek (near Warburton):* Upper Yarra Draught Horse Festival. *Lakes Entrance:* Larger than Lakes Festival. *Lorne:* Pier to Pub Swim; Mountain to Surf Foot Race. *Maryborough:* Highland Gathering. *Metung (near Lakes Entrance):* Regatta. *Mornington Peninsula:* Wine and Food Festival. *Murtoa:* New Year's Day Race Meeting. *Orbost:* Australian Wood Design Exhibition. *Portland:* Foreshore Carnival. *Portsea (near Sorrento):* Swim Classic. *Sale:* Bush Races (bush horse race). *Terang:* New Year's Day Family Picnic; Australian Stockhorse Weekend. *Warburton:* Upper Yarra Draughthorse Festival. *Yarrawonga:* Rowing Regatta.

FEBRUARY

Melbourne: Australian Masters (golf tournament); Formula 500 (motor racing); Autumn Racing Carnival; Chinese New Year Festival. *Ballarat:* Super Southern Swap Meet. *Beechworth:* Drive Back in Time (vintage car rally). *Buchan:* Canni Creek Races. *Buninyong (near Ballarat):* Gold King Festival. *Cohuna:* Aquatic Festival; Bridge to Bridge Swim. *Colac:* Otway Harvest Festival. *Edenhope:* Henley-on-Lake Wallace. *Echuca:* Southern 80 Ski Race; Riverboats, Food, Jazz and Wine Festival. *Foster:* Agricultural Show. *Geelong:* Australian International Air Show (odd-numbered years). *Halls Gap:* Grampians Jazz Festival. *Hamilton:* Beef Expo. *Hanging Rock (near Woodend):* Vintage Car Rally. *Healesville:* Coldstream Country and Western Festival. *Heathcote:* Eppalock Gold Cup (power-boat race). *Kyneton:* Country Music Festival. *Leongatha:* Cycling Carnival. *Maldon:* Camp Draft. *Mooroopna (near Shepparton):* Fruit Salad Day. *Paynesville:* Jazz Festival. *Portland:* Fishing Competition; Go Kart Street Grand Prix; Yachting Regatta. *Seymour:* Alternative Farming Expo. *Shepparton:* Bush Market Day. *Traralgon:* Music in the Park. *Warrnambool:* Wunta Fiesta. *Wodonga:* Sports Festival.

MARCH

Public holiday: Labour Day. *Melbourne:* Australian Formula One Grand Prix; Moomba Festival (incl. International Dragon Boat Festival); Food and Wine Festival. *Apollo Bay:* Music Festival. *Ararat:* Jailhouse Rock Festival. *Bairnsdale:* Riviera Festival. *Ballarat:* Begonia Festival; Antique Fair. *Bendigo:* Madison 10 000 Cycling Race. *Casterton:* Vintage Car Rally; Polocrosse Championships. *Colac:* Food and Wine Festival. *Corryong:* Man From Snowy River Festival. *Dromana (near Mornington):* Maize Maze Festival. *Eaglehawk (near Bendigo):* Dahlia and Arts Festival. *Edenhope:* Gourmet Food Day; Races. *Euroa:* Let's Go Irish Week. *Geelong:* Highland Gathering. *Harcourt (near Castlemaine):* Apple Festival. *Healesville:* Australian Car Rally Championship; Grape Grazing. *Horsham:* Fishing Competition; Art Is (community festival). *Inverloch:* Jazz Festival. *Koo-wee-rup:* Potato Festival. *Kyabram:* Rodeo. *Lancefield (near Woodend):* Woodchopping Competition. *Maffra:* Gippsland Harvest Festival; Mardi Gras. *Mansfield:* Harvest Festival. *Mildura:* Arts Festival. *Moe:* Jazz Festival; Blue Rock Classic (cross-country horse race). *Mount Beauty:* Conquestathon Fun Climb. *Myrtleford:* Tobacco, Hops and Timber Festival. *Nagambie:* Goulburn Valley Vintage Festival. *Numurkah:* Art Show. *Omeo:* Picnic Races. *Paynesville:* Marlay Point–Paynesville Yacht Race. *Port Fairy:* Folk Festival. *Portland:* Dahlia Festival. *Robinvale:* 80 Ski Classic. *Rutherglen:* Tastes of Rutherglen. *Seymour:* Rafting Festival. *Sorrento:* Street Festival. *Swan Hill:* Redgum Festival. *Thorpdale (near Moe):* Potato Festival. *Traralgon:* Music in the Park (contd). *Wedderburn:* Gold Festival. *Yarra Glen:* Grape Grazing Festival. *Yea:* Autumn Fest.

EASTER

Public holidays: Good Friday; Easter Monday. *State-wide:* Easterbike (various locations). *Alexandra:* Art Show. *Beechworth:* Golden Horseshoes Festival. *Benalla:* Art Show; Garden Expo. *Bendigo:* Fair (features Chinese dragon). *Buchan:* Rodeo. *Hopetoun:* Country Music Festival. *Lake Boga (near Swan Hill):* Yacht Club Regatta. *Lake Bolac:* Yachting Regatta. *Maldon:* Fair. *Mallacoota:* Festival of the Great Southern Ocean. *Mangalore (near Seymour):* National Air Show. *Omeo:* Rodeo and Market. *Patchewollock (near Hopetoun):* Easter Sports. *Quambatook (near Kerang):* Australian Tractor Pull Championship. *Rutherglen:* Easter in Rutherglen. *Stawell:* Easter Gift (foot race); Easter Festival. *Torquay:* Bells Beach Surfing Classic. *Warracknabeal:* Y-Fest. *Wonthaggi:* Coal Skip Fill. *Wunghnu (near Numurkah):* Tractor Pull Festival. *Yarram:* Tarra Festival.

APRIL

Public holiday: Anzac Day. *State-wide:* Heritage Week. *Melbourne:* International Comedy Festival. *Avoca:* Pyrenees Vignerons Gourmet Food and Wine Race Meeting. *Bairnsdale:* East Gippsland Agricultural Field Days. *Ballarat:* Eureka Jazz Festival. *Bendigo:* Bendigo by Bike; Chrysanthemum Championships; Wine Festival. *Bright:* Autumn Festival. *Castlemaine:* State Festival (odd-numbered years). *Colac:* Country Music Festival. *Daylesford:* Fair. *Dimboola:* Wimmera German Fest. *Echuca:* Barmah Muster. *Emerald:* Great Train Race. *Geelong:* Alternative Farmvision. *Numurkah:* Splashdown (fishing competition). *Ouyen:* Autumn Art Show. *Smeaton (near Creswick):* Food, Wine and Jazz Festival. *Tallangatta:* Dairy Festival. *Yarra Glen:* Music Viva Yarra Valley Festival.

MAY

Melbourne: Next Wave Festival (even-numbered years). *Bairnsdale:* Australasian Street Grand Prix. *Cobram:* Rotary Art Show. *Cowes:* Motor Racing. *Daylesford:* Hepburn Swiss–Italian Festival. *Halls Gap:* Grampians Gourmet Weekend. *Lake Goldsmith (near Beaufort):* Steam Rally. *Stratford (near Maffra):* Shakespeare Celebration. *Warrnambool:* Racing Carnival.

JUNE

Public holiday: Queen's Birthday. *Cobram:* Antique Fair. *Donald:* Scottish Dancing Country Weekend. *Echuca:* Steam, Horse and Vintage Car Rally. *Geelong:* National Wool Week; National Celtic Folk Festival. *Kilmore:* Celtic Festival. *Mornington:* Queen's Birthday Wine Weekend. *Murtoa:* Cup (horse race). *Rutherglen:* Winery Walkabout; Country Fair. *Swan Hill:* Racing Cup Carnival.

JULY

Melbourne: Le Boite Winter Festival (choral singing); International Film Festival. *Ballarat:* Winter Festival. *Bendigo:* National Model Engineers Annual Exhibition. *Bright:* Winter Wonderland Festival. *Camperdown:* One Act Play Festival. *Daylesford:* Mid-Winter Festival. *Hamilton:* Eisteddfod. *Mallacoota:* Blues Festival. *Mildura:* International Balloon Fiesta. *Swan Hill:* Italian Festa. *Warburton:* Winterfest.

AUGUST

Melbourne: International Film Festival (contd.); Le Boite Winter Festival (choral singing) (contd). *Ballarat:* Royal South Street Eisteddfod. *Casterton:* Woodturning Demonstration Exhibition. *Hamilton:* Sheepvention. *Maryborough:* Golden Wattle Festival. *Olinda:* Rhododendron Festival. *Speed (near Ouyen):* Mallee Machinery Field Days.

SEPTEMBER

State-wide: Opening of Australia's Open Garden Scheme. *Melbourne:* Australian Football League and Association Finals; Royal Melbourne Show. *Anglesea:* Angair Wildflower Festival. *Ararat:* Cymbidium Orchid Festival. *Ballarat:* Royal South Street Eisteddfod (contd). *Geelong:* Momenta Arts. *Kyneton:* Daffodil and Arts Festival. *Leongatha:* Daffodil and Floral Festival. *Maryborough:* Golden Wattle Festival (contd). *Mildura:* Country Music Festival. *Nhill:* Little Desert Festival. *Numurkah:* Kart Titles (go-kart championships). *Olinda:* Rhododendron Festival (contd). *Rutherglen:* Wine Show. *Silvan (near Olinda):* Tesselaar's Tulip Festival. *Wedderburn:* Historic Engine Exhibition.

OCTOBER

Melbourne: Lygon Street Festa; Oktoberfest; Spring Racing Carnival (incl. Caulfield Cup); Melbourne Festival; Fringe Festival. *Alexandra:* Picnic Races. *Ararat:* Golden Gateway Festival; Orchid Festival. *Ballarat:* Royal South Street Eisteddfod (contd). *Bendigo:* Bendigo Heritage Uncorked; Orchid Club Spring Show. *Bright:* Alpine Spring Festival. *Broadford (near Kilmore):* Scottish Festival. *Chiltern:* Art Show. *Colac:* Garden Expo; Go Colac, Go Country Festival (includes Ferret Cup). *Cowes:* Grand Prix Motorcycle Race. *Creswick:* Brackenbury Classic Fun Run. *Euroa:* Wool Week. *Geelong:* Agricultural Show; Racing Carnival. *Halls Gap:* Wildflower Exhibition. *Harcourt (near Castlemaine):* Spring Orchid Festival. *Harrietville:* Bluegrass Festival. *Horsham:* Spring Garden Festival. *Maldon:* Vintage Car Hill Climb; Folk Festival. *Maryborough:* Gourmet, Grapes and Gardens Weekend. *Mildura:* Sunraysia Oasis Rose Festival. *Moe:* Cup (horse race). *Mutoa:* Big Weekend. *Myrtleford:* International Festival (even-numbered years). *Nhill:* Garden Walk. *Newham (near Woodend):* Macedon Ranges Budburst Wine Festival. *Olinda:* Rhododendron Festival (contd). *Ouyen:* Mallee Wildflower Festival. *Port Fairy:* Spring Music Festival. *Pyramid Hill:* Pioneer Machinery Display. *Rainbow:* Iris Festival. *Seymour:* Cup (horse race). *Tallangatta:* (or Nov.) Art Exhibition; Fifties Festival. *Warrnambool:* Melbourne–Warrnambool Cycling Classic. *Wodonga:* Wine and Food Festival.

NOVEMBER

Public holiday: Melbourne Cup Day (Vic metro. only). *Melbourne:* Spring Racing Carnival (incl. Melbourne Cup and Oaks Day). *Alexandra:* Picnic Races; Rose Festival. *Bacchus Marsh:* Cup Day in the Park. *Ballarat:* Royal South Street Eisteddfod (contd); Springfest Extravaganza; Ballarat Cup. *Beechworth:* Celtic Festival. *Benalla:* Rose Festival. *Bendigo:* National Swap Meet; Racing Carnival. *Casterton:* Street-car Drag Racing. *Castlemaine:* Festival of Gardens (odd-numbered years). *Cobram:* Sun Country Doll, Bears and Collectables Show; Harness Racing Meeting. *Dimboola:* Rowing Regatta. *Dunkeld:* Dunkeld Cup (horse race). *Healesville:* Gateway Festival. *Lake Goldsmith (near Beaufort):* Steam Rally. *Maldon:* Folk Festival (contd). *Mansfield:* Mountain Country Festival. *Maryborough:* Energy Breakthrough. *Milawa:* Brown Brothers Wine and Food Weekend. *Mildura:* Sunraysia Jazz and Wine Festival. *Mornington:* Tea Tree Festival. *Mornington Peninsula:* Peninsula Wine and Music Gala. *Nagambie:* Shiraz Challenge (wine competition). *Olinda:* Rhododendron Festival (contd). *Ouyen:* Farmers Festival. *Portland:* Three Bays Marathon. *Shepparton:* Strawberry Festival; Spring Car Nationals. *St Arnaud:* Festival. *Wallington (near Queenscliff):* Strawberry Fair. *Wangaratta:* Festival of Jazz and Blues. *Whitfield and Cheshunt (near Milawa:* King Valley Virgin Wine, Food and Arts Festival. *Wodonga:* World Cup Show Jumping. *Yarram:* Seabank Fishing Contest.

DECEMBER

Public holidays: Christmas Day; Boxing Day. *Apollo Bay:* Aquathon. *Bendigo:* Tram Spectacular. *Broadford (near Kilmore):* Hells Angels Concert. *Daylesford:* Highland Gathering. *Eildon:* Christmas Eve Gala Night. *Horsham:* Kannamaroo Rock'n'Roll Festival. *Lakes Entrance:* New Year's Eve Fireworks. *Lancefield (near Woodend):* Dog Show. *Lorne:* Falls Festival. *Nagambie:* Rowing Regatta. *Nariel (near Corryong):* Folk Music Festival. *Port Fairy:* Moyneyana Festival. *Skipton:* Rose Festival. *Woodend:* Five Mile Creek Festival.

Note: The information given here was accurate at the time of printing. However, as the timing of events held annually is subject to change and some events may extend into the following month, it is best to check with the local tourism authority or event organisers to confirm the details. The calendar is not exhaustive. Most towns and regions hold sporting competitions, arts and craft exhibitions, agricultural and flower shows, music festivals and other such events annually. Details of these events are available from tourism outlets.

Melbourne

Melbourne prides itself on its reputation as the world's most livable city, and it is easy to see why. Melbourne has a modern skyline with stunning new buildings, but at ground level you will find clanging trams, elegant Victorian gold-rush architecture, and restaurants everywhere. Add tree-lined boulevards, magnificent public gardens, excellent shopping, plus world-class sporting venues and you will have some idea of the city.

VISITOR INFORMATION
Melbourne Visitor Information Centre
Melbourne Town Hall,
cnr Swanston and Little Collins sts
Melbourne
(03) 9658 9955
Information booth
Bourke St Mall, Melbourne
Victorian Tourism Information Service
13 2842
www.melbourne.org
Melbourne organises a Greeter Service:
visitors are matched to Melbourne residents
of similar interests for an introductory tour.
Greeters are available in thirty languages.
Three days' notice is required. Book at
Melbourne Visitor Information Centre.

There's always something happening in Melbourne. The major festivals include the Melbourne Festival (an arts festival), the Comedy Festival, the Food and Wine Festival and the Film Festival. If you are interested in sport, the sporting year starts with the Australian Open tennis; the Australian Formula One Grand Prix follows; the cricket season leads into the football season, then there is the Spring Carnival horseracing, culminating with the Melbourne Cup in November. The year ends with a cricket Test Match that traditionally begins on Boxing Day at the Melbourne Cricket Ground (MCG).

Melbourne is multicultural, with residents from many countries, particularly Asia and Greece; it has one of the largest Greek-speaking populations in the world. This cosmopolitan influence is reflected in Melbourne's bustling markets, delicatessens and restaurants. Eating out is a great Melbourne pastime.

Situated at the head of Port Phillip and centred on the north bank of the Yarra River, Melbourne's population is about 3.3 million. The suburbs spread in all directions, particularly down the east coast of the bay and towards the Dandenongs, the picturesque mountains east of Melbourne. The Yarra River has become a focus for Melburnians: there are barbecues and picnic tables overlooking the river near the Botanic Gardens, and a bike path runs along the riverbank from the city into the Yarra Valley. The Yarra is an integral part of the Moomba Festival in March, with dragonboat racing, fireworks and waterskiing drawing huge crowds. The popular Southgate and the Crown Entertainment Complex are the stars of the south bank, along with the beautiful riverside public gardens.

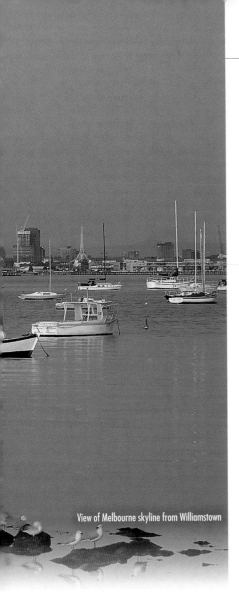

View of Melbourne skyline from Williamstown

A good way to explore the city is on the City Explorer or the City Wanderer, the latter extending as far as the Westgate Bridge and Williamstown. View more than 50 attractions from their upper decks or, alternatively, break your journey at any point and rejoin later. Both buses operate daily and tickets are available from the Visitor Information Centre, or your bus driver.

The city centre has plenty of carparking, mainly as short-term parking meters and undercover carparks. At peak times it can be difficult to find an unoccupied meter, and inexpensive long-term parking is not so easy to locate centrally. Outside the centre, however, there is usually no problem finding a parking spot.

The Yarra River has a variety of tour boats, including water taxis and ferries. Many are moored at Southgate or Princes Bridge, and destinations include Williamstown and St Kilda. There are sightseeing trips around the bay and the river, and along the Maribyrnong River departing from Dynon Bridge in Footscray.

Cycling is popular, particularly alongside the Yarra River, and you can hire a bicycle at Princes Bridge to explore the Yarra Bike Trail.

MELBOURNE BY AREA

CITY CENTRE

Flinders Street Station, on the corner of Flinders and Swanston streets, is an excellent place to begin. A busy terminus, it is a popular meeting place. Diagonally opposite is **St Paul's Anglican Cathedral**, built 1880–91. This Gothic-style building has a sandstone exterior whilst the interior is banded with limestone and bluestone.

The area between St Paul's and the Yarra River is **Federation Square**, intended to be a contemporary focus for the city, with the Museum of Australian Art and the Australian Centre for the Moving Image. **Young & Jacksons Hotel** is also on this intersection. It was once notorious for 'Chloe', a nude painting that shocked Victorians at the turn of the century. 'Chloe' now hangs upstairs.

Take the free burgundy-and-cream-coloured City Circle tram (they depart about every 10 minutes between 10 a.m. and 6 p.m.) west down Flinders Street to the Old Customs House. Restored to its original grandeur, the Long Room in

EXPLORING MELBOURNE

The city centre is easy to explore, with its wide streets laid out in a grid system. Public transport is excellent, particularly the tram system. There are free City Circle trams around the perimeter of the central grid, in both directions. Normal tram services criss-cross the city on their way to the suburbs. Tickets are available at railway stations and shops displaying a Metcard flag throughout Melbourne, as well as a limited choice from vending machines on the trams; tickets are valid for suburban trains, trams and buses.

There are two main railway stations: Spencer Street services country and suburban destinations, while Flinders Street is the main terminus for the suburban lines. Trains from Flinders Street go round an underground loop that can be used instead of the City Circle tram to explore Melbourne. Buses cover major routes that are not reached by trams or trains.

NOT TO BE MISSED

IN MELBOURNE	Map Ref.
MELBOURNE AQUARIUM The magic of marine life	210 C9
MELBOURNE MUSEUM A superb introduction to Melbourne and Australia	210 F3
MELBOURNE ZOO An essential stop for animal lovers	213 K7
QUEEN VICTORIA MARKET Always bustling, noisy and fun	210 B4
RIALTO TOWERS Stunning 360° views of the city from the Observation Deck of Australia's tallest building	210 C8
ROYAL BOTANIC GARDENS Considered to be among the best in the world	210 I12
SCIENCEWORKS Exciting and award-winning interactive science and technology museum, with new Planetarium	212 I9
SOUTHGATE & CROWN ENTERTAINMENT COMPLEX Something for everyone – shop, wine and dine or have a flutter	210 E9
WILLIAMSTOWN Take a ferry from St Kilda to this fascinating historic suburb	212 I11

GETTING AROUND

Airport shuttle bus
Skybus (03) 9335 3066

Motoring organisation
Royal Automobile Club of Victoria (RACV)
13 1955

Car rental
Avis 1800 225 533; Budget 13 2727; Delta
13 1390; Hertz 13 3039; Thrifty 1300 367 227

Public transport
The Met (trams, including free City Circle
trams, suburban trains) 13 1638

Tourist bus
City Explorer, City Wanderer (03) 9563 9788

Taxis
Black Cabs Combined 13 2227; Embassy
13 1755; Melbourne Combined (wheelchair only)
13 1323; North Suburban 13 1119; Silver Top
13 1008; West Suburban (03) 9689 1144

Water taxi
Whaleboat Water Taxi (Yarra River, Tues.–Sun.)
0416 068 655

Boat trips
Melbourne River Cruises (03) 9614 1215;
Southbank Cruises (03) 9646 5677; Williamstown
Bay and River Cruises (03) 9692 9555; Penguin
Waters Cruises (03) 9386 2986; Canoe Capers
(03) 9742 2699

Bicycle hire
Dial-a-Bike (03) 9500 1808; Fitzroy Cycles
(03) 9636 3511; Hire a Bicycle 019 429 000;
St Kilda Cycles (03) 9534 3074

Riverside scene

particular is worth a look as it is a magnificent example of Victorian architecture, with a superb tessellated tile floor, wonderful ionic columns and architraves. The Old Customs House is now the **Immigration Museum** and **Hellenic Antiquities Museum**. You can search genealogical records and passenger lists at the Discovery Centre for information on migrant forbears.

On the river just west of this spot is the **Melbourne Aquarium**, where state-of-the-art technology allows visitors to view the underwater world of approximately 270 marine species from the Southern Ocean and Australia's inland waterways.

From the Aquarium, take the City Circle tram to Spencer Street. As the tram turns into Spencer Street, you can see, through the arches of the railway bridge, the **World Trade Centre** and **Melbourne Convention Centre**, which host trade displays. Tucked behind these is the **Victoria Police Museum**, in the Victoria Police Centre on Flinders Street. This museum houses memorabilia from some of Victoria's most famous criminal cases, including Ned Kelly's armour,

and displays of state-of-the-art police equipment. Rejoin the City Circle tram (or walk) to the Collins Street stop in Spencer Street. Walk a block along Collins Street to the **Rialto Towers**, and take the lift to its Observation Deck on level 55 for a magnificent view of the city. A 20-minute film of major Melbourne and Victorian tourist attractions is shown here every half-hour. The elaborate Rialto Towers building and its neighbours on Collins Street were retained as a facade to this towering hotel and office complex, the tallest building in Australia.

Rejoin the tram again on its clockwise route to **Flagstaff Gardens**. These were the city's first public gardens, and were used as a signalling station to inform settlers of the arrival and departure of ships at Williamstown. Before this the area was a pioneer graveyard; today it is a pleasant place to relax under shady trees. Facing the park, in King Street, you can see **St James' Old Cathedral** (1839). Built of sandstone and bluestone, it contains two unusual pews set high in the walls, resembling boxes at a theatre; Victoria's first Governor, Governor La Trobe, sat in one and faced the Chief Justice of Victoria.

The old **Royal Mint Building** on the corner of Latrobe and William streets, a splendid building built in 1872, is home to the Royal Historical Society of Victoria. Its wrought-iron gates still bear elaborate coats of arms. Further down William Street is the **Supreme Court of Victoria** and the **Law Courts**.

Continue down Latrobe Street to **Melbourne Central**, a huge retail complex featuring a 20-storey glass cone that encloses a historic shot tower – where lead shot was made by dropping molten metal into water – and a large clock with an 'Australiana' theme which attracts

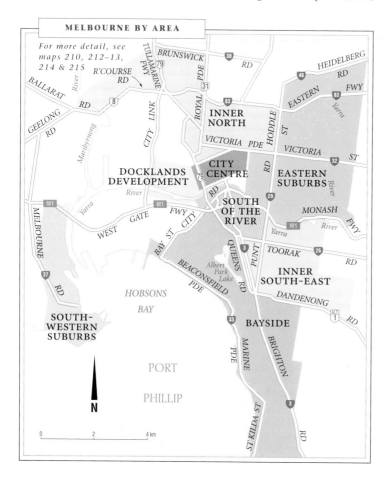

MELBOURNE BY AREA

*For more detail, see
maps 210, 212–13,
214 & 215*

visitors on the hour to see its display. **Daimaru**, Melbourne's most recent department store, is here and you can reach Melbourne's best-known department store, **Myer**, through a walkway over Lonsdale Street.

The **State Library of Victoria**, with its magnificent domed roof, is on the corner of Latrobe and Swanston streets. Just behind the library, in Russell Street, is the temporary home of the National Gallery of Victoria under renovation until 2002. Just north of the crossroads on Swanston Street is the unusual facade of **Storey Hall**, part of RMIT University. Two doors along, the RMIT Gallery has changing exhibitions of contemporary art.

Nearby, left down Russell Street, is the **Old Melbourne Gaol** and **Penal Museum**, a grim reminder of the past with its chillingly macabre exhibits, including the gallows where bushranger Ned Kelly swung. The gaol's claustrophobic atmosphere becomes even more dramatic during after-dark tours. A little further along Latrobe Street, on the corner of Exhibition Street, is the National Philatelic Centre and **Post Master Gallery**, for those interested in stamps.

The tram then takes you to Victoria Parade near the corner of Nicholson Street. A short walk along Victoria Parade leads to Gisborne Street and the Eastern Hill Fire Station – headquarters of the Melbourne Fire Brigade, which houses the **Fire Services Museum** (open Friday and Sunday). In Melbourne's early days, the site was one of the highest spots, and a fire-watch could be kept from the lookout tower. **St Patrick's Cathedral** also fronts Gisborne Street. Built of massive bluestone, it dominates the north-east corner of the city. Further south is Parliament Place, and on your left the elegant Tasma Terrace, which houses the head office of the National Trust where you can gather information on their properties.

Continue south to Spring Street, the centre of State government. At the top of Bourke Street is the **Parliament of Victoria**, a classical-style building; when Parliament is not sitting there are free guided tours. Across the street is **The Windsor Hotel**, grandest of Melbourne's hotels, and a block to the north is the beautifully restored **Princess Theatre**.

Victorian Arts Centre spire

MELBOURNE ON FOOT

Aboriginal Heritage Walk
With an Aboriginal guide, explore the culture of the Bunurong and Woiwurrung people in their traditional camping place, now the Royal Botanic Gardens; bookings essential; charge applies

Art and About
Tours through Melbourne's cultural precincts and galleries (Mon.–Fri.); bookings essential

Chinatown Heritage Walk
Includes Chinese Museum; bookings essential; charge applies

Chocolate Indulgence
Walk around major chocolate outlets; bookings essential; charge applies

City Pub Walks
Young locals introduce you to Melbourne nightlife; bookings essential; charge applies

Melbourne Cemetery
Melbourne's history brought to life; bookings essential; charge applies

Melbourne City Walks – Historic and Heritage
Seven self-guide walks providing an insight into the city's history and architecture

Murders and Mysteries Tour
Night tour examining some of the murders and unsolved mysteries around Melbourne; bookings essential; charge applies

Queen Victoria Market – Foodies Dream Tour
Tour of this famous market; bookings essential; charge applies

Royal Botanic Gardens
Guided walk, free of charge

For further information, contact the **Melbourne Visitor Information Centre**

ENTERTAINMENT

*Melbourne has entertainment for every taste. There's the **Victorian Arts Centre** on St Kilda Road for theatre, opera and ballet, and next to it the **Melbourne Concert Hall** for classical music. In the city, the **Princess Theatre**, the **Regent Theatre** and the **Athenaeum Theatre** show musicals and popular theatrical productions, while more experimental theatre is alive at smaller venues. If you are looking for nightlife, you will find lots of wine bars and jazz bars in town, especially in Flinders Lane, Little Collins Street and Swanston Street. There are also nightclubs in **South Yarra** and **Commercial Road**, Prahran. The young at heart may be amused at **Luna Park**, the funfair at St Kilda.*
*During the summer there are open-air performances of theatre in the parks and gardens, concerts at the **Sidney Myer Music Bowl**, and twilight jazz at the **Melbourne Zoo**. The **Crown Entertainment Complex** includes everything from nightclubs to cinemas. Melburnians love going to the cinema, and, apart from the large chains, there are numerous independent screens. The Age newspaper includes a supplement on Fridays, EG, that lists everything going on in town. Use it to find what bands are playing, as Melbourne pubs host all kinds of gigs: rock, jazz, country and folk. Stand-up comedy is also a tradition in pubs; check EG for venues.*

The **Old Treasury Museum** stands just south of MacArthur Street. Built in 1853, it has been refurbished and houses Melbourne Exhibition, an exhibition on Melbourne's fine architecture and colourful social history; and Built on Gold, a display in the historic basement gold vaults. Nearby are the **Treasury Gardens**, a delightful park full of huge old trees; beside its lake is the J. F. Kennedy Memorial.

From Spring Street wander west down Collins Street. You will pass **The Melbourne Club**, mecca to the Establishment, on your right. Opposite is **Collins Place**, an impressive multi-storey complex with many shops and a Sunday market. Continue down the hill past the exclusive shops until you reach **St Michael's Uniting Church** and, opposite this, the **Grand Hyatt Melbourne** hotel complex, with its interesting food hall and shopping plaza. **The Scots Church** is just over the road and, if you continue west, the graceful porticoed **Melbourne Baptist Church** is a little further on.

The **Melbourne Town Hall** stands on the corner of Collins and Swanston streets (as does a statue dear to Melburnians, the statue of the famous explorers Burke and Wills); the Melbourne Visitor Information Centre is in the town hall. On the right,

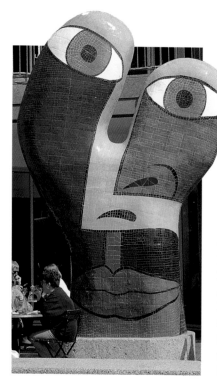

Southgate sculpture

just before the next major intersection, is the **Block Arcade** on Collins Street. This elegant precinct is the oldest arcade in Australia, and has a mosaic floor, glass and iron-lace roof and stylish shops. The arcade leads to Block Place and Little Collins Street and another gracious arcade, the **Royal Arcade**, where large gilded statues of Gog and Magog strike the hour. Do not miss the magnificent **ANZ Bank** building on the corner of Collins and Elizabeth streets, a wonderful example of 19th-century Gothic Revival architecture, with an elaborate carved facade. Its palatial banking hall, with gold leaf, pilasters and mouldings, is a reminder of a vanished era. Inside are historical displays in the **ANZ Banking Museum** (open Monday to Friday).

Turn north along Bourke Street. It becomes a mall at Elizabeth Street, and you can sit and watch the buskers. Be careful when crossing the mall, though, as trams run through it. The mall has humorous sculptures, and a Half-Tix booth where you can buy reduced-price theatre tickets for the day's performances. There is also a visitor information booth, and shopping and sightseeing tram tours depart from here (bookings are essential). As well, the mall is home to the **General Post Office** and two department stores, **Myer** and **David Jones**. These huge shops extend over several blocks, and vie with each other for fine window displays, especially at Christmas.

Further along Bourke Street, towards Parliament of Victoria, you will find a mixture of bookshops and bistros. The coffee bar at **Pellegrini's** is an old favourite, while on the Spring Street corner is the up-beat **Hard Rock Cafe**. For a different perspective, walk along Little Bourke Street, one block north. Between Spring and Swanston streets is Melbourne's **Chinatown**, packed with fascinating restaurants and shops. In the heart of Chinatown, at Cohen Place off Little Bourke Street, the colourful **Chinese Museum** is worth a visit. You can see a 92-metre-long dragon that walks Melbourne's streets at Moomba and Chinese New Year, and the basement has a fascinating glimpse of life on the goldfields for Chinese immigrants last century.

Yarra River and Melbourne skyline

For a different cultural experience, visit Lonsdale Street between Swanston and Russell streets. Cafes playing Greek music and shops selling pastries make this a mini-Athens. Further east towards Spring Street is the **Koorie Heritage Centre**, which provides an insight into Aboriginal cultural life in Victoria. You will find commercial galleries of Aboriginal art at the top end of Flinders Lane.

DOCKLANDS DEVELOPMENT

The vast area that was Melbourne's docklands is being redeveloped, and will be a major new waterfront area, with a promenade, parks, restaurants and sporting facilities, and a mixture of houses and businesses surrounding a marina.

Closest to the city is the **Colonial Stadium**, with a retractable roof and seating for 52 000. The Stadium is designed to convert from a sporting area to an entertainment venue, and promises to be the focus for this exciting addition to the varied life of the city.

SOUTH OF THE RIVER

The south side of the Yarra River has many attractions. The ***Polly Woodside*** is a restored 1885 square-rigged sailing ship that stands in a wooden-walled dry dock. It is run by the National Trust, and there is an interesting maritime

museum here. Next to the *Polly Woodside* is the **Melbourne Exhibition Centre**, with its striking entrance angled upward over the water. Walking east along the riverbank, you next reach the **Crown Entertainment Complex**, which contains a casino as well as shops, restaurants, nightclubs and cinemas. Walk into the magnificent atrium at its east end (the Crown Towers hotel) where music, lights and water are choreographed in a dazzling display. Continuing east you reach **Southgate**, an exciting development of restaurants, shops, wine bars and outdoor eating areas. Melburnians flock to this spot to sip cappuccinos as they watch the world go by. Many river cruises and ferries depart from the dock here.

The Southgate promenade ends at St Kilda Road, where the arts precinct begins. The **Melbourne Concert Hall** is used for classical music and large concerts. It also houses the **Performing Arts Museum**, which offers a programme of regularly changing exhibitions covering the whole spectrum of performing arts. Alongside the Concert Hall, the **Victorian Arts Centre**, with its distinctive spire that is lit at night, contains three theatres: the State Theatre, used for opera, ballet and large musicals; the Playhouse, for drama; and the George Fairfax Studio, for experimental productions. The Performing Arts

HISTORY

Melbourne was founded in 1835, when John Batman and John Pascoe Fawkner sailed from Tasmania and settled at the mouth of the Yarra River. Gold was discovered in 1851 in Victoria, and Melbourne grew quickly over the next 30 years, as wealth poured into it. Many of its gracious wide streets were laid out at this time, resulting in a legacy of elegant mansions and well-proportioned terrace houses, with cast-iron verandahs and balconies, that give charm to Melbourne's streetscape today. The trams that are so much a part of Melbourne were introduced early, horsedrawn at first, and electrified early this century.

PARKS AND GARDENS

Melburnians are extremely proud of their extensive parks and public gardens, some of which are listed below.

Map Ref.

ALBERT PARK
Venue of the Formula One Grand Prix, with lake, cafes and playground — 213 K10

BRIMBANK PARK
Showcase for native plants; children's farm — 212 G5

BURNLEY GARDENS
Horticultural gardens with superb displays — 213 M9

CARLTON GARDENS
Site of the Royal Exhibition Building — 210 F3

ELTHAM LOWER PARK
Miniature steam-train rides — 213 P5

FAWKNER PARK
Oasis in 19th-century tradition — 213 L10

FITZROY GARDENS
With Captain Cook's Cottage; the Fairy Tree; and Model Tudor Village — 210 H6

FLAGSTAFF GARDENS
Historical associations and shady trees — 210 B6

GASWORKS PARK
Sculptures, playground and native garden in a park setting — 213 K10

JELLS PARK
127 hectares with the large Wildlife Lake; watch the waterbirds — 213 R12

KINGS DOMAIN
Huge park south of the river containing the Sidney Myer Music Bowl and Shrine of Remembrance — 210 G10

MUSEUM OF MODERN ART AT HEIDE
Sculpture gardens around museum lead down to the Yarra River — 213 O6

ROYAL BOTANIC GARDENS
Melbourne's showpiece — 210 I12

ROYAL PARK
Large park with many sporting facilities and the Melbourne Zoo — 213 K7

TREASURY GARDENS
At dusk you can see many possums — 210 G7

WATTLE PARK
Bushland retreat with many native birds — 213 O10

WESTERFOLDS PARK
Large park beside the Yarra River — 213 P5

YARRA BEND PARK
Last refuge of bushland in inner-city Melbourne; boathouses with canoe hire — 213 L7

Museum has exhibitions in the foyer of the Victorian Arts Centre. Nearby, in Sturt Street, **The C.U.B. Malthouse** contains two more theatres. Next door to the Victorian Arts Centre is the massive bluestone **National Gallery of Victoria**, which is undergoing major renovations until 2002. Some of its collection is on display at the former Museum of Victoria in Russell Street, while some is touring Victoria's regional centres.

Across St Kilda Road is the **Floral Clock**; behind it stretches a superb series of parks. Alexandra Gardens is on the water's edge, Queen Victoria Gardens in front of you and the trees of Kings Domain behind. In the latter is the **Sidney Myer Music Bowl**, used in summer for outdoor concerts; **Government House**, with its prominent white tower (open to visitors on the third Sunday in October); and the majestic, pyramid-style **Shrine of Remembrance**, which dominates St Kilda Road. Kings Domain is also home to **La Trobe's Cottage**, on Dallas Brooks Drive. This quaint cottage was Victoria's first Government House. It was imported from England by the first Governor (La Trobe) in prefabricated sections. It is now a National Trust property, furnished with many of La Trobe's belongings. Adjacent is the **Australian Centre for Contemporary Art**.

Immediately north are the wonderful **Royal Botanic Gardens**, established in 1846 and covering more than 35 hectares. There are several entrances, but the most interesting is **Observatory Gate** in Birdwood Avenue. With lush, landscaped gardens and lawns, attractive trees and shrubs and ornamental lakes, the gardens are a peaceful retreat. The rainforest fern-gully is home to fruit bats. In the gardens are tearooms, a cafe, a gift shop and a garden shop, a Visitors Centre – guided walks depart from here at 11 a.m. and 2 p.m. daily, Sunday to Friday – and the restored Old Observatory which offers star-viewing as part of its night tours. On summer evenings, the gardens host various theatrical performances and a moonlit cinema. Alexandra Avenue, on the river side of the Botanic Gardens, is one of Melbourne's prettiest streets. Barbecues are dotted along the riverbank and provide a focus for Melburnians to gather and watch the rowing crews at training.

AFL Grand Final, Melbourne Cricket Ground

INNER SOUTH-EAST

Toorak and **South Yarra** are areas of fine shopping, great food and vibrant life, with expensive houses tucked away. **Fawkner Park**, off Toorak Road, offers a refuge in 19th-century tradition, with orderly avenues, playing ovals and lawns. Take a tram along **Toorak Road** – known for its elegant boutiques carrying designer labels, expensive restaurants and gourmet food shops – to the **Como Centre**, at the Chapel Street intersection, which has a large food plaza, shops and a cinema.

Chapel Street is the haunt of the younger crowd, and is lined with bistros, cafes and trendy fashion outlets. The **Jam Factory** is a shopping precinct developed within an old factory. On the opposite side of Chapel Street, on the corner of Commercial Road, the traditional **Prahran Market** springs to life on Tuesdays, and Thursdays to Saturdays. A block south is **Greville Street**, a funky mix of clubs and shops.

High Street is the next main road crossing Chapel Street, and a tram will take you east along High Street to **Armadale**, centre of the antique trade. There are also art and craft galleries, and designer clothes shops stretching for several blocks along High Street. Turning north along Orrong or Kooyong roads will bring you back to Toorak; the area bounded by Malvern Road to the south, and the river to the north, is full of imposing gates and high walls screening huge mansions.

The National Trust mansion **Como** is at the north end of Williams Road. It is set in pleasant gardens and is a perfect example of 19th-century colonial grandeur. Parkland stretches from the house down to the river, and from here you can see **Herring Island**. A constructed island, formed when the river's path was altered, it is now an environmental sculpture park, but is accessible only by water. A punt service operates from Como Landing at weekends, 12 noon to 6 p.m.

INNER NORTH

The suburbs of **North Melbourne**, **Carlton** and **Fitzroy** are mainly residential, but with many interesting sights. Carlton has one of the largest concentrations of Victorian houses in Melbourne. Its shady wide streets and squares of restored terraces can make you forget you are within walking distance of a modern city. **Brunswick Street** in Fitzroy is, by contrast, alive with young style: boutiques and bookshops sit next to pubs and restaurants. At the city end is the **Mary MacKillop Foundation**, where there is memorabilia and information about Australia's beatified nun.

From Brunswick Street you can cut through to **Carlton Gardens**, and its domed **Royal Exhibition Building**. Built for the Great Exhibition of 1880, trade and public exhibitions are still held here. In Carlton Gardens you will also find the new **Melbourne Museum**. Adjacent is the **IMAX Theatre** where you can enjoy movies on an immense screen. **Lygon Street** lies a block west of Carlton Gardens. Known locally as 'little Italy', it is lined with restaurants,

delicatessens, bookshops and boutiques. Also on Lygon Street is the **Trades Hall** building (1859), the world's oldest operating trade union building.

Carlton is the home of the **University of Melbourne**. In its grounds – a mixture of original ivy-clad buildings and modern blocks – are three museums. The **Ian Potter Museum of Art** is on Swanston Street and the **Grainger Museum**, a collection of memorabilia, including instruments, belonging to the composer Percy Grainger, is on Royal Parade. The **Medical History Museum** is in the Medical building near the corner of Grattan Street and Royal Parade. Nearby is the leafy suburb of **Parkville**, another pocket of gracious Victorian terraces.

South of the university on Victoria Street is the **Queen Victoria Market** – a Melbourne institution. Here you will find a huge variety of all sorts of food – meat, vegetables, breads and cheeses – plus clothing, plants and souvenirs. It is open Tuesdays and Thursdays to Sundays.

Further north lies **Royal Park**, home of many sporting facilities and the **Melbourne Zoo**. The zoo prides itself on making the enclosures as large and natural as possible. See the magnificent collection of butterflies in the walk-through butterfly house, and lions at play from the safety of a 'people cage' – an enclosed bridge that takes you through the lions' enclosure. The primates have also been housed in extensive, natural environments into which humans gaze from small

SPORT

*If you love sport, you'll love Melbourne. There's always something to watch, and to take part in. The facilities are superb, with the **Melbourne Cricket Ground** the venue for the Australian Football League (AFL) and cricket, including World Series Cricket, and a Test Match that starts every Boxing Day. Alongside, **Melbourne Park**, a wonderful multipurpose venue with a retractable roof, hosts the Australian Open tennis in January and basketball matches throughout the year. Nearby **Olympic Park** is home to the Melbourne Storm rugby league team. The Australian Formula One Grand Prix is raced in **Albert Park**, around the lake, every March. Throughout the winter months you'll see eager football supporters dressed in their team colours every weekend cheering on their Australian Rules team – Melbourne has nine teams. In late October, Melbourne goes to the races in a big way for the Spring Racing Carnival, culminating in the Melbourne Cup at **Flemington** racecourse, which brings the State to a halt on the first Tuesday in November. Albert Park has recently been redeveloped, its new facilities including the state-of-the-art **Melbourne Sports and Aquatic Centre**, as well as a public golf course and driving range, while the **Docklands** now have a new stadium with retractable roof.*

St Kilda Pier and kiosk

West Gate Bridge

galleries. To finish your tour of the northern suburbs, take a cruise on the **Maribyrnong River**; boats leave from near the Dynon Bridge, Footscray.

BAYSIDE

Melbourne's seaside suburbs are diverse. Directly south-west out of the city along City Road is **Port Melbourne**. Once a working-class area with light industry, this area is being redeveloped and the houses restored. **Station Pier**, now the departure point for the *Spirit of Tasmania*, was the introduction to Australia for many thousands of migrants.

Beaconsfield Parade, which runs along the Port Phillip foreshore, takes you to the suburb of **South Melbourne** with its leafy streets and trendy outdoor cafes. The Chinese Temple of See Yup Society in Clarendon Street, a 19th-century temple, is still a place of worship. Further around the bay from South Melbourne lies **Albert Park**. The Albert Park Lake, formed as a result of draining a swamp, is covered with small boats at weekends, with joggers, walkers and cyclists circling its perimeter all week. The park is the venue for the Australian Formula 1 Grand Prix each March, but the grandstands are temporary so for much of the year there is no evidence of Formula 1. The park is home to many sports, with facilities for badminton, table tennis and soccer, and the **Melbourne Sports and Aquatic Centre**, the nation's largest integrated sport and leisure facility.

Next around the bay is the cosmopolitan **St Kilda**. Roller-bladers weave between walkers, and the **St Kilda Pier** is always busy. On the foreshore you will find South Pacific St Kilda, a fitness complex with heated indoor pool, shops and restaurant. Other restaurants overlook the foreshore, and in nearby **Fitzroy Street**, grand old hotels have been restored as stylish cafes, cinemas and restaurants. Nearby, along the beach are the funfair **Luna Park**, and the enormous **Palais Theatre**. And on Sundays art and craft stalls appear on The Esplanade, which winds around to Acland Street famous for its luscious cakes. Just around the corner is the St Kilda Botanical Garden. A short distance away is the **Jewish Museum of Australia**, in Alma Road.

South of St Kilda lie Hampton and **Brighton**. Brighton Beach has a colourful line of bathing boxes, and is a favourite with Melburnians in summer. Elwood, the next suburb, is a quiet family area. Inshore, at Hotham Street in Elsternwick stands **Rippon Lea**, a National Trust property. This Romanesque mansion, open daily, has beautiful English-style landscaped gardens and strutting peacocks. Yet further around the bay is **Black Rock** with its family atmosphere, and the additional attraction of **HMVS *Cerberus*** offshore. The *Cerberus* was commissioned by Victoria in 1866, to counter the threat of a Russian attack. Its naval career over, it was scuttled as a breakwater in 1926.

SOUTH-WESTERN SUBURBS

South-west of the city lies Melbourne's oldest suburb, **Williamstown**. To reach it, take a ferry or the West Gate Freeway. The **West Gate Bridge** is a marvel of modern engineering, taking you over the wide river to **Spotswood**. The award-winning science and technology museum, **Scienceworks**, is here. There are hands-on, high-tech exhibitions, a new Planetarium, Australia's first plane and car, and the opportunity to see the Victorian sewage pumping station that serviced Melbourne. Scienceworks is fascinating and well worth a visit.

The route to Williamstown takes you through Newport, where there is a **Railway Museum** on Champion Road. Open only weekend afternoons, it contains an extraordinary collection of old steam locomotives. Williamstown itself, a former maritime village, has many quaint seafront pubs, churches and cottages. It was somewhat cut off from Melbourne until the West Gate Bridge was built, and retains an independent atmosphere. At weekends you can tour HMAS *Castlemaine*, a World War II minesweeper restored by the Maritime Trust, and see model ships, early costumes and relics at the **Maritime Museum**.

EASTERN SUBURBS

The **Fitzroy Gardens**, on Wellington Parade, is a good spot to begin an exploration of Melbourne's east. A Model Tudor Village, the Fairies Tree – with its carved trunk – and Captain Cook's Cottage are just some of its attractions. The cottage, the home of Captain Cook's family in Yorkshire, was re-erected here in 1934 to commemorate Melbourne's centenary.

Across Wellington Parade is the tiny suburb of Jolimont and the **Melbourne Cricket Ground** – the MCG. Holding about 100 000 people, this complex is the focus for much of Melbourne's sport, and major concerts are held here too. Outside the Members' entrance is the **Australian Gallery of Sport**, which celebrates Australian sporting history. There is also an **Olympic Museum** and, in the Members' Pavilion, a **Melbourne Cricket Club Museum**. A footbridge over the railway takes you to **Melbourne Park**, home of The Australian Open tennis tournament; the **Melbourne Sports and Entertainment Centre** (known as the Glasshouse) is close by.

Four major roads head east out from the city centre, each catering to particular tastes. The most southerly, **Swan Street**, is a centre for Greek culture and home to a horticultural college whose gardens are superb. Parallel to Swan Street is **Bridge Road**, a mecca for the fashion-conscious, with its many designer-label factory outlets. Further north again, **Victoria Street** is the Vietnamese area of Melbourne, and dozens of restaurants offer affordable and interesting food. Finally, **Johnston Street** takes you over the Yarra River into Studley Park and the huge **Yarra Bend Park** which runs north past the Eastern Freeway. Raheen, a grand mansion on Studley Park Road, is now owned privately but was originally built as the Catholic archbishop's palace. Turn down Yarra Boulevard to drive along the river. **Studley Park Boathouse** is a pleasant spot for a rest, and you can hire a canoe here. North-east over the Eastern Freeway is the **Museum of Modern Art at Heide**; set in the tranquil parklands of Bulleen, and one of Australia's most renowned art spaces, it houses a collection of the great Australian Modernists and new artists.

The magnificent, wide, tree-lined avenues; the understorey of Victorian-era facades; the shopping and eating precincts both riverside and in the inner suburbs; the huge areas of beautiful parkland in the heart of the city; the international cultural and sporting events: all justify Melbourne's plaudit as the 'world's most liveable city'.

RESTAURANTS AND CAFES

Melbourne prides itself on the variety and standard of its restaurants and cafes. Many restaurants are BYO – bring your own wine or beer (there is usually a small charge for corkage).

Map Ref.

SOUTHGATE & THE CROWN ENTERTAINMENT COMPLEX
A variety of modern cafes, bistros, takeaways and restaurants along the riverbank   210 E9

LITTLE BOURKE STREET, CITY
The heart of Chinatown, with terrific Chinese restaurants at all price ranges   210 E6

LYGON STREET, CARLTON
Italian pasta, pizza and gelati, in traditional style   210 E4

VICTORIA STREET, ABBOTSFORD
A bustling road full of inexpensive Vietnamese establishments   213 L8

BRUNSWICK STREET, FITZROY
Trendy cafes and bistros for up-to-the-minute style   213 K8

TOORAK ROAD & CHAPEL STREET, PRAHRAN
The place to be seen, in drop-dead stylish surroundings   213 L10

SWAN STREET, RICHMOND
For authentic Greek cuisine   213 L9

ACLAND STREET, ST KILDA
Cafe society and luxury cakes   213 K11

FITZROY STREET, ST KILDA
Almost a hundred restaurants in this cosmopolitan strip   213 K11

Tram in East Melbourne

DAY TOURS
from Melbourne

Some of Australia's most beautiful and interesting tours start from Melbourne and include stunning scenery, historic towns, wine-growing regions and wildlife experiences. The areas surrounding Melbourne are as varied as its climate: whether your preference is sea and sand, mountains and wooded hills, animals or historical excursions, there is a trip to suit you.

SOVEREIGN HILL

111 km to Ballarat via Western Freeway `M8`
Sovereign Hill, Ballarat, is arguably the world's most authentic reconstruction of a 19th-century goldmining township. The first gold was discovered in the 1850s, and the cities and towns that developed reached their peak of affluence in the 1880s. **Ballarat**, one of the major cities of the region, was also the site of the 1854 Eureka rebellion, when miners refused to pay government licence fees

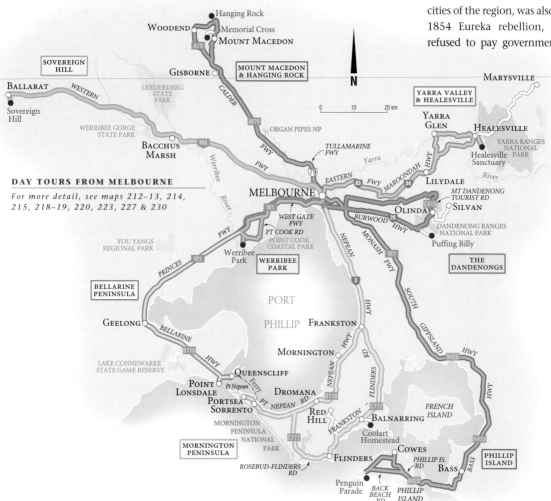

DAY TOURS FROM MELBOURNE

For more detail, see maps 212–13, 214, 215, 218–19, 220, 223, 227 & 230

National Rhododendron Gardens, Dandenong Ranges

and fought troops and police at the Eureka Stockade.

Leave Melbourne from its north-western end via Flemington Road, turning left onto Racecourse Road and eventually onto Ballarat Road, which becomes the Western Freeway. The drive along the Western Freeway passes the orchards near **Bacchus Marsh** and the turn-offs to Lerderderg State Park and Werribee Gorge State Park. As you approach Ballarat, look out for the turn-off on the left to Sovereign Hill.

At this re-creation of life on the gold-fields visitors can pan for gold, shop in Main Street, ride on a Cobb & Co. coach, watch a spectacular sound-and-light show on the Eureka rebellion and stay in 1850s-style accommodation. The site is divided into three parts: the Red Hill Gully diggings, which bring to life how the gold was mined; the re-creation of a goldmining township; and the Mining Museum with its guided tunnel tours.

From Sovereign Hill, drive north to Ballarat's town centre. Many areas retain much of the charm of the gold-boom era. Don't miss the Eureka Stockade Centre and the Eureka Exhibition in Eureka Street, where you can immerse yourself in the rebellion. **See also:** individual entries in A–Z listing for towns in bold type.

YARRA VALLEY AND HEALESVILLE

61 km to Healesville via Eastern Freeway ⑧₃, Springvale Road ④₀ and Maroondah Highway ③₄

In the past two decades the Yarra Valley has established itself as a premier wine-growing area, and wineries dot the landscape. The gentle slopes, temperate climate and reliable rainfall mean Yarra Valley grapes are very high quality, and produce award-winning vintages.

Leave Melbourne on the Eastern Freeway and continue along until it ends at Springvale Road. Turn right along Springvale Road for 2 kilometres, then left onto Maroondah Highway. Beyond Lilydale the valley unfolds and orchards and dairy farms dominate the landscape. At the junction of Maroondah and Melba highways is a small estate surrounded by high hedges. Dame Nellie Melba retired here once her singing days were over.

Stay on the Maroondah Highway and just past Coldstream evidence of the wine industry begins: St Huberts Vineyard is on your left, followed by Domaine Chandon, a magnificent winery constructed by Moet & Chandon, French champagne makers. There are tours, tastings of their delicious sparkling wines and spectacular views over the valley. More wineries follow, including Oakridge Estate, Badger's Brook (weekends only), and Eyton on Yarra which has a fine restaurant. Nearby are Warramate and Coldstream Hills vineyards. All these wineries welcome visitors for tastings and cellar-door sales.

Maroondah Highway leads to **Healesville**, where you can pick up a brochure on the area's wineries from the information centre in Harker Street. If you visit Healesville on a Sunday or public holiday, enjoy an open-air trolley ride towards Yarra Glen on the Yarra Valley Tourist Railway.

Take Badger Creek Road out of Healesville to reach Healesville Sanctuary, where all of Australia's distinctive fauna are displayed in one huge natural enclosure. Highlights include the World of the Platypus exhibit, and the awe-inspiring display Where Eagles Fly.

Nocturnal animals in their natural environment can also be observed during the Eco-Centre night walks at Badger Weir Park on Badger Weir Road, near the sanctuary. Another attraction for the family is Hedgend Maze, on Albert Road just off Badger Creek Road.

To return to Melbourne, take the Yarra Glen Road to **Yarra Glen**, passing other wineries, including Tarrawarra Estate, along the way. Visit the historic Gulf Station just north of Yarra Glen, on the Melba Highway, to see how a 19th-century farm worked (open Wednesday to Sunday and public holidays).

Return south along Melba Highway, past another winery, Yering Station. Nearby is Yarra Valley Dairy, off McMeikans Road, who specialise in handmade cheeses.

For a scenic extension of the tour, continue out of Healesville along the Maroondah Highway through the splendid mountain ash forests and fern gullies of **Yarra Ranges National Park** to Black Spur, and on to **Marysville**. The road twists and turns, but it is worth the drive. There are lookouts and picnic facilities along the way.

See also: National Parks and individual entries in A–Z listing for towns and parks in bold type.

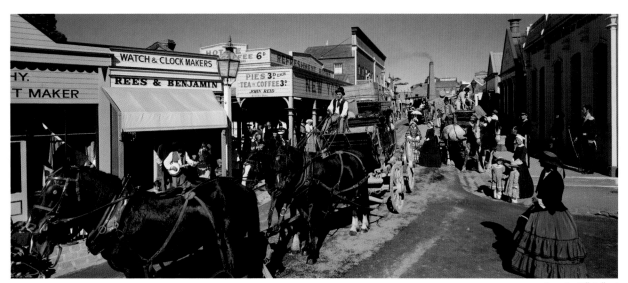

Sovereign Hill, Ballarat

PHILLIP ISLAND

142 km to Cowes via the Monash Freeway [M1] *, South Gippsland Highway* [M420] *, Bass Highway* [A420] *and Phillip Island Road* [B420] Phillip Island, at the entrance to Western Port, is renowned for its fascinating penguin parade. Koalas and seals also vie for the visitor's attention. By way of contrast, each October brings the roar of motorbikes competing in the Australian 500 cc Motorcycle Grand Prix.

Depart Melbourne on the Monash Freeway, turning onto the South Gippsland Highway and, later, the Bass Highway. Wildlife Wonderland, with its Giant Earthworm Museum, is on the southern outskirts of Bass.

Just across the San Remo bridge, stop at the Visitor Information centre at Newhaven. Half a kilometre on, turn right for Churchill Island (reached by bridge), where the historic 1862 homestead and gardens are open to the public. Just before the bridge you can visit the Big Flower Farm, which has a huge computerised glasshouse. Churchill Island also has walking trails.

Return to the Phillip Island Road and turn off to the famous surf beach at Cape Woolamai. A two-hour walk leads to the highest point on the island, from where there are breathtaking views of the coastline. The sand dunes all along the cape are the home of many short-tailed shearwaters (muttonbirds); at dusk in summer, you can see thousands of these birds returning to their burrows.

Koalas and a treetop boardwalk feature at the Koala Conservation Centre, near Five Ways. Further along Phillip Island Road towards Cowes and on your left is Phillip Island Wildlife Park, set in 32 hectares of bushland. Waterbirds can be spotted in the Rhyll swamp and bird sanctuary on the northern side of the island.

Cowes, the main town on the island and a popular summer resort, has sheltered beaches, safe for swimming, yachting and other water sports. From Cowes, take a cruise to Seal Rocks, at the south-west tip of the island, where over 10 000 fur seals sunbathe on the rocks in the breeding season.

But the greatest attraction for visitors is the parade of little (fairy) penguins on Summerland Beach, near the southwestern corner of the island. The penguins spend their day at sea catching whitebait. At sunset they return in small groups and waddle up the beach to their sand-dune burrows; visitors watch under subdued floodlights and no photography is permitted beyond the Visitor Centre. The Phillip Island Penguin Reserve is open daily (inquiries and bookings (03) 5956 8300).

Nearby, at the far south-western corner, is a big rock outcrop, The Nobbies. At high tide, see the Blow Hole in action. The Seal Rocks Sea Life Centre overlooks The Nobbies and offers visitors an interpretation of marine life in the region.

Retrace your route past Summerland Beach, then turn right down Back Beach Road. Between Berrys Beach and Pyramid Rock roads is an old chicory kiln. There are remnants of these kilns around the island, recognisable by their high-pitched roofs and chimneys. A kilometre further is the Grand Prix Circuit (for motorcycle racing) and Visitor Centre. The road soon rejoins the Phillip Island Road for your return to Melbourne. **See also:** individual entries in A–Z listing for towns in bold type.

THE DANDENONGS

50 km to Olinda via Burwood Highway [26] *and Mount Dandenong Tourist Road* [C415] The **Dandenong Ranges** are renowned for their beauty; spectacular hills and gullies are crowded with creepers, tree ferns and soaring mountain ash. The area is also famous for its beautiful gardens and its great variety of European trees, particularly attractive in spring and autumn. Many excellent restaurants, art and craft galleries, antique shops and plant nurseries add to the Dandenongs' charm.

Leave Melbourne via Toorak Road, which becomes Burwood Highway, and continue along the highway until you reach Ferntree Gully. A few hundred metres past Ferntree Gully, the Mount Dandenong Tourist Road branches to the left.

If you want to ride on Puffing Billy, continue to Belgrave along Monbulk Road. Puffing Billy, a Melbourne institution, is a narrow-gauge steam train. It runs several times daily (except Christmas Day) to **Emerald** and Gembrook along a restored line.

Turning onto Mount Dandenong Tourist Road, from the Burwood Highway, the road climbs steeply through the **Dandenong Ranges National Park**, with many hairpin bends. Around Ferny Creek you may see evidence of the 1997 bushfire that engulfed the area. The next township is Sherbrooke, a stronghold for the elusive lyrebird. Just past Sherbrooke, turn right onto Sherbrooke Road, which leads to the Alfred Nicholas Memorial Gardens. The 13 hectares of gardens, with ornamental lake, is well worth a visit. Nearby is another fine public garden – Pirianda Gardens, with a mixture of native and exotic plants.

Return to the Mount Dandenong Tourist Road and continue to Sassafras and then **Olinda**, where tearooms and craft shops ensure a pleasant stop. Turn right onto Olinda–Monbulk Road and then left onto Falls Road to visit the 43-hectare National Rhododendron Gardens. In spring the thousands of azaleas and rhododendron bushes are a blaze of colour. A little further south-east along Olinda–Monbulk Road is the Cloudehill garden and winery.

Spring is also the season to enjoy Tesselaar's Tulip Festival at Silvan, still further south-east along Olinda–Monbulk Road. Along the way, stop at the R. J. Hamer Forest Arboretum, with its thousands of native and exotic trees.

Return to Mount Dandenong Tourist Road and just past Olinda, turn left along Ridge Road to Mt Dandenong Lookout with its superb views over Melbourne. Just past the lookout is the William Ricketts Sanctuary. Ricketts, who died in 1993, sculpted Aboriginal figures and symbolic scenes in clay.

The Mount Dandenong Tourist Road passes Kalorama – notice the magnificent view east over the Silvan Reservoir – and then winds down to Montrose, where you join Canterbury Road for the return to Melbourne. **See also:** National Parks and individual entries in A–Z listing for parks and towns in bold type.

MORNINGTON PENINSULA

100 km to Portsea via Nepean Highway ③ *and Point Nepean Road* B110
The promontory separating Port Phillip and Western Port is a mix of countryside and seaside towns with safe bayside beaches and ocean surf beaches. Be safe: swim only at surf beaches controlled by the Surf Lifesaving Association, and then only between the flags. The peninsula has many wineries, especially on its ridge, with cellar-door sales. Berries grow well too, and in season you can pick your own.

Take St Kilda Road out of the city centre; it becomes the Nepean Highway and follows the foreshore of Port Phillip through Frankston and **Mornington**, then skirts inland near Mount Martha. Here you can visit The Briars Homestead, an 1840s homestead whose first owner collected artifacts connected with Napoleon.

The Highway returns to the sea at Dromana, where, set back from the road, is Heronswood, a delightful exhibition garden and homestead. Just past Dromana, take the turn-off to Arthur's Seat. Here there is a chairlift to the top of the hill from which there are magnificent views across Port Phillip and Bass Strait. Return to the foreshore and continue on to McCrae, with its historic 1844 homestead, the first building on the peninsula.

From McCrae take the Point Nepean Road to **Sorrento**, near the site of Victoria's first official European settlement. From Sorrento you can see across the bay to **Queenscliff**, and if you are lucky you may spot bottlenose dolphins frolicking in the waters; a regular ferry from Sorrento crosses to Queenscliff.

Four kilometres further along is Portsea, an exclusive holiday destination. Beyond Portsea, the road takes you to Point Nepean in **Mornington Peninsula National Park**, where forts were built to protect Port Phillip. The national park stretches along the south coast of the peninsula, taking in Cape Schanck and its historic 1858 limestone lighthouse. Be careful: occasional freak waves make walking on the rocks around the lighthouse hazardous. There are self-guide coastal walks between Bushranger Bay and the lighthouse, and at London Bridge, an unusual natural arch on Portsea surf beach.

To drive to Cape Schanck Lighthouse, retrace the route to just before Rosebud, then take the Boneo Road which becomes the Rosebud–Flinders Road, and take the turn-off to the lighthouse. The Rosebud – Flinders Road leads to **Flinders**, a quiet holiday resort facing Western Port and Phillip Island. From Flinders drive past Shoreham and Point Leo – another surf beach – to Balnarring. If you detour inland towards Red Hill, just after Shoreham, you will find Ashcombe Maze, a huge hedge maze, and at Red Hill, if you are there on the first Saturday of the months September to May, you will find yourself in the thick of a terrific market.

At Balnarring turn right for the small township of Somers and the Coolart Homestead. This mansion, built in the 1890s, has 27 rooms, and its gardens include a lagoon with a prolific wetland bird population.

Rejoin the Frankston–Flinders road for Melbourne. **See also:** National Parks and individual entries in A–Z listing for parks and towns in bold type.

WERRIBEE PARK

35 km to Werribee Park via West Gate Freeway and Princes Freeway M1
Just outside Werribee, an outer suburb of Melbourne, is Werribee Park, a large

Little (fairy) penguins, Phillip Island

estate with a magnificent Italianate mansion of some sixty rooms, built in the 1870s for the Chirnside brothers, who had established a pastoral empire in the western district. Now owned by the Victorian government, Werribee Park is open daily.

Leave Melbourne on the West Gate Freeway; the West Gate Bridge over the Yarra River is a superb engineering feat. Further along the freeway is the turnoff to Werribee Park.

The two-storey mansion is made of sandstone, with a tower and colonnade. Inside it is opulent, with many pillars, and gold leaf around the mouldings. The gardens have a formal parterre, while the lake has a grotto on its island.

Next to the mansion is the Victoria State Rose Garden, with 4500 types of roses. In late spring and early summer it is not to be missed. Victoria's Open Range Zoo is close by; climb aboard a safari bus and drive through enclosures to see the giraffes, zebras, white rhinos, cheetahs, antelopes and hippos.

Drive back along K Road towards Werribee, then turn right for Point Cook, which is at the end of Aviation Road. Point Cook RAAF Base museum is the premier aviation museum in Australia. A platform gives a view of 16 historic aircraft, lovingly restored. Next to the airbase is Point Cook Coastal Park, where you can picnic and watch wetland species, including pelicans, while children play on a nautical theme playground. Take Point Cook Road north to rejoin the freeway for Melbourne.

BELLARINE PENINSULA

103 km to Queenscliff via the West Gate Freeway, Princes Freeway **M1** *, Bellarine Highway* **B110**

This tour around the peninsula passes through numerous seaside villages that are busy in summer with holiday visitors.

Leave Melbourne on the West Gate Freeway and take the Princes Freeway to **Geelong**. Look right for the signs to Little River; the You Yangs, a range of granite peaks, rise steeply from the volcanic plain nearby. Geelong, Victoria's second largest city, is the starting place for exploring the Bellarine Peninsula.

Leave Geelong on the Bellarine Highway. If you are interested in birds, take the turnoff to Lake Connewarre State Game Reserve, where there are many wetland species. If there are kids on board, Country Connection Adventure Park and A Maze'N Things (a timber maze, with mini-golf and a cafe) are located near Wallington.

Continue along the Bellarine highway to **Queenscliff**, at the south-east end of the peninsula, one of Melbourne's favourite seaside resorts. From Queenscliff you can see across to the Mornington Peninsula, and watch huge tankers and container ships sailing into Port Phillip; you can also catch a car or passenger ferry to **Sorrento**.

Point Lonsdale is close to Queenscliff, but faces the ocean and The Rip; it has a surf back beach, as well as a sandy front beach. Visit the lighthouse that guides ships into Port Phillip through the dangers of The Rip; tours on Sunday mornings, book through the Queenscliff Maritime Centre. **See also:** individual entries in A–Z listing for towns in bold type.

MOUNT MACEDON AND HANGING ROCK

70 km to Hanging Rock via Tullamarine Freeway and Calder Freeway **M79**

This day tour is one of contrasts: a marvellous geological formation, superb European-style gardens and a mysterious Australian icon.

Leave Melbourne on the Tullamarine Freeway, which becomes the Calder Freeway. At Organ Pipes National Park there is a short walk from the carpark to Jacksons Creek, where you see extraordinary lava formations that resemble huge organ pipes running vertically up the 22-metre cliff. A stone mosaic, the Tessellated Pavement, and the Rosette Rock are also fascinating.

Continue north-west along the Calder Freeway past Gisborne, then turn right for Mount Macedon and Hanging Rock. After Macedon the road starts to climb. At the turn of the century, wealthy Melburnians built summer houses on the cool slopes and surrounded them with extensive gardens. At the mountain top (via Cameron Drive) is a huge cross, a memorial to the fallen in World War I, and superb views. A bush trail leads to the outcrop called The Camel's Hump.

Hanging Rock is about 12 kilometres north; the route is well signposted. The Rock imprinted itself on Australian psyches with the novel and subsequent film *Picnic at Hanging Rock*, which tell of the mysterious disappearance of a group of schoolgirls. Today the Rock is a popular spot for a picnic and a climb to the top to soak in its atmosphere. The reserve around the Rock is home to koalas and wallabies. Hanging Rock is also the venue for picnic races on New Year's Day and Australia Day.

From Hanging Rock return to Melbourne via **Woodend**, a historic country town on the Calder Freeway. **See also:** individual entries in A–Z listing for towns in bold type.

Colourful bollards near Cunningham Pier, Geelong

Great Ocean Tour

Geelong to Port Fairy (345 km)

The Great Ocean Road winds through some of the most dramatic scenery in Australia. It is a journey of contrasts, with a magnificent vista around every corner: massive rock formations sculpted by the waves, stunning surf beaches, and ancient rainforests. Shortly after Port Campbell, the route passes Victoria's top whale-watching spot en route to the quaint fishing village of Port Fairy. You should allow about three days to complete the tour and return to Geelong. There are numerous holiday cottages, B & Bs, motels and camping grounds all along the coast – Apollo Bay and Port Fairy would make ideal overnight stops.

❶ Port city

The tour begins in **Geelong**, set on the shores of Corio Bay, 72 kilometres from Melbourne. This large, industrial, port city has exported wool and other produce from Victoria's rich western district since the 1830s. Some of the historic bluestone warehouses remain along the waterfront, and one of these has been restored to house the fascinating National Wool Museum. Geelong's attractive Waterfront Geelong, stretching from Cunningham Pier to the art deco pavilion at Eastern Beach, is an ideal stopping place – cafes, restaurants and grassy picnic spots overlook the bay.

National Wool Museum
26 Moorabool Street
Geelong
Open: 9.30 a.m.–5 p.m. daily
Phone: (03) 5227 0701

❷ Making waves

Take the Princes Highway and join the Surf Coast Highway on the southern outskirts of Geelong. Your next destination is **Torquay**, mecca for surf enthusiasts and home of the Surfworld Surfing Museum. Visitors to the museum can make waves (in an 8-metre tank), listen to their favourite surf music and view the historic surfboard collection. Many big-name manufacturers of surfing gear are based here, including Rip Curl, Quicksilver and Rojo. If you are in the market for some discount beach gear, take a wander through the busy factory outlets adjacent to the museum.

Surfworld Surfing Museum
Beach Road
Torquay
Open: 9 a.m.–5 p.m. weekdays;
10 a.m.–4 p.m. weekends/public holidays
Phone: (03) 5261 4219

Loch Ard Gorge

❸ Hang ten

After Torquay, the Surf Coast Highway becomes the Great Ocean Road. Two kilometres from town, turn left along **Bells Beach** Road to the world-famous surf beach of the same name. Over Easter, this is the setting for one of the coveted international titles, the Bells Beach Surfing Classic. From the cliff-top car park you can usually see distinct swell lines moving towards the shore. On a good day the waves are an impressive 3–4 metres high.

If you are tempted to test the water yourself, the company, Go Ride a Wave operates regular 2-hour classes for beginners at Anglesea and Torquay; phone (03) 5263 2111 for details.

❹ Kangaroos

From Bells Beach Road, take Jarosite Road to return to the Great Ocean Road and head towards **Anglesea**. The beach at Anglesea is patrolled during the summer school holidays and on weekends from November to the end of Easter (see signs on beach for details of patrol times). If you want to stretch your legs, turn left down Purnell Street, soon after you enter town, and stop at the car park. A 3.5-kilometre circuit walk extends from here, along the cliff-top and back through heathland alongside the Anglesea Recreation Reserve.

No trip to Anglesea is complete without a visit to the golf course, where kangaroos graze the greens. From the Great Ocean Road, turn right along Noble Street after crossing the bridge and follow the signs to Anglesea Golf Club.

❺ History of the road

Return to the Great Ocean Road and turn right towards Lorne. Soon after leaving Anglesea, you crest Point Roadknight and are rewarded with a spectacular view of the coastline stretching out ahead.

After passing through Aireys Inlet, you come to the **Memorial Arch**, dedicated to those who died in World War I. The Great Ocean Road was initially a post-war project devised to employ returned soldiers; these men were later joined by the unemployed during the Great Depression of the 1930s. The connection with World War I is evident in many of the names given to features along the route – Artillery Rocks and Shrapnel Gully are two examples. It is hard to comprehend that picks, shovels and crowbars were the main tools used to carve the road out of the rocky coastline.

❻ Waterfalls

As you continue towards Lorne, the road hugs the cliffs and shoreline, with a dramatic meeting of land and sea at each bend. Lorne is a popular holiday town on the shores of Loutit Bay – and scenic, with the Otway Ranges forming a striking backdrop. The main street is a cosmopolitan mix of cafes, restaurants and shops, an ideal place to stop. Enjoy a caffe latte or an ice-cream, and watch the throng of holidaymakers.

Nearby, in the leafy, emerald folds of the Otway Ranges, is **Erskine Falls**. Take the signposted turn-off from the centre of town and follow the road as it winds up through the forest. After 8 kilometres, branch off to the Erskine Falls car park. From here it is only a short walk through the rainforest to a viewing platform overlooking the falls; follow the steps down the side of the gully to see the falls from beneath.

Otway rainforest

7 Rainforest rest

Return to the Great Ocean Road and continue south-west towards Apollo Bay. The route winds along the shore and there are lookouts at Mount Defiance, Wye River and Cape Patton. After 45 kilometres of superb coastal scenery, you arrive at Apollo Bay, where rolling hills extend down to the sea. The town is the base for the local fishing fleet, and you can buy fresh seafood down at the harbour.

After Apollo Bay, the Great Ocean Road leaves the coast, temporarily, to wind through the cool green of Otway National Park. The road is lined with a forest of tree ferns and giant mountain ash trees. No drive along the Great Ocean Road is complete without pausing at one of the beautiful pockets of rainforest, either **Maits Rest** or Melba Gully State Park (near Lavers Hill). Maits Rest is 17 kilometres from Apollo Bay on the left. An easy 40-minute boardwalk

The Twelve Apostles

circuit leads into the heart of a mossy gully, past tree ferns and ancient myrtle beech trees.

8 To the lighthouse

Continue along the Great Ocean Road for a few kilometres before turning left along Lighthouse Road to Cape Otway. The **Cape Otway Lighthouse** stands dramatically on a cliff 100 metres above the sea. Built by convicts in 1848, this remote lighthouse was accessible only by sea, until the road was completed in 1937. It is now open to the public and the historic keeper's quarters are available for accommodation (bookings must be made well in advance).

Cape Otway Lighthouse
Lighthouse Road
Cape Otway
Open: 9 a.m.–4.30 p.m. daily
Phone: (03) 5237 9240

9 The Twelve Apostles

Return to the Great Ocean Road and continue on towards Lavers Hill. The road winds inland for 29 kilometres before reaching Lavers Hill, where you can turn left to visit the other beautiful pocket of rainforest, Melba Gully State Park. Follow the signs to the car park. A boardwalk winds through the damp, mysterious world of the rainforest, across the Johanna River and past a 300-year-old tree with its impressive 27-metre girth.

After almost 40 kilometres of forest and farmland, the Great Ocean Road returns to the coast near Princetown. From this point, the road runs parallel to the

precipitous cliff-line of Port Campbell National Park. Over the years, strong waves have eroded the limestone headlands, creating huge rock stacks. For your first views of these dramatic rock formations, pull in at the lookout above Gibson Steps. If you are feeling energetic, take the steps to the base of the cliff and enjoy a stroll along the magnificent beach – the sheer size of the formations and the height of the cliff are even more apparent.

Shortly after Gibson Steps, prepare to turn left to **The Twelve Apostles** lookout. The view of these famous rock forms is one of the great highlights of the Great Ocean Road. The Twelve Apostles have a sculptural quality that makes them irresistible to amateur and professional photographers alike.

Surf Coast action

10 Shipwreck coast

Return to the Great Ocean Road and take the signposted turn-off to **Loch Ard Gorge**. The narrow gorge, which is a short walk down steep steps from the car park, was named after the ill-fated clipper *Loch Ard*, which was dashed against the rocks in 1878. Of the 54 people on board, only two survived: Tom Pearce, a crew member only 18 years old, and Eva Carmichael, a passenger of the same age, who was eventually washed into the gorge and saved by Tom. The cemetery above the gorge contains the graves of those who drowned.

11 London Bridge

Return to the Great Ocean Road and continue through the town of Port Campbell before taking the signposted turn-off to another famous sight, **London Bridge**. This was, until recently, a bridge with two 'spans' along which visitors could walk, as the water foamed beneath. In 1990 one span collapsed, leaving a couple of tourists stranded; they had to be rescued by helicopter.

12 Whale-watching

Just after Peterborough, as the Great Ocean Road turns inland again, the Bay of Islands can be seen. It contains smaller rock stacks than The Twelve Apostles, but nevertheless is a delightful sight. The tour continues though dairy country to join the Princes Highway just before **Warrnambool**.

SOUTHERN

N

If you are touring between June and September, a detour to Logans Beach is a must. Southern right whales swim from their Antarctic feeding grounds to give birth just off the beach here, and visitors are often rewarded with the sight of huge cows swimming with their calves. The turn-off along Simpson Street to Logans Beach is signposted during the whale-watching season.

Return to the Princes Highway and continue to the centre of Warrnambool. Turn left down Banyan Street to visit Flagstaff Hill Maritime Museum. The museum is a re-creation of a 19th-century port based around an original lighthouse. There are displays of Aboriginal history and other displays of shipwreck artifacts, restored ships, a working blacksmith and a shipwright.

Flagstaff Hill Maritime Museum
Merri Street
Warrnambool
Open: 9 a.m.– 5 p.m. daily
Phone: (03) 5564 7841

⑬ Extinct volcano
Twelve kilometres west of Warrnambool, to the right of the Princes Highway, is **Tower Hill State Game Reserve**, an extinct volcano with a lake in its crater. At one stage the area around the lake was heavily over-grazed, but extensive revegetation in recent years has resulted in a haven for

birdlife (around 200 species). The reserve is also a habitat for many kangaroos, koalas and emus. A one-way road circles the lake, past lookout points and pleasant picnic areas.

⑭ Fishing village
The final leg of the tour takes you a further 16 kilometres along the Princes Highway to **Port Fairy**, one of Victoria's earliest ports. The town is an enchanting mixture of historic whitewashed houses and a busy waterfront. Over 50 of the town's buildings have been classified by the National Trust. You can buy fresh seafood from the jetty on the Moyne River where the local fishing fleet moors. Alternatively, if you have come equipped, there is surf fishing on East Beach and estuary fishing on the river. For the birdwatcher, Griffiths Island, at the head of the river, is home to a huge colony of short-tailed shearwaters (muttonbirds). Between September and April as many as 15 000 birds can be seen flying in to roost every evening.

Returning to Geelong
The most direct route back to Geelong is via the Princes Highway (213 kilometres). If you have the time, there are various interesting alternative routes. One option is to retrace your steps back to the Great Ocean Road and take one of the many roads leading inland to the Princes Highway, through the dairy country around Cobden; consider stopping at Timboon Farmhouse Cheese to taste the local produce en route. Another option is to return to Lavers Hill and wind your way back to the Princes Highway through the forests of the Otway Ranges, but beware of logging trucks and take care to avoid unsealed roads after rain.

Southern right whale

Cape Otway Lighthouse

VICTORIA from A to Z

Goulburn River near Alexandra, late afternoon

Alexandra

Pop. 1859

MAP REF. 217 O1, 239 J11

Alexandra is a farming and holiday centre, 26 km W of Eildon. The nearby Goulburn River is one of the State's most important trout fisheries. **In town:** Timber and Tramway Museum in former railway station, Station St. In Downey St: National Trust-classified post office and adjacent law courts; Alexandra Potters (closed Sun.). Rotary Park, Grant St. Bush Market, Perkins St, 2nd Sat. each month (Sept.–June). Jan., Mar., Oct. and Nov.: Picnic Race Races. Easter: Art Show. June: Truck, Bus and Ute Show. Oct.: Open Gardens Weekend. Nov.: Agricultural Show; Rose Festival. **In the area:** Trout-fishing in Goulburn, Acheron and Rubicon rivers. Self-guide tourist drives, brochure available. Excellent walks at Lake Eildon National Park, 16 km E. Bonnie Doon, 37 km NE near Lake Eildon, a good base for trail-riding, bushwalking, water sports and scenic drives. McKenzie Nature Reserve, southern edge of town, virgin bushland with abundance of winter and spring orchids. Coach Stop Gallery, 8 km S. At Taggerty, 18 km S: Willowbank Gallery; bush market 4th Sat. each month. Cathedral Range State Park, 3 km S of Taggerty, for camping, bushwalking and rock climbing. **Visitor information:** 45a Grant St; (03) 5772 1100, freecall 1800 652 298.

Anglesea

Pop. 1995

MAP REF. 216 E12, 223 C11, 233 Q9

This attractive seaside town on the Great Ocean Road offers excellent swimming and surfing. The golf course is well known for the tame kangaroos that graze there. **In town:** Melaleuca Gallery, Great Ocean Rd. Coogoorah Park, on Anglesea River, a bushland reserve with waterways, islands, boardwalks, bridges and picnic areas. Viewing platform, behind town in Coalmine Rd, overlooks open-cut brown-coal mine and power station. Sept.: Angair Wildflower Festival. **In the area:** J. E. Loveridge Lookout, 1 km W. Point Roadknight beach, 2 km SW. Angahook–Lorne State Park, access from Anglesea or Aireys Inlet (11 km SW on Great Ocean Rd). At Aireys Inlet: lighthouse and horseriding. Further south, Memorial Arch, commemorating construction of Great Ocean Rd. 35-km Surf Coast Walk, from Jan Juc (south of Torquay) to Moggs Creek (south of Aireys Inlet); brochure available. Ironbark Basin Reserve, 7 km NW north off Point Addis Rd, for walks, birdlife and cliff-top views of coastline. Point Addis Koori Cultural Walk, brochure available. **Visitor information:** Jums Barbecued Chickens, 77 Great Ocean Rd; (03) 5263 2390. **See also:** Great Ocean Tour p. 159.

Apollo Bay

Pop. 979

MAP REF. 221 G12, 233 N12

The Great Ocean Road leads to this attractive coastal town, the centre for a rich dairying and fishing area and an active crayfish and abalone fishing fleet. The wooded mountainous hinterland offers memorable scenery and there is excellent sea and river fishing in the area. The rugged and beautiful coastline has been the scene of many shipwrecks in the past. **In town:** Self-guide walks, leaflet available. Bass Strait Shell Museum, Noel St. Old Cable Station Museum, Great Ocean Rd (2–5 p.m. weekends, school and public holidays). Market on foreshore each Sat. Jan.: Beach Horse Races. Mar.: Music Festival. Dec.: Aquathon (swimming and running race). **In the area:** Historical and scenic guided and self-guide drive, walking and mountainbike tours; details from information centre. Carisbrook Falls, 14 km NE on Great Ocean Rd; nearby walking tracks to spectacular views. Grey River Scenic Reserve, 24 km NE. Marriners Lookout, 1.5 km NW, for views across Skenes Creek and Apollo Bay. Crows Nest Lookout, 5 km NW, on Tuxion Rd. Paradise Scenic Reserve in beautiful Barham River Valley, 10 km NW. Beauchamp Falls, 20 km NW; scenic walk from picnic area to falls. Triplet Falls, 70 km NW via Ferguson in former timber-milling country; 450 m or 900 m walks with steep steps. In Otway National Park, 13 km SW: excellent bushwalking through park to sea; scenic Elliot River and adjacent Shelly Beach; Maits Rest rainforest boardwalk; 300-yr-old National Trust-registered native beech tree; historic Cape Otway Lighthouse (1848), 34 km SW. Melba Gully State Park, 56 km W near Lavers Hill, features fern gullies, myrtle beech trees, also glowworm habitat; self-guide rainforest walk. **Visitor information:** 155 Great Ocean Rd; (03) 5237 6529. **See also:** Great Ocean Tour p. 159.

Ararat

Pop. 6890

MAP REF. 226 B8, 233 K2, 235 K13

The Ararat gold boom came in 1857. It was short-lived and sheep farming became the basis of the town's economy. Today the town is the commercial centre of a prosperous farming and winegrowing region. The area also produces fine merino wool. The first vines in the district were planted by French settlers in 1863 and the town of Great Western, 17 km NW of Ararat, gave its name to some of Australia's most famous wines. **In town:** Historical walk/drive, brochures available. Beautiful bluestone buildings in Barkly St: post office, town hall, civic square and war memorial. Also in Barkly St, Ararat Art Gallery, a regional gallery specialising in wool and fibre pieces by leading artists.

National Parks

Although it is Australia's smallest mainland State, Victoria houses over 100 national, State, wilderness and regional parks. Victoria's parks protect representative samples of most of the State's land and vegetation types: from alps, grasslands and mallee to rainforests, tall forests, coasts, volcanic plains and heathlands. Spring and summer are the best seasons to visit parks noted for their wildflowers. In summer, sun lovers can head for parks along the coast to swim, surf, canoe, boat or fish. Autumn beckons the bushwalker, and winter means skiing at alpine parks.

AROUND MELBOURNE

At **Organ Pipes National Park**, only 20 kilometres north-west of Melbourne, there are fascinating rock formations: hexagonal basalt columns rising more than 20 metres above Jacksons Creek. These 'organ pipes' were formed when lava cooled in an ancient river bed. While this is the best-known feature of the small 121-hectare park, it is also excellent for picnics, walks and bird-observing. Nearby is the 704-hectare **Woodlands Historic Park**, which features the Woodlands Homestead, brought from Britain as a timber kit home and erected here in 1843. A favourite of bushwalkers, 40 kilometres north-east of Melbourne, is **Kinglake National Park**, where wooded valleys, fern gullies and timbered ridges provide a perfect setting for two beautiful waterfalls, Masons and Wombelano falls. From a lookout, visitors can enjoy a view of the Yarra Valley, Port Phillip Bay and the You Yangs Range.

Just 35 kilometres east of Melbourne is the green wonderland of the 3215-hectare **Dandenong Ranges National Park**. This park includes tree-fern gullies in which huge fronds of ferns form a canopy overhead, screening the sun and creating a cool, moist environment in which mosses, delicate ferns and flowers, including over 30 orchid species, all thrive. There are more than 20 native animal species, including echidnas, platypuses, ringtail possums and sugar gliders; kookaburras, rosellas and cockatoos often visit picnic areas. The spectacular rufous fantail can be seen in the summer months. There are over 100 bird species, but

MacKenzie Falls, Grampians National Park

make sure you identify them by sight, because the lyrebird can mimic many of their calls.

Mornington Peninsula National Park is probably the most interesting park close to Melbourne: in addition to its popular surf beaches, for more than 100 years the Point Nepean area of the park was out of bounds. It had associations with early settlement, quarantine, shipping and defence. As one of Victoria's major Bicentennial projects, an information centre, walking tracks, displays and other facilities were provided during 1988-9. Today the park has a total area of 2686 hectares and stretches from Point

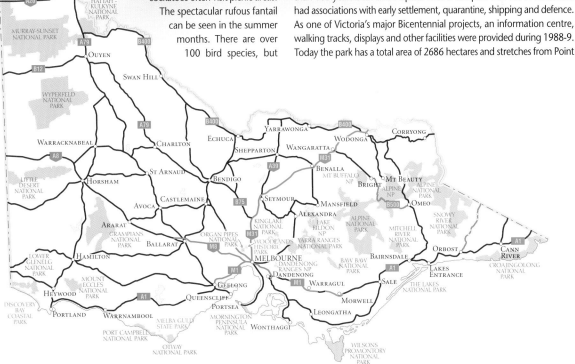

Nepean to Cape Schanck. To prevent overcrowding and damage to the environment, visitor numbers are limited in the Point Nepean section and bookings for day visits (with a park-use fee) are required. Vehicles are not permitted to the tip of Point Nepean, so walk, cycle or take the transporter. Highlights of the point are Fort Nepean, the cemetery with burials dating from the 1850s, and the fascinating Cheviot Hill and Pisterman's Track walks.

Yarra Ranges National Park is north-east of Melbourne. The majestic eucalypts and lush tree-fern glades of the Black Spur on the Maroondah Highway form a dramatic gateway to Marysville, Lake Mountain, Alexandra and Eildon. Further south, along the Yarra Valley via Warburton, is the sub-alpine environment of Mt Donna Buang. The park includes some of Melbourne's water catchment areas, generally closed to public access. The moist forests of the Yarra Ranges are of national botanical significance, and they provide vital habitats for unique animals. In particular, the forests of mountain ash – the world's tallest flowering plant – provide the habitat for Leadbeater's possum, an endangered species that is hollow-dependent. Long thought to be extinct, Leadbeater's possum was rediscovered in these forests in 1961.

COASTAL PARKS

Wilsons Promontory National Park in Gippsland is the best-known coastal park and one of the most popular in Victoria. The Prom, as it is known, has something for everyone. Amenities and accommodation, including camping and caravan sites and cabins, are located at Tidal River, as are the visitor information centre and park office. Leaflets for 150 kilometres of walking tracks are available here, and visitors should also inquire about the long but rewarding Lighthouse Walk (walker accommodation is available at the lighthouse). Other natural attractions include secluded bays and magnificent stretches of beaches, granite outcrops, and spectacular wildflowers that begin blooming in late winter and continue through spring. Wilsons Promontory is very popular, particularly in summer. Campsites are available only by ballot for the Christmas and Easter holiday periods.

The unusual rock structures found at **Port Campbell National Park** – including The Twelve Apostles, The Arch and Loch Ard Gorge – are majestic formations sculpted out of soft limestone cliffs by the relentless sea. While it is the spectacular coastal scenery that makes this park so popular, it is also an interesting park for birds, with around 100 species being recorded. The park was a popular place with Aboriginal people too, if the number of shell middens along the coast is an indication. And it is especially notorious for being part of the 'Shipwreck Coast'. Further west is **Discovery Bay Coastal Park**, which offers a rugged coastline and a broad range of fauna environments. The park is an important habitat for the endangered hooded plover, which nests in exposed situations above high-tide line.

Closer to Melbourne are the beautiful lush tree-fern gullies and towering mountain-ash forests of **Otway National Park** and the special **Melba Gully State Park** near Lavers Hill. Because of the treacherous waters of Bass Strait, a lighthouse was the first piece of 'civilisation' at Cape Otway; it was opened in 1848. Cottages adjacent to the lighthouse can be booked for accommodation. Activities include sightseeing all year (even in winter storms), while camping, surfing, fishing and walking are best in spring and summer.

Eastern Victoria, with its mild and fairly wet climate, has vast areas of dense forest. These are attractive to bushwalkers and campers, who will find here a wide range of trees — mainly eucalypts, but also native pines, banksias and paperbarks.

Some of the most attractive coastal scenery close to any major regional centre can be found in and around **The Lakes National Park**. The park is surrounded by the waters of the extensive Gippsland Lakes system, ideal for sailing, boating and fishing. The 2390-hectare park harbours a large population of kangaroos and more than 140 bird

Tidal River in Wilsons Promontory National Park

species. Camping, picnicking and a network of walking tracks cater for those who are land-based.

Croajingolong National Park has 87 500 hectares of coastline and hinterland stretching from Sydenham Inlet to the New South Wales border. The area contains remote rainforest, woodland, ocean beaches, rocky promontories, inlets and coves. Several rare species of wildlife can be found here, such as the smoky mouse and the ground parrot, and in spring the visitor will see an array of wildflowers. There is a wide range of activities for visitors at Croajingolong, with camping areas, a holiday centre at Mallacoota, and other towns along the Princes Highway offering accommodation and fine food.

IN THE NORTH-EAST OF THE STATE

The **Alpine National Park**, created in December 1989 and currently covering approximately 645 000 hectares, is the State's largest national park. Stretching along the Great Dividing Range, the park links with Kosciuszko National Park in New South Wales and its neighbour Namadgi National Park in the Australian Capital Territory in a grouping of national parks that encompasses almost all of south-east Australia's alpine areas. The park protects the habitats of a variety of flora and fauna, including the rare mountain pygmy possum (the world's only exclusively subalpine marsupial). The Alps are renowned for their sublime landscapes, features characterised by Mount Bogong and Mount Feathertop (Victoria's highest mountains) and the unique Bogong High Plains. During spring and summer the high plains are carpeted with wildflowers; more than 1100 native plant species are found in the park, including 12 found nowhere else in the world. The park is ideal for bushwalking, horseriding and cross-country skiing. Both Falls Creek and Mount Hotham ski resorts are surrounded by the Alpine National Park. In the summer months most roads provide easy access for vehicles, allowing a range of scenic drives with short walks to lookouts and other points of interest. Some huts in the park, popular places for walkers to visit, are being restored for their historic value.

Mount Buffalo National Park, north-west of Bright, encompasses Mount Buffalo plateau with its granite tors and rounded boulders. In milder weather, the park, with its bubbling streams and cascading waterfalls, offers visitors over 80 kilometres of marked walking tracks. The wildflowers on the undulating snow plains are at their best between

November and March. Wombats, wallabies, lyrebirds, rosellas and gang-gang cockatoos may be seen. In winter, skiers can enjoy excellent cross-country and beginners' downhill skiing.

Canoeists will enjoy shooting the rapids or exploring the gorges of **Snowy River National Park** or **Mitchell River National Park**, both in East Gippsland, while bushwalkers can hike through beautiful forests.

Baw Baw National Park covers the granite Baw Baw plateau at the southern end of Victoria's high country, and sections of the Thomson and Aberfeldy river valleys. This park offers good cross-country skiing in winter: Baw Baw Alpine Village abuts the park. Numerous walking tracks are popular in summer, including a 20-kilometre section of the Australian Alps Walking Track, which extends from Walhalla to Cowombat Flat on the New South Wales border. In summer, visitors can take short walks to the track and to the plateau, or follow cross-country ski trails. Colourful wildflowers bloom on the plateau in summer. The park is home to Leadbeater's possum and the Baw Baw frog (both endangered species), as well as wombats, wallabies, echidnas, platypuses, gliders and several types of snakes and lizards. Crimson rosellas, yellow-tailed black cockatoos, gang-gangs and lyrebirds are common.

Lake Eildon National Park centres on Lake Eildon, and offers boating, sailing, water skiing, fishing and swimming, and a number of walking tracks, including a nature trail near Devil Cove. The park's western boundary, along the Puzzle Range, provides scenic views over nearby peaks and Coller Bay. There are many kangaroos and wallabies in the park. Crimson rosellas, cockatoos, galahs and kookaburras visit the camping grounds, and around the lake there are cormorants, pelicans, ducks, swans, herons and ibis.

IN THE WEST OF THE STATE
The 167 200-hectare **Grampians National Park** offers marvellous scenery, wildlife and tourist facilities. The park is famous for its rugged sandstone ranges, waterfalls, wildflowers and varied birds and mammals, as well as its Aboriginal rock-art sites. The peaks rise to over 1000 metres and form the western edge of the Great Dividing Range. The Grampians are best seen on foot: there are many walking tracks, from short well-marked trails in the Wonderland section near Halls Gap, to challenging walks across the semi-alpine landscape of the Major Mitchell Plateau.

Mount Eccles National Park, in south-west Victoria, is one of several parks that contain rock formations of great geological interest. An extinct volcano, a lava canal, lava cave and the Stony Rises are exceptional features. In the middle of the crater of Mount Eccles is the appropriately named Lake Surprise. West of this park is **Lower Glenelg National Park**, surrounding the tranquil Glenelg River and offering good walks and fishing.

The surprise for most visitors to **Little Desert National Park** is to discover that it is neither little (at 132 647 hectares) nor a desert. It is best known for its amazing displays of wildflowers in spring; more than 600 flowering-plant species are found here, including more than 40 ground orchids. Another special feature of the Little Desert

is that mallee fowl are found here. These birds build mounds for eggs and the mounds can be as much as 5 metres in diameter and 1.5 metres high.

Wyperfeld National Park in the north-west contains hundreds of species of plants and birdlife, and is a great park to visit in the spring, autumn and winter. In good rainfall years there are colourful spring wildflowers, and in the autumn and winter the visitor will enjoy crisp, clear days – perfect for bushwalking and birdwatching.

The vast **Murray–Sunset National Park** contains semi-arid environments from riverine floodplains to heathlands, salt lakes and woodlands, which support a tremendous variety of wildlife, particularly birdlife. It is the second largest national park in the State covering 633 000 hectares. This park is also best visited in the cooler months of the year.

Another park in the north-west of the State is **Hattah–Kulkyne National Park**. Typically, summers here are long, hot and dry; rainfall is usually less than 300 millimetres per year. The animals of this area have evolved strategies for avoiding or tolerating heat and dryness: some burrow, others just rest during the heat of the day; some birds catch thermals to cooler air. After rainfall and flooding from the Murray River, the serenely beautiful Hattah Lakes system transforms the park into a bird haven and a wonderful wildflower landscape.

For more information on Victoria's national parks, contact the Parks Victoria Information Centre; 13 1963. Web site www.parkweb. vic.gov.au

The Cathedral, Mount Buffalo

Oth Art gallery, Birdwood Ave. Chinese Gold Discovery Memorial, Lambert St. Langi Morgala Folk Museum, Queen St, displays Aboriginal weapons and artifacts. Alexandra Park and Botanical Gardens, Vincent St, features orchid glasshouse display, walk-in fernery and herb garden. J-Ward, Old Ararat Gaol, off Lowe St; guided tours. Gum San ('Hill of Gold') Chinese Museum, Western Hwy, commemorates 600 Chinese miners who discovered gold (1857) on Canton Lead. Mar.: Jailhouse Rock Festival. Sept.: Cymbidium Orchid Festival. Oct.: Orchid Festival; Golden Gateway Festival. **In the area:** Green Hill Lake, a constructed lake 4 km E off Western Hwy, ideal for fishing and water sports. Langi Ghiran State Park, 14 km E off Western Hwy, has scenic walks and children's playground. At Buangor, 23 km SE, century-old Buangor Hotel and old Cobb & Co. changing station (c. 1860); 18 km further on, Mt Buangor State Park includes Fern Tree Waterfalls. One Tree Hill Lookout, 5 km NW, for 360° views. Wineries, most open for tastings and cellar-door sales, *north-west of town:* Garden Gully Vineyard, 15 km; Seppelt Great Western Winery, 17 km, established 1865 and specialising in dry red and sparkling wines (underground cellars National Trust-classified); Best's wines, 19 km; *east of town:* Kimbarra Wines, 1.5 km; Mt Langi Ghiran Wines, 20 km; *south of town:* Montara Winery, 3 km; *west of town:* Cathcart Ridge Winery, 6 km; The Gap, 35 km. **Visitor information:** Railway Station, 91 High St; (03) 5352 2096, freecall 1800 657 158. Web site www.ararat. asn.au/tourism.htm **See also:** The Golden Age p. 171; Vineyards and Wineries p. 207.

Avoca   Pop. 968

MAP REF. 226 H6, 235 M12

In the Central Goldfields region, Avoca was established with the discovery of gold in the area in 1852. Located at the junction of the Sunraysia and Pyrenees hwys, the surrounding Pyrenees Range foothills offer attractive bushwalking and possible sightings of kangaroos, wallabies and koalas. **In town:** Self-guide walk, leaflet available. Early National Trust-classified bluestone buildings: old gaol, Davy St; powder magazine, Camp St; courthouse (now a museum) and one of State's earliest pharmacies, Lalor's (1854), still operating on original site in High St. Also in High St.: bakery in old State Bank building; Albion House; and The Avoca

Museum. Pyrenees Waterfalls and picnic area, Vinoca Rd. Market at RSL Hall, High St, 2nd Sat. each month. Mar. and Apr.: Petanque Tournaments (French bowls). Apr.: Pyrenees Vignerons Gourmet Food and Wine Race Meeting. Oct.: Avoca Cup (horse race). **In the area:** Mt Lonarch Arts, 10 km S, gallery and studio. Cemetery, northern outskirts of town, has early Chinese burial sites. At Elmhurst, 26 km SW, Oasis Crystal Gallery for local art and craft. Fishing: Avoca River, near town; Wimmera River 42 km W. A number of wineries in the area; details from information centre. **Visitor information:** High St; (03) 5465 3767. **See also:** The Golden Age p. 171; Vineyards and Wineries p. 207.

Bacchus Marsh   Pop. 11 279

MAP REF. 216 G5, 227 Q13, 230 A3, 233 R4

The trees of the Avenue of Honour provide an impressive entrance from the east to Bacchus Marsh, 49 km W of Melbourne. This long-established town is in a fertile valley, once marshland, between the Werribee and Lerderderg Rivers. **In town:** Manor House, Manor St, home of town's founder, Captain Bacchus; privately owned. In Main St: original blacksmith's shop and cottage; courthouse, lockup and National Bank (all National Trust-classified); Border Inn (1850), thought to have been State's first service stop for Cobb & Co. coaches travelling to goldfields. In Gisborne Rd: Holy Trinity Anglican Church (1877); Express Building Art Gallery. Ra Ceramics and Crafts, Station St. Big Apple Tourist Orchard, Avenue of Honour. June: Rotary Art Show. Nov.: Cup Day in the Park. Dec.: Woodchop. **In the area:** Lerderderg Gorge, 10 km N, for picnics, bushwalking and swimming. Long Forest Flora Reserve, 2 km NE, features bull mallee, some specimens centuries old. Merrimu Reservoir and Wombat State Forest, both about 10 km NE. At Melton, 14 km E, Willows historic homestead. Maddingley open-cut coal mine, 3 km S. At Brisbane Ranges National Park, 16 km SW: steep-sided Anakie Gorge, walking tracks and wildflowers in spring. Werribee Gorge, 10 km W, day walks and picnic area. At Ballan, 20 km NW, Vintage Machinery and Vehicle Rally in Feb. At Blackwood, 31 km NW: Mineral Springs Reserve; Garden of St Erth open garden (check times), in former cemetery dating back to 1855; Shindig Festival on Australia Day Sat. (Jan.); Easter Festival. Wineries and vineyards: St Anne's Vineyard on

Western Fwy, 6 km W, has a bluestone cellar built from remains of old Ballarat gaol; Craiglee Winery and Goonawarra Vineyard, Sunbury, 47 km NE; Wildwood Vineyard, Bulla, 9 km SE. **Visitor information:** Shire Offices, Main St; (03) 5367 2111.

Bairnsdale   Pop. 10 890

MAP REF. 231 P4, 240 F13

Located on the river flats of the Mitchell River, this East Gippsland trade centre and holiday town is at the junction of the Princes Hwy, the Great Alpine Rd and the road east to Lakes Entrance, making it an excellent base for touring the region. **In town:** Self-guide heritage walks. Historical Museum (1891), Macarthur St, contains items of local historic interest. St Mary's Church, Main St, features wall and ceiling murals by Italian artist Francesco Floreani. Krowathunkooloong, Aboriginal Keeping Place and Museum, Dalmahoy St, houses history, heritage and culture of East Gippsland Koories; canoe tree in Howitt Park, Princes Hwy, 4-m-long scar made around 170 years ago when bark was stripped from tree to make a canoe — both included in Bataluk Cultural Trail, brochure available. Adjacent to post office, Port of Bairnsdale site and river walk. Boardwalk across part of McLeod Morass, a bird wetland habitat on southern outskirts of town, access from Macarthur St. Market at Howitt Park, Princes Hwy, 4th Sun. each month. Mar.: Riviera Festival. Apr.: East Gippsland Agricultural Field Days. May: Australasian Street Grand Prix. Nov.: Agricultural Show. **In the area:** Self-guide scenic drives and walks, and 4WD tours; details from information centre. Mitchell River empties into Lake King at Eagle Point, 12 km S, where it forms the silt jetties that stretch 8 km into lake; view from Eagle Point Bluff. Jolly Jumbuk Country Craft Centre, 5 km E on Princes Hwy, has woollen products for sale. Nicholson River Winery, 10 km E. Metung, 30 km SE, a picturesque fishing village on shores of Lake King. Historic Dargo township, 93 km NW. Scenic drive through high plains to Hotham Heights, 80 km N of Dargo (unsealed road, check conditions); stunning in spring when wattles bloom. Mitchell River National Park, near Lindenow, 15 km W, features excellent bushwalking tracks and Den of Nargun, Aboriginal cultural site in gorge and part of Bataluk Cultural Trail. **Visitor information:** 240 Main St; (03) 5152 3444. **See also:** Gippsland Lakes p. 186.

Wildlife-Watching

Victoria has some marvellous wildlife-watching opportunities. Besides the ever-popular penguins at Phillip Island there are many interesting encounters to be had, including picnicking among kangaroos, peeking at a mallee fowl as it tends its nesting mound, and watching thousands of short-tailed shearwaters (muttonbirds) fly home to their roosts at dusk.

IN MELBOURNE

Thanks to Melbourne's wonderful gardens and reserves, native animals can still be seen in the city. The lake in the **Botanic Gardens**, in the inner suburb of South Yarra, is a habitat for black swans, cormorants, ducks, moorhens and coots. An indigenous fruit bat, the grey-headed flying-fox, also roosts in the gardens.

Melbourne's possums have adapted well to their urban environment. There are two varieties: the ringtail with its white-tipped tail, and the larger brushtail possum. Brushtails are the more brash of the two, and can often be seen rummaging after dark in the **Fitzroy** and **Alexandra gardens**.

Westgate Park is an unlikely bird sanctuary in an industrial area under the busy eastern approach to the Westgate Bridge. This does not discourage seabirds and waterbirds from using this valuable wetland: ducks, coots, pelicans and swans share the sanctuary, and ibis breed on one of the park's islands between July and October. **Jells Park** in Wheelers Hill is another prime suburban birdwatching site, particularly in September when migratory Japanese snipe arrive at the lake. A bird hide allows the snipe to be viewed undisturbed.

Melbourne is on the shores of **Port Phillip**, which is home to schools of bottlenose dolphins and seals. Dolphin- and seal-viewing boat tours operate from the bayside towns of Sorrento and Queenscliff. Cruises also leave for Pope's Eye Marine Reserve, within the bay, to view Australasian gannets. Pope's Eye and other nearby navigation structures are the only fabricated structures in the world where gannets nest.

Also within the bay is a colony of little (fairy) penguins. Cruises leave in daylight hours from Southbank and St Kilda pier to view the penguins at the St Kilda breakwater.

AROUND MELBOURNE

The most famous penguin-watching spot is a couple of hours south of Melbourne at **Phillip Island**. At Summerland Beach the little (fairy) penguins come ashore each evening to their burrows in the sand dunes. At the visitors centre, nesting penguins can be spied on through peepholes in their specially designed nesting boxes. From May to July, these birds can be seen nest-building; from August to January, eggs are laid and chicks raised. February to April are good months to see the penguins moulting.

Koalas can also be seen in their natural habitat from raised walkways at the Koala Conservation Centre on the island. Cruise trips leave from Cowes to Seal Rocks on the south-western tip of the island, allowing close-up views of Australia's largest colony of breeding fur seals. At San Remo, pelicans get a fish meal daily on the waterfront.

South-west of Melbourne near Lara is **Serendip Wildlife Reserve**. This grassland and wetland habitat has viewing hides, and is a good location to see native birds. Visitors can see waterbirds such as spoonbills, grebes and ducks, as well as several species of birds of prey.

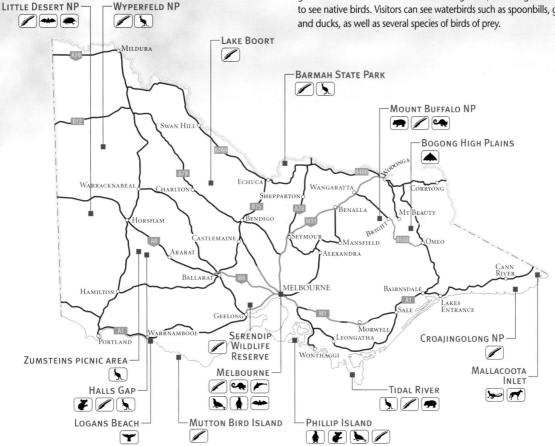

ON THE SOUTH-WEST COAST

Just off the coast near Port Campbell is **Mutton Bird Island**, a bird colony free from introduced predators. Thousands of migratory short-tailed shearwaters (muttonbirds) arrive from the north Pacific and nest on the island between September and April. Their evening fly-ins are a spectacular sight.

The most famous visitors to the south-west coast are southern right whales. After spending the summer months in the plankton-rich sub-Antarctic waters, they return to breeding grounds at **Logans Beach** just east of Warrnambool between June and September. Southern right whales are slowly increasing in numbers after being decimated by commercial whaling earlier in the century. While there is no guarantee of spotting a whale, these months offer the best chance of seeing one of these huge but graceful mammals close to shore.

Eastern grey kangaroos are a common sight in the Grampians

IN THE GRAMPIANS

The rugged sandstone ranges of the Grampians offer some of the best opportunities for wildlife-watching in south-western Victoria. Koalas can be seen around **Halls Gap**, and boisterous flocks of long-billed corellas arrive each evening to roost in the eucalypts opposite the town's shops. Eastern grey kangaroos are common in grassland around the town, particularly at dawn and dusk. For a closer look at our national symbol, visit **Zumsteins picnic area** in Grampians National Park. Kangaroos graze there freely throughout the day. During school holidays, night wildlife-watching walks are conducted in the park – several species are likely to be seen by torchlight, including gliders, owls, kangaroos, ringtail and brushtail possums, and wallabies.

IN THE MALLEE

North of the Grampians is **Wyperfeld National Park**. Follow the Lake Brambruk Nature Walk to see emus, kangaroos, soaring wedge-tailed eagles, and the endangered regent parrot. Wyperfeld's best-known bird is the threatened mallee fowl. The male builds a large nesting mound comprising a core of organic material covered by a layer of sand. With a little patience there is a good chance of seeing a mallee fowl at its mound, particularly October–March. **Little Desert National Park** also has mallee fowl, along with small insectivorous bats which can be seen flying on summer evenings, and a healthy population of short-beaked echidnas.

AROUND THE MURRAY AND IN THE NORTH-CENTRAL REGION

Barmah State Park in north-central Victoria provides a unique bird habitat. Floods are common between July and October; a good time for boat tours to look for waterbirds. Eastern grey kangaroos can be readily seen throughout the forest, though you will need a torch and some patience to glimpse the less-common nocturnal marsupials.

Lake Boort is a haven for birdlife in the north-central region, and is a significant breeding ground. In spring several species raise their young in the logs and rushes around the lake.

IN THE NORTH-EASTERN HIGHLANDS

One of Victoria's most popular native species is the common wombat, and a good place to see this burrowing marsupial is in **Mount Buffalo National Park**. They venture out at dusk to graze on snow grass flats. The chalet within the park attracts the colourful crimson rosellas.

An equally colourful but much smaller park resident is the flame robin, the male having a bright red breast. Lake Catani within the park is a good location to see the retiring lyrebird. Bring a torch to the lake and search for ringtail possums after dark in the surrounding eucalypts.

The Bogong moth played an important part in the lives of local Aborigines before European settlement. Each summer Aboriginal groups trekked to the high country to feast on the insects. Thousands of the moths still inhabit the **Bogong High Plains** in summer, and the best places to find them are in rock crevices.

ON THE EASTERN COAST

The Mallacoota region offers wildlife-watchers a good chance to see large tree goannas, particularly along the picnic sites at **Mallacoota Inlet**. The elusive dingo can occasionally be spotted along beaches in the area, and their tracks can be seen in the sand. There is a large bird population in **Croajingolong National Park** – over 300 species. Glossy black cockatoos are attracted to the native casuarina trees along the walking track to Genoa Peak within the park. King parrots and lyrebirds can also be seen.

AT WILSONS PROM

Wilsons Promontory National Park has no shortage of wildlife. Eastern grey kangaroos and emus graze on grassland at **Tidal River**, and blond-coloured wombats emerge at dusk at Norman Beach. This is also a good area for short-tailed shearwaters (muttonbirds). Kookaburras and flame robins are easily seen, while Easter is prime-time for flocks of rainbow lorikeets as they arrive to feed on flowering coastal banksias.

For a good introduction to Victorian wildlife visit Healesville Sanctuary, just east of Melbourne. A range of native wildlife is on display in natural surroundings. The platypus display offers an intimate view of this unique animal, and the birds of prey enclosure has daily feeding demonstrations. The Department of Natural Resources and Environment publishes a booklet, *Wildlife Watching in Victoria*, which is an invaluable guide to over 90 viewing sites. For more information on wildlife-watching in national parks, contact the Parks Victoria Information Line; 13 1963. Web site www.parkweb.vic.gov.au **See also:** National Parks p. 163; The Prom p. 181; The Grampians p. 182 and individual entries in A–Z listing for towns and parks in bold type.

WILDLIFE-WATCHING ETHICS

Do not disturb wildlife or wildlife habitats. Keep the impact of your presence to a minimum. Use available cover or hides wherever possible.

Do not feed wildlife, even in urban areas. (Note: supervised feeding is allowed at some locations.)

Be careful not to introduce exotic plants and animals – definitely no pets.

Stay on defined trails.

Ballarat

Pop. 64 831

MAP REF. 216 C4, 225, 227 K11, 233 O3, 238 A13

Ballarat is Victoria's largest inland city, situated in the Central Highlands. Its inner areas retain much of the charm of its gold-boom era, with many splendid original buildings still standing. Ballarat was just a small rural township in 1851, when its rich alluvial goldfields were discovered. Within two years it had a population of nearly 40 000. Australia's only civil battle occurred here in 1854, when miners refused to pay Government licence fees and fought with police and troops at the Eureka Stockade. Today Ballarat is a bustling city featuring many galleries, museums, and antique and craft shops. It has excellent recreational facilities, and beautiful gardens and parks, making it most attractive to visitors. The begonia is the city's floral emblem. **In town:** In Lydiard St: Fine Art Gallery, Australia's largest and oldest regional gallery, has comprehensive collection of Australian art including works by Lindsay family; Her Majesty's Theatre (1875), oldest intact, purpose-built theatre in Australia; Craig's Royal Hotel and George Hotel for dining and accommodation in old-world surroundings. Lake Wendouree, used for water sports, and paddle-steamer tours with commentary on history of city. At Botanic Gardens adjoining the lake area: Robert Clarke Horticultural Centre, showcase for famous begonias; Adam Lindsay Gordon Cottage; Tramway Museum, featuring vintage trams; Prime Ministers' Avenue, displaying busts of Australian prime ministers; elegant statuary pavilion nearby. Vintage Tramway, via Wendouree Pde (rides weekends, public and school holidays). In Eureka St: award-winning historic Montrose Cottage (1856), first masonry cottage built on the goldfields; unique $4 million Eureka Stockade Centre, with interpretive information about the famous battle. Ballarat Wildlife and Reptile Park, cnr York and Fussell sts, features native animals in natural habitat. Sovereign Hill, in Main St, is a major tourist attraction; it is a world-class reconstruction of a goldmining settlement, and features orientation centre and working displays; 'Blood on the Southern Cross', a night sight-and-sound spectacular re-creating the Eureka rebellion; Proctor's Wheelwright Factory, a working replica

Rows of lavender at Yuulong Lavender Estate, near Ballarat

of wooden carriage-wheel production; panning for gold; re-created shops and businesses; barbecue facilities, kiosk, restaurant and licensed hotel; accommodation. Adjoining Sovereign Hill, Gold Museum features exhibits of gold history, large collection of gold coins and display of the uses of gold 'today and tomorrow'. Trash and Trivia Market at Showgrounds, Creswick Rd, each Sun. Pleasant Street Market, 4th Sun. each month. Jan.: Organs of the Ballarat Goldfields. Feb.: Super Southern Swap Meet. Mar.: Begonia Festival; Antique Fair. Apr.: Eureka Jazz Festival. July: Winter Festival. Aug.–Nov.: Royal South Street Eisteddfod. Nov.: Springfest Extravaganza; Ballarat Cup. **In the area:** On western edge of city, Avenue of Honour (22 km) and Arch of Victory, honouring those who fought in World War I. Kirks and Gong Gong reservoirs, both 5 km NE, for picnics. Ballarat Exhibition and Entertainment Centre, 8 km E, an authentic working woolshed with demonstrations by shearers, classers and working sheepdogs. Nearby, Kryal Castle, reconstruction of a medieval castle offering family entertainment. Lake Burrumbeet, 22 km NW, for water sports and excellent trout fishing; scenic picnic spots on shore. At Yendon, 15 km SE, Yuulong Lavender Estate (check opening times). Well-known Yellowglen Winery, 24 km SW at Smythesdale. Berringa Mines Historic Reserve, 8 km SE of Smythesdale. At Buninyong, 13 km S: Flora and Bird

Park, with raised walkway and 60 parrot aviaries; Clayfire Gallery; Timeless Timber Gallery; market 1st Sun. each month; in Feb., Gold King Festival celebrates early history of town. Enfield State Park, 16 km S near Enfield, features 61 species of orchid and some remains of goldworkings. Mt Buninyong Lookout, 13 km SE, for good views. Lal Lal Falls (30 m) on Moorabool River, 18 km SE. Nearby, Lal Lal Blast Furnace, beautiful archaeological remains from 19th century. **Visitor information:** cnr Sturt and Albert sts; (03) 5332 2694, freecall 1800 648 450. **See also:** The Golden Age p. 171; Vineyards and Wineries p. 207.

Beaufort

Pop. 1039

MAP REF. 226 F10, 233 M3

This small town on the Western Hwy, midway between Ballarat and Ararat, has a gold-rush history, like so many towns in this area. The discovery of gold at Fiery Creek swelled its population in the late 1850s to nearly 100 000. Today Beaufort is primarily a centre for the surrounding pastoral and agricultural district. **In town:** Historic courthouse, Livingstone St, open by appt. Turn-of-century band rotunda, Neill St. **In the area:** Mt Cole State Forest, 16 km NW via Raglan, for bushwalks, native flora and fauna, picnic and camping facilities. At Lake Goldsmith, 14 km S, Steam Rally held in May and November. **Visitor information:** Shire Offices, 5 Lawrence St; (03) 5349 2000.

Beechworth   Pop. 2953

MAP REF. 239 O6, 240 A3
Once the centre of the great Ovens gold-mining region, Beechworth lies 24 km off the Hume Fwy, between Wangaratta and Wodonga. This is one of Victoria's best-preserved and most beautiful gold towns, magnificently sited in the foothills of the Alps. The whole town has been classified as historically important by the National Trust. The rich alluvial goldfield at Woolshed Creek was discovered by a local shepherd during the 1850s, and a total of 4 121 918 ounces of gold was mined in 14 years. A story is told of Daniel Cameron, campaigning to represent the Ovens Valley community: he rode through the town at the head of a procession of miners from Woolshed, on a horse shod with golden shoes. Sceptics claim they were merely gilded, but the tale is an indication of what Beechworth was like during the boom, when its population was 42 000 and it boasted 61 hotels and a theatre at which international celebrities performed. **In town:** Use of local honey-coloured granite in fine 1850s government buildings (especially in Camp and Ford sts), and in the powder magazine (1860) in Gorge Rd on northern outskirts of town. In Albert Rd: Harness and Carriage Museum, run by National Trust; Tanswell's Hotel, restored lacework building; Ned Kelly's cell, under Shire Offices; Beechworth Gaol (1859), still used as a prison. In Ford St: historic former Bank of Australasia, now a restaurant; Berringa Antiques and Buckland Gallery. In Camp St: Beechworth Galleries and Beechworth Bakery. In Loch St: Robert O'Hara Burke Memorial Museum, displays relics of gold rush and features 16 mini-shops depicting town's main street as it was more than 100 years ago. Bicycle hire, horseriding and maps for walking tours and gem/gold fossicking available. Market at Town Hall gardens, Ford St, 4 times a year (check dates). Feb.: Drive Back in Time (vintage car rally). Easter: Golden Horseshoes Festival. Nov.: Celtic Festival. **In the area:** Cemetery on northern outskirts of town: Chinese burning towers; Chinese cemetery. Beechworth Historic Park (surrounds town): Woolshed Falls historical walk through former alluvial goldmining sites; Gorge Scenic Drive (5 km) starts north of town; gold-fossicking in limited areas. Fletcher Dam, Beechworth Forest Drive, 3 km SE towards historic village

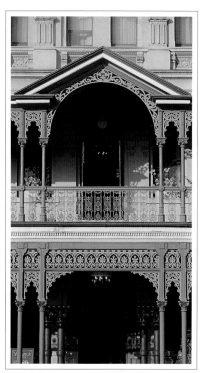
Shamrock Hotel, Bendigo

of Stanley. Kelly's Lookout, Woolshed Creek, about 4 km N. Mt Pilot Lookout, 5 km N, for panoramic views of Murray Valley; signposted Aboriginal cave paintings nearby. **Visitor information:** Ford St; (03) 5728 3233.

Benalla   Pop. 8582

MAP REF. 228 A2, 239 K7
This small city, just off the Hume Fwy, is 40 km SW of Wangaratta. During the late 1870s Benalla experienced the activities of the notorious Kelly Gang, who were eventually captured at nearby Glenrowan in 1880. Benalla is also the home town of Sir Edward ('Weary') Dunlop, and Michael J. Savage, NZ Prime Minister in the 1940s. **In town:** Lake Benalla, created in the Broken River, has good recreation and picnic facilities, and is a haven for birds; self-guide walk around lake, brochure available. In Bridge St: Botanical Gardens, with splendid rose gardens and memorial statue in honour of Sir Edward ('Weary') Dunlop; Art Gallery, on shores of lake, features important Ledger Collection of Australian paintings. In Mair St: a 3-dimensional ceramic mural; The Creators Gallery at information centre, for paintings, pottery and craft; Costume and Pioneer Museum, has Ned Kelly's cummerbund on display. At aerodrome on northern outskirts of town: centre for Gliding Club of Victoria;

hot-air ballooning and glider flights. Market, Fawckner Dr., 4th Sat. each month. Easter: Art Show; Garden Expo. Nov.: Rose Festival; Agricultural Show. **In the area:** Reef Hills Regional Park, 4 km S on Midland Hwy: 2040 ha of forest with wide variety of native flora and fauna. At Swanpool, 23 km S, 1950s-style cinema showing classic films. Pleasant day trip south-east to King Valley and spectacular Paradise Falls. Winton Motor Raceway, 10 km NE. **Visitor information:** 14 Mair St; (03) 5762 1749. Web site www.benalla.net.au

Bendigo   Pop. 59 936

MAP REF. 224, 227 P2, 235 Q9, 238 C8
One of Victoria's most famous gold-mining cities, and sited at the junction of four highways, Bendigo is central for trips to other gold towns nearby. The gold rush began here in 1851 and gold production continued for 100 years. The affluence of the period can still be seen today in many splendid public and commercial buildings. **In town:** Self-guide heritage walk, brochure available. Bus tours, in red London-style buses, of major attractions. Shamrock Hotel (1897), cnr Pall Mall and Williamson St, Bendigo's famous landmark (tours). Sacred Heart Cathedral, largest outside Melbourne, Wattle St. Alexandra Fountain at Charing Cross. In Pall Mall: renaissance-style post office (1887), now information centre; and law courts (1896). In View St: Bendigo Art Gallery (1890); Capital Theatre (1873); and National Trust-classified Dudley House (1859). Central Deborah Gold Mine, Violet St, in working order; surface interpretive display and underground tours. Vintage Trams (taped commentary), run from mine on 8-km city trip (includes stop at Tram Depot Museum displaying 30 vintage trams). Golden Dragon Museum, Bridge St, features Chinese history of goldfields, largest display of Chinese processional regalia in the world (including world's oldest imperial dragon 'Loong' and longest imperial dragon 'Sun Loong', more than 100 m long) and classical Chinese gardens adjacent to museum. Lookout tower, cascade and Conservatory Gardens in Rosalind Park, Barnard St. Discovery Science and Technology Centre, Railway Pl., has more than 100 hands-on displays. Bendigo Woollen Mills, Lansell St West (tours). Markets each Sun. at Showgrounds, Holmes St, and cnr Rotis

The Golden Age

The cities and towns of the goldfields region of Victoria came to a peak of affluence in the 1880s, an affluence built on the first gold discoveries in the 1850s. The towns display all the frivolity and grandeur of Victorian architecture, having grown during a period when it was believed that gold and wealth would be a permanent benefit in Victoria.

The two major cities of the region are Ballarat and Bendigo, but there are many other towns in the area. They all have historic houses and public buildings, and many have other trappings of the past — statues, public gardens (some with lakes), bandstands and grand avenues of English trees. Spring and autumn are the best seasons to visit this region, because then there are not the extremes of summer and winter temperatures, and the flowers and foliage are at their best.

It is a quiet region now. The remaining small towns serve the surrounding rich pastoral district, and secondary industries and services centre on the two cities. It was once, however, an area of frantic activity. Gold was found at Clunes in 1851 and within three months 8000 people were on the diggings in the area between Buninyong and Ballarat. Nine months later 30 000 people were

A show of colour at Conservatory Gardens, Bendigo

on the goldfields and four years later 100 000. The population of the city of Melbourne dwindled and immigrants rushed to the diggings from Great Britain, America and many other countries. Ships' crews, and sometimes even their captains, abandoned their vessels and trekked to the diggings to try their luck. Tent cities sprang up on the plains as men dug and panned for gold. The communities were remarkable: there were shanty towns, the streets crowded day and night with hawkers and traders; there were pubs and dancing-rooms, and continuous sounds of music and revelry.

There were remarkable finds of huge nuggets in the early days, but finally the amount of gold obtained by panning in the rivers and by digging grew less and less. As the surface gold was worked out, expensive company-backed operations followed: mining in deep shafts, then the ore stamped and crushed in steam-powered plants on the surface. The success of these methods heralded a new era, that of the company mines, outside investors and stock-exchange speculation. It led to a much more stable workforce and to the well-established communities that slowly evolved into the towns of the region today. As the pastoral and industrial potential began to

be realised and fully exploited, it was the perfect scene for expansion and optimism.

The years between 1870 and 1890 saw the towns embellished with fine civic buildings, mansions, solid town houses, churches, hotels and all the trappings of affluence. Thus Ballarat, Bendigo, Castlemaine and to a lesser extent Clunes, Creswick, Daylesford and Maldon became extraordinary *nouveau riche* visions of the current British taste.

Gold was discovered in **Ballarat** in 1851, and the city of Ballarat was laid out to the west of the diggings within twelve months of the first discovery of gold. The design included a magnificent chief thoroughfare, Sturt Street, wide enough for future plantations and monuments. The primitive buildings of early settlement were gradually replaced by boom-style architecture in the 1880s; many superb buildings survive to this day.

A visit to the Red Hill Gully Diggings at Sovereign Hill will show you something of the life of those early days. Without doubt, Sovereign Hill is the major attraction in Ballarat. This re-created goldmining township is a fascinating place for a day's outing that would appeal to the whole family.

Red Hill Gully Diggings at Sovereign Hill, Ballarat

A turn-off to the south near Ballarat leads to Buninyong, the scene of one of the first gold strikes in Victoria. Gold was discovered here at Hiscock's Gully in 1851. The impressive township of Buninyong with its grand tree-lined main street has a number of striking buildings: the Crown Hotel and white-walled Uniting Church are of the 1860s, while the combined council chambers and courthouse of 1886 are in rich Italianate design, unified by a central clock tower.

North of Ballarat, on the Midland Highway is **Creswick**, a picturesque valley town with a wonderfully ornate town hall. The bluestone tower of St John's Church dominates the town's western hill and across the valley is a Tudor-style hospital building which is now a school of forestry.

Turn off the highway to **Clunes** where gold was discovered in July 1851. It proved difficult to get supplies to this remote township, so the rush was limited and the later discoveries at Buninyong and Ballarat quickly diverted attention from this area.

On the Western Highway, 133 kilometres north-west of Ballarat, past **Ararat** (where a gold rush began in 1857), is **Stawell**. Gold was discovered at the present site of Stawell in 1853; by 1857 there was a population of 30 000, and the township was proclaimed in 1858. Goldmining continued until 1920.

North-east of Ballarat up the Midland Highway is **Daylesford**, another former goldmining town set in wooded hills around Wombat Hill Botanical Gardens and Lake Daylesford. On the hill are groves of rhododendrons, exotic trees and a lookout tower that provides a view of Mount Franklin (a perfectly preserved volcanic crater) and Mount Tarrangower. The Convent Gallery in town is housed in a former girls' school (1891), surrounded by beautiful gardens. Several kilometres north of Daylesford is the famed Hepburn Spa, which attracted visitors in the 19th century for its medicinal properties and is still popular with tourists.

Further north on the road to Bendigo is **Castlemaine**, a larger town and one of the most picturesque in the region. The streetscape in the centre of the town has remained virtually unaltered since the early days, for the prosperity of the 1860s diminished and the town settled down to a quieter rural life.

Nearby **Maldon** has been declared a Notable Town by the National Trust. The winding streets are flanked by low buildings, with deep verandahs shading the bluestone pavements laid in 1866.

Bendigo is the jewel of the region and is Victoria's most outstanding example of a boom town. Its gardens alone stand as a testament to the city's past wealth. Gothic- and classical-style buildings have been designed in vast proportions, richly ornamented and combined with the materials of the age, cast iron and cast cement.

The goldfields region can be enjoyed in three days or three weeks, according to time and taste. Several companies organise gold-fossicking excursions, including instruction in the use of metal detectors. A great way to see the region is via the Goldfields Tourist Route, a 450-kilometre triangle road route linking Ballarat, Ararat, Stawell, **Avoca**, **Maryborough**, Bendigo, Castlemaine and Daylesford. Free maps marking the route are available at the Victorian Visitor Information Centre, Melbourne Town Hall, cnr Little Collins and Swanston sts, Melbourne, all RACV offices and various visitor information centres throughout the goldfields region.

More detailed information can be obtained from the Bendigo Visitor Information Centre, Old Post Office, 51–67 Pall Mall; (03) 5444 4433, freecall 1800 813 153. Web site www.bendigo.vic.gov.au Alternatively, call Ballarat Visitor Information Centre, cnr Sturt and Albert sts; (03) 5532 2694, freecall 1800 648 450. Web site www.ballarat.com **See also:** individual entries in A–Z listing for towns in bold type. **Map references:** 224–7.

and Strickland rds; craft market, Pall Mall Rd, 4th Sun. each month. Mar.: Easter Festival: Madison 10 000 Cycling Race. Easter: Fair (first held 1871; features Chinese dragon). Apr.: Bendigo by Bike; Chrysanthemum Championships; Wine Festival. July: National Model Engineers Annual Exhibition. Oct.: Bendigo Heritage Uncorked; Orchid Club Spring Show. Nov.: National Swap Meet (Australia's largest meet for vintage car and bike enthusiasts); Racing Carnival. Dec.: Tram Spectacular. **In the area:** Excellent wineries, art, ceramics and antiques. Guided goldfields prospecting tours and self-guide Goldfields Tourist Route; details from information centre. Fortuna Villa mansion (1871), Chum St, 2 km S (open Sun.). One Tree Hill observation tower, 4 km S, panoramic views. At Mandurang, 8 km SE: historic wineries; Orchid Nursery; Tannery Lane Pottery; Rupertswood Country Home Open Garden (check open weekends). Arakoon Resort, 18 km SE, aquatic fun park (check opening times). Sedgwick's Camel Farm, 20 km SE at Sedgwick, offers rides and treks (check opening times). Bendigo Cactus Gardens (established 1937), National Trust-classified, 3 km NE at White Hills. At Epsom, 6 km NE: Bendigo Pottery, Australia's oldest working pottery (tours and sales); Wings and Things (part of pottery complex); Sun. market. National Trust-classified Chinese Joss House, 1 km N at Emu Point, temple built by Chinese miners. Iron Bark Riding Centre, 4 km N. At Whipstick State Park, 21 km N: wildlife, old goldmining areas (take care around old gold workings), bushwalking, cycling, gold-panning in gullies after rains; nearby, Hartland's Eucalyptus Factory and Historic Farm (tours Sun.), built 1890 to process eucalyptus oil obtained from surrounding scrub. At Eaglehawk, 6.5 km NW, site of goldrush in 1852: reminders of mining days; fine examples of 19th-century architecture, many National Trust-classified; self-guide heritage tour, brochure available; Dahlia and Arts Festival held each Mar. Balgownie Estate winery, 10 km NW (open Mon.–Sat.). Chateau Leamon winery, 10 km SW (open Wed.–Mon.). Goldfields Mohair Farm at Lockwood, 11 km SW (open daily, guided tours Mon.–Fri.). **Visitor information:** Old Post Office, 51–67 Pall Mall; (03) 5444 4445, freecall 1800 813 153. Web site www.bendigo.vic.gov.au **See also:** The Golden Age p. 171; Vineyards and Wineries p. 207.

Splendid views from Mount Buffalo National Park, near Bright

Birchip   Pop. 800

MAP REF. 120 F13, 235 K4

On the main rail link between Melbourne and Mildura, Birchip gets its water supply from the Wimmera–Mallee stock and domestic channel system. **In town:** In Cumming Ave: Big Red (Mallee bull); Historical Society Museum in old courthouse (open by appt). **In the area:** Sites of historic interest within Shire are indicated by markers; leaflet available. Junction of two major irrigation channels constructed in early 1900s, 1 km N. Sections of original Dog Fence, a vermin-proof barrier constructed in 1883 between Murray River near Swan Hill and South Australian border, 20 km N. Tchum Lake, 9 km E, facilities for motor boats, caravans and camping. **Visitor information:** Shire Offices, 22 Cumming Ave; (03) 5492 2200.

Boort   Pop. 805

MAP REF. 120 H13, 235 O5

A pleasant rural and holiday town on the shores of Lake Boort. The lake is popular for water sports, has good picnic facilities and beaches, and offers redfin-fishing. There is prolific native birdlife in the area; each spring several species raise their young around the lake. **Visitor information:** Boort Lake Caravan Park, Durham Ox Rd; (03) 5455 2064. **See also:** Wildlife-Watching p. 167.

Bright   Pop. 1898

MAP REF. 229 L5, 239 P8, 240 C6

In the heart of the beautiful Ovens Valley and at the foothills of the Victorian Alps, Bright is an attractive tourist centre. The town offers easy access to the ski resorts of Mt Hotham, Mt Buffalo and Falls Creek, and a number of ski-hire shops in the town stay open late during the winter season. The discovery of gold was responsible for the town's beginnings; remains of alluvial goldfields can still be seen. The area is excellent for bushwalking, horseriding, mountain-bike riding and trout-fishing, and is a photographer's delight, particularly in autumn. **In town:** Avenues of deciduous trees, planted in 1930s, particularly beautiful in spring and autumn. In Gavan St: Gallery 90; local art and craft at information centre; Centenary Park with deep weir (ideal for swimming in summer), children's playground and picnic facilities. Country Collectables, Ireland St. Bright Art Gallery and Cultural Centre, Mountbatten Ave. Historical Museum, old railway station, Station Ave. Lotsafun Amusement Park, entrance Mill Rd. Ovens River flows through town; picnic and camping spots alongside. Variety of safe, well-marked walking tracks in Bright area, including Canyon Walk along Ovens River where remains of gold workings can be seen; leaflets available. Hang-gliding, paragliding and 4WD tours. Craft market, Burke St, 3rd Sat. each month. Apr.: Autumn Festival. July: Winter Wonderland Festival. Oct.: Alpine Spring

Festival. **In the area:** Wandiligong, National Trust-classified hamlet in scenic valley, 6 km SE; linked to Bright by road, and walking and cycle track; hedge maze. Scenic drives in the area to: Tower Hill Lookout, 4 km NW; Huggins Lookout, 2 km S; Clearspot (stunning views), 13 km S; from Great Alpine Rd south-east to Mt Hotham, superb views of Mt Feathertop, the Razor Back and Mt Bogong. At Porepunkah, 6 km NW at junction of Ovens and Buckland rivers, Boyntons of Bright winery; further 10 km, Snowline Deer and Emu Farm in Hughes Lane, Eurobin. Mount Buffalo Chalet, 33 km W within Mount Buffalo National Park; also within the park, wildlife including ringtail possums at Lake Catani, wombats and crimson rosellas. **Visitor information:** 119 Gavan St; (03) 5755 2275, freecall 1800 500 117. **See also:** Alpine Country p. 190.

Buchan Pop. 134

MAP REF. 113 B13, 240 I11

This small town, set in the heart of Gippsland mountain country north-east of Bairnsdale, is well known for its limestone caves. **In town:** Tours of Royal and Fairy Caves, conducted daily (adventure tours also available); spring-fed swimming pool at Buchan Caves Reserve. Conorville Heritage Model Village, Main St: model buildings from 1780 to 1914, including miniature sculptures of people; also full-sized furnished 1840s bark-house replica. Feb.: Canni Creek Races. Easter: Rodeo. Nov.: Flowers and Craft Show. **In the area:** 4WD and rafting trips; self-drive Forest Snowy Drive east of town, brochure available. Schoolhouse (1865), at Suggan Buggan, 64 km N. South of Suggan Buggan, Eagle Loft Gallery, for local art and craft. Alpine National Park, surrounding Suggan Buggan, for spectacular mountain scenery. Outstanding views from lookout over Little River Gorge, 70 km N on road to McKillops Bridge (large bridge over Snowy River); Little River Falls near gorge. **Visitor information:** General Store, Main St; (03) 5155 9202. Web site www.buchan.com.au

Camperdown Pop. 3153

MAP REF. 221 C5, 233 L8

This south-western town on the Princes Hwy has the English-style charm of gracious buildings and avenues of elms. The centre for a rich pastoral district, Camperdown is also a base for fishing in the volcanic crater lakes nearby. **In town:** Historical Heritage Trail, brochure available. Clock tower (1896), cnr Manifold and Pike sts. Also in Manifold St: Historical Society Museum; courthouse; post office. Craft market at Finlay Ave or Theatre Royal, 1st Sun. each month. July: One Act Play Festival. **In the area:** At Mt Noorat, near Noorat, 21 km W: Alan Marshall Memorial Walking Track, off Glenormiston Rd, 3-km summit and return (1 hr) or crater-rim 1.5-km circuit (30 min.); excellent views over Western District. Mt Leura, 1 km S, extinct volcano next to the perfect cone shape of Mt Sugarloaf; lookout offers views over numerous crater lakes and volcanoes, north across plains to the Grampians. At Cobden, 13 km S, Cobden Miniature Trains, operates 3rd Sun. each month. Lake Corangamite, 13 km E, Victoria's largest salt lake. Excellent fishing lakes including Bullen Merri, 3 km W; and Purrumbete, 15 km SE, well-stocked with Quinnat salmon, also has excellent water-sports facilities, picnic spots and caravan park. **Visitor information:** Fragrant Cottage, Old Courthouse Building, Manifold St; (03) 5593 3390.

Cann River Pop. 246

MAP REF. 113 E13, 241 N11

A popular stop for Sydney–Melbourne motorists using the Princes Hwy. Excellent fishing, bushwalking and camping in the rugged hinterland. **In the area:** Lind National Park, 15 km W, includes Euchre Valley Nature Drive through warm-temperate rainforest, brochures from Parks Victoria. Coopracambra National Park, 30 km N near NSW border. Croajingolong National Park, main access 45 km S, stretches from Sydenham Inlet to NSW border; incorporates Point Hicks Lighthouse Reserve at Point Hicks, and Tamboon, Wingan and Mallacoota inlets. **Visitor information:** Snowy River–Orbost Visitor Centre, 13 Lochiel St, Orbost; (03) 5154 2424, or Parks Victoria; 13 1963 (ask for Cann River office). Web site www.parks.vic.gov.au

Casterton Pop. 1731

MAP REF. 232 C4

Given the Roman name meaning 'walled city' because of lush hills surrounding the valley, Casterton is on the Glenelg Hwy, 42 km E of the South Australian border. The Glenelg River flows through the town. Overlooking the town is a large

illuminated scout emblem carved into a hillside. **In town:** Signposted town walk, brochure available. Historical museum in old railway buildings, cnr Jackson and Clarke sts (open by appt). Alma and Judith Zaadstra Fine Art Gallery, Henty St. On eastern edge of town, Mickle Lookout. Visitor information centre displays local art and craft. Mar.: Vintage Car Rally; Polocrosse Championships. May: Race Cup (horseracing). June: Kelpie Working Dog Auction. Aug.: Woodturning Demonstration Exhibition. Nov.: Street-car Drag Racing. Dec.: Christmas Lights Festival (bus tours available). **In the area:** Long Lead Swamp, 11 km W on Penola Rd, has waterbirds, kangaroos and emus, and trail-bike track. National Trust-classified Warrock Homestead (1843), 26 km N, unique collection of 33 buildings erected by founder, George Robertson; open working day on Easter Sun. Bilston's Tree, 30 km N on Glenmia Rd, 50 m high and arguably world's largest red gum tree in terms of timber mass. Baileys Rocks, 50 km N in Dergholm State Park, unique green-coloured giant granite boulders. Other interesting geological formations: The Hummocks, 12 km NE; The Bluff, 20 km SW, exposed geological formations dating back 150 million years, surrounded by excellent scenery; nearby, slab cottage (1870), school (1875) and picnic facilities (open Sun. and public holidays). **Visitor information:** Shiels Tce; (03) 5581 2070.

Castlemaine Pop. 6690

MAP REF. 227 O6, 235 Q11, 238 C10

Castlemaine epitomises the goldmining towns of north-western Victoria. The town lies at the intersection of the Pyrenees and Midland hwys, 119 km from Melbourne. In the 1850s and 1860s enormous quantities of gold were found in its surface fields – this gold boom saw Castlemaine grow rapidly and many of its fine old buildings were constructed then. **In town:** Midland Hotel, Templeton St, and Imperial Hotel, Lyttleton St, have splendid iron lacework verandahs. Also in Lyttleton St: courthouse, town hall, regional art gallery and museum. Theatre Royal, Hargraves St. Buda Historic Home and Garden, Urquhart St, home from late 1850s of silversmith and jeweller Ernest Leviny and his family, with preserved home and gardens of the era. Restored 19th-century Castlemaine Market Building

(1862-63), Mostyn St, has Diggings Interpretive Centre and other regular exhibitions. Botanic Gardens, Parker St, designed by Baron von Mueller, who also designed the Melbourne Botanic Gardens. Old Castlemaine Gaol, Bowden St. Apr.: Castlemaine State Festival (odd-numbered years). Nov.: Festival of Gardens (odd-numbered years). **In the area:** Mt Alexander Diggers Trails, for gold rush sites; booklet available. At Wesley Hill, 2.5 km E, market each Sat. At Harcourt, 9 km NE: Skydancers Orchid and Butterfly Gardens, a walk-through nursery and butterfly house; Harcourt Valley Vineyard (Wine Festival each Easter Sunday); Blackjack Vineyards; Mt Alexander wineries; Spring Orchid Festival each October; Apple Festival each March. On Mt Alexander, 19 km NE, koala reserve. Historic Forest Creek Gold Mine, on road to Chewton (4 km SE), tours and gold panning. At Chewton: Wattle Gully goldmine; Dingo Farm (puppy time July–Aug.); market each Sat. At Fryerstown, 11 km SE: ruins of Duke of Cornwall mine; Herons Reef Cultural Heritage Gold Diggings (tours, check opening times). Chinese cemetery and mineral springs at Vaughan, 14 km S. Big Tree, a giant red gum over 500 years old, 14 km SW at Guildford. At Newstead, 16 km SW: winery, pottery. At Strathlea, Kyirong Emu farm, 24 km SW on Strathlea Rd, emu farming from chick to product (by appt). **Visitor information:** Market Building, Mostyn St; (03) 5470 6200. Web site www.mountalexander.vic.gov.au/tourism **See also:** The Golden Age p. 171.

Charlton

Pop. 1096

MAP REF. 235 M6

A supply centre for a rich wheat district, Charlton is set on the banks of the Avoca River, at the intersection of the Calder and Borung hwys in north-central Victoria. **In town:** Fishing in Avoca River; Travellers Rest picnic area, on banks of river. Walking track along river, from town to weir (about 2 km one-way). Easter: Lions Market. Oct.: Art Show. **In the area:** Wooroonook Lake, 12 km W, for swimming and boating. Bish Deer Farm, further 18 km W. At Wycheproof, 30 km NW: Mt Wycheproof, a mere 43 m high and smallest mountain in world; Centenary Park and Willandra Historical Museum. Wychitella State Forest, 27 km E, for a variety of native flora and fauna, including the lowan (mallee fowl). **Visitor information:** 1 High St; (03) 5491 1755.

McKillops Bridge, north of Buchan

Chiltern

Pop. 1080

MAP REF. 121 P13, 239 O4, 240 A2

Halfway between Wangaratta and Wodonga, Chiltern is 1 km off the Hume Fwy. It was once a goldmining boom town with 14 suburbs. Many of its attractive buildings have been classified by the National Trust. **In town:** In Conness St: Athenaeum Museum (1866), features heritage display; Dow's Pharmacy (1868), National Trust-owned chemist shop with its original features; Stephen's Motor Museum, for motoring memorabilia. In Main St: Famous Grapevine, formerly Grape Vine Hotel, boasts the largest grapevine in Australia (in Guinness Book of Records, planted 1867); National Trust-classified Federal Standard newspaper office, dates from goldmining era (1860–61) (open by appt for groups). Picnic spots with barbecues at Lake Anderson, via Main St. Walking track from lake-shore over bridge to National Trust-classified 'Lake View', Victoria St, home of author Henry Handel Richardson (open weekends, public and school holidays). Self-guide historical walk, leaflet available. Aug.: Antique Fair. Oct.: Art Show. **In the area:** Chiltern Box-Ironbark National Park, surrounding town, for spring wildflowers, bushwalking and picnicking; tourist drives and guided walking tours available. Magenta open-cut mine, 2 km E. Near Barnawartha, 10 km NE, Koendidda historic homestead and gardens and B&B. Pioneer Cemetery, 2 km N. **Visitor information:** Gilmours Corner, 47 Conness St; (03) 5726 1611.

Clunes

Pop. 846

MAP REF. 216 C2, 227 J8, 233 O2, 235 O13, 238 A11

The first registered gold strike in the State was made at Clunes on 7 July 1851 when James Esmond announced his discovery of 'pay dirt'. The town, 36 km N of Ballarat, has several National Trust-classified bluestone buildings, and the verandahed elegance of Fraser St is worth noting. Surrounding the town are a number of extinct volcanoes, and a good view of these can be obtained about 3 km S, on the road to Ballarat. **In town:** In Bailey St: town hall and courthouse (1870); Bottle Museum in former South Clunes State School; Queens Park, established over 100 years ago on banks of Creswick Creek; old post office (1873), now second-hand bookshop (open weekends). Butter Factory Gallery, Cameron St, sculpture and art gallery. In Fraser St: The Weavery, handwoven fabrics; Museum, open weekends, public and school holidays. Nov.: Agricultural Show. **In the area:** Clunes Homestead Furniture, 1 km NW on Talbot Rd. At Talbot, historic town 18 km NW: many 1860–70 buildings, particularly in Camp St and Scandinavian Cres.; Arts and Historical Museum in former Primitive Methodist Church (1870); Bull and Mouth restaurant in old bluestone building (1860s), formerly hotel. At Mt Beckworth, 8 km W, scenic reserve. **Visitor information:** Clunes Museum, Fraser St; (03) 5345 3592. **See also:** The Golden Age p. 171.

The Pinnacles, on Cape Woolamai, south-east of Cowes

Cobram
Pop. 3865

MAP REF. 121 M13, 239 J3

Magnificent wide sandy beaches are a feature of the Murray River at Cobram, so picnicking, fishing and water sports are popular. This is an area of fast-growing industry and is also fruit-growing country; the clingstone variety of peach was developed here. **In town:** Log Cabin, opposite information centre in Punt Rd, historic cottage built in Yarrawonga 1875 and moved piece by piece. Rotary dairy, 200 cows, on outskirts of town; open at milking time, 4–5 p.m. daily. Market in Punt Rd, 1st Sat. each month. Jan.: Peaches and Cream Festival (odd-numbered years). May: Rotary Art Show. June: Antique Fair. Oct.: Agricultural Show: Open Gardens Display. Nov.: Sun Country Doll, Bears and Collectables Show; Harness Racing Meeting. **In the area:** Wineries open for tastings and sales include: Heritage Farm Wines, 5 km W on Murray Valley Hwy, with 116-m woodcarving depicting scenes of early Murray River life; Monichino Wines, 30 km W on Berry's Rd, Katunga; Strathkellar Wines, 8 km E and Fyffefield Wines, 15 km E, both on Murray Valley Hwy. Strawberry-picking in season, 5 km W at Koonoomoo. At Strathmerton, 16 km W: Cactus Country, Australia's largest cacti gardens. Just east of town, Quinn Island on Murray River; self-guide nature walk. Binghi Boomerang Factory at Barooga, 4 km NE. Sportavia Soaring Centre at Tocumwal airport, 20 km NW. **Visitor information:** The Old Grain Store, cnr Station St and Punt Rd; (03) 5872 2132. **See also:** The Mighty Murray p. 201.

Cohuna
Pop. 1979

MAP REF. 121 J12, 235 Q3, 238 C2

Located on the Murray Valley Hwy, Cohuna is surrounded by dairy farms. The town is beside Gunbower Island, formed by the Murray River on the far side and Gunbower Creek just across the highway from the town. This island is covered in red gum and box forest, which provides a home for abundant birdlife as well as kangaroos and emus. The forest is subject to flooding and a large part of the island has breeding rookeries during the flood periods. **In town:** Cohuna Historical Museum, Sampson St. Feb.: Aquatic Festival; Bridge to Bridge Swim. Mar.: Agricultural Show. **In the area:** 2-hr cruises in the *Wetlander* along Gunbower Creek. On Gunbower Island: birdlife, picnic/barbecue facilities and walking tracks (map at local shops). Major Mitchell Trail, 1700-km signposted trail that retraces this explorer's footsteps from Mildura to Wodonga via Portland; from Cohuna, signposted trail along Gunbower Creek, down to Mt Hope. Kow Swamp, 23 km S, a bird sanctuary; picnic spots and good fishing at Box Bridge. Mt Hope (110 m), about 28 km S, for good views and spring wildflowers. Cohuna Grove Cottage, 4 km SE on Murray Valley Hwy, local art and craft. Kraft factory and shop (open a.m. Mon.–Fri.), 16 km SE at Leitchville. Torrumbarry Weir, 40 km SE; during winter, entire weir structure is removed from the river; in summer, water-skiing above the weir. Mathers Waterwheel Museum, 9 km W on Brays Rd, has memorabilia. **Visitor information:** Golden River Tourism, 25 Murray St, Barham; (03) 5453 3100.

Colac
Pop. 9793

MAP REF. 216 B11, 221 G7, 233 N9

Colac is situated on the eastern edge of the volcanic plain that covers much of the Western District of Victoria. It is the centre of a prosperous, closely settled agricultural area and is sited on the shores of Lake Colac, which has good fishing and a variety of water sports. **In town:** In Gellibrand St: Historical Centre, (open Thurs., Fri., Sun. p.m.); Botanic Gardens. Barongarook Creek has prolific birdlife and walking track alongside, leading from Princes Hwy to Lake Colac on northern outskirts of town (good redfin fishing in lake). Self-guide town walk leaflet and information on full-day mountain scenic drive available. At information centre, recreation area with picnic/barbecue facilities. Market in Memorial Sq, Murray St, 3rd Sun. each month. Feb.: Otway Harvest Festival. Mar.: Food and Wine Festival. Apr.: Country Music Festival. Oct.: Garden Expo; Go Colac, Go Country Festival (includes Ferret Cup). **In the area:** Irrewarra Homestead, 10 km N on Colac–Ballarat Rd; natural ice-creams. Red Rock Lookout, 22 km N near Alvie; 30 volcanic lakes can be seen from here, including Lake Corangamite, Victoria's largest saltwater lake. Floating Island Reserve, 18 km W off Princes Hwy, a lagoon with islands that change position. Burtons Lookout, 13 km S, views of Otway hinterland; Wanawong Gardens at lookout. Red Rock Winery, 15 km S (check opening times). Gellibrand Pottery, 30 km S. Otway Ranges, about 30 km S, features beautiful winding roads, lush mountain scenery and waterfalls. Tarndwarncoort Homestead, 15 km E, has wool display and sales. At Birregurra, 20 km E, interesting old buildings. **Visitor information:** cnr Murray and Queen sts; (03) 5231 3730.

Coleraine
Pop. 1084

MAP REF. 232 E4

Situated 34 km NW of Hamilton, the Coleraine area was first settled by Europeans in 1838 for pastoral grazing. Today the primary products are fine-wool sheep and beef cattle. **In town:** Historic railway station, Pilleau St, now information centre; local arts and crafts. In Whyte St, both open by appt: Matthew Cooke's Blacksmiths Shop (1888), and Historical Society in Old Courthouse. Also in Whyte St: Chocolate Factory, open daily for tastings; Eucalyptus Discovery Centre. At

Point's Arboretum, southern outskirts of town on Coleraine–Portland Rd: largest number of eucalyptus species in Australia; also other native plants; prolific birdlife; lookout and picnic area. Apr.: Autumn Festival. Aug.: Art Show. **In the area:** Self-guide scenic day trips, brochure available. Historic homesteads: National Trust-classified Warrock Homestead (1843), 20 km W towards Casterton; Glendinning Homestead with wildlife sanctuary near Balmoral, 49 km N. Gardens of Glendinning Homestead and Mistydown Perennials (also at Balmoral); brochure available, check opening times. Wannon Falls, 14 km SE, and Nigretta Falls, 24 km SE. **Visitor information:** Old Railway Station, Pilleau St; (03) 5575 2733.

Corryong   Pop. 1215

MAP REF. 113 B8, 240 G2

Corryong is situated at the gateway to the Snowy Mountains. The district offers superb mountain scenery and excellent trout-fishing in the Murray River and its tributaries. **In town:** Two Feet Tour, brochure available. Jack Riley, reputedly 'the Man from Snowy River', came from these parts; his grave is in Corryong cemetery. The Man from Snowy River Folk Museum, Hanson St, features Riley's hut and classic clothing and ski collections. Large wooden galleon, Murray River Hwy. Mar.: Man from Snowy River Festival. Apr.: Bush Festival. **In the area:** Horse trail rides and 4WD tours; details from information centre. Scenic drive west from Corryong. Scenic views: Players Hill Lookout, 1 km SE; Mt Mittamatite and Emberys Lookout, 10 km N; lookout with views over Kosciuszko National Park at Towong, 12 km NE; Sassafras Gap, 66 km S. Canoeing and mountain-bike excursions from Walwa, 47 km NW. Emu Farm, 4 km W on Murray Valley Hwy. At Burrowa–Pine Mountain National Park, 27 km W: Cudgewa Bluff Falls, excellent scenery and bushwalking tracks. At Nariel, 45 km SW: trout-fishing in Nariel Creek; Folk Music Festival in Dec. Upper Murray Fish Farm, 38 km S. **Visitor information:** Hanson St; (02) 6076 2277.

Cowes   Pop. 3060

MAP REF. 217 L12, 219 O11, 230 E9

This is the main town on Phillip Island, a popular resort area in Western Port linked to the mainland by a bridge at San Remo. Cowes is situated on the northern side of the island; it has safe beaches for children, and a popular jetty for fishing and swimming. Market, Settlement Rd, each Sun. Apr.: Superbike Championships. May: Motor Racing. Oct.: Grand Prix Motorcycle Race. **In the area:** Summerland Beach, on southern shore, about 11 km SW, famous for its nightly penguin parade (no photography beyond the Visitor Centre). Colonies of fur seals year-round on Seal Rocks, 13 km SW, also short-tailed shearwaters (muttonbirds) Oct.–Apr.; Seal Rocks Sea Life Centre at nearby Nobbies offers marine displays and activities, and seal-watching. Phillip Island Vineyard and Winery, 9 km SW on Berrys Beach Rd, for tastings, sales and casual dining. Rhyll swamp and bird sanctuary, 8 km E. On Phillip Island Rd: Phillip Island Wildlife Park has native fauna in natural environment, 3 km S; Koala Conservation Centre features elevated boardwalk. Grand Prix Circuit and Visitor Centre, 6 km SE on Back Beach Rd, venue for Grand Prix Motorcycle Race. A Maze 'N Things, 7 km SE: large timber maze, optical illusion rooms, maxi mini golf. Cape Woolamai, 16 km SE: 2- and 4-hr walks from surf beach, around southern end of cape, past The Pinnacles. Australian Dairy Centre at Newhaven, 16 km SE, museum and cheese factory. At Churchill Island, 2 km from Newhaven, historic homestead and walking tracks. Feed pelicans, 11.30 a.m. on foreshore opposite San Remo Fishing Co-op. Wildlife Wonderland, 9 km from San Remo, including the Giant Earthworm Museum and Wombat World. Walks on island, maps available. **Visitor information:** Phillip Island Rd, Newhaven; (03) 5956 7447 or freecall 1300 366 422 (tickets for Phillip Island attractions available here). **See also:** Day Tours from Melbourne p. 154.

Creswick   Pop. 2327

MAP REF. 216 C3, 227 K9, 233 O2, 235 O13, 238 A12

Creswick is situated 18 km N of Ballarat on the Midland Hwy. One of the richest alluvial goldfields in the world was discovered here. **In town:** Mullock heaps on Ullina Rd (take care around old gold workings). Historical Museum, Albert St. Gold Battery, Battery Cres. Cemetery, Clunes Rd, with early miners' graves and Chinese section. In Melbourne Rd: Koala Park; St Georges Lake. Oct.: Brackenbury Classic Fun Run. **In the area:** Creswick Landcare Nursery, 1 km E. World of Dinosaurs, 1.5 km E off Midland Hwy, has life-size models. Gold panning in Slaty Creek, 4 km E. Tangled Maze, a maze formed by climbing plants, 5 km E. At Smeaton, 16 km NE: Smeaton House (1850s); Anderson's Mill (1860s), Food, Wine and Jazz Festival held here each Apr.; Tuki Trout Farm. **Visitor information:** Vincent St, Daylesford; (03) 5348 1339. **See also:** The Golden Age p. 171.

Daylesford   Pop. 3287

MAP REF. 216 E2, 227 N9, 233 Q2, 235 Q13, 238 B12

Daylesford and Hepburn Springs, 4 km N, together constitute a spa town, with 65 documented mineral springs, many with hand pumps. Daylesford rambles up the side of Wombat Hill, at the top of which are the Botanical Gardens. **In town:** Hepburn Springs Spa Complex, in the Mineral Springs Reserve, Forest Ave, offers public and private baths, flotation tanks, massage and a sauna. Convent Gallery with beautiful gardens, in former girls' school (1891), Daly St. Nearby, Wombat Hill Botanical Gardens and lookout tower. In Vincent St: Alpha Hall Galleria, in former silent movie house (open Thurs.– Mon.); historical museum in former School of Mines (open weekends). Central Springs Spa Reserve and Lake Daylesford, Central Springs Rd; Tipperary Walking Track from here to Mineral Springs Reserve, leaflet available. Market near railway station, Sun. a.m.; during market, Central Highlands Tourist Railway runs hourly rail-motor services between Daylesford and Musk, 7 km SE, and ganger's trolleys operate to Wombat Forest hourly every Sun. Jan.: Glenlyon Sports Day and Daylesford Gift (horse race). Apr.: Fair. May: Hepburn Swiss–Italian Festival. July: Mid-Winter Festival. Nov.: Agricultural Show. Dec.: Highland Gathering. **In the area:** Lyonville spring, 15 km SE. Loddon Falls, 10 km NE. Breakneck Gorge, 5 km N. Mt Franklin, an extinct volcano, 13 km N. Yandoit, a settlement of Swiss–Italian heritage, 18 km NW. Sailors Falls, 5 km S. **Visitor information:** Vincent St; (03) 5348 1339. **See also:** The Golden Age p. 171.

Derrinallum   Pop. 265

MAP REF. 221 C2, 233 L6

A small rural town servicing the local pastoral farming community and surrounded by volcanic plains. **In the area:** Significant dry-stone walls, immediately west of town. Mt Elephant, 2 km SW, a scoria cone of volcanic origin rising high above surrounding plains. At Darlington,

Little Desert National Park, near Dimboola

19 km SW: Elephant Bridge Hotel, a 2-storey bluestone building, National Trust-classified. Lake Tooliorook, 6 km SE, for fishing and water sports. **Visitor information:** Fragrant Cottage, Old Courthouse Building, Manifold St, Camperdown; (03) 5593 2288.

Dimboola
Pop. 1557

MAP REF. 234 F7
This is a peaceful town on the tree-lined Wimmera River, 36 km NW of Horsham. **In town:** Walking track along Wimmera River. Apr.: Wimmera German Fest. Oct.: Agricultural Show. Nov.: Rowing Regatta. **In the area:** At Little Desert National Park, 6 km SW: self-guide walks, including Pomponderoo Hill Nature Walk (1 km) from Horseshoe Bend picnic and camping area at river's edge; short-beaked echidnas; occasional sightings of endangered mallee fowl. At Wail, 11 km SE, well-stocked Natural Resource League forest nursery (open Mon.–Fri.). Ebenezer Mission Station (founded 1859), near Antwerp on Jeparit Rd, 15 km N: historic site with ruins and restored church. Pink Lake, coloured salt lake, 9 km NW. At Kiata, 26 km W, mallee fowl can be seen in Lowan Sanctuary all year. **Visitor information:** Mog's Menagerie, 119 Lloyd St; (03) 5389 1290.

Donald
Pop. 1383

MAP REF. 235 K7
At the junction of the Sunraysia and Borung hwys, Donald is situated on the Richardson River. **In town:** In Wood St: historic police station (1874);

shepherd's hut (1850). Steam Train Park, cnr Hammill and Walker sts, site of old J524 class steam locomotive. Agricultural museum, Hammill St. Historic water pump by lake in caravan park. Bullocks Head Lookout, Byrne St: unusual growth on box tree, resembling bull's head, beside Richardson River. Scilleys Island has walking tracks and wildlife; access by footbridge from Sunraysia Hwy. Kooka's Country Cookies, Sunraysia Hwy, has tours and sales. Self-guide walks, brochure available. Market in Byrne St, 3rd Sat. each month. June: Scottish Dancing Country Weekend. Labour Day Weekend Lawn Tennis Championship. **In the area:** Glengar River Sanctuary, 2 km NE on Borung Hwy, contains grave of first woman settler in district. Mt Jeffcott, 20 km NE, for flora, kangaroos and views of Lake Buloke. Good fishing in Richardson River. River flows into Lake Buloke, 10 km N, a wetlands area. Watch-em Lake, 35 km N, good fishing and water sports. Lake Batyo Catyo and Richardson River Weir offer good fishing, both 20 km S. **Visitor information:** Bev and Guildy's Cafe, 75 Wood St; (03) 5497 1155.

Drysdale
Pop. 1474

MAP REF. 216 H9, 223 H7, 230 B6
This is primarily a service centre for the local farming community on the Bellarine Peninsula. **In town:** In High St: Old Courthouse Museum, home of the Bellarine Historical Society; Drysdale Community Crafts. Community Market at Recreation Reserve, Duke St, every 3rd Sun. (Sept.–Apr.). **In the area:** Lake Lorne picnic area, 1 km SW. Nearby Bellarine

Peninsula Railway offers steam-train rides between Drysdale and Queenscliff, weekends and summer holidays; locomotives and carriages dating back to 1870s on display. Soho Nursery and Fine Arts Gallery, 6 km E. Local wineries include: Scotchmans Hill Winery, 8 km NE on Scotchmans Road; historic Spray Farm Winery, Portarlington Rd (open weekends and public holidays), has Summer Concert Series Jan.–Feb. in natural amphitheatre. At Portarlington, a popular seaside resort 8 km NE: historic flour mill (1857), restored by National Trust, with historical displays; Lavender Cottage Gallery; public reserve; safe bay for children to swim. At St Leonards, a small beach resort, 13 km E: Edwards Point Wildlife Reserve; memorial commemorates landing by Matthew Flinders in 1802, and John Batman and his party in 1835. **Visitor information:** A Maze'N Things, 1570 Bellarine Hwy, cnr Grubb Rd, Wallington; (03) 5250 2669.

Dunkeld
Pop. 444

MAP REF. 232 H4
On the Glenelg Hwy, 32 km NE of Hamilton, Dunkeld is the southern gateway to the Grampians and is convenient for trips to the Chimney Pots, a landmark in the Grampians National Park, 25 km N. **In town:** Self-guide walk or drive of historic places of interest, leaflet available. Historical museum in old church, Templeton St, features history of area's Aborigines, local wool industry and explorer Major Mitchell's journeys; open weekends or by appt. Arboretum, Old Ararat Rd, has exotic species from worldwide, brochure available. Nov.: Dunkeld Cup (horse race). **In the area:** Walking tracks to top of Mt Sturgeon (3 km N) and Mt Abrupt (8 km N); both climbs steep, but very good views. Easier walk to Mt Piccaninny, 4.5 km N. Freshwater Lake Reserve, 8 km N. **Visitor information:** Glenelg Hwy; (03) 5577 2558.

Dunolly
Pop. 668

MAP REF. 227 J3, 235 O10
A small town in north-central Victoria, in the heart of the gold country and on the Goldfields Tourist Route. 'Welcome Stranger', considered to be the largest nugget ever discovered, was found 15 km NW at Moliagul. The district has produced more nuggets than any other goldfield in Australia; 126 were unearthed in the town itself. **In town:** Restored courthouse, Market St, has display relating to historic

gold discoveries in area (open by appt). Next door, original lockup (1859) and stables. In Broadway: handsome original buildings; Goldfields Historical and Arts Society collection, includes replicas of some of town's most spectacular nuggets (open weekends). **In the area:** Self-guide bike rides and gold-focussed town tours of region, leaflets available. Countryside abounds with colourful spring wildflowers and native fauna. Gold-panning in local creeks. Laanecoorie Reservoir, 16 km E, for swimming, boating, waterskiing, camping and picnic facilities. Tarnagulla, 16 km NE, a small mining town with splendid Victorian architecture; mine (not open to public) and flora reserve nearby. At Moliagul, 15 km NW: monuments mark spot where 'Welcome Stranger' nugget found in 1869; birthplace of Rev. John Flynn, founder of Royal Flying Doctor Service; Welcome Stranger Discovery Walk, leaflet available. **Visitor information:** Railway Station Complex, Station St, Maryborough; (03) 5460 4511, freecall 1800 356 511.

Echuca
Pop. 10 014

MAP REF. 121 K13, 238 E4

Echuca and its twin town Moama, across the river in NSW, are at the junction of the Murray, Campaspe and Goulburn rivers. Now a city and once Australia's largest inland port, Echuca took its name from an Aboriginal word meaning 'meeting of the waters', while Moama means 'place of the dead'. A historic iron bridge joins the two. **In town:** Port of Echuca, restored to the period of its heyday with its massive red gum wharf; paddle-steamer *Pevensey* (renamed *Philadelphia* for TV mini-series *All the Rivers Run*); D26 logging barge, PS *Alexander Arbuthnot*; PS *Adelaide*; all available for cruises. Also part of the Port's attractions, all in Murray Esplanade: Star Hotel, underground bar with escape tunnel; Bridge Hotel, built by Henry Hopwood, founder of Echuca, who ran original punt service; Red Gum Works, has woodturning demonstrations; award-winning Sharp's Magic Movie House and Penny Arcade; carriage rides; port tour. In High St: Echuca Historical Society Museum (1867) in former police station; World in Wax museum. National Holden Museum, Warren St. Port of Call Wine Centre, Redcliffe St. Cruises on paddlewheelers *Canberra* and *Pride of the Murray*; accommodation and cruises on paddlesteamer *Emmylou*; MV *Mary Ann* cruising restau-

rant. Houseboat, boat and canoe hire. Feb.: Southern 80 Ski Race from Torrumbarry Weir to Echuca; Riverboats, Food, Jazz and Wine Festival. Apr.: Barmah Muster. June: Steam, Horse and Vintage Car Rally. **In the area:** Camping, fishing, water sports and bushwalking. In Moama: Gumnutland model village; Silverstone Go-Kart Track; Horseshoe Lagoon reserve. At Barmah State Park 39 km NE: Dharnya Aboriginal Interpretative Centre, has excellent historical display of culture of local Yorta Yorta people; wetlands cruises, fishing, swimming, canoes and barbecue pontoons for hire at Barmah Lake. Near Mathoura, 40 km N: Moira Forest Walkway and Bird Observatory. Picnic Point recreational area, 11 km E of Mathoura. **Visitor information:** Old Pumphouse, cnr Heygarth St and Cobb Hwy; (03) 5480 7555. Web site www.echucamoama.com **See also:** The Mighty Murray p. 201; Vineyards and Wineries p. 207.

Edenhope
Pop. 776

MAP REF. 234 C11

On the Wimmera Hwy, just 30 km from the border with South Australia, Edenhope is situated on the shores of Lake Wallace, a haven for waterbirds. When full, the lake is popular for water sports and fishing. **In town:** Cairn, beside lake in Lake St, commemorating visit of first all-Aboriginal cricket team to England; team was coached by T. W. Willis, who was also the founder of Australian Rules football. Feb.: Henley-on-Lake Wallace. Mar.: Gourmet Food Day; Races. **In the area:** At Harrow, one of Victoria's oldest inland towns, 32 km SE: historic buildings including Hermitage Hotel (1851) and log gaol (1862); cemetery contains grave of first Aboriginal cricketer, Johnny Mullagh; National Bush Billycart Championship in Mar. Rocklands Reservoir, part of Wimmera–Mallee irrigation system, for fishing and boating; 65 km E. About 50 km W, over SA border, Naracoorte Caves Conservation Park. **Visitor information:** 98 Elizabeth St; (03) 5585 1509.

Eildon
Pop. 703

MAP REF. 217 P2, 228 A12, 239 K11

Built to irrigate a vast stretch of northern Victoria and to provide hydro-electric power, Lake Eildon is the State's largest constructed lake and is a popular resort area, surrounded by the beautiful foothills of the Alps within Lake Eildon National

Park. Various self-guide walks and drives and horseriding. Excellent recreational facilities around the foreshores, two major boat harbours, launching ramps, picnic grounds and many lookout points. Power boat and houseboat hire at boat harbours. Dec.: Christmas Eve Gala Night. **In the area:** Signposted Lake Eildon Wall Lookout, 1 km N. Lake cruises from Eildon Boat Harbour. Eildon Pondage and Goulburn River, for excellent fishing (no closed season for trout in Lake Eildon). Lake Eildon National Park, surrounding town, has several walking tracks, and camping and picnicking at Jerusalem Inlet. Mt Pinninger (503 m), 3 km E, for panoramic views of Mt Buller, the Alps and lake. Snobs Creek Fish Hatchery, 6 km SW; millions of trout bred to stock waterways. Just past hatchery, Snobs Creek Falls. Eildon Deer Park nearby, on Goulburn Valley Hwy. Rubicon Falls, 18 km SW via Thornton. Scenic drive to Lake Eildon National Park, 16 km NW: walks including popular Candlebark Gully Nature Walk. **Visitor information:** Main St; (03) 5774 2909.

Emerald
Pop. 4673

MAP REF. 217 M7, 220 C13, 230 F5

The Puffing Billy steam railway runs from Belgrave to Gembrook via Emerald, the first European settlement in the Dandenong Ranges. **In town:** Many galleries and craft shops. At Emerald Lake, on Emerald Lake Rd: Environmental Centre, walking tracks, barbecues, paddleboats, model railway, kiosk and tearooms; scenic trails. Apr.: Great Train Race (runners attempt to race Puffing Billy from Belgrave to Emerald Lake Park). **In the area:** Many scenic walking tracks, brochures available. At Menzies Creek, 4 km NW: Puffing Billy Steam Museum (open weekends, and public holidays and Wed.); Cotswold House, fine food and views; Cardinia Reservoir Park, for good views, picnic spots and native fauna including kangaroos roaming freely; nearby Lake Aura Vale, for sailing and picnics. Sherbrooke Art Gallery in Monbulk Rd, Belgrave, 11 km NW. Australian Rainbow Trout Farm at Macclesfield, 8 km N. At Gembrook, 14 km E: The Motorist Cafe and Museum, Main St, heritage vehicles; market last Sat. each month at railway station. Bimbimbie Wildlife Park at Mount Burnett, 12 km SE. Trail horseriding available at Sherbrooke Equestrian Park, 3 km W on Wellington Rd. **Visitor**

Puffing Billy makes its way through the Dandenongs, near Emerald

information: Dandenong Ranges Tourism, 1211 Burwood Hwy, Upper Ferntree Gully; (03) 9758 7522. Web site www.pbr.org.au **See also:** Day Tours from Melbourne p. 154.

Euroa   Pop. 2697

MAP REF. 238 I8
A small town 151 km NE of Melbourne, just off the Hume Fwy, Euroa is a good base for exploring the Strathbogie Ranges and tablelands. The Kelly gang staged a daring robbery here in 1878, rounding up some 50 hostages at the nearby Faithfull Creek station and then making off with money and gold worth almost £2000. **In town:** Several historic buildings, including National Bank and post office in Binney St. In Kirkland Ave: Seven Creeks Park for fishing; Farmers Arms Historical Museum, includes Ned Kelly and Eliza Forlonge history (open Fri.–Mon. p.m.). Miniature steam-train rides, Turnbull St (last Sun. each month). Parachuting School, Drysdale Rd (open weekends). Wildflower walks in spring, leaflet available; open gardens spring and autumn. Mar.: Let's Go Irish Week. Oct.: Agricultural Show; Wool Week. **In the area:** Forlonge Memorial, off Strathbogie Road, 10 km SE, commemorates Eliza Forlonge, who with her sister imported first merino sheep into Victoria. Scenic drive to Gooram Falls (20 km SE) and around Strathbogie Ranges. Polly McQuinns, historic river crossing and reservoir, 20 km SE on Strathbogie Rd. Balloon Flights Victoria, 10 km SW. At Longwood, 14 km SW: historic buildings, especially White Heart Hotel; Lavender Art Gallery; horse-drawn carriage rides. At Locksley, 20 km SW, gliding and parachuting. Mt Wombat Lookout, 25 km SW, spectacular views of surrounding country and Alps. Faithfull Creek Waterfall, 9 km NE. At Violet Town, 24 km NE, Stone Crop art gallery. **Visitor information:** Strathbogie Ranges Tourism at BP Service Centre, Tarcombe St; (03) 5795 3677.

Flinders   Pop. 501

MAP REF. 217 J12, 219 J11, 230 D9
Flinders is the most southerly town on the Mornington Peninsula. In clear weather there are spectacular clifftop views across the bay to French Island and The Nobbies and Seal Rocks on Phillip Island. **In town:** Several historic buildings, including Bimbi (1870s), the earliest remaining dwelling in Flinders; and Wilga (1880s), fine Victorian-era home with large hedge; both in King St. Flinders Golf Links, Wood St, on West Head with spectacular views across Bass Strait. **In the area:** Ace Hi horseriding and wildlife park, 11 km W. Cape Schanck lighthouse (1859), 15 km W. At Main Ridge, 11 km NW: Sunny Ridge Strawberry Farm, Mornington–Flinders Rd, pick-your-own berries in season; Pig and Whistle, an authentic English pub, Purves Rd. At Red Hill 17 km N: The Cherry Farm, Arkwells Lane, picturesque setting, pick-your-own cherries and berries; variety of galleries on Mornington–Flinders Rd; community market first Sat. each month (Sep.–May); Red Hill Truck Show and Festival in Jan. Also in the Red Hill area, several wineries with cellar-door sales. At Shoreham, 6 km NE, Ashcombe Maze and Water Gardens, Red Hill Rd, hedge mazes surrounded by gardens (closed Aug.). The Barn Art and Craft Centre at Merricks, 13 km NE on Bittern–Dromana Rd, has numerous local craft displays (open Wed.–Mon.). At Balnarring 17 km NE: Emu Plains Market, 3rd Sat. each month, (Nov.–May); Coolart Homestead, with historical displays, gardens, wetlands bird observation area; several wineries with cellar-door sales. Surfing at Point Leo, 5 km E of Shoreham. **Visitor information:** Peninsula Visitor Centre, Point Nepean Rd, Dromana; (03) 5987 3078, freecall 1800 804 009. Web site www. travelbook.com.au/vic/mornpen/index. html **See also:** Day Tours from Melbourne p. 154; Vineyards and Wineries p. 207.

Foster   Pop. 1049

MAP REF. 231 J10
A picturesque small town within easy reach of Corner Inlet, Waratah Bay and Wilsons Promontory on the south-east coast of Victoria, and about 170 km E Melbourne. **In town:** In Main St: Historical Museum, in old post office; Stockyard Gallery. Kaffir Hill Walk from town car park, scenic nature walk past old goldmining sites. Feb.: Agricultural Show. **In the area:** Foster North Lookout, 6 km NW. Scenic drive to Fish Creek, 11 km SW; 2 km SE of town, Fish Creek Potters. Cape Liptrap, 46 km SW, excellent views of rugged coastline and Bass Strait. Good surf beach at Sandy Point, 22 km S; surrounding protected waters of Shallow Inlet popular for fishing, windsurfing and swimming. Wilsons Promontory National Park, 32 km S, has spectacular scenery, abundant flora and fauna, magnificent beaches, many walks, and camping at Tidal River. Turtons Creek, 18 km N, old gold-rich area; lyrebirds sometimes seen in tree-fern gullies nearby. Pleasant beaches: Waratah Bay, 34 km SW; Walkerville, 36 km SW; Port Franklin, 12 km SE. **Visitor information:** Stockyard Gallery, Main St; (03) 5682 1125, freecall 1800 630 704.

Geelong   Pop. 125 382

MAP REF. 216 F9, 222, 223 E7, 230 A6, 233 R7
Geelong, on Corio Bay, is the largest
provincial city in Victoria. It is a major
manufacturing and processing centre, and
has a strong tradition in wool selling and
storage. The Corio Bay area was first settled
in the 1830s and, apart from a rush to the
diggings during the gold boom, Geelong
has grown and prospered steadily. It is a
pleasant and well-laid-out city with lovely
views across the bay. **In town:** National
Wool Museum, in historic bluestone woolstore cnr Moorabool and Brougham sts,
features sound and audio-visual displays,
re-created shearers' quarters and mill-
worker's cottage. Interesting buildings
(more than 100 with National Trust classifications) include Merchiston Hall (1856),
Osborne House (1858), and Corio Villa
(1856). Open to the public: The Heights
(1855), 14-roomed prefabricated timber
mansion surrounded by delightful gardens, Aphrasia St, Newtown; Barwon
Grange (1855), Fernleigh St, Newtown.
Christ Church, Moorabool St, oldest
Anglican church in Victoria in continuous
use. Customs House, Brougham St. Ford
Discovery Centre, cnr Brougham and
Gheringhap sts, history of Ford cars, with
interactive displays (closed Tues). Geelong
Art Gallery, large regional gallery;
Performing Arts Centre; both in Little
Malop St. Wintergarden, McKillop St,
historic building housing gallery, nursery,
antiques and gift shop. Pottage Crafts,
Moorabool St. Waterfront Geelong,
restored promenade on Eastern Beach;
swimming in fully restored 1930s sea-
bathing complex. Beachfront Scenic Drive.
Botanic Gardens, Garden St in Eastern
Park, overlooking Corio Bay. Johnstone
Park, cnr Mercer and Gheringhap sts.
Queens Park, Queens Park Rd, Newtown,

The Prom

Wilsons Promontory,
at the southern-
most tip of the main-
land, is one of Victoria's
largest and most spect-
acular national parks.
'The Prom', as it is affectionately known to
Victorians, has an impressive range of
landscapes, including tall forested ranges,
luxuriant tree fern valleys, open heaths, salt
marshes and long drifts of sand dunes. Its
wide, white sandy beaches are truly
magnificent, some dominated by spectacular
granite tors and washed by a rolling surf.
There is a safe swimming beach at Norman
Bay near the main camping area at Tidal
River. At the aptly named Squeaky Beach, the
sand squeaks underfoot.

Two lookouts in particular offer magnificent
views across the Prom, the sea and offshore
islands: Sparkes Lookout, off the main road to
Tidal River, and the lookout at the Mount
Oberon summit.

Birds and other wildlife abound on the
Prom: lorikeets, rosellas, kookaburras and
blue wrens are in evidence, even in the main
general store area at Tidal River village; and
for the more dedicated and patient
birdwatcher, sightings of beautiful firetails
and emu-wrens can be the reward.

Emus feed unperturbed on the open grassland by the side of
the main road at the park entry area at Yanakie Isthmus, and
kangaroos and wallabies seem unimpressed by their human
observers; drive carefully to avoid them. At night, wombat-spotting
by torchlight is a favourite pastime with children staying in the Tidal
River area.

There are more than 150 kilometres of walking tracks in the Wilsons
Promontory National Park. Some cover short walks, such as the nature
trail in Lilly Pilly Gully, where the vegetation varies from bushland
inhabited by koalas, to rainforest with ancient tree ferns and trickling
streams. Other longer walks can be taken to such places as Sealers

Refuge Cove, a beautiful cove on the eastern side of the Prom

Cove, Refuge Cove or to South East Point, where there is a lighthouse
dating from 1859. Cottages adjacent to the lighthouse can be booked
for accommodation.

At the visitor information centre and park office at Tidal River,
brochures are available detailing walking tracks and the flora and fauna
of the park. During summer and Easter, there are talks, guided walks
and spotlight tours as well as children's nature activities. Permits are
required for all overnight hikes.

For further information and bookings, contact the Wilsons Promontory
National Park, Park Office, Tidal River; (03) 5680 9555. Web site
www.parkweb.vic.gov.au **Map reference:** 231 K12.

has walks to Buckley Falls. Balyang Bird Sanctuary, Shannon Ave, Newtown. Extensive walking tracks and bike paths alongside Barwon River. Boat ramps on Corio Bay beaches. Good river and bay fishing. Steampacket Gardens Market on foreshore at Eastern Beach, 1st Sun. each month. Jan.: Waterfront Festival. Feb.: Australian International Air Show (odd-numbered years). Mar.: Highland Gathering. Apr.: Alternative Farmvision. June: National Wool Week; National Celtic Folk Festival. Sept.: Momenta Arts Geelong. Oct.: Agricultural Show; Racing Carnival. **In the area:** 14 wineries (details from information centre); Norlane Water World, 7 km N. You Yangs, 20 km N, a range of distinctive granite hills in You Yangs Regional Park, has walking tracks, picnic grounds and information centre. Nearby, Serendip

Sanctuary, once purely a wildlife research station, now open to public, has nature trails, bird hides and visitors' centre. Anakie, a township at foot of Brisbane Ranges, 29 km N. Brisbane Ranges National Park, 34 km N: has many species of ferns and flowering plants, and native fauna, including koalas; Discovery Walk leads to Anakie Gorge (leaflet available). Nearby Fairy Park, with miniature houses and scenes from fairytales. Mt Anakie Winery; Staughton Vale winery; both north of Anakie on Staughton Vale Rd. Steiglitz, 10 km NW of Anakie, once a gold town, now almost deserted, has restored courthouse (1875), open Sun. Fyansford, 4 km W on outskirts of city, one of oldest settlements in region: historic buildings including Swan Inn, Balmoral Hotel (1854) and Fyansford Hotel; information board at

Common Reserve has interpretative material on history, flora and fauna of region; Monash Bridge across Moorabool River thought to be one of first reinforced-concrete bridges in Victoria. Brownhill Observation Tower, 10 km SW at Ceres, excellent view of surrounding areas. At Moriac, 22 km SW, horse-drawn caravan hire. **Visitor information:** National Wool Museum, 26–32 Moorabool St; (03) 5222 2900, freecall 1800 620 888. Web site www.greatoceanrd.org.au **See also:** Wildlife-Watching p. 167.

Glenrowan   Pop. 343

MAP REF. 228 D1, 239 M6

Glenrowan, 220 km NE of Melbourne, is the famous site of the defeat of Ned Kelly and his gang by the police in 1880.

The Grampians

The massive sandstone ranges of the Grampians in western Victoria provide some of the State's most spectacular scenery. Rising in peaks to heights of over 1000 metres, they form the western extremity of the Great Dividing Range. For many thousands of years, several Aboriginal groups occupied the area. More recently, the explorer Major Mitchell climbed and named the highest peak Mt William in July 1836, and gave the name 'The Grampians' to the ranges because they reminded him of the Grampians in his native Scotland.

In 1984 these ranges became a national park. The park offers good scenery, wildlife and tourist facilities. The scenic drives are on good roads; bushwalking and rock-climbing are popular. The western and northern Grampians have Aboriginal rock-art sites and the Brambuk Aboriginal Cultural Centre, near Hall's Gap, interprets indigenous culture. Lake Bellfield provides for fishing, canoeing and kayaking, and there is trout-fishing in the lake and in Fyans Creek.

There is plenty of wildlife to be seen: koalas and kangaroos are numerous, and echidnas, possums and platypuses can be found, while more than 200 bird species have been identified.

Apart from their grandeur, the Grampians are best known for the beauty and variety of their wildflowers. There are more than 1000 species of indigenous ferns and flowering plants, and they are at their most colourful from August to November. The Halls Gap Wildflower Exhibition is held each October.

Halls Gap, which takes its name from a pioneer pastoralist who settled in the eastern Grampians in the early 1840s, is the focal point of the area and offers a wide variety of accommodation.

The Grampians, rugged sandstone ranges in western Victoria

For information on accommodation, contact the Stawell and Grampians Tourism Information Centre, 50–52 Western Hwy, Stawell; (03) 5358 2314, freecall 1800 246 880. For park information contact the Grampians National Park Visitors Centre, Grampians Rd, Halls Gap; (03) 5356 4381 or call the Parks Victoria Information Line, 13 1963. Web site www.parkweb. vic.gov.au **See also:** National Parks p. 163 and individual entries in A–Z listing for towns in bold type. **Map references:** 232 H1, 234 H12.

In town: Self-guide Historic Ned Kelly Trail, brochures available. Historic Siege St, site of Kelly's last stand against police. On Gladstone St (Old Hume Hwy): Ned Kelly Memorial Museum and Homestead; Kate's Cottage, gifts and souvenirs behind huge 6-m high statue of Ned Kelly set in cottage gardens; Kellyland, engrossing computer-animated show of Ned Kelly's capture; Cobb and Co and Museum. White Cottage Herb Garden, Hill St. **In the area:** Nearby wineries: Baileys of Glenrowan, Taminick Gap Rd (just NW of town); Auldstone Cellars and Booths Taminick Cellars, both on Booths Rd, Taminick, 10 km NW; HJT Vineyards, Keenan Rd (near Lake Mokoan). **Visitor information:** Kate's Cottage, Gladstone St (Old Hume Hwy); (03) 5766 2448. **See also:** Vineyards and Wineries p. 207.

Halls Gap   Pop. 256

MAP REF. 232 I1, 234 I12
Beautifully sited in the heart of the Grampians, this little village is adjacent to Lake Bellfield and surrounded by the Grampians National Park and a network of scenic roads. **In town:** Long-billed corellas arrive each evening to roost opposite shops. Feb.: Grampians Jazz Festival. May: Grampians Gourmet Weekend. Oct.: Wildflower Exhibition. **In the area:** The region is noted for its wildflowers. Bushwalking, camping, rock climbing and abseiling in national park, one of largest in State; Visitors Centre, 2.5 km S on Dunkeld Rd. Brambuk Aboriginal Cultural Centre, 2 km S: displays; art exhibitions; information on shelters, art and other significant sites; tours. The Gap Vineyard, 2 km E. Lake Fyans, 17 km E, for swimming, fishing, yachting and water-skiing. At Roses Gap Recreation Park, Roses Gap Rd, 21 km N in Northern Grampians section of park: scenic walks, fitness track, accommodation and camping. Also within Grampians National Park: Boroka Lookout, Reids Lookout and The Balconies, 12 km NW; MacKenzie Falls, 17 km NW; eastern grey kangaroos at Zumsteins picnic area, 22 km NW; school holiday activities. Wartook Pottery and Restaurant, 20 km NW. **Visitor information:** Stawell and Grampians Visitor Information Centre, 50–52 Western Hwy, Stawell; (03) 5358 2314, freecall 1800 246 880. Web site www.ngshire.vic.gov.au **See also:** National Parks p. 163; Wildlife-Watching p. 167; The Grampians p. 182.

Hamilton   Pop. 9248

MAP REF. 232 F5
Known as the 'Wool Capital of the World', Hamilton is a prosperous and stylish city less than an hour's drive from the coastal centres of Portland, Port Fairy and Warrnambool to the south and the Grampian Ranges to the north. **In town:** Big Woolbales Complex, Coleraine Rd, focuses on wool industry, and has wool-shed memorabilia and craft centre. Hamilton Country Spun Woollen Mill and Factory, Peck St, has sales and tours (Mon.–Fri.). HIRL (Hamilton Institute of Rural Learning), North Boundary Rd, has nature trail and breeding area for eastern barred bandicoots (open Mon.–Wed.). Historical and scenic walks and drives, brochures available. Land-care tours, bookings essential (contact information centre). Hamilton Art Gallery, Brown St, fine regional gallery, contains Herbert Shaw Collection. Lake Hamilton, Ballarat Rd, for water sports and fishing; sandy beach, jogging and cycling tracks and picnic facilities. On banks of lake, Sir Reginald Ansett Transport Museum, Glenelg Hwy, has historical collection and memorabilia; Ansett transport industry began in Hamilton 1931. Botanical Gardens (established 1870), French St, has native animal enclosure, free-flight aviary and historic band rotunda. Hamilton Pastoral Museum, in former St Luke's Lutheran Church, on Glenelg Hwy (check times). Hamilton History Centre, Gray St, features histories of early Western District families. Hamilton is the starting point for Mary MacKillop Pilgrims Drive; grave of Mary's father in cemetery on Henty Hwy. Feb.: Beef Expo. Apr.: Southern Grampians Autumn Festival (even-numbered years). July: Eisteddfod. Aug.: Sheepvention (sheep and wool inventions and farmdog championships). **In the area:** Nigretta Falls, 15 km NW, has viewing platform nearby. Wannon Falls, 19 km W. Mt Eccles National Park, 35 km S near Macarthur, features 3 extinct volcanoes: Mt Eccles (with crater Lake Surprise, camping and koalas), Mt Rouse (at Penshurst), and Mt Napier (not accessible). Byaduk Caves (lava caves) en route to park. Grampians tour (good day trip from Hamilton) to Dunkeld, Grampians National Park, Halls Gap, Ararat and back via Glenthompson. At Cavendish, 25 km N, 3 beautiful private gardens, brochure available. **Visitor information:** Lonsdale St; (03) 5572 3746, freecall 1800 807 056. Web site www.sthgrampians.vic.gov.au

Harrietville   Pop. 186

MAP REF. 229 M8, 239 Q9, 240 C7
This former goldmining village, tucked into the foothills of Mt Hotham and Mt Feathertop, is a convenient accommodation centre for skiers at Mt Hotham and summer holidaymakers. **In town:** On Great Alpine Rd: Pioneer Park, an open-air museum and picnic area; Tavare Park, with swing bridge and picnic/barbecue facilities. Bush market, 2nd Sun. in Jan. and Easter Sun. Jan.: Classical Music Competition; Ride-on Mower Grand Prix. Oct.: Bluegrass Festival. **In the area:** Lavender Farm, at northern edge of town on Great Alpine Rd (closed in winter). Summer bushwalking in high mountain country of Alpine National Park, which surrounds town (note that weather conditions can be harsh and change suddenly); walking tracks to Mt Feathertop (1922 m), 20 km return; Mt Hotham (1868 m), 65 km return. Hotham Heights Alpine Village, 31 km SE, has summer bushwalking (Australian Alps Walking Track passes through village) in Bogong High Plains and Dargo High Plains, and winter downhill and cross-country skiing. Dinner Plain Alpine Village, 43 km SE, has summer bushwalking and horseriding, and winter cross-country skiing. Bright Waters Trout Farm and, nearby, Mountain Fresh Trout Farm, 5 km N, offer fishing and educational displays. **Visitor information:** General Store, Great Alpine Rd; (03) 5759 2553. **See also:** Alpine Country p. 190.

Healesville   Pop. 6368

MAP REF. 217 N5, 220 E6, 230 F3
Surrounded by mountain forest country, Healesville is a short drive from Melbourne along the Maroondah Hwy. It has been a popular resort town since the turn of the century, as the climate is cool and pleasant in summer and the area offers excellent bushwalks and beautiful scenic drives. **In town:** Open-air trolley rides, Healesville railway station to Yarra Glen (Sun. and public holidays). Market, River St, 1st Sun. each month. Feb.: Coldstream Country and Western Festival. Mar.: Australian Car Rally Championship; Grape Grazing. Nov.: Gateway Festival. **In the area:** World-famous Healesville Sanctuary, 4 km S on Badger Creek Rd: 32-ha reserve housing a variety of native birds and animals in largely natural bushland setting, yet displays enable animals to be seen in close proximity; picnic/barbecue facilities, kiosk and bistro. En route to Healesville

Close encounter with a falcon at Healesville Sanctuary

Sanctuary: HCP Antique Emporium, a large, undercover antique market; Hedgend Maze, Albert Rd; pottery, lapidary and art gallery at Nigel Court; Corranderrk Aboriginal Cemetery, 3 km S. Mallesons Lookout, 8 km S, views of Yarra Valley through to Melbourne. Yarra Ranges National Park, just east of town: majestic mountain ash forests and fern gullies; within park, superb drive through forest over Black Spur, picnic facilities at top; Badger Weir Park, 7 km SE, majestic park in natural setting; Tuscany Gallery, 5 km E; Donnelly's Weir Park, 4 km N, start of 5000-km Bicentennial National Trail to Cooktown (Qld) for horseriders and walkers; Mt St Leonard, 14 km N, fine views from summit. Maroondah Reservoir Park, 3 km NE: magnificent park in forested setting, walking tracks and lookout nearby. At Toolangi, 20 km NW: Singing Garden of C. J. Dennis, a beautiful, formal garden; Sculpture Studio, sculpture from recycled timbers, and pottery. There are around 30 wineries in the area open for cellar-door sales and tastings; Yarra Valley wine tours. **Visitor information:** Yarra Valley Visitor Information Centre, old courthouse, Harker St; (03) 5962 2600. **See also:** Day Tours from Melbourne p. 154; Wildlife-Watching p. 167; Vineyards and Wineries p. 207.

Heathcote

Pop. 1565

MAP REF. 238 E9
In attractive countryside on the McIvor Hwy, Heathcote is set along the McIvor Creek, 47 km SE of Bendigo. **In town:** Courthouse Crafts, in old courthouse, High St, has historical display, art and craft. Pink Cliffs, Pink Cliffs Rd, off

Hospital Rd, brilliant mineral staining created by eroded spoil from gold sluices. Old Heathcote Hospital (1859), Hospital St. McIvor Range Reserve, off Barrack St. Heathcote Winery, High St. Easter: Rodeo. Nov.: Agricultural Show. **In the area:** Bushwalking tracks in surrounding forests, details from information centre. Lake Eppalock, 10 km W, one of the State's largest lakes; Eppalock Gold Cup (power boat race) each Feb. Mount Ida Lookout, 4 km N, excellent views. Central Victorian Yabby Farm, 5 km S: catch your own yabbies, farm tours, picnic/barbecue facilities. Wineries nearby: Zuber Estate, 2 km N; Wild Duck Creek Estate, 10 km W; Jasper Hill and Huntleigh Vineyards, 6 km N; McIvor Creek Wines, 5 km SE; and Eppalock Ridge Vineyards, 22 km NW. **Visitor information:** Cnr High and Barrack sts; (03) 5433 3121. **See also:** Vineyards and Wineries p. 207.

Hopetoun

Pop. 670

MAP REF. 120 E12, 234 H3, 236 H13
This small Mallee town, south-east of Wyperfeld National Park, was named after the seventh Earl of Hopetoun, first Governor-General of Australia. Hopetoun was a frequent visitor to the home of Edward Lascelles, who was largely responsible for opening up the Mallee area. **In town:** In Evelyn St, 2 National Trust-classified homes: Hopetoun House (1891) built for Lascelles; Corrong homestead (1846), home of first European settler in area, Peter McGinnis. Mallee Mural and leadlight window in Shire Offices, Lascelles St, depict history of the Mallee. Lake Lascelles, end Austin St, for boating, swimming and picnics. Easter: Country

Music Festival. Oct.: Agricultural Show. **In the area:** Wyperfeld National Park, 50 km W: information centre in park, Brambruck Nature Walk, occasional sightings of threatened mallee fowl. At Patchewollock, 35 km NW, Easter Sports and Camel Cup (part of Warracknabeal Y-Fest). **Visitor information:** Gateway Beet, 75 Lascelles St; (03) 5083 3001.

Horsham

Pop. 12 591

MAP REF. 234 G9
Situated at the junction of the Western, Wimmera and Henty hwys, Horsham is generally regarded as the capital of the Wimmera region. It is a popular base for tours to Little Desert National Park, the Grampians and Mt Arapiles. **In town:** Botanic Gardens, cnr Baker and Firebrace sts. Horsham Regional Art Gallery, Wilson St, features Mack Jost collection of Australian art. May Park, Dimboola Rd. Apex Adventure Island, in Barnes Rd, a children's playground. In Golf Course Rd: Horsham Rocks and Gems and Country Crafts; The Wool Factory, producing top quality, extra-fine wool from Saxon-Merino sheep (tours daily). Attractive picnic spots and viewing places for spectacular sunsets alongside Wimmera River. Historic River Walk and self-guide town tour, brochures available. Market, at showgrounds, McPherson St, 2nd Sun. each month. Mar.: Wimmera Machinery Field Days; Fishing Competition; Art Is (community festival). Sept.: Agricultural Show. Oct.: Spring Garden Festival. Dec.: Kannamaroo Rock'n'Roll Festival. **In the area:** Water sports and good fishing for redfin and trout in lakes in area, including: Green Lake, 13 km SE; Pine Lake, 16 km SE; Taylors Lake, 18 km SE; Toolondo Reservoir, 44 km SW, home of the fighting brown trout; and Rocklands Reservoir, 90 km S, on Glenelg River, built to supplement Wimmera–Mallee irrigation scheme. Black Range Cashmere and Thryptomene Farm, 40 km S; 4WD tours available, bookings essential, contact information centre. Grampians National Park, 50 km SE, for rugged sandstone ranges, wildflowers, waterfalls, wildlife and Aboriginal rock-art sites. At Jung, 10 km NE, market last Sat. each month. Do See View Farm, 15 km NW: operating farm, native flower walk, Clydesdale horses, blacksmith's shop. Little Desert National Park, 40 km NW. **Visitor information:** 20 O'Callaghan Pde; (03) 5382 1832, freecall 1800 633 218.

Inglewood   Pop. 699

MAP REF. 235 O8, 238 A7

North along the Calder Hwy from Bendigo is the 'Golden Triangle' town of Inglewood. Sizeable gold nuggets were found in this area during the Gold Rush last century and are still being unearthed in the region today. Inglewood is also known as the birthplace of Australian aviator Sir Reginald Ansett. **In town:** Old eucalyptus oil distillery, Calder Hwy, northern end of town. Old courthouse, Southey St, has historical memorabilia (open by appt). In Verdon St: Tivey House (1883) and town hall (1887) with chiming clock. Blue Mallee Crafts, Brooke St. Old Inglewood Cemetery, Calder Hwy. Oct.: Blue Eucalyptus Festival (even-numbered years). **In the area:** Blanche Barkly Winery, 10 km SW on Kingower–Rheola Rd; Passing Clouds winery, 11 km W at Kingower; Kangderaar Vineyard, 15 km SW at Rheola. Kooyoora State Park, 16 km W, features well-known Melville Caves, once haunt of notorious bush-ranger Captain Melville. At Bridgewater on Loddon, 8 km SE: fishing, water-skiing, parachute jumping at weekends; Old Loddon Vines vineyard, Water Wheel Vineyards; horse-drawn caravans for hire. **Visitor information:** Loddon Shire Council, High St, Wedderburn; (03) 5494 1200. **See also:** Vineyards and Wineries p. 207.

Inverloch   Pop. 2448

MAP REF. 230 G10

This is a small seaside resort on Anderson Inlet, east of Wonthaggi. It has long stretches of excellent beach with good surf and is very popular during the summer months. **In town:** In the Esplanade: Environment Centre, for books and natural products; Shell Museum. Mar.: Jazz Festival. **In the area:** Adjacent to town, Anderson Inlet, most southerly habitat of mangroves; nearby, Townsend Bluff and Maher's Landing for birdwatching. Inverloch–Cape Paterson scenic road to the south-west through Bunurong Marine Park, offers views equal to those on Great Ocean Rd. At Cape Paterson, spear fishing and surfing. Tarwin River, 20 km SE, offers good fishing. Beaches, natural bushland and wildlife at Venus Bay nearby. **Visitor information:** Community Centre, 3 Reilly St; (03) 5674 1169.

Jeparit   Pop. 403

MAP REF. 234 F6

This little town in the Wimmera, 37 km N of Dimboola, is 5 km SE of Lake Hindmarsh, the largest natural freshwater lake in Victoria. Sir Robert Menzies, long-serving Prime Minister, was born here 1894. **In town:** Sir Robert Menzies Spire, Sands Ave. Menzies Square, cnr Charles and Roy sts, site of dwelling where Menzies was born. Wimmera–Mallee Pioneer Museum, Charles St, at southern entrance to town: 4-ha complex of colonial buildings furnished in period, and displays of restored farm machinery; Wimmera River walk (6 km return) from museum, brochures available. Mar.: Museum Open Day. Oct.: Agricultural Show. **In the area:** Safe beaches, fishing, water-skiing, sailing and camping at Lake Hindmarsh, 5 km NW. Wildflowers, native fauna and walking tracks at Wyperfeld National Park, 44 km N. **Visitor information:** Wimmera–Mallee Pioneer Museum, Charles St; (03) 5397 2101.

Kaniva   Pop. 765

MAP REF. 234 C7

Kaniva in the west Wimmera, 43 km from Bordertown, SA, is just north of Little Desert National Park, which is noted for its wildflowers in spring. **In town:** Historical town walks, brochure available. Shoe Museum (shoes displayed in various shop windows). Historical museum, Commercial St, has large collection of items of local history (open by appt). On western outskirts of town, Rotary Fauna Park with nature walk and bird hide. Tours to Little Desert, Big Desert and farms; details from information centre. **In the area:** Billy-Ho Bush Walk, a 3-km self-guide walk in Little Desert National Park, begins some 10 km S; numbered pegs allow identification of various species of desert flora, brochure available. Mooree Reserve, 20 km SW. At Serviceton, 25 km W, National Trust-classified railway station (1889) (key from Serviceton General Store). **Visitor information:** 41 Commercial St; (03) 5392 2418.

Kerang   Pop. 3883

MAP REF. 120 I12, 235 P3, 237 P13, 238 A2

Some 30 km from the Murray River and 60 km from Swan Hill, Kerang is the centre of a productive rural area and lies at the southern end of a chain of lakes and marshes. Some of the world's largest breeding-grounds for ibis and other waterfowl are found in these marshes. The ibis is closely protected because of its value in controlling locusts and other pests. **In town:** Lester Lookout Tower, cnr Murray Valley Hwy and Shadforth St, houses Gemstone Museum. Historical Museum, Riverwood Dr., features cars and farm machinery. Easter: Quilters Exhibition. Oct.: Woodworking Expo. **In the area:** Apex Park recreation area near the first of the three Reedy Lakes (8 km NW); the second has a large ibis rookery. Lakes Meran, Reedy, Kangaroo and Charm for water sports; and others have excellent fishing. Gunbower State Forest, 25 km N: significant red gum habitat, flora and fauna. At Murrabit, 27 km N on the Murray and surrounded by picturesque river forests: historic building and sawmill; country market, 1st Sat. each month. Lake Boga, 42 km NW, for good sandy beaches and water sports. At Easter, Australian Tractor Pull Championship at Quambatook, 40 km SW. **Visitor information:** Golden Rivers Tourism, 25 Murray St, Barham (NSW); (03) 5453 3100, freecall 1800 621 882. **See also:** The Mighty Murray p. 201.

Kilmore   Pop. 2710

MAP REF. 217 J2, 238 F11

Kilmore, 60 km north of Melbourne on the Northern Hwy, is Victoria's oldest inland town, first settled by Europeans in 1841. It is known for its historic buildings and its horseracing. **In town:** Fine old buildings, including Whitburgh Cottage (1857), Piper St; Post Office, Sydney St, and Court House, Powlett St, (both 1860s); several Sydney St shops and hotels (1850s). Old Kilmore Gaol, Sutherland St: restaurant, tours; closed Mon. Hudson Park, cnr Sydney and Foote sts, has cable-tram rides and picnic/barbecue facilities. Market at Old Kilmore Gaol, 2nd Sat. each month. June: Celtic Festival. **In the area:** Tramways Museum at Bylands, just south of town: extensive display of cable cars and early electric trams; tram rides through surrounding countryside. At Broadford, 14 km NW: historic precinct in High St; Scottish Festival each Oct.; Hells Angels Concert each Dec. Nearby: Mt Piper Walking Track (1 hr return, wildlife and wildflowers); Strath Creek, for Strath Creek Falls and drive through Valley of a Thousand Hills. **Visitor information:** Library, 12 Sydney St, Kilmore; (03) 5782 1322.

Gippsland Lakes

Many people regard the Gippsland Lakes as the most outstanding holiday area in Victoria. Dominated by Australia's largest system of inland waterways, it certainly lives up to all the superlatives accorded it. With the foothills of the high country just to the north and the amazing stretch of the Ninety Mile Beach separating the lakes from the ocean, the region offers a variety of natural beauty and recreational activities. Here the choice really is yours — lake, river or ocean fishing, boating, cruising, surfing, swimming, birdwatching or just sitting by the water's edge.

Within easy reach of the Lakes area the high country begins, so it is possible to vary a waterside trip with days exploring the alpine reaches (some minor roads may be closed in winter) and some of the fascinating little old townships such as **Omeo**, Briagolong and Dargo. The road across the Dargo High Plains and the Great Alpine Road leading to Mount Hotham passes through some stunning country. Check your car thoroughly before you set off — service stations are scarce along the way.

Wellington, King, Victoria, Reeve and Coleman — these five lakes cover more than 400 square kilometres and stretch parallel to the Ninety Mile Beach for almost its entire length. **Sale**, at the western edge of the region, is the local base for the development of the Bass Strait oil and gas fields. Both Sale and **Bairnsdale**, further east on the banks of the Mitchell River, make excellent bases for holidays on the lakes or for alpine trips. The main resort towns are **Lakes Entrance**, at the mouth of the Lakes; **Paynesville**, a mecca for boating and fishing enthusiasts; Metung, a departure point for cruising holidays on the lakes; and Loch Sport, nestled between **The Lakes National Park**, Ninety Mile Beach and Lake Victoria.

The Lakes National Park, the **Mitchell River National Park**, and the hills and valleys of the alpine foothills to the north, all provide plenty of opportunities for bushwalking, for enjoying nature or for simply enjoying the peace.

For further information on the Gippsland Lakes area, contact local visitor information centres: at Lakes Entrance, cnr Esplanade and Marine Pde, (03) 5155 1966, freecall 1800 637 060; at Bairnsdale, 240 Main St, (03) 5152 3444; at Sale, Princes Hwy, (03) 5144 1108; at Paynesville, Esplanade, (03) 5156 7479. **See also:** National Parks p. 163 and individual entries in A–Z listing for parks and towns in bold type. **Map reference:** 231 Q5.

The township of Lakes Entrance at the mouth of the Gippsland Lakes

Koo-wee-rup
Pop. 1118

MAP REF. 217 M10, 230 F7

Well known for its Potato Festival held on 3rd Sat. each Mar., this town near Western Port is in the middle of Australia's largest asparagus-growing district. **In town:** Historical Society Museum, Rossiter Rd (open Sun.). Mar.: Potato Festival. **In the area:** Bunyip Byways Tourist Trails, maps available. Bayles Flora and Fauna Park, 8 km NE. At Tynong, 20 km NE: Victoria's Farm Shed (farm animals and shearing displays); Gumbaya Park, in landscaped bushland. At Pakenham, 13 km N: Military Vehicle Museum, Army Rd; Berwick–Pakenham Historical Society Museum, John St. At Cardinia, 11 km NW, Australian Pioneer Farm offers opportunity to shear sheep and milk cows. Royal Botanic Gardens, 22 km NW at Cranbourne, native gardens. Fishing and boating at Tooradin, 10 km W, on Sawtell's Inlet. On South Gippsland Hwy towards Tooradin: Harewood House (1850s), has original furnishings (open weekends); Swamp Observation Tower offers views of surrounding swamp and Western Port. Market, 4th Sun. each month, at Grantville, 30 km S. **Visitor information:** Newsagency, 277 Rossiter Rd; (03) 5997 1456.

Korumburra
Pop. 2739

MAP REF. 217 O12, 230 H8

Korumburra is known for a large species of a local worm, the giant Gippsland earthworm. Situated on the South Gippsland Hwy, the town is 118 km SE of Melbourne. The area surrounding the town is given to dairying and agriculture, and the countryside is hilly. **In town:** Coal Creek Heritage Village, cnr South Gippsland Hwy and Silkstone Rd, a re-creation of 19th-century coal-mining village on original site of Coal Creek mine. **In the area:** South Gippsland Railway tourist train offers rides through 40 km of countryside linking Leongatha, Korumburra, Loch and Nyora (departure times from information centre). Gooseneck Pottery, 9 km SE at Ruby. Top Paddock Cheeses, 6 km NW at Bena, has tastings and sales of traditional, curd and soft cheeses. At Loch, 14 km NW: antiques, art and craft. At Poowong, 18 km NW: Poowong Pioneer Chapel, fine example of German architecture; Mudlark Pottery. At Arawata, 12 km NE, Quitters Barn, for craft, coffee shop and accommodation. **Visitor information:** South Gippsland

Visitor Information Centre, cnr South Gippsland Hwy and Silkstone Rd; (03) 5655 2233, freecall 1800 630 704.

Kyabram
Pop. 5738

MAP REF. 238 G5

A prosperous town in the Murray–Goulburn area, just 40 km NW of Shepparton, Kyabram is located in a rich dairying and fruit-growing district. **In town:** Community-owned waterfowl and fauna park on Lake Rd has five ponds with waterbirds and 15 ha of open-range parklands with native fauna. The Stables, adjacent to fauna park, for pottery and crafts. Mar.: Rodeo. Oct.: Bush Market Day. **Visitor information:** Fauna park, 75 Lake Rd; (03) 5852 2883. **See also:** The Mighty Murray p. 201.

Kyneton
Pop. 3757

MAP REF. 216 G1, 233 R1, 235 R12, 238 D11

Little more than an hour's drive from Melbourne along the Calder Hwy, Kyneton is a well-preserved, attractive town with several interesting bluestone buildings. Farms around the town prospered during the gold rushes, supplying large quantities of fresh food to the Ballarat and Bendigo diggings. **In town:** In Piper St: Kyneton Museum in former bank (c.1865), drop-log cottage in grounds (open Fri.–Sun.); Steam Mill, restored to operational condition (check opening times); Meskills Woolstore, has wool spinning mill, and yarn and garments for sale. Botanic Gardens, Clowes St, an 8-ha area above river with 500 specimen trees. Historic buildings: town's churches; mechanics institute, Mollison St; old police depot, Jenning St. Campaspe River Walk, leaflet available. Feb.: Country Music Festival. Mar.: Autumn Flower Show. Sept.: Daffodil and Arts Festival. Nov.: Kyneton Cup (horse race). **In the area:** Two-storey bluestone mills on either side of town; both on Calder Hwy. Upper Coliban, Lauriston and Malmsbury reservoirs, all nearby. At Malmsbury, 10 km NW: historic bluestone railway viaduct; historic Botanic Gardens; Bleak House (1850s), with rose garden; The Mill (1861), National Trust-classified, has gallery, restaurant and accommodation; wineries in the area. At Trentham, 22 km SW: historic foundry; Jargon Crafts; Minifie's Berry Farm, pick-your-own in season; Firth Park in Wombat State Forest. Carlsruhe Gallery and Campaspe Art Gallery at

Carlsruhe, 5 km SE. Art and craft gallery at Tylden, 13 km W. Trentham Falls, 20 km SE. Turpins and Cascade falls with picnic area and walk, 22 km N near Metcalfe. **Visitor information:** Jean Haynes Playground, High St; (03) 5422 6110 (closed Tues. and Thurs.).

Lake Bolac
Pop. 235

MAP REF. 233 J5

In the Western District plains area, this small town on the Glenelg Hwy is by a 1460-ha freshwater lake that has sandy beaches around a 20-km shoreline and is good for fishing (eels, trout, perch and yellow-belly), boating and swimming. There are several boat-launching ramps. Easter: Yachting Regatta. **Visitor information:** Lake Bolac Motel, Glenelg Hwy; (03) 5350 2218.

Lakes Entrance
Pop. 5248

MAP REF. 231 R5, 240 H13

This extremely popular holiday town is at the eastern end of the Gippsland Lakes, the largest inland network of waterways in Australia, covering an area of more than 400 sq. km. The lakes are separated from the ocean by a thin sliver of sand dunes forming a large part of the Ninety Mile Beach, which stretches south to Seaspray. A bridge across the Cunningham Arm gives access to the surf beach from Lakes Entrance. The town caters well for both seaside recreation and exploration of the mountain country to the north. It is the home port for a large fishing fleet and many pleasure craft. **In town:** Fisherman's Co-operative, Bullock Island, has viewing platform and fish for sale. Seashell Museum, The Esplanade. Jan.: Larger than Lakes Festival. Dec.: New Year's Eve Fireworks. **In the area:** Sightseeing cruises of lakes; boat hire; fishing charters; beach fishing; joy flights; Bataluk Cultural Trail, which covers Aboriginal heritage in the East Gippsland area, self-guide brochure available. Lake Bunga, 3 km E, has nature trail on foreshore. Kinkuna Country Family Fun Park, 3.5 km E on Princes Hwy. East Gippsland Carriage Co., 30 km E, has carriage tours. Lake Tyers (6–23 km NE, depending on access point): sheltered waters ideal for fishing, swimming and boating; cruises depart from Fishermans Landing; Lake Tyers Forest Park, for walking, wildlife, picnicking and camping. Braeburne Park Orchards, 6 km N. Woodsedge Art Centre, 8 km N on Baades Rd; gallery, furniture workshop and glass-blowing demonstrations. Wyanga Park Vineyard and Winery, 10 km N; also reached by boat trip from town. Nyerimilang Heritage Park, 10 km NW: 1920s homestead, farm buildings and East Gippsland Botanic Gardens; Rose Pruning Day here in July features demonstrations (clippings given to the public). At Swan Reach, 14 km NW: Rosewood Pottery; Malcolm Cameron Studio Gallery (open weekends). Good views from Jemmy's Point, 1 km W. At Metung, 15 km W: Chainsaw Sculpture Gallery has chainsaw sculpture and display of Annemieke Mein's embroidery art; boat hire; marina regatta in Jan. each year. **Visitor information:** cnr Esplanade and Marine Pde; (03) 5155 1966, freecall 1800 637 060. **See also:** Gippsland Lakes p. 186; Vineyards and Wineries p. 207.

Leongatha   Pop. 4144

MAP REF. 217 P13, 230 H9

Located near the foothills of the Strzelecki Ranges, Leongatha is a large dairying area and a good base for trips to Wilsons Promontory, the seaside and fishing resorts on the coast. **In town:** In McCartin St: Historic Society Museum (check opening times); Art and Craft Gallery. Mushroom Crafts and Pottery, Bair St. Jan.: South Gippsland Food and Wine Festival. Feb.: Cycling Carnival; South Gippsland Golf Classic. Mar.: Riverfest. Sept.: Daffodil and Floral Festival; Rotary Art Show. **In the area:** Canoeing and abseiling adventures. South Gippsland Railway tourist train, from Leongatha to Korumburra, Loch and Nyora; departure times from information

centre. Firelight Museum, 9 km N, features antique lamps and firearms. About 21 km N, excellent scenic driving along Grand Ridge Rd to Tarra–Bulga National Park (120 km E). Mossvale Park, 16 km NE: impressive park plantation of exotic trees, good picnic/barbecue facilities; soundshell is venue for Victorian State Orchestra performance each Feb. At Mirboo North, 26 km NE: Grand Ridge Brewing Company, viewing of beer-brewing process and sales; Colonial Bank Antiques; Erinae Lavender Garden and Tea Rooms. Brackenhurst Rotary Dairy, 5 km E on Christoffersens Rd, has 300 cows (milked from 3.30 p.m. daily), also museum. Craft shop at Meeniyan, 16 km SE. Gooseneck Pottery, 9 km NW at Ruby. **Visitor information:** CAB, Michael Place Complex; (03) 5662 2111 (weekdays), freecall 1800 630 704.

Lorne   Pop. 1082

MAP REF. 216 D13, 223 A13, 233 P10

The approaches to Lorne along the Great Ocean Road, whether from east or west, are quite spectacular. The town is one of Victoria's most attractive coastal resorts. It has a year-round mild climate and the superb mountain scenery of the Otways nearby. Captain Loutit, of the schooner *Apollo*, gave the district the name of Loutit Bay. The village of Lorne was established in 1871, became popular with pastoralists from inland areas, and developed rather in the style of an English seaside resort. When the Great Ocean Road opened in 1932, Lorne grew more popular; however, the town itself has remained relatively unspoiled, with good beaches, surfing, and excellent bushwalking in the hills.

In town: Teddy's Lookout, at edge of George St behind town, has excellent bay views. Foreshore reserve. Shipwreck Walk along beach. Paddle boats for hire. Qdos Contemporary Art Gallery, Allenvale Rd. Lorne Fisheries on pier; daily supplies from local fleet. Jan.: Pier to Pub Swim; Mountain to Surf Foot Race. Dec.: Falls Festival. **In the area:** Surrounding town: Angahook–Lorne State Park, features Erskine Falls (9 km NW of town) and many walking tracks, including one to Kalimna and Phantom waterfalls from Sheoak Picnic area (about 4 km from town). Scenic drives: west in the Otway Ranges; southwest or north-east along Great Ocean Rd. Cumberland River Valley, 4 km SW, has walking tracks and camping ground. Mt Defiance, 10 km SW; narrow stretch of the road with excellent roadside viewingpoint. Wye River, 17 km SW, for fishing and surfing. Gentle Annie Berry Gardens, 26 km NW via Deans Marsh, pick-your-own (open Nov.–Apr.). **Visitor information:** 144 Mountjoy Pde; (03) 5289 1152. Web site www.greatoceanrd.org.au **See also:** Great Ocean Tour p. 159.

Maffra   Pop. 4033

MAP REF. 231 M5

The area around Maffra supports intensive farming, made possible by the Macalister Irrigation Scheme. **In town:** Maffra Sugar Beet Historic Museum, River St (open Sun. p.m.). Mineral and gemstone display at information centre, Johnson St. All Seasons Herb Gardens, Foster St. Feb.: Scotfest. Mar.: Gippsland Harvest Festival; Mardi Gras. Easter: Tennis Tournament. **In the area:** 'Traralgon to Stratford'

Fishing boats at Lakes Entrance

brochure available, describes attractions in area. Lake Glenmaggie, 21 km N of Heyfield, popular water-sports venue. Spectacular scenic drives along forest road north (closed in winter), which follows Macalister Valley to Licola (54 km N of Heyfield), and to Mt Tamboritha (20 km NE of Licola) in Alpine National Park; or to Jamieson (145 km NW of Heyfield, check road conditions), with access to snowfields or Lake Eildon. 4WD tours into high country, bookings essential, at information centre. At Briagolong, 26 km NE, historic hotel and mechanics institute. Lake Tali Karng, located in Alpine National Park, 60 km NE of Licola, is a major focus for bushwalking in season. At Stratford, 9 km E: Avon River for picnics; Aboriginal Bataluk Heritage Trail; Shakespeare Celebration held here in May. Australian Wildlife Art Gallery and Sculpture, 25 km E, on Princes Hwy near Munro. Trail-riding tours in surrounding area. **Visitor information:** Courthouse, 8 Johnson St; (03) 5141 1811.

Maldon   Pop. 1255

MAP REF. 227 M5, 235 P11, 238 B10
In 1996 the National Trust declared Maldon a 'Notable Town', the first in Australia. Situated 18 km NW of Castlemaine in central Victoria, Maldon is very popular with tourists, especially during the Maldon Easter Fair, and in spring when the wildflowers are in bloom. The quartz reef goldmines in the area were among Victoria's richest, and at one stage 20 000 men worked on the Tarrangower diggings. Enthusiasts still search for gold in the area. **In town:** Anzac Hill, southern end of High St, for good view of town. Many notable buildings, some constructed of local stone: Maldon Hospital (1860), cnr Adair and Chapel sts; post office (1870), High St; old council offices, High St (now Museum); Dabb's General Store, with faithfully restored old storefront, Main St. National Trust properties: former Denominational (Penny) School, Camp St; Welsh Congregational Church, cnr Camp and Church sts. The Beehive Chimney (1862), south end of Church St. Victorian Goldfields Railway runs steam trains from railway station, Hornsby St (Sun., Wed., public and school holidays). Town walking tour, leaflet available. Feb.: Camp Draft. Easter: Fair. Oct.: Vintage Car Hill Climb. Oct.–Nov.: Folk Festival. **In the area:** Bushwalks and intriguing rock formations. Panoramic views from Mt Tarrangower Lookout Tower, 2 km W. Carman's Tunnel, 2 km SW, a reminder of hardships of

Railway station at Maldon, a National Trust-classified town

goldmining days. Cairn Curran Reservoir, 10 km SW, for water sports and fishing; picnic facilities, sailing club near spillway. 'Porcupine Township', 3 km NE, a reconstructed goldmining town. Goldmining dredge beside road to Bendigo, 4 km NE. Nuggetty Ranges and Mt Moorol, 2 km N. **Visitor information:** High St; (03) 5475 2569. Web site www.mountalexander.vic. gov.au/tourism **See also:** The Golden Age p. 171.

Mallacoota   Pop. 982

MAP REF. 113 G13, 241 Q11
In far east Gippsland, at the mouth of a deep inlet of the same name, Mallacoota is a seaside and fishing township and a popular holiday centre with good swimming along Foreshore Reserve. **In town:** Easter: Festival of the Great Southern Ocean. July: Blues Festival. **In the area:** Birdwatching; lake and river cruises; scenic drives and walks; network of bushwalking tracks; leaflets available from Parks Victoria, cnr Allan and Buckland drs. At Croajingolong National Park, surrounding town: over 300 bird species; glossy-black cockatoos along walking track to Genoa Peak, magnificent views from peak; Shepherd Creek Camp Ground has flora and fauna, short walks and picnic area. Gabo Island Lightstation Reserve, 11 km W, scenic day trip or stay in Lightkeeper's Residence. Gipsy Point, 16 km NW, a quiet holiday retreat overlooking Genoa River. Bastion Point, 2 km SE, and Betka, 5 km S, are good surfing beaches. **Visitor information:** Snowy River–Orbost Visitor Centre, 13 Lochiel St, Orbost; (03) 5154

2424, or call Parks Victoria, 13 1963 (ask for Mallacoota office). Web site www. parkweb.vic.gov.au **See also:** National Parks p. 163; Wildlife-Watching p. 167.

Mansfield   Pop. 2526

MAP REF. 228 C10, 239 L10
A popular inland town at the junction of the Midland and Maroondah hwys, Mansfield is 3 km E from the northern arm of Lake Eildon. It is the nearest sizeable town to Mt Buller Alpine Village and Mt Stirling Alpine Resort. **In town:** Self-guide historical walk, brochure available. Troopers' Monument, cnr High St and Midland Hwy, monument to the 3 police officers shot by Ned Kelly at Stringybark Creek, near Tolmie, in 1878; graves can be seen in Mansfield cemetery. Nearby, National Trust-classified courthouse. Highton Manor (1896), Highton La. Balloon trips leave from Highton Manor, advance bookings essential, details from information centre. Bush market, 4 times a year (check date). Balloon Festival (check dates). Mar.: Harvest Festival. Nov.: Mountain Country Festival. **In the area:** Camel treks and horse trail-riding. Road over mountains to Whitfield in the King River Valley (62 km NE) passes through spectacular scenery, including Powers Lookout, 48 km NE, for views over King River Valley (former vantage point for bushranger Harry Power). Lake William Hovell, 85 km NE, for boating and fishing. Mt Samaria State Park, 14 km N, for scenic drives, camping and bushwalking. At Lake Nillahcootie, 20 km NW: boating, fishing, canoeing and sailing.

Alpine Country

To the east and north-east of Melbourne, the gently rounded peaks of the Victorian Alps stretch, seemingly endlessly towards the New South Wales border. They are a majestic sight, especially when covered in snow. These blue ranges are not high enough to have a permanent cover of snow, but the expanses of rolling mountains are ideal in winter for both cross-country and downhill skiing.

The skiing season officially opens on the Queen's Birthday long weekend each June and closes in October. Each year, thousands of people flock to the snow for the enjoyment of skiing, for snowboarding or just for the beauty of nature.

Cattlemen's huts in the Alpine National Park and the High Plains are tourist attractions and there is bountiful fishing in the lakes and trout streams. Tennis, rock climbing, sailing, swimming, canoeing and water-skiing are popular sports in the summer. Many riding schools in the valleys provide for those who want to explore the countryside on horseback. For the more energetic, bushwalking in this beautiful rugged country is a must.

In spring and summer the alpine wildflowers are a delight. More than 1100 plant species are found in the national park, including twelve exclusive to the park. Despite their summer beauty, however, the alps can still be dangerous and claim the life of an ill-prepared bushwalker. Make sure you have the necessary equipment and knowledge and always tell someone where you are going and when you expect to be back.

Victoria's ski resorts are all located within easy reach of Melbourne.

Mount Donna Buang, 95 km from Melbourne, via Warburton. Sightseeing and novice skiing.

Lake Mountain, 120 km from Melbourne, via Healesville. Sightseeing and cross-country skiing.

Mount Baw Baw, 177 km from Melbourne, via Drouin. Beginners, novices and cross-country skiing.

Mount St Gwinear nearby, is popular for cross-country skiing.

Mount Buller, 221 km from Melbourne, via Mansfield. For beginners to advanced skiers. Ski hire and instruction.

Mount Stirling, 250 km from Melbourne, near Mount Buller. Cross-country skiing. Most trails start at Telephone Box Junction. Visitor centre with public shelter, ski hire and trail maps.

Mount Buffalo, 331 km from Melbourne, via Myrtleford. Includes Dingo Dell (6 km) and Cresta (10 km). Beginners, families and cross-country skiing. Ski hire and instruction.

Falls Creek, 356 km from Melbourne, via the Snow Road through Oxley. Protected ski runs for novices, intermediate and advanced skiers; good cross-country skiing. Ski hire and instruction.

Mount Hotham, 367 km from Melbourne, via the Snow Road through Oxley. For experienced downhill skiers. Also cross-country skiing. Ski hire and instruction available.

Dinner Plain, a 10-minute ski-shuttle ride from Mount Hotham. Offers ski hire, cross-country skiing, and horseriding in summer.

Mount Hotham Airport, 20 km from Mount Hotham and 10 km from Dinner Plain, allows quick access to these ski resorts from Melbourne, Sydney and Adelaide.

For information on snow conditions, contact the recorded service; 1902 240 523. Web site www.snowreport.vic.gov.au **See also:** Safe Skiing p. 611. **Map references:** 228–9; for Lake Mountain, 230 H2; for Mount Donna Buang, 230 G3; and for Mount Baw Baw, 231 J4.

Striking views from Mount Hotham

Houseboat hire, watersports and fishing at Lake Eildon, 15 km S. To the south, Delatite, Howqua, Jamieson and Goulburn rivers are popular for trout fishing and gold-fossicking. Historic buildings at old goldmining town of Jamieson, 37 km S on Jamieson River. Mt Skene, 48 km SE of Jamieson, has wildflowers Dec.–Feb. (road closed in winter). Delatite Winery, on Stoneys Rd, 7 km SE. At Merrijig, 19 km SE, Rodeo each Mar. Craig's Hut, 50 km E, used for filming *The Man from Snowy River* (no vehicle access in winter). Alpine National Park, 60 km E, for bushwalking and 4-wheel driving. **Visitor information:** Old Railway Station, Maroondah Hwy; (03) 5775 1464. **See also:** Alpine Country p. 190; Vineyards and Wineries p. 207.

Maryborough Pop. 7381

MAP REF. 227 J5, 235 O11

First sheep farming, then the gold rush, and now secondary industry have contributed to the development of this small city on the northern slopes of the Great Dividing Range, 70 km N of Ballarat. Maryborough is in the centre of an agricultural and forest area. **In town:** Pioneer Memorial Tower, Bristol Hill. Worsley Cottage (1894), Palmerston St, a historical museum (open Sun.). Old railway station (1892), Station St, now a complex housing information centre, antique gallery and woodwork shop. Central Goldfields Art Gallery, in old fire station, Neill St. Phillips Gardens, Alma St. Imposing Civic Square buildings, Clarendon St. Self-guide Historic Buildings Drive, brochure available. Markets, Maryborough–Dunolly Rd, 1st and 3rd Sun. each month. Jan.: Highland Gathering. Aug.–Sept.: Golden Wattle Festival (includes Gumleaf-Playing Championship). Oct.: Gourmet, Grapes and Gardens Weekend. Nov.: Energy Breakthrough (energy expo). **In the area:** Self-guide Golden Way Tourist Drive, brochures available. Aboriginal wells, 4 km S. At Carisbrook, 7 km E, Tourist Market, 1st Sun. each month in Chaplins Rd. **Visitor information:** Railway station complex, Station St; (03) 5460 4511, freecall 1800 356 511. **See also:** The Golden Age p. 171.

Marysville Pop. 626

MAP REF. 217 O4, 220 I3, 230 G2, 239 J13

The peaceful sub-alpine town of Marysville owes its existence first to gold, as its site was on the route to the Woods Point goldfields, and later to timber milling. It is

Autumn trees, Marysville

34 km NE of Healesville, off the Maroondah Hwy. The town is surrounded by attractive forest-clad mountain country and is a popular year-round resort. **In town:** In Murchison St: Old Fashioned Lolly Shop; Country Touch pottery; Hidden Talents, local art and crafts. Bruno's Art and Sculpture Garden, Falls Rd. Sawyer's Marysville Museum, Darwin St, features vintage cars and accessories. Nicholl's Lookout, Cumberland Rd, for excellent views of surrounding area. Market, Murchison St, 2nd Sun. each month. **In the area:** Numerous bushwalking tracks lead to a variety of beauty spots: 3-min walk to Steavenson Falls from Falls Rd (walk and falls illuminated at night); 4-km loop walk in Cumberland Memorial Scenic Reserve, 16 km E; 2-hr walk to Keppel's Lookout; 30-min walk to Mt Gordon (begins 2 km W of town). Lady Talbot Forest Drive through surrounding area, brochure available. Lake Mountain, 19 km E: accessible walking and cross-country skiing trails and tobogganing. Big River State Forest, 30 km E: camping, good fishing and gold-fossicking. At Buxton, 11 km N: zoo; trout farm; Australian Bush Pioneer's Farm, at foot of Mt Cathedral; nearby, Cathedral Range State Park. **Visitor information:** Murchison St; (03) 5963 4567. Web site www.mmtourism.com.au **See also:** Day Tours from Melbourne p. 154.

Milawa Pop. 120

MAP REF. 228 G1, 239 N6

Milawa is 16 km SE of Wangaratta on what is known as the Snow Road, which links Oxley, Milawa and Markwood with Wangaratta to the west and the Great Alpine Rd to the east. Brown Brothers Vineyard has operated here since 1889, producing quality wines. **In town:** Milawa Mustards, off Snow Rd, has a wide range of mustards and attractive cottage garden. Milawa Cheese Company, Factory Rd, for specialist cheeses. Nov.: Brown Brothers Wine and Food Weekend. **In the area:** Numerous wineries in immediate and surrounding areas, details from information centre. At Oxley, 4 km W: Blue Ox Blueberry Farm; Churchworks; Earthly Gems; King River Cafe. At Whitfield, 46 km S, and Cheshunt, 51 km S, King Valley Virgin Wine, Food and Arts Festival in Nov. **Visitor information:** Wangaratta and Region Visitors Information Centre, cnr Handley St and Tone Rd, Wangaratta; (03) 5721 5711. **See also:** Vineyards and Wineries p. 207.

Mildura Pop. 24 142

MAP REF. 120 D7, 236 G3

Sunny mild winters and picturesque locations on the banks of the Murray River make Mildura and neighbouring

Boat harbour at Mornington

towns popular tourist areas. Mildura, 557 km N of Melbourne, is a pleasant city that developed with the expansion of irrigation. Alfred Deakin, statesman and advocate of irrigation, persuaded the Chaffey brothers, Canadian-born irrigation experts, to visit this region. They selected Mildura as the first site for development. The project was fraught with setbacks, but by 1900 the citrus-growing industry was established and, with the locking of the Murray completed in 1928, Mildura soon became a city. **In town:** In Deakin Ave: The Alfred Deakin Centre, has interactive exhibitions and displays of region; statue of W. B. Chaffey, Mildura's first mayor. Mildura Arts Centre complex, Cureton Ave, includes Rio Vista, original Chaffey home, now museum displaying colonial household items; Sculpture Trail in gardens surrounding the centre. Langtree Hall (1889), Walnut Ave, is Mildura's first public hall (open Tues.–Sun.). Paddle-steamers leave from Mildura Wharf, end of Madden Ave, for river trips: PS *Melbourne*, 2-hr round trips; PS *Avoca*, luncheon and dinner cruises; PS *Coonawarra*, 3-, 5- and 6-day cruises; PV *Rothbury*, day cruise to Trentham Winery (each Thurs.). Snakes and Ladders, 17th St, fun park featuring dunny collection. Mildura Lock Island and Weir. Aquacoaster waterslide, cnr Seventh St and Orange Ave. Dolls on the Avenue, Benetook Ave. Pioneer Cottage, Hunter St. The Citrus Shop, Deakin Ave, for local citrus products. Mar.: Arts Festival. July: International Balloon Fiesta. Sept.: Country Music Festival. Oct.: Sunraysia Oasis Rose Festival. Nov.: Sunraysia Jazz and Wine Festival. **In the area:** Many vineyards: Lindemans Karadoc Winery,

20 km S, largest winery in Southern Hemisphere; Milburn Wine Co., south off Calder Hwy; Trentham Estate, south off Sturt Hwy; Mildara Wines, 9 km W. Woodsie's Gem Shop and Murray Gum Pottery, 6 km SW. Sunbeam Dried Fruits, 6 km S at Irymple (tours). Red Cliffs, 15 km S, important area for citrus and dried fruit industries; 'Big Lizzie' steam traction engine in town. Bushwalking and birdwatching in Hattah–Kulkyne National Park, 70 km S. Angus Park Promotion Centre, 10 km SE, dried fruits and confectionery. In NSW: Orange World, 6 km N, offers tours of citrus-growing areas; Australian Inland Botanic Gardens, 6 km N (open Sun.–Fri); Mungo National Park, 104 km NE, World Heritage Area with Walls of China, a huge crescent of dunes. In Vic.: Tulkland Kumbi Aboriginal Galleries, 18 km N (open Mon.–Fri); Golden River Zoo, 3 km NW, with native and exotic species in natural surroundings. Several self-guide drives, maps available. **Visitor information:** The Alfred Deakin Centre, 180–190 Deakin Ave; (03) 5021 4424. **See also:** NSW National parks, p. 42; The Mighty Murray p. 201; Vineyards and Wineries p. 207.

Moe
Pop. 15 558

MAP REF. 217 R10, 231 J7

Situated on the Princes Hwy, 134 km SE of Melbourne, Moe is a rapidly-growing residential city in the La Trobe Valley and a gateway to the alpine region. **In town:** Pioneer township, Lloyd St, re-creation of 19th-century community with over 30 restored buildings brought from surrounding areas, and fine collection of fully restored horse-drawn vehicles.

Cinderella Dolls, Andrew St. Picturesque race track, Waterloo Rd. Self-guide walks in and around Moe, brochure available. Craft and produce market at Heritage Park, 2nd Sun. each month. Jan.: Modelling and Hobby Exhibition. Feb.: Woodworking Festival. Mar.: Jazz Festival; Blue Rock Classic (cross-country horse race). Oct.: Moe Cup (horse race). **In the area:** Edward Hunter Heritage Bush Reserve, 3 km S via Coalville St. Trafalgar Lookout and Narracan Falls near Trafalgar, 10 km W. Blue Rock Dam, 20 km NW, for fishing, swimming and sailing. Scenic road northeast: leads to picturesque old mining township of Walhalla, Thomson Reservoir nearby, and through mountains to Jamieson, 147 km further north (check road conditions in winter). Mt Baw Baw, 77 km N, for cross-country and downhill skiing; Baw Baw plateau is excellent for bushwalking, with abundant wildflowers in summer. At Thorpdale (known for its potatoes), 22 km SW: potato bread from bakery, Potato Festival each Mar. **Visitor information:** Gippsland Heritage Park, Lloyd St; (03) 5127 3082.

Mornington
Pop. 13 692

MAP REF. 217 K10, 219 J3, 230 D7

Mornington retains its small-town character while being easily accessible from Melbourne. It offers an excellent base from which to explore the Mornington Peninsula. **In town:** Historic Mornington pier, first built in 1850s. Studio City Pop and Media Museum, Cool Stores, Moorooduc Hwy: film, television, radio and pop-music memorabilia. Mornington Peninsula Regional Gallery, Dunns Rd, has print and drawing collections, including works by Dobell, Drysdale and Nolan (open Tues.–Sat.). Motorised trolley rides operate from Bungower Road level crossing each Sun. p.m. In Tyabb Rd: National Antique Centre; World of Motorcycles Museum. Local historical display, housed in old post office, cnr Main St and The Esplanade. Self-guide town walk, brochures available. Street market on Main St each Wed., and Mornington Racecourse craft market on 2nd Sun. each month. June: Queen's Birthday Wine Weekend. Nov.: Tea Tree Festival. **In the area:** Ballam Park (1845), 14 km NE on Cranbourne Rd at Frankston, French farmhouse-style homestead (open Sun.). At Baxter, 14 km NE: Mulberry Hill, Golf Links Rd, former home of artist Sir Daryl Lindsay and Joan Lindsay, author of *Picnic at Hanging Rock* (open Sun. p.m.). At Tyabb, 16 km E, Tyabb

Packing House, Mornington–Tyabb Rd, for antiques and collectables. Several wineries between Tyabb and Hastings, with cellar-door sales, including Barak Estate, Ermes Estate, Stumpy Gully Vineyard and Moorooduc Estate. Several festivals celebrate Peninsula produce, including Wine and Food Festival in Jan. and Peninsula Wine and Music Gala in Nov. At Hastings, 21 km SE on Western Port: fauna park; wetlands area and 2-km coastal wetlands walk through most southerly mangroves in world. Coastline between Mornington and Mount Martha (7 km S), features sheltered sandy bays. At Mount Martha, historic The Briars (1866): has gardens; significant collection of Napoleonic artifacts and furniture; wetland areas and bird hides; bushland walks. At Dromana, 16 km SW: 20-min scenic chairlift ride up the mountain to Arthurs Seat State Park (check operating times); picnic facilities at top of chairlift, as well as several walks (Arthurs Seat Discovery Day held here in Feb.); historic Seawinds Park, with gardens, sculptures, short walks and sweeping views; Arthurs Seat Maze; Pine Ridge Car and Folk Museum; riding school for horserides; Maize Maze Festival held at Dromana in Mar. **Visitor information:** Peninsula Visitor Centre, Point Nepean Rd, Dromana; (03) 5987 3078, freecall 1800 804 009. **See also:** Vineyards and Wineries p. 207.

Morwell   Pop. 13 823

MAP REF. 231 J7

Morwell, 150 km SE of Melbourne, is situated in the heart of the La Trobe Valley. This valley contains one of the world's largest deposits of brown coal. Morwell is an industrial town with a number of secondary industries. **In town:** PowerWorks, off Princes Hwy, dynamic displays on electrical industry. In Commercial Rd: La Trobe Regional Gallery; Rose Garden, with over 200 varieties. Market, La Trobe Rd, each Sun. **In the area:** Scenic day tours, brochure available. Views of La Trobe Valley from routes along Strzelecki Ranges and Baw Baw mountains. Hazelwood Pondage, 5 km S, has warm water, ideal for year-round water sports. Morwell National Park, 12 km S, has good walking tracks. At Yinnar, 12 km SW, Arts Resource Collective in old butter factory. Narracan Falls, 27 km W. Lake Narracan, 15 km NW, for fishing and waterskiing. **Visitor information:** PowerWorks Visitors Centre, Commercial Rd; (03) 5135 3415.

Mount Beauty   Pop. 1649

MAP REF. 229 N5, 239 Q8, 240 D6

Situated in the Upper Kiewa Valley, 338 km NE of Melbourne, Mount Beauty was originally an accommodation town for workers on the Kiewa Hydro-electric Scheme in the 1940s. An ideal holiday centre, the town lies at the foot of Mount Bogong, Victoria's highest mountain (1986 m). There is ski hire, coach services and parking for Falls Creek skiers. In summer, the area is one of Australia's premier mountain-bike locations; the town also services bushwalkers heading for the high plains. **In town:** Heritage Museum, at information centre. Markets, Main St, each Sat. Mar.: Conquestathon Fun Climb of Mt Bogong. **In the area:** Good water sports and fishing at Mount Beauty Pondage, 250 m N of Main St. Bogong, 15 km SE; walks around nearby Lake Guy. Scenic drive to Falls Creek, 30 km SE, and the Bogong High Plains (not accessible in winter beyond Falls Creek); at Falls Creek, winter skiing and Kangaroo Hoppett (cross-country ski race) each Aug. Tawonga Gap, 13 km NW, features scenic lookout over 2 valleys. Walks, mountain-bike hire, horseriding and hang-gliding. **Visitor information:** Bogong High Plains Rd; (03) 5754 4531. **See also:** Alpine Country p. 190.

Murtoa   Pop. 839

MAP REF. 234 I9

Murtoa is situated around picturesque Lake Marma, 31 km E of Horsham on the Wimmera Hwy. It is in the centre of Victoria's wheat belt. **In town:** Huge wheat-storage silos and facilities. Many buildings c. 1880. Original shopping centre (c. 1900), McDonald St. Four-storey railway water tower (1886), Soldiers Ave, now a museum with James Hill's 1885–1930 taxidermy collection of some 500 birds and animals (open Sun. p.m.). Lake Marma, around which is a walking track, offers birdwatching and spectacular sunsets. Stick Shed (1941) built from 640 unmilled tree trunks, Wimmera Hwy on eastern side of town. Jan.: New Year's Day Race Meeting. June: Murtoa Cup (horse race). Oct.: Big Weekend (includes Agricultural Show, race meeting, Arts Show, vintage machinery demonstrations and Poets on the Pier). **In the area:** Barrabool Forest Reserve, 7 km S, has wildflowers in spring (difficult access in winter). **Visitor information:** Marma Gully Antiques, 50 Marma St; (03) 5385 2422.

Myrtleford   Pop. 2705

MAP REF. 229 J2, 239 O7, 240 B5

On the Great Alpine Rd, 46 km SE of Wangaratta, the town of Myrtleford is surrounded by an area that produces hops, timber, vegetables, fruit, chestnuts and wine. It also has some of the largest walnut groves in the Southern Hemisphere. **In town:** The Phoenix Tree, in Lions Park on highway, sculptured butt of a red gum, crafted by Hans Knorr. The Big Tree, Smith St, a huge old red gum. Town's original school, Albert St, now restored (open Thurs., Sun. or by appt). Myrtleford Mart, Myrtle St, for bric-a-brac. Swing bridge over Myrtle Creek, Standish St. Reform Hill Lookout, end of Halls Rd; scenic walking track from Elgin St leads to lookout. Rotary Park, Myrtle St, and Apex Park, Standish St, both delightful picnic spots and rest areas. Jan Mitchell Art Gallery, Power St. Michelini Wines, Great Alpine Rd. Street Life market, Great Alpine Rd, each Sat. (Jan.–Apr.). Mar.: Tobacco, Hops and Timber Festival. Oct.: International Festival (even-numbered years). Dec.: Boxing Day Rodeo. **In the area:** Wineries: Rosewhite Vineyards and Winery, 8 km SE, Happy Valley Rd (open weekends, public holidays and Jan.); at Gapsted, 8 km NW, Victorian Alps Winery. Also at Gapsted, Valley Nut Groves has tours and sales. Near Eurobin, 16 km SE: Red Deer and Emu Farm; Leita Berry Farm, for homemade jams and berries in season (Dec.–Mar.); Bisinella Rose Farm. Nug Nug Quarter Horse Stud and Dingo Breeding, 16 km S (open by appt). Good fishing at Lake Buffalo (25 km S), Ovens River and Buffalo River. **Visitor information:** Ponderosa Cabin, 29–31 Clyde St; (03) 5752 1727. **See also:** Alpine Country p. 190.

Nagambie   Pop. 1335

MAP REF. 238 G8

Between Seymour and Shepparton on the Goulburn Valley Hwy, Nagambie is on the shores of Lake Nagambie, which was created by the construction of the Goulburn Weir in 1891. Rowing regattas, and speedboat and water-ski tournaments are held here throughout the year. **In town:** Several National Trust-classified buildings. In High St: Colonial Doll Shop; The Nut House, for Australian nuts and Australian-made products. Boat hire available. Self-guide walking tour, brochure available. Mar.: Goulburn Valley Vintage Festival. Nov.: Shiraz Challenge (competition for the best shiraz). Dec.: Rowing

Regatta. **In the area:** David Traeger Wines, on Goulburn Valley Hwy, southern side of town. National Trust-classified buildings at Chateau Tahbilk Winery, 6 km SW. Mitchelton Winery, 10 km SW off Goulburn Valley Hwy, also has 60-m observation tower and scenic river cruises on the Goulburn River (check times). Paul Osicka's Wines, Graytown, 24 km W. Days Mill, 18 km N of Murchison, flour mill with buildings dating from 1865. Plunketts Winery and Cafe at Avenel, 20 km SE. Self-guide bicycle tours of surrounding area, brochures available. **Visitor information:** 145 High St; (03) 5794 2647. Web site www.mcmedia.com.au/nagambie **See also:** Vineyards and Wineries p. 207.

Natimuk   Pop. 479

MAP REF. 234 F9

This Wimmera town, 27 km W of Horsham, is close to the striking Mt Arapiles, a 369-m sandstone monolith that has been described as 'Victoria's Ayers Rock'. A drive to the summit, in Mount Arapiles–Tooan State Park, reveals a scenic lookout. The mountain was first climbed by Major Mitchell in 1836, and today is popular with rock-climbing enthusiasts. Brigitte Muir, the first Australian woman to climb Mt Everest, used it as a training ground. **In town:** In Main St: Arapiles Historical Society Museum, in old courthouse (open by appt); Arapiles Craft Shop for local craft. Self-guide heritage trail, brochures available. **In the area:** Lake Natimuk, 2 km N, for water sports. Duffholme Museum, 21 km W. Mount Arapiles–Tooan State Park, 12 km SW. Toolondo Reservoir, 30 km S, for excellent trout fishing. Banskia Hill Flower Farm, 10 km E. **Visitor information:** Natimuk Hotel, Main St; (03) 5387 1300.

Nhill   Pop. 1890

MAP REF. 234 D7

The name of this town is possibly derived from the Aboriginal word *nyell*, meaning 'white mist on water'. A small wheat town on the Western Hwy, exactly halfway between Melbourne and Adelaide, it claims to have the largest single-bin silo in the Southern Hemisphere (in Davis Ave). The town is the starting point for tours of the Little Desert. **In town:** Historical Society Museum, McPherson St (open by appt). In Victoria St: cottage of John Shaw Neilson, lyric poet (in Jaypex Park, open by appt); boardwalk from Jaypex Park to Nhill Lake, with bird hide; Draughthorse Memorial to

famous Clydesdales, indispensable in opening up Wimmera region (in Goldsworthy Park); Lowana Craft Shop, for local craft. National Trust-classified post office (1888), Nelson St. Self-guide historical walk and drive, brochures available. Miniature Railway, at various locations, see by appt. Mar.: Country Music Festival. Sept.: Little Desert Festival. Oct.: Garden Walk. **In the area:** Little Desert National Park, 18 km S. Nearby, Little Desert Lodge operates day tours of Little Desert; Little Desert Wildflower Exhibition held here in Oct. Mallee Dam, 20 km SW, is important location for native birdwatching and has bird hide. Prolific birdlife also seen on Hermans Hill Tourist Walk through mallee and heathland to hill overlooking Big Desert Wilderness Park, brochure available. Big Desert Wilderness Park, 52 km NW via Yanac, on track north to Murrayville; exploration of this remote park by walking tracks and 4WD (but roads impassable in wet weather, check conditions); tours available. **Visitor information:** Victoria St; (03) 5391 3086.

Numurkah   Pop. 3128

MAP REF. 121 M13, 238 I4

Numurkah, 37 km N of Shepparton on the Goulburn Valley Hwy, is only half an hour from some sandy beaches and excellent fishing spots on the Murray River. The town is in an irrigation area concentrating on dairying, and was originally developed through the Murray Valley Soldier Settlement Scheme. **In town:** In Melville St: Steam and Vintage Machinery Display; historical museum (open Sun. p.m.); Court House Crafts. Marie's House of Dolls, Meiklejohn St. Mar.: Art Show. Apr.: Splashdown (fishing competition). Sept.: Kart Titles (go-kart championships). **In the area:** Glenarron, 8 km N, a tourist dairy farm. Monichino's Winery at Katunga, 11 km N. At Strathmerton, 26 km N, Cactus Country, cactus and succulent garden (2 ha). Ulupna Island flora and fauna reserve, 21 km N near Strathmerton, has large koala population; Red Gum Wildlife Tours of Ulupna Island. Barmah State Park, 40 km NW, largest red gum forest in Southern Hemisphere; safari tours. Morgan's Beach Caravan Park, at edge of forest on bank of Murray River, offers bushwalking and horseriding (horses for hire, facilities for visitors' horses). Historic buildings set on banks of Broken Creek at Nathalia, 24 km W. At Wunghnu 5 km S: Institute Tavern in restored Mechanics Institute (c. 1880); Tractor Pull Festival

at Easter. Crafty Characters Cottage at Brookfield, 6 km SE (open Sat. or by appt). **Visitor information:** Goulburn Valley Hwy, Wunghnu; (03) 5862 3458.

Ocean Grove   Pop. 9144

MAP REF. 216 G10, 223 G9, 230 A7, 233 R8

At the mouth of the Barwon River, Ocean Grove offers fishing and surfing, while nearby Barwon Heads offers safe family relaxation along the shores of its protected river. Both holiday towns are linked by a bridge over the Barwon River estuary, and are popular in the summer months as they are the closest ocean beaches to Geelong, 26 km NW. **In town:** Ocean Grove Nature Reserve, Grubb Rd. **In the area:** Jirrahlinga Koala and Wildlife Sanctuary, Taits Rd, Barwon Heads. Mangrove swamps in Lake Connewarre State Game Reserve, 7 km N. At Wallington, 8 km N: A Maze'N Things, timber maze with mini-golf and cafe; Koombahla Park Equestrian Centre; Country Connection Adventure Park; Bellarine Adventure Golf. **Visitor information:** A Maze'N Things, 1570 Bellarine Hwy (at Grubb Rd), Wallington; (03) 5250 2669.

Olinda   Pop. 949

MAP REF. 214 F11, 217 M7, 220 B11, 230 E4

This picturesque town in the centre of the Dandenong Ranges is well known for its gardens and galleries. Devonshire teas are a tradition in the Dandenongs, and there are a number of tea rooms and cafes in Olinda and the surrounding area. **In town:** Several galleries, including Touchstone Gallery, Monash Ave; Olinda Art Gallery, Parsons La. Feb.: Jazz Festival. Aug.–Nov.: Rhododendron Festival. **In the area:** On Olinda–Monbulk Rd: National Rhododendron Gardens, superb displays of rhododendrons and azaleas in season; R. J. Hamer Arboretum, walking tracks amongst 100 ha of rare and exotic trees; Cloudehill Gardens, has excellent landscaped gardens and program of twilight concerts in summer. Nearby, several walks and picnic areas among mountain-ash forest in Dandenong Ranges National Park; lyrebirds occasionally seen along walking tracks; rosellas feed from your hand. At Sherbrooke, 4 km S, Alfred Nicholas Gardens, featuring quaint ornamental lake and boathouse; George Tindale Memorial Garden, flowering plants under mountain ash trees. At Upwey, 28 km S, Burrinja Gallery, memorial to artist Lin Onus, has Aboriginal and

Oceanic sculptures and paintings. Mount Dandenong Lookout, 2 km N, spectacular views over Melbourne. William Ricketts Sanctuary, 3 km N, sculptures by the well-known Australian artist and conservationist, in native bushland setting. Kawarra Australian Plant Garden, 4.5 km N at Kalorama, extensive native plant collection. At Wandin North, 15 km NE, Mont De Lancey (1882): historic house and garden; museum; chapel; open Wed.–Sun. and public holidays. At Silvan, 15 km NE: tulip farms; Silvan Reservoir, surrounding area has walking tracks and picnic facilities; Silvan Winery, open for tastings on weekends and public holidays; Tesselaar's Tulip Festival held here each Sept.–Oct. At Kallista, 6 km S, Grants Picnic Ground, good spot to feed rosellas; craft market held here 1st Sat. each month. **Visitor information:** Dandenong Ranges Tourism, 1211 Burwood Hwy, Upper Ferntree Gully; (03) 9758 7522. Web site www.accomguidedandenong-ranges.net.au **See also:** Day Tours from Melbourne, p. 154; National Parks p. 163.

Omeo   Pop. 298

MAP REF. 113 A12, 240 F8
The high plains around historic Omeo were opened up in 1835 when overlanders from the Monaro region moved their stock south to these lush summer pastures. Its name is an Aboriginal word meaning 'mountains', and the township is set in the heart of the Victorian Alps at an altitude of 643 m. It is a base for winter traffic approaching Mt Hotham and Dinner Plain along the Great Alpine Rd from Bairnsdale, 121 km S, and for summer and autumn bushwalking expeditions to the Bogong High Plains. Omeo was damaged by earthquakes in 1885 and 1892 and was half destroyed by the Black Friday bushfires of 1939. Nevertheless, several old buildings remain. **In town:** In the A. M. Pearson Historical Park, Day Ave: old courthouse (1861), now museum; present courthouse (1892); log gaol (1858); stables; blacksmiths. Also in Day Ave: post office (1891); Commercial Bank (1890); Colonial Bank (1889); school (1866); 19th-century timber buildings including DNRE office, CWA Hall and Petersens Gallery; Cuckoo Clocks, has traditional German clocks and artifacts. Pioneer Cemetery, cnr Great Alpine Rd and Omeo Hwy. Dec.–Jan.: Omeo Plains Mountain Festival. Mar.: Picnic Races. Easter: Rodeo and Market. Nov.: Agricultural and Pastoral Show. **In the area:** High-country horseback and 4WD

Cloudehill Gardens, Olinda

tours; llama tours; bushwalking; trout fishing; skiing and whitewater rafting (in spring) on Mitta Mitta and Cobungra rivers; scenic drives, brochure available; Wineries and Riverside Drive. Omeo has a gold-rush history; high cliffs left after sluicing for gold, stone walls and tunnel openings can be seen at the Oriental Claims, 1.5 km W on Great Alpine Rd; walks; gold-panning popular along Livingstone Creek. Remains of State's first hydro-electric plant (power for Cassilis goldfield), 25 km W off Victoria Falls Rd. At Cassilis, 15 km S: Mt Markey Winery, Cassilis Rd; markets held next to historic cemetery (check dates). Blue Duck Inn (1890s) is a base for fishing at Anglers Rest, 29 km NW. Just beyond Benambra, 21 km NE, Lake Omeo, huge scenic salt lake in extinct volcano, has abundant bird life. Taylors Crossing suspension bridge, part of Australian Alps Walking Track, 44 km NE, off Tablelands Rd. National Trust-classified Hinnomunjie Bridge over Mitta Mitta River, 37 km N. Scenic drives: Tambo River valley between Swifts Creek and Bruthen (97 km S), especially beautiful in autumn; to Benambra then Corryong, 144 km NE; Omeo Hwy through Mitta Mitta to Tallangatta (172 km NW); from Omeo through Dinner Plain to Mt Hotham. Note: scenic drives cross State forests (be alert for timber trucks) or alpine areas (check road conditions in winter). **Visitor information:** Cuckoo Clocks, Day Ave (Great Alpine Rd); (03) 5159 1552. Web site www.omeo.net/region

Orbost   Pop. 2150

MAP REF. 241 J12
Situated on the banks of the legendary Snowy River, Orbost is on the Princes Hwy, surrounded by spectacular coastal and

mountain territory. **In town:** Information centre, Lochiel St, has audiovisual display explaining complex nature of rainforest ecology. In Forest Rd: Old Pump House, behind Slab Hut; hut (1872) relocated from its original site 40 km away; Historical Museum; Croajingolong Mohair Farm, has garments, yarns, fleeces, fabrics and leathergoods; Snowy River Country Craft; Lorna's doll display. Netherbyre Gemstone and Art Gallery, cnr Browning and Carlyle sts. Jan.: Australian Wood Design Exhibition. Nov.: Craft Expo. **In the area:** Raymond Creek Falls, 42 km N, 40-min return walk to falls; further 1-hr walk to Snowy River; check road conditions. Beautiful Bonang Rd, unsealed in parts, leads north-east through mountains to Delegate in NSW. Walking in Snowy River National Park, 25 km NW, and Errinundra National Park, 54 km NE. Latter has rainforest boardwalk; check road conditions in wet weather; 4WD tours. Tranquil Valley Tavern, on banks of Delegate River near NSW border, about 115 km NE. Spectacular drive to Buchan, 58 km NW, leads to Little River Falls and McKillop's Bridge on the Snowy River. Scenic coastal drive to Marlo (where Snowy River meets the sea) and Cape Conran (30 km E) starts just west of Orbost, returns to Princes Hwy near Cabbage Tree Creek. Cabbage Tree Palms Flora Reserve, 27 km E. At Marlo, 14 km S: galleries; Slab Hut; Bush Races in Jan.; Triathlon in Jan. or Mar. Bemm River Scenic reserve, 40 km E off Princes Hwy: 1-km signposted Rainforest Walk; picnic facilities. Bemm River, on Sydenham Inlet, 58 km E, popular centre for bream anglers. Baldwin Spencer Trail, a 262-km scenic driving circuit following route of explorer; incorporates Snowy River estuary and Errinundra National Park. **Visitor information:** 13 Lochiel St; (03) 5154 2424. Web site www.lakesandwilderness.com.au

Moyne River borders the coastal fishing village of Port Fairy

Ouyen   Pop. 1251

MAP REF. 120 E10, 236 H9
At the junction of the Calder and Mallee hwys, Ouyen is 107 km s of Mildura, north-east of the Big Desert area. **In town:** Apr.: Autumn Art Show. Oct.: Mallee Wildflower Festival. Nov.: Farmers Festival. **In the area:** Hattah–Kulkyne National Park, 34 km N, with abundant wildlife, birdwatching, bushwalking, canoeing, and wildflowers in spring. Pink lakes are outstanding subjects for photography in Murray–Sunset National Park, 60 km w. At Patchewollock, 41 km sw, Easter Sports (with camel-racing). At Speed, 39 km s, Mallee Machinery Field Days each Aug. **Visitor information:** Oke St; (03) 5092 1000.

Paynesville   Pop. 2661

MAP REF. 231 Q5
A popular tourist resort 18 km SE of Bairnsdale on the McMillan Straits, Paynesville is a mecca for fishing and boating enthusiasts, and is noted for yachting and speedboat racing as well as water-skiing. **In town:** In the Esplanade: St Peter-by-the-Lake church (1961), incorporating seafaring symbols; Community Craft Centre. Market at Gilsenan Reserve, 2nd Sun. each month. Feb.: Jazz Festival. Mar.: Marlay Point–Paynesville Yacht Race. **In the area:** At Eagle Point, 2 km NW, Australian Power Boat Racing Championships held each Easter. Rotamah Island Bird Observatory, 8 km s by boat. Ninety Mile Beach, 10 km s by boat; ferry crosses Straits to Raymond Island. On Raymond

Island: Koala Reserve; Riviera Meadows, an animal farm specialising in miniature breeds. The Lakes National Park, to the east, 5 km by boat to Sperm Whale Head; otherwise via Loch Sport. Lake cruises and organised scenic tours of lakes. Boat charter and hire. Dolphins in lakes. **Visitor information:** Community Craft Centre, Esplanade; (03) 5156 7479. **See also:** Gippsland Lakes p. 186.

Port Albert   Pop. 248

MAP REF. 231 L10
This tiny historic town on the south-east coast, 120 km SE of Morwell, was the first established port in Victoria. Sailing boats from Europe and America once docked at the large timber jetty here. Boats from China brought thousands of Chinese to the Gippsland goldfields. Originally established for trade with Tasmania, Port Albert was the supply port for Gippsland pioneers until the railway from Melbourne to Sale was completed (1878). Today, Port Albert is a commercial fishing port, its sheltered waters popular with anglers and boat owners. Ninety Mile Beach, popular with surfers and anglers, begins north-east of the town. **In town:** Historic buildings in Tarraville Rd: original government offices and stores; Bank of Victoria (1861), now Maritime Museum with photographs and relics of the area. Warren Curry Art Gallery, also in Tarraville Rd, features Australian country-town streetscapes. Port Albert Hotel, Wharf St, first licensed in 1842 and one of the oldest hotels still operating in State. **In the area:** At Tarraville, 5 km NE, Christ Church (1856), first church in

Gippsland. Swimming at Manns Beach, 10 km NE. Surfing at Woodside on Ninety Mile Beach, 34 km NE. Wildlife sanctuary on St Margaret Island, 12 km E. **Visitor information:** The Court House, Rodger St, Yarram; (03) 5182 6553.

Port Campbell   Pop. 281

MAP REF. 221 A10, 233 K11
This small crayfishing village and seaside resort is situated in the centre of Port Campbell National Park and on a spectacular stretch of the Great Ocean Rd. **In town:** Historical Museum, Lord St (open school holidays). Loch Ard Shipwreck Museum, Lord St, has relics from the *Loch Ard* wrecked in 1878 at nearby Loch Ard Gorge. Signposted self-guide Discovery Walk (2.5 km). Good fishing from rocks and pier; boat charters for fishing and diving. Market, Lord St, each Sun. in summer. **In the area:** Mutton Bird Island, just off coast, attracts short-tailed shearwaters (muttonbirds) Sept.–Apr.; best viewing at dawn and dusk. Port Campbell National Park surrounds town; its coastal features include London Bridge, one section of which has now fallen down (6 km w), The Arch (5 km w), Loch Ard Gorge (7 km SE) and world-famous Twelve Apostles (12 km SE). Walking tracks in park (Parks brochure available), scenic drives, and historic shipwreck sites (for divers only). Glenample, 12 km E on Great Ocean Rd, first homestead in area; survivors of Loch Ard recuperated there (check opening times). Gibson Steps, 13 km SE, cut into limestone cliff face, provide access to beach and Twelve Apostles. Otway Deer and Wildlife Park, 20 km E. Picturesque road leads north to pretty timbered township of Timboon, 19 km N, centre of dairy area. Nearby, pick-your-own berries (in season) at Berry World. Just south of Timboon is Timboon Farmhouse Cheese, for cheese tastings and sales. **Visitor information:** Parks Victoria Office, Morris St; (03) 5598 6382. **See also:** Great Ocean Tour p. 159; Wildlife-Watching p. 167.

Port Fairy   Pop. 2625

MAP REF. 232 G9
The home port for a large fishing fleet and an attractive, rambling holiday resort, Port Fairy is 28 km w of Warrnambool, with both ocean and river as its borders. The town's history goes back to whaling days. At one time it was one of the largest ports in Australia. Over 50 of its small cottages and bluestone buildings are National

Trust-classified. This charming old-world fishing village is popular with heritage lovers and holiday-makers. **In town:** Self-guide historical walks, brochures available. History Centre, Gipps St, in old court-house. Battery Hill, end Griffith St, old fort and signal station at mouth of river. National Trust-classified buildings: splendid timber home of Captain Mills, Gipps St; Mott's Cottage, Sackville St. Other attractive buildings: Old Caledonian Inn, Bank St; Seacombe House and ANZ Bank building, Cox St; St John's Church of England (1856), Regent St; Gazette Office (1849), Sackville St. Hot Glass Studio, Regent St. Mar.: Folk Festival. Oct.: Spring Music Festival. Dec.: Moyneyana Festival (holiday and family festival). **In the area:** Mahogany Walk to Warrnambool, 6–7 hrs one-way (return by bus); brochures available. Griffiths Island, connected to east of town by causeway, has lighthouse and short-tailed shearwater (muttonbird) rookeries; spectacular nightly return of the short-tailed shearwaters to island (Sept.–Apr.). Australia's only mainland colony of short-tailed shearwaters at Pea Soup Beach and South Beach, on southern edge of town. Lady Julia Percy Island, 22 km off coast, home of fur seals; accessible only by experienced boat operators in calm weather. Lake Yambuk, 17 km W. Mt Eccles National Park, 56 km NW. Tower Hill State Game Reserve, 14 km E, fascinating area with an extinct volcano and crater lake with islands; nature walk starts at Natural History Centre within reserve. **Visitor information:** 22 Bank St; (03) 5568 2682. Web site www.greatoceanrd.org.au **See also:** Great Ocean Tour p. 159.

Portland   Pop. 9664

MAP REF. 232 D9

Portland, situated 72 km E of the South Australian border, is the most western of Victoria's major coastal towns and is the only deep-water port between Melbourne and Adelaide. It was the first permanent settlement in Victoria, founded by the Henty family in 1834. Today it is an important industrial and commercial centre, and a popular year-round destination with beaches, surfing, fishing and out-standing coastal and forest scenery. **In town:** Number of self-guide and guided walks in and around Portland, including the Walk in the Footsteps of Mary MacKillop, around sites significant during this beatified nun's time in Portland (also guided tours). Portland Maritime Discovery Centre at information centre,

Lee Breakwater Rd: 13-m sperm whale skeleton (sit inside the rib cage); original lifeboat used to rescue 19 survivors from shipwreck of *Admella* (1859). Adjacent is wreck of *Regia*, lying in 2 m of water. Botanical Gardens (1857), Cliff St. More than 200 early buildings, some National Trust-classified: customs house and court-house in Cliff St; Steam Packet Inn (1842) and Mac's Hotel in Bentinck St. History House, Charles St, a historical museum and family research centre in old town hall (1863). Edward Henty's homestead Burswood, Cape Nelson Rd. Fawthrop Lagoon, Glenelg St, has prolific birdlife. Powerhouse Car Museum, Percy St. Good views from Watertower Lookout, Clifton Crt, requires climbing 133 steps (displays of memorabilia on the way) to 360° view, excellent position for whale-watching; also from Portland Battery, Battery Hill. Portland Aluminium Smelter (guided tours, check times). Kingsley Winery (tastings and sales outlet), Bancroft St. Jan.: Foreshore Carnival. Feb.: Fishing Competition; Go Kart Street Grand Prix; Yachting Regatta. Mar.: Dahlia Festival. Nov.: Three Bays Marathon. **In the area:** Cape Nelson State Park, 11 km SW, offers spectacular coastal scenery and National Trust-classified light-house (check opening times). Discovery Bay Coastal Park, 19 km W, has rugged coastline and habitat for endangered hooded plover. Barrett's Gorae West Wines, 20 km W. Safe swimming and surfing at Cape Bridgewater, 21 km SW; nearby, petrified forest (formed by sand engulfing an ancient forest), blowholes and freshwater springs; 2–hr return walk (or take boat trip) to see Australian fur seals from viewing platform; walks to Cape Duquesne and Discovery Bay, both further west. For the more energetic, the 250-km Great South West Walk, a scenic circular track from information centre through national parks and State forests to Discovery Bay and Cape Nelson (can be covered in easy stages). Mt Richmond National Park, 25 km NW. Lower Glenelg National Park, 44 km NW via Kentbruck, has spectacular gorges, wildflowers, native birds and animals, and excellent fishing. Along coastal road is charming hamlet of Nelson, 70 km NW; here, launch trips to Glenelg River mouth (at Discovery Bay), also good water-skiing area. Nearby Princess Margaret Rose Caves (tours). Narrawong State Forest, 18 km NE. At Heywood, 28 km N, Bower Birds Nest Museum. **Visitor information:** Lee Breakwater Rd; (03) 5523 2671, freecall 1800 035 567.

Pyramid Hill   Pop. 527

MAP REF. 120 I13, 235 Q5, 238 B4

A small country town 32 km SW of Cohuna and 101 km N of Bendigo, Pyramid Hill was named for its unusually shaped hill, 187 m high. **In town:** Historical Museum, McKay St (open Sun. or by appt). A climb to the top of Pyramid Hill provides scenic views of the surrounding irrigation and wheat district and wildflowers in spring; there is also a Braille walking trail for the visually impaired. Trips to Pyramid Hill Salt mines, 10 km SW, bookings essential, contact information centre. Oct.: Pioneer Machinery Display; Agricultural Show. Nov.: Sidewalk Sale (local produce and festival events). **In the area:** Terrick Terrick State Park, 20 km SE: large Murray Pine forest reserve with numerous granite outcrops (southernmost outcrop called Mitiamo Rock); walks; variety of birdlife and other fauna. Mt Hope, 16 km NE, named by explorer Major Mitchell, has wildflowers in spring. **Visitor information:** Newsagency, 12–14 Kelly St; (03) 5455 7036.

Queenscliff   Pop. 3832

MAP REF. 216 H10, 218 B5, 223 I9, 230 B7

Queenscliff, 30 km SE of Geelong on the Bellarine Peninsula, was established as a commercial fishing centre in the 1850s and still has a large fishing fleet based in its harbour. The town looks out across the famous and treacherous Rip at the entrance to Port Phillip. **In town:** Queenscliff Maritime Centre, Weeroona Pde, explores town's long association with the sea. Adjacent, Marine Studies Centre offers summer holiday pro-gramme for visitors. Fort Queenscliff (1882), King St, built during the Crimean War, includes Black Lighthouse (1861), White Lighthouse (1862). Other historic buildings include: Vue Grand Hotel, Hesse St; Ozone and Queenscliff hotels, Gellibrand St. Historical tours leave from pier. In Hesse St: Queenscliffe Arcade, for local art and craft; Seaview Gallery in Seaview House. In Hobson St: Hobson's Choice Gallery; The Grand Ballroom Gallery. Bellarine Peninsula Railway oper-ates steam train between Queenscliff (station in Symonds St) and Drysdale (8 km NW) on weekends and summer holidays; also display of historic locomo-tives and carriages at station. Regular passenger ferry service operates between Queenscliff and Portsea across bay in summer and school holidays. Daily vehicle and passenger ferry service between Queenscliff and Sorrento (about 45 min.). Fishing charters, seal- and dolphin-watching trips, and swimming with dolphins and seals; details from information centre. Market at Princes Park, Gellibrand St, last Sun. of month (Sept.–May). Nov.: Music Festival. **In the area:** Point Lonsdale, 6 km SW, seaside holiday and tourist resort; market 2nd Sun. each month. Marine life viewing at Harold Holt Marine Reserve, which includes Mud Island and coastal reserves. Lake Victoria, 1 km W of Point Lonsdale. At Wallington, 15 km NW: A Maze'N Things; horseriding at Australian Equestrian Academy; Country Connection Adventure Park; pick-your-own fruit and vegetable farms (in season); Strawberry Fair in Nov. **Visitor information:** 55 Hesse St; (03) 5258 4843

Rainbow
Pop. 562

MAP REF. 120 D13, 234 F4

This Wimmera township, 69 km N of Dimboola, is near Lake Hindmarsh, popular for fishing, boating and water-skiing. **In town:** Murals on buildings, Federal St; self-guide mural walk, brochure available. Pasco's Cash Store (1928), Federal St, an original country general store. National Trust-classified Yurunga Homestead (1910), Gray St (on northern edge of town), has large collection of antiques and original fittings. Oct.: Iris Festival; Agricultural Show (includes harness racing). **In the area:** Historic fisherman's hut, 10 km SW at Lake Hindmarsh. Lutheran church (1901), 10 km W at Pella, has old pipe organ, only one other of its kind in State. Lake Albacutya Park, 12 km N, lake only fills when Lake Hindmarsh overflows. Wyperfeld National Park, 30 km N via sealed road north from Yaapeet: walks, bike trails and car tours, extended 4WD tours, brochures available at park entrance. **Visitor information:** Shell Service Station, cnr Federal and Tavern sts; (03) 5395 1026.

Robinvale
Pop. 1758

MAP REF. 120 F8, 237 J6

This small riverside town on the NSW border, 83 km SE of Mildura, is almost entirely surrounded by bends in the Murray River. The area around town is ideal for the production of dried fruit and wine grapes. Water sports and fishing are popular along the river. **In town:** In Moore St: McWilliams Wines;

Lexia Room, features historical exhibits. In Bromley Rd: Rural Life Museum (open by appt); at information centre, local almonds for sale. Mar.: 80 Ski Classic; Tennis Tournament. **In the area:** Euston Weir and lock on Murray, 3 km downstream. Robinvale Wines, Greek-style winery, 5 km S on Sea Lake Rd. Hattah–Kulkyne National Park, 66 km SW, walks and drives, brochures available. **Visitor information:** Kyndalyn Park Information Centre, Bromley Rd; (03) 5026 1388. **See also:** Vineyards and Wineries p. 207.

Rochester
Pop. 2553

MAP REF. 238 E6

On the Campaspe River, 29 km S of Echuca, Rochester is the centre for a rich dairying and tomato-growing area. A small, busy town, it has some attractive older buildings and boasts the largest dairy factory in Australia. **In town:** In Moore St: The 'Oppy' Museum (open Mon.–Fri.); opposite, statue of Sir Hubert Opperman, champion cyclist; antique shop. Historical Plaque Trail, Cemetery Walk and Campaspe River Walk; brochures available. **In the area:** Random House homestead, amid 4 ha of gardens beside river in Bridge Rd, on eastern edge of town. Campaspe Siphon, 3 km N, an engineering achievement, where the Waranga–Western irrigation channel runs under the Campaspe River. District channels are popular with anglers for redfin and carp. Pleasant lakes in district, popular for fishing and water sports, including Greens Lake and Lake Cooper (14 km SE). At Elmore, 17 km S: Campaspe Run Rural Discovery Centre, tells story of Koori and European settler history and heritage; Elmore Field Days held in Oct. **Visitor information:** Railway Station, Moore St; (03) 5484 1860.

Rushworth
Pop. 976

MAP REF. 238 G7

Rushworth, 20 km W of Murchison, off the Goulburn Valley Hwy, still shows traces of its gold-rush days. Many of the town's attractive original buildings still stand, witness to the days when Rushworth was the commercial centre for the surrounding mining district. **In town:** Nearly all the buildings in High St are National Trust-classified: St Pauls Church of England; band rotunda; former Imperial Hotel (now a private residence); Glasgow Buildings; the Whistle Stop. Also in High St, History

Museum in Mechanics Institute (1913) (open by appt). **In the area:** Rushworth State Forest, 3 km S, largest natural ironbark forest in world. At Whroo Historic Area, 7 km S: Balaclava Hill open-cut goldmine, camping, visitor centre display, Whroo cemetery and Aboriginal waterhole (all with visitor access). Further south, remnants of deserted goldmining towns Angustown, Bailieston and Graytown. At Murchison, 20 km E: Italian War Memorial and chapel; Meteorite Park, site of meteorite fall in 1969; nearby, Longleat Winery and Campbell's Bend picnic reserve. At Waranga Basin, 6 km NE: water sports, fishing, camping and excellent picnic facilities. **Visitor information:** Shire of Campaspe, 33 High St; (03) 5856 1207.

Rutherglen
Pop. 1904

MAP REF. 121 O13, 239 N4

Rutherglen is the centre of one of the most important winegrowing areas in Victoria. There is a cluster of vineyards surrounding the town, with winegrowing country stretching south to the Milawa area. **In town:** Main St, a fully preserved example of late-19th-century small-town architecture. Historical walking, bike or drive tour of town, maps available. Common School Museum, just behind Main St, for local memorabilia in fully restored 1800s schoolroom. Walkabout Cellars, Main St. Bush market in Main St, 4th Sun. each month. Mar.: Tastes of Rutherglen. Easter: Easter in Rutherglen. June: Winery Walkabout; Country Fair. Sept.: Wine Show. Nov.: Campbell's Spring Picnic; Tour de Muscat (cycling). **In the area:** National Trust-classified castle-like building at All Saints Estate Winery, 10 km NW; All Saints Live Concert here in Jan. Other wineries include Anderson, Bullers (with bird park), Campbells, Chambers, Cofield, Fairfield, Gehrig Estate, Jones, Morris, Mount Prior, Pfeiffer, St Leonards, Stanton and Killeen, Sutherland Smith and Warrabilla; check opening times. Old customs house at Wahgunyah, 10 km NW, relic of days when duty was payable on goods coming from NSW. Lake Moodemere Vineyards, 6 km W. Further 2 km W is Lake Moodemere, good for water sports, with canoe trees around lake; fauna reserve nearby. **Visitor information:** cnr Drummond and Main sts; (02) 6032 9166. **See also:** The Mighty Murray p. 201; Vineyards and Wineries p. 207.

St Arnaud
Pop. 2638

MAP REF. 235 L9

This old goldmining town is on the Sunraysia Hwy between Donald and Avoca, and is surrounded by forest and hill country. Many of the town's historic iron-lacework decorated buildings are National Trust-classified and together form a nationally recognised historic streetscape. **In town:** In Napier St: Queen Mary Gardens, Shire Hall (1902); courthouse (1866); Crown Lands Office (1876); Old Post Office (1866), now B&B and restaurant. Police lock-up (1862), Jennings St. Oct.: Agricultural Show. Nov.: Festival. **In the area:** Good fishing in Avoca River and at Teddington Reservoir, 28 km s. St Peter's Church (1869), made of pebbles, at Carapooee, 11 km SE. Self-guide drive in surrounding area, map available. **Visitor information:** The Old Post Office, 2 Napier St; (03) 5495 2313.

Sale
Pop. 13 366

MAP REF. 231 N6

Sale is the main administrative city in Gippsland. In nearby Bass Strait, there is a concentration of offshore oil development. Just over 200 km E of Melbourne on the Princes Hwy, Sale is convenient for exploration of the whole Gippsland Lakes area, which extends from Wilsons Promontory to Lakes Entrance, and is bordered to the north by the foothills and mountains of the Great Divide and, most of the way along the coast, by the famous Ninety Mile Beach. **In town:** Port of Sale, thriving during the days of the paddle-steamers. In Foster St: Lake Guthridge, with fauna park and adventure playground; historical museum; Gippsland Regional Arts Gallery; bronze of Mary MacKillop in St Mary's Church. Also in Foster St, Ramahyuck Aboriginal Corporation, has locally produced art and craft, and is part of Bataluk Cultural Trail which begins in Sale; Howitt Bike Trail also begins in Sale; details and brochures available for both. Attractive buildings: Our Lady of Sion Convent; clock tower; Victoria Hall; Criterion Hotel, with beautiful lacework verandahs. RAAF base, Raglan St, home of the famous Roulettes aerobatic team. Sale Common and State Game Refuge, protected wetlands area with boardwalk, on south-east edge of town. Jan.: Bush Races (bush horse race). Feb.: Sale Cup (horse race). Nov.: Agricultural Show. **In the area:** Holey Plains State Park, 14 km SW, has fossils in limestone quarry wall, and lake for swimming. Vintage

The impressive All Saints Estate Winery, near Rutherglen

Tractor Pull each Mar. at Longford, 7 km s. Seaspray, 32 km s on Ninety Mile Beach, offers excellent surfing and fishing; as do Golden and Paradise beaches, 35 km SE, and Loch Sport, a further 30 km; nearby, The Lakes National Park and Rotamah Island Bird Observatory, 15 km from Loch Sport. Marlay Point, 25 km E on shores of Lake Wellington, has extensive boat launching facilities; yacht club here sponsors overnight yacht race to Paynesville each Mar. Popular rivers for fishing include the Avon, close to Marlay Point, and the Macalister, Thomson and La Trobe, especially at Swing Bridge (1883), 5 km s of Sale. **Visitor information:** Central Gippsland Information Centre, Princes Hwy; (03) 5144 1108. Web site www.wellington.vic.gov.au **See also:** Gippsland Lakes p. 186.

Seymour
Pop. 6294

MAP REF. 238 G10

Seymour is a commercial, industrial and agricultural town on the Goulburn River, 89 km N of Melbourne. The area was recommended by Lord Kitchener during his visit in 1909 as being suitable for a military base. Nearby Puckapunyal was an important training place for troops during World War II and is still a major army base. **In town:** In Emily St: Royal Hotel, featured in Russell Drysdale's famous 1941 painting 'Moody's Pub'; The Old Courthouse (1864), for local art; Fine Art Gallery in The Old Post Office; Old Goulburn Bridge (1891), preserved as historic relic; walking track alongside Goulburn River. Goulburn Park, cnr Progress and Guild sts, has picnic and swimming areas. Seymour Railway Heritage Centre, Railway Pl., has restored

steam engine and carriages for viewing (by appt). Self-guide historical walk, brochure available. Mobby's Market, Wimble St, every 2nd Sun. Feb.: Alternative Farming Expo. Mar.: Rafting Festival. Oct.: Seymour Cup. **In the area:** Wineries: Somerset Crossing Vineyards, 2 km s; Hankin's Wines, 5 km NW on Northwood Rd; Hayward's Winery, 12 km SE near Trawool. Army Tank Museum at Puckapunyal army base, 10 km W. Historic railway station in scenic Trawool Valley, 5 km SE. At Mangalore, 5 km N, National Air Show held Easter Sunday. **Visitor information:** The Old Courthouse, Emily St; (03) 5799 0233. Web site www.mitchellshire.vic.gov.au **See also:** Vineyards and Wineries p. 207.

Shepparton
Pop. 31 945

MAP REF. 238 I6

The 'capital' of the rich Goulburn Valley, this thriving, well-developed city, 172 km N of Melbourne, has 4000 ha of orchards within a 10-km radius and 4000 ha of market gardens along the river flats nearby. The area is irrigated by the Goulburn Irrigation Scheme. **In town:** Art Gallery, Welsford St, features Australian paintings and ceramics. Parkside Gardens and Aboriginal Keeping Place, Parkside Dr., has displays and dioramas (check opening times). Historical Museum in Historical Precinct, High St (open even-dated Sun. p.m.). Emerald Bank Heritage Farm, Goulburn Valley Hwy, shows farming in the 1930s. Redbyrne Pottery, Old Dookie Rd. Victoria Park Lake, Tom Collins Dr. SPC cannery, Andrew Fairley Ave, has direct sales, and guided tours during fruit season (Jan.–Apr.). Reedy Swamp Walk, at end of Wanganui Rd, for prolific birdlife.

Fruit Connection, at rest stop on causeway, has arts and crafts. Trash and treasure market, Melbourne Rd, each Sun; craft market in Queens Gardens, Wyndham St, 3rd Sun. each month. Jan.: International Dairy Week. Feb.: Bush Market Day. Nov.: Strawberry Festival; Spring Car Nationals (car competitions). **In the area:** Several vineyards in surrounding region. Tallarook State Forest, 5 km SW. Taste of Tatura (food and wine festival) each Mar. at Tatura, 13 km SW. At Kialla, 5 km S: Boxwood Pottery, Elm Vale Nursery. Mud Factory Pottery, 6 km S on Goulburn Valley Hwy. Belstack Strawberry Farm, on Goulburn Valley Hwy, Kialla West, 9 km S (by appt); Belstack Strawberry Fair in Nov. Ardmona Kids Town, 3 km W on Peter Ross-Edwards Causeway. At Mooroopna, 5 km W: craft market, 1st Sun. each month; Fruit Salad Day in Feb.; Lemnos-Campbells soup cannery and Ardmona fruit cannery have direct sales. **Visitor information:** 534 Wyndham St; (03) 5831 4400, freecall 1800 808 839. **See also:** Vineyards and Wineries p. 207.

Skipton   Pop. 453

MAP REF. 226 F13, 233 M4
This small township on the Glenelg Hwy, 51 km SW of Ballarat, is situated in an important pastoral and agricultural district. The town was a major centre for merino sheep sales in the 1850s. **In town:** Eel factory, Cleveland St, nets eels in region's lakes and rivers and exports them, mainly to Germany. National Trust-classified bluestone Presbyterian Church (1872), Montgomery St, has unusual gargoyles. May and Nov.: Lake Goldsmith Steam Rally (vintage vehicles). Dec.: Rose Festival. **In the area:** Mooromong, 11 km NW, notable historic homestead (open by appt). Mt Widderin Cave, 6 km S, volcanic cave with large underground chamber that was once a dance venue (tours by appt). Kaolin Mine, 10 km E (open by appt). **Visitor information:** Roadhouse, Glenelg Hwy; (03) 5340 2131.

Sorrento   Pop. 1328

MAP REF. 216 I11, 218 D7, 223 I10, 230 B8
Situated on a thin strip of land between Port Phillip and Bass Strait, Sorrento was the site of Victoria's first European settlement in 1803. Lack of water initially forced its abandonment, though the area has been a popular seaside holiday destination since the 1870s. The township is close to historic Point Nepean and to major surf and bayside beaches. **In town:** Collins Settlement Historic Site on Sullivan Bay, marking the State's first European settlement, includes early settlers' graves. Several self-guide walks around the township, passing jetties, boat sheds and sandstone cliffs; brochures available. Sorrento Hotel, Hotham Rd; Continental Hotel, Ocean Beach Rd; and Koonya Hotel, The Esplanade; all fine examples of early Victorian architecture. Nepean Historical Society Museum and Heritage Gallery, Melbourne Rd, houses collection of artifacts and memorabilia in the National Trust-classified Mechanics Institute (1877). Adjacent is Watt's Cottage (1869), constructed of wattle and daub, and the Pioneer Memorial Garden. A vehicular and passenger ferry operates between Sorrento and resort town of Queenscliff across the bay; ferries depart adjacent to Sorrento pier and return daily. Craft market at Sorrento Primary school, cnr Kerferd and Coppin rds, last Sat. each month. Mar.: Street Festival. **In the area:** Cruises to fabricated Pope's Eye Marine Reserve, where gannets nest; dolphin and seal cruises. Portsea, 4 km NW, opulent holiday township with safe swimming on its bayside beach and good jetty-fishing. Portsea Swim Classic held here in Jan. Mornington Peninsula National Park, including Sorrento, Rye and Portsea back beaches, features: wild coastline and excellent surfing; London Bridge, at Portsea back beach, a unique rock formation; Point Nepean; Fort Nepean, the fort's guns fired the first allied shots in both world wars (access to the point and the fort by daily transport service departing Portsea, except on Bike and Hike Day, 4th weekend of each month, when the 10-km return trip is made on foot or by bicycle); former Quarantine Station (1859) on Point Nepean, built following deaths from smallpox on a vessel anchored in nearby Weeroona Bay (tour includes quarantine and army health services museums each Sun. and public holidays). At Blairgowrie, 4 km E, swim-with-dolphins tours (Sept.–May). McCrae homestead (1844), 17 km E, drop-slab National Trust property (open p.m.). At the bayside resort town of Rosebud, 15 km E: summer fishing launches, depart from Rosebud pier; safe family beaches. Cruises depart from Rye pier, just south of Rosebud, to seal colonies in Port Phillip. **Visitor information:** Peninsula Visitor Centre, Point Nepean Rd, Dromana; (03) 5987 3078; freecall 1800 808 009. **See also:** Wildlife-Watching p. 167; Vineyards and Wineries p. 207.

Stawell   Pop. 6272

MAP REF. 216 A5, 235 J11
North-east of Halls Gap and 129 km NW of Ballarat on the Western Hwy, Stawell is well sited for tours to the Grampians. It is the home of the Stawell Easter Gift, Australia's most famous professional foot race. **In town:** Self-guide historic city tour, maps available. Big Hill, local landmark and goldmining site; at summit, Pioneers Lookout indicates positions of famous mines. Old cyanide vats, Leviathans Rd, last used in 1935 to extract gold from tailings. Casper's World in Miniature Tourist Park, London Rd, has scale working models of famous world features such as Eiffel Tower, dioramas and commentaries. In Main St: Stawell Gift Hall of Fame Museum, Central Park; Fraser Park, has various items of mining equipment on display. Pleasant Creek Court House Museum, Western Hwy. Stawell Ironbark Forest, northern outskirts of town, off Newington Rd, has spring wildflowers, including rare orchids. Market, Sloane St, 1st Sun. each month. Easter: Easter Gift (professional foot race); Easter Festival. June: State Ballooning Championships. **In the area:** Scenic flights, 4WD tours and balloon flights. Bunjil's Shelter, 11 km S off Pomonal Rd, Aboriginal rock paintings in ochre. The Sisters Rocks, 3 km SE, huge granite tors beside Western Hwy. Wineries at Great Western, Ararat and Halls Gap. At Great Western, a picturesque wine village 19 km SE, The Diggings pottery. Overdale Station, 10 km E on Landsborough Rd, guided tours by appt. National Trust property, Tottington Woolshed, 55 km NE on road to St Arnaud, rare example of 19th-century woolshed. Deep Lead Flora and Fauna Reserve, 6 km W, off Western Hwy. Lake Fyans, 17 km SW, for sailing. Lake Bellfield, 30 km SW, offers fishing, canoeing and kayaking. Lake Wartook, in Grampians National Park, 60 km W and Lake Lonsdale, 12 km NW, for all water sports. **Visitor information:** Stawell and Grampians Visitor Information Centre, 50–52 Western Hwy; (03) 5358 2314, freecall 1800 246 880. **See also:** The Golden Age p. 171; The Grampians p. 182; Vineyards and Wineries p. 207.

Swan Hill   Pop. 9385

MAP REF. 120 H11, 237 N11
In 1836 when the explorer Thomas Mitchell camped on the banks of the Murray, he named the spot Swan Hill because the black swans had kept him

The Mighty Murray

As a present-day explorer, a trip following the course of the Murray River is an opportunity to discover a rich cross-section of Australian country and its history, as well as the infinite variety of natural beauty and wildlife the river itself supports.

THE SOURCE
The Murray has its source on Cowombat Flat, near Native Dog Flat, just south of the border of New South Wales and Victoria in Alpine National Park. Here it is just a gurgling mountain stream.

THE UPPER MURRAY
The upper reaches of the river flow through the scenic area around Jingellic and Walwa, and on to the beautiful Lake Hume near **Albury** and **Wodonga** before continuing past **Corowa**, the birthplace of Federation, and into Lake Mulwala.

LAKES, BEACHES AND RED GUMS
As it flows from the aquatic playgrounds of Lakes Hume and Mulwala, the Murray becomes a wide and splendid river. Lined with magnificent red gums in the region around **Cobram**, the riverbanks are transformed into wide sandy beaches. This is ideal holiday country with pleasant resort towns: **Yarrawonga**, **Mulwala**, **Barooga** and **Tocumwal**.

WINE COUNTRY
Victoria's main winegrowing area is centred around **Rutherglen** and extends to the wineries of Cobram and the Ovens and Goulburn valleys. Most of the wineries welcome visitors and many offer tours.

THE HEYDAY OF THE RIVERBOATS
Notable river towns like **Echuca**, **Swan Hill** and **Wentworth** have carefully preserved much of the history of the colourful riverboat era. The Port of Echuca, the Swan Hill Pioneer Settlement and the historic Murray Downs homestead are a must if you are in the area. Children especially will delight in the 'living museum' aspect of these river towns, with their original buildings, paddle-steamers and old wharves faithfully restored.

WILDLIFE
The Murray's abundant bird and animal life is protected by national parks and in a number of sanctuaries and reserves stretching from the banks of the river. Spoonbills, herons, eagles, harriers and kites abound.

The **Hattah–Kulkyne National Park**, near Mildura, includes a section of the river frontage and the Hattah Lakes system. Many bird species have been recorded here. Red kangaroos can be regularly seen: a rare experience in Victoria. The other major park near the river, **Murray–Sunset National Park**, includes a section of the riverine plains of the Murray and supports a varied array of native fauna including the mallee fowl. Near Picnic Point in the Moira State Forest, near Mathoura, waterbirds and wildlife abound and can be seen from the observatory in this beautiful red gum forest. At **Kerang**, which lies at the beginning of a chain of lakes and marshes, you can see huge breeding grounds for the splendid ibis. **Kyabram** has a widely known community-owned fauna and waterfowl park which is open daily, and almost all of Gunbower Island is a protected sanctuary for wildlife.

SUNRAYSIA
The beautiful climate of **Mildura** supports flourishing citrus and winegrowing industries as well as attracting countless holidaymakers to the Sunraysia area. Upstream is Red Cliffs, a town founded after World War I by returned soldiers, who turned it into a model irrigation town, and the surrounding areas into prosperous winelands. At the junction of the Murray and the Darling lies **Wentworth** (in New South Wales), one of the oldest of the river towns, with a historic gaol and the beautifully preserved paddle-steamer *Ruby*. From Wentworth, holidaymakers can cruise along the Darling River in MV *Loyalty*.

RIVERLAND
The Murray crosses into South Australia and at **Renmark** begins its splendid flow down to its mouth at Lake Alexandrina. The banks are lined with such historic river towns as Renmark, **Morgan** and **Murray Bridge**. **Goolwa** at its mouth has a strong tradition of shipbuilding, originating from the busy riverboat days. Renmark, like Mildura, is famous for its year-round sunshine. This South Australian stretch of the Murray offers splendid river scenery and birdlife, excellent fishing and water sports, and the chance to enjoy the many wineries in the area.

Further information is available from the visitor information centres in the various towns along the river, including Swan Hill, (03) 5032 3033, freecall 1800 625 373; Mildura, (03) 5021 4424; Cobram, (03) 5872 2132; Echuca, (03) 5480 7555; or Yarrawonga, (03) 5744 1989. Web site www.murrayoutback.org.au **See also:** National Parks p. 163 and individual entries in A–Z listing for parks and towns in bold type.

Paddlesteamers on the Murray River at Echuca

awake all night. The township became a busy 19th-century river port and today it is a pleasant city and major holiday centre on the Murray Valley Hwy, 335 km NW of Melbourne. The climate is mild and sunny, and the river and nearby lakes offer good fishing, boating and water sports. **In town:** Australia's first heritage museum, The Pioneer Settlement, at end of Gray St on Little Murray River, features local Aboriginal culture and life in the last century, staff in period costume, old-fashioned transport and Sound and Light tour (bookings essential); daily Murray cruises on paddle-steamer, PS *Pyap*. Regional Gallery of Contemporary Art, opposite Pioneer Settlement. Burke and Wills Fig Tree, Curlewis St, considered largest in Australia, commemorates explorers' visit. Self-guide walk, brochure available. Market, Curlewis St, 3rd Sun. each month. Mar.: Redgum Festival. June: Racing Cup Carnival. July: Italian Festa. **In the area:** Lakeside Nursery and Gardens, 10 km NW, with over 300 roses on view. Buller's winery at Beverford, 11 km NW. Historic Tyntyndyer homestead (c. 1846), National Trust-classified, 20 km NW on Murray Valley Hwy (open public and school holidays or by appt). Market at Nyah, 27 km NW, 2nd Sat. each month. Pheasant farm and aviaries at Nowie North, 32 km NW. At Tooleybuc, 46 km N (in NSW): tranquil riverside atmosphere, fishing, picnicking, riverside walks, Bridgekeepers Cottage for craft and dolls. Murray Downs homestead, 2 km NE over bridge into NSW on Moulamein Rd, is historic sheep, cattle and irrigation property (check opening times); daily river cruises from Murray Downs River Cruises wharf on MV *Kookaburra*. At Lake Boga, 17 km SE: re-built Catalina flying boat and museum in original communications war bunker; Imperial Egg Gallery, collection of egg artwork; lake nearby ideal for water sports, with Yacht Club Regatta each Easter. Best's St Andrew's Vineyard near Lake Boga. **Visitor information:** 306 Campbell St; (03) 5032 3033, freecall 1800 625 373. **See also:** The Mighty Murray p. 201; Vineyards and Wineries p. 207.

Tallangatta
Pop. 952

MAP REF. 239 Q5, 240 D2
When the old town of Tallangatta was submerged in 1956 for the construction of the Hume Weir, many of its buildings were moved to a new location 8 km W, on the shores of Lake Hume. Today, situated 42 km SE of Wodonga on the Murray

Valley Hwy, the town has the benefit of this large lake and boasts an attractive inland beach. It is the easternmost main Mitta River town and is directly north of the beautiful alpine region of Victoria. **In town:** The Hub, Towong St, for art and craft; also houses Lord's Hut, the only remaining slab hut in the district. Self-guide walks and drives; leaflets available. Apr.: Dairy Festival. Oct. or Nov.: Art Exhibition; Fifties Festival. **In the area:** Laurel Hill Trout Farm at Eskdale, 33 km S. Scenic drives include: to Cravensville; from Mitta Mitta along Omeo Hwy; to Tawonga and Mount Beauty. At Mitta Mitta, 60 km S: remnants of large open-cut gold mine; Baratralia Emu Farm. Australian Alps Walking Track passes over Mt Wills, 48 km S of Mitta Mitta. Lake Dartmouth, 58 km SE, for good trout fishing and boating. Traron Alpacas, 15 km E at Bullioh, has alpacas and other animals, yarns and garments for sale, and Paulownia trees (Chinese trees grown for shade or fodder). Gold-panning tours to Granya, 28 km NE. **Visitor information:** The Hub, 35–37 Towong St; (02) 6071 2611.

Terang
Pop. 1867

MAP REF. 221 A6, 233 K8
Terang, located on the Princes Hwy in a predominantly dairy-farming area, is a well-laid-out town with grand avenues of deciduous trees, recognised by the National Trust. The town is well-known for its horseracing facilities and events. **In town:** Early 20th-century commercial architecture. In High St: Gothic-style sandstone Presbyterian church; cottage crafts shop in old courthouse. District Historical Museum, Princes Hwy, features old railway station and memorabilia. Self-guide historical town walk, brochure available. Lions walking track (4.8 km) beside dry lake beds and National Trust-classified trees (entrance behind Civic Centre, High St). Jan.: New Year's Day Family Picnic; Australian Stockhorse Weekend. **In the area:** Intricately constructed dry stone walls, built 1860s, are a common sight in district. Lake Keilambete, 4 km NW, 2.5 times saltier than the sea, reputed to have therapeutic properties, contact information centre. Noorat, 6 km N, birthplace of Alan Marshall, author of *I Can Jump Puddles*; Alan Marshall Walking Track, a gentle climb to summit of extinct volcano with excellent views of crater, surrounding district and across to Grampians. Noorat Agricultural Show in Nov. Glenormiston

Agricultural College, 4 km further N, tastefully developed around historic mansion. Model Barn Australia, 5 km E on Robertson Rd, collection of model cars, boats and planes (open by appt). Ralph Illidge Wildlife Sanctuary, 17 km S. Demo Dairy, 3 km W on Princes Hwy, demonstrates dairy-farming practices (open 1st Mon. each month). Hopkins Falls, 33 km W, spectacular after good rains. **Visitor information:** Clarke Saddlery, 105 High St; (03) 5592 1164. Web site www.ansonic.com.au/tdpa

Torquay
Pop. 5984

MAP REF. 216 F11, 223 E10, 233 Q9
This popular resort is 21 km S of Geelong, close to the Bells and Jan Juc surfing beaches. The Torquay Surf Lifesaving Club is the largest in the State. Torquay also marks the eastern end of the Great Ocean Road, a spectacular drive south-west to Anglesea and beyond. **In town:** On Surfcoast Hwy: Mary Elliott Pottery; surfing products and Surfworld Surfing Museum. Craft Cottage, Anderson St. Barbara Peake's Studio, Sarabande Cr. Pieces Gallery, Bell St. Large sundial, Fishermans Beach foreshore. Tiger Moth World vintage aeroplane flights, Blackgate Rd, offers joyflights. Easter: Bells Beach Surfing Classic. **In the area:** Bicycle track along Surfcoast Hwy, Grovedale to Anglesea; various walks and scenic drives; brochures available. Horserides at Sea Mist, 22 km NW on Wensleydale Station Rd, Moriac. Museum of early Australian horse-drawn carriages near Bellbrae, 5 km W. At Bellbrae: Pottery Studios, Fast 'n' Fun, radio-controlled models, Spring Creek Trail Rides. **Visitor information:** Surfworld Surfing Museum, cnr Surfcoast Hwy and Beach Rd; (03) 5261 4219. **See also:** Great Ocean Tour p. 159.

Traralgon
Pop. 18 993

MAP REF. 231 K7
Situated on the Princes Hwy, 172 km SE of Melbourne, Traralgon is one of the La Trobe Valley's main cities, the others being Moe and Morwell. **In town:** Walking tours and heritage drive, leaflets available. Old post office and courthouse, cnr Franklin and Kay sts. On Princes Hwy: band rotunda and miniature railway at Victory Park. Feb.–Mar.: Music in the Park. Nov.: Traralgon Cup (horse races). **In the area:** Loy Yang power station, 5 km S (tours, contact Morwell

visitor centre). At Toongabbie, 19 km NE, Festival of Roses held in Nov. **Visitor information:** The Old Church, Southside Central, Princes Hwy; (03) 5174 3199, freecall 1800 621 409.

Walhalla   Pop. 15

MAP REF. 231 K5

This tiny goldmining town is tucked away in dense mountain country in Gippsland. The drive from Moe, 46 km S, takes in some spectacular scenery. Walhalla is set in a narrow, steep valley, with sides so sheer that its cemetery has graves that have been dug lengthways into the hillside. It was connected to electricity in 1998; which time generators were used. **In town:** Historic buildings and relics of gold-boom days. Signposted heritage town walk. Excellent local walks, including to cricket ground, perched on top of 200-m hill, and historic cemetery. Long Tunnel Extended Gold Mine, one of the most successful in the State (guided tours, check times). Rotunda (1896). Old Fire Station (1901), hand-operated fire engine and fire memorabilia. Post office (1886). Old bakery (1865), oldest surviving building in town, near hotel. Museum (1894), gold-era memorabilia. Windsor House (1890). Walhalla Goldfields Railway, runs Sat., Sun. and public holidays. Gold-panning in Stringers Creek which runs through town. **In the area:** 4WD tours to gold-era 'suburbs'. Walhalla Mountain River Trail, scenic drive linking Walhalla, Traralgon and Moe, brochure available. Australian Alps Walking Track (655 km) commences at Walhalla. Deloraine Gardens, terraced gardens just north of town. Walking and downhill and cross-country skiing in Baw Baw National Park, on western outskirts of town. Scenic road between Walhalla and Jamieson (140 km N), check road condition in wet weather. Rawson, 8 km SW, built for construction of nearby Thomson Dam; Mountain Trail Rides. At Erica, 12 km SW: timber industry display at Erica Hotel; Mountain Saddle Safaris; King of the Mountain Woodchop held each Jan. Thomson River, 4 km S, for excellent fishing, canoeing and white-water rafting (rafting tours). Moondarra State Park, 30 km S. Boola Boola Winery, 5 km SE on Tyers Rd. **Visitor information:** Regional Visitor Information Centre, The Old Church, Southside Central, Princes Hwy, Traralgon; (03) 5174 3199, freecall 1800 621 409. **See also:** Gippsland Lakes p. 186.

Airworld Aviation Museum near Wangaratta

Wangaratta   Pop. 15 527

MAP REF. 239 M6

Wangaratta's proximity to the high country, winery regions and the Murray River, make it an ideal town from which to explore north-eastern Victoria. The surrounding fertile area produces wool, wheat, tobacco, kiwifruit, walnuts, chestnuts, hops and wine grapes. **In town:** Numerous bike trails, leaflet available. In cemetery, Tone Rd, grave of bushranger Daniel 'Mad Dog' Morgan; his headless body was buried here, the head having been sent to Melbourne for examination. At information centre, cnr Tone Rd and Handley St: Mrs Stell's House in Miniature (one-sixth scale 1950s-style mansion); history of Kelly Gang. Paddys market at Council car park, Ovens St, each Sun. a.m. Oct.: Agricultural Show. Nov.: Festival of Jazz and Blues. **In the area:** Airworld Aviation Museum, 7 km S, said to be Australia's largest collection of antique civil aircraft in flying condition. Road to Moyhu, 27 km S, leads to beautiful King Valley and Paradise Falls. Network of minor roads allows exploration of unspoiled area and tiny townships of Whitfield (50 km S), Cheshunt and Carboor. King Valley scenic drive runs beside King River to Whitfield and Powers Lookout (74 km S). Newton's Prickle Berry Farm at Whitfield. At Warby Range State Park, 12 km W: good vantage points, picnic spots and variety of bird and plant life. Interesting old gold township Eldorado, 20 km NE: has largest gold dredge in the Southern Hemisphere, built in 1936; historical museum; potteries.

Nearby, Reids Creek, popular with anglers, gem-fossickers and gold-panners. Wombi Toys at Whorouly, 25 km SE. **Visitor information:** cnr Tone Rd and Handley St; (03) 5721 5711. **See also:** Vineyards and Wineries p. 207.

Warburton   Pop. 2446

MAP REF. 217 O6, 220 H9, 230 G3

Warburton was established with the gold finds of the 1880s; however, by the turn of the century it had found its niche as a popular tourist town with fine guest houses. It is surrounded by the foothills of the Great Dividing Range and is only a 90-minute drive from Melbourne. **In town:** At information centre, Warburton Hwy: 6m-diameter old-style operating waterwheel; historical display; arts and crafts; wood-fired bakery. Several art and craft, and old wares shops. Riverside Walk (5 km return), access behind information centre. River Walk (9 km return), from Signs Bridge on Warburton Hwy. Jan.: Upper Yarra Draughthorse Festival. June: Film Festival. July: Winterfest (wood festival). Nov.: Strawberry Festival. **In the area:** Bushwalks, horseriding, birdwatching and fishing; opportunities to spot platypuses; details from information centre. Multi-use Rail Trails follow former railway tracks, leaflet available. Tommy Finn's Trout Farm, 2 km W. Yarra Junction Historical Museum, 10 km W. Mt Donna Buang, 17 km NW in Yarra Ranges National Park, popular day-trip destination from Melbourne, often snow-covered in winter; lyrebirds, increasing in number, may be seen at

Lake Pertobe, Warrnambool

dawn and dusk in summer; Donna Buang Rainforest Gallery has treetop viewing platform and walkway; popular nightwalks. Upper Yarra Dam, 23 km NE. Along Warburton Hwy, an attractive area of vineyards: Yarra Burn Winery, McWilliams Lillydale Vineyard, Five Oaks Vineyard and Brahams Creek Winery. The Acheron Way begins 1 km E of Warburton, giving access to views of Mt Donna Buang, Mt Victoria and Ben Cairn, on the scenic 37-km drive north to St Fillans. Walk into History, from Powelltown (25 km S) to Warburton East, leaflet available; this is a branch of the Centenary Trail. Between Powelltown and Noojee, rainforest gully walk to Ada Tree, a giant mountain ash. Upper Yarra Draught Horse Festival in Jan. at Hoddles Creek, 15 km SW. Yellingbo State Fauna Reserve, 25 km SW. **Visitor information:** 3400 Warburton Hwy; (03) 5966 5996. **See also:** Vineyards and Wineries p. 207.

Warracknabeal   Pop. 2493

MAP REF. 234 H6
Situated at the intersection of the Borung and Henty hwys, 378 km NW of Melbourne, Warracknabeal is in the centre of a rich grain-growing area. The Aboriginal name means 'the place of the big red gums shading the watercourse'. **In town:** Historical Centre, Scott St, includes pharmaceutical collection, a wide variety of clocks, and antique furnishings of child's nursery (open p.m.). Black Arrow Tour of historic buildings (self-guide drive or walk) and other walks including the Yarriambiack Creek Walk; leaflets available. National Trust-classified buildings: post office (1907) and Warracknabeal Hotel (1872), with its beautiful iron lacework, both in Scott St; original log lock-up (1872), Devereaux St, built when town acquired its first permanent policeman. Lions Park, on Yarriambiack Creek, has picnic spots, and flora and fauna park. Easter: Y-Fest (golf, horseracing, vintage machinery, country music, Patchewollock Sports and Camel Cup). **In the area:** North Western Agricultural Machinery Museum, 3 km S on Henty Hwy, displays of farm machinery from last 100 years. **Visitor information:** 119 Scott St; (03) 5398 1632.

Warragul   Pop. 9011

MAP REF. 217 P10, 230 H6
Much of Melbourne's milk comes from this prosperous dairy-farming area 106 km SE of Melbourne. It is also an important commercial centre. **In town:** West Gippsland Arts Centre, Civic Place. Lillico Garden Railway, Copelands Rd. Mar.: Gippsland Field Days. **In the area:** Wild Dog Winery, 5 km S on Warragul–Korumburra Rd (open daily by appt). Near Drouin, 8 km W: Oakbank Angoras and Alpacas; Fruit and Berry Farm. Gumbaya Park, 35 km W, a family fun park. Wildflower sanctuary at Labertouche, 16 km NW. At Neerim South, 17 km N: Tarago River Cheese Company; picnic/barbecue facilities at nearby Tarago Reservoir; scenic drives through nearby mountain country. Further 12 km N at Nayook: Fruit and Berry Farm; Country Farm Perennials Nursery and Gardens. At Noojee, 10 km NE of Nayook: Alpine Trout Farm; trestle bridge. Darnum Musical Village, 8 km E on Princes Hwy, complex of buildings housing collection of musical instruments dating back to 1400s; visitors can play them. Yarragon, 13 km SE, has good shopping for antiques, crafts, gourmet food and boutique wines; Dairy Fest held in Nov. At Childers, 31 km SE: Sunny Creek Fruit and Berry Farm; Windrush Cottage. Mt Worth State Park, 19 km SE. Nature reserves and picnic spots: Glen Cromie (Drouin West), Glen Nayook (south of Nayook) and Toorongo Falls (just north of Noojee). Gourmet Deli Trail, guides visitors on a food trip around this scenic region via various farms, cheese producers, wineries, nurseries, restaurants and food outlets; brochure available. **Visitor information:** The Old Church, Southside Central, Princes Hwy, Traralgon; (03) 5174 3199, freecall 1800 621 409.

Warrnambool   Pop. 26 052

MAP REF. 232 I9
Warrnambool is 257 km SW of Melbourne on Lady Bay, where the Princes Hwy meets the Great Ocean Road. This beautiful seaside city has first-class sporting, cultural and entertainment facilities and well-maintained parks and gardens. Over 100 ships were wrecked on the coast near

Warrnambool, the most famous being the Loch Ard in 1878 which claimed all but two lives of those on board. **In town:** Self-guide Heritage Walk, 3 km, brochure available. Flagstaff Hill Maritime Museum, Merri St: a reconstructed 19th-century Maritime Village; Flagstaff Hill tapestry, with themes of Aboriginal history, sealing, whaling, exploration, immigration and settlement; famous earthenware Loch Ard Peacock, recovered from *Loch Ard* wreck. In Timor St: Performing Arts Centre; Art Gallery. In Gilles St: Customs House Gallery; History House, with local memorabilia (open 1st Sun. each month or by appt). Botanic Gardens, Botanic Rd, designed by Guilfoyle in 1879. Fletcher Jones Gardens, Raglan Pde. Lake Pertobe Adventure Playground, Pertobe Rd; swimming beach opposite. Portugese Padrao, Cannon Hill, monument to Portugese explorers. The Potter's Wheel, Liebig St. Thunder Point Reserve, end Macdonald St. Middle Island, off Pickering Point, colony of little (fairy) penguins, Aboriginal middens. Unusually designed Wollaston Bridge (over 100 years old), on northern outskirts of town. Kid's Country Treasure Map (available at information centre) provides informative way for the whole family to enjoy Warrnambool. Horseriding trail rides, mainly on beach. Cruises on Hopkins River. National Trust-classified Hopkins River Boathouse, off Otway Rd. Blue Hole, at mouth of river, for fishing, surfing and rock pools. Sun. market at showgrounds, Koroit St. Feb.: Wunta Fiesta (family entertainment and stalls). May: Racing Carnival. Oct.: Melbourne–Warrnambool Cycling Classic; Spring Orchid Show. **In the area:** Annual visit of rare southern right whales, usually June–Sept. (viewing platform just east of town at Logans Beach). Allansford Cheeseworld, 10 km E, for cheese tasting and sales. At Cudgee, 17 km E, Cudgee Creek Wildlife Park: deer; crocodiles and other native fauna; aviary; barbecue facilities. In late spring, early summer at Hopkins Falls, 13 km NE, hundreds of baby eels can be seen migrating up the falls. Warrnambool Trout Farm, 4 km N on Wollaston Rd: catch-your-own; fish cleaned by staff; fish-feeding; seafood products for sale. At Koroit, 18 km NW: National Trust-classified historic buildings, botanic gardens. Mahogany Walk from Warrnambool–Port Fairy (22 km), along beach dunes. Helicopter and joy flights along coast. **Visitor information:** 600 Raglan Pde; (03) 5564 7837. **See also:** Great Ocean Tour p. 159; Wildlife-Watching p. 167.

Wedderburn   Pop. 708

MAP REF. 235 N7

Once one of Victoria's richest gold-mining towns in the 'Golden Triangle', Wedderburn is on the Calder Hwy, 74 km NW of Bendigo. Many large nuggets have been unearthed in the area, and gold is still found around the town. **In town:** At northern edge of town: Hard Hill area, former gold diggings and Government Battery, Wilson St; Kuku-Yalanji, Wallaby Dr., an Aboriginal art and craft gallery. In High St: Museum and General Store (1910), original building furnished and stocked as it was at turn of century; coach-building factory; old bakery, converted into a pottery. Self-guide town walks, brochure available. Mar.: Gold Festival. Aug.: Wool Expo. Sept.: Historic Engine Exhibition. **In the area:** Fossickers Drive, takes in goldmining and Aboriginal sites, wineries, Melville Caves and bushwalk starting points; brochure available. Christmas Reef Mine, 3 km E, a working tourist mine. Mount Korong, 16 km SE, for rock-scrambling and bushwalking. Wychitella Forest Reserve, 16 km N, wildlife sanctuary in mallee forest. At Korong Vale, 13 km NW, The Chandelier Man, manufacturer of crystal chandeliers. **Visitor information:** Shire Offices, High St; (03) 5494 1200.

Welshpool   Pop. 138

MAP REF. 231 K10

Welshpool is a small dairying town and nearby Port Welshpool is a deep-sea port servicing fishing and oil industries. Barry Beach Marine Terminal, 8 km S of the South Gippsland Hwy, services the offshore oil rigs in Bass Strait. **In the area:** Excellent fishing and boating. At Port Welshpool, Maritime Museum. Agnes Falls, 19 km NW, highest falls in State. Scenic drive west with panoramic views from Mt Fatigue, off South Gippsland Hwy. Near Toora, 11 km W, Franklin River Reserve has nature walk. **Visitor information:** cnr South Gippsland Hwy and Silkstone Rd, Korumburra; (03) 5655 2233, freecall 1800 630 704.

Winchelsea   Pop. 1027

MAP REF. 216 D10, 223 A8, 233 P8

This town is on the Barwon River, 37 km W of Geelong. It originated as a watering-place and shelter for travellers on the road to Colac from Geelong. **In town:** On Princes Hwy: Barwon Bridge, with its graceful stone arches, opened 1867 to handle

increasing westward traffic; Alexandra's Antiques and Art Gallery; Barwon Hotel (1842), housing museum of Australiana; Old Shire Hall, beautiful restored turn-of-the-century bluestone building, now popular tearooms with craft and woodwork for sale in gallery; old library (1893), now art gallery. **In the area:** National Trust property, Barwon Park homestead, 3 km N on Inverleigh Rd (open Sun. and Wed.). Country Dahlias gardens, 5 km S on Mathieson Rd (open Feb.–Apr.). Killarney Park Lavender Farm, 6 km S (open Sept.–May). **Visitor information:** Old Shire Hall Art Gallery, Princes Hwy; (03) 5267 2769.

Wodonga   Pop. 25 825

MAP REF. 121 P13, 239 P4, 240 B2

Wodonga is the Victorian city – Albury, the NSW city – in a twin-city complex astride the Murray in north-east Victoria. Albury–Wodonga, with the attractions of the Murray and nearby Lake Hume, makes a good base for a holiday. **In town:** National Museum of Australian Pottery, South St, displays work of 19th-century potters. Gateway Village, Lincoln Causeway, includes working craft shops, information centre and restaurant. Behind village, self-guide Wiradjuri Walkabout river walk highlights Aboriginal culture; canoe trees, fish and tortoise carvings in trunks; brochure available. Also on Lincoln Causeway: Palatinat Boutique Brewery; Harveys Fish Farm, offers catch-your-own Australian native fish; minigolf; water playground and restaurant. Sumsion Gardens, Church St, a beautiful lakeside park. In Melrose Dr., largest outdoor tennis centre in Australia. Border Country Fair at Gateway Village, 2nd Sun. each month. Feb.: Sports Festival. Mar.: Wodonga Show. Oct.: Wine and Food Festival. Nov.: World Cup Show Jumping. **In the area:** Winery and fishing tours, hot-air ballooning, trail-riding and canoe hire; details from information centre. Kids Play World, indoor play centre with cafe and restaurant, Young St, Albury. Jindera Museum, 16 km NW of Albury, pioneer museum with old-style store and storekeeper's house. At Bonegilla, 12 km W of Wodonga, Festival held in Oct. (odd-numbered years). Military Museum, 4 km SE at Bandiana. Hume Weir, 15 km E; Hume Weir Trout Farm. Mt Granya State Park, 56 km E, offers spectacular views of alps. Nearby touring areas include: Upper Murray, mountain valleys of north-east Victoria; Murray Valley; Riverina district.

The Old Stone Bridge, Yackandandah

Visitor information: Gateway Information Centre, Lincoln Causeway; (02) 6041 3875, freecall 1800 800 743. Web site http://albury.wodonga.com/tourism **See also:** The Mighty Murray p. 201.

Wonthaggi   Pop. 5887

MAP REF. 230 G10

Once the main supplier of coal to the Victorian Railways, Wonthaggi, situated 8 km from Cape Paterson in Gippsland, is South Gippsland's largest town. It began as a tent town in 1909 when the coal mines were opened up by the State government following industrial unrest in the NSW coalfields. The mines operated until 1968. **In town:** Easter: Coal Skip Fill. **In the area:** State Coal Mine, 1.5 km S on Cape Paterson Rd, features tours of reopened Eastern Area Mine, with experienced former coalminer as guide, and museum of mining activities. Cape Paterson, 8 km S in Bunurong Marine Park, for surfing, swimming, snorkelling and scuba-diving. Scenic drive to beaches at Inverloch, 12 km SE. George Bass Coastal Walk from Kilcunda, 11 km NW; brochures available for this and other walks in the area. **Visitor information:** Watts St; (03) 5672 2484.

Woodend   Pop. 2974

MAP REF. 216 G2, 230 A1, 233 R2, 238 D12

Woodend is situated on the Calder Hwy, an hour's drive north of Melbourne. It acquired its name from its position at the end of the Black Forest. During the gold rushes (1850s), travellers sought refuge from mud, bogs and bushrangers at the 'wood's end' around Five Mile Creek. The main danger for today's travellers is 'black ice' in winter; hazard warning lights are installed on the Calder Hwy. **In town:** On Calder Hwy: Bluestone bridge (1862) crossing Five Mile Creek, on northern outskirts of town; St Mary's Anglican Church (1864); clock tower, built as WW I memorial; Insectarium of Victoria, insect and invertebrate research and interpretation centre. Courthouse (1870), Forest St (check opening times). The Bulb Shop, High St, has rare bulbs. Craft market, 3rd Sun. each month (Oct.–May). Dec.: Five Mile Creek Festival. **In the area:** Black gum trees (*Eucalyptus aggregata*); Woodend region is only place in State where these trees are found. Hanging Rock, 8 km NE, a massive rock formation made famous by *Picnic at Hanging Rock*, film of Joan Lindsay's novel by the same name; Picnic Cafe; picnic races held nearby on New Year's Day and Australia Day; vintage car rally each Feb. At Lancefield, 25 km NE: historic buildings, wineries, horseriding; Woodchopping Competition in Mar.; Dog Show in Dec. At Monegeetta, 15 km S of Lancefield, Mintaro homestead (1882), replica (but smaller) of Melbourne's Government House (not open to the public). Mt Macedon (1013 m), 10 km E on Mount Macedon Rd, has huge WW I memorial cross at summit; area around renowned for its beautiful gardens, many open

autumn and spring. The Camels Hump, 12 km E off Mount Macedon Rd, has 12-km signposted walk to summit. Scenic drives and bushwalks in Macedon Regional Park. At Macedon, 8 km SE, Church of the Resurrection has stained-glass windows designed by Leonard French. At Gisborne, 16 km SE: Gisborne Steam Park; craft outlets. Barringo Wildlife Reserve at New Gisborne, 17 km SE. Llapaca Picnics, 20 km W on McGiffords Rd, Fernhill: organised scenic walk with picnic supplied and carried by llama or alpaca (by appt, contact information centre). At Carlsruhe, 10 km NW: galleries, crafts and antiques. Over 15 wineries in region (maps available): close to town is Hanging Rock Winery, at Newham (10 km NE); Macedon Ranges Budburst Wine Festival held last weekend in Oct. **Visitor information:** High St, beside Five Mile Creek; (03) 5427 2033. Web site www.macedon-ranges.vic.gov.au

Yackandandah   Pop. 592

MAP REF. 239 P5, 240 B3

Located about 28 km S of Wodonga, this exceptionally attractive town, with avenues of English trees and traditional verandahed buildings, has been classified by the National Trust. Yackandandah is in the heart of the north-east goldfields (gold was discovered here in 1852), but today it is better known for its historic buildings. **In town:** Number of original buildings in High St: post office; several banks and general stores; Bank of Victoria (1865), now historical museum (open Sun. and school holidays). Self-guide walking tour, brochure available. Also in High St: Ray Riddington's Premier Store and Gallery; The Old Stone Bridge (1857). Art and craft from: Yackandandah Workshop, cnr Kars and Hammond sts; Wildon Thyme, High St. Numerous antique shops, including Finders Bric-a-Brac and Old Wares, Frankly Speaking (both in High St); Vintage Sounds Restorations, Windham St (old and antique gramophones, telephones and radios). Rosedale Garden and Tea Rooms, Kars St. Jan.: Lavender Harvest Festival. Mar.: Folk Festival. June: Vintage Engine Swap Meet. **In the area:** Tours of Kars Reef Goldmine, and gold-panning (licence required); details from information centre. Creeks in Yackandandah area still yield alluvial gold to amateur prospectors. Lavender Patch Plant Farm, 4 km W on Beechworth Rd. Picturesque Indigo Valley, 6 km NW; scenic drive leads

Vineyards and Wineries

Viticulture developed in Victoria following the 1850s gold rush. Unsuccessful diggers began planting vines as a source of income. Earlier, William Ryrie and his two brothers had taken up Yering Station, near Yarra Glen, as a grazing property and first planted vines there in 1838. By 1868 more than 1200 hectares of vines had been established in the State. The light, dry wines produced in these vineyards won wide acclaim, but the event of phylloxera saw the industry decline until the early 1960s, when it began to develop into what it is today.

One of the oldest regions is in the north-east, 270 kilometres from Melbourne. **Rutherglen** and the other nearby wine-making towns of Wahgunyah, **Glenrowan** and **Milawa** produce wine unique to the region's climate and soils. Many of the wineries are still managed by the descendants of the founders. The region is famed for its rich flavoursome reds, and for the exotic range of fortified wines such as Rutherglen muscat, Rutherglen tokay and its famous port-style wine. On the June long weekend, a winery walkabout enables wine-lovers to visit the vineyards and sample some of these fine wines. It is advisable to book accommodation in advance at this time.

Vineyard in the Yarra Valley region

West along the Murray, the towns of **Echuca**, **Swan Hill** and **Mildura** are part of the Murray Valley and north-west region known for the production of wines for everyday drinking.

About 200 kilometres west of Melbourne, between Stawell and Ararat, is the little town of Great Western, where the Seppelt and Best wineries developed in the 1860s. Since then they have consistently produced fine wines, including the renowned champagne-style Great Western Special Reserve from the Seppelt winery. The vineyards of Great Western are also noted for their rich red and full-flavoured white table wines.

At **Ararat**, Trevor Mast's Mt Langi Ghiran Wines and the Montara Winery, both produce excellent wine with their own individual character.

To the north-east of Great Western is the region of the Pyrenees with the towns of **Avoca**, Redbank and Moonambel. Here are the Taltarni, Mt Avoca, Redbank, Blue Pyrenees, Summerfield, Peerick, St Ignatius, Berrys Bridge, Dalwhinnie and Warrenmang wineries.

Stretching from **Shepparton** along to **Nagambie**, **Seymour** and **Mansfield** is the picturesque Goulburn Valley region with a contrast from the historic, classified buildings of Chateau Tahbilk to the modern wineries of Delatite and Mitchelton. One acclaimed wine variety is the Marsanne, a distinct and rather unusual white wine.

One of the two oldest regions near Melbourne is the Yarra Valley region, which is centred round **Yarra Glen**, Lilydale, Coldstream and **Healesville** (in the central part of the region), Cottles Bridge and St Andrews (at the northern end), and Seville and **Warburton** (to the south). This region's premium wine has had a rebirth after starting in the early 1850s and petering out as late as the 1920s. There is a wide range of wines, from sparkling wine to quality reds and white table wines.

Wineries of particular interest include Domaine Chandon for its sparkling wines and splendid tasting room, and Fergusson, Eyton on Yarra, Yarra Burn, Yering Station and De Bortoli, some of which have restaurants. There are many other wineries worth visiting, including Bianchet for the merlot and verduzzo wines, and St Huberts, one of the first wineries in the re-birth of the district. Grape Grazing, a food and wine festival, is held every March.

Another wine-producing region close to Melbourne is the Mornington Peninsula. A cool-climate winegrowing district, its vineyards nestle between farming and coastal hamlets and often have spectacular views. The main spread covers the area from Dromana, through Red Hill and across the Peninsula to Merricks and Balnarring, with **Mornington**, Main Ridge and Mt Martha offering several vineyards. Most vineyards are open weekends and public holidays for cellar-door tastings and sales; some are open by appointment only. The wine producers in this area organise the June long-weekend Queen's Birthday Wine Weekend at the Regional Gallery in Mornington.

North of Melbourne's Tullamarine Airport, wineries dot the landscape with pockets of vines stretching from the Sunbury area into the Macedon Ranges; some were established in the 1860s, others more recently. They include Knight's Granite Hills, Wildwood, Hanging Rock, Virgin Hills, Craiglee, Goonawarra, Cleveland, Cope-Williams, Flynn and Williams — each with its own distinct quality and character.

The Heathcote–Bendigo region is, like so many of Victoria's wine regions, goldmining country that gave up much hidden wealth in the period 1850–1900. Today there are many wineries scattered around the townships of **Heathcote**, Kingower, **Bendigo** and Bridgewater on Loddon. Wineries include Passing Clouds, Jasper Hill, Paul Osicka's, Zuber Estate, Water Wheel, Chateau Leamon and Mildara's Balgownie Estate.

In the last 30 years Victoria's wine industry has changed from an industry in decline, with about 25 commercial wineries, to a flourishing concern with more than 300 commercial wineries and 100 smaller ones. Most larger wineries are open daily for tastings and sales; some of the smaller ones have restricted opening times, so check before visiting. A number of wineries stage cultural events, in particular music concerts and festivals.

Tourism Victoria publish an excellent guide, *Wine Regions of Victoria*, describing more than 200 wineries; a copy of the guide as well as further information on Victoria's wine regions can be obtained from the Victorian Visitor Information Centre, Melbourne Town Hall, cnr Little Collins and Swanston sts, Melbourne, (03) 9658 9955. Web site www.wineries.tourism.vic.gov.au **See also:** individual entries in A–Z listing for towns in bold type. **Map reference:** 220, for Yarra Valley region.

through rolling hills along valley floor to Barnawatha. At Allans Flat, 10 km NE: The Vienna Patisserie, for coffee, ice-cream and quality Austrian cakes (closed Tues.); Park Wines; Schmidt's Strawberry Winery. At Leneva, 16 km NE, Wombat Valley Tramways small-gauge railway (Easter or by appt for groups). Kirbys Flat Pottery and Gallery, 4 km S on Kirbys Flat Rd (open weekends or by appt weekdays). **Visitor information:** The Athenaeum, High St; (02) 6027 1988.

Yarra Glen   Pop. 1232

MAP REF. 217 M5, 220 B6, 230 E3

Yarra Glen is situated in the heart of the picturesque Yarra Valley wine country, a favourite touring destination from Melbourne. **In town:** National Trust-classified Yarra Glen Grand hotel (1888), Bell St. Craft Market at racecourse, 1st Sun. each month. Mar.: Grape Grazing Festival. Apr.: Music Viva Yarra Valley Festival. May: Yarra Valley Expo. **In the area:** Hot-air balloon flights and champagne breakfast, details from information centre. Gulf Station (1854), 2 km NE, National Trust-owned pastoral property, remaining virtually unchanged since early pioneering days; farming implements, original breeds of cattle, sheep, horses, turkeys and ducks; open Wed.–Sun. and public holidays. At Dixons Creek, 9 km NE: De Bortoli Wines & Restaurant has excellent Yarra Valley views; Allinda Winery (open Sat., Sun., public holidays). Fergusson Winery and Restaurant, 7 km N of Yarra Glen in Wills Rd. Several other wineries in area, and also in Panton-Hill–St Andrews area to the west. Kinglake National Park, 26 km N: walking tracks, waterfalls, lyrebirds and wombats, and picnic areas. Ponyland Equestrian Centre, 7 km W: trail rides, riding lessons, overnight and weekend rides. Sugarloaf Reservoir Park, 10 km W: sailing, fishing, walking, barbecues and picnic areas. Yarra Valley Dairy, 4 km S, handmade specialty cheeses and clotted cream. **Visitor information:** Yarra Valley Healesville Visitor Information Centre, old courthouse, Harker Street; Healesville; (03) 5962 2600. **See also:** Vineyards and Wineries p. 207.

Yarram   Pop. 1807

MAP REF. 231 L9

This established South Gippsland town, 225 km by road from Melbourne, has some interesting original buildings and a pleasant golf course inhabited by relatively tame kangaroos. Situated between the Strzelecki Ranges and Bass Strait, it is a gateway to both rainforest and the coast. **In town:** Tarra Spinning Wheels, Alberton Rd, has spinning wheels, boat wheels, beds and general wood turning. Restored Regent Theatre (1930), Commercial Rd; cinema operates weekends and school holidays. Easter: Tarra Festival. Nov.: Seabank Fishing Contest. **In the area:** Good bush camping, details from information centre. Historic towns: Alberton, 6 km S, has early settlers' graves in cemetery. At Tarraville, 11 km SE, Christ Church (1856) and maritime museum in old bank building. Beaches patrolled in summer: Woodside Beach, 29 km E; Seaspray, 68 km NE. Fishing beaches: Manns, 16 km SE; McLoughlins, 29 km E. Native animal zoo, 19 km E at Woodside. Australian Omega Navigation Facility with 432-m-high steel tower, 30 km N. In the Strzelecki Ranges, 27 km NW: Tarra–Bulga National Park, has hilly, beautiful rainforest, dense mountain ash, myrtle and sassafras, spectacular fern glades, splendid river and mountain views, the occasional koala as well as rosellas and lyrebirds; wagon rides through ranges; Tarra Bulga Visitor Centre at Balook, Grand Ridge Rd, has interpretive displays. In the Tarra Valley, north-west of town: Eilean Donan Gardens and Riverbank Nursery; splendid gardens; 2 caravan parks; horseriding nearby. 46-km circuit drive from Yarram through Hiawatha: Minnie Ha Ha Falls on Albert River; nearby, picnic facilities and camping; gypsy wagons for hire. Won Wron Forest, 16 km N on Hyland Hwy, has wildflowers in spring. **Visitor information:** The Court House, Rodger St; (03) 5182 6553.

Yarrawonga   Pop. 3435

MAP REF. 121 N13, 239 K3

A pleasant stretch of the Murray and the attractive Lake Mulwala have made this border town and Mulwala (in NSW) extremely popular holiday resorts. The 6000-ha lake was created in 1939 during the building of the Yarrawonga Weir, which controls the irrigation waters in the Murray Valley. **In town:** Around the lake and along the river: sandy beaches and still waters, ideal for water sports; abundant birdlife. The Yarrawonga and Mulwala foreshore areas: shady willows, water-slides, barbecues and boat ramps. At information centre, Irvine Pde: Old Yarra Mine Shaft houses a large collection of gems, minerals and fossils. Canning A.R.T.S. Gallery, Belmore St, has art and craft, including local art. Tudor House Clock Museum, Lynch St. Bush market at railway station, Sharp St, 2nd and 4th Sun. each month. Rotary Market at Showgrounds, 3rd Sun. each month. Jan.: Rowing Regatta; Powerboat Racing; Rockalonga Concert. Oct.: Linga Longa Festival. Dec.: Murray Marathon. **In the area:** Daily cruises on *Paradise Queen* or *Lady Murray*, depart Bank St. Canoe and boat hire, horseriding available. Ovens River and winery tours, bookings at information centre. Fishing in Murray River. Fyffefield Winery, 19 km W on Murray Valley Hwy. **Visitor information:** Irvine Pde; (03) 5744 1989. **See also:** The Mighty Murray p. 201.

Yea   Pop. 960

MAP REF. 217 M1, 238 I11

This town, 58 km N of Yarra Glen, stands beside the Yea River, a tributary of the Goulburn River. Set in pastoral and dairy-farming land, it is well situated for touring around Mansfield, Eildon and the mountains, and to the gorge country between Yea and Tallarook, as well as south-east to Marysville. There are some beautiful gorges and fern gullies close to the Yea–Tallarook Road. **In town:** Heritage Walk, brochure available. In High St: Beaufort Manor (1870s); General Store (1887), now a restaurant. On eastern outskirts of town, Wetlands Walk, glider possums and a variety of birds. Market, Main St, 1st Sat. each month (Sept.–May, a.m.). Mar.: Autumn Fest. Nov.: Agricultural Show. **In the area:** Many scenic drives in area (best time is Aug.–Sept., when wattles are in bloom), leaflets available. In Murrindindi Reserve, 11 km SE: Murrindindi Cascades and wildlife including wombats, platypuses, lyrebirds. Pick-your-own fruit at Berry King Farm, Two Hills Rd, 28 km S at Glenburn. Kinglake National Park, 30 km S, for beautiful waterfalls, tall eucalypts, fern gullies and impressive views. Spectacular Wilhelmina Falls, 32 km S via Melba Hwy. Flowerdale Winery, 23 km SW on Whittlesea–Yea Rd. Ibis rookery at Kerrisdale, 17 km W. Grotto, a beautiful old church, in the hills 27 km N at Caveat. Mineral springs at Dropmore, 47 km N off back road to Euroa. Several good campsites along Goulburn River. **Visitor information:** Old Railway Station, Station St, Mansfield; (03) 5797 2663.

Victoria

LOCATION MAP

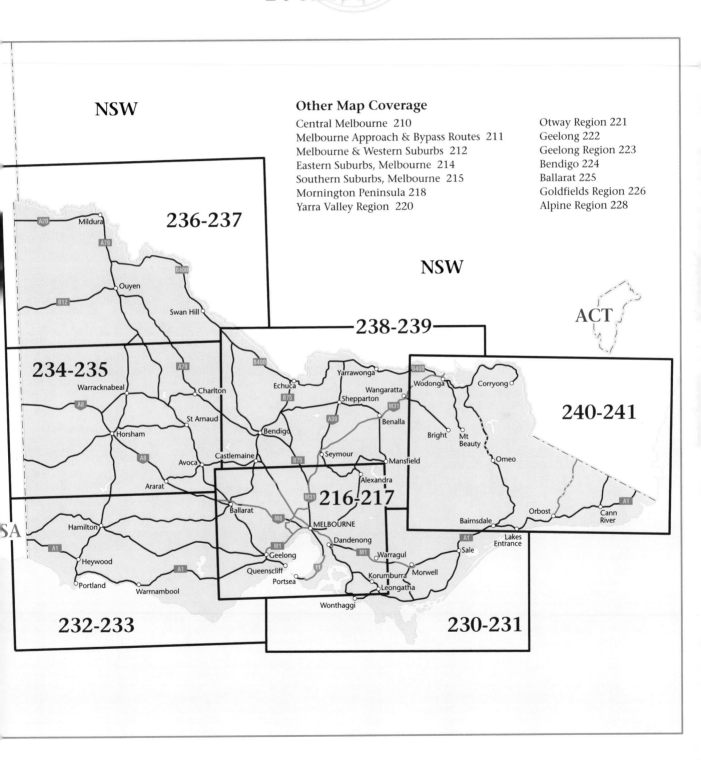

NSW

Other Map Coverage

Central Melbourne 210
Melbourne Approach & Bypass Routes 211
Melbourne & Western Suburbs 212
Eastern Suburbs, Melbourne 214
Southern Suburbs, Melbourne 215
Mornington Peninsula 218
Yarra Valley Region 220

Otway Region 221
Geelong 222
Geelong Region 223
Bendigo 224
Ballarat 225
Goldfields Region 226
Alpine Region 228

NSW

ACT

236-237

238-239

240-241

234-235

216-217

232-233

230-231

Mildura
Ouyen
Swan Hill
Warracknabeal
Charlton
Echuca
Yarrawonga
Wangaratta
Shepparton
Wodonga
Corryong
St Arnaud
Horsham
Bendigo
Benalla
Bright
Mt Beauty
Castlemaine
Avoca
Seymour
Mansfield
Omeo
Ararat
Alexandra
Ballarat
MELBOURNE
Hamilton
Dandenong
Bairnsdale
Orbost
Cann River
Heywood
Geelong
Warragul
Sale
Lakes Entrance
Queenscliff
Portsea
Korumburra
Morwell
Portland
Warrnambool
Leongatha
Wonthaggi

SA

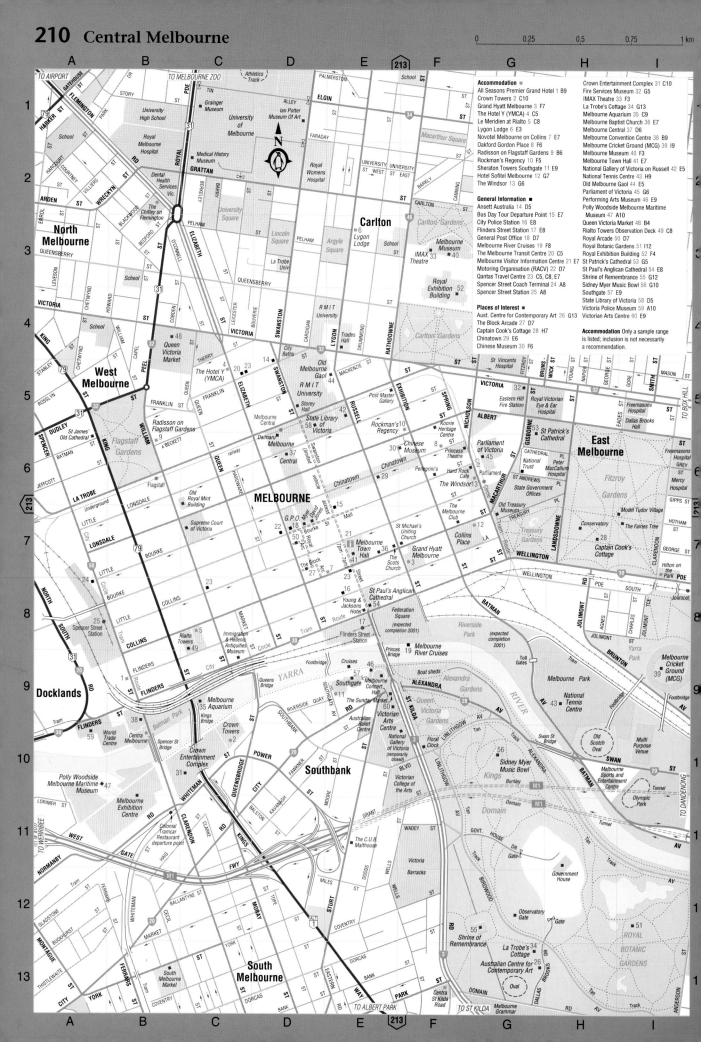

0   0.25   0.5   0.75   1 km

A   B   C   D   E   F   G   H   I

TO AIRPORT
Athletics Track
TO MELBOURNE ZOO
School

1

HABKER ST
GATEHOUSE ST
FLEMINGTON
STORY
PDE
TIN
Grainger Museum
ALLEY
Ian Potter Museum Of Art
ELGIN
PALMERSTON
School ST
213
34

University High School
University of Melbourne
FARADAY
Macarthur Square

2

ARDEN ST
HARCOURT ST
COURTNEY ST
VILLIERS ST
WRECKYN ST
BLACKWOOD
ROYAL PARK
RD
GRATTAN
Medical History Museum
Royal Womens Hospital
BARKLY ST
UNIVERSITY ST WEST
UNIVERSITY ST EAST
CANNING
CARLTON
46

Dental Health Services Vic.
Royal Melbourne Hospital

Accommodation ■
All Seasons Premier Grand Hotel 1 B9
Crown Towers 2 C10
Grand Hyatt Melbourne 3 F7
The Hotel Y (YMCA) 4 C5
Le Meridien at Rialto 5 C8
Lygon Lodge 6 E3
Novotel Melbourne on Collins 7 E7
Oakford Gordon Place 8 F6
Radisson on Flagstaff Gardens 9 B6
Rockman's Regency 10 F5
Sheraton Towers Southgate 11 E9
Hotel Sofitel Melbourne 12 G7
The Windsor 13 G6

Crown Entertainment Complex 31 C10
Fire Services Museum 32 G5
IMAX Theatre 33 F3
La Trobe's Cottage 34 G13
Melbourne Aquarium 35 C9
Melbourne Baptist Church 36 E7
Melbourne Central 37 D6
Melbourne Convention Centre 38 B9
Melbourne Cricket Ground (MCG) 39 I9
Melbourne Museum 40 F3
Melbourne Town Hall 41 E7
National Gallery of Victoria on Russell 42 E5
National Tennis Centre 43 H9
Old Melbourne Gaol 44 E5
Parliament of Victoria 45 G6
Performing Arts Museum 46 E9
Polly Woodside Melbourne Maritime
    Museum 47 A10
Queen Victoria Market 48 B4
Rialto Towers Observation Deck 49 C8
Royal Arcade 50 E7
Royal Botanic Gardens 51 I12
Royal Exhibition Building 52 F4
St Patrick's Cathedral 53 G5
St Paul's Anglican Cathedral 54 E8
Shrine of Remembrance 55 G12
Sidney Myer Music Bowl 56 G10
Southgate 57 E9
State Library of Victoria 58 D5
Victoria Police Museum 59 A10
Victorian Arts Centre 60 E9

General Information ■
Ansett Australia 14 D5
Bus Day Tour Departure Point 15 E7
City Police Station 16 E8
Flinders Street Station 17 E8
General Post Office 18 D7
Melbourne River Cruises 19 F8
The Melbourne Transit Centre 20 C5
Melbourne Visitor Information Centre 21 E7
Motoring Organisation (RACV) 22 D7
Qantas Travel Centre 23 C5, C8, E7
Spencer Street Coach Terminal 24 A8
Spencer Street Station 25 A8

Places of Interest ■
Aust. Centre for Contemporary Art 26 G13
The Block Arcade 27 D7
Captain Cook's Cottage 28 H7
Chinatown 29 F6
Chinese Museum 30 F6

Accommodation
Only a sample range is listed; inclusion is not necessarily a recommendation.

3

North Melbourne
Queensberry ST
BERKELEY ST
O'CONNELL ST
ELIZABETH ST
ROYAL PDE
PELHAM
BEDFORD ST
CHETWYND ST
University Square
Lincoln Square
Argyle Square
La Trobe Univ
Lygon Lodge
6
School
Carlton
Lygon Lodge
IMAX Theatre 33
Melbourne Museum 40
52
Royal Exhibition Building
QUEENSBERRY
PELHAM
CARLTON

4

KING ST
VICTORIA ST
LEVESON ST
HOWARD ST
CHETWYND
WILLIAM ST
School
CAPEL ST
PEEL ST
COBDEN ST
LEICESTER ST
BOUVERIE ST
SWANSTON ST
CARDIGAN
LYGON ST
DRUMMOND
RATHDOWNE ST
VICTORIA
RMIT University
Trades Hall
Carlton Gardens
Carlton Gardens
32
79
48
Queen Victoria Market

5

West Melbourne
STANLEY ST
ROSSLYN ST
DUDLEY ST
KING ST
31
32
PEEL ST
FRANKLIN ST
QUEEN ST
ELIZABETH ST
Radisson on Flagstaff Gardens
9
The Hotel Y (YMCA)
4
20 23
14
SWANSTON
City Baths
Old Melbourne Gaol 44
RMIT University
MACKENZIE ST
Post Master Gallery
EXHIBITION ST
RUSSELL
SPRING ST
NICHOLSON ST
VICTORIA
ALBERT
St Vincents Hospital
32
Eastern Hill Fire Station
Royal Victorian Eye & Ear Hospital
Freemasons Hospital
Dallas Brooks Hall
GISBORNE ST
BRUNSWICK ST
YOUNG ST
NAPIER ST
GEORGE ST
GORE ST
SMITH ST
MASON
TO BOX HILL

6

Flagstaff Gardens
St James' Old Cathedral
BATMAN ST
JEFFCOTT ST
LA TROBE
WILLIAM ST
Flagstaff
Storey Hall
42
State Library of Victoria
58
Daimaru
Melbourne Central
Swanston
Chinese Museum
30
Rockman's Regency
10
Koorie Heritage Centre
8
Chinatown
Princess Theatre
Pellegrini's
Hard Rock Cafe
The Windsor 13
Parliament of Victoria
45
National Trust
Parliament
ST ANDREWS PL
State Government Offices
Old Treasury Museum
PETER MacCALLUM Hospital
CATHEDRAL PL
St Patrick's Cathedral
53
East Melbourne
Freemasons Hospital
GREY
Mercy Hospital
GIPPS ST
HOTHAM

7

213
LONSDALE
LITTLE LONSDALE
79
Old Royal Mint Building
Supreme Court of Victoria
QUEEN ST
HARDWARE
MELBOURNE
G.P.O.
18
22
BOURKE
50
Royal
The Block Arc
27
23
David Jones
15
Mall
21
St Michael's Uniting Church
The Scots Church
36
41
Melbourne Town Hall
3
Grand Hyatt Melbourne
12
Collins Place
The Melbourne Club
COLLINS
LA
MACARTHUR ST
WELLINGTON
Treasury Gardens
The Melbourne
TREASURY PL
28
Conservatory
The Fairies Tree
Captain Cook's Cottage
Fitzroy Gardens
Model Tudor Village
LANDSDOWNE ST
CLARENDON ST
GEORGE ST
Hilton on the Park
PDE
SOUTH
Jolimont

8

NORTH ST
SOUTH ST
50
24
25
Spencer Street Station
LITTLE COLLINS
Tram
COLLINS
LITTLE BOURKE
Circle
Tram
MARKET ST
23
Route
5
49
Rialto Towers
Immigration & Hellenic Antiquities Museum
City Circle
Tram Route
30
Federation Square (expected completion 2001)
17
Flinders Street Station
Young & Jacksons Hotel
54
St Paul's Anglican Cathedral
16
BATMAN AV
Riverside Park
WELLINGTON PDE
JOLIMONT
AGNES
CHARLES
JOLIMONT TCE
BRUNTON AV
Melbourne Cricket Ground (MCG)
39

9

Docklands
FLINDERS RD
20
31
FLINDERS
FLINDERS
World Trade Centre
59
38
World Trade Centre
Central Melbourne
1
Queens Bridge
YARRA
Batman Park
Kings Bridge
Melbourne Aquarium
35
Crown Towers
2
SOUTHBANK
RIVERSIDE QUAY
SOUTHGATE AV
57
46
11
The Sunday Market
Southgate
9
Boat sheds
Princes Bridge
19
Melbourne River Cruises
Cruises
ST KILDA RD
ALEXANDRA
Queen Victoria Gardens
Alexandra Gardens
RIVER
AV
43
National Tennis Centre
Melbourne Park
Footbridge
AV
Footbridge
Melbourne Cricket Ground (MCG)
39

10

Docklands
RD
20
31
Crown Entertainment Complex
Melbourne Exhibition Centre
Spencer St Bridge
WHITEMAN ST
Centra Melbourne
QUEENSBRIDGE ST
CITY RD
POWER ST
FANKNER ST
MOORE ST
Crown Towers
2
Australian Ballet Centre
Victorian Arts Centre
60
National Gallery of Victoria (temporarily closed)
Southbank
Floral Clock
3
LINLITHGOW
Victorian College of the Arts
BLVD
56
Sidney Myer Music Bowl
Kings Domain
LINLITHGOW AV
ALEXANDRA AV
SWAN ST
BATMAN AV
Melbourne Sports and Entertainment Centre
Old Scotch Oval
Multi Purpose Venue
Olympic Park
20
Tunnel
TO DANDENONG

11

TO WERRIBEE
WEST GATE
NORMANBY
M1
Colonial Tramcar Restaurant departure point
Polly Woodside Melbourne Maritime Museum
47
LORIMER ST
CLARENDON ST
KINGS WAY
WHITEMAN ST
CLARKE ST
HAIG ST
KAVANAGH ST
BALSTON ST
GRANT ST
WADEY ST
The C.U.B. Malthouse
Victoria Barracks
GOVT. HOUSE DR
Gate
Government House
Domain
M1
Tan
The Domain
AV
Tunnel
BIRDWOOD
Track

12

GLADSTONE ST
FERRARS ST
BUCKHURST ST
Tram
20
WHITEMAN ST
CECIL ST
MORAY ST
TOPE ST
DODDS ST
WELLS ST
STURT ST
Victoria Barracks
55
Observatory Gate
Gate
51
ROYAL BOTANIC GARDENS
BIRDWOOD
Track

13

South Melbourne
MONTAGUE ST
THISTLETHWAITE ST
CITY RD
YORK ST
COVENTRY ST
FERRARS ST
South Melbourne Market
Tram
MARKET ST
CLARENDON ST
YORK ST
DORCAS ST
BANK ST
EASTERN RD
PARK WAY
STURT ST
COVENTRY ST
MILES ST
ALT 1
DORCAS RD
TO ALBERT PARK
BANK ST
School
3
Melbourne Grammar
Shrine of Remembrance
La Trobe's Cottage
34
Australian Centre for Contemporary Art
26
Oval
Centra St Kilda Road
TO ST KILDA
DOMAIN
DALLAS BROOKS DR
BIRDWOOD
AV
Track
ROYAL BOTANIC GARDENS

A   B   C   D   E   F   G   H   I
213

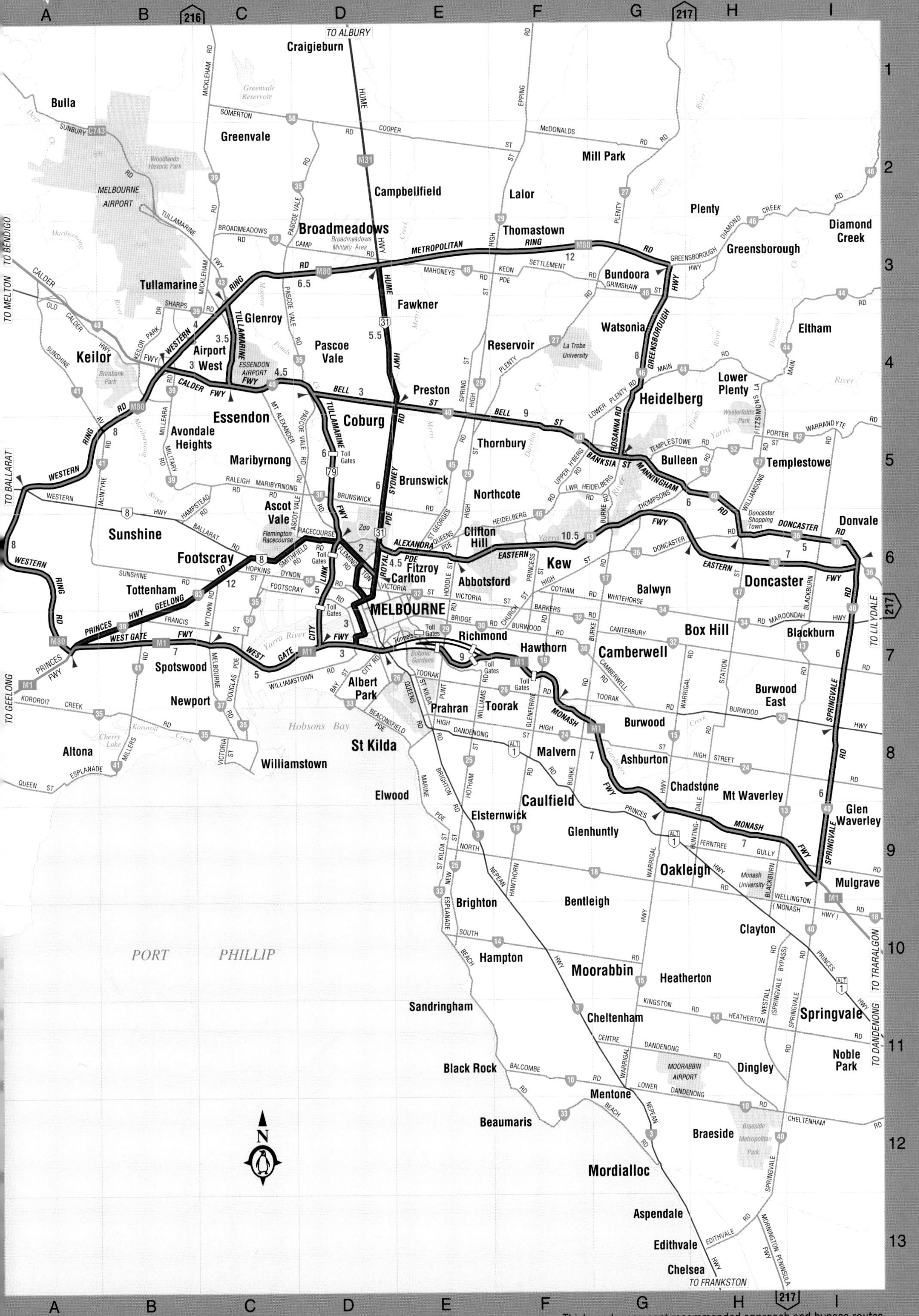

0 2 4 6 8 km

A | B | C | D | E | F | G | H | I

TO ALBURY

Craigieburn

Bulla

Greenvale

SUNBURY C743

Woodlands
Historic Park

MELBOURNE
AIRPORT

Campbellfield

Broadmeadows

Broadmeadows
Military Area

Mill Park

Lalor

Thomastown

METROPOLITAN RING

Plenty

Diamond
Creek

Tullamarine

WESTERN RING

Glenroy

Airport
West

ESSENDON
AIRPORT

Pascoe
Vale

Fawkner

HUME HWY

Reservoir

La Trobe
University

Bundoora

Watsonia

GREENSBOROUGH HWY

Greensborough

Eltham

Keilor

CALDER FWY

Essendon

Avondale
Heights

Maribyrnong

Coburg

Preston

BELL ST

Thornbury

Heidelberg

Lower
Plenty

Westerfolds
Park

Templestowe

WESTERN RING RD

Sunshine

Ascot
Vale

Flemington
Racecourse

Zoo

Brunswick

Northcote

Clifton
Hill

Kew

Balwyn

Bulleen

Doncaster
Shopping
Town

MANNINGHAM RD

DONCASTER RD

Donvale

Footscray

Tottenham

GEELONG

Fitzroy
Carlton

MELBOURNE

Abbotsford

EASTERN FWY

Doncaster

SPRINGVALE RD

TO LILYDALE

WEST GATE FWY

Spotswood

Newport

CITY FWY

Richmond

Hawthorn

Camberwell

Box Hill

Blackburn

Burwood
East

Altona

Williamstown

Albert
Park

Prahran

Toorak

MONASH

Malvern

Burwood

Ashburton

Chadstone

Mt Waverley

Glen
Waverley

St Kilda

Elwood

Caulfield

Elsternwick

Glenhuntly

MONASH FWY

Mulgrave

PORT   PHILLIP

Brighton

Bentleigh

Oakleigh

Monash
University

Clayton

TO TRARALGON

Hampton

Moorabbin

Heatherton

Springvale

Sandringham

Cheltenham

MOORABBIN
AIRPORT

Dingley

Noble
Park

Black Rock

Mentone

Braeside

Braeside
Metropolitan
Park

Beaumaris

Mordialloc

N

Aspendale

Edithvale

Chelsea

TO FRANKSTON

Hobsons Bay

Thick roads represent recommended approach and bypass routes.

PORT   PHILLIP

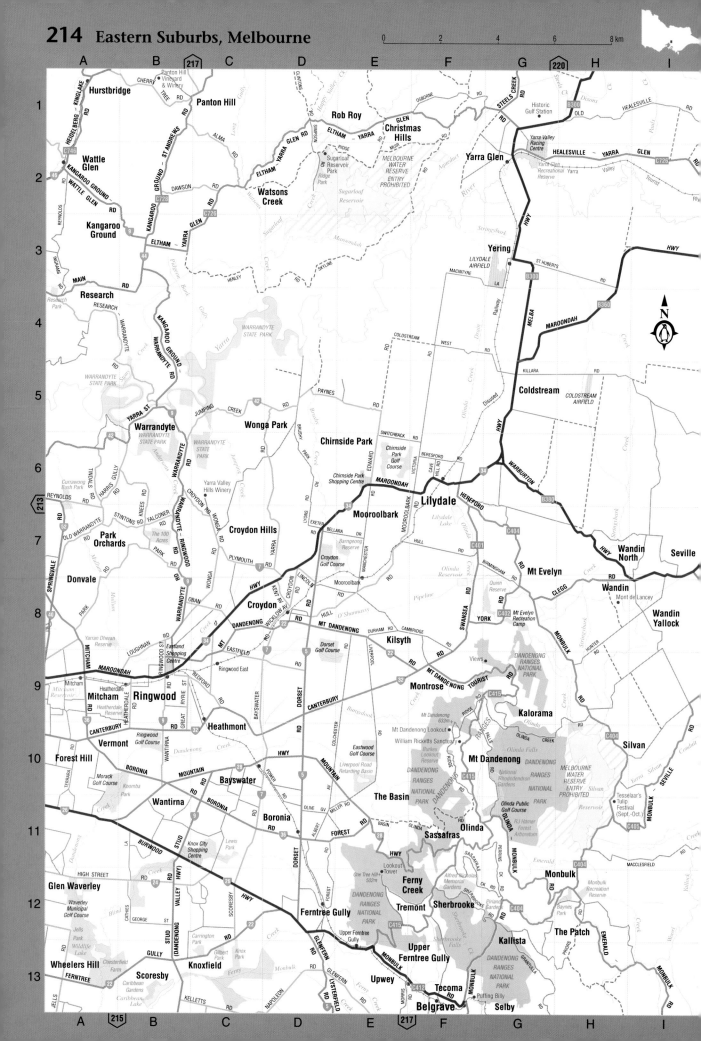

0 2 4 6 8 km

Column A
St Kilda St
North Brighton
Brighton
Middle Brighton
DENDY
Brighton Municipal Golf Course
ESPLANADE
SOUTH
WERE ST
BEACH
Hampton
Moorabbin
Picnic Point
Sandringham
Black Rock
Beaumaris Bay
Ricketts Point
LUDSTONE
HIGHETT
BAY RD
HMVS "Cerberus" Breakwater
Half Moon Bay

Column B
Ormond
McKinnon
Bentleigh
Highett
Beaumaris
Mentone
Parkdale
Mordialloc
Aspendale
Edithvale
Chelsea
Bonbeach
Carrum
Patterson Lakes
Seaford
Frankston
Sandringham Municipal Golf Course
Victoria Golf Course
Royal Melbourne Golf Course
Rossdale Golf Course
Chelsea Golf Course
Patterson River Country Club Golf Course
Long Island Country Club Golf Course

Column C
Oakleigh
Cheltenham
Braeside
New Cheltenham Cemetery
Southland Shopping Centre
Kingston Centre
Kingston Heath Golf Course
Cheltenham Golf Course
Woodlands Golf Course
Epsom Training Track
Braeside Park
WARRIGAL RD
LOWER DANDENONG

Column D
Notting Hill
Clarinda
Heatherton
Dingley
Moorabbin Airport
Moorabbin Municipal Golf Course
Kingswood Golf Course
Southern Golf Course
CLAYTON RD
KINGSTON RD
HEATHERTON RD
BOUNDARY RD
GOVERNOR RD
WELLS RD
Chelsea Heights
Chelsea Multi-Purpose Reserve

Column E
Ferntree Gully
Metropolitan Golf Course
Huntingdale Golf Course
Commonwealth Golf Course
Yarra Yarra Golf Course
Clayton
Westall
The Grange Reserve
Spring Valley Golf Course
Spring Park Golf Course
Cheltenham
Keysborough Golf Course
Mornington Peninsula Fwy
National Water Sports Centre

Column F
Monash University
Monash Medical Centre
MONASH HWY
PRINCES HWY
WELLINGTON RD
POLICE RD
Springvale
Sandown Racecourse and Motor Raceway
Springvale Crematorium & Cemetery
Burden Park
Ross Reserve
Noble Park
Keysborough
Keysborough Reserve
Parkmore Shopping Centre
Melbourne Water
Bangholme
Gaelic Park Sports Complex
Melbourne Water
Patterson River
Carrum Downs
THOMPSON RD

Column G
Wheelers Hill
Brandon Park Shopping Centre
Mulgrave
Waverley Park (AFL)
Springvale
Dandenong & District Hospital
Greaves Reserve
Dandenong
Dandenong South
Lyndhurst
Skye
Skye Recreation Reserve
Centenary Park Golf Course
Department of Agriculture
The Pines Flora & Fauna Reserve
Karingal
Langwarrin
Cranbourne South
Peninsula Country Club Golf Course

Column H
Scoresby
Caribbean Gardens
Caribbean Lake
Waverley Golf Course
Tirhatuan Park Golf Course
Dandenong Police Paddocks Reserve
Churchill Park Golf Course
Doveton
Booth Reserve
Betula Reserve
General Motors
Carrum Downs Recreation Reserve
STUD RD
DANDENONG VALLEY HWY
FRANKSTON–DANDENONG RD
CRANBOURNE RD

Column I
Knoxfield
Chesterfield Farm
Wildlife Lake
Gilbert Park
KELLETTS RD
TAYLORS RD
CHURCHILL NATIONAL PARK
Endeavour Hills
Amstel Golf Course
M1
A780
M420

Port Phillip
PORT PHILLIP

Grid columns: A B C D E F G H I
Grid rows: 1–13

TO AVOCA
Lamplough
Amherst
Talbot
Majorca
Strathlea
Strangways
Yapeen
Guildford
Fryerstown
Taradale
TO BENDIGO
Langley
Edgecombe
Baynton
Lillicur
Green Hill Creek
Caralulup
Tullaroop Reservoir
Campbelltown
Yandoit
Franklinford
Vaughan
Tarilta
Glenluce
Malmsbury
RANGE
Ben More
Evansford
Burnbank
Dunach
Glengower
Mooroolbark
Shepherds Flat
Mt Franklin
Drummond
Denver
Lauriston
Pipers Creek
Carlsrühe
Kyneton
Cobaw
Newham
Hanging Rock
Rochford
Romsey
Lancefield
Nulla Nulla

Lexton
Waubra
Glendaruel
Tourello
Coghills Creek
Hepburn Springs
Daylesford
Musk Vale
Bullarto
Lyonville
Little Hampton
Fern Hill
Woodend
Mount Macedon
Macedon
Monegeetta

SUNRAYSIA
Learmonth
Creswick
Springmount
Newlyn
Dean
Rocklyn
Leonards Hill
Trentham
Newbury
Barrys Reef
New Gisborne
Riddells Creek

WESTERN HWY
Trawalla
Burrumbeet
Cardigan Village
Miners Rest
Mount Rowan
Clarkes Hill
Spargo Creek
Blackwood
Greendale
Gisborne

GREAT
Mena Park
Haddon
WENDOUREE
BALLARAT
Sebastopol
Bungaree
Wallace
Gordon
Millbrook
Ballan
Bacchus Marsh
Melton

DIVIDING
Snake Valley
Smythesdale
Cambrian Hill
Mount Helen
Buninyong
Napoleons
Scotsburn
Mount Egerton
Mount Wallace
Darley
Rockbank

GLENELG
Scarsdale
Newtown
Linton
Happy Valley
Piggoreet
Durham Lead
Clarendon
Lal Lal
Mount Doran
Ballark
Glenmore
Rowsley
Parwan
Exford

Mannibadar
Cape Clear
Berringa
Enfield
Grenville
Mount Mercer
Elaine
Morrisons
Durdidwarrah
Balliang East
Tarneit

Bradvale
Willowvale
Illabarook
Dereel
Woodburne
Meredith
Steiglitz
Sheoaks
Anakie
Balliang
One Tree Hill
HOPPERS CROSSING

Rokewood Junction
Corindhap
Rokewood
Lethbridge
Maude
Anakie East
YOU YANGS REGIONAL PARK
Little River
WERRIBEE

TO HAMILTON
Berrybank
Duverney
Cressy
Shelford
Teesdale
Bannockburn
Gheringhap
Lara
AVALON AIRFIELD
Kirk Point

Wingeel
Murgheboluc
Inverleigh
Batesford
CORIO
Point Wilson

Lake Corangamite
Cundare
Barpinba
Eurack
Dreeite
Fyansford
Ceres
GEELONG
Eastern Beach
National Wool Museum
Portarlington
Bellarine
Indented Head
St Leonards

Beeac
Warrion
Ombersley
Gnarwarre
Mount Moriac
BELMONT
MARSHALL
Leopold
Clifton Springs
Drysdale

Coragulac
Cororooke
Lake Colac
Winchelsea
Moriac
Freshwater Creek
Mount Duneed
Ocean Grove
Marcus Hill
Queenscliff

Alvie
Warncoort
Birregurra
Wurdiboluc
Connewarre
Barwon Heads
Point Lonsdale
Portsea

Pirron Yallock
Colac
Elliminyt
Bambra
Bellbrae
Torquay
Jan Juc
Bells Beach
Sorrento
Blairgowrie

Larpent
Whoorel
Deans Marsh
Anglesea
Point Addis
MORNINGTON PENINSULA

Irrewillipe
Yeodene
Pennyroyal
Boonah
Benwerrin
Aireys Inlet
Fairhaven
Eastern View

Kawarren
Gerangamete
Barwon Downs
Murroon
Forrest
Gellibrand
Lorne

CARLISLE STATE PARK
Carlisle River
Wimba
TO APOLLO BAY
The Spit

BASS STRAIT

For more detail on Goldfields Region see pages 226–227

For more detail on Geelong Region see page 223

N
PENGUIN

0 10 20 30 km

J K L M N O P Q R

MELBOURNE

TO SEYMOUR · TO SEYMOUR · TO MANSFIELD

Broadford · Glenaroua · Kerrisdale · Highlands · Yarck · Fawcett · Piries · Boorolite · Macs Cove

Sunday Creek · Tyaak · Strath Creek · Homewood · Cathkin · Molesworth · Alexandra · Goughs Bay · Howqua

Reedy Creek · Waterford Park · Flowerdale · Hazeldene · Devlins Bridge · Glenburn · Limestone · Acheron · Thornton · Eildon · Snobs Creek · Jamieson · Kevington · Ten Mile

Bylands · Wandong · Heathcote Junction · Upper Plenty · Murrindindi · Taggerty · Rubicon · Cambarville · Enoch Point · Knockwood

Wallan · Kalkallo · Donnybrook · Beveridge · Glenvale · Merrigan · Humevale · Kinglake West · Kinglake · Castella · Buxton · Narbethong · Marysville · Mt Lake Mountain Ski Area · Gaffneys Creek · A1 Mine Settlement · Wood's Point

Whittlesea · Woodstock · Yan Yean · Arthurs Creek · Mittons Bridge · Kinglake Central · Kinglake East · Toolangi · St Fillans · Granton · Cambarville

Craigieburn · Mernda · Cottles Bridge · St Andrews · Smiths Gully · Christmas Hills · Dixons Creek · Mt Slide · Black Spur · McMahons Creek

Thomastown · South Morang · Hurstbridge · Wattle Glen · Panton Hill · Watsons Creek · Yarra Glen · Yering · Healesville · Healesville Sanctuary · Upper Yarra Dam · Upper Yarra Reservoir

Greensborough · Watsonia · Warrandyte · Coldstream · Seville · Woori Yallock · Don Valley · Millgrove · Warburton East · Warburton · Big Pats Creek

Coburg · Heidelberg · Templestowe · Lilydale · Wandin North · Wandin · Launching Place · Yarra Junction · Wesburn · Loch Valley

Melbourne · Kew · Box Hill · Croydon · Yellingbo · Gladysdale · Hoddles Creek · Three Bridges · Powelltown · Tanjil Bren · Mt Baw Baw

St Kilda · Caulfield · Glen Waverley · Ferntree Gully · Silvan · Olinda · Monbulk · Macclesfield · Nangana · Noojee · Icy Creek · Fumina · Mt Baw Baw Alpine Village

Brighton · Oakleigh · Upwey · Belgrave · The Patch · Menzies Creek · Avonsleigh · Clematis · Cockatoo · Gembrook · Alpine Trout Farm · Nayook · Neerim Junction

Sandringham · Picnic Point · Springvale · Lysterfield · Emerald · Harkaway · Maryknoll · Tonimbuk · Neerim · Neerim East

Mordialloc · Dandenong · Endeavour Hills · Narre Warren · Upper Beaconsfield · Beaconsfield · Officer · Garfield North · Labertouche · Jindivick · Neerim South · Crossover · Hill End

Chelsea · Lyndhurst · Berwick · Pakenham · Nar Nar Goon · Tynong · Bunyip · Drouin West · Tarago · Rokeby · Willow Grove

Seaford · Carrum Downs · Cranbourne · Clyde · Cardinia · Garfield · Iona · Longwarry · Drouin · Brandy Creek · Buln Buln · Shady Creek · Tanjil South

Frankston · Pelican Point · Cranbourne South · Tooradin · Koo-wee-rup · Bayles · Modella · Drouin South · Warragul · Nilma · Darnum · Westbury · Moe

Mornington · Baxter · Pearcedale · Cannons Creek · Monomeath · Catani · Ripplebrook · Ellinbank · Yarragon · Trafalgar · Newborough · Narracan

Mount Martha · Moorooduc · Somerville · Warneet · Lang Lang · Heath Hill · Athlone · Seaview · Allambee · Coalville · Thorpdale

Safety Beach · Tyabb · Western Port · Nyora · Poowong · Poowong East · Trida · Childers · Delburn

Rosebud · Red Hill · Balnarring · Bittern · French Island · The Gurdies · Loch · Strzelecki · Allambee South · Boolarra

Flinders · Red Hill South · Merricks · Hastings · Crib Point · Stony Point · Grantville · Corinella · Korumburra · Ruby · Mirboo North

Shoreham · Somers · Tankerton · French National Park · Coronet Bay · Kernot · Bena · South Gippsland · Mirboo

Cowes · Ventnor · Rhyll · Newhaven · Glen Forbes · Jumbunna · Leongatha · Koonwarra · Boolarra

Phillip Island · Koala Conservation Centre · Churchill Island · San Remo · Cape Woolamai · Bass · Kilcunda · Dalyston · Woolamai · Kongwak · Outtrim · Leongatha South · Dumbalk

Seal Rocks · The Nobbies · Penguin Parade · Cape Woolamai · Archies Creek · TO WONTHAGGI · TO INVERLOCH · TO FOSTER

GREAT DIVIDING RANGE · YARRA RANGES NATIONAL PARK · BAW BAW NP · STRZELECKI · SOUTH GIPPSLAND · LAKE EILDON NATIONAL PARK · CATHEDRAL RANGE STATE PARK

For more detail on Melbourne suburbs see pages 212–215
For more detail on Mornington Peninsula see pages 218–219
For more detail on Yarra Valley Region see page 220

A B C D E F G H I

1

Bellarine
Spray Farm Winery
Indented Head
Indented Head
C125

Scotchmans Hill Winery

BELLARINE

2

MURRADOC
PENINSULA
St Leonards
South Red Bluff

223

The Bluff

PORTARLINGTON RD

3

C126

Mannerim

EDWARDS POINT WILDLIFE RESERVE

Spirit of Tasmania Ferry
Station Pier to Devonport

PORT   *PHILLIP*

4

QUEENSCLIFF 11

Swan
Bay

Queenscliff Golf Course

Swan Island

Edwards Point

Duck Island

Bellarine Peninsula Railway

Devil Cat Ferry
Station Pier to George Town
(December to April)

5

BELLARINE HWY
B110
Queenscliff
Queenscliff Station
Maritime Centre
Black Lighthouse
Fort Queenscliff
White Lighthouse

4

Mud
Islands

MOUNT PL
Martha Poin
Droma
Bo
Saf

6

Point Lonsdale
Point Lonsdale

The Rip
Fort Nepean
Point Nepean
MORNINGTON PENINSULA NP
Cheviot Beach
Nepean Bay
Observatory Point
Ticonderoga Bay

Vehicle

Passenger
Passenger

Ferry
Ferry

Safety B

7

COMMONWEALTH LAND
MORNINGTON
London Bridge
Portsea Surf Beach
PENINSULA
Weeroona Bay
Portsea Golf Course
Portsea
Collins Bay
Point King

Sorrento
Sorrento Golf Course

Capel   Sound

ARTHURS SEAT STATE PARK: Originally named after a similar mountain near Edinburgh, Scotland during the first European exploration of Port Phillip. Take a 20-minute ride on the chairlift for spectacular views of the peninsula and bay. Enjoy a short walk to scenic Flinders Lookout and to historic Seawinds Park.

Dromana
Heronswood

PENINSULA

McCrae
McCrae Homestead
6
Eastern Lighthouse

Arthurs Seat Chairlift
Arthurs Seat 909m

ARTH
SEA
STA
PAR

8

MORNINGTON PENINSULA NATIONAL PARK: This magnificent park extends from the tip of Point Nepean to Cape Schanck. A transporter service operates, taking visitors to Cheviot Beach, Observatory Point and historic Fort Nepean. Numerous walking tracks provide easy access to London Bridge, Cape Schanck Lighthouse and endless spectacular coastal scenery.

NATIONAL PARK
The Sisters
Collins Settlement Historic Site
Sullivan Bay
Sorrento Back Beach
Jubilee Point
Diamond Bay
Koonya Beach
Spray Point
Canterbury Jetty Rd
White Cliffs
Observation Hill
Blairgowrie
19
Rye
Tootgarook
B110
DUNDAS ST
3
MORNINGTON
Rosebud West
NEPEAN
Rosebud
11
ARTHURS
Rosebud Golf Course
Rosebud Country Club
C777
ARTHURS SEAT STATE PARK
PURVES
18
21
14

JETTY
Main Creek

Koreen Point
Pearces Beach
The Divide
BROWNS
The Dunes Golf Links
Eagle Ridge Golf Course
BROWNS
4
TRUEMANS
RD
30
SHA
Main Ridge
25

9

10

VISITOR INFORMATION:
Cowes (Phillip Island Rd, Newhaven)
Flinders, Mornington & Sorrento
(Point Nepean Rd, Dromana)

SANDY
7
RD
St Andrews
Capri Beach

BONEO
MORNINGTON

Rye Ocean Beach

Boags Rocks
Gunnamatta Surf Beach

PENINSULA

MORNINGTON PENINSULA NATIONAL PARK

25

National Golf Course
Cape Schanck
Cape Schanck Golf Course

School Hill 184m
25

MEAKINS
C777
ROSEBUD
FLINDERS

11

N

12

Cape Schanck Lighthouse
Bushranger Bay
Cape Schanck
Picnic Point
Simmons Bay
The Arch
Cairns Bay
The Blo

13

BASS   *STRAIT*

A B C D E F G H I

HISTORIC HOMES: The Mornington Peninsula has an array of magnificently preserved historic homesteads. Visit Coolart at Balnarring, a century-old mansion nest in landscaped gardens, or the simple 1884 drop-slab c McCrae homestead. The Briars, an 1860s homestead a Mount Martha, houses a significant collection of Napo artefacts and furniture.

FRANKSTON
TO MELBOURNE
CRANBOURNE
Cranbourne South
LANGWARRIN
Ballam Park Homestead
BROWNS
Langwarrin Flora & Fauna Reserve
ROBINSONS
WARRANDYTE
TO DANDENONG
Devon Meadows
Five Ways
MANKS
SOUTH GIPPSLAND HWY
Daveys Bay
Pelican Point
Canadian Bay
Mt Eliza
Sunnyside Beach
Schnapper Point
Mornington Golf Course
Frankston Reservoir
HUMPHRIES
Baxter Park
Mt Eliza 160m
BAXTER
Baxter
BAXTER – TOORADIN
PEARCEDALE
Pearcedale
QUEENS RD
HASTINGS
WESTERNPORT
CRAIG
Cannons Creek
BAXTER – TOORADIN
Warneet
WARNEET
Tooradin
TO KORUMBURRA
Blind Bight
Watson Inlet
Quail Island
Mornington
Fishermans Beach
ESPLANADE
MORNINGTON
Mornington Racecourse
Civic Reserve
Craft Market
BENTONS
CRAIGIE
Fossil Beach
The Briars Homestead
ERAMOSA ROAD
Studio City Pop & Media Museum
WEST
Somerville
ERAMOSA ROAD EAST
BUNGOWER
Mooroduc
MORNINGTON
TYABB
Tyabb
Western Port Airfield
BHP Steel Western Port Works
BAYVIEW
Bembridge 9 Hole Golf Course
WESTERN PORT
Scrub Point

FRENCH ISLAND: Named in 1802 by Captain Bauclin, leader of a French scientific expedition, this naturally protected island of state parkland provides the perfect habitat for rare white-breasted sea eagles, potoroos and koalas.

Devilbend Golf Course & Rec Res
The Briars Homestead
GRAYDENS
Devilbend Reservoir
HODGINS
Bittern Reservoir
Warringine Ck
COOLART
BOES
Hastings
Long Point
Long Island
FRENCH ISLAND
FRENCH ISLAND NATIONAL PARK
Mt Wellington 98m
Hastings Bight
Sandstone Island
Fairhaven
BITTERN
DROMANA
Red Hill
TUBBARUBBA
MYERS
STUMPY GULLY
Bittern
Balnarring Racecourse
Emu Plains Market
HENDERSONS
WOOLLEYS
Crib Point
The Pinnacles 66m
FRENCH ISLAND
Red Hill Market
BITTERN DROMANA RD
FRANKSTON
SOUTH BEACH
DISNEY
Crib Point
Stony Point
Passenger
Red Hill South
MERRICKS
STANLEYS
Balnarring
Merricks North
SANDY POINT
Coolart Reserve
Coolart Homestead
HMAS Cerberus
Hanns Inlet
(PROHIBITED AREA)
Tankerton
Tankerton Jetty
Merricks
POINT LEO RD
Merricks Beach
Point Summer
Balnarring Beach
Somers Beach
South Beach
Somers
Western Port Beach
Sandy Point
Tortoise Head
Ashcombe Maze
FLINDERS
Point Leo
Point Leo
Shoreham
C777
Shoreham Beach

ASHCOMBE MAZE: Wander through the large green hedge maze with one kilometre of pathways, or wind your way through the beautiful rose maze of over 1200 colourful and fragrant roses. The tea room and extensive gardens provide perfect places for relaxation.

WESTERN PORT
Flinders
Kennon Cove
West Head
Seal Rocks
Penguin Rock
McHaffie Point
Cowes
CHURCH ST
Cowes Golf Course
Observation Point
Rhyll Inlet
VENTNOR RD
Ventnor
Phillip Island Wildlife Park
PHILLIP ISLAND
COWES
RHYLL
Rhyll
Fishermans Point
Bird Sanctuary
Koala Res
PHILLIP ISLAND NATURE PARK
VENTNOR
BACK BEACH
BEACH
THE GAP RD
Five Ways
A Maze 'N Things
B420
Koala Conservation Centre
NEWHAVEN
PHILLIP ISLAND
Cat Bay
Swan Lake
Phillip Island Vineyard & Winery
BERRYS BEACH RD
Grand Prix Circuit & Visitor Centre
Churchill Island
Swan Bay
Australian Dairy Centre
Woody Point
Newhaven
San Remo
Phillip Is Penguin Reserve
Point Grant
The Nobbies
The Blowhole
Seal Rocks
Seal Rocks Sea Life Centre
Penguin Parade
Summerland Beach
Berrys Beach
PYRAMID ROCK
Pyramid Rock
PHILLIP ISLAND NATURE PARK
Storm Bay
Cunningham Bay
Phillip Is Airfield
Cape Woolamai
The Narrows

PHILLIP ISLAND: This year-round tourist destination with its diverse coastline is an excellent weekend getaway. Visit the rugged terrain of The Nobbies and view the seal colony at Seal Rocks. Wander through various sections of Phillip Island Nature Park. Every evening the little (fairy) penguins parade up Summerland Beach providing a delightful natural wildlife spectacle.

0 2 4 6 8 10 km

KINGLAKE NATIONAL PARK: Home to numerous lyrebirds and wombats, Kinglake National Park was established to protect the wet eucalypt forests on the Great Dividing Range. Tranquil walks through fern gullies and forested spurs take you to the Wombelano Falls.

TOOLANGI-BLACK RANGES: Toolangi, once home of C.J. Dennis, author of *The Sentimental Bloke*, is a mountainous berry-producing area nestled in the Black Ranges State Forest. Picturesque roadways provide easy access to the spectacular Wilhelmina Falls and Murrindindi Cascades. There are excellent riding tours available in the area, taking you along rugged mountain tracks and tranquil river paths. Trout and blackfish can be caught in the Murrindindi River.

GULF STATION: Now owned by the National Trust, Gulf Station at Yarra Glen is one of Victoria's oldest pastoral properties, dating back to the 1850s. Visitors can step back in time and explore the original timber buildings and cottage gardens.

HEALESVILLE SANCTUARY: Home to over 200 of Australia's unique birds, animals and reptiles, including some endangered species. Open every day of the year, the sanctuary is recognised as Victoria's top wildlife park. Spend the day venturing among friendly kangaroos, emus and wombats in 31 hectares of natural bushland.

SILVAN RESERVOIR: Located on the edge of beautiful Olinda, Stonyford picnic ground at Silvan Reservoir provides excellent barbecue facilities. Stop along the Monbulk Road for breathtaking views of the region.

PUFFING BILLY: This superbly restored vintage steam train ambles its way from the ferny stands of Belgrave through the cool rainforest to Gembrook.

VISITOR INFORMATION:
Healesville (Harker St)
Marysville (Murchison St)
Warburton (Warburton Hwy)

WINERIES:
Allinda Winery 1 C5
Badgers Brook Winery 2 D7
Bianchet Winery 3 A7
Brahams Creek Winery 4 H8
Britannia Falls Winery 5 G9
Coldstream Hills 6 D8
De Bortoli Wines 7 C4
Domaine Chandon 8 C6
Eyton on Yarra 9 D7
Fergusson Winery & Restaurant 10 C5
Five Oaks Vineyard 11 C10
Kellybrook Winery & Restaurant 12 A7
Lirralirra Estate 13 A8
Long Gully Estate 14 D5
Lovey's Estate 15 C5
McWilliams Lillydale Vineyards 16 D9
Oakridge Estate 17 C7
Paternoster 18 D13
St Huberts Vineyard 19 C7
Shantell Vineyard 20 C4
Steels Creek Estate 21 B4
Tarrawarra Estate 22 D6
Warramate Vineyard 23 D7
Yarra Burn Winery & Restaurant 24 F9
Yarra Ridge 25 B6
Yarra Track Winery 26 C6
Yering Station - Yarrabank Vineyards 27 B6

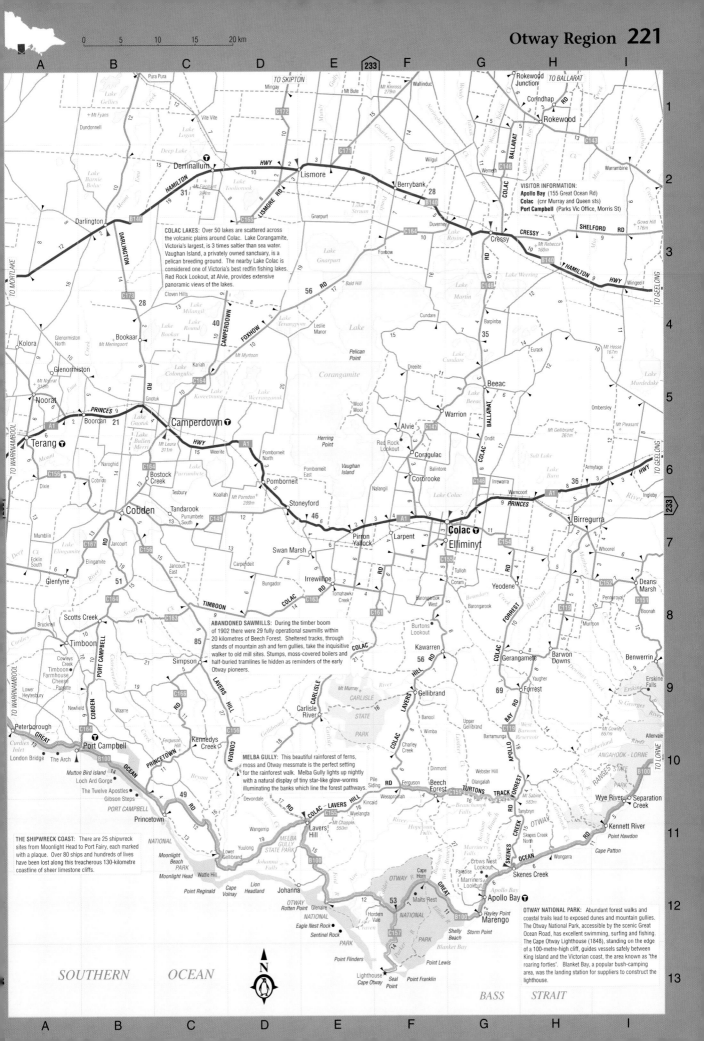

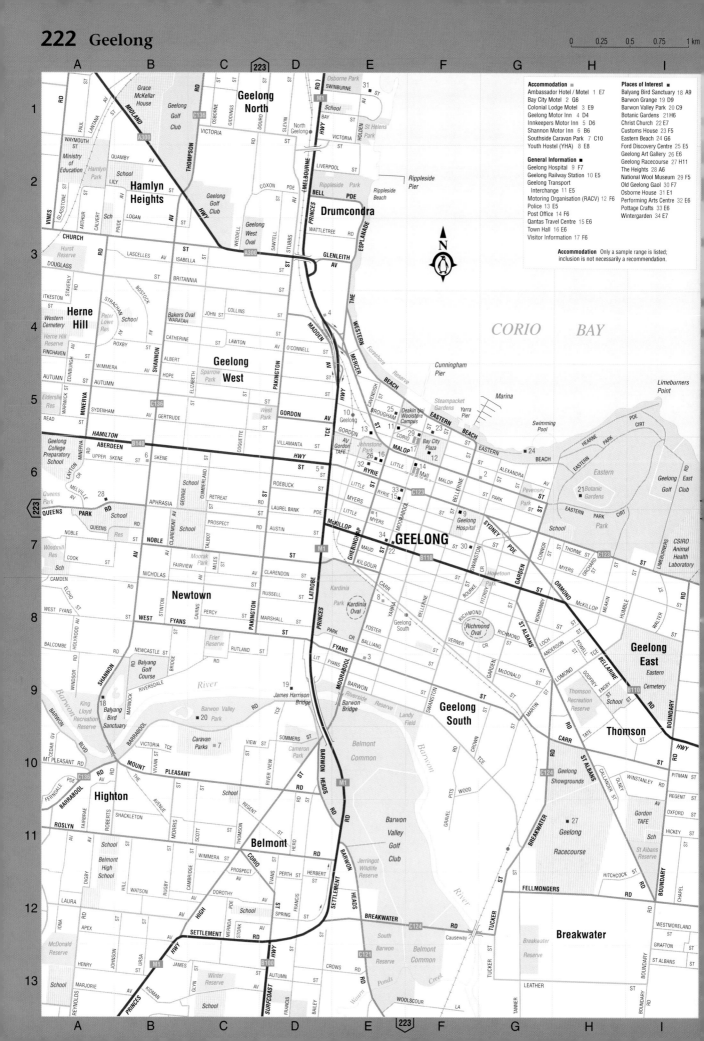

Accommodation ■
Ambassador Hotel / Motel 1 E7
Bay City Motel 2 G6
Colonial Lodge Motel 3 E9
Geelong Motor Inn 4 D4
Innkeepers Motor Inn 5 D6
Shannon Motor Inn 6 B6
Southside Caravan Park 7 C10
Youth Hostel (YHA) 8 E8

General Information ■
Geelong Hospital 9 F7
Geelong Railway Station 10 E5
Geelong Transport
  Interchange 11 E5
Motoring Organisation (RACV) 12 F6
Police 13 E5
Post Office 14 F6
Qantas Travel Centre 15 E6
Town Hall 16 E6
Visitor Information 17 F6

Places of Interest ■
Balyang Bird Sanctuary 18 A9
Barwon Grange 19 D9
Barwon Valley Park 20 C9
Botanic Gardens 21 H6
Christ Church 22 F5
Customs House 23 F5
Eastern Beach 24 G6
Ford Discovery Centre 25 E5
Geelong Art Gallery 26 E6
Geelong Racecourse 27 H11
The Heights 28 A6
National Wool Museum 29 F5
Old Geelong Gaol 30 F7
Osborne House 31 E1
Performing Arts Centre 32 E6
Pottage Crafts 33 E6
Wintergarden 34 E7

Accommodation Only a sample range is listed;
inclusion is not necessarily a recommendation.

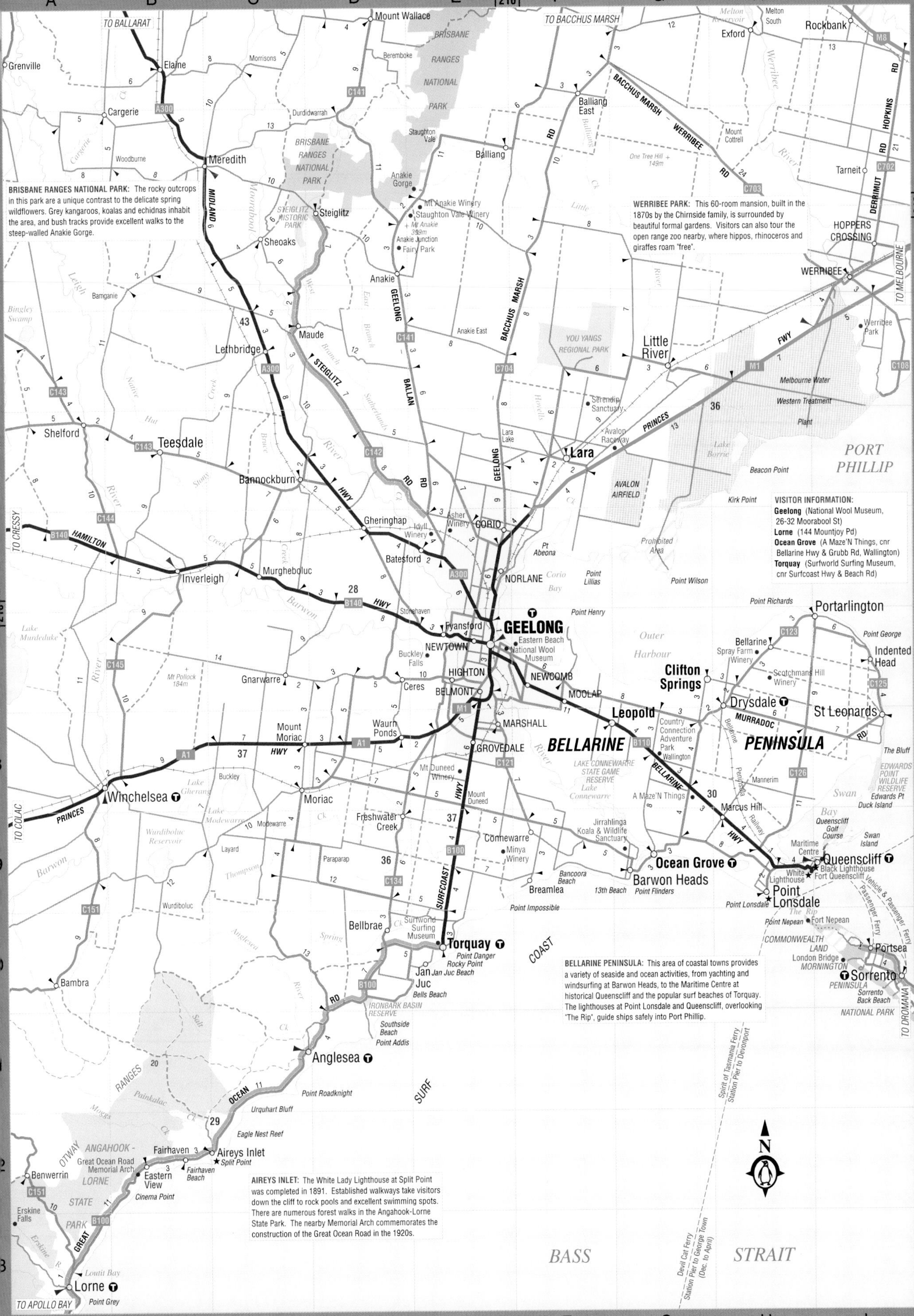

0 2.5 5 7.5 10 km

A B C D E 216 F G H I

BRISBANE RANGES NATIONAL PARK: The rocky outcrops in this park are a unique contrast to the delicate spring wildflowers. Grey kangaroos, koalas and echidnas inhabit the area, and bush tracks provide excellent walks to the steep-walled Anakie Gorge.

WERRIBEE PARK: This 60-room mansion, built in the 1870s by the Chirnside family, is surrounded by beautiful formal gardens. Visitors can also tour the open range zoo nearby, where hippos, rhinoceros and giraffes roam "free".

VISITOR INFORMATION:
Geelong (National Wool Museum, 26-32 Moorabool St)
Lorne (144 Mountjoy Pd)
Ocean Grove (A Maze'N Things, cnr Bellarine Hwy & Grubb Rd, Wallington)
Torquay (Surfworld Surfing Museum, cnr Surfcoast Hwy & Beach Rd)

BELLARINE PENINSULA: This area of coastal towns provides a variety of seaside and ocean activities, from yachting and windsurfing at Barwon Heads, to the Maritime Centre at historical Queenscliff and the popular surf beaches of Torquay. The lighthouses at Point Lonsdale and Queenscliff, overlooking "The Rip", guide ships safely into Port Phillip.

AIREYS INLET: The White Lady Lighthouse at Split Point was completed in 1891. Established walkways take visitors down the cliff to rock pools and excellent swimming spots. There are numerous forest walks in the Angahook-Lorne State Park. The nearby Memorial Arch commemorates the construction of the Great Ocean Road in the 1920s.

Place names (selected):
TO BALLARAT, Grenville, Elaine, Cargerie, Woodburne, Meredith, Bamganie, Steiglitz, Sheoaks, Anakie, Maude, Lethbridge, Shelford, Teesdale, Bannockburn, Gheringhap, Inverleigh, Murgheboluc, Gnarwarre, Batesford, Fyansford, Ceres, Stonehaven, GEELONG, NEWTOWN, HIGHTON, BELMONT, NEWCOMB, MOOLAP, Leopold, Clifton Springs, Drysdale, Portarlington, Indented Head, St Leonards, Mount Wallace, Morrisons, Durdidwarrah, Beremboke, Balliang, Balliang East, Anakie East, Lara, Little River, Serendip Sanctuary, Avalon Raceway, Avalon Airfield, Kirk Point, Point Richards, Point George, Bellarine, PENINSULA, Marcus Hill, Queenscliff, Point Lonsdale, Portsea, Sorrento, Mount Moriac, Waurn Ponds, MARSHALL, GROVEDALE, Moriac, Buckley, Freshwater Creek, Connewarre, Paraparap, Winchelsea, Wurdiboluc, Modewarre, Layard, Bellbrae, Torquay, Jan Juc, Anglesea, Fairhaven, Aireys Inlet, Eastern View, Benwerrin, Lorne, TO APOLLO BAY, TO COLAC, TO CRESSY, Hamilton, PRINCES HWY, SURFCOAST HWY, GREAT OCEAN ROAD, Barwon Heads, Ocean Grove, Breamlea, TO MELBOURNE, Werribee, Hoppers Crossing, Tarneit, Rockbank, Exford, Melton, Melton South, TO BACCHUS MARSH

PORT PHILLIP
Outer Harbour
Corio Bay
BASS STRAIT
YOU YANGS REGIONAL PARK
LAKE CONNEWARRE STATE GAME RESERVE
ANGAHOOK-LORNE STATE PARK
OTWAY RANGES
BRISBANE RANGES NATIONAL PARK

N

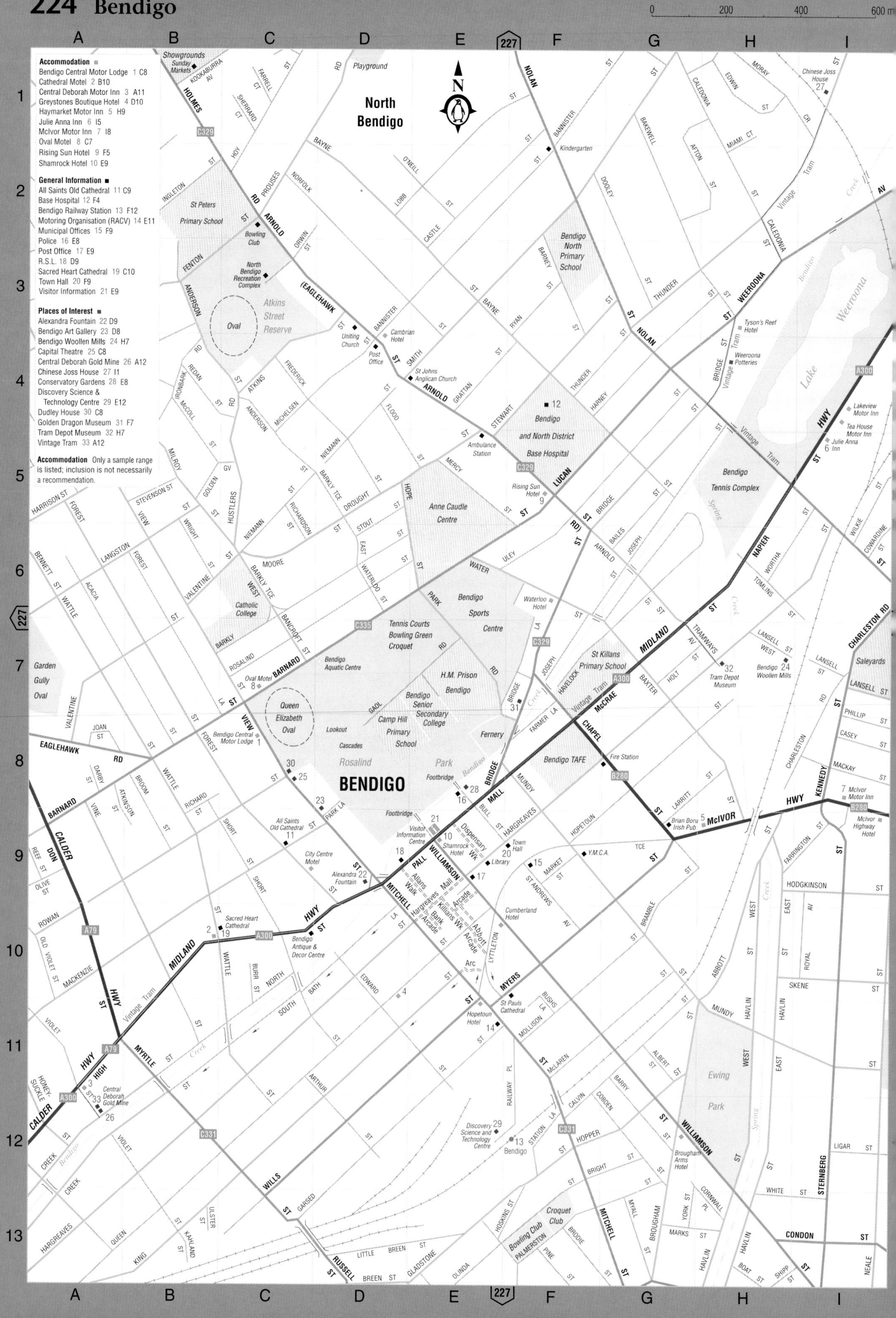

0 200 400 600 m
Accommodation
Bendigo Central Motor Lodge 1 C8
Cathedral Motel 2 B10
Central Deborah Motor Inn 3 A11
Greystones Boutique Hotel 4 D10
Haymarket Motor Inn 5 H9
Julie Anna Inn 6 I5
McIvor Motor Inn 7 I8
Oval Motel 8 C7
Rising Sun Hotel 9 F5
Shamrock Hotel 10 E9
General Information
All Saints Old Cathedral 11 C9
Base Hospital 12 F4
Bendigo Railway Station 13 F12
Motoring Organisation (RACV) 14 E11
Municipal Offices 15 F9
Police 16 E8
Post Office 17 E9
R.S.L. 18 D9
Sacred Heart Cathedral 19 C10
Town Hall 20 F9
Visitor Information 21 E9
Places of Interest
Alexandra Fountain 22 D9
Bendigo Art Gallery 23 D8
Bendigo Woollen Mills 24 H7
Capital Theatre 25 C8
Central Deborah Gold Mine 26 A12
Chinese Joss House 27 I1
Conservatory Gardens 28 E8
Discovery Science & Technology Centre 29 E12
Dudley House 30 C8
Golden Dragon Museum 31 F7
Tram Depot Museum 32 H7
Vintage Tram 33 A12
Accommodation Only a sample range is listed; inclusion is not necessarily a recommendation.
North Bendigo
BENDIGO
Rosalind Park
Queen Elizabeth Oval
Lake Weeroona
Bendigo Tennis Complex
Bendigo Sports Centre
Anne Caudle Centre
Bendigo and North District Base Hospital
H.M. Prison Bendigo
Bendigo Senior Secondary College
Camp Hill Primary School
Bendigo TAFE
St Killians Primary School
Bendigo North Primary School
St Peters Primary School
Atkins Street Reserve
Garden Gully Oval
Ewing Park
Saleyards
Showgrounds
Playground
MIDLAND HWY
CALDER HWY
McIVOR HWY
NAPIER ST
McCRAE ST
HIGH ST
PALL MALL
MITCHELL ST
WILLIAMSON ST
ARNOLD ST
NOLAN ST
BARNARD ST
VIEW ST
MYRTLE ST
WILLS ST
RUSSELL ST
KENNEDY ST
CHARLESTON RD
EAGLEHAWK RD
A B C D E F G H I
1 2 3 4 5 6 7 8 9 10 11 12 13

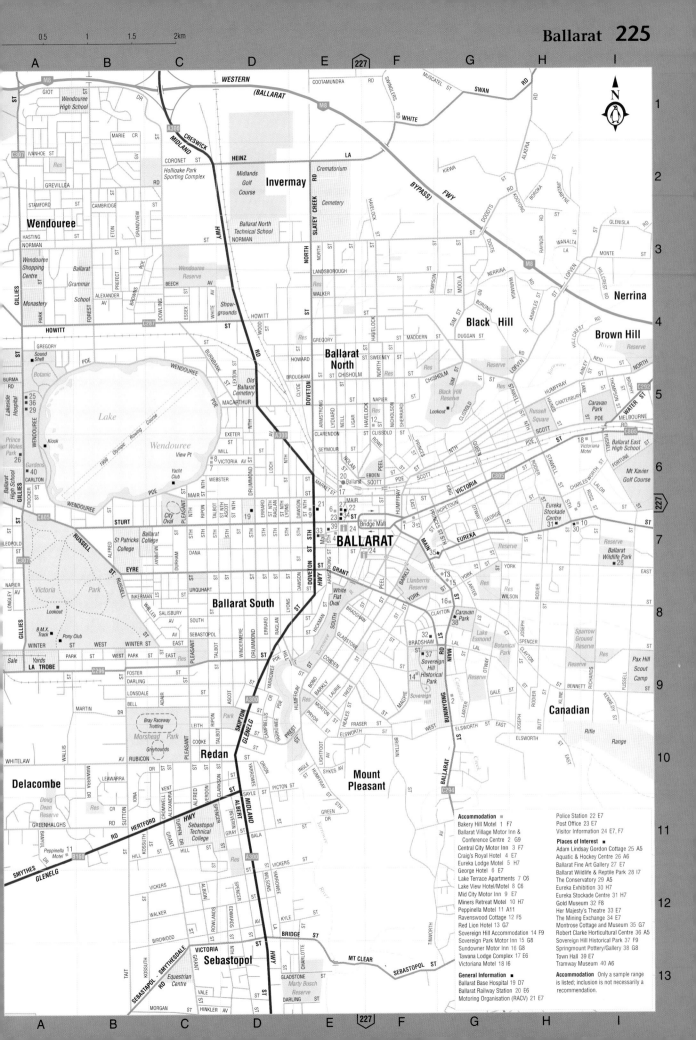

Scale: 0.5 | 1 | 1.5 | 2km

Suburbs and localities
Wendouree, Invermay, Ballarat North, Black Hill, Nerrina, Brown Hill, Ballarat, Ballarat South, Canadian, Redan, Mount Pleasant, Delacombe, Sebastopol

Accommodation ■
Bakery Hill Motel 1 F7
Ballarat Village Motor Inn & Conference Centre 2 G9
Central City Motor Inn 3 F7
Craig's Royal Hotel 4 E7
Eureka Lodge Motel 5 H7
George Hotel 6 E7
Lake Terrace Apartments 7 C6
Lake View Hotel/Motel 8 C6
Mid City Motor Inn 9 E7
Miners Retreat Motel 10 H7
Peppinella Motel 11 A11
Ravenswood Cottage 12 F5
Red Lion Hotel 13 G7
Sovereign Hill Accommodation 14 F9
Sovereign Park Motor Inn 15 G8
Sundowner Motor Inn 16 G8
Tawana Lodge Complex 17 E6
Victoriana Motel 18 I6

General Information ■
Ballarat Base Hospital 19 D7
Ballarat Railway Station 20 E6
Motoring Organisation (RACV) 21 E7

Police Station 22 E7
Post Office 23 E7
Visitor Information 24 E7, F7

Places of Interest ■
Adam Lindsay Gordon Cottage 25 A5
Aquatic & Hockey Centre 26 A6
Ballarat Fine Art Gallery 27 E7
Ballarat Wildlife & Reptile Park 28 I7
The Conservatory 29 A5
Eureka Exhibition 30 H7
Eureka Stockade Centre 31 H7
Gold Museum 32 F8
Her Majesty's Theatre 33 E7
The Mining Exchange 34 E7
Montrose Cottage and Museum 35 G7
Robert Clarke Horticultural Centre 36 A5
Sovereign Hill Historical Park 37 F9
Springmount Pottery/Gallery 38 G8
Town Hall 39 E7
Tramway Museum 40 A6

Accommodation Only a sample range is listed; inclusion is not necessarily a recommendation.

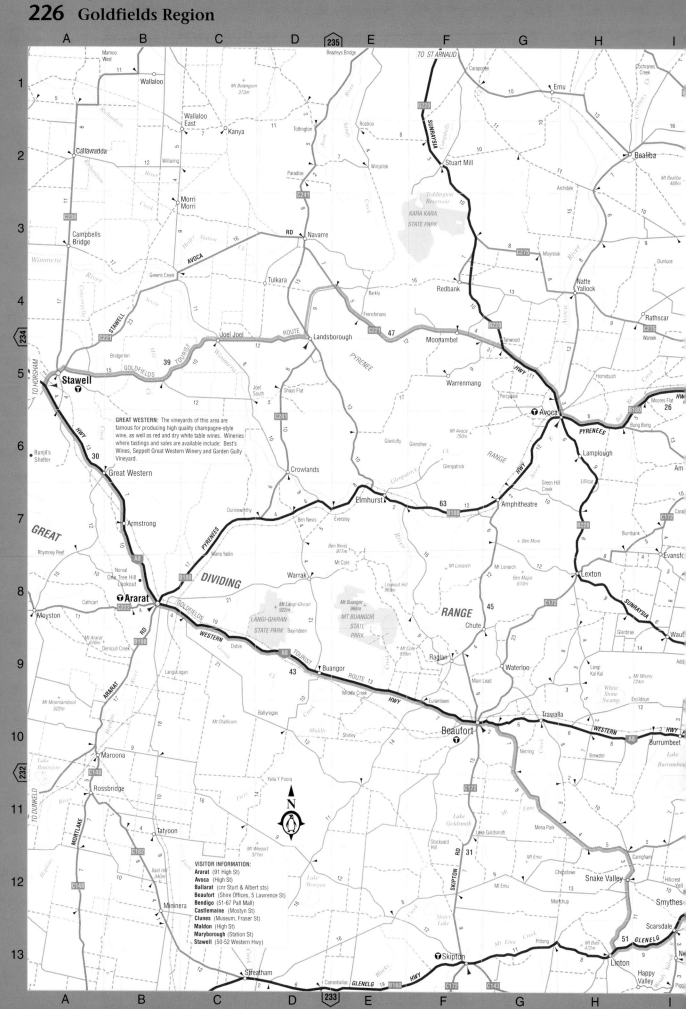

GREAT WESTERN: The vineyards of this area are famous for producing high quality champagne-style wine, as well as red and dry white table wines. Wineries where tastings and sales are available include: Best's Wines, Seppelt Great Western Winery and Garden Gully Vineyard.

VISITOR INFORMATION:
Ararat (91 High St)
Avoca (High St)
Ballarat (cnr Sturt & Albert sts)
Beaufort (Shire Offices, 5 Lawrence St)
Bendigo (51-67 Pall Mall)
Castlemaine (Mostyn St)
Clunes (Museum, Fraser St)
Maldon (High St)
Maryborough (Station St)
Stawell (50-52 Western Hwy)

0 5 10 15 20 25 km

J K L M N O P Q R

1

TO INGLEWOOD TO KERANG
235
WHIPSTICK STATE PARK
TO ECHUCA HWY
Woodvale
Arnold West
Arnold
Leichardt
B260
Myers Flat
Huntly 8
Bagshot
B240
Marong
A79 14
EAGLEHAWK
Golden Dragon Museum
MIDLAND
EPSOM
A300
Fosterville

Murphys Creek
Llanelly
Newbridge
GOLDFIELDS TOURIST ROUTE 37
Spring
Maiden Gully
HWY
Bendigo Pottery
WHITE HILLS
BENDIGO'S VINTAGE TRAM: Visitors can take a tram ride through the historic centre of Bendigo and enjoy a potted history provided by a recorded commentary.

2

BENDIGO
Tarnagulla
B240
ST. ARNAUD RD
23
KANGAROO FLAT
Central Deborah Gold Mine
B280 9
McIVOR
Longlea
Junortoun
HWY
Axedale
TO HEATHCOTE

For more detail on Bendigo see page 224

Laanecoorie
MARYBOROUGH
Woodstock
Lockwood
Goldfields Mohair Farm
RD
Mandurang
Strathfieldsaye

3

Dunolly
Bromley
Eddington
GOLDFIELDS REGION: The cities and towns of this region came to a peak of style and affluence in the 1880s, a wealth built on the first gold discoveries in the 1850s.
29
A790
A79
Lockwood South
Mandurang South
Sedgwick
Eppalock
Lake Eppalock
238

Bet Bet
Betley
Baringhup
Bradford
Nuggetty
Ravenswood
CALDER
Mandurang
Sedgwick's Camel Farm
Pilchers Bridge
Myrtle Creek

4

Havelock
51
Lookout
Mt Tarrengower 570m
Porcupine Flat
Walmer
Ravenswood South
Harcourt North
Sutton Grange
Lyal
Mia Mia
C326

Timor
C277
C288
Maldon Historic Town
Perkins Reef
Barkers Creek
HWY
Harcourt
Mt Alexander 741m
Myrtle Creek
C327
Redesdale

5

Maryborough
Old Railway Station
Carisbrook
PYRENEES
Welshmans Reef
Gowar
CASTLEMAINE
MIDLAND
CALDER
Market Building Buda Historic Home and Garden
Golden Point
Faraday
35
Metcalfe
Mia Mia

C287
B180
47
Moolort
Joyces Creek
Newstead
Chewton
34
B180
Elphinstone
Barfold
Glenhope

6

Daisy Hill
Craigie
Majorca
Strathlea
Campbells Creek
Yapeen
Fryerstown
Taradale
A79

Dunach
Mt Cameron 417m
Campbelltown
C238
Sandon
Clydesdale
Vaughan
Irishtown
Glenluce
Malmsbury Reservoir
Malmsbury
Langley
C326
Sidonia

7

C288
Glengower
Strathlea
C285
Guildford
ROUTE A300
Tarilta
Glenluce
CALDER
Lauriston
Edgecombe
Pastoria

MARYBOROUGH
Clunes
BALLARAT
C291
Yandoit
40
Franklinford
Mt Franklin
Porcupine Ridge
Loddon Falls
Denver
C316
Drummond
Lauriston
Kyneton
Pipers Creek
Carlsruhe

8

Smeaton
Shepherds Flat
Mineral Springs
Mt Franklin
Glenlyon
Spring Hill
Lauriston Reservoir
Upper Coliban Res
The Jim Jim 746m
216

Broomfield
Allendale
Kingston
Hepburn Springs
Daylesford
Convent Gallery
Wheatsheaf
Little Hampton
Tylden
33
Newham
Hanging Rock

9

Coghills Creek
Ascot
MIDLAND
A300
Eganstown
Sailors Falls
Blampied
Musk Vale
Coomoora
Musk
Lyonville
C317
Trentham Falls
RANGE
Fern Hill
C317
Woodend
Memorial Cross
Camels Hump
Mt Macedon 1013m

Creswick
GOLDFIELDS
Springmount
46
Newlyn
Bullarto
Trentham
Newbury
MACEDON RD
Mount Macedon

10

GREAT
Dean
For more detail on Ballarat see page 225
Rocklyn
Leonards Hill
Bullarto South
Barrys Reef
Mineral Springs Reserve
Blackwood
Rosslynne Reservoir
CALDER
Macedon
M79

Mount Rowan
White Swan Res
Mollongghip
Barkstead
30
Korweinguboora
Garden of St Erth
New Gisborne
FWY

11

WESTERN
Windermere
Miners Rest
C287
WENDOUREE
NERRINA
Leigh Creek
M8
Bullarook
Bolwarrah
Blakeville
C318
Ballan North
Greendale
Bullengarook East
Gisborne
C705

BALLARAT
Eureka Stockade Centre
Clarkes Hill
Monsabool Reservoir
Spargo Creek
Cleavers Hill 665m
Bunding
LERDERDERG STATE PARK
Mt Bullengarook 673m
Mt Gisborne 643m

12

SEBASTOPOL
Sovereign Hill
Ballarat Exhibition & Entertainment Centre
Kryal Castle
Bungaree
Wallace
WESTERN
Gordon
Ballan
M8
Korobeit
Mt Blackwood 736m
32
Bullengarook
C704
Toolern Vale
C705

MAGPIE
Mount Clear
Dunnstown
Millbrook
Mt Steiglitz 638m
25
Myrniong
Lerderderg Gorge
Merrimu Reservoir

13

Ross Creek
Cambrian Hill
Mount Helen
Buninyong Flora & Bird Park
Navigators
MT BUNINYONG: An extinct volcanic crater that rises 745 metres above sea level. A sealed road leads up to the lookout which offers stunning 360° views.
Mt Egerton
Ballan
WERRIBEE GORGE STATE PARK
Parwan
Avenue of Honour
Melton
FWY
M8

Napoleons
Buninyong
MIDLAND
Scotsburn
Yendon
Yuulong Lavender Estate
Mt Buninyong 745m
Lal Lal Falls
Ingliston
The Highlands
Coimadai
Jurunjung
Darley
TO MELBOURNE

EIGN HILL: This re-created gold-township is one of Victoria's major attractions and should not be missed.
Clarendon
Durham Lead
Lal Lal Reservoir
Bungal
Yaloak Vale
Fiskville
Bacchus Marsh

ENFIELD STATE PARK
C146
TO GEELONG

GARDENS: There are many fine historic and public gardens scattered throughout the region. Public gardens of particular note include the Botanic Gardens of Castlemaine, Daylesford and Malmsbury, and the Queen Mary Gardens at St Arnaud. Many of the cities and towns of the region have spectacular seasonal displays; Ballarat is famous for its begonias.

DIVIDING

J K L M N O P Q R
216

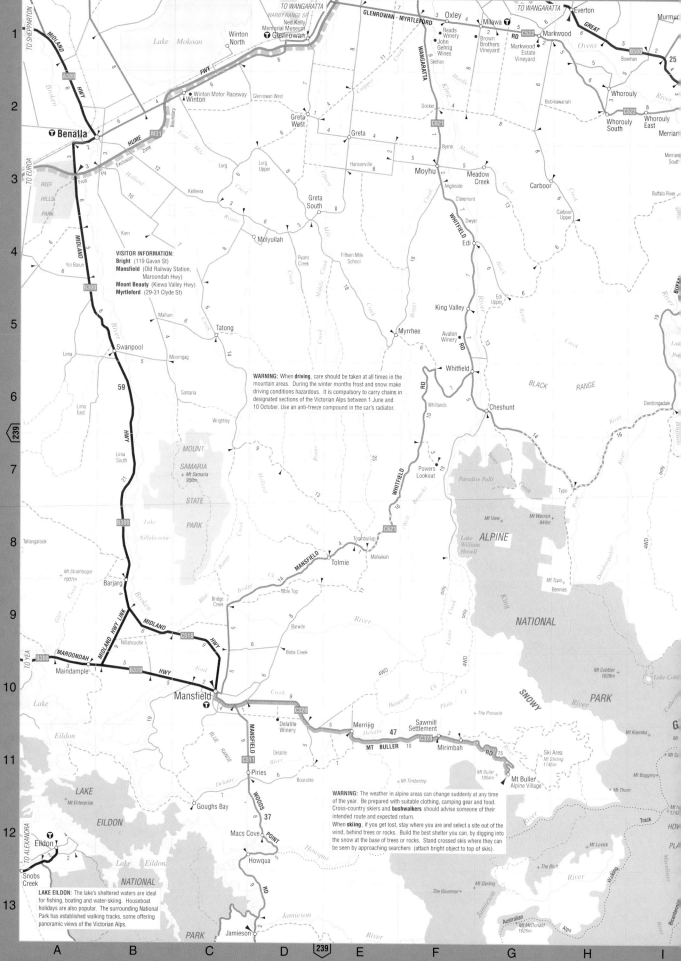

VISITOR INFORMATION:
Bright (119 Gavan St)
Mansfield (Old Railway Station, Maroondah Hwy)
Mount Beauty (Kiewa Valley Hwy)
Myrtleford (29-31 Clyde St)

WARNING: When **driving**, care should be taken at all times in the mountain areas. During the winter months frost and snow make driving conditions hazardous. It is compulsory to carry chains in designated sections of the Victorian Alps between 1 June and 10 October. Use an anti-freeze compound in the car's radiator.

WARNING: The weather in alpine areas can change suddenly at any time of the year. Be prepared with suitable clothing, camping gear and food. Cross-country skiers and **bushwalkers** should advise someone of their intended route and expected return.
When **skiing**, if you get lost, stay where you are and select a site out of the wind, behind trees or rocks. Build the best shelter you can, by digging into the snow at the base of trees or rocks. Stand crossed skis where they can be seen by approaching searchers (attach bright object to top of skis).

LAKE EILDON: The lake's sheltered waters are ideal for fishing, boating and water-skiing. Houseboat holidays are also popular. The surrounding National Park has established walking tracks, some offering panoramic views of the Victorian Alps.

0 5 10 15 20 km

Mt Stanley 1051m

TO WODONGA

Tallandoon
OMEO
TO TALLANGATTA

C528
Dederang

Mudgegonga

C527
5

KIEWA
C531
Gundowring Upper
Gundowring Junction

Little Snowy Creek

Eskdale
C543
15
HWY

Mitta Mitta
Mt Misery 1403m

C544
Dartmouth
Banimboola

10
Barwidgee Creek

yrtleford

Running Creek

C534
Kancoona

The Pinnacles

Rosewhite
VALLEY
RD

Mt Tawonga 1271m

Mt Dorchap 1056m

Lake Banimboola

RD
5
Ovens
HAPPY
Rosewhite Vineyards
9
38
VALLEY
18
Kancoona South
Mongans Bridge
Coral Bank
25

Mt Elmo 1101m

Granite Flat

C543

B500
GREAT
11
32
Happy Valley
ALPINE
Eurobin
Havilah

Mullindolingong

Redbank

Mt Yorke 1262m

HWY

ALPINE NATIONAL PARK: Stretching along the Great Dividing Range, this park joins the Kosciuszko National Park in New South Wales and its neighbour Namadgi National Park in the Australian Capital Territory. It protects the habitats of a variety of flora and fauna, including the rare mountain pygmy possum. During spring and summer the high plains are carpeted with wildflowers; more than 1100 native plant species are found in the park, including 12 found nowhere else in the world.

Lightning Creek

26
RD
B500
Mt Porepunkah 1193m

C531
Tawonga

Mt Emu 1361m

Bogong Saddle

OMEO

MOUNT
Mt McLeod 1529m
C535
rson Peak 1539m
10
Boyntons of Bright Winery
Porepunkah

Tawonga Gap
Germun
31
C536
TAWONGA
RD
Tawonga South

BUFFALO
BUFFALO
Mount Buffalo Chalet
Lake Catani

Bright
6
Germantown
BRIGHT

Mount Beauty

ALPINE

Christmas Creek

HWY

ATIONAL
Eagle Point 1477m

Pyramid Hill

UPPER
18
30
Bogong

Mt Bogong 1986m

Big Hill

Australian

PARK
MT
11
Ski Area

Freeburgh

KIEWA

Spion Kopje 1834m
Mt Nelse North 1885m
Mt Nelse 1882m

240

The Horn 1724m

Buckland

Wandiligong

GREAT
10

VALLEY
C531
15

Big
Alps

WANDILIGONG VALLEY: Classified by the National Trust, this beautiful valley is easily accessible from the township of Bright. Wandiligong was once a thriving goldmining town and a number of historic buildings have been preserved. Beyond the town is a huge apple orchard and the much-photographed Wandiligong poplars, at their most beautiful in autumn.

Smoko

ALPINE
RD

Falls Creek Alpine Village

Mt Fainter North

Marm Point 1819m

Walking
Track

Sunnyside

For downhill skiers, facilities are available otham, Dinner Plain, Falls Creek, Mt Buller Buffalo. For cross-country skiers, there is a riety of touring country ranging from well-trails near the resorts to winter wilderness Away from the resorts there are few marked

56
RD
B500
Trout Farm

Mt Fainter South

Mt McKay 1842m

NATIONAL

Glen Valley

Harrietville

Mt Feathertop 1922m

Mt Niggerhead

Rocky Valley Reservoir

Middle

C543
RD

Shannonvale

RIVER

Mt Jim

BOGONG

HIGH

WARNING: Road closed during snow season.

Mt Bundara
Mt Cope 1837m

Buckety Plain

HIGH
PLAINS
37

11

Anglers Rest

GREAT

Mt Loch 1882m

RANGE

Cobungra

BOGONG HIGH PLAINS: Considered to contain some of the most awe-inspiring mountain scenery in Victoria, this area is particularly splendid in spring and early summer when wildflowers cover the plains. Scattered across the plains are historic huts used by the cattlemen of the lower valley during the summer months. At the end of summer, the cattle are mustered and then taken down to the valley for winter.

TO OMEO

ALPINE
RD
21
Mt Hotham 1861m
Hotham Heights Alpine Village

Track
Mt Higginbotham 1842m

PARK

B500
GREAT

Dinner Plain Alpine Village

Mt Sugarloaf 1511m
Mt St Bernard

10

ALPINE
12
RD
23

DIVIDING

The Twins 1703m
Mt Freezeout

Cobungra

Mt Tabletop 1588m

B500

Mt Parslow 1494m

Cobungra

Catherine Station

Mt Murray 1640m

MOUNTAINS

Mt Blue Rag 1703m

AUSTRALIAN ALPS WALKING TRACK: This 655-km track, one of the finest long-distance bushwalking tracks in the country, stretches between Walhalla in Victoria and Canberra in the Australian Capital Territory. To walk the Victorian section of the track takes about 30 days. The track passes through remote areas and many sections should only be attempted by seasoned bushwalkers. During summer, water is in short supply in some areas; taking a compass and a map is essential.

DARGO
HIGH
PLAINS

Walking

Alps

INE

Australian

NATIONAL

Treasures Homestead

DARGO
McMillan

Mt Phipps 1402m

Basalt Knob

N

WARNING: Road closed during snow season.

HIGH

Mt Birregun 1463m

National
Trail

PARK

Bicentennial

BICENTENNIAL NATIONAL TRAIL: Extends from Healesville in Victoria to Cooktown in Queensland and passes through the Alpine National Park.

J K L M N 240 O P Q R

0 10 20 30 40 50 km

J K L 239 M N O P 240 Q R

1

RANGE
ALPINE
NATIONAL
PARK

Jamieson
+ Mt McDonald 1625m
Swifts Creek
Doctors Flat
Big Hill 675m
Ensay North
Brookville
Mt Delusion 1399m
ys Creek
Mt Skene 1571m
ine Settlement
Mt Baldhead 1377m
Ensay
Reedy Flat
Ensay South
121

Wood's Point
atlock
Mt Kent 1563m
Crooked River
Dargo
Mt Tamboritha 1640m
Mt Wellington 1635m
Waterford
Mt Djoandah 610m
Mt Dow 1000m
Stirling
Tambo Crossing
Mt Elizabeth 942m
B500
31

Lake Tali Karng
Castle Hill 1448m
Castleburn
EAST
Deptford
GIPPSLAND
Tabberabbera
Morris Peak 789m

AVON
WILDERNESS
PARK
Licola
Mt Selma 1457m
Gable End 1570m
Mt Useful 1432m
Red Jacket
Jericho
Cobbannah
MITCHELL RIVER NATIONAL PARK
Bullumwaal
Mt Alfred 503m
Little Dick 320m
ALPINE

3

Aberfeldy
Ben Cruachan 839m+
Mt Taylor 475m
Clifton Creek
Wiseleigh
Bruthen
Tambo Upper
Colquhoun

Thomson Reservoir
en
Beardmore
Culloden
Iguana Ck
Wuk Wuk
Mount Taylor
Sarsfield
GREAT
Mossiface
Swan Reach

BAW BAW
Mt St Gwinear Ski Area
Lake Glenmaggie
Glenaladale
Woodglen
Calulu
Lucknow
East Bairnsdale
Nicholson
A1
74
Kalinga

Talbot Peaks 1519m
54
Stockdale
Walpa
Lindenow
Wy Yung
Hillside
PRINCES
22
Kalimna West

4

arkers Corner
Coongulla
Valencia Creek
Briagolong
Lindenow South
Bairnsdale
Aboriginal Museum
HWY
20
Nungurner
Kalimna
Lakes Entrance

BAW BAW NATIONAL PARK
Walhalla
Glenmaggie
Newry
Boisdale
Bushy Park
Fernbank
A1
Eagle Point
Metung
GIPPSLAND LAKES COASTAL PARK

Rawson
Erica
Heyfield
Maffra West Upper
PRINCES
69
Delvine
Forge Creek
Paynesville
GIPPSLAND LAKES

5

ONDARRA STATE PARK
Moondarra
Seaton
Dawson
Tinamba
Maffra
Llowalong
Munro
32
14
Goon Nure
Lake King
THE LAKES NATIONAL PARK

Moondarra Reservoir
Coopers Creek
Swing Bridge
Cowwarr
Denison
Nambrok
9
Stratford
Airly
Perry Bridge
Meerlieu
Bengworden

Tanjil South
Toongabbie
Winninddoo
16
17
30
Montgomery
Clydebank
Lake Wellington
Loch Sport

6

TYERS PARK
Glengarry
Kilmany
Fulham
Cobains
Marlay Point
Seacombe
Lake Coleman
GIPPSLAND LAKES COASTAL PARK

Narracan Lake
Yallourn North
Tyers
HWY
26
Kilmany South
Wurruk
Sale
The Heart

Moe
Newborough
PRINCES
A1
65
Rosedale
Longford
Dutson
Paradise Beach

7

Open Cut Mine
Morwell
Traralgon
HYLAND
Flynn
28
24
25
Golden Beach

Hazelwood
Open Cut Mine
Traralgon South
Loy Yang
Loy Yang Power Station
Willung
35
Stradbroke West
Flamingo Beach

nnar
Churchill
Jeeralang North
Callignee North
Callignee
Gormandale
Stradbroke
B440

8

arra
Budgeree
Jumbuk
Balook
Carrajung
Willung South
Carrajung South
Seaspray
GIPPSLAND
Mile

MORWELL NATIONAL PARK
Blackwarry
40
TARRA-BULGA NATIONAL PARK
Macks Creek
Won Wron
Gifford
Darriman
Ninety

Ryton
Hiawatha
Madalya
Devon North
C482
Greenmount
19
Woodside
31

9

GIPPSLAND
Gunyah
Yarram
Jack River
Hunterston
Woodside Beach

Wonyip
Binginwarri
Alberton West
Alberton
McLoughlins Beach

Mt Best
Whoorra
Gelliondale
163
Tarraville
Manns Beach

Hazel Park
Agnes
SOUTH
28
Langsborough
Mann
Port Albert

Toora
Welshpool
Hedley
Port Albert

10

Port Franklin
Port Welshpool
NOORAMUNGA MARINE AND WILDLIFE RESERVE

ER INLET
RINE AND
STAL PARK
Corner
Inlet

TASMAN

11

Entrance Point
Mt Hunter 348m
WILSONS PROMONTORY MARINE PARK

SEA

Mt Roundback 314m
WILSONS PROMONTORY NATIONAL PARK

12

Tidal River
Mt Vereker 637m
Mt La Trobe 759m
Mt Wilson 709m
Lookout
WILSONS PROMONTORY

N

Glennie
South East Point
WILSONS PROMONTORY MARINE RESERVE

13

J K L M N O P Q R

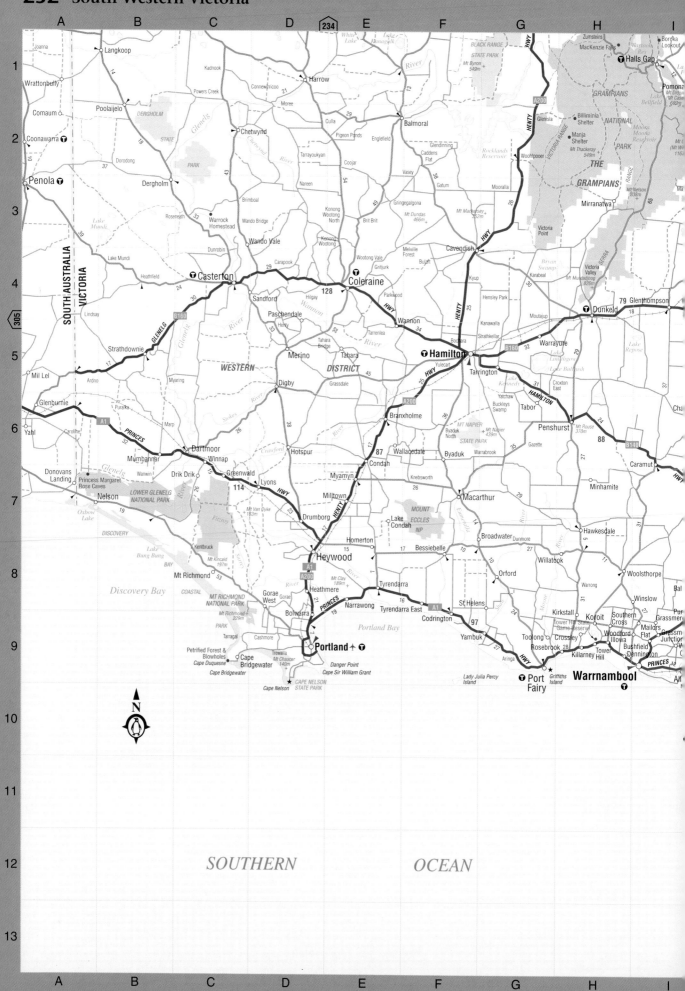

0 10 20 30 40 50 km

BASS STRAIT

For more detail on Goldfields Region see pages 226 - 227

For more detail on Ballarat see page 225

For more detail on Geelong Region see page 223

For more detail on Otway Region see page 221

BALLARAT
Geelong
Bacchus Marsh
Ararat
Beaufort
Colac
Camperdown
Daylesford
Kyneton
Woodend
Torquay
Ocean Grove
Lorne
Apollo Bay
Port Campbell
Winchelsea
Anglesea
Leopold
Lara
Little River

Great Western · Armstrong · Crowlands · Elmhurst · Amphitheatre · Lamplough · Amherst · Talbot · Majorca · Daisy Hill · Strathlea · Campbelltown · Yandoit · Guildluce · Glenluce · Vaughan · Yapeen · Taradale · Langley · Barfold · Malmsbury · Lauriston · Carlsruhe · Tylden

Warrak · Dunneworthy · Eversley · Lexton · Evansford · Clunes · Ullina · Lawrence · Smeaton · Kingston · Allendale · Broomfield · Glengower · Glenlyon · Little Hampton · Rowsley · Trentham · Newbury · Blackwood · Bullengarook East

Armstrong · Buangor · Raglan · Chute · Waterloo · Waubra · Learmonth · Creswick · Hepburn Springs · Dean · Newlyn · Spargo Creek · Bullarto · Blackwood · Greendale

Beaufort · Trawalla · Burrumbeet · Cardigan Village · Gardigan · Miners Rest · Bullarook · Bolwarra · Bolwarrah · Blakeville · Bunding · Myrniong

Maroona · Rossbridge · Tatyoon · Skipton · Snake Valley · Smythesdale · Scarsdale · Haddon · Ross Creek · Buninyong · Mt Helen · Dunnstown · Navigators · Millbrook · Gordon · Wallace · Bungaree · Ballan · Gordon

Willaura · Mininera · Streatham · Westmere · Linton · Happy Valley · Newtown · Napoleons · Scotsburn · Yendon · Lal Lal · Mt Egerton · Fiskville · Glenmore · Mount Wallace · Bacchus Marsh · Parwan

Lake Bolac · Wickliffe · Mannibadar · Bradvale · Willowvale · Cape Clear · Berringa · Illabarook · Dereel · Piggoreet · Enfield · Durham Lead · Clarendon · Garibaldi · Grenville · Elaine · Durdidwarrah · Balliang · Balliang East

Derrinallum · Lismore · Berrybank · Cressy · Rokewood Junction · Corindhap · Rokewood · Mount Mercer · Cargerie · Meredith · Steiglitz · Sheoaks · Maude · Anakie · Anakie East · Little River

Darlington · Cloven Hills · Bookaar · Kolora · Glenormiston North · Kariah · Duverney · Shelford · Bannockburn · Teesdale · Lethbridge · Murgheboluc · Inverleigh · Batesford · Corio · Lara

Noorat · Glenormiston · Gnotuk · Camperdown · Pomborneit · Stoneyford · Beeac · Warrion · Alvie · Coragulac · Cororooke · Wingeel · Gnarwarre · Fyansford · Geelong · Marshall · Leopold · Ocean Grove

Terang · Garvoc · Cobden · Tandarook · Swan Marsh · Larpent · Colac · Elliminyt · Birregurra · Winchelsea · Moriac · Mount Moriac · Ceres · Waurn Ponds · Freshwater Creek · Bellbrae · Breamlea · Barwon Heads · Torquay

Panmure · Laang · Ecklin South · Glenfyne · Scotts Creek · Irrewillipe · Carpendeit · Pirron Yallock · Warncoort · Yeodene · Bambra · Deans Marsh · Boonah · Anglesea · Aireys Inlet · Fairhaven · Eastern View

Nullawarre · Nirranda · Curdie Vale · Nirranda South · Timboon · Cowleys Creek · Brucknell · Simpson · Barongarook West · Barwon Downs · Kawarren · Gerangamete · Murroon · Benwerrin · Lorne · Separation Creek

Peterborough · Newfield · Waarre · Paaratte · Kennedys Creek · Carlisle River · Gellibrand · Wimba · Forrest · Mt Cowley · Wye River · Kennett River

Port Campbell · London Bridge · The Arch · Loch Ard Gorge · The Twelve Apostles · Gibson Steps · Princetown · Chapple Vale · Beech Forest · Weeaproinah · Tanybryn · Skenes Creek · Cape Patton

Moonlight Head · Point Reginald · Lavers Hill · Yuulong · Johanna · Glenaire · Hordern Vale · Paradise · Apollo Bay · Marengo · Cape Otway · Blanket Bay

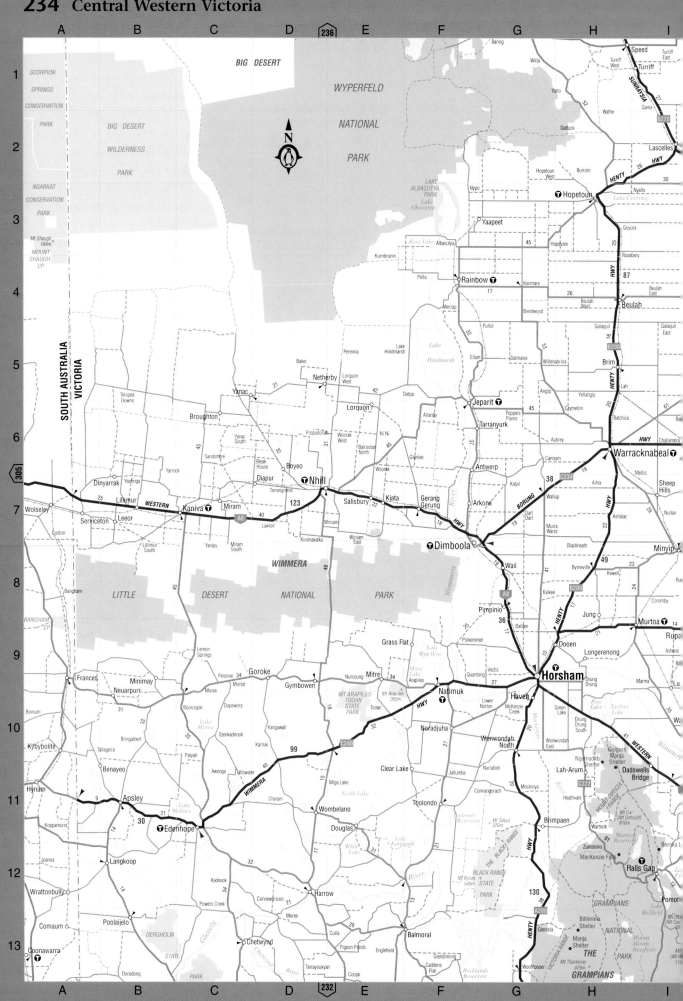

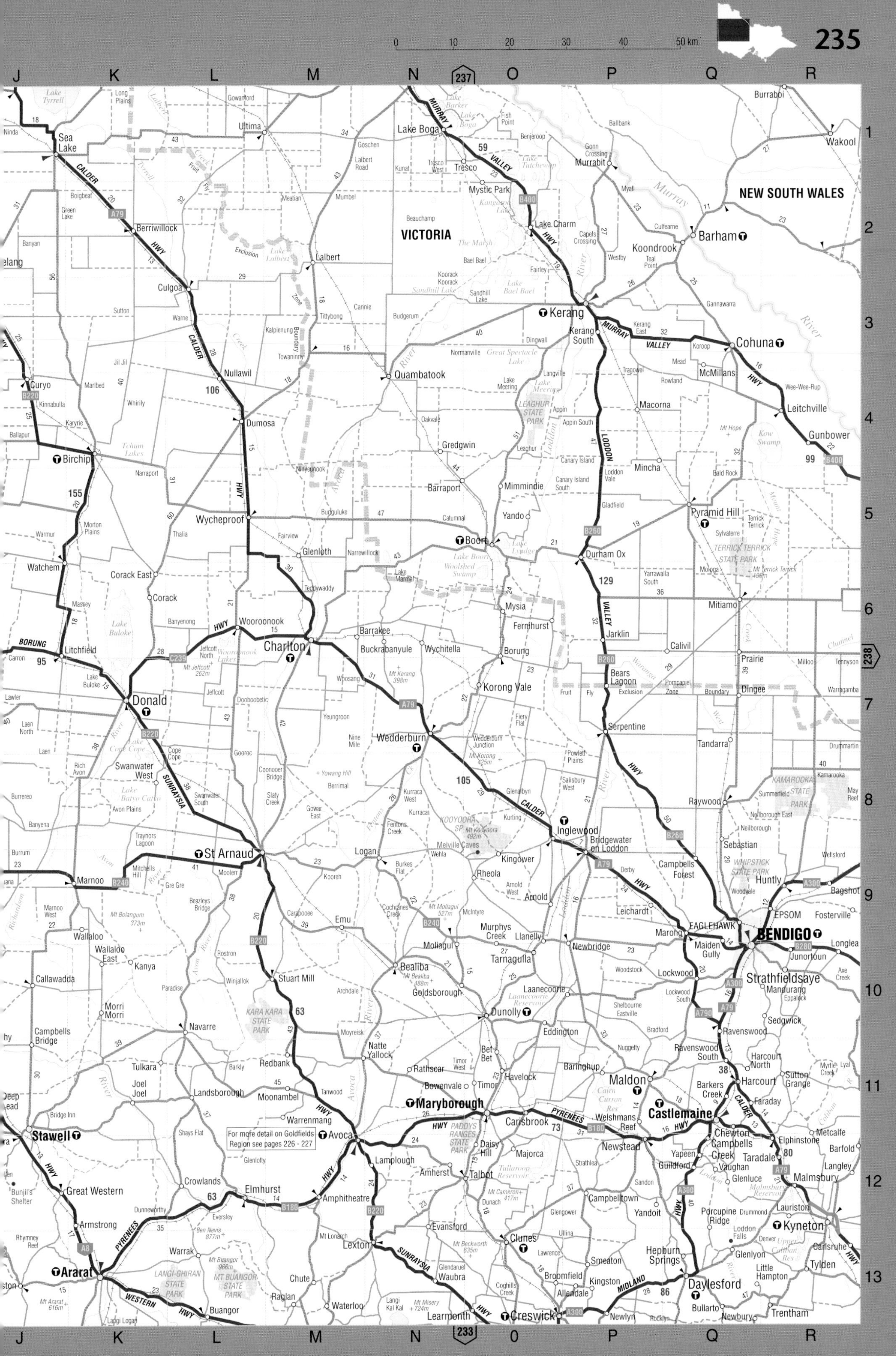

50 km

J K L M N O P Q R

VICTORIA

NEW SOUTH WALES

1

2

3

4

5

6

7

8

9

10

11

12

13

Sea Lake
Lake Tyrrell
Long Plains
Gowanford
Ultima
Lake Barker
Lake Boga
Lake Boga
Fish Point
Burraboi
Wakool

Berriwillock
Culgoa
Nullawil
Lalbert
Quambatook
Lake Boga
Tresco
Mystic Park
Lake Charm
Murrabit
Barham
Koondrook

Kerang
Kerang South
Cohuna
Leitchville
Gunbower

Birchip
Dumosa
Gredgwin
Barraport
Mimmindie
Yando
Macorna
Mincha
Pyramid Hill

Wycheproof
Glenloth
Boort
Durham Ox
Mysia
Fernhurst
Jarklin
Calivil
Prairie
Dingee
Mitiamo

Charlton
Wooroonook
Barrakee
Buckrabanyule
Wychitella
Borung
Korong Vale
Bears Lagoon
Serpentine

Donald
Litchfield
Wedderburn
Wedderburn Junction
Tandarra
Raywood

St Arnaud
Logan
Inglewood
Bridgewater on Loddon
Sebastian
Huntly
Bagshot

Marnoo
Emu
Rheola
Kingower
Arnold
Leichardt
Eaglehawk
Epsom
Fosterville
Maroha

Stuart Mill
Bealiba
Moliagul
Murphys Creek
Tarnagulla
Llanelly
Newbridge
BENDIGO
Strathfieldsaye

Navarre
Goldsborough
Dunolly
Laanecoorie
Woodstock
Lockwood
Ravenswood

Redbank
Moonambel
Bet Bet
Eddington
Baringhup
Maldon
Harcourt
Sutton Grange

Stawell
Landsborough
Rathscar
Timor
Havelock
Barkers Creek
Castlemaine

Great Western
Avoca
Maryborough
Carisbrook
Newstead
Chewton
Taradale
Malmsbury

Ararat
Crowlands
Elmhurst
Amphitheatre
Lexton
Talbot
Clunes
Guildford
Vaughan
Kyneton

Creswick
Learmonth
Waubra
Smeaton
Campbelltown
Hepburn Springs
Daylesford

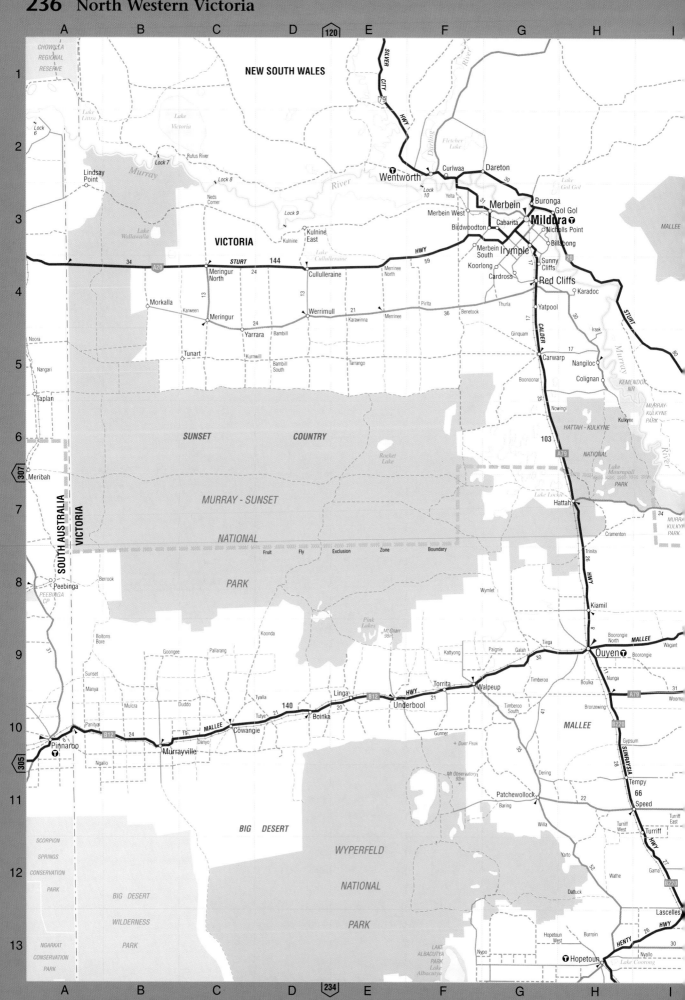

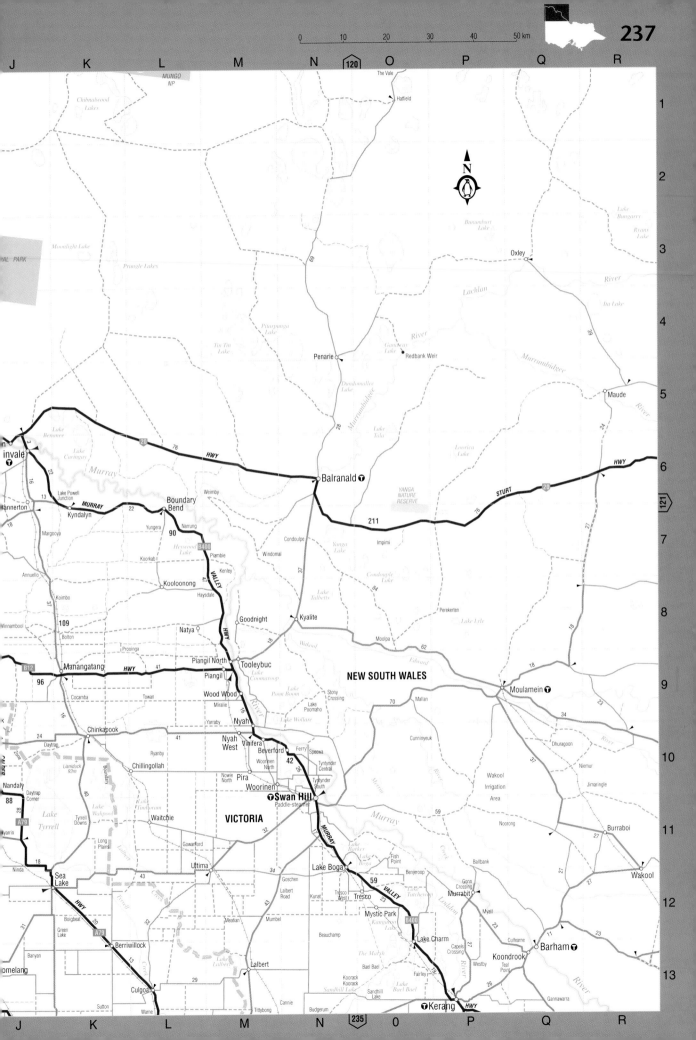

0 10 20 30 40 50 km

J   K   L   M   N   O   P   Q   R

MUNGO NP

Chibnalwood Lakes

The Vale

120

Hatfield

Moonlight Lake

AL PARK

Bunumburt Lake

Ryans Lake

Lake Bangarry

Pringle Lakes

Oxley

Lachlan

River

Itta Lake

Tin Tin Lake

Pitarpunga Lake

River

Murrumbidgee

39

Gannocary Lake

Dundomallee Lake

Penarie

Redbank Weir

Maude

invale

3

20 76 HWY

Lake Benanee

Murray

Lake Caringay

Lake Iala

Lake Lowrica

River

24

STURT HWY

20

121

Balranald

Weimby

22

13

MURRAY

Boundary Bend

YANGA NATURE RESERVE

211

76

STURT

annerton

Kyndalyn

22 Narrung

90

Yungera

Condoulpe

Windomal

18

Margooya

Hexwood Lake

B400

Piambie

Koorkab

VALLEY

Kenley

Condouple Lake

Perekerten

Lake Lyle

18

Annuello

Kooloonong

47

Haysdale

Lake Talbetts

37

Koimbo

109

Natya

HWY

Goodnight

18

Kyalite

Wakool

Edward

62

River

18

Winnambool

Bolton

Prooinga

Piangil North

Tooleybuc

Moolpa

B12

Manangatang

HWY 41

Piangil

Lake Coonatoop

NEW SOUTH WALES

Moulamein

96

Cocamba

Towan

Wood Wood

Lake Poon Boon

Stony Crossing

70

Mallan

34

23

Miralie

River

Dhuragoon

Niemur

16

Chinkapook

41

Yarraby

Nyah

Lake Wollare

Cunninyeuk

Jimaringle

24

Daytrap

Ryanby

Nyah West

Vinifera

Speewa

31

Wakool Irrigation Area

27

Lamiduck 93m

Boundary

Chillingollah

Beverford

Ferry

42 26

Tyntynder Central

Nandaly

40

Nowie North

Pira

Woorinen North

Tyntynder South

Murray

59

Burraboi

88

Daytrap Corner

Tyrrell Downs

Woorinen

Swan Hill

Paddle-steamer

Noorong

27

A79

yarrin

Lake Tyrrell

Long Plains

Waitchie

VICTORIA

Lake Barker

Lake Boga

Ballbank

Wakool

Ninda

18

Sea Lake

Gowanford

32

Ultima

34

Lake Boga

Fish Point

Benjeroop

Gonn Crossing

27

31

Boigbeat

Goschen

Lalbert Road

Kunat

Tresco West

59

VALLEY

Murrabit

Myall

23

Green Lake

20

A79

Lalbert

43

Tresco

23

B400

Culfearne

11

Barham

omelang

Banyan

Berriwillock

13

Meatian

Mumbel

Mystic Park

Kangaroo Lake

Westby

Koondrook

Teal Point

23

Culgoa

Sutton

Warne

29

Lalbert

Beauchamp

The Marsh

Bael Bael

Koorack

Lake Bael Bael

Capels Crossing

Loddon

River

26

Gannawarra

Budgerum

Cannie

Tittybong

Sandhill Lake

Koorack

Sandhill Lake

Fairley

Kerang

HWY

235

J   K   L   M   N   O   P   Q   R

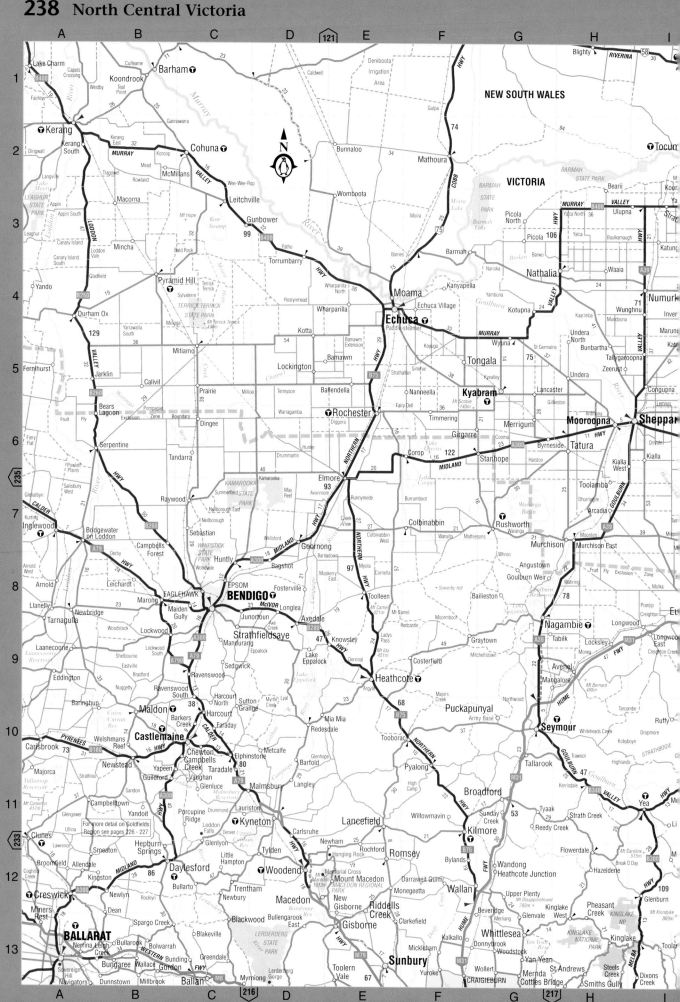

0 10 20 30 40 50 km

J K L M N O P Q R

1
Rand 121
Daysdale
Bulgandry
WIESNERS SWAMP NR
Alma Park
Morven
Wooloona
Berrigan
22
Culcairn
Holbrook
29

2
RIVERINA
37
Savenake
217
Sangar
Coreen
38
Walbundrie
35
Walla Walla
OLYMPIC
41
Gerogery
Woomargama
HWY
58
Rennie
22
Lowesdale
Oil Tree Lagoon
Brocklesby
Burrumbuttock
Gerogery West
31
20
53

3
Buraja
13
Baldale
Fruit Fly Exclusion Zone Boundary
NEW SOUTH WALES
RIVERINA
27
Howlong
58
Bungowannah
Jindera
Ettamogah Pub
Wirlinga
Lake Hume
Bungil
Wymah
Barooga
B400
59
Murray River
Mulwala
Corowa
Wahgunyah
Great Northern
Browns Plains
Albury
Talgarno
Bellbridge
Bethanga
MT GRANYA STATE PARK
Granya
Mt Granya 871m

4
Yarrawonga
Burramine
21
Bundalong
VALLEY 128
27
Rutherglen
Indigo
18
Barnawartha
28
FWY M31
Wodonga
Bandiana
VICTORIA
Boneglla
Ebden
Jarvis Ck
Old Tallangatta
Georges Creek
120

5
Katamatite
Telford
Boomahnoomoonah
Brimin
Esmond
Chiltern
Middle Indigo
Woorage North
Baranduda
Leneva
Staghorn Flat
Huon
Kiewa
Tangambalanga
MURRAY VALLEY
The Cascade
Tungamah
29
Almonds
Yeerip
Killawarra
Springhurst
68 HUME
CHILTERN BOX - IRONBARK NP
PILOT RANGE
Wooragee
C315
Indigo Upper
Allans Flat
Osbornes Flat
Kergunyah
91
C543

6
St James
Lake Rowan
Boweya
Peechelba
Boorhaman
Boralma
M31
Londrigan
Byawatha
Eldorado
Carraragarmungee
Reids Ck
Beechworth
Silver Creek
Stanley
Bruarong
Mt Stanley 1051m
Kergunyah South
Glen Ck
Mt Big Ben 1158m
Dederang
C531
Tallandoon
Eskdale
29
208
240
Dookie
Devenish
Thoona
Warby Range State Park
Mt Warby 500m
Wangaratta
Tarrawingee
C315
Everton
ALPINE
Murmungee
Mudgegonga
Mt Tawonga 1271m
Little Snowy Creek
Mitta Mitta

7
66
HWY 20
Goorambat
Glenrowan
Airworld Aviation Museum
18
Oxley
Milawa
Markwood
Ovens
24
74
Gapsted
39
Whorouly
Merriang
Myrtleford
Rosewhite
Coral Bank
KIEWA VALLEY
35
Mullindolingong
Benalla
Winton
Greta West
Greta
Meadow Creek
Whorouly South
Ovens
B500
Havilah
Tawonga

8
Baddaginnie
REEF HILLS PARK
Molyullah
Ryans Creek
Edi
Edi Upper
MOUNT BUFFALO NATIONAL PARK
Nug Nug
Eurobin
Anderson Peak 1539m
Tawonga Gap
Tawonga South
31
ALPINE
Mt Bogong 1986m
94
HUME
23
MIDLAND
Karn
Lurg
King Valley
Myrrhee
Mount Buffalo Chalet
Mt Buffalo 1724m
Ski Area
Eagle Peak 1024m
Porepunkah
Bright
Freeburgh
Mount Beauty

9
Strathbogie
B300
Warrenbayne
Swanpool
Moornag
Wrightley
Whitfield
Cheshunt
Dandongadale
Buckland
Smoko
Bogong
C531
Falls Creek Alpine Village
Rocky Valley Reservoir
Mt Wombat 799m
Boho South
Lima
Tatong
38
Powers Lookout
Typo
Mt Warrick 944m
ALPINE
Abbeyard
Harrietville
Mt Feathertop 1922m
NATIONAL
BOGONG
HIGH
PLAINS
37

10
Merton
HWY B300
Bonnie Doon
Maindample
Mansfield
Mt Strathbogie 1007m
Tallangalook
Dry Creek
Barjarg
Bobs Creek
Tolmie
24
NATIONAL PARK
Mt Cobbler 1628m
Catherine River
Mt Murray 1640m
ALPINE
Mt Hotham 1868m
Hotham Heights Alpine Village
Dinner Plain Alpine Village
111
Mt Tabletop 1588m
RANGE
HIGH
PARK
Kanumbra
76

11
Alexandra
B340
Eildon
LAKE EILDON NP
LAKE EILDON
19
C320
Merrijig
Mirimbah
Ski Area
Mt Stirling 1745m
Mt Buller 1804m
Mt Buller Alpine Village
SNOWY
Mt Howitt 1742m
Mt McDonald 1625m
DARGO HIGH PLAINS
Mt Phipps 1402m
Cobungra
Thornton
VALLEY
26
Snobs Creek
Goughs Bay
Macs Cove
Howqua
DIVIDING
HOWITT PLAINS
For more detail on Alpine Region see pages 228 - 229

12
Acheron
Taggerty
Rubicon
Jamieson
Kevington
37
Mt Terrible 1335m
Mt Skene 1571m
HOWITT
RANGE
Mt Kent 1563m
Crooked River
Mt Birregun 1463m
Buxton
CATHEDRAL RANGE STATE PARK
TORBRECK RANGE
Mt Torbreck 1514m
41
ALPINE
Mt Tamboritha 1640m
NATIONAL

13
MAROONDAH HWY
Narbethong
Black Spur
Marysville
B360
Granton
Mt Strickland 1219m
YARRA RANGES NATIONAL PARK
GREAT
Lake Mountain 1470m Ski Area
Mt Duffy 1028m
C511
Gaffneys Creek
A1 Mine Settlement
Mt Matlock 1372m
Mt Wellington 1635m
Castle Hill 1448m
PARK
Mt Tambo
Dargo
Waterford

J 217 K L M N 231 O P Q R

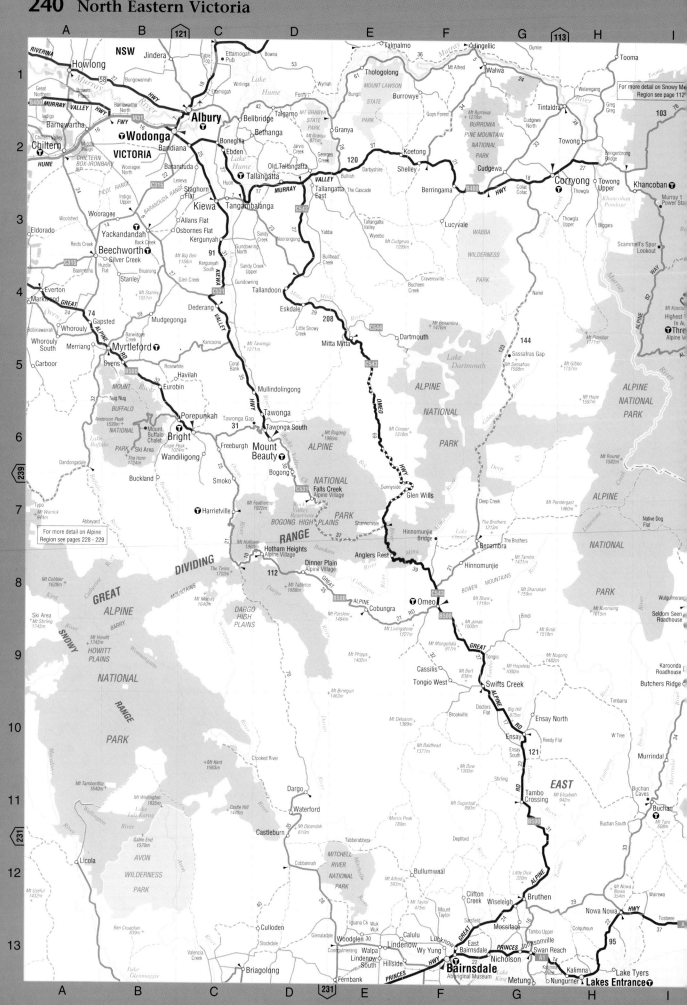

0 10 20 30 40 50 km

J K L M N 113 O P Q R

1
RANGE
Timut Pond Reservoir
abramurra
Anglers Reach
SNOWY
Adaminaby
Rosedale
18
MOUNTAINS
24
O'Neill Lagoon
Mt Flinders 1484m
Bredbo
HWY
Mt Dowling 1198m
Bald Mtn 1469m
DEUA
NATIONAL
Bergalia

2
Old Adaminaby
33
MONARO
Railway
23
McInally Mtn 1085m
Peak View
Badja Mill
PARK
River
Bodalla
Nerrigundah
146
1
18
Eucumbene
Lake Eucumbene
Buckenderra
27
HWY
Bunyan
22
Numeralla
Tuross Falls
Belowra
Tuross
Eurobodalla
Dalmeny
Wagonga

3
Mt Jagungal 161m
uthega pine Village
Sawpit Creek
26
Lake Jindabyne
Kiah Lake
29
28
33
Cooma
Cooma West
MONARO
23
Rock Flat
Disused
42
WADBILLIGA
NATIONAL
Wandella
Peak Alone 954m
Narooma
Corunna Lake
Central Tilba
18
Tilba Tilba
Smiggin Holes
Alpine Village
Perisher
Alpine Village
te Pass
illage 34
WAY
East Jindabyne
Berridale
Jindabyne
18
Buckleys Lake
39
River
HWY
Cobargo
18
HWY
WALLAGA LAKE NP
13

4
PARK
Snowy
River
Dalgety
15
Maffra
Nimmitabel
Mt Kydra 1236m
Quaama
Brogo Dam
BIAMANGA NATIONAL PARK
Bermagui
Bermagui South
Lake Jillamatong
36
Beloka
Paupong
Numbla Vale
River
Mt Cooper 1018m
30
SNOWY
108
18
Bemboka
MTNS
29
HWY
1
Brogo
34
Tanja
MIMOSA ROCKS NATIONAL PARK

5
WARNING: During the winter months (June to October), travellers should check prevailing conditions before departure.
Ingebyra
Beards Lake
Bungarby
Gunning Grach
HWY
83
21
Ando
SOUTH EAST FOREST NATIONAL PARK (Bemboka Section)
Numbugga
Morgans Crossing
Bega
Kalaru
Tathra

6
lace Craigie Lookout
Byadbo Mtn 1237m
Mt Alexander 1075m
Rodney
Mt Rix 988m
Bukalong
Bibbenluke
Cathcart
SOUTH EAST FOREST NATIONAL PARK (Tantawangalo Section)
20
Bimbaya
Candelo
Kameruka
21
Princes
20
Wolumla
15
20
32
Kalaru
BOURNDA NATIONAL PARK
SOUTH

7
77
River
Little River
Mulligans Mtn 908m
Jimenbuen
Tombong
Adams Pk
Black Lake
20
16
Bombala
35
Rocky Hall
Wyndham
20
Yellow Pinch Dam
28
Pambula
15
Tura Beach
Merimbula
Pambula Beach

8
NEW SOUTH WALES
VICTORIA
Deddick
Carrowidgin
Amboyne Crossing
Tubbut
Delegate River
36
Delegate
Mila
Craigie
Quinburra
23
Maharatta
SOUTH EAST FOREST NATIONAL PARK (Coolangubra Section)
Burragate
Towamba
SOUTH EAST FOREST NATIONAL PARK (Yowaka Section)
Nethercote
19
Eden
East Boyd
BEN BOYD NATIONAL PARK
PACIFIC

9
McKillops Bridge
SNOWY RIVER
NATIONAL
Mt Bowen 1320m
Bonang West
Bonang
Bendoc
Haydens Bog
Mt Delegate 1308m
Dellicknora
45
MONARO
29
Platts
BONDI GULF NP
Pericoe
Mt Imlay 886m
12
Kiah
Wonboyn Lake
Twofold Bay
Boydtown
OCEAN

10
PARK
Martins Creek
69
C612
Goongerah
ERRINUNDRA NATIONAL PARK
Mt Jersey 759m
Broom Mtn 1010m
24
Mt Ellery 1291m
Errinundra
Combienbar
Mt Canterbury 1059m
Buldah
88
HWY
42
Kowat
Coopracambra 958m
COOPRACAMBRA NATIONAL PARK
Wroxham
Wangarabell
57
Narrabarba
32
158
1
Timbillica
Mt Nagha 543m
Wonboyn Lake
Disaster Bay
Green Cape
NADGEE NATURE RESERVE
SOUTH
For more detail on South Coast see page 111

11
Sardine Creek
Mt Kuark 91m
B23
Mt Kaye 1002m
Chandlers Creek
Weeragua
Noorinbee North
Noorinbee
CANN
VALLEY
Genoa
A1
HWY
Gipsy Point
Fairhaven
Lake Barracoota
Cape Howe

12
GIPPSLAND
Mt Buck 507m
Club Terrace
LIND NP
PRINCES
Tonghi Creek
21
Cann River
ALFRED NATIONAL PARK
Karlo Creek
A1
23
Mallacoota
Mallacoota Inlet
Gabo Island
TASMAN
N

13
Orbost
Brodribb River
Tabbara
26
Cabbage Tree Creek
75
Bellbird Creek
19
9
23
Mt Cann 530m
Bemm River
CROAJINGOLONG NATIONAL PARK
Mt Everard 371m
Tamboon
CROAJINGOLONG NATIONAL PARK
Wingan Inlet
Little Rame Head
SEA
Marlo
14
Lake Curlip
CAPE CONRAN COASTAL PARK
Pearl Point
Sydenham Inlet
Tamboon Inlet
Point Hicks (Cape Everard)
Rame Head
Point Ricardo
Cape Conran

SOUTH AUSTRALIA

Remarkable Rocks, Kangaroo Island

S outh Australia offers a quality of grandeur and an energetic spirit quite different from that of the other States. It has a landscape of extraordinary beauty, a diverse, vibrant community, and a bounty of fine local food and wine.

For many years, South Australia has maintained its reputation as the Festival State, although many visitors come here primarily to see and experience the wonderful natural attractions.

South Australia is the driest State in the driest continent; two thirds is near-desert and eighty-three per cent receives an annual rainfall of less than 250 millimetres. These are facts easily forgotten when you feast your eyes on the lush green of the Barossa Valley or explore the rugged beauty of the Flinders Ranges.

South Australia's original settlement began as the result of one man's vision for a model colony. Edward Gibbon Wakefield believed that the difficulties in the Australian colonies stemmed from the fact that land was too easy to obtain. He argued that land should be sold at 2 pounds an acre, thereby attracting those with capital to invest in the colony and providing employment for those who had only their labour to offer. This in turn would encourage investment and the development of resources. In 1834, these ideas were put to the test in the Gulf St Vincent area.

Today, South Australia's economy continues to rely mainly on primary industries such as agriculture and fishing. Mining is another significant industry. Olympic Dam is one of the world's largest copper mines and probably the biggest uranium mine. The Leigh Creek coalfields supply the fuel for the majority of the State's power needs. At Coober Pedy, beautiful, multicoloured opals are uncovered and exported at a rate unequalled anywhere in Australia.

The fame of South Australia's wines also extends well beyond Australian shores. The Barossa, McLaren Vale, Riverland, Clare Valley, Langhorne Creek, Adelaide Hills and Coonawarra wine regions all have distinct specialities determined by soil and climate. In the famous Barossa Valley region, there are close to 50 wineries. The valley was originally settled by German Lutherans who planted orchards, olive groves and vineyards.

The coastal areas of South Australia enjoy a pleasant year-round Mediterranean climate, while the northern part of the State has a desert climate which is ideal for winter travel, but is less hospitable in the summer. Adelaide, the capital, with its average rainfall of 530 millimetres, enjoys a mid-summer average maximum temperature of 28°C

NOT TO BE MISSED	
IN SOUTH AUSTRALIA	**Map Ref.**
ADELAIDE HILLS Cleland Wildlife Park, historic towns, galleries and beautiful scenery	300 D10
BAROSSA WINE REGION Australia's most famous wine-producing area	300 E4
COOBER PEDY Opal mining town	301 R11
COORONG NATIONAL PARK Known for its birdlife	305 D5
INNES NATIONAL PARK Impressive coastal scenery and wildflowers in spring	306 G10
KANGAROO ISLAND Unique scenery, unusual rock formations and native fauna	306 F11
'LITTLE CORNWALL' Kadina, Moonta, Wallaroo; rich mining history	306 I6
MOUNT GAMBIER Caves and crater lakes, particularly the beautiful Blue Lake	305 H12
VICTOR HARBOR Coastal resort town; take horse-drawn tram to Granite Island	307 L11
WHALERS WAY (PORT LINCOLN) Stunning cliff-top drive near Port Lincoln	306 D9
WILPENA POUND Extraordinary dish-shaped geological formation in the Flinders Ranges	303 E8

and a mid-winter average maximum of 15°C. Almost seventy per cent of the population lives here, making South Australia the most urbanised of all the States.

South of Adelaide is the substantial seaside town of Victor Harbor. A little further on is Coorong National Park, renowned for its prolific birdlife, near the mouth of the Murray River at Lake Alexandrina. The Murray River is the lifeline of the State. It enters South Australia at Chowilla Regional Reserve on the Victorian border and completes its 2600-kilometre journey across the country on reaching the Southern Ocean at Goolwa. Along the riverbanks are many historic towns, extensive citrus orchards and vegetable crops all maintained by irrigation. Unfortunately, the bounties of irrigation have come at a price – the rising water table has led to salinity problems and much work is now being done to combat this.

North of Adelaide are the attractive, unspoilt coastlines of the Yorke and Eyre peninsulas. Port Lincoln, on the Eyre Peninsula, is a popular base for game-fishing and the Yorke Peninsula towns of Wallaroo, Moonta and Kadina – known collectively as 'Little Cornwall' – are well worth a visit.

For those leaving the coast and travelling further north, the Stuart Highway is completely sealed, making it possible to drive from Port Augusta to central Australia on an all-weather road. If you feel the call of adventure, take time to explore the opal town of Coober Pedy. Temperatures often exceed 40°C in Coober Pedy in the summer (hence most of the town is built underground), so make sure you plan your trip during the cooler months. Certain precautions should be taken before negotiating other roads in the desert regions of the State (see: Outback Motoring p. 603).

The spectacular Flinders Ranges, just north-west of Augusta, have passable roads, although some are unsealed. Wilpena Pound and Arkaroola are the main holiday bases in the ranges.

Jenke Vineyard cellars near Tanunda

CLIMATE GUIDE

ADELAIDE

	J	F	M	A	M	J	J	A	S	O	N	D
Maximum °C	29	29	26	22	19	16	15	16	18	21	24	27
Minimum °C	17	17	15	13	10	9	8	8	9	11	13	15
Rainfall mm	20	21	24	44	68	72	67	62	51	44	31	26
Raindays	4	4	5	9	13	15	16	16	13	11	8	6

VICTOR HARBOR REGION

	J	F	M	A	M	J	J	A	S	O	N	D
Maximum °C	24	24	23	21	19	16	15	16	18	20	22	23
Minimum °C	16	16	15	12	10	8	8	8	9	11	12	14
Rainfall mm	22	20	23	43	62	71	74	67	55	46	28	23
Raindays	4	4	6	10	14	15	16	16	14	11	8	6

BAROSSA VALLEY

	J	F	M	A	M	J	J	A	S	O	N	D
Maximum °C	29	29	26	22	17	14	13	14	17	20	24	27
Minimum °C	14	14	12	9	7	5	4	5	6	8	10	12
Rainfall mm	18	19	24	42	61	52	66	63	58	50	28	22
Raindays	5	3	5	9	13	12	16	16	13	11	8	6

WILPENA REGION

	J	F	M	A	M	J	J	A	S	O	N	D
Maximum °C	31	31	27	24	17	14	13	15	20	24	27	29
Minimum °C	16	16	13	9	6	4	3	3	5	9	11	14
Rainfall mm	34	25	20	19	51	57	67	50	33	35	14	25
Raindays	3	3	2	3	8	8	9	7	5	6	4	4

VISITOR INFORMATION
South Australian Travel Centre
1 King William Street, Adelaide
(08) 8303 2033; freecall 1300 655 276
www.visit-southaustralia.com.au

CALENDAR OF EVENTS

JANUARY
Public holidays: New Year's Day; Australia Day. *Adelaide:* Schützenfest; Blessing of the Waters (at Glenelg); Tour Down Under (cycling). *Goolwa:* Milang to Goolwa Freshwater Classic Yacht Race. *Kingston S.E.:* Cape Jaffa Food and Wine Festival; Fishing Contest; Lobster Fest.; Yachting Regatta. *Penola:* Vignerons Cup. *Port Germein (near Port Pirie):* Festival of the Crab. *Port Lincoln:* Tunarama Festival. *Port MacDonnell:* Bayside Festival. *Port Vincent (near Minlaton):* Yacht Race. *Robe:* Lions Regatta. *Streaky Bay:* Perlubie Sports Day; Family Fish Day Contest; Aquatic Carnival. *Victor Harbor:* Granite Island Regatta; Regional Art Show. *Wallaroo:* New Year's Day Regatta. *Wilmington:* Rodeo.

FEBRUARY
Adelaide: Adelaide Festival of the Arts (even-numbered years); Adelaide Fringe Festival (runs parallel to Adelaide Festival); Womadelaide (odd-numbered years); International Provincial Rugby Sevens. *Barossa Valley:* Barossa Under the Stars. *Berri:* Rodeo; Speedboat Spectacular. *Burra:* Rock 'n' Roll Festival. *Kingscote:* Racing Carnival. *Loxton:* Mardi Gras. *Mount Compass (near Victor Harbor):* Cow Race. *Mount Gambier:* Country Music Festival. *Peterborough:* Rodeo. *Port Lincoln:* Lincoln Week Regatta. *Tanunda:* Oompah Fest.

MARCH
Adelaide: Adelaide Festival of the Arts (contd); Adelaide Fringe Festival (contd); Glendi Festival. *Adelaide Hills:* Hills Harvest Festival. *Burra:* Twilight Jazz Affair. *Clare:* Clare Valley Cup. *Goolwa:* Wooden Boat Festival (odd-numbered years). *Kapunda:* Celtic Music Festival. *Port Augusta:* Outback Surfboat Carnival. *Waikerie:* International Food Fair. *William Creek (east of Coober Pedy):* Race Meeting and Gymkhana (weekend before Easter).

EASTER
Public holidays: Good Friday; Easter Saturday; Easter Monday. *Andamooka:* Family Fun Day. *Barmera:* Lake Bonney Yachting Regatta. *Barossa Valley:* Vintage Festival (odd-numbered years). *Berri:* Carnival. *Ceduna:* Horseracing Carnival. *Clare:* Easter Races. *Coober Pedy:* Opal Festival. *Jamestown:* Bilby Hunt. *Kadina:* Bowling Carnival. *Victor Harbor:* Craft Fair. *Waikerie:* Horse and Pony Club Easter Horse Show. *Whyalla:* Australian Amateur Snapper Fishing Championship.

APRIL
Public holiday: Anzac Day. *Adelaide:* 500 in Adelaide (V8 supercar race). *Clare:* Spanish Festival. *Laura (near Crystal Brook):* Folk Fair. *Maitland:* Agricultural Show. *Port Augusta:* Antique and Craft Fair. *Port Pirie:* Regional Masters Games. *Streaky Bay:* Cup Race Meeting. *Victor Harbor:* Triathlon. *Yankalilla:* Rodeo.

MAY
Public holiday: Adelaide Cup Day. *Adelaide:* Adelaide Cup Racing Carnival. *Blinman:* Land Rover Jamboree. *Burra:* Antique and Decorating Fair. *Clare:* Gourmet Weekend. *Hawker:* Horseracing Carnival. *Mannum:* Houseboat Hirers' Open Days. *Mount Gambier:* Generations in Jazz. *Naracoorte:* Swap Meeting; Young Riders Equestrian Event. *Oodnadatta:* Race Meeting and Gymkhana. *Penola:* Festival. *Stansbury:* Sheepdog Trials. *Strathalbyn:* Settlers Celebration (even-numbered years). *Waikerie:* Riverland Rock 'n' Roll Festival. *Yorke Peninsula (Kadina/Moonta/Wallaroo):* Kernewek Lowender (odd-numbered years).

JUNE
Public holiday: Queen's Birthday. *Barmera:* SA Country Music Festival and Awards. *Coober Pedy:* Glendi Festival. *Gawler:* Horse Trials. *McLaren Vale:* Sea and Vines Festival. *Marree:* Picnic Races. *Port Augusta:* Cup Carnival (horseracing). *Victor Harbor:* Whale Season Launch.

JULY
Marree: Australian Camel Cup. *Willunga:* Almond Blossom Festival.

AUGUST
Balaklava: Balaklava Cup. *Barossa Valley:* Gourmet Barossa. *Innamincka:* Races. *Kadina:* Agricultural Show. *Port Augusta:* Camel Cup. *Strathalbyn:* Collectors, Hobbies and Antique Fair.

SEPTEMBER
Adelaide: Royal Adelaide Show; Bay to Birdwood Run (vintage car rally; even-numbered years); Birdwood Classic (post-1945 car rally; odd-numbered years). *Adelaide Hills:* Hills Affare (food and wine). *Barossa Valley:* Gourmet Barossa (contd). *Ceduna:* Agricultural Show. *Hawker:* Art Exhibition. *Keith:* Market Day. *Murray Bridge:* International Pedal Prix. *Paskeville (near Kadina):* Yorke Peninsula Field Days (odd-numbered years). *Port Pirie:* Blessing of the Fleet. *Streaky Bay:* Agricultural Show.

OCTOBER
Public holiday: Labour Day. *Adelaide:* Tasting Australia (odd-numbered years); Adelaide International Horse Trials (sometimes Nov.); SA Football League Finals. *Andamooka:* Opal Festival. *Balaklava:* Garden and Gallery Festival (even-numbered years). *Barmera:* Sheepdog trials. *Beachport:* Festival by the Sea. *Bordertown:* Clayton Farm Vintage Field Day. *Ceduna:* Oyster-Fest. *Coober Pedy:* Horse races. *Coonawarra:* Cabernet Celebration. *Curdimurka (west of Marree):* Outback Ball (even-numbered years). *Edithburgh:* Gala Day. *McLaren Vale:* Continuous Picnic; Wine Bushing Festival. *Murray Bridge:* 110km Waterski Race. *Port Pirie:* Festival of Country Music. *Renmark:* Rose Festival. *Strathalbyn:* Glenbarr Scottish Festival. *Victor Harbor:* Folk and Music Festival. *Yorke Peninsula:* Yorke Surfing Classic.

NOVEMBER
Adelaide: Christmas Pageant. *Berri:* Art and Craft Fair. *Clare:* Spring Festival. *Goolwa:* Cocklefest. *Kapunda:* Agricultural Show; Antique and Craft Fair. *Loxton:* Loxton Lights Up (Christmas lights). *Murray Bridge:* Steam and Riverboat Rally. *Port Pirie:* Cycling and Athletics Carnival. *Robe:* Village Fair (incl. Blessing of the Fleet and Art and Craft Festival). *Streaky Bay:* Camel Cup Races.

DECEMBER
Public holidays: Christmas Day; Boxing Day; Proclamation Day. *Adelaide:* Proclamation Day Celebrations (at Glenelg). *Barmera:* Christmas Pageant and Fireworks. *Jamestown:* Christmas Pageant. *Mount Gambier:* Carols by Candlelight. *Naracoorte:* Carols by Candlelight. *Renmark:* Christmas Pageant.

Note: The information given here was accurate at the time of printing. However, as the timing of events held annually is subject to change and some events may extend into the following month, it is best to check with the local tourism authority or event organisers to confirm the details. The calendar is not exhaustive. Most towns and regions hold sporting competitions, art and craft exhibitions, agricultural and flower shows, music festivals and other such events annually. Details of these events are available from local tourism outlets.

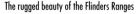
The rugged beauty of the Flinders Ranges

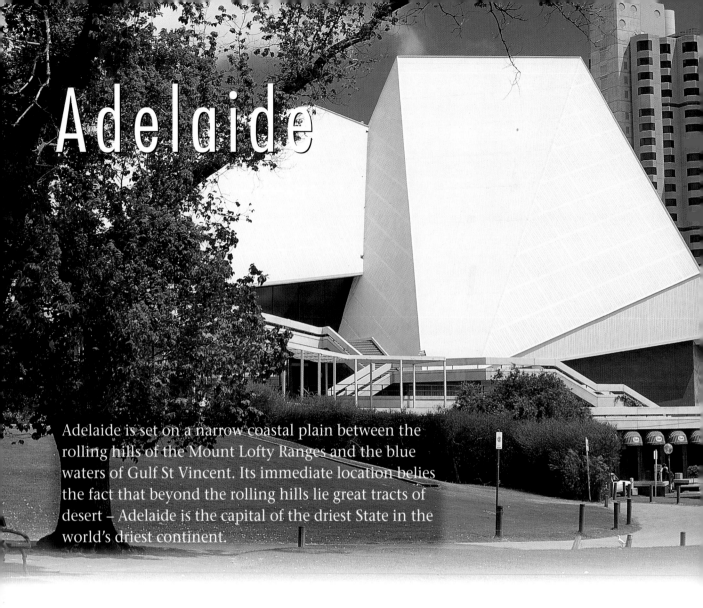

Adelaide

Adelaide is set on a narrow coastal plain between the rolling hills of the Mount Lofty Ranges and the blue waters of Gulf St Vincent. Its immediate location belies the fact that beyond the rolling hills lie great tracts of desert – Adelaide is the capital of the driest State in the world's driest continent.

The city of Adelaide flanks the wide curves of the splendid River Torrens. It is a well-planned city, thanks to Colonel Light, the first Surveyor-General. It is the only major metropolis in the world where the city's centre is completely encircled by parkland. It has a population of almost 1.1 million, but feels smaller and, despite its bustle and cosmopolitan character, it remains a friendly and open place. The city offers visitors a regular calendar of festivals, a well-preserved history, a large and varied arts program, the warmth and light of the South Australian outdoors, and some of the best wining and dining opportunities in Australia.

EXPLORING ADELAIDE

Adelaide's city centre is compact and easily negotiated on foot. For those who like some help getting around, or those wishing to travel further out, there is a safe, clean and efficient public transport system. The **Explorer Tram** offers visitors the chance to tour the city's attractions at a leisurely pace and with the benefit of a recorded commentary. This tram replica has many stopping points and visitors can board and alight as they wish. A fleet of **Popeye** motor launches cruise the River Torrens and also provide an ideal means of transport to the Adelaide Zoo. The **Trans Adelaide's O-Bahn** is the longest guided busway in the world. The busway runs alongside the river, from the city to Modbury, through its own landscaped park. The historic **Glenelg tram** is the most famous of Adelaide's tourist rides. It departs Victoria Square regularly for a return trip to Adelaide's premier seaside suburb. The MV *Port Princess*, operating from Port Adelaide, carries visitors down the Port River, taking in historic sites and beaches and providing a chance to see dolphins. Car travel is recommended for

Adelaide Festival Centre

touring some of the farther-flung regions; the roads are excellent and provided you have a road map, navigation should not be a problem.

ADELAIDE BY AREA

CITY CENTRE

The centre of Adelaide is a well-planned area of wide streets, low buildings and plenty of open public areas. An exploration of the city should start at **Rundle Mall**, the city's major shopping precinct. It is a pleasant tree-lined area where shoppers can sit and watch the passing parade and regular street entertainment. There are department stores, boutique outlets, and arcades off the mall, including the historic **Adelaide Arcade** (1885), a fine example of the highly decorative style of Victorian retail architecture.

From Rundle Mall enter King William Street and head south. On the right-hand side is **Edmund Wright House** (1878)

distinguished by its elaborate Renaissance facade. Travelling exhibitions from the National Museum of Australia are held here and it is also the home of the State History Centre. Further along and across Pirie Street is the **Adelaide Town Hall** (1863), also in the Renaissance style and modelled on buildings in Genoa and Florence; it is much admired for its magnificent tower and classic portico entrance. King William Street opens out into Victoria Square, an elegant public space that captures something of the essence of Light's vision of an ordered, open city. The historic **General Post Office** and **Treasury Building**, which claim the north-west and north-east corners respectively, are well worth a look. The Post Office was constructed in 1867 and is a fairly typical, large, Victorian-era building. The Treasury, parts of which date back to 1839, now houses a museum that charts the fascinating history of exploration and surveying in South Australia. On the eastern side of Victoria Square, in Wakefield Street, is **St Francis Xavier's Cathedral**. Dating from 1856, it is Australia's oldest Catholic cathedral.

Head west across Victoria Square into Grote Street to reach the **Central Market**. This busy marketplace has some of the best (and cheapest) fresh food anywhere in Australia, with vendors specialising in superb local produce such as olive oil, nuts, herbs and smallgoods. Cafes and restaurants in the area offer cuisines from around the world. Nearby is **Chinatown** with its good produce shops and restaurants; also nearby is **Gouger Street**, a must for the legendary seafood of South Australia (you will be amazed at the prices).

Just north of here and towards Hindley Street is known locally as the West End. This area has some interesting old buildings including **Her Majesty's Theatre** on Grote Street; **Queen's Theatre** in Waymouth Street, Australia's oldest mainland theatre; and old **Wests Coffee Palace Building** in the heart of Hindley Street. **Hindley Street** is the western extension of Rundle Mall and is the city's most pleasantly inelegant and lively precinct. Here you will find nightclubs and bars as well as a top selection of ethnic restaurants, with a heavy concentration on Middle Eastern Food.

NOT TO BE MISSED

IN ADELAIDE   Map Ref.

ADELAIDE CASINO
In a beautifully restored railway station   294 E8

ADELAIDE FESTIVAL CENTRE
One of the best performance venues in the world   294 E7

ART GALLERY OF SOUTH AUSTRALIA
A superb overview of Australian art   294 F8

BOTANIC GARDENS
Join a free tour of these beautiful formal gardens with their exotic and native species   294 G7

CENTRAL MARKET
Bustling market with local produce   294 D10

GLENELG
Board a tram to this seaside resort with its old-world feel   296 C10

LIGHT'S VISION
Share Light's vision of the city from this spot   294 D6

RUNDLE STREET
Enjoy the vibrant, cosmopolitan cafe strip   294 G8

ST PETER'S CATHEDRAL
Visit one of Australia's finest cathedrals   294 E6

TOP EVENTS

Schützenfest (Jan.)
The longest-running cultural festival in Australia

Tour Down Under (Jan.)
Cycling event featuring the world's top pros

Womadelaide (Feb., odd-numbered years)
Vibrant world music in Botanic Park

Adelaide Festival of the Arts and **Adelaide Fringe Festival**
(Feb.–Mar., even-numbered years)
This highly regarded international festival claims the city for three weeks

Glendi Festival (Mar.)
Greek culture, food, song and dance

500 in Adelaide (Apr.)
V8 supercar race on a modified Grand Prix circuit

Bay to Birdwood Run
(Sept., even-numbered years)
The largest historic motor-vehicle run in the Southern Hemisphere

Tasting Australia (Oct., odd-numbered years)
Sample the latest innovations in food and wine

For further details visit the web site
www.visit-southaustralia.com.au

HISTORY

Colonel William Light, a soldier and surveyor, chose the site of the city of Adelaide, named for Queen Adelaide, consort of William IV, in 1836. He placed the settlement in the midst of good wheat-growing country and on the edge of Gulf St Vincent from where produce could be shipped, via Port Adelaide, to the rest of the continent and the world. Light envisaged a well-ordered garden city, and the results may be seen today in the wide streets, elegant open squares and the wide swathe of parkland that surrounds Adelaide's centre. Socially and culturally, Adelaide has always been something of a mixed bag. It is regarded as a conservative city, a place that reflects the interests of the first English landholders who settled the surrounding districts, established the major public institutions – including an uncommon number of churches – and who more or less came to represent something of an unofficial aristocracy. Equally strong, however, is its identity as a progressive city, demonstrated by its embrace of multiculturalism, promotion of the arts and advancement of social reforms.

The area around the eastern end of Rundle Street is known as the East End, the city's busiest cafe precinct. This is where Adelaide looks and feels like a large Mediterranean town, with acres of outdoor tables, wide pavements, plenty of streetlife and even the odd grapevine bedecking a verandah here and there. By contrast you will also find here an English pub, a cigar bar and an Imax Cinema. The shops in this area generally tend towards the out-of-the-ordinary in terms of their products, be it music, books, clothes or flowers. One block south of the East End Markets, in Grenfell Street, is **Tandanya – National Aboriginal Cultural Institute**. This was the first institution in Australia devoted to Aboriginal culture. It houses a permanent collection of Aboriginal art, hosts a range of exhibitions of artworks and artifacts and offers performance space for dance and theatre.

NORTH TERRACE

Many of the city's most important cultural institutions sit shoulder to shoulder on this gracious tree-lined boulevard. Visitors can stroll easily between churches, galleries and museums, and still have the energy for a flutter at the casino as the day ends. The **Botanic Hotel** (1878), at the eastern end, is the grandest of Adelaide's historic hotels. Fully and faithfully restored, it offers fine or casual dining. A short stroll, heading west, is **Ayers House** (1855), an elegant 19th-century residence and one of the first grand homes to be built in Adelaide. Originally owned by Henry Ayers, seven times premier and early mining magnate, Ayers House is open to the public and contains a small museum and a restaurant. The **University of Adelaide** is another North Terrace cultural landmark, offering a mix of classic and contemporary architecture set in superbly landscaped grounds that stretch from North Terrace down to the River Torrens. On campus is the **Museum of Classical Archaeology**, which boasts a collection of more than 500 objects, some of which date back to the third millennium; behind the museum lies **Elder Hall**, a fine concert venue with a spectacular pipe organ.

Alongside the museum is the **Art Gallery of South Australia**, which was established in 1871 and houses a

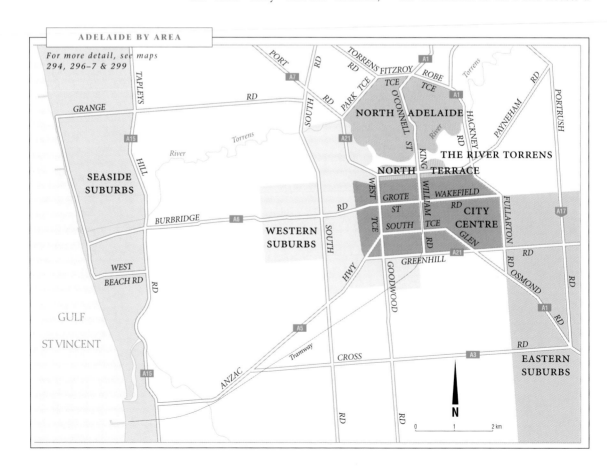

collection that offers a stunning overview of the history of Australian art from the 18th century on. Of particular interest are the works of many distinguished artists from South Australia, including Margaret Preston and Stella Bowen. Next door, the **South Australian Museum** has the world's largest collection of anthropological Aboriginal artifacts, arranged in a series of educative and culturally relevant exhibits, as well as an extraordinary range of artifacts from the Pacific Islands and Ancient Egypt.

The **State Library** is situated around the corner from North Terrace in Kintore Avenue. The Mortlock Library within houses an important South Australian collection of books, maps and other archives. The Institute, also part of the library, is responsible for the Bradman Collection, comprising more than 100 items of cricket memorabilia belonging to that giant of test cricket, Don Bradman, or 'The Don' as he is known. Behind the library is the **Migration Museum**, located in the magnificent old buildings of what was once the Destitute Asylum. The exhibits chart the hopes and fears of generations of migrants, the social policies that helped or hindered them, and the material circumstances of their lives before, during and after arrival.

Near the corner of King William Street and North Terrace lies **Government House**. Construction of the building began in 1839, and constant renovations and enlargements took place throughout the 19th century; it stands today as Adelaide's oldest building. Across King William Street is **Parliament House**, South Australia's seat of government. The west wing of the building was completed in 1889, while the east wing did not open until 1939. The most striking feature of this classically inspired building are the ten Corinthian columns at the front, a popular adornment for large public buildings in Australia towards the end of the 19th century.

Back behind Parliament House lies **Adelaide Casino**, looking increasingly elegant when compared with some of the Las Vegas-like ventures that have

Light's Vision on Montefiore Hill

RESTAURANTS AND CAFES

Adelaide claims more restaurants and cafes per capita than any other city in Australia. A good starting point is the local publication *Dine* (produced by Wakefield Press). **Map Ref.**

EAST END
Precinct at the east end of Rundle Street featuring many cheap, good cafes serving a variety of cuisine **294 G8**

HINDLEY STREET
Middle Eastern restaurants, excellent seafood and good coffee **294 C8**

GOUGER STREET
Best range of Asian restaurants in town; exceptional seafood **294 C10**

HUTT STREET
Streetside cafes open for breakfast, lunch and dinner **294 G11**

NORTH ADELAIDE
Head for O'Connell and Melbourne streets for fine dining and great outdoor cafes **294 D3 & E5**

SEASIDE
Jetty Road in Glenelg, Henley Square in Henley and beautiful beachfront restaurants in the suburbs of Grange and Semaphore offer a range of eating options

PARKS AND GARDENS
The belt of parkland that circles the city centre is one of Adelaide's best features. As well as containing a labyrinth of trails and paths, and a large number of picnic and sporting grounds, there are a few special gardens. **Rymill Park**, *on the east side of the city, has a children's rowing lake with boats for hire; to the south of the city are the* **Himeji Gardens**, *designed along classic Japanese lines and including a traditional lake and examples of dry mountain gardens; also south are the* **Veale Gardens**, *which feature a formal rose garden, rockeries and fountains; and the jewel: the* **Botanic Gardens**.
On the outer fringe of the city are native bushland areas, perfect for a family day out. **Belair National Park**, *one of the world's oldest national parks, contains recreation areas, walking tracks and the old summer residence of the Governor of South Australia.* **Morialta Conservation Park** *features a rugged gorge, ideal for the adventurer, and many walking tracks through some beautiful country. In the southerly seaside suburb of Hallet Cove is* **Hallet Cove Conservation Park**, *established to preserve glacial features of the coastal landscape estimated to be more than 270 million years old. The self-guide walk leads visitors through a prehistoric spectacle of encrusted fossils, folded rocks and evidence of giant ice sheets.*

St Peter's Cathedral and Pennington Gardens

ENTERTAINMENT

*In Adelaide you immediately notice the number and quality of the city's old pubs. Some are friendly 'locals' where you can get a local beer on tap and join in a conversation, particularly if you mention Australian Rules Football. Others incorporate restaurants, wine bars and dance floors. The **Stag Hotel** in Rundle Street is in a beautifully restored heritage building with a restaurant and bar, and the **Austral Hotel** in Rundle Street is also well worth a look. The best bar in town for its general ambience and its offerings of local wines is in the old **Botanic Hotel** on the corner of North Terrace and East Terrace. The nearby **Adelaide Casino**, centrally located on North Terrace, is a good spot for a bit of after-dinner fun, or drop in at the **Oxford Hotel** or the **Royal Oak Hotel**, both in O'Connell Street, North Adelaide. Thanks to the demands of its enormous arts festival, Adelaide has many excellent performance-arts spaces, ranging from dugout warehouses to the acoustic perfection of the Festival Centre spaces. Adelaide has its own theatre company, an internationally renowned classical music quartet, a symphony orchestra and probably the most innovative modern dance company in Australia. For cinema goers, the city offers an **Imax cinema** as well as big blockbuster complexes and smaller arthouse cinemas, some of them tourist attractions in their own right. For a full guide to what's on, there is a lift-out entertainment guide in the Adelaide Advertiser on Thursdays.*

ADELAIDE ON FOOT

Botanic Gardens
Guided walks (including Aboriginal trails); self-guide walks

City Parks
Walking and cycling trails in parkland around city and along the River Torrens

East End
Self-guide heritage walk, 'Light on Adelaide', produced by the National Trust

Glenelg
Self-guide heritage walk in Your Guide to Glenelg booklet

North Adelaide
Self-guide heritage walk in O'Connell Street brochure

Port Adelaide
Self-guide heritage walk

St Kilda
Various guided and self-guide walks through mangrove area near town; bookings essential

For further information and bookings, contact the South Australian Travel Centre

sprung up in some east-coast cities. Housed within the beautifully restored old Adelaide Railway Station, the casino prides itself on being at the boutique end of the market. It forms the eastern end of a large entertainment complex that includes the **Adelaide Convention Centre**, **Exhibition Hall** and the appropriately luxurious **Hyatt Regency**. **Holy Trinity Church** (on the south side of North Terrace) is the oldest church in South Australia; construction began in 1838, just two years after the arrival of the Europeans. It provides a wonderful example of very early South Australian colonial architecture. Further along are the **Lion Arts Centre** and **Jam Factory Craft and Design Centre**, near the corner of North Terrace and Morphett Street. These two institutions between them offer something of an overview of the cultural life of South Australia. There are performance and gallery spaces, a cinema, and tours around studios where you can see artists working at their various crafts.

THE RIVER TORRENS

Since the days of early settlement, the River Torrens has provided an essential focus for a city set 10 kilometres from the coastline. Flanked by parkland and a series of must-see attractions, the river has developed as the chief artery of central Adelaide's leisure and entertainment activity. An extensive network of trails and paths provides scenic opportunities for cycling and walking. **Elder Park**, on the southern riverbank, is a popular picnic spot, and its 1882 Rotunda is an Adelaide icon.

The **Adelaide Festival Centre** graces the rise of Elder Park and provides superb views across the river. It serves as a central venue during the Adelaide Festival and is considered to have some of the finest performance space in the world. There is a spectacular environmental sculpture in the Southern Plaza, and the many contemporary tapestries and paintings throughout the building are well worth a look. The South Australian Theatre Museum, also housed here, has a display charting the history of the performing arts.

East of Elder Park are the **Botanic Gardens**, 16 hectares of native and exotic plant species set among artificial lakes and attractions such as the Palm House (an extensive 19th-century glasshouse) and the **Bicentennial Conservatory** (considered to be the largest in the Southern Hemisphere). During February, in odd-numbered years, the gardens host Womadelaide, an international music event. Further north is the **Adelaide Zoo**, which runs along the banks of the River Torrens and can be reached via one of the fleet of Popeye river launches from an Elder Park landing stage. Reptiles and mammals from around the world can be seen. Of special interest is the large variety of native birdlife, including many unusual land and water species.

NORTH ADELAIDE

North Adelaide is set in the large belt of parkland that surrounds the city centre. Head north along King William Road and across the Adelaide Bridge to reach this pretty historic inner suburb, and explore some of the attractions along the way. On the western side of King William Road is the **Adelaide Oval**, said to be one of the most picturesque sporting ovals in the world. The Adelaide Oval Cricket Museum is housed in one of the grandstands, and is a must for enthusiasts. Just off Montefiore Road on Montefiore Hill is **Light's Vision**, where the figure of Colonel Light is immortalised in bronze. From this vantage point visitors can gaze over the city of Adelaide with its broad streets and rolling parklands, and see the lay of the land as Light did when he stood on this spot to map out the city. **St Peter's Cathedral** (foundation stone laid in 1869) in King William Road, is one of Australia's finest ecclesiastical buildings, an exceptional example of the Gothic Revival craze that swept through the colonial cities during this period.

Pennington Gardens provide a perfect backdrop, and make a lovely spot for a picnic. There are many fine old colonial buildings in North Adelaide, from the stately homes and grand hotels with lacework balconies to the tiny stone cottages. In particular, the area around O'Connnell Street, which is the northern extension of King William Road, preserves many fine examples of 19th-century public architecture. It is also one of Adelaide's best shopping and dining precincts.

SEASIDE SUBURBS

The sheltering curve of Gulf St Vincent creates a massive body of calm, clean water fronted by more than 60 kilometres of quiet sandy beaches within the Adelaide metropolitan area. Add to this a near-perfect climate of dry, warm days, and you have a city with great seaside value. This magnificent suburban coastline provides everything you need for a family day out or a more extended stay. There are boats for hire, jetties to fish from, cafes and restaurants offering a wide range of cuisine, promenades and piers for those evening strolls and, if it should rain, there are plenty of indoor attractions for entertainment.

Glenelg, the most famous and easily reached Adelaide beach, is a must for the family – particularly if a visit to **Magic Mountain**, the giant seaside waterslide and amusement centre on Anzac

The seaside suburb of Glenelg

SHOPPING	
	Map Ref.
MELBOURNE STREET, NORTH ADELAIDE Some of the city's most exclusive shops	294 E5
MAGILL ROAD, STEPNEY For antiques and second-hand treasures	297 J4
THE PARADE, NORWOOD A boulevard bursting with great delis, coffee shops, home design stores and bookshops	297 J5
KING WILLIAM ROAD, HYDE PARK Many stylish specialty shops, cafes and boutiques	296 I6
GLEN OSMOND ROAD, EASTWOOD Offers a wide variety of top-label fashions at reduced prices	294 F11
EAST END, RUNDLE STREET Has experienced a retail rebirth; offers good, but not expensive, boutique shopping	294 G8

MARKETS	
	Map Ref.
ORANGE LANE MARKET, NORWOOD Features second-hand goods, homemade produce and local crafts (Sat. & Sun.)	297 K5
BRICKWORKS MARKET, THEBARTON Sells produce and bric-a-brac (Fri.–Sun.)	296 F4
JUNCTION MARKETS, KILBURN A popular market featuring fresh produce (Sat. & Sun.)	298 H11
FISHERMANS WHARF MARKET, PORT ADELAIDE Offers produce and quality bric-a-brac (Sun.)	298 C11
TORRENS ISLAND OPEN MARKET, MOORHOUSE ROAD Fresh fish can be bought direct from the boats (Sun.)	298 D8

SPORT

*For the sports enthusiast, Adelaide offers horseracing at **Victoria Park**, **Morphettville** and **Cheltenham**; greyhound racing at **Angle Park**; tennis, squash, swimming and golf. Pools, water slides, fountains, river rapids, waterfalls, and gym, spa and sauna facilities are a feature of the **Adelaide Aquatic Centre** in North Adelaide. The **City of Adelaide Golf Links** in North Adelaide commands splendid views of the city. **Adelaide Oval**, on King William Road, is a venue for interstate and international cricket matches, and Australian Rules Football which is also played at the **Football Park Stadium** in West Lakes. The **Memorial Drive Tennis Courts** have hosted international players since 1929. The parkland along the river is a perfect place for cycling, walking and jogging.*

The Rotunda, in Elder Park

Highway, is on the agenda. A popular way to reach Glenelg from the city is to take the tram south-west from Victoria Square right to the edge of the beach. Lunch at the magnificent **Stamford Grand**, perhaps, and stroll along the foreshore to see the grand old houses dating back to the time when Glenelg was established as a resort for Adelaide's wealthy. Take a look at the excellent replica of HMS *Buffalo*, the boat that brought the first European settlers to found a new colony. Attached is a museum where the seafaring tales are retold through the exhibits of illustrations, maps, logbooks and other fascinating relics. Or visit the **Old Gum Tree** in McFarlane Street, where the first Europeans came ashore and proclaimed the colony of South Australia.

Continuing north along the coast is West beach, home to the **Woolshed**, which provides a wonderful insight into the shearing history of Australia and includes a children's animal nursery and a restaurant. Next along the coast are **Henley Beach** and **Semaphore**, sharing a relaxed, small seaside village atmosphere, with their generous piers, cafes, and fish and chip shops. Just north of Henley Beach is the suburb of Grange where you will find **Sturt House** (1840), once home to Captain Charles Sturt, who pursued (unsuccessfully) the mythical inland sea, and mapped (successfully) much of Australia's eastern inland river system. The furnished cottage recreates for the visitor an idea of colonial Adelaide. Further north is the **Semaphore Railway**, 2 kilometres of coast-hugging railway line, which takes visitors from **Fort Glanville**, the oldest fort in South Australia, to Semaphore.

If you travel a couple of kilometres inland from here you will reach **Port Adelaide**. This area at the mouth of the Adelaide River was the centre for export trade in Adelaide throughout much of the 19th century, and it remains a well-preserved reminder of the waterfront architecture and culture of that era. There are many significant buildings, including the police station, courthouse, town hall, and various shipping and transport buildings. The **South Australian Maritime Museum** in Lipson Street offers a wealth of memorabilia, chronicling a time when

the sea was South Australia's only link with the rest of the world. There is a re-creation of 19th-century dock life, hands-on replicas of parts of old sailing boats, and a re-creation of the third-class quarters on an immigrant ship of the 1850s. Also in Lipson Street is the **Port Dock Railway Museum**, housing the largest under-cover collection of locomotives, carriages and freight vehicles in Australia. Back towards the water, at the end of Commercial Road, is the **South Australian Military Museum**. There are cruises and fishing trips available from Queens Wharf and McLaren Wharf, near the **Fishermans Wharf Market**. A few blocks north in Ocean Steamers Road is the **Aviation Museum**, which houses the Woomera rocket collection.

St Kilda is located to the north of the city on the outer edge of Torrens Reach. This area is known for its mangrove vegetation and there is an excellent 1.7-kilometre walk along the **St Kilda Mangrove Trail Boardwalk**. While there, stop at the **Australian Electric Transport Museum** which charts the history of the time (1908–58) when trams were the main form of transport in Adelaide. The **St Kilda Adventure Playground** at the end of St Kilda Road is an engineering feat of flying foxes, swings, dips and ships, and is probably one of the best of its kind in Australia.

WESTERN SUBURBS

The inner western suburbs have their share of attractions. The **Historic Adelaide Gaol** is adjacent to Bonython Park, a stroll away from the city. Built in 1840 and last used in 1988, the gaol is open on Sundays and provides a rare glimpse of colonial penal architecture.

In Thebarton, and offering a great family day, is **Mount Thebarton Snow and Ice**. This ice arena boasts the world's first artificial ski slope and a large skating rink. Another one for the young, and the young at heart, is **Kart-Mania** at Richmond, providing safe indoor 'kart' racing and interactive computer games. Another high-tech attraction is the **Investigator Science and Technology Centre** at Wayville, on the inner south-west corner of the city. Packed with hands-on displays, this centre combines a genuine opportunity for some science education with a healthy dose of pleasure.

EASTERN SUBURBS

Heritage lovers might like to head south-east to the suburb of Springfield, where the magnificent **Carrick Hill** is open to the public. The house, built to look like an English manor, was home to Sir Edward Hayward, a prominent retailer. It contains an impressive art collection, plenty of solid oak and English furniture, and is set in a lovely formal garden created in 1939 and inspired by some of the great gardens of England. North-east in Magill is the **Penfolds Magill Estate**, the original vineyard and winery of one of Australia's best-known wine companies, and producers of the nation's most famous red, Grange Hermitage. Tours are available, and occasionally wine clinics are held, where you can bring your aged bottles in for an update and reseal. The tasting and sales facility is in the former distillery, and the restaurant on the property is one of the best in Adelaide.

Surrounded by parkland, Adelaide, with its elegant stone buildings and wide avenues, combines the vitality of a large modern city with an easy-going Australian lifestyle.

DAY TOURS
from Adelaide

Within half an hour of driving in any direction, the suburbs of Adelaide are left behind for a countryside of rolling hills, vineyards which produce some of the best wines in Australia, wild beaches, rugged cliffs, swathes of native bushland, small farms and historic towns.

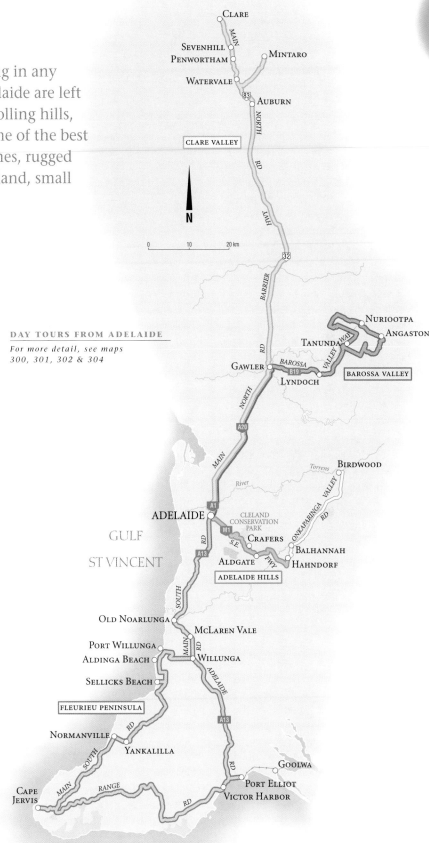

DAY TOURS FROM ADELAIDE

For more detail, see maps 300, 301, 302 & 304

BAROSSA VALLEY

78 km to Nuriootpa via Main North Road A1 A20 *and Barossa Valley Way* B19

A must for visitors to Adelaide is the Barossa, Australia's premier wine-producing region. The district boasts around 50 wineries and many historic buildings, galleries, cafes and restaurants.

To begin your journey, head north from Adelaide along the Main North Road. The Barossa region begins at **Gawler**, a heritage-listed town with fine examples of colonial and Victorian architecture. From here there are many wineries leading off the route, most clearly signposted, so stop and taste at leisure. At Gawler turn east along the Barossa Valley Way to **Lyndoch**, which features an interesting ironstone pub, then on to **Tanunda**. The Barossa Wine and Visitor Centre is here; pick up a guide to the wineries and see the excellent displays on the local wine industry.

From Tanunda continue north along Barossa Valley Way then turn left into Seppeltsfield Road through Marananga, Seppeltsfield and Greenock. At Greenock, head east along Greenock Road to **Nuriootpa**, then south, back along Barossa Valley Way for a short distance before turning left onto the road to **Angaston**. Here the interesting architectural mix of German and English heritage is clearly evident in town. Some of the big wineries, including Yalumba and Saltram, are nearby. From Angaston take the Mengler Hill Scenic Drive which offers some wonderful rustic views of grapevines and rolling hills, best appreciated from Mengler Hill Lookout (watch out for it on the right). Continue through the township of Bethany to Barossa Valley Way and the return journey to Adelaide.

If you plan to eat at one of the many restaurants in the area, book well ahead, particularly on weekends and holidays. On a day trip you can visit about 10 wineries, so find out which ones might interest you. The larger, more commercial wineries are inundated on weekends and holidays. For those who wish to stay overnight, there is a wide range of accommodation, including some excellent B&Bs and historic boutique hotels.

The region is also renowned for its festivals. The major festival is the Barossa Valley Vintage Festival, which starts on Easter Monday each odd-numbered year. In August–September, Gourmet Barossa offers visitors the opportunity to sample and enjoy fine wines and gourmet food. The award-winning Barossa Music Festival is held in October, and Barossa Under the Stars, an open-air concert with internationally acclaimed artists, takes place in February. **See also:** Vineyards and Wineries p. 277; and individual entries in A–Z listing for towns in bold type.

CLARE VALLEY

161 km to Mintaro and Clare via Main North Road **A1** **A20** **32** *and Barrier Highway* **83**
The Clare Valley is a beautiful winegrowing region noted for its rieslings and full-bodied cabernet sauvignons. There are some 30 wineries in this peaceful and relaxed little pocket of the world. Because of its proximity to the Barossa, many are tempted to see the Clare Valley as part of that region, but the two are very different – where the Barossa is home to some of the biggest wineries in the country, Clare is very much a boutique winery area.

Take Main North Road, bypassing the township of Gawler, to Auburn, the first of the Clare Valley's wine townships.

Further north, just past the next township of Leasingham, is the turn-off to **Mintaro**, a place that seems to have escaped modernisation. The village contains a series of small stone buildings,

including the pub, Reilly Wines, Old Devonshire House, the Pay Office Cottage and Mintaro Mews. The magnificent Martindale Hall, just outside the village, is a large 19th-century residence; you can stay there, or just pay a visit.

Return to the highway and continue north to explore the towns of Watervale, Penwortham and Sevenhill and the surrounding wineries. The Sevenhill Cellars winery is where the first grapevines were planted in 1848 by two Jesuit priests who were keen to maintain a steady supply of sacrificial wine. Continue to the town of **Clare**, the commercial and cultural centre of the region. The town began in 1842 and is named after County Clare in Ireland. There are some interesting historic attractions to explore around the town, and information on heritage walks is available from the information centre at the town hall.

There are many charming parks and picnic spots throughout the area, as well as some excellent restaurants (book ahead) and some lovely country-style accommodation. **See also:** Vineyards and Wineries p. 277; and individual entries in A–Z listing for towns in bold type.

FLEURIEU PENINSULA

180 km to Cape Jervis and Port Elliot via South Road **A13** *and Range Road*
The Fleurieu Peninsula starts near the southern coast of Adelaide and stretches down to Cape Jervis, taking in some extraordinarily beautiful country on the way. There are two major areas of interest:

the superb winegrowing region of McLaren Vale with its rustic wineries and lovely historic villages; and the coastal scenery, which ranges from soaring cliffs and roaring surf to wide sandy beaches and gentle coves and bays.

Take South Road to Old Noarlunga and turn left to McLaren Vale. **McLaren Vale** is the centre of the winegrowing region; here you can pick up a map of the area from the information centre in Main Road. There are more than 60 wineries in the area, often in picturesque bush settings, ranging from boutique outfits to some of the big names in the business: Hardy's Tintara Wines, Edwards and Chaffey, Chapel Hill and Wirra Wirra, to name a few. All are well signposted and most have wine-tastings and cellar-door sales. McLaren Vale is one of the best shiraz-producing regions; other successes are grenache and chardonnay.

The region is also a top spot for Australian-grown olives, and some wineries, for example Coriole, do a good sideline in olive products, including excellent olive oil. Almonds, herbs and goats are among other small thriving concerns in the area.

From McLaren Vale take Main Road to **Willunga**, about five minutes away, and discover beautifully preserved old buildings and good shopping for antiques and crafts. Take Aldinga Road east out of town and turn right onto Main South Road for about a kilometre before turning left along Port Road, past some superb historic residences to Port Willunga. This pretty holiday village is where the coastal section

Vineyards in the Barossa region

of the tour begins. Gulf St Vincent fronts this stretch of coastline, so the waters are generally calm and protected. Beach fishing is popular here. Continue down the coast to Aldinga and Sellicks beaches, both very pretty if a little suburbanised. The road then cuts inland and passes through a beautiful hilly stretch – the last of the Mount Lofty Ranges before they drop to the sea. Continue east to the town of **Yankalilla** and on through Normanville to Second Valley, a picturesque spot which, with its protected cove, interesting rock platform and old pier, is the perfect place to unpack that picnic.

The road then winds down to Cape Jervis. This small settlement sits right at the tip of the peninsula and commands a clear view across Backstairs Passage, the strip of water between the peninsula and Kangaroo Island. This is the departure point for the vehicular ferry to the island. From Cape Jervis take Range Road (partly unsealed), which cuts across the bottom of the peninsula to **Victor Harbor**, a village established as a whaling outpost in the 1830s and now one of the State's most popular holiday spots. There are some very good beaches here and plenty of attractions, including the little (fairy) penguin colony on Granite Island (joined to the mainland by a causeway) and some magnificent historic sites. A steam train connects Victor Harbor to the historic townships of **Port Elliot** and **Goolwa**. Do a round trip and return to the city via the Adelaide Road. **See also:** Wildlife-Watching p. 268; Kangaroo Island p. 273;

Vineyards and Wineries p. 277; and individual entries in A–Z listing for towns in bold type.

ADELAIDE HILLS

28 km to Hahndorf via the South Eastern Freeway M1
The Adelaide Hills rise in the south-east out of the flat coastal plain of the city. There are two distinct aspects to the character of this region: the magnificent stretch of native bushland, preserved with conservation zones, right along the eastern border of the outer suburbs; and a provincial blend of farm buildings, vineyards, orchards and market gardens that would call to mind images of Europe if it were not for the clarity of light and sense of openness that are characteristic of the South Australian landscape.

Take the South Eastern Freeway up into the hills, then turn off onto Mount Lofty Summit Road to Mount Lofty. At 727 metres, Mount Lofty is Adelaide's highest point. There is a lookout, an information centre, a summit restaurant, and sensational views over Adelaide and the hills district. From here it's a short trip to Cleland Wildlife Park. Set within the eucalypt paradise of the Cleland Conservation Park, this sanctuary displays a variety of Australian wildlife. Return on the Mount Lofty Summit Road, cross over the freeway and head towards the township of Crafers to explore a network of towns that bear a very English-village character. They include Stirling, which has beautiful trees and historic homes; Aldgate, nestled in a

picturesque valley; and Bridgewater, with its historic water wheel (1860), now part of the restored mill that houses the winemaking and maturation plant for Petaluma's sparkling wines. The restaurant at Bridgewater has a remarkable interior and is the best in the hills area if not the whole of Adelaide.

Rejoin the freeway and head east, taking the turn-off to the town of Hahndorf. This is a most distinctive country town. Silesian and Prussian Lutheran refugees settled it in 1839, seeking escape from religious persecution. Today it stands as a little bit of 19th-century rural Prussia grafted onto the South Australian landscape. The main street, lined with elms, has galleries, boutique shops and restaurants. Hillstowe Wines' cellar-door sales take place from a faithfully restored 1840s cottage and nearby is the recently restored Old Mill. One of the most interesting sites, just outside the town on the road north to Oakbank, is The Cedars, home, studio and garden of Sir Hans Heysen, who depicted the area's beauty so well. Guided tours are available Sunday to Friday. Return to the South Eastern Freeway to head back to Adelaide.

Alternatively, those with an interest in vintage cars can continue north to Birdwood. Take the Balhannah Road north out of Handorf to Balhannah. From here join the Onkaparinga Valley Road to Lobethal and turn off onto the Mount Torrens Road to Birdwood. The main attraction here is the National Motor Museum, which houses the most important motor vehicle collection in Australia.

CLASSIC TOUR
Outback Adventure
Quorn to Blinman via Wilpena Pound and Arkaroola (710 km)

This journey through the Flinders and Gammon ranges provides a taste of the outback via well-maintained roads, enabling a conventional vehicle to be used. These rugged ranges to the north-east of Port Augusta have much to offer: extraordinary rock formations, Aboriginal art sites, a fascinating pastoral history and opportunities for bushwalking, camping and wildlife-watching.

The tour will take at least a week to complete; those with less time could drive to Wilpena and return to Quorn in three or four days.

Before European settlement, the Flinders and Gammon ranges were occupied by the Wailpi, Kuyani, Jadliaura, Piladappa and Pangkala Aboriginal groups. The local ochre and stone was highly prized, making this area a centre for the great north–south trade routes. Today, the local Aborigines live and work in Nepabunna, Leigh Creek and Port Augusta. They identify themselves collectively as the Adnyamathanha, which means 'hills people'. This tour takes you past a number of Adnyamathanha art sites.

AN ADNYAMATHANHA CREATION STORY

Akurra is a giant water snake who has a beard, mane and very sharp fangs. He is the creator and keeper of all permanent waterholes and springs (awi). Akurra lived in the Gammon Ranges. One day he travelled to the plains looking for water. When he came across Lake Frome and Lake Callabonna, he drank them dry.

Because the water was salty Akurra became bloated and his trip back to the ranges was very slow. The heat from the sun warmed his bloated belly and made rumbling sounds that can still be heard over a great distance. As he went Akurra carved out the gorges in which creeks run and made waterholes and springs and finally Ikara (Wilpena Pound) and Ngarri Mudlanha (St Mary Peak).*

*Reproduced from Flinders Ranges National Park: Yura Yarta (Visitor Information, National Parks and Wildlife Service, South Australia, July 1998)

❶ Old railway town
The tour commences in **Quorn**, an old railway town built to service the wheatlands in the 1880s. The wheat failed, and the railway closed. Today, the 19th-century buildings make an attractive picture, with original awnings and ironwork balconies. If you are a railway enthusiast, time your visit to coincide with a trip on the restored steam train that runs along the narrow-gauge Pichi Richi Railway to Stirling North; phone ahead for operating times.

Pichi Richi Railway
Quorn Railway Station
Quorn
Phone: (08) 8395 2566

Kanyaka Homestead Historic Site

❷ Rock wallabies
Leave Quorn via the road that leads to Port Augusta; just after the railway crossing, turn right onto the unsealed road which passes The Dutchmans Stern Conservation Park. You can visit this popular bushwalking area by taking the 2-kilometre detour, just over 6 kilometres from the turn-off. Otherwise, continue to the **Warren Gorge** turn-off, and take the short track down to a pebbly creek bed enclosed by towering cliffs. Warren Gorge is one of the prettiest gorges in the Flinders

Ranges and an ideal campsite. A gentle stream runs through the gorge for most of the year. If you are here at dawn or dusk you are most likely to catch a glimpse of the colony of endearing yellow-footed rock wallabies that inhabit the gorge.

❸ The ruins of a dream
Return to the road and continue north, past stands of native pines and dry creekbeds lined with river red gums, towards **Kanyaka Homestead Historic Site**. You will

pass the turn-offs to Buckaringa and Middle gorges, and Proby's Grave. Hugh Proby founded Kanyaka Station in 1851 at the age of 24; a year later he drowned while attempting to cross the flooded Willochra Creek. The property, which once employed 70 families, was completely abandoned by 1888, after years of drought and flood. Today you can see the sturdy remains of the homestead on your left, just 7 kilometres after joining the sealed Hawker Road. From the

homestead you can drive a kilometre along the creekbed to see the remains of the once-substantial woolshed, a poignant reminder of the sheer scale of this pastoral operation – in 1864, some 40 000 sheep were shorn here.

❹ Charcoal and ochre
Continue north along Hawker Road. Just past the ruins of Wilson Railway Station, turn left onto the unsealed road that leads to **Yourambulla Caves**, one of the

The natural beauty of the Flinders Ranges

Adnyamathanha art sites. There are two rock shelters, both about 30 minutes' walk from the car park (some ladder-climbing involved). As you make the ascent to the shelters, the expansive Willochra Plain opens out below. The largest shelter features mainly charcoal drawings and the other has yellow ochre paintings, including hand stencils.

5 Panoramic views
Continue on to the township of Hawker. The town centre, just off the main road, is a convenient stopping point for fuel and supplies. Like Quorn, this old railway town is now largely dependent on tourism for its survival.

From the main road, turn left along the unsealed road to **Jarvis Hill Lookout**. A marked 1-kilometre loop walk takes you from the car park to the summit of Jarvis Hill and provides panoramic views of the Flinders Ranges and the flat, arid landscape from which they emerge. These marvellous contortions of the earth's crust can be explained as the product of millions of years of geological activity, or in terms of the Adnyamathanha creation stories.

6 Dreamtime serpent
Return to the Hawker–Wilpena Road and continue north. You will pass several lookouts before reaching the turn-off to **Arkaroo Rock**. This important rock-art site, on the slopes of Rawnsley Bluff, just inside the boundary of the Flinders Ranges National Park, is named

after Akurra, the Adnyamathanha Dreamtime serpent. A 2-kilometre walking track leads to the sandstone rock where you will see snake lines, circles and representations of birds painted in charcoal and ochre.

7 Natural amphitheatre
Just north of the Arkaroo Rock turn-off is Rawnsley Bluff Lookout, offering great views of Rawnsley Bluff and the Elder Range. The country becomes increasingly timbered as you approach Wilpena, with rocky outcrops on the left and undulating hills on the right. Turn left at the Wilpena junction. Before you reach the camping and accommodation area, there is a Visitor Information Centre (camping permits can be obtained here) and general store. There is so much to see and do in the area that you should plan to stay at least a couple of nights.

To reach the famous dish-shaped formation known as **Wilpena Pound** you can either catch a shuttle bus from the Visitor Information Centre, or walk from the car park (45 minutes) to Pound Gap. From here, a walking trail (30 minutes) follows the creek to a restored hut built by the Hill family in 1902. The Hills came here to grow wheat and farm sheep and cattle, only to leave in 1914 after a drought-breaking flood washed away their access road. Before the arrival of the Hills, the area was used as a stock enclosure or 'pound'.

The walking track continues up Wangarra Hill for breathtaking views of the natural amphitheatre with its jagged rim. It is believed

that the name 'Wilpena' derives from an Adnyamathanha word for 'cupped hand' or 'bent fingers', and, on viewing the pound, you will see how appropriate that description is. Native vegetation has regenerated and wattles and she-oaks flourish within the pound. At dawn and dusk you are likely to see euros (a type of kangaroo) on the slopes.

8 A special place
While you are staying at Wilpena, take a drive to **Sacred Canyon**, another Adnyamathanha art site. As you walk through this narrow, steep-walled canyon it is not hard to imagine the spiritual significance of the site. The walls have been engraved with images of animal tracks, human figures and waterholes; a rock shelter at the end of the gorge has been painted with ochre.

To reach Sacred Canyon, drive past the Visitor Information

Centre to the Wilpena junction and turn left along the unsealed road. One kilometre after the distinctive Cazneaux Tree, immortalised by photographer Harold Cazneaux in 1937, a road branches off to the right and winds through native pines to Sacred Canyon car park. The canyon entrance is an easy 10-minute walk from here.

9 Sheltered oasis
Drive north from Wilpena on the Wilpena–Blinman Road (unsealed), then take the signposted turn-off to **Bunyeroo Gorge**. The roadside vegetation is varied and interesting: river red gums and blue gums grow along the creek beds, and native pines dominate the plains. In spring, the ubiquitous weed Salvation Jane (Paterson's Curse) adds its purple hues to the landscape. Kangaroos can be seen at dawn and dusk and there is a rich variety of birdlife. Emus, corellas, galahs, honeyeaters and wedge-tailed eagles are some of the species you might see as you drive along. Look out for reptiles too: geckos, blue-tongued lizards, bearded dragons and snakes.

Stop at Bunyeroo Valley Lookout for views across to Wilpena Pound and the vast horizontal layers of the Heysen Ranges. The road descends steeply to follow Bunyeroo Creek. The car park is at the head of Bunyeroo Gorge; continue along the creek on foot. As the water supply is permanent, the gorge is full of plant and animal life. Massive cliffs tower above the river red gums, providing shelter from the harsh environment.

10 Picturesque
Continue about 11 kilometres until you reach a crossroad. Turn right, then left after 500 metres to

Bunyeroo Valley

Brachina Gorge

reach the road to **Aroona Valley**. Sir Hans Heysen painted some of his best-known landscapes while living in an old hut (recently restored) on various expeditions to this picturesque valley. He would explore the surrounding area on foot and set up his fold-away easel to paint the river red gums and multi-hued hillsides that so inspired him. The ruins of Aroona homestead, occupied from 1851 to 1862, are located on the nearby ridge, about 100 metres from the hut.

⑪ Geological trail
Retrace your steps to the cross-road and continue in a westerly direction to **Brachina Gorge**, one of Heysen's favourite subjects. The road is narrow and traverses the creek bed through the

centre of the gorge. Magnificent gums grow beside the creek and the fresh green leaves are in stark contrast to the red sawtooth ridges. Roadside interpretive signs reveal the fascinating geological story of the gorge, layer by layer. Fossils at the western end of the gorge date as far back as 500–1000 million years.

⑫ Abandoned town
Head in a westerly direction to the Hawker–Leigh Creek Road (sealed). Turn right towards Parachilna and

Leigh Creek. If you have time, take a detour at **Parachilna** to see the spectacular scenery alongside the dirt road to Parachilna Gorge. Otherwise continue north past Red Range to Beltana Roadhouse. The old township of **Beltana** is off to the right.

Beltana was established to service the busy Sliding Rock copper mine (1871–7). It was also a focal point during the construction of the Trans Continental Railway in the 1880s; up until 1956, when the line was diverted, it was a railway town. In 1983, the Hawker–Leigh Creek Road was realigned to bypass

Beltana, resulting in the closure of the town's last business. It is now classified as a State Historic Site. Brochures for self-guide walks are available from the roadhouse. Residents still occupy some of the buildings, but the streets have a sense of eerie quiet, and the encroaching saltbush adds to the atmosphere of abandonment.

⑬ Open-cut coalmine
Return to the roadhouse and continue north to **Leigh Creek**, a modern township established to service the open-cut coalmine 22 kilometres north. The original town was built on the coalfield, but when the mine expanded in the 1970s the inhabitants were relocated to this new, purpose-built town.

A 2-kilometre train transports 9000 tonnes of coal from Leigh Creek to Port Augusta each day. You can see the workings of this massive mine on a 3-hour tour that departs each Saturday at 1 p.m., between late March and late October; inquire about additional tours during school holidays. Meet your tour bus at the tourist bay on the main road, 200 metres south of Leigh Creek (no bookings required).

Before you leave Leigh Creek, remember to stock up on

Map labels

To Lyndhurst

Leigh Creek Coalfield
Mt Coffin +835m
Leigh Creek
COPLEY
❼ LEIGH CREEK ⑬
Moolooloo North
Maynards Well
Mt Jeffery 727m
Angepena
Patsy Springs 45
Yankaninna
GAMMON RANGES
GAMMON RANGES NATIONAL
Mt McKinley 1051m
Italowie Gorge
NEPABUNNA
Hawker Hill 756m
18
Mt Painter 790m
Balcanoona
Park Headquarters
⑭ ARKAROOLA
Wooltana
32

Sliding Rock Ck
Warraweena
NORTH
ADNYAMATHANHA
ABORIGINAL
LAND
Wertaloona
39

Beltana Roadhouse
Beltana
BELTANA ⑫
Puttapa
Mt Stuart
Nantawarrina
Narrina
Patawarta Hill 1009m
RED RANGE
RANGES
Mulga View
Wearing Gorge
26
⑮ Mt Chambers Gorge
Mt Chambers 433m
9
Mt Frome +394m
29

PARACHILNA
Parachilna Gorge
11
Commodore
Brachina Gorge ⑪
Aroona Valley ⑩
Great Wall of China
FLINDERS RANGES
Oraparinna
18
Eregunda Valley
BLINMAN ⑯
Wirrealpa
Wirrealpa Ck
35
21
HEYSEN RANGES
22

N
27
Bunyeroo Gorge ⑨
NATIONAL PARK
Bunyeroo Valley Lookout
Willow Springs
Stokes Hill Lookout
29

St Mary Peak 1165m
❼ WILPENA ⑦
Wilpena Pound
Arkaroo Rock ⑥
Rawnsley Bluff
Mt Aleck 1128m
Sacred Canyon ⑧
Rawnsley Bluff Lookout
15
11
17

Moralana
Ck
ELDER RANGE
Arkaba
42
Wonoka
23
FLINDERS
To Cradock

Jarvis Hill Lookout ⑤
Yourambulla Caves ④
Wilson Railway Station (ruins)
Yappala
HAWKER ❼
To Cradock
17
10
7

Kanyaka Homestead Historic Site
Proby's Grave
Middle Gorge
Buckaringa Gorge
Mt Arden 839m
Warren Gorge ②
③
Gordon
37
7
47
30

THE DUTCHMANS STERN CP
QUORN ❼ ①
WILLOCHRA PLAINS
SOUTH FLINDERS

To Port Augusta   To Wilmington

provisions, water and fuel. The next section of the tour – around 250 kilometres – is through rugged country, without facilities.

Leigh Creek Coalfield
Leigh Creek
Phone: (08) 8675 4320

14 Remote and rugged

Drive north to Copley, then turn right along the unsealed road towards Gammon Ranges National Park. The scenery becomes very wild and rugged. Acacias dominate the plains and there are native pines on some slopes, with porcupine grass on the higher ground and river red gums and melaleucas in the gorges.

After Nepabunna Community, the road enters Gammon Ranges National Park and passes through pretty Italowie Gorge. On reaching Balcanoona, where the park headquarters are located, turn left for Arkaroola Wilderness Sanctuary.

Most visitors stay at least two nights at **Arkaroola**, as there are plenty of activities and places to explore. For a breathtaking introduction to the geology and wildlife of this remote region, take the famous Ridgetop Tour. This 4-hour tour reaches dizzy heights and offers views of Lake Frome. Other guided tours include a bush tucker and bush medicine walk with an Adnyamathanha guide. Scenic flights provide another perspective of this magnificent terrain.

There are numerous walking trails, including some gentle walks through the nearby gorges. Dawn and dusk are the best times to sit quietly by a waterhole and watch as the animals come to drink. Once the sun has gone down, you

Ridgetop Tour

can view the clear desert sky through the powerful telescope at the Arkaroola Observatory.

Arkaroola Wilderness Sanctuary
Phone: 1800 676 042

15 Ancient engravings

Retrace your steps to Balcanoona then continue south. Once you leave the national park, the landscape flattens out and the road passes through pastoral stations and across several creeks. After 39 kilometres the road branches; take the right fork to **Mount Chambers Gorge**. En route, you will pass through Wearing Gorge – its cool shade is welcoming. A little further along on the left is the turn-off to Mount Chambers Gorge. Drive into the narrowing gorge; you will have to ford the creek several times and, unless there has been rain, you should be able to reach the

most spectacular part of the gorge, known as Main Bend, in a conventional vehicle. Be prepared to walk a little, though, if the track has deteriorated.

From here, walk north-east along the creekbed for about 500 metres to a gallery of Aboriginal engravings thought to be thousands of years old. A 45-minute walk leads from the gallery through the gorge to a waterhole called Three Sisters Waterhole. This beautiful pool, surrounded by river red gums, is surmounted by the rock formation that gives the place its name. As you walk along, keep an eye out for galahs, little corellas and wedge-tailed eagles. After rain, you might be treated to the gorgeous crimson of Sturt's desert pea in bloom.

16 Old copper town

Return to the main track and turn left, then right at Wirrealpa and on through the Eregunda Valley to **Blinman**. After rain, the valley is a tapestry of wildflowers and the birdlife is prolific.

At 610 metres above sea level, Blinman is South Australia's highest town. In 1869 this was a thriving coppermining town with a population of 1500. Since the mine closed in 1907 it has maintained a much quieter existence. The stories on the gravestones in Blinman cemetery give testimony to the harsh conditions of this once-thriving outback town. Just north-east of town is the Blinman Mine Historic Site. An interesting self-guide trail through the site takes about an hour to complete.

Returning to Hawker and on to Adelaide

From Blinman, head south for Wilpena. You will pass the Great Wall of China on the left. It is a wall-like limestone ridge, but you won't confuse it with the real thing! Drive through the Flinders Ranges National Park, stopping at Stokes Hill Lookout for sweeping views of distant ranges. From Wilpena take the Hawker–Wilpena Road to Hawker.

From Hawker, you can drive to Adelaide via Quorn and Port Pirie (425 kilometres), or take a more scenic route, via Cradock, Orroroo, Jamestown and the towns of the Clare Valley wine region (376 kilometres).

Kangaroo at waterhole

BE PREPARED

Beyond Wilpena, much of the tour is on unsealed roads. These roads are suitable for two-wheel drive vehicles but not all are safe for trailers or caravans. There are many creek crossings in the Flinders Ranges. Heavy rain can cut access and unsealed roads become treacherous after rain. Phone the Northern Roads Condition Hotline on 1300 361 033 before departure.

Wilpena and Arkaroola have camping and tourist accommodation and there are plenty of bush camps along the route, as well as farm-based accommodation and hotels/motels in larger centres. September and October are popular months, so remember to book ahead. Allow a leisurely pace, avoiding strenuous bushwalks, if you are taking this tour at the height of summer. Fire bans are enforced in the national parks from November to April, so campers should bring a portable gas stove (you may not gather firewood at any time).

The Flinders and Gammon ranges are popular bushwalking areas, but do not attempt long walks without preparing thoroughly: the terrain is difficult and water scarce.

To ensure you are prepared for outback driving, read the section on Outback Motoring on page 603.

SOUTH AUSTRALIA from A to Z

Historic Collingrove near Angaston

Aldinga Beach   Pop. 4638

MAP REF. 301 E4, 302 A11, 305 B3, 307 K10
A holiday town 49 km S of Adelaide, near the Fleurieu Peninsula, known for its good fishing, surfing, and diving. **In town:** Gnome Caves, Aldinga Beach Rd, for children. Aldinga Market, Old Coach Rd, 1st Sat. each month. **In the area:** Self-guide historic walk around Aldinga and Willunga, brochure available. Aldinga Bay Winery, 3 km SE. At Aldinga, 4 km NE: St Ann's Anglican Church (1866); Uniting Church (1863). McLaren Vale, 16 km NE, centre of winegrowing region; more than 60 wineries. Sellicks Beach, 8 km S, boat access and good fishing. Maslin Beach, 10 km N, Australia's first nude bathing beach. At Port Willunga, 3 km NW: wreck of *Star of Greece* (1888) visible at low tide; Star of Greece Cafe, overlooking wreck. Bush trails through Aldinga Scrub Conservation Park, 1.6 km from Aldinga, brochures available. Off-shore, Aldinga Aquatic Reserve has a rare reef formation and good diving. Lookout, 6 km SW, views of Gulf St Vincent. Lookout, 23 km SW, views of Myponga Reservoir. **Visitor information:** Aldinga Bay Holiday Village, Esplanade; (08) 8556 5019. **See also:** Day Tours from Adelaide p. 253; Vineyards and Wineries p. 277.

Andamooka   Pop. 506

MAP REF. 308 G4
Andamooka, surrounded by opal fields, is about 600 km N of Adelaide, to the west of the saltpan Lake Torrens. The road to Andamooka from the turn-off at Roxby Downs is now sealed. The town is off the beaten track, summer conditions are harsh, the weather is severe and water is precious. Many people live in dugouts to avoid the heat. Visitors need a precious-stone prospecting permit from the Mines Department in Adelaide before staking out a claim. Looking for opals on mullock dumps requires permission from claim owners. There are tours, including underground, and showrooms with opals for sale. **In town:** Andamooka Heritage Trail and other self-guide walks/drives, brochures available. In Main St: Duke's Bottle House, made of empty beer bottles; Andamooka Gems and Trains, mineral specimens, model railway; quaint 1930s miners' cottages, next to creek bed. Market, Sun. of long weekends (May, June, Oct.). Art and craft market, 1st Sun. each month. Easter: Family Fun Day. Oct.: Opal Festival. **In the area:** Self-guide walk/drive, brochure available. **Visitor information:** 275 Opal Creek Boulevard; (08) 8672 7007. **See also:** The Outback p. 278.

Angaston   Pop. 1862

MAP REF. 300 G4, 304 I5, 307 M8
Angaston is high in the Barossa Valley; within 79 km of the coast, it is 361 m above sea level. The town is named after 1830s Barossa Valley settler, George Fife Angas. **In town:** Angas Park Fruit Co., Murray St, dried fruit and nuts. A & H Doddridge Blacksmith Shop (1873), Murray St, once the industrial heart of the village, now restored, tools of trade on display. For local art and craft, Bethany Arts and Crafts, Washington St. The Lego Man, Jubilee Ave, collection of Lego models dating back to 1959. Feb.: Barossa Under the Stars (concert with international performers). Easter: Barossa Vintage Festival (odd-numbered years). Aug.–Sept.: Gourmet Barossa. Oct.: Barossa Music Festival. **In the area:** Good view of Barossa Valley from Mengler's Hill Lookout, 8 km SW. Saltram Wine Estate, 1 km W. Yalumba Winery, 2 km S. Collingrove homestead (1850), 7 km SE, National Trust property once owned by Angas pioneering family; viewing and accommodation (meals by prior arrangement only). Henschke Cellars, 10 km SE. Eden Valley and Mountadam wineries at Eden Valley, 19 km SE. At Springton, 27 km SE: Grand Cru Estate; Herbig Tree, large hollow river red gum, first home of the Herbig family (information board, historic photos); Herbig Homestead Heritage Centre (open by appt); Merindah Mohair Farm. Yookamurra Sanctuary, 54 km NE, for local wildlife and plant species (check opening times); guided walks and tours and accommodation (bookings essential). **Visitor information:** Barossa Wine and Visitor Centre, 66 Murray St, Tanunda; (08) 8563 0600, freecall 1800 812 662. **See also:** Day Tours from Adelaide p. 253; Vineyards and Wineries p. 277.

Ardrossan   Pop. 1081

MAP REF. 307 J7
Ardrossan, 148 km NW of Adelaide, is the largest port on Yorke Peninsula's east coast. An important outlet for wheat, barley and dolomite, it is an attractive town with excellent crabbing (blue crabs) and fishing from the jetty. **In town:** Ardrossan and District Historical Museum, Fifth St. The stump jump

plough (late 1800s) was invented here; restored plough on display on cliffs in East Tce. **In the area:** Salt and dolomite mines. BHP Lookout, 2 km S, excellent views of Gulf St Vincent. For keen divers, *Zanoni* wreck off coast, 20 km SE (permission essential, from Department for Environment, Heritage and Aboriginal Affairs, Heritage South Australia, (08) 8204 9245). Clinton Conservation Park, 40 km N, tidal shallows attract migratory waterbirds. **Visitor information:** Ardrossan Bakery, 39 First St; (08) 8837 3015. Web site www.classiccountry.org.au/ardrossan.html **See also:** The Yorke Peninsula p. 281.

Arkaroola   Pop. 24

MAP REF. 303 H1, 309 M3

Arkaroola is a remote settlement, founded 1968, in the northern Flinders Ranges, about 660 km N of Adelaide. It is set on Arkaroola Wilderness Sanctuary, a privately owned property of 61 000 ha. The area is crossed by incredible quartzite ridges, deep gorges and rich mineral deposits, and is a haven for birdlife and rare marsupials. **In town:** Astronomical Observatory, access by tour only. Guided bush tucker, bush medicine and Dreamtime walking tour. Various self-guide walks. **In the area:** At nearby Gammon Ranges National Park, ruins of Cornish-style Bolla Bollana Smelters (1861). Scenic waterholes Bolla Bollana, and Nooldoonooldoona, 12 km NW. Weetootla Gorge, 31 km SW, permanent springs. Italowie Gorge, 42 km SW, 4WD vehicles required; experienced bushwalkers only. Big Moro Gorge, with rock pools, 59 km S (Aboriginal Land Permit required for entry, contact Nepabunna Community Council, (08) 8648 3764); access to gorge may require 4WD. Mt Chambers Gorge, 98 km S, has Aboriginal rock carvings. Marked walking trails, self-guide brochures available. 4WD tours: Ridgetop Tour, spectacular 42-km trip across Australia's most rugged mountains including Mt Painter and Mt Gee, breathtaking views of Yudnamutana Gorge and Lake Frome (salt lake); other 'tagalong' tours (your own 4WD in an organised convoy). Scenic flights, guided tours. **Visitor information:** Arkaroola Travel Centre, 37e Dulwich Ave, Dulwich (Adelaide suburb); (08) 8431 7900. Web site www.arkaroola.on.net **See also:** Outback Adventure p. 256; National Parks p. 262.

Balaklava   Pop. 1441

MAP REF. 307 K6

Balaklava, on the banks of the River Wakefield 91 km N of Adelaide, was named after a battle in the Crimean War. **In town:** National Trust Museum, May Tce, has relics of district's early days of European settlement (check opening times). Court House Gallery and Shop, Edith Tce, community art gallery. Urlwin Park Agricultural Museum, Short Tce. Lions Club Walking Trail along Wakefield River, brochure available. Racecourse, Racecourse Rd, major country racecourse. Aug.: Balaklava Cup. Sept.: Agricultural Show. Oct.: Garden and Gallery Festival (even-numbered years). **In the area:** Weekend glider joy-flights. Devils Gardens, 7 km NE on Auburn Rd, and The Rocks Reserve, 10 km E; both with picnic facilities. Beachside town of Port Wakefield, 26 km W at head of Gulf St Vincent. **Visitor information:** Country Gardens Coffee Shoppe, 14 Edith Tce; (08) 8862 2123. Web site www.classiccountry.org.au/balaklava.html

Barmera   Pop. 1837

MAP REF. 307 P7

The sloping shores of Lake Bonney make a delightful setting for this Riverland town, 214 km NE of Adelaide. Lake Bonney is ideal for swimming, water-skiing, sailing, boating and fishing. The surrounding irrigated areas are mainly vineyards but there are also apricot and peach orchards and citrus groves. Soldier settlement after WW I marked the start of the town. **In town:** Donald Campbell Obelisk, Queen Elizabeth Dr., commemorates Campbell's attempt on world water-speed record in 1964. Rocky's Country Hall of Fame, Barwell Ave. Bonneyview Wines, Sturt Hwy, has restaurant and wine-tasting. Canoe tours, jetski hire. Easter: Lake Bonney Yachting Regatta. June: SA Country Music Festival and Awards. Oct.: Sheepdog trials. Dec.: Christmas Pageant and Fireworks. **In the area:** At North Lake, 10 km NW, ruins of Napper's Old Accommodation House (1850) preserved by National Trust. Loch Luna Game Reserve, 16 km NW. At Overland Corner, 19 km NW on Morgan Rd: hotel (1859), now also National Trust museum; self-guide historical walk. Highway Fern Haven, 5 km E on Sturt Hwy, rare ferns in tropical setting. At Cobdogla, 5 km W: Irrigation and Steam Museum, with the only working

Humphrey Pump in the world, photos and memorabilia of Loveday Internment Camp (self-guide drive to remains of camp site, 3 km SW), brochure available, as well as steam rides, historic displays and picnic areas; Chambers Creek, for canoeing and prolific birdlife; Easter Sunday Craft Expo. Moorook Game Reserve, 16 km SW, includes Wachtels Lagoon with birdlife and walking trail. Nearby, Yatco Lagoon abounds with a variety of birdlife. **Visitor information:** Barwell Ave; (08) 8588 2289.

Beachport   Pop. 441

MAP REF. 305 F11

First settled as a whaling station in the 1830s, Beachport is 51 km S of Robe. Rivoli Bay nearby provides safe swimming as well as shelter for lobster boats. One of the State's longest jetties stretches into Rivoli Bay and is popular with anglers. **In town:** Old Wool and Grain Store, Railway Tce, now National Trust Museum with whaling, shipping and local history exhibits. Artifacts Museum, McCourt St, Aboriginal heritage displays. Centenary Park, in town centre, has barbecues, tennis courts, playgrounds and skateboard track. Heritage walk, maps from National Trust Museum; other walking trails, maps from District Council. Oct.: Festival by the Sea. **In the area:** At Lake George, 4 km N: waterbirds, windsurfing and fishing. Beachport Conservation Park, between Lake George and the Southern Ocean, features Aboriginal shell middens and Jack and Hilda McArthur Walk; 1.2-km signposted flora trail around Wolley Lake (accessed from Five Mile Drift Rd). Bowman Scenic Drive from base of lighthouse to Woolleys Rock (5 km N) for spectacular views of Southern Ocean; on the way, swim in Pool of Siloam, a lake with high salt content and reputed therapeutic benefits. Woakwine Cutting, 10 km N on Robe Rd, extraordinary drainage project, with observation platform and machinery exhibit. **Visitor information:** Wattle Range Council, 24 McCourt St; (08) 8735 8029.

Berri   Pop. 3912

MAP REF. 307 Q7

The commercial centre of the Riverland region, Berri is 227 km NE of Adelaide. Once a wood-refuelling stop for paddle-steamers and barges that plied the Murray River, the town was proclaimed in 1911. This is fruit- and vine-growing

National Parks

Nowhere else in Australia can wildlife be seen in such close proximity and in such profusion as in the parks of South Australia. To protect its valuable native animals and plants, and to conserve the natural features of the landscape, this State has set aside over 20 per cent of its total area as national parks and other conservation areas.

From the harsh beauty of the outback to the tranquillity of coastal and inland waterways, South Australia's parks and reserves have much to offer those who enjoy camping, bushwalking and wildlife-watching.

The range of climatic zones enables visitors to spend time in these parks and reserves throughout the year; coastal parks are cool in summer and autumn, while mountain areas are ideal in winter and spring. In summer, however, many of the State's parks are very hot and have a high fire danger. If planning to visit during the peak fire season, check bushfire danger and fire restrictions. Contact National Parks and Wildlife, South Australia, (08) 8204 1910, for more details.

AROUND ADELAIDE

Cleland Wildlife Park is located in the natural bushland of **Cleland Conservation Park**, on the slopes of Mount Lofty overlooking Adelaide. Here visitors are able to walk freely among the animals, which are housed in areas similar to their native habitat.

Within Adelaide's southern suburbs is **Belair National Park**, established with great foresight in 1891. The park features a wide range of recreational facilities such as ovals, tennis courts, picnic shelters, barbecues and a playground. Visitors can also take one of the self-guide walks or join a tour of Old Government House.

The Cazneaux Tree, near Wilpena in the Flinders Ranges National Park

IN THE SOUTH-EAST OF THE STATE

Coorong National Park, one of the State's finest, is 185 kilometres from Adelaide, south of the Murray River mouth. Named from the Aboriginal word *karangh*, meaning 'narrow neck', the Coorong is a series of saltwater lagoons fed by the Murray and separated from the sea by Younghusband Peninsula. The park contains wetlands of international importance. There are six island bird sanctuaries, which are prohibited to the public. These islands house rookeries of pelicans, crested terns and silver gulls. More than 200 species of birds have been recorded in the Coorong. You can take the pleasant drive along the coast road beside the waterway, stopping to camp or picnic. The ocean beach is a favourite haunt of anglers. At dusk, kangaroos and wombats can be seen feeding on the grassed open areas in the park.

Bool Lagoon Game Reserve is on the southern plains of South Australia, near Naracoorte. The lagoon's natural cycle of flooding and drying makes a perfect breeding ground for waterbirds. In spring, when the water is deepest, thousands of black swans crowd the lagoon. In summer and autumn, when the water is shallow, waterfowl and waders flock to feed on the rich plant life. Bool Lagoon is also the largest permanent ibis rookery in Australia. Dense thickets of paperbark and banks of reeds in the reserve's central reaches provide a safe breeding ground. Boardwalks allow access to wildlife without disturbing the environment.

The World Heritage-listed **Naracoorte Caves** are in a small conservation park in the south-east of the State. These impressive caves enclose a wonderland of stalagmites, stalactites, shawls, straws and other calcite formations. Four of the limestone caves, including Blanche Cave, the first to be discovered (1845), are open for inspection through guided or adventure tours. The Wonambi Fossil Centre, (08) 8762 2340, gives visitors the chance to see life-like representations of extinct animals, such as the giant browsing kangaroos, a hippopotamus-sized wombat and a marsupial lion, that roamed the area 200 000 years ago.

IN THE SOUTH-WEST OF THE STATE

Flinders Chase National Park, encompassing most of the western end of Kangaroo Island, protects pristine natural vegetation including mallee, forests and stunted coastal plants. Bushwalkers can enjoy trails along creeks to secluded beaches, or follow the rugged coastline to observe the full force of the Southern Ocean. Lighthouses and keepers' cottages provide cultural interest. Visitors are provided with opportunities to see kangaroos, koalas, fur seals, echidnas and platypuses. **Seal Bay Conservation Park**, also on Kangaroo Island, allows visitors to see

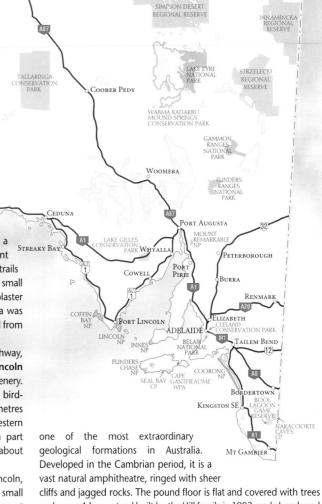

Australian sea-lion breeding colonies. The neighbouring **Cape Gantheaume Wilderness Protection Area** is a popular area for experienced bush-walkers. Camping is available in the adjacent Cape Gantheaume Conservation Park areas. More information is available from National Parks and Wildlife, 37 Dauncey St, Kingscote; (08) 8553 2381.

On the south-west tip of Yorke Peninsula is **Innes National Park**, where the ground is blanketed with wildflowers in spring and birdwatching is a favourite pastime. As well as native bushland and magnificent coastal scenery, there are many excellent fishing spots. Walking trails lead to the coast and to the historic ruins of Inneston (1913). This small settlement once housed miners who dug for gypsum, used for plaster and chalk; for many years nearly every schoolchild in Australia was taught with the aid of blackboard chalk mined here and shipped from Stenhouse Bay. Camping and accommodation are available.

The Eyre Peninsula, bordered to the north by the Eyre Highway, contains a number of parks. **Coffin Bay National Park** and **Lincoln National Park** feature wilderness areas and spectacular coastal scenery. Both parks provide excellent opportunities for bush camping, bird-watching and bushwalking. Coffin Bay National Park is 50 kilometres west of Port Lincoln and includes Coffin Bay Peninsula. The western coastline faces the Great Australian Bight while the eastern part has sheltered sandy beaches and islands. Inquire locally about safe swimming.

Lincoln National Park, a 15-kilometre drive south of Port Lincoln, occupies a large part of Jussieu Peninsula and is surrounded by small islands. At its northern tip, on Stamford Hill, the Flinders Monument commemorates exploration by Matthew Flinders in 1802. From this hill visitors can enjoy spectacular views of the surrounding area.

Diverse bird habitats are provided by salt lakes, dry mallee and western myall vegetation at **Lake Gilles Conservation Park**, also on Eyre Peninsula.

IN THE NORTH OF THE STATE

The Flinders Ranges, extending for 430 kilometres, contain three national parks. **Mount Remarkable National Park** lies in a rugged and dense area of the southern Flinders Ranges. Mount Remarkable itself rises to 960 metres, and provides spectacular views of the surrounding country. The rock is red quartzite and glows a beautiful red at sunset. Two creeks flow through the park, providing water for river red gums, white cypress pines and brilliant wildflowers in spring. Alligator Gorge, the weathered red cliffs of which are a photographer's delight, and Mambray Creek, have a number of well-marked walking trails.

The **Flinders Ranges National Park** is one of the major national parks in Australia. The Wilpena section, in the south, comprises Wilpena Pound and the Wilpena Pound Range, covering 10 000 hectares. The pound is one of the most extraordinary geological formations in Australia. Developed in the Cambrian period, it is a vast natural amphitheatre, ringed with sheer cliffs and jagged rocks. The pound floor is flat and covered with trees and grass. A homestead built by the Hill family in 1902, and abandoned after floods in 1914, stands as a reminder of the difficulties of farming in this environment. Rock paintings at Arkaroo Rock indicate that this was a significant area in Aboriginal mythology. Twenty-five kilometres north of Wilpena is the Oraparinna section of the park; this was a sheep station last century, at one time maintaining more than 20 000 sheep.

Further north the **Gammon Ranges National Park**, an arid, isolated region of rugged ranges and deep gorges, provides visitors with the experience of an extensive wilderness area. The mountains sparkle with exposed formations of quartz, fluorspar, hematites and ochres (fossicking is not permitted in geological sites). The Gammon Ranges are a sanctuary for many species of native fauna, including the western grey kangaroo, the big red kangaroo, the euro or hill kangaroo and the yellow-footed rock wallaby. Nearby, the remote settlement of Arkaroola offers motel accommodation and a serviced camping ground.

Further north, in the State's arid lands, over 9 million hectares have been set aside to protect the unique desert environment. All parks and reserves in this vast desert area require a Desert Parks Pass; they include Lake Eyre National Park, Witjira National Park, Innamincka Regional

Reserve, Simpson Desert Conservation Park and Regional Reserve, **Strzelecki Regional Reserve**, **Tallaringa Conservation Park**, **Wabma Kadarbu Mound Springs Conservation Park** and **Unnamed Conservation Park**. Passes can be obtained from the Marree Outback Roadhouse; (08) 8675 8360, The Environment Shop in Adelaide or at 9 Mackay St, Port Augusta; (08) 8648 5300. The pass is valid for 12 months from the date of purchase. It enables visitors to enter the parks as many times as they wish and to camp for 5 nights at a time in any one location. The pass is supplied with the *Desert Parks South Australia Handbook*, which also includes detailed information and maps on each park and reserve.

Lake Eyre, the central feature of the park of the same name, is one of the world's greatest salinas or salt lakes and is 15 metres below sea level at its lowest point. Ironically, it is the hub of a huge internal drainage system while located in the driest part of the Australian continent. Vegetation is sparse, but after heavy rains, when the area floods, the ground is carpeted with colourful wildflowers, the lake teems with fish and birds flock to the area. Care needs to be taken when visiting this area; access to the park is by 4WD and campers must be fully self-sufficient.

Witjira National Park, 170 kilometres north of Oodnadatta, is an area of vast desert, gibber plains, sand dunes, saltpans and mound springs, upwellings of the Great Artesian Basin. Visitors may explore this extremely arid environment from the park's oasis, Dalhousie Springs.

The **Innamincka Regional Reserve** covers much of the flood-prone country around the Cooper and Strzelecki creeks up to the Queensland border. These arid wetlands, which comprise a series of semi-permanent overflow lakes, hold many surprises for birdwatchers.

The **Simpson Desert Conservation Park**, which is for the more adventurous park visitor, consists of spectacular red sand dunes, which in places can run parallel for hundreds of kilometres, as well as salt lakes, flood-out plains, hummock grasslands, gibber desert, gidgee woodland, tablelands and mesas. Access to the park is by 4WD only.

IN THE WEST OF THE STATE

Situated along the Eyre Highway in the far west corner of the State, the **Nullarbor National Park** offers spectacular views of the Great Australian Bight. The park itself is entirely desert, with patches of mallee scrub and some ground cover of bluebush and saltbush; it is renowned for its unique desolate beauty. The Nullarbor Plain's substratum of limestone has been eroded to form one of the largest underwater cave systems in the world, popular with experienced potholers and cave divers. Access to the caves is available only through arrangement with the Far West District Office, 11 McKenzie St, Ceduna; (08) 8625 3144. The park is home to several nocturnal species, including a large population of southern hairy-nosed wombats.

Many of South Australia's national parks charge camping and entrance fees. For information on camping restrictions, fees, annual and short-term passes, and other details relating to the State's national parks, contact The Environment Shop, 77 Grenfell St, Adelaide (GPO Box 1047, Adelaide SA 5001); (08) 8204 1910. Web site www.parksweb.sa.gov.au

The Great Australian Bight forms the southern boundary of the Nullarbor National Park

country, dotted with peaceful picnic and fishing areas. **In town:** Earth Works, Sturt Hwy, for local art and craft. Berri Art Gallery, Wilson St. Water Tower Lookout (17 m), Fiedler St, for panoramic views of river and town. Nearby, sculpture and cave memorial to Jimmy James, Aboriginal tracker. Houseboats and canoes for hire, contact information centre. Feb.: Rodeo; Speedboat Spectacular (subject to river condition). Easter: Carnival. Nov.: Art and Craft Fair. **In the area:** On Sturt Hwy: dried fruit and confectionery at Angas Park Kiosk, 3 km W; Berri Estates winery and distillery, largest winemaking facility in Southern Hemisphere, 13 km W. Murray River National Park, 10 km SW, features Kia Kia Nature Trail for bushwalkers. Martin's Bend, 2 km E, popular for water-skiing and picnicking. Berrivale Orchards, 4 km N on Sturt Hwy, has educational audiovisual on Riverland's history and various stages in fruit-processing (open Mon.–Fri., Sat. a.m.). Wilabalangaloo flora and fauna reserve, 5 km N, off Sturt Hwy: walking trails, spectacular scenery, museum and paddlewheeler (check opening times). Rollerama roller-skating centre nearby. At Monash, 12 km NW on Morgan Rd, Monash Adventure Playground, features maze, flying fox, rope bridge. Nearby, Norman's Winery. **Visitor information:** 24 Vaughan Tce; (08) 8582 1655.

Blinman Pop. 30

MAP REF. 305 E5, 309 K6
Blinman, 478 km N of Adelaide and 30 km from the Flinders Ranges National Park, is the sole survivor of numerous mining townships surveyed in the area in the 19th century. The town was a thriving coppermining centre 1860–75 and 1882–1907. Blinman's population peaked at 1500 in 1869. **In town:** Historic buildings in Mine Rd: pug and pine miners' cottages (c. 1870), school (1883), police station and cells (1885), memorial hall (1896), hotel (1869). May: Land Rover Jamboree. Oct.: Picnic Gymkhana and Races. **In the area:** Mawson (bike) Trail (Adelaide to Blinman) ends here, brochures from Recreation SA, (08) 8416 6677. Blinman Mine Historic Site, just NE of town: 1-km self-guide walk (approx. 1 hr), signs explaining history and geology of the site, brochure available. Great Wall of China, limestone ridge, 10 km S on Wilpena Rd. Further south, beautiful Aroona Valley and ruins of old Aroona

Old copper mine, Burra

homestead; nearby Brachina Gorge. Scenic Glass Gorge, beautiful wildflowers in spring, and Parachilna Gorge, both between Blinman and Parachilna; nearby, the Blinman Pools, fed by a permanent spring. Scenic drive east through Eregunda Valley, then north-east to Mt Chambers Gorge with its rock pools and Aboriginal carvings, then north-west to view spectacular Big Moro Gorge off Arkaroola Rd (Aboriginal Land Permit required, contact Nepabunna Land Council, (08) 8648 3764; access to gorge may require 4WD). **Visitor information:** Post office, Mine Rd; (08) 8648 4874. **See also:** Outback Adventure p. 256; National Parks p. 262.

Bordertown Pop. 2337

MAP REF. 305 H6
Bordertown is a quiet town on the Dukes Hwy, 274 km SE of Adelaide. In 1852 it became an important supply centre for the goldfields of western Victoria. Today the area produces wool, cereals, meat and vegetables. **In town:** Robert J. L. Hawke, former Australian Prime Minister, was born here. His childhood home, in Farquhar St, includes memorabilia (open Mon.–Fri.). Apex park, Woolshed St. **In the area:** Bordertown Wildlife Park, Dukes Hwy, has native birds and animals, including pure white kangaroos. Historic Clayton Farm, 3 km S, features vintage farm machinery and thatched buildings (open p.m. Sun.–Fri.). Clayton Farm Vintage Field Day, held Oct. long weekend. At Mundulla, 10 km SW: Mundulla

Hotel (1884), National Trust building with restaurant, tearooms and craft shop. At Padthaway, 42 km SW, 1882 homestead housing Padthaway Estate winery (meals and accommodation). Nearby, picnic areas among magnificent red gums and stringybarks at Padthaway Conservation Park. Bangham Conservation Park, 30 km SE, near the town of Frances, significant habitat for the red-tailed black cockatoo. **Visitor information:** Council Chambers, 43 Woolshed St; (08) 8752 1044.

Burra Pop. 1008

MAP REF. 307 L5
Nestled in Bald Hills Range, 154 km N of Adelaide, this former coppermining centre is one of the country's best-preserved mining towns. Copper was discovered in 1845 and extraction valued almost $10 million before the mine closed in 1877. The district of Burra Burra is now noted for stud merino sheep, and Burra is the market town for surrounding farms. *Breaker Morant* was filmed here in 1980. **In town:** Burra Heritage Passport allows a walk or drive around 11 km of heritage buildings, museums, mine shafts and lookout points. Daily bus tours of town and its mining history; bookings essential. Antique shops, Commercial St. Burra Creek miners' dugouts, alongside Blyth St, where over 1500 people lived during the boom; 2 dugouts preserved. Cemetery, off Spring St. Heritage and cemetery walks, details from information centre. Burra Mine Open Air Museum, off

Market St, with Enginehouse Museum built 1858 and reconstructed 1986 near archaeological excavation of 30-m entry tunnel to Morphett's Shaft; also features ore dressing tower, powder magazine and offers views of open-cut mine and town. Market Square Museum, opposite information centre. Malowen Lowarth Cottage, Kingston St, old miner's cottage. In Bridge Tce: underground cellars of old Unicorn Brewery; Paxton Square Cottages (1850), 33 two-, three- and four-roomed cottages built for Cornish miners, now visitor accommodation. In Burra North: antique shops; police lockup and stables (1849), Tregony St; Redruth Gaol (1857), off Tregony St; Ryan's Deer Farm, opposite gaol, includes animal nursery; Bon Accord Mine buildings (1846), Railway Tce, now a museum complex. Picturesque spots on Burra Creek for swimming, canoeing and picnicking. Feb.: Rock'n'Roll Festival. Mar.: Twilight Jazz Affair. May: Antique and Decorating Fair. **In the area:** Chatswood Farm Gallery, 14 km s at Hanson. Scenic 90-km Dares Hill Drive, begins 30 km N near Hallett (maps available). Barracas Park Alpacas, eastern outskirts of town (off Paradise St). Burra Trail Rides, 4 km E. Mongolata gold mine, 27 km E, tours by appt. Burra Gorge, 27 km SE. **Visitor information:** Visitor Centre, 2 Market Sq.; (08) 8892 2154. Web site www.classiccountry.org.au/burra.html

Ceduna   Pop. 2599

MAP REF. 315 N9

Near the junction of the Flinders and Eyre hwys, Ceduna is the last major town before you cross the Nullarbor east–west; the place to check your car and stock up on food and water before the long drive. Ceduna is set on Murat Bay with its sandy coves, sheltered bays and offshore islands. It is an ideal base for swimming, diving, fishing, water-skiing, windsurfing and boating. The port at Thevenard, 3 km SW, handles bulk grain, gypsum and salt. The fishing fleet is noted for its large whiting hauls. Snapper, salmon, tommy ruff and crab are other catches. There was a whaling station on St Peter Island in the 1850s. According to map references in Swift's *Gulliver's Travels*, the tiny people of Lilliput might well have lived on St Peter Is. (visible from Thevenard) or the Isles of St Francis. **In town:** Old Schoolhouse National Trust Museum, Park Tce, pioneering items and artifacts from atomic testing at Maralinga (open Mon.–Sat.). Sea Dragon Art Gallery, cnr Day and

O'Loughlin Tce, works by local artists (check opening times). Easter: Horse-racing Carnival. Sept.: Agricultural Show. Oct.: Oyster-Fest. **In the area:** Paul's Fish Factory at Thevenard Boat Haven, fresh seafood (best prior to 9 a.m.). At Denial Bay, 13 km W: McKenzie Ruins, site of original settlement; Clear Water Oyster Farm, tours. Picnicking, surfing and safe fishing: west of town at Denial Bay and Davenport Creek, with its pure white sandhills; and to the south-east at Decres Bay, Laura Bay and Smoky Bay (boat charter for diving and fishing available at Ceduna). Southern right whales can be seen June–Oct. along coast west of Ceduna particularly at Head of Bight, 300 km W (daytrips, contact information centre). At Penong, 73 km W: more than 40 windmills which draw town's water from underground; Penong Woolshed museum with local crafts; Goanywea camel day-rides and safaris (May–Oct.). Amazing sand dunes and excellent surf at Cactus Beach, 94 km W. Spectacular coastline includes prominent headland at Point Brown, 56 km SE, noted for its surf beaches, salmon fishing and coastal walks. **Visitor information:** Ceduna Gateway Visitor Information Centre, 58 Poynton St (closed p.m. weekends); (08) 8625 2780, freecall 1800 639 413. Web site www.epta.com.au **See also:** Wildlife-Watching p. 268; The Eyre Peninsula p. 284.

Clare   Pop. 2815

MAP REF. 307 L5

Set in rich agricultural and pastoral country, this charming town was first settled by Europeans in 1842; it was named after County Clare in Ireland. The area is famed for its prize-winning table wines. Wheat, barley, honey, stud sheep and wool are other important regional industries. The first vines were planted by Jesuit priests at Sevenhill in 1848; today Sevenhill Cellars still produces table and sacramental wines. **In town:** Gift Horse Gallery, 130 Main Rd. National Trust museum in old police station (1850), cnr Victoria Rd and Neagles Rock Rd (open weekends and holidays). Stately Wolta Wolta homestead (1846), West Tce, built by pastoralist John Hope, still owned by Hope family; rebuilt after Ash Wednesday fires (open by appt). Lookouts at Billy Goat Hill, from Wright St; Neagles Rock, Neagles Rock Rd. Maynard Memorial Park, Pioneer Ave. Town walk, self-guide leaflets available.

Mar.: Clare Valley Cup. Easter: Easter Races. Apr.: Spanish Festival. May: Gourmet Weekend. Nov.: Spring Festival. **In the area:** More than 30 wineries (most open for inspection and cellar-door sales, check opening times); *around Clare*: Tim Adams Wines, Jim Barry Wines, Knappstein Wines, Emerald Estate, Eldredge Wines; *in Polish Hill River district*, 12 km SE: Pike's Polish Hill River Estate, Paulett Wines and The Wilson Vineyard; *at Mintaro*, 19 km SE: Mintaro Cellars and Reilly's Cottage; *at Sevenhill*, 7 km S: Sevenhill Cellars established 1851 and featuring monastery buildings, including historic St Aloysius Church, Stringy Brae Wines, Waninga Wines, Skillogalee Wines, Jeanneret Wines and Mitchell Winery; *around Penwortham*, 10 km S: Penwortham Wines and Pearson Wines; *around Watervale*, 12 km S: Clos Clare, Crabtree of Watervale, Olssen Wines, Stephen John Wines, Quelltaler Estate and Tim Gramp Wines; *around Auburn*, 26 km S: Taylors Wines and Grosset Wines. Also at Watervale, 12 km S, Murray Edwards Studio. Also at Auburn, 26 km S: Riesling Trail, scenic bike and walking path along old Clare railway line between Clare and Auburn; birthplace of poet C. J. Dennis in 1876; many historic buildings (accommodation in some), maintained by National Trust (self-guide walk leaflets available); Auburn Railway Station (1918) transformed into Mt Horrocks Wines cellar-door outlet. At Blyth, 13 km W: flora and fauna in Padnainda Reserve; Medika Gallery, originally a Lutheran church (1886), specialising in Australian bird and flower paintings. Scenic drive 12 km S to Spring Gully Conservation Park featuring rare red stringybarks. Bungaree Station homestead (1841), historic merino sheep station 12 km N: group tours, accommodation. Geralka Rural Farm, 25 km N, working farm (tours). **Visitor information:** Town Hall, 229 Main North Rd; (08) 8842 2131. Web site www.classiccountry.org.au/clare.html **See also:** Day Tours from Adelaide p. 253; Vineyards and Wineries p. 277.

Coffin Bay   Pop. 396

MAP REF. 306 C8

A picturesque holiday town and fishing village, on the shores of a beautiful estuary 51 km NW of Port Lincoln, Coffin Bay offers sailing, water-skiing, swimming and fishing. The coastal scenery is magnificent. Oysters cultivated in Coffin Bay are among the best in the country. The bay's name was bestowed by Matthew Flinders in 1802 to honour his friend Sir Isaac Coffin. **In town:** Oyster Farm, also known for its lobster, The Esplanade. Oyster Walk, 12-km walkway along foreshore from lookout (excellent view of Coffin Bay) to Long Beach; brochure available. Charter boats and boat hire. **In the area:** Coffin Bay National Park and Kellidie Bay Conservation Park surround township; abundant wildflowers in both parks in spring. Yangie Trail drive, 10 km S via Yangie Bay Lookout (magnificent coastal views to Point Avoid). Farm Beach, 50 km N; further 5 km N, Gallipoli Beach, location for film *Gallipoli* (1981). Further 50 km N, scenic stretch of Flinders Hwy between Mount Hope and Sheringa. **Visitor information:** Beachcomber Agencies, The Esplanade; (08) 8685 4057. Web site www.epta.com.au **See also:** The Eyre Peninsula p. 284.

Coober Pedy   Pop. 2762

MAP REF. 313 R11

In the heart of South Australia's outback, 845 km N of Adelaide on the Stuart Hwy, is the opal-mining town of Coober Pedy. This is the last stop for petrol between Cadney Homestead (151 km N) and Glendambo (252 km S) on the Stuart Hwy. The name Coober Pedy is Aboriginal for 'white man's hole in the ground': many people live in dugouts (at a constant 24°C) for protection from the severe summer temperatures (often reaching 45°C), and the cold winter nights. Futhermore, there is no local timber for building. The countryside is desolate and harsh, and the town has reticulated water from a bore 23 km N. Opals were discovered here in 1915; today there are thousands of mines. **In town:** Demonstrations of opals being cut and polished; jewellery and stones for sale. On eastern edge of town: Big Winch Lookout, Italian Club Rd; Old Timers Mine, Crowders Gully Rd, a mine museum and interpretive centre with self-guide walks. In Hutchison St: Umoona underground mine and museum, has interpretive section and underground mine tours; underground churches, including St Peter and St Pauls; Desert Cave, an international underground hotel with shopping complex. Underground Catacomb Church, Catacomb Rd. Guided tours of mines and town. Easter: Opal Festival. June: Glendi

Festival (celebration of Greek culture). Oct.: Horse races. **In the area:** *Opal fields pocked with diggings; beware of unprotected mine shafts. Avoid entering any field area unless escorted by someone who knows the area.* For safety reasons, visitors to the mines are advised to join a tour. Trespassers on claims can be fined a minimum of $1000. Opal Quest Mine, 2 km SW, tours. Underground Pottery, 2 km W, features local pottery. The Breakaways, 30 km N: 40-sq. km reserve featuring unique landscape, used as backdrop in many films and commercials (passes to reserve from information centre and other outlets in town); return via road past part of dog fence, a 5300-km fence stretching across Australia, built to protect sheep properties in the south from wild dogs. Arckaringa Hills, 234 km N, richly coloured hills in an area known as the Painted Desert; also noted for its flora and fauna. At William Creek, 170 km E: hotel; Race Meeting and Gymkhana held weekend before Easter. **Visitor information:** Council Offices, Hutchison St; (08) 8672 5298, freecall 1800 637 076. Web site www.opalcapitaloftheworld.com.au **See also:** The Outback p. 278.

Coonalpyn   Pop. 233

MAP REF. 305 F4, 307 O12

This tiny town, 180 km SE of Adelaide, is a good place to break your journey along the Dukes Hwy. In the cooler months it is also a base from which to explore the Mt Boothby (30 km SW) and Carcuma (20 km NE) conservation parks, and to see grey kangaroos, echidnas, emus and mallee fowl. Summer access to both parks is discouraged because of heat and fire danger. Check bushfire danger and fire restrictions before entering parks; for Mt Boothby Conservation Park, (08) 8575 1200; for Carcuma Conservation Park, (08) 8757 2261. **In town:** Dog Exercise Park, signed on hwy, safe stop for pets. Tunnel Vision, under railway line in subway leading to Dog Park, mural depicting town's history. Daisy Patch Nursery, cnr George and Richards tces, for native plants. Oct.: Agricultural and Horticultural Show (includes Antique Tractor Pull). **In the area:** Scenic 26-km loop drive, maps available. Tintinara homestead, 37 km S, historic buildings. **Visitor information:** Peg's Place, 27 Dukes Hwy; (08) 8571 1272.

Coonawarra   Pop. 40

MAP REF. 234 A13, 305 H10

The European settlement of Coonawarra goes back to 1890 when John Riddoch subdivided 2000 acres (800 ha) of his vast landholding for orchards and vineyards. Although the vines flourished and excellent wines were made, demand was not high until the 1950s and 1960s, when the region became an important winegrowing area. The terra rossa soil and dedicated viticulturalists and winemakers combine to produce award-winning white and red table wines. **In town:** Art gallery at Chardonnay Lodge, Penola Rd. Oct.: Cabernet Celebration. **In the area:** Wineries, most open for tastings and sales, including (N to S): S. Kidman Wines, Rymill Winery, Redman Wines, Brands

Underground home at Coober Pedy

Wildlife-Watching

It is worth taking the time to spot some of South Australia's wildlife: look at migratory bats in Naracoorte Caves, in the rocky Flinders Ranges for yellow-footed rock wallabies, or out to the Southern Ocean for a glimpse of southern right whales.

AROUND ADELAIDE

Victor Harbor, on the Fleurieu Peninsula just south of Adelaide, should be the first stop for keen whale-watchers. More than 25 whale and dolphin species swim off the South Australian coast, and the South Australian Whale Centre at Victor Harbor has an interpretive display explaining the life-cycles of these popular mammals. The centre's Whale Information Network tracks the movements of migratory whales and offers Statewide information on the best whale-watching localities. Southern right whales can be seen along the Fleurieu Peninsula coastline from June to October. Connected by causeway to Victor Harbor is Granite Island, a haven for little (fairy) penguins. There is an interpretive centre on the island as well as year-round penguin-viewing walks at sunset.

Kangaroo Island also has a healthy population of little (fairy) penguins; interpretive centres and guided tours operate at Penneshaw and Kingscote. Guided tours also operate at Seal Bay to see the colony of Australian sea-lions, while Admirals Arch in Flinders Chase National Park is the spot to encounter New Zealand fur seals as they rest ashore after fishing excursions.

Pelicans are a familiar sight along the south-eastern coast

IN THE SOUTH OF THE STATE

Bent-wing bats migrate each spring from south-eastern Australia to the Bat Cave in **Naracoorte Caves Conservation Park**, where they join the cave's resident bats. The Bat Cave Teleview Centre provides a unique view of the bats' activities. Infra-red cameras in the caves are connected to monitors in the centre, allowing visitors to view the tiny mammals without disturbing them. Each evening between November and February thousands of bats fly from the cave to feed on insects.

Bool Lagoon Game Reserve lies 17 kilometres south of Naracoorte. The lagoon is a vital habitat and essential drought refuge for many rare and endangered bird species. Its cycle of flooding and drying is perfect for the breeding patterns of waterbirds. In spring black swans crowd the lagoon. Take the Tea-tree Boardwalk into the heart of the lagoon, where ibis and spoonbills nest in the foliage. In summer and autumn migratory birds, such as sharp-tailed sandpipers,

greenshanks and godwits, can be found in the exposed shallows. Bourne's Bird Museum, 10 kilometres west of Bool Lagoon, has a huge display of mounted birds for close-up viewing (closed Tuesdays and July–August).

Also in the south-east is the **Coorong National Park**, which curves 145 kilometres along the coast. Here, 238 species of native birds live amongst the narrow saltwater lagoons, sand dunes, saltpans, claypans and bush. Take binoculars to view pelicans, crested terns and silver gulls. Pied oystercatchers feed along the beaches – their flattened bills allow them to dig up and open cockles. Flocks of tiny red-necked stints migrate to the Coorong lagoon from Siberia via Japan each year.

ALONG THE NORTHERN COASTLINE

Motorists heading north to make the Nullarbor crossing should consider taking the coastal route and stopping to meet the only permanent colony of Australian sea-lions on the mainland. Visitors to **Point Labatt Conservation Park**, south of Streaky Bay, can see these wonderful sea mammals resting and playing at remarkably close range.

Between May and October, Nullarbor travellers have the opportunity of viewing southern right whales from one of the best cliff-based whale-watching sites in the world. Twelve kilometres east of the Nullarbor Roadhouse on the Eyre Highway, a signposted turn-off extends from the endless bluebush plain to the sheer Bunda Cliffs at the Head of Bight. From this point, visitors are rewarded with intimate views of southern right whales in their chosen breeding ground, now protected as part of the **Great Australian Bight Marine Park**. These massive creatures are possibly the most boisterous of the great whales: their antics make entertaining viewing. The road and whale-watching area is on Yalata Aboriginal Land. Whale-watching permits are required and these can be purchased from the White Well Ranger Station near the viewing platform.

INLAND

Mount Remarkable National Park lies on the southern edge of the Flinders Ranges. Just outside the park there are red kangaroos in the plains surrounding Mambray Creek. Adelaide rosellas, little corellas and kookaburras are also residents, their riotous calls breaking the peace of the plains. Within the park, sugar gums and native pines in Mambray Creek Gorge offer shelter for euros. From a distance these may be confused with grey kangaroos, but euros are stockier and have darker paws, hindfeet and tail-tips. Look also for the yellow-footed rock wallaby.

For a good overview of South Australian wildlife, visit the Cleland Wildlife Park at Mount Lofty, just outside Adelaide. Here it is possible to view dingoes, koalas, kangaroos and wallabies; walk through the extensive aviaries; or join a guided night walk to spot nocturnal animals. For more information on wildlife-watching in national parks, contact The Environment Shop, 77 Grenfell St, Adelaide (GPO Box 1047, Adelaide SA 5001); (08) 8204 1910. Web site www.parksweb.sa.gov.au **See also:** Outback Adventure p. 256, National Parks p. 262, Kangaroo Island p. 273 and The Coorong p. 274.

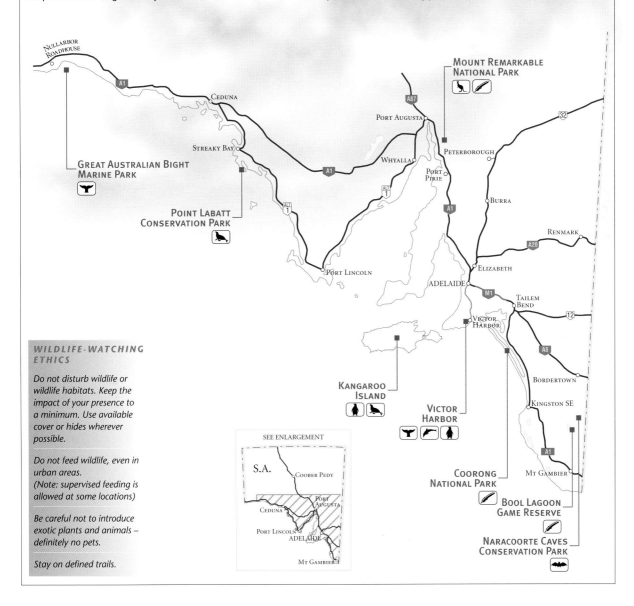

WILDLIFE-WATCHING ETHICS

Do not disturb wildlife or wildlife habitats. Keep the impact of your presence to a minimum. Use available cover or hides wherever possible.

Do not feed wildlife, even in urban areas.
(Note: supervised feeding is allowed at some locations)

Be careful not to introduce exotic plants and animals – definitely no pets.

Stay on defined trails.

Cooper Creek near Innamincka

Laira Wines, Wynns Coonawarra Estate, Rouge Homme Wines, Zema Estate, Mildara Wines, Majella Wines, St Mary's Vineyard (15 km E), Katnook Estate, Highbank Wines, Leconfield Coonawarra, Bowen Estate, Balnaves of Coonawarra, The Blok Estate, Hollick Wines, Wetherall Wines, Punters Corner, Lindemans Wines. **Visitor information:** 27 Arthur St, Penola; (08) 8737 2855. **See also:** Vineyards and Wineries p. 277.

Cowell   Pop. 748

MAP REF. 306 G5

A pleasant township 108 km S of Whyalla, Cowell is on the almost landlocked Franklin Harbor. One of the world's major jade deposits is in the district. The sandy beach at Cowell is safe for swimming; fishing is excellent. Oyster farming is a local industry and fresh oysters can be purchased year-round. **In town:** Old post office and attached residence (1888), Main St, now Franklin Harbor National Trust Historical Museum. On Lincoln Hwy: open-air agricultural museum; Cowell Jade Motel, has displays and sales of local jade jewellery. Boats for hire. **In the area:** Franklin Harbor Conservation Park, south of town, has good fishing spots. Swimming and excellent fishing locations abound, including around Gibbon Point, 15 km S. Arno Bay, 48 km S, popular holiday town with sandy beaches and jetty for fishing. **Visitor information:** Council Offices, Main St; (08) 8629 2019. Web site www.epta.com.au **See also:** The Eyre Peninsula p. 284.

Crystal Brook   Pop. 1323

MAP REF. 307 J4

Once part of a vast sheep station, this town, 25 km SE of Port Pirie, is now a service centre for the sheep, beef and cereal industries of the region. **In town:** National Trust Museum, Brandis St, has local history collection in first two-storeyed building in town, originally a butcher's shop and bakery; underground bakehouse behind building. Crystal Crafts, Bowman St, for local craft. Picnicking in creekside parks. Aug.: Agricultural Show. **In the area:** Bowman Park, 5 km E: surrounds ruins of Bowman family property Crystal Brook Run (1847); Steakhouse Restaurant and opportunities for wildlife-watching. Heysen Walking Trail through Bowman Park. At Gladstone, set in rich rural country in Rocky River Valley 21 km NE: tours of Gladstone gaol (1881); Trend Drinks Factory, home of Old Style Ginger Beer (tours). At Laura, boyhood town of C. J. Dennis the author of *The Songs of a Sentimental Bloke*, 32 km N: cottage crafts; art galleries; historic buildings; self-guide walking tour, leaflet at Biles Art Gallery, Herbert St (open Sat., Sun., public holidays); Beetaloo Valley and Reservoir (west of Laura), pleasant picnic spot Apr.–Nov. and venue for Folk Fair in Apr. Near Wirrabara, 50 km N: scenic walks through pine forests; picnic grounds; Old Tree Nursery, est. 1877. At Redhill, 25 km S: riverside walk; museum; craft shop; antique shop. Koolunga, 10 km E of Redhill, has cottage industry (potters and painters) outlets and picnic areas. Salt lakes around Snowtown, 50 km S. Nearby on Lochiel–Ninnes Rd, lookout with superb views of inland lakes and country-side. **Visitor information:** Port Pirie Regional Tourism and Arts Centre, Mary Elie St; (08) 8633 0439, freecall 1800 000 424.

Edithburgh   Pop. 400

MAP REF. 306 I10

Located on the foreshore at the south-eastern tip of Yorke Peninsula, Edithburgh overlooks Gulf St Vincent and Troubridge Island. **In town:** Native Flora Park, Ansty Tce. In Edith St: Edithburgh Museum, features historical maritime collection (check opening times). In Blanche St: Bakehouse Arts and Crafts, for local crafts; 9-hole golf course. Town jetty, end of Edith St, built 1873. Boat ramp adjacent caravan park. Natural tidal pool, excellent for swimming. Fishing and offshore diving tours; diving trail to *Clan Ranald* wreck, brochures available. Nature walks; south to Sultana Point and north to Coobowie, brochures available. Oct.: Gala Day. **In the area:** Nearby Sultana Point, 2 km S, for fishing and swimming. Scenic drive south-west along coast to Innes National Park. Coobowie, 5 km N, a popular coastal town. Tours to Troubridge Island Conservation Park (30 min. by boat), home to penguins, black-faced shags and crested terns. **Visitor information:** Edithburgh Caravan Park; (08) 8852 6056. Web site www.classiccountry.org.au/edithburgh. html **See also:** The Yorke Peninsula p. 281.

Elliston   Pop. 217

MAP REF. 306 B5

Nestled in a range of hills on the shore of Waterloo Bay, 332 km SW of Port Augusta, Elliston is the centre for a cereal-growing, mixed-farming and fishing community. Known for its rugged and scenic coastline, excellent fishing and safe swimming beaches, Elliston is a popular holiday destination. **In town:** Town hall mural, Main St, representing history of town and district. **In the area:** Just north of town: clifftop walk at Waterloo Bay; good surfing near Anxious Bay. Walkers Rocks, 15 km N, has good beaches, rock fishing and camping area. Talia Caves, 40 km N. Camel Beach, 50 km N, good salmon-fishing. Lock's Well Beach and Sheringa Beach to south, for surf fishing. Scenic drives north and south of town offer superb views of magnificent coastline; good views also from Cummings Monument Lookout, just off hwy near Kiana, 52 km S. Flinders Is., 35 km offshore (limited accommodation). **Visitor information:** District Council, Beach Tce; (08) 8687 9177. Web site www.epta.com.au **See also:** The Eyre Peninsula p. 284.

Gawler   Pop. 15 484

MAP REF. 300 D5, 307 L8
Settled by Europeans in 1839, Gawler, 40 km NE of Adelaide, is a historic town and the centre for a thriving agricultural district. It is also the gateway to the famous Barossa Valley. **In town:** Self-guide historical walks/drives, brochures available. Historic buildings: Gawler Mill, Bridge St; old telegraph station, Murray St. Eagle Foundry (1870), King St, once a busy manufacturer of castings for agricultural implements and cast-iron lacework, now B&B. Para Para (1862), Penrith Ave, historic residence (not open to the public). Anglican Church, has interesting pipe organ (open Sun. or by appt). Church Hill Heritage Area (adjacent to Murray St), provides a fascinating 'snapshot' of town planning in the 1830s. Dead Man's Pass Reserve, end Murray St, has picnic facilities and walking trails. Gawler South Markets, each Thurs., Adelaide Rd. June: Horse Trials. Aug.: Agricultural Show. **In the area:** Restored Willaston post office, 2 km N. Roseworthy Agricultural Museum, 15 km N on Roseworthy campus of University of Adelaide, is a dryland farming museum featuring vintage farm implements, engines and working tractors (open Wed. and 3rd Sun. each month, tours by appt). Astronomical Society of SA's observatory at Stockport, 30 km N, has public viewing nights. Scholz Park Museum (open by appt), 54 km N, at Riverton. Wellington Hotel at Waterloo, 76 km N (near Manoora), once Cobb & Co. staging post. **Visitor information:** 2 Lyndoch Rd; (08) 8522 6814. Web site gawler.sa.gov.au **See also:** Day Tours from Adelaide p. 253.

Goolwa   Pop. 3723

MAP REF. 301 I7, 305 C3, 307 L11
Goolwa is a rapidly growing holiday town on the last big bend of the Murray River, 12 km from its mouth near Lake Alexandrina. Once a key port in the golden days of the riverboats, the area

has a strong tradition of shipbuilding, trade and fishing. Today the area is ideal for boating, fishing and aquatic sports, and popular with birdwatchers and photographers. **In town:** Historic buildings in B. F. Laurie Lane, off Cadell St: distinctive railway superintendent's house (1852), known as 'the round-roofed house'; RSL Club, in former stables of Goolwa Railway (1853). In Cadell St, display of first horse-drawn railway carriage used in SA between Goolwa and Port Elliot from 1854. Steam Ranger, steam-train rides between Goolwa and Victor Harbor. National Trust Museum, Porter St, in former blacksmith's shop dating from 1870s. Next door, in rebuilt cottage, Goolwa Print Room. Two hotels, the Goolwa in Cadell St and the Corio in Railway Pl., date from 1850s. Signal Point River Murray Interpretive Centre, The Wharf, interactive display of river and district before European settlement, and impact of local development. Self-guide walk, brochure available. South Coast Regional Arts Centre, wharf precinct, in restored original police station. Clydesdale wagon rides (weekends and school holidays); boat trips to The Coorong via Murray River (Oct.–June) depart from wharf. Armfield Slip, Admiral Tce, has working exhibition of boatbuilding. Market 1st and 3rd Sun. each month, Jaralde Park, The Wharf. Jan.: Milang to Goolwa Freshwater Classic Yacht Race. Mar.: Wooden Boat Festival (odd-numbered years). Nov.: Cocklefest. **In the area:** Excellent fishing. Bird sanctuary east of Goolwa, has swans, pelicans and other waterfowl, also bird hide. Nearby, the Barrages, desalination points that prevent salt water from reaching the Murray River. MV *Aroona*, MV *Spirit of the Coorong*, MV *Wetlands Explorer* and MV *Coorong Pirate* cruise to mouth of the Murray, The Coorong, the Barrages and the Lower Murray; details (08) 8555 2203. On Hindmarsh Is. (via ferry), Captain Sturt Lookout and monument, location of first European sighting of mouth of Murray River. Scenic flights; airport 5 km N. At Currency Creek, 8 km N: Canoe Tree; Currency Creek Winery (with restaurant and fauna park); creekside park and walking trail. Tooperang Trout Farm, 20 km NW. **Visitor information:** Signal Point River Murray Interpretive Centre, The Wharf; (08) 8555 1144. **See also:** Day Tours from Adelaide p. 253.

Hawker   Pop. 319

MAP REF. 303 D10, 309 J9
This outback town is 369 km N of Adelaide. Once a railway town, it is now the centre for the Southern Flinders Ranges, a unique area that attracts visitors from both Australia and overseas to marvel at the colouring and grandeur of the many ranges. **In town:** Museum at Hawker Motors, cnr Wilpena and Cradock rds. Historic buildings: post office (1882), Hawker Hotel (1882), both in Elder Tce; old railway station complex (1885), Leigh Creek Rd. Heritage walks through town, scenic flights and 4WD tours. May: Horseracing Carnival. Sept.: Art Exhibition. **In the area:** Entry points for Heysen Trail (walkers) and Mawson Trail (cyclists). Moralana Scenic Drive, 42 km N, joins roads to Wilpena and Leigh Creek. Opportunities for station holidays in surrounding area. Walking trail, scenic lookout at Jarvis Hill, 7 km SW. Rock paintings at Yourambulla Caves, 12 km S. Ruins at Kanyaka Homestead Historic Site, 28 km S, off main road to Quorn; nearby, Kanyaka Death Rock overlooks permanent waterhole, once an Aboriginal ceremonial ground. Ruins of Wilson Railway Station, Hookina and Wonoka. **Visitor information:** Hawker Motors, cnr Wilpena and Cradock rds; (08) 8648 4014. Web site www.hawker.mtx.net **See also:** Outback Adventure p. 256; National Parks p. 262.

Innamincka   Pop. 9

MAP REF. 311 Q7, 534 H10
This tiny settlement, 1027 km NE of Adelaide, is built around a hotel and trading post on the Strzelecki Track, and is on the banks of the Cooper Creek. *Motorists intending to travel along the track should ensure road conditions are suitable by phoning the Northern Roads Condition Hotline on 1300 361 033 before departure; also read the section on Outback Motoring (p. 603). There are no supplies or petrol between Lyndhurst and Innamincka.* **In town:** Rebuilt Australian Inland Mission hostel, now houses National Parks office. Boat and canoe hire. Aug.: Races. **In the area:** Picturesque Cullyamurra Waterhole on Cooper Creek, 16 km NE, has Aboriginal rock carvings and excellent fishing. Memorials to explorers Burke and Wills near Innamincka; famous 'Dig Tree' is best known, 71 km across border in Qld. Coongie Lakes, a haven for wildlife, 103 km NW (road conditions can vary

Kernewek Lowender, biennial Cornish festival, Kadina

Creative Arts Network, personalised learning experiences with local residents (available throughout region, contact information centre). Easter: Bowling Carnival. May: Kernewek Lowender, a Cornish festival held in conjunction with Wallaroo and Moonta (odd-numbered years). Aug.: Agricultural Show. **In the area:** Yorke Peninsula Field Days at Paskeville, 19 km SE, in Sept. (odd-numbered years). **Visitor information:** Moonta Station Visitor Information Centre, Old Moonta Railway Station, Kadina Rd, Moonta; (08) 8825 1891. Web site www.classiccountry.org.au/kadina.html **See also:** The Yorke Peninsula p. 281.

Kapunda   Pop. 2195

MAP REF. 300 E3, 307 L7

Kapunda is situated 80 km N of Adelaide on the edge of the Barossa Valley. Copper was discovered here in 1842 and Kapunda became Australia's first coppermining town. The population rose to 5000 and there were 16 hotels. A million pounds' worth of copper was dug out before the mines closed in 1878. **In town:** Historic Ford House, Main St, an 1860s general store with unusual vaulted iron roof, now B&B. In Hill St: Kapunda Museum (1870s); Bagot's Fortune, mine interpretation centre with mining history displays. Kapunda Gallery, cnr Main and Hill sts, a significant regional gallery. High School's main building on West Tce, off Clare Rd, formerly residence of famous cattle king Sir Sidney Kidman. 'Map Kernow' (Sons of Cornwall), 8-m tall bronze statue at southern entrance to town, end of Main St, commemorates early miners, many of whom migrated from Cornwall in England. Kapunda Railway Station, Railway Tce, now B&B. Heritage trail and historic mine walking trail, maps available. Finishing point for Bicycle Federation of Australia trials held Aug.–Sept. Mar.: Celtic Music Festival. Nov.: Agricultural Show; Antique and Craft Fair. **In the area:** Pines Reserve, 6 km NW, nature reserve and wildlife. Historic local stone buildings at Tarlee, 16 km NW. Scholz Park Museum (open by appt) and heritage-listed railway station (check opening times) at Riverton, 30 km NW. Anlaby Station, 16 km NE, historic Dutton Homestead and gardens with fine coach collection (check opening times). Scenic drive 26 km NE through sheep, wheat and dairy country to Eudunda. **Visitor information:** 76 Main St; (08) 8566 2902. Web site www.kaptour.mtx.net

considerably, 4WD recommended). **Visitor information:** Trading Post; (08) 8675 9900 or National Parks and Wildlife Service; (08) 8675 9909. **See also:** The Outback p. 278.

Jamestown   Pop. 1430

MAP REF. 307 L3, 309 K13

Jamestown is a well-planned country town 205 km N of Adelaide. The surrounding country produces stud sheep and cattle, cereals, dairy produce and timber. **In town:** Self-guide town and cemetery walks, brochures available. Heritage murals, Ayr St. Railway Station Museum, Irvine St (check opening times). Parks along banks of Belalie Creek for picnics; banks floodlit at night. Easter: Bilby Hunt. Oct.: Agricultural Show. Dec.: Christmas Pageant. **In the area:** Scenic drive through Bundaleer Forest Reserve, 9 km S, has wildlife, walking trails; continue towards New Campbell Hill for panoramic views of plains, towards Mt Remarkable and The Bluff (self-guide drive and walk brochures available). Near Spalding, 34 km S: series of open waterways with picnic areas and trout fishing opportunities; Geralka Rural Farm, 49 km S, working commercial

farm (tours). Appila Springs, scenic picnic spot 8 km from Appila, 24 km NW. **Visitor information:** Country Retreat Caravan Park, 103 Ayr St; (08) 8664 0077. Web site www.classiccountry.org.au/jamestown.html

Kadina   Pop. 3536

MAP REF. 306 I6

The largest town on Yorke Peninsula, Kadina is the chief commercial centre for this agriculturally rich region. The town's history includes the boom coppermining era during the 1800s and early 1900s, when Cornish miners flocked to the area; the community is still proud of its ancestry. **In town:** Historic hotels: the Wombat, the Kadina, both in Taylor St; Royal Exchange, Digby St, with iron-lace balconies and shady verandahs. National Trust Kadina Heritage Museum, Matta Rd (access from Kadina–Moonta Rd or Russell St): Matta House (1863), former home of manager of Matta Matta Copper Mine; agricultural machinery; blacksmith's shop; printing museum; old Matta mine; the Kadina Story, a display of town history (check opening times). Banking and Currency Museum, Graves St, unique private museum (check opening times).

Kangaroo Island

Only 120 kilometres south-west of Adelaide, Kangaroo Island, the third largest Australian island, shows nature in its wildest and purest form. A walk through bush or along coastal cliffs may provide glimpses of wallabies, koalas, echidnas or, of course, kangaroos; there are also many species of birds and wildflowers.

Visitors can fly to the island from Adelaide (Emu Airways and Kendell Airlines) or go by ferry. The vehicular ferries *Sealion 2000* and *The Navigator* operate from Cape Jervis to Penneshaw. Tours are available and hire vehicles include cars and bicycles. A bus service operates between Kingscote and the airport. A ferry shuttle bus operates twice daily between Penneshaw and Kingscote. Kangaroo Island's waters offer excellent fishing; game-fishing charters are available.

At the four main towns, **Kingscote**, American River, Parndana and Penneshaw, there is a range of accommodation from hotels and motels, through flats and cottages, to camping, cabins and bed-and-breakfasts. Many farms also provide bed and breakfast accommodation.

American River, nestled in a pine-fringed bay, is ideal for fishing and canoeing. Pelican Lagoon is a sanctuary for birds and fish. Penneshaw overlooks the passage separating the island from the mainland. Little (fairy) penguins promenade on the rocks here at night. Penguin-watching tours leave from the Penguin Interpretive Centre.

The coastline of the island varies from the several kilometres of safe swimming beach at Emu Bay in the north to the rugged cliffs and roaring surf of the south. However, in the south, D'Estrees Bay's wide deserted beach is ideal for fishing, collecting shells and exploring. **Cape Gantheaume** and **Seal Bay conservation parks** are located on this exposed southern coast. Seal Bay has a permanent colony of Australian sea-lions. New Zealand fur seal colonies are found near Admirals Arch on Cape du Couedic. Also on the south coast are limestone formations in

Australian sea-lions, Seal Bay

the caves at Kelly Hill Conservation Park. At Cape Borda, on the north-west tip of the island, is one of the most picturesque of Australia's old lighthouses; there are guided tours daily, arranged through National Parks and Wildlife, South Australia, at Cape Borda. Other attractive spots along the northern coast include the rugged rocks at Harveys Return; Western River Cove with its idyllic white beach; a superb protected bay at Snelling Beach; and Stokes Bay, where a secret tunnel leads to the beach. On the western end of the island, which is dominated by the soaring eucalypt forests of the **Flinders Chase National Park**, are two of the island's natural wonders: Admirals Arch, a huge arch where on sunny afternoons stalactites can be seen in silhouette against a background of the deep blue Southern Ocean, and the Remarkable Rocks, huge, unusually shaped granite boulders.

For further information contact the Kangaroo Island Visitor Information Centre, Howard Drive, Penneshaw; (08) 8553 1185. Web site www.tourkangarooisland.com.au **See also:** Wildlife-Watching p. 268. For details on parks and towns in bold type, see National Parks p. 262 and individual entries in A–Z town listings. **Map references: 301 A11, 306 F11.**

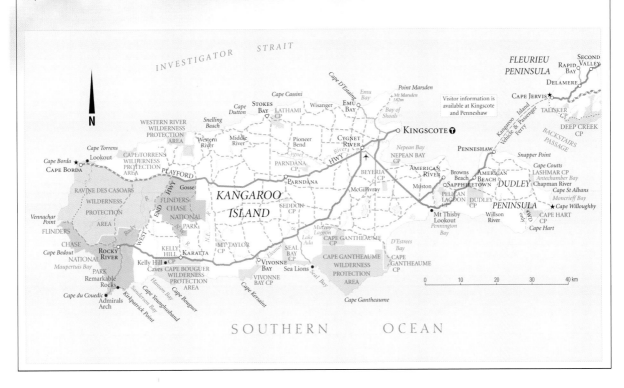

Keith

Pop. 1089

MAP REF. 305 G6, 307 P13

Keith is a farming town on the Dukes Hwy, 241 km SE of Adelaide, in the centre of the former Ninety Mile Desert (now Coonalpyn Downs). The area has been transformed from infertile pasture to productive farming by the use of modern farming methods. **In town:** National Trust-classified buildings in Heritage St: former Congregational Church (1910), with 11 locally made leadlight windows depicting the town's life and pioneering history; The Old Manse. Also in Heritage St, Keith Water Feature (water sculpture). Sept.: Market Day, local art and craft. **In the area:** Mount Rescue Conservation Park, 16 km N, a vast expanse of sandplain with heath, pink gums, Aboriginal campsites and burial grounds and an abundance of native wildlife. Old Settlers Cottage (1894), 2 km NE on Emu Flat Rd. Ngarkat Conservation Park, 25 km NE, has variety of flora and fauna. Mt Monster Conservation Park, 10 km S, for scenic views and diverse wildlife. **Visitor information:** Council Chambers, 43 Woolshed St, Bordertown; (08) 8752 1044.

The Coorong

The Coorong National Park curves along the southern coast of South Australia for 145 kilometres, extending from the mouth of the Murray River in the north, almost to the township of **Kingston S.E.** in the south. A unique area, it has an eerie isolation, a silence broken only by the sounds of birds wheeling low over the scrub and dunes, and the pounding of waves from the Southern Ocean.

The Coorong proper is a shallow lagoon, a complex system of low-lying saltpans and claypans. Never more than 3 kilometres wide, the lagoon is divided from the sea by the towering white sandhills of Younghusband Peninsula, known locally as the Hummocks. One of the best natural bird sanctuaries in Australia, the Coorong is home to 238 bird species including pelicans, cormorants, ibis, swans and terns.

Access to the park is gained by leaving the Princes Highway at Salt Creek and following the old road along the shore. Noonameena, Mark Point and Long Point in the northern section can be accessed from the turnoff at Meningie. Explore the unspoiled stretches of beach where the rolling surf washes up gnarled driftwood and beautiful shells. Year-round access to the beach is from a point further south known as 42 Mile Crossing; the final 1.3 kilometres is suitable for 4WD or walking.

For those who wish to explore in comfort, **Meningie** in the north and the fishing port of Kingston S.E. in the south have a range of accommodation and can be used as touring bases. Camping is permitted in the **Coorong National Park** in designated areas only. Permits may be obtained from local commercial outlets (look for the pelican logo), from self-registration stations in the park or from the Coorong Shop in Meningie. The area is rich in history as well as being a naturalists' haven; pick up the *Coorong Tattler* for details. Fishing, boating and walking are popular activities.

For further information, contact National Parks and Wildlife, South Australia, at Meningie; (08) 8575 1200. Web site www.parksweb. sa.gov.au **See also:** Wildlife-Watching p. 268. For details on parks and towns in bold type, see National Parks p. 262 and individual entries in A–Z town listing. **Map references:** 305 E5, 307 N13.

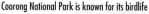

Coorong National Park is known for its birdlife

Kimba
Pop. 677

MAP REF. 306 F3, 308 E13

A small town on the Eyre Hwy, 155 km SW of Port Augusta, Kimba is a gateway to the outback. This is sheep- and wheat-growing country. **In town:** On Eyre Hwy: historical museum featuring Pioneer House (1908), school and blacksmith's shop; the Big Galah, 8 m high; locally mined and crafted jade (including rare black jade, mined here at world's only known site) at Kimba Halfway Across Australia Gem Shop. Pug 'n' Pine Gallery, High St, for local craft. Sept.: Agricultural Show. **In the area:** Sturt Desert Pea nursery on Eyre Hwy, 1 km W. Walking trail 1 km NE of town, meanders through 3 km of bushland to White's Knob Lookout (360° views). Lake Gilles Conservation Park, 20 km NE, habitat for mallee fowl. Caralue Bluff, 20 km SW, for rock climbing, good flora and fauna. At base of Darke Peak, 40 km SW, memorial to John Charles Darke, explorer who was speared to death in 1884; excellent views from summit. Pinkawillinie Conservation Park, 45 km W, habitat for small desert birds, emu and western grey kangaroo. Gawler Ranges, north-west, vast wilderness area; check road conditions and read section on Outback Motoring. **Visitor information:** Kimba Halfway Across Australia Gem Shop, Eyre Hwy; (08) 8627 2112, (08) 8627 2766. Web site www.epta.com.au

Kingscote
Pop. 1529

MAP REF. 306 I12

The largest town on Kangaroo Island, 120 km SW of Adelaide, Kingscote was the first official European settlement in the State (1836). Travel to the island from the mainland is by vehicular ferry from Cape Jervis (45 min) or by air from Adelaide (30 min). **In town:** Cairn on foreshore marks State's first post office. Hope Cottage, Centenary Ave, National Trust Folk Museum. St Alban's Church, Osmond St, has stained-glass windows and pioneer memorials. Town's cemetery, Seaview Rd, is oldest in State. Rock pool, for swimming. Penguin tours depart from Ozone Seafront Hotel, The Foreshore. Fishing from jetty for squid, tommy ruff, trevally, garfish, whiting and snook. Feb.: Racing Carnival. Oct.: Agricultural Show. **In the area:** At Parndana, 38 km SW, Kangaroo Island Easter Fair. Eucalyptus oil distillery, 20 km S on Willsons Rd, off South Coast Rd. Clifford's Honey Farm, 25 km S. Mt

Thisby Lookout, 50 km S, for spectacular views. Jumbuck shearing demonstrations, 29 km E, cnr Hog Bay and Three Chain rds. American River, a fishing village about 50 km E. At Penneshaw, on the north-east coast of Dudley Peninsula, where vehicular ferry arrives from Cape Jervis: Folk Museum in former old Penneshaw School; penguin tours, depart from Penguin Interpretive Centre; Dudley, Cape Hart and Pelican Lagoon conservation parks on peninsula. Antechamber Bay, about 20 km SE of Penneshaw, excellent for bushwalking, fishing and swimming. Island Pure, 12 km W at Cygnet River, a sheep-milk dairy. Gum Creek Marron Farm, 24 km W. At Stokes Bay, 62 km W, natural rock tunnel leads to rock pool (ideal for swimming). On western end of island: Flinders Chase National Park, sanctuary for some of Australia's rarest wildlife; Cape Borda Lighthouse, north-west; Remarkable Rocks and Admirals Arch, south-west (boardwalk for viewing New Zealand fur seals at Admirals Arch). Guided tours available for Seal Bay, Kelly Hill Caves, Cape Borda and Cape Willoughby lighthouses. **Visitor information:** Kangaroo Island Visitor Information Centre, Howard Dr., Penneshaw; (08) 8553 1185. **See also:** National Parks p. 262; Wildlife-Watching p. 268; Kangaroo Island p. 273.

Kingston S.E.
Pop. 1431

MAP REF. 305 F8

Located at the southern end of the Coorong National Park on Lacepede Bay, Kingston S.E. is a farming and fishing town and seaside resort. The shallow lakes and lagoons in the area are a haven for birdlife and a delight for naturalists and photographers. **In town:** Unusual sundial, on island in creek, adjacent to Apex Park, in East Tce. Aboriginal burial ground, Dowdy St. In Holland St: historic post office (1867); Power House engine, Lions Park. National Trust Pioneer Museum (1872), Cooke St. Cape Jaffa Lighthouse (built 1860s, dismantled and re-erected in 1970s), Marine Pde. Boat ramp, Maria Creek. Fresh lobsters in season (Oct.–Apr.). Giant 'Larry Lobster' at entrance to town, Princes Hwy. Jan.: Cape Jaffa Food and Wine Festival; Fishing Contest; Lobster Fest; Yachting Regatta. **In the area:** Butchers Gap Conservation Park, 6 km SW, has a variety of birdlife; walking trails and picnic areas. Scenic drive south-west to Cape Jaffa, a small fishing village. The Granites, 18 km N, unique rock

formations. Mt Scott Conservation Park, 20 km E, part of former coastal dune system. Jip Jip Conservation Park, 50 km NE, features prominent outcrop of unusually shaped granite boulders. **Visitor information:** The Big Lobster, Princes Hwy; (08) 8767 2555. **See also:** National Parks p. 262; Wildlife-Watching p. 268; The Coorong p. 274.

Leigh Creek
Pop. 1006

MAP REF. 303 D3, 309 J4

Located in the Flinders Ranges, Leigh Creek is the second-largest town north of Port Augusta. The large open-cut coalfield eventually consumed the original township, about 13 km N, and in 1982 residents moved to the new township. A tree-planting scheme transformed the new site into an attractive oasis. **In the area:** Viewing area for coal workings, 3 km from turn-off to coalfields, north on Hawker–Marree Hwy; free tours on Sat., late Mar.–late Oct., and school holidays. Copley Hotel, 6 km N. Lyndhurst (39 km N) and Marree (119 km N), respective end points of Strzelecki and Birdsville tracks. At Lyndhurst, unique gallery of sculptures by well-known talc-stone artist 'Talc Alf'. A further 5 km N of Lyndhurst are the colourful Ochre Cliffs, where Aborigines used to dig for ochre (colours range from white to reds, yellows and browns). Aroona Dam, 4 km W, in steep-sided valley with richly coloured walls; scenic picnic area near gorge. Gammon Ranges National Park, 64 km E, wilderness area. 'Almost ghost' town of Beltana 27 km S, declared a historic reserve; Picnic Race Meeting and Gymkhana in Sept. Sliding Rock Mine ruins, 60 km S; access track rough in places. Lakes Eyre, Frome and Torrens, all dry saltpans that occasionally fill with water; Desert Parks Pass required for Lake Eyre National Park (see National Parks for contact numbers and addresses). *As with all outback driving, care must be taken; check road conditions with Northern Roads Condition Hotline on 1300 361 033 before departure.* **Visitor information:** Leigh Creek Coalfield; (08) 8675 4320. **See also:** Outback Adventure p. 256; National Parks p. 262.

Loxton
Pop. 3310

MAP REF. 307 Q7

Known as the Garden City of the Riverland region, Loxton is 251 km NE of Adelaide. The surrounding irrigated land supports citrus, wine, dried-fruit, wool and wheat industries. The area was first named Loxtons Hut, after a boundary rider built a pine and pug hut here. The largest war-service settlement scheme in the State was carried out here after WW II. **In town:** Art galleries and craft shops, have local paintings and handcrafts. Heritage Walk, main street, brochures available. Loxton Historical Village, on riverfront, with over 30 re-created buildings (including Loxton's hut), and machinery and implements from late 1880s to mid-1900s. Nearby, pepper tree grown from seed brought by Loxton over 110 years ago. Nature trail along riverfront. Canoes for hire. Feb.: Mardi Gras. Sept.: Riverland Field Days. Oct.: Agricultural Show. Nov.: Loxton Lights Up (Christmas lights throughout town, self-guide tour map available). **In the area:** In Bookpurnong Rd, in Loxton North: Medea Cottage, fresh and preserved local produce; Australian Vintage, wine-tasting, sales. Picnics on riverbank, map available. Lock 4, 14 km N, on Murray River. **Visitor information:** Loxton Tourism and Art Centre, Bookpurnong Tce; (08) 8584 7919.

Lyndoch   Pop. 1137

MAP REF. 300 E6, 304 C9, 307 L8

At the southern end of the Barossa Valley and an hour's drive from Adelaide, Lyndoch is one of the oldest towns in the State. Early industry was farm-oriented, and four flour mills operated. The Para River was used to operate a flour mill in the mid-1800s. Vineyards were established from the 1840s, but wine production remained limited until the 1890s. **In town:** Stone mill wheel (1855), on display in Flebig Square. Self-guide historical walk, featuring buildings from mid-1800s, including many built from locally quarried hard ironstone; brochure available. Feb.: Barossa Under the Stars (concert with international performers). Aug.–Sept.: Gourmet Barossa. **In the area:** Helicopter and balloon flights. Wineries, most open for tastings and cellar-door sales, include *to the north of town*: Kies Family Winery, Burge Family Winemakers, Charles Cimicky Wines, and Chateau Yaldara Estate (tours); *east of town*: Kellermeister Wines and Barossa Settlers; *south of town*: Twin Valley Estate; *west of town*: Wards Gateway Cellar and Tait Wines. *At Rowland Flat*, 5 km NE: Jenke Vineyard Cellars, Miranda Wines, Orlando Wines and Liebichwein.

Goldfields Walk, starts 10 km SW near cnr Goldfields and Para Wirra rds, brochure available. Barossa Reservoir and Whispering Wall, 8 km SW, acoustic phenomenon allowing messages whispered at one end to be audible at the other end, 140 m away. At Kersbrook, 22 km S: historic buildings; trout farm. Lyndoch Lavender Farm, 6 km SE, over 30 varieties of lavender; shop, picnic/barbecue facilities (open Sept.–Feb.). **Visitor information:** Barossa Wine and Visitor Centre, 66 Murray St, Tanunda; (08) 8563 0600, freecall 1800 812 662. **See also:** Day Tours from Adelaide p. 253; Vineyards and Wineries p. 277.

McLaren Vale   Pop. 2313

MAP REF. 300 A13, 301 F4, 302 E8, 305 B2, 307 K10

Centre of the McLaren winegrowing region, in which over 60 wineries flourish, McLaren Vale is 42 km S of Adelaide. Winemaking really began in 1853 when Thomas Hardy bought Tintara Vineyards. Today, Hardy's is the largest winery in the area. **In town:** Historic buildings: Hotel McLaren and Congregational Church, both in Main Rd; Salopian Inn, Willunga Rd. Almond Train, Main Rd, variety of local almond produce housed in restored railway carriage. June: Sea and Vines Festival. Oct.: Continuous Picnic; Wine Bushing Festival. **In the area:** McLaren Vale walk, brochure available; many historic buildings are now restaurants, wineries, tearooms and galleries. Tourist Route 60, scenic drive through wine region; starts at information centre, brochure available. Most wineries open for tastings and cellar-door sales. At Hardy's Tintara Wines, on Main Rd, huge heritage-listed Moreton Bay fig tree in grounds and Dridans Fine Arts housed in former cellar. Salopian Inn, 1 km S, restaurant in historic building. McLaren Vale Olive Grove, 3 km N, has olive-growing, processing, bottling, sales and tours. Coriole Vineyards, 5 km NE, sells a range of fine oils and vinegars. At Old Noarlunga, 5 km NW: colonial buildings, walk brochures available; good swimming and fishing at nearby beaches, nude swimming at southern end of Maslin Beach. At Hackham, 13 km NW, Lakeside Leisure Park. At Hallett Cove, 21 km NW, glacier tracks. **Visitor information:** Main Rd; (08) 8323 9944, freecall 1800 628 410. **See also:** Day Tours from Adelaide p. 253; Vineyards and Wineries p. 277.

Maitland   Pop. 999

MAP REF. 306 I7

Maitland is in the heart of Yorke Peninsula and is the centre for this rich agricultural area. Wheat, barley, wool and beef cattle are the main primary industries. Parks surround the town centre and provide pleasant picnic spots. **In town:** St John's Anglican Church (1876), cnr Alice and Caroline sts, stained-glass depicting Biblical stories in Australian settings. Lions Bicycle Adventure Park, off Elizabeth St. Maitland National Trust Museum, in former school, cnr Gardiner and Kilkerran tces, displays local history (check times). Self-guide heritage walk with interpretive signs, leaflet from District Council, Elizabeth St. Apr.: Agricultural Show. **In the area:** Coastal town of Balgowan, 15 km W, has safe, sandy beaches and is popular with anglers. **Visitor information:** Moonta Station Visitor Information Centre, Kadina Rd, Moonta; (08) 8825 1891. Web site www.classiccountry.org.au/maitland.html **See also:** The Yorke Peninsula p. 281.

Mannum   Pop. 1966

MAP REF. 300 I9, 305 D1, 307 M9

Mannum, 82 km E of Adelaide, is one of the oldest towns on the Murray River. Wool, beef and cereals are produced in the region, and the town is the starting point for the Adelaide water-supply pipeline. Picturesque terraced banks overlook the river. The *Mary Ann*, the first paddle-steamer on the Murray, left Mannum in 1853 and the first steam car was built in town in 1894 by David Shearer. **In town:** Mary Ann Reserve, a popular recreation reserve riverbank; PS *River Murray Princess* is moored here between cruises. Historic Leonaville homestead (1883), River La., built by town's first private developer, Gottlieb Schuetze. PS *Marion* built in 1897, located in Arnold Park, Randell St. Twin ferries to eastern side of river and scenic upriver drive. Lookout, off Purnong Rd to east. River cruises available weekends in summer. Self-guide scenic and historic walks, brochures available. May: Houseboat Hirers' Open Days. **In the area:** Excellent scenic drive from Wongulla to Cambrai; begins 20 km N. Choni Cottage country collectables, 10 km NW on Palmer Rd. Kia Marina, 8 km NE, largest river marina in State (boats and houseboats for hire). Water sports at Walker Flat, 26 km NE. Scenic drive north-east to Purnong, runs parallel to Halidon Bird Sanctuary

Vineyards and Wineries

South Australia produces more than 50 per cent of the wines and 95 per cent of the brandy made in Australia. Kilometres of vineyards stretch over valleys, plains and hillsides throughout several key winegrowing regions: the Barossa, McLaren Vale, Clare Valley, Riverland, Adelaide Hills, Coonawarra, Langhorne Creek and around Padthaway. New areas emerging include the Southern Eyre Peninsula, Kangaroo Island, Wrattonbully, Mount Benson, Adelaide Plains and Mount Gambier.

The **Barossa**, encompassing Barossa Valley and Eden Valley, Australia's most famous wine-producing area, is located about 55 kilometres north-east of Adelaide. It is a warm and intimate place of charming old towns, with vineyards spreading across undulating hills in well-tended, precise rows.

Grape vines at the Coonawarra, in the State's far south-east

The Barossa Valley was named in 1837 by Colonel Light in memory of Barrosa in Spain, where he fought a decisive battle in 1811. The recorded spelling 'Barossa' was an error that was never rectified. The district was settled in 1839 by English and Germanic settlers. Today the Barossa has a distinctive culture and atmosphere that derives from this Germanic concentration in the mid-19th century and is evidenced in the vineyards, stone buildings, restaurants, bakeries and Lutheran churches that dot the region.

The Barossa produces a wide variety of wines, in particular fragrant riesling and smooth, berry-flavoured shiraz. Chardonnay is a relative newcomer that has proved to be highly successful. Some of the most famous wineries of the Barossa are Yalumba, Orlando, Penfolds, Seppelt, Wolf Blass and Peter Lehmann. Some wineries are still run by members of the same families that established them last century. Others have been taken over by big international companies, but the distinctive qualities of the region's wine remain. There are many medium-size wineries making excellent wines, such as Grant Burge, Bethany, Basedow, Krondorf, Henschke, and many boutique wineries specialising in producing quality wines, including Barossa Settlers, Elderton, Rockford, Turkey Flat, Gnadenfrei Estate, Charles Cimicky and St Hallett.

The **McLaren Vale** region on the Fleurieu Peninsula, just south of Adelaide, is noted for its velvety shiraz, remarkably full-bodied cabernet sauvignon and, more recently, variously flavoured chardonnays. Nestled in the gentle folds of the Mount Lofty Ranges with a westerly view to the sea lies the township of McLaren Vale, the centre of this winegrowing area. There are more than 60 wineries in the region, among them Coriole, Chapel Hill, d'Arenberg, Dennis, Hardy's Tintara, Edwards and Chaffey, Haselgrove and Wirra Wirra, and they range from very large to very small. In most of the wineries, the person at the cellar door is the person who makes the wine — meet your maker at McLaren Vale!

The vineyards of the **Clare Valley** are about 130 kilometres north of Adelaide and produce fine table wines, including much of Australia's quality riesling. Winemaking in the valley dates back to 1852, and most of the current wineries are small family-owned operations. Four of the better-known wineries are Taylors, Leasingham, Sevenhill and Jim Barry.

Near the Victorian border is the **Riverland** region, famous for a wide range of products from golden chardonnay and old-vine grenache to ouzo and brandy. The well-known wineries include Kingston Estate at Kingston-on-Murray and Angove's near Renmark.

Winemaking is rapidly expanding throughout the **Adelaide Hills**, where the first vintage was produced in 1841. From ancient soils of moderate to low fertility the region produces fine sparkling and still wines of intense flavour and balance. Wineries include Karl Seppelts Grand Cru Estate, Gumeracha Cellars, Hillstowe and Petaluma.

The **Coonawarra** in the far south-east is best known for its award-winning red and white table wines from a small area of unique, rich, volcanic soil. The Coonawarra boasts Australia's most expensive viticultural real estate and produces most of the country's great cabernet sauvignon. The established wineries of the area are Wynns, Mildara, Redman and Rouge Homme. Newer wineries include The Blok Estate, Rymill, Balnaves and Hollicks. Padthaway Estate, just north of the Coonawarra, is another regular port of call for wine-lovers.

The **Langhorne Creek** region is 70 kilometres south of Adelaide, between the foothills of the Mount Lofty Ranges and Lake Alexandrina. It is a rapidly expanding wine region and produces mostly red wines with soft tannins. Bleasdale Vineyards is the best-known winery.

The **Southern Eyre Peninsula** winegrowing region is one of the State's newest. Located around Port Lincoln and North Shields are the two major wineries in this area: Boston Bay Winery and Delacolline Estate. **Kangaroo Island** established its first vineyard in 1987 and produces grapes for red wine. There is no winery on the island.

Most of the South Australian wineries are open for inspection, tastings and cellar-door sales.

For further information about hours of inspection and winery tours, contact the South Australian Travel Centre, 1 King William Street, Adelaide; (08) 8303 2033, or the information centre for each region. For more specialist information on South Australian wineries, contact the South Australian Wine and Brandy Industry Association, 555 The Parade, Magill; (08) 8331 0042. **Map references:** 302, for McLaren Vale region; 304, for Barossa Valley.

The Outback

Motorists contemplating travel in the outback should prepare their vehicles and familiarise themselves with expected conditions in advance.

The outback of South Australia covers a vast area and is one of the most remote areas of the world; conditions are harsh, the climate extreme and distances are daunting.

The countryside is usually dry, barren and dusty, but freak rains and heavy floods can transform the land. The enormous, salt Lake Eyre, dry creek beds and waterholes fill, wildflowers bloom and birdlife flocks to the area.

The main road to the Northern Territory, the Stuart Highway, is a sealed road. From **Port Augusta** to **Alice Springs** the road covers a distance of 1227 kilometres. Turn off the highway to visit **Woomera**, the mining town of **Roxby Downs**, Olympic Dam (mine tours available) and the opal-mining town of **Andamooka**.

Petrol, food and supplies are available at Port Augusta, Pimba, Glendambo, Coober Pedy, Cadney Homestead, Marla and Kulgera just over the Northern Territory border.

The notorious Birdsville Track starts at **Marree**, once a supply outpost for Afghan camel traders, and follows the route originally used to drove cattle from south-west Queensland to the railhead at Marree. The track lies between the Simpson Desert, with its giant sand dunes, and the desolate Sturt's Stony Desert. Artesian bores line the route, pouring out 64 million litres of salty boiling water every day. The road is well maintained; however, care should be taken during and after heavy rains. *Petrol and supplies are available at Marree and Mungerannie Hotel, and at Birdsville over the Queensland border.*

The Oodnadatta Track runs from Marree to **Oodnadatta** and continues on to join the Stuart Highway at Marla, 212 kilometres west. *Fuel is available only at Marree, William Creek, Oodnadatta and Marla.*

The Strzelecki Track begins at Lyndhurst; a harsh, dusty road, it stretches 459 kilometres to the almost deserted outpost of **Innamincka**, with *no stops for petrol or supplies.*

Motorists intending to travel in the outback should be prepared and well equipped (read the section on Outback Motoring p. 603). Many of the roads in the outback are unsealed with sandy patches. Heavy rain can cut access for several days. Motorists are advised to ring the Northern Roads Condition Hotline on 1300 361 033 for information before departure.

For further information on the area, contact Flinders Ranges and Outback South Australia Tourism, 41 Flinders Tce, Port Augusta 5700, freecall 1800 633 060. Web site www.flinders.outback.on.net **See also:** individual entries in A–Z listing for details on towns in bold type. **Map references:** 308–13.

Castle Rock, near Coober Pedy

for 15 km. Mannum Waterfalls Reserve, 10 km S, for picnics and scenic walks. **Visitor information:** Arnold Park, Randell St; (08) 8569 1303.

Marree
Pop. 85

MAP REF. 308 I1, 310 I13

Marree is a tiny outback town 645 km N of Adelaide at the junction of the legendary Birdsville and Oodnadatta tracks. There are remnants of date palms planted by Afghan traders who drove their camel trains into the outback in the 1800s and played a significant role in opening up the outback. Desolate salt-bush country surrounds the town, now a service centre for the north-east. **In town:** Replica of early bush mosque. Mosaic sundial. Camel sculpture, made out of railway sleepers. June: Picnic Races. July: Australian Camel Cup. **In the area:** 2 km W from town centre, historic ceme-tery. *As with all outback driving, care must be taken when attempting the Birdsville and Oodnadatta tracks. These tracks are unsealed with sandy patches. Heavy rain in the area can cut access for several days. Motorists are advised to ring the Northern Roads Condition Hotline on 1300 361 033 for information before departure.* Also read section on Outback Motoring (p. 603); daily road information available from information centre. On the Birdsville Track, fuel avail-able only at Marree, Mungerannie Hotel (204 km N) and Birdsville (516 km N). On the Oodnadatta Track, fuel available only at Marree, William Creek (202 km NW), Oodnadatta (405 km NW) and Marla (617 km NW). Lake Eyre National Park, 90 km N, accessible via Muloorina Station; Desert Parks Pass required (avail-able information centre, and see section on National Parks). Ruins of railway sidings from original Ghan line to Alice Springs at Curdimurka Siding and Bore, about 90 km W; setting for Outback Ball in Oct. (even-numbered years). Wabma Kadarbu Mound Springs Conservation Park, 130 km W, features a series of mound springs, including Coward Springs, The Bubbler, Blanche Cup and Hamilton Hill (extinct); Desert Parks Pass required (available information centre, and see section on National Parks); pro-lific birdlife at Coward Springs, an extensive pond formed by warm water bubbling to the surface; nearby old date palms and remnants of old plantation. **Visitor information:** Outback Road-house, Oodnadatta Track; (08) 8675 8360. **See also:** The Outback p. 278.

Melrose
Pop. 205

MAP REF. 307 J2, 309 J12

Melrose, a quiet settlement at the foot of Mt Remarkable, 268 km N of Adelaide, is the oldest town in the Flinders Ranges. **In town:** In Stuart St: old police station and courthouse (1862), now National Trust Museum featuring colonial furniture and farm implements (2 p.m.–5 p.m. daily); Mt Remarkable Hotel (1857); Bluey's Blacksmith Shop (1865), now B&B and coffee shop; Serendipity Gallery. In Nott St: North Star Hotel (1854); Melrose Inn (Royal Exchange Hotel, 1857), National Trust property (not open to public). Ruins of Jacka's Brewery (1877), former flour mill. Self-guide historic walk, brochure available. Pleasant walks and picnic spots along creek. Scenic views from Monument and Melrose Mine, Joe's Rd. Further on, Cathedral Rock. **In the area:** Walking trail with superb views (5 hrs return) from town to top of Mt Remarkable (956 m); map available. Mt Remarkable National Park, 2 km W. Near Murray Town, 14 km S: scenic look-outs at Box Hill, Magnus Hill and Baroota Nob; scenic drive west through Port Germein Gorge; 3 km SW is Murratana sheep property specialising in breeding sheep with coloured wool (visitors welcome). Booleroo Steam Traction Preservation Society's Museum, Booleroo Centre, 15 km SE (open by appt). **Visitor information:** Caravan Park, Joes Rd; (08) 8666 2060. Web site www.lga.sa.gov.au/ dcmr **See also:** National Parks p. 262.

Meningie
Pop. 918

MAP REF. 305 D4, 307 M12

Meningie is set on the edge of the fresh-water Lake Albert and the northern tip of the vast saltpans of the Coorong National Park, 159 km S of Adelaide. Fishing is a major industry. The area abounds with birdlife, including ibis, pelicans, cormorants, ducks and swans. Sailing, boating, water-skiing and swimming are popular. **In the area:** Camp Coorong, 12 km S, museum and cultural centre; bush tucker tours. At The Coorong, south and west: inland waterways, islands, ocean beach and wildlife; 4WD tours. Scenic drive west following Lake Albert, adjacent to Lake Alexandrina which is the largest permanent freshwater lake in the country (50 000 ha). Poltalloch homestead, 30 km NW, one of the oldest in the region; accommodation and tours. Further west, channel between lakes is

crossed by ferry service at Narrung. **Visitor information:** Melaleuca Centre, 76 Princes Hwy; (08) 8575 1259. **See also:** National Parks p. 262; The Coorong p. 274.

Millicent
Pop. 4717

MAP REF. 305 G11

A thriving commercial and industrial town 50 km from Mt Gambier, Millicent is in the middle of a huge tract of land reclaimed in the 1870s. Today rural and fishing industries contribute to the area's prosperity, with pine forests supporting a pulp mill, paper mill and sawmill. **In town:** On northern edge of town, gum trees surround a swimming lake and picnic area. Award-winning Living History Museum and Admella Gallery, housed in original primary school (1873), Mt Gambier Rd. **In the area:** Nangula Country Market, 7 km SE, 2nd Sun. each month (not Jan.). Tantanoola, 21 km SE, home of famous 'Tantanoola Tiger' (a Syrian wolf shot in the 1890s); 'tiger' now stuffed and displayed in the Tantanoola Tiger Hotel. Underground caves, 20 km SE in Tantanoola Caves Conservation Park, fascinating limestone formations. National Trust Woolshed (1863) at Glencoe, 29 km E. Scenic pine-forest drive to Mount Burr, 10 km NE. Millicent Wildlife Park and Nursery, 2 km N: native birds and animals, beautiful gardens, rare plants for sale. Lake McIntyre, 5 km N: prolific birdlife, native fish and yabbies, walking trail, viewing platforms, bird hide, picnic/barbecue facilities. Fresh farm flowers, 20 km N at Furner. Massive sand dune system and fascinating flora and fauna in Canunda National Park, 27 km W (accessed from Millicent and Southend); self-guide walks, leaflets avail-able. **Visitor information:** 1 Mt Gambier Rd; (08) 8733 3205.

Minlaton
Pop. 733

MAP REF. 306 I9

Located 209 km W of Adelaide on the Yorke Peninsula, Minlaton was originally called Gum Flat because of the giant eucalypts in the area. Pioneer aviator Capt. Harry Butler, pilot of the *Red Devil*, a 1916 Bristol monoplane, was born here. **In town:** In Main St: Harry Butler Memorial; fauna park; National Trust Museum (check opening times); Harvest Corner Information and Craft, for local crafts. **In the area:** Gum Flat Homestead

The picturesque Blue Lake, Mount Gambier

Gallery, 1 km E: pioneer homestead, local artists' work. At Port Vincent, 25 km E: good swimming, yachting, water-skiing; Yacht Race in Jan. Gipsy Waggon holidays at Brentwood, 14 km SW. Scenic Port Rickaby and Bluff Beach, 16 km NW. **Visitor information:** Harvest Corner Information and Craft, 59 Main St; (08) 8853 2600. Web site www. classiccountry.org.au/minlaton.html **See also:** The Yorke Peninsula p. 281.

Mintaro Pop. 80

MAP REF. 307 L5
The township nestles among rolling hills and rich agricultural land, 19 km SE of Clare. A Heritage Town, Mintaro is a timepiece of early colonial architecture. Many buildings display the fine slate for which the district is world-renowned; the quarry opened in 1854. **In town:** Early colonial buildings, 18 with heritage listings. Heritage walk, brochure available. Two historic cemeteries. **In the area:** Magnificent classical architecture of Martindale Hall (1880), 3 km SE; location for film *Picnic at Hanging Rock*

(1975), now offers accommodation and dining. **Visitor information:** Town Hall, 229 Main North Rd, Clare; (08) 8842 2131. **See also:** Day Tours from Adelaide p. 253.

Moonta Pop. 2898

MAP REF. 306 I6
The towns of Moonta, Kadina and Wallaroo form the corners of the 'Copper Coast' or 'Little Cornwall'. Moonta is a popular seaside town 163 km NW of Adelaide, with pleasant beaches and good fishing at Moonta Bay. A rich copper-ore deposit was discovered here in 1861 and soon thousands of miners, including many from Cornwall, flocked to the area. The mines were abandoned in the 1920s with the slump in copper prices and rising labour costs. **In town:** Stone buildings, charming Queen Square and picturesque town hall opposite the square in George St. All Saints Church (1873), cnr Blanche and Milne tces. Galleries and gift shops. Self-guide walks/drives in town and around mines, maps available. Twilight Market at Old

Moonta Railway Station, Sat. evenings in Jan. May: Kernewek Lowender, prize-winning Cornish festival held in conjunction with nearby towns of Kadina and Wallaroo (odd-numbered years). Sept.: Agricultural Show. **In the area:** Moonta Mines, a State Heritage Area, 2 km SE, on Verran Tce: old primary school (1878), now Moonta Mines National Trust Museum, features mining artifacts and history of local Cornish miners; Cornish miner's cottage (1870) furnished in period style; pump house, shafts, tailings heaps, ruins of mines offices; Moonta Mines Railway tours through mines area (check opening times). Wheal Hughes Mine, 3 km N on Wallaroo Rd, tours 1 p.m. daily (book at information centre; subject to weather conditions and maintenance). Moonta Wildlife Park at Moonta Bay, 5 km W. **Visitor information:** Moonta Station Visitor Information Centre, Old Moonta Railway Station, Kadina Rd; (08) 8825 1891. Web site www. classiccountry.org.au/moonta.html **See also:** The Yorke Peninsula p. 281.

Morgan Pop. 492

MAP REF. 307 N6
Once one of the busiest river ports in the State, Morgan is on the Murray River, 164 km NE of Adelaide. **In town:** Antique shops, Railway Tce. Self-guide trail covers historic sites: the impressive wharves (1877), standing 12 m high, constructed for the riverboat industry; customs house and courthouse near railway station, reminders of town's thriving past. Picnic/barbecue facilities, with children's play area, near customs house. Dockyards on Oval Rd (tours by appt). Port of Morgan Historic Museum in old railway buildings on riverfront, off High St (open by appt). PS *Mayflower* (1884), still operating; details from museum's caretaker. Houseboats for hire. **In the area:** Morgan Conservation Park, across river. Fossicking for fossils near township. White Dam Conservation Park, 9 km NW. On Renmark Ave: Engineering and Water Supply Pumping Station, 2 km E (tours by appt); Nor-West Bend private museum, 8 km E (open by appt); Riverland Camel Farm and Trail Ride, 13 km E (day and overnight trips). Free ferry across river, on road to Waikerie (operates 24 hours). **Visitor information:** Morgan Roadhouse, Fourth St; (08) 8540 2205. Web site www.riverland. net.au/~morgansa/

Mount Gambier Pop. 22 037

MAP REF. 305 H12

In 1800 Lieutenant James Grant sighted an extinct volcano and named it Mount Gambier. The city, 460 km SE of Adelaide, is in the centre of the largest softwood pine plantation in the Commonwealth and surrounded by rich farming, horticulture, viticulture and dairy country. The Hentys built the first dwelling in 1841 and by 1850 there was a weekly postal service to Adelaide. The white Mount Gambier stone used in most buildings, together with fine parks and gardens, make an attractive environment. **In town:** Historic buildings: town hall (1862), Commercial St; Old Post Office (1865), Bay Rd; many old hotels. Heritage walks, leaflets available. Open caves: Cave Garden, Bay Rd; Umpherston Sinkhole, Jubilee Hwy East; Engelbrecht Cave, Jubilee Hwy. Old Courthouse Law and Heritage Centre, Bay Rd, a National Trust museum. Lewis'

Museum, Pick Ave. In Jubilee Hwy East: the Lady Nelson Visitor and Discovery Centre, has full-scale replica of *Lady Nelson* as part of centre's structure; Dimjalla Park, fun park. Riddoch Art Gallery, in complex of 19th century buildings, Commercial St East. Market, each Sat., Fletcher Jones Complex. Feb.: Country Music Festival. May: Generations in Jazz. Dec.: Carols by Candlelight. **In the area:** Christmas Lights drive, map available. On the outskirts of town: crater lakes, particularly Blue Lake (average depth 70 m), which changes from sombre winter blue to brilliant turquoise each Nov. then reverts at end of summer; nearby scenic 5-km drive offers lookouts, wildlife reserve, picnic areas and boardwalks; Pumping Station at Blue Lake, daily tours down through pumping station to lake level. Timber mill tours; bookings essential. Blue Lake Papermill 2 km E, in Pollard Close, old way of making paper (tours). Tarpeena Fairy Tale Park, 22 km N on Penola Rd. Glencoe Woolshed

(1863), 23 km NW, National Trust building (open Sun. p.m. or by appt). Haig's Vineyard, 4 km S. Mount Schank, 17 km S, excellent views of surrounding district from summit. Glenelg River cruises from Nelson (Vic.), 36 km SE; tours of spectacular Princess Margaret Rose Cave. Several gardens in area, details from information centre. **Visitor information:** Lady Nelson Visitor and Discovery Centre, Jubilee Hwy East; (08) 8724 9750. Web site www.mountgambiertourism.com.au

Murray Bridge Pop. 12 831

MAP REF. 300 I12, 305 D2, 307 M10

Murray Bridge, which overlooks a broad sweep of the Murray River, is South Australia's largest river town. When settled in the 1850s it was a centre for the riverboat traders. Now water sports, river cruises and excellent accommodation make Murray Bridge a perfect holiday spot. The South Eastern Fwy

The Yorke Peninsula

Yorke Peninsula was put on the map by the discovery of rich copper-ore deposits in 1861 and the influx of thousands of miners, many from Cornwall. Today, it is one of the world's richest wheat and barley regions.

The drive down the highway on the east coast is mainly within sight of the sea. Many of the east-coast towns have excellent fishing from long jetties once used for loading grain ships. Fishing from the beach and rocks is also excellent, as is surf fishing.

The west coast is lined with safe swimming beaches and beautiful coastal scenery. **Port Victoria** was once the main port of call for sailing ships transporting grain. Further north is **Moonta** with its old stone buildings and mining history.

Innes National Park with its diverse birdlife and impressive coastal scenery is on the southern tip of the peninsula. Pondalowie Bay is a must for surfers.

For further information on the Yorke Peninsula, contact the local information centres: at Moonta (Moonta Station Visitor Information Centre, Old Moonta Railway Station, Kadina Rd, (08) 8825 1891); at Minlaton (Harvest Corner Information and Craft, 59 Main St, (08) 8853 2600). Web site www.classiccountry.org.au **See also:** National Parks p. 262 and individual entries in A–Z listing for details on parks and towns in bold type. **Map reference:** 306 H8.

Innes National Park

provides access to Adelaide, 80 km away. **In town:** Captain's Cottage Museum, Thomas St. In Jervois Rd: Dundee's Wildlife Park; Puzzle Park, a funpark for adults as well as children. Heritage and Cultural Community Mural, 3rd St. Pomberuk Aboriginal Art Gallery, Adelaide Rd. Riverside reserves: Sturt Reserve, offering fishing, swimming, picnic and playground facilities; Hume Reserve, Hume Rd; Long Island Reserve, Long Island Rd. Sims Park, Lookout Dr., for views of town. Charter and regular cruises on MV *Barrangul* and PS *Captain Proud*; charter cruises on PS *Proud Mary*. Town and riverside walk. Sept.: International Pedal Prix, novelty bikes, endurance event. Oct.: 110 km Waterski Race. Nov.: Steam and Riverboat Rally. **In the area:** Monarto Zoological Park, 10 km W off Old Princes Hwy, open-range zoo with many endangered species. Willow Point Winery, 10 km S on Jervois Rd. Riverglen Marina, 11 km S, has houseboats for hire. At the historic railway town of Tailem Bend, 25 km SE: excellent views across Murray River; children's playground featuring old steam locomotive; Old Tailem Town Pioneer Village, 5 km N; scenic drive via ferry across river to Jervois, then south-west to Wellington where river meets lake; restored courthouse (1864) complex at Wellington. Mypolonga, 14 km N, centre for surrounding beautiful citrus and stone-fruit orchard area and rich dairying country. Australia's largest clock, 8 km NW on Palmer Rd. At Avoca Dell, 5 km upstream: boating, waterskiing, mini-golf, good picnic and caravan facilities. Thiele Reserve, east of river, good for water-skiing. Other riverside reserves are at Swanport, 5 km SE; White Sands, 10 km SE. Lookouts: White Hill, west on Princes Hwy; east at Swanport Bridge. **Visitor information:** Murray Bridge Information Centre, 3 South Tce; (08) 8532 6660. Web site www.rcmb.sa.gov.au

Naracoorte   Pop. 4674

MAP REF. 305 H9
Situated 330 km SE of Adelaide, Naracoorte dates from the 1840s. The area is renowned for its World Heritage-listed limestone caves. Beef cattle, sheep, grains and wine grapes are the main primary industries. **In town:** The Sheep's Back wool museum, craft gallery and information centre in former flour mill (1870), MacDonnell St. Naracoorte

Museum and Snake Pit, Jenkins Tce, museum collection and live snakes (closed mid-July to end Aug.). Mini Jumbuk Factory, Ormerod St, for Visitor Centre and display gallery, including woollen products. Restored locomotive on display in Pioneer Park. Regional Art Gallery, Smith St. Jubilee Park, off Park Tce: nature park, walks, swimming lake. May: Swap Meeting; Young Riders Equestrian Event. Oct.: Agricultural Show. Dec.: Carols by Candlelight. **In the area:** At Naracoorte Caves Conservation Park, 12 km SE: World Heritage-listed Wonambi Fossil Centre, has life-like representations of large extinct animals in rainforest environment; Blanche Cave and Alexandra Cave, have spectacular stalagmites and stalactites; high-tech bat-viewing in new interpretive centre; guided and self-guide cave tours and adventure tours. Tiny Train Park, 3 km S, mini-train rides and mini-golf. Wrattonbully wine district, 15 km E. Bool Lagoon Game Reserve, 17 km S, wetland area of international significance and haven for ibis and numerous water-bird species; boardwalks and bird hide. Coonawarra wine region, located 40 km S. Padthaway and Keppoch wine districts, about 40 km NW. Lucindale 26 km W, Lucindale Show in February. Bourne's Bird Museum, 27 km SW, huge display of mounted birds (check opening times). **Visitor information:** The Sheep's Back, MacDonnell St; (08) 8762 1518, freecall 1800 244 421. **See also:** National Parks p. 262; Wildlife-Watching p. 268.

Nuriootpa   Pop. 3486

MAP REF. 300 F4, 304 G4, 307 M8
The Para River runs through Nuriootpa, its course marked by fine parks and picnic spots. The town is the commercial centre of the Barossa Valley. **In town:** Coulthard Reserve, off Penrice Rd. Pioneer settler's home, Coulthard House, Murray St (not open). Luhrs Pioneer German Cottage, Light Pass Rd. St Petri Church, First St. Feb.: Barossa Under the Stars (concert with international performers). Easter: Barossa Vintage Festival (odd-numbered years). Sept.: Gourmet Barossa. Oct.: Barossa Music Festival. **In the area:** Wineries, *south of town:* Elderton Wines, Hamilton's Ewell Vineyards, Yunbar Estate, Tarac Distillers (tastings), Penfolds Wines, Kaesler Wines; *west of town:* Branson Wines, Heritage Wines, Viking Wines, Gnadenfrei Estate Winery,

Seppelt Wines (tours), Greenock Creek Cellars; *north-east of town:* The Willows Vineyard, Wolf Blass Wines; *south-east of town:* Barossa Cottage Wines; also other wineries in Barossa Valley; most wineries are open for tastings and cellar-door sales. **Visitor information:** Barossa Wine and Visitor Centre, 66 Murray St, Tanunda; (08) 8563 0600, freecall 1800 812 662. **See also:** Vineyards and Wineries p. 277.

Oodnadatta   Pop. 160

MAP REF. 310 B6
A tiny but widely known outback town 1050 km NW of Adelaide, Oodnadatta is an old railway town with a well-preserved sandstone station (1890), now a museum. It is believed that the name Oodnadatta originated from an Aboriginal term meaning 'yellow blossom of the mulga'. Fuel and supplies available. May: Race Meeting and Gymkhana. **In the area:** Witjira National Park, gateway to Simpson Desert, 180 km N; hot thermal ponds at Dalhousie Springs; nearby, Dalhousie ruins (of early pastoral station); camping and accommodation at Mt Dare homestead; camping at Dalhousie Springs (permits from information centre). The Oodnadatta Track runs from Marree through Oodnadatta and joins the Stuart Hwy at Marla, 212 km W. Scenic drive to Painted Desert, 100 km SW. **Visitor information:** Pink Roadhouse, Ikaturka Tce; (08) 8670 7822, freecall 1800 802 074. **See also:** The Outback p. 278.

Penola   Pop. 1189

MAP REF. 232 A3, 305 I10
One of the oldest towns in the south-east of the State, Penola, 50 km N of Mount Gambier, has fine examples of 1850s slab- and hewn-timber cottages. Penola is noted for its association with Mary MacKillop a Josephite nun who in 1866 established here Australia's first school to cater for any child, regardless of income or social class. In 1994 she was beatified (the second-last step in the process of being declared a saint by the Vatican). Several Australian poets are also associated with Penola: Adam Lindsay Gordon, John Shaw Neilson and Will Ogilvie left poetry inspired by the landscape and lifestyle encountered here. **In town:** In Petticoat La.: heritage buildings and art and craft shops. Stone classroom in which Mary MacKillop taught, cnr Portland St and Petticoat La.; interpretive

centre behind classroom. At information centre: details of bike trails and self-guide walk; John Riddoch Interpretive Centre featuring local history displays; Hydrocarbon Centre featuring hands-on and static displays of gas process. Jan.: Vignerons Cup. May: Penola Festival. **In the area:** Yallum Park homestead (1880), 8 km W, historic homestead built by John Riddoch; founder of Coonawarra wine industry. Signposted woodland and wetland walk at Penola Conservation Park, 10 km W. Coonawarra region, 10 km N, more than 20 wineries; most open for tastings and sales. **Visitor information:** 27 Arthur St; (08) 8737 2855.

Peterborough   Pop. 1855

MAP REF. 307 L2, 309 K12

Peterborough is an old railway town 250 km N of Adelaide, surrounded by grain-growing and pastoral country. It is the principal town on the Port Pirie to Broken Hill railway line. **In town:** Steamtown, open daily: historic rolling stock, unique roundhouse and turntable; narrow-gauge steam-train trips during winter (check operation times). Rann's Museum, Moscow St, 19th-century exhibits including farm implements. The Gold Battery, end Tripney Ave, an ore-crushing machine (open by appt). Saint Cecilia, Callary St, gracious home (with splendid stained glass) once a bishop's residence, offering accommodation, dining and murder-mystery nights. In Queen St: Ley's Museum, exhibition of antiques; Victoria Park, has constructed lake and islands. Guided bus tour of town. Self-guide drives and town walk, brochures available. Feb.: Rodeo. **In the area:** Terowie, 24 km SE, old railway Historic Town with several historic buildings, including Terowie Hotel (1874), Church of St Michael and St John (1877) and Pioneer Cottages (1882), brochure available. At Magnetic Hill, 8 km W of Black Rock, a vehicle with the engine turned off can roll uphill! **Visitor information:** Main St; (08) 8651 2708.

Pinnaroo   Pop. 606

MAP REF. 120 A11, 236 A10, 305 I3, 307 R10

This little township on the Mallee Hwy is only 6 km from the Victorian border. **In town:** In Mallee Tourist and Heritage Centre, Railway Tce Sth: Australia's largest cereal collection (1300 varieties); Historical Museum; working printing

Naracoorte Caves, a World Heritage-listed area, south-east of Naracoorte

museum; farm-machinery museum; Gum Family Collection of farm machinery. Animal park and aviary with native birds, South Tce. **In the area:** Walking trail in Karte Conservation Park, 30 km NW on Karte Rd. Peebinga Conservation Park, 42 km N on Loxton Rd. In Scorpion Springs Conservation Park, 28 km S, walking trail at Pine Hut Soak. Pertendi walking trail, 49 km S. Near Lameroo, 39 km W: Byrne pug and pine homestead (1898), Yappara Rd, contact information centre to gain entry); Baan Hill Reserve, 20 km SW, natural soakage area surrounded by sandhills and scrub; Billiatt Conservation Park, 37 km N. **Visitor information:** Council Offices, Day St; (08) 8577 8002.

Port Augusta   Pop. 13 914

MAP REF. 303 A13, 308 I11

A thriving industrial city at the head of Spencer Gulf and in the shadow of the Flinders Ranges, Port Augusta is the most northerly port in South Australia, 308 km from Adelaide. It is a supply centre for the outback areas and the large sheep stations of the district. Port Augusta is an important link on the Indian–Pacific railway and a stopover for the famous Ghan train to Alice Springs, which departs from Adelaide. It is also a popular stopping point for motorists en route to Flinders Ranges and the outback. The city has played a part in the State's development since the State Electricity Trust built major power stations here. Fuelled by coal from the huge open-cut mines at Leigh Creek, the stations generate more than a third of the State's electricity. **In town:** In Flinders Tce: multi-award-winning Wadlata Outback Centre, introduces sights and sounds of Flinders Ranges and the outback; Fountain Gallery, open during exhibitions. Homestead Park Pioneer Museum, Elsie St, has picnic areas, recreation of a blacksmith's shop, old steam train and crane, and rebuilt 130-year-old pine-log Yudnappinna homestead. Royal Flying Doctor Service Base, Vincent St, open weekdays. School of the Air, Power Cres., tours during school-term time. Curdnatta Art and Pottery Gallery in town's original railway station, Commercial Rd (check

The Eyre Peninsula

The Eyre Peninsula is a vast region stretching from Whyalla in the east to the Western Australian border in the west, and, in a north-south direction, from the Gawler Ranges to Port Lincoln. Spencer Gulf borders the eastern edge of the peninsula, along which are located a number of small coastal towns featuring sheltered waters, safe swimming, white sandy beaches and excellent fishing from either shore or boat. The peaceful resort towns of **Cowell**, Arno Bay and Port Neill are charming. Cowell has the added attraction of being one of the world's major sources of black and green jade.

Whyalla is the second largest city in South Australia and acts as an important gateway to Eyre Peninsula. Located near the top of Spencer Gulf, this bustling, industrially based city also offers a wide range of attractions for the visitor.

The southern Eyre Peninsula includes the tourist resort towns of **Tumby Bay**, famous for its fishing and the beautiful Sir Joseph Banks Group of islands nearby; the jewel in the crown, the city of **Port Lincoln**, nestled on blue Boston Bay; and **Coffin Bay**, with its magnificent sheltered waters.

In stark contrast to the sheltered waters of Spencer Gulf, the west coast is exposed to the full force of the Southern Ocean and offers some of the most spectacular coastal scenery to be found in Australia. This coast is punctuated by a number of bays and inlets and, not surprisingly,

several resort towns have flourished where shelter can be found from precipitous cliffs and pounding surf. **Elliston**, Venus Bay, Port Kenny, **Streaky Bay**, Smoky Bay and **Ceduna** — all offer the visitor a diverse range of coastal scenery, good fishing and other water-related activities. The only known mainland breeding colony of Australian sea-lions (at Point Labatt), and Murphy's Haystacks, windworn granite formations over 1500 million years old, are both south of Streaky Bay.

Ceduna provides a vital service and accommodation facility for traffic across Australia, and acts as a gateway information centre for visitors approaching the region from the west.

The hinterland of Eyre Peninsula encompasses the picturesque Koppio Hills in the south, the vast grain-growing tracts of the central region and the eternal beauty of the Gawler Ranges in the north.

The Nullarbor is a vast treeless plain, bordered in the south by towering limestone cliffs that drop sheer to the pounding Southern Ocean. Here schools of southern right whales can be seen along the coastline between June and October on their annual breeding migration. Sightings occur regularly and are on the increase.

For more information on the area, contact the Eyre Peninsula Tourism Association, Jobomi House, Liverpool St, Port Lincoln; (08) 8682 4688. Web site www.epta.com.au **See also:** Wildlife-Watching p. 268. For details on towns in bold type, see individual entries in A–Z town listing. **Map reference: 306, 308 & 315.**

Massive limestone cliffs on the edge of the Nullarbor

opening times). Self-guide heritage walk, includes town hall (1887), Commercial Rd; courthouse (1884) with cells built of Kapunda marble, cnr Jervios St and Beauchamp's La.; St Augustine's Church (1882), Church St, with magnificent stained glass (brochure available). Australian Arid Lands Botanic Gardens, Stuart Hwy, northern outskirts of town. Northern Power Station, northern outskirts (tours Mon.–Fri., 11 a.m. and 1 p.m.). Scenic views and picnic facilities: McLellan Lookout, Whiting Pde, site of Matthew Flinders' landing in 1802; Water Tower Lookout (1882), Mitchell Tce. Matthew Flinders Lookout, end of McSporran Cres., provides excellent view of Gulf and Flinders Ranges. Mar.: Outback Surfboat Carnival. Apr.: Antique and Craft Fair. June: Cup Carnival (horseracing). Aug.: Camel Cup. **In the area:** Scenic drive north-east to splendid Pichi Richi Pass, historic Quorn, and Warren Gorge; see the same sights by train on Pichi Richi Railway, 33-km round trip operating from Quorn (Easter–Nov., check days of operation). Mt Remarkable National Park, 63 km SE, features rugged mountain terrain, magnificent gorges and abundant wildlife. Historic Melrose, 65 km SE, oldest town in Flinders Ranges. **Visitor information:** Wadlata Outback Centre, Flinders Tce; (08) 8641 0793. Web site www.epta.com.au **See also:** Outback Adventure p. 256; Wildlife-Watching p. 268; The Outback p. 278.

Port Broughton   Pop. 628

MAP REF. 307 J4

On the extreme north-west coast of Yorke Peninsula, Port Broughton is 169 km from Adelaide. Set on a protected inlet, the town is a major port for fishing boats and is noted for its deep-sea prawns. **In town:** Safe swimming beach along foreshore. Heritage Museum, Edmund St, has local historical displays. In Harvey St: Shandele porcelain dolls made and on display; Council Office Museum in old school building, has displays relating to history of local government in the area. Historical walking trail, brochure available. **In the area:** Fisherman's Bay, 10 km N, a popular fishing, boating and holiday spot. **Visitor information:** Council Offices, Bay St; (08) 8635 2107. Web site www.classiccountry.org.au/ptbroughton.html

First light at Port Augusta

Port Elliot   Pop. 1427

MAP REF. 301 H8, 305 C3, 307 L11

Only 5 km NE of Victor Harbor, Port Elliot is a charming historic town with the main focus on its scenic Horseshoe Bay. The town was established in 1854, the same year Australia's first public horse-drawn railway operated between Goolwa and Port Elliot. **In town:** In The Strand: National Trust historical display at railway station (1911); council chambers (1879); police station (1853); St Jude's Church (1854); spectacular views from Freeman's Knob at end of The Strand. Port Elliot Art Pottery, Main Rd. Scheduled stop for steam-train rides on Steam Ranger, operating between Victor Harbor and Goolwa. Self-guide town walks, brochure available. Market 1st and 3rd Sat. each month, Primary School, North Tce. **In the area:** Crows Nest Lookout, 6 km N, excellent views of coast. North-east between town and Middleton, Basham Beach Regional Park has scenic coastal trails with interpretive signage. At Middleton, 6 km NE, Heritage Bakery; old flour mill, largest building in town; further 5 km, Middleton Winery. **Visitor information:** Dodd & Page Land Agents, 51 The Strand; (08) 8554 2029. **See also:** Day Tours from Adelaide p. 253.

Port Lincoln   Pop. 11 678

MAP REF. 306 D8

Port Lincoln, originally considered as a site for the State's capital, is on attractive Boston Bay, which is three times the size of Sydney Harbour. The port, 250 km due west of Adelaide across St Vincent and Spencer gulfs, was reached by Matthew Flinders in 1802 and settled by Europeans in 1839. With its sheltered waters, Mediterranean climate, scenic coastal roads and farming hinterland, Port Lincoln is a popular holiday destination. It is also the base for Australia's largest tuna fleet and tuna-farming industry, and an export centre for wheat, wool, fat lambs, live sheep, frozen fish, lobster, prawns, abalone and tuna. The coastline is deeply indented, offering magnificent scenery, sheltered coves, steep cliff faces and impressive surf beaches. **In town:** Boston Bay for swimming, water-skiing, yachting and excellent fishing. Mill Cottage Museum (1867) and Settler's Cottage Museum, both in picturesque Flinders Park. Old Mill Lookout, Dorset Pl., offers views of town and bay. Lincoln Hotel (1840), Tasman Tce, oldest hotel on Eyre Peninsula. Axel Stenross Maritime Museum, Lincoln Hwy, north end of town; nearby, First Landing site. Rose-Wal Memorial Shell Museum in grounds of Eyre Peninsula Old Folks Home, Flinders Hwy. Arteyrea Gallery, Washington St, community art centre. M. B. Kotz Collection of Stationary Engines, Baltimore St. Parnkalla Walking Trail, winds around edge of harbour, brochure available. Lincoln Cove, off Ravendale Rd, includes marina, leisure centre with waterslide, holiday charter boats and base for commercial fishing

Commercial fishing fleet moored at Lincoln Cove, Port Lincoln

fleet. Yacht and boat charters for game-fishing, diving, day fishing and to view sea-lions, dolphins and birdlife around Sir Joseph Banks Group of Islands and Dangerous Reef. Regular launch cruises of Boston Bay to visit commerical tuna farm. *Dangerous Reef Explorer* for group charter to Dangerous Reef, off Boston Island, home for large sea-lion colony, and Boston Bay. Apex Wheelhouse, original wheelhouse from tuna boat *Boston Bay*, adjacent to Kirton Point Caravan Park, Hindmarsh St. Jan.: Tunarama Festival (celebrates opening of tuna season). Feb.: Lincoln Week Regatta. **In the area:** Winter Hill Lookout, 5 km NW on Flinders Hwy. Glen-Forest Animal Park, 15 km NW, has native animals and bird-feeding (check opening times). Wildflowers in spring, 30 km NW near Wanilla. Boston Bay Winery, 6 km N on Lincoln Hwy; Delacolline Estate Winery, Whillas Rd, 1 km W, (both offer sales on weekends or by appt). At Poonindie, 20 km N, church (1850) with two chimneys. At Koppio, 38 km N: Koppio Smithy Museum (open Tues.–Sun. and school holidays) also houses fencing equipment museum; Glendarra Rose Garden (late Oct.–May); Tod Reservoir museum with heritage display, nearby picnic area. At Lincoln National Park, 20 km S: wildlife, network of walking trails; Flinders

Monument on Stamford Hill for views; Flinders Tablet in Memory Cove, a plaque in memory of crew members lost in seas nearby during Flinders' 1802 voyage (gate key and permit from information centre). Whalers Way, a privately owned, scenic cliff-top tourist drive on southernmost tip of Eyre Peninsula: stunning coastal scenery from Flinders Lookout (permit from information centre). On road to Whalers Way: Constantia Designer Craftsmen, world-class furniture factory and showroom (guided tours); historic Mikkira sheep station (keys and permit from information centre). For boating enthusiasts: Spilsby and Thistle islands (accommodation) and Boston Island; Thistle and Wedge islands (both privately owned), popular with bluewater sailors and anglers. **Visitor information:** 66 Tasman Tce; (08) 8683 3544. Web site www.epta.com.au **See also:** The Eyre Peninsula p. 284.

Port MacDonnell Pop. 662

MAP REF. 305 H13
Port MacDonnell, 28 km S of Mount Gambier, is a quiet fishing town that was once a thriving port. The rock-lobster fishing fleet here is the largest in the State. **In town:** Maritime Museum, Meylin St, features salvaged artifacts from

shipwrecks and photographic history of town. Jan.: Bayside Festival. **In the area:** 'Dingley Dell' (1862, but restored), 2 km W, home of poet Adam Lindsay Gordon, now a museum. Opposite, start of Germein Reserve boardwalk, an 8-km return walk through wetlands. Cape Northumberland Lighthouse, on coastline west of town. Devonshire teas at Ye Olde Post Office Tea Rooms at Allendale East, 6 km N. Walking track to summit of Mt Schank, 10 km N, crater of extinct volcano. Nearby Mt Schank Fish Farm sells fresh fish and yabbies. Heading east, good surf-fishing at Orwell Rocks. Sinkholes for experienced cave divers at Ewens Ponds, 7 km E, and Picaninnie Ponds conservation parks, 20 km E. **Visitor information:** Lady Nelson Visitor and Discovery Centre, Jubilee Hwy East, Mount Gambier; (08) 8724 9750.

Port Pirie Pop. 13 633

MAP REF. 307 J3, 308 I13
The city of Port Pirie, 227 km N of Adelaide on Spencer Gulf, is near the Southern Flinders Ranges. Situated on the tidal Port Pirie River, the city is a major industrial and commercial centre. The first European settlers came in 1845; wheat farms and market gardens were established around the region's sheep

industry. Broken Hill Associated Smelters began smelting lead in 1889 and today the largest lead smelters in the world treat thousands of tonnes of concentrates annually from the silver, lead and zinc deposits at Broken Hill, NSW. Wheat and barley from the mid-north of the State are exported from here and there is a thriving fishing industry. The ocean is close by and swimming, water-skiing, fishing and yachting are popular sports on the river. **In town:** Regional Tourism and Arts Centre, Mary Elie St, features local and touring art exhibitions, craft shop and cafe. National Trust Museum Buildings, Ellen St, includes Victorian pavilion-style railway station. On waterfront: loading and discharging of Australian and overseas vessels. Northern Festival Centre in Memorial Park, off Gertrude St, venue for local and national performances. Self-guide walks, brochures available: National Trust walking tours; Journey Landscape, a 1.6-km nature trail representing changes in vegetation from Broken Hill to Port Pirie. Mary Elie St Market each Sun. Apr.: Regional Masters Games. Sept.: Blessing of the Fleet and associated festivals, celebrate role of Italians at turn of century in establishing local fishing industry. Oct.: Festival of Country Music. Nov.: Cycling and Athletics Carnival. **In the area:** Weeroona Island, 13 km N, a good fishing, holiday area accessible by car. Port Germein, a beachside town 24 km N, with jetty said to be longest in Southern Hemisphere; Festival of the Crab held here in Jan. **Visitor information:** Regional Tourism and Arts Centre, Mary Elie St; (08) 8633 0439, freecall 1800 000 424. Web site www.classiccountry.org.au/ ptpirie.html

Port Victoria   Pop. 311

MAP REF. 306 H7

A tiny township on the west coast of Yorke Peninsula, Port Victoria was once the main port for sailing ships carrying grain from the area. **In town:** Geology trail along foreshore, booklet available from information centre explains coastline's ancient volcanic history. Swimming and jetty fishing, from original 1888 jetty at end of Main St. National Trust Maritime Museum, Main St (open Sun., public holidays, or by appt). **In the area:** Conservation Islands are breeding areas for several bird species. Wardang Island, Aboriginal reserve, 10 km off coast; permission required from Point Pearce

Community Council. Wardang Island Maritime Heritage Trail for scuba divers, includes visits to 8 wrecks; waterproof self-guide leaflet available. **Visitor information:** Moonta Station Visitor Information Centre, old Moonta Railway Station, Kadina Rd, Moonta; (08) 8825 1891. Web site www.classiccountry.org. au/portvictoria.html **See also:** The Yorke Peninsula p. 281.

Quorn   Pop. 1038

MAP REF. 303 B12, 308 I10

Nestled in a valley in the Flinders Ranges, 345 km N of Adelaide, Quorn was established as a railway town on the Great Northern Railway in 1878. Built by Chinese and British workers, the line was closed in 1957. Part of the line through Pichi Richi Pass has been restored as a tourist railway taking passengers on the scenic 33-km round trip. **In town:** Historic buildings; self-guide historic walk, leaflet available. In Railway Tce.: Quorn Mill (1878), originally a flour mill, now motel and restaurant; Quornucopia Gallery, large collection of Norman Lindsay paintings, and Bruse's Dining Hall; railway station, departure point for Pichi Richi Railway (Easter–Nov., check days of operation). Nairana Craft Centre, First St. Sept.: Agricultural Show. Oct.: Campdraft and Field Days. **In the area:** Colourful rocky outcrops of The Dutchmans Stern Conservation Park, 8 km W; walking trails in park. Junction Gallery, 16 km N on Yarrah Vale Rd. Warren Gorge, 23 km N, popular with climbers. Proby's Grave, 35 km N; Hugh Proby was the first settler at Kanyaka sheep station. Buckaringa scenic drive, 36 km N, through ranges north of town (signposted). Bruce, 22 km SE, features 1870s architecture. Scenic drive 10 km S to Devils Peak, Pichi Richi Pass, Mt Brown Conservation Park and picturesque Waukarie Creek, 16 km away; good walking trails in area. **Visitor information:** Railway Station, Railway Tce, (08) 8648 6419. Web site www. flindersrangescouncil.sa.gov.au/tourism **See also:** Outback Adventure p. 256.

Renmark   Pop. 4366

MAP REF. 307 Q6

Renmark is at the heart of the oldest irrigation area in Australia, 260 km NE of Adelaide on the Sturt Hwy. In 1887 the Canadian Chaffey brothers were granted 250 000 acres (100 000 ha) to test their irrigation scheme. Today lush orchards

and vineyards thrive with Murray River water and there are canneries, wineries and fruit-juice factories. Wheat, sheep and dairy cattle are other local industries. **In town:** Historic Renmark Hotel, Murray Ave, community-owned and run. National Trust Museum 'Olivewood', former Chaffey homestead, cnr Renmark Ave (Sturt Hwy) and 21st St. Display of old hand-operated wine press, Renmark Ave. Chaffey original wood-burning irrigation pump on display outside Renmark Irrigation Trust Office (original Chaffey Bros. office), Murray Ave. PS *Industry* (1911), now floating museum, moored behind information centre; cruises available 1st Sun. of each month. Riverland Fruit Co-op packing shed, Renmark Ave, near 19th St, sales of local products (group tours). Zenith Art Gallery, Ral Ral Ave; Ozone Art Gallery, Ral Ral Ave. Big River Rambler cruises depart from Town Wharf, 2 p.m. daily. Houseboat hire. Renmarket, on Town Wharf, 1st Sat. each month. Oct.: Rose Festival. Dec.: Christmas Pageant. **In the area:** Self-guide tourist drive to historic sites and wineries (includes town walk), brochure available. Bookmark Biosphere Reserve: conservation and ecological research; 900 000 hectares north and south of town, including Calperum Pastoral Lease and Chowilla Reserve. On Sturt Hwy: Renmano Winery, 5 km SW; unique collection of fauna, particularly reptiles, at Bredl's Wonder World of Wildlife, 7 km SW. Ruston's Roses, 4000 varieties, 7 km SW off Sturt Hwy (open Oct.–May). Angove's winery and distillery, Bookmark Ave, 5 km SW. On Loch 5 Rd: SA Water Corporation Loch 5 and Weir, 2 km SE; Margaret Dowling National Trust Park, 3 km SE, area of natural bushland. At Paringa, 4 km E: suspension bridge (1927); Bert Dix Memorial Park; the Black Stump, root system of river red gum estimated to be about 500 years old; houseboats for hire. Dunlop Big Tyre spans Sturt Hwy at Yamba Roadhouse, 16 km SE; also fruit fly inspection point (no fruit allowed into SA). Scenic drive 40 km E into Vic. to see spring blossoms at Lindsay Point Almond Park. Headings Lookout tower, 16 km NE, for excellent views of surrounding irrigated farmland and river cliffs. Murtho Forest Reserve, 19 km NE. Danggali Conservation Park, 60 km N: vast area of mallee scrub, bluebush and black oak woodland, and wildlife. **Visitor information:** Visitor Information Centre, Murray Ave; (08) 8586 6704.

Robe
Pop. 816

MAP REF. 305 F9

A small, historic town on Guichen Bay, 336 km s of Adelaide, Robe is a fishing port and holiday centre. The rugged, windswept coast has many beautiful and secluded beaches. Lagoons and salt lakes surround the area and wildlife abounds. In the 1850s, Robe was a major wool port. During the gold rush, 16 500 Chinese disembarked here and travelled overland to the Victorian goldfields to avoid the Poll Tax. **In town:** National Trust buildings and art and craft, especially in Smillie and Victoria sts. Historic Interpretation Centre in Library building, Victoria St, has displays and leaflets on self-guide heritage walks/drives. Old Customs House (1863, includes museum) in Royal Circus (check opening times). Karatta House, summer residence of Governor Sir James Fergusson in 1860s, off Christine Dr. (not open to public). Caledonian Inn (1858), Victoria St, accommodation and meals. Robe House, Hagen St: old Governor's residence, now B&B. Crayfish fleet anchors in Lake Butler (Robe's harbour); fresh crays and fish Oct.–Apr. Jan.: Lions Regatta. Nov.: Robe Village Fair, includes Blessing of the Fleet and Art and Craft Festival. **In the area:** Long Beach (17 km long), 2 km N. Yabbi Farm, 12 km N on Kingston Rd, yabbies for sale (or catch your own). Historic home Lakeside (1884), now offers accommodation and caravan park, 2 km SE on Main Rd. Water-skiing on adjacent Lake Fellmongery. Narraburra Woolshed, 14 km SE, sheepshearing and sheepdog demonstrations. Beacon Hill, 2 km s, panoramic views. Little Dip Conservation Park, 13 km s, features a complex moving sand-dune system, salt lakes, freshwater lakes and abundant wildlife. The Obelisk at Cape Dombey, 3 km W. **Visitor information:** Robe Library, Victoria St; (08) 8768 2465. Web site www.robe.sa.gov.au

Roxby Downs
Pop. 2446

MAP REF. 308 F4

A modern township built to accommodate employees of the Olympic Dam mining project, Roxby Downs is 85 km N of Pimba, which is just off Stuart Hwy, 568 km N of Adelaide. A road from Roxby Downs joins the Oodnadatta Track just south of Lake Eyre South, 125 km N of Roxby. **In town:** At information centre, Richardson Pl.: maps, history, photo gallery. **In the area:** Olympic Dam Mining Complex, 15 km N: over 2 million tonnes of ore mined annually to obtain refined copper, uranium oxide, gold and silver; surface tours mid-Mar.–mid-Nov. (bookings at Olympic Dam Tours; (08) 8671 0788). Heritage Centre and Missile Park, 90 km s at Woomera. **Visitor information:** Council Offices, Richardson Pl.; (08) 8671 0010. Web site www.roxby.net.au/~mucorodo./index.htm **See also:** The Outback p. 278.

Stansbury
Pop. 524

MAP REF. 306 I9

Situated on the lower east coast of Yorke Peninsula and with scenic views of Gulf St Vincent, Stansbury was originally known as Oyster Bay because the bay was one of the best oyster beds in the State. In days gone by, ketches shipped grain across the gulf from Stansbury to Port Adelaide. A popular holiday destination, the bay is excellent for water sports, including diving and water-skiing. **In town:** School House Museum, in first Stansbury school (1878), North Tce. Jetty fishing. May: Sheepdog Trials. **In the area:** Coastal walking trail, brochures at post office and stores. Lake Sundown, 15 km NW, one of many salt lakes in area; photographer's delight at sunset. Kleines Point Quarry, 5 km s, State's largest limestone quarry; a.m. tours of quarry including inspection of ship being loaded with limestone (bookings essential; (08) 8852 4104). **Visitor information:** Moonta Station Visitor Information Centre, Old Moonta Railway Station, Kadina Rd, Moonta; (08) 8825 1891. Web site www.classiccountry.org.au/stansbury.html **See also:** The Yorke Peninsula p. 281.

Strathalbyn
Pop. 2962

MAP REF. 301 I4, 305 C3, 307 L10

An inland town with a Scottish heritage, on the Angas River, Strathalbyn is 58 km s of Adelaide and a Heritage township. The Soldiers Memorial Gardens follow the river through town, offering shaded picnic grounds. **In town:** National Trust Museum, in old police station and courthouse, Rankine St. St Andrew's Church (1848), Alfred Pl. Old Provincial Gas Company (1868), South Tce. Antique and art and craft shops. May: Strathalbyn Settlers Celebration (even-numbered years). Aug.: Collectors, Hobbies and Antique Fair. Oct.: Glenbarr Scottish Festival; Agricultural Show. **In the area:** Lookout, 7 km SW, for views over town and district. Lakeside holiday town of Milang, 20 km SE, an old riverboat town; Port Milang Historical Railway Station, a local history museum. Langhorne Creek, 15 km E: centre for winegrowing district; museum; Vintage Affair held in May. Pottery at Paris Creek, near Meadows, 15 km NW. Iris gardens, 2 km W of Meadows (open Oct.–Mar.). Old gold diggings at Jupiter Creek Goldfields, 35 km NW. **Visitor information:** Old Railway Station, South Tce; (08) 8536 3212.

Streaky Bay
Pop. 1101

MAP REF. 315 P12

Streaky Bay, 727 km NW of Adelaide, is a holiday town, fishing port and agricultural centre for the cereal-growing hinterland. Matthew Flinders, the explorer, named the bay for the streaking effect caused by seaweed. The town is almost surrounded by small bays and coves, sandy beaches and towering cliffs. Crayfish and many species of fish abound, and fishing from boat or jetty is good. **In town:** At information centre: fishing information and interesting shark replica. Powerhouse Restored Engine Centre, Alfred Tce, display of old working engines (open Tues. and Fri. or by appt). National Trust Museum in Old School House (1901), Montgomery Tce (check opening times). Hospital Cottage (1864), first building in Streaky Bay, now private residence. St Canutes Catholic Church (1912), Poochera Rd. Jan.: Family Fish Day Contest; Aquatic Carnival; Perlubie Sports Day. Apr.: Cup Race Meeting. Sept.: Agricultural Show. Nov.: Camel Cup Races. **In the area:** Magnificent coastal scenery and rugged cliffs; snorkelling and diving areas. Scenic drive via Cape Bauer and the Blowhole, 20 km NW, offers spectacular cliff-top views across the bight. Half-day tourist drive south-east along coast. Point Labatt Conservation Park, 55 km SE, has only permanent colony of Australian sea-lions on the mainland. Murphy's Haystacks, 40 km SE, two sculptural groups of ancient pink granite rocks (private property; entry by donation at gate). Port Kenny, 62 km SE on Venus Bay, offers excellent fishing. Further 14 km s, fishing village of Venus Bay; nearby, breathtaking views from Needle Eye Lookout. Bairds Grave Monument, 25 km s. Felchillo Oasis, 20 km NE, includes quandong (bush tucker) orchard and nursery, fauna park and example of alternative power generation. **Visitor information:** Streaky Bay Motel, 13–15 Alfred Tce; (08) 8626 1126.

Web site www.epta.com.au **See also:** Wildlife-Watching p. 268; The Eyre Peninsula p. 284.

Swan Reach   Pop. 255

MAP REF. 307 N8
Swan Reach is a quiet little township on the Murray River, about 100 km E of Gawler. Citrus, grapes, almonds and Geraldton Wax flowers are grown in the area. Picturesque river scenery and excellent fishing make the town a popular holiday destination. **In the area:** Murray River Educational Nature Tours, by appt; (08) 8570 2212. Swan Reach (11 km W) and Ridley (5 km S) conservation parks, abound with wildlife including wombats, emus and kangaroos. Punyelroo Caravan Park, 7 km S, offers fishing, boating and water-skiing. At Nildottie, nearby junction of Marne and Murray rivers, 14 km S, Ngaut Ngaut Aboriginal Conservation Park. Water sports at Walker Flat, 26 km S. Yookamurra Sanctuary, 21 km NW, a conservation project including eradication of feral animals and restocking with native animals (guided walks and overnight accommodation, bookings essential). Murray Aquaculture Yabby Farm, 1.5 km E. **Visitor information:** Mannum Tourist Information Centre, Randall St, Mannum; (08) 8569 1303.

Tanunda   Pop. 3499

MAP REF. 300 F5, 304 F6, 307 L8
The town of Tanunda is the heart of the Barossa wine region. It was the focal point for early German settlement, growing out of the village of Langmeil, established 1843, part of which can be seen in the western areas of town. **In town:** Fine examples of Lutheran churches. Historical museum in former post and telegraph office (1865), Murray St, features collections specialising in German heritage. Barossa Wine and Visitor Centre, incorporates Wine Interpretation Centre, 66 Murray St. Story Book Cottage and Whacky Wood (for children), Oak St. Barossa Kiddypark, Menge St, family funpark with rides. Award-winning Kev Rohrlach Collection, Barossa Valley Way, Tanunda Nth, displays range from pioneering heritage to satellites; Barossa Market held in grounds each Sun. Chateau Tanunda Estate Winery, Basedow Rd. The Woodcutters Haven, Buring Rd: rocking-horses, woodcarving items. Heritage Town Walk, brochure available. Feb.: Oompah Fest; Barossa Under the Stars. Easter: Barossa Vintage Festival. Sept.: Gourmet Barossa. Oct.: Barossa Music Festival. **In the area:** Local wineries, *to the north:* Basedow Wines, Veritas Winery, Langmeil Winery, Richmond Grove Barossa Winery, Stanley Bros Winery, Peter Lehmann Wines, Chateau Dorrien Wines; *to the south:* Turkey Flat Vineyard, Glaetzer Wines, St Hallet Wines, Grant Burge Wines, Rockford Wines, Charles Melton Wines, Krondorf Wines. Bethany, first German settlement in Barossa, 4 km S, pretty village with creekside picnic area, pioneer cemetery, attractive streetscapes, winery (Bethany Wines) and walking trail along Rifle Range Rd. Norm's Coolie Sheep Dogs, south off Barossa Valley Way (performances 2 p.m. Mon., Wed., Sat.). The Keg Factory, makers of kegs, barrel furniture and wine racks, St Hallet Rd. At Kersbrook, 40 km S: historic buildings; trout farm. **Visitor information:** Barossa Wine and Visitor Centre, 66 Murray St; (08) 8563 0600, freecall 1800 812 662. **See also:** Day Tours from Adelaide p. 253; Vineyards and Wineries p. 277.

Tumby Bay   Pop. 1151

MAP REF. 306 E7
Tumby Bay is a pretty coastal town 49 km N of Port Lincoln on the east coast

Unloading the day's catch of southern bluefin tuna at Streaky Bay

of Eyre Peninsula. The town is known for its long crescent beach and white sand. **In town:** C. L. Alexander National Trust Museum, in old timber schoolroom on West Tce (open Fri. and Sat. p.m.). Police station (1871), Tumby Tce. For local art and craft: Rotunda Art Gallery, Tumby Tce; Briar Craft Shop, Wibberley Tce; Tumby Cottage Crafts, North Tce. Mangrove boardwalk, Berryman Cres., a 70-m walk, signs explain ecology of mangroves. **In the area:** Rock and surf fishing. At Lipson Cove, 10 km NE, visitors can walk to Lipson Island at low tide. Rugged, beautiful scenery and fishing at Ponta and Cowley's beaches, 15 km NE; catches include snapper, whiting and bream. At Port Neill, 42 km NE: grassed foreshore for picnics; safe swimming beach; Vic and Jill Fauser's Museum; Port Neill Lookout, 1 km N. Fishing, sea-lions, dolphins and birdlife at Sir Joseph Banks Group of Islands, south-east off coast; charter tours. Trinity Haven Scenic Drive leads south along coast. Island Lookout for spectacular views, 3 km S. Shoalmarra, 5 km S, quandong bush tucker farm (open Tues. for tours or by appt). Excellent fishing at Thuruna, 10 km S. **Visitor information:** Hales MiniMart, 1 Bratten Way; (08) 8688 2584. Web site www.tumbybay.aust.com **See also:** The Eyre Peninsula p. 284.

Victor Harbor   Pop. 7343

MAP REF. 301 G8, 305 B4, 307 L11

A popular coastal town and regional 'capital' of the Fleurieu Peninsula, Victor Harbor is 84 km S of Adelaide. Established in the early days of whaling and sealing (1830s), the town overlooks historic Encounter Bay, protected by Granite Island. **In town:** Historic buildings: Congregational Church (1869), Victoria St; Mount Breckan (1879), Renown Ave; Adare House (1852), The Drive; Old Customs House (1867), now National Trust Discovery Centre, Flinders Pde, history of coast and whaling (check opening times); St Augustine's Church (1869), Burke St; Telegraph Station Art Gallery, in former telegraph station (1866); Old Goods Shed (1890), Railway Tce. SA Whale Centre, Railway Tce, has displays to aid conservation of the 25 species of whale and dolphin in southern Australian waters. Whale-watching, June–Oct. The Steam Ranger, a restored tourist railway service, operates between Victor Harbor and Goolwa, via Port Elliot, departs from Railway Tce, near causeway. Jan.: Granite Island Regatta; Regional Art Show. Easter: Craft Fair. Apr.: Triathlon. June: Whale Season Launch. Oct.: Folk and Music Festival. **In the area:** On Granite Island, joined to mainland by 630-m causeway (walk or take horse-drawn tram, which has operated since 1894); little (fairy) penguin rookeries (guided tours available at sunset); Fairy Penguin Interpretive Centre. The Bluff (Rosetta Head), facing Encounter Bay; worth 100-m climb for views. Waitpinga Beach, 17 km SW. Spectacular Deep Creek Conservation Park, 50 km SW, features impressive flora and fauna, rugged cliffs and section of Heysen Walking Trail. Located alongside, Talisker Conservation Park, site of historic silver-lead mine has old mine buildings and diggings. At tip of Fleurieu Peninsula, Cape Jervis, 70 km SW, offers panoramic views to Kangaroo Island. Hindmarsh Falls, 15 km NW, has pleasant walks and spectacular waterfalls. Spring Mount Conservation Park, 14 km NW. Inman Valley: Glacier Rock, 19 km NW, shows effect of glacial erosion (said to be the first recorded discovery of glaciation in Australia); Galloway Yabbie products. Hindmarsh and Inman rivers, north and west of town respectively: good fishing, peaceful picnic spots on-shore. Greenhills Adventure Park, 3.5 km N on banks of Hindmarsh River. Urimbirra Wildlife Park, 5 km N. Next door, Wild Rose Miniature Village. Opposite, Nangawooka Flora Reserve with more than 1200 species of Australian plants. At Mt Compass, 24 km N: pottery; Cow Race held here each Feb. Nearby, strawberry and blueberry farms, begonia farm and nursery, Tooperang Trout Farm and deer and pheasant farms. **Visitor information:** 10 Railway Tce; (08) 8552 5738. **See also:** Day Tours from Adelaide p. 253; Wildlife-Watching p. 268.

Waikerie   Pop. 1798

MAP REF. 307 O6

Waikerie, the citrus centre of Australia, is surrounded by an oasis of irrigated orchards and vineyards in mallee-scrub country in the Riverland. Situated 170 km NE of Adelaide, the town has beautiful views of river gums and sandstone cliffs along the Murray River. There is abundant birdlife along the river and in the mallee scrub. **In town:** Waikerie Citrus-packing House, Sturt Hwy, one of the largest in Australia. Rain Moth Gallery, Peake Tce. Lions Park, on riverfront, picnic/barbecue facilities. Harts Lagoon, Ramco Rd, a wetland area with bird hide. Houseboat hire. Mar.: International Food Fair. Easter: Horse and Pony Club Easter Horse Show. May: Riverland Rock 'n' Roll Festival. Sept.: Riverland Field Days. **In the area:** On Sturt Hwy: clifftop lookout and walk, northern outskirts of town; The Orange Tree, 2 km E, fruit products and river-viewing platform. Area internationally acclaimed as a glider's paradise; joy rides and courses at Gliding Club, 4 km E off Sturt Hwy. Devlin's Pound, 11 km E, part of river where Devlin's ghost sighted. Holder Bend Reserve and Maize Island Conservation Park, 6 km NE via causeway. Waikerie Golf Course, 12 km W. Pooginook Conservation Park, across river then 20 km NE, birdwatching, no facilities, 4WD tracks only. Crystallised gypsum fossils in abundance at Broken Cliffs on northern side of river near Lock 2, 15 km NE on Taylorville Rd. At Blanchetown, 42 km W: first of Murray River's 6 SA locks; lookout at Blanchetown Bridge; floating restaurant. 11 km W of Blanchetown, Brookfield Conservation Park, home of southern hairy-nosed wombat. **Visitor information:** The Orange Tree, Sturt Hwy; (08) 8541 2332.

Wallaroo   Pop. 2516

MAP REF. 306 I6

Situated 154 km NW of Adelaide, Wallaroo is a key shipping port for Yorke Peninsula, exporting barley and wheat. Processing of rock phosphate is another major industry. The safe beaches and excellent fishing make the area a popular tourist destination. In 1859 vast copper-ore deposits were discovered. A smelter was built, thousands of Cornish miners arrived and the area boomed until the 1920s, when copper prices dropped and the industry slowly died out. The nearby towns of Moonta and Kadina form part of 'Little Cornwall', and there are many reminders of its colourful past. **In town:** At cemetery, Moonta Rd, grave of Caroline Carleton; author of *Song of Australia*. National Trust Wallaroo Heritage and Nautical Museum, Jetty Rd, maritime exhibits in town's original post office (1865). Historical walks, brochure available at museum or town hall (guided tours Sun.). Historic buildings: old railway station, Owen Tce; in Jetty Rd, customs house (1862), and Hughes chimney stack (1865), which contains over 300 000 bricks and is more than 7 m square at its base. Wallaroo–Kadina Tourist Train operates from Wallaroo railway station, John Tce (2nd Sun. each month and during school holidays). Jan.: New Year's Day Regatta. May: Kernewek Lowender, Cornish festival held in conjunction with Moonta and Kadina (odd-numbered years). **In the area:** Several charming old Cornish-style cottages in district. Bird Island, 10 km S, noted for crabbing. **Visitor information:** Moonta Station Visitor Information Centre, Old Moonta Railway Station, Kadina Rd, Moonta; (08) 8825 1891. Web site www.classiccountry.org.au/wallaroo.html **See also:** The Yorke Peninsula p. 281.

Whyalla   Pop. 23 382

MAP REF. 306 I2, 308 H13

Whyalla, northern gateway to Eyre Peninsula, has grown from a small settlement, Hummock Hill (1901), to the largest provincial city in the State. It is known for its heavy industry, particularly the enormous iron and steel works, and ore mining in the Middleback Ranges. A shipyard operated here 1939–78. Whyalla is a modern city with safe beaches, good fishing and boating, and excellent recreational facilities. The area enjoys a sunny Mediterranean-type climate. **In town:** Whyalla Maritime Museum, Lincoln Hwy: 650-tonne corvette *Whyalla*, the largest permanently land-locked ship in Australia (entry includes guided tour of ship); collection of models, including 'OO' gauge model railway; Matthew Flinders Room. Next door, Tanderra Craft Village (check opening times). Mount Laura Homestead Museum (National Trust), includes Telecommunications Museum, Ekblom St (check opening times). Whyalla Art Gallery, Darling Tce. Foreshore area, includes safe beach, jetty for recreational fishing, landscaped picnic/barbecue area, and marina with boat-launching facilities. Hummock Hill Lookout, Queen Elizabeth Dr. Flinders Lookout, Farrel St. Ada Ryan Gardens, Cudmore Tce: mini-zoo, picnic facilities under shady trees. Park and wetlands with picnic/barbecue area, Broadbent Tce. Guided bus tour of steel works Mon., Wed., Sat. or by arrangement; book at information centre (for safety, visitors must wear long-sleeve top, trousers and closed footwear). Large, arid-lands wildlife and reptile sanctuary, south-east on Lincoln Hwy, near airport (open sunrise to sunset). Whyalla Scenic Drive, brochure available. Easter: Australian Amateur Snapper Fishing Championship. **In the area:** Cuttlefish spawning (May–Aug.) and temperate waters offer diverse marine ecosystem for divers to explore. Port Bonython, 34 km E. At Point Lowly, 36 km E: lighthouse (1882), oldest building in area (not open to public); scenic coastal drive along Fitzgerald Bay to Point Douglas. Whyalla Conservation Park, 10 km N off Lincoln Hwy, includes 30-min walking trail over Wild Dog Hill. **Visitor information:** Lincoln Hwy; (08) 8645 7900, freecall 1800 088 589. Web site www.whyalla.sa.gov.au **See also:** The Eyre Peninsula p. 284.

Willunga
Pop. 1622

MAP REF. 300 B13, 301 F4, 302 E11, 305 B3, 307 K10

A historic town, surveyed in 1839, Willunga was named from the Aboriginal word willa-unga, meaning 'the place of green trees'. The town is at the southern edge of the McLaren Vale winegrowing region and is also a major almond-growing centre. **In town:** The Willunga Walk, historic walk, brochures available. Historic pug cottages and fine examples of Colonial architecture. National Trust police station and courthouse (1855),

One of Willunga's many historic buildings

High St. Anglican church, with Elizabethan bronze bell, St Andrews Tce. Quarry (1842), Delabole Rd, operated for 60 years, now National Trust site. Markets, 2nd Sat. each month, Scout Grounds, Aldinga Rd. July: Almond Blossom Festival. **In the area:** Cowshed Gallery at Yundi, 9 km SE: Mt Magnificent Conservation Park, 12 km SE: western grey kangaroos in bushland; scenic walks; picnic areas and good views from the summit. Kyeema Conservation Park, 14 km NE, for birdlife, good hiking and camping. **Visitor information:** McLaren Vale and Fleurieu Visitor Centre, Main Rd, McLaren Vale; (08) 8323 9944, freecall 1800 628 410. **See also:** Day Tours from Adelaide p. 253.

Wilmington
Pop. 261

MAP REF. 307 J1, 308 I11

A tiny settlement formerly known as Beautiful Valley, Wilmington is 292 km N of Adelaide in the Flinders Ranges. **In town:** In Main St: police station (1880), now a private residence; old coaching stables (1880) at rear of Wilmington Hotel (1879); early 20th-century billiard rooms (open by appt). Butter Factory (1898), adjacent to school, off Main St (now a private residence). Jan.: Rodeo. **In the area:** Views of Spencer Gulf at Hancocks Lookout, 8 km W, off road to Port Augusta; highest point of Horrocks Pass, named after explorer John Horrocks, who descended through the pass in 1846.

Bruce, historic railway town, 35 km N: 1880s architecture, railway line used by Pichi Richi Railway Society. Mount Remarkable National Park, 13 km S, features clear mountain pools, dense vegetation and abundant wildlife; Mambray Creek and spectacular Alligator Gorge in park. Historic Melrose, 24 km S, oldest town in Flinders Ranges. Booleroo Steam and Traction Preservation Society's Museum (open by appt), Booleroo Centre, 48 km SE. Hammond, historic railway town, 26 km NE, 1870s architecture. At Carrieton, 56 km NE: historic buildings; Aboriginal carvings, further 9 km along Belton Rd; scenic drive to deserted Johnburgh. **Visitor information:** Wilmington General Store, Main St; (08) 8667 5155.

Wilpena
Pop. 20

MAP REF. 303 E8, 309 K7

Wilpena, 429 km N of Adelaide, consists of a resort and caravan/camping park near the entrance to Wilpena Pound. The pound, part of the Flinders Ranges National Park, is a vast natural amphitheatre surrounded by peaks that change colour with the light. The only entrance is through a narrow gorge and across Sliding Rock. In 1902 the Hill family (wheat farmers) built a homestead inside the pound, but abandoned their farm after a flood washed away the access road in 1914. **In the area:** Resort is powered by largest solar power system in Southern

Historic mining town in Innes National Park, south-west of Yorketown

Hemisphere (tours). Organised tours, self-guide drives, 4WD tours, scenic flights, bushwalking and mountain climbing in surrounding countryside; brochures available. Numerous walking trails in Wilpena Pound, including one to St Mary Peak, the highest point (1165 m). Aboriginal rock carvings and paintings at Arkaroo Rock on slopes of Rawnsley Bluff, 20 km S, and at Sacred Canyon, 19 km E. At Rawnsley Park station, 20 km S on Hawker Rd, demonstrations of sheep-drafting and shearing (Sept.– Oct.). Appealinna homestead (1851), 16 km N, off Blinman Rd, ruins of house built of flat rock from creek bed. Scenic drives: Stokes Hill Lookout, 12 km NE; Bunyeroo and Brachina gorges, Aroona Valley, 5 km NW; Moralana Scenic Drive, 25 km S; Wangarra Lookout, 10 km SW (also accessible by 12-km walking track). **Visitor information:** Wilpena Pound Resort; (08) 8648 0004. Web site www.wilpenapound.on.net **See also:** Outback Adventure p. 256.

Woomera   Pop. 1349

MAP REF. 308 F6
Established in 1947 as a site for launching British experimental rockets, Woomera was until 1982 a prohibited area to visitors. The town, 490 km NW of Adelaide, is still administered by the Defence Department. **In town:** Missile Park and Heritage Centre, cnr Dewrang

and Banool sts, displays of rockets, aircraft and weapons. Old Guard Gate, Old Pimba Rd, opal sales. Breen Park picnic area, Girrahween Ave. **Visitor information:** Eldo Hotel, Kotara Cres.; (08) 8673 7867. **See also:** The Outback p. 278.

Wudinna   Pop. 527

MAP REF. 306 C3, 308 B13
Wudinna is located on the Eyre Hwy, 571 km NW of Adelaide. The township is the gateway to the Gawler Ranges and has become an important service centre for the Eyre Peninsula. The countryside surrounding Wudinna is often referred to as Granite Country because of the many unusually shaped outcrops that dominate the landscape. **In the area:** Airport: sealed strip, daily services to Adelaide. Mt Wudinna, thought to be second largest granite outcrop in Southern Hemisphere, 10 km NE: at summit (261 m), scenic views; at base, recreation area; 30-min return interpretive walking trail. Nearby, Turtle Rock, turtle-shaped ancient granite rock. Signposted tourist drives to all major rock formations in the area. Prolific wildlife and wildflowers in spring. At Minnipa, 37 km NW: Dryland Farming Research centre; Pildappa Rock (wave rock); Tcharkuldu Rock. At Koongawa, 50 km E, Darke's Memorial on site where explorer John Charles Darke was speared to death in 1844. Ucontitchie Hill, 38 km SW, interesting geological feature.

Visitor information: Council Offices, Burton Tce; (08) 8680 2002. Web site www.epta.com.au

Yankalilla   Pop. 434

MAP REF. 301 D7, 305 B3, 307 K11
A growing settlement just inland from the west coast of Fleurieu Peninsula, Yankalilla is 35 km W of Victor Harbor. **In town:** In Main St: Uniting Church (1878); Bungala House and the Olde Peppertree Store, for gifts and pottery; Yankalilla Hotel, country-style counter meals; historical museum. Apr.: Rodeo. **In the area:** Seaside town of Normanville, 4 km W. Bay Tree Farm, 14 km SW on Cape Jervis Rd, has herbs, flowers, afternoon teas in farm setting. Paradise Wirrina Cove Resort, 10 km SW, family resort. Second Valley, 17 km SW, peaceful picnic spot with jetty for fishing. Cape Jervis, 35 km S, departure point for vehicular ferries to Kangaroo Island. Glacier Rock, a 500 million-year-old Cambrian quartzite, 22 km E. Steep hillsides and gullies, and western grey kangaroos at Myponga Conservation Park, 9 km NE. At Myponga, 14 km NE: historic buildings; Myponga Reservoir, ideal barbecue/picnic setting and lookout; further 4 km NE, Begonia Farm (open Oct.–Apr.). **Visitor information:** Main St; (08) 8558 2999. **See also:** Day Tours from Adelaide p. 253.

Yorketown   Pop. 692

MAP REF. 306 I9
The principal town at the southern end of Yorke Peninsula, Yorketown services the surrounding cereal-growing district. Yorketown is surrounded by extensive inland salt lakes (some pink), which are still worked. **In the area:** At Innes National Park, 77 km SW: rugged coastal scenery and peaceful hinterland; Inneston, historic mining town in park, managed as historic site by the Department for Environment, Heritage and Aboriginal Affairs; Yorke Surfing Classic each Oct. Many shipwrecks along this section of coast including *The Ethel* (remains of wreck near Inneston). Surfing at Daly Head, 50 km W. South of Daly Head, blowhole. At Corny Point, on north-western tip of Peninsula, 55 km NW: lighthouse, lookout, camping, fishing. **Visitor information:** District Council, 15 Edithburgh Rd; (08) 8852 1433. Web site www.classiccountry.org.au/yorketown.html **See also:** The Yorke Peninsula p. 281.

South Australia

LOCATION MAP

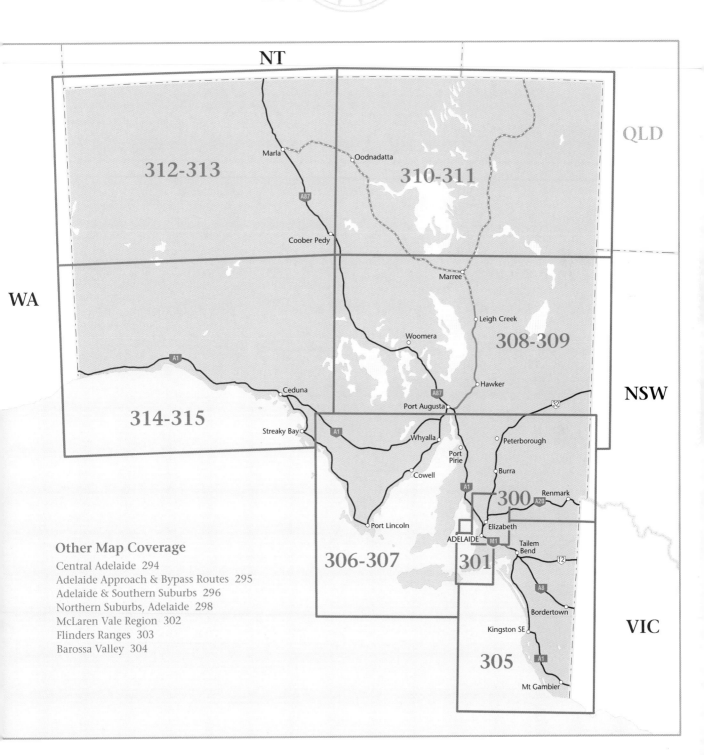

NT

QLD

WA

NSW

VIC

312-313

310-311

308-309

314-315

306-307

300

301

305

Marla

Oodnadatta

Coober Pedy

Marree

Leigh Creek

Woomera

Hawker

Ceduna

Streaky Bay

Port Augusta

Whyalla

Port Pirie

Cowell

Port Lincoln

Peterborough

Burra

Renmark

Elizabeth

ADELAIDE

Tailem Bend

Bordertown

Kingston SE

Mt Gambier

A87

A1

A87

A1

32

A20

M1

12

A8

A1

Other Map Coverage

Central Adelaide 294
Adelaide Approach & Bypass Routes 295
Adelaide & Southern Suburbs 296
Northern Suburbs, Adelaide 298
McLaren Vale Region 302
Flinders Ranges 303
Barossa Valley 304

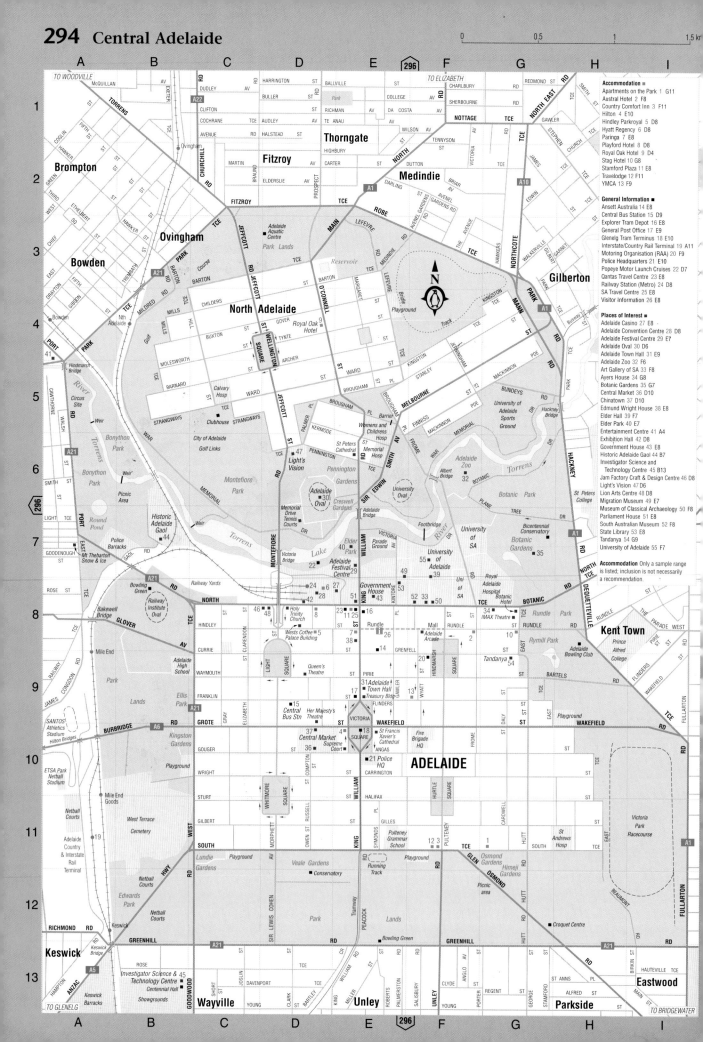

Accommodation ■
Apartments on the Park 1 G11
Austral Hotel 2 F8
Country Comfort Inn 3 F11
Hilton 4 E10
Hindley Parkroyal 5 D8
Hyatt Regency 6 D8
Paringa 7 E8
Playford Hotel 8 D8
Royal Oak Hotel 9 D4
Stag Hotel 10 G8
Stamford Plaza 11 E8
Travelodge 12 F11
YMCA 13 F9

General Information ■
Ansett Australia 14 E8
Central Bus Station 15 D9
Explorer Tram Depot 16 E8
General Post Office 17 E9
Glenelg Tram Terminus 18 E10
Interstate/Country Rail Terminal 19 A11
Motoring Organisation (RAA) 20 F9
Police Headquarters 21 E10
Popeye Motor Launch Cruises 22 D7
Qantas Travel Centre 23 E8
Railway Station (Metro) 24 D8
SA Travel Centre 25 E8
Visitor Information 26 E8

Places of Interest ■
Adelaide Casino 27 E8
Adelaide Convention Centre 28 D8
Adelaide Festival Centre 29 E7
Adelaide Oval 30 D6
Adelaide Town Hall 31 E9
Adelaide Zoo 32 F6
Art Gallery of SA 33 F8
Ayers House 34 G8
Botanic Gardens 35 G7
Central Market 36 D10
Chinatown 37 D10
Edmund Wright House 38 D8
Elder Hall 39 F7
Elder Park 40 E7
Entertainment Centre 41 A4
Exhibition Hall 42 D8
Government House 43 E8
Historic Adelaide Gaol 44 B7
Investigator Science and
  Technology Centre 45 B13
Jam Factory Craft & Design Centre 46 D8
Light's Vision 47 D6
Lion Arts Centre 48 D8
Migration Museum 49 E7
Museum of Classical Archaeology 50 F8
Parliament House 51 E8
South Australian Museum 52 F8
State Library 53 E8
Tandanya 54 G9
University of Adelaide 55 F7

Accommodation Only a sample range
is listed; inclusion is not necessarily
a recommendation.

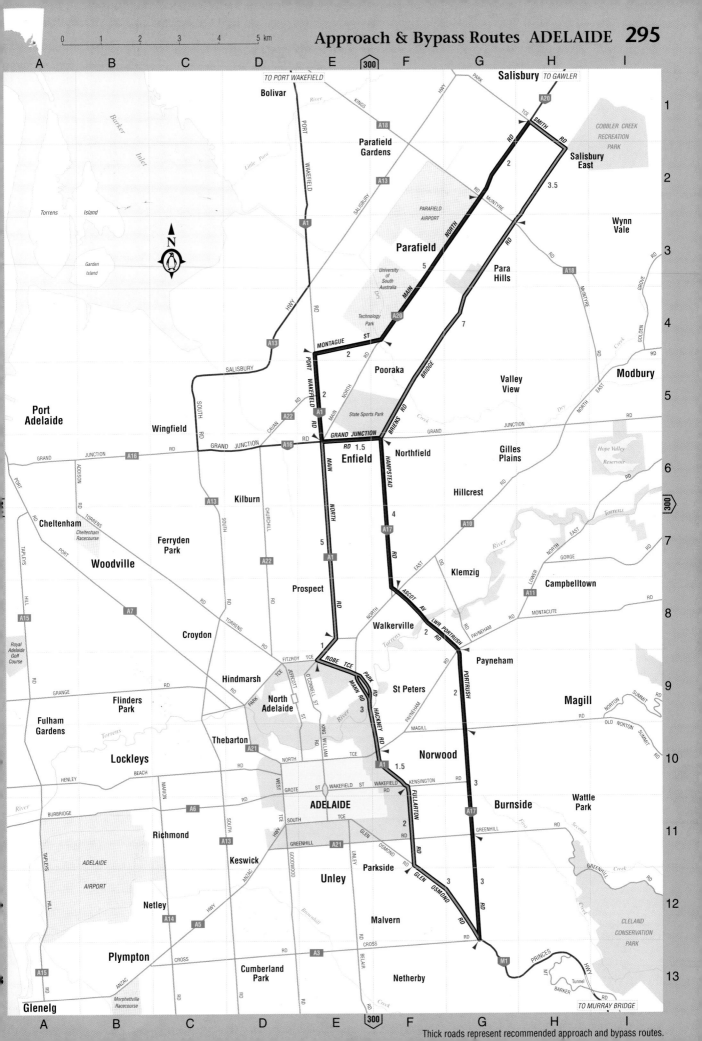

Thick roads represent recommended approach and bypass routes.

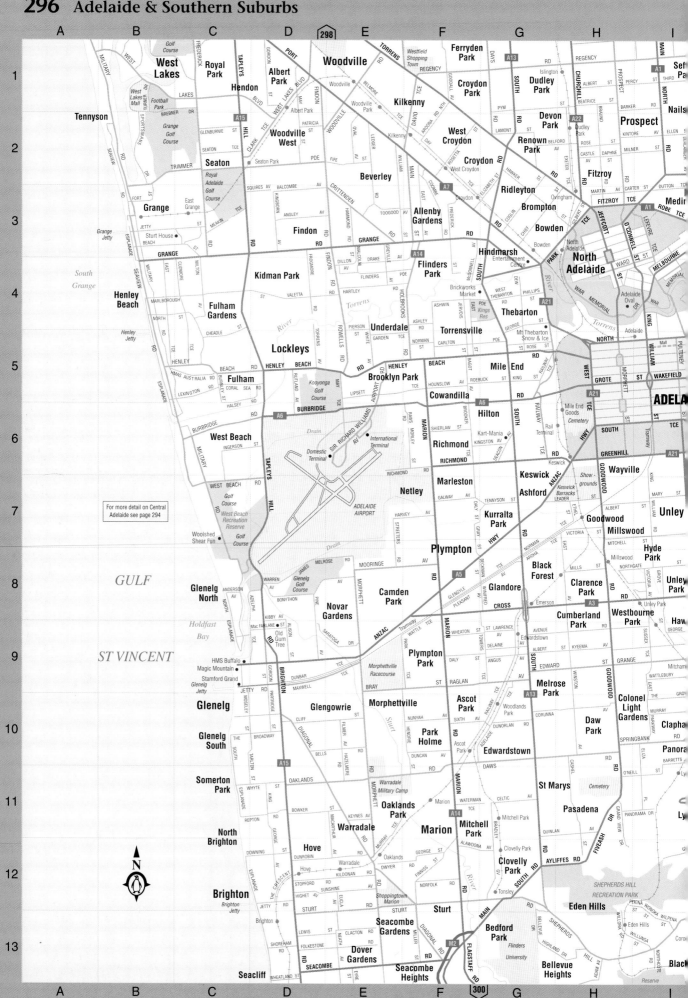

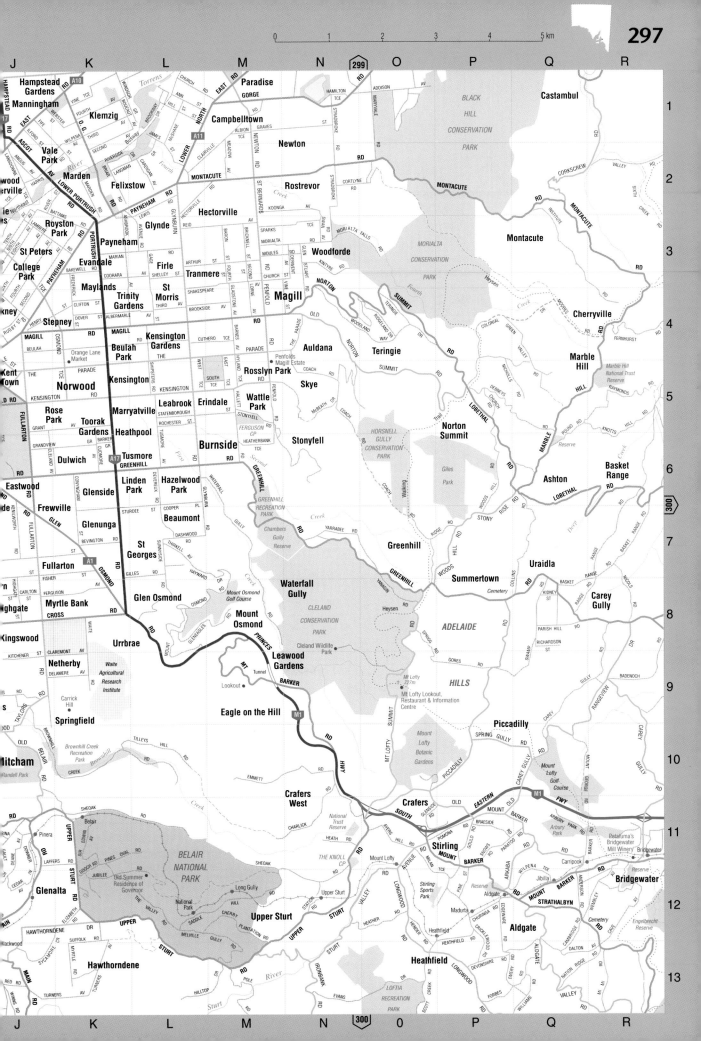

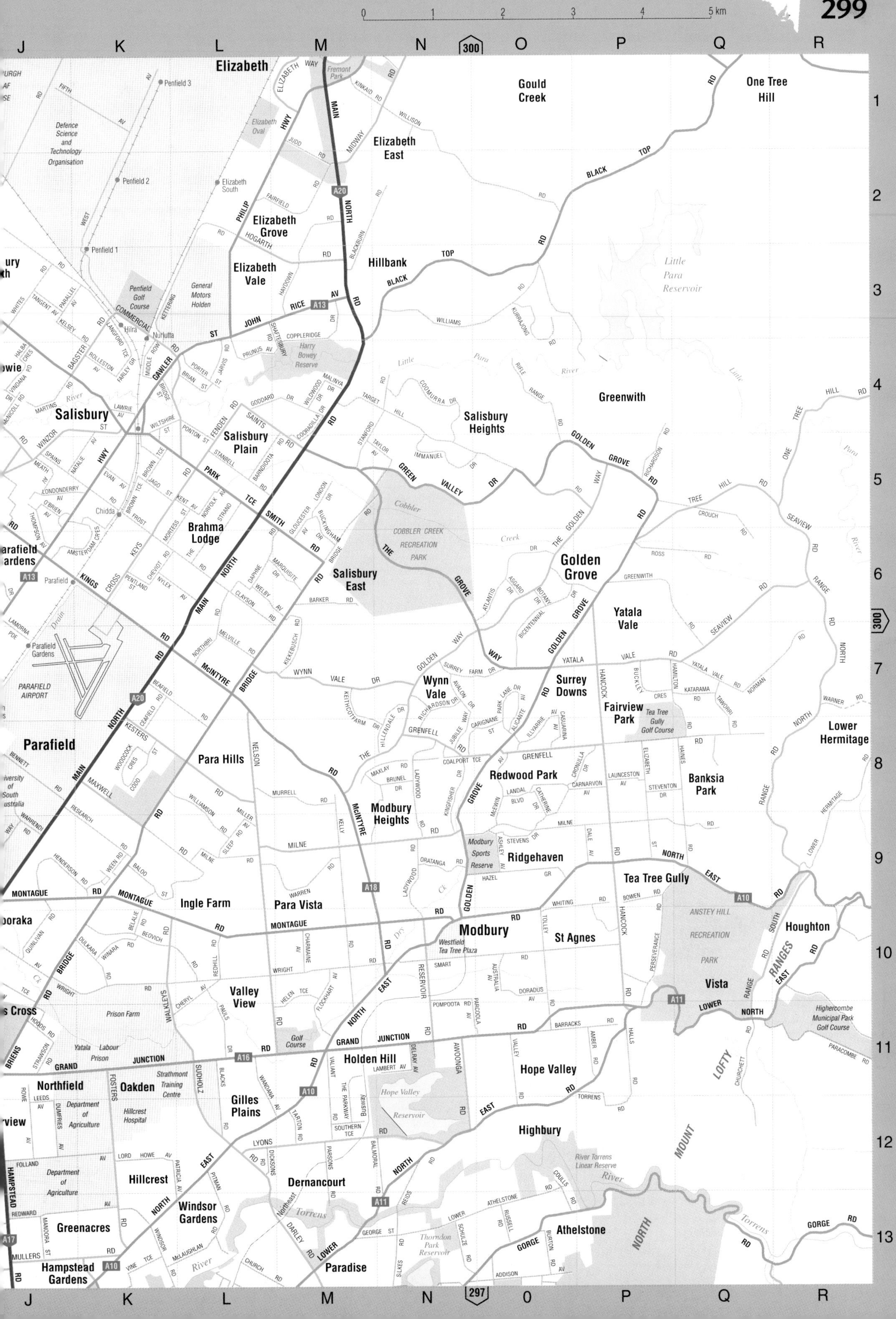

0 1 2 3 4 5 km

J K L M N 300 O P Q R

Elizabeth

Gould Creek

One Tree Hill

1

Defence Science and Technology Organisation

Penfield 3

Elizabeth Oval

Elizabeth East

2

Penfield 2

Elizabeth Grove

Elizabeth Vale

Hillbank

Little Para Reservoir

3

Penfield 1

Penfield Golf Course

General Motors Holden

Harry Bowey Reserve

Little Para River

Greenwith

4

Salisbury

Salisbury Plain

Salisbury Heights

Golden Grove

5

Brahma Lodge

Cobbler Creek Recreation Park

The Grove

Golden Grove

6

Parafield Gardens

Salisbury East

Yatala Vale

7

Parafield

Parafield Airport

Para Hills

Wynn Vale

Surrey Downs

Fairview Park

Tea Tree Gully Golf Course

Lower Hermitage

8

Modbury Heights

Redwood Park

Banksia Park

9

Montague

Ingle Farm

Para Vista

Modbury Sports Reserve

Ridgehaven

Tea Tree Gully

Anstey Hill Recreation Park

10

Para Vista

Modbury

St Agnes

Vista

Houghton

Highercombe Municipal Park Golf Course

11

Northfield

Oakden

Gilles Plains

Valley View

Holden Hill

Hope Valley Reservoir

Hope Valley

Highbury

12

Hillcrest

Windsor Gardens

Dernancourt

Athelstone

13

Hampstead Gardens

Greenacres

Paradise

Thorndon Park Reservoir

River Torrens Linear Reserve

J K L M N 297 O P Q R

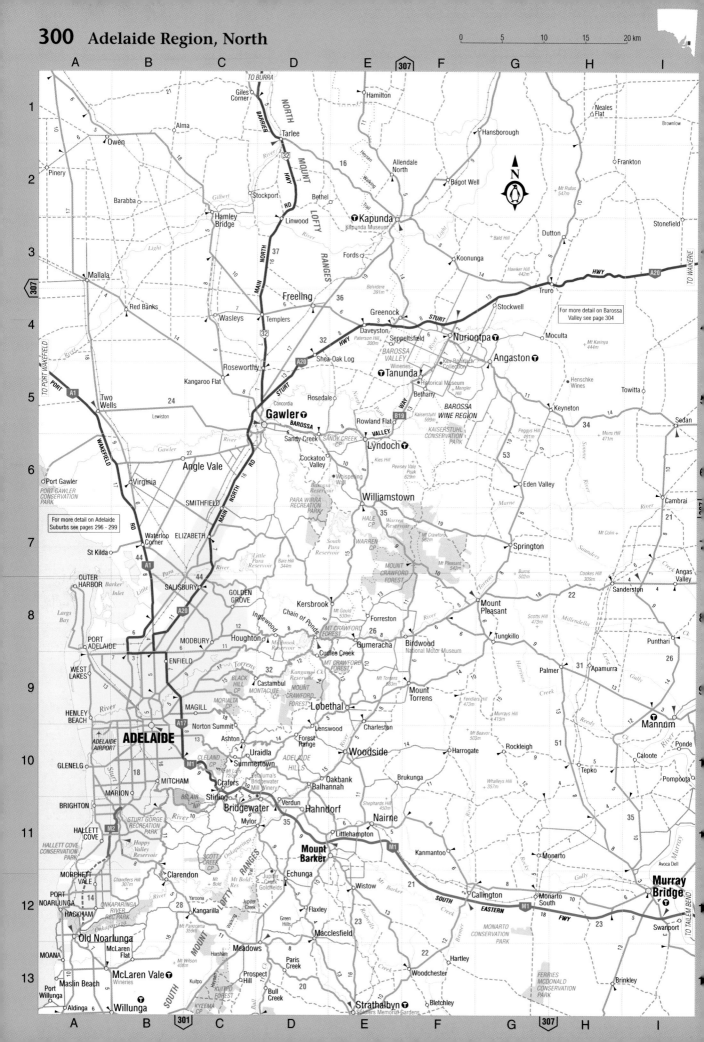

0   5   10   15   20 km

A   B   C   D   E   F   307   F   G   H   I

N

TO BURRA

Giles Corner
Alma
Owen
Pinery
Barabba
Hamley Bridge
Stockport
Bethel
Linwood
Tarlee
Hamilton
Allendale North
Bagot Well
Hansborough
Neales Flat
Frankton
Brownlow
Stonefield

Mt Rufus 547m

Mallala
Red Banks
Wasleys
Templers
Freeling
Roseworthy
Kangaroo Flat
Fords
Greenock
Daveyston
Seppeltsfield
Shea-Oak Log
Koonunga
Nuriootpa
Stockwell
Truro
Moculta
Dutton
Mt Karinya 444m

For more detail on Barossa Valley see page 304

TO PORT WAKEFIELD
Two Wells
Lewiston
Concordia
Rosedale
Tanunda
Bethany
Historical Museum
Angaston
Henschke Wines
Towitta
Keyneton
Sedan

BAROSSA WINE REGION
KAISERSTUHL CONSERVATION PARK

Port Gawler
Virginia
Angle Vale
Gawler
Sandy Creek
Cockatoo Valley
Rowland Flat
Lyndoch
Williamstown
Eden Valley
Springton
Cambrai

PORT GAWLER CONSERVATION PARK
PARA WIRRA RECREATION PARK

For more detail on Adelaide Suburbs see pages 296 - 299

St Kilda
Waterloo Corner
Smithfield
Elizabeth
Kersbrook
Forreston
Gumeracha
Birdwood
Mount Pleasant
Tungkillo
Punthari
Apamurra
Palmer
Sanderston
Angas Valley

OUTER HARBOR
Largs Bay
PORT ADELAIDE
WEST LAKES
Enfield
Modbury
Golden Grove
Houghton
Inglewood
Chain of Ponds
Cudlee Creek
Castambul
Mount Torrens
Lobethal
Charleston
Lenswood
Woodside
Harrogate
Rockleigh
Tepko
Caloote
Ponde
Pompoota
Mannum

HENLEY BEACH
Magill
Norton Summit
Ashton
Uraidla
Summertown
Forest Range
Oakbank
Balhannah
Brukunga
Monarto

ADELAIDE
ADELAIDE AIRPORT
GLENELG
Mitcham
Crafers
Stirling
Bridgewater
Mylor
Verdun
Hahndorf
Nairne
Kanmantoo
Monarto

MARION
BRIGHTON
BELAIR NP
Littlehampton
Mount Barker
Callington
Monarto South
Murray Bridge

HALLETT COVE
HALLETT COVE CONSERVATION PARK
STURT GORGE RECREATION PARK
Happy Valley Reservoir
Echunga
Wistow
Avoca Dell
Swanport

MORPHETT VALE
PORT NOARLUNGA
HACKHAM
Clarendon
Kangarilla
Flaxley
Green Hills
Macclesfield
Hartley
Woodchester
Bletchley
Brinkley

ONKAPARINGA RIVER REC PARK
SCOTT CREEK CP

MOANA
Old Noarlunga
McLaren Flat
Meadows
Paris Creek
Prospect Hill
Bull Creek
Strathalbyn

Port Willunga
Maslin Beach
Aldinga
McLaren Vale
Willunga
Kuitpo
KUITPO FOREST
KYEEMA CP

SOUTH MOUNT LOFTY RANGES

FERRIES MCDONALD CONSERVATION PARK

301   C   D   E   F   G   307   H   I

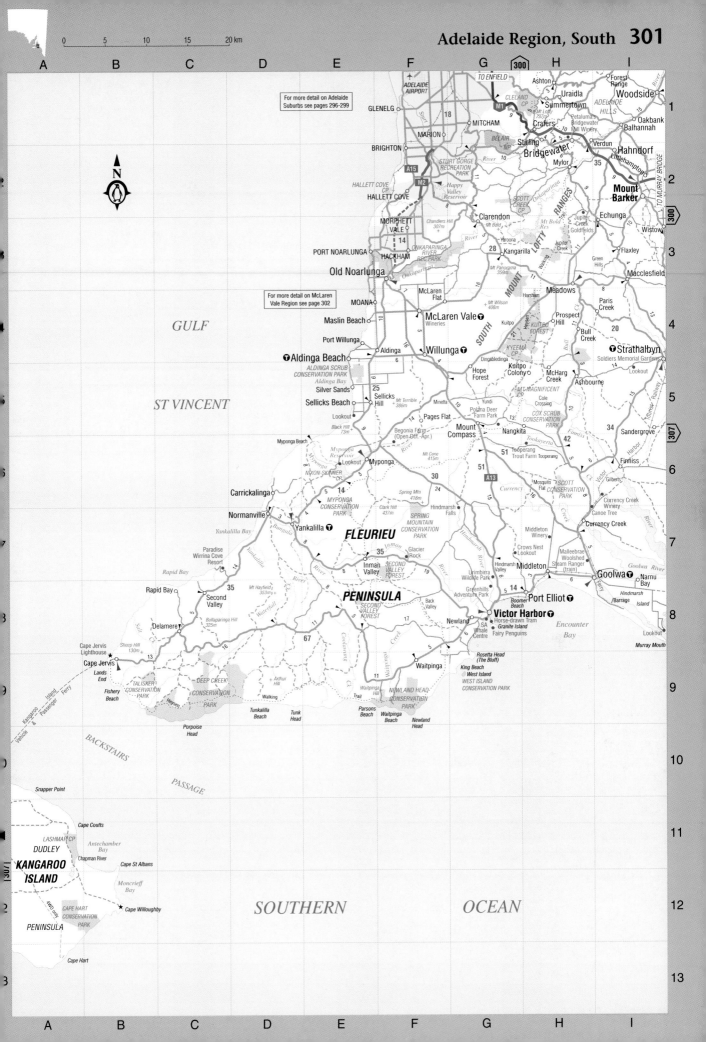

0   5   10   15   20 km

GULF

ST VINCENT

For more detail on Adelaide
Suburbs see pages 296-299

GLENELG

MARION

BRIGHTON

ADELAIDE
AIRPORT

TO ENFIELD

Ashton
Uraidla
Summertown

Forest
Range

Woodside

*ADELAIDE
HILLS*

Oakbank
Balhannah

MITCHAM

Crafers
Stirling

Bridgewater

Petaluma's
Bridgewater
Mill Winery

Verdun
Hahndorf

Mylor

Littlehampton

*CLELAND
CP*

*BELAIR
NP*

*STURT GORGE
RECREATION
PARK*

*HALLETT COVE
CP*

HALLETT COVE

MORPHETT
VALE

Happy
Valley
Reservoir

Chandlers Hill
307m +

Clarendon

*SCOTT
CREEK
CP*

Mt Bold
Res

SOUTH

LOFTY

RANGES

Mount
Barker

Echunga

Jupiter
Creek
Goldfields

Wistow

PORT NOARLUNGA

HACKHAM

*ONKAPARINGA
RIVER
REC PARK*

Old Noarlunga

For more detail on McLaren
Vale Region see page 302

MOANA

Maslin Beach

Port Willunga

Aldinga Beach

Silver Sands

Sellicks Beach

McLaren
Flat

McLaren Vale

Wineries

Aldinga

Willunga

25

Sellicks
Hill

MOUNT

Yarroona

Kangarilla

28

Meadows

Paris
Creek

Prospect
Hill

*KUITPO
FOREST*

Bull
Creek

Macclesfield

Strathalbyn

Soldiers Memorial Gardens

20

Lookout

34

Sandergrove

Finniss

Mt Panorama
359m

Mt Wilson
408m

Dingabledinga

Hope
Forest

Kuitpo
Colony

McHarg
Creek

Ashbourne

*KYEEMA
CP*

Lookout

Black Hill
73m

Pages Flat

Minetta

Mt Terrible
386m

*MT MAGNIFICENT
CP*

Cole
Crossing

14

Mypamga Beach

*Myponga
Reservoir*

Lookout

Myponga

Begonia Farm
(Open Oct.-Apr.)

Yundi

Nangkita

Polina Deer
Farm Park

13

*COX SCRUB
CONSERVATION
PARK*

42

Finniss

307

*NIXON-SKINNER
CP*

Mt Cone
415m

Mount
Compass

51

Tooperang
Trout Farm Tooperang

Carrickalinga

14

*MYPONGA
CONSERVATION
PARK*

Spring Mtn
418m

30

24

Clark Hill
437m

Hindmarsh
Falls

*SPRING
MOUNTAIN
CONSERVATION
PARK*

Mosquito
Flat

*SCOTT
CONSERVATION
PARK*

Currency Creek
Winery

Canoe Tree

Currency Creek

Normanville

Yankalilla Bay

3

Yankalilla

FLEURIEU

35

Bungala

Yankalilla

Inman

Glacier
Rock

*SECOND
VALLEY
FOREST*

19

Middleton
Winery

Middleton

Crows Nest
Lookout

Hindmarsh
Valley

Urimbirra
Wildlife Park

Hindmarsh

Malleebrae
Woolshed
Steam Ranger
(train)

Goolwa

Goolwa River

Narnu
Bay

Rapid Bay

Paradise
Wirrina Cove
Resort

14

PENINSULA

Inman
Valley

8

8

Greenhills
Adventure Park

Back
Valley

14

Port Elliot

*Hindmarsh
Island*

Barrage

Rapid Bay

35

Second
Valley

Mt Hayfield
353m +

Bullaparinga Hill
325m

Waterfall

*SECOND
VALLEY
FOREST*

17

Newland

Victor Harbor

*SA
Whale
Centre*

Horse-drawn Tram

Granite Island

Fairy Penguins

Boomer
Beach

*Encounter
Bay*

Lookout

Delamere

5

67

Salt

16

Sheep Hill
130m

13

Coolawang

11

Arthur
Hill

Waitpinga

Waitpinga

King Beach

Rosetta Head
(The Bluff)

West Island

Murray Mouth

Cape Jervis
Lighthouse

Cape Jervis

Lands
End

*TALISKER
CONSERVATION
PARK*

*DEEP CREEK
CONSERVATION
PARK*

Heysen

Walking

11

*Waitpinga
Hill*

Trail

*NEWLAND HEAD
CONSERVATION
PARK*

*WEST ISLAND
CONSERVATION
PARK*

Fishery
Beach

Tunkalilla
Beach

Tunk
Head

Parsons
Beach

Waitpinga
Beach

Newland
Head

Kangaroo Island Vehicle & Passenger Ferry

Porpoise
Head

BACKSTAIRS

PASSAGE

Snapper Point

Cape Coutts

LASHMAR CP

DUDLEY

Antechamber
Bay

Chapman River

Cape St Albans

**KANGAROO
ISLAND**

*Moncrieff
Bay*

*CAPE HART
CONSERVATION
PARK*

4WD only

Cape Willoughby

PENINSULA

Cape Hart

SOUTHERN

OCEAN

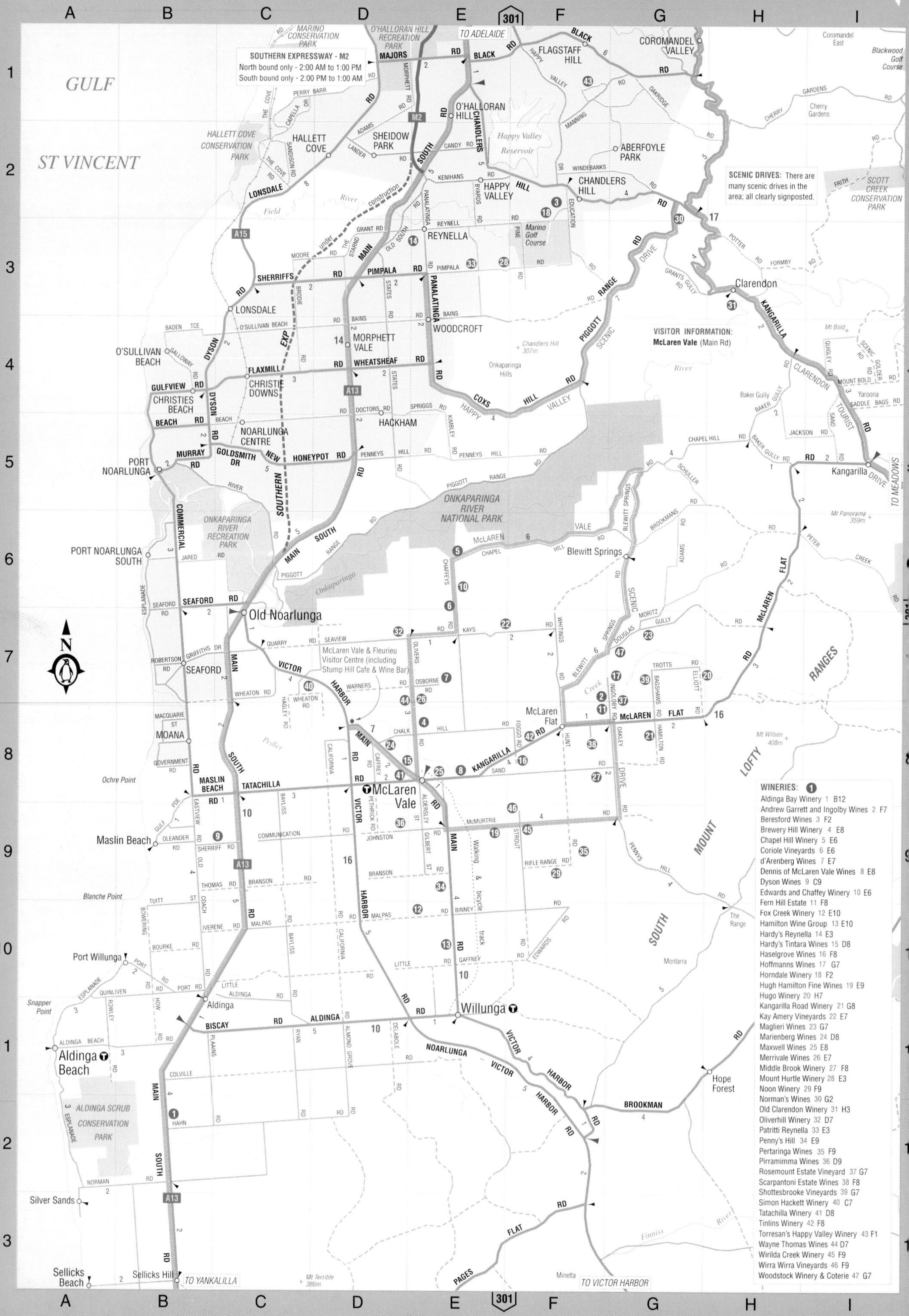

0 1 2 3 4 5 km
SOUTHERN EXPRESSWAY - M2
North bound only - 2:00 AM to 1:00 PM
South bound only - 2:00 PM to 1:00 AM
SCENIC DRIVES: There are many scenic drives in the area; all clearly signposted.
VISITOR INFORMATION:
McLaren Vale (Main Rd)
McLaren Vale & Fleurieu Visitor Centre (including Stump Hill Cafe & Wine Bar)
GULF
ST VINCENT
TO ADELAIDE
TO YANKALILLA
TO VICTOR HARBOR
TO MEADOWS
O'Halloran Hill
Hallett Cove
Sheidow Park
Happy Valley
Reynella
Lonsdale
Woodcroft
Morphett Vale
O'Sullivan Beach
Christies Beach
Christie Downs
Noarlunga Centre
Hackham
Port Noarlunga
Port Noarlunga South
Old Noarlunga
Seaford
Moana
Maslin Beach
McLaren Vale
McLaren Flat
Blewitt Springs
Clarendon
Kangarilla
Coromandel Valley
Flagstaff Hill
Aberfoyle Park
Chandlers Hill
Port Willunga
Aldinga
Aldinga Beach
Willunga
Hope Forest
Silver Sands
Sellicks Beach
Sellicks Hill
Onkaparinga River National Park
Onkaparinga River Recreation Park
Aldinga Scrub Conservation Park
Hallett Cove Conservation Park
Marino Conservation Park
O'Halloran Hill Recreation Park
Scott Creek Conservation Park
Mount Lofty Ranges
WINERIES:
Aldinga Bay Winery 1 B12
Andrew Garrett and Ingolby Wines 2 F7
Beresford Wines 3 F2
Brewery Hill Winery 4 E8
Chapel Hill Winery 5 E6
Coriole Vineyards 6 E6
d'Arenberg Wines 7 E7
Dennis of McLaren Vale Wines 8 E8
Dyson Wines 9 C9
Edwards and Chaffey Winery 10 E6
Fern Hill Estate 11 F8
Fox Creek Winery 12 E10
Hamilton Wine Group 13 E10
Hardy's Reynella 14 E3
Hardy's Tintara Wines 15 D8
Haselgrove Wines 16 F8
Hoffmanns Wines 17 G7
Horndale Winery 18 F2
Hugh Hamilton Fine Wines 19 E9
Hugo Winery 20 H7
Kangarilla Road Winery 21 G8
Kay Amery Vineyards 22 E7
Maglieri Wines 23 G7
Marienberg Wines 24 D8
Maxwell Wines 25 E8
Merrivale Wines 26 E7
Middle Brook Winery 27 F8
Mount Hurtle Winery 28 E3
Noon Winery 29 F9
Norman's Wines 30 G2
Old Clarendon Winery 31 H3
Oliverhill Winery 32 D7
Patritti Reynella 33 E3
Penny's Hill 34 E9
Pertaringa Wines 35 F9
Pirramimma Wines 36 D9
Rosemount Estate Vineyard 37 G7
Scarpantoni Estate Wines 38 F8
Shottesbrooke Vineyards 39 G7
Simon Hackett Winery 40 C7
Tatachilla Winery 41 D8
Tinlins Winery 42 F8
Torresan's Happy Valley Winery 43 F1
Wayne Thomas Wines 44 D7
Wirilda Creek Winery 45 F9
Wirra Wirra Vineyards 46 F9
Woodstock Winery & Coterie 47 G7

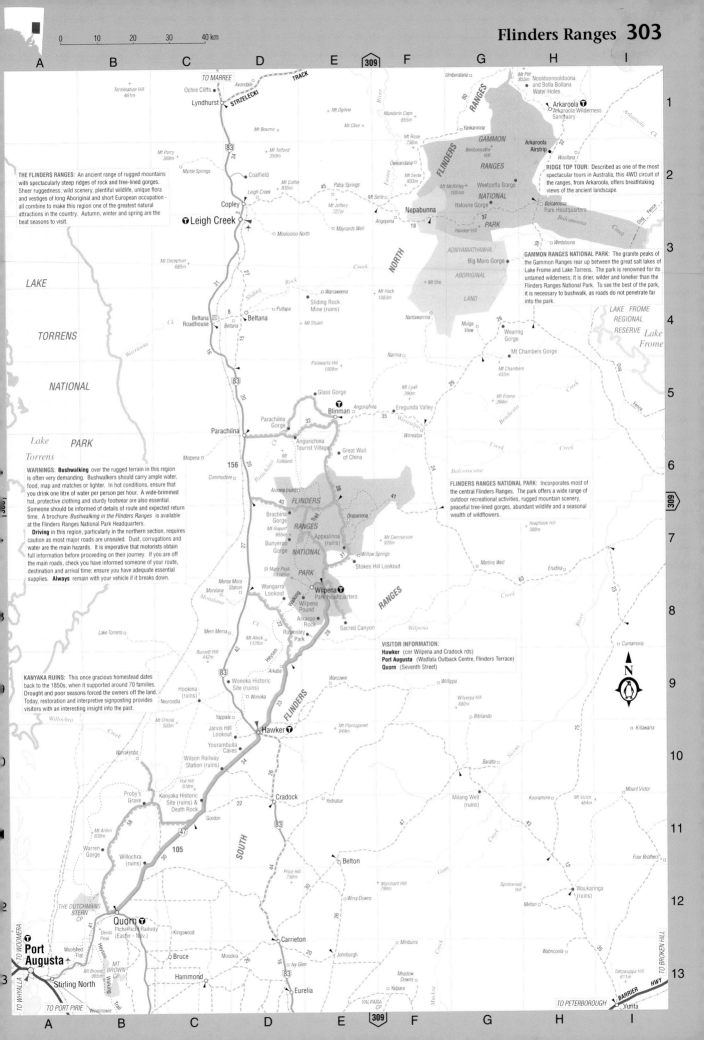

THE FLINDERS RANGES: An ancient range of rugged mountains with spectacularly steep ridges of rock and tree-lined gorges. Sheer ruggedness, wild scenery, plentiful wildlife, unique flora and vestiges of long Aboriginal and short European occupation - all combine to make this region one of the greatest natural attractions in the country. Autumn, winter and spring are the beat seasons to visit.

WARNINGS: Bushwalking over the rugged terrain in this region is often very demanding. Bushwalkers should carry ample water, food, map and matches or lighter. In hot conditions, ensure that you drink one litre of water per person per hour. A wide-brimmed hat, protective clothing and sturdy footwear are also essential. Someone should be informed of details of route and expected return time. A brochure *Bushwalking in the Flinders Ranges* is available at the Flinders Ranges National Park Headquarters.
   Driving in this region, particularly in the northern section, requires caution as most major roads are unsealed. Dust, corrugations and water are the main hazards. It is imperative that motorists obtain full information before proceeding on their journey. If you are off the main roads, check you have informed someone of your route, destination and arrival time; ensure you have adequate essential supplies. **Always** remain with your vehicle if it breaks down.

KANYAKA RUINS: This once gracious homestead dates back to the 1850s, when it supported around 70 families. Drought and poor seasons forced the owners off the land. Today, restoration and interpretive signposting provides visitors with an interesting insight into the past.

RIDGE TOP TOUR: Described as one of the most spectacular tours in Australia, this 4WD circuit of the ranges, offers breathtaking views of the ancient landscape.

GAMMON RANGES NATIONAL PARK: The granite peaks of the Gammon Ranges rear up between the great salt lakes of Lake Frome and Lake Torrens. The park is renowned for its untamed wilderness; it is drier, wilder and lonelier than the Flinders Ranges National Park. To see the best of the park, it is necessary to bushwalk, as roads do not penetrate far into the park.

FLINDERS RANGES NATIONAL PARK: Incorporates most of the central Flinders Ranges. The park offers a wide range of outdoor recreational activities, rugged mountain scenery, peaceful tree-lined gorges, abundant wildlife and a seasonal wealth of wildflowers.

VISITOR INFORMATION:
Hawker (cnr Wilpena and Cradock rds)
Port Augusta (Wadlata Outback Centre, Flinders Terrace)
Quorn (Seventh Street)

0 1 2 3 4 5 km

VISITOR INFORMATION:
Tanunda (66 Murray St)

WALKING TRAILS: The famous 1500-km Heysen Trail begins near Cape Jervis and ends in the Flinders Ranges. The Barossa section, which passes through vineyards, is particularly picturesque. Other trails have been organised in the region including one along Rifle Range Road (near Bethany F6); all are clearly marked.

N

Koonunga

TO KAPUNDA

TO BLANCHETOWN

Freeling

Stockwell

Belvidere 391m+

Greenock

Daveyston

Light Pass

Plush Corner

Shea-Oak Log

Nuriootpa

Luhrs Pioneer German Cottage

Marananga

Penrice

Seppeltsfield

Paterson Hill 300m

Kroemers Crossing

Kev Rohrlach Collection

Bethany Arts & Crafts

Angas Park Fruit Co.

Tappa Pass

Angaston

Nuraip

Tanunda

Tanunda Pottery Shop

Vine Vale

Gomersal

Barossa Kiddypark

Historical Museum

Bethany

Story Book Cottage and Whacky Wood

Mengler Hill Lookout

Rosedale

Collingrove Homestead National Trust Property

The Keg Factory

Schreiberau

Moorooroo

Kaiserstuhl 599m+

KAISERSTUHL CONSERVATION PARK

Rowland Flat

Sandy Creek

Warpoo

Lyndoch

Cockatoo Valley

Kies Hill

Lyndoch Lavender Farm

Pewsey Vale Peak 629m

Pewsey Vale

Goldfields Walk

Whispering Wall

Barossa Reservoir

Williamstown

PARRA WIRRA RECREATION PARK

Red Gum Flat

HALE CONSERVATION PARK

WARREN CONSERVATION PARK

MOUNT CRAWFORD FOREST

Mt Crawford 562m

TO BIRDWOOD

SPRINGTON

FESTIVALS:

Barossa Vintage Festival: (Biennial, odd years): A week-long festival beginning Easter Monday to celebrate the grape harvest. Highlights include grape-picking, wine tasting, entertainment and processions.

Barossa Under the Stars: An annual event held in February, featuring an open air concert with internationally acclaimed artists performing in a natural amphitheatre.

Gourmet Barossa: An annual event held in August/September featuring delectable cuisine and excellent wines.

Barossa Music Festival: A 16-day festival of classical music held in October each year. It attracts musicians from around the country and overseas.

WINERIES: 1

Barossa Cottage Wines 1 G5
Barossa Settlers 2 D9
Basedow Wines 3 F6
Bethany Wines 4 F7
Branson Wines 5 D4
Burge Family Winemakers 6 C8
Charles Cimicky Wines 7 C8
Charles Melton Wines 8 F7
Chateau Dorrien Wines 9 F5
Chateau Tanunda Estate 10 F6
Chateau Yaldara Estate 11 C8
Elderton Wines 12 G4
Glaetzer Wines 13 E6
Gnadenfrei Estate Winery 14 E4
Grant Burge Wines 15 E7
Greenock Creek Cellars 16 D4
Hamiltons Ewell Vineyards 17 G5
Heritage Wines 18 E4
Jenke Vineyard Cellars 19 D8
Kaesler Wines 20 G4
Kellermeister Wines 21 D8
Kies Family Winery 22 C8
Krondorf Wines 23 F7
Langmeil Winery 24 F5
Liebichwein 25 E8
Miranda Wines 26 D8
Mountadam Vineyard 27 G10
Orlando Wines 28 D8
Penfolds Wines 29 G4
Peter Lehmann Wines 30 F5
Richmond Grove Barossa Winery 31 F5
Rockford Wines 32 E7
St Hallett Wines 33 E7
Saltram Wine Estates 34 H5
Seppelt Wines 35 D4
Stanley Bros Winery 36 F5
Tait Wines 37 B8
Tarac 38 F4
Tarchalice Winery 39 G5
The Willows Vineyard 40 H3
Turkey Flat Vineyard 41 E6
Twin Valley Estate 42 D10
Veritas Wines 43 F5
Viking Wines 44 E4
Wards Gateway Cellar 45 B8
Wolf Blass Wines 46 H3
Yalumba Wines 47 I6
Yunbar Estate 48 G5

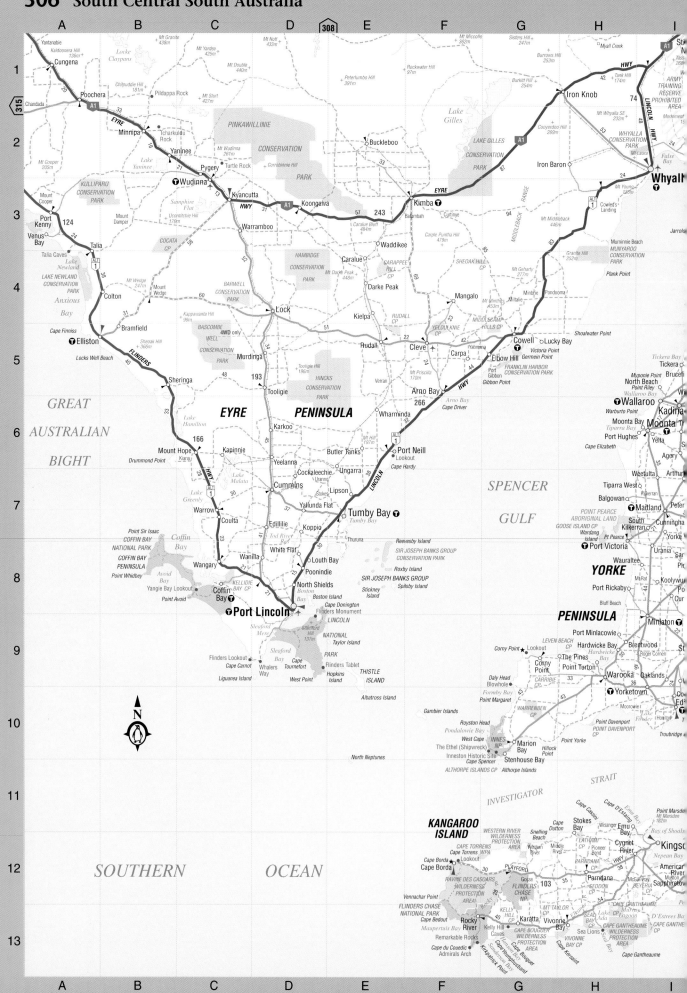

0 20 40 60 80 100 km

J K L M N O P Q R

1

Hammond Eurelia Yalpara Meadow Downs Tattawuppa Hill 6 km Oulnina Hill 710m Oulnina Park Wadnaminga Browns Hill 152m

Wilmington Willowie Morchard Orroroo Yunta Dare Hill 452m Hunt Creek RANGE

2

Melrose Booleroo Pekina Black Rock Dawson Nackara Nantabibbie Oodla Wirra Doughboy Hill 602m Alderman Reservoir Wrights Hill 517m

Booleroo Centre Peterborough Minvalara Yongala Ucolta Nackara Hill 661m

3

Wirrabara Hornsdale Appila Stone Hut Belalie Terowie Yatina DANGGALI CONSERVATION

Nelshaby Laura Jamestown Caltowie Whyte Yarcowie Ugloob Mount Bryan East PARK

4

Napperby Warnertown Gladstone Georgetown Huddleston Canowie Hallett Mt Bryan 932m Curoona SOUTH AUSTRALIA NEW SOUTH WALES 120

Crystal Brook Narridy Gulnare Spalding Mount Bryan Mt Cone 793m Tracy CHOWILLA REGIONAL RESERVE

5

Merriton Redhill Koolunga Yacka Andrews Leighton Burra Hanson Stein Hill 612m Redbanks

Wokurna Collinsfield Lake View Rochester Hilltown CLARE VALLEY WINE REGION Blyth Farrell Flat

6

Snowtown Bumbunga Blyth Clare Penwortham Merildin Black Springs Emu Downs Geranium Plain Morgan Eba Cadell Lock 2 POOGINOOK CONSERVATION PARK Cooltong MURRAY RIVER NP Lindsay Point

Port Wakefield Halbury Watervale Leasingham Manoora Brady Creek Robertstown Australia Plains Qualco Taylorville Overland Corner Renmark Paringa Lake Littra

7

Port Clinton Balaklava Rhynie Saddleworth Julia Tarnma Peep Hill Bower Mount Mary Ramco Lowbank Waikerie Barmera Monash Glossop Berri Taldra Morkalla A20

Avon Owen Tarlee Riverton Marrabel Hamilton Hansborough Neales Flat Brownlow Blanchetown New Well Boolgun Kingston-on-Murray Moorook Lyrup Loxton North

8

Long Plains Hamley Bridge Kapunda Dutton Stonefield STURT Notts Well Maggea Yinkanie New Residence Winkie Loxton

Windsor Freeling Greenock Nuriootpa Truro BROOKFIELD CONSERVATION PARK Swan Reach Nildottie Bakara Wunkar Pyap Myrla MURRAY-SUNSET NATIONAL PARK 236

Two Wells Gawler Angaston Tanunda Keyneton Sedan Punyelroo Bakara Galga Caliph Pata Nadda Veitch

9

Port Adelaide Angle Vale Williamstown Eden Valley Cambrai Black Hill Wongulla Copeville Mindarie Cobera Malpas Paruna Meribah

ADELAIDE ELIZABETH SALISBURY Birdwood Mount Pleasant Forster Purnong Teal Flat Kalyan Wanbi Alawoona BILLIATT CONSERVATION PARK Peebinga Berrook

GLENELG Kersbrook Gumeracha Palmer Apamurra Younghusband Bowhill Perponda Sandalwood Halidon Karte PEEBINGA CP

10

Balhannah Lobethal Woodside Tepko Mannum Coolcha Kilpalie Kilpalie Borrika Kringin Boltons Bore Goongee

PORT NOARLUNGA Hahndorf Nairne Callington Monarto South Murray Bridge Wynarka Karoonda Kulkami Yurgo Marama Mulpata Karte Parilla Pinnaroo Murrayville

Old Noarlunga McLaren Vale Macclesfield Woodchester Woods Point Tailem Bend Sherlock Buccleuch Geranium Lameroo MALLEE HWY B12

11

Aldinga Beach Willunga Strathalbyn Belvidere Langhorne Creek Wellington Cooke Plains Peake Jabuk Parrakie Wilkawatt

Sellicks Beach Myponga Nangkita Finniss Milang Raukkan Narrung Malinong Yumali Coomandook DUKES CARGUMA CONSERVATION PARK

Normanville Yankalilla Goolwa Ashville Ki Ki Carcuma SCORPION SPRINGS CONSERVATION PARK

12

Rapid Bay Second Valley Port Elliot Waltowa Coonalpyn One Tree Hill 140m NGARKAT CONSERVATION PARK BIG DESERT WILDERNESS PARK

DEEP CREEK CP Victor Harbor Meningie Culburra Tintinara Mt Shaugh 184m Mt Shaugh

FLEURIEU PENINSULA YOUNGHUSBAND Noonameena Camp Coorong MOUNT BOOTHBY CP 195 Coombe 133

13

DUDLEY PENINSULA LASHMAR CP Magrath Flat Mt Boothby 130m MOUNT RESCUE CONSERVATION PARK Mt Rescue 129m

CAPE HART CONSERVATION PARK COORONG PENINSULA Woods Well 218 MESSENT CONSERVATION PARK PRINCES HWY Keith A8 Brimbago

SOUTHERN OCEAN Policemans Point Salt Creek NATIONAL PARK SOUTH AUSTRALIA VICTORIA 234

For more detail on Adelaide Region see pages 300 & 301

GULF ST VINCENT

J K L M N O P Q R

309 305

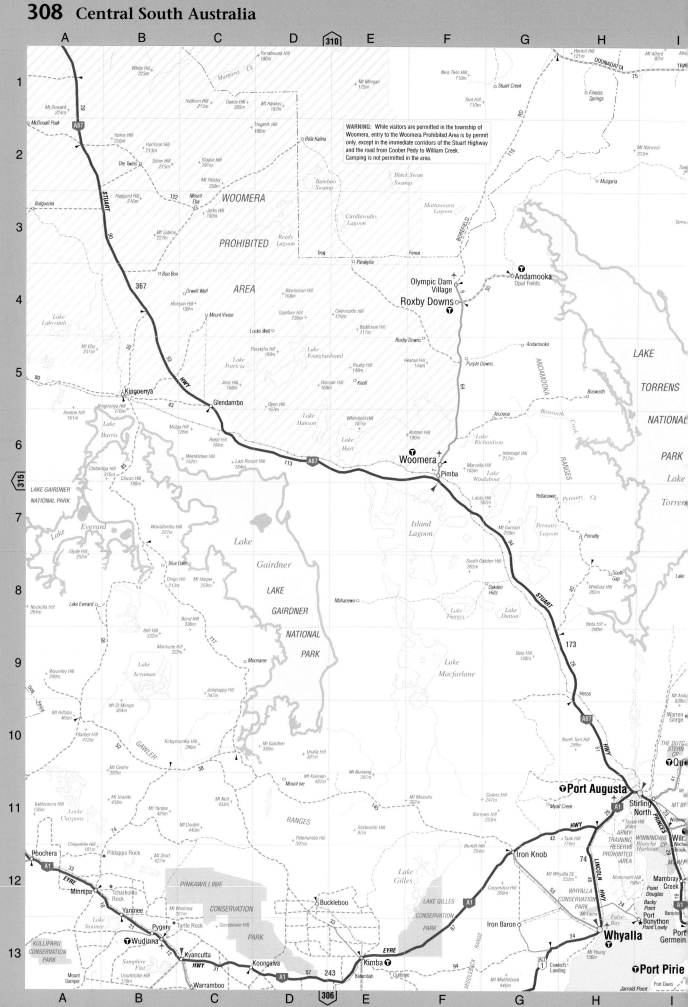

WARNING: While visitors are permitted in the township of Woomera, entry to the Woomera Prohibited Area is by permit only, except in the immediate corridors of the Stuart Highway and the road from Coober Pedy to William Creek. Camping is not permitted in the area.

0 20 40 60 80 100 km

J K L M N 311 O P Q R

1

Mundowdna
Marquee Hill +111m
Lake Pinnaric
Wilpoorinna
79
Farina (ruins)
83
118
re Cliffs
yndhurst
Avondale
Mt Lyndhurst 286m +
STRZELECKI
Mount Lyndhurst
34
Mt Ogilvie +
Mt Bourne +
Copley
45
Leigh Creek
350m
Leigh Creek
Mt Telford +
Mt Coffin +835m
Leigh Creek
Mt Jeffery +727m
Maynards Well
NORTH
Beltana house
Beltana
Sliding Rock Ck
Sliding Rock Mine (ruins)
Mt Stuart +
47
20
Patawarta Hill +1009m
Narrina
Commodore
156
Parachilna
Blinman
35
Mt Hack +1083m
Nantawarrina
26
Great Wall of China
Balcoorana
Mt Lyall +390m
Mt Chambers Gorge
Mt Chambers +433m
Wirreala
Wirrealpa
Creek
Aroona (ruin)
FLINDERS
RANGES
Oraparinna
Mt Caernarvon +920m
Reaphook Hill +388m
Mt Rupert +655m
NATIONAL
St Mary Peak 1165m +
PARK
Wilpena
Wilpena Pound
Martins Well
Erudina
Wangarra Lookout
Moralana
RANGES
89
Rawnsley Park
Wilpena
Creek
Curnamona
Burnett Hill +442m
Mt Aleck +1128m
Arkaba
51
Wonoka Historic Site (ruins)
FLINDERS
Mt Plantagenet +949m
Wilyerpa Hill 880m +
Willippa
Bibliando
Killawarra
Old Telechie
Hawker
Yourambulla Caves
34
26
105
Cradock
Yednalue
22
Gordon
83
Mt Victor +464m
Mount Victor
Plumbago
Bimbowrie
Belton
Marchant Hill +799m
Spotswood Hill +
Waukaringa (ruins)
Four Brothers
Weekeroo Hill +568m
Weekeroo
Outalpa Hill +496m
Outalpa
44
Carrieton
Johnburgh
Waiawera
HWY
Olary
Mingary
24
Tepco
Aroona
Hammond
156
Eurelia
Yalpara
Meadow Downs
Mannahill
221
4A
Wadnaminga
Maldorky Hill +428m
Ballara
Broams Hill 152m +
Mutooroo
Burta
Willowie
56
Morchard
Orroroo
12
Yunta
41
BARRIER
32
Quinina Hill 710m
Quinina Park
Dare Hill +452m
Paratoo
Manunda
Oalia
BENDA
RANGE
Olary
Boolcroo
Pekina
Black Rock
Dawson
Nackara
Nackara Hill 661m +
Ulcolta
elrose
Boolcroo Centre
Wepowie
Nantabibbie
Dodla Wirra
Doughboy Hill +602m
Alderman Reservoir
Wrights Hill 517m +
Murray Town
Minvalara
Tarcowie
Yatina
56
14
Wirrabara
Hornsdale
Yongala
Peterborough
Appila
Mannanarie
Gumbowie
Belalie
Boikevie Hill +539m
Ironback Hill +378m
Faraway Hill +216m
Stone Hut
by
Laura
Caltowie
Jamestown
Whyte Yarcowie
Terowie
PANDAPPA CONSERVATION PARK
Hills Lagoon
DANGGALI CONSERVATION PARK
own
Gladstone

Mount Hopeless
Lake Callabonna
Dog
Fence
Mt Gardiner +374m
Mount Freeling
Mt Livingston 616m +
Ck
Mt Fitton +
Moolawatana
Mt Babbage 369m +
Mt Neil 571m
Mt Thomas 689m +
Mt Pitt 855m +
Mt Painter +790m
Nooldoonooldoona and Bolla Bollana Water Holes
Mt Rose 756m +
Arkaroola
Arkaroola Wilderness Sanctuary
GAMMON
RANGES
Weetootla Gorge
Mt Serle 933m
Wooltana
FLINDERS
Mt McKinlay 1051m +
55
NATIONAL
Balcanoona
Park Headquarters
Nepabunna
Wertaloona
ADNYAMATHANHA
Big John Ck
39
ABORIGINAL
LAND
Frome Downs

Hawker Gate House
Winnathee Creek
Smithville House
Lake Want
118
Lake Wallace
Starvation Lake
Turleys Gate
Pine View
Packsaddle
Sanpah
Boghams Gate
Teilta
Lake Culberta
Lake Carnanto
Lake Maljanapa
Lake Karpi
Lake Moko
Lake Millyera
Lake Tarkarooloo
Eurinilla
Dog Fence
Lake Namba
Lake Yentanwena
Morphetts Ck
Benagerie
Mulyungarie
MUNDI MUNDI PLAIN
Umberumberka Reservoir
Silverton Historic Town
49
HWY
32
BARRIER
Cockburn
Mooleulooloo
Wompinie
Donarta
Harry Ck
Pine Ck
West Boundary Zone Exclusion
Fruit Fly

SOUTH AUSTRALIA
NEW SOUTH WALES

Lake Frome

LAKE FROME

REGIONAL

RESERVE

WARNINGS: In outback Australia, long distances separate some towns. Travellers should familiarise themselves with prevailing conditions before departure and take care to ensure their vehicle is roadworthy. Adequate supplies of petrol, water and food should be carried at all times.

In central Australia, rainfall can make some roads impassable. Full information on road conditions should be obtained from local authorities before departure.

If visitors intend diverting off public roads within Aboriginal Land areas, a permit is required from the relevant Aboriginal authority.

For more detail on Flinders Ranges see page 303

N

Tattawuppa Hill 611m +

J K L M N 307 O P Q R

2
3
4
5
6
7
8
9
10
11
12
13

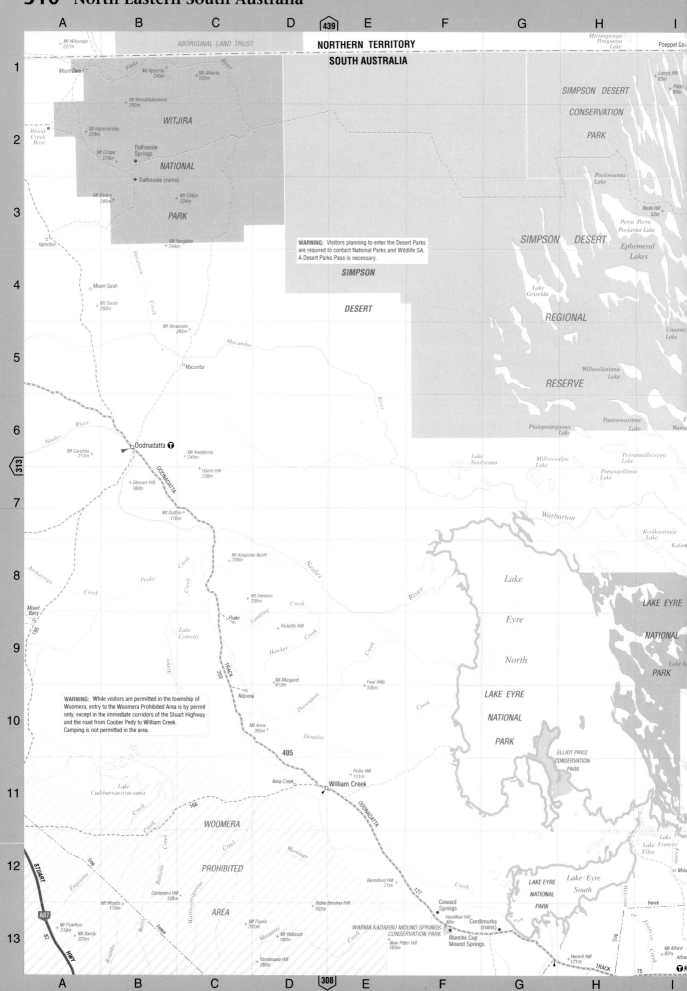

A B C D 439 E F G H I

ABORIGINAL LAND TRUST

NORTHERN TERRITORY

SOUTH AUSTRALIA

Poeppel Co

1

Mt Wilyunpa
227m

Mount Dare

Finke

River

Mt Apperda
245m

Mt Alinerta
222m

Miramponga
Pongunna
Lake

Larrys Hill
63m

Pitari
60m

SIMPSON DESERT

CONSERVATION

PARK

2

Blood
Creek
Bore

WITJIRA

Mt Hammersley
229m

Mt Wieahlakimione
292m

Dalhousie
Springs

NATIONAL

Mt Crispe
279m

Poolowanna
Lake

3

Hamilton

Mt Emery
289m

PARK

Dalhousie (ruins)

Mt Dillon
234m

Stevenson

Mt Yangalee
244m

SIMPSON DESERT

Perra Perra
Poolanna Lake

Beale Hill
53m

Ephemeral

Lakes

4

Mount Sarah

Mt Sarah
260m

Creek

Macumba

WARNING: Visitors planning to enter the Desert Parks
are required to contact National Parks and Wildlife SA.
A Desert Parks Pass is necessary.

SIMPSON

DESERT

Lake
Griselda

REGIONAL

Umaroo
Lake

5

Macumba

Mt Alexander
285m

Willawilaninna
Lake

RESERVE

6

313

Neules

River

Mt Carulina
211m

Oodnadatta

Mt Areebinna
245m

Hanns Hill
238m

River

Lake
Nootyeana

Pialopotingoona
Lake

Pantoowarinna
Lake

Warre

Millyeewilpa
Lake

Peeramudlayeppa
Lake

Pompapillinna
Lake

7

OODNADATTA

Stewart Hill
180m

Mt Dutton
176m

Warburton

Koolkootinnie
Lake

Kalan

8

Arckaringa

Creek

Peake

Creek

Creek

Mt Kingston North
209m

Neales

River

Lake

Eyre

LAKE EYRE

NATIONAL

9

198

Mount
Barry

Creek

Lake
Conway

Aimee

Peake

Mt Denison
238m

Lambing

Ricketts Hill

Creek

Hawker

Creek

Creek

North

Creek

PARK

Lake M

10

WARNING: While visitors are permitted in the township of
Woomera, entry to the Woomera Prohibited Area is by permit
only, except in the immediate corridors of the Stuart Highway
and the road from Coober Pedy to William Creek.
Camping is not permitted in the area.

TRACK
203

Mt Margaret
412m

Nilpinna

Mt Anna
265m

405

Davenport

Douglas

Four Hills
105m

Creek

LAKE EYRE

NATIONAL

PARK

ELLIOT PRICE
CONSERVATION
PARK

11

Lake
Cadibarrawirracanna

166

Creek

Creek

Anna Creek

Ruby Hill
111m

William Creek

OODNADATTA

12

STUART

A87

82

Engenina

Dog

Baluna

Watturaragamia

Creek

WOOMERA

PROHIBITED

AREA

Campeera Hill
158m

Creek

Worriner

Creek

Beresford Hill
71m

127

Coward
Springs

Hamilton Hill
40m

Curdimurka
(ruins)

LAKE EYRE
NATIONAL
PARK

Lake Eyre
South

Lake
Frances

Lake
Ellen

Creek

Welcome

or

Fence

Mulli

13

HWY

Mt Pearhyn
216m

Mt Sandy
223m

Mt Woods
170m

Bramby

Baltin

Fence

Mt Purvis
291m

Margaret

Mt Riddoch
182m

Yarrabouna Hill
180m

Bidina Boudna Hill
162m

New Peter Hill
163m

WABMA KADARBU MOUND SPRINGS
CONSERVATION PARK

Blanche Cup
Mound Springs

Creek

Dog

Hermit Hill
121m

TRACK

75

Mt Alford
82m

Attra

A B 308 C D E F G H I

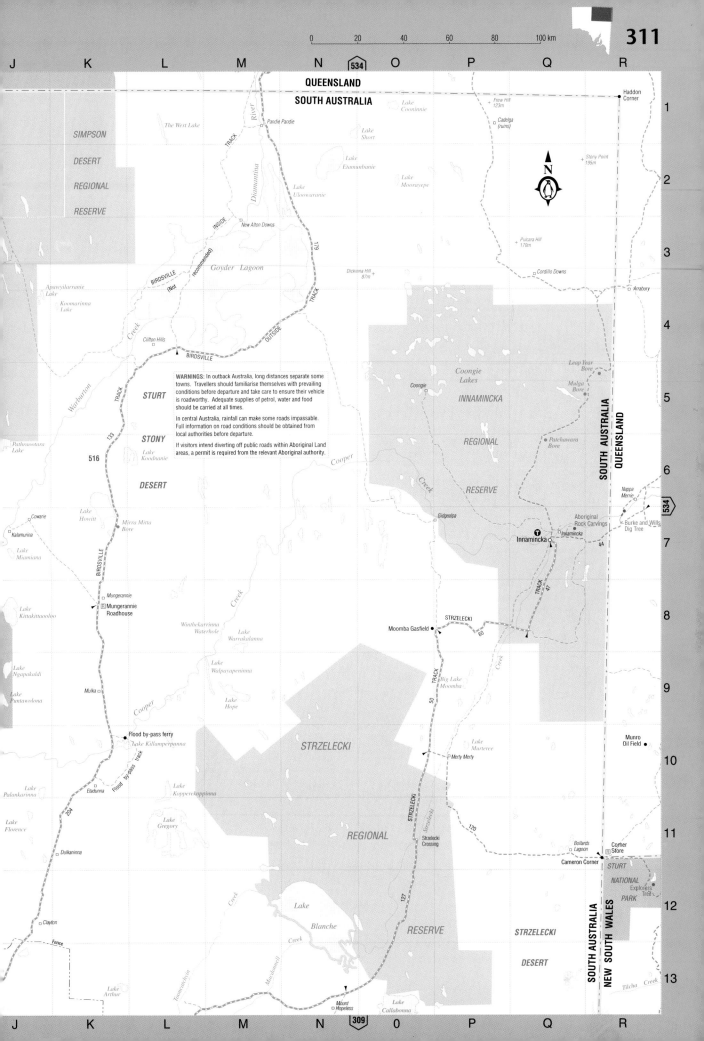

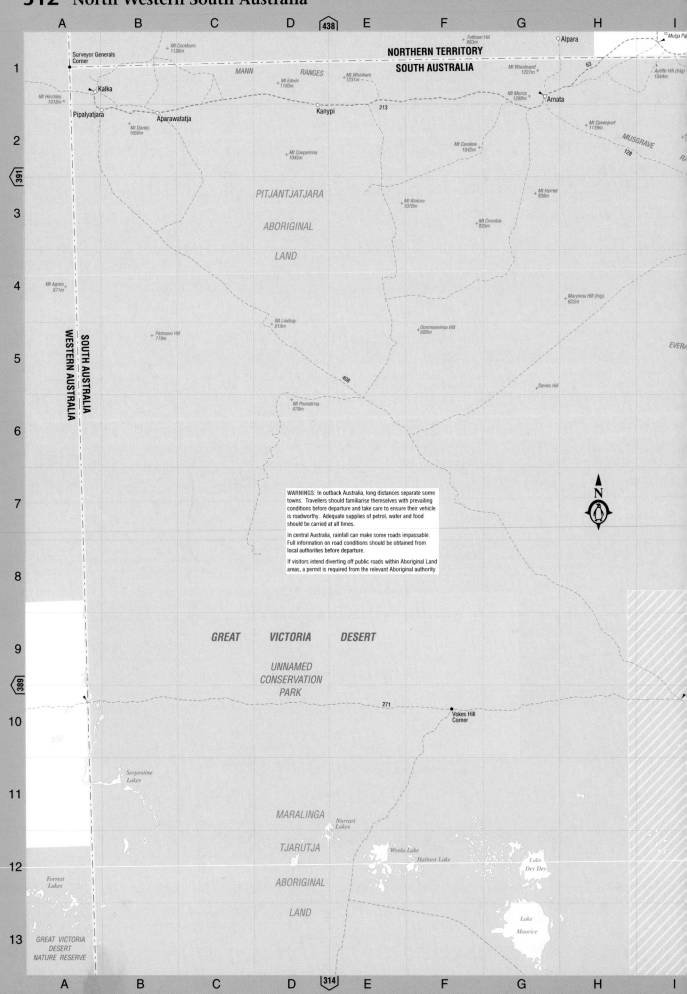

NORTHERN TERRITORY

SOUTH AUSTRALIA

Surveyor Generals Corner

Mt Hinckley
1018m +

Mt Cockburn
1138m +

▲ Mulga Pa

Feltham Hill
863m +

○ Alpara

Mt Woodward
1227m +

63

Ayliffe Hill
1044m +

Kalka

Pipalyatjara

Mt Davies
1058m +

Aparawatatja

Mt Edwin
1193m +

Kanypi

Mt Whinham
1231m +

213

Mt Morris
1288m +

○ Amata

Mt Davenport
1139m +

MUSGRAVE

128

391

PITJANTJATJARA

Mt Cooperinna
1045m +

Mt Caroline
1042m +

Mt Harriet
938m +

ABORIGINAL

Mt Kintore
1070m +

Mt Crombie
835m +

LAND

Mt Agnes
671m +

Maryinna Hill (trig)
622m +

Mt Lindsay
819m +

Oenmooninna Hill
600m +

EVER

Permano Hill
719m +

408

Davies Hill +

Mt Poondinna
678m +

N

WARNINGS: In outback Australia, long distances separate some towns. Travellers should familiarise themselves with prevailing conditions before departure and take care to ensure their vehicle is roadworthy. Adequate supplies of petrol, water and food should be carried at all times.

In central Australia, rainfall can make some roads impassable. Full information on road conditions should be obtained from local authorities before departure.

If visitors intend diverting off public roads within Aboriginal Land areas, a permit is required from the relevant Aboriginal authority.

GREAT   VICTORIA   DESERT

389

**UNNAMED
CONSERVATION
PARK**

271

Vokes Hill
Corner

Serpentine
Lakes

MARALINGA

Nurrari
Lakes

TJARUTJA

Wyola Lake

Halinor Lake

Lake
Dey Dey

Forrest
Lakes

ABORIGINAL

LAND

Lake
Maurice

GREAT VICTORIA
DESERT
NATURE RESERVE

438

314

SOUTH AUSTRALIA

WESTERN AUSTRALIA

MANN   RANGES

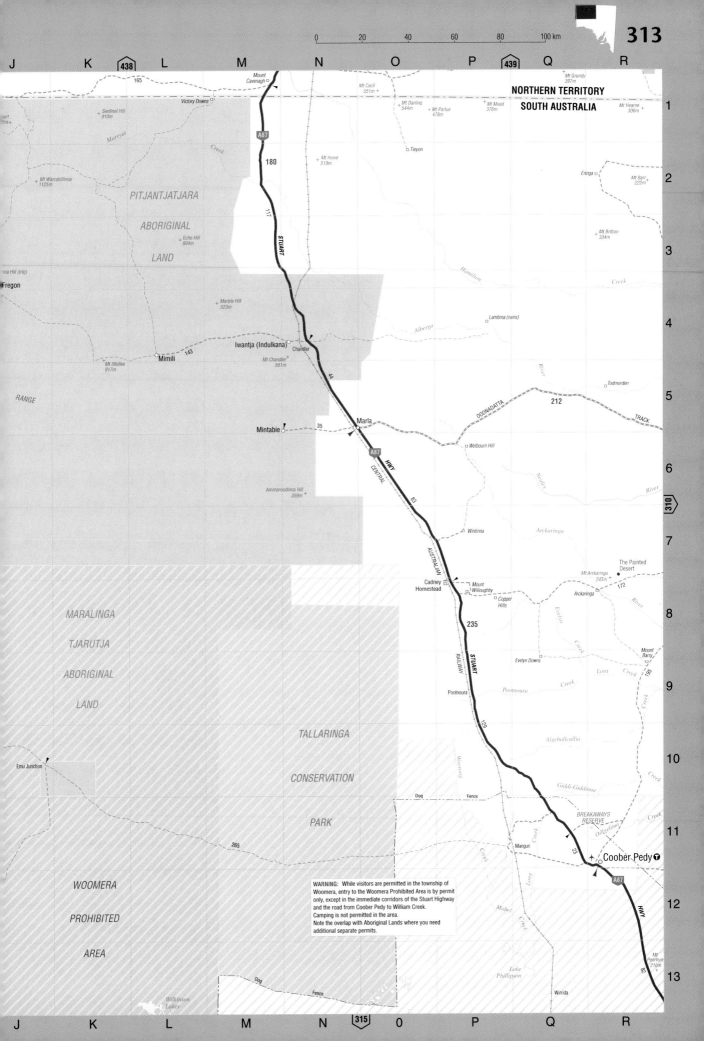

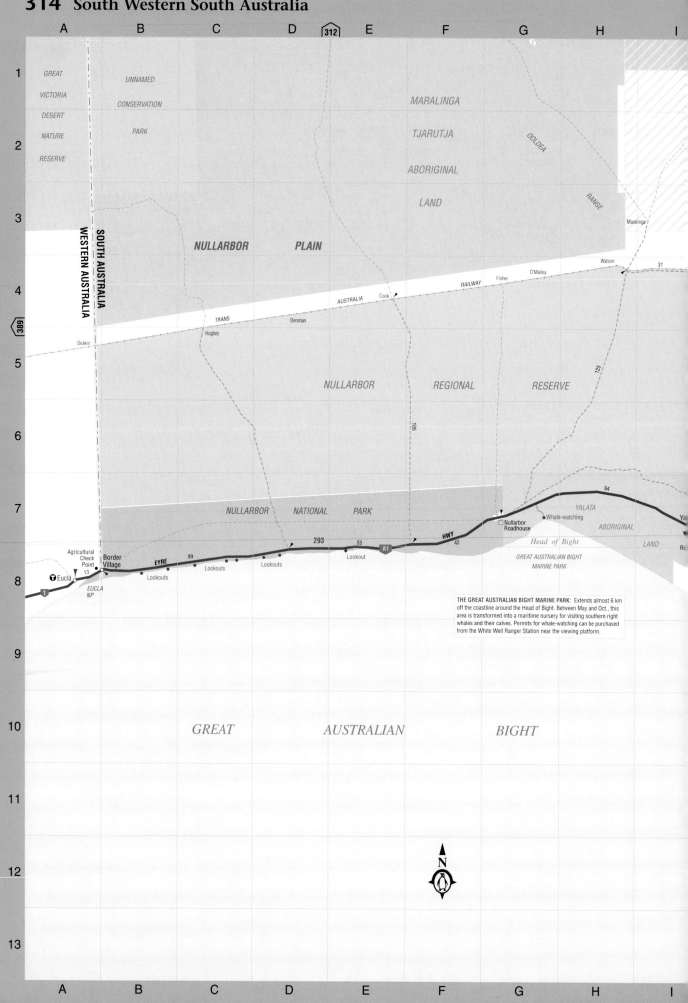

THE GREAT AUSTRALIAN BIGHT MARINE PARK: Extends almost 6 km off the coastline around the Head of Bight. Between May and Oct., this area is transformed into a maritime nursery for visiting southern right whales and their calves. Permits for whale-watching can be purchased from the White Well Ranger Station near the viewing platform.

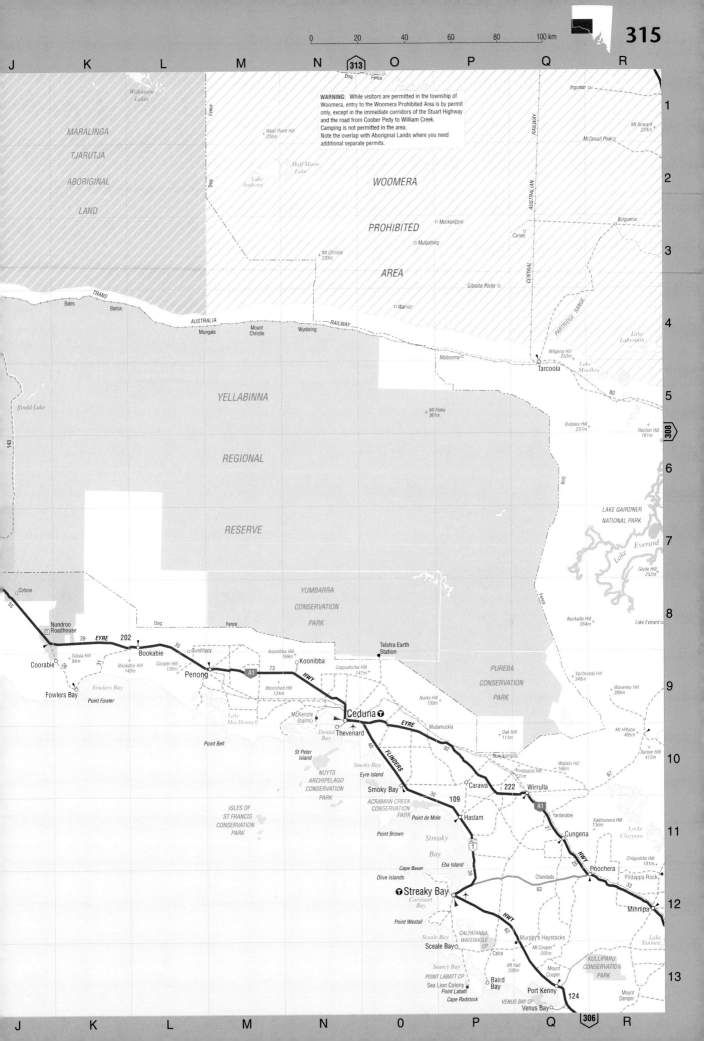

WESTERN AUSTRALIA

Mulla Mulla in the Hamersley Range

W estern Australia, the largest of the Australian States and Territories, covering roughly one-third of the Australian continent, has less than one-tenth of the nation's population. For the traveller, this vast State offers varied and magnificent scenery.

Even a casual glance at a map of Australia will quickly reveal that a car-touring holiday in Western Australia requires a great deal of thought and advance planning. The south-west region can be easily and pleasantly covered by car, but to travel the unique north and north-east requires more time and careful planning.

The Dutch had mapped the western coastline of Australia as early as the sixteenth century, yet it was not until 1826 that a British party from Sydney landed at King George Sound (Albany) and then only for fear of possible French colonisation. Three years later Perth, the first non-convict settlement in the country, was founded by Captain James Stirling. Due mainly to the ruggedness and sheer size of the land, the West struggled to develop until 1892, when gold was discovered at Coolgardie and the first economic boom for the region began. Today it is an immensely rich mineral State, its thriving economy still growing.

The climate in the north of the State is tropical, and as you travel south the climate becomes subtropical and then temperate – the beautiful city of Perth has the best climate of any Australian capital with a midwinter average maximum temperature of 18°C, a year-round average maximum of 24°C and an average of almost eight hours of sunshine a day.

It is easy to assume from a map that Perth is a coastal city; in fact, it is 19 kilometres inland, up the beautiful Swan River, home of the black swan. A city of over one million people, Perth is large enough to offer excitement and variety, yet compact enough to be seen quite easily. King's Park is only a short drive from the city centre, and nearby ocean beaches offer the visitor year-round swimming and surfing.

Nearby Rottnest Island is small and sandy, and only 20 kilometres off the coast of Fremantle. Regular air and ferry services from Perth will take you to this popular holiday island. Reefs and shipwrecks attract skindivers to this area.

The southern corner of this State is aptly described as the garden of Western Australia. Hardwood forests of massive karri and jarrah trees soar above the hundreds of different species of wildflowers that bloom from

NOT TO BE MISSED	
IN WESTERN AUSTRALIA	Map Ref.
BUNGLE BUNGLES Magnificent beehive-shaped rock formations in Purnululu National Park	385 P8
KARIJINI NATIONAL PARK Breathtaking gorges and crystal clear waterholes	390 B5
KALGOORLIE-BOULDER For its flamboyant architecture from the gold-boom days	388 I6
MARGARET RIVER For magnificent coastal and river scenery, caves and craft outlets – and excellent wine	381 C7
NAMBUNG NATIONAL PARK A moonscape of coloured quartz studded with limestone pillars, some 4 metres high	388 B6
NINGALOO REEF Snorkel on the coral reef and swim with the gentle whalesharks	387 B4
SHARK BAY Where wild dolphins swim into the shallows at Monkey Mia	387 A9
VALLEY OF THE GIANTS A beautiful drive near Walpole; allow time to take the Tree Top Walk through the giant stands of karri and tingle trees	382 H12
WILDFLOWERS A brilliant display across the State each spring	

September to November. Great surfing beaches, coastal panoramic views and wineries add to the attractions of the south-west region, with such popular locations as Margaret River, Busselton, Yallingup and Albany. Further east is Esperance, renowned for its stunning beaches, as is nearby Cape Le Grand National Park which also features wildflowers in season. The Margaret River region is a must, whether or not you are interested in wine. The region is fertile and beautiful, and the vineyards flourish on the rich loam that is perfect for grape-growing.

North-east of this well-vegetated corner, and 597 kilometres from Perth, is the one-time gold-boom area of Kalgoorlie-Boulder, surrounded by small historic mining towns such as Coolgardie and Broad Arrow. Further east you reach the Nullarbor Plain, famous for its almost treeless landscape, stretching as far as the eye can see. Further north are the Great Victoria and Gibson deserts.

Along the Brand Highway, 424 kilometres north of Perth, is the coastal town of Geraldton where you can sample freshly caught crays. Between Perth and Geraldton is the unique Pinnacle Desert in Nambung National Park, as well as vibrant displays of spring wildflowers. Magnificent beaches, excellent fishing and coral reefs are the main attractions along the coast north of Geraldton. Kalbarri National Park is renowned for its splendid flora and fauna, and its spectacular coastal gorges and cliffs. At Monkey Mia on Shark Bay, wild dolphins come close to the shore to be fed. Carnarvon, renowned for its succulent prawns, is an industrial fishing port at the mouth of the Gascoyne River. Ningaloo Marine Park protects the 260-kilometre coral reef near Coral Bay. Nearby, the town of Exmouth is world famous for its year-round fishing, and its beaches.

The Pilbara region has some of the country's most spectacular gorges in Karijini National Park. This is where Western Australia's second economic boom began, with the exploitation of the Hamersley Range, which stretches for 320 kilometres and is literally a mountain of iron.

Magnificent coastline near Esperance

CLIMATE GUIDE

PERTH

	J	F	M	A	M	J	J	A	S	O	N	D
Maximum °C	30	31	29	25	21	19	18	18	20	22	25	27
Minimum °C	18	19	17	14	12	10	9	9	10	12	14	17
Rainfall mm	8	12	19	45	123	184	173	136	80	54	21	14
Raindays	3	3	4	8	14	17	18	17	14	11	6	4

ALBANY REGION

	J	F	M	A	M	J	J	A	S	O	N	D
Maximum °C	25	25	24	22	19	17	16	16	17	19	21	24
Minimum °C	14	14	13	12	10	8	8	7	8	9	11	12
Rainfall mm	27	24	28	63	102	103	124	106	82	78	48	25
Raindays	8	9	11	14	18	19	21	21	18	15	13	10

KALGOORLIE REGION

	J	F	M	A	M	J	J	A	S	O	N	D
Maximum °C	34	32	30	25	20	18	17	18	22	26	29	32
Minimum °C	18	18	16	12	8	6	5	5	8	11	14	17
Rainfall mm	22	28	19	19	28	31	26	20	15	16	18	15
Raindays	3	4	4	5	7	8	9	7	5	4	4	3

DERBY REGION

	J	F	M	A	M	J	J	A	S	O	N	D
Maximum °C	36	35	35	35	33	31	30	32	35	36	37	37
Minimum °C	26	26	25	22	19	16	14	16	20	23	25	26
Rainfall mm	182	155	110	32	22	10	6	1	0	2	17	84
Raindays	12	10	8	2	1	1	1	0	0	0	2	6

CALENDAR OF EVENTS

JANUARY
Public holidays: New Year's Day; Australia Day. *Perth:* Classic Perth (golf); Hopman Cup (tennis); Perth Cup (horseracing); Skyworks. *Busselton:* Beach Festival; Festival; Australia Day Yacht Regatta. *Denmark:* Pantomime. *Esperance:* Sailboard Classic. *Fremantle:* Sardine Festival. *Geraldton:* Windsurfing Classic. *Hopetoun:* Summer Festival. *Mandurah:* Festival. *Narrogin:* State Gliding Championships.

FEBRUARY
Perth: Chinese New Year Festival; Festival of Perth. *Boyup Brook:* Country Music Awards. *Dwellingup:* Log Chop Day. *Esperance:* Offshore Angling Classic. *Katanning:* Triathlon. *Margaret River:* Leeuwin Estate Concert. *Mandurah:* Crab Festival.

MARCH
Public holiday: Labour Day. *Perth:* Festival of Perth (contd). *Australind:* Ocean Festival. *Brookton:* Old Time Motor Show (even-numbered years). *Bunbury:* Show. *Busselton:* Blue-water Classic (fishing). *Carnamah:* Wimbledon of the Wheatbelt. *Geraldton:* Sea Jazz Spectacular. *Harvey:* Harvest Festival. *Kalbarri:* Sport Fishing Classic; Cycle Races and Triathlon. *Margaret River:* Margaret River Masters (surfing). *Mount Barker:* Machinery Field Day; Porongurup Wine Summer Festival. *Nannup:* Music Festival. *Pingelly:* Autumn Alternative Agricultural Show.

EASTER
Public holidays: Good Friday; Easter Monday. *Albany:* Great Southern Wine Festival. *Brookton:* King of the Hill (off-road car racing); Wildflower Show (odd-numbered years). *Denmark:* Brave New Works. *Dongara:* Horse Races. *Donnybrook:* Apple Festival. *Lancelin:* Dune Buggy Championships.

APRIL
Public holiday: Anzac Day. *Balingup:* Small Farm Field Day. *Broome:* Rotary Dragon Boat Classic. *Busselton:* Heritage Week. *Exmouth:* Billfish Bonanza. *Margaret River:* Margaret River Masters (contd). *Mundaring:* Mundaring Hills Festival.

MAY
Boyup Brook: Autumn Art Affair. *Broome:* Fringe Arts Festival. *Carnarvon:* Fremantle–Carnarvon Yacht Race (even-numbered years). *Eucla:* Golf Classic. *Fremantle:* Fremantle–Carnarvon Yacht Race (even-numbered years); Rhythm and Blues Festival. *Gingin:* British Car Day. *Toodyay:* Moondyne Festival.

JUNE
Public holiday: Foundation Day. *Perth:* Celebrate WA. *Broome:* Fringe Arts Festival (contd). *Geraldton:* Batavia Celebrations. *Karratha:* Pilbara Pursuit Jetboat Classic. *Kununurra:* Dam to Dam Regatta. *Manjimup:* 15 000 Motocross. *Wagin:* Foundation Day. *York:* Country Music Festival.

JULY
Perth: Marathon. *Derby:* Boab Festival. *Exmouth:* Exmo Week; Arts and Crafts Show. *Fitzroy Crossing:* Rodeo. *Halls Creek:* Agricultural Show. *Marble Bar:* Cup Race Weekend.

AUGUST
Perth: City to Surf Fun Run. *Avon Valley National Park (near Toodyay):* Avon Descent (white-water classic). *Balingup (near Donnybrook):* Tulip Festival. *Beverley:* Agricultural Show. *Broome:* Shinju Matsuri; Opera Under the Stars; Sailfish Tournament. *Carnarvon:* Festival; Arts Festival. *Collie:* Collie to Donnybrook Cycle Race. *Denham:* Fishing Fiesta. *Dampier (near Karratha):* Game-Fishing Classic. *Dwellingup:* Forest Heritage Festival. *Halls Creek:* Races. *Karratha:* FeNaCLNG Festival. *Katanning:* Prophet Mohammad's Birthday. *Mullewa:* Wildflower Show; Agricultural Show. *Nannup:* Flower and Garden Month. *Newman:* Fortescue Festival. *Northam:* Avon River Festival. *Perenjori:* Bush Bouquet Craft Festival. *Pingelly:* Art and Tulip Festival. *Port Hedland:* Spinifex Spree. *Roebourne:* Royal Show; Roebourne Cup and Ball. *Tom Price:* Nameless Festival. *Walyunga National Park (near Mundaring):* Avon Descent. *Wyndham:* Races (horses). *York:* Daffodil Festival; Agricultural Show.

SEPTEMBER
Public holiday: Queen's Birthday. *Perth:* Football League Finals; Kings Park Wildflower Festival; Perth Royal Show. *Augusta:* Spring Flower Show. *Beverley:* Duck Race. *Boyup Brook:* Country Music Weekend. *Bridgetown:* Blackwood Classic (powerboats). *Broome:* Shinju Matsuri (contd); Fly Billfish Tournament. *Carnamah:* Agricultural Show. *Coolgardie:* Coolgardie Day; Art Exhibition. *Corrigin:* Agricultural Show. *Cranbrook:* Wildflower Display. *Exmouth:* Gulf Aquafest. *Harvey:* Spring Markets. *Kalgoorlie:* Kalgoorlie Cup; Spring Festival. *Kojonup:* Country and Wildflower Festival. *Kulin:* Charity Rally. *Mingenew:* Lions Expo. *Northampton:* Agricultural Show. *Perenjori:* Agricultural Show. *Ravensthorpe:* Wildflower Show; Spring Festival. *Southern Cross:* Agricultural Show. *York:* Jazz Weekend.

OCTOBER
Perth: Perth Royal Show (contd). *Augusta:* Spring Flower Show (contd). *Boyup Brook:* Blackwood River Marathon Relay; Spring Garden Expo. *Bridgetown:* Blackwood River Marathon Relay. *Busselton:* West Coast Golf Open. *Cranbrook:* Wildflower Display (contd). *Esperance:* Agricultural Show; Festival of the Wind (even-numbered years). *Eucla:* Eucla Shoot. *Fremantle:* Blessing of the Fleet. *Geraldton:* Sunshine Festival. *Harvey:* Agricultural Show. *Kojunup:* Agricultural Show. *Kulin:* Bush Races Weekend (at Jilakin Rock). *Leonora:* Art Prize. *Merredin:* Vintage Car Festival (odd-numbered years). *Narrogin:* Spring Festival; Agricultural Show; Orchid Show. *Northam:* Multicultural Festival. *Northampton:* Airing of the Quilts; Festival Day. *Northcliffe:* Mountain Bike Championship. *Porongurup:* Wildflower Weekend. *Swan Valley:* Spring in the Valley (wine). *Walpole:* Wildflower Week. *York:* Flying 50s (car rally).

NOVEMBER
Perth: Rally Australia. *Australind:* Wine Festival (even-numbered years). *Beverley:* Harvest Festival (at Avondale Discovery Farm). *Bridgetown:* Blues at Bridgetown; Festival of Country Gardens. *Broome:* Mango Festival. *Cranbrook:* Art Show. *Darlington (near Mundaring):* Arts Festival. *Dongara:* Blessing of the Fleet. *Exmouth:* Gamex (game fishing). *Fitzroy Crossing:* Barra Splash. *Fremantle:* Festival Fremantle. *Jurien Bay:* Marine Expo and Blessing of the Fleet. *Kalbarri:* Blessing of the Fleet. *Margaret River:* Wine Region Festival. *Manjimup:* Forest and Horticultural Expo. *Rockingham:* Spring Festival. *Wickepin:* Art and Craft Show (even-numbered years).

DECEMBER
Public holidays: Christmas Day; Boxing Day. *Perth:* Christmas Pageant. *Cervantes (near Jurien Bay):* Slalom Carnival (windsurfing). *Derby:* Boxing Day Sports. *Katanning:* Caboodle. *Lancelin:* Ledge Point Ocean Race (windsurfing). *Rockingham:* Christmas Regatta; Cockburn Yachting Regatta. *Yallingup:* Longboard Classic.

Note: The information given here was accurate at the time of printing. However, as the timing of events held annually is subject to change and some events may extend into the following month, it is best to check with the local tourism authority or event organisers to confirm the details. The calendar is not exhaustive. Most towns and regions hold sporting competitions, regattas and rodeos, art, craft and trade exhibitions, agricultural and flower shows, music festivals and other events annually. Details of these events are available from local tourism outlets.

At the State's very top is the Kimberley region, with the King Leopold Range in the west and Purnululu National Park in the east. The region's economy is based on diamond mining and the more traditional cattle industry. A visit to this remote, dramatic region with its gorges and rivers is a unique experience – in keeping with many areas of Australia's largest State.

VISITOR INFORMATION
*Western Australian Tourist Centre (WATC)
cnr Forrest Pl. & Wellington St, Perth
(08) 9483 1111 or freecall 1300 361 351
www.westernaustralia.net*

Aerial view of the Kimberley region

Perth

With a Mediterranean-type climate and coastal river setting, Perth is ideal for an outdoor lifestyle. Clean surf beaches, tranquil forests and well-kept parklands all lie within easy reach of the city centre.

VISITOR INFORMATION
Western Australian Tourist Centre (WATC)
cnr Forrest Pl. & Wellington St, Perth
(08) 9483 1111 or freecall 1300 361 351
www.perthwa.com.au

HISTORY
Perth was founded by Captain James Stirling in 1829, three years after a British party from Sydney landed at King George Sound (Albany) to abate fears of French colonisation. The progress of the isolated Swan River settlement, made up of free settlers, was slow. It was not until the first shipment of convicts arrived in 1850 that the colony found its feet. The convicts were soon put to work building roads, bridges and fine public buildings, and in 1856 Perth was proclaimed a city. Gold discoveries in the State in the 1880s gave Perth another boost and, more recently, the huge diamond finds in the Kimberley and the reopening of goldmines in the Kalgoorlie region have stimulated new growth.

Perth is a cosmopolitan city with a population of more than 1.3 million. The Swan River winds through the suburbs, widening to lake size near the city centre. The 404-hectare Kings Park contrasts dramatically with Perth's modern skyline, and the serene blue hills of the Darling Range form a more distant backdrop.

EXPLORING PERTH

The city centre is compact and easy to explore. A free, regular bus service known as CAT (Central Area Transit) System operates around central Perth; the blue CAT runs in a north–south loop and the red CAT operates in an east–west loop. You can also travel free with Transperth bus or train within the Free Transit Zone in the city centre. Transperth produces a handy *Tourist Guide and Map*, which shows the Free Transit Zone.

A good way to discover the city is on the Perth Tram Co. tours, which operate daily. These replicas of the city's first trams extend east to Burswood International Resort Casino and west to the University of Western Australia. You can break your journey at any point. On weekdays, Trams West operates a 'tram' tour (the vehicle is actually a bus) around the streets of historic Subiaco and out to Lake Monger.

EXPLORING THE SWAN RIVER

The Swan River foreshores, on both the city side and around South Perth, provide pleasant walking and cycling trails; obtain a Bikewest *Touring Perth and Kings Park by Bike* map for details. Bicycles can be hired just off Riverside Drive near the Causeway, at the Barrack Street Jetty and at Kings Park.

If you are touring by car, the circuit route around the Swan River foreshore is a must. Follow the Canning Highway along the southern side of the river, and business area is linked by malls, overpasses and underground walkways. **London Court**, an arcade with the appearance of a quaint Elizabethan street, runs from Hay Street Mall to St Georges Terrace. At the Hay Street entrance, knights joust above a replica of Big Ben every 15 minutes, while St George and the Dragon do battle above the clock over the St Georges Terrace entrance.

Looking in a westerly direction along St Georges Terrace, the older buildings are largely overshadowed by modern office buildings; however, you can see the cast-iron verandahs of the **BankWest** building (formerly the Palace Hotel, 1895), the decorative brickwork of the **Cloisters** (1859) and the gothic-style **Old Perth Boys School** (1846). At the end of St Georges Terrace, not far from the perspex skirt of the modern **QV1 Building**, is **Barracks Archway**. The central arch is all that remains of the Pensioners' Barracks, a structure that originally had two wings, with 120 rooms. This building housed the British soldiers who guarded the convicts in the mid-1800s. Across the road (the other side of the Mitchell Freeway) is Western Australia's **Parliament House**. Weekday tours are available; bookings essential.

For a stroll through the oldest part of Perth, start at the **Central Government Building** near the north-east corner of St Georges Terrace and Barrack Street. Perth was founded here with a tree-felling ceremony in 1829. Convicts and hired labour commenced work on the Central Government Building in 1874. At one stage, it housed the General Post Office, and a plaque on the building's east corner marks the point from which all distances in the State are measured.

Cross St Georges Terrace and walk through the **Stirling Gardens** to Perth's oldest surviving building, the **Old Court House**. Built in 1836, it is now home to the Frances Burt Law Museum. Back on St Georges Terrace, look out for Perth's Tudor-style **Government House** (1859). Across the road, on the Pier Street corner, you will see the **Deanery** (1859) and **St George's Cathedral** (1879); this Anglican church features a rich jarrah ceiling, perhaps the finest in Perth.

Perth skyline from Kings Park

then cross over at Stirling Bridge and return via the Stirling Highway.

Ferries and cruise boats depart regularly from the Barrack Street Jetty to various destinations, including Fremantle, South Perth and the Swan Valley wine region. Dinner cruises are a popular way to see the city light up at night.

PERTH BY AREA
CITY CENTRE
The centre of Perth is a well-balanced mixture: elegant colonial buildings sit comfortably alongside the steel and glass giants from the heady days of the 1980s; old-fashioned friendliness mingles with a sharp-edged competitiveness.

Most of Perth's shops and arcades are in the blocks bounded by St Georges Terrace and William, Wellington and Barrack streets, centering around **Hay Street Mall**, **Murray Street Mall** and **Forrest Place Mall**. Perth's shopping

NOT TO BE MISSED

IN PERTH	Map Ref.
FERRY TRIP Past the exclusive waterside suburbs to Fremantle	372 D8
KINGS PARK Bushland reserve with good views of city	372 A7
LAKE MONGER To see black swans and other waterbirds	374 F1
NORTHBRIDGE For its lively arts precinct	372 C4
PERTH MINT Lift a gold bar and watch a gold pourer at work	372 F7
PERTH ZOO Beautiful butterflies and animals of the night	372 C12
OCEAN BEACHES To surf, swim or relax by the sparkling sea	372 & 374

PERTH ON FOOT
Guntrips Walking Tours
2-hour guided walks around city and Kings Park; bookings essential

Heritage Walk
2-hour guided walk of central business district; bookings essential

Perth Heritage Trails
Self-guide heritage trails

Perth Walking Tours
2-hour guided heritage walks; bookings essential

For further information and bookings, contact WATC

TOP EVENTS

Classic Perth (Jan.)
Premier international golf tournament

Hopman Cup (Jan.)
Prestigious international tennis event

Festival of Perth (Feb.–Mar.)
International arts festival

Kings Park Wildflower Festival (Sept.)
*Australia's premier native plant and
wildflower exhibition*

Rally Australia (Nov.)
*Four days of action-packed, world-class
motor sport*

*For further details visit the web site
www.westernaustralia.net/whats_on/
index.shtml*

SPORT

*Perth's sporting facilities are an excellent
indication of this city's obsession with
sport. Cricket and football are the
mainstays, with baseball, basketball and
hockey gaining in popularity. Golf
courses abound and the national passion
for horseracing is well represented by the
centrally located racecourses, **Ascot** and
Belmont Park. Night pacing is at
Gloucester Park near the famous **WACA**
cricket ground. In Mt Claremont is
Challenge Stadium, a multipurpose
venue. The city's pride are its two
national Australian Football League
teams, the West Coast Eagles and the
Fremantle Dockers; the **Subiaco Oval** is
their home ground. Sailing is Perth's
grandest obsession, with a yacht club at
every bend in the river.*

Continue along Pier Street to the National Trust-classified Murray Street Precinct, which includes the **Former Government Printer's Office**, the **Old Fire Brigade Building** which now houses a fire museum, and **Kirkman House** (with its massive fig tree). This harmonious group of buildings is a legacy of the wealth of the gold era. At the eastern end of Murray Street, in Victoria Square, is the gothic-style **St Mary's Cathedral** (1863).

To complete your historic ramble, return along Murray Street and turn left into Barrack Street. The decorative **Perth Town Hall** (1867) with its distinctive clocktower is on the corner of Hay and Barrack streets.

NORTHBRIDGE

The inner-city suburb of **Northbridge** is connected to the city centre via an extensive walkway that crosses Perth Railway Station and leads directly to the **Perth Cultural Centre** complex. The **Art Gallery of Western Australia**, home to a fine display of Western Australian art, is located here. So, too, is the **Perth Institute of Contemporary Arts** (PICA) where you can sample the latest in visual and performance art. On weekends, the **Galleria Art and Craft Markets** create a colourful atmosphere in the Cultural Centre Mall. Across the mall

is the excellent **Western Australian Museum**, which includes the original Perth Gaol (1856) and an 1860s cottage.

On Friday and Saturday nights, the streets west of the Perth Cultural Centre provide popular places to eat, drink and go nightclubbing. Many of the restaurants and bars open out into the streets to take advantage of the mild Perth evenings.

EAST OF THE CITY CENTRE

Towards the eastern end of Hay Street is the **Perth Mint** (1899) with its imposing facade built from Rottnest Island limestone – one of the best examples of Perth gold-boom architecture. Here, visitors can see the world's largest collection of natural gold specimens and watch gold being poured.

Queens Gardens, at the corner of Hay and Plain streets, is on the site of the former brickworks, source of the lovely mellow bricks used in many of Perth's Colonial buildings. In 1899 the clay pits were transformed into ornamental lily ponds and garden beds.

Those interested in cricket will want to pay homage to the **Western Australian Cricket Association (WACA) Oval**, in Nelson Crescent. Every Tuesday at 10 a.m. regular tours are conducted around the museum and the 'Wacca' ground; phone (08) 9265 7222.

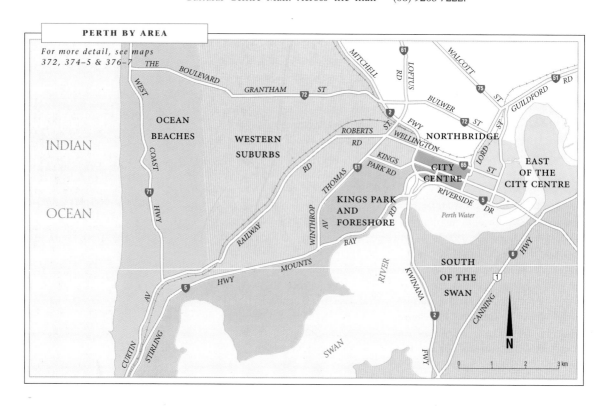

PERTH BY AREA

*For more detail, see maps
372, 374–5 & 376–7*

Across the Swan are the beautifully landscaped gardens of **Burswood Park**, an adventurous blend of native and exotic plants. The Atrium Lobby in the **Burswood International Resort Casino** is one of the city's modern architectural highlights. This 47-metre high pyramid of shimmering glass contains a tropical garden and waterfall.

KINGS PARK AND FORESHORE

Just minutes from the city centre, **Kings Park** is one of Perth's major attractions. Within this huge natural bushland reserve there are landscaped gardens and walkways, lakes, children's playgrounds and a war memorial. During spring, the **Botanic Gardens** on Mount Eliza Bluff are ablaze with wildflowers.

Drive along the river past Kings Park to the suburb of Crawley and the **University of Western Australia**, with its Mediterranean-style buildings and landscaped gardens. Within the university grounds you will find the Brendt Museum of Anthropology and the Lawrence Wilson Art Gallery. Nearby, the grassy Matilda Bay shoreline has shady spots and views back up the river and towards the city. The **Royal Perth Yacht Club** is located near Pelican Point.

Continuing along the river foreshore towards the ocean, you will pass through the exclusive waterfront suburbs – **Nedlands, Dalkeith, Claremont, Peppermint Grove** and **Mosman Park** – with their charming village-style shopping areas, fashionable galleries and foreshore restaurants. **Claremont Museum**, once the Freshwater School (1862), has an interesting social history display.

WESTERN SUBURBS

Just west of the city on the edge of Kings Park is the popular shopping, cafe and market area **Subiaco**, one of Perth's oldest suburbs.

In West Perth at the City West shopping complex are the **Scitech Discovery Centre**, which features a hands-on science and technology display, and the massive screen of the **Omni Theatre**. Just north of West Perth in Leederville is **Lake Monger**, the best place in Perth to see Western Australia's famous black swans.

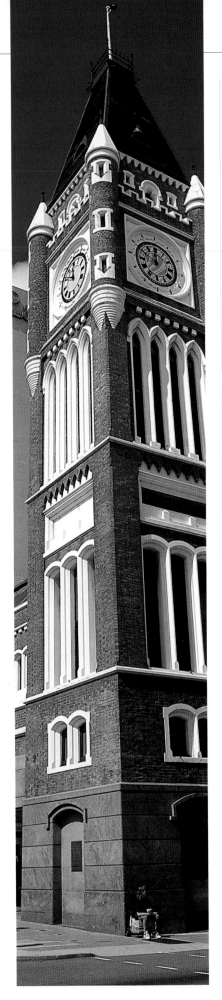

Perth Town Hall clocktower

SHOPPING

	Map Ref.
DEPARTMENT STORES Myer and Aherns are the two major ones	372 D5 & D6
LONDON COURT Mock-Tudor arcade with souvenir and jewellery stores	372 D6
SQUARES & MALLS Hay Street Mall; Murray Street Mall; Forrest Place Mall	372 D5 & D6
KING STREET High fashion, galleries and cafes with style	372 C6
SUBURBAN VILLAGE-STYLE SHOPPING STRIPS Claremont (Bay View Terrace)	374 D6
Cottesloe (Napoleon Street, off Leake Street)	374 C7
Subiaco (Rokeby Road)	374 F3

MARKETS

	Map Ref.
CANNING VALE SUNDAY MARKETS, CANNING VALE Huge undercover flea market	375 K12
GALLERIA ART & CRAFT MARKET, PERTH CULTURAL CENTRE, NORTHBRIDGE Handcrafted items (Sat. & Sun.)	372 D5
SCARBOROUGH FAIR MARKETS, SCARBOROUGH BEACH Specialty stalls and a food hall (Sat. & Sun.)	376 B10
STATION STREET MARKETS, SUBIACO Eclectic array of goods and live entertainment (Sat. & Sun.)	374 F2
SUBIACO PAVILION MARKETS, SUBIACO Art and craft stalls in restored warehouse adjacent to station (Thurs.–Sun.)	374 F3

ENTERTAINMENT

*It is worth timing your visit to experience a performance in **His Majesty's Theatre**, Australia's only remaining Edwardian theatre. Other major venues include the **Perth Concert Hall** in St Georges Terrace, the **Perth Entertainment Centre** off Wellington Street and the splendid Art Deco **Regal Theatre** in Subiaco. For avant-garde theatre, try the small performance venues in **Northbridge**. **Burswood International Resort Casino**, is another lively night-time destination. Alternatively, why not make the most of Perth's glorious weather and check out the outdoor theatre and cinema venues during summer.*

For entertainment details check the West Australian newspaper on Thursdays or pick up a free copy of the X-Press gig guide.

RESTAURANTS AND CAFES

One of the highlights of Perth is the opportunity to taste seafood straight from the clear waters of the Indian Ocean, accompanied by a superb range of fresh fruit and vegetables, and complemented by quality Western Australian wines or locally brewed beers.

Map Ref.

BARRACK ST JETTY
Brunch or dinner by the river — 372 C7

KING STREET (IN THE CITY CENTRE)
International cafe-style fare — 372 C6

LEEDERVILLE (ALONG OXFORD STREET)
The inner-city alternative — 374 G2

NORTHBRIDGE
Italian and Asian cuisine at reasonable prices — 372 C4

NORTHERN FORESHORE
Quality seafood and glorious views — 374

SOUTH PERTH
Bright modern cafes overlooking the river — 372 C12

SUBIACO
Street cafes, stylish pubs and fine restaurants — 374 F3

GALLERIES AND MUSEUMS

Map Ref.

WESTERN AUSTRALIAN MUSEUM
Comprehensive collection including some of Perth's oldest buildings — 372 E4

ART GALLERY OF WESTERN AUSTRALIA
Collection of Australian and international works — 372 E5

CREATIVE NATIVE
Aboriginal art and craft, traditional and modern — 372 C5

CRAFTWEST
Craft by leading Western Australian artists — 372 C5

ARTIST IN RESIDENCE GALLERY
An Aboriginal art gallery where you can watch the current resident artist at work — 372 A7

PERTH INSTITUTE OF CONTEMPORARY ARTS (PICA)
Vibrant contemporary art and performance space — 372 D5

OCEAN BEACHES

Swimming and surfing are part of the joy of Perth and several beautiful Indian Ocean beaches – including Cottesloe, Swanbourne (a nude bathing beach), City, Floreat, Scarborough, Trigg and North beaches – are close to the city.

A drive along the foreshore to **Cottesloe** is full of surprises: the distinctive Norfolk Island pines, the colonial splendour of the Indiana Tea House and the Spanish-style Cottesloe Civic Centre with its magnificent gardens.

Further north at **Scarborough**, you will find wonderful weekend stalls at the Scarborough Fair Markets, adjacent to the five-star Rendezvous Observation City. Hillarys Boat Harbour at **Sorrento Quay** features recreational facilities, a marine retail village and a world-class oceanarium, Underwater World. Ferries depart daily from here for Rottnest Island and there are whale-watching tours from September to November. Near Hillarys Boat Harbour is Marmion Marine Park, offering fishing, snorkelling, diving and Little Island, a wildlife reserve where visitors can watch sea-lions and whales.

SOUTH OF THE SWAN

There is a host of interesting attractions south of the Swan River. South Perth is home to **Perth Zoo**, with its magnificent garden environment, butterfly house and Australian animal exhibits. The trip can be combined with a visit to the **Old Mill**, on the South Perth foreshore. This picturesque whitewashed windmill, built in 1838, now houses an interesting collection of early colonial artifacts.

On the other side of Canning River is **Wireless Hill Park**, a natural bushland area with beautiful spring wildflowers. Three lookout towers provide views of the Swan River and the city skyline. The **Telecommunications Museum** is housed in the original Wireless Station and is open weekends. Further south, black swans and other waterbirds can be seen at **Bibra Lake** in the suburb of the same name. Also at Bibra Lake is the State's biggest theme park, **Adventure World**, which is open October to April and offers among its attractions a wildlife park, animal circus, rides and Australia's largest swimming pool.

Bannister Road, in the south-east suburb of Canning Vale, is the location of Western Australia's biggest undercover marketplace, the **Canning Vale Sunday Markets**. Nearby in Baile Road you will find the **Swan Brewery**, renowned for its Swan and Emu beers. Tours of this state-of-the-art brewery are available; bookings essential, phone (08) 9350 0222.

Closer to the coast, in Spearwood, there are two other attractions: **Cables Water Ski Park**, a water-ski fun park, and the **Stock Road Markets**, held under cover at weekends.

Perth is a modern capital in a splendid natural setting. Renowned for its outdoor and easy going lifestyle, this compact city offers a host of urban pleasures.

'Tram' tours through Kings Park

Fremantle

VISITOR INFORMATION
Fremantle Tourist Bureau
Fremantle Town Hall
cnr William and Adelaide sts
(08) 9431 7878

GETTING TO FREMANTLE
FROM PERTH
By car
A drive of 20–30 minutes, either via Stirling Hwy on north bank of Swan River, or via Canning Hwy on south bank.
By train
A 30-minute journey from Perth Railway Station, Wellington St. Trains depart every 15 minutes on weekdays, less frequently at weekends.
By bus
Many buses and routes link both cities. Timetables and route details from Wellington St Bus Station in Perth, TransPerth, or Fremantle Town Hall.
By ferry
Various ferry operators travel twice daily between Perth and Fremantle, departing Barrack St Jetty, Perth.
Combined travel packages
Two packages, Tourist Trifecta organised by Trams West and Tourist Quartet organised by Fremantle Trams, combine ferry travel and train tours. The Quartet package includes bus or train back to Perth.

GETTING AROUND
Car rental
Avis 1800 225 533; Budget 13 2727; Hertz 13 3039
Public transport
Transperth 13 6213
Taxis
Swan 13 1008; Black and White 13 1924
Scooter hire
Scootabout (08) 9336 3471
Bicycle hire
Fleet Cycles (08) 9430 5414
Tourist tram
Fremantle tram (departs from Fremantle Town Hall) (08) 9339 8719

Although now linked to Perth by suburbs, Fremantle ('Freo' to the locals) has a feel that is quite different, in both its architecture and its atmosphere. It stands at the mouth of the Swan River, 19 kilometres south-west of Perth, and was the site of the first European settlement in Western Australia.

Today Fremantle is a major port and fishing centre with unusually well-preserved nineteenth-century port streetscape. It is also a place to stay, to unwind, and to watch the world go by. You can visit historic buildings, shop at the famous market, take a tram ride, or rest at a cafe and wait for the arrival of the 'Fremantle doctor', the cool, refreshing, afternoon wind that blows in from the ocean. Fremantle combines the bustle of a port with the relaxed feeling of a holiday destination.

European settlers first arrived in 1829, and Fremantle grew slowly, its existence dependent on whaling and fishing. Its population was boosted with the arrival of British convicts in 1850. They constructed the forbidding Fremantle Prison, now open to the public, and the imposing lunatic asylum, now the Fremantle Arts Centre and History Museum. Many heritage houses, terraces and cast-iron balconies have survived from this era.

Fremantle was at the centre of the world stage in 1987 when it hosted the America's Cup series of yacht races, in defence of the cup won by *Australia II* – a Fremantle yacht – in 1983. Preparations for this huge event included the restoration of many old buildings in Fremantle, and the boost to its tourist economy has lasted to the present.

EXPLORING FREMANTLE

The centre of Fremantle is compact, so exploring on foot is an option, although the Fremantle Arts Centre and History Museum are outside the city centre. If you are driving, there are a number of carparks along the foreshore on Marine Terrace and the Esplanade, and in the city centre, as well as metered street parking.

For train travellers to Fremantle, the station is close to the city centre and the wharves. If you arrive by ferry, you can catch the tourist 'tram' into town. The replica tram (actually a bus) is a great way to see Fremantle. It departs from the

The Round House

TOP EVENTS

Sardine Festival (Jan.)
Taste freshly caught sardines from
the waters of Fremantle

Blessing of the Fleet (Oct.)
Traditional Italian blessing of the
fishing fleet

Festival Fremantle (Nov.)
Streets come to life with food, music,
theatre, dance, and exhibitions

For further details visit the web site
www.fremantle.wa.gov.au

Town Hall hourly (10 a.m.–4 p.m.), passes the popular sights and has a commentary. For the more energetic, bicycle and scooter hire are available.

FREMANTLE BY AREA

HISTORIC CENTRE

To explore the historic centre, start at the **Fremantle Town Hall** in Kings Square, on the corner of William and Adelaide streets. The **Fremantle Tourist Bureau** is here, so you can pick up information on the city's attractions before you set out. The town hall, built in 1887, has a clock tower. Nearby in Adelaide Street is **St John's Anglican Church** with its stone bell-tower.

From the town hall, walk along High Street towards the sea, past the shops, and turn right into Henry Street, which ends at Phillimore Street. Turn left down Phillimore Street to three imposing buildings: the Georgian-style **Old Customs House**, built in 1853, one of the oldest buildings in Fremantle; the **Old Fremantle Fire Station** (now a restaurant) and,

alongside, the **Chamber of Commerce**, with stained-glass panels around its door. Turn left along Cliff Street and go past the lavish, Victorian-era **Lionel Samson Building** on your way to the Western Australian Maritime Museum at the far end.

Between 1851 and 1862 convicts built the Commissariat store, which now houses the **Western Australian Maritime Museum**. Its most popular exhibit is the reconstructed stern of the *Batavia*, wrecked off the Western Australian coast in 1629, which looms above the visitor. The Batavia room contains a stone portico that was being transported to Java when the wreck occurred.

From the Western Australian Maritime Museum stroll along Marine Terrace to Fremantle's **Old Courthouse** (1883), on the corner of Mouat Street and Marine Terrace and now part of the University of Notre Dame. The **Esplanade Hotel Fremantle**, overlooking The Esplanade Reserve on Marine Terrace, is a grand old hotel with a lovely wooden verandah reminiscent of the 1890s gold-rush era. Retrace back to Collie Street to visit **Artisans of the Sea**, where there is a pearling industry heritage display and award-winning Kailis Broome pearl jewellery. Turn left onto Pakenham Street and second on the right is Bannister Street. Here you will find the **Bannister Street Craft Workshops**, where a cooperative of artisans create, display and sell their work.

At the end of Bannister Street, turn right into Market Street and along **South Terrace**, the cappuccino strip, an ideal place to take a break at a cafe or restaurant. The **Sail and Anchor Hotel** was Western Australia's first pub brewery and serves specialty beers – it even has a banana beer!

In this strip you will also find the **Fremantle Markets** in a gorgeously restored Victorian building. It is one of Fremantle's most popular attractions, and contains a diversity of stalls:

FREMANTLE BY AREA

For more detail, see map 380

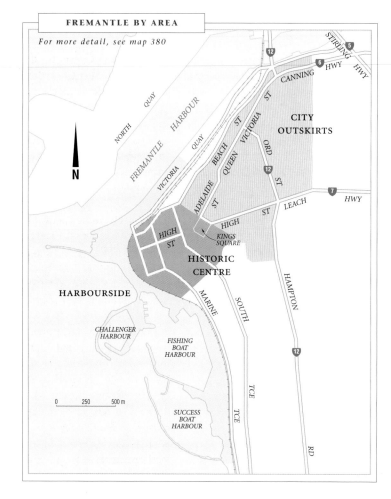

produce, books, clothes, pottery and crafts. The markets are open Friday to Sunday.

From the markets walk up Henderson Street to the **Fremantle Police Station and Courthouse**, a limestone building dating from the 1890s. Nearby are the **Warders' Quarters**, a row of cottages built by convicts in 1851.

HARBOURSIDE

At the port of Fremantle the industrial activities are across the river on the northern side, but there are plenty of boats on this side of the Swan in the Harbourside area. Furthest south is **Success Boat Harbour**, home to the yachts of the Fremantle Sailing Club. Alongside is **Fishing Boat Harbour**, where the 500-strong fishing fleet moors. Restaurants line the wharves here, giving you a chance to sample the deliciously fresh catch, particularly lobster. North of this is **Challenger Harbour**, built for the America's Cup.

If you continue north to the end of Bathers Beach you will come to the area known as Arthur Head, and dominating the hill here, behind a limestone-retaining wall, is the Round House. The **Round House** actually has twelve sides, constructed around a central yard, and is the oldest building in the State, built in 1830 as a gaol. At 1 p.m. daily, the Round House's signal station fires a cannon – the time gun – and a time ball is activated. There are Fremantle Heritage Guides on site daily, between 10 a.m. and 5 p.m. November to April, and between 10.30 a.m. and 3.30 p.m. May to October.

From here it is a short stroll past the shipyards to the river and the sheds

The Old Customs House

that line **Victoria Quay**. **A Shed** houses a cafe; and **E Shed** a market (open Friday to Sunday) and more cafes. Also on the riverfront is the towering Fremantle **Port Authority** building; at 1.30 p.m. on weekdays you can catch the guided tour to the Observation Deck for a great view.

The *Leeuwin*, a traditional square-rigger and the largest tall ship in Australia, has a berth at Victoria Quay. It takes people on weekend, day and half-day cruises, during which they can experience being part of the crew – a terrific adventure.

CITY OUTSKIRTS

The first convicts arrived in Fremantle in 1850 and were immediately set to work to build a prison. The limestone used in the building of the prison was quarried on site. Huge, forbidding and full of history, the **Fremantle Prison** was in use until 1991. Now, visitors can experience

the grim atmosphere as part of a guided tour. The entrance is in The Terrace, and can be reached via steps and a walkway around Fremantle Oval from Parry Street.

Hampton Road (which becomes Ord Street), at the far side of the prison, will take you to **Samson House** (1888), on the corner of Ellen Street. This gracious mansion has been restored to elegance and is open on Sunday afternoons (1 p.m. to 5 p.m.).

Further along Ord Street is the magnificent limestone **Fremantle Arts Centre and History Museum**. Also built by convicts, it was the old female lunatic asylum. With its steeply pitched roofs and Gothic arcades it is a striking building. It offers contemporary art exhibitions, an interesting display on the history of Fremantle, a ghost walk and a garden area with a cafe.

Close by, in Burt Street, the **Army Museum of Western Australia** is open Saturday and Sunday afternoons, while the **World of Energy**, with its fascinating interactive displays, is in Quarry Street on the way back to town from the Fremantle Arts Centre and History Museum.

From Fremantle's Victoria Quay you can catch a ferry to Rottnest Island, a favourite beach spot for Western Australians. With its relaxed, almost Mediterranean atmosphere, its architecture, its working port and fishing-boat harbour, its renowned markets and its cafe-lined South Terrace, Fremantle attracts large numbers of visitors and locals, particularly at weekends: it is the playground for Perth.

Marina at Fremantle

DAY TOURS
from Perth

Perth is a wonderful base for day touring –
whether you head for the coast or the
hills, there is so much to see and do. For a
day in the country, make the gradual
ascent into the Darling Range, or meander
through the Swan Valley, famous for its
vineyards and charming towns. The short
trip north to Yanchep National Park is
another option, often combined with a leisurely
drive back alongside the sparkling Indian
Ocean. Rottnest Island, one of Perth's premier
day-trip destinations, provides a welcome break
for the tired motorist – this low, sandy island,
just 20 kilometres west of Fremantle, can be
accessed only by air or sea.

Turquoise waters surrounding Rottnest Island

DAY TOURS FROM PERTH
*For more detail, see maps
374–5, 376–7 & 378*

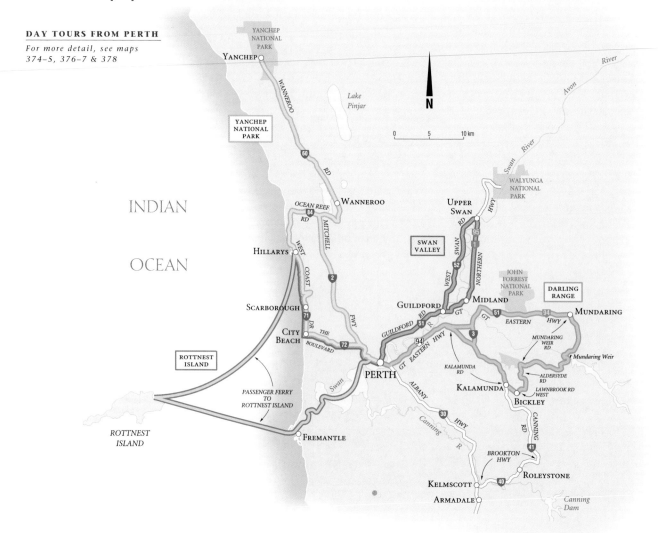

INDIAN

OCEAN

YANCHEP
NATIONAL
PARK

YANCHEP

WANNEROO RD

YANCHEP
NATIONAL
PARK

60

Lake
Pinjar

OCEAN REEF
RD

Wanneroo

MITCHELL

84

Hillarys

WEST

COAST

2

Scarborough

71

CITY
BEACH

DR

THE

BOULEVARD

72

FWY

ROTTNEST
ISLAND

PASSENGER FERRY
TO
ROTTNEST ISLAND

ROTTNEST
ISLAND

Swan

R

FREMANTLE

N

0   5   10 km

WALYUNGA
NATIONAL
PARK

Swan River

Avon River

UPPER
SWAN

WEST SWAN RD

NORTHERN HWY

95
1

SWAN
VALLEY

52

JOHN
FORREST
NATIONAL
PARK

DARLING
RANGE

Guildford

GUILDFORD RD

51

GT

GT

Midland

EASTERN

3

51

HWY

MUNDARING
WEIR
RD

Mundaring

94

Mundaring Weir

PERTH

GT EASTERN HWY

94

KALAMUNDA
RD

ALBANY

HWY

30

Canning R

KALAMUNDA
RD

Kalamunda

ALDERSYDE
RD

LAWNBROOK RD
WEST

Bickley

CANNING RD

CANNING RD

41

BROOKTON
HWY

40

ROLEYSTONE

KELMSCOTT

ARMADALE

Canning
Dam

DARLING RANGE

42 km to Mundaring Weir via Great Eastern Highway and Bypass 94 *, and Mundaring Weir Road*

Pack your picnic basket and leave the city behind! This tour follows the Great Eastern Highway into the gently undulating hills of the Darling Range. For a fresh perspective on Perth, stop at **Greenmount National Park** and take in the views. Further into the hills, **John Forrest National Park** is another worthwhile diversion, with shady picnic areas, lookouts, a pretty rock pool and walking trails through the jarrah forest.

Along the way there are tearooms and craft shops if you wish to make a stop. At **Mundaring** turn off at Mundaring Weir Road, which leads to the weir. The rolling lawns and bushland surrounding the weir make the reserve an ideal lunch spot. The C. Y. O'Connor Museum at Mundaring Weir provides an insight into the challenge of supplying water to the goldfields during the 1890s.

To visit the fertile valley of Bickley, turn off at Aldersyde Road. Orchards and vineyards line the road and there are plenty of opportunities to sample the local produce.

At Kalamunda you can go back in time at the History Village Museum. This folk museum contains early settlers' cottages, and original railway yards complete with steam locomotive. From Kalamunda, return to Perth via Williams Street, which becomes Zig Zag Scenic Drive. This section is lovely, particularly in spring when the roadside wildflowers are in bloom.

Those who wish to spend more time exploring the hills will find a cluster of interesting attractions further south around Armadale. One of the Darling Range's top attractions is Araluen Botanic Park at Roleystone. The park's terraced gardens are spectacular in spring when the special Tulip Time display draws many visitors. **See also:** National Parks p. 336 and individual entries in A–Z listing for parks and towns in bold type.

SWAN VALLEY

28 km to Upper Swan via Guildford Road 51 *and Great Northern Highway* 1 95

The Swan Valley, home to some of Australia's top vineyards, is a picturesque day-tour destination from Perth. Follow the Swan River inland along Guildford Road (or the Great Eastern Highway) to historic Guildford. The Old Courthouse, Gaol and Museum is open on Sunday afternoons. Inside is a treasure chest of farm and cooperage tools, fashions of yesteryear and old household items. Next door is the Guildford Village Potters Gallery, which has an on-site pottery workshop. The village also boasts the Rose and Crown Hotel (1841), the oldest trading hotel in the State.

After exploring Guildford, continue north-east to West Midland and visit Woodbridge House (1855), overlooking the Swan River. This fine example of late-Victorian architecture has been restored and furnished by the National Trust.

To take in some of the region's natural beauty, extend your journey along the Great Northern Highway to Walyunga National Park, a popular picnic and walking area. Here, the Avon River flows through lovely bushland, renowned for its wildflower display in spring.

For a shorter trip, turn left off the Great Northern Highway near Upper Swan, and loop back along West Swan Road 52 . A signposted diversion, right off West Swan Road, leads to Whiteman Park, a popular attraction with wildlife, sheepshearing, camel rides, a vintage tramline, a mussel pool and picnic and barbecue area. West Swan Road passes many of the finest vineyards in Australia. Houghton Wines, Evans and Tate and Sandalford are just a few familiar labels you will come across. In the heart of this winegrowing country, on the western bank of the Swan River, is the charming All Saints Church, the oldest church in the State.

YANCHEP NATIONAL PARK

39 km to Yanchep National Park via Mitchell Freeway 2 *, Ocean Reef Road* 84 *and Wanneroo Road* 60

Yanchep National Park has long been a favourite day-trip destination from Perth. A highlight of the park is Crystal Cave, one of Western Australia's most accessible caves. Visitors can take regular guided tours through the cave, which features stalactites hanging over an underground pool.

There is plenty to do above ground as well. Picnic spots overlook the waters of Loch McNess, the park's picturesque centrepiece. Lake cruises operate Monday to Sunday (by appointment), and public holidays, and rowing-boats are available daily for hire. Birdwatching is popular, as the lake's islands provide a haven for waterbirds, and there are many other species to be found in the surrounding bushland. The park also supports a colony of koalas, wild kangaroos and a magnificent range of wildflowers in spring.

The most direct route to Yanchep National Park is via the Mitchell Freeway. A railway runs down the centre of the freeway and the quirky railway station buildings along the line are in themselves a feature.

Turn off along the Ocean Reef Road to join Wanneroo Road, near the beautifully land-scaped satellite town of Joondalup.

For a change of scenery, return along West Coast Drive ⑪, via Hillarys Boat Harbour and past the white sandy

Quokka, Rottnest Island

beaches of the Indian Ocean, and take time to enjoy the glorious sunsets for which this coastline is famous. Hillarys Boat Harbour is a haven for boats and has a waterside shopping village complete with cafes and restaurants. Nearby at Underwater World, a submerged tunnel gives visitors the opportunity to come face to face with thousands of marine animals. There is also a touch pool and a dolphin sanctuary. **See also:** National Parks p. 336 for parks in bold type.

ROTTNEST ISLAND

Access by ferry from Barrack Street Jetty, Hillarys Boat Harbour or Fremantle; flights also operate from Perth

'Terrestrial paradise' – that was how Dutch explorer Willem de Vlamingh described **Rottnest Island** when he landed there in 1696. Vlamingh named the island Rotte-nest (Rat's Nest) in reference to the island's marsupial

residents, the quokkas, which he believed to be a type of rat. Visitors today can still enjoy the peace, beauty and unique natural features of the island; there are also many places of historic interest which add to Rottnest's charm.

Only 11 kilometres long and about 5 kilometres wide, Rottnest Island has an attractive coastline with many small bays and coves, white beaches and turquoise waters. Ferries arrive at Main Jetty in Thomson Bay. The Visitor Centre is clearly visible as you approach the Settlement – stop to pick up a map and plan your day. The museum, located behind the Settlement shopping mall, provides an excellent introduction to the island's historical and natural features.

Cars are not permitted on Rottnest, which contributes to the wonderful sense of peace. There are various ways to explore the island: you can hire

a bicycle; take a special 2-hour coach tour, conducted twice daily; catch the Bayseeker bus which does a circuit of the main beaches, or walk. There are free, guided walks daily, covering the history of the early settlement, as well as self-guide walks and bicycle trails. A train operates several times daily on a 7-kilometre route from the historic settlement area to the Oliver Hill Battery, where there is a walking tour of the World War II Gun Emplacements.

Rottnest boasts many sheltered swimming spots – the Basin, Longreach Bay, Parakeet Bay and Geordie Bay are some of the best. Surfers head for the western end, where the most popular breaks are at Strickland Bay and Cathedral Rocks. If you enjoy snorkelling, there is an underwater trail on Pocillopora Reef off the south of the island. Scuba diving is also available. Visit the Dive, Surf and Ski Shop near the Main Jetty for underwater equipment and diving information. The *Underwater Explorer*, a glass-bottomed cruiser, leaves regularly from Main Jetty, for glimpses of shipwrecks, reefs and a startling array of fish.

While there is no shortage of things to see and do on Rottnest, many visitors prefer to simply laze in the sunshine, linger over lunch at the Dome Cafe, or enjoy a relaxing drink in the beer garden at the Quokka Arms.

If you decide to stay more than a day – and you are sure to be tempted – there is a range of accommodation, including lodge rooms, units, cabins, hostels and a camping area. For further information, contact the Rottnest Visitor Centre, Main Jetty; (08) 9372 9752. **See also:** Wildlife-Watching p. 340.

Cape to Cape

Busselton to Cape Leeuwin via Cape Naturaliste (188 km)

Travelling from Cape Naturaliste to Cape Leeuwin takes you on a route that runs between the coast and a picturesque landscape of forest, farmland and wineries, and through Leeuwin–Naturaliste National Park. A limestone ridge stretches from cape to cape, and water has hollowed out vast caverns underground. A visit to one or more of these caves is sure to be a highlight of your tour. Allow at least two days to take in the sights between Busselton and Augusta; those with a special interest in either caves or wineries should allow at least one extra day. If you are touring between June and December, you may also be treated to the sight of whales along the coast.

❶ The longest jetty

The tour starts in **Busselton**, located on the shore of magnificent Geographe Bay, 228 kilometres south of Perth. The sea here is generally placid, in contrast to the wilder coastline between the capes. Dolphins swimming in the bay may be sighted from the picturesque 2-kilometre wooden jetty, the longest in Australia. When the jetty was built in 1865, it serviced the American whaling ships; later, it was extended to take a railway line for the loading of timber. Today, a small tourist train chugs along the jetty on the hour between 10 a.m. and 4 p.m.

❷ To the lighthouse

From Busselton, head west along the Bussell Highway, then turn right onto Caves Road and on to the popular holiday town of Dunsborough. Skirt the town centre and turn right onto Cape Naturaliste Road, which leads to the lighthouse. Peppermint and banksia trees shade the road, gradually giving way to cycads, grass trees and coastal heath. Between mid-September and the end of October the heath is a carpet of pinks, reds and purples.

Cape Naturaliste Lighthouse (1906), which was the last staffed lighthouse in Western Australia, is now automated. Visitors can climb the steep steps to the top of the tower where the prismatic lens is in constant rotation. At the entrance to the lighthouse grounds there is a small, interesting display on the history and technology of lighthouses .

If you are here in season, the easy 800-metre stroll to the whale-watching platform is a must. Humpbacks often swim close to shore as they round the cape on their annual migration from the Antarctic to the Kimberley coast in the north of the State (April to June), returning south from October to December. Southern right whales sometimes venture this far north to calve in the shallow waters (June to September).

For those who wish to explore the natural wonders of the cape, there is a network of well-marked walking trails. The wild seas and lunar landscape of the western headland are in stark contrast to the scenic coastline and sheltered waters of Bunker Bay to the east.

Bunker Bay

Humpback whale

Cape Naturaliste Lighthouse
Phone: (08) 9755 3955
Open: 9.30 a.m.–3.30 p.m. daily;
extended hours in summer and
school holidays

❸ Surf and salmon

Drive back along Cape Naturaliste Road, then turn left onto Eagle Bay Road. The road winds along the rocky coastline, offering extended vistas of Geographe Bay, and eventually rejoins Cape Naturaliste Road. At Dunsborough, turn onto Caves Road. Just past Ngilgi Cave, there is a road on the right that leads to the internationally renowned Yallingup surf beach. The beaches from here to the south have powerful surf and fearful names, such as Guillotines, Gallows and Suicides. This section of coast is also excellent fishing territory.

Return to Caves Road, head south for a short distance and turn right onto the road leading to **Canal Rocks**. This canal-like rock formation, which extends for many metres out into the surf, was caused by an ancient fault. The fault line is best viewed from the Rotary Lookout on the cliff.

For a close encounter with the ocean, you can follow the boardwalk, which has been built out across the rocks, but beware, the waves can be dangerous. Between May and June, Canal Rocks attracts large numbers of enthusiastic anglers. At this time of year huge schools of Australian salmon swim north on their annual spawning run.

❹ The moon's bathing place

Rejoin Caves Road and continue south through the heart of the Margaret River wine region. The scenery is a patchwork of emerald-green pasture and vineyards; enticing cellar-door and B&B signs line the road.

Six kilometres after you have passed the turn-off to Gracetown, turn right onto Ellensbrook Road which leads to **Ellensbrook** (1857). This wattle and daub homestead was the first home of the Bussell family, after whom Busselton was named. The homestead, which is set by a bubbling brook, was the hub of a beef and dairy cattle lease that stretched 30 kilometres along the coast. A signposted 1.3-kilometre circuit walk winds past Meekadarribee Waterfall and Grotto. At the grotto there is an enchanting storybook display outlining an Aboriginal legend that describes the grotto as 'the moon's bathing place'.

Ellensbrook

Ellensbrook Road, off Caves Road
Margaret River
Phone: (08) 9755 9015
Open: 10 a.m.–4 p.m. daily;
walking trail open daily

⑤ Wild and free

Rejoin Caves Road and continue south through wine country before turning left along Wallcliffe Road to Margaret River. Here there is a wide range of accommodation in and around the town, making it an ideal base for touring the region's wineries and caves.

Wine barrels

At Margaret River, take the Bussell Highway to the southern outskirts of town and turn right along Boodjidup Road to reach **Eagles Heritage**, a rehabilitation centre for injured birds of prey. Here you can see about 20 of the 24 Australian raptor species, depending on releases into the

wild, and there are free-flight displays of these magnificent birds at 11 a.m. and 1.30 p.m. daily. A 1-kilometre walk winds around the park, through the magnificent bushland setting.

As you continue along Boodjidup Road towards Caves Road, you will pass the turn-off to two of the area's leading wineries, Leeuwin Estate and Voyager Estate, both of which are open for tastings and cellar-door sales.

Eagles Heritage

Boodjidup Road
Margaret River
Phone: (08) 9757 2960
Open: 10 a.m.–5 p.m. daily

⑥ Underground wonders

From Boodjidup Road turn left onto Caves Road, which winds through farmland for about 4 kilometres until it reaches a section of Leeuwin–Naturaliste National Park. Two caves are nearby: Mammoth Cave to the left, about a kilometre on, and Lake Cave on the right after another 2 kilometres.

Frances Bussell is credited with the discovery of Lake Cave; she came across the crater-like entrance while searching for lost cattle in 1851. At the mouth of Lake Cave is **CaveWorks**, a fascinating interpretive centre with a dynamic working cave model.

CaveWorks

Off Caves Road
Phone: (08) 9757 7411
Open: 9 a.m.–5 p.m. daily

WINERIES

The Margaret River wine region has been compared favourably with the French Bordeaux district. The first vines were planted as recently as 1967, at Vasse Felix, but more wineries soon followed. Over 15% of Australia's premium wines are now produced in the area.

Many wineries are open to the public for tasting and cellar-door sales, while others have restaurants and tours of their premises. A good starting point is the Margaret River Regional Wine Centre in Cowaramup (open Mondays–Saturdays 10 a.m.–8 p.m., Sundays 12 noon–6 p.m.). Here you can pick up information about all the wineries and taste the local produce.

There are now more than forty wineries in the Margaret River region, many of which are marked on the road map on page 381. Amberley Estate, Leeuwin Estate, Vasse Felix, Cape Mentelle, Brookland Valley Vineyard and Voyager Estate are just some of the wineries with fine reputations and facilities for visitors. There are more unusual ones too: Serventy Organic Wines grows organic grapes for its vintages, while The Berry Farm has a range of fruit wines, from sparkling strawberry to pink plum port, as well as a selection of vinegars and jams. Bootleg Brewery is a must for those who enjoy their beer.

⑦ Karri forests to Hamelin Bay

Rejoin Caves Road and, 3 kilometres south of CaveWorks, turn right onto Boranup Drive, an unsealed road that winds through karri forest for 14 kilometres before meeting up again with Caves Road. Take care after heavy rain and watch for oncoming traffic.

The forest here is regenerating from extensive logging, which took place between 1890 and 1910. In the late 19th century, Maurice Coleman Davies created a vast business empire from these giant trees. Today, the largest trees in the forest are around 50 metres tall and wildflowers carpet the ground in spring. Boranup Lookout, at the southern end of this scenic drive, provides panoramic views of the coast and the Leeuwin–Naturaliste ridge.

After rejoining Caves Road, continue south before turning right to **Hamelin Bay**. At the end of the road is a windswept beach with crumbling limestone cliffs. The skeleton of an old jetty is all that remains of what was once a focal point in international trade.

Cape Leeuwin Lighthouse

At the height of Davies' timber empire, massive amounts of jarrah and karri were transported from Hamelin Bay to London, Sydney and South Africa. The port's exposure to the treacherous north-west winds resulted in 11 wrecks. There is now a wreck trail for experienced divers just offshore, and the beach is popular for fishing and swimming. Watch out for stingrays around the old jetty.

❽ Historical themes

Return to Caves Road and continue south, past the entrance to Jewel and Moondyne caves, to join the Bussell Highway on the outskirts of **Augusta**. Along with Busselton, Augusta is one of the oldest settlements in the State. The Augusta Historical Museum explores a number of interesting themes: the life of the early pastoralists, the timber and whaling industries, and the story of the 'group settlers' – English migrants who cleared the land for farming in the 1920s.

For superb views of Augusta's riverside setting, the karri forests and the coast, make a short detour west from the centre of town along Hillview Road (10 km return).

Augusta Historical Museum
Blackwood Avenue
Augusta
Phone: (08) 9758 1695
(Leeuwin Souvenirs)
Open: 10 a.m.–12 noon daily;
also 2 p.m.–4 p.m. Sept.–Apr.
and school holidays

❾ A view of two oceans

From Augusta continue south to the tip of Cape Leeuwin; the Bussell Highway becomes Blackwood Avenue in Augusta, then Leeuwin Road.

Cape Leeuwin was named by Captain Matthew Flinders in 1801 when he set out from this point to charter the entire east coast. Stop at the Matthew Flinders Memorial at the Groper Bay turn-off, particularly if you are travelling between July and September, when you may sight whales offshore.

Continue towards **Cape Leeuwin Lighthouse**; just before you reach it you will see on the right the unusual sight of a wooden waterwheel apparently turning to stone. It once supplied water to the keepers from an underground spring. Minerals from the spring have precipitated onto the wood, resulting in a limestone coating that is gradually covering the structure.

The Cape Leeuwin Lighthouse, the final destination on your cape to cape tour, is located on Western Australia's south-western tip. Commissioned by Davies in 1895, the limestone tower overlooks both the Indian and Southern oceans. You can climb to the top for even more spectacular views of the two oceans, but be prepared for blustery conditions.

Cape Leeuwin Lighthouse
Phone: (08) 9758 1920
Open: 9 a.m.–4 p.m. daily

Jewel Cave

CAVES

As you travel from cape to cape you are passing over an extensive network of limestone caves, five of which are regularly open to the public:
Ngilgi Cave – the largest cave in the area; 'adventure' caving; self-guide tours with access to a guide in the main chamber
Mammoth Cave – contains the remains of an extinct wombat-like creature; self-guide tour with CD headset
Lake Cave – features a reflective lake-like stream; guided tours
Jewel Cave – includes the largest straw stalactite in any tourist cave; guided tours
Moondyne Cave – guided 'adventure' caving with helmets, lamps and overalls

The CaveWorks entrance fee includes admission to one of either Jewel, Lake, Mammoth or Moondyne caves; phone CaveWorks for opening hours and tour details; (08) 9757 7411. Contact Ngilgi Cave directly for details; (08) 9755 2152.

Hamelin Bay

Continuing on, or returning to Perth

To return to Perth from Cape Leeuwin, drive north along the Bussell Highway, through Augusta, Margaret River, Busselton and Bunbury (143 kilometres).

Alternatively, drive north from Augusta to Karridale. Turn right along the Brockman Highway, over Alexandra Bridge and on to Nannup. From there, continue across the Great Australian Bight to South Australia or follow the Balingup Road through Donnybrook and on to Bunbury and Perth (370 kilometres).

WESTERN AUSTRALIA from A to Z

Lighthouse at Albany

Albany   Pop. 20 493

MAP REF. 383 N12, 386 H13, 388 F12

Picturesque Albany is the State's oldest town. On the edge of King George Sound and the magnificent Princess Royal Harbour, the town is 408 km S of Perth. Albany dates from 1826, when a military post was established to give the British a foothold in the west. Whaling was important in the 1840s; in the 1850s Albany became a coaling station for steamers from England. As WA's most important holiday centre, it offers visitors a wealth of history and coastal, rural and mountain scenery. Its harbours, weirs and estuaries provide excellent fishing. **In town:** Colonial Buildings Historic Walk, brochure available. Old Post Office-Intercolonial Communications Museum, cnr Stirling Tce and Spencer St. Victorian shopfronts in Stirling Tce. In Residency Rd: Residency Museum (1850s), originally home of Resident Magistrates, now houses historical and environmental exhibits; Old Gaol and Museum (1851) has two gaols in one. Vancouver Arts Centre, Vancouver St. House of Gems, Frenchman Bay Rd. Old Farm (1836), Middleton Rd, Strawberry Hill, site of first Government farm in WA. Faithfully restored Patrick Taylor Cottage (1832), Duke St, has extensive collection of period costume and household goods.

Princess Royal Fortress (commissioned 1893), off Forts Rd, on Mt Adelaide, Albany's first federal fortress. Mt Adelaide Forts Heritage Trails, starting cnr Apex Dr. and Forts Rd; self-guide leaflets available. On Princess Royal Dr.: the *Amity*, full-scale replica of brig that brought Major Lockyer and convicts to establish Albany in 1826; Amity Crafts, for local art and craft. Desert Mounted Corp Memorial statue, on Apex Dr. near top of Mt Clarence; spectacular view here and at John Barnesby Memorial Lookout, on Melville Dr., at Mt Melville. Southern right whale-watching cruises, daily from town jetty (July–mid-Oct.). Easter: Great Southern Wine Festival. **In the area:** Fishing at: Jimmy Newhill's Harbour, 20 km S; Frenchman Bay, 25 km S; Emu Point, 8 km NE; Oyster Harbour, 15 km NE. *To the north:* Deer-O-Dome deer farm (6 km); Mt Romance Emu Farm (12 km); Porongurup National Park (37 km), featuring huge granite peaks and easy walking tracks to splendid views; Stirling Range National Park (80 km) for climbing and bushwalking, breathtaking scenery, brilliant wildflowers in spring, some unique to area. *To the west towards Denmark:* West Cape Howe National Park (30 km) one of south coast's most popular parks for walking, fishing, swimming and hang-gliding, and has one of best

lookouts on coast; Torbay Head in parks southernmost point in WA. Care should be taken when exploring the coast; king waves can be dangerous and have been known to rush in unexpectedly, with fatal consequences. *To the south:* Torndirrup National Park (17 km) for spectacular coastal views, The Gap and Natural Bridge, the Blowholes. *To the south-east:* On Vancouver Peninsula: Point Possession Heritage Trail with views, interpretive plaques; brochures available. Also on peninsula is Camp Quaranup (20 km), site of old quarantine station, historical walk south on Geake Point. Albany Whaleworld at the old Cheyne's Beach Whaling Station (25 km) which ceased operation in 1978; in its heyday, the Station's chasers took up to 850 whales per season. *To the east:* Two Peoples Bay Marron Farm (20 km); Nanarup (20 km) and Little Beach (40 km) have sheltered waters; Willowie Game Park (30 km); Two Peoples Bay Nature Reserve (40 km), noted for the noisy scrub-bird (*Atrichornis clamosus*), thought to be extinct, redis-covered 1961. **Visitor information:** Old Railway Station, Proudlove Pde; (08) 9841 1088, freecall 1800 644 088. **See also:** The South-West p. 335; Western Wildflowers p. 364.

Augusta   Pop. 1087

MAP REF. 379 C13, 381 D12, 386 B11, 388 B11

The town of Augusta overlooks the mouth of the Blackwood River, the waters of Flinders Bay and rolling, heavily wooded countryside. Augusta is one of the oldest settlements in WA and a popular holiday town. Jarrah, karri and pine forests supply the district's 100-year-old timber industry. **In town:** In Blackwood Ave: Augusta Historical Museum; Lumen Christi Catholic Church. Crafters Croft, Ellis St, for art and craft. Sept.–Oct.: Spring Flower Show. **In the area:** Picturesque coastline; excellent swimming and surfing; fishing in river and ocean. Marron (freshwater lobster) in season, fishing licence required, available post office, Blackwood Ave. Augusta–Busselton Heritage Trail; pamphlet available. Cruises on Blackwood River and Hardy Inlet. Views from Hillview Lookout and golf course, 6 km NW. Jewel Cave, famous for its colourful limestone formations, and Moondyne Cave, for guided adventure tours; both 8 km NW.

The South-West

The south-west corner of Western Australia is a lush green land. Its gently rolling hills are crossed by rivers winding through deep-sided valleys. The soils are fertile and the farms prosperous. Along the coast, there are many beautiful bays ideal for swimming and fishing. At Cape Leeuwin, near **Augusta**, in the far south-west, the roaring Indian and Southern oceans join forces. The hinterland features karri and jarrah forests, picturesque orchards, and seasonal wildflower displays. The countryside is dotted with orchards and many wildflowers in season.

Pinjarra, 84 kilometres south of Perth, is one of the State's oldest districts. It has interesting historic buildings and makes a good base for touring the surrounding area.

Near **Harvey** there is fine agricultural land and the undulating farms stretch to the foothills of the Darling Range. North-west of Harvey is Yalgorup National Park, where the lakes attract a wide variety of birdlife.

The coast of the south-west is fascinating: an unusual mixture of craggy outcrops and promontories, sheltered bays with calm waters and beaches pounded by rolling surf. The length of the coast, together with the many rivers and estuaries, makes the south-west an angler's paradise. The Murray, Harvey and Brunswick rivers and their tributaries are only some of the streams annually stocked with trout.

The main port for the south-west, **Bunbury** rests on Geographe Bay looking out over the Indian Ocean. It is a perfect holiday town. One of the oldest towns in the State, **Busselton**, sited on the Vasse River, has a wealth of pioneer houses, many restored and open to the public.

Margaret River on the river of the same name, offers beaches, caves, magnificent scenery and world-class wineries. The **Leeuwin–Naturaliste National Park** combines a scenic rugged coast with magnificent wildflowers and the tall timbers of karri and jarrah forests. **Yallingup** is known for its excellent surf and spectacular limestone caves.

Bridgetown, **Donnybrook** and Greenbushes are small townships tucked away in green, hilly orchard country. Goldmining flourished briefly here at the turn of the century. **Manjimup** and **Pemberton** are world famous for their surrounding karri and jarrah forests. Here some of the world's tallest trees reach straight up, often to 80 and 90 metres. The Beedelup, Scott, Warren and Brockman national parks are nearby, and were introduced to protect the unique environment.

The south-west region has an important historical heritage. **Albany** was the first town in Western Australia, established two and a half years before the Swan River colony. Major Edmund Lockyer landed here in 1826 to claim the western half of the continent as British territory.

Albany is the unofficial capital of the area, and retains a charming English atmosphere from the colonial days. The town looks out over the magnificent blue waters of Princess Royal Harbour and King George Sound. There are numerous scenic drives around the coast to the Gap,

Two Peoples Bay, east of Albany

the Natural Bridge and the Blowholes. There are also white sandy beaches and secluded bays. The fishing is superb. **Denmark**, a holiday destination, lies on the banks of the tranquil Denmark River, and the little village of Nornalup nestles near the Frankland River. Near Nornalup is the awe-inspiring Valley of the Giants, best seen from the Tree Top Walk which is 40 metres above the ground.

The vineyards around **Mount Barker** produce award-winning wines. The skyline is dominated by the Stirling and Porongurup mountain ranges, both protected by national park status. The Porongurup Range has granite peaks dominating giant hardwood trees, and a maze of wildflowers and creepers. There are many easy climbs, rewarded by splendid views.

Limestone caves at Yallingup

The high, jagged peaks of the Stirling Range (the highest is Bluff Knoll at 1073 metres) tower over virgin bushland. The peaks can sometimes be seen shrouded in mist, and on occasion even tipped with snow. There are more than 100 bird species in the **Stirling Range National Park** and native animals are plentiful. Look also for the beautiful wild orchids, Stirling banksia and mountain bells.

Small towns, including Tambellup with its colonial buildings, and thriving towns such as **Katanning**, **Kojonup**, **Cranbrook**, Gnowangerup and Jerramungup are all surrounded by peaceful rural farmland.

See also: National Parks p. 336 and individual entries in A–Z town listing for details on parks and towns in bold type. **Map references:** 381, for Margaret River; 382–3, for Albany region.

National Parks

The national parks of Western Australia are tourist attractions in themselves: their colourful gorges, towering forests and spectacular displays of wildflowers create a paradise for photographers and a wonderland for bushwalkers and campers. Visitor fees apply to some of the State's national parks; contact the Department of Conservation and Land Management for details on passes.

AROUND PERTH

There are many national parks around Perth that are well worth a visit. At **Nambung National Park**, 230 kilometres north of Perth on the coast, unusual rock formations are to be found. Here a moonscape of coloured quartz is studded with fantastic limestone pillars ranging in size from stony 'twigs' to 4-metre-high columns. This is the unique Pinnacle Desert, a favourite subject for photographers. **Yanchep National Park**, about 50 kilometres north of Perth on a belt of coastal limestone, has forests of massive tuart trees. Islands on Loch McNess, within the park, are waterfowl sanctuaries. Yanchep is also famed for its underground limestone caves and spring wildflowers.

Some 80 kilometres north-east of Perth is **Avon Valley National Park**; its most popular attractions are upland forests and river valleys, as well as beautiful wildflowers in season. The highest point in the park is Bald Hill, which provides panoramic views of the Avon River. After winter rains, a tributary of the Avon, Emu Spring Brook, spills 30 metres down in a spectacular waterfall.

A cluster of national parks to the east of Perth includes **John Forrest National Park**, which was Western Australia's first proclaimed national park. With the Darling Escarpment within its boundaries, the park features granite outcrops, dams and waterfalls, creeks and rock pools. Other nearby national parks are **Kalamunda**, **Greenmount**, **Gooseberry Hill** and **Lesmurdie Falls**, all within 20 to 25 kilometres of Perth. The Bibbulmun Track, a walking trail that links the forests, east of Perth, to the area once occupied by the Bibbulmun people of the south-west, begins its 950-kilometre route in Kalamunda National Park.

Proclaimed as the State's first flora and fauna reserve in 1894, **Serpentine National Park** is about 60 kilometres south of Perth and a firm favourite of day trippers who picnic at the falls area in the park. Jarrah and marri forests, and wildflowers in spring, are some of the park's attractions.

IN THE SOUTH OF THE STATE

Leeuwin–Naturaliste National Park extends along the rugged south-west coast. There are over 100 limestone caves in the area, some containing fossils of marsupials, no longer found on the mainland. The park is home to rare ospreys and rufous bristlebirds, as well as the more common sea birds. Whales can occasionally be seen offshore.

Along the lower south-west coast of the State is **Walpole–Nornalup National Park**, 15 861 hectares of wilderness in which creeks gurgle under tall eucalypts, rivers meander between forested hills and inlets rich in fish create a haven for anglers and boating enthusiasts. A network of roads and walking tracks, through forests of karri and tingle, attracts bushwalkers and birdwatchers. Here visitors can follow the Tree Top Walk through the Valley of the Giants.

About 100 kilometres east is **West Cape Howe National Park**, the spectacular coastline of which includes the gabbro cliffs of West Cape Howe and the granite of Torbay Heads, fronting the cold waters of the Southern Ocean. Extensive coastal heath, swamps, lakes and karri forest

The magnificent domes of Purnululu National Park

cover the inland area, and the park is popular with anglers, bushwalkers, rock-climbers and hang-gliders.

The South Western Highway bisects **Shannon National Park**, 358 kilometres south of Perth. Within the park is the former timber-milling town site of Shannon, now a camping area. The remainder of the park consists of towering karri and jarrah forests, surrounding the Shannon River. Visitors can take the Great Forest Trees Drive through the forest and tune into 100 FM at the signposted 'radio stops'; self-guide books are available from the Department of Conservation and Land Management.

Stirling Range National Park, 450 kilometres south-east of Perth, is one of Australia's outstanding reserves. Surrounded by a flat, sandy plain, the Stirling Range rises abruptly to over 1000 metres, its jagged peaks veiled in swirling mists. The cool, humid environment created by these low clouds contributes to the survival of 1000 flowering plant species, some of which, like the mountain bells, are found nowhere else in the world.

Brilliant displays of wildflowers are also a feature of the nearby **Porongurup National Park**, where the granite domes of the Porongurup Ranges are clothed in a forest of karri trees.

Spectacular coastal scenery is the main attraction of the **Torndirrup National Park** on the Flinders Peninsula, 460 kilometres south of Perth. Also on the south coast are other outstanding parks, including **Cape Le Grand National Park**, with its magnificent bays and beaches, protected by granite headlands, located 40 kilometres east of Esperance.

Two other parks are near Esperance, both to the west of the town. **Stokes National Park** hugs the coastline around Stokes Inlet and features long sandy beaches and rocky headlands backed by sand dunes and low hills. Stokes Inlet and its associated lakes support a rich variety of wildlife. Inland from Stokes lies **Peak Charles National Park**. A walk to the ridge of this ancient granite peak allows sweeping views of its companion, Peak Eleanora, and the dry sandplain heaths and salt-lake systems of the surrounding country.

One of the loveliest sections of the south coast of Western Australia is **Fitzgerald River National Park**, a World Biosphere Reserve, through which the rugged Barren Range stretches from west to east. The park's 330 000 hectares comprise gently undulating sandplains, river valleys, precipitous cliff edges, narrow gorges, and beaches for swimming and rock-fishing. The park contains many rare species of flora and fauna.

IN THE NORTH OF THE STATE

North of Geraldton the visitor will discover the wild beauty of ancient landscapes, unsurpassed at **Kalbarri National Park**. Here, the lower reaches of the Murchison River wind through spectacular gorges to the Indian Ocean. Sea cliffs in layers of multi-coloured sandstone loom over the crashing white foam at Red Bluff.

Cape Range National Park, near Exmouth, is cut by deep gorges but remains arid for most of the year. Vegetation is sparse, except around the creek and after cyclonic storms have flooded the area. Yardie Creek, the only permanent water in the area, is a landlocked river that occasionally breaks through the sandbar and meets the sea. River tours operate regularly from March to December.

In the Pilbara, 1400 kilometres north of Perth, is **Karijini National Park**. It is in the Hamersley Range and part of a massive block of weathered rock over 450 kilometres long. Within this huge, spectacular park are many well-known gorges, including Dales Gorge, its strata in horizontal stripes of blue, mauve, red and brown dating back almost 2000 million years. A trail in the park winds up to Mt Bruce, the State's second highest point. Interpretive displays along the trail provide an insight into the Aboriginal heritage, as well as the flora and fauna, of the area. Further north, still in the Pilbara, **Millstream–Chichester National Park** encompasses almost 200 000 hectares of clay tablelands and sediment-capped basalt ranges. At Millstream, on the Fortescue River, natural freshwater springs have created an oasis featuring waterlilies, Millstream palms and paperbarks. In contrast, there are the Chichester Ranges: rolling hills, hummocks of spinifex, white-barked snappy gums on the uplands, and pale coolibahs along the usually dry watercourses.

In the far north of Western Australia are the national parks of the Kimberley region. The largest of these parks, **Geikie Gorge**, is 20 kilometres north-east of Fitzroy Crossing and has an area of 3136 hectares. The multi-coloured cliffs are reflected in the placid waters of the Fitzroy River, which flows through the gorge. The area is too rugged for extensive walking, but organised boat trips go up the river through the gorge, enabling visitors to see one of Australia's most beautiful waterways.

Other national parks nearby are **Windjana Gorge** and **Tunnel Creek**, both north-west of Geikie Gorge. Tunnel Creek

River tour, Cape Range National Park

is a permanent watercourse that flows underground for 750 metres. It is possible to walk through the high, wide tunnel to a small river beach beyond; some deep wading may be necessary, and carry a torch.

South of Lake Argyle is the spectacular **Purnululu National Park**, with its tiger-striped, beehive-shaped domes, deep gullies and unique palms. Access is by 4WD vehicle only. Because of the fragility of internal roads in wet conditions, this park is closed from October to May.

Mirima National Park, only 2.5 kilometres east of Kununurra, has features typical of the Kimberley: banded sandstone outcrops similar to those of the Bungle Bungle massif, boab trees, red soil dotted with eucalypts, and black kites circling overhead. Aboriginal rock paintings are also a feature of the park.

For further information on Western Australia's national parks, contact the Department of Conservation and Land Management, 50 Hayman Rd, Como (Locked Bag 104, Bentley Delivery Centre, WA 6983); (08) 9334 0333. Web site www.calm.wa.gov.au

At Karridale, 14 km NW, Alan Fox Glass Studio. Alexandra Bridge, 10 km N, a charming picnic spot with towering jarrah trees and beautiful wildflowers in spring. Boranup Maze, 18 km N. Boranup Lookout, 19 km N: fine views of Leeuwin–Naturaliste National Park; pleasant picnic spot. Winery at Hamelin Bay, 18 km NE. The Landing Place, 3 km S, where first European settlers landed in area. Whale Rescue Memorial, 4 km S, commemorating the rescue of a large pod of pilot whales beached here in 1986. Matthew Flinders Memorial, 5 km S. Cape Leeuwin, 8 km SW, most south-westerly point of Australia and where Indian and Southern oceans meet; at cape, limestone lighthouse (1895) and old water wheel. **Visitor information:** Blackwood Ave; (08) 9758 0166. Web site www. margaretriverwa.com **See also:** Cape to Cape p. 331.

Australind   Pop. 5694

MAP REF. 379 G4, 386 C8, 388 C10

This popular holiday town is 11 km NE of Bunbury on the Leschenault Estuary. Fishing, crabbing, swimming and boating on the estuary and the Collie River are the main attractions. **In town:** In Paris Rd: Henton Cottage (1841), now real estate agency; restored Church of St Nicholas (1842), thought to be smallest church in WA. Featured Wood Gallery, Piggot Dr. (off Paris Rd), traditional wood furniture and craft (open Thurs.–Mon.). Pioneer Memorial, on Old Coast Rd. Scenic 2-km drive along Cathedral Ave, a shaded avenue of paperbark trees. Mar.: Ocean Festival. Nov.: Wine Festival (even-numbered years). **In the area:** Leschenault Inlet Fishing Groyne, built along old pipeline, 1 km S; excellent fishing spot. Australind–Bunbury Tourist Drive: coastal scenery, good crabbing and picnic spots; brochure available. Cemetery, 2 km N, has pioneer graves and beautiful wildflowers in season. Pleasant beach towns to the north: Binningup (26 km) and Myalup (30 km). **Visitor information:** Harvey Tourist and Interpretative Centre, South Western Hwy, Harvey; (08) 9729 1122.

Balladonia   Pop. 10

MAP REF. 389 L8

Balladonia is on the Eyre Hwy, 191 km E of Norseman. At this point, the road crosses undulating dryland forest through the Fraser Range. Visitors can see claypans typical of the region and stone fences built

in the 1800s. **In town:** At Roadhouse, Cultural Heritage Museum, includes display on crashlanding of Skylab debris near town 1979. **In the area:** Arid desert woodland, one of the world's oldest landscapes, seashells millions of years old. Wildflowers in spring. Balladonia Station homestead (1886), 22 km E behind old telegraph station, has a gallery of paintings depicting local history (open by appt). Newmans Rocks, 50 km W on Eyre Hwy, rocky outcrops and granite sheets. **Visitor information:** Roadhouse; (08) 9039 3453. **See also:** Crossing the Nullarbor p. 348.

Beverley   Pop. 787

MAP REF. 386 F4, 388 D8

On the Avon River, 130 km E of Perth, is the town of Beverley. **In town:** Picnic spots beside Avon River. In Vincent St: Aeronautical Museum, shows development of WA aviation and includes biplane built 1929 by local aircraft designer Selby Ford; Courthouse (1897) designed by architect George Temple Poole (check opening times, Shire Council). In Hunt Rd: Dead Finish (1872), one of oldest buildings in town and town centre hotel until the coming of the railway in 1886 (open Sun. or by appt); Barry Ferguson's Garage, has display of old hand-operated machinery. St Mary's Anglican Church (1890), John St, fine stained-glass windows. Aug.: Agricultural Show. Sept.: Duck Race (with plastic ducks). **In the area:** The Avon Ascent, self-guide drive tour of the Avon Valley; leaflet available. Magnificent view from Seaton Ross Hill, Top Beverley Rd, on northern outskirts of town. Restored St Paul's Church (consecrated 1862), opposite original town site, 5 km NW. Beverley Gliding Club, 2 km W, dual-seat glider flights over town and valley (Fri.–Sun., bookings essential). Avondale Discovery Farm, 6 km NW, has range of historic farm implements, an agricultural museum and Clydesdale horses; Harvest Festival each Nov. Restored church, St John's in the Wilderness (consecrated 1895), 27 km SW. County Peak lookout, 35 km SE, offers bushwalking, picnic area and spectacular views from summit. **Visitor information:** Aeronautical Museum, Vincent St; (08) 9646 1555.

Boyup Brook   Pop. 553

MAP REF. 382 E2, 386 E9, 388 D11

A small town near the junction of Boyup Creek and the Blackwood River, Boyup

Brook is a centre for the district's sheep, dairy-farming and timber industries. Blackboys, huge granite boulders, shaded pools, charming cottages and farms are scenic features. **In town:** Pioneers Museum, Jayes Rd (check opening times). Sandy Chambers Art Studio, Gibbs St, for artworks; aviaries and camels outside. Stagline Woollen Clothing, Henderson St. Old Flax Mill, on Blackwood River off Barron St, now caravan park. Haddleton Flora Reserve, Arthur River Rd. Carnaby Collection of beetles and butterflies at information centre. Bicentennial Walk Trail, historical walk; leaflet available. Feb.: Country Music Awards. May: Autumn Art Affair. Sept.: Country Music Weekend. Oct.: Blackwood River Marathon Relay (running, canoeing, horseriding, cycling, swimming to Bridgetown); Spring Garden Expo. **In the area:** Visits to farms (wheat, sheep, pig, Angora goat, deer); Boyup Brook Flora Drives, leaflet available. Glacial rock formations at Glacier Hill, 18 km S. Blackwood Crest winery at Kulikup, 40 km E. Gregory Tree blazed by explorer Captain Gregory in 1845, 15 km NE. School and teacher's house (1900) at Dinninup, 21 km NE. At Wilga, 22 km NW, vintage engines and old timber mill. Stormboy Jumpers, 20 km W on Jayes Rd, for locally produced woollen goods (open by appt). Scotts Brook Winery at Mayanup, 14 km SE, tasting and sales (open by appt). Norlup Homestead, 27 km SE, off Norlup Rd (open by appt). **Visitor information:** cnr Bridge and Able sts; (08) 9765 1444. Web site www.avon.net. au/tourism/beverley/index.htm **See also:** The South-West p. 335.

Bremer Bay   Pop. 221

MAP REF. 388 G11

Bremer Bay, a popular holiday destination 181 km NE of Albany, was named in honour of the captain of HMS *Tamar*, Sir Gordon Bremer. The town was built around the Old Telegraph Station at the mouth of Wellstead Estuary (named after John Wellstead, an 1850s settler). **In town:** Fishing, boating, surfing, scuba diving, water-skiing and bay cruises. Rammed-earth buildings, including hotel/motel, Franton Way; church in John St, overlooking estuary. Wellstead Homestead, Wellstead Rd, has historic vehicles and heirlooms, Ann Crawford Gallery (tours by appt). **In the area:** At Fitzgerald River National Park, 17 km N: abundant wildflowers (June–Nov.); Quaalup Homestead, built by John Wellstead (1858), restored as museum, also offers meals, self-guide park walks; at Point Ann, 45 km NE, whale-watching (July–Nov.). At Fishery Beach, 6 km W, good boat-launching facilities. At Peppermint Grove, 3 km S: first residence in area, built by John Wellstead (1850), now houses Peppermint Grove Museum with historic farm equipment and vintage cars and motorbikes. **Visitor information:** Roadhouse, Gnombup Tce; (08) 9837 4093. Web site www.sage.alphawest.net.au/~bremertc/index.html **See also:** The South-West p. 335.

Bridgetown Pop. 2123

MAP REF. 382 C3, 386 D10, 388 D11
Bridgetown is in undulating country in the south-west corner of WA. Here the Blackwood River, well stocked with trout, curves through some of the prettiest country in the State. The first European settlers arrived in 1857 and soon the first apple trees were planted. **In town:** In Hampton St: Bridgetown Pottery; Brierley Jigsaw Gallery (at information centre); Gentle Era craft shop; St Paul's Church (1911), with paintings by local artists; Memorial Park, a peaceful picnic area. Bridgedale (1862), on South Western Hwy near bridge and overlooking river, constructed of local clay and timber by first European settler John Blechynden; restored by National Trust. Also on South Western Hwy, Blackwood River Park for picnics and river walks. Markets, fortnightly on Sun., at Blackwood River Park. Sept.: Blackwood Classic (powerboat event).

Oct.: Blackwood River Marathon Relay (running, canoeing, swimming, horse-riding and cycling the 58.3-km course between Boyup Brook and Bridgetown). Nov.: Blues at Bridgetown; Festival of Country Gardens. **In the area:** Wild-flowers and apple blossom in spring. Geegelup Heritage Trail (52 km) retraces history of agriculture, mining and timber. Scenic drives through rolling green hills, orchards and valleys into noted karri and jarrah timber country. Fine views: Sutton's Lookout, off Phillips St; Hester Hill, 5 km N. Greenbushes Historical Park, at Greenbushes, 18 km N: displays of tin-mining industry; Gwalia Mine Site Lookout. Bushwalking and picnicking at Bridgetown Jarrah Park, 15 km W and at Karri Gully, a further 5 km W. **Visitor information:** Hampton St; (08) 9761 1740. **See also:** The South-West p. 335.

Brookton Pop. 526

MAP REF. 386 F5, 388 D8
An attractive town 137 km SE of Perth near the Avon River, in fertile farming country, Brookton was founded in 1884 when the Great Southern Railway line opened. **In town:** In Robinson Rd: Old Railway Station, houses information centre and art and craft shop; Old Police Station Museum (inquire at information centre); St Mark's Anglican Church (1895). Lions Picnic Park, off Corrigin Rd, on bank of Avon River, at eastern entrance to town. Mar.: Old Time Motor Show (even-numbered years). Easter:

King of the Hill (off-road car racing). **In the area:** Brookton Pioneer Heritage Trail, includes places significant to Nyongah Aboriginal people; brochure available. Nine Acre Rock, 12 km E on Brookton– Kweda Rd, one of the largest natural granite outcrops in the area; nearby remnants of pioneer Jack Hansen's home. Christmas Tree Well Picnic Area, 60 km E. Yenyening Lakes Nature Reserve, 35 km NE: salt lake popular for picnics and for water-skiing and sailing (if adequate water); profusion of wildflowers in spring. Boyagin Rock, 18 km SW, picnic area with scenic views and rare flora and fauna. **Visitor information:** Old Railway Station, Robinson Rd; (08) 9642 1316.

Broome Pop. 11 368

MAP REF. 392 G9
Situated on the coast at the southern tip of the Kimberley, Broome enjoys wide beaches, turquoise water and a warm, sunny climate. Closer to Bali than to Perth, and with a major airport, the town is lively and cosmopolitan. The discovery of pearling grounds off the coast in the 1880s led to the foundation of Broome township in 1883. By 1910 Broome was the world's leading pearling centre. The industry suffered when world markets collapsed in 1914 but stabilised in the 1970s as cultured-pearl farming developed. With increasing tourism, Broome is again rapidly expanding. **In town:** Self-guide heritage trail (2 km) introduces buildings and

Camel riding on Cable Beach, near Broome

Wildlife-Watching

Besides the wonderful variety of birds and marsupials, much of Western Australia's wildlife can be found in the State's clear coastal waters. There are some exciting encounters to be had: try a beachside meeting with Monkey Mia's dolphins, or a boat trip to see Ningaloo Reef's mysterious whale sharks. The adventurous can even don snorkel and mask to swim with tropical fish or manta rays.

IN PERTH

Swan Estuary Marine Park is a welcome sight for migratory birds each spring. Sections of Perth's picturesque waterway have been set aside, including Alfred Cove, Pelican Point and Milyu. Between August and November the birds touch down on the warm mudflats of the estuary, and they stay until late March. Some of the smallest visitors are red-necked stints; they arrive from their breeding grounds in Arctic Siberia, weighing only 30–40 grams.

Perth also has some rather unusual wildlife-watching locations. Only 4 kilometres north of Perth city centre visitors to Lake Monger can stand among a variety of birdlife including dozens of black swans, attracted by a constructed breeding island at the western end of the lake. Golfers at **Joondalup public golf course** in the city's northern outskirts look out for western grey kangaroos when teeing off. Kangaroos are quite common on local golf courses.

AROUND PERTH

Rottnest Island, a short ferry ride from the port of Fremantle, is a 'must-see' for wildlife-watchers. The island was named after its marsupial quokkas were mistaken for rats by the early Dutch explorer Vlamingh. Dusk and dawn are the best times to glimpse these animals, though sharp-eyed tour-bus drivers can often find them through the day. Good quokka spotting locations are around the bakery at Thomson Bay and at Watsons Glade near the road to Jeannies Lookout (eastern arm).

The stunning turquoise waters surrounding the island will provide memorable experiences. At Pocillopora Reef off the south of the island is an underwater snorkelling trail which should not be missed. The reef, named after its beautiful pink coral, is alive with marine-life. Snorkellers can fin through coral landscapes, following illustrated underwater plaques that explain the reef's plants and animals. Each stopping point has handles for snorkellers to hold while they read – fortunately there is one breath's worth of information per plaque.

Off the coast of Rockingham to the south, visitors to **Penguin Island** can see a breeding colony of about a thousand little (fairy) penguins and may catch sight of dolphins in the surrounding waters of Shoalwater Marine Park, where marine life is abundant.

Perth-based wildlife-watchers have several good mainland parks and reserves within a short drive. **Avon Valley National Park** has a healthy population of echidnas; their long trench-like diggings can be seen throughout the park. Late afternoon is a good time to see the park's western grey kangaroos as they move into the open after having spent

Dolphin at Monkey Mia, near Denham

their day in thick bushland. Euros are also present, although these sure-footed kangaroos prefer the steeper rocky country.

John Forrest National Park, just east of Perth, is good for bird-watching. Unusually named and brilliantly coloured 'twenty eight' parrots can be seen in the woodlands, along with less common red-capped parrots. Rufous and golden whistlers are noisy residents, and New Holland honeyeaters enjoy the spring wildflower season. Also, keep an eye out for racehorse goannas on the park's roads and tracks.

IN THE NORTH OF THE STATE

A classic wildlife experience is interacting with bottlenose dolphins at **Shark Bay**, north of Perth. They often swim into the shallows at Monkey Mia to make contact with humans and receive offerings of fish.

The best time to meet these marine mammals is between 8 a.m. and 1 p.m., when they are fed under the supervision of park rangers. The dolphins may feel more sociable on some days than others. Part of the attraction of Monkey Mia is that the dolphins set the day's agenda and visitors respond, rather than forcing the animals to perform on cue.

Shark Bay supports a variety of marine life besides dolphins; sea turtles, school sharks, manta rays and dugongs flourish in the area. At Eagle Bluff, 20 kilometres south of Denham, school sharks and turtles can sometimes be seen in the clear green waters below. Boat tours leave from Monkey Mia to view the dugongs or 'sea cows' which graze among the seagrass beds. Dugongs feature unusual flattened snouts designed to shovel through the sand in search of the choicest plants. A catamaran also leaves from Denham to spot a variety of marine life, including the giant yet harmless manta rays.

Further north again near Exmouth is Ningaloo Reef, Western Australia's largest coral reef and one of its most spectacular features. The diversity of marine life is incredible and is protected by **Ningaloo Marine Park**. March to late May are the best months to view the park's most famous visitors, the whale sharks. These are huge but docile fish with beautifully mottled backs and flattened heads. They swim with their mouths open to filter the tiny marine organisms on which they feed. While the complete life-cycle of the world's largest fish is a mystery, it is now believed that their arrival corresponds with the recently discovered phenomenon of mass coral-spawning at Ningaloo (March to April). The spawning results in an abundance of food for the sharks. Fortunately for whale shark-watchers, when the fish arrive they cruise slowly just under the surface and can be seen from boat cruises and air flights from Exmouth.

August to November is a good time for humpback whale-watching cruises at Ningaloo as the whales travel to their Antarctic feeding grounds and north-west shelf breeding area. Humpbacks are the show-ponies of the whale world. It is hard to believe how active these huge mammals are until you see 30 tonnes of whale launching itself from the water or splashing its mighty tail – humpbacks are anything but shy. Cruises leave regularly from Exmouth during the whale season.

Another reason to visit during these months is the arrival of large schools of manta rays at the reef. They are more elusive than humpbacks, though once a school is located, snorkellers on tour boats out of Exmouth can swim among these harmless plankton-feeders.

Extending to the shores of Ningaloo Marine Park is **Cape Range National Park**, and within this park is a rich tidal inlet called Mangrove Bay. The bay is home to some of the park's 125 bird species, particularly waders such as ibis and heron, which emerge onto the exposed flats at low tide. A bird hide provides a discreet viewpoint, and a stroll along the boardwalk gives a fascinating perspective on inlet life. There is also a fauna hide at Mangrove Bay, built alongside a waterhole that is a magnet for wildlife. Keep an eye out here for emus, euros and flocks of galahs. Also in the park is Yardie Creek Gorge, where regular cruises operate. Bring binoculars to spot ospreys and herons nesting on the cliff-faces, and the numerous black-footed rock wallabies.

ON THE SOUTH-WEST COAST

Southern right whales spend time off the southern coast around **Albany** each year from July to mid-October. Albany's association with whales has not always been a friendly one, with commercial whaling ceasing only in 1978. Whale numbers are now on the increase, and

Whaleworld near Albany provides a good introduction to the behaviour and life cycles of these magnificent marine mammals.

Whale-watching cruises depart daily from Albany's wharf in season. For land-based spotters there is the platform at Point Ann in Fitzgerald River National Park. If whales are about, Point Ann offers the best chance to see one. With luck you may see a mother whale with her calf.

For more information on wildlife-watching in national parks and reserves contact the Department of Conservation and Land Management, 50 Hayman Rd, Como (Locked Bag 104, Bentley Delivery Centre, WA 6983); (08) 9334 0333. Web site address www.calm.wa.gov.au **See also:** National Parks p. 336.

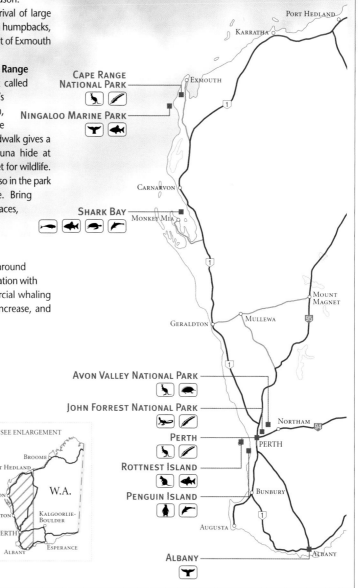

places of interest including: Chinatown, with Pearl Emporium, a reminder of Broome's early multicultural mix; Historical Society Museum, in Old Customs House, Saville St; Library, Haas St. In Hamersley St: Captain Gregory's House, now art gallery (access through Matso's Store); Bedford Park, relics of Broome's history; Courthouse (former Cable House). Crocodile Park, Cable Beach Rd. Shell House, Guy St, contains one of largest shell collections in Australia. Sun Pictures, Carnarvon St, opened 1916 and believed to be oldest operating outdoor cinema in the world. In Dampier Tce, restored original pearl luggers; former divers conduct maritime history tours daily. On Port Dr.: Chinese Cemetery; Japanese Cemetery (graves of early Japanese pearl divers). Pioneer Cemetery in Lions Pioneer Park. Floatplane scenic flights over Buccaneer Archipelago. Market, each Sat. at Courthouse. Apr.: Rotary Dragon Boat Classic. May–June: Fringe Arts Festival. May–July: Broome Race Round (4 horseracing days). Aug.: Opera Under the Stars; Sailfish Tournament. Aug.–Sept.: Shinju Matsuri (Festival of the Pearl, recalls Broome's heyday). Sept.: Fly Billfish Tournament. Nov.: Mango Festival. **In the area:** Beaches ideal for swimming and shell-collecting; good fishing all year. Staircase to the Moon: natural phenomenon, visible at most full moons during dry season (Apr.–Oct.); caused by moonlight reflecting off mudflats at extreme low tides over Roebuck Bay (dates and times from information centre); markets often held on town beach, Robinson St, to coincide with the phenomenon. Hovercraft *Spirit of Broome* visits local beaches. Safaris, cruises, scenic flights, short tours. Charter boats: 6- to 10-day Kimberley expeditions to coral reefs, Rowley Shoals, Prince Regent River and waterfalls at Kings Cascades. Day tours to: former Lombadina Mission, 200 km NE; Cape Leveque, 220 km NE. Cable Beach, 3 km NW, is 22 km long, named after underwater cable linking Broome to Java. At Gantheaume Point, 5 km SW, giant dinosaur tracks believed to be 130 million years old; can be seen 30 m from base of cliff at very low tide. At Roebuck Bay, 18 km E: Buccaneer Rock, at entrance to Dampier Creek, landmark to Capt. William Dampier and HMAS *Roebuck*; Broome Bird Observatory. Willie Creek Pearl Farm, 35 km N, tours available. **Visitor information:** cnr Bagot Rd and Broome Hwy; (08) 9192 2222. Web site www.ebroome.com/tourism **See also:** The Kimberley p. 356.

Bunbury   Pop. 24 945

MAP REF. 379 F4, 386 C8, 388 C10

Bunbury, known as 'Harbour City', serves as the major port, commercial and regional centre for the south-west. Situated 185 km S of Perth on the Leschenault Estuary, at the junction of the Preston and Collie rivers, it is a popular tourist area, with a warm temperate climate, beautiful beaches and the Darling Range in the distance. Originally called Port Leschenault, Bunbury was settled by Europeans in 1838, and the whalers who anchored in Koombana Bay provided a market for pioneer farmers. Today the port is the main outlet for the thriving timber industry, mineral sands and produce of the fertile hinterland. **In town:** 12-km heritage trail from old railway station, Wellington St. King Cottage (1880), Forrest Ave, a historical museum with displays of domestic life at turn of century (check opening times). Tree-lined pathways lead to Boulter's Heights Lookout, Haig Cres., for views of city and surrounds. Basaltic rock, on foreshore, at end of Clifton St (off Ocean Dr.); formed by volcanic lava flow 150 million years ago. Lighthouse, at end of Ocean Dr., painted in black and white check, has lookout at base. Marlston Hill Lookout, Apex Dr., original lighthouse site and whale-spotting point for early whaling fleet. Lighthouse Beach pathway follows coastline from the lighthouse to original harbour breakwater. In Victoria St: cafe strip with art and craft shops. Galleries in Wittenoom and Victoria sts. Harbour City Markets, cnr Victoria and Carey sts, open daily. Rose Hotel (1865), cnr Stephens and Victoria sts, grand heritage building with period furnishings. Paisley Centre (1887), Arthur St, originally the Bunbury Boys School, attended by three early WA premiers (not open to public). Centenary Gardens, cnr Wittenoom and Prinsep sts in city centre, a peaceful picnic spot. Estuary foreshore has picnic/barbecue facilities, playground and boat ramp. Miniature railway, Forrest Park, Blair St (3rd Sun. each month). Excellent beaches; surf club at Ocean Beach. Drive along breakwater to Koombana Bay, modern harbour facilities, popular for water-skiing and boating; in Koombana Dr., Dolphin Discovery Centre, offers chance to wade or swim with dolphins under ranger guidance; opposite, beginning of mangrove cave and shipwreck trail (with interpretive signage) through the southernmost mangrove colony in WA. Good deep-sea fishing and fishing for bream, flounder, tailor and whiting in bay. Succulent blue manna crabs in season in estuary. Variety of birdlife in bush near waters of inlet. Big Swamp Wildlife Park, Prince Phillip Dr., displays over 100 species of native birds, mammals and reptiles. Historic jetty in outer harbour, busy international trading hub from the 1860s–1960s, currently under restoration. Tours of city sights; night bush tours; dolphin cruises. Mar.: Show. **In the area:** South West Museum, 12 km S. Killerby Wines, 17 km S. At Capel, 27 km S, Capel Vale Wines. Restored St Mark's (1842), 5 km SE at Picton, second oldest church in WA, retains some original timber structure. Wansborough Wines, 27 km SE, open weekends; nearby, Joshua Creek Fruit Wines, tastings Sat., Sun., public holidays. King Tree Winery, 35 km SE, open p.m. Bunbury–Australind Tourist Drive along Old Coast Rd; coastal scenery, good crabbing and picnic spots; brochure available. **Visitor information:** Old Railway Station, Carmody Pl.; (08) 9721 7922, freecall 1300 656 202. Web site www.bunburytourism.org.au **See also:** The South-West p. 335.

Busselton   Pop. 10 642

MAP REF. 379 D7, 381 F3, 386 B9, 388 C10

First settled by Europeans in the 1830s, and one of the oldest towns in WA, Busselton is a seaside holiday destination at the centre of a large rural district. It is situated 228 km S of Perth, on the shores of Geographe Bay and the picturesque Vasse River. Inland are jarrah forests, logged by the local timber industry, as well as dairy and beef cattle farms, and vineyards. Fishing is important, particularly crayfish and salmon in season. **In town:** Prospect Villa (1855), Pries Ave, now a B&B. Opposite, Ballarat Engine, first steam locomotive in WA. St Mary's (1844), Peel Tce, oldest stone church in State. Villa Carlotta (1897), Adelaide St, boarding-school for 50 years, now guest house. Jetty, on beachfront near Queen St, longest timber jetty (2 km) in the Southern Hemisphere; partially destroyed by Cyclone Alby in 1978, still popular with anglers; small train runs along jetty. Nearby on beachfront: Entertainment Park with giant

Coastline near Carnarvon

water slide; Nautical Lady Entertainment Centre with Jetty Point tower and nautical museum. Old Courthouse, Queen St, restored gaol cells, arts complex, tearooms. In Peel St: Old Butter Factory Museum, on riverbank, displays old butter- and cheese-making equipment; Vasse River Parkland, with barbecue/picnic facilities. In Layman Rd: Wonnerup House (1859), a National Trust Museum and fine example of colonial Australian architecture furnished in period style; restored old school and teacher's house, built of local timber. Archery Park and Minigolf, Bussell Hwy. Geographe Bay has good sheltered beaches for swimming, diving, fishing, boating and dolphin-watching. Western coast ideal for surfing. Jan.: Australia Day Yacht Regatta; Beach Festival; Busselton Festival. Mar.: Bluewater Classic (fishing). Apr.: Heritage Week (at Wonnerup House). Oct.: West Coast Golf Open. **In the area:** Numerous vineyards and wineries. Scenic drive west, excellent views of rugged coast. Wildflower, scenic, canoe and 4WD tours; diving and deep-sea fishing cruises; whale-watching cruises and flights (Oct.–Dec.). Augusta– Busselton Heritage Trail, pamphlets available. Bunyip Craft Centre, 7 km E at Ludlow. Whistle Stop, a miniature

railway on Vasse Hwy, 11 km SE. Tuart Forest National Park, 12 km NE, only natural tuart forest in the world; forest walks and picnic sites in magnificent setting. **Visitor information:** Cnr Peel Tce and Causeway Rd; (08) 9752 1288. **See also:** Cape to Cape p. 331; The South-West p. 335. Web site www.capeweb.com.au/escape

Caiguna
Pop. 10

MAP REF. 389 N8

Caiguna is the first stop for petrol and food after the long drive from Balladonia, 182 km W. This section of the Eyre Hwy is one of the longest straight stretches of sealed road in Australia. **In the area:** South of town, Nuytsland Nature Reserve, scenic area bounded by sheer cliffs fronting the Southern Ocean. **Visitor information:** John Eyre Motel; (08) 9039 3459. **See also:** Crossing the Nullarbor p. 348.

Carnamah
Pop. 338

MAP REF. 388 C5

Carnamah is a small, typically Australian country town, 290 km N of Perth. Wheat and sheep are the local industries. **In town:** Historical Society Museum, McPherson St, displays old farm

machinery. Mar.: Wimbledon of the Wheatbelt. Sept.: Agricultural Show. **In the area:** McPherson homestead (1880), 1 km E, grounds open to the public, house open by appt. Tathra National Park, 50 km SW, renowned for variety of wildflowers in spring. Lake Indoon, 61 km SW, for water-skiing. At Three Springs, 23 km NW, open-cut talc mine tours. Cockatoo Canyon, 36 km W of Three Springs, bush reserve popular with wildflower enthusiasts. **Visitor information:** Shire Offices, McPherson St; (08) 9951 1055.

Carnarvon
Pop. 6357

MAP REF. 387 B8

Carnarvon, at the mouth of the Gascoyne River, 904 km N of Perth, is the commercial centre of the Gascoyne region. The district was seen in 1616 by Dutch navigator Dirk Hartog. Another explorer, Willem de Vlamingh, landed at Shark Bay in 1697. By the 1880s a number of Europeans had settled in the region. Today, sheep, beef cattle and fishing are important industries and the Gascoyne River has been tapped for irrigation for the extensive tropical fruit and vegetable plantations. The USA National Aeronautics and Space Administration (NASA) operated nearby at Browns Range 1964–74. Carnarvon has warm winters and takes on a tropical appearance when the bougainvilleas and hibiscus flower. **In town:** The main street (c. 1880s) was 40 m wide, built to enable camel trains to turn; it is now divided by trees and gardens. Jubilee Hall (1887), Francis St. Pioneer Park, Olivia Tce. Tropical Bird Park, Angelo St. Rotary Park, North West Coastal Hwy. Heritage walk trail, 20 historic landmarks around town; map available. Courtyard markets at civic centre, Robinson St, 1st Sat. each month. May: Fremantle–Carnarvon Yacht Race (even-numbered years). Aug.: Carnarvon Festival; Arts Festival. **In the area:** Excellent fishing for snapper or groper, game-fishing for marlin or sailfish; charter boat available. On Babbage Island, connected to township by causeway: Carnarvon Maritime Heritage Precinct incorporating museum at old lighthouse keeper's cottage; travel by steam train from One Mile Jetty to town bridge and return; prawning factory at old whaling station, tours in season, usually mid-Apr.–late-Oct.; Pelican Point, near southernmost tip of the island, for picnics, swimming and fishing. Westoby Banana Plantation, 5 km E, tours available (closed Tues.). Mammoth 29-m diameter reflector ('The Big Dish'), 8 km E, part of old NASA station, views of town and plantations from base. Rocky Pool, 55 km E along Gascoyne Rd, picnic area and deep billabong ideal for swimming. Munro's Banana Plantation, 10 km N via hwy and South River Rd, has fruit and vegetables for sale in season (tours Sun.–Fri.). Bibbawarra artesian bore, 16 km N, where hot water surfaces at 65°C; picnic area nearby. Bibbawarrah Trough adjacent to bore, 180 m long, believed to be the longest in the Southern Hemisphere. Miaboolya Beach, 22 km N, has good fishing, crabbing and swimming. Blowholes, 73 km N, 20 m high; about 1 km S, a superb sheltered beach with oysters on rocks, but beware of king waves and tides. Cairn commemorating loss of HMAS *Sydney* in 1941, 80 km N (via blowholes). A further 20 km N, Cape Cuvier, natural port with 60-m cliff where ships can be seen loading salt and gypsum. **Visitor information:** Robinson St; (08) 9941 1146.

Cocklebiddy   Pop. 9

MAP REF. 389 O8
This tiny settlement is on the Eyre Hwy, between Madura and Caiguna, 310 km

The Nullarbor cliffs, south of Cocklebiddy

from the SA border. **In the area:** Cocklebiddy Cave, just north-west, for adventure caving (directions at information centre). South of town, a dirt track leads to escarpment for magnificent views of Southern Ocean; from here 4WD necessary to reach both Eyre Bird Observatory and Post Office Historical Society Museum in old telegraph station building (tours available, 24-hr notice required, contact information centre). Whale-watching at Eyre Bird Observatory (Aug.–Oct.) **Visitor information:** Wedgetail Inn; (08) 9039 3462. **See also:** Crossing the Nullarbor p. 348.

Collie   Pop. 7194

MAP REF. 386 D8, 388 C10
Collie, the centre of the State's only coal-producing region, has been important in WA's development. In dense jarrah forest, 202 km S of Perth near the winding Collie River, the town has an abundance of parks and gardens. There are fine views on the Coalfields Hwy approach. **In town:** Central Precinct Historic Walk, brochure available. In

Throssell St: Collie Mosaic Footpath; tourist coal mine, guided tours daily; Coalfields Museum, in old Roads Board buildings, displays coal-industry and area history; Steam Locomotive Museum; old police station (1926); post office (1898); art gallery, at Shire Office, has local art. Courthouse (1913), cnr Wittenoon and Pendleton sts. Impressive Norman-style All Saints' Anglican Church (1915), Venn St. Soldiers Park, on banks of Collie River, Steer St, has shady trees and lawns, for picnics. Suspension bridge, River Ave. Minninup Pool, off Mungalup Rd, in bushland; wildflowers in season. Market at Westrail Reserve, Forrest St, 1st Sun. each month (except winter). **In the area:** Tours of Bunnings Timber Mill, 2 km E. Collie River Scenic Drive, offers views of jarrah forest and wildflowers in season, brochures available. Wellington Dam and Honeymoon Pool, 18 km W, in heart of Collie River Irrigation Scheme, offers fishing and bushwalking, and grassy picnic spots on shore. Beautiful picnic area surrounds Harris Dam, 14 km N. Muja Power Station, 24 km SE; tours available.

(*Muja* is the Aboriginal word for the bright yellow Christmas tree that grows in area.) Glen Mervyn Dam, 18 km S, offers canoeing, marroning and water-skiing. **Visitor information:** Throssell St; (08) 9734 2051. Web site www.collierivervalley.org.au

Coolgardie   Pop. 1258

MAP REF. 388 I6

The old goldmining town of Coolgardie is 550 km E of Perth and 39 km SW of Kalgoorlie–Boulder. After alluvial gold was found at Fly Flat in 1892, Coolgardie grew in 10 years to a boom town of 15 000 people, 23 hotels, 6 banks and 2 stock exchanges. The main street was wide enough for camel trains to turn, splendid buildings were erected and ambitious plans made. Sadly, the gold soon petered out. By 1985 there were only 700 people; however, with tourism the population is increasing. **In town:** Series of historic markers documenting historic points of interest; index to markers is in Bayley St, next to information centre. Historic buildings in Bayley St: Old Courthouse (1898), now houses bottle collection and most comprehensive prospecting museum in WA; post office (1898); old gaol; Denver City Hotel (1898), with handsome verandahs; Ben Prior's Open-air Museum, displays include wagons, horse- and camel-drawn vehicles. Railway Station (1896), Woodward St, now a museum with a transport exhibition and display of famous Varischetti mine rescue. Warden Finnerty's house (1895), McKenzie St, striking example of early Australian architecture and furnishings. Adjacent, C. Y. O'Connor Dedication, a fountain and water course in memory of O'Connor, who masterminded the Coolgardie Water Scheme. St Anthony's Convent, Lindsay St, now boarding-school. Gaol Tree, Hunt St, used for restraining prisoners in early gold-rush days. Lions Bicentennial Lookout, near southern end of Hunt St. Lindsay's Pit Lookout, over open-cut goldmine, Ford St. Sept.: Coolgardie Day; Art Exhibition. **In the area:** Cemetery, 1 km W, evokes harsh early days of gold rush. Coolgardie Camel Farm, 4 km W. Kurrawang Emu Farm, 20 km E. Burra Rock, 55 km S, originally called Woodline Dam (built 1890s to supply water for mining-industry locomotives), popular picnic area. **Visitor information:** Bayley St; (08) 9026 6090. **See also:** The Goldfields p. 352.

Coral Bay   Pop. 936

MAP REF. 387 B5

The Ningaloo Reef system approaches the shore at Coral Bay, 150 km S of Exmouth. Unspoilt white beaches offer good swimming, snorkelling, boating and fishing. **In the area:** Ningaloo Marine Park, just off beach; reef comprises 220 species of coral and supports 500 varieties of fish. Good views of reef from coral-viewing vessels. Diving equipment for hire. Coastal 4WD track to secluded beaches, for the adventurous; map available. Marine wildlife-watching tours: whale sharks (Mar.–June), humpback whales (June–Nov.) and manta rays (all year). Numerous shipwreck sites at Pt Cloates, 8 km N. **Visitor information:** Coral Bay Arcade, Robinson St; (08) 9942 5988. Web site www.gta.asn.au

Corrigin   Pop. 703

MAP REF. 386 H5, 388 E8

Rich farming country surrounds Corrigin, 230 km SE of Perth. **In town:** In Kunjin St: pioneer museum; miniature railway. RSL monument, Gayfer St, is a Turkish mountain gun from Gallipoli. Art and craft shop, Walton St. Sept.: Agricultural Show. **In the area:** Lookout, 3 km W, on signposted Wildflower Scenic Drive. Dog cemetery, 5 km W. Kunjin Farm, 18 km W, for emus and alpacas. Yealering Lake, 40 km SW and Gorge Rock, 20 km SE, for picnics. **Visitor information:** Shire Offices, Lynch St; (08) 9063 2203.

Cranbrook   Pop. 283

MAP REF. 383 L6, 386 H11, 388 E11

In the 1800s sandalwood for incense was exported from Cranbrook to China. Today this attractive town, near the Stirling Range foothills, 320 km SE of Perth, is a sheep- and cereal-growing centre. **In town:** Station House Museum (1889), Gathorne St, restored and furnished 1930s-style. Wildflower Walk, 300 m, to Stirling Gateway on Salt River Rd, orchids in spring. Sept.: Wildflower Display. Nov.: Art Show. **In the area:** Wildflower Drive and Frankland Heritage Trail, brochures available. Sukey Hill Lookout, 5 km E off Salt River Rd, expansive views of farmland, salt lakes and Stirling Range. Stirling Range National Park, 10 km SE, almost 1000 species of flowering plants, 100 unique to the area; best time for wildflowers is Aug.–Nov. Quality

table wines produced in Frankland River region, 50 km W; Alkoomi, Frankland Estate and Marribrook wineries open to public. Also in region, largest plantings of olive trees in the State. Big Poorarecup Lagoon (known locally as Lake Poorarecup), 40 km SW, for swimming and water-skiing; picnic facilities and camping on foreshore. **Visitor information:** Shire Offices, Gathorne St; (08) 9826 1008. **See also:** Western Wildflowers p. 364.

Cue   Pop. 241

MAP REF. 387 H13, 388 E1, 390 B13

Cue, 650 km NE of Perth on the Great Northern Hwy, was a boom town and centre for the Murchison goldfields, as its well-kept stone buildings testify. **In town:** National Trust-classified buildings in Austin St: bandstand built over well, water from which was said to have started a typhoid epidemic; impressive government offices. Former Masonic Lodge (1899), Dowley St, built largely of corrugated iron. **In the area:** Gem-fossicking; heritage trail, including old hospital ruins. Day Dawn, 5 km W, original town site on gold reef; town disappeared when reef died out in 1930s, mine manager's house is last remaining building; the new open-cut mine can be seen from here. Big Bell, 30 km W, large mine opened in 1989 (access restricted). Walga Rock, 50 km W, a monolith 1.5 km long and 5 km around base (second largest in Australia) with largest gallery of Aboriginal rock paintings in WA. Spectacular variety of wildflowers. **Visitor information:** Apr.–Oct. only: Robinson St, (08) 9963 1216.

Denham   Pop. 1140

MAP REF. 387 B10

Two peninsulas form the geographical feature of Shark Bay, 833 km from Perth. Denham is the most westerly town in Australia and the centre for the Shark Bay region. Dirk Hartog, the Dutch navigator, landed on an island at the bay's entrance in 1616. Town named after Capt. H. M. Denham, Royal Navy hydrographer who surveyed region in 1858. Pearling developed as the main industry and the population was a mixture of Malays, Chinese and Europeans. Until recently, Shark Bay was known only for its fishing, but today it is renowned for the wild dolphins which come inshore nearby at Monkey Mia. **In town:** Shark Bay

Fisheries, Dampier Rd (check opening times). Stone on which Capt. Denham carved his name is in Pioneer Park, Hughes St; originally on Eagle Bluff, but relocated after falling into sea. Aug.: Fishing Fiesta. **In the area:** Monkey Mia, 26 km NE, where wild dolphins come inshore to be fed; local centre and rangers provide information on these wonderful animals. Aquaria, aquatic wildlife park, 25 km NE on Monkey Mia Rd. Shark Bay Heritage Trail; coastal scenery. Catamarans MV *Hartog Explorer* and *Sea Eagle* offer cruises. Safaris and coach tours. Boat trips (weekends), also charter flights, to historic Dirk Hartog Island (homestead and backpackers' accommodation available on island). Francois Peron National Park, 7 km N, includes Peron homestead with its famous 'hot tub' of hot artesian water. Eagle Bluff, 20 km S, habitat of sea eagle. Nanga Bay Resort, 50 km S, huge sheep station with motel units, restaurant, tourist facilities, sailboard and dinghy hire on beach. Shell Beach, 50 km S, 110-km stretch of unique Australian coastline comprising countless tiny shells. Striking scenery at Zuytdorp Cliffs, 160 km S and extending further south to Kalbarri (4WD access only). On shores of Hamelin Pool, 100 km SE: historic displays in Flint Cliff Telegraph Station and Post Office Museum (1894); remarkable stromatolites, sedimentary rocks formed of fossilised blue-green algae in nature reserve. Spectacular coastal scenery at Steep Point, westernmost point on mainland (260 km W by road, 4WD only). **Visitor information:** 71 Knight Tce; (08) 9948 1253. Web site www.gta. asn.au/sharkbay

Denmark
Pop. 1978

MAP REF. 383 K12, 386 G13, 388 E12
This beautiful century-old former timber town, 54 km W of Albany, is at the foot of Mt Shadforth, overlooking the tranquil Denmark River and Wilson Inlet. The town offers excellent fishing, sandy white beaches and scenic drives through farming country and karri forests. **In town:** Kurrabup Aboriginal Art Gallery, McLeod Rd. In Mitchell St: Historical Museum; Cottage Industries Shop. Denmark Gallery, Strickland St. Art, craft and antiques at Old Butter Factory, North St. Pentland Alpaca Stud and Tourist Farm, Scotsdale Rd. Jassi Skincraft, Glenrowan Rd, off Mt Shadforth Scenic Drive. Mt Shadforth Lookout, top of Mohr Dr., for magnificent views. Berridge and Thornton

parks, both along riverbank in Holling Rd, offer shaded picnic areas. Michael Cartwright Art Gallery, McNabb Rd. Craft market with entertainment, on riverbank in Dec., Jan. and Easter (check dates at information centre). Jan.: Pantomime (in Berridge Park). Easter: Brave New Works (new performance art). **In the area:** Brochures available for Mt Shadforth and Scotsdale scenic drives, featuring wineries, galleries, lookouts and forest walks; Mokare and Wilson Inlet Heritage Trail (walk); tours of wineries, forest and wildflowers; cruises of Denmark River and Wilson Inlet; pony trekking. Wineries include: Howard Parks Wines, 2 km N; Matilda's Meadow Winery and Restaurant, 4 km N; Misty Creek Wines and Restaurant, 5 km W; Tinglewood Wines, 8 km W; Karriview Wines, 11 km W; Mariner's Rest Wines, 13 km W. Eden Gate Blueberry Farm, 25 km E, spray-free fruit and blueberry wines. Whale-watching (on cliff) at Lowlands Beach, 28 km E (July–Oct.), also fishing and swimming. Jonathan Hook Ceramics, Lantzke Rd, 5 km NW. The Edge Gallery and Coffee House, 14 km NW. Bridgart's Orchard, 9 km W, for fresh fruit and preserves. Kurrabup Aboriginal Art Gallery, 18 km W. Bartholomew's Meadery, 20 km W, features honey, honey wines, other bee products and live beehive display. Parry's Beach, 25 km W, for fishing (salmon in season). Spiral Studio Pottery, 32 km W. Majestic Merino Wool Craft Shop, 38 km W. Aqua Blue Marron Farm, 40 km W. Lookout at top of Monkey Rock, 10 km SW. Lights Beach, 13 km SW, with back beach, swimming and fishing. At William Bay National Park, 17 km SW: Greens Pool, natural sea pool, ideal for fishing, swimming and snorkelling; waterfall enters ocean at Madfish Bay, spectacular coastal views. West Cape Howe National Park, 30 km SW, for walking, fishing and swimming, includes WA's most southerly point (Torbay Head). Ocean Beach, 8 km S, for good surfing. **Visitor information:** Strickland St; (08) 9848 2055.

Derby
Pop. 3236

MAP REF. 384 B9, 393 J7
Derby is an administrative centre for several Aboriginal communities and a hinterland rich in pastoral and mineral wealth. Near King Sound, 223 km NE of Broome, the town is an ideal base for exploring the outback regions of the Kimberley. Roads have been greatly improved, including the Gibb River Rd,

spanning the 647 km from Derby to the junction of the Great Northern Hwy between Wyndham and Kununurra. However, as rain closes some roads in the area Nov.–Mar., check conditions before setting out on any excursion. **In town:** In Loch St: Botanic Gardens; Old Derby Gaol; Wharfinger House Museum, with photographic display. In Clarendon St: Kimberley School of the Air; Royal Flying Doctor Service. Ngunga Craft Shop, Stanley St. Derby Wharf, to see the extraordinary difference in level between high and low tides. Market, Clarendon St, every Sat. May–Sept. July: Boab Festival (rodeo, mardi gras, mud football). Dec.: Boxing Day Sports. **In the area:** Charter boats to various locations, including Buccaneer Archipelago and Walcott Inlet. Charter flights over Kimberley coast, King Leopold Ranges, Cockatoo and Koolan islands and horizontal, reversible waterfall. Crabbing tours (just out of town). Pigeon Heritage Trail, from Derby to Windjana Gorge and Tunnel Creek National Park. Prison Tree, 7 km S, boab tree reputedly used as prison in early days. Close by, Myall's Bore, a 120-m-long cattle trough. Fitzroy River empties into King Sound, 48 km S. Camel tours from Udialla Bush Camp, 110 km SW (bookings essential, at information centre). Tours to: spectacular Windjana Gorge, 145 km E in Windjana Gorge National Park; remarkable Tunnel Creek in Tunnel Creek National Park, 184 km E, where flying foxes can be seen late in the year if you wade through tunnel with torch; also Pigeon's Cave, hideout of 1890s Aboriginal outlaw. King Leopold Ranges, 200 km E. Sir John Gorge, 350 km E (4WD access only). Lennard Gorge, 190 km NE (4WD access only). Adcock Gorge, 270 km NE, rock pools and falls early in year. Barnett River Gorge, 340 km NE (4WD recommended). Mitchell Plateau, 580 km NE via Gibb River Rd and Kalumburu Rd, features spectacular Mitchell Falls, King Edward River and Surveyor's Pool; in this remote region, visitors must be entirely self-sufficient (read section on Outback Motoring p. 603 before departure). **Visitor information:** 1 Clarendon St; (08) 9191 1426. Web site www.comswest.net.au/ ~derbytb **See also:** The Kimberley p. 356.

Dongara
Pop. 1874

MAP REF. 388 B4
Dongara and nearby Port Denison are coastal towns, 359 km N of Perth. Dongara has beaches, reef-enclosed bays

William Bay, south-west of Denmark

and an abundance of rock lobster. There is good fishing around Port Denison. **In town:** Historic buildings in Waldeck St: Anglican rectory (1882) and church (1884); old police station (1870); Royal Steam Flour Mill (1894). Russ Cottage (1870), Point Leander Dr. Main street, Moreton Tce, shaded by 90-year-old Moreton Bay fig trees. In cemetery, Dodd St, headstones date from 1874. Heritage Trail, Old Mill to historic Priory Lodge, brochure available. Easter: Horse Races. Easter Sat.: Craft market at old police station. Nov.: Blessing of the Fleet. **In the area:** Fisherman's Lookout, near Leander Point, Port Denison, for views of harbour. At Eneabba, 81 km SE, RGC Mineral Sands: open-cut, hydrolic and dredge mining, with advanced revegetation scheme; tours Wed., public and school holidays. Holiday towns south-west of Eneabba: Leeman, 38 km, Green Head, 50 km. Western Flora Caravan Park, 60 km S, noted for spring wildflowers in bushland and river setting. **Visitor information:** Old Police Station Building, 5 Waldeck St; (08) 9927 1404.

Donnybrook   Pop. 1635

MAP REF. 379 H6, 386 C8, 388 C10
The township of Donnybrook, the home of Granny Smith and Lady Williams apples, is in the oldest apple-growing area in WA, 210 km S Perth. Gold was found here in 1897, but mined for only four years. Donnybrook stone has been used in construction State-wide. **In town:** On South Western Hwy, Anchor and Hope Inn (1865), once staging post for mail coaches, now

a restaurant; Cadenza Gallery, wood-turning products. Arboretum, junction Irishtown Rd and South Western Hwy. Trigwell Place, near river at southern end of town on South Western Hwy, has picnic/barbecue facilities and playground. Easter: Apple Festival. **In the area:** Old Goldfields Orchard and Cider Factory, 5 km S. Several scenic drives, maps available. Glen Mervyn Dam, 30 km NE, onshore picnic/barbecue facilities. Cedar Shed Pottery, 10 km SE. Old Stables Pottery, 25 km SE; nearby, Blackwood Inn, old staging post, now restaurant and accommodation. At Balingup, 30 km SE: several art and craft outlets, including Old Cheese Factory; Tinderbox, herbs and herbal remedies; Birdwood Park Fruit Winery; Small Farm Field Day each Apr.; Tulip Festival each Aug.; several B&Bs; further 2 km SE, Golden Valley Tree Park. At Boyanup, 12 km NW, Boyanup Transport Museum. **Visitor information:** Stationmaster's Cottage, South Western Hwy; (08) 9731 1720.

Dunsborough   Pop. 1154

MAP REF. 379 C7, 381 C2, 386 B9, 388 B10
Dunsborough is a quiet town on Geographe Bay, west of Busselton, popular for its beaches. **In town:** For local art, Dunsborough Gallery, Naturaliste Tce. Bush Cottage Crafts, Commonage Rd. Rivendell Gardens, Wildwood Rd, has winery, cottage gardens, cafe. Market at Dunsborough Hall, cnr Gibney St and Gifford Rd, 2nd Sat. each month. Lions Market, Lions Park, some Sats (check dates). Nov.: Margaret River Wine Festival.

In the area: Whale-watching boat charters Sept.–Dec.; scuba diving, snorkelling and canoeing; wildflowers, craft and tours of wineries. Scenic coastline to NW of town: Meelup, 5 km; Eagle Bay, 8 km; Bunker Bay, 12 km; Sugar Loaf Rock, 13 km. At Cape Naturaliste, 13 km NW: Lighthouse and Museum; whale-watching platform (best time Sept.–Dec.); several walking tracks with spectacular views of coastline. Wreck of HMAS *Swan*, off Point Picquet, just south of Eagle Bay, submerged Dec. 1997; dive site, tour bookings and permits at information centre. Wise Winery, 6 km NW. Bannamah Wildlife Park; Country Life, farm with animals and hayrides; both 1 km W on Cowes Rd. Torpedo Rock, 10 km W. Several wineries in the south-west. Quindalup Fauna Park, 4 km E. **Visitor information:** Seymour Boulevard; (08) 9755 3299 Web site www.capeweb.com.au/escape **See also:** Cape to Cape p. 331.

Dwellingup   Pop. 399

MAP REF. 378 D11, 386 D6, 388 C9
This small town, 24 km SE of Pinjarra and 109 km from Perth, was rebuilt after the 1961 bushfire. The impressive jarrah forests nearby supply the local timber mill. Bauxite is mined in the area. **In town:** In Marrinup St: country-style meals at Community Hotel, last community hotel in WA; photographic exhibition, depicting 1961 bushfire and local lifestyles, at information centre. Forest Heritage Centre, Acacia Rd, has timber-related exhibits, tree-tops walk, forest trails and wood products.

Crossing the Nullarbor

The trip from Adelaide to Perth along the Eyre Highway is one of Australia's great touring experiences. It is far from monotonous, with breathtaking views of the Great Australian Bight from the road in many places. There is nothing quite like a long straight road stretching as far as the eye can see.

If you are planning a return journey, it is well worth considering driving one way and putting the car on the train for the return. Train bookings need to be made well in advance, even at off-peak times. (**See also:** Planning Ahead p. 587.)

The Eyre Highway is bitumen for its entire length. The highway is well signposted, with indications of the distance to the next town with petrol and other services.

If the journey is undertaken at a sensible pace, it can be surprisingly relaxing, especially during the quieter times of the year. The standard of accommodation along the way is good and reasonably priced, with a friendly atmosphere in the bars and dining rooms of the large motel/roadhouses that are strategically situated along the highway. Many friendships have been made during the trip across the Eyre Highway as the same carloads of travellers meet at stopping-places each night.

The highway is well-maintained, but take care when overtaking, especially in damp conditions when the spray from the vehicle in front completely cuts visibility ahead. Semitrailer drivers are usually courteous, though, and signal when it is safe to overtake. The setting sun can make driving somewhat unpleasant for drivers travelling in a westerly direction. Remember to watch out for kangaroos, particularly at dusk or after rain. Also, do not forget the time changes you will encounter on the way! (**See also:** Time Zones p. 592.)

Above all, it is most important to have a safe, reliable car. The settlements along the highway are mainly motels and roadhouses; you could have a long wait for mechanical or medical help.

The journey proper begins at **Port Augusta**, 308 kilometres north-east of Adelaide, at the head of Spencer Gulf. Port Augusta is a provincial city that services a vast area of semi-arid grazing and wheat-growing country to the north and west. As you head out of the city on the Eyre Highway, you see the red peaks of the Flinders Ranges soaring above the sombre bluebush plains; these are the last hills of any size for 2500 kilometres. Through the little towns of **Kimba** and Kyancutta the scenery can vary from mallee scrub to wide paddocks of wheat. This area was once called Heartbreak Plains, a reminder of the time when farmers walked off their land in despair, leaving behind crumbling stone homesteads that today dot the plains.

The highway meets the sea at **Ceduna**, a small town of white stone buildings and limestone streets set against a background of blue-green sea. The waters of the Great Australian Bight here are shallow and unpredictable, but they yield Australia's best catches of its most commercially prized fish, whiting. On the outskirts of Ceduna is a warning sign about the last reliable water. This marks the beginning of the deserted, almost treeless land that creeps towards the Nullarbor Plain.

The highway stays close to the coast, and alongside there is always a little scrub and other vegetation.

The name 'Nullarbor' is a corruption of the Latin words meaning 'no trees' and the name is apt. Geologists believe that the completely flat plain was once the bed of a prehistoric sea, which was raised by a great upheaval of the earth.

West of Ceduna the traveller will find Penong, a town of 100 windmills, and the breathtaking coastal beauty around Point Sinclair and Cactus Beach. Then on to Nundroo and south to the abandoned settlement of Fowlers Bay, once an exploration depot for Edward John Eyre and now a charming ghost town best known for its fishing.

The Eyre Highway links Port Augusta in South Australia and Norseman in Western Australia

From May to October, travellers will often be rewarded with sightings of the majestic southern right whale on its annual migration along the southern part of the Australian continent. Head of Bight is an important mating and breeding ground. To reach the interpretive centre and viewing platform, take the signposted turn off the highway, 12 kilometres east of Nullarbor Roadhouse; whale-watching permits can be purchased at the interpretive centre.

Between Nullarbor Roadhouse and Border Village are five of Australia's most spectacular coastal lookouts where travellers can see giant ocean swells pounding the towering limestone cliffs that make up this part of the Great Australian Bight. Fuel, refreshments and accommodation are all available at Penong, Nundroo Roadhouse, Nullarbor Roadhouse and Border Village.

There is a checkpoint for westbound travellers at the SA–WA border; visitors should ensure that they are not carrying fruit, vegetables, honey, used fruit and produce containers, plants or seeds. After crossing the border, the road leads through the sandplains of **Eucla** and past Mundrabilla and **Madura** Pass roadhouses.

The road continues through tiny **Cocklebiddy** and **Caiguna** and past **Balladonia** Roadhouse, until it reaches the first real town in over 1200 kilometres, **Norseman**, an ideal stopping-place.

From here you turn north to **Kalgoorlie-Boulder** or south to **Esperance** on the coast. At Kalgoorlie-Boulder you will see one of the longest-established goldmining centres in Western Australia. Set in vast dryland eucalypt forest, the town is picturesque in frontier style. Esperance, on the other hand, offers coastal scenery including long, empty beaches. Nearby, wildflowers enhance the countryside in spring.

As you travel west from Kalgoorlie-Boulder, the undulating forest and wildflower scrub continue for a further 250 kilometres until the road reaches the wheat- and wool-growing lands surrounding the towns of **Southern Cross** and **Merredin**. The farmland becomes increasingly rich as it rises into the Darling Range, the beautiful, wooded mountain country that overlooks Perth. At the end of this long journey Perth glitters like a jewel on the Indian Ocean – a place of civilisation and style, of beaches, waterways and greenery.

See also: individual entries in the South Australian A–Z town listing or in the Western Australian A–Z town listing for details on towns in bold type.

Forest Ranger Tour, steam-train ride to Perth and return (May–Oct., check dates). Etmilyn Forest Tramway, old-style steam train, goes from railway station into jarrah forest (check times). Feb.: Log Chop Day. Aug.: Forest Heritage Festival. **In the area:** Lane-Poole Reserve, 10 km S in jarrah forest, with Baden Powell Pool, a popular recreational area. Loop walk, starts 3 km SW and passes scenic Marrinup Falls. Oakly Dam and Falls, 7 km SW. **Visitor information:** Marrinup St; (08) 9538 1108.

Esperance   Pop. 8647

MAP REF. 389 J10
Wide sandy beaches, a scenic coastline and the Recherche Archipelago are all attractions near Esperance, on the south coast of WA. The town, 720 km from Perth via Wagin, is the port and service centre for the agricultural and pastoral hinterland. In 1863 the first permanent European settlers came to this area. The town boomed in the 1890s as a port for the goldfields. From the 1950s the heath plains were converted into fertile pasture and farms. **In town:** Municipal Museum, James St, has old machinery, furniture, farm equipment; also display of Skylab, which fell to earth over Esperance in 1979. Art and craft at The Cannery Arts Centre, Norseman Rd. Mermaid Marine Leather, Wood St, produces and sells fashion leathers from discarded fish skins. Charter boats and dive instruction at Esperance Diving and Fishing, The Esplanade. Fishing and seal-watching from Tanker Jetty. 10-km waterfront walk and bicycle path. Beach-fishing excursions and horseriding. Jan.: Sailboard Classic. Feb.: Offshore Angling Classic. Oct.: Agricultural Show; Festival of the Wind (even-numbered years). Dec.–Mar.: Turf Racing (horse-racing). **In the area:** Great Ocean Dr., 39-km loop road along spectacular coastline; passes Windfarms, supplier of 17 per cent of town's electricity, Salmon Beach (5 km W) and Ten Mile Lagoon (16 km W); map available. Whale-watching (June–Nov.) as southern right whales visit coastal bays and protected waters to calve. Rotary Lookout or Wireless Hill, 2 km W, for views of bay, town and Recherche Archipelago. Pink Lake, 5 km W, a pink saltwater lake. Twilight Cove, 12 km W, for sheltered swimming. Views of bay

and islands from Observatory Point and Lookout, 17 km W. Monjingup Lake Reserve, 20 km W. Dalyup River Wines, 42 km W (open weekends and public holidays). Recherche Archipelago (Bay of Isles), 105 small unspoiled islands providing haven for seals and sea lions. Daily cruises (3 hrs 30 min) around Cull, Button, Charlie, Woody and other islands; landing permitted only on Woody Island. Full-day cruises to Woody Island, developed as tourist attraction (overnight camping facilities). Cape Le Grand National Park, 56 km E, has spectacular coastline, attractive beaches (Lucky Bay, Hellfire Bay, Thistle Cove), coastal and bush walks (brochures available) and displays of wildflowers in spring; also Whistling Rock, a rock that 'whistles' under certain wind conditions, and magnificent view from Frenchmans Peak. Cape Arid National Park, 120 km E, for fishing and camping; 4WD routes. Helms Arboretum, 15 km N. Telegraph Farm, 21 km N on South Coast Hwy, has proteas, deer, buffalo and native animals (farm tours). Speddingup Wildflower Sanctuary, 35 km N, guided walks through magnificent wildflowers in season. **Visitor information:** Museum Village, Dempster St; (08) 9071 2330. **See also:** Crossing the Nullarbor p. 348.

Eucla   Pop. 30

MAP REF. 314 A8, 389 R7
Eucla is 13 km from the WA–SA border, on the Eyre Hwy. There is a quarantine checkpoint for westbound travellers at the border; they should ensure they are not carrying fruit, vegetables, honey, used fruit and produce containers, plants or seeds. **In town:** Local history museum at information centre. May: Golf Classic. Oct.: Eucla Shoot. **In the area:** Cross on escarpment, 5 km S, dedicated to all Eyre Hwy travellers; illuminated at night. Bureau of Meteorology Weather Station, 1 km E (open to public 9.30 a.m.–1.30 p.m. daily). Highway westward from Eucla descends to coastal plain via Eucla Pass. Midway down Pass (about 200 m), track to left leads to sand-covered ruins of old telegraph station and former town site, 4 km S. **Visitor information:** Motor Hotel; (08) 9039 3468. **See also:** Crossing the Nullarbor p. 348.

Exmouth   Pop. 3058

MAP REF. 387 C3
One of the newest towns in Australia, Exmouth was founded 1967 as a support town for the Harold E. Holt US Naval Communications Station, the main source of local employment. Excellent year-round fishing and nearby beaches have made Exmouth a major tourist destination. The town is on the north-eastern side of North West Cape, the nearest point in Australia to the continental shelf, so there is an abundance of marine life in surrounding waters. In March 1999 Exmouth was hit by Cyclone Vance. **In town:** Ningaloo Impressions Gallery and Studio, Eurayle St. Sun. mall market (Apr.–Sept.). Apr.: Billfish Bonanza. July: Exmo Week; Arts and Crafts Show. Sept.: Gulf Aquafest. Nov.: Gamex (world-class game-fishing). **In the area:** Turtle-nesting Nov.–Jan.; coral-spawning Mar.–Apr.; boat cruises and air flights to see whale sharks Mar.–June; humpback whales can be seen Aug.–Nov. from lighthouse, 17 km N, and from regular whale-watching boat tours; snorkellers can swim with manta rays located by cruise boats. Swimming, snorkelling, fishing; fishing-boat charter; coral-viewing boat cruises; safari tours of cape, national parks and naval base; dive courses and dive trips. In Cape Range National Park, south of town: Shothole Canyon, a spectacular gorge accessed via Shothole Canyon Rd; Charles Knife Canyon, accessed via Charles Knife Rd (spectacular views); Yardie Creek Gorge, with deep-blue water and multi-coloured rock; Milyering Visitor Centre, 52 km SW; abundant wildlife, picnic spots, scenic lookouts and walking trails. Ningaloo Marine Park, 14 km W of cape, largest fringing coral reef in Australia; 500 fish species identified and 220 reef-building coral species. Panoramic views from Vlaming Head Lighthouse, 17 km N. Wreck of SS *Mildura*, 100 m off shore. **Visitor information:** Murat Rd; (08) 9949 1176; freecall 1800 287 328. Web site www.gta.asn.au

Fitzroy Crossing   Pop. 1147

MAP REF. 384 G11, 393 L9
In the Kimberley, where the Great Northern Hwy crosses the Fitzroy River, is the settlement of Fitzroy Crossing, 254 km inland from Derby. Once a sleepy hamlet, the town has grown as a result of Aboriginal settlement, mining by Western Metals at Cadjebut, 80 km SE,

China Wall near Halls Creek

and an increase in visitors to the nearby Geikie Gorge National Park. July: Rodeo. Nov.: Barra Splash (barramundi fishing competition). **In the area:** Check road conditions before setting out on any excursions Dec.–Mar. as area is prone to flooding. Various scenic flights, bookings essential. Picturesque waterholes surrounding town support abundance of fish and other wildlife. Magnificent Geikie Gorge, 18 km NE in Geikie Gorge National Park, offers variety of wildlife, including sawfish, barramundi, stingrays (adapted to fresh water) and freshwater crocodiles; cruises, including Aboriginal Heritage Cruise (May–Nov.). Tours to Windjana Gorge, 153 km NW. Tunnel Creek National Park, 110 km NW, features creek tunnel through mountain range; 4WD access only, tours available. Windjana Gorge National Park, 145 km NW, rock pools supporting variety of fish and birdlife, and walking trails; 4WD access only, tours available. **Visitor information:** cnr Great Northern Hwy and Flynn Dr.; (08) 9191 5355. **See also:** National Parks p. 336.

Gascoyne Junction Pop. 38

MAP REF. 387 D8
Located 170 km E of Carnarvon, at the junction of the Gascoyne and Lyons rivers, this town is the administration centre for the surrounding region.

In town: Old Roads Board Museum, memorabilia of area (check opening times). The old-fashioned pub is a good rest stop. **In the area:** Scenic Kennedy Range National Park, 60 km N. Mt Augustus National Park, 294 km NE, features walks and drives; brochures available. **Visitor information:** Junction Hotel; (08) 9943 0504.

Geraldton Pop. 25 243

MAP REF. 388 A3
The port and administration centre for the mid-west region, Geraldton is 424 km N of Perth on Champion Bay. A year-round sunny climate and a mild winter make it one of the State's most popular holiday destinations. The flourishing city has interesting museums, white, sandy beaches and good fishing. The area has rich agricultural land, magnificent spring wildflowers and picturesque countryside. The Houtman Abrolhos Islands, named in the 16th century, lie 64 km off the coast and are used mainly as a base for rock-lobster fishing. **In town:** Heritage trail, brochure available. In Cathedral Ave: Queens Park Theatre, surrounded by gardens; St Francis Xavier Cathedral, designed by Mons. John C. Hawes, architect of some fine buildings in and around Geraldton. On Marine Tce: Sir John Forrest Memorial; Geraldton Museum (includes maritime display building), features relics from shipwrecks off coast. Art Gallery, cnr Durlacher St and Chapman Rd. Old Gaol Craft Centre, Bill Sewell Complex, Chapman Rd. Lookout and wishing-well on Waverley Heights, Brede St. Point Moore Lighthouse (1878), Willcock Dr. Excellent fishing from town's breakwater. At Fisherman's Wharf in season (Nov.–June), watch impressive hauls of lobster being unloaded. Lobster factory tours. Jan.: Windsurfing Classic. Mar.: Sea Jazz Spectacular. June: Batavia Celebrations. Oct.: Sunshine Festival. **In the area:** For good fishing: Sunset Beach, 6 km N; Drummond Cove, 10 km N; mouth of Greenough River, 10 km S. Banks of Greenough River, favourite place for picnics; market here 3rd Sun. each month; Greenough River Walk, starts at river mouth; safe swimming for children in river; daily river cruises. Greenough, 24 km S, restored by National Trust to 1880s look (guided tours). Ellendale Bluffs and Pool, 45 km SE, a permanent waterhole at base of steep rock face. Mill's Park Lookout, 15 km NE on Waggrakine Cutting, offers excellent views over Moresby Range and coastal plain towards Geraldton. Chapman Valley, 35 km NE, a farming district noted for its spectacular spring wildflowers. Chapman Valley Wines, tastings daily. **Visitor information:** Bill Sewell Complex, cnr Bayley St and Chapman Rd; (08) 9921 3999.

Gingin Pop. 549

MAP REF. 386 C2, 388 C7
Situated 83 km N of Perth and 30 km from the coast, Gingin is mainly a centre for mixed farming, horticulture, and cattle and sheep breeding. As a day trip from Perth it offers alternative return trips through coastal centres or inland via the scenic Chittering Valley. The town is built around a loop of Gingin Brook, which rises from nearby springs and flows strongly all year. **In town:** Fine examples of traditional Australian architecture in village-like atmosphere. In Weld St: St Luke's Anglican Church (1860s), Granville (1871), Uniting Church (1868), and Dewar's House (1886). In Brockman St: Philbey's Cottage (1906), now a real estate agency. Uniforms of the World Museum, Brook St (closed Mon.). Granville Scenic Park, Weld St, has barbecue facilities. Adjacent to park, Jim Gordon V. C. Trail, a delightful 30-min walk along Gingin Brook. Apr.: Gingin Expo (horticulture and primary production). May: British Car

Day. **In the area:** Gingin Cemetery, northern outskirts of town on Dewar Rd, has prolific display of kangaroo paws in spring. Neergabby Pottery, 25 km W. At Bullsbrook, 30 km S: The Maze; Bullsbrook Antiques and Cottage Crafts. Golden Grove Citrus Orchard and Observatory at Lower Chittering, 30 km SE. Colamber Bird Park, just east of town on Mooliabeenie Rd. At Bindoon, 24 km E: Neroni Wines; Chittering Valley Estate; Kay Road Art and Craft Gallery. **Visitor information:** Shire Offices, 7 Brockman St; (08) 9575 2211. Web site www.iinet.net.au/~ginginwa

Guilderton   Pop. 174

MAP REF. 386 B2, 388 C7
Located at the mouth of the Moore River, 94 km N of Perth, Guilderton is a popular day trip from Perth and a holiday destination. There is excellent fishing in both river and sea, and safe swimming for children. Dutch relics have been found here, possibly from the wreck of the *Vergulde Draeck* (Gilt Dragon) in 1656. **In town:** Cruises on Moore River, depart Edward St. **In the area:** Seabird, 20 km N, a small but growing fishing village with a safe beach. **Visitor information:** Caravan Park, 2 Dewar St; (08) 9577 1021.

Halls Creek   Pop. 1263

MAP REF. 385 N11, 393 P9
In the heart of the Kimberley, 2832 km from Perth, at the edge of the Great Sandy Desert, is Halls Creek, site of WA's first gold find in 1885. In the period 1885–87, 10 000 men came to the Kimberley goldfields then gradually drifted away, leaving 2000 on the diggings. Today beef cattle is the main industry. **In town:** Russian Jack Memorial, Thomas St, tribute to miner who pushed his sick friend in a wheelbarrow from Halls Creek to Wyndham for medical help. July: Agricultural Show. Aug.: Races. **In the area:** Aboriginal dreamtime places, brochures available from Kimberley Language Resource Centre, Terone St. Scenic flights to Purnululu National Park, bookings essential, at information centre. China Wall, 6 km E, a natural quartz formation. Prospecting at Old Halls Creek, 16 km E; mud-brick ruins of original settlement; caravan park. Caroline Pool, 10 km E, near old town site off Duncan Rd, for swimming and picnicking (best Oct.–May). Fishing,

swimming and picnicking at Palm Springs (41 km E), and Sawpit Gorge (43 km E), both on Black Elvire River. Purnululu National Park, 160 km NE, has spectacular Bungle Bungle rock formations. Wolfe Creek Meteorite Crater, 148 km S, almost 1 km wide, and 49 m deep; second largest meteorite crater in world. **Visitor information:** Apr.–Sept.: Great Northern Hwy; (08) 9168 6262. **See also:** The Kimberley p. 356.

Harvey   Pop. 2570

MAP REF. 379 H2, 386 C7, 388 C10
The thriving town of Harvey, 139 km S of Perth, is set in some of the best agricultural country in Australia. Bordered by the Darling Range and the Indian Ocean, the fertile plains are perfect for dairying. The irrigation storage dams and recreation areas are popular with tourists. **In town:** Historical Society Museum, in old railway station (1914), Harvey St (open 2–4 p.m. Sun.). Information centre has local industry displays, Moo Shoppe and local craft. Stirling Cottage, behind information centre, replica of 1880s home of May Gibbs (author of *Snugglepot and Cuddlepie*). Internment Camp Memorial Shrine, South Western Hwy, built by prisoners of war in 1940s; obtain key from information centre. Mar.: Harvest Festival. Sept.: Spring Markets. Oct.: Agricultural Show. **In the area:** Weir, 3 km E, off Weir Rd; Weir Walk, a 1-km trail alongside Harvey River. Scenic drive around north-west side of Stirling Dam (venue for world canoe championships), 17 km E, leads to Harvey Falls and Trout Ladder. Logue Brook Dam, 15 km NE, for swimming, water-skiing and trout fishing. Hoffmans Mill, 25 km NE, has picnic and camping facilities. At Yarloop, 15 km N: historic steam-age Workshops Museum; heritage trail, details from museum. Myalup and Binningup beaches, 25 km W off Old Coast Rd, are wide and sandy, ideal for swimming, fishing and boating. **Visitor information:** South Western Hwy; (08) 9729 1122. **See also:** The South-West p. 335.

Hopetoun   Pop. 319

MAP REF. 388 H11
Hopetoun is a peaceful holiday town overlooking the Southern Ocean. 49 km S of Ravensthorpe, the town offers rugged, beautiful coastal scenery and year-round

wildflowers. Once called Mary Ann Harbour, Hopetoun has a colourful history. **In town:** White, sandy beaches, sheltered bays, excellent fishing. Chatterbox Crafts, Veal St, for local art and craft. Jan.: Summer Festival. **In the area:** Scenic drives, brochures available. Lookout at Table Hill, 1 km N, offers 360° views over town and ocean and has cairn to explorer John Eyre. Dunn's Swamp, 5 km N, for picnics, bushwalking and birdwatching. Lookout at No Tree Hill, 27 km NW offers views across to Eyre Range. Fitzgerald River National Park, 10 km W, includes the Barrens, a series of rugged mountains, undulating sandplains and steep narrow gorges; East Mt Barren Footpath, walk to summit (2–3 hrs return); Hamersley Inlet, a scenic picnic and camping spot. Take care fishing from rocks – king waves can roll in unexpectedly and take lives. **Visitor information:** Chatterbox Crafts, Veal St; (08) 9838 3100. Web site www.comswest.net.au/~hopetel **See also:** National Parks p. 336.

Hyden   Pop. 150

MAP REF. 388 F8
Hyden is 351 km E of Perth, in the semi-arid eastern wheat area of WA. **In the area:** Fascinating rock formations, especially Wave Rock, 4 km E, a 2700 million-year-old granite outcrop rising 15 m, like a giant wave about to break. At Wave Rock: Wildlife Park; coffee shop; caravan park with cabins; Pioneer Town, with collection of Australiana; lacework (from 1600s) at information centre; 1 km E of centre, salt lakes for swimming and picnics, good reflections of rock. Other rock forma-tions within walking distance of Wave Rock: Hippos Yawn; The Breakers; The Falls. Scenic flights from airfield, 5 km E, bookings essential. Aboriginal rock paintings at Mulka's Cave, 18 km N of Wave Rock. Nearby, The Humps, another unusual granite formation. **Visitor information:** Wave Rock Visitors Centre, Wave Rock Rd, 4 km E of town; (08) 9880 5182. Web site www.promaco.com.au/mapping/ hyden

Jurien Bay   Pop. 636

MAP REF. 388 B6
Located 266 km N of Perth on a sheltered bay, Jurien Bay is a lobster-fishing centre. The town is also a

The Goldfields

The land that boasted the first goldmining boom in Western Australia is almost as forbidding as that of the far north-west. This is the vast region to the east of Perth that contains the famous towns of Kalgoorlie-Boulder, Coolgardie, Norseman, Kambalda, Leonora, Gwalia and Laverton with Kalgoorlie-Boulder the main centre.

The western gold rush began in 1892 with strikes around Coolgardie. The town sprang up from nowhere and enjoyed a boisterous but short life. In 1900 there were 15 000 people, today **Coolgardie** has a population of 1258. The grand old courthouse is used now as a museum and has a record of life on the fields as it once was.

In 1893 Irishman Paddy Hannan made a bigger strike of gold at Kalgoorlie. The area became known as the Golden Mile, reputedly the richest square mile in the world.

The modern **Kalgoorlie-Boulder** is a major goldmining centre, producing more than half of the gold mined in Australia. At Hannans North Historic Mining Reserve visitors can don a hard hat and cap lamp, and go below the surface, where guides explain the hardships endured by the miners in their search for gold. To the south is Kambalda, a new boom town, founded on rich nickel deposits.

Most of the towns north of Kalgoorlie are alive again as a result of the current goldmining operations. Deep underground mines are being replaced by massive open-cuts, which create their own adjacent table top mountains of overburden. The renovated State Hotel, at Gwalia, just outside **Leonora**, is a fine example of the former prosperity of this region and old miners' cottages provide an insight into the lifestyles of early miners in the same town.

Kanowna once boasted a population of 12 000. Now all that remains is old and new mine workings, and historic markers describing what used to be. Siberia, Niagara and Bulong are the exotic names of some of the towns that flourished and died in a few short years. Nevertheless, mining is once again active in most of these areas.

See also: individual entries in A–Z town listing for towns in bold type.

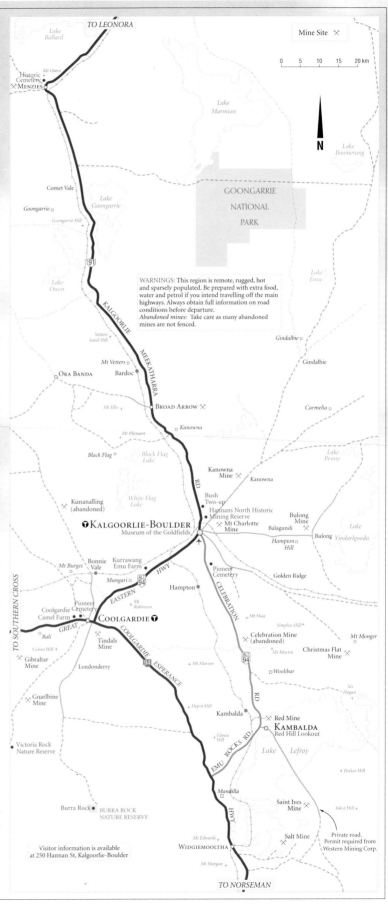

Mine Site

WARNINGS: This region is remote, rugged, hot and sparsely populated. Be prepared with extra food, water and petrol if you intend travelling off the main highways. Always obtain full information on road conditions before departure.
Abandoned mines: Take care as many abandoned mines are not fenced.

Visitor information is available at 250 Hannan St, Kalgoorlie-Boulder

holiday destination because of its magnificent safe swimming beaches, excellent climate and reputation as an angler's paradise. Jurien Bay boat harbour, a 17-ha inland marina, has excellent boating facilities. **In town:** Tours of rock-lobster processing factory, Roberts Rd, in fishing season. Nov.: Marine Expo and Blessing of the Fleet (start of rock-lobster season). **In the area:** Spectacular sand dunes along coast. Cockleshell Gully, 31 km N, has great diversity of flora and fauna. Stockyard Gully National Park, 50 km N (4WD access only), has walk through 300-m Stockyard Gully Tunnel along winding underground creek (torch necessary, tours available). Lesueur National Park, 25 km E, noted for variety of spring wildflowers. At Cervantes, 55 km S, Slalom Carnival (windsurfing) held in Dec. Nearby is Nambung National Park, featuring The Pinnacles, thousands of spectacular calcified spires, 1–4 m high and around 30 000 years old, scattered over 400 ha of multi-coloured sand (coach tours daily); check road conditions before leaving Jurien Bay if taking coastal track (main signposted route further inland recommended). 2-km walking trail through heathlands of Badgingarra National Park; Badgingarra Shears Competition each Aug. **Visitor information:** Shire Offices, Bashford St; (08) 9652 1020. Web site www.promaco.com.au/mapping.twcc

Kalbarri   Pop. 1788

MAP REF. 387 C13, 388 A2
This popular holiday town is between Geraldton and Carnarvon, 591 km N of Perth. The town's picturesque Murchison River estuary setting, its year-round sunny climate, the spectacular gorges of Kalbarri National Park, its excellent fishing and the brilliance of more than 500 wildflower species all attract a growing number of tourists. **In town:** In Grey St: Recollections, a doll and marine museum; Gemstone Mine. In Porter St: Kalbarri Entertainment Centre; bicycle hire available. Pelican feeding on foreshore (8.45 a.m.). Mar.: Cycle Races and Triathlon; Sport Fishing Classic. Nov.: Blessing of the Fleet. **In the area:** Majestic coastal gorges and precipitous red cliffs dropping to Indian Ocean. *River Queen* ferry cruises; camel safaris; coach, 4WD, and abseiling adventure tours; canoe safaris; joy

flights. Kalbarri Big River Ranch, 3 km E, for horseriding. At Kalbarri National Park, a large area of magnificent virgin bushland surrounding town: Meanarra Lookout, 7 km E; spectacular Murchison River gorges, 30 km E; coastal views from Hawks Head Lookout and Ross Graham Lookout, both 39 km E; abundance of wildlife and native flora; no camping. Rainbow Jungle and Tropical Bird Park, 3.5 km S. Red Bluff, 4 km S, for swimming, fishing and rock-climbing. Cairn at Wittecarra Creek, 4 km S, marking site of first permanent landing of Europeans in Australia (two Dutchmen sent ashore for their part in *Batavia* mutiny in 1629). Views from the Loop and Z Bend lookouts, 30 km NE. **Visitor information:** Grey St; (08) 9937 1104, freecall 1800 639 468. Web site www.wn.com.au/kalbarrionline **See also:** National Parks p. 336; Western Wildflowers p. 364.

Kalgoorlie-Boulder
Pop. 28 087

MAP REF. 388 I6
At the heart of WA's largest goldmining area is the city of Kalgoorlie-Boulder, 597 km E of Perth and located on the Golden Mile, reputed to be the richest square mile in the world. Over 1300 tonnes of gold have been mined from this small area. Paddy Hannan found gold in 1893; by 1902 the population was 30 000, with 93 hotels. Fortunes were made overnight; impressive stone buildings and wide streets are reminders of this golden era. Miners set up tents on the Golden Mile near the Great Boulder Mine; this camp became the town of Boulder. Tree plantings dating from the late 1800s are a distinctive feature; many of the 50 species are eucalypts from the surrounding woodlands. One of the greatest difficulties facing miners in this semi-desert area was lack of water. Determination and the brilliant scheme of engineer C. Y. O'Connor saved the day. A pipeline was completed in 1903, carrying water 563 km from a reservoir near Perth. Goldmining continues today in a climate of fluctuating gold prices. The Kalgoorlie-Boulder region is also important for high-quality wool. **In town:** Heritage walk along Hannan and Burt sts, brochures available. Fine examples of early Australian architecture in Hannan St: Exchange, Palace and

Australia hotels; Government buildings; Kalgoorlie Post Office; distinctive Kalgoorlie Town Hall (1908), featuring original statue of Paddy Hannan, impressive staircase, and paintings by local artists. Also in Hannan St: Museum of the Goldfields, incorporating the British Arms Hotel (1899), with display recalling heyday of gold-rush; replica statue of Hannan; Desert Art Shop. Goldfields Aboriginal Art Gallery, Dugan St. Paddy Hannan's Tree, Outridge Tce, marks site of first gold find in Kalgoorlie. School of Mines Mineral Museum, Egan St, includes world-class display of most minerals found in WA. In Cassidy St, Goldfields Arts Centre has regular exhibitions. At Hannans North Historic Mining Reserve, Broad Arrow Rd, underground and surface tours, gold-pouring demonstrations. Super Pit Lookout, off Eastern Bypass Rd. In Burt St: Boulder Town Hall (1908), has unique Goatcher curtain and miners' monument; Goldfields War Museum has personal war memorabilia and outdoor armoured vehicle display. Picturesque Cornwall Hotel (1898), Chesapeake St. Royal Flying Doctor Base, at airport (off Gatacre St): serves one of largest areas in Australia; tours weekdays; scenic flights over goldfields and Super Pit Lookout. Hammond Park, Lyall St, a wildlife sanctuary with lake and model of Bavarian castle. Karlkurla Bushland Park, off Riverina Way in Hannans; guided tours Apr.–Oct. Mt Charlotte Reservoir and Lookout, off Sutherland St; reservoir is storage for Kalgoorlie's vital fresh-water supply. The Loopline, a tourist railway line around the Golden Mile; timetable at information centre. Sept.: Kalgoorlie Cup; Spring Festival. **In the area:** Carpet of wildflowers in season. City is an ideal base for visiting old gold-mining towns in district (all within a day's drive, all active, tours July–Oct.): Coolgardie, 37 km SW; Broad Arrow, 38 km N; Ora Banda, 54 km NW; Kookynie, 200 km N; Leonora-Gwalia, 235 km N. Scenic flights, and bush tours including Aboriginal tours with local Wongi people; WA's only legal Bush Two-up (a gambling game), 7 km N of Kalgoorlie-Boulder on eastern side of road to Menzies. Rowles Lagoon, 34 km NW, excellent for water sports. Kurrawang Emu Farm, 18 km W, also features Aboriginal artifacts (closed Sun., tours available).

Visitor information: 250 Hannan St; (08) 9021 1966. Web site www.kalbldtc. com.au **See also:** Crossing the Nullarbor p. 348; The Goldfields p. 352.

Karratha Pop. 10 057

MAP REF. 387 G1

This modern town was established on Nickol Bay in 1968 as a result of expansion of the Hamersley Iron Project. There was a lack of suitable land at Dampier and a need for a new regional centre. The town grew further when Woodside Petroleum developed the immense offshore gas reserve on the North West Shelf, and Karratha now has the best facilities in the Pilbara. Karratha's warm winter temperatures make it a good place to escape the cold. **In town:** Excellent views from TV Hill lookout, Millstream Rd. June: Pilbara Pursuit Jetboat Classic. Aug.: FeNaCLNG Festival (annual show). **In the area:** Scenic flights, day tours and safari tours of Pilbara outback. Jaburara Heritage Trail, 3-hr walk, features Aboriginal rock carvings and artifact scatters. At Dampier, 22 km N: Hamersley Iron deepwater port (tours Mon.–Fri.); salt-harvest ponds near port; water sports and boat hire; Game-fishing Classic held Aug. Near Dampier: North West Shelf Gas Project Visitors Centre (8 km NW on Burrup Peninsula), and Aboriginal rock carvings nearby. Chichester Range Camel Trail and Millstream–Chichester National Park, 124 km S. **Visitor information:** 4548 Karratha Rd; (08) 9144 4600. **See also:** The Hamersley Range p. 367.

Katanning Pop. 4035

MAP REF. 383 L1, 386 H9, 388 E10

A thriving town 186 km N of Albany, Katanning's well-planned streets have some impressive Federation buildings. The countryside is given over to grain-growing and pastoral activities, and is noted for its fine merino sheep. **In town:** Self-guide scenic and heritage walks, brochure available. Old Mill Museum (1889), cnr Clive St and Austral Tce, features outstanding display of vintage roller flour-milling process. Majestic Kobeelya mansion (1902), Brownie St, a country retreat now owned by Baptist Church (open by appt). All Ages Playground, Clive St, has miniature steam railway. Old Winery ruins, Andrews Rd, being restored. In Dore St, largest country-based sheep-selling facility in WA; regular sales on Wed. throughout year; ram sale in Aug. Metro Meats meatworks, Wagin Rd (tours by appt, contact Metro Meats or information centre). Market at Blyth's Tree Farm, Prosser St (Sun. a.m., check dates). Feb.: Triathlon. Aug.: Prophet Mohammad's Birthday. Dec.: Caboodle. **In the area:** Katanning–Piesse Heritage Trail, a 20-km drive/walk trail. Lakes surrounding town are excellent for swimming, boating and water-skiing. **Visitor information:** Flour Mill, cnr Austral Tce and Clive St; (08) 9821 2634. **See also:** The South-West p. 335.

Kojonup Pop. 1035

MAP REF. 383 J2, 386 G9, 388 E11

Situated on the Albany Hwy, 154 km NW of Albany, Kojonup takes its name from the Aboriginal word 'kodja', meaning 'stone axe'. In 1837, when surveying the road from Albany to the newly established Swan River settlement, Alfred Hillman was guided to the Kojonup Spring by local Aborigines. Later, a military outpost was set up on the site, and this marked the beginning of the town. **In town:** In Spring St: Kojonup Spring and picnic area; Military Barracks (1845), Barracks Pl., houses Kojonup Pioneer Museum (open Sun. p.m. or by appt). Elverd's Cottage (1851), Soldier Rd, has display of pioneers' tools and implements. On Albany Hwy: Sundial in Hillman Park; Kojonup Brook Walk, a walk alongside stream and featuring swing bridge. Walsh's Cattle Complex, Broomehill Rd, has regular cattle sales. Farrar Reserve, Blackwood Rd, noted for its wildflower display in Spring. Myrtle Benn Memorial Flora and Fauna Sanctuary, Tunney Rd. Heritage Harness Display, Railway Shed, Benn Pde (next to information centre). Feb.: Rodeo. Sept.: Country and Wildflower Festival. Oct.: Agricultural Show. **In the area:** Variety of flora (includes more than 60 orchid species) and fauna (especially birds). Outlets for locally made jarrah furniture, hand-turned grass-tree articles, woollen jumpers. Proandra Flowers, 20 km W, a protea farm. Lake Towerrining, 40 km NW, ideal for boating, onshore camping. Australian Bush Heritage Funds Reserve at Cherry Tree Pool, 16 km N, offers walk through *Eucalyptus wandoo* and wildflowers. **Visitor information:** Old Railway Station, Benn Pde; (08) 9831 1686. **See also:** The South-West p. 335.

Kulin Pop. 360

MAP REF. 386 I6, 388 F9

A centre for the sheep and grain farms of the district, Kulin is 283 km SE of Perth. *Eucalyptus macrocarpa* is a spectacular feature of local flora. **In town:** Kulin Herbarium, specialising in wildflowers from local area, tours by appt. On Kondinin–Wickepin Rd, Cooperative Bulk Handling Facility (huge grain-storage bins); tours, bookings essential. Sept.: Charity Rally (for pre-1977 cars). **In the area:** Several species of native orchids. Several wildflower walks/drives; brochure available. Jilakin Rock and Lake, 15 km E, a salt lake with salt plants, and wildflowers in spring; Kulin Bush Races Weekend held here in Oct. Buckley's Breakaway (pit with coloured hollows caused by granite decomposing to kaolin), 58 km E; also unusual coloured rock formations and wildflowers in area. Hopkins Nature Reserve, 20 km NE, an important flora conservation area. Historic Kondinin Cottage, 32 km NW at Kondinin, National Trust-classified mudbrick settler's cottage, offering antiques, collectables, rural craftwork and afternoon teas. **Visitor information:** Kulin Woolshed, Johnston St; (08) 9880 1275 or Shire Offices, Johnston St; (08) 9880 1204. Web site www.kulin.com.au

Kununurra Pop. 4884

MAP REF. 385 P2, 393 Q5

Kununurra is situated alongside Lake Kununurra on the Ord River. Adjoining is the magnificent Mirima National Park. The town supports several industries, including agriculture and mining, and is the major site for the Argyle Diamond Mine (the largest producing diamond mine in the world) and the Ord River Irrigation Area. **In town:** Sales of pink diamonds from the Argyle Diamond Mine, and other gems, at various outlets. Diversion Gallery, River Fig Ave, for fine Kimberley artworks. June: Dam to Dam Regatta. **In the area:** Kununurra is major starting point for flights and ground tours to: remarkably coloured and shaped Bungle Bungles in Purnululu National Park to the south; Argyle Diamond Mine in the south-west (access via tour only); Mitchell Plateau and Kalumburu in the north-west Kimberley. Minibus tours of local attractions, charter flights and bush camping. Good fishing; barramundi a prized catch. Mirima National Park, 2 km E (no camping). 2 km N: Warringarri Aboriginal Arts; Kelly's Knob Lookout, for views of surrounding

Early Australian architecture in Hannan St, Kalgoorlie-Boulder

irrigated land. Barra Barra Banana Farm, 9 km N, tastings and sales (daily May–Oct.). Top Rockz Gallery, 10 km N, exhibits gemstones and precious metals (open May–Sept.). Melon Farm, 12 km N. Ivanhoe Crossing, 12 km N, for fishing. Middle Springs, 30 km N; Black Rock Falls, 32 km N, flows only in wet season. Cruises on Lake Kununurra and upstream into the Everglades and gorges for teeming birdlife. El Questro Station, 100 km SW, features Aboriginal rock art, rugged scenery, hot springs, fishing and boating (camping and accommodation available). Sleeping Buddha (Elephant Rock), 10 km S. Zebra Rock Gallery, 16 km S. Scenic Lake Argyle, 72 km S in Carr Boyd Range, largest body of fresh water in Australia, created by Ord River Dam, which transformed mountain peaks into islands. Argyle Homestead Museum, lake cruises, caravan park and accommodation at Lake Argyle Tourist Village. **Visitor information:** Coolibah Dr.; (08) 9168 1177. **See also:** The Kimberley p. 356.

Lake Grace   Pop. 575

MAP REF. 388 F9
A pleasant town with good facilities, situated 252 km N of Albany in the peaceful countryside of the central south wheat belt, Lake Grace derives its name from the shallow lake just west of the settlement. **In town:** In Stubbs St: mural depicting pioneer women, in Lake Grace Plaza; restored Inland Mission hospital, last in WA; old railway buildings. **In the area:** Roe Heritage Trail, retraces part of J. S. Roe's explorations in 1848. Lookout, 5 km W. **Visitor information:** Shire Council; (08) 9865 1105.

Lake King   Pop. 29

MAP REF. 388 G9
With a tavern and several stores, Lake King is a crossroads stopping-place for visitors travelling across arid country and through Frank Hann National Park to Norseman. **In the area:** Colourful wildflowers in season, 5 km W. Lake King, 5 km W, a saltwater lake. At Pallarup, 15 km S: pioneer well; Lake Pallarup. Mt Madden cairn and lookout, 25 km SE, also picnic area. Frank Hann National Park, 32 km E, good representation of inland sandplain heath flora. Park is traversed by Lake King–Norseman Rd, a formed gravel road; check road conditions before departure. *Note: No visitor facilities or supplies available between Lake King and Norseman.* **Visitor information:** Australia Post Agency, 13 Ravensthorpe Rd; (08) 9874 4015.

Lancelin   Pop. 597

MAP REF. 386 B1, 388 B7
This little fishing town on the shores of Lancelin Bay is 127 km N of Perth. A natural breakwater extends from Edward Island to Lancelin Island, providing a safe harbour and a perfect breeding ground for fish. There are rock lobsters on the offshore reefs outside the bay. Long stretches of white sandy beach provide ideal swimming for children. Lancelin is becoming known as the sailboard mecca of WA and each Dec. large numbers of international and interstate windsurfers take part in the Ledge Point Ocean Race. Jan.: Ledge to Lancelin Windsurfing Race. Sept.: Lily Festival and Market Day. Easter: Dune Buggy Championships. **In the area:** Large off-road area for dune buggies at northern end of town. Whale-watching Oct.–Mar. Ledge Point, 15 km S, a community built around fishing industry; good beach fishing. Dive trail to 14 shipwrecks (c. 1760), map available. Eco cruise around islands. Self-guide wildflower drives, maps available. Track (4WD only) leads 76 km N to Nambung National Park; check road conditions at information centre before setting out; map available; alternative bitumen-road route is 166 km. **Visitor information:** 102 Gingin Rd; (08) 9655 1100.

Laverton   Pop. 644

MAP REF. 389 J3
Laverton, was officially gazetted in 1900 and, situated 360 km NE of Kalgoorlie on the edge of the Great Victoria Desert, is

The Kimberley

Until relatively recently the Kimberley region in the far north of Western Australia was only for hardened pioneers and prospectors. Now the National Highway puts it on Australia's travel map and it can offer both excitement and adventure.

There are two seasons in the Kimberley. The long dry period in winter brings delightful weather, while the wet season brings higher temperatures, with monsoonal rains usually falling between December and March.

On the west side, the gateway to the Kimberley is the old pearling town of **Broome**. In the boisterous days of the early 1900s, the pearling fleet numbered some 400 luggers with 3000 crewmen. Today cosmopolitan Broome is rapidly expanding to become one of Western Australia's most popular tourist destinations. There are many points of interest near town, including a set of dinosaur tracks believed to have been embedded in limestone 130 million years ago, and fascinating reminders of Broome's heady days as the world's leading pearling centre.

Further north-east is **Derby**, on King Sound near the mouth of the Fitzroy River, a centre for the beef cattle industry of the Fitzroy Valley and the King Leopold Ranges. Just 7 kilometres south of the town is a centuries-old boab tree. Shaped like an inverted wineglass and

Boab tree near Kununurra

14 metres in diameter, it is hollow and is reputed to have been used as a cell for prisoners.

Derby is a useful base for excursions to **Windjana Gorge** and **Tunnel Creek** in the Napier Range, and **Geikie Gorge** near the town of **Fitzroy Crossing**. Fitzroy Crossing is a centre for local Aboriginal communities and also has a range of accommodation and camping facilities. The river gorges here are among the most colourful and spectacular in northern Australia.

The old gold settlement of **Halls Creek**, 16 kilometres from the site of the present town, was the scene of the first gold rush in Western Australia in 1885. Scores of diggers perished of hunger and thirst, and very little gold was found.

Just east of Halls Creek is the China Wall, a natural white quartz outcrop above a placid creek. Wolfe Creek Meteorite Crater, 148 kilometres south of Halls Creek, is the second largest in the world. The meteorite is believed to have struck the earth about one million years ago.

The most northerly town and safe port harbour in Western Australia is **Wyndham**, the terminus of the Great Northern Highway and now also the port for the Ord River Irrigation Area as well as for the east Kimberley cattle stations. A 100-kilometre route from Wyndham to **Kununurra** winds through spectacular ancient gorge country.

Kununurra, a lively town with excellent facilities, is the base for Lake Argyle, **Mirima National Park** and **Purnululu National Park**. Purnululu is the location of the most unusual geological formations: thousands of bee-hive shaped mounds striped in black and orange. Ground access is by 4WD only. Due to the fragility of the roads during wet conditions, the park is closed from October to March. South of Lake Argyle is the Argyle Diamond Mine, the world's largest. Kununurra is linked to Darwin by the National Highway.

For further information contact the Kununurra Tourist Bureau, Coolibah Drive, Kununurra; (08) 9168 1177. **See also:** National Parks p. 336 and individual entries in A–Z town listing for parks and towns in bold type. **Map references:** 384–5, 393 L6.

THE ORD RIVER

The development of the Ord River Scheme was a far-sighted move to develop the tropical north of Western Australia. During the wet season, the rivers of the Kimberley become raging torrents and at times the Ord River empties more than 50 million litres a second into the sea. With the end of the wet season, the rich seasonal pastures die and the land becomes dry again. The Ord River Dam was built to harness this tremendous wealth of water for agriculture.

Lake Argyle is the main storage reservoir. It is the largest constructed lake in Australia. This vast expanse of water is dotted with islands that were once peaks rising above the surrounding valleys. The water of the Ord is now capable of irrigating 72 000 hectares of land.

The area is becoming increasingly attractive to tourists. Surrounding Lake Argyle are rugged red slopes, a haven for native animals, such as the bungarra lizard, the brush-tailed wallaby and the euro. There are lake cruises, bushwalks and a picnic area.

The original Durack homestead from Argyle Downs Station is also to be found here; once the residence of the cattle-pioneering Durack family, the homestead was reconstructed on its present site when the original homestead was covered by the waters of Lake Argyle. The homestead is a fascinating memorial to the early settlers of the district.

surrounded by numerous old mine workings and modern mines including new nickel and gold projects. With an annual rainfall of around 200 mm, summers are hot and dry; Apr.–Oct. is the recommended time to travel. **In town:** In Craiggie St: Courthouse, Old Police Station and Gaol, and Railway Station. **In the area:** Wildflowers Aug.–Sept. Windarra Heritage Trail, 28 km NW on Old Windarra Minesite Rd, includes rehabilitated mine site and has interpretive plaques along route. Great Victoria Desert escorted 4WD tours (Apr.–Nov.), bookings at information centre. Empress Springs, 305 km NE near Tjukayirla Roadhouse; site discovered by explorer David Carnegie in 1896. From Laverton to Ayers Rock via Outback Hwy (1200 km), all roads are unsealed but regularly maintained. The following points should be noted:

• Permit required to travel through Aboriginal Reserves and Communities; obtained from Aboriginal Affairs Department, Perth, or the Central Land Council in Alice Springs.
• Water is scarce.
• Supplies at Laverton. Fuel, supplies and accommodation at Tjukayirla Roadhouse (305 km), Warburton, and Warakurna Roadhouse.
• Credit card facilities are not necessarily available at desert stops.
• Check road conditions before departure, at the Laverton Police Station or Laverton Shire Offices. Roads can be closed due to heavy rain.
Visitor information: Shire Offices, MacPherson Pl.; (08) 9031 1202. **See also:** The Goldfields p. 352.

Leonora   Pop. 1143

MAP REF. 388 I3
Leonora, 243 km N of Kalgoorlie, has a typical country town appearance, with wide streets and verandahed shopfronts. The town is the busy centrepoint of, and railhead for, the north-eastern goldfields, with mining of gold, copper and nickel at Laverton, 120 km NE, and Leinster, 134 km NW. Most of the surrounding country is flat mulga scrub, but there are brilliant wildflowers in Aug. and early Sept. after good rains. Oct.: Art Prize. **In the area:** Three major gold producers, including famous Sons of Gwalia. At Gwalia, 2 km S: renovated State Hotel (1903), fine example of former prosperity; old mine offices now house a museum depicting miners' lifestyle; several old houses restored to

show conditions in which early miners' families lived; 1-km heritage trail. Small goldmining town of Menzies, 110 km S, has historical cemetery. Kookynie, 92 km SE, a small town with old mine workings; Grand Hotel offers warm welcome. Malcolm, 20 km E; good picnic spot alongside Malcolm Dam. **Visitor information:** Gwalia Museum; (08) 9037 7210 or Shire Offices, Tower St; (08) 9037 6044. **See also:** The Goldfields p. 352.

Madura   Pop. 15

MAP REF. 389 P8
The Hampton Tablelands form a backdrop to Madura, 195 km from the WA–SA border, on the Eyre Hwy. The settlement dates from 1876 when horses for the Indian Army were bred here. Now it is surrounded by private sheep stations. **In the area:** Blowholes at The Pass, 1 km N. Spectacular views from escarpment lookout, 1 km W on hwy. **Visitor information:** Madura Pass Oasis Motel and Roadhouse; (08) 9039 3464. **See also:** Crossing the Nullarbor p. 348.

Mandurah   Pop. 35 945

MAP REF. 378 B9, 386 C5, 388 C9
This popular holiday destination is on the coast, 74 km S of Perth. The Murray, Serpentine and Harvey rivers meet here, forming the vast inland waterway of Peel Inlet and the Harvey Estuary. This river junction was once a significant meeting site for Aboriginal groups who travelled here to barter tools and other objects; the town's name is derived from the Aboriginal word *Mandjar*, meaning trading place. Today the river and the Indian Ocean offer excellent yachting, boating, swimming, water-skiing and fishing. **In town:** Heritage Art and Historic Heritage walks, brochures available. Hall's Cottage (1832), Leighton Rd, a small whitewashed cottage (open Sun. p.m.). Christ Church (1870), cnr Pinjarra Rd and Sholl St, features hand-carved furniture. Community Museum, in old school building (1898), Pinjarra Rd (open Tues. and Sun.). Peel Discovery Centre, Mandurah Tce, interactive exhibition of the history and natural wonders of the region. Old Mandurah Traffic Bridge, cnr Mandurah Tce and Pinjarra Rd, excellent crabbing and fishing. Parrots in Bellawood Park, Furnissdale Rd. Estuary cruises depart information centre. Boat hire available. Dolphins sometimes seen in estuary.

Waters also attract abundance of birdlife. King Carnival Amusement Park, in Hall Park (weekends and school holidays, a.m.). Jan.: Festival. Feb.: Crab Festival. **In the area:** Good beaches at Halls Head, just over Old Mandurah Traffic Bridge. Mandurah Wreck Trail for divers; brochure available. Bavarian Castle Fun Park, Old Coast Rd, 2 km S. Further south, Dawesville Channel between inland waterways and ocean; good fishing from bridge. Erskine Conservation Park, 5 km S, features 1-km nature trail with boardwalk over wetlands. Bouvard Gallery at Melros, 15 km SW, sculptures depicting Australian folklore. In Yalgorup National Park, 45 km S: lakes Clifton and Preston, two long, narrow lakes parallel to coast. Wineries at Cape Bouvard, Mt John Rd (22 km S); Peel Estate and Baldivis Estate Winery, Fletcher Rd, Baldivis (20 km N). At Karnup, 12 km N, Linga Longa Park and Marapana Wildlife World, wildlife and recreation parks. Houseboat hire at South Yunderup, 12 km SE. Peel Pottery at Halls Head, 3 km E. Western Rosella Bird Park, 5 km E, has native birds in natural settings. Also 5 km E, Murray Mandurah Markets, weekends and Mon. public holidays. **Visitor information:** Mandurah Tce; (08) 9550 3999.

Manjimup   Pop. 4390

MAP REF. 382 D6, 386 D10, 388 D11
Fertile agricultural country and magnificent karri forests surround Manjimup, 307 km S of Perth. This is the commercial centre of the State's south-west and one of its most diversified horticultural regions. Quality fruit and vegetables are grown for the local and Asian markets; the area is particularly well-known for its apples. Timber is the main industry, while wine, wool and dairy food are smaller, but growing in importance. **In town:** Manjimup Regional Timber Park, cnr Edward and Rose sts: information centre; Blacksmith's Shop; Timber Museum with original sawmill steam loco; Age of Steam Museum; Historic Hamlet; Fire Tower Lookout; gallery and tearooms; picnic/barbecue facilities; timber tours available. June: 15 000 Motocross. Nov.: Forest and Horticultural Expo. **In the area:** Wildflowers Sept.–Nov. Abseiling, rock-climbing, bushcraft, horseriding adventures, horse-drawn picnic excursions, forest discovery tours and safari tours. Diamond Tree Fire Lookout, 9 km S, a 52-m-high karri

White sandy beaches are a feature of the Margaret River region

tree in use 1941–74 (can be climbed by visitors); nearby, children's adventure trail and picnic/barbecue area. Swimming at Fonty's Pool, 10 km S, originally dammed in 1925 for irrigation; picnicking in landscaped surrounds. Collect walnuts and chestnuts in season (Apr.–May) at Fontanini's Nut Farm, next to Fonty's Pool. Tours of Bunnings Diamond Woodchip Mill, 12 km S. Black George's Winery and Alpaca Centre, 12 km S on South Western Hwy, features historic cottage, alpaca stud and wine-tasting. Nyamup, 20 km SE, old mill town redeveloped as a tourist village. Southern Wildflowers farm, 33 km SE at Quinninup. King Jarrah, 4 km E, a 47-m-high tree estimated to be 300–400 years old; heritage trail begins here. Perup Forest Ecology Centre, 50 km E, night spotlight walks to see rare, endangered and common native animals. Pioneer cairn, 9 km NE. Pioneer cemetery, 10 km NE. The 19-km round trip to Dingup, north-east of Manjimup, passes through farmland and forest; at Dingup, church (1896); historic house (1870). Curragundi Wildlife Park, 2 km N (closed Tues.). One Tree Bridge, 22 km W, a karri tree felled in 1904 to cross Donnelly River; pleasant walk along river's edge to the Four Aces (four magnificent karri trees,

300–400 years old). Donnelly River Holiday Village, 28 km W, features horseriding and abundant wildlife. **Visitor information:** cnr Rose and Edward sts; (08) 9771 1831. **See also:** The South-West p. 335.

Marble Bar   Pop. 318

MAP REF. 390 D2

Known as the hottest town in Australia because of its consistently high temperatures, Marble Bar lies 200 km SE of Port Hedland (last 43 km of road is unsealed). This typical WA outback town takes its name from the unique bar of red jasper that crosses the Coongan River, 4 km W of town. Alluvial gold was discovered at Marble Bar in 1891, and in 1931 at Comet Mine. Today the major industries are goldmining and pastoral production. **In town:** Government buildings (1895), General St, built using locally quarried stone. State Battery site (1910), Newman–Tabba Rd (not open to public). July: Cup Race Weekend. **In the area:** Beautiful scenery, especially in winter and after rain when spinifex country is transformed by flowering plants; rugged ranges, rolling plains, steep gorges and deep rock pools. Jasper deposit at Marble Bar Pool, 4 km W. Nearby, Chinaman's Pool, an ideal picnic

spot. Flying Fox Lookout, 6 km SW, spectacular when river is running. Corunna World War II RAAF Base, 40 km SE. Old goldmines at Nullagine, 111 km SE. Good swimming at Coppin's Gap, 68 km NE and Kitty's Gap, further 6 km. **Visitor information:** BP Garage, 1 Francis St; (08) 9176 1041. **See also:** The Hamersley Range p. 367.

Margaret River   Pop. 2846

MAP REF. 379 C10, 381 C7, 386 A10, 388 B11

This pretty township is on the Margaret River near the coast, 280 km from Perth. The area is noted for its world-class wines, magnificent coastal scenery, excellent surfing beaches and spectacular cave formations. **In town:** Historic steam train in Rotary Park, Bussell Hwy; starting point for heritage walks, brochures available. On Bussell Hwy: Old Settlement Historical Museum; Margaret River Gallery; Margaret River Pottery. Melting Pot Glass Studio, Boodjidup Rd. Grange on Farrelly (1885), Farrelly St, inn and restaurant, formerly homestead. Mar.–Apr.: Margaret River Masters (surfing). Nov.: Margaret River Wine Region Festival. **In the area:** Wineries include Cowaramup (10 km N) and Willyabrup (20 km N); regional wine directory available. Leeuwin Estate

Winery, 8 km S, has restaurant with contemporary Australian paintings and picnic/barbecue facilities; venue for Leeuwin Estate Concert each Feb. Eagles Heritage, 5 km S, has large collection of birds of prey. Bellview Shell Museum, 6 km S at Witchcliffe. Boranup Gallery, 20 km S on Caves Rd, Boranup. Boranup Eco Walks, guided bushwalks through Leeuwin–Naturaliste National Park. Trout fishing and marron delicacies at Margaret River Marron Farm, 9 km SE. Pioneer Settlers Memorial, 14 km SE. The Berry Farm and Winery, 15 km SE. Cheese outlets on Bussell Hwy: Fonti's and Margaret River Cheese Factory, 4 km N. At Cowaramup, 10 km N: Margaret River Regional Wine Centre; Utopiary Studio for art and craft (closed Tues.); Cowaramup Pottery. Ellensbrook homestead (1857), a National Trust property, 15 km NW. Prevelly, on coast 8 km W; Greek Chapel at Prevelly Park. Mammoth Cave, 21 km SW, features fossil remains of prehistoric animals; 4 km on is Lake Cave and CaveWorks, with dynamic working cave model, and boardwalk offering spectacular views of collapsed cavern. Other coastal areas include Gracetown, 15 km NW; Redgate, 10 km S; Hamelin Bay, 34 km S. Augusta–Busselton, Margaret River and Hamelin Bay heritage trails, brochures available. Adventure tours offering abseiling, caving, dolphin-watching and canoeing; details from information centre. **Visitor information:** cnr Tunbridge Rd and Bussell Hwy; (08) 9757 2911. Web site www.margaretriver.wa.com **See also:** Cape to Cape p. 331.

Meekatharra   Pop. 1270

MAP REF. 387 I11, 390 C12
Meekatharra lies 768 km NE of Perth on the Great Northern Hwy. Gold, copper and other minerals are mined in the area, and there are huge sheep and cattle stations. Meekatharra was once important as the railhead for cattle that had travelled overland from the Northern Territory or East Kimberley. **In town:** In Main St: State Battery relics; Royal Flying Doctor Service base (open 9 a.m.–2 p.m. Mon.–Fri.). School of the Air, High St (open to public during school terms 8 a.m.–10.30 a.m.). Old Courthouse, Darlot St. **In the area:** Old goldmining towns, relics of mining equipment, mine shafts; several mines, including Peak Hill (no access), have reopened. Peace Gorge (The Granites),

5 km N. Bilyuin Pool, 88 km NW, for swimming (no water in summer). Mt Gould, 156 km NW; nearby, restored police station. Mt Augustus National Park, 360 km NW: Mt Augustus, a sandstone and quartz massif that rises out of arid shrubland; good walks and drives. **Visitor information:** Shire Offices, Main St; (08) 9981 1002. Web site www. meekashire.wa.gov.au

Merredin   Pop. 2911

MAP REF. 386 I2, 388 F7
A main junction on the Kalgoorlie–Perth railway line, this important wheat centre is 259 km E of Perth. In the late 1800s Merredin grew up as a shanty town as miners stopped on their way to the goldfields. Now, forty percent of the State's wheat is grown within a 100-km radius of the town. **In town:** Cummins Theatre (1926), Bates St, oldest theatre outside Perth. Military Museum, East Barrack St, has World War II collection; also departure point for Merredin Peak Heritage Trail (self-guide drive or walk, brochure available) featuring wildflowers in season, and sites of historical and geological interest. Old Railway Station Museum, Great Eastern Hwy. CBH wheat storage and transfer depot, Gamenya Ave, is largest horizontal storage depot in Southern Hemisphere, capacity 220 000 tonnes. Oct.: Vintage Car Festival (odd-numbered years). **In the area:** Pumping Station No. 4 (1902), 3 km W, designed by C. Y. O'Connor, a fine example of early industrial architecture; station closed 1960 to make way for electrically driven stations. Lookout over Edna May Goldmine, 32 km E at Westonia. At Kellerberrin, 55 km W: folk museum; scenic lookout at top of Kellerberrin Hill; Durakoppin Wildlife Sanctuary, 27 km N of Kellerberrin, and Gardner Flora Reserve, 35 km SW. Totadgin Dam Reserve, 16 km SW of Merredin; Totadgin Rock has wave formation similar to Wave Rock. At Bruce Rock, 50 km SW: museum, craft centre and Australia's smallest bank. Good views from summit of Kokerbin Rock, 90 km SW. Picnics and bushwalking near Hunts Dam, 5 km N. Lake Chandler, 45 km N. Mangowine homestead, 40 km NW at Nungarin, a National Trust property. Museum, 140 km NW at Koorda; several wildlife reserves in vicinity. **Visitor information:** Barrack St; (08) 9041 1666. **See also:** Crossing the Nullarbor p. 348.

Mingenew   Pop. 313

MAP REF. 388 B4
The little town of Mingenew is in the wheat district of the mid-west, 378 km N of Perth. **In town:** In Main St: Mingenew Hotel, a restored colonial building (c. 1900); Old Railway Station with local art and craft (check times). Heritage-listed Schools Inn Bed and Breakfast (c. 1900), William St. Museum, Victoria St, in original school building, displays pioneer relics (check times). Views of surrounding wheat-growing area from Mingenew Hill lookout and Pioneer Memorial, off Mingenew–Mullewa Rd. Sept.: Lions Expo (includes wildflower display). **In the area:** Wildflower walks, include spider orchids; brochure available. Picnic spots at Depot Hill, 15 km W. At Coalseam Conservation Park, 32 km NE, the State's first coal shafts; Irwin Gorge, riverbed rocks for rockhunters and wildflowers in spring. **Visitor information:** Schools Inn B&B, 26 William St; (08) 9928 1149.

Morawa   Pop. 692

MAP REF. 388 C4
Renowned for its grain harvests, Morawa is in the mid-west, 362 km N of Perth. The surrounding area has an abundance of wildflowers in spring. **In town:** In Prater St: Historical Museum (open by appt); St David's Anglican Church. Tiny Catholic church, Davis St, claimed to be smallest in world; part of Mons. Hawes Heritage Trail. **In the area:** Wildflower and historical walks and drives, brochures available. Gliding flights and lessons, book at information centre. Koolanooka Mine Site and Lookout, 19 km E. Koolanooka Springs Reserve, 24 km E, ideal for picnics. Bilya Rock Reserve, 5 km W, with 20-min walk around rock. **Visitor information:** Shire Council, Prater St; (08) 9971 1204.

Mount Barker   Pop. 1648

MAP REF. 383 M9, 386 H12, 388 E12
Situated in the Great Southern district of WA, Mt Barker is 360 km from Perth, with the Stirling Range to the north and the Porongurups to the east. The area was visited by Europeans in 1829 and settlers arrived in the 1830s. Vineyards were first established here in the late 1960s. Today, Mount Barker is a major wine-producing area. **In town:** On Albany Hwy: historic police station and gaol (1868), now

museum (open Sat., Sun. and school holidays); Old Station House Craft Shop. Plantagenet Cottage Craft, Mt Barker Rd. Banksia Farm, western end of town (cnr Pearce and Marmion sts). Shire Art Gallery, Lowood Rd, exhibitions include local artists. Heritage trail, 30-km drive through town and surrounds; map available. Mar.: Machinery Field Day; Porongurup Wine Summer Festival. Oct.: Porongurup Wildflower Weekend. **In the area:** Self-guide scenic and historical St Werburghs Way Tourist Drive, map available. Several wineries. Lookout on summit of Mt Barker, 5 km SW, pinpointed by 168-m-high television tower, has excellent views of Stirling Range across to Albany. St Werburgh's Chapel (1872), 12 km SW, a small privately owned mud-walled chapel overlooking Hay River Valley. Craft at Narrikup Country Store, 16 km S. Porongurup National Park, 24 km E, features granite peaks, karri forests and brilliant seasonal wildflowers. Tall peaks, picturesque plains and over 1000 species of native flora at Stirling Range National Park, 80 km NE. Historic town of Kendenup, 16 km N, location of WA's first gold find. **Visitor information:** Unit 6, Lot 622 Albany Hwy; (08) 9851 1163. Web site comswest.net.au/ ~mtbarkwa **See also:** The South-West p. 335; Western Wildflowers p. 364.

Mount Magnet　Pop. 747

MAP REF. 388 E2

The goldmining town of Mount Magnet, a popular stopping-place for motorists driving north to Port Hedland, is in a pastoral farming area 562 km from Perth on the Great Northern Hwy. There are spectacular wildflowers in the area in spring. **In town:** Heritage walk, 1.4 km, brochure available. Pastoral Museum, Hepburn St, has pioneering and mining artifacts. **In the area:** Tourist drive (37 km) includes views of old open-cut goldmine from lookout, and takes in features such as The Granites and various ghost towns; map available. Fossicking for gemstones, but take care as there are dangerous old mine shafts in the area. The Granites, 7 km N, has Aboriginal rock art and picnic spot nearby. Ghost town of Lennonville, 11 km N. Near Sandstone, 166 km E: The Brewery, a historic constructed cave formerly used for beer storage; London Bridge, a rock formation. **Visitor information:** Hepburn St; (08) 9963 4172.

Mullewa　Pop. 591

MAP REF. 388 B3

Gateway to the Murchison goldfields, Mullewa is 99 km NE of Geraldton. **In town:** Kembla Zoo, Stock Rd. In Maitland Rd: Our Lady of Mount Carmel Church; Monsignor John C. Hawes Priesthouse Museum. Water Supply Reserve, Lovers La., features native plants. Aug.: Wildflower Show; Agricultural Show. **In the area:** Mons. Hawes Heritage Trail (drive then walk), begins at signboard in Jose St and extends through the Mid-West and Murchison. Waterfalls after heavy rain, 5 km N near airport. Tallering Peak and Gorge, 58 km N, has spectacular wildflowers in spring. Bindoo Hill Glacier Bed, 40 km NW. Tenindewa Pioneer Well (1900s), a stone-lined well, 18 km W. Butterabby grave site, 18 km S, burial-place of Aborigines hanged there after clash with European settlers. St Mary's Agricultural School, 40 km SE near Tardun. Tallering Station, 40 km NE, has gallery featuring Aboriginal and other local art and craft, and accommodation and camping (open Apr.–Oct.). **Visitor information:** Jose St; (08) 9961 1505 (May–Nov.) or Shire Offices, cnr Padbury and Thomas sts; (08) 9961 1007.

Mundaring　Pop. 1912

MAP REF. 378 E4, 388 C8

Mundaring is situated on the Great Eastern Hwy, 34 km E of Perth. The picturesque Mundaring Weir is the water source for the goldfields 500 km to the east. The original dam was opened in 1903, and the original pumping station was used until 1955. The hilly bush setting makes the weir a popular picnic spot. **In town:** Fred Jacoby Park, Mundaring Weir Rd, has picnic/barbecue facilities. Sculpture Park, Jacoby St, with sculptures by WA artists. Arts Centre, Great Eastern Hwy, has program of varied exhibitions. Apr.: Mundaring Hills Festival. **In the area:** Several heritage trails, including Farming Heritage Trail and John Forrest Heritage Trail. Lake Leschenaultia, 12 km NW, for swimming and canoeing; walks, camping and picnic/barbecue facilities, and miniature scenic railway on shore. Walyunga National Park, 30 km NW, a beautiful bushland park and location for Avon Descent, a major whitewater canoeing event held Aug. Old Mahogany

Inn (1842), 3 km W, WA's oldest residential inn. Mount Olive Stained Glass Studio, 6 km W. John Forrest National Park, 6 km W, on high point of Darling Range; picnic spot beside natural pool at Rocky Pool. Quatre Sessions Heritage Rose Garden, 9 km W, one of State's largest private collections. At Darlington, 10 km W: Darling Estate Winery, Nelson Rd (open Thurs.–Sun.); Arts Festival held each Nov. At Mundaring Weir, 8 km S: C. Y. O'Connor Museum (1880s), housed in former pumphouse, depicts the mammoth project of connecting the weir to the goldfields; features models of pipeline. Nearby, Hills Forest Activity Centre offers activities such as abseiling and bushcraft, and performances by Aboriginal dance groups and bush bands (details at information centre). Kalamunda National Park, 23 km S, has walking trails through jarrah forest, including first section of the 950-km Bibbulmun Track. History Village, nearby at Kalamunda, a collection of historic buildings (open Sat.–Thurs.). Carosa Vineyard, 7 km E at Mt Helena (open Sat. and Sun.). **Visitor information:** 7225 Great Eastern Hwy; (08) 9295 0202. **See also:** Day Tours from Perth p. 328.

Nannup　Pop. 521

MAP REF. 379 G10, 382 A4, 386 C10, 388 C11

Nannup is in the Blackwood Valley, 290 km S of Perth. The surrounding countryside is lush, gently rolling pasture alongside jarrah and pine forests. **In town:** Heritage trail (2.5 km) and river walk, brochures available. In Brockman St: Old Police Station (1922), now information centre and surrounded by Blythe Family Gardens; Arboretum (planted 1926). In Warren Rd: art and craft centre; Bunnings Timber Mill, largest jarrah sawmill in State (tours Mon., Wed. and Fri.); Nannup Temptations and Crafty Creations, for jarrah goods; Country Mayde, for local craft; Old Templemore Antique Shop, converted historic house, specialises in antique tools; Gemstone Museum (closed Wed.). Blackwood Winery. Market 2nd Sat. each month, Warren Rd. Mar.: Music Festival. Aug.: Flower and Garden Month. **In the area:** Self-guide wildflower (in spring), waterfall (in winter) and forest walks; scenic drives through jarrah forest and pine plantations, including 40-km Blackwood Scenic Drive; brochures available. Blackwood River for canoeing and trout fishing. Hillbrook tulip farm, 1 km S (open July–Sept.). Carlotta Crustaceans marron farm, 14 km S off Vatte Hwy. Donnelly River Wines, 45 km S. Barrabup Pool, 10 km W, largest of a number of pools ideal for swimming and fishing. Tathra, 14 km NE, fruit winery and restaurant. **Visitor information:** 4 Brockman St; (08) 9756 1211. Web site richie.comp. west.net.au/~nannuptb

Narrogin   Pop. 4491

MAP REF. 386 G6, 388 E9
The centre of prosperous agricultural country, Narrogin is 192 km SE of Perth on the Great Southern Hwy. Sheep, pigs and cereal farms are the major industries. The town's name is derived from an Aboriginal word *Gnarojin*, meaning waterhole. **In town:** In Egerton St: History Hall, with local history collection; Courthouse Museum (1894), originally a school, later district courthouse (open Mon.–Sat. or by appt). Foxes Lair, Williams Rd, 45 ha of natural bushland. Lions Lookout, Kipling St, for excellent views. In Federal St: Gallery (open Feb.–Nov.); Restoration Group Museum, displays cars, stationary engines and other machinery (check opening times). Gnarojin Park, in town centre next to Narrogin Brook: picnic/barbecue facilities; pathway marked with 100 locally designed commemorative tiles relating to local history, brochure available. Jan.: State Gliding Championships. Oct.: Spring Festival; Agricultural Show; Orchid Show. **In the area:** Heritage trail, brochure available. Yilliminning and Birdwhistle rocks, 11 km E, unusual rock formations. Dryandra Woodland, 30 km NW, features walking trails and fauna including numbats and mallee fowl; 'Sounds of Dryandra' (tune into 100 FM for information at signposted 'radio stops'), features information on Aboriginal culture and local wildlife; map available. **Visitor information:** Egerton St; (08) 9881 2064.

New Norcia   Pop. 75

MAP REF. 386 D1, 388 C6
In 1846 Spanish Benedictine monks established a mission at New Norcia, 132 km N of Perth in the secluded Moore Valley, in an attempt to help the local Aboriginal population. The

Great Northern Highway near Newman

handsome Spanish-inspired buildings come as a surprise, surrounded by farms and bushland. New Norcia still operates as a monastery and is Australia's only monastic town. Visitors may join the monks at daily prayers. **In town:** Self-guide heritage trail (2 km), includes inspection of oldest operating flour mill in WA (1879) (mill has interpretive display), abbey church, cemetery, hotel (1927), Bishops Well, Rosendo Salvado Statue; or guided 2-hr tour of town; guide booklet available. Benedictine community's Museum and Art Gallery, Great Northern Hwy, has priceless religious art, both Australian and European, and Spanish artifacts (many the gifts of Queen Isabella of Spain); museum displays history of monks' involvement with local indigenous population; shop sells local food products, including olive oil pressed at the monastery. Group accommodation for up to 250 in old convent and college buildings (advance bookings required). Daily tours of monastery, including interiors. Salvado Restaurant, in Roadhouse, Great Northern Hwy, style resembles monastery refectory. **In the area:** At Mogumber, 24 km SW, one of State's highest timber and concrete bridges. Historic hotel at Bolgart, 49 km SE. Former Wyening Mission, 50 km SE, a historic site (open by appt, inquire at information centre). Piawaning, 31 km NE, has magnificent stand of eucalypts north of town. **Visitor information:** Museum and Art Gallery, Great Northern Hwy; (08) 9654 8056. Web site www. newnorcia. wa.edu.au

Newman   Pop. 4790

MAP REF. 390 D6
This town was built by Mt Newman Mining Co. for employees involved in the extraction of iron ore. Mt Newman ships its ore from Port Hedland; a 426-km railway connect the towns. In 1981 responsibility for the town was handed over to the local shire. **In town:** Mt Whaleback Mine, largest iron ore open-cut mine in world, tours depart from information centre Mon.–Sat. At information centre: BHP Iron Ore Silver Jubilee Museum and Gallery, mining museum. Radio Hill Lookout, off Newman Dr., good views over town; walking trail and climb from museum to lookout. Aug.: Camp Draft and Rodeo; Fortescue Festival. **In the area:** Opthalmia Dam, 15 km N, for swimming; picnic/barbecue facilities. Good views from Mt Newman, 20 km N. Kalgans Pool, 51 km NW (day trip, 4WD access only). Eagle Rock Falls, 69 km NW, has permanent pools and picnic spots nearby (road to falls requires 4WD). Aboriginal rock carvings, rock pools and waterholes at Punda (4WD only), 75 km NW, and Wanna Munna, 70 km W. **Visitor information:** cnr Fortescue Ave and Newman Dr.; (08) 9175 2888. **See also:** The Hamersley Range p. 367.

Norseman   Pop. 1516

MAP REF. 389 J8
Norseman, 195 km S of Kalgoorlie, is the last large town on the Eyre Hwy for travellers heading east towards SA. Gold put Norseman on the map in the early

1890s with one of the richest quartz reefs in Australia. The town is steeped in gold-mining history, reflected in its colossal tailings dumps. The area is popular with amateur prospectors and gemstone collectors; gemstone fossicking permits are available from information centre. **In town:** Historical Collection, Battery Rd, includes mining tools and household items. Heritage Mining Park, Prinsep St, open-plan park with displays, stream and picnic facilities. Post office (1896), cnr Prinsep and Ramsay sts. Heritage trail (33 km), follows Cobb & Co. route, including a graduated descent into the old Iron Duke Mine site. In Roberts St: statue commemorating horse called Norseman, who allegedly pawed the ground and unearthed a nugget of gold, thus starting a gold rush in area; Dollykissangel, toy museum. Beacon Hill Lookout, Mines Rd, offers good views of surrounding salt lakes (spectacular at sunrise and sunset). **In the area:** Dundas Rocks, 22 km S, over 2 million years old; excellent picnic area and old Dundas town site nearby. Bromus Dam, 32 km S, freshwater dam with picnic area nearby. Peak Charles, in Peak Charles National Park, 50 km S then 40 km W off hwy; energetic climbers are rewarded with magnificent views. Gemstone leases on Eyre Hwy and off Kalgoorlie Hwy. Mt Jimberlana, 5 km E of town, walking trail to summit and views. Buldania Rocks, 28 km E, has picnic area and beautiful spring wildflowers. To south-west, Frank Hann National Park, 50 km E of Lake King township, traversed by Lake King–Norseman Rd; check road conditions before departure; no visitor facilities or supplies between Norseman and Lake King. Cave Hill Nature Reserve, 55 km N, then 50 km W (on unsealed road, excercise care, especially when wet): spectacular granite outcrops, caves, waterholes, wildlife. **Visitor information:** 68 Roberts St; (08) 9039 1071. **See also:** Crossing the Nullarbor p. 348; The Goldfields p. 352.

Northam
Pop. 6300

MAP REF. 378 H2, 386 E3, 388 D7
The regional centre of the fertile Avon Valley at the junction of the Avon and Mortlock rivers, Northam is on the Great Eastern Hwy, 99 km E of Perth. Settled in 1836, it is now an important supply point for the eastern wheat belt and a major railway centre. **In town:** In Wellington St: Old police station (1866); courthouse

(1896); town hall (1897); Avon Valley Arts Society Gallery. Flour Mill (1871), Newcastle St. In Fitzgerald St: Old Railway Station Museum (open Sun.); Shamrock Hotel (1886), fully renovated. At information centre, Heaton Ave, WW II migrant exhibition. Footbridge over Avon River, adjacent to information centre, one of the longest swing bridges in Australia. White swans and much native birdlife can be seen between Peel Tce bridge and weir. Morby Cottage (1836), Old York Rd, Northam's first house, built by the pioneer Morrells (open Sun.). National Trust-classified Sir James Mitchell House (1905), cnr Duke and Hawes sts. Northam–Katrine Heritage Trail, history of early settlers in town, brochure available. Aug.: Avon Descent (white-water classic); Avon River Festival. Oct.: Multicultural Festival. **In the area:** Muresk University of Technology, 10 km S, former early farming property. Hot-air ballooning Apr.–Nov., Northam Airfield, 2 km NE. At Dowerin, 58 km NE: museum; craft centre; Hagbooms Lake; Field Days here in Aug. In spring, wild-flowers abound near Wubin, 190 km N. Avonlea Alpaca Tourist Farm, 12 km NW (check opening times). Aronbrook Valley Winery at Clackline, 19 km NE, open for tastings by appt. **Visitor information:** Heaton Ave; (08) 9622 2100. Web site www.avon.net.au/tourism/northam/~index.htm

Northampton
Pop. 842

MAP REF. 388 A3
Northampton is a heritage-listed town nestled among gentle hills in the valley of Nokarena Brook, 51 km N of Geraldton. Inland there is picturesque country with vivid wildflowers in spring. The drive west leads to the coast, with beaches for swimming and fishing. **In town:** Heritage Walk, brochure available. In Hampton Rd: Chiverton House Museum (open Thurs.–Mon.); Old Convent, now heritage accommodation, and Church of Our Lady in Ara Coeli, designed by Mons. Hawes. Gwalla church site and cemetery, Gwalla St. Miners' cottages (1860s), Brook St. Market at Kings Park, cnr Essex St and Hampton Rd, 1st Sat. each month. Sept.: Agricultural Show. Oct.: Airing of the Quilts Festival Day (quilts hung in main street, raffle and judging). **In the area:** Wildflower tours in spring. Alma School House (1915), 12 km N. Near coast at Port Gregory, 47 km NW: Lynton Station, including ruins of labour-hiring depot for convicts (in use 1853–56); Lynton House,

(not open to public), a squat building with slits for windows, probably erected as protection from hostile Aborigines; Sanford House (1853). Hutt Lagoon, near Port Gregory, appears pink in midday sun. At Horrocks Beach, 20 km W, pleasant bays, sandy beaches, good fishing and surfing. **Visitor information:** Hampton Rd; (08) 9934 1488.

Northcliffe
Pop. 239

MAP REF. 382 C9, 386 D12, 388 D12
Magnificent virgin karri forests surround the little township of Northcliffe, 31 km S of Pemberton in the extreme south-west corner of the State. Unique flora and fauna is found in this area. **In town:** In Wheatley Coast Rd: Pioneer Museum, has historical relics and photographs; at information centre, large rock and mineral collection, Aboriginal Interpretation Room, and photographic folio of native flora and birds; Northcliffe Art and Craft. South West Timber Trekking Company, off Wheatley Coast Rd, offers horseriding along forest tracks. Mountain bike hire, contact information centre. Oct.: Mountain Bike Championship. **In the area:** Pemberton Tramway, tram-cars based on 1907 Fremantle trams operate daily in summer through tall-forest country between Northcliffe and Pemberton; depart from information centre. Adjacent to town, Forest Park has Hollow Butt Karri and Twin Karri walking trails, and picnic areas. Warren River, 8 km N, trout fishing and sandy beaches. Petrene Estate Vineyard, 2 km E, has cellar-door sales. Mt Chudalup, 10 km S, a giant granite outcrop with walking trail to summit for views. Point D'Entre-casteaux, 27 km S; cliffs popular with rock climbers. Windy Harbour and Salmon Beach, 29 km S. Bibbulmun Track links the three national parks: D'Entrecasteaux (5 km S), Warren (20 km NW) and Shannon (30 km E). Great Forest Tree Drive through Shannon National Park, east of town; picnic spots and signposted walks in park, brochure available. Boorara Tree (once a fire lookout) and Lane-Poole Falls, 18 km SE. **Visitor information:** Wheatley Coast Rd; (08) 9776 7203.

Onslow
Pop. 588

MAP REF. 387 D3
Onslow, on the north-west coast, is the base for off-shore gas and oil fields. The town was originally at the Ashburton River mouth, but was moved to Beadon

Karri forest near Northcliffe

Bay in 1925 after constant cyclones caused the river to silt up. Onslow was a bustling pearling centre and in the 1890s gold was discovered. During WW II, US, British and Dutch submarines refuelled here, and the town was bombed twice. In 1952 it was the mainland base for Britain's nuclear experiments at Montebello Islands. **In town:** Ian Blain Memorial Walkway, a signposted scenic walk; map available. Heritage trail, brochure available. Goods Shed Museum, Second Ave, items of historical interest. Karijini Aboriginal Corporation, Third Ave, art gallery. **In the area:** Remains of old town site, 48 km SW, brochure available. Excellent fishing; boat charters to Mackerel and Montebello islands June–Sept. Native fauna, including emus, red kangaroos, sand goannas and a variety of birdlife. The Sturt desert pea and Ashburton pea are among the many wildflowers that bloom in spring. Termite mounds, 10 km S on Onslow Access Rd, with interpretive display. **Visitor information:** Second Ave; (08) 9184 6644. **See also:** The Hamersley Range p. 367.

Pemberton   Pop. 994

MAP REF. 382 C7, 386 D11, 388 C11
Pemberton, 335 km S of Perth, is in a quiet valley surrounded by towering karri forests with some of the tallest hardwood trees in the world and, in spring, brilliant flowering plants. Pemberton is known as a centre for high-quality woodcraft. **In town:** Craft outlets include Peter Kovacsy Studio in Jamieson St; Fine Woodcraft Gallery, Dickinson St. In Brockman St: Karri Visitors Centre, includes museum with collection of historic photographs and forestry equipment, and Karri Forest Discovery Centre; Pemberton Sawmill, tours Mon.–Fri. Pemberton Tramway, tramcars based on 1907 Fremantle trams, operate daily through tall-forest country between Pemberton and Northcliffe; depart from railway station, Railway Cres.; steam train Easter–Nov., runs weekends and holidays. On Pump Hill Rd: Forest Park and Pool, offers walking trails and picnic spots; Trout and Marron Hatchery, supplies WA rivers and dams, tours available. **In the area:** Forest Industry tours into logging and regrowth areas; walking trails; scenic bus tours; 4WD adventure tours; horseriding; fishing in rivers (inland fishing licence required for trout and marron); self-guide forest drives. Tours of wineries: Warren Vineyard, Conte Rd; Gloucester Ridge, Burma Rd; Mountford Wines, Bamess Rd; Salitage, Vasse Hwy. Moon's Crossing, 18 km SE, for picnics (4WD access in winter). In Gloucester National Park, 1 km S: The Cascades for picnics, bushwalking and fishing; Gloucester Tree, signposted off Brockman St, tallest fire lookout in world (over 61 m high with 153 rungs spiralling upwards), open for climbing during daylight hours. Brockman Saw Pit, 13 km S, restored to show timber-sawing in 1860s. King Trout Farm, 8 km SW. Warren National Park, 9 km SW, includes some of best accessible virgin karri forest, also Marianne North Tree (tree was subject of painting by artist) and Dave Evans Bicentennial Tree, lookout tree with picnic facilities and walking tracks nearby. Eagle Springs marron farm, 18 km W. Nearby, Beedelup National Park, features falls, suspension bridge, magnificent wildflowers in spring and a giant karri tree with a hole cut through it. Donnelly River Wines, 35 km NW. Lavender and Berry Farm, 4 km N, off Vasse Hwy. Big Brook Dam and Arboretum, 7 km N. Founders Forest, 10 km N on Smiths Rd, has karri re-growth trees over 120 years old. Rosebank Cottage Crafts, 4 km NE, off Vasse Hwy. Piano Gully Vineyard, 24 km NE, off South Western Hwy. **Visitor information:** Karri Visitors Centre, Brockman St; (08) 9776 1133, freecall 1800 671 133. Web site www. pemberton.tourist.com.au **See also:** The South-West p. 335.

Perenjori   Pop. 600

MAP REF. 388 C4
Located on the Wubin–Mullewa Hwy, 352 km NE of Perth, Perenjori is on the fringes of the Murchison goldfields and the great sheep stations of the west. **In town:** Historical Museum and Tourist Bureau, Fowler St (open July–Oct., closed Sun.). Historic Catholic Church, Carnamah Rd, designed by Mons. Hawes. Aug.: Bush Bouquet Craft Festival. Sept.: Agricultural Show. **In the area:** Wildflowers in season (July–Sept.).

Western Wildflowers

Parakeelya near Cue

The sandplains, swamps, flats, scrub and woodlands of south-western Australia light up with colour in spring as the 'wildflower State' puts on its brilliant display. The plains can become carpeted, almost overnight, with the gold of everlastings or feather flowers, or the red and pinks of boronia and leschenaultia. The banksia bushes throw up their red and yellow cylinders along the coast and in the woodlands, grevilleas spill their flowers down to the ground and orchids proliferate. Flowering gums on the south coast become a mass of red and the felty kangaroo paws invade the plains.

There are over 9000 named species and 2000 unnamed species of wildflowers in Western Australia, giving the State one of the richest floras in the world. Around 75 per cent of them are unique to the region, although they may have family connections with other plants of northern or eastern Australia. Isolation by the barrier of plain and desert that separates the west from the eastern States has caused plants on both sides to pursue their own evolution; some families of plants are unique to the west.

On even a short trip to Perth, visitors can see a wide variety of Western Australian wildflowers. At King's Park close to the city, wildflower species give a brilliant display between August and October. Visitors in any part of the south-west at that time will see wildflowers all around them. Only 25 kilometres east of Perth on the Great Eastern Highway is **John Forrest National Park**, on the edge of the Darling Range escarpment. On these undulating hills and valleys the undergrowth of the jarrah forest is rich in flowering plants; red and green kangaroo paw, swamp river myrtle, blue leschenaultia and pink calytrix are the most common. Fifty kilometres north of Perth is **Yanchep National Park**, a place of coastal limestone and sandy plains, covered with wildflowers.

There are many places further north that are worth visiting; one is **Kalbarri National Park**, 670 kilometres north of Perth, at the mouth of the Murchison River. The park contains magnificent flowering trees and shrubs of banksia, grevillea and melaleuca, while the ground beneath is covered with many species, such as leschenaultia, twine rushes and sedges. Further inland, after good rains in spring, the old goldfields around **Cue** are rich with parakeelya and blue pincushions.

Prolific displays of wildflowers can also be found throughout the wheat belt, forests and sandplains of the south-west. Dryandra Woodland, near **Narrogin** in the south-west, has magnificent woodlands of wandoo and powderbark, with brown mallet and bush thickets. An important sanctuary for the mallee fowl and numbat, this forest contains a number of species of dryandra.

Another interesting area of Western Australia is **Stirling Range National Park**, 450 kilometres south of Perth and near the Porongurup Range. There are banksias here, as well as dryandra, cone bushes, cats paws and a number of mountain bells, which have red or pink flower heads. The bare granite domes and the boulders of the Porongurup Range tower over slopes of karri and flowering trees such as B*anksia grandis* and creepers such as the native clematis.

There are many coastal parks around **Albany**. **Torndirrup National Park** is an area of coastal hills and cliffs and such scenic features as the Gap, the Blowhole and the Natural Bridge. In the stunted, windswept coastal vegetation there are many wildflowers, including the endemic giant-coned *Banksia praemorsa* and the Western Australian Christmas tree with its brilliant orange flowers.

Twenty-five kilometres east of Albany is the peaceful and beautiful Two Peoples Bay Nature Reserve, which has thickets of mallee, banksia and peppermint, together with many flowering shrubs and plants. Along the coast west of Albany is **Walpole–Nornalup National Park**, where dense karri forest mingles with red tingle, jarrah, marri, casuarina and banksia trees, and many wildflowers including the kangaroo paw, the potato orchid and the babe-in-cradle orchid.

Although most wildflowers occur in the south-west of the State, northern areas also have displays peculiar to climatic changes and times of rainfall. While enjoying Western Australia's brilliant native flora, visitors should remember that wildflowers are protected under the State's *Native Flora Protection Act 1950*.

For further information on national parks and wildflower display areas, contact the Western Australian Tourist Centre; (08) 9483 1111, freecall 1300 361 351 or the Department of Conservation and Land Management, 50 Hayman Rd, Como (Locked Bag 104, Bentley Delivery Centre, WA 6983); (08) 9334 0333. Web site www.calm.wa.gov.au
See also: National Parks p. 336 and individual entries in A–Z town listing for parks and towns in bold type.

Numerous scenic drives, brochures available. Perenjori–Rothsay Heritage Trail (180 km), recalls early goldmining days. Many gemstones for fossickers in this mineral-rich region. Goldmines in surrounding area (4WD access only); take care as unfenced pits make the area dangerous. Aboriginal Stones at Damperwah Soak, 40 km NE (4WD access only). Salt lakes with variety of waterbirds, including Mongers Lake (lookout near lake), 50 km NE. **Visitor information:** Fowler St (July–Oct.); (08) 9973 1105.

Pingelly   Pop. 756

MAP REF. 386 F5, 388 D9

On the Great Southern Hwy, 154 km SE of Perth, Pingelly is part of the central southern farming district. The cutting of sandalwood was once a local industry, but today sheep and wheat are the major produce. **In town:** In Parade St: Community Craft Centre; Courthouse Museum. Apex Lookout, Stone St, for fine views of town and country. Mar.: Autumn Alternative Agricultural Show. Aug.: Art and Tulip Festival. **In the area:** Moorumbine Heritage Trail, 1-hr walk through old town of Moorumbine. Historic St Patrick's Church (1873), 10 km E at Moorumbine. Tuttanning Flora and Fauna Reserve, 21 km E. Pingelly Heights Observatory, 4 km SE. **Visitor information:** Shire Offices, 17 Queen St; (08) 9887 1066.

Pinjarra   Pop. 1892

MAP REF. 378 C10, 386 C6, 388 C9

Pinjarra is a pleasant drive 84 km S of Perth along the shaded South Western Hwy. The town has a picturesque setting on the Murray River in one of the earliest established districts in WA. The Alcoa Refinery, north-east of town on the South Western Hwy, is the largest alumina refinery in Australia. **In town:** Pinjarrah Heritage Trail, 30-min river walk featuring historic sites and buildings. In Henry St: St John's Church (1862), made of mud bricks; Heritage Rose Garden, including war memorial; Liveringa (1874), early home of McLarty family; Old School (1896); Teacher's House. Edenvale (1888), George St, house built by McLarty family, now restored and housing information centre, arts and crafts and tearoom. Suspension bridge across the Murray River, picnic facilities

on either side. **In the area:** Hotham Valley Tourist Railway, steam-train rides Pinjarra–Dwellingup each Wed. May–Oct. Alcoa Scarp Lookout, 14 km E, for good views of coastal plain, surrounding farming area and Alcoa Refinery. Athlone Angora Stud and Goat Farm, 16 km E. Alcoa Refinery, 4 km NE (bus tours Wed.). At North Dandalup, 10 km NE, Whittakers Mill, for bushwalking, camping and barbecues. North Dandalup Dam, 16 km N then 6 km E: coastal views from lookout; recreation lake and picnic area. Award-winning Tumbulgum Farm, 38 km N at Mundijong, features native and farm animals, Aboriginal culture, farm shows and WA products sales. Old Blythewood (1860s), 4 km S, a former post office, coaching inn and family home (check opening times). Lake Navarino Forest Resort and Waroona Dam, 33 km S, for water sports, fishing, walking and horseriding. **Visitor information:** Edenvale, George St; (08) 9531 1438. **See also:** The South-West p. 335.

Port Hedland   Pop. 12 846

MAP REF. 390 C1, 392 B13

Port Hedland's remarkable growth has been due to the iron ore boom, which started in the early 1960s. The town was named after Captain Peter Hedland, who reached the harbour in 1863. Today Port Hedland handles the largest iron ore export tonnage of any Australian port. Iron ore from some of the world's biggest mines is loaded on to huge ore carriers. The 2.6-km-long trains operated by BHP Iron Ore arrive nine times daily. Salt production is another major industry, with about 2 million tonnes exported per annum. **In town:** Self-guide historic town walk/drive, brochure available. Town tour Mon., Wed., Fri., numbers permitting. Observation Tower, at information centre, Wedge St. Lions Park, cnr Athol and Darlots sts, has pioneer relics. BHP industrial tours (Mon.–Fri.); book at information centre. Don Rhodes Mining Museum, Wilson St. At Two Mile Ridge, opp. fire brigade in Wilson St, Aboriginal carvings in limestone ridge (obtain key from Aboriginal Affairs, open Mon.–Fri.). Historic St Matthew's Church (1917), Edgar St, view by appt. Old Port Hedland cemetery, Stevens St, has graves of early gold prospectors and

Japanese pearl divers. Markets, Wedge St, 2nd Fri. each month (evenings). Aug.: Spinifex Spree. Late June–early July: Black Rock Stakes and Pub to Port (wheelbarrow race, stalls and street party). **In the area:** Stairway to the Moon, a natural wonder, when full moon rises over shoreline at low tide; best alongside caravan park at Cooke Point. Picnic, fish and swim at Pretty Pool, next to Cooke Point Caravan Park. (Poisonous stone fish frequent coast, especially Nov.–Mar.; make local inquiries before swimming in sea.) At Cargill Salt, 8 km S, giant cone-shaped mounds of salt awaiting export. At airport, 15 km S: Royal Flying Doctor Base, open to public 9 a.m.–1 p.m. Mon.–Fri.; School of the Air, visitors welcome, a.m. only. Whale-watching trips June–Oct.; scenic harbour and sunset cruises. Excellent fishing; charter boat hire. Birdlife is abundant; watch for bustards, eagles, herons, cockatoos, galahs, ibises, pelicans and a variety of parrots. **Visitor information:** 13 Wedge St; (08) 9173 1711. **See also:** The Hamersley Range p. 367.

Ravensthorpe   Pop. 354

MAP REF. 388 H10

Ravensthorpe, situated 533 km SE of Perth, is the centre of the Phillips River Goldfield. Copper mining was also important here, reaching a peak in the late 1960s; the last copper mine shut in 1972. Many old mine shafts can be seen around the district. Wheat, sheep and mixed farming are the local industries. **In town:** Historic buildings: Anglican Church, Dunn St; Old Mine Manager's House, Carlisle St. In Morgans St: Dance Cottage (museum); Palace Hotel; restored Commercial Hotel (now Community Centre). Also in Morgans St, Rangeview Park features local plant species. Sept.: Wildflower Show, features over 700 local species; Spring Festival. **In the area:** Scenic drives, brochures available. Rock-collecting, check locally to avoid trespass. Ravensthorpe Range, 3 km N, and Mt Desmond, 10 km SE, for views. WA Time Meridian at first rest bay west of town. Eremia Camel Farm, 2 km SE, offers rides and bush tucker. Fitzgerald River National Park, 46 km S, now Biosphere Reserve for UNESCO. Old copper smelter, 3 km SE. **Visitor information:** Morgans St; (08) 9838 1277. Web site www.wn.com.au/ ourstate/goldfields.htm

Rockingham   Pop. 49 917

MAP REF. 378 B7, 386 C4, 388 C8

At the southern end of Cockburn Sound, 47 km S of Perth, Rockingham is a coastal city and seaside destination. Established in 1872 as a timber port, the harbour fell into disuse with the opening of the Fremantle inner harbour in 1897. Today its magnificent golden beaches and protected waters are Rockingham's main attraction. **In town:** Museum, Kent St, features local history exhibits. Lookout and WW II coastal battery at Cape Peron, Point Peron Rd. In Civic Blvd.: Art Gallery; Art and Craft Centre. The Granary, Rockingham Rd, northern outskirts of town, displays history of WA's grain industry; tours by appt). At nearby Kwinana Beach: hull of wrecked SS *Kwinana*; jetskiing (jetskis for hire). Markets Sun., Flinders La. Nov.: Spring Festival. Dec.: Christmas Regatta; Cockburn Yachting Regatta. **In the area:** Old Rockingham and Rockingham–Jarrahdale heritage trails. Penguin Island, has a colony of little (fairy) penguins; Penguin Experience Island Discovery Centre (open Sept.–May). Mersey Point Jetty at Shoalwater, departure point for cruises and island tours. Three Island Tour to Penguin, Seal and Bird islands. Garden Island, home to HMAS *Stirling*, naval base; access by private boat during the day (causeway link to mainland closed to public). Offshore reefs and wrecks, popular with dive enthusiasts; diving excursions and cruises available. Shoalwater Bay Islands Marine Park, extends from just south of Garden Island to Becher Point; cruises of park, including swim with dolphin tours (Oct.–May). Near Lake Richmond, 4 km SW, walks, freshwater flora and fauna, and domed thrombalites (unlayered stromatolites). Sloan's Cottage (1911), 2 km W at Leda, restored pioneer cottage (open Mon.–Fri.). Marapana Wildlife World, 15 km S, drive-through deer and wildlife park. Wineries: Baldivis Estate, 15 km SE; Peel Estate, 17 km SE. Scenic drive 48 km SE to Serpentine Dam, WA's major water conservation area; noted for brilliant wildflowers in spring, gardens and bushland; nearby, Serpentine Falls. WA Water Ski Park, at Baldivis, 5 km E, constructed water-ski complex. Self-guide Nature Reserve Environmental Walk, nearby at Karnup; brochure available. Tumbleggum Farm, 29 km E at

Mundijong: Aboriginal culture; native and farm animals; farm shows; WA product sales. **Visitor information:** 43 Kent St; (08) 9592 3464.

Roebourne   Pop. 958

MAP REF. 387 G1, 390 A2

Named after John Septimus Roe, the State's first surveyor-general, Roebourne was established 1864 and is the oldest town on the north-west coast. It was developed as the north-west's capital and was once the administrative hub for the area north of Murchison River. As the centre for the early mining and pastoral industries in the Pilbara, it was connected, by tramway, to the pearling port of Cossack, and later to Point Samson, for the transport of passengers and goods. **In town:** Old stone buildings (some National Trust-classified): police station, Queen St; post office (1887), Sholl St; in Hampton St, hospital (1887) and courthouse (1887); Holy Trinity Church (1894), Withnell St; in Roe St, Union Bank (1889) and Victoria Hotel (1866), last of town's five original pubs; Old Roebourne Gaol (1886), Queen St, now information centre and museum. Good views from Mt Welcome, Fisher Dr. Aug.: Royal Show; Roebourne Cup and Ball. **In the area:** Emma Withnell Heritage Trail (52 km), historical drive taking in Roebourne, Cossack and Point Samson; brochure available. Wickham, 12 km N, Robe River Iron Associates company town: processes and exports Pannawonnica iron ore; tour of plant, port (at Cape Lambert) and historic Cossack departs from information centre, bookings essential. Wickham Expo here in May. Cossack (once called Tien Tsin), 14 km N: first port in the north-west; ghost town, but almost completely restored; historic buildings (open Apr.–Christmas); interesting cemetery; boat hire; Cossack Art Awards held July. Point Samson, 19 km N: good swimming, fishing and skindiving; fishing trawlers moored here; boat ramp; boat hire and fishing charter; offshore game-fishing. Fishing at Cleaverville, 25 km N. Millstream Springs, 150 km S, former camel watering holes, now offer safe swimming in freshwater springs; walking trails nearby; old homestead now information centre. **Visitor information:** Old Gaol, Queen St; (08) 9182 1060. **See also:** The Hamersley Range p. 367.

Southern Cross   Pop. 1147

MAP REF. 388 G7

A small, flourishing town on the Great Eastern Hwy, 368 km E of Perth, Southern Cross is the centre of a prosperous agricultural and pastoral area and a significant gold-producing area. The town's wide streets were designed to allow camel trains to turn, and were named after stars and constellations. **In town:** First courthouse in eastern goldfields (1893), Antares St, now a history museum. Other historic buildings: post office (1891), Antares St; Railway Tavern (1890s), Spica St. Restored Palace Hotel (1912), Orion St. Sept.: Agricultural Show. **In the area:** Wildflowers on sandplains in spring. Goldmining activities at Marvel Loch, 35 km S; Bullfinch, 36 km N. Hunt's Soak, 7 km N, a picnic area. Koolyanobbing, 52 km N, built for miners extracting iron ore; mining of the rich iron ore recommenced in 1994 following closure in 1983. Interesting rock formations with adjacent areas ideal for picnics at Frog Rock (30 km S), and Baladjie Rock (50 km NW). **Visitor information:** Shire Offices, Antares St; (08) 9049 1001. **See also:** Crossing the Nullarbor p. 348.

Tom Price   Pop. 3872

MAP REF. 387 H4, 390 B5

The huge iron-ore deposit now known as Mt Tom Price was discovered in 1962, after which the Hamersley Iron Project was established. A mine, two towns (Dampier and Tom Price) and a railway between the towns all followed quickly. Today the town is an oasis in the dry countryside. The nearby Karijini National Park, and a chance to tour an open-cut mining operation, make the town a popular stopping-place. Aug.: Nameless Festival. **In the area:** Hamersley Iron open-cut iron ore mine, tours departing from information centre, Central Rd. In Karijini National Park, 50 km E: Dales Gorge, with permanent waterfalls; Kalamina Gorge and Pool, the most accessible gorge; Joffre, Hancock, Weano and Red gorges join below Oxer Lookout; Hamersley Gorge, with permanent pools for swimming and coloured folds in rock; trail with interpretive signs on Aboriginal heritage and flora and fauna winds up to Mt Bruce. *To the north-east is Wittenoom, no longer habitable as there is still a significant health risk from microscopic asbestos fibres created by the milling process at the asbestos mine*

The Hamersley Range

Stretching over 300 kilometres through the heart of the mineral-rich Pilbara, the Hamersley Range forms a rugged, wild and enticing landscape.

The mountains slope gently up from the south to the flat-topped outcrops and Western Australia's highest peak, Mt Meharry. In the north they rise majestically from golden spinifex plains.

The iron-ore boom in the area has created employment opportunities in this land of sand spinifex, mulga scrub and massive red mountains. Model mining-company towns have sprung up. Gardens, swimming pools, golf courses and communal activities help compensate for the isolation and harsh climate.

Dampier, on King Bay, is a modern iron-ore company town, with a major salt industry nearby. Offshore is the North West Shelf Gas Project, which is the largest single resource development undertaken in Australia; it includes a 1500-kilometre pipeline. Another side to the town is the Dampier Archipelago, comprising 42 islands of which 25 are incorporated into flora and fauna reserves. Fishing, diving, swimming, boating, camping and bushwalking are allowed around and on several of these outcrops.

Roebourne, the oldest town in the north-west, has been a centre for the pastoral, copper and pearling industries. The old pearling port of Cossack is nearby. To the south, the fishing village of **Onslow** and its offshore islands is the perfect holiday retreat. **Karratha** is a modern town and regional centre, as is Wickham. Wickham's port at Cape Lambert has the tallest and second-longest open-ocean wharf in Australia, standing 18.5 metres above water and 3 kilometres long. At **Port Hedland**, streamlined port facilities cope with more iron ore tonnage than any other port in the country. Ore mined inland at Tom Price, Newman, Paraburdoo and other centres is railed on giant trains to the ports for export.

Fishing in the Port Hedland area is good, with many world records being set. Swimming in the sea can be dangerous, because sharks, sea snakes and poisonous stone fish frequent the waters; always make local inquiries before you swim. **Marble Bar**, considered to be the hottest place in Australia and keeping alive the tradition of the great Australian outback, is 200 kilometres south-east of Port Hedland.

Although the main activity in the area is centred on the mining towns of **Tom Price**, Paraburdoo, **Newman** and others, visitors will find many other areas of interest. Spectacular gorges have been carved by watercourses, some with wide, crystal-clear pools. Lush green vegetation thrives and the gorges are cool oases in the harsh climate.

Tom Price is a good base from which to explore the beauty of the Hamersley Range, in particular, **Karijini National Park**. The breathtaking Dales Gorge is 45 kilometres long. Fortescue Falls and Hamersley Gorge with its folded bands of coloured rock, are other highlights of the park.

One particularly enchanting oasis in the Hamersley Range area is **Millstream–Chichester National Park**, on the Fortescue River, inland

Iron ore mined at Tom Price being railed to the coast for export

from Roebourne. Thousands of birds flock to this delightful spot, where ferns, lilies, palms and rushes grow in abundance. There are two long, deep, natural pools. The springs produce over 36 million litres of water a day from an underground basin, which is piped to Roebourne, Dampier, Karratha, Wickham and Cape Lambert. In contrast to Karijini National Park, the scenery in Millstream–Chichester National Park varies from magnificent views over the coastal plain to the deep permanent river pools of tropical Millstream. This attractive spot offers excellent swimming conditions and pleasant camping areas.

The Hamersley Range is rugged, exciting country, and is enticing and often beautiful. Keep in mind, however, that you are travelling in remote areas. Read the section on Outback Motoring p. 603 before departure. Old roads are being improved and new ones constructed in an effort to open up one of the oldest landscapes in the world.

For further information contact Tom Price Tourist Bureau, Central Rd, Tom Price; (08) 9188 1112. Web site address www.pilbara.com **See also:** National Parks p. 336 and individual entries in A–Z town listing for parks and towns in bold type. **Map references:** 387 G3, 390 A4.

Ironstone rocks and spinifex in the Hamersley Range

Valley of the Giants Tree Top Walk, near Walpole

which was closed in 1966. Some mine tailings potentially dangerous especially around old Wittenoom township and Wittenoom Gorge; entry to this area is strongly discouraged. Kings Lake, 2 km W, constructed lake; nearby, park with picnic/barbecue facilities. Remarkable views of district around Tom Price from Mt Nameless Lookout, 6 km W, via walking trail or 4WD track. Aboriginal carvings, 10 km S. **Visitor information:** Central Rd; (08) 9188 1112. Web site www.pilbara.com **See also:** The Hamersley Range p. 367.

Toodyay   Pop. 674

MAP REF. 378 G1, 386 E2, 388 D7
The National Trust-classified town of Toodyay is nestled in the Avon Valley, 85 km NE of Perth, and surrounded by picturesque farming country and virgin bushland. **In town:** Many historic buildings in or near Stirling Tce,

particularly Stirling House (1908), now tearooms, and Toodyay Antiques. Connor's Mill (1870s), now housing information centre, displays a steam-driven flour mill, still in working order. In Clinton St: Old Newcastle Gaol Museum (1865), where infamous bushranger Moondyne Joe was imprisoned; police stables (1870), opposite, convict-built with random rubble stone. Duidgee Park, Harper Rd, popular picnic spot on riverbank, has miniature railway and walking track. Pelham Reserve Lookout, Duke St. Market, Stirling Tce, each Sat. May: Moondyne (colonial and convict) Festival. **In the area:** Windmill Hill Cutting, 6 km SE, deepest railway cutting in Australia. Coorinja Winery, 4 km S, dates from 1870 (open Mon.–Sat.). Hoddywell Archery and Caravan Park, 8 km S. Emu farm, 15 km SW, one of the oldest in Australia. Enchantmentland, 4 km W on Beaufort Rd: dioramic

nursery-rhyme display in 2-acre garden; Australiana; dolls' houses and gifts. Trout farm, 12 km SW, offers fishing and sales. Avon Valley National Park, 25 km SW, for spectacular scenery, seasonal wildflowers and wildlife-watching; Avon Descent, a white-water canoe race, held here in Aug. Cartref Park, 16 km NW, 2 ha of English gardens and landscaped native plants with prolific birdlife. **Visitor information:** Connor's Mill, Stirling Tce; (08) 9574 2435. Web site www.avon.net.au/~toodyay

Wagin   Pop. 1337

MAP REF. 386 G8, 388 E10
The prosperous countryside around Wagin supports grain crops, and pastures for sheep, cattle and emu. Located 177 km E of Bunbury, Wagin is an important railway-junction town. **In town:** Wagin Historical Village, Kitchener St, has huge collection of early pioneer artifacts set in 20 authentic old buildings. Heritage trails through historical village or fine Victorian buildings and shopfronts in Tudhoe and Tudor sts. Giant Ram (7 m high), Arthur River Rd, in park with ponds and waterfalls. Regular horse-trotting meets at Trotting Grounds, Kitchener St. Mar.: Woolorama, attended by sheep farmers nation-wide, attracts more than 28 000 people. June: Foundation Day. **In the area:** Corralyn Emu Farm, 4 km N. Mt Latham, 6 km W, for bushwalking and summit views. Puntapin, 6 km SE, a rock formation used as water catchment; wildflowers abound in spring. Lake Norring (intermittent), 13 km SE, for swimming, sailing and water-skiing. Lake Dumbleyung, 18 km E, where Donald Campbell established new world water-speed record in 1964; swimming, boating, birdwatching. At Dumbleyung, 40 km E, signposted bush trails. At Kukerin, 79 km E: Tracmach Vintage Fair Sept.–Oct. Wheatbelt Wildflower Drive, includes Tarin Rock Nature Reserve. **Visitor information:** Shire Offices, Arthur Rd; (08) 9861 1177 or Wagin Historical Village, Showgrounds, Kitchener St; (08) 9861 1232. **See also:** The South-West p. 335.

Walpole   Pop. 337

MAP REF. 382 G12, 386 F13, 388 D12
The forest meets the sea at Walpole. Trees in the surrounding Walpole–Nornalup National Park include karri, jarrah and

the giant red tingle. The region is known for its wildflowers in season as well as its wildlife. **In town:** Pioneer Cottage in Pioneer Park, South Coast Hwy, opened 1987 to commemorate district pioneers; cottage follows design of early pioneer homes. Daily ferry trips on Nornalup Inlet, depart jetty off Boronia Ave. Houseboat hire, Boronia St. Oct.: Wildflower Week. **In the area:** Coalmine Beach Heritage Trail; Knoll Drive, 3 km E. At Walpole–Nornalup National Park: Valley of the Giants, 16 km E, famous for its Tree Top Walk, 38 m above the forest floor, and a boardwalk through a grove of veteran tingle trees known as the Ancient Empire. Giant Tingle Tree, off Hilltop Rd, 8 km SE; Circular Pool, on Frankland River, 11 km NE. Thurlby Herb Farm, 13 km N, features herb gardens, herbal produce, tearooms. Mt Frankland National Park, 29 km N. Fernhook Falls, 32 km NW. For bushwalkers, Nuyts Wilderness area, 7 km W, and other walking trails. Ocean, river and inlet for anglers. Peaceful Bay, 28 km SE. **Visitor information:** Pioneer Cottage, Pioneer Park; (08) 9840 1111. **See also:** National Parks p. 336; Western Wildflowers p. 364.

Wanneroo   Pop. 9864

MAP REF. 378 B3, 388 C8
Just a short drive from Perth, the district around Wanneroo stretches along 50 km of varied coastline. **In town:** Botanic Golf, Burns Beach Rd, tee off in a botanical garden. **In the area:** On West Coast Dr. at Hillarys Boat Harbour: Underwater World, with submerged tunnel, touch pool and Microworld display; whale-watch tours (Sept.–Nov.). In Prindiville Dr., 8 km S: Gumnut Factory, craft outlet and Gumnut Land Model Village Railway; Wanneroo Weekend Markets, Wangara, 8 km S, huge market in carnival-like atmosphere Sat. and Sun. In Wanneroo Rd, Conti Estate Wine Cellars. Cameleer Park Camel Farm, 10 km NE, has camel rides. Carabooda Estate Wines, 20 km N. **Visitor information:** Gumnut Factory, 30 Prindiville Dr., Wangara; (08) 9409 6699.

Wickepin   Pop. 249

MAP REF. 386 G6, 388 E9
Wickepin dates from the 1890s, when the first European settlers arrived. The town is set in farming country, 214 km SE of Perth. Albert Facey's autobiography *A Fortunate*

Life details much of Wickepin's pioneering lifestyle. **In town:** Good examples of Edwardian architecture in Wogolin Rd. Nov.: Art and Craft Show (even-numbered years). **In the area:** Wildflowers in spring. Albert Facey Heritage Trail, brochure available from Wickepin Shire Council. Toolibin Lake Reserve, 20 km S, has wide variety of waterfowl. Malyalling Rock, 15 km NE, unusual rock formation. Tiny town of Yealering, and Yealering Lake, 30 km NE. Sewell's Rock Nature Reserve, 44 km NE via Yealering, ideal for picnics and nature walks. **Visitor information:** Newsagency and Milkbar, 28 Wogolin Rd; (08) 9888 1070.

Wyndham   Pop. 868

MAP REF. 385 N1, 393 P4
Wyndham is the most northerly town and safe port harbour in WA. There are two main areas: the original Wyndham Port, on Cambridge Gulf, and Wyndham ('Three Mile'), on the Great Northern Hwy, the residential and shopping area. The meatworks, Wyndham's main industry, closed in 1985. Today Wyndham services nearby Aboriginal communities, the pastoral industry, mining exploration and tourism. Wyndham Port now handles live cattle shipment to South-East Asia and stores and exports raw sugar and molasses produced at Kununurra. **In town:** Wyndham Heritage Walk, short walk from Museum to Port, brochure available. Historic buildings in Port Town historic precinct, main street (O'Donnell St): old Shire Hall, now Boab Art and Craft Gallery; Durack's Wool Store; courthouse, now historic museum; Anthon's Landing. Warriu Park Aboriginal Monument in town centre. Port display next to Marine and Harbours offices, near wharf. Crocodile-spotting from wharf. Daily feeding of crocodiles, alligators and komodo dragons at Zoological Gardens and Crocodile Park, Barytes Rd, Wyndham Port. Wyndham Caravan Park, off Great Northern Hwy, has huge boab tree, 1500–2000 years old. Aug. (1st and 2nd Sat.): Wyndham Races (horseracing). **In the area:** Self-guide drive, brochure available. To south-west on King River Rd: Aboriginal rock paintings (18 km); Prison Tree, boab tree 2000–4000 years old, once used by local police as a lock-up, (22 km); check road conditions before departure. Horse treks from Diggers Rest Station, 33 km W. Five

Rivers Lookout, 5 km N atop Bastion Range, for spectacular views of Kimberley landscape, mountain ranges, Cambridge Gulf, Wyndham Port and rivers. Afghan cemetery, 1 km E. Parry CK Road, begins 14 km SE: 4WD route to Kununurra, via Ord River and Ivanhoe Crossing; camping and fishing en route. Abundant wildlife at Marglu Billabong, 15 km SE, part of Parry Lagoons Nature Reserve, 70 sq km of wetlands. The Grotto, 36 km E (2 km off road), a rock-edged waterhole, estimated to be 100 m deep, offering a cool, shaded oasis and safe year-round swimming. Sealed road leading to Wyndham passes through splendid gorge country. El Questro Station, 100 km S: vast cattle station, includes Emma Gorge (1.6-km walking track from parking area to gorge) for swimming; numerous touring and accommodation options available. **Visitor information:** Kimberley Motors, 6 Great Northern Hwy; (08) 9161 1281. **See also:** The Kimberley p. 356.

Yalgoo   Pop. 80

MAP REF. 388 D3
Yalgoo lies 216 km E of Geraldton along an excellent road through typical Australian outback country. Alluvial gold was discovered here in the 1890s. Traces of gold are still found in the district, which encourages fossicking by locals and visitors. **In town:** Courthouse Museum, Gibbons St. Restored Dominican Convent Chapel (1922), Henty St. **In the area:** Abundant native wildlife in the area and prolific wildflowers in season (July–Sept.). Joker's Tunnel, 12 km SE on Paynes Find Rd, carved through solid rock by early prospectors, named after Joker mining syndicate. Chinaman Rock, 43 km N on Cue Rd, interesting granite outcrop. **Visitor information:** Shire Offices, 15 Shamrock St; (08) 9962 8042.

Yallingup   Pop. 175

MAP REF. 379 B7, 381 C2, 386 A9, 388 B10
Yallingup is known for its excellent surf and magnificent limestone caves. **In town:** Caves House Hotel, off Caves Rd, built by government as holiday hotel in 1903. Early visitors arrived from Busselton via horse and buggy along dirt road, a journey of 2 hours. Hotel was rebuilt 1938 after a fire, using locally milled timber; now

Town Hall, York

has award-winning accommodation and restaurant. Dec.: Yallingup Longboard Classic. **In the area:** Ngilgi (Yallingup) Caves, 2 km E. Goanna Gallery, 8 km SE, for local art and craft. Shearing Shed, Wildwood Rd, 10 km SE, has shearing demonstrations and wool shop (check opening times). Rivendell Gardens, 10 km SE, jam and pickle sales at winery. Canal Rocks and Smith's Beach, 5 km SW, offer fishing, surfing and swimming. Gunyulgup Gallery and Yallingup Gallery, both 9 km SW. Wineries in the surrounding region include: Hunts Foxhaven Estate, 3 km S; Wildwood Winery, 5 km S; Cape Clairault Wines, 10 km S; Willyabrup Valley district, 20 km S; Happ's Vineyard and Pottery, 8 km SE; Abbey Vale Vineyards, 11 km SE; further 8 km, Bootleg Brewery; Amberley Estate Winery, 5 km E. **Visitor information:** Seymour Boulevard, Dunsborough; (08) 9755 3299. **See also:** Cape to Cape p. 331; The South-West p. 335.

Yanchep
Pop. 1790

MAP REF. 378 A1, 386 C2, 388 C7
Yanchep is a quiet beachside holiday spot, only 51 km N of Perth. **In the area:** In Yanchep National Park, 5 km E, covering 2842 ha of natural bushland: Gloucester Lodge Museum has displays of local history including park history (check opening times); historic Yanchep Inn for refreshments; popular koala-viewing area; Yonderup and Crystal caves, featuring magnificent limestone formations; launch cruises on freshwater Loch McNess (Sun.), rowing-boats for hire; walking trail through Loch McNess wetland. Aboriginal cultural tours through park and Balga Mia Village; bookings essential, at information centre. Wild Kingdom, 3 km NE, a wildlife park and zoo. Marina at Two Rocks, 6 km NW. Caraboda Estate Wines, 10 km S. Wreck of *Alkimos*, south of Yanchep, said to be guarded by ghost. Picturesque Gnangara Lake, 30 km SE, with picnic facilities

around the shore. **Visitor information:** Information Office, Yanchep National Park; (08) 9561 1004. Web site www.calm.wa.gov.au **See also:** Day Tours from Perth p. 328; National Parks p. 336; Western Wildflowers p. 364.

York
Pop. 1923

MAP REF. 378 I4, 386 F3, 388 D8
First settled by Europeans in 1831, York is on the banks of the Avon River in the fertile Avon Valley, 97 km from Perth. The town has a wealth of historic buildings, carefully preserved. **In town:** Heritage trails, booklet available. In Avon Tce: Old Gaol and Courthouse, and Police Station, built of local stone in 1895; Settlers' House (1850), restored two-storey mud-brick building, now offering old-world accommodation; Castle Hotel, Imperial Inn and The York, fine examples of early coaching inns; Romanesque Town Hall (1911); Mill Gallery, featuring recycled jarrah craftwork; Loder Antiques; York Motor Museum, one of Australia's best collections of veteran, classic and racing cars (and some bicycles and motorcycles); Talking Points Antique Toy Train Museum, open Sun. and by appt; Sandalwood Yards and Tipperary School, old sandalwood storage area and now site of relocated school (1874). Avon Valley Historical Rose Garden, Osnaberg Rd, roses in season. In Brook St: Old York Hospital, with original shingle roof; Residency Museum (1843), displaying colonial furniture and early photographs. Old-world costumes at The Needle and I, cnr Georgiana and Macarthy sts (appt only). Fine churches: Holy Trinity (consecrated 1858), Suburban Rd; St Patrick's Church (1886), South St; Uniting Church (1888), Grey St. In Low St: Suspension Bridge (originally 1906) across river; picnic/barbecue facilities at Avon Park; market also in Avon Park (check times). June: Country Music Festival. Aug.: Daffodil Festival; Agricultural Show. Sept.: Jazz Weekend. Oct.: Flying 50s (car rally). **In the area:** Mt Brown Lookout, 3 km SE; follow signs from Castle Hotel to Pioneer Dr. and then to Mt Brown. Miniature Village, 3 km S on Great Southern Hwy. Picnic area overlooking river at Gwanbygine Park, 10 km S. Near Quairading, 64 km E, Toapin Weir and panoramic views from Mt Stirling. **Visitor information:** 81 Avon Tce; (08) 9641 1301.

Western Australia

LOCATION MAP

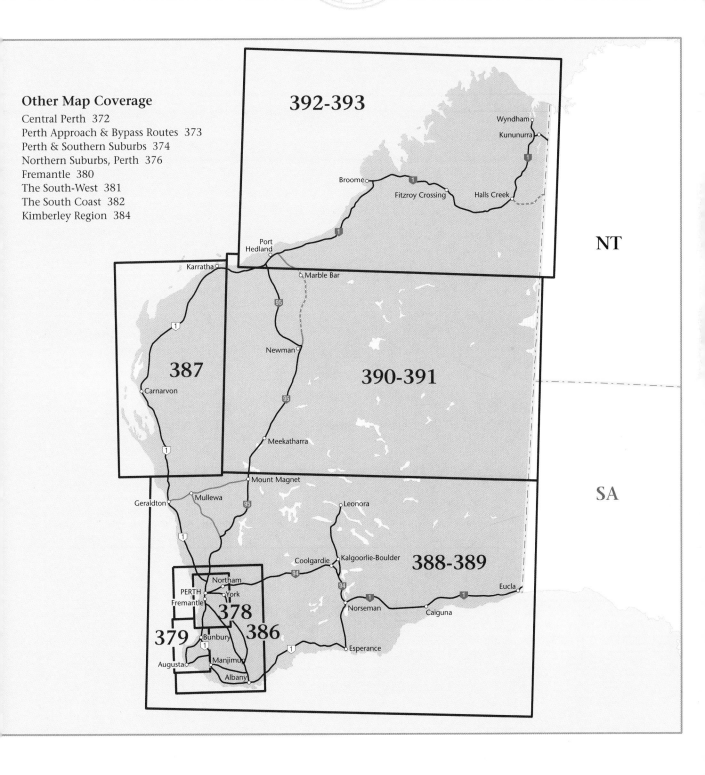

Other Map Coverage

Central Perth 372
Perth Approach & Bypass Routes 373
Perth & Southern Suburbs 374
Northern Suburbs, Perth 376
Fremantle 380
The South-West 381
The South Coast 382
Kimberley Region 384

392-393

Wyndham
Kununurra

Broome
Fitzroy Crossing
Halls Creek

Port Hedland

NT

Karratha
Marble Bar

387

Newman

390-391

Carnarvon

Meekatharra

Mount Magnet

SA

Geraldton
Mullewa

Leonora

Coolgardie
Kalgoorlie-Boulder

388-389

Eucla

Northam
PERTH
Fremantle
York
378

Norseman
Caiguna

379
Bunbury
386
Augusta
Manjimup
Albany

Esperance

0 0.25 0.5 0.75 1 km

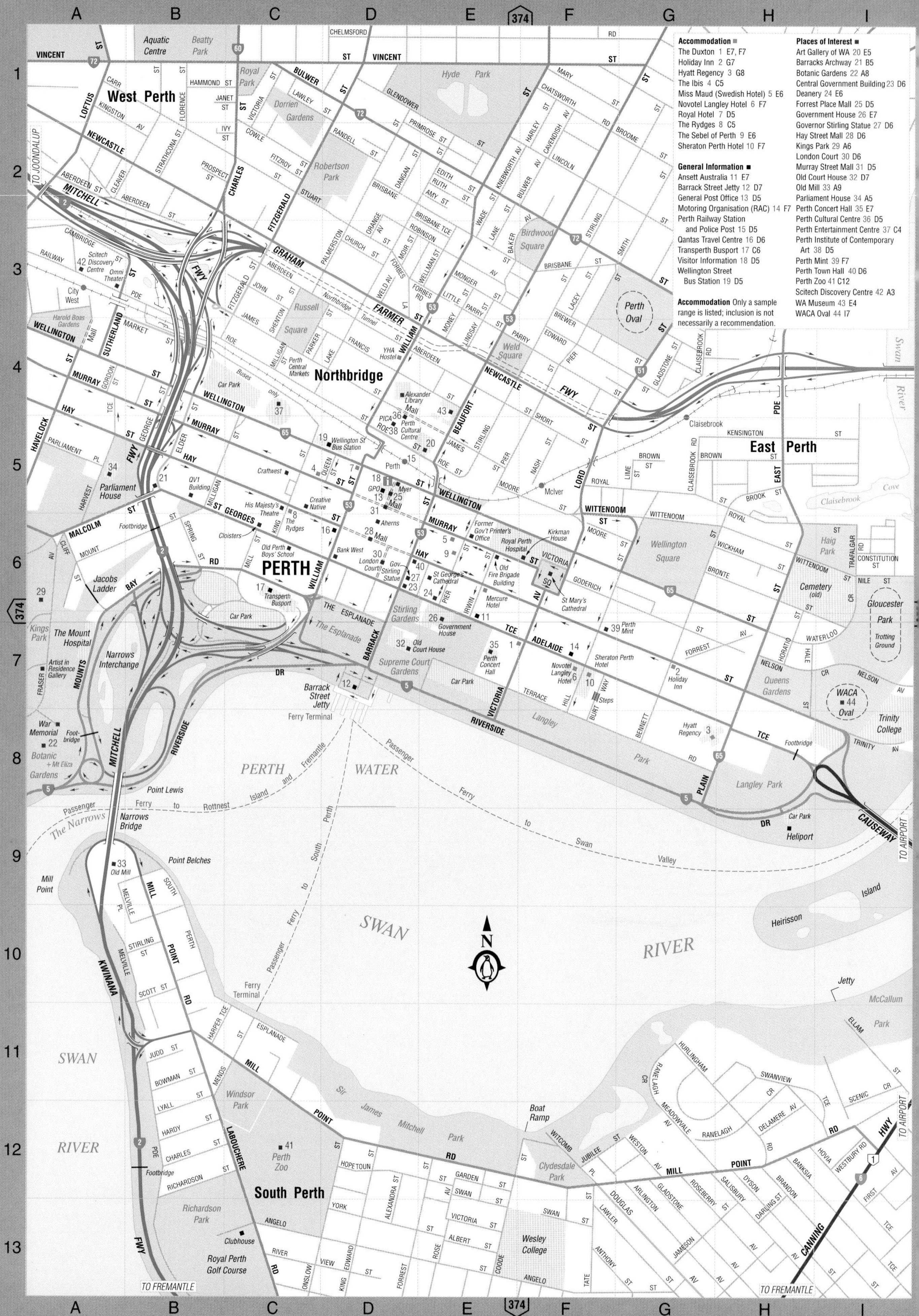
Accommodation
The Duxton 1 E7, F7
Holiday Inn 2 G7
Hyatt Regency 3 G8
The Ibis 4 C5
Miss Maud (Swedish Hotel) 5 E6
Novotel Langley Hotel 6 F7
Royal Hotel 7 D5
The Rydges 8 C5
The Sebel of Perth 9 E6
Sheraton Perth Hotel 10 F7
General Information
Ansett Australia 11 E7
Barrack Street Jetty 12 D7
General Post Office 13 D5
Motoring Organisation (RAC) 14 F7
Perth Railway Station and Police Post 15 D5
Qantas Travel Centre 16 D6
Transperth Busport 17 C6
Visitor Information 18 D5
Wellington Street Bus Station 19 D5
Accommodation Only a sample range is listed; inclusion is not necessarily a recommendation.
Places of Interest
Art Gallery of WA 20 E5
Barracks Archway 21 B5
Botanic Gardens 22 A8
Central Government Building 23 D6
Deanery 24 E6
Forrest Place Mall 25 D5
Government House 26 E7
Governor Stirling Statue 27 D6
Hay Street Mall 28 D6
Kings Park 29 A6
London Court 30 D6
Murray Street Mall 31 D5
Old Court House 32 D7
Old Mill 33 A9
Parliament House 34 A5
Perth Concert Hall 35 E7
Perth Cultural Centre 36 D5
Perth Entertainment Centre 37 C4
Perth Institute of Contemporary Art 38 D5
Perth Mint 39 F7
Perth Town Hall 40 D6
Perth Zoo 41 C12
Scitech Discovery Centre 42 A3
WA Museum 43 E4
WACA Oval 44 I7
West Perth
Northbridge
PERTH
East Perth
South Perth
PERTH WATER
SWAN RIVER
Heirisson Island
TO JOONDALUP
TO FREMANTLE
TO AIRPORT

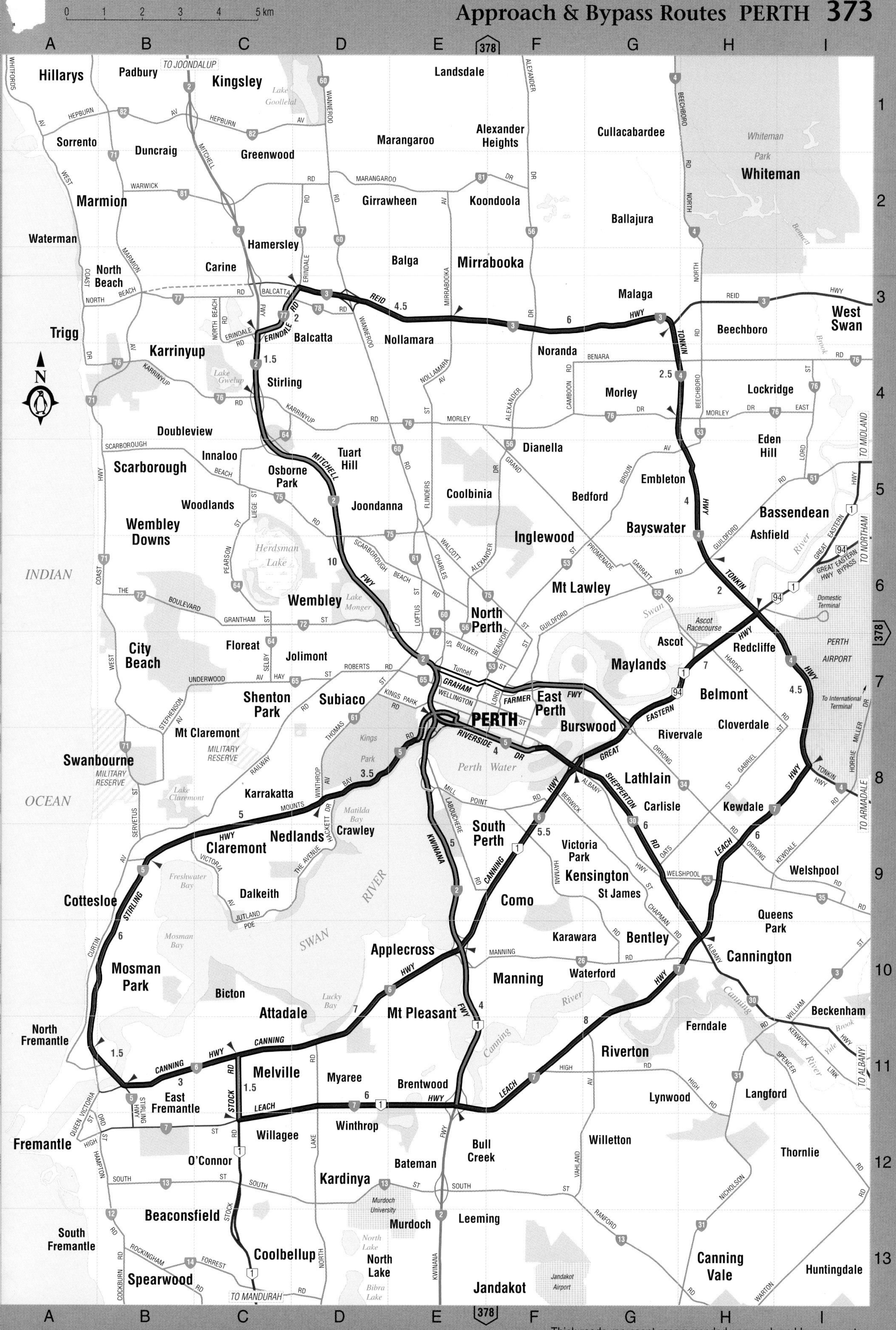

0 1 2 3 4 5 km

A B C D E 378 F G H I

Hillarys Padbury **Kingsley** Landsdale
TO JOONDALUP Lake Goollelal
1

Sorrento Duncraig Greenwood Marangaroo Alexander Heights Cullacabardee *Whiteman Park* **Whiteman**

Marmion Girrawheen Koondoola Ballajura
2

Waterman Hamersley Balga Mirrabooka Malaga Beechboro **West Swan**

North Beach Carine Balcatta Nollamara Noranda Beechboro
3

Trigg **Karrinyup** **Balcatta** Stirling Morley Lockridge

Doubleview Tuart Hill Dianella Bayswater Embleton Eden Hill **Bassendean**
5

Scarborough Innaloo Osborne Park Joondanna Coolbinia Bedford Ashfield

Woodlands **Wembley Downs** Mt Lawley Ascot Racecourse
6

City Beach Floreat Jolimont Wembley North Perth Ascot Redcliffe PERTH AIRPORT

Shenton Park Subiaco **Maylands** **Belmont** Cloverdale
7

Swanbourne Mt Claremont Karrakatta **PERTH** East Perth Burswood Rivervale **Lathlain** Kewdale Welshpool

Cottesloe **Claremont** Nedlands Crawley **South Perth** Victoria Park **Kensington** St James **Bentley** Queens Park **Cannington** Beckenham
9

Mosman Park Bicton Dalkeith Applecross Como Karawara Waterford Ferndale

North Fremantle Attadale Mt Pleasant Manning **Riverton** Lynwood Langford Thornlie
11

East Fremantle Melville Myaree Brentwood Winthrop Willetton

Fremantle Willagee **Kardinya** Bateman Bull Creek **Canning Vale** Huntingdale

O'Connor Leeming
12

Beaconsfield Murdoch University Murdoch **Jandakot**

South Fremantle **Spearwood** **Coolbellup** North Lake Bibra Lake Jandakot Airport
13

TO MANDURAH

A B C D E 378 F G H I

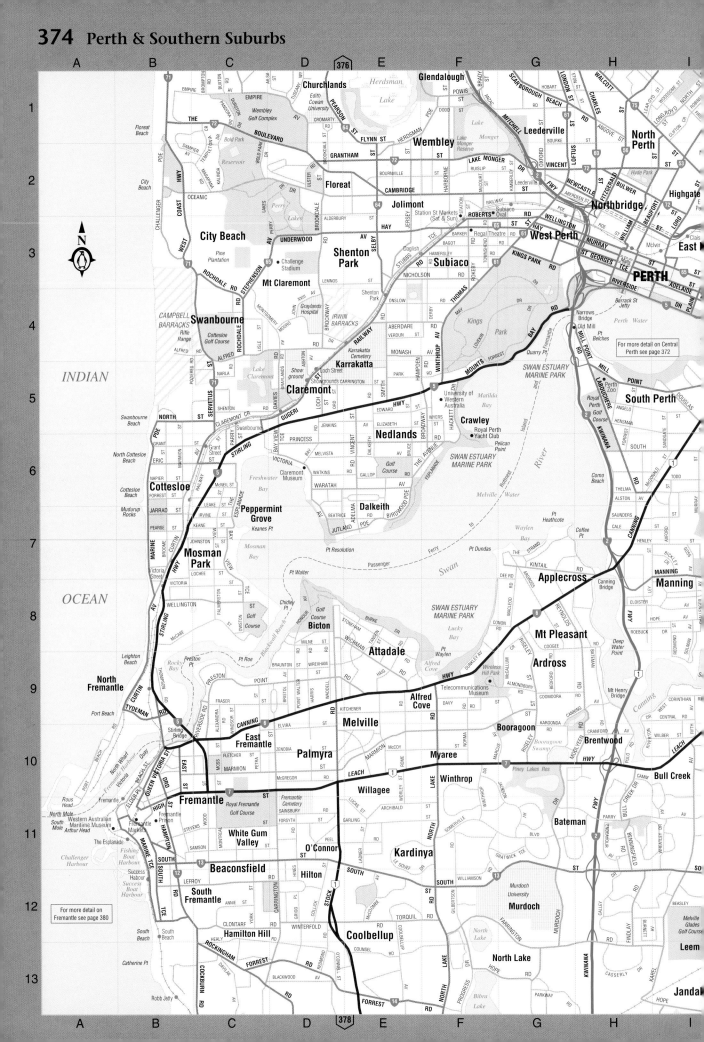

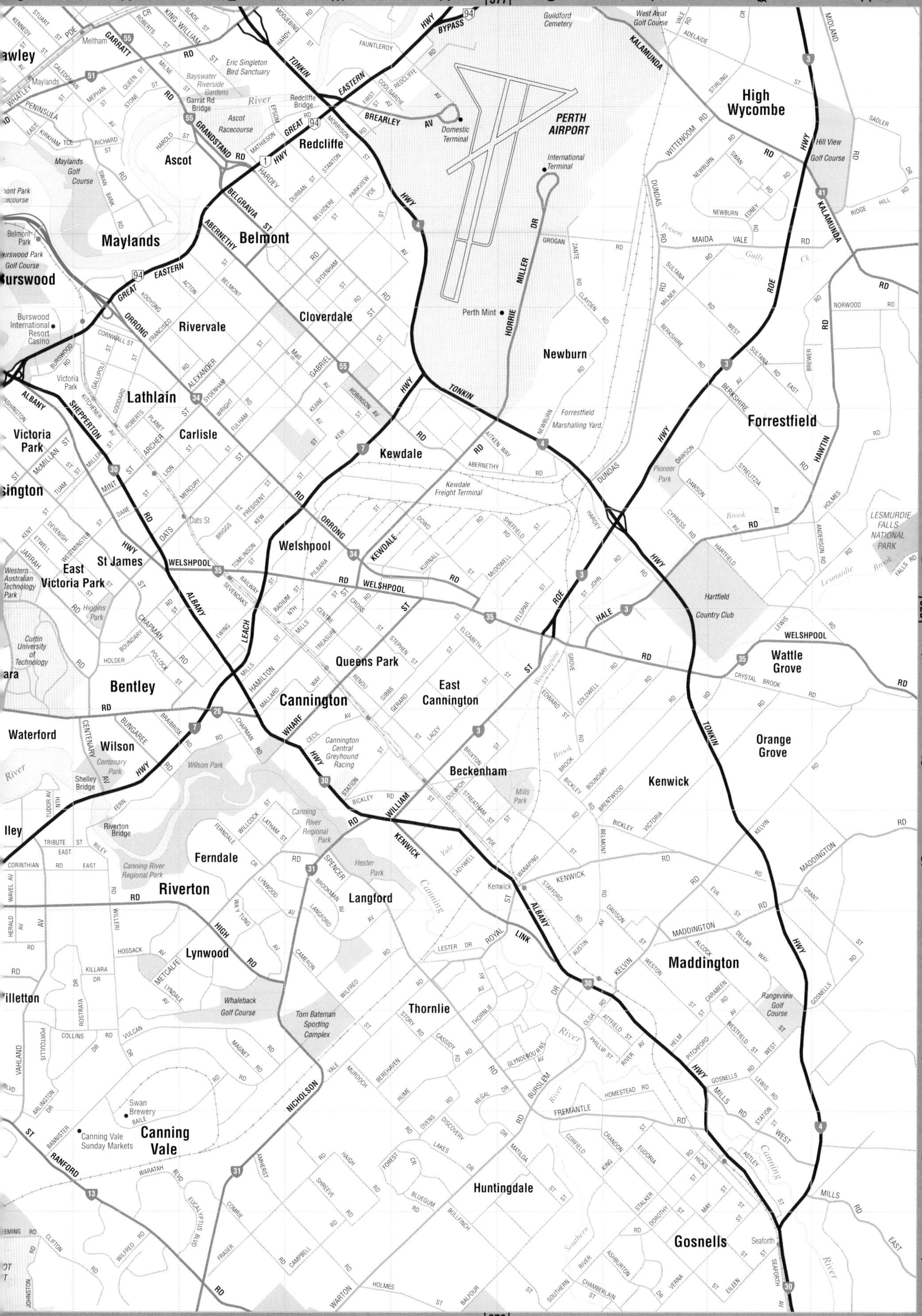
0 1 2 3 km
J K L M N O P Q R
377
378
1 2 3 4 5 6 7 8 9 10 11 12 13
High Wycombe
PERTH AIRPORT
Domestic Terminal
International Terminal
Guildford Cemetery
West Aviat Golf Course
Eric Singleton Bird Sanctuary
Bayswater Riverside Gardens
Garrat Rd Bridge
Redcliffe Bridge
Ascot Racecourse
Maylands Golf Course
Maylands
Ascot
Redcliffe
Belmont
Burswood
Burswood International Resort Casino
Rivervale
Cloverdale
Perth Mint
Newburn
Hill View Golf Course
Forrestfield
Lathlain
Victoria Park
Carlisle
Kewdale
Kewdale Freight Terminal
Forrestfield Marshalling Yard
Pioneer Park
LESMURDIE FALLS NATIONAL PARK
Welshpool
St James
East Victoria Park
Western Australian Technology Park
Higgins Park
Curtin University of Technology
Hartfield Country Club
Queens Park
Bentley
Cannington
East Cannington
Wattle Grove
Waterford
Wilson
Centenary Park
Shelley Bridge
Wilson Park
Cannington Central Greyhound Racing
Beckenham
Mills Park
Orange Grove
Kenwick
Riverton Bridge
Canning River Regional Park
Ferndale
Riverton
Hester Park
Langford
Lynwood
Maddington
Rangeview Golf Course
Whaleback Golf Course
Tom Bateman Sporting Complex
Thornlie
Willetton
Swan Brewery
Canning Vale Sunday Markets
Canning Vale
Huntingdale
Gosnells
Seaforth
TONKIN HWY
GREAT EASTERN HWY
ROE HWY
ALBANY HWY
LEACH HWY
WELSHPOOL RD
KALAMUNDA RD
NICHOLSON RD
RANFORD RD

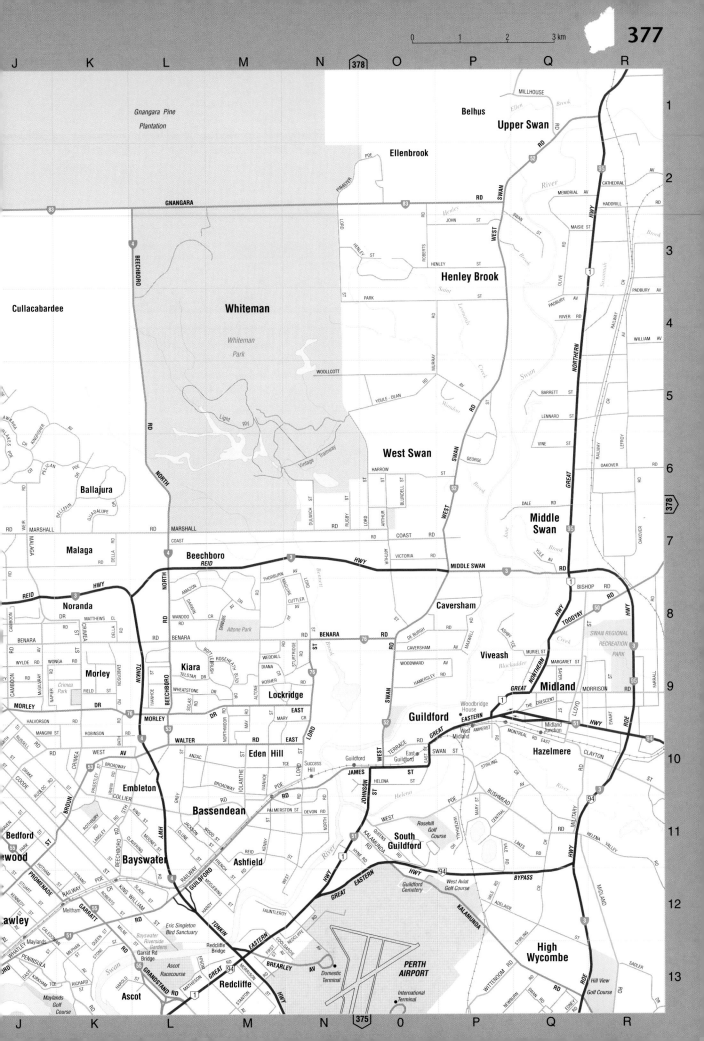

Map scale: 0 5 10 15 20 25 km

For more detail on Perth Suburbs see pages 374 - 377

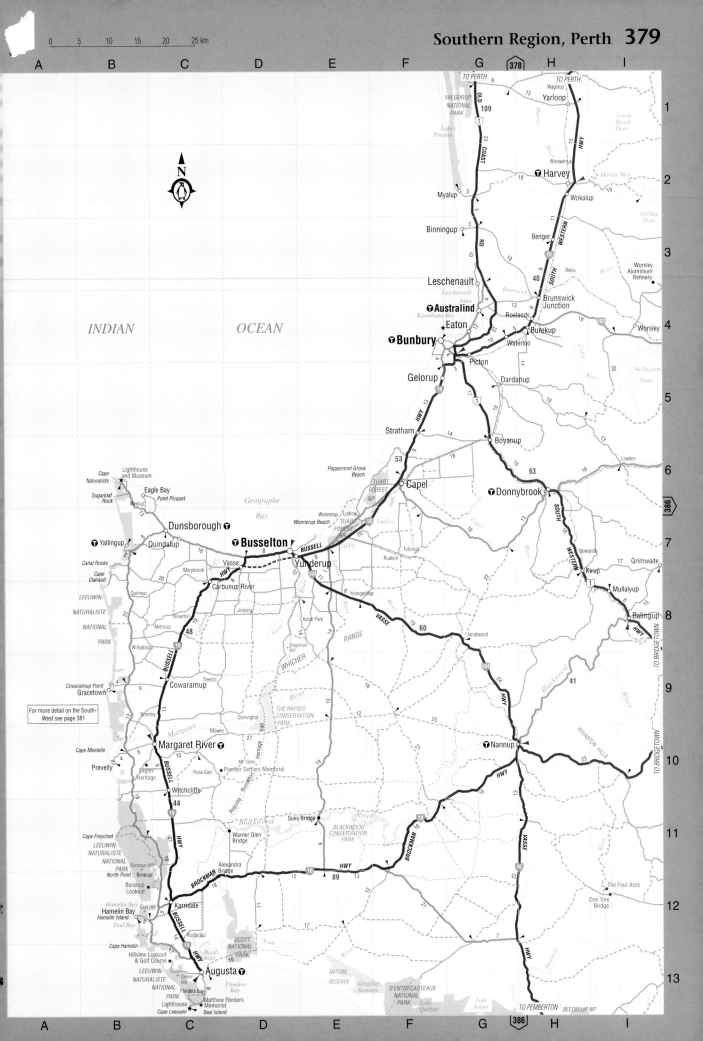

0 5 10 15 20 25 km

A   B   C   D   E   F   G   H   I

TO PERTH
TO PERTH
YALGORUP NATIONAL PARK
Wagerup
Yarloop
Logue Brook Dam
OLD
109
Lake Preston
COAST
23
15
Myalup
3
Warawarrup
Harvey
Wokalup
Binningup
2
SOUTH WESTERN HWY
Benger
10
19
11
20
40
Beela
Worsley Aluminium Refinery
Leschenault
Brunswick
Brunswick Junction
Australind
13
6
Koombana Bay
Roelands
19
107
Worsley
Eaton
22
5
Burekup
Bunbury
10
Waterloo
4
Picton
11
Gelorup
3
Dardanup
20
Wellington Dam
HWY
13
1
19
5
Stratham
14
Boyanup
1
INDIAN   OCEAN
53
9
18
15
63
16
Lowden
Peppermint Grove Beach
TUART FOREST NP
Capel
Donnybrook
SOUTH
Cape Naturaliste
Lighthouse and Museum
Eagle Bay
Point Picquet
Meelup
13
Geographe Bay
Wonnerup
Wonnerup Beach
Ludlow
TUART FOREST NP
10
Ludlow
18
WESTERN
18
13
Newlands
17
Grimwade
Sugarloaf Rock
Dunsborough
Quindalup
16
8
Busselton
BUSSELL
Yunderup
Abba
20
Ruabon
Tutunup
River
Kirup
1
Mullalyup
Yallingup
Vasse
HWY
River
104
11
6
Yoongarillup
River
Balingup
HWY
Canal Rocks
Marybrook
10
River
Cape Clairault
Carbunup River
Vasse
VASSE
19
60
Jarrahwood
24
41
HWY
LEEUWIN-NATURALISTE NATIONAL PARK
Quinnup
20
Yelverton
Jindong
Acton Park
Chapman Hill
RANGE
104
Blackwood River
48
Metricup
WHICHER
16
HWY
Willyabrup
BUSSELL
10
Treeton
River
Cowaramup Point
Gracetown
4
9
Cowaramup
13
Bramley
Osmington
THE RAPIDS CONSERVATION PARK
12
23
Nannup
WHISTON HILLS
For more detail on the South-West see page 381
Margaret
Mowen
Heritage
Trail
Buscotton
10
HWY
Margaret River
27
Mt Yates
19
18
13
23
Cape Mentelle
Prevelly
4
5
BUSSELL
Rosa Glen
Pioneer Settlers Memorial
VASSE
Eagles Heritage
Witchcliffe
44
18
Blackwood
Sues Bridge
BLACKWOOD CONSERVATION PARK
River
HWY
BROCKMAN
22
10
The Four Aces
Cape Freycinet
LEEUWIN-NATURALISTE NATIONAL PARK
North Point
Boranup Hill
Boranup
Warner Glen Bridge
10
Alexandra Bridge
12
HWY
89
13
One Tree Bridge
Boranup Lookout
18
21
Hamelin Bay
East Hill
Karridale
11
17
HWY
Hamelin Island
Foul Bay
5
BUSSELL
Kudardup
Scott
SCOTT NATIONAL PARK
Cape Hamelin
14
10
HWY
15
NATURE RESERVE
Gingilup Swamps
D'ENTRECASTEAUX NATIONAL PARK
Lake Quitjup
HWY
Hillview Lookout & Golf Course
Green Hill
Augusta
Flinders Bay
Lake Jasper
BEEDELUP NP
LEEUWIN-NATURALISTE NATIONAL PARK
Flinders Bay
Lighthouse
Matthew Flinders Memorial
Cape Leeuwin
Seal Island
TO PEMBERTON

386

TO BRIDGETOWN

386

1 2 3 4 5 6 7 8 9 10 11 12 13

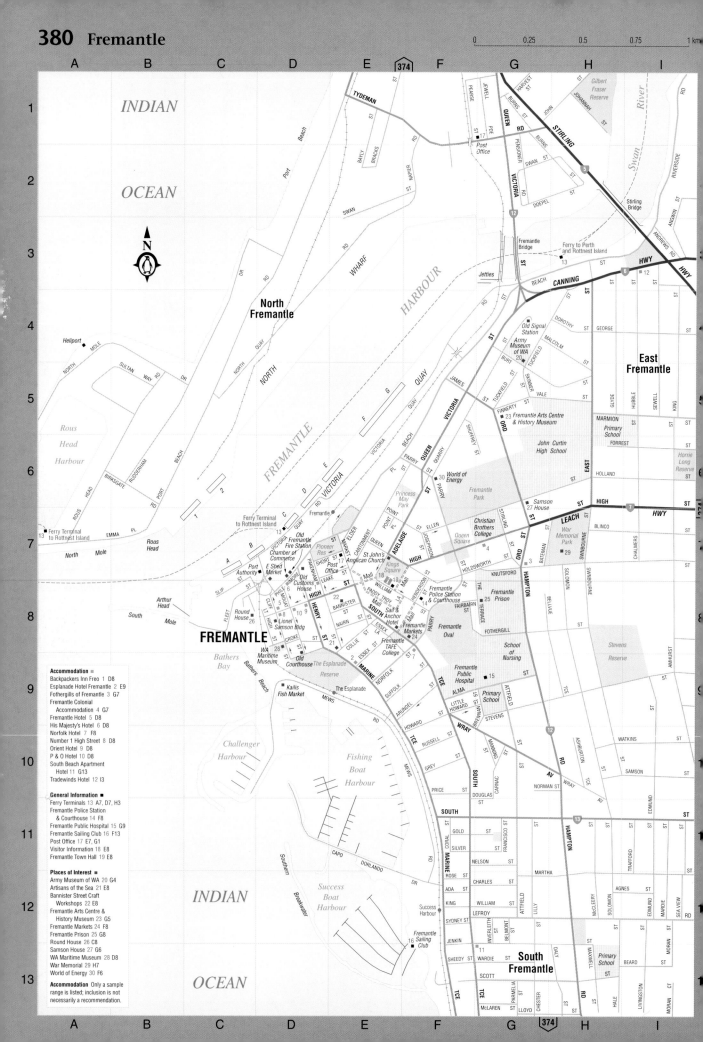

0   0.25   0.5   0.75   1km

A   B   C   D   E   374 F   G   H   I

INDIAN

OCEAN

North
Fremantle

Rous
Head
Harbour

FREMANTLE

East
Fremantle

Bathers
Bay

Challenger
Harbour

Fishing
Boat
Harbour

Success
Boat
Harbour

INDIAN

OCEAN

South
Fremantle

Accommodation ■
Backpackers Inn Freo 1 D8
Esplanade Hotel Fremantle 2 E9
Fothergills of Fremantle 3 G7
Fremantle Colonial
 Accommodation 4 G7
Fremantle Hotel 5 D8
His Majesty's Hotel 6 D8
Norfolk Hotel 7 F8
Number 1 High Street 8 D8
Orient Hotel 9 D8
P & O Hotel 10 D8
South Beach Apartment
 Hotel 11 G13
Tradewinds Hotel 12 I3

General Information ■
Ferry Terminals 13 A7, D7, H3
Fremantle Police Station
 & Courthouse 14 F8
Fremantle Public Hospital 15 G9
Fremantle Sailing Club 16 F13
Post Office 17 E7, G1
Visitor Information 18 E8
Fremantle Town Hall 19 E8

Places of Interest ■
Army Museum of WA 20 G4
Artisans of the Sea 21 E8
Bannister Street Craft
 Workshops 22 E8
Fremantle Arts Centre &
 History Museum 23 G5
Fremantle Markets 24 F8
Fremantle Prison 25 G8
Round House 26 C8
Samson House 27 G6
WA Maritime Museum 28 D8
War Memorial 29 H7
World of Energy 30 F6

Accommodation Only a sample
range is listed; inclusion is not
necessarily a recommendation.

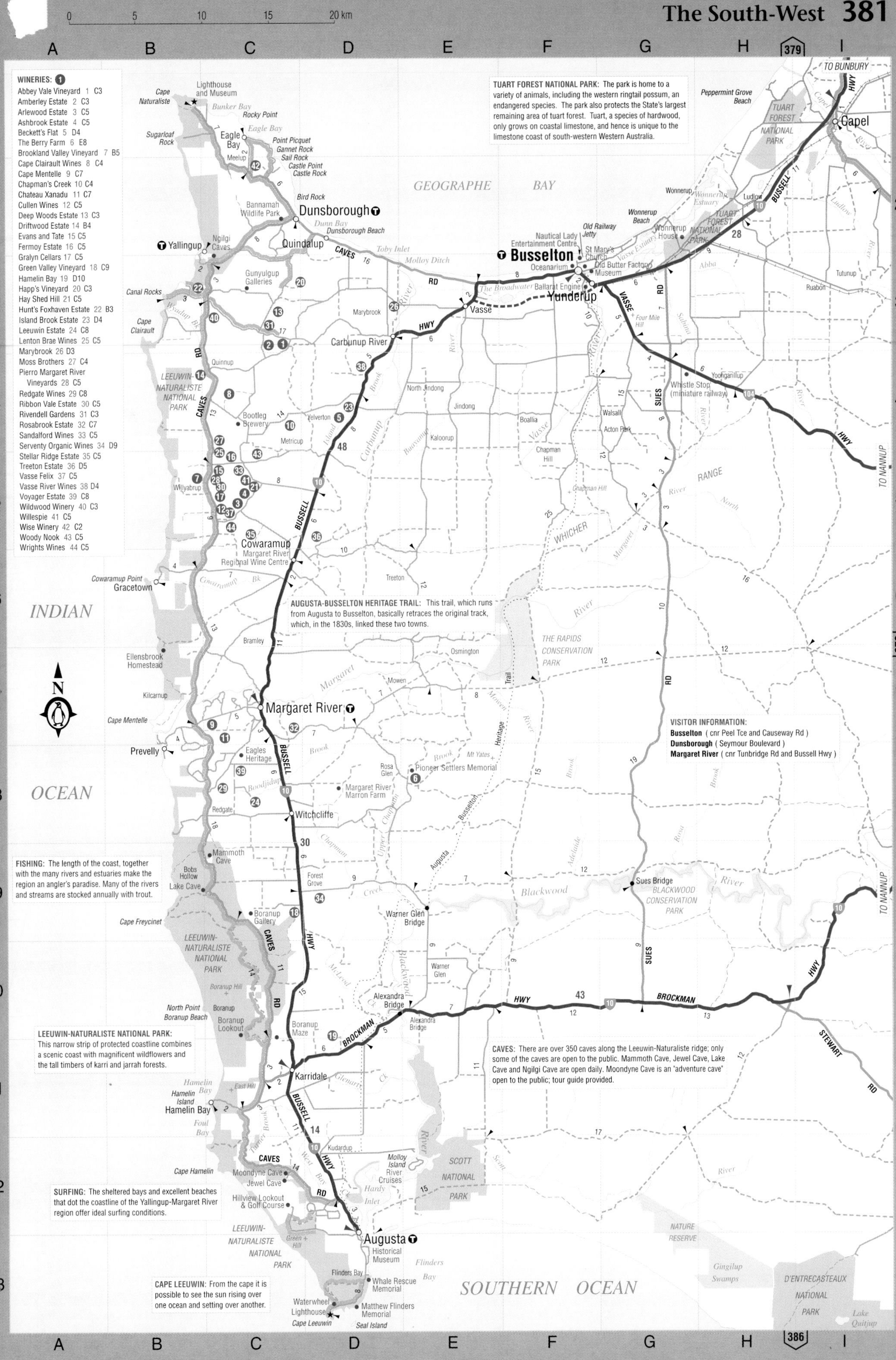

0 5 10 15 20 km
WINERIES:
Abbey Vale Vineyard 1 C3
Amberley Estate 2 C3
Arlewood Estate 3 C5
Ashbrook Estate 4 C5
Beckett's Flat 5 D4
The Berry Farm 6 E8
Brookland Valley Vineyard 7 B5
Cape Clairault Wines 8 C4
Cape Mentelle 9 C7
Chapman's Creek 10 C4
Chateau Xanadu 11 C7
Cullen Wines 12 C5
Deep Woods Estate 13 C3
Driftwood Estate 14 B4
Evans and Tate 15 C5
Fermoy Estate 16 C5
Gralyn Cellars 17 C5
Green Valley Vineyard 18 C9
Hamelin Bay 19 D10
Happ's Vineyard 20 C3
Hay Shed Hill 21 C5
Hunt's Foxhaven Estate 22 B3
Island Brook Estate 23 D4
Leeuwin Estate 24 C8
Lenton Brae Wines 25 C5
Marybrook 26 D3
Moss Brothers 27 C4
Pierro Margaret River Vineyards 28 C5
Redgate Wines 29 C8
Ribbon Vale Estate 30 C5
Rivendell Gardens 31 C3
Rosabrook Estate 32 C7
Sandalford Wines 33 C5
Serventy Organic Wines 34 D9
Stellar Ridge Estate 35 C5
Treeton Estate 36 D5
Vasse Felix 37 C5
Vasse River Wines 38 D4
Voyager Estate 39 C8
Wildwood Winery 40 C3
Willespie 41 C5
Wise Winery 42 C2
Woody Nook 43 C5
Wrights Wines 44 C5
TUART FOREST NATIONAL PARK: The park is home to a variety of animals, including the western ringtail possum, an endangered species. The park also protects the State's largest remaining area of tuart forest. Tuart, a species of hardwood, only grows on coastal limestone, and hence is unique to the limestone coast of south-western Western Australia.
AUGUSTA-BUSSELTON HERITAGE TRAIL: This trail, which runs from Augusta to Busselton, basically retraces the original track, which, in the 1830s, linked these two towns.
VISITOR INFORMATION:
Busselton (cnr Peel Tce and Causeway Rd)
Dunsborough (Seymour Boulevard)
Margaret River (cnr Tunbridge Rd and Bussell Hwy)
FISHING: The length of the coast, together with the many rivers and estuaries make the region an angler's paradise. Many of the rivers and streams are stocked annually with trout.
LEEUWIN-NATURALISTE NATIONAL PARK: This narrow strip of protected coastline combines a scenic coast with magnificent wildflowers and the tall timbers of karri and jarrah forests.
CAVES: There are over 350 caves along the Leeuwin-Naturaliste ridge; only some of the caves are open to the public. Mammoth Cave, Jewel Cave, Lake Cave and Ngilgi Cave are open daily. Moondyne Cave is an "adventure cave" open to the public; tour guide provided.
SURFING: The sheltered bays and excellent beaches that dot the coastline of the Yallingup-Margaret River region offer ideal surfing conditions.
CAPE LEEUWIN: From the cape it is possible to see the sun rising over one ocean and setting over another.
TO BUNBURY
Capel
TUART FOREST NATIONAL PARK
Peppermint Grove Beach
GEOGRAPHE BAY
Cape Naturaliste
Lighthouse and Museum
Bunker Bay
Rocky Point
Sugarloaf Rock
Eagle Bay
Point Picquet
Gannet Rock
Sail Rock
Castle Point
Castle Rock
Bird Rock
Bannamah Wildlife Park
Dunsborough
Dunn Bay
Dunsborough Beach
Yallingup
Ngilgi Caves
Quindalup
Toby Inlet
Molloy Ditch
Gunyulgup Galleries
Canal Rocks
Cape Clairault
Marybrook
Vasse
Carbunup River
Busselton
Nautical Lady Entertainment Centre
Old Railway Jetty
St Mary's Church
Old Butter Factory Museum
Oceanarium
Ballarat Engine
The Broadwater
Yunderup
Wonnerup
Wonnerup Beach
Wonnerup House
Ludlow
Tutunup
Ruabon
Abba
Four Mile Hill
Yoongarillup
Whistle Stop (miniature railway)
TO NANNUP
Quinnup
LEEUWIN-NATURALISTE NATIONAL PARK
North Jindong
Jindong
Boallia
Walsall
Acton Park
Bootleg Brewery
Yelverton
Metricup
Kaloorup
Chapman Hill
Chapman Hill
RANGE
WHICHER
Willyabrup
Cowaramup
Margaret River Regional Wine Centre
Treeton
Cowaramup Point
Gracetown
INDIAN
OCEAN
Bramley
Osmington
THE RAPIDS CONSERVATION PARK
Ellensbrook Homestead
Kilcarnup
Mowen
Margaret River
Cape Mentelle
Prevelly
Eagles Heritage
Rosa Glen
Mt Yates
Pioneer Settlers Memorial
Margaret River Marron Farm
Redgate
Witchcliffe
Heritage Trail
Augusta Busselton
Mammoth Cave
Bobs Hollow
Lake Cave
Forest Grove
Warner Glen Bridge
Sues Bridge
BLACKWOOD CONSERVATION PARK
Blackwood
River
Boranup Gallery
Cape Freycinet
Warner Glen
Boranup Hill
North Point
Boranup
Boranup Beach
Boranup Lookout
Boranup Maze
Alexandra Bridge
Karridale
Hamelin Bay
Hamelin Island
East Hill
Foul Bay
Kudardup
Cape Hamelin
Moondyne Cave
Jewel Cave
Molloy Island
River Cruises
Hardy Inlet
SCOTT NATIONAL PARK
Hillview Lookout & Golf Course
Green Hill
Augusta
Historical Museum
Flinders Bay
Whale Rescue Memorial
Matthew Flinders Memorial
Waterwheel
Lighthouse
Cape Leeuwin
Seal Island
SOUTHERN OCEAN
NATURE RESERVE
Gingilup Swamps
D'ENTRECASTEAUX NATIONAL PARK
Lake Quitjup
CAVES RD
BUSSELL HWY
VASSE HWY
SUES RD
BROCKMAN HWY
STEWART RD
379
386

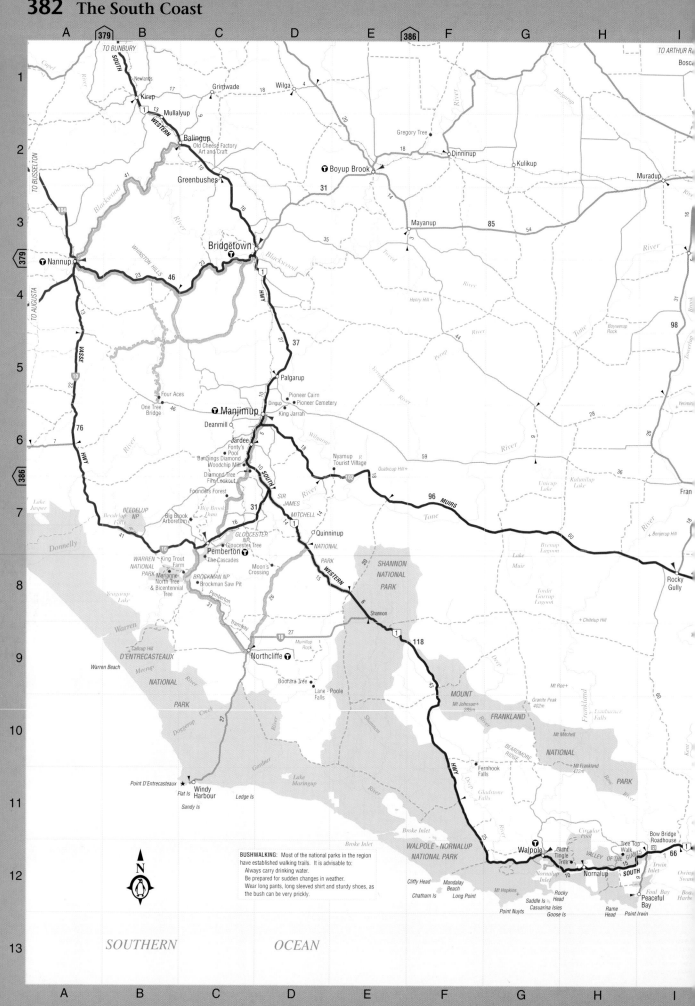

SOUTHERN OCEAN

BUSHWALKING: Most of the national parks in the region
have established walking trails. It is advisable to:
Always carry drinking water.
Be prepared for sudden changes in weather.
Wear long pants, long sleeved shirt and sturdy shoes, as
the bush can be very prickly.

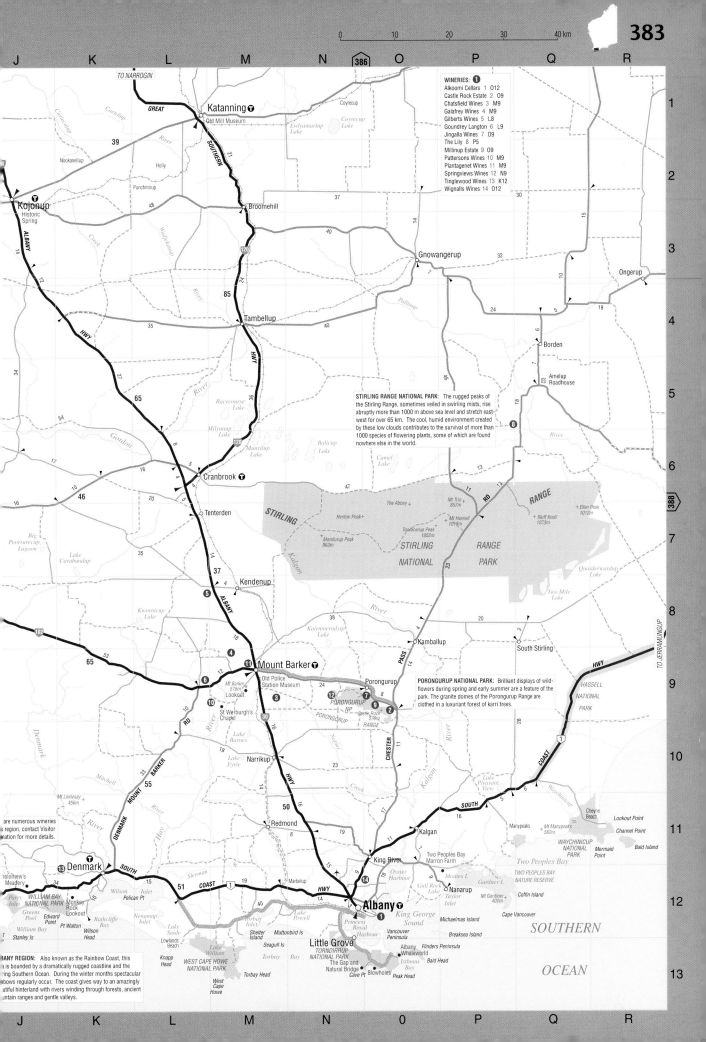

10   20   30   40 km

J   K   L   M   N   386   O   P   Q   R

WINERIES: ❶
Alkoomi Cellars 1 O12
Castle Rock Estate 2 O9
Chatsfield Wines 3 M9
Galafrey Wines 4 M9
Gilberts Wines 5 L8
Goundrey Langton 6 L9
Jingalla Wines 7 O9
The Lily 8 P5
Millinup Estate 9 O9
Pattersons Wines 10 M9
Plantagenet Wines 11 M9
Springviews Wines 12 N9
Tinglewood Wines 13 K12
Wignalls Wines 14 O12

TO NARROGIN

GREAT

Katanning
Old Mill Museum

39

Nookanellup

Holly

Punchimirup

Coyrecup

Covrecup Lake

Ewlyamartup Lake

SOUTHERN

21

Broomehill

37

40

Gnowangerup

14

32

10

15

Ongerup

Kojonup
Historic Spring

48

120

24

85

ALBANY

12

HWY

27

35

River

24

Tambellup

40

46

24

5

Borden

19

34

65

120

36

Racecourse Lake

Milyunup Lake

Munrulip Lake

Balicup Lake

Camel Lake

6

Amelup Roadhouse

18

8

54

17

46

16

10

20

5

Cranbrook

47

STIRLING

Henton Peak+

The Abbey +

Mt Trio 857m

Toolbrunup Peak 1052m

Mt Hassell 1078m

RD

RANGE

+ Ellen Peak 1012m

Bluff Knoll 1073m

11

13

River

Quarderwardup Lake

388

16

Big Poorrarecup Lagoon

Lake Carabundup

35

Tenterden

14

37

Mondurup Peak 863m

STIRLING

RANGE

NATIONAL

PARK

23

20

Two Mile Lake

102

Kworncup Lake

Kendenup

5

4

ALBANY

18

River

Kairnmerndyip Lake

38

River

8

4

Kamballup

PASS

14

9

South Stirling

3

HWY

TO JERRAMUNGUP

65

53

4

11

Mount Barker

Old Police Station Museum

12

Porongurup

24

7

8

9

PORONGURUP NP

Castle Rock 576m

2

HASSELL

NATIONAL

PARK

6

Denmark

RD

Mt Barker 576m Lookout

10

St Werburgh's Chapel

30

16

PORONGURUP RANGE

CHESTER

28

COAST

1

33

BARKER

MOUNT

55

Lake Barnes

River

19

Lake Eyrie

Narrikup

23

Nomir

Kalgan

17

River

Lake Pleasant View

6

Manypeaks

Mt Manypeaks 562m

WAYCHINICUP NATIONAL PARK

Cheyne Beach

Lookout Point

Channel Point

Bald Island

Mermaid Point

50

16

Redmond

8

19

11

Kalgan

SOUTH

16

are numerous wineries region, contact Visitor nation for more details.

Denmark

SOUTH

51

COAST

15

19

1

14

HWY

Marbelup

15

14

King River

Two Peoples Bay Marron Farm

14

Oyster Harbour

Nanarup

Moates L

Gardner L

Two Peoples Bay

TWO PEOPLES BAY NATURE RESERVE

Mt Gardner 401m

Coffin Island

Cape Vancouver

SOUTHERN

olomew's Meadery

34

WILLIAM BAY NATIONAL PARK

Monkey Rock Lookout

Wilson Head

Pelican Pt

Nenamup Inlet

Lake Saide

Lowlands Beach

Albany Whaleworld

Gull Rock Lake

Michaelmas Island

OCEAN

Greens Pool

Edward Point

Pt Walton

Wilson Pt

Rathcliffe Bay

William Bay

Stanley Is

Lake William

Torbay Inlet

Shelter Island

Muttonbird Is

Seagull Is

Torbay Head

Albany

Princess Royal Harbour

King George Sound

Breaksea Island

Flinders Peninsula

Cape Vancouver

ANY REGION: Also known as the Rainbow Coast, this is bounded by a dramatically rugged coastline and the ring Southern Ocean. During the winter months spectacular bows regularly occur. The coast gives way to an amazingly utiful hinterland with rivers winding through forests, ancient ntain ranges and gentle valleys.

WEST CAPE HOWE NATIONAL PARK

West Cape Howe

Knapp Head

Torbay Bay

Little Grove

TORNDIRRUP NATIONAL PARK

The Gap and Natural Bridge

Cave Pt

Blowholes

Peak Head

Vancouver Peninsula

Bald Head

Isthmus Bay

STIRLING RANGE NATIONAL PARK: The rugged peaks of the Stirling Range, sometimes veiled in swirling mists, rise abruptly more than 1000 m above sea level and stretch east-west for over 65 km. The cool, humid environment created by these low clouds contributes to the survival of more than 1000 species of flowering plants, some of which are found nowhere else in the world.

PORONGURUP NATIONAL PARK: Brilliant displays of wildflowers during spring and early summer are a feature of the park. The granite domes of the Porongurup Range are clothed in a luxuriant forest of karri trees.

1
2
3
4
5
6
7
8
9
10
11
12
13

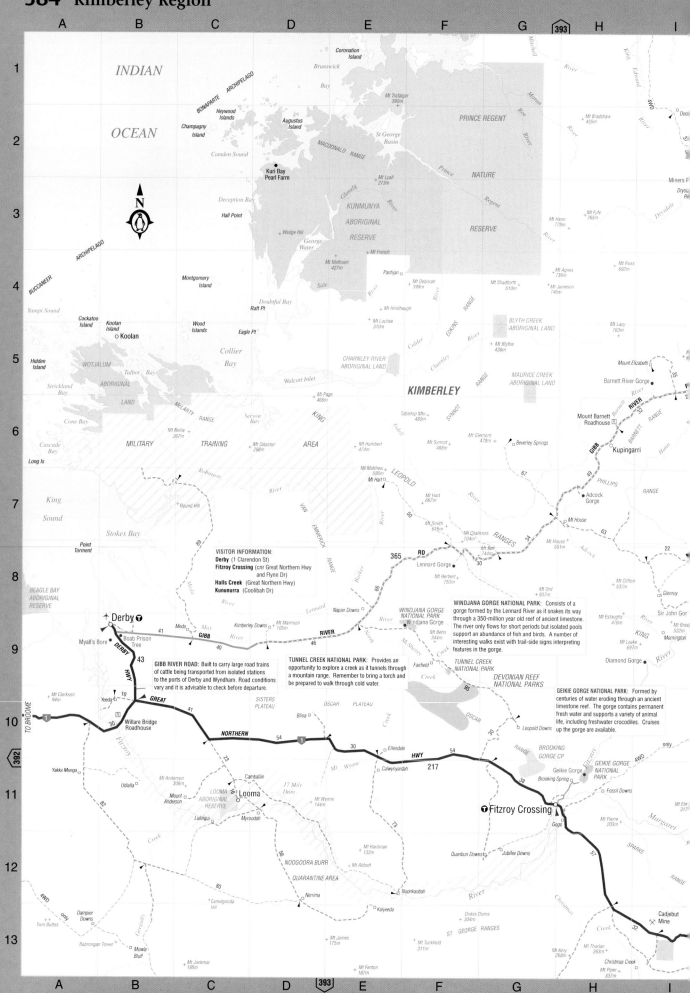

INDIAN

OCEAN

Coronation Island

Brunswick Bay

BONAPARTE ARCHIPELAGO

Heywood Islands

Champagny Island

Augustus Island

Mt Trafalgar 390m

St George Basin

PRINCE REGENT

Camden Sound

MACDONALD RANGE

NATURE

Kuri Bay Pearl Farm

Mt Lyall 213m

Deception Bay

Glenelg River

KUNMUNYA

Hall Point

ABORIGINAL

Prince Regent

RESERVE

Mt Hann 779m

Mt Fyfe 765m

Wedge Hill

George Water

RESERVE

Mt French

Mt Methuen 427m

Mt Russ 692m

Mt Bradshaw 455m

Montgomery Island

Pantijan

Mt Agnes 736m

Mt Jameson 746m

Mt Deborah 399m

Mt Shadforth 510m

BUCCANEER

Doubtful Bay

Raft Pt

Sale River

Mt Hindhaugh

RANGE

EDKINS

BLYTH CREEK ABORIGINAL LAND

Mt Lacy 763m

Yampi Sound

Cockatoo Island

Koolan Island

Wood Islands

Eagle Pt

Mt Lochee 310m

Calder River

Mount Elizabeth

ARCHIPELAGO

Koolan

Charnley River

Barnett River Gorge

Collier Bay

CHARNLEY RIVER ABORIGINAL LAND

KIMBERLEY

MAURICE CREEK ABORIGINAL LAND

Hidden Island

WOTJALUM

Talbot Bay

Walcott Inlet

Mt Page 466m

SYNNOT RANGE

Barnett RIVER

Mount Barnett Roadhouse

Strickland Bay

ABORIGINAL

Secure Bay

KING

Tabletop Mtn 480m

Mt Blythe 436m

Kupingarri

Cone Bay

LAND

McLARTY RANGE

Isdell River

Mt Glemont 478m

Beverley Springs

GIBB

BARNETT RANGE

Mt Nellie 267m

Mt Disaster 266m

Mt Humbert 474m

Mt Synnot 488m

PHILLIPS

Cascade Bay

MILITARY

TRAINING

AREA

Adcock Gorge

RANGE

Long Is

Robinson River

Mt Matthew 586m

LEOPOLD

Mt House

King Sound

VAN

EMMERICK RANGE

Round Hill

Mt Hart

Mt Hart 667m

RD

Mt Chalmers 704m

Mt House 551m

Stokes Bay

RANGES

Adcock River

Mt Smith 616m

Mt Bell 744m

Point Torment

VISITOR INFORMATION:
Derby (1 Clarendon St)
Fitzroy Crossing (cnr Great Northern Hwy and Flynn Dr)
Halls Creek (Great Northern Hwy)
Kununurra (Coolibah Dr)

365

Lennard Gorge

Mt Herbert 753m

Mt Ord 937m

Mt Clifton 537m

Glenroy

Sir John Gor

BEAGLE BAY ABORIGINAL RESERVE

Media River

Lennard River

Napier Downs

WINDJANA GORGE NATIONAL PARK

Windjana Gorge

Mt Behn 344m

WINDJANA GORGE NATIONAL PARK: Consists of a gorge formed by the Lennard River as it snakes its way through a 350-million year old reef of ancient limestone. The river only flows for short periods but isolated pools support an abundance of fish and birds. A number of interesting walks exist with trail-side signs interpreting features in the gorge.

Mt Estaughs 476m

Mt Leake 697m

KING

Mornington

Derby

Meda

Kimberley Downs

Mt Marmion 105m

RIVER

North River

Diamond Gorge

Myall's Bore

Boab Prison Tree

DERBY HWY

GIBB

40

46

TUNNEL CREEK NATIONAL PARK: Provides an opportunity to explore a creek as it tunnels through a mountain range. Remember to bring a torch and be prepared to walk through cold water.

Fairfield

TUNNEL CREEK NATIONAL PARK

43

GIBB RIVER ROAD: Built to carry large road trains of cattle being transported from isolated stations to the ports of Derby and Wyndham. Road conditions vary and it is advisable to check before departure.

Creek

DEVONIAN REEF NATIONAL PARKS

Mt Clarkson 94m

Yeeda

10

GREAT

41

SISTERS PLATEAU

OSCAR PLATEAU

95

GEIKIE GORGE NATIONAL PARK: Formed by centuries of water eroding through an ancient limestone reef. The gorge contains permanent fresh water and supports a variety of animal life, including freshwater crocodiles. Cruises up the gorge are available.

TO BROOME

Willare Bridge Roadhouse

30

NORTHERN

54

Blina

Creek

OSCAR

30

RANGE

BROOKING GORGE CP

Leopold Downs

GEIKIE GORGE NATIONAL PARK

only

Yakka Munga

23

Camballin

17 Mile Dam

Mt Wynne

Ellendale

HWY

54

Geikie Gorge

Brooking Spring

Fossil Downs

Udialla

Mt Anderson 306m

Looma

Calwynyardah

217

38

Mt Ell 317

82

Mount Anderson

LOOMA ABORIGINAL RESERVE

Mt Wynne 144m

Fitzroy Crossing

Mt Pierre 203m

Margaret

Lulugui

Myroodah

73

Gogo

57

RANGE

4WD

80

NOOGOORA BURR

Mt Hardman 132m

Mt Abbott

Quanbun Downs

Jubilee Downs

Dampier Downs

QUARANTINE AREA

Nerrima

Noonkanbah

River

Twin Buttes

Camelgooda Hill

Kalyeeda

Dukes Dome 304m

Christmas

Cadjebut Mine

Babrongan Tower

Mowla Bluff

Mt Jariemai 185m

Mt James 175m

Mt Tuckfield 311m

ST GEORGE RANGES

Mt Fenton 187m

Mt Amy 268m

Mt Thorian 263m

32

Mt Piper 337m

Christmas Creek

J K L M N O P Q R

1

DRYSDALE RIVER NATIONAL PARK

OOMBULGURRI ABORIGINAL LAND

NOOGOORA BURR QUARANTINE AREA

OKSOW HILLS

Mt Connection 191m

Carlton Hill

2

BOAB: A symbol of the region, the boab, sometimes called the 'bottle tree', produces furry brown nuts on which local artists carve scenes or animals.

Wyndham

Prison Tree only

4WD

52

4WD

Home Valley

Mt Cockburn North 496m

COCKBURN RANGE

34

41

PARRY LAGOONS NATURE RESERVE

VICTORIA

38

43

Kununurra

MIRIMA NATIONAL PARK

Emu Creek (Gulgagulaeng)

36

99

HWY

MIRIMA NATIONAL PARK: A rugged area of ancient sandstone hills and valleys of special significance to the Aboriginal people. The park has several pleasant walking trails which offer spectacular views of both the park and Kununurra.

KEEP RIVER NATIONAL PARK

3

GIBB 284

Ellenbrae 165

Ellenbrae Creek

RIVER

Durack

RANGE

Emma Gorge

El Questro Station

Dunham Pilot Dam

Lake Kununurra

Ord River

34

20

Mt Hensman 384m

Mt Brooking 379m

Lake Argyle Tourist Village

Ord Dam

Newry

TO KATHERINE

4

44

Pimple Peak

Pentecost Downs

FACE RANGE

BLUFF

Chapman Creek

Salmond River

RANGES

Pentecost River

Dunham River

SAW RANGES

117

Dunham River

CARR BOYD RANGE

Lake Argyle

Rosewood

The Twins 318m

38

5

ARGYLE DIAMOND MINE: Largest producing diamond mine. The pink diamonds from the mine along with other precious gems can be purchased at various outlets in Kununurra.

151

HWY

Glenhill

Argyle Diamond Mine

Lissadell

29

Ord

Spring Creek

Mt Quirk 323m

80

RD

Mt Mary

Waterloo

6

WARNINGS: In outback Australia, long distances separate some towns. Travellers should familiarise themselves with prevailing conditions before departure and take care to ensure their vehicle is roadworthy. Adequate supplies of petrol, water and food should be carried at all times.

In northern Australia, rainfall during the wet season (October to March) can make some roads impassable. Full information on road conditions should be obtained from local authorities before departure.

If visitors intend diverting off public roads within Aboriginal Land areas, a permit is required from the relevant Aboriginal authority.

Beware of crocodiles in rivers, estuaries and coastal areas.

Chamberlain

DURACK

Wilson River

Castlereagh Hill

Bow River

34

Turkey Creek Roadhouse

Warmun

Turkey Ck

Mt Jarrad

Texas Downs

32

Bow River

West Baines River

253

436

7

VIOLET HILL ABORIGINAL LAND

Mt Lush 778m

Mt Remarkable 748m

Mabel Downs

55

163

NORTHERN

OSMOND RANGE

Osmond River

Mt John 526m

Mt Buchanan 417m

Mt Elder

Mistake Creek

36

Negri

8

72

Tableland

4WD only

Mt King 950m

28

Ord

Bedford Downs

74

Mt Ranford

River

4WD only

RANGE

DIXON

PURNULULU

NATIONAL

PARK

DUNCAN

90

NORTHERN TERRITORY
WESTERN AUSTRALIA

Nelson Springs

Mt Panton 340m

9

LEOPOLD

Little Fitzroy River

Mt Warton 37m

Fitzroy River

NARRIE RANGE

71

Mt Laptz 245m

Lansdowne

4WD only

52

GREAT

Tullewa Hill

Mt Wells 983m

Springvale

14

Alice Downs

Old Turner

PURNULULU NATIONAL PARK: The Bungle Bungles in Purnululu National Park are considered one of Australia's greatest natural wonders. The ecology of the park is very delicately balanced as the striped rock formations have a skin of beach lichen and orange silica which if broken, exposes the soft sandstone underneath to erosion. The southern end of the park contains the spectacular beehive formations and awe-inspiring gorges. Vehicle access is limited to 4WD only.

Kirkimbie

HWY

10

old

Little

Panton R

Little Ponton

34

Mt Coghlan 622m

Saunders Creek

Nicholson

RD

BUNTINE

11

Ball 4m

fred

Mt Cummings

O'Donnell

RANGE

MUELLER

Mt Amhurst 719m

Moola Bulla

Mt Barrett 692m

22

Halls Creek

China Wall

Burks Park

Sophie Downs

29

Mt Flora 458m

Elvire River

Flora Valley

80

Wallamunga

12

Mt Ramsay 421m

Margaret River

11

Fairbairn 8m

Louisa Downs

Mount Amhurst

Glidden

Mt Cummings

16

Lamboo

Koongie Park

34

41

HWY

NORTHERN

47

Mt Dockrell 500m

Ruby Plains

Black

Palm Spring

DUNCAN

55

173

30

Canning Stock Route Heritage Trail

47

Mt Wittenoom 428m

Gordon Downs

GARDNER RANGE

13

98

GREAT 295

Mary River

Wolfe Creek

TANAMI

RD

DENISON PLAINS

CANNING STOCK ROUTE: Once the longest and loneliest stock route, the 1500-km track enabled the beef cattle from the Kimberley region to be driven to the southern goldfields.

Downs

J K L M N O P Q R

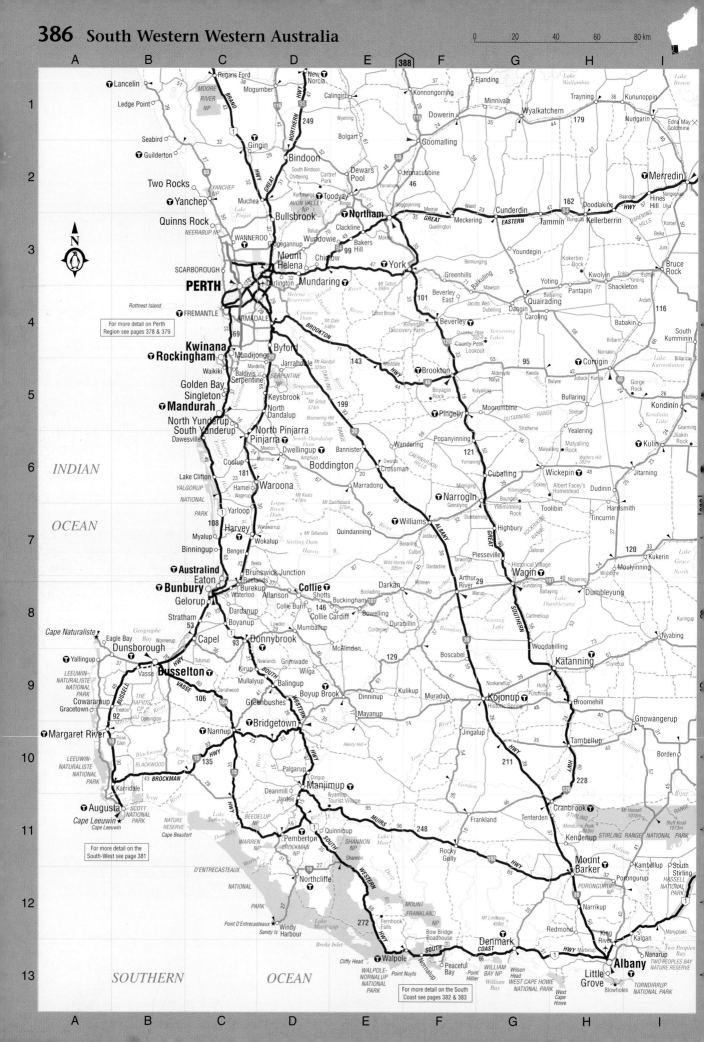

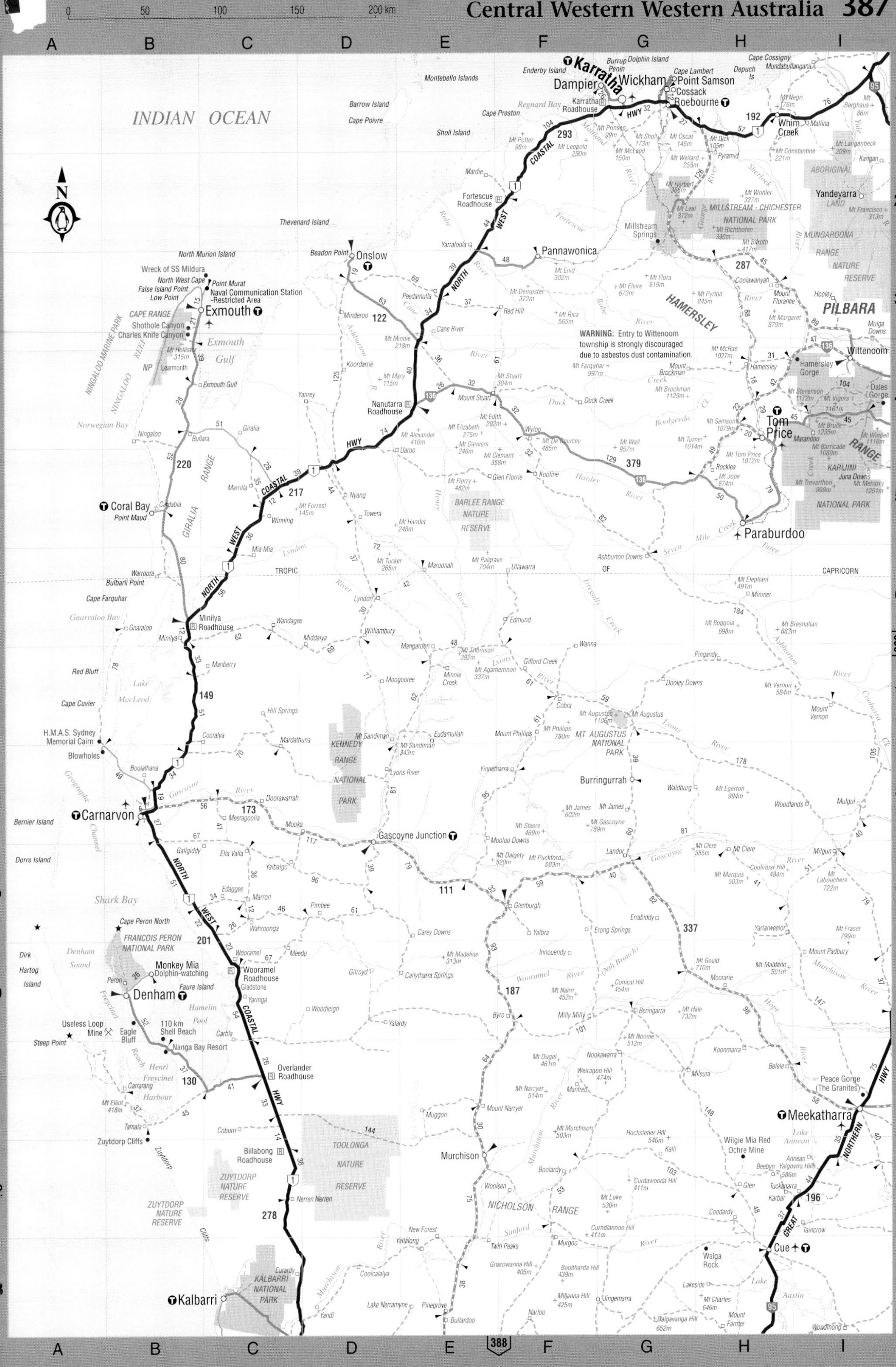

0   50   100   150   200 km

INDIAN OCEAN

N

Karratha
Dampier
Wickham
Point Samson
Cossack
Roebourne
Karratha Roadhouse
Burrup Penin
Dolphin Island
Enderby Island
Cape Lambert
Cape Cossigny
Depuch Is
Mundabullangana
Whim Creek
192

Montebello Islands
Barrow Island
Cape Poivre
Sholl Island
Cape Preston
Regnard Bay

Mt Negri
176m
Berghaus
86m
Mallina
Mt Langenbeck
209m
Kangan

Fortescue Roadhouse

Pannawonica

MILLSTREAM - CHICHESTER NATIONAL PARK
Millstream Springs
Mt Richthofen
390m

HAMERSLEY

PILBARA
Wittenoom
Hamersley Gorge

WARNING: Entry to Wittenoom township is strongly discouraged due to asbestos dust contamination.

Onslow
Beadon Point
Peedamulla
Cane River
Red Hill

Exmouth
North West Cape
Point Murat
Naval Communication Station -Restricted Area
North Murion Island
Wreck of SS Mildura
False Island Point
Low Point
Learmonth
Exmouth Gulf

CAPE RANGE
Shothole Canyon
Charles Knife Canyon
Mt Hollins 315m

NINGALOO MARINE PARK
NP

Nanutarra Roadhouse

Tom Price
Mt McRae 1027m
Mount Brockman
Mt Brockman 1129m

KARIJINI NATIONAL PARK

Paraburdoo
379

Coral Bay
Point Maud
Cadabia

GIRALIA RANGE

TROPIC OF CAPRICORN

Warroora
Bulbarli Point
Cape Farquhar
Minilya Roadhouse

BARLEE RANGE NATURE RESERVE

Gnaraloo Bay
Gnaraloo
Red Bluff
Cape Cuvier

Lake MacLeod

149

Manberry

Hill Springs
Mardathuna

KENNEDY RANGE NATIONAL PARK

MT AUGUSTUS NATIONAL PARK
Mt Augustus 1106m
Mt Augustus 780m

Burringurrah

H.M.A.S. Sydney Memorial Cairn
Blowholes
Boolathana

Carnarvon
173
Meeragoolia
Mooka
Gascoyne Junction
111

Mt James 602m
Mt Gascoyne 789m

Bernier Island
Dorre Island
Shark Bay

FRANCOIS PERON NATIONAL PARK
Cape Peron North
201
Monkey Mia Dolphin-watching
Faure Island
Denham
Wooramel Roadhouse
Gladstone
Yaringa
187
337

Dirk Hartog Island
Steep Point
Useless Loop Mine
Eagle Bluff
110 km Shell Beach
Nanga Bay Resort
130
Overlander Roadhouse
Zuytdorp Cliffs
Tamala

TOOLONGA NATURE RESERVE
144

Murchison

NICHOLSON RANGE

Meekatharra
Peace Gorge (The Granites)
196

Billabong Roadhouse
278

ZUYTDORP NATURE RESERVE

Cue

Kalbarri
KALBARRI NATIONAL PARK

GREAT NORTHERN HWY

Walga Rock

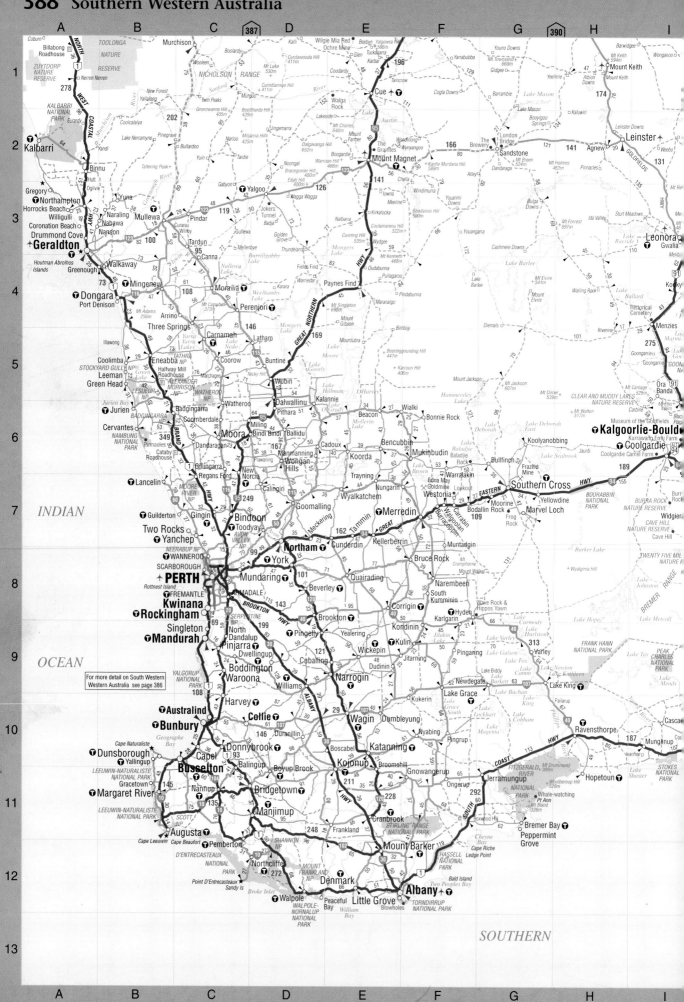

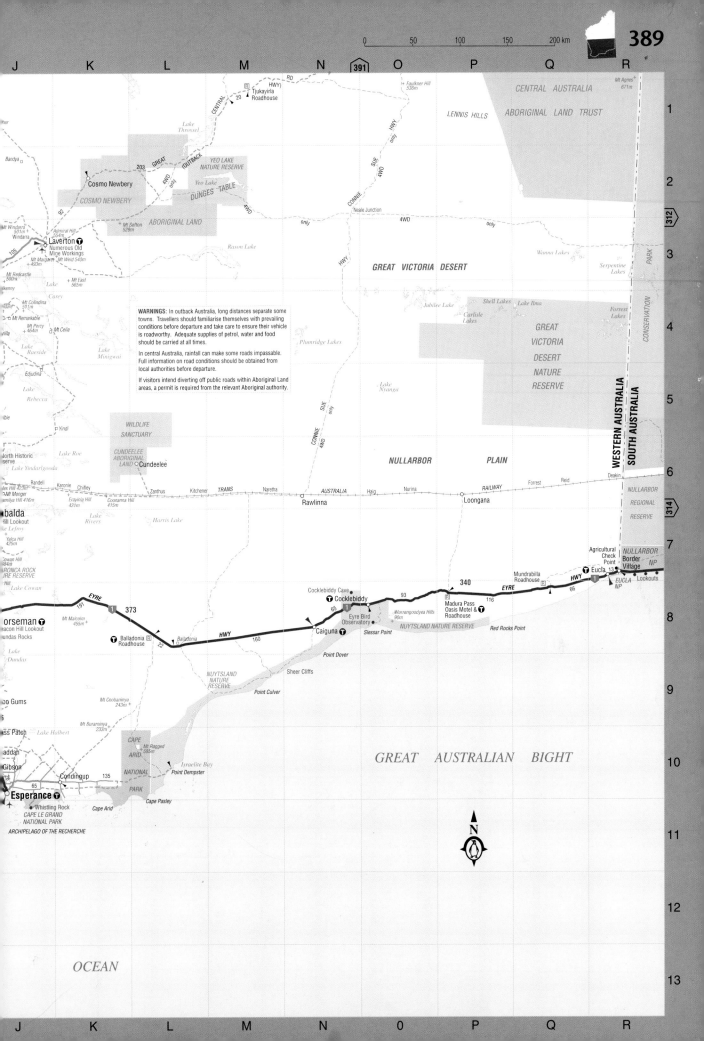

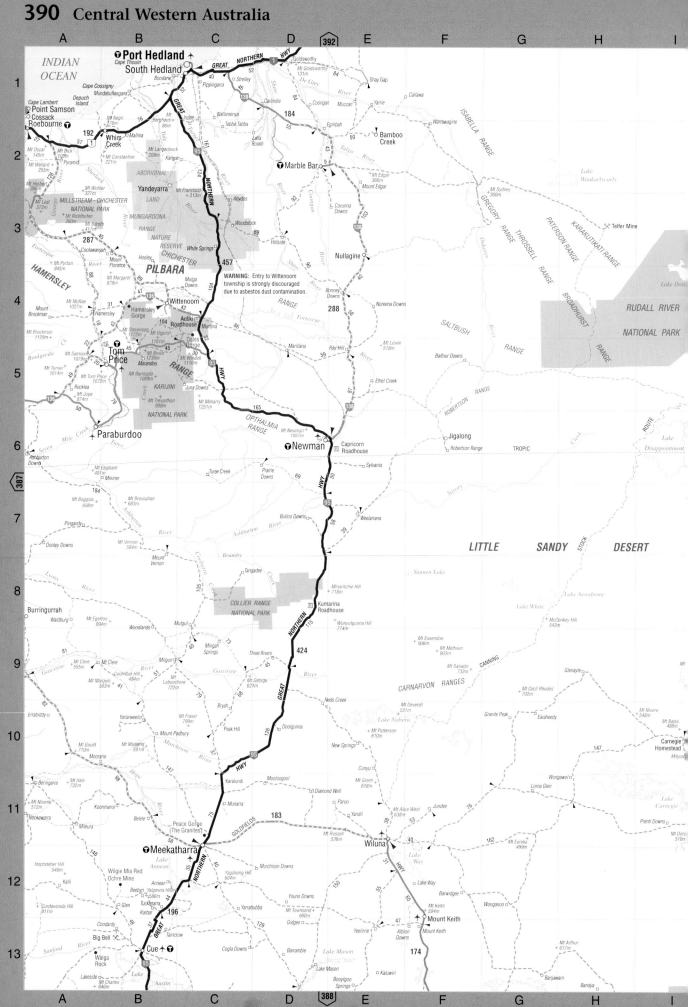

0   50   100   150   200 km

J   K   L   M   N   O   P   Q   R

WARNINGS: In outback Australia, long distances separate some towns. Travellers should familiarise themselves with prevailing conditions before departure and take care to ensure their vehicle is roadworthy. Adequate supplies of petrol, water and food should be carried at all times.

In central Australia, rainfall can make some roads impassable. Full information on road conditions should be obtained from local authorities before departure.

If visitors intend diverting off public roads within Aboriginal Land areas, a permit is required from the relevant Aboriginal authority.

393

1
2
3
4
5
6
7
8
9
10
11
12
13

KEARNEY

ABORIGINAL

LAND

Lake Gregory

Lake Jeavons
Lake Dennis
Lake Lucas
Lake White
Lake Wills
Lake Hazlett

Mt Cornish
363m
Mt Romily
353m

Mt Crown Head
419m
Mt Elliott
418m

ROUTE

Percival Lakes

Tobin Lake

Lake Auld

Lake George

Lake Mackay

infred

CANNING

STOCK

Gary Junction

OF

CAPRICORN

Windy Corner

Kiwirrkurra

Mt Webb
532m

Mt Tietkens
546m

Ininti

438

Kintore
Mt Leisler
901m

Lake Macdonald

GIBSON   DESERT

Lake Cobb

CENTRAL AUSTRALIA
ABORIGINAL LAND TRUST

Lake Hopkins

WESTERN AUSTRALIA
NORTHERN TERRITORY

Mt Madley
533m

Lake Cohen

McPhersons Pillar
530m

Lake Hancock

GIBSON DESERT

Lake Newell

NATURE RESERVE

Lake Earnham

Mt Taylor
1001m

Kaltukatjara
(Docker River)

Lake Jones

MUNGILLI
CLAYPAN
NATURE
RESERVE

Mt Lampe
497m

Charlies Knob
551m

HWY   Everard Junction

Mt Everard
544m

Warakurna
18
Giles
Meteorological
Station

Warakurna
Roadhouse

29

76

PETERMANN

RANGES

GUNBARREL

Mt William Lambert
517m

Mt Johnson
534m

452

Mt Beadell
530m

Notabilis Hill
468m

Thryptomene Hill
439m

Mt Samuel
519m

BAKER

RANGE

Lake Breaden

Jackie Junction

JAMESON

RANGE

215

336

Mt Harvest
558m

Bentley Hill
581m

RANGE

248

105

Blackstone

Mt Gosse
885m

Surveyor
Generals
Corner

Mt Cockburn
1138m

SUTHERLAND

RANGE

Mt Worsnop
461m

Boyd
Lagoon

WARBURTON

Warburton
Roadhouse

Warburton

Mt Talbot 623m

Mt Rawlinson
670m

Mt Elvire
603m

Mt Palgrave
539m

Mt Scott 668m

BARROW

RANGE

Mt Aloysius
1085m

55

Mt Hinckley
1018m

Kalka

Aparawatatja

Mt Davies
1058m

Pipalyatjara

Lake Gillen

IDA   RANGE

RD

HWY

4WD
only

565

CENTRAL

209

(OUTBACK

SUE

Mt Eveline
631m

Mt Eliza
646m

Mt Gooper
670m

CENTRAL   AUSTRALIA

312

ke Wells

Calachini Hills
543m

Empress
Spring

59

Tjukayirla
Roadhouse

GREAT

20

Faulkner Hill
536m

Mt Agnes
671m

Permano Hill
719m

WESTERN AUSTRALIA
SOUTH AUSTRALIA

Lake Throssel

CONNIE

LENNIS HILLS

ABORIGINAL   LAND   TRUST

YEO LAKE
NATURE RESERVE

389

J   K   L   M   N   O   P   Q   R

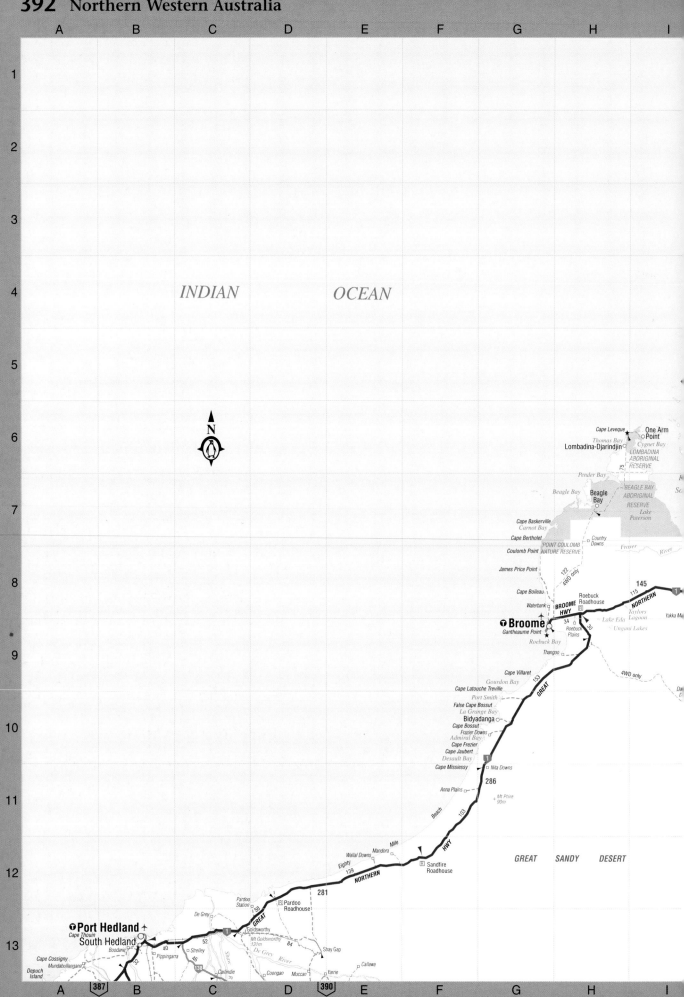

INDIAN   OCEAN

N

Cape Leveque → One Arm Point
Thomas Bay   Cygnet Bay
Lombadina-Djarindjin   LOMBADINA ABORIGINAL RESERVE

Pender Bay

Beagle Bay   Beagle Bay   BEAGLE BAY ABORIGINAL RESERVE
                                 Lake Paterson

Cape Baskerville
Carnot Bay
Cape Bertholet   POINT COULOMB   Country Downs
Coulomb Point   NATURE RESERVE   Fraser River

James Price Point   122
                                                4WD only

Cape Boileau   145
                                                115
Waterbank   BROOME   Roebuck   NORTHERN
               HWY   Roadhouse
⊕ Broome   34   Taylors
Gantheaume Point   Roebuck   30   Lagoon
                          Plains   Lake Eda
                          Roebuck Bay   Ungani Lakes
                Thangoo

Cape Villaret   4WD only
Gourdon Bay   153
Cape Latouche Treville   GREAT
Port Smith
False Cape Bossut
La Grange Bay
Bidyadanga
Cape Bossut
Frazier Downs
Admiral Bay
Cape Frezier
Cape Jaubert
Desault Bay
Cape Missiessy   Nita Downs
                      286
Anna Plains   Mt Phire 90m

                 Beach   103

                                       GREAT   SANDY   DESERT

Mile
Wallal Downs   Mandora   HWY
Eighty   139   Sandfire Roadhouse
                NORTHERN
                            281

Pardoo Station   50
De Grey   GREAT   Pardoo Roadhouse
Goldsworthy
⊕ Port Hedland   52   Mt Goldsworthy 84
Cape Thouin   40   131m   Shay Gap
South Hedland   Boodarie De Grey River
Cape Cossigny Mundabullangana Pippingarra 46 Callawa
Depuch Island   Carlindie   Coongan Muccan Yarrie

387   138   390

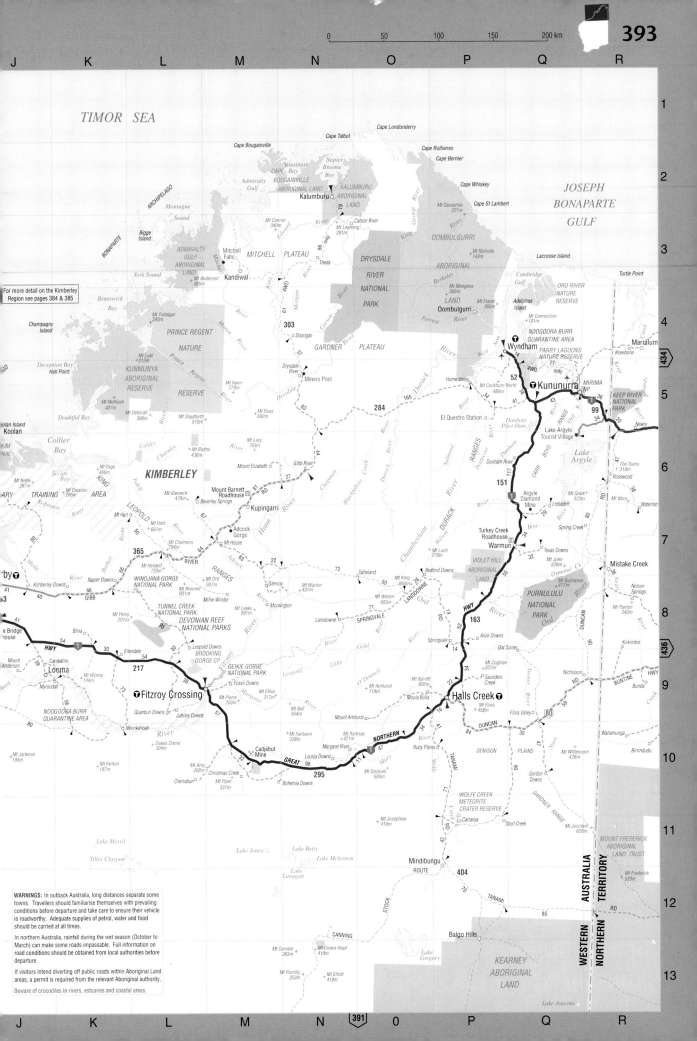

TIMOR SEA

JOSEPH
BONAPARTE
GULF

KIMBERLEY

WARNINGS: In outback Australia, long distances separate some
towns. Travellers should familiarise themselves with prevailing
conditions before departure and take care to ensure their vehicle
is roadworthy. Adequate supplies of petrol, water and food
should be carried at all times.

In northern Australia, rainfall during the wet season (October to
March) can make some roads impassable. Full information on
road conditions should be obtained from local authorities before
departure.

If visitors intend diverting off public roads within Aboriginal Land
areas, a permit is required from the relevant Aboriginal authority.

Beware of crocodiles in rivers, estuaries and coastal areas.

WESTERN AUSTRALIA / NORTHERN TERRITORY

NORTHERN TERRITORY

Uluru (Ayers Rock)

ustralia's Northern Territory is known as a place of vast, wild beauty and remarkable extremes. The landscape of the Red Centre, dominated by rugged ranges, open plains and red dunes, exists in complete contrast with the tropical waterfalls and mangrove wetlands of the Top End.

Six times the size of Great Britain, the Northern Territory has a population similar to that of Newcastle in New South Wales. Among numerous places of interest it boasts the famous Red Centre, the world's largest monolith Uluṟu (Ayers Rock), and many of the best Aboriginal rock-art sites in the continent.

There are only three main highways that take motorists into the Northern Territory: the Barkly Highway from Mount Isa in Queensland, the Stuart Highway from South Australia and the Victoria Highway from the extreme north-east of Western Australia.

Given the enormous distances involved, you may well decide to fly, either to Darwin or to Alice Springs, and then hire a car to travel around the area. Alternatively, airlines, coach companies and many tour operators offer day and extended coach tours, coach camping tours, and adventure and safari trek tours, all of which allow you to discover this unique, relatively uninhabited and exciting Territory in experienced hands.

If you are going it alone by car, you should research your trip before setting out; read the section on Outback Motoring (p. 603) and bear in mind that the dry season is definitely the most pleasant weather for touring. Always make detailed enquiries about conditions before leaving sealed roads. The Stuart, Arnhem, Kakadu, Victoria and Barkly highways are now all-weather roads, sealed for their entire length. Even so, any driving at night should be undertaken with care because of the danger from wildlife and cattle wandering across the road.

The first, unsuccessful, attempt to settle this huge, forbidding region was not on the mainland at all, but on Melville Island in 1824. It was not until 1869 that a town called Palmerston, later to become Darwin, was established. Originally the Territory was part of

New South Wales, when that State's western boundary extended to the 129th east meridian. Later, the Territory was annexed to South Australia and it did not come under Commonwealth control until 1911. In July 1978 the Territory attained self-government.

In terms of monetary value, the Territory's main industry is mining with an emphasis on gold, bauxite, manganese ore, copper, silver and uranium. The tourist industry ranks second, and beef-cattle farming is significant, even though sixteen hectares or more are often required to support one animal.

The dry season, between May and October, is a good time to visit; Darwin's average monthly rainfall during this period is only 21 millimetres. Between November and April, Darwin has an

NOT TO BE MISSED	
IN THE NORTHERN TERRITORY	**Map Ref.**
ALICE SPRINGS DESERT PARK A spectacular showcase of Central Australia's flora and fauna	433 N4
KINGS CANYON Soaring 300-metre sandstone walls and views of the valley below	438 F9
LITCHFIELD NATIONAL PARK Superb scenery and spring-fed waterfalls	430 C8
NITMILUK (KATHERINE) GORGE Cruise through this fascinating river canyon	434 G10
ORMISTON GORGE The jewel in the West MacDonnell Ranges	432 I4
TERRITORY WILDLIFE PARK Drive south-east from Darwin to see excellent displays of native fauna in natural bushland	430 D4
UBIRR Outstanding rock-art galleries in Kakadu National Park	431 Q2
ULUṞU (AYERS ROCK) The Red Centre's most famous landmark	438 E12

average monthly rainfall of 256 millimetres, the rain falling mainly in the afternoon and overnight. July is the Northern Territory's coolest month when Darwin's average maximum temperature is 30° C. In Alice Springs the average maximum in July is 20° C, cooling at night to around zero.

The Northern Territory's two main centres, Darwin and Alice Springs, are more than 1500 kilometres apart. Darwin was largely rebuilt after Cyclone Tracy in 1974. It is known for its relaxed lifestyle and beautiful beaches, and makes a perfect jumping-off spot for exploring the Top End region.

East of Darwin is Kakadu National Park, which is rich in natural and cultural heritage. The section of Arnhem Land east of Kakadu can be explored by extended coach tour or adventure tour. Many Aboriginal lands require entry permission from an Aboriginal Land Council.

South of Darwin is the superb wilderness area of Litchfield National Park. Further south is Katherine, with its spectacular Nitmiluk Gorge. From Katherine, the Stuart Highway continues via Tennant Creek to Alice Springs.

Alice Springs has been immortalised on film and in snapshots countless times. No other town, or even tiny settlement, is nearer to the geographic centre of the country. In 1872 Alice Springs was simply a repeater station for the Overland Telegraph Service; today it is not only the centre for the outback cattle industry, but also a lively tourist centre with a permanent population of approximately 22 000.

Uluṟu (Ayers Rock), 450 kilometres to the south-west in Uluṟu–Kata Tjuṯa National Park, is the world's biggest monolith: one huge rock, 9 kilometres in circumference and rising 348 metres above the plain on which it stands.

CLIMATE GUIDE

DARWIN

	J	F	M	A	M	J	J	A	S	O	N	D
Maximum °C	32	31	32	33	32	31	30	31	32	33	33	33
Minimum °C	25	25	24	24	22	20	19	21	23	25	25	25
Rainfall mm	406	349	311	97	21	1	1	7	19	74	143	232
Raindays	21	20	19	9	2	0	1	1	2	7	12	16

ALICE SPRINGS REGION

	J	F	M	A	M	J	J	A	S	O	N	D
Maximum °C	36	35	32	28	23	20	19	22	27	31	33	35
Minimum °C	21	21	17	13	8	5	4	6	10	15	18	20
Rainfall mm	36	42	37	14	17	15	16	12	9	21	26	37
Raindays	5	5	3	2	3	3	3	2	2	5	6	5

Jim Jim Falls, Kakadu National Park

VISITOR INFORMATION
Northern Territory Tourist Commission
freecall 1800 621 336
www.nttc.com.au

Central Australian Tourism Industry Association
cnr Gregory Tce and Todd St, Alice Springs
(08) 8952 5800
www.catia.asn.au/catia

Darwin Region Tourism Association
cnr Mitchell and Knuckey sts, Darwin
(08) 8981 4300

Kata Tjuṯa (The Olgas)

CALENDAR OF EVENTS

JANUARY
Public holidays: New Year's Day; Australia Day. *Alice Springs:* Lasseter's Indoor Challenge.

EASTER
Public holidays: Good Friday; Easter Monday. *Darwin:* Corroborree Park Challenge (fishing competition). *Borroloola:* Fishing Classic.

APRIL
Public holiday: Anzac Day. *Alice Springs:* Racing Carnival (horseracing); Country Music Festival. *Timber Creek:* Fishing Competitions.

MAY
Public holiday: May Day. *Darwin:* Arafura Sports Festival (odd-numbered years); Fred's Pass Rural Show including Litchfield Gift (foot race); Touring Car Championships. *Alice Springs:* Bangtail Muster. *Mataranka:* Back to the Never Never Festival; Art Show. *Pine Creek:* Gold Rush Festival; Races. *Tennant Creek:* Cup Day; Go-Kart Grand Prix. *Timber Creek:* Fishing Competitions (contd); Rodeo.

JUNE
Public holiday: Queen's Birthday. *Darwin:* Greek Glenti Festival. *Adelaide River:* Bush Race Meeting; Show. *Alice Springs:* Finke Desert Race. *Batchelor:* International Skydiving and Parachuting Championships (sometimes held in July). *Katherine:* Barunga Sport and Cultural Festival; Katherine Cup; Canoe Marathon. *Pine Creek:* Rodeo.

JULY
Darwin: Royal Darwin Show (regional public holiday); Darwin Cup Carnival; International Guitar Festival (odd-numbered years); Rodeo and Country Music Concert (sometimes held in Aug.). *Alice Springs:* Camel Cup; Agricultural Show. *Katherine:* Agricultural Show (regional public holiday). *Nhulunbuy:* National Aboriginal and Islander Day of Celebration. *Tennant Creek:* Agricultural Show (regional public holiday).

AUGUST
Public holiday: Picnic Day. *Darwin:* Beer Can Regatta; Darwin Cup Carnival (contd); Fringe Festival; NT championship; National Aboriginal Art Award (sometimes held in Sept.). *Alice Springs:* Rodeo. *Borroloola:* Agricultural Show (regional public holiday); Rodeo. *Jabiru:* Wind Festival. *Katherine:* Flying Fox Festival. *Mataranka:* Rodeo.

SEPTEMBER
Darwin: Festival of Darwin; Fringe Festival (contd). *Daly Waters:* Rodeo. *Katherine:* Flying Fox Festival (contd). *Tennant Creek:* Desert Harmony Festival (arts and culture festival). *Timber Creek:* Races (horseracing).

OCTOBER
Alice Springs: Henley-on-Todd Regatta; Masters Games (mature-age athletic carnival, even-numbered years).

NOVEMBER
Alice Springs: Corkwood Festival (art, craft, music and dance).

DECEMBER
Public holidays: Christmas Day; Boxing Day.

Note: The information given here was accurate at the time of printing. However, as the timing of events held annually is subject to change and some events may extend into the following month, it is best to check with the local tourism authority or event organisers to confirm the details. The calendar is not exhaustive. Most towns and regions throughout the Territory hold sporting competitions; regattas; rodeos; art, craft and trade exhibitions; agricultural and flower shows; music festivals and other events annually. Details of these events are available from local tourism outlets.

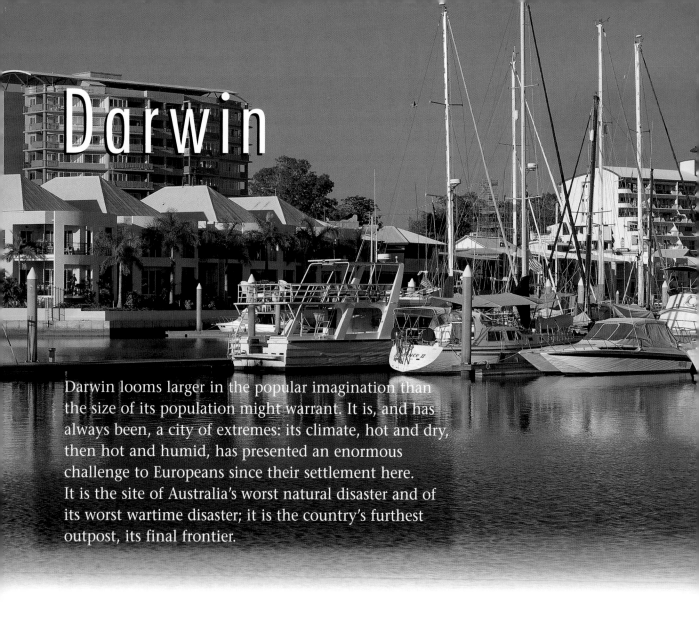

Darwin

Darwin looms larger in the popular imagination than the size of its population might warrant. It is, and has always been, a city of extremes: its climate, hot and dry, then hot and humid, has presented an enormous challenge to Europeans since their settlement here. It is the site of Australia's worst natural disaster and of its worst wartime disaster; it is the country's furthest outpost, its final frontier.

VISITOR INFORMATION
Darwin Region Tourism Association
cnr Mitchell and Knuckey sts, Darwin
(08) 8981 4300

GETTING AROUND
Airport shuttle bus
Darwin Airport Shuttle (08) 8981 5066
Motoring organisation
Automobile Association of the
Northern Territory (AANT) (08) 8981 3837
Car rental
Avis (08) 8981 9922; Brits-Australia
(08) 8981 2081; Budget (08) 8981 9800;
Hertz (08) 8941 0944
Public transport
Darwin Bus Service (08) 8924 7666
Bus tours
Tour Tub (08) 8981 5233;
Darwin Discovery Service (08) 8932 6222
Taxis
Darwin Radio Taxis (08) 8981 9835
Boat cruises
City of Darwin Cruises 018 890 429;
Darwin Pearl Lugger Cruises (08) 8942 3131;
Spirit of Darwin (08) 8981 3711

Twice rebuilt, Darwin has a spacious, ordered feel thanks to the wide streets, newish, low buildings and expansive, manicured lawns. But it is also a city with a magnificent tropical chaos as streets give way to mangrove estuaries, brightly coloured foliage and huge ocean tides.

Darwin is about the size of a provincial country town (population 86 600), with all the facilities you would expect of a capital city, such as major cultural and social institutions, great restaurants, international hotels and a range of leisure activities. Culturally and ethnically it is Australia's most diverse city. The mix includes southern transients on northern assignments; tourists from as far away as Europe on extended stays; Aboriginal communities to whom the site of Darwin once belonged; the stayers, the settlers who have lived through successive disasters (and who have kept coming back); and the large immigrant communities, most hailing from nearby South-East Asia and China.

The climate of the Top End is legendary. The temperatures sit for most of the year in the low thirties. Between May and October the climate is dry and still. In November the Wet arrives and the city is subjected to months of high humidity, monsoonal rain (400 millimetres in January alone) and some random madness on the part of the residents as they wait for the worst to pass. That said, there are many who come especially for this season. The human population drops, the wildlife population expands, and the landscape of the city and surrounds turns a lush tropical green.

EXPLORING DARWIN

Darwin is a very easy city to negotiate either by car or on foot. The streets are well signed and traffic is light even at peak times. The **Tour Tub** is a service that

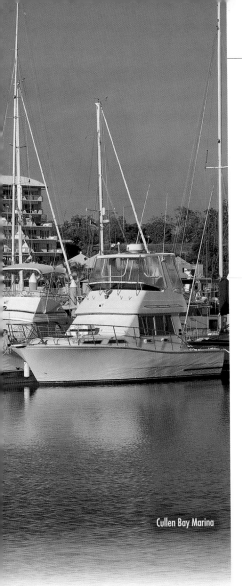

Cullen Bay Marina

provides a bus tour of the city's top sights, departing daily from the north end of Smith Street Mall. The service completes a loop every hour, and you can get on and off as you please. Another service, the **Darwin Discovery Service**, will pick you up from your accommodation and take you further afield. The extensive network of paths around town, along with the benefit of a fairly flat terrain, makes Darwin a terrific place to explore by bicycle. A tour of the harbour is a must. Cullen Bay Marina is the departure point for cruises around Fannie Bay, Stokes Hill Wharf and Frances Bay, and for ferry trips to Mandorah on the Cox Peninsula. The Darwin Bus Service provides a vital link between the city centre and outlying suburbs; the main terminal is on Harry Chan Avenue. If you are planning to hire a car, it is important to check the stipulations for driving on unsealed roads, particularly if you are travelling beyond Darwin.

DARWIN BY AREA

CITY CENTRE

Start your exploration of Darwin in **Smith Street Mall**, the city's retail heart. Within this pleasant area of plazas, modern shops and giant tropical trees is the **Victoria Hotel**, built in the 1890s. Still a fully operational hotel and popular with visitors and locals alike, it now has a small shopping complex.

Walk south down Smith Street, beyond the mall, to the corner of Harry Chan Avenue and **Brown's Mart**, now home to the Darwin Theatre Company. It was built in 1883, making it Darwin's oldest surviving commercial structure. Visitors with thespian aspirations can participate in the workshops held regularly. Opposite, lie the ruins of the **Palmerston (Darwin) Town Hall**, which was built in 1883 and survived a devastating cyclone in 1897 and the bombings of World War II, before being destroyed by Cyclone Tracy in 1974.

Continue south along Smith Street, towards the harbour, to **Christ Church Cathedral**. The original church was built in 1902. It served as the Garrison Church during the war, was hit by Japanese fire in 1942 and was destroyed by Cyclone Tracy in 1974. The new Christ Church incorporates the original porch, which serves as a memorial to the victims of the cyclone, and an incredible altar that was hewn from a jarrah log believed to be more than 400 years old. Behind the church, in the back courtyard of Darwin City Council's Civic Centre, you will find the 'Tree of Knowledge', an ancient spreading banyan tree (Aboriginal name, *dura-munkamani*), bearing an inscription that says it has served as a meeting place for 'travellers, wise old-timers and free-thinking young people'.

Walk back towards the city, passing the Magistrates Court and along Bennett Street, before turning into Woods Street to visit the **Chinese Temple**. Rebuilt in 1978 from the remains of the original temple constructed in 1887, it serves to mark the long history and cultural impact of the Asian population in Darwin. Visitors are welcome, but remember that the temple is still used for religious purposes.

NOT TO BE MISSED

IN DARWIN	Map Ref.
AQUASCENE Hand-feed Darwin's many fish species	427 B7
BICENTENNIAL PARK Take a stroll here at sunset	427 C8
CROCODYLUS PARK For a safe encounter with these prehistoric monster reptiles	430 D2
CULLEN BAY MARINA Wonderful views and waterfront dining	428 B10
DARWIN BOTANIC GARDENS Lush tropical gardens	430 D1
DECKCHAIR CINEMA Dry-season screenings of alternative films under the stars (May–Oct.)	430 I9
HARBOUR CRUISE Explore the beautiful Darwin coastline	428 B10
MINDIL BEACH SUNSET MARKET Exotic foods, arts and crafts, a tropical sunset and great music (in the dry season, May–Oct.)	430 B1
MUSEUM & ART GALLERY OF THE NORTHERN TERRITORY Features one of the most significant Aboriginal collections in the country, and the Cyclone Tracy Exhibition	428 D7
PARLIAMENT HOUSE Darwin's most imposing modern building	430 F10

RESTAURANTS AND CAFES

Popular dining precincts include **Cullen Bay Marina**, **Stokes Hill Wharf** *and* **Mitchell Street** *in the city. The quality and variety of food available at restaurants is generally excellent given the size of the city. The diverse multicultural population guarantees excellent opportunities for ethnic dining. And in the dry season (May–Oct.), don't forget the* **Mindil Beach Sunset Market** *for superb ethnic food at affordable prices. There is a good section on dining out in the local visitors' guide,* Darwin and the Top End Today, *available from the Darwin Region Tourism Association.*

THE ESPLANADE

The Esplanade runs north–south along the western foreshore of the city centre. Large international hotels and some lovely old tropical-style houses are perfectly positioned to catch those incomparable Darwin sunsets. **Bicentennial Park** fronts the foreshore. It has extensive walking trails, brilliant views from the many lookout points and a series of memorial sites, many commemorating World War II, as well as a steady population of joggers, power walkers and late afternoon strollers. Start your exploration at the southern end. On the corner of the Esplanade and Herbert Street is the **Hotel Darwin**, well worth a visit for its 'wartime

Parliament House, in State Square

in the tropics' atmosphere. Further along the Esplanade is **Old Admiralty House**, built in 1937 to a design by Beni Burnett, whose work set a benchmark for housing in the Top End for at least two decades. Across Knuckey Street is **Lyons Cottage** (B.A.T. House), which is run by the Museum and Art Gallery of the Northern Territory. It was built in 1925 to house staff from the British and Australian Telegraph Company. It now operates as a museum with exhibits on the history of the city. At the northern end of the Esplanade, off Doctors Gully Road, is **Aquascene**. Visitors gather here to handfeed the hundreds of fish of many different coastal species, which turn up at high tide, in time for breakfast or dinner.

STATE SQUARE

This grassy pocket perched on the sea cliffs is the Territory's place of governance. **Parliament House** dominates the square. Opened in 1994, it is a huge white structure drawing for inspiration on the architecture of the warm climes, namely Asia and the Middle East. The building, which also houses the **Northern Territory Library**, opens to the public daily, with tours on Saturdays; bookings essential. Also in State Square is the **Supreme Court** (entrance off Mitchell Street), which was built in 1990 and features a foyer with an extraordinary floor mosaic designed by the Aboriginal artist Nora Napaltijari. **Liberty Square**, the grassy apex between these buildings, was the site of a popular uprising against the tyrannical Administrator in 1918, an event that is second only to the Eureka Stockade in terms of the history of the country's insurrections. The **Overland Telegraph Memorial**, located near the southern corner of Liberty Square between Parliament House and the Supreme Court, marks the

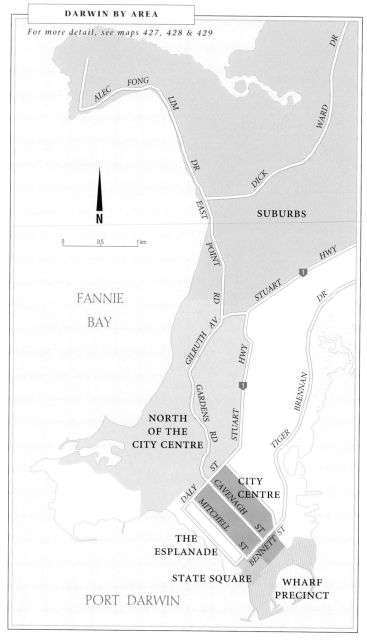

DARWIN BY AREA

For more detail, see maps 427, 428 & 429

ALEC FONG LIM DR

WARD DR

DICK WARD DR

EAST POINT RD

SUBURBS

GILRUTH AV

STUART HWY

TIGER BRENNAN DR

FANNIE BAY

GARDENS RD

STUART ST

NORTH OF THE CITY CENTRE

DALY ST

CAVENAGH ST

MITCHELL ST

BENNETT ST

CITY CENTRE

THE ESPLANADE

STATE SQUARE

WHARF PRECINCT

PORT DARWIN

N

0   0,5   1 km

centenary of other key events in Darwin's history: the completion of the Overland Telegraph line between Adelaide and Darwin, and the laying of the overseas cable to Java, Indonesia. Across the Esplanade are the lush tropical gardens of **Government House**. Built in 1883, the elegant gabled colonial residence is Darwin's oldest building. It is open to the public once a year.

At the south-east end of the Esplanade, on the corner of Smith Street, lies the **Old Police Station and Courthouse**, dating back to 1884. It was built for the South Australian Government in the days when the Territory was administered by South Australia. Nowadays the building is used as the office of the Northern Territory Administrator.

WHARF PRECINCT

Stokes Hill Wharf, which stretches out into the harbour immediately below the city centre, was once the main port for the city and, with some revamping, has become a popular leisure area. There are food outlets, a pearl store, and a bar and restaurant. A facility for servicing cruise ships can also be found here. The potential of this magnificent site has not been fully realised, but there are plans afoot for future development of the wharf precinct.

Start your exploration of the Wharf Precinct at **Survivors Lookout** on the southern side of the Esplanade. The lookout marks the spot where the battles of World War II were witnessed and reported by teams of journalists and photographers. A set of steps leads down to Hughes Avenue, then to Kitchener Drive where you will find the **World War II Oil Storage Tunnels**. This network of five concrete tunnels was built to store oil for the navy after the above-ground storage tanks were bombed by the Japanese. One tunnel is open to the public and features photographs and stories of the tumultuous war years. Continue down Kitchener Drive to the entrance to Stokes Hill Wharf. Here you will find the **Indo Pacific Marine**, where local coral ecosystems have been re-created in a series of self-maintaining exhibits. In the same building is the **Australian Pearling Exhibition**, which

Sailing is popular on Fannie Bay

SPORT AND RECREATION

*Sporting interests are well served in Darwin. There are three public golf courses (**Marrara, Gardens Park** and **Palmerston**), a motor sports complex (**Hidden Valley**) and a racecourse (**Fannie Bay**). The city also has facilities for all the major ball sports, the main facility being the popular **Marrara Sporting Complex** near the airport. Swimming pools are located at **Parap, Casuarina, Nightcliff** and **Palmerston**. Swimming in the sea is not recommended between October and May – dangerous box jellyfish are common in the waters off Darwin. Always check first with locals, regardless of what time of year. Sailing and other water sports are very popular in Darwin – just don't fall in. Fishing is huge in the Top End, and yes, you can hook a barra in the Darwin vicinity. There are some great game-fishing opportunities in the outer harbour area. Obtain a copy of the locally produced freebie, Fishing Territory, to get you on your way. Contact Darwin Region Tourism Association with any inquires about hire, charter and experienced guides.*

SHOPPING

*Darwin's shopping is particularly varied. The main shopping precincts are the city centre (**Smith Street Mall** and **Knuckey Street**) and the northern suburbs' **Casuarina Shopping Square**. A highlight of Darwin shopping is the fine selection of Top End Aboriginal and Islander art and craftwork, ranging from traditional items such as baskets and boomerangs to modern garments featuring indigenous designs.
There are a few markets around town, including the **Mindil Beach Sunset Market** (Thurs. evenings May to Oct.; Sun. evenings June to Sept.) and the **Parap Market** (Sat., 8 a.m.–2 p.m.), noted for its stalls of tropical fruit and Asian food. Other markets include the **Palmerston Night Markets** (Fri. evenings: outside in Frances Mall Apr. to Oct.; inside Palmerston Shopping Centre Nov. to Mar.); **Rapid Creek Markets** (Sun. mornings); **Nightcliff Markets** (Sun. 8 a.m.–2 p.m.); and **Mitchell Street Nite Markets** (nightly).*

DARWIN ON FOOT

Casuarina Coastal Reserve
Marked walking trail along this
beautiful coastal stretch

Darwin Botanic Gardens
Self-guide walks through different
environments; pamphlets available
from information centre at Geranium
Street entrance to gardens

The 'Discovering Darwin' series
Eight self-guide walks, including
wharf precinct, Esplanade, city
centre, northern suburbs, East Point
and Fannie Bay

Historic walk
Excellent walk covering city's historic
attractions provided in the official
visitor's guide, Darwin and the
Top End Today

For further information, contact the
Darwin Region Tourism Association

GALLERIES AND MUSEUMS

	Map Ref.
AUSTRALIAN AVIATION HERITAGE CENTRE Exhibits include a massive B52 bomber and a Wessex helicopter	429 I12
AUSTRALIAN PEARLING EXHIBITION Story of pearling in northern Australia	427 I11
EAST POINT MILITARY MUSEUM Artillery, warplanes and WW II history	428 B2
FANNIE BAY GAOL MUSEUM Discover the history of Darwin from 1883 to 1979	428 D5
INDO PACIFIC MARINE Explore the wonders of the tropical ocean floor	427 I11
MUSEUM & ART GALLERY OF THE NORTHERN TERRITORY Excellent Aboriginal and regional art collections and Cyclone Tracy Exhibition	428 D7

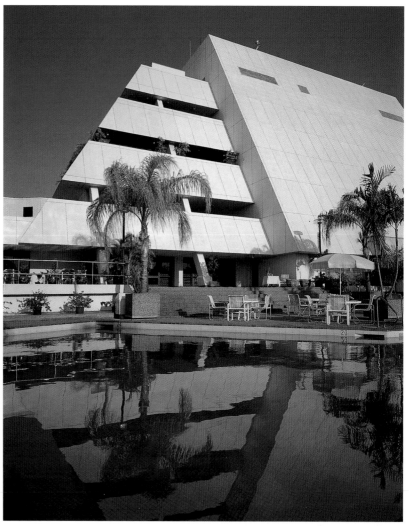

Darwin's international casino, near Mindil Beach

features exhibits on the history and science of this important Territory industry, and some superb examples of the produce. To the north is the outdoor **Deckchair Cinema** which, during the rain-free period of May to October, offers a program of alternative films beneath a tropical starlit sky.

NORTH OF THE CITY CENTRE

The **Cullen Bay Marina** is to the immediate north-west of the city and is the departure point for harbour cruises and ferries. It is also establishing itself as a leisure precinct, with restaurants, cafes, apartments, small shops and a pleasant boardwalk area. Just west of the marina is the Myilly Point Heritage Precinct, a small group of pre-World War II houses constructed for senior public servants. One of these is **Burnett House** (named after the architect Beni Burnett) now headquarters for the National Trust. As

you head north along Gilruth Avenue, the streets and buildings give way to sprawling parkland, of which the **Darwin Botanic Gardens** are a part. The gardens, which occupy 42 hectares of land, date back to a vegetable patch established in the 1870s by a German settler. These days the gardens boast a superb tropical collection, with some 1500 species in all. There are impressive orchid and palm collections, and a self-guide Aboriginal plant-use trail.

Also accessed from Gilruth Avenue is Mindil Beach, home of the **Mindil Beach Sunset Market** – the penultimate Darwin experience. The exotic smells of food from many cultures, carried on the warm air of the early evening, seem to draw together the grand themes of life at the Top End. Live entertainment, a variety of art and craft stalls and spectacular beach fireworks add the final touches to the spectacle. The market operates Thursday

Government House

nights between May and October, and Sunday nights June to September. **Mindil Beach** is a lovely 2-kilometre stretch of white sand where people stroll, play and picnic. The water is incredibly inviting, but off-limits from September to April when the box jellyfish come in – or as the locals say, 'Don't swim in the sea during the months where there's an "r" in the spelling'. **MGM Grand Darwin**, located near the shore of Mindil Beach, is a large complex offering luxury accommodation, restaurants and discos; it also houses Darwin's international casino.

Follow Gilruth Avenue into East Point Road, then turn into Conacher Street to reach the **Museum and Art Gallery of the Northern Territory** set on the cliff top overlooking Fannie Bay. Within the modern building the collection focuses on the life, history and culture of the Territory. The collection of Aboriginal paintings and artifacts held here is regarded as one of the best in the world. The complex also features a Cyclone Tracy gallery, which captures the experience and aftermath of Australia's worst natural disaster, and the 'Sweet and Sour' exhibit, recognising the contribution of Chinese families to Darwin's history. Next door to the gallery is **Territory Craft**, which houses a variety of exhibitions year-round.

SUBURBS

Heading north away from the city along East Point Road is the **Fannie Bay Gaol Museum**, housed in what was Darwin's prison between 1883 and 1979. The displays relate to the region's history, and there are remnants of prison history on display, including old cells and gallows. There are some lovely beaches and picnic spots in the area.

Continue along East Point Road into Alec Fong Lim Drive to reach **East Point Reserve**, with its walking and cycling paths, and picnic areas. It features a saltwater man-made lake, Lake Alexander, which offers crocodile-free swimming and windsurfing, and access to mangrove swamps, a dominant ecosystem in the Darwin area. The lookout at Dudley Point provides sensational views across Fannie

Bay towards central Darwin. The **East Point Military Museum**, at the western end of East Point Reserve, features artillery, war planes, archival footage of the Japanese bombings and an impressive photographic collection. Outside the museum are the gun turrets that were erected during World War II to protect the northern coastline from the Japanese onslaught.

Military history is also on display at the **Australian Aviation Heritage Centre**, located north-east of Darwin along the Stuart Highway in Winnellie. This museum houses an impressive list of exhibits including a massive B52 bomber (one of only two outside the US) and the wreckage of a Zero fighter shot down over Darwin in 1942.

Crocodylus Park is at the end of McMillans Road not far from the airport. The park is a research centre as well as a public education forum featuring a museum, crocodile-feeding displays and a variety of wildlife. Further north past the airport is the **Casuarina Coastal Reserve**, where there is a long white sandy beach backing onto dunes, mangrove and monsoon vine thickets, and patches of rainforest. A walking and cycling track runs along the reserve to Nightcliff. Sites of interest include World War II artillery observation posts and a registered Aboriginal Sacred Site, Old Man Rock (*Dariba Nunngalinya*).

Darwin has a relaxed and tropical atmosphere all its own and, despite the extremes of climate, distance and isolation, exerts a perverse attraction on both its inhabitants and visitors to this 'last frontier'.

TOP EVENTS

Touring Car Championships (May)
V8 Supercars in a three-day contest

Royal Darwin Show (July)
Three-day premier event

International Guitar Festival
(July, odd-numbered years)
Internationally renowned artists perform

Darwin Cup Carnival (July–Aug.)
The city's premier horserace

Darwin Rodeo and Country Music Concert
(July or Aug.)
Three days of yee-ha, Top End style

Darwin Beer Can Regatta (Aug.)
'Darwin-style' boat race with a difference

Darwin Fringe Festival (Aug.–Sept.)
Three weeks of cultural activities in tropical venues

National Aboriginal Art Award (Aug. or Sept.)
Acknowledges the finest indigenous art

Festival of Darwin (Sept.)
A feast of visual and performing arts

For further details visit the web site
www.nttc.com.au

CITY BY NIGHT

Darwin is a live-it-up place, and boasts increasingly varied night-time activities. There are plenty of clubs, pubs and theme bars, and, of course, the MGM Grand Casino, with its special offering of jazz on the lawns on certain Sundays (check details with MGM). For more jazz, go to Cullen Bay for Jazz on the Lawn, every Sunday. The Deckchair Cinema is popular with night owls, while Mitchell Street – a lively quarter with theme pubs, bars and cafes – is the spot to go for a nightcap. Try the Discovery nightclub there. The Darwin Theatre Company has an excellent reputation and performances can be seen at Brown's Mart, or the Darwin Entertainment Centre – also the venue for interstate and international performances. Friday's edition of the Northern Territory News publishes a roundup of what's on in the 'Gig Guide'.

DAY TOURS
from Darwin

While Kakadu National Park is the main reason most people visit the Top End, there are many attractions closer to Darwin that can be visited as part of a day trip. Litchfield National Park with its dramatic waterfalls is less than two hours' drive from Darwin. If crocodiles are on your agenda there are tours that include a crocodile farm and a boat cruise with jumping crocodiles. More fauna can be seen at the Territory Wildlife Park, Howard Springs or Fogg Dam. Mary River Wetlands offers both flora and fauna and a spot of fishing.

LITCHFIELD NATIONAL PARK

170 km to Wangi Falls via Stuart Highway and Litchfield Park Road

Litchfield National Park, less than two hours from Darwin, provides a great opportunity for visitors to experience the extraordinary natural environment of the Top End. The park is generally accessible by conventional vehicle throughout the year; during the wet season check with the ranger; (08) 8976 0282.

Leave Darwin on the Stuart Highway and turn right along Batchelor Road to **Batchelor**. Then take Litchfield Park Road through the park; all the attractions are marked along the way.

The magnetic termite mounds are the first point of interest. These giant structures always point north, and grouped together they present an extraordinary scene. A further 10 kilometres on, there is an optional 4WD diversion (closed in the wet season) to the Lost City.

Litchfield's best-known waterfalls – Florence, Tolmer and Wangi – are all accessed via Litchfield Park Road, athough flooding may cause them to be closed seasonally. The deep pools below these falls are generally crocodile-free and therefore safe for camping. Swimming is not permitted at Tolmer Falls but Wangi and Florence falls are both suitable for swimming, Wangi being especially popular – although the water can be cold at both places. There are short and extended walking tracks, and excellent picnic and barbecue facilities at Wangi and Florence falls, with a kiosk at Wangi. Buley Rockhole is also excellent for swimming and rock-hopping.

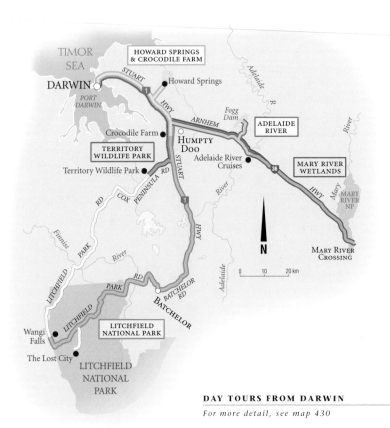

DAY TOURS FROM DARWIN

For more detail, see map 430

Fogg Dam, a sanctuary for wildlife

An alternative route back to Darwin is to continue along the Litchfield Park Road, and turn right along the Cox Peninsula Road to rejoin the Stuart Highway near Noonamah. Note that 42 kilometres of the latter route is unsealed, which may be a problem for those in hire cars. **See also:** National Parks p. 410 and individual entries in A–Z listing for parks and towns in bold type.

HOWARD SPRINGS AND CROCODILE FARM

49 km to Howard Springs and Crocodile Farm via Stuart Highway 🛡
These two spots make for a terrific day trip from Darwin and are very accessible from the Stuart Highway.

Take the signposted turn-off to reach Howard Springs, a spring-fed pool set within a monsoon rainforest in Howard Springs Nature Park. A kiosk and picnic area are nearby. Many species of birds can be found in the surrounding area.

Darwin Crocodile Farm is 18 kilometres south on the Stuart Highway. This is Australia's first and largest crocodile farm – it boasts 7000 crocodiles. There are tours, feeding displays and the chance to purchase food items made from the livestock.

ADELAIDE RIVER

88 km to Fogg Dam and Adelaide River via Stuart 🛡 *and Arnhem* 🟥 *highways*
Take the Stuart Highway out of Darwin and turn left onto Arnhem Highway. Drive past Humpty Doo to Fogg Dam, a left-hand turn off the highway and along a sealed road. Fogg Dam was built in the late 1950s to service the short-lived rice-growing plantations near Humpty Doo. When the crops failed, the area became a sanctuary for wildlife. This is an excellent place to experience the prolific wildlife of the Territory. During the day the creatures tend to retreat, but at sunrise and sunset you can witness an incredible spectacle as the birds and animals move between their feeding grounds and sleeping spots.

Further east along the Arnhem Highway, turn left to visit the Window on the Wetlands Visitor Centre. The centre provides an overview of the conservation value of wetlands and views of the surrounding floodplains. Return to the highway and continue east for 3 kilometres, where you can board a cruise boat for an air-conditioned tour of the Adelaide River, famous for its jumping crocodiles and superb scenery.

MARY RIVER WETLANDS

108 km to Mary River Crossing via Stuart 🛡 *and Arnhem* 🟥 *highways*
The wetlands extend from the Adelaide River Crossing on the Arnhem Highway through to the border of Kakadu National Park and are preserved within Mary River National Park. Monsoon and paperbark forests and freshwater billabongs teem with wildlife, and the birdlife is sensational.

Take the Stuart Highway and branch off along the Arnhem Highway. Continue to Mary River Crossing, about 3 kilometres west of the Bark Hut Inn. A picnic area and a boat ramp make this a good starting point for an exploration of the area. Fishing is popular, barramundi being the prize catch. If you wish to spend more time exploring the park, there is a network of unsealed roads (many 4WD only) leading to picnic areas, bird-watching spots and boat-access points. North Rockhole is a particularly popular point for accessing the channels of the Mary River, and Couzen's Lookout offers views of the Mary River and floodplains. Tours, cruises and accommodation are available at Wildman Wilderness Lodge and Mary River Park. During the wet season, flooding may cause road closures. Information on tracks and road conditions is available from the Wildman Region Office; (08) 8978 8986.

TERRITORY WILDLIFE PARK

58 km to Territory Wildlife Park via Stuart Highway 🛡 *and Cox Peninsula Road*
This award-winning park comprises over 400 hectares of bushland and features hundreds of unique animal and bird species. Take the Stuart Highway out of Darwin and turn right onto the Cox Peninsula Road to access the park. As you approach the park you will pass Berry Springs Nature Park, well worth a visit on your return.

The Territory Wildlife Park's exhibits are connected by a 4-kilometre path; stroll or catch the shuttle train. The park provides a thorough introduction to the amazing range of creatures that inhabit this part of Australia.

Berry Springs Nature Park is an ideal place for a picnic and a cooling swim. The park features a spring-fed oasis that provides safe, crocodile-free swimming, set within beautiful natural bushland.

CLASSIC TOUR
Dreamtime Trail
Alice Springs to Glen Helen Gorge (187 km)

This tour from Alice Springs into the West MacDonnell Ranges is a journey into the Dreamtime landscape of the Arrernte Aboriginal people. Here, amid some of the most spectacular gorge scenery in Australia, you will also discover a unique array of flora and fauna. Although the two-wheel drive version of the tour could be completed in a single day, this would leave little time to explore the natural wonders on offer. Ideally, allow for an overnight stop at Glen Helen Resort or stay at one or more of the camping areas along the tour. Relax, watch the sunset and take in the grandeur of the star-filled outback sky.

BE PREPARED
Before setting out, ensure you have plenty of fuel; *petrol (leaded and unleaded) and diesel are available only at Glen Helen Resort and Hermannsburg. While a limited amount of drinking water is available throughout West MacDonnell National Park and kiosk facilities are available at Standley Chasm and Glen Helen Resort, you are strongly advised to carry sufficient water for your party.*

To ensure that you are prepared for outback driving, read the section on Outback Motoring on page 603.

❶ The lore of the land
The outback town of Alice Springs, starting point for your tour, holds remarkable sway in the popular imagination. If possible, spend a few days here to get a feel for the area, its history and its people.

Many of the geographic features you will see on this tour are important and sacred places for the Arrernte people, having strong associations with various ancestral beings. While in Alice Springs, visit the **Aboriginal Art and Culture Centre** for an insight into the customs, history and art of the Pwerte Marnte Marnte (Southern Arrernte) people.

Aboriginal Art and Culture Centre
86 Todd Street
Alice Springs
Phone: (08) 8952 3408
Open: 8.15 a.m.–7 p.m. daily
(until 9 p.m. Fri. & Sat.)

❷ The colours of the outback
From Alice Springs head west on Larapinta Drive. Two kilometres along on your left is the

Ghost gums, a feature of the West MacDonnell Ranges
Left: Thorny devil, a creature of the desert

Araluen Centre for Arts and Entertainment which houses a permanent collection of works by Albert Namatjira and other artists from the Hermannsburg school of landscape painters. These paintings capture the vibrant colours of the country: the subtle blue and purple hues of the ranges contrasting with the rich orange of the rocks and the stark, white trunks of the ghost gums. Each year in late June and early July, the Araluen Centre presents The Desert Mob Art Show, featuring recent works by Central Australian artists. The stained-glass windows in the foyer of the centre are also a feature, telling the Honey Ant Dreaming story.

Araluen Centre for Arts and Entertainment
Larapinta Drive
Alice Springs
Phone: (08) 8951 1120
Open: 10 a.m.–5 p.m. daily

❸ Animals of the desert
The next stop, also on the left, is at the **Alice Springs Desert Park**, 4 kilometres further along Larapinta Drive. The Desert Park provides an excellent introduction to the plants, animals and habitats you are likely to see along this tour. A 1.6-kilometre path winds through three arid zone habitats: Desert Rivers, Sand Country and Woodlands. The nocturnal house provides a rare opportunity to see many of the animals that would otherwise remain hidden, living underground or emerging only at night. If possible, time your visit to include the Birds of Prey exhibition, daily at 10 a.m. and 3.30 p.m. in the Nature Theatre. You need to allow three hours to fully explore the Desert Park.

Alice Springs Desert Park
Larapinta Drive
Alice Springs
Phone: (08) 8951 8788
Open: 7.30 a.m.–6 p.m. daily

❹ Into the ranges
The outback beckons, so continue west on Larapinta Drive. Just 300 metres along on the left is a sign for John Flynn's Grave. Flynn, the founder of the Royal

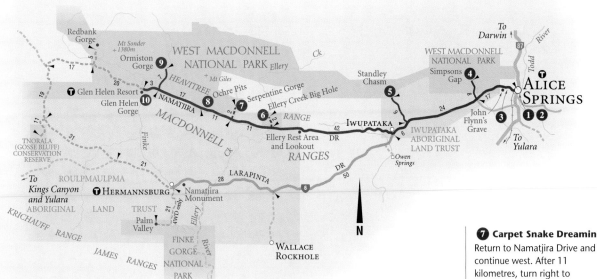

Flying Doctor Service, was buried here, in the foothills of Mt Gillen. Continue west for 10 kilometres, then turn right to visit **Simpsons Gap**.

The gap is located within West MacDonnell National Park. A short walk from the car park along a sandy creek bed lined with huge river red gums is a small waterhole. The creek has cut an impressive gap through the ridge, leaving red cliffs towering several hundred metres above the waterhole. Aboriginal legend associates this place with the Perentie (Goanna) Dreaming. A resident population of about 20 black-footed rock wallabies can often be seen on the boulder-strewn eastern slope of the Gap. Swimming is not permitted here but there are plenty of opportunities to enjoy a refreshing dip further along the tour.

Simpsons Gap
Larapinta Drive
Open: 8 a.m.–8 p.m. daily

❺ A midday marvel
Return to Larapinta Drive and continue west until you reach the turn-off on the right to **Standley Chasm**. The chasm, located on Iwupataka Aboriginal land, is part of the Termite Ancestress Dreaming. A 20-minute walk, past cycads and ferns that flourish in this protected environment, brings you to a narrow cleft in the range. The chasm is spectacular at midday when the sun transforms it into a glowing red corridor. Dingoes and rock wallabies are frequent visitors.

Standley Chasm
Larapinta Drive
Open: 8 a.m.–6 p.m. daily

❻ Birds at the Big Hole
Return to Larapinta Drive and continue west until the road branches. Take the right branch, Namatjira Drive, and after 32 kilometres, stop at the lookout on

the left (Ellery Rest Area and Lookout) and enjoy the great views to the south. A further 10 kilometres along, take the turn-off to **Ellery Creek Big Hole**. As you follow the gravel road to the waterhole, look at the rocks around you. What were once horizontal layers are now vertical, displaying the fascinating geological history of the area.

A short walk from the car park brings you to this beautiful waterhole, surrounded by river red gums and backed by red cliffs on which the rare MacDonnell Ranges cycad grows. The pool is a popular swimming and picnic spot. The permanent water also attracts a variety of birds, including spotted bowerbirds, Port Lincoln parrots, white-plumed honeyeaters, pied butcherbirds and white-faced herons. The Dolomite Walk, a 3-kilometre loop, starts near the waterhole on the west of the creek.

❼ Carpet Snake Dreaming
Return to Namatjira Drive and continue west. After 11 kilometres, turn right to **Serpentine Gorge**. The gorge winds through the rocks just like a snake, thus it is no surprise that it is part of the local Carpet Snake Dreaming. It is possible to swim at the first waterhole but not at the higher ones: these are protected habitats for rare plants and animals, including the Centralian flannel-flower. Found only around here, it has a white flower and seems to grow straight out of the cliff walls.

When the water level is low, you can walk along the creek to the gorge (1-hour return). There is also a steep climb to a lookout on the east of the gorge from the first pool (30-minute return) which rewards you with spectacular views of Serpentine Gorge and the mountains to the south.

❽ Red and yellow paints
Return to Namatjira Drive and continue west for another 11 kilometres before turning right to go to the **Ochre Pits**. Ochre plays an important part in traditional Aboriginal life. It can be mixed with water or animal fat to

The colours of the West MacDonnell Ranges

produce a paste or paint and is used to decorate the body during ceremonies and to heal various ailments. Rock paintings are also done with ochre.

Follow the path 300 metres along the creek to the deposit. The exposed ochre pit represents 700 million years of geological history. Ranging from deep red through to bright yellow and pure white, the colourful layers are caused by the presence of iron oxide in varying quantities. The white ochre has little or no iron oxide and a high level of kaolin, a white clay mineral. The Arrernte bushtrack (3-hour return) commences at the end of the Ochre Pits and leads to Inarlanga Pass, a remote and spectacular gorge; signs along the track explain local Aboriginal land management and customs.

9 Emu Dreaming

Return to Namatjira Drive, continue west for another 17 kilometres, then take the turn-off on the right to **Ormiston Gorge**. The cliffs in this gorge are the highest you will see; their breathtaking scale dwarfs the visitor. Ormiston Gorge is part of the local Emu Dreaming, and the waterhole here is sacred. There is a visitor centre here; check the

Standley Chasm

information board for ranger-conducted activities.

Two walks start at the gorge. The Ghost Gum Walk (1 hour) is memorable for the startling white tree trunks against the red cliffs. This walk takes you along the creek and up on to the ridge behind the gorge. The other walk takes you into Ormiston Pound, a bowl in the mountains formed by

erosion. This is a longer walk (4 hours), but it rewards you with wonderful views over the pound and the gorge. It is a loop and, for maximum scenic enjoyment, an anti-clockwise direction is recommended.

If you are planning an overnight stop, Ormiston Gorge is welcoming, with a camping area, toilets, solar-heated showers and gas barbecues.

10 Finally, the Finke

Return to Namatjira Drive and continue west to Glen Helen Resort. At **Glen Helen Gorge**, about 700 metres from the resort and car park, the Finke River has cut through layers of sandstone to produce a rather unusual formation. The permanent waterhole in the gorge is one of the few along the Finke River system. Surrounded by reeds, the waterhole is a haven for ducks, herons and waders; ospreys, jabirus and crakes are occasional visitors. Swimming is allowed. There are no marked trails, but you can climb over the ridge to the south side of the waterhole, and then walk to the next ridge to see the Organ Pipes. This unusual geological formation consists of a series of vertically uplifted sandstone columns that look just like the pipes of an organ.

Ochre Pits

Returning to Alice Springs

If you are travelling in a two-wheel drive vehicle, retrace your journey along Namatjira Drive and Larapinta Drive.

Four-wheel drive parties have a longer option (265 km), returning to Alice Springs via Redbank Gorge, Tnorala (Gosse Bluff) Conservation Reserve and Hermannsburg. You must pick up a Meerenie Tour Pass to enter Tnorala (Gosse Bluff) Conservation Reserve; these are available at visitor information centres in Alice Springs and at Glen Helen Resort.

Before leaving Glen Helen Resort, check road conditions for the unsealed section of Namatjira Drive. After 20 kilometres take the turn-off on the right to Redbank Gorge, to see the narrow chasm formed by the icy waters of Redbank Creek. Further west is Tnorala (Gosse Bluff) Conservation Reserve. Tnorala is a spectacular crater, kilometres across, produced by a comet impact 130 million years ago. From Tnorala, return to Alice Springs via Hermannsburg – site of a historic Lutheran missionary settlement where Albert Namatjira painted – and Larapinta Drive.

A popular extension of the four-wheel drive return option is to turn south from Hermannsburg to Finke Gorge National Park, where you will find a shady camping area with toilets and solar showers. The rough four-wheel drive track along the creek bed is impassable after rain. Finke Gorge features spectacular outcrops of sandstone that have been weathered into extraordinary shapes. Within the gorge is an area known as Palm Valley, where palm-like cycads and rare red fan palms create a prehistoric atmosphere.

NORTHERN TERRITORY from A to Z

Adelaide River   Pop. 279

MAP REF. 430 E8, 434 E7

A small settlement in pleasant country, 112 km SE of Darwin on the Stuart Hwy, Adelaide River was the location for 30 000 Australian and American soldiers during World War II. **In town:** Charlie the Buffalo (of *Crocodile Dundee* fame) at Adelaide River Inn, Stuart Hwy. June: Bush Race Meeting; Show. **In the area:** War Cemetery, just north of town, has graves of 434 servicemen. Historic Mount Bundy Station, 3 km NE, offers rural experience, fishing, walking, swimming and a wide range of accommodation. Robin Falls, 15 km S, flow most of the year. Daly River Roadhouse and area, 114 km SW, for good fishing, local Aboriginal arts and crafts, and native flora and fauna. **Visitor information:** Darwin Region Tourism Association, Beagle House, cnr Mitchell and Knuckey sts, Darwin.

Aileron   Pop. 10

MAP REF. 438 I6

A popular rest stop on the Stuart Hwy, Aileron is 133 km N of Alice Springs. **In town:** At Roadhouse: Aboriginal art, native wildlife, Sunday roast lunch, playground, picnic/barbecue facilities. **In the area:** Ryans Well Historical Reserve, 7 km SE. **Visitor information:** Roadhouse, Stuart Hwy; (08) 8956 9703.

Alice Springs   Pop. 22 488

MAP REF. 433 N4, 439 J8

Alice Springs, at the heart of the Red Centre and almost 1500 km from the nearest capital city, is en route to many attractions including Uluṟu (Ayers Rock). More than 350 000 visitors a year pass through this well-maintained town in the scenic MacDonnell Ranges. The area has a strong beef-cattle industry, and more recent industries include cut-flowers, camel meat and date-growing. The Todd River, which runs through town, is dry except after heavy rains; for the Henley-on-Todd Regatta held annually in Oct. the boats are carried or fitted with wheels. Between May and Sept. days are warm and nights can be cold. For the rest of the year daytime temperatures rise to the high 30s but nights are milder. Rains, usually brief, can come at any time of year. Alice Springs

Todd Mall, in Alice Springs

has an interesting pioneering history that began when the town site was seen by William Whitfield Mills in 1871, when surveying for the Overland Telegraph Line. He named the Todd River after the SA Superintendent of Telegraphs, Sir Charles Todd, and a nearby waterhole Alice Springs after Lady Todd. The first European settlement was at the repeater station, built for transmitting messages across the continent. In 1860 John McDouall Stuart had passed about 50 km W of the site. He named Central Mt Sturt after Captain Sturt, who had commanded an earlier expedition; however, the SA Government renamed the mountain in Stuart's honour. Pastoralist John Ross also helped look for a route for the telegraph line. Until 1880 the repeater station was the only reason for a handful of Europeans being in this remote area, then the Government sent surveys north seeking sites for railheads. The township of Stuart, 3.2 km from the telegraph station, was gazetted in 1880 but the railway remained unbuilt. Supplies were maintained by camel train from Port Augusta. Even the discovery of gold at Arltunga, 113 km NE, did little to develop Stuart. The Federal Government took control of NT from SA in 1911; from that time the township developed slowly. The Australian Inland Mission stationed Sister Jane Finlayson there in 1916 and the needs of the area led to the establishment of Adelaide House nursing hostel in 1926. The railway was completed in 1929 and the service became known as *The Ghan*, after the Afghan camel drivers. As the township grew there was confusion between Stuart and Alice

Springs, only 3 km apart, so the name Stuart was dropped. **In town:** In Todd Mall: Flynn Memorial Church, in memory of founder of Royal Flying Doctor Service; Adelaide House, originally hospital now museum housing pedal-radio equipment used by Flynn, and other memorabilia; Sounds of Starlight Theatre, musical journey through Central Australia, Apr.–Nov. (check session times at information centre); various outlets for Aboriginal art and artifacts. Aboriginal Art and Culture Centre, Todd St. Royal Flying Doctor Service base, Stuart Tce (tours daily). In Hartley St: Panorama 'Guth', a 360° landscape painting of Central Australia; National Pioneer Women's Hall of Fame, Old Courthouse Building; Minerals House, featuring geological and mineral displays (open Mon.–Fri.). Old Stuart Gaol, Parsons St. Museum of Central Australia, cnr Larapinta Dr and Memorial Ave. Technology, Transport and Communications Museum, Memorial Dr. Araluen Arts Centre, Larapinta Dr., for performing and visual arts; magnificent stained-glass window by local artist Wenten Rubuntja. *At the northern end of town:* Anzac Hill, Wills Tce, for excellent views of town; School of the Air, Head St. *At the western end of town:* Alice Springs Desert Park, Larapinta Dr., features desert animals and plants and information about their traditional use by Aboriginal people; film and interactive displays. *Across the river:* Lasseter's Casino, Barrett Dr.; Olive Pink Botanic Gardens, cnr Barrett Dr., Australia's only arid-zone botanic garden. Self-guide town walks, brochure available. Market at Todd Mall, 2nd Sun. Mar.–Dec.,

National Parks

There are more than 90 parks, reserves and protected areas in the Northern Territory. The major ones are in two groups: one group at the Top End, the other in Central Australia from Tennant Creek through to Yulara.

AT THE TOP END

The splendid **Kakadu National Park** is leased by the traditional Aboriginal owners to Parks Australia. Here the visitor can see Aboriginal rock art and the magnificent scenery of the Arnhem Land escarpment, go bushwalking or take a boat cruise through wetlands.

Litchfield National Park is 100 kilometres south of Darwin. Waterfalls cascade from the sandstone plateau of Tabletop Range and create beautiful pools for year-round swimming. Monsoonal rainforests contrast with treeless black-soil plains where magnetic termite mounds dot the landscape. Tjaynera Falls (Sandy Creek), and the Lost City with its fascinating sandstone formation, are on 4WD tracks. Swimming, photography, wildlife observation and bushwalking are all popular activities. On the way to this park, do not miss the Territory Wildlife Park, where you can see native fauna in a bush setting; the nocturnal house, aquarium and huge walk-through aviary are popular attractions.

Gurig National Park, on the Cobourg Peninsula, is Aboriginal land managed by agreement with the Parks and Wildlife Commission of the Northern Territory. Because the approach route is also through Aboriginal land, a permit is necessary. The park can be reached by 4WD, but road access is May–October only. This isolated park is rich in Aboriginal culture as well as containing lonely ruins of early European attempts at settlement.

Located 29 kilometres north-east of Katherine is **Nitmiluk National Park**. This fascinating river canyon, with its Aboriginal rock paintings, can be seen from a walking track, canoe or tour boat. In the dry season (May–October), anglers catch barramundi and other fish in the gorge's deep pools. **Elsey National Park**, 112 kilometres south-east of Katherine, is alongside the Roper River. The park includes Mataranka Hot Springs, a swimming area believed to have therapeutic powers.

On the Victoria Highway south-west of Katherine is **Flora River National Park**, home of the Wardaman people and interesting for its riverine forest. Further along the highway lie **Gregory National Park**, in two sections and one of the largest parks in the Territory, and **Keep River National Park**. Both feature tropical and semi-arid plant life, spectacular range and gorge scenery, significant Aboriginal sites and evidence of early European pastoral history. Boat tours can be arranged at Victoria River Wayside Inn and Timber Creek, both on the Victoria River.

IN CENTRAL AUSTRALIA

South of Tennant Creek is **Devils Marbles Conservation Reserve**. The large spherical boulders were formed by the weathering of granite outcrops on a wide quartz plain. Devils Marbles are particularly attractive at sunset, when they glow a deep red. The reserve has no marked walking tracks but the flat plain and sparse vegetation allow easy walking. Further east is **Davenport Range National Park**, accessible by four-wheel drive or high clearance vehicles only. Offering permanent waterhole ecology, the park is isolated and visitors should advise their travel plans; (08) 8964 1959, or at Wauchope or Tennant Creek.

The best known park in the Centre is World Heritage-listed **Uluru–Kata Tjuta National Park**, which contains the monolith Uluru (Ayers Rock) and Kata Tjuta (The Olgas). The area is of vital cultural and religious significance to Anangu (the traditional Aboriginal owners), whose ancestors have lived in the area for at least 30 000 years.

Anangu encourage visitors to seek alternatives to climbing Uluru, out of respect for its sacred status. A good alternative is the 9-km circuit walk or guided coach tour around the rock base to see significant traditional sites, such as the Mutitjulu Rock shelter, containing Aboriginal paintings, and Kantju Gorge. Walks are conducted by Aboriginal guides. Visitors who decide to climb the rock should be aware that the journey to the 348-metre summit is strictly for those with a good head for heights. It should not be attempted by anyone who is unfit or unwell, or in hot weather; casualties are common.

Further west, the great domes of Kata Tjuta are separated by deep clefts, many of which support an abundance of wildlife such as euros, very much at home in this rocky country. The

Palm Valley in Finke Gorge National Park

name Kata Tjuṯa means 'many heads'. There are several walks, such as Valley of the Winds and Olga Gorge, which take from one to four hours. Keep to the marked tracks and carry plenty of water.

In the **West MacDonnell National Park** lie the MacDonnell Ranges, the land of the Arrernte Aboriginal people. The park is a paradise for photographers and artists. There are spectacular gorges offering crimson and ochre rock walls bordering deep blue pools, and slopes covered with spring wildflowers. Close to Alice Springs is Simpsons Gap, only 25 kilometres west. There are several walking tracks, as well as seasonal ranger-guided tours, through rocky gaps and along steep-sided ridges overlooking huge gums and timbered creek flats. A bicycle path linking Alice Springs to Simpsons Gap provides a different way to see this part of the MacDonnell Ranges. Other well-known scenic spots include Ormiston Gorge and Pound, where fish bury themselves in the mud as a string of waterholes shrink to puddles, then wait for the rains. The deepest part of Ormiston Creek is a magnificent permanent pool the Arrernte link to the Emu Dreaming story (Kwartetweme). At the far end of the gorge, the walls are curtained by a variety of ferns and plants, including the lovely Sturt's desert rose and the relic *Macrozamia* or cycad.

Finke Gorge National Park, a scenic wilderness straddling the Finke River, includes the picturesque Palm Valley. This valley is a refuge for cycads and the rare red fan palm *Livistona mariae*, estimated to be about 5000 years old. The park is particularly rugged and visitors who do not join tours are advised to use a 4WD.

Between Finke Gorge and Uluṟu lies **Watarrka National Park**, including the amazing Kings Canyon. Waterholes, rock formations and wildlife provide excellent photographic and bushwalking opportunities.

Note: In national parks, reserves and other areas, it is essential to heed local advice on the dangers of swimming. Both saltwater and freshwater crocodiles are found throughout waterways in the Top End. The saltwater crocodile is particularly dangerous and can be found in both salt water (including the sea) and fresh water. Heed local warning advice and warning signs. In the Centre daytime heat can be extreme, especially in summer. Avoid walking in the heat of the day and always carry plenty of water.

For more information about Kakadu and Uluṟu, contact Parks Australia, 7th Floor, TCG Centre, 80 Mitchell St, Darwin NT 0800 (postal address GPO Box 1260, Darwin NT 0801); (08) 8946 4300. For information about the Territory's other parks and reserves, contact the Parks and Wildlife Commission of the Northern Territory, PO Box 496, Palmerston NT 0830; (08) 8999 5511. Web site www.nt.gov. au/paw **See also:** Day Tours from Darwin p. 404, Dreamtime Trail p. 406 and The Top End p. 419. Note detailed map of Kakadu National Park on page 431.

Wildlife-Watching

A visit to the Territory without wildlife-spotting would be incomplete. Mary River crocodiles attract attention from wildlife lovers, as do the bird-friendly billabongs of Kakadu. Further south, Central Australia is home to dingoes, kangaroos, thorny devils and a host of other reptiles.

IN DARWIN

Aquascene, at **Doctors Gully**, attracts hundreds of fish to its shallow waters for a free meal each high tide. Milkfish, catfish, batfish and many other species compete for offerings. There is no need to bring snorkel and mask as these wild fish can be hand-fed as you wade among them.

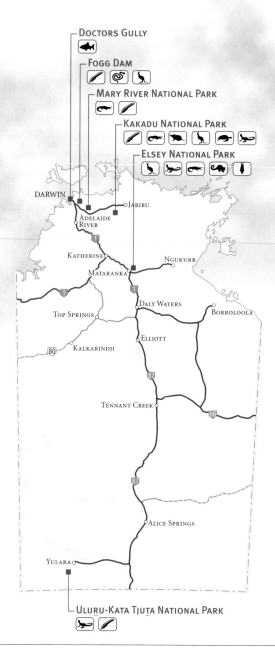

The jacana, a resident of the Top End wetlands

AT THE TOP END

It is tempting to head straight for Kakadu, but those who stop along the way will have some wonderful wildlife-watching experiences. **Fogg Dam** was constructed east of Darwin in the 1950s for an ill-fated rice-growing scheme, and was an unexpected gift to the Territory's bird population. It is now a peaceful conservation reserve with bird-viewing platforms and boardwalks through paperbark swamps and rainforest. You are likely to encounter comb-crested jacanas as they step nimbly over waterlilies, as well as pairs of green pygmy-geese among the reeds. Harmless water pythons and wallabies are often seen in the evenings. Nearby on the Arnhem Highway is the Window on the Wetlands Visitor Centre, which offers an overview of the area's ecology.

Further east is **Mary River National Park**, a fascinating mix of salt and freshwater habitats. There is no shortage of saltwater crocodiles here,

WILDLIFE-WATCHING ETHICS

Do not disturb wildlife or wildlife habitats. Keep the impact of your presence to a minimum. Use available cover or hides wherever possible.

Do not feed wildlife, even in urban areas.
(Note: supervised feeding is allowed at some locations.)

Be careful not to introduce exotic plants and animals – definitely no pets.

Stay on defined trails.

and a river cruise is the best way to see them. A close-up view of these oversized reptiles explains why there are no 'swim-with-the-croc' tours. Boat tours operate regularly through both the fresh-water and salt-water sections. For birdwatchers, the Mary River floodplains are also home to a large population of sea eagles and egrets. Pelicans, jabirus, jacanas, spoonbills and kingfishers are often seen as well.

Kakadu National Park is world-renowned for its ecological and cultural significance. It is the temporary or permanent home to one-third of Australian bird species so it makes good sense to begin with a bird checklist. This can be obtained from the Bowali Visitor Centre.

Two of the best birdwatching sites within the park are Mamukala and Yellow Water (Ngurrungurrudjba). Towards the end of the dry season between August and October, these and other billabongs become welcome oases for Kakadu's birds. Large flocks of magpie geese, plumed whistling-ducks and many other waterbirds crowd in as the surrounding country dries out. The opportunity to see this wonderful parade of birds should not be missed. Bring your binoculars to the bird hide at Mamukala, or enjoy the spectacle from the raised croc-proof boardwalk at Yellow Water. Regular boat cruises through Yellow Water provide an opportunity to spot saltwater crocodiles as well as birds.

Campers may see brown bandicoots at night and wallabies and wallaroos in the park's open grassy areas. Northern short-necked turtles may rest on logs at the water's edge, and many kinds of monitor lizards can be spotted around billabongs and on road verges.

Near Mataranka on the Stuart Highway is **Elsey National Park**, famous for its rejuvenating thermal pool. When the sun is high overhead the pool is the best place to be – time your wildlife-spotting for the early morning and late afternoon. At these cooler times of day the animals are at their most active. Wallabies and goannas can be seen, as well as water monitors and occasional freshwater crocodiles along the river – treat the latter with the same respect as their notorious saltwater cousins. Evening is a good time to glimpse a possum or flying fox in the trees.

IN CENTRAL AUSTRALIA

Much of Central Australia's wildlife is right at your feet. Larger animals are less common, though insects and lizards flourish in the harsh desert environment. Their tiny tracks criss-cross the sand and tell a fascinating tale of the previous night's adventures and activities.

In **Uluru–Kata Tjuṯa National Park** birds are always a welcome sight against the deep-blue skies. Cockatoos, ringneck parrots and budgerigars keep an eye out for birds of prey such as kestrels and whistling kites. Honeyeaters are at home in the park, as are flocks of tiny zebra finches.

The Territory Wildlife Park south of Darwin brings together the Territory's wildlife at one location. Barramundi and turtles swim overhead at the walk-through aquarium tunnel, and eleven aviaries cover different habitats. For a close-up view of Central Australian wildlife the Alice Springs Desert Park should not be missed. This park showcases a range of common and rare Central Australian plants and animals. In its desert nocturnal house tiny mammals, bats and birds go about their business, oblivious of curious visitors. For more information on wildlife-watching in national parks and reserves, contact the Parks and Wildlife Commission of the Northern Territory, PO Box 496, Palmerston NT 0830; (08) 8999 5511. Web site www.nt.gov.au/paw **See also:** National Parks p. 410 and The Top End p. 419.

Water monitors can be spotted in Elsey National Park

Mereenie Loop links Alice Springs with major attractions

and Thurs. evenings in summer. Jan.: Lasseter's Indoor Challenge (several competitions including backgammon, bridge and scrabble). Apr.: Racing Carnival; Country Music Festival. May: Bangtail Muster. June: Finke Desert Race. July: Camel Cup; Agricultural Show. Aug.: Rodeo. Oct.: Henley-on-Todd Regatta; Masters Games (mature-age athletic carnival), even-numbered years. Nov.: Corkwood Festival (art, craft, music and dance). **In the area:** Great variety of tours covering scenic attractions, Aboriginal culture and specialist interests; by bus or coach, train, limousine, 4WD safari, Harley-Davidson motorcycle, camel, horse, aircraft, helicopter or hot-air balloon. *To the north:* Alice Springs Telegraph Station Historical Reserve (3 km) with original stone buildings and equipment, historical display, guided tours, bushwalking and wildlife. *To the north-east:* At Gemtree (135 km), Mud Tank zircon field offers prospecting for zircons, guided fossicking tours and your gems cut at the caravan park. *To the east:* Pitchi Richi Sanctuary (2 km), an open-air museum displaying William Ricketts clay sculptures; Frontier Camel Farm (7 km) features camel rides, reptile house and museum displays highlighting importance of camels and Afghans to the area; nearby, Mecca Date Gardens, Australia's first commercial date farm; Alice Springs Winery, NT's only commercial winery (11 km); Emily Gap (13 km) and Jessie Gap (18 km) nature parks. *To the south:* Old Timers' Museum (5 km) features exhibits of 1890s era; Transport Heritage Centre (10 km) has re-creation of a 1930s railway siding and display showing ingenuity used to overcome outback hardships; Ghan Preservation Society rail museum at MacDonnell Siding (10 km) features the

Old Ghan which runs on 23.5 km of private line between MacDonnell Siding and Ewaninga; Ewaninga Rock Carvings Conservation Reserve, (35 km SE), an Aboriginal cultural site with rock engravings; Chambers Pillar Historical Reserve (149 km) includes 50-m high rock pillar which served as a landmark feature for the Centre's early pioneers and explorers. *To the south-west:* Camel Outback Safaris (93 km) offers camel and trail rides; Henbury Meteorites Conservation Reserve (147 km). *To the west:* Grave site of Rev. John Flynn (5 km); Simpsons Gap (25 km), also linked to Alice Springs by sealed bicycle path; Standley Chasm (50 km). Ellery Creek Big Hole (93 km); Serpentine Gorge (104 km); Ochre Pits (119 km), natural quarry once mined by Aborigines; Ormiston Gorge (132 km); Glen Helen Gorge (133 km); the nearby Glen Helen Resort, used as a base by many to explore the area; Hermannsburg (125 km); Palm Valley, in Finke Gorge National Park (140 km, 4WD access only); Redbank Gorge (170 km, 4WD access only); Tnorala (Gosse Bluff) meteor crater (210 km, 4WD access only, permit required, note permit for Mereenie Loop allows access to Tnorala); most of these are in West MacDonnell National Park; as is Larapinta Trail, a well-marked walking track through the West MacDonnell Ranges. Mereenie Loop links Alice Springs, Kings Canyon and Uluru (Ayers Rock) via the West MacDonnell Ranges and Glen Helen; permit required because section of the route passes through Aboriginal Land. **Visitor information:** Central Australian Tourism Industry Association, Gregory Tce (south end of Todd Mall); (08) 8952 5800. **See also:** Dreamtime Trail p. 406; The Red Centre p. 415; Aboriginal Art p. 420.

Barkly Homestead Pop. 15

MAP REF. 437 N11
Barkly Homestead is a comfortable fuel or accommodation stop at the junction of Barkly and Tablelands hwys, 187 km E from the junction of Stuart and Barkly hwys.

Barrow Creek   Pop. 10

MAP REF. 439 J4
Located on the Stuart Hwy, 285 km N of Alice Springs, Barrow Creek was originally a telegraph station and a rest stop for cattle-droving on the North–South Stock Route. **In town:** Old Telegraph Station (1872). Barrow Creek Hotel (1932). **Visitor information:** Barrow Creek Hotel; (08) 8956 9753.

Batchelor   Pop. 645

MAP REF. 430 D7, 434 E7
The former town for Rum Jungle, Australia's first uranium mine (now closed), Batchelor is the gateway to Litchfield National Park. **In town:** Coomalie Cultural Centre, Batchelor College, cnr Awilla Rd and Nurudina St, has display of Aboriginal works and culture. Mini replica of Karlstein Castle of Bohemia, Rum Jungle Rd. Scenic flights, parachuting and gliding, at airport. June (or July): International Skydiving and Parachuting Championships. **In the area:** Lake Bennett Wilderness Resort, Chinner Rd, 18 km NE: fishing, abseiling, swimming, windsurfing, boat hire, walks, restaurant, range of accommodation. Rum Jungle Lake, 10 km W, for swimming. Litchfield National Park, 40 km W, a wilderness area with rivers, spectacular waterfalls (Wangi, Sandy Creek, Florence and Tolmer), bushwalks, fauna, magnetic termite mounds, pockets of scenic rainforest, secluded waterholes and camping grounds. **Visitor information:** Tarkarri Rd; (08) 8976 0444. **See also:** Day Tours from Darwin p. 404.

Borroloola   Pop. 551

MAP REF. 435 O13, 437 O3
A small settlement on the McArthur Riverbanks and once one of the larger and more colourful frontier towns, Borroloola is now popular with fishing and 4WD enthusiasts. Although an Aboriginal community, no permit is required to visit the town. **In town:** Museum in old police station (1886), Robinson Rd. Fishing charters.

The Red Centre

The first priority for most visitors to the Red Centre is Uluru (Ayers Rock). About 450 kilometres south-west of Alice Springs, the world's greatest monolith rises majestically 348 metres above a wide, sandy floodplain covered in spinifex and desert oak. The rock is 9 kilometres in circumference and, with the movement of the sun during the day, it changes colour through shades of fiery red, delicate mauve, blue, pink and brown. When rain falls it veils the rock in a torrent of silver.

Yulara, about 20 minutes' drive north of Uluru, is a self-contained township; it has accommodation, a supermarket, and other shops and services. Ayers Rock Resort at Yulara offers a range of accommodation: the top-class Sails in the Desert Hotel, the Outback Pioneer Hotel and Lodge, the Desert Gardens four-star resort, Spinifex Lodge, Emu Walk self-contained serviced apartments, and well-equipped camping grounds. If you can, allow for a stay of at least two days; this will give you time to explore Uluru and see a sunrise and a sunset there, and to visit Kata Tjuta (The Olgas) – the two most famous attractions in **Uluru–Kata Tjuta National Park**.

Kata Tjuta (The Olgas)

An excellent way to familiarise yourself with the region is to spend an hour or so at the Yulara Visitors Centre. Displays depict the geology, history, flora and fauna of the region, and there is a spectacular collection of photographs. Audiovisual shows are held regularly. For a comprehensive introduction to the park and its culture, visit the award-winning Uluru–Kata Tjuta Cultural Centre on the road to Uluru. The form of this splendidly-designed building is based on the shape of two ancestral beings: Kuniya (python) and Liru (poisonous snake).

According to Aboriginal legends, Uluru and Kata Tjuta were created and given their distinctive forms during the Tjukurpa or creation period. At the base of Uluru there are cave paintings and carvings made over many thousands of years by Anangu (traditional owners) belonging to the Luritja, Yankunytjatjara and Pitjantjatjara language groups. It is not difficult to appreciate that this is a sacred place since ancient times for its traditional owners.

The 1.6-kilometre climb to the top of Uluru follows a religious track, and Anangu prefer visitors to respect this and take some of the other discovery walks in the park and near the rock itself. Taking the 9-kilometre circuit walk around the base of Uluru, you will see rock art, as well as the Mutitjulu Waterhole. Tours include the Mala Walk (conducted by national park rangers) and the Kuniya and Liru walks (conducted by Aboriginal guides). Self-guide walks are also an option; maps are available at the Uluru–Kata Tjuta Cultural Centre on the road to Uluru.

If you do decide to climb the rock, do not attempt to do so if the weather is hot. You also need to be fit and well, and have a good head for heights – the track is exposed and steep, and casualties are common.

Some 50 kilometres to the west are Kata Tjuta (The Olgas), a cluster of rounded, massive rocks that are equally mysterious. They too are dramatic and vividly coloured. Mount Olga, the tallest dome of Kata Tjuta, is 546 metres above the Valley of the Winds that runs through the rock system.

A good way to see many of the tourist attractions in the Red Centre is to start from **Alice Springs**. You can take advantage of the various tours that operate from there, or take your own vehicle. A few tourist destinations require 4WD; check before you set out. The Mereenie Loop (4WD recommended) links Alice Springs with Kings Canyon and Uluru, via the West MacDonnell Ranges, and Glen Helen. It allows most of the attractions to the west and south of Alice Springs to be incorporated in a circular route without major backtracking. As the Mereenie Loop passes through Aboriginal land, a permit is required. Check road conditions with Visitor information before departure.

The Alice Springs Telegraph Station Historical Reserve is only 3 kilometres north of Alice Springs. The original Alice Springs settlement's stone buildings have been restored by the Parks and Wildlife Commission of the Northern Territory and furnished with artifacts from early this century. There is also a historic display. Guided tours are available half-hourly. A small waterhole, the original water source for the settlement, from which Alice Springs obtained its name, is nearby.

The telegraph station was built to link Port Augusta to Darwin, the link continuing by submarine cable to Java. Completed in 1872, the line was used until 1932, when operations were transferred to the site at the corner of Parsons Street and Railway Terrace in Alice Springs. Alice Springs Desert Park, on the western outskirts of town, is another must-see attraction. The park provides an excellent introduction to the animals of the Red Centre.

An interesting day tour from Alice Springs is to visit the attractions of the **West MacDonnell National Park**. The beautiful Standley Chasm, 50 kilometres west, is managed by the Angkerle Aboriginal Corporation. This colourful cleft in the West MacDonnells is only 5 metres wide. At midday when the sunlight reaches the floor of the chasm, turning the walls a blazing red, it is a memorable sight. On the way, Simpsons Gap, 25 kilometres west of Alice Springs, can be visited. A sealed bike track links Alice Springs to Simpsons Gap.

Further west, about 133 kilometres from Alice Springs on the Finke River, are Glen Helen and Ormiston gorges. Their colours were captured by the famous Aboriginal artist Albert Namatjira; they also lend themselves to photography, as does the sunrise on Mount Sonder to the west. **Glen Helen Resort** is a homestead-style accommodation base for the West MacDonnells.

A 4WD day tour from Alice Springs will also take you to Palm Valley and the Finke River Gorge, 155 kilometres south-west. The Finke River is one of the oldest water-courses in the world and to walk along its bed is an unforgettable experience. Palm Valley, with its rock pools, cycads and red fan palms unique to the area, is yet another of the wonders of the Red Centre. The plant life has such a prehistoric appearance that to enter the valley is like taking a trip back in time. These two attractions can also be visited by taking a two-day tour from Alice Springs. Also well worth a visit is the restored mission at **Hermannsburg**, birthplace of the artist Albert Namatjira, 125 kilometres west of Alice Springs, on the way to Palm Valley – arrive for their splendid morning tea, lunch or afternoon tea.

Kings Canyon, 333 kilometres south-west of Alice Springs in **Watarrka National Park**, is one of the most interesting and scenic areas of the Centre. The climb to the rim of the canyon is fairly arduous, but well worth the effort. Even more spectacular views can be obtained by crossing via the small, railed Cotterills Bridge, near the old, nerve-racking tree-trunk bridge. The Lost City and the Garden of Eden are superb sights here. The Kings Canyon Resort and Kings Creek Camping Ground provide accommodation in this area.

East of Alice Springs in the East MacDonnell Ranges are Corroboree Rock, which is of significance to Eastern Arrernte Aboriginal people; the scenic Trephina Gorge; N'Dhala Gorge, which has a variety of flora and ancient rock engravings; and Ruby Gap Nature Park, a picturesque bush camping area only accessible to high-clearance 4WD.

The Arltunga Historical Reserve, 117 kilometres east of Alice Springs beyond Trephina Gorge, preserves memorabilia of the goldmining era in the region. Little evidence remains of the shanty town that grew up after 1887 when alluvial gold was found. You can explore the stone ruins, scattered workings, grave-stones and go down a mine. At the Visitor Centre there are historical exhibits, with a gaol and restored police station 2 kilometres away. There is a private camping ground next to the reserve and the hotel offers meals and has antiques on display. Fossicking in the area is good. **Ross River** Homestead, 91 kilometres east of Alice Springs, offers a range of outback experiences and comfortable accommodation.

Thirty-four kilometres south of Alice Springs are the ancient Ewaninga Rock Carvings or petroglyphs. Signs along a short walk explain Aboriginal use of this area.

About 133 kilometres south-west of Alice Springs is a turn-off from the Stuart Highway leading to the Henbury meteorite craters. The Henbury craters are believed to have been formed several thousand years ago when a falling meteor broke into pieces and hit the earth. The largest of the 12 craters is 180 metres wide and 15 metres deep; while the smallest is 6 metres wide and only a few centimetres deep.

Valley of the Domes, Kings Canyon

The Mereenie Loop

The Mereenie Loop links Glen Helen to **Kings Canyon** in the far south-west. The road is mainly gravel or dirt and a 4WD vehicle is strongly recommended. As a section of the road passes through Aboriginal Land, a permit is required; these are obtainable in **Alice Springs** (contact information centre), Kings Canyon and Yulara. This route links Alice Springs with Kings Canyon and Uluru (Ayers Rock) via the West MacDonnell Ranges, and Glen Helen, without major backtracking.

Heading west from Alice Springs and along Namatjira Drive, this route passes the major attractions of the **West MacDonnell National Park**, including Simpsons Gap, Standley Chasm, Ellery Creek Big Hole and Serpentine and Ormiston gorges, before reaching Glen Helen. An alternative route to access the Mereenie Loop from Alice Springs is to continue on Larapinta Drive via **Hermannsburg** and, if travelling by 4WD, it is possible to divert to Palm Valley in **Finke Gorge National Park**.

After Glen Helen, the route leads south-west to Kings Canyon in **Watarrka National Park**. After Glen Helen it is possible to divert to Tnorala (Gosse Bluff), a spectacular crater formed 130 million years ago; a separate permit is required to enter the Tnorala Conservation Reserve which is included in the Mereenie Tour Pass.

From Watarrka visitors can travel via Luritja Road and Lasseter Highway to **Yulara** and **Uluru–Kata Tjuta National Park**. A minimum of two days should be allowed for the journey. Hotel-style accommodation is available at Kings Canyon Resort and Yulara, or inquire about camping locations at information centre. Various informative Aboriginal cultural tours are available at certain landmarks along the way. **See also:** Aboriginal Cultural Tours p. 423. For details on parks and towns in bold type, see National Parks p. 410 and individual entries in A–Z town listing. **Map references:** 432 D5, 438 F9.

For further information about the attractions of the Red Centre, contact the Central Australian Tourism Industry Association, cnr Gregory Tce and Todd St, Alice Springs; (08) 8952 5800. Web site www.catia.asn.au/catia **See also:** Dreamtime Trail p. 406. For details on parks and towns in bold type, see National Parks p. 410 and individual entries in A–Z town listing. **Map reference:** 432–3.

Scenic flights over town and the islands of the Sir Edward Pellew group. Easter: Fishing Classic. Aug.: Agricultural Show; Rodeo. **In the area:** Cape Crawford, 110 km SW: base for seeing Bukalara Rock Formations (60 km E), mass of chasms winding through ancient sandstone formations (in very remote area, guide recommended); and Lost City, accessible only by helicopter, visitors must be accompanied by a guide. Limmen Bight Fishing Camp, 250 km NW: range of accommodation; check wet-season road access. **Visitor information:** McArthur River Caravan Park, Robinson Rd; (08) 8975 8734.

Daly Waters   Pop. 349

MAP REF. 436 I3
Situated 4 km N of the junction of Stuart and Carpentaria hwys, Daly Waters became the first international refuelling stop for Qantas in 1935. **In town:** Historic hotel (1930), Stuart St. Sept.: Rodeo. **In the area:** Airport museum, 1 km NE, off Stuart Hwy at Old Daly Waters aerodrome. Tree, 1 km N, reputedly marked with letter S by explorer John McDouall Stuart. Other stopping-places on Stuart Hwy: Dumarra, 44 km S and 8 km S of Buchanan Hwy turnoff; Larrimah, 93 km N, historic WW II sites. **Visitor information:** Daly Waters Hotel, Stuart St; (08) 8975 9927.

Elliott   Pop. 432

MAP REF. 437 J6
Elliott, on the Stuart Hwy, 254 km N of Tennant Creek, was named after Captain Elliott, the officer in charge of a camp for troops during World War II. The town is a green, shady spot with good facilities. **In town:** Site of World War II camp on southern outskirts of town. **In the area:** At Newcastle Waters, an old droving town 24 km NW: bronze statue 'The Drover'; historic buildings; no services. **Visitor information:** Elliott Hotel, Stuart Hwy; (08) 8969 2069.

Glen Helen   Pop. 5

MAP REF. 432 I5, 426 H8
On Namatjira Drive, 132 km W of Alice Springs, the small homestead-style resort of Glen Helen is an excellent base for exploring the superb scenery of West MacDonnell National Park. **In the area:** At Glen Helen Gorge, 300 m E, walk along Finke River bed, between towering cliffs. Helicopter flights to surrounding areas including Mt Sonder. In West MacDonnell

Historic mission buildings, Hermannsburg

National Park: Ormiston Gorge, 12 km NE, the 'jewel of the MacDonnell Ranges'; Ochre Pits, 21 km E, natural ochre quarry once mined by Aborigines for painting and ceremonial decoration; Serpentine Gorge, 35 km E, narrow winding gorge with beautiful scenery, wildlife and walking trails; Ellery Creek Big Hole, 45 km E, large waterhole with high red cliffs and sandy creek fringed with river redgums; further east towards Alice Springs are Standley Chasm and Simpsons Gap; Redbank Gorge, 24 km NW, accessible by 4WD only. Larapinta Walking Trail winds through heart of West MacDonnell Ranges; it currently extends 80 km and can be walked in total (registration necessary) or in part (some sections are overnight walks). Mereenie Loop links Glen Helen to Kings Canyon in far south west; permit required. **Visitor information:** Glen Helen Resort, Namatjira Dr.; (08) 8956 7489.

Hermannsburg   Pop. 462

MAP REF. 432 I6, 438 H9
This Aboriginal community, 125 km W of Alice Springs, occupies the site of a former mission station established by German Lutherans in 1877. For many years it was the home of painter Albert Namatjira. The Arrernte Aboriginal community have owned freehold title to the land since 1982: visitors to town are restricted to the shop, petrol station and historic precinct. **In town:** Historic precinct: Strehlow's House (1897), now Kata-Anga Tea Rooms, known for their apple strudel; old manse (1888), now a gallery housing watercolour paintings by Aboriginal artists of the Hermannsburg school (guided tours);

remains of mission station, including schoolhouse (1896) and tannery (1941); museum in the Old Colonists House (1885) displays historic items from missionary era. **In the area:** Monument to Albert Namatjira on Larapinta Dr., 2 km E. Cultural tours and camping at Wallace Rockhole Aboriginal community, 46 km SE. Finke Gorge National Park, 20 km S (4WD access only), features red fan palms (*Livistona mariae*) in Palm Valley, and amazing rock formations: 'amphitheatre', 'sphinx' and 'battleship'. Tnorala (Gosse Bluff) meteorite crater, 35 km W (Mereenie Loop Pass required for access). **Visitor information:** Kata-Anga Tea Rooms; (08) 8956 7402. **See also:** Dreamtime Trail p. 406; The Red Centre p. 415.

Jabiru   Pop. 1696

MAP REF. 431 P4, 434 H6
A mining town within the Kakadu National Park, 280 km from Darwin on the Arnhem Hwy, Jabiru's services are designed to limit the effect of the town on the surrounding World Heritage-listed National Park. **In town:** Gagudju Crocodile Hotel, Flinders St, a 250-m crocodile-shaped building; design was approved by the Gagudju people, to whom the crocodile is a totem. Frontier Kakadu Lodge and Caravan Park, Jabiru Dr., laid out in traditional Aboriginal circular motif. Jabiru Olympic Swimming Pool, Civic Dr., largest in NT; nearby, 9-hole golf course. Fishing and safari tours. Aug.: Wind Festival. **In the area:** Note that this area experiences extreme heat Sept.–Jan. and that 4WD roads are usually accessible only in the dry season. Tourist walk (1.5 km) from town

centre through bush to Bowali Visitor Centre. Nourlangie Rock, 34 km S, has significant Aboriginal rock art around its base. Yellow Water near Cooinda, 55 km SE, a billabong with prolific flora and fauna; waterbirds best seen by a boat cruise (departs near Gagudju Lodge, Cooinda). Nearby, Warradjan Aboriginal Cultural Centre built in shape of a Warradjan (pig-nosed turtle): offers insight into Aboriginal culture in Kakadu region; Aboriginal craft gallery. Further south, Jim Jim Falls and Twin Falls (both 4WD access only), after rains (Nov.–Apr.) the two largest falls in park. North of Jabiru is another renowned Aboriginal rock-art site, Ubirr, in Kakadu National Park, with galleries featuring a range of styles; ranger-guided walks and tours, dry season only. From Ubirr, exceptional sunset views across East Alligator River flood plains. Further north-east at Oenpelli, Injalak Art and Craft Centre (permit required, visitors welcome). Ranger Uranium Mine, 6 km E, daily tours May–Oct. At airport, scenic flights over unique Kakadu territory: see virtually inaccessible sandstone formations standing 300 m above vast flood plains; seasonal waterfalls; wetland wilderness; remote beaches and ancient Aboriginal rock-art sites. **Visitor information:** 6 Tasman Plaza; (08) 8979 2548. **See also:** National Parks p. 410; The Top End p. 419.

Katherine   Pop. 7979

MAP REF. 434 G10

Katherine is on the southern side of the Katherine River, 310 km SE of Darwin. Katherine River was named after a daughter of one of the sponsors of John McDouall Stuart. Stuart first saw it in 1862. The town's economic mainstays are the Mt Todd goldmine, tourism, and the Tindal

RAAF airbase, 28 km SE. In some of NT's most promising agricultural and grazing country, Katherine is the centre of scientific experiments designed to improve the beef-cattle industry. **In town:** Katherine Museum, Gorge Rd (check opening times). Railway Station Museum, Railway Tce, has displays of history of railways in the area (check opening times); old steam engine adjacent to museum. School of the Air, Giles St (open weekdays Apr.–Oct., check visiting times). O'Keefe House, Riverbank Dr., one of the oldest houses in town. Self-guide Pioneer Walk around town. NT Rare Rocks, Zimmin Dr., rock and gem displays. Katherine Orchid Nursery, Stutterd St, 25 000 orchids; open Wed.–Sat. Self-guide Arts and Crafts Trail, brochure available. Market, Warburton St, each Sat. (Apr.–Sept.). Tick Markets, Lindsay St, 1st Sat. each month, Apr.–Sept. June: Burunga Sport and Cultural Festival; Katherine Cup; Canoe Marathon. July: Agricultural Show. Aug.–Sept.: Flying Fox Festival (community festival, theatre and music). **In the area:** Heli tours, scenic flights, 4WD safaris, barramundi fishing tours, horse trail-rides. Nitmiluk Gorge in Nitmiluk National Park, 29 km NE, has ancient rock walls dotted with caves; Aboriginal paintings thousands of years old decorate both faces of the gorge above the floodline. Numerous reptile and amphibian species here; kangaroos and wallabies congregate in higher reaches. Self-guide walk, brochure available. The best way to see the gorge is by flat-bottomed boat; hire a canoe and camp in the gorge overnight, or take a guided tour; daily cruises (book at information centre); no private motorboats allowed in gorge May–Oct. Weather is hot (yet countryside is at its best) Nov.–Mar., but there is little humidity for the remaining months, when it is warm during the day and cool at

night. Also in park, Edith Falls, 62 km N; surrounding area ideal for bushwalking, picnicking and camping. Springvale homestead (1878), 8 km W on Shadforth Rd: oldest remaining homestead in NT, built by Alfred Giles; market each Sun., Apr.–Sept. Flora River Nature Park, 86 km SW, for interesting mineral formations, pools and cascades along river, and camping. Natural hot springs, 3 km S on Victoria Hwy, on banks of Katherine River. Cutta Cutta Caves Nature Park, 27 km SE (cave tours daily). Elsey National Park near Mataranka homestead, 112 km SE, features thermal pool believed to have therapeutic powers. Old Gallon Licensed Store (1847) (now private residence), 2 km E on Giles St, marks original site of township. Manyallaluk Aboriginal Corporation based at Eva Valley station, 100 km NE, operates Aboriginal cultural tours. **Visitor information:** cnr Lindsay St and Katherine Tce; (08) 8972 2650. Web site nttc.com.au **See also:** The Top End p. 419; Aboriginal Art p. 420.

Kings Canyon   Pop. 50

MAP REF. 438 F9

Kings Canyon, an enormous natural amphitheatre with 100-m sheer rock faces, is the main feature of Watarrka National Park, 333 km SW of Alice Springs. Kings Canyon Resort is situated in the park and provides a base from which to explore the region. Aboriginal tours and scenic helicopter flights available. **In the area:** 6-km circuit Rim Walk of Kings Canyon, features boardwalk through prehistoric cycads in lush Garden of Eden; unusual rock formations, particularly The Lost City; views across canyon. From same starting point, Kings Creek Walk, 1 hr return, up centre of canyon. Giles Walk, 13 km, from Kings Canyon to Kathleen Springs, for experienced walkers. Also within park, Carmichael Crag (3 km N) displays majestic colours, particularly at sunset. Mereenie Loop to Glen Helen (permit required). **Visitor information:** Kings Canyon Resort; (08) 8956 7442. **See also:** The Red Centre p. 415.

Mataranka   Pop. 667

MAP REF. 434 I11

This small town is 106 km SE of Katherine. **In town:** Self-drive Discovery Trail of town and surrounding area, brochure available at information centre. On Stuart Hwy: Stockyard Gallery, for NT artists' works including leather sculpture; Territory Manor, daily feeding of barramundi,

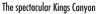
The spectacular Kings Canyon

The Top End

Ubirr, a major rock-art site in Kakadu National Park

Darwin is a major tourist destination with its warm weather, excellent beaches and abundance of fish, but its real attraction is as a base for exploring the wild and fascinating country at the 'Top End'. Here you see wide billabongs covered with lilies, clouds of magpie geese wheeling above the trees, crocodiles sunning themselves on muddy banks, plunging waterfalls in the wet season, spectacular cliff and rock features, and caves and cliffs bearing the Aboriginal rock art of the past.

A number of parks and conservation reserves protect and manage the features of the region and make them accessible to travellers. One of the most spectacular of these is **Kakadu National Park**, in the vast and wild country along the East and South Alligator rivers.

Kakadu has World Heritage status; it is considered to be of outstanding national and international significance for both its natural features and its cultural heritage. Its western boundary is 140 kilometres from Darwin, and the park encompasses an area of 1 307 300 hectares (almost 20 000 square kilometres). The majority of land within the park is owned by the Aboriginal people, and has been leased to Parks Australia under a joint management agreement for all visitors to enjoy.

Kakadu contains a wealth of archaeological and rock-art sites that provide insights into Aboriginal culture. The park's traditional owners are willing to share their knowledge and understanding of their land so that visitors will appreciate the importance of Kakadu and share responsibility for its protection.

Kakadu is unique in that it encompasses an entire river catchment, the South Alligator River system, and within it are found all the major habitat types of the Top End. The park is rich in vegetation, ranging from pockets of rainforest through dwarf shrubland to open forest and swamps. The abundant wildlife includes many animals unique to the area, such as the banded pigeon, the oenpelli python and the black wallaroo. Features in the park include Yellow Water (Ngurrungurrudjba), a spectacular wetlands area with prolific birdlife, particularly in the dry season, and Ubirr and Nourlangie Rock, where there is Aboriginal rock art. A spectacular point in the park is Jim Jim Falls, 215 metres high and with a sheer drop of 152 metres of water pouring (in the wet season) over a rugged escarpment (4WD dry season access only).

North of Jim Jim Falls is the East Alligator River, a well-known fishing ground where barramundi can be caught and where the river reaches wind through spectacularly beautiful country. Visits to some isolated locations in the park are subject to a permit system to limit visitor numbers because of the sensitive nature of those areas.

As crocodiles are present in the park, swimming is not recommended and those who fish from the banks of rivers or from boats should take care.

Spectacular **Litchfield National Park** is just a 2-hour drive south from Darwin. It offers stunning sandstone formations, magnetic termite mounds, four major year-round waterfalls, as well as year-round swimming. There are delightful short walks, camping sites within the park and, for the adventurous, a 4WD track to the park's remote southern region is open during the dry season.

Small parks close to Darwin are Berry Springs Nature Park, 65 kilometres south, and Howard Springs Nature Park, 35 kilometres south-east. Berry Springs is noted for its warm water, pleasant and safe swimming, and its birdlife. Adjacent to Berry Springs is the Territory Wildlife Park, where visitors can see animals and birds of the area in a bush setting, including a large walk-through aviary; shuttle trains assist visitor access. At Howard Springs the pool is surrounded by rainforest; again, the park abounds in birds and other wildlife.

Along the Stuart Highway, 320 kilometres south-east of Darwin, are the town of **Katherine** and the spectacular **Nitmiluk National Park**. Here the river flows between the brilliantly coloured walls of the gorge, which reach a height of 60 metres. A boat tour through the gorge is guaranteed to be a highlight of any holiday.

A further 112 kilometres south-east of Katherine is **Elsey National Park**, which includes the Mataranka Hot Springs Reserve, where thermal springs are surrounded by lush tropical forest and the water is permanently at body temperature.

Four-wheel drive wildlife safaris can be arranged in Darwin; an ideal way to see the country and experience something of life in the Top End. There are major roads to all these Top End attractions. However, if you are contemplating an unguided tour of the region, it is vital to recognise that, should you stray into unknown areas, you may experience difficulties. It is important to plan carefully. **See also:** Outback Motoring p. 603.

For further information on Kakadu, contact Kakadu National Park, PO Box 71, Jabiru NT 0886; (08) 8938 1100. A visitor guide to the park is available from Parks Australia, 7th Floor, TCG Centre, 80 Mitchell St, Darwin NT 0800; or from Park Headquarters. For further information on the Top End contact the Darwin Region Tourism Association, Beagle House, cnr Mitchell and Knuckey sts; (08) 8981 4300. **See also:** National Parks p. 410 and individual entries in A–Z town listing for details on parks and towns in bold type. **Map references:** 430–1, 434–5.

Aboriginal Art

Art is one of the essential elements in Aboriginal culture, often using symbols to communicate ideas that cannot be expressed in any other way. Rich and complex beliefs embodied in the Dreaming are expressed in art with many layers of meaning in a variety of contexts, from the sacred and secret realm of ceremony to the more public domain. Aboriginal art takes many forms, from the enduring rock engravings and paintings and the more ephemeral forms including body decoration, to bark and ground paintings and contemporary art.

There is an enormous regional diversity; for example, in the desert regions ground paintings have been the tradition, whereas in Arnhem Land bark paintings are made. Rock art is the oldest surviving type of Aboriginal art and is widely distributed throughout the continent. The most extensive and possibly the oldest rock art in the world can be found in the sandstone country of the Quinkin Reserves around Laura in far north Queensland, the Arnhem Land plateau (including Kakadu), the Victoria River district in the Northern Territory and the Kimberley in north-western Western Australia. Simple engraved lines are found in caves in south-eastern Australia and the Nullarbor Plain, and engravings and petroglyphs ranging from simple designs to cryptic symbols are distributed across the continent from Sydney through southern Australia to the Pilbara in Western Australia.

Aboriginal contemporary artists continue the cultural traditions that are thousands of years old. In recent years there has been a flowering of traditional and contemporary themes applied to ceramics, fabrics, paintings and prints.

The following includes some of the places where rock art can be seen, as well as the major Aboriginal galleries and shops where paintings and artifacts can be viewed or purchased.

'X-ray' art at Nourlangie Rock in Kakadu National Park

Aboriginal Galleries and Shops
Darwin: Aboriginal Fine Arts, 1st Floor, cnr Mitchell and Knuckey sts • Cultural Images, Transit Centre, Mitchell St • Ampiji, Darwin Airport • Framed the Darwin Gallery, cnr Geranium St and Stuart Hwy • Indigenous Creations, cnr Smith and Knuckey sts, and Shop 1, 31 Smith St Mall • Raintree Aboriginal Art Gallery, Shop 1, 18 Knuckey St • Riji Dij, Shop 3, Anthony Plaza • Shades of Ochre Aboriginal Art Gallery, Shop 2, Parap Pl., Parap.
Kakadu National Park: Marrwuddi Gallery, Bowali Visitor Centre, Kakadu Hwy • Warradjan Cultural Centre, Cooinda Rd, Yellow Water.
Katherine: Framed the Katherine Gallery, 34 Katherine Tce • Mimi Aboriginal Arts and Crafts, Shop 9, Southgate Complex, Lindsay St.

AT THE TOP END
Western Arnhem Land, which includes Kakadu National Park, is the major rock-art area in the Top End. Kakadu has representation of all the diverse rock-art styles to be found in western Arnhem Land and the two most accessible sites for visitors are Ubirr and Nourlangie Rock. Some of the sites have been dated at 60 000 years, and others go back even earlier. The earliest images include hand stencils and grass prints (made by dipping clumps of grass in pigment then throwing them against a rock wall to produce an image). Some of the most spectacular sites in western Arnhem Land can be seen via a number of exclusive safari camps; contact the Darwin Region Tourism Association for details.

Eastern Arnhem Land is one of the traditional strongholds for bark paintings. The Buku-Larrnggay Mulka Arts and Culture Centre at Yirrkala near Nhulunbuy, and the Nambara Arts and Crafts Centre, in Nhulunbuy, have outstanding collections. Traditionally bark painting was transient and the designs were secret or sacred. The designs are complex and identify ancestral beings and their relationship to each other and the landscape against a background of intricate crosshatching. The production of bark paintings for sale involved the use of non-secret designs and techniques that preserved both bark and pigments. Eastern Arnhem Land has numerous art and craft centres in remote communities that can be accessed by special charters; contact the Darwin Region Tourism Association for details.

The Museum and Art Gallery of the Northern Territory in Darwin has an extensive collection of Aboriginal art and artifacts. It also hosts the prestigious National Aboriginal Art Award in late August or early September each year.

IN CENTRAL AUSTRALIA
Ground painting was once a widespread practice in Central Australia, and is still practised occasionally today. The paintings are used for storytelling and ceremonial purposes, and the designs, based on significant landscape features and mythological creatures, are painted on prepared earth, usually with ochre, and the background filled with dots. Ground painting formed the basis for 'dot painting' which is practised today using western mediums.

Aboriginal Galleries and Shops
Alice Springs: Aboriginal Art and Culture Centre, 86–88 Todd St • Aboriginal Desert Art Gallery, 87 Todd Mall • Aboriginal Dreamtime Gallery, 71 Todd Mall • Arunta Art Gallery and Book Shop, 70 Todd St • Gallery Gondwana, 43 Todd St Mall • Jukurrpa Artists, cnr Stott and Leichhardt tces • Mbantua Gallery, Gregory Tce • The Original Dreamtime Art Gallery, 63 Todd Mall • Papunya Tula Artists Pty Ltd, 78 Todd St • Pmara Yultha Karta, cnr Memorial Ave and Larapinta Dr. • Warumpi Arts, Shop 7, 105 Gregory Tce.
Tennant Creek: Ngalipanyanga Art Gallery, Irvine St.
Yulara: Maruku Arts and Crafts, Uluṟu–Kata Tjuṯa Cultural Centre, within park on road to Uluṟu • Mulgara Gallery, foyer of Sails in the Desert Hotel, Ayers Rock Resort.

For further information about Aboriginal art sites and Aboriginal galleries and shops: in the Top End, contact Darwin Region Tourism Association, cnr Mitchell and Knuckey sts; (08) 8981 4300; in Central Australia, contact Central Australian Tourism Industry Association, cnr Gregory Tce and Todd St, Alice Springs; (08) 8952 5800.

Aboriginal Lands

Tnorala (Gosse Bluff), a spectacular crater on Aboriginal land near Glen Helen

In the Northern Territory, Commonwealth and Northern Territory laws do not permit people to enter Aboriginal land unless they have been issued with a permit.

It should be noted that, as a general rule, Land Councils have been asked by traditional owners not to issue entry permits for unaccompanied tourist travel. This does not affect visitors travelling on organised tours on to Aboriginal land where tour bookings include the necessary permit.

If there is a likelihood of a need to enter Aboriginal land for any reason, including fuel, travellers should seek permits from the relevant Land Councils. When making an application for entry to any Aboriginal land, applicants must state the reason for entry, dates and duration of intended stay, names of persons travelling, vehicle details, and itinerary and routes to be used while on these lands. Permits can be issued only after consultation and approval of the traditional owners and relevant Aboriginal communities. Processing permit applications can take two weeks – this is something to bear in mind when planning your trip. It is the right of traditional owners of Aboriginal land to refuse entry permits.

All public roads that cross Aboriginal lands are exempt from the permit requirements; the exemption covers the immediate road corridor only. If travellers are unsure about the status of roads on which they are driving, they should seek advice from the Land Councils before departure. Some towns within Aboriginal land are also exempt from the provisions.

A pass is required to travel on the Mereenie Loop, which links Glen Helen with Kings Canyon and passes through Aboriginal land. Passes may be obtained from the Central Australian Tourism Industry Association office in Alice Springs, or from Hermannsburg or Kings Canyon. Travellers also receive an information brochure.

A number of tourist ventures operate on Aboriginal land; they include tourist camps and outlets for artworks and artifacts. For details contact Northern Territory Tourist Commission, 67 Stuart Hwy, Alice Springs; (08) 8951 8555.

The relevant land councils, to whom applications for permits and any inquiries must be directed in writing, are:

Alice Springs and Tennant Creek regions:
Central Land Council Permits
33 Stuart Hwy, Alice Springs
(PO Box 3321 Alice Springs NT 0871)
(08) 8951 6320
Web site www.clc.org.au

Darwin, Nhulunbuy and Katherine regions:
Northern Land Council
9 Rowling St, Casuarina
(PO Box 42921 Casuarina NT 0811)
(08) 8920 5100

Melville and Bathurst islands:
Tiwi Land Council
PO Box 38545
Winnellie NT 0821
(08) 8981 4898

Trephina Gorge Nature Park, near Ross River

9.30 a.m. and 1 p.m.; Museum of the Never Never, outdoor displays of railway history, Overland Telegraph and bush workshop; giant termite mound. May: Back to the Never Never Festival; Art Show. Aug.: Rodeo. **In the area:** Elsey National Park, 5 km E: thermal pool in lush tropical forest, popular for swimming; walking tracks through pockets of rainforest; camping area; barramundi fishing on Roper River; canoe hire; departure point for walking trail to Mataranka Falls at Twelve Mile Yards. Mataranka Homestead Tourist Resort, near thermal pool, has camping and replica of Elsey homestead. Elsey Cemetery, 20 km S, graves of outback pioneers immortalised by Jeannie Gunn (lived at Elsey Station homestead 1902–03, wrote the book *We of the Never Never)*; nearby, cairn marking site of original homestead. **Visitor information:** Stockyard Gallery, Stuart Hwy; (08) 8975 4530. **See also:** The Top End p. 419.

Nhulunbuy   Pop. 3695

MAP REF. 435 P5
Nhulunbuy is on the north-eastern tip of Arnhem Land, on the Gove Peninsula. The whole of the peninsula is held as freehold by the Yolngu people. *Intending visitors must obtain a permit from the Northern Land Council (contact (08) 8920 5100) beforehand; rules apply. Allow 2 weeks for processing.* Originally built as a service town for the bauxite-mining industry, Nhulunbuy is now the administrative centre for the Arnhem Region as well. Access is by a year-round daily jet air service from Darwin or Cairns. Local car hire. *A recreation permit is required for travel outside the Nhulunbuy Town Lease (contact (08) 8987 3992).* **In town:** Gayngaru (Town Lagoon)

self-guide nature walk. July: National Aboriginal and Islander Day of Celebration. **In the area:** At Nambara Arts and Crafts, Melville Bay Rd, 15 km NW: traditional and contemporary Aboriginal art and craft. Buku-Larrnggay Mulka, at Yirrkala Community, Melville Bay Rd 20 km SE: renowned community based Aboriginal art museum; no permit required for museum visit. Stunning beaches with tropical-blue water, accessible by permit (fee applies). Boat charters for game-, reef- and barramundi-fishing. Also water sports, birdwatching, croc-spotting, Yolngu guides, guided 4WD, and bauxite mine tour (Fri.). **Visitor information:** Westall St; (08) 8987 1777. Web site www1.octa4.net.au/ealta

Noonamah   Pop. 8

MAP REF. 430 E4, 434 E6
Noonamah is on the Stuart Hwy, 43 km S of Darwin. **In the area:** Over 7000 crocodiles at Crocodile Farm, just north of town; feeding displays and tours. Howard Springs Nature Park, 23 km NW, for safe swimming, bird-watching and picnicking. On Cox Peninsula Rd: Berry Springs Nature Park, 14 km SW, safe swimming in spring-fed pool in monsoon forest; alongside, Territory Wildlife Park, has native fauna in 400-ha bushland setting viewed via walking trails or motorised open train; 4 km W of Wildlife Park, Lakes Resort, has watersports, waterski and jetski hire, and accommodation. South of Lakes Resort on Pipeline Rd, Southport Siding Exotic Fruit Farm: orchard tours, sales, wildlife. Majestic Orchids, orchid-growing area, 24 km SW. Tumbling Waters Deer Park, 26 km SW. Manton Dam, 25 km S, for water sports and picnicking on foreshore. **Visitor information:** Hotel; (08) 8988 1054.

Pine Creek   Pop. 521

MAP REF. 430 I13, 434 F8
Pine Creek, on the Stuart Hwy, 90 km NW of Katherine, experienced a brief gold rush in the 1870s; today the town is experiencing a resurgence following the reopening of goldmining. **In town:** Numerous historic buildings; trail brochure available. Miners Park, Main Tce, has historic mining machinery. Railway Station museum and historic steam train used in film *We of the Never Never*, off Main Tce (check opening times). Museum and Library, Railway Tce, has display on Overland Telegraph. Mine Lookout, off Moule St. At Gun Alley Gold Mining, Gun Alley: restored steam ore crusher, gold-panning tours. Bird Park, tropical birds in lush garden setting. Old Timers Rock Hut, Jenson St, has rock and mineral display. May: Gold Rush Festival; Races. June: Rodeo. **In the area:** Gold fossicking (licence required). Copperfield Recreation Reserve at Copperfield Dam, 6 km SW, foreshore ideal for picnics. Umbrawarra Gorge, 22 km SW: good swimming, rock-climbing and walking. Bonrook Lodge and station, 6 km SE, wild horse sanctuary. Edith Falls, 67 km SE in northwestern end of Nitmiluk National Park, for swimming and bushwalking in area. The Rock Hole, 65 km NE via Kakadu Hwy, a secluded waterhole (4WD access only). Gunlom (Waterfall Creek), 113 km NE via Kakadu Hwy, beautiful falls and permanent waterhole in Kakadu National Park. Butterfly Gorge Nature Park (4WD access only), 113 km NW, named for butterflies that settle in rock crevices. **Visitor information:** Diggers Rest Motel, 32 Main Tce; (08) 8976 1442. **See also:** Day Tours from Darwin p. 404.

Renner Springs   Pop. 11

MAP REF. 437 J8
A roadside stop on the Stuart Hwy, 160 km N of Tennant Creek, Renner Springs was named after Frederick Renner, doctor to workers on the Overland Telegraph. Dr Renner discovered springs when he observed bird flocks gathering there. The source of the springs is unknown. Fuel, supplies and meals at Renner Springs Desert Inn. Picnic/barbecue facilities.

Ross River   Pop. 30

MAP REF. 433 P4, 439 K8
At Ross River is Ross River Homestead, in a ranch-style outback setting with cabins, backpacker accommodation, camping and

Aboriginal Cultural Tours

For over 60 000 years the Aboriginal people have developed a unique understanding of the relationship between the physical and spiritual world. Today a number of Aborigines work professionally to share their knowledge with visitors. There is a wide range of Aboriginal cultural

tours available throughout the Northern Territory, each offering the Aboriginal perspective of their particular area.

For further information on Aboriginal cultural tours in the Northern Territory contact the Northern Territory Holiday Information HELPLINE; 1800 621 336.

Location	Tour operator	Features
AT THE TOP END		
KAKADU NATIONAL PARK	Guluyambi East Alligator River Cruises	• cruise along East Alligator River • spectacular contrasting scenery • landscape interpreted by Aboriginal guide
	Magela Cultural and Heritage Tours	• journeys through the more remote and restricted areas of the park as guests of the Bunidji people • small groups only • Jabiru-based cultural tour during wet season
ARNHEM LAND	Davidson's Safaris	• wilderness experience • operates all seasons • extensive rock-art galleries • insights into Aboriginal culture and bush foods
	Dreamtime Safaris	• Talabon people demonstrate traditional dance, arts and crafts and storytelling • exclusive, luxury camp
	The Arnhemlander Aboriginal Cultural Tour	• visit rock-art sites, Mikinj Valley • learn bush skills, food gathering and preparation • visit Injalak Arts and Crafts centre at Oenpelli • most tours accompanied by an Aboriginal guide
	Umorrduk Safaris	• rock-art galleries • interpretation of land, history and mythology of Aboriginal culture • exclusive safari camp
	Wadda Safaris	• camp with tour guide • walkabout with local Aboriginal people • swim in secluded waterholes
BATHURST ISLAND (80 km N of Darwin)	Tiwi Tours	• cultural tours of Bathurst Island (1–2 days) • visit island communities • explore the island's natural features
KATHERINE Springvale Station Homestead (8 km W)	Aboriginal Corroboree	• traditional Aboriginal dance performance • historic homestead
Eva Valley (100 km NE)	Manyallaluk Aboriginal Corporation	• various tours from 1-day cultural experience to 2-day camp-outs and 5-day tours from Darwin • caravan-park and cabin facilities available for self-drive visitors
Nitmiluk National Park (30 km N)	Travel North	• 2½ hour Aboriginal-guided bush tour • learn bush skills, food gathering and bush medicine • traditional corroboree at historic Springvale station homestead
Mataranka and surrounding area	Far Out Adventures	• personalised charters for small groups into areas of natural and cultural significance
IN CENTRAL AUSTRALIA		
	Spencer Tours	• range of short and extended tours • specialises in personally designed private tours • experienced guides offer insights into Aboriginal and pastoral heritage
	Desert Tracks	• tours vary from 1 to 8 days • specialise in small group visits to Aboriginal communities in the spectacular Pitjantjatjara lands
	Rod Steinert Tours	• learn about spiritual beliefs, kinship system, weaponry, bush tucker • see a corroboree
	Vast Visual Arts and Specialist Tours	• personally designed art, culture and nature tours
Hermannsburg	Hermannsburg Tour	• first Aboriginal mission in NT • visit Historic Precinct and Kata-Anga Tea Rooms
Wallace Rockhole	Wallace Rockhole Community	• rock-art tours with local Arrernte guides • camping facilities
Oak Valley	Oak Valley Tours	• day tour • ancient rock art
Uluru-Kata Tjuta National Park	Anangu Tours	• local Anangu guides offer insights into their history, knowledge and lifestyle

caravan park, 83 km E of Alice Springs. The homestead offers a range of outback activities, from boomerang-throwing and whip-cracking with billy tea and damper as refreshment, to feeding kangaroos, horse and camel treks, and overnight safaris. **In the area:** Trephina Gorge Nature Park, 17 km NW, has scenic walking tracks, camping and picnic facilities. N'Dhala Gorge Nature Park (4WD access only), 11 km SW, features Aboriginal rock engravings, walking tracks and ancient fossil deposits. Corroboree Rock Conservation Reserve, 33 km SW, has signposted walk

explaining significance of rock to Eastern Arrernte people. Arltunga Historical Reserve (4WD access only), 45 km NE: old goldmining town with stone ruins, scattered workings and gravestones; police station and gaol have been restored; visitor centre displays local history. Nearby, gold panning and metal-detecting in declared fossicking area; fossicking permits at Arltunga Hotel. Further east, Ruby Gap Gorge (4WD access only) on the intermittent Hale River. **Visitor information:** Ross River Homestead, Ross Hwy; (08) 8956 9711. **See also:** The Red Centre p. 415.

Tennant Creek   Pop. 3856

MAP REF. 437 K10

According to legend, the town of Tennant Creek was founded when a beer wagon broke down at the site. The town is 506 km N of Alice Springs, on the Stuart Hwy. Gold and copper deposits account for its development today as a centre for the Barkly Tablelands. **In town:** National Trust Museum in historic Tuxworth Fullwood House, Schmidt St, features photographic collection and displays of early mine buildings and equipment (open

Fishing in the Territory

Fishing for barramundi on the lower Daly River, south of Darwin

Whether you are fishing in salt water or fresh water, the Territory provides some of the best fishing in Australia. The coast has sheltered bays, estuaries, mangrove-lined creeks, offshore reefs and islands, and much of the fishing is easily reached from population centres. The inland has huge areas of wetlands, with rivers, billabongs and flood plains. Note that it is an unwritten rule of the north that you retain fish only for the table, and catch and release the others.

Some of the best blue-water fishing in Australia is available straight out of Darwin. You can fish from the shore or wharves of the city; explore the coastal estuaries, mangroves and sandbars; venture along the coast or to the offshore reefs by boat; or organise a charter to go game-fishing. The fishing on the east coast of Arnhem Land, based on the Gove Peninsula and Groote Eylandt, is legendary, but access is difficult. The popular fish are giant trevally, queenfish (leatherskin), mackerel, cobia and tuna. Black jewfish and fingermark (golden snapper) are taken from the harbour wharves, and sweetlip, coral trout and stripey are found around the reefs.

Freshwater fishing in the Territory is best just after the wet, and at the end of the dry when the receding waters and increasing water

temperatures mobilise the fish into an aggressive feeding pattern. In Darwin itself, as well as throughout the Territory, there are many operators of guided fishing tours. To the east of Darwin lies Kakadu National Park, which contains several major rivers, although fishing is prohibited in certain parts of the park. The Mary and Adelaide rivers' wetlands, the McArthur River at Borroloola and the Victoria River west of Katherine are popular places for catching barramundi. Fishing in inland waters away from major population centres is not for the inexperienced. Much of the Territory is rugged and during the wet season the country can only be traversed on the few sealed highways and all-weather gravel roads.

Anglers should watch out for crocodiles in the tidal estuary waters and inland waters and observe basic safety measures. Cleaning fish close to the waterline or wading in the water are not advised.

For further information on fishing in the Territory, contact the Department of Primary Industry and Fisheries Recreational Fishing Office, PO Box 990, Darwin NT 0801; (08) 8999 2372. Web site www.nt.gov.au/dpif/fishing.shtml

May–Sept., check times). Travellers Rest Area in Purkiss Reserve, Ambrose St, has picnic area and swimming pool nearby. Scenic drives; heritage walk; leaflets available. May: Cup Day (horseracing); Go-Kart Grand Prix. July: Agricultural Show. Sept.: Desert Harmony Festival (arts and culture festival). **In the area:** Tours of goldmining areas, including night tour of early goldmine. Gold fossicking. Battery Hill, 1.5 km E on Peko Rd, features one of three 10-stamp batteries still operational in Australia, modern underground mine with working machinery, displays, films, and nature walk. Past the Battery, Ben Allen Lookout offers views of town and area. Juno Horse Centre, 10 km E, for horseriding and cattle drives. Nobles Nob, 16 km E, once richest open-cut goldmine in world. Mary Ann Dam, 5 km NE, for water sports. Restored telegraph station (1875), 12 km N. Three Ways Roadhouse and Hotel, junction of Stuart and Barkly hwys, 25 km N; nearby, John Flynn Memorial. Attack Creek Historical Reserve, 73 km N; memorial marks encounter between John McDouall Stuart and local Aborigines. The Pebbles, 16 km NW, miniatures of Devil's Marbles (huge 'balancing rocks' found 106 km S). **Visitor information:** Battery Hill Visitor Information Centre, Peko Rd; (08) 8962 3388.

Ti Tree
Pop. 50

MAP REF. 438 I5
A rest stop on the Stuart Hwy, Ti Tree is 192 km N of Alice Springs. **In town:** Opposite Roadhouse, Gallereaterie: local Aboriginal art (exhibitions, sales), eatinghouse. Ti Tree Park, with picnic area and playground. **In the area:** Central Mt Stuart Historical Reserve, 18 km N, includes monument at base of mountain marking the spot as the centre of Australia. **Visitor information:** Roadhouse, Stuart Hwy; (08) 8956 9741.

Timber Creek
Pop. 556

MAP REF. 434 D13, 436 D2
Timber Creek is 285 km SW of Katherine on the Victoria Hwy. **In town:** National Trust Museum, off hwy, has displays of historical artifacts (open Apr.–Aug.). Boat tours, cruises, fishing tours and scenic flights. Conservation Commission Headquarters, Victoria Hwy, provides road and park information for visitors travelling into Gregory or Keep River national parks. Apr.–May: Fishing competitions. May: Rodeo. Sept.: Timber Creek Races (horseracing). **In the**

Gregory National Park, west of Timber Creek

area: Gregory National Park, 15 km W, features Limestone Gorge, Aboriginal and European heritage sites and boab trees. Keep River National Park, 175 km W, features rugged scenery, Aboriginal rock art and wildlife; most trails 4WD only. For both parks, check with Conservation Commission for access details. Jasper Gorge, 48 km SW, a scenic gorge with permanent waterhole. **Visitor information:** Timber Creek Hotel, Victoria Hwy; (08) 8975 0722. **See also:** National Parks p. 410.

Victoria River
Pop. 6

MAP REF. 434 E12, 436 E2
Victoria River is a rest stop located where the Victoria Hwy crosses the mighty Victoria River. Victoria River Roadhouse complex: boat tours, fishing trips (both from Wayside Inn); range of accommodation. Scenic bushwalks in area, particularly Joe's Creek Walk, 10 km W. **Visitor information:** Wayside Inn, Victoria Hwy; (08) 8975 0744.

Wauchope
Pop. 7

MAP REF. 437 K13, 439 K2
Wauchope is on the Stuart Hwy, 114 km S of Tennant Creek. The historic hotel once served the old Wolfram Mines. **In the area:** Devil's Marbles, 8 km N, large, precariously balanced granite boulders. Wycliffe Well (1872), 17 km S, opposite Wycliffe Hotel. Davenport National Park, 118 km W: Aboriginal

heritage and waterhole ecology isolated area, high clearance or 4WD access only, advise travel; (08) 8964 1959 or Wauchope Hotel. **Visitor information:** Wauchope Hotel, Stuart Hwy; (08) 8964 1963.

Yulara
Pop. 2754

MAP REF. 432 B12, 438 E11
Situated on the outskirts of Uluru–Kata Tjuta National Park, this town is the location for the world-class Ayers Rock Resort, offering full visitor facilities and airconditioned accommodation in all price brackets (advance bookings essential). **In town:** Visitors Centre has displays of geology, history, flora and fauna of the region; also spectacular photographic collection. Tours include Uluru Experience Night Sky Show, which offers night-sky viewing and narration of Aboriginal and European interpretations of the night sky; book tours at information centre or reception in accommodation areas. **In the area:** On approach road to Uluru, Uluru–Kata Tjuta Cultural Centre, designed in shape of two snakes, has displays and sales of Aboriginal culture and arts. Uluru (Ayers Rock), 20 km SE, Australia's famous sandstone monolith: Aboriginal rock-art sites; spectacular sunrises and sunsets; guided tours around base of Uluru, highlighting its Aboriginal significance. Kata Tjuta (The Olgas), 50 km W, the Centre's other famous landmark: Valley of Winds walk; views; flora and fauna. **Visitor information:** Visitors Centre; (08) 8956 2240. **See also:** The Red Centre p. 415.

Northern Territory

LOCATION MAP

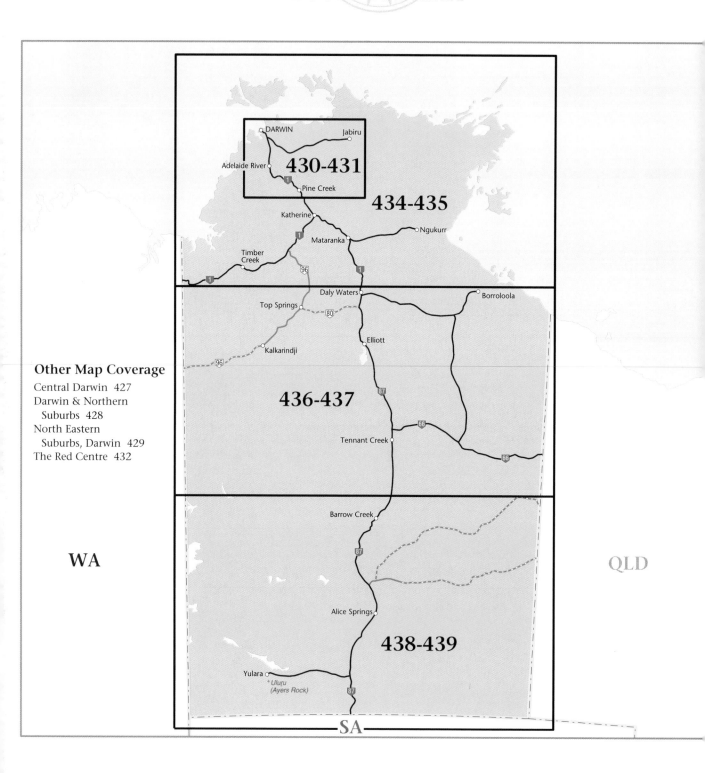

Other Map Coverage

Central Darwin 427
Darwin & Northern
  Suburbs 428
North Eastern
  Suburbs, Darwin 429
The Red Centre 432

WA

QLD

SA

DARWIN
Jabiru
Adelaide River
430-431
Pine Creek
434-435
Katherine
Mataranka
Ngukurr
Timber
Creek
96
1
Daly Waters
Borroloola
Top Springs
80
Elliott
Kalkarindji
96
436-437
87
66
Tennant Creek
66
Barrow Creek
87
Alice Springs
438-439
Yulara
* Uluru
(Ayers Rock)
87

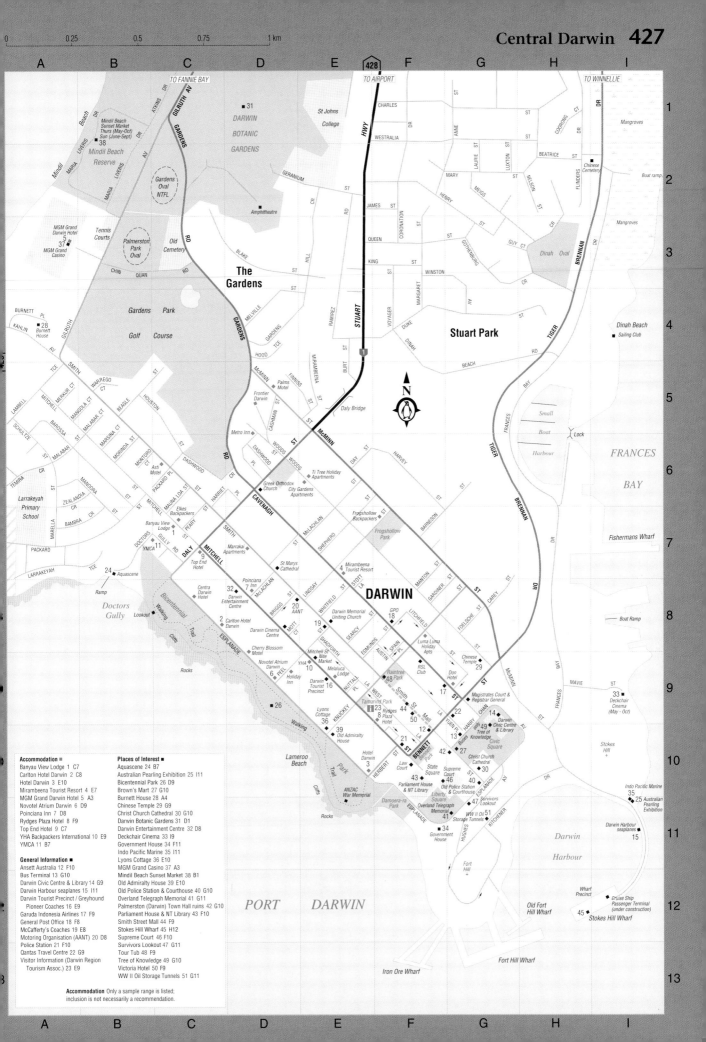

0   0.25   0.5   0.75   1 km

A B C D E F G H I

TO FANNIE BAY

■ 31

DARWIN BOTANIC GARDENS

St Johns College

428

TO AIRPORT

TO WINNELLIE

Mindil Beach Sunset Market Thurs (May-Oct) Sun (June-Sept)
■ 38

Mindil Beach Reserve

Mangroves

Chinese Cemetery ■

Boat ramp

Gardens Oval NTFL

Amphitheatre

Mangroves

MGM Grand Darwin Hotel
■ 5
■ 37
MGM Grand Casino

Tennis Courts

Palmerston Park Oval

Old Cemetery

Dinah Oval

Dinah Beach Sailing Club

The Gardens

Stuart Park

Gardens Park Golf Course

Small Boat Harbour

Lock

FRANCES BAY

■ 28 Burnett House

Frontier Darwin

Metro Inn

Palms Motel

Daly Bridge

N

Asti Motel

Larrakeyah Primary School

Greek Orthodox Church

City Gardens Apartments

Ti Tree Holiday Apartments

Fishermans Wharf

Elkes Backpackers

Frogshollow Backpackers

Frogshollow Park

Boat Ramp

Banyau View Lodge 1

YMCA 11

Marrakai Apartments

Top End Hotel 9

Aquascene

Ramp

St Marys Cathedral

Miramabeena Tourist Resort 4

DARWIN

Doctors Gully

Lookout

Walking

Centra Darwin Hotel

32 ■

Poinciana Inn 7

Darwin Entertainment Centre

Cherry Blossom Motel

2 Carlton Hotel Darwin

Darwin Cinema Centre

20 AANT

19

Darwin Memorial Uniting Church

GPO 18

Litchfield

Luma Luma Holiday Apts

Chinese Temple 29

Boat Ramp

Novotel Atrium Darwin
6

YHA 10

Mitchell St Nite Market

Melaluca Holiday Inn

Raintree Park 48

RSL Club

Don Hotel

Darwin Tourist Precinct 16

17

Chinese Cinema (May - Oct) 33

26 ■

Lyons Cottage 36

Rydges Plaza Hotel 8

44

Magistrates Court & Registrar General

14

Darwin Civic Centre & Library 49 Tree of Knowledge

22

27

50

12

Civic Square

Old Admiralty House 39

13

42

Christ Church Cathedral 30

Stokes Hill

Hotel Darwin 3

21

Law Court

State Square

Supreme Court

46

40

Bennett

Herbert

Lameroo Beach

Parliament House & NT Library

43

Old Police Station & Courthouse

Liberty Square

Overland Telegraph Memorial 41

Survivors Lookout 51 WW II Oil Storage Tunnels

Indo Pacific Marine 35

ANZAC War Memorial

Damoera-ra Park

Government House 34

25 Australian Pearling Exhibition

Darwin Harbour seaplanes 15

Rocks

Government House

Darwin Harbour

Fort Hill

PORT DARWIN

Old Fort Hill Wharf

Wharf Precinct

Cruise Ship Passenger Terminal (under construction)

45 Stokes Hill Wharf

Iron Ore Wharf

Fort Hill Wharf

Accommodation ■
Banyau View Lodge 1 C7
Carlton Hotel Darwin 2 C8
Hotel Darwin 3 E10
Mirambeena Tourist Resort 4 E7
MGM Grand Darwin Hotel 5 A3
Novotel Atrium Darwin 6 D9
Poinciana Inn 7 D8
Rydges Plaza Hotel 8 F9
Top End Hotel 9 C7
YHA Backpackers International 10 E9
YMCA 11 B7

General Information ■
Ansett Australia 12 F10
Bus Terminal 13 G10
Darwin Civic Centre & Library 14 G9
Darwin Harbour seaplanes 15 I11
Darwin Tourist Precinct / Greyhound
 Pioneer Coaches 16 E9
Garuda Indonesia Airlines 17 E8
General Post Office 18 F8
McCafferty's Coaches 19 E8
Motoring Organisation (AANT) 20 D8
Police Station 21 F10
Qantas Travel Centre 22 G9
Visitor Information (Darwin Region
 Tourism Assoc.) 23 E9

Places of Interest ■
Aquascene 24 B7
Australian Pearling Exhibition 25 I11
Bicentennial Park 26 D9
Brown's Mart 27 G10
Burnett House 28 A4
Chinese Temple 29 G9
Christ Church Cathedral 30 G10
Darwin Botanic Gardens 31 D1
Darwin Entertainment Centre 32 D8
Deckchair Cinema 33 I9
Government House 34 F11
Indo Pacific Marine 35 I11
Lyons Cottage 36 E10
MGM Grand Casino 37 A3
Mindil Beach Sunset Market 38 B1
Old Admiralty House 39 E10
Old Police Station & Courthouse 40 G10
Overland Telegraph Memorial 41 G11
Palmerston (Darwin) Town Hall ruins 42 G10
Parliament House & NT Library 43 F10
Smith Street Mall 44 F9
Stokes Hill Wharf 45 H12
Supreme Court 46 F10
Survivors Lookout 47 G11
Tour Tub 48 F9
Tree of Knowledge 49 G10
Victoria Hotel 50 F9
WW II Oil Storage Tunnels 51 G11

Accommodation Only a sample range is listed;
 inclusion is not necessarily a recommendation.

0 0.25 0.5 0.75 1 km

429

DARWIN AIRPORT

East Point Military Museum

East Point Reserve

East Point

Lake Alexander

Rocks

Dudley Point Lookout

Ludmilla

BAGOT ABORIGINAL COMMUNITY

Ludmilla Primary School

RAAF Base

The Narrows

Dwyer Park

Mangroves

Waratah Sports Club

Fannie Bay Racecourse

Richardson Park (Rugby League)

Ross Smith Memorial

Fannie Bay Gaol Museum

Trailer Boat Club
Boat Ramp
Sailing Club

Vesteys Beach

FANNIE BAY

Fannie Bay

Olympic Pool

Primary School

Parap

Parap Market (Saturday)

Water-ski Club
Boat Ramp

Museum and Art Gallery of the Northern Territory

Darwin Bowling Club

Bullocky Point
Rocks

Darwin High School

The Gardens

Sacred Heart College

Botanic Gardens

St Johns College

Primary School

Mindil Beach Sunset Market

Mindil Beach

Gardens Oval NTFL

Amphitheatre

MGM Grand Darwin

Tennis Courts

Old Cemetery

Stuart Park

Chinese Cemetery
Boat Ramp

Dinah Oval

Dinah Beach

CHARLES DARWIN NATIONAL PARK

Myilly Point
Rocks

Myilly Point Park

Burnett House

Darwin Harbour Cruises

Cullen Bay Marina

Passenger Ferry

Ferries to Mandorah

Lock

Emery Point

Gardens Park

Golf Course

Small Boat Harbour

Larrakeyah

LARRAKEYAH ARMY BASE

Elliott Point

Daly Bridge

DARWIN

Aquascene
Ramp

Doctors Gully

Rocks Cliffs

Lyons Cottage

Old Admiralty House
Lameroo Beach

Parliament House

Government House

Deckchair Cinema

Indo Pacific Marine and Australian Pearling Exhibition

FRANCES BAY

For more detail on Central Darwin see page 427

Fort Hill

Stokes Hill Wharf

Darwin Harbour

PORT DARWIN

Iron Ore Wharf

Fort Hill Wharf

0   0.25   0.5   0.75   1 km

TIMOR   SEA

BEAGLE   GULF

N

Casuarina Coastal Reserve

Royal Darwin Hospital
Lee Point

Surf Life Saving Club
Dripstone Caves

Memorial to No. 31 Squadron

Tiwi
Tiwi Park
Tiwi Campus NTU
Dripstone High School

Brinkin

Nakara
Nakara Park
Nakara Primary School

Wanguri Park
Wanguri Primary School
Wanguri

Leanyer

Northern Territory University

Casuarina Shopping Square
Swimming Pool Gsell Park

Casuarina

Wagaman
Wagaman Primary School
Wagaman Park

Rocks
Picnic Area
Footbridge
RAPID   CREEK

Rapid Creek

Alawa Primary School
Alawa

Casuarina Senior College

Jabiru

Wulagi

Swimming Pool
Nightcliff High School

Rapid Creek Primary School

Recreation Reserve

Mangroves

Jingili
Jingili Primary School
Jingili Park

Darwin Water Gardens

Moil Primary School
Moil Park
Moil

Yanyula
Anula Primary School

Jetty
Boat Ramp
Rocks
Casuarina

Nightcliff
Primary School
Nightcliff Oval

Rapid Ck Markets (Sunday)

Anula

Rocks

Nightcliff Markets (Sunday)

TROWER

Millner Primary School

Orchid Park
Cemetery

McMILLANS

Marrara Park
Rugby
Baseball

Darwin Golf Club

Coconut Grove

Caravan Park

Tong Luck

Millner

Kimmorley Bridge

Recreation Reserve

Indoor Stadium
Aths Tck
Football
Hockey
Soccer
Cricket

Marrara

Mangroves

Darwin Tennis Centre
Velodrome

COLLOPY

Marrara Sporting Complex

General Aviation Apron
SLADE CT
PEDERSON

DARWIN AIRPORT

Ludmilla

Darwin Airport Terminal

BAGOT ABORIGINAL COMMUNITY

Benwerrin

Camara

Ludmilla Primary School

RAAF Base

Mangroves

Fannie Bay Racecourse

Richardson Park (Rugby League)

The Narrows

Australian Aviation Heritage Centre

Ross Smith
Olympic Pool
Primary School

HWY

Winnellie

Showgrounds & Greyhound Track

Parap
Parap Market (Sat)

CHARLES DARWIN NATIONAL PARK

A   B   C   D   E   F   G   H   I

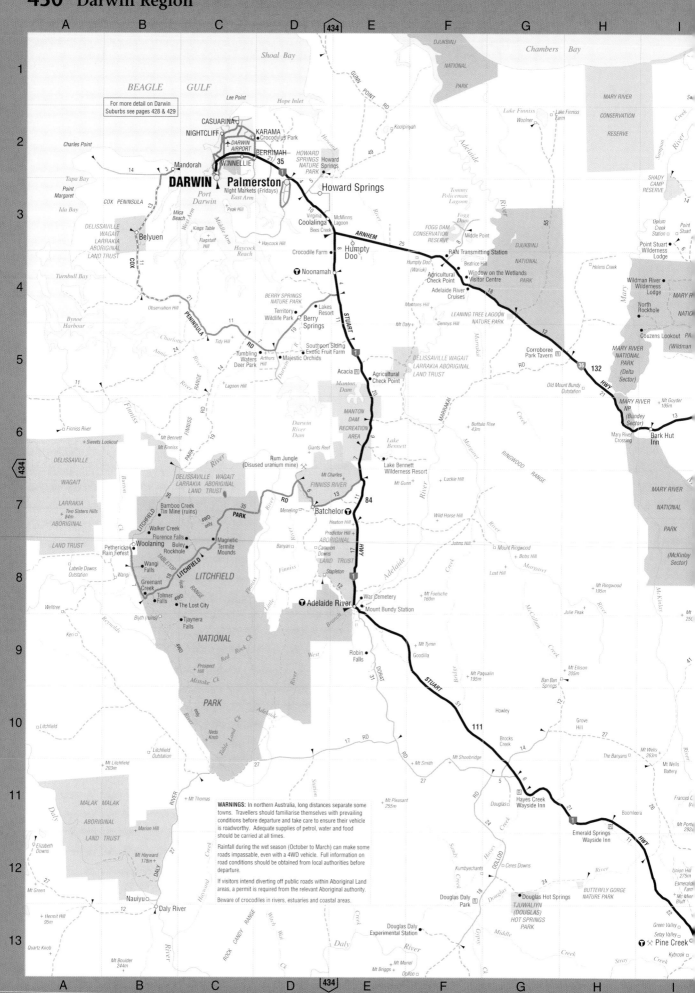

WARNINGS: In northern Australia, long distances separate some towns. Travellers should familiarise themselves with prevailing conditions before departure and take care to ensure their vehicle is roadworthy. Adequate supplies of petrol, water and food should be carried at all times.

Rainfall during the wet season (October to March) can make some roads impassable, even with a 4WD vehicle. Full information on road conditions should be obtained from local authorities before departure.

If visitors intend diverting off public roads within Aboriginal Land areas, a permit is required from the relevant Aboriginal authority.

Beware of crocodiles in rivers, estuaries and coastal areas.

For more detail on Darwin
Suburbs see pages 428 & 429

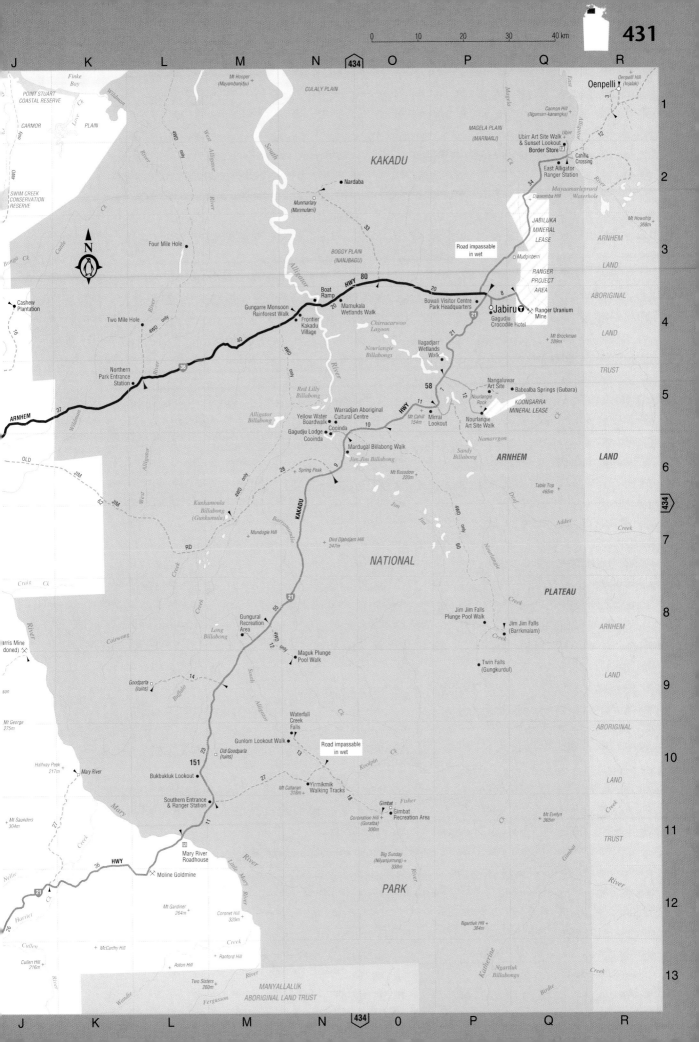

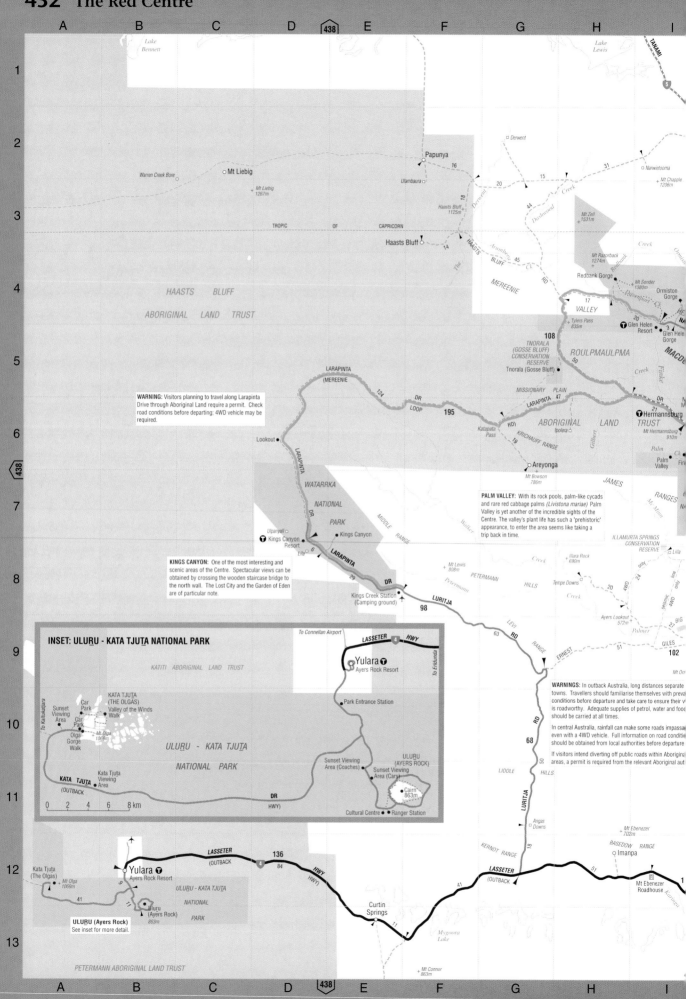

WARNING: Visitors planning to travel along Larapinta Drive through Aboriginal Land require a permit. Check road conditions before departing; 4WD vehicle may be required.

KINGS CANYON: One of the most interesting and scenic areas of the Centre. Spectacular views can be obtained by crossing the wooden staircase bridge to the north wall. The Lost City and the Garden of Eden are of particular note.

PALM VALLEY: With its rock pools, palm-like cycads and rare red cabbage palms (Livistona mariae) Palm Valley is yet another of the incredible sights of the Centre. The valley's plant life has such a 'prehistoric' appearance, to enter the area seems like taking a trip back in time.

WARNINGS: In outback Australia, long distances separate towns. Travellers should familiarise themselves with prevai conditions before departure and take care to ensure their v is roadworthy. Adequate supplies of petrol, water and foo should be carried at all times.

In central Australia, rainfall can make some roads impassa even with a 4WD vehicle. Full information on road conditi should be obtained from local authorities before departure

If visitors intend diverting off public roads within Aborigina areas, a permit is required from the relevant Aboriginal aut

INSET: ULURU - KATA TJUTA NATIONAL PARK

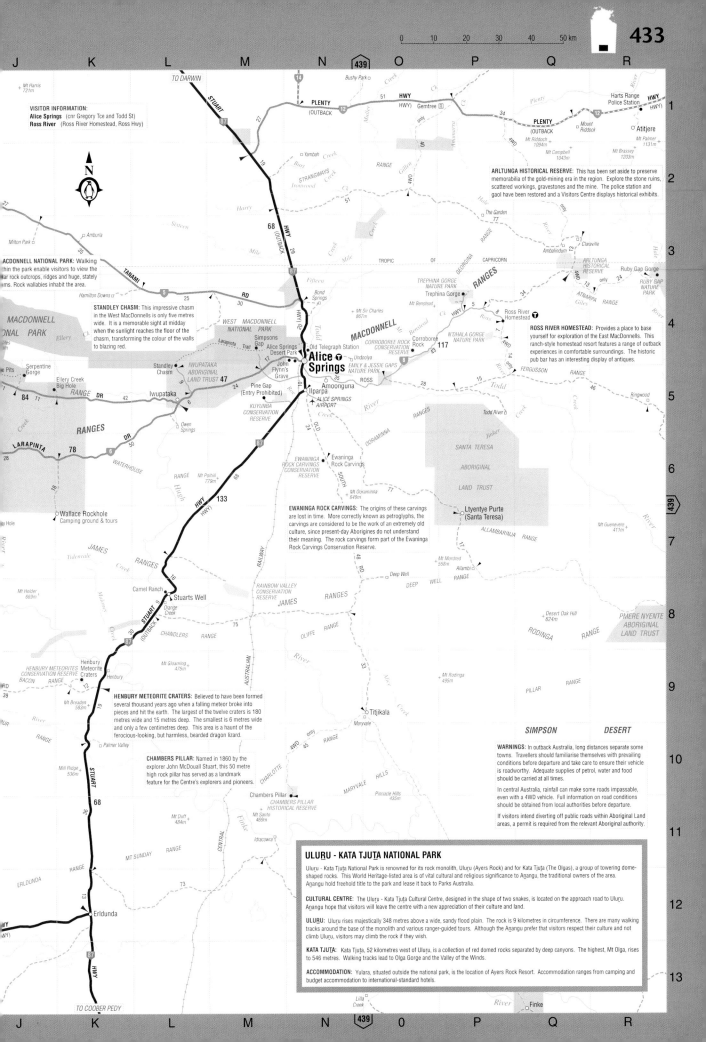

0 10 20 30 40 50 km

J K L M N O P Q R

VISITOR INFORMATION:
Alice Springs (cnr Gregory Tce and Todd St)
Ross River (Ross River Homestead, Ross Hwy)

ARLTUNGA HISTORICAL RESERVE: This has been set aside to preserve memorabilia of the gold-mining era in the region. Explore the stone ruins, scattered workings, gravestones and the mine. The police station and gaol have been restored and a Visitors Centre displays historical exhibits.

[MAC]DONNELL NATIONAL PARK: Walking [wit]hin the park enable visitors to view the [simil]ar rock outcrops, ridges and huge, stately [gu]ms. Rock wallabies inhabit the area.

STANDLEY CHASM: This impressive chasm in the West MacDonnells is only five metres wide. It is a memorable sight at midday when the sunlight reaches the floor of the chasm, transforming the colour of the walls to blazing red.

ROSS RIVER HOMESTEAD: Provides a place to base yourself for exploration of the East MacDonnells. This ranch-style homestead resort features a range of outback experiences in comfortable surroundings. The historic pub bar has an interesting display of antiques.

EWANINGA ROCK CARVINGS: The origins of these carvings are lost in time. More correctly known as petroglyphs, the carvings are considered to be the work of an extremely old culture, since present-day Aborigines do not understand their meaning. The rock carvings form part of the Ewaninga Rock Carvings Conservation Reserve.

HENBURY METEORITE CRATERS: Believed to have been formed several thousand years ago when a falling meteor broke into pieces and hit the earth. The largest of the twelve craters is 180 metres wide and 15 metres deep. The smallest is 6 metres wide and only a few centimetres deep. This area is a haunt of the ferocious-looking, but harmless, bearded dragon lizard.

CHAMBERS PILLAR: Named in 1860 by the explorer John McDouall Stuart, this 50 metre high rock pillar has served as a landmark feature for the Centre's explorers and pioneers.

WARNINGS: In outback Australia, long distances separate some towns. Travellers should familiarise themselves with prevailing conditions before departure and take care to ensure their vehicle is roadworthy. Adequate supplies of petrol, water and food should be carried at all times.

In central Australia, rainfall can make some roads impassable, even with a 4WD vehicle. Full information on road conditions should be obtained from local authorities before departure.

If visitors intend diverting off public roads within Aboriginal Land areas, a permit is required from the relevant Aboriginal authority.

ULURU - KATA TJUTA NATIONAL PARK

Uluru - Kata Tjuta National Park is renowned for its rock monolith, Uluru (Ayers Rock) and for Kata Tjuta (The Olgas), a group of towering dome-shaped rocks. This World Heritage-listed area is of vital cultural and religious significance to Anangu, the traditional owners of the area. Anangu hold freehold title to the park and lease it back to Parks Australia.

CULTURAL CENTRE: The Uluru - Kata Tjuta Cultural Centre, designed in the shape of two snakes, is located on the approach road to Uluru. Anangu hope that visitors will leave the centre with a new appreciation of their culture and land.

ULURU: Uluru rises majestically 348 metres above a wide, sandy flood plain. The rock is 9 kilometres in circumference. There are many walking tracks around the base of the monolith and various ranger-guided tours. Although the Anangu prefer that visitors respect their culture and not climb Uluru, visitors may climb the rock if they wish.

KATA TJUTA: Kata Tjuta, 52 kilometres west of Uluru, is a collection of red domed rocks separated by deep canyons. The highest, Mt Olga, rises to 546 metres. Walking tracks lead to Olga Gorge and the Valley of the Winds.

ACCOMMODATION: Yulara, situated outside the national park, is the location of Ayers Rock Resort. Accommodation ranges from camping and budget accommodation to international-standard hotels.

TO DARWIN

TO COOBER PEDY

Alice Springs

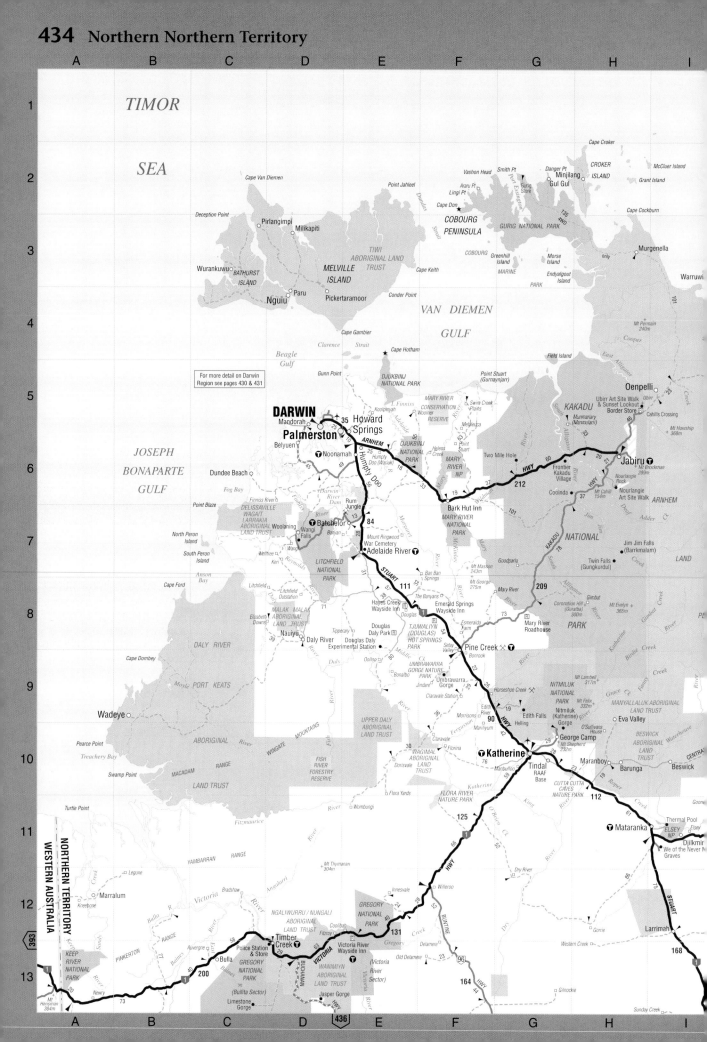

TIMOR

SEA

JOSEPH

BONAPARTE

GULF

Cape Van Diemen

Deception Point

Pirlangimpi

Milikapiti

TIWI
ABORIGINAL LAND
TRUST

Wurankuwu

BATHURST
ISLAND

MELVILLE
ISLAND

Paru

Nguiu

Pickertaramoor

Conder Point

Point Jahleel

Cape Keith

Cape Van Diemen

Cape Don

COBOURG
PENINSULA

Smith Pt

Araru Pt
Lingi Pt

Vashon Head

Port Essington

Gung
Store

GURIG NATIONAL PARK

Danger Pt
Minjilang
Gul Gul

CROKER
ISLAND

McCluer Island

Grant Island

Cape Croker

Cape Cockburn

COBOURG

Greenhill
Island

MARINE

Morse
Island

Endyalgout
Island

PARK

only

Mt Permain
240m

Murgenella

Warruwi

Cooper

VAN DIEMEN

GULF

Clarence Strait

Cape Gambier

Cape Hotham

Point Stuart

Field Island

East Alligator

Mt Howship
368m

Oenpelli

Beagle
Gulf

Gunn Point

Cape Hotham

I. Finniss

DJUKBINJ
NATIONAL PARK

MARY RIVER
CONSERVATION
RESERVE

Swim Creek
Plains

Point Stuart
(Gurnaynjarr)

Ubirr Art Site Walk
& Sunset Lookout
Border Store

Ubirr

Cahills Crossing

KAKADU

Mt Cahill
154m

ARNHEM

For more detail on Darwin
Region see pages 430 & 431

DARWIN
Mandorah
Palmerston
Belyuen

Howard
Springs

35

Koolpinyah

Adelaide River

Woolner

Wildman

Munmariary
(Mannulari)

Frontier
Kadaku
Village

Nourlangie
Rock

Two Mile Hole

HWY

60

212

Jabiru

Mt Brockman
289m

20 21

Noonamah

ARNHEM

DJUKBINJ
NATIONAL
PARK

Humpty
Doo (Waruk)

MARY
RIVER
NP

Helens
Creek

Point
Stuart

HWY

Cooinda

37

Nourlangie
Art Site Walk

NATIONAL

Dundee Beach

Fog Bay

Point Blaze

Rum
Jungle

Darwin
River
Dam

Bark Hut Inn

MARY RIVER
NATIONAL
PARK

19

101

McKinlay

Goodparla

KAKADU

78

LAND

Jim Jim Falls
(Barrkmalam)

Twin Falls
(Gungkurdul)

Batchelor
Wangi
Falls

84

13

Banyan

Wangi

Mount Ringwood
War Cemetery
•Adelaide River

Ban Ban
Springs

Mt Masson
243m

Mt George
275m

Goodparla

Mary River

209

Coronation Hill
(Guratba)
300m

Mt Evelyn
365m

Gimbat

Gimbat Creek

North Peron
Island

DELISSAVILLE
WAGAIT
LARRAKIA
ABORIGINAL
LAND TRUST

Welltree

Keri

LITCHFIELD
NATIONAL
PARK

31

STUART

111

The Banyans

Hayes Creek
Wayside Inn

Emerald Springs
Wayside Inn

Douglas

Setay
Valley

73

Mary River
Roadhouse

PARK

South Peron
Island

Cape Ford

Litchfield
Outstation

Litchfield

71

MALAK
MALAK
ABORIGINAL
LAND TRUST

Elizabeth
Downs

Douglas
Daly Park

TJUWALIYN
(DOUGLAS)
HOT SPRINGS
PARK

Bonrook

Esmeralda
Farm

Katherine

Anson
Bay

39

Nauiyu

Daly River

Douglas Daly
Experimental Station

Ooloo

UMBRAWARRA
GORGE NATURE
PARK

Pine Creek

22

Bonrook

Horseshoe Creek

NITMILUK
NATIONAL
PARK

Mt Lambell
317m

Mt Felix
332m

MANYALLALUK ABORIGINAL
LAND TRUST

Cape Dombey

DALY RIVER

Daly River

Daly

Bonalba

Jindare

Umbrawarra
Gorge

Claravale Station

26

Edith
River

19

Edith Falls

Helling

Nitmiluk
(Katherine)
Gorge

O'Sullivans
House

Eva Valley

Wadeye

Moyle River

PORT KEATS

WINGATE

MOUNTAINS

UPPER DALY
ABORIGINAL
LAND TRUST

Fish

River

96

Morrisons

Ferguston

Marilynn

90

HWY

42

29

George Camp

Mt Shephard
232m

ABORIGINAL
LAND
TRUST

CENTRAL

Pearce Point

Treachery Bay

Swamp Point

MACADAM

RANGE

LAND TRUST

ABORIGINAL

River

FISH
RIVER
FORESTRY
RESERVE

30

WAGIMAL
ABORIGINAL
LAND
TRUST

Florina

Dorisvale

Flora Yards

Caravale

Claravale

76

Manbulloo

Katherine

Tindal
RAAF Base

23

Maranboy

Barunga

Beswick

CUTTA CUTTA
CAVES
NATURE PARK

19

112

Roper

61

Goone

Turtle Point

Fitzmaurice

River

Wombungi

FLORA RIVER
NATURE PARK

Katherine

King

59

O'Brien Ck

52

125

66

HWY

Dry River

Thermal Pool

•Mataranka

ELSEY
NP

Djilkmir

We of the Never Never
Graves

YAMBARRAN RANGE

Legune

Kneebone

Bradshaw

Angalarri River

Mt Thymanan
304m

Willeroo

Innesvale

GREGORY
NATIONAL
PARK

24

28

52

BUNTINE

Dry

STUART

Elsey

86

75

Larrimah

Marralum

Bulla
R

Bulla

RANGE

Victoria

River

58

Coolibah

Fitzroy

NGALIWURRU / NUNGALI
ABORIGINAL
LAND TRUST

131

Victoria River
Wayside Inn

Delamere

Old Delamere

23

96

HWY

164

44

Western Creek

Gorrie

168

Gilnockie

PINKERTON

KEEP
RIVER
NATIONAL
PARK

20

Newry

73

Mt
Hensman
384m

Aupvergne

Police Station
& Store
Timber
Creek

•Bulla

200

GREGORY
NATIONAL
PARK
(Bullita Sector)

Limestone
Gorge

53

29

BUCHANAN

VICTORIA

WANIMIYN
ABORIGINAL
LAND TRUST

Jasper Gorge

Gregory

River

(Victoria
River
Sector)

HWY

Sunday Creek

393

436

ARAFURA   SEA

0   50   100   150 km

N

Cape Wessel ★

WESSEL ISLANDS

Marchinbar Island

Drysdale Island

Guluwuru Island

Braithwaite Point

ELCHO ISLAND

Mooroongga Is

HOWARD ISLAND

Point Napier

Point Wilberforce

Cape Stewart

Maningrida
166
Ji-Marda
Milingimbi

Galiwinku

Bremer Island

Gunyangara Nhulunbuy
19 Yirrkala
27

Rorruwuy

35

Ngangalala
81
Ramingining

Castlereagh Bay

Gapuwiyak Landing Ground

Arnhem Bay

GOVE PENINSULA

Cape Arnhem

Old Arafura

ARNHEM LAND

112

Gapuwiyak

Gurrumuru

Manmoyi

Mirrngadja Village

River

RD

FREDERICK HILLS
172

Garrthalala

Point Alexander

ABORIGINAL

Gullawangay

Birany Birany

ARNHEM 160

Cape Grey

Gandar

Maldjanga

River

Mann

Liverpool

MITCHELL

CENTRAL

RANGE

Koolatong

Baniyala

Cape Shield

LAND

PARSONS

83

RANGE

Annie

Creek

BATH

RANGE

Walker

River

Isle Woodah

Cape Barrow

GULF

776

Bulman
Mt Marumba

TRUST

RD

116

Vanderhon

Harris

Creek

Cape Barrow

Milyakburra ★
★

Alyangula

Umbakumba

OF

CARPENTARIA

Mountain Valley

Mainoru

Mt Furner 188m

Phelp

Creek

GROOTE EYLANDT

Bickerton Island

Angurugu

DOWNERS

RANGE

Limmen Bight

COLLERA

156

Numbulwar

Tasman Point

Cape Beatrice

Lake Allen

MITNS

Roper Bar
HWY
63 Roper Bar Store
198

Ngukurr
24
St Vidgeon (ruins)
91

Port Roper

River

Maria Island

WARNINGS: In northern Australia, long distances separate some towns. Travellers should familiarise themselves with prevailing conditions before departure and take care to ensure their vehicle is roadworthy. Adequate supplies of petrol, water and food should be carried at all times.

Rainfall during the wet season (October to March) can make some roads impassable, even with a 4WD vehicle. Full information on road conditions should be obtained from local authorities before departure.

If visitors intend diverting off public roads within Aboriginal Land areas, a permit is required from the relevant Aboriginal authority.

Beware of crocodiles in rivers, estuaries and coastal areas.

Roper
47 Roper Valley
Mt Harriet 187m

39

PORT

ROPER RD
44

MARRA ABORIGINAL LAND TRUST

Towns

NATHAN

RIVER

208

Miniyeri

HODGSON DOWNS LEASE

River

Arnold

Limmen Bight River Fishing Camp

SIR EDWARD PELLEW GROUP

96
Maryfield (ruins)

Hodgson River

ALAWA ABORIGINAL LAND TRUST

Nathan River

Roose

West Island

North Island

BARRANYI (NORTH ISLAND) NATIONAL PARK

Bing Bong

WADA WADALLA LEASE

SW Is

Centre Island

Vanderlin Island

18
Nutwood Downs

Minamia

Cox

RD

River

Limmen Bight

Batten Creek

King Ash Bay

651

NARWINBI ABORIGINAL LAND

Manangoora

Garawa
Borroloola
Mara
26

Wandangula
26

437

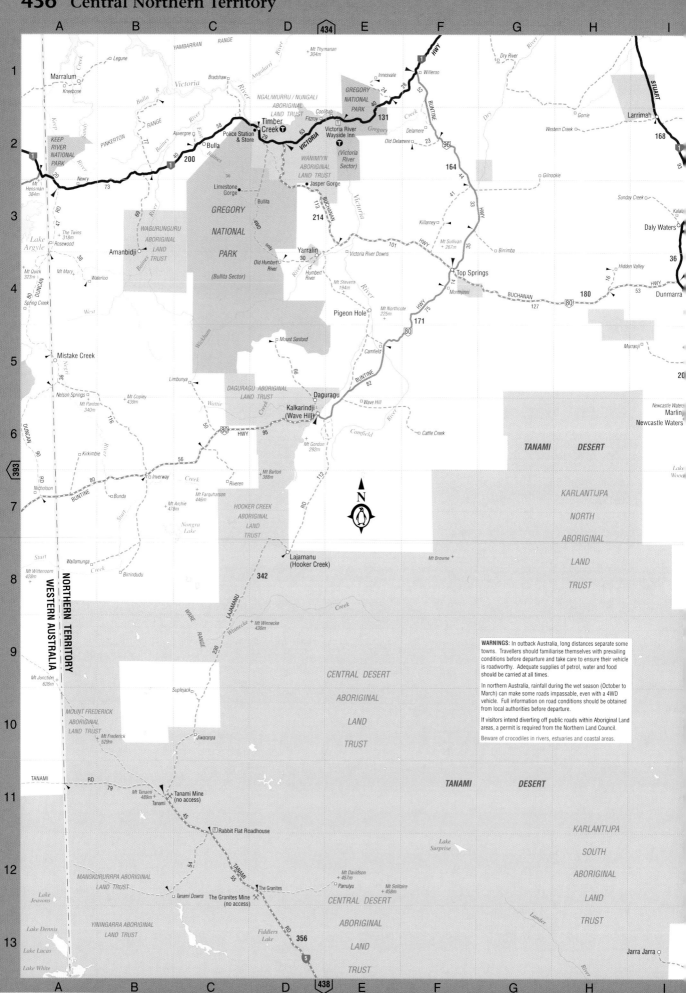

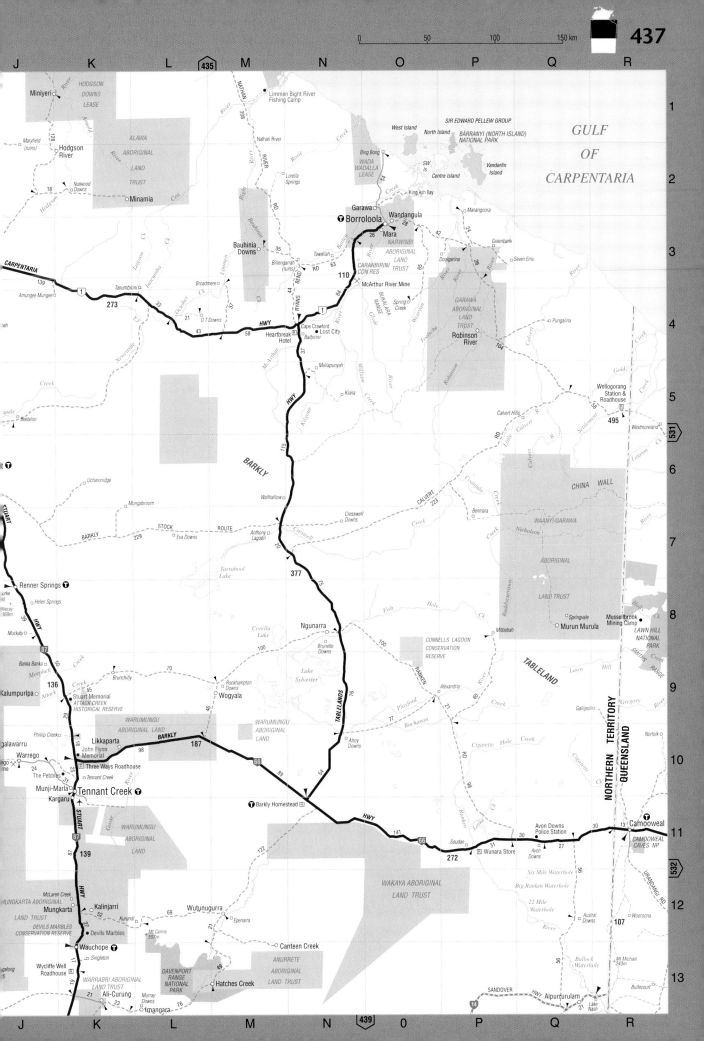

50 100 150 km

J K L M N O P Q R

WAKAYA ABORIGINAL LAND TRUST

1

'ARTA ABORIGINAL LAND TRUST
McLaren Creek
Mungkarta
Kalinjarri
52 Kurundi
69 Wutunugurra
Epenarra
21
Six Mile Waterhole
Big Ranken Waterhole
22 Mile Waterhole
Austral Downs
Wooroona
107

DEVILS MARBLES CON RES
Devils Marbles
Wauchope
Singleton
Canteen Creek
Mt Cairns 597m
7
49
ANURRETE ABORIGINAL LAND TRUST
56
Bullock Waterhole
Mt Michael 243m
Bullecourt

2

Wycliffe Well Roadhouse
WARRABRI ABORIGINAL LAND TRUST
Ali-Curung
23
DAVENPORT RANGE NATIONAL PARK
Hatches Creek
Murray Downs
76
100 Elkedra
Elkedra River
147 HWY
Alpururulam
Lake Nash
Georgina Downs
Georgina
SANDOVER
14
Headingly

3

110
WARRABRI ABORIGINAL LAND TRUST
Imangara
33
41
95
60
Annitowa
37
OORATIPPRA ABORIGINAL LAND
Stokes
Woodroffe
Mountain Waterhole
Urandangi
93

Tara
Barrow Creek
30
ALYAWARRA ABORIGINAL LAND TRUST
Antarrengeny
Ampilatwatja
24
Ammaroo
579
157
10
15
Argadargada
Mt Hogarth 338m
Manners Creek
532

4

Wilora
Mt Tops 705m
Mt Octy 696m
HWY
Sandover River
Ooratippra
River

Atneltyey
ANGARAPA ABORIGINAL LAND TRUST
Irrwelty
Arawerr
135
14
Derry Downs
45
TARLTON DOWNS ABORIGINAL LAND
Tobermorey
HWY (OUTBACK HWY)
5

ABORIGINAL TRUST
25
Mt Skinner 677m
Atartinga
Utopia
Bundey
MacDonald Downs
14
Arapunya
Lucy Creek
12
101
DOWDHUE (OUTBACK HWY)
HWY

Chianina
Red Cliff 658m
Waite River
18
33
Delny
Mount Swan
16
Dneiper
Arthur
DULCIE RANGE NATIONAL PARK
Mt Sainthill 549m
Tarlton Downs
43
Marqua

6

Sandover 82
Mueller Creek
Alcoota
29
Mt Swan 633m
37
Huckitta
Old Jinka Homestead
PLENTY (OUTBACK
95
Mt Reinecke 283m
Mt Woods 265m
Mt Wooldridge 288m

Bushy Park
51
Engawala
34
Harts Range Police Station
55
12
30
486
75
Jervois
18
Mt Winnecke 258m

PLENTY (OUTBACK
Gemtree
4WD
Mt Riddoch 1094m
Mt Campbell 1043m
Mount Riddoch
Atitjere
Mt Palmer 1131m
Mt Brassey 1203m
58
HWY HWY
41
Atula
Western Plenty
ATNETYE

7

Yambah
STRANGWAYS RANGE
The Garden
77
Quartz Hill 1043m
HARTS RANGE
Indiana
TROPIC OF
CAPRICORN
ABORIGINAL

Bond Springs
TREPHINA GORGE NATURE PARK
HWY MACDONNELL
ARLTUNGA HISTORICAL RESERVE
Mt Ruby 853m
Carter Knoll
RUBY GAP NATURE PARK
LAND

Alice Springs
Mt Sir Charles 867m
Ross River Homestead
Claraville
Hale
Illogwa
TRUST

8

ROSS
35
Amoonguna
N'DHALA GORGE NATURE PARK
89
Ringwood
Ethabuka

Ewaninga Rock Carvings
SANTA TERESA ABORIGINAL LAND TRUST
Todd River
62
Limbla
Numery
Todd

9

Mt Ooramina 649m
Ltyentye Purte (Santa Teresa)
Little Well
River
Creek

RAINBOW VALLEY CONSERVATION RESERVE
OLD
Allambi
Todd River Downs
PMERE NYENTE ABORIGINAL LAND TRUST
Mumbleberry Lake
Lake Torquinie

10

75
SOUTH 33
Mt Rodinga 495m
217
SIMPSON
534

For more detail on The Red Centre see pages 432 & 433

Titjikala
CHAMBERS PILLAR HISTORICAL RESERVE
119
MAC CLARK (ACACIA PEUCE) CONSERVATION RESERVE
DESERT
Muncoonie Lake West

11

Macumba only
Horseshoe Bend
River
River

76
Finke
34
36
Finke
31
95
16
Andado
Old Andado
SIMPSON DESERT
NATIONAL
12

Lilla Creek
60
Mt Peebles 262m
New Crown
River
PARK

147
Mt Grundy 397m
Mt Wilyunpa 227m
PMER ULPERRE INGWEMIRNE ABORIGINAL LAND TRUST
Larrys Hill 63m
Pitan Hill 60m
Poeppel Corner

13

NORTHERN TERRITORY
SOUTH AUSTRALIA
Mt Parlue 478m
Mt Mead 376m
Mt Hearne 306m
Mount Dare
Mt Apperda 245m
Mt Alimerta 222m
WITJIRA
SIMPSON DESERT
SIMPSON DESERT

Tieyon
Blood Creek Bore
Eringa
Mt Wheahlakimurne 292m
Mt Hammersley 229m
NATIONAL PARK
REGIONAL RESERVE
CONSERVATION PARK
Lake Thomas

J K L M N O 310 P Q R

NORTHERN TERRITORY
QUEENSLAND

TOKO RANGE
TOOMBA RANGE

WARNINGS: In outback Australia, long distances separate some towns. Travellers should familiarise themselves with prevailing conditions before departure and take care to ensure their vehicle is roadworthy. Adequate supplies of petrol, water and food should be carried at all times.

In central Australia, rainfall can make some roads impassable, even with a 4WD vehicle. Full information on road conditions should be obtained from local authorities before departure.

If visitors intend diverting off public roads within Aboriginal Land areas, a permit is required from the relevant Aboriginal authority.

QUEENSLAND

Palm Cove in the tropical north

Queensland is ideal holiday country, evoking dreams of long, golden days, tropical islands set in jewel-blue seas and the chance to relax outdoors. In recent years, it has also come to be known as one of the world's top eco-tourism destinations.

Although the coastal region is the area most popular with visitors, Queensland's hinterland is lushly beautiful and its protected areas, with many species of flora and fauna unique to the State, total more than seven million hectares.

In 1821 Sir Thomas Brisbane, then Governor of New South Wales, sent John Oxley, his Surveyor-General, to explore the country north of the Liverpool Plains. The area was at that time almost unknown to Europeans. Oxley's task was to find a site for a penal settlement and he decided on Moreton Bay. In 1824 troops and convicts arrived at what is now Redcliffe, but a lack of fresh water and opposition from the Aborigines persuaded them to move south and they settled at the present site of Brisbane. By 1859 the settlement was established and the free settlers were urging separation from New South Wales; on 10 December of that year, the State of Queensland was proclaimed.

Having gained legislative independence, the new population of just 23 000 set about achieving economic independence. Fortunately the new State was well endowed with excellent farming land, and wool and beef production were soon established on the western plains and tablelands. It was not long before sugar production, worked by Kanaka labour from the Pacific Islands, became much more important, and it is still significant.

As well as being blessed with fertile land that produces grain, sugar, dairy food, wool, mutton, beef, cotton, peanuts and timber, Queensland has rich mineral deposits; the vast Mount Isa mining complex in the west produces copper, lead and zinc in large quantities.

Queensland's attraction as a holiday destination is very much due to its climate. In the west, the climate is similar to that of the Red Centre, with fierce summer daytime heat. On the coast the temperature rarely exceeds 38°C and for seven months of the year the weather is extremely pleasant. If you are unused to high humidity, however, the period from December to April can be uncomfortable.

Four geographic and climate regions run north to south, neatly dividing the State. In the west is the Great Artesian Basin, flat and hot. Parched and bare during drought, it becomes grassy after rain, thanks to a complex system of boreholes that distribute water through channels and allow grazing. The tablelands to the east are undulating and sparsely timbered, broken up by meandering rivers.

NOT TO BE MISSED	
IN QUEENSLAND	Map Ref.
CARNARVON NATIONAL PARK Beautiful park with magnificent gorge and Aboriginal art	524 F2
DARLING DOWNS An area of beauty and prosperity — rural Australia at its best	525 M9
GOLD COAST HINTERLAND Spectacular scenery in Numinbah Valley and at Springbrook	519 B12
GREAT BARRIER REEF Best seen by boat; your own, a charter boat or a cruise boat	527 M3
THE *GULFLANDER* TRAIN Ride between Normanton and old goldmining town of Croydon	528 C8
KURANDA SCENIC RAILWAY Spectacular train ride from Cairns to Kuranda; return via Skyrail Rainforest Cableway	529 M6
NOOSA NATIONAL PARK Beautiful coastal park offering memorable views and walks	520 H1
SUNSHINE COAST HINTERLAND Mountain scenery and charming villages	520 C8
THEME PARKS ON THE GOLD COAST Dreamworld, Movie World and Sea World — fun for all the family	519 C1, C3, F4

The backbone of Queensland is the Great Dividing Range – most spectacular in its extreme north and south, where it comes closest to the coast.

The State's highway and road system is good in the south-east and in areas close to the larger northern towns, but in more remote areas roads can be narrow and poorly graded, and conditions deteriorate during drought or heavy rain.

The two main towns of the tropical northern region are Townsville and Cairns. The more northerly Cairns is a major holiday centre and makes an excellent base for deep-sea fishing and for exploring the region, with its lush sugar plantations, mountainous jungle country and the wilds of the Cape York Peninsula. The Atherton Tableland is a rich volcanic area west of Cairns, with superb lakes, waterfalls and fern valleys. Stretching along this coastline are some of Queensland's famed islands including Lizard (north of Cooktown), Green, Fitzroy, Dunk, Bedarra, Hinchinbrook, Orpheus and Magnetic. Further south are the beautiful Whitsunday Islands and Great Keppel, South Molle, Heron, Lady Musgrave, Lady Elliot, and Fraser islands. If you are planning an island holiday, make sure your choice fits in with the idea of a tropical paradise. Many islands are extensively developed for tourism; others remain relatively untouched. Beyond, and protecting them from the South Pacific, is the outer Great Barrier Reef, the world's largest and most famous coral formation.

South of the Reef is the Sunshine Coast. This scenic coastal region, with its leisurely pace and its wide variety of natural attractions and sporting facilities, offers an alternative to the more commercialised Gold Coast.

Brisbane, Australia's third-largest capital city, is built on both sides of the Brisbane River. The Gold Coast, 75 kilometres to the south, is the heart of holiday country. Inland is rich agriculturally, mainly sugarcane and dairy farming, its setting a sharp contrast with the tropical north or the mining areas of Mount Isa.

VISITOR INFORMATION
Tourism Queensland
Level 36, Riverside Centre,
123 Eagle Street, Brisbane
(07) 3406 5400

Lamington National Park in the Gold Coast hinterland

CLIMATE GUIDE

BRISBANE

	J	F	M	A	M	J	J	A	S	O	N	D
Maximum °C	29	29	28	27	24	21	21	22	24	26	27	29
Minimum °C	21	21	20	17	14	11	10	10	13	16	18	20
Rainfall mm	169	177	152	86	84	82	66	45	34	102	95	123
Raindays	14	14	15	11	10	8	7	7	7	10	10	11

COOLANGATTA REGION

	J	F	M	A	M	J	J	A	S	O	N	D
Maximum °C	28	28	27	25	23	21	20	21	22	24	26	26
Minimum °C	20	20	19	17	13	11	9	10	12	15	17	19
Rainfall mm	184	181	213	114	124	122	96	103	49	108	137	166
Raindays	14	15	16	14	10	9	7	9	9	11	11	13

MACKAY VALLEY

	J	F	M	A	M	J	J	A	S	O	N	D
Maximum °C	30	29	28	27	24	22	21	22	25	27	29	30
Minimum °C	23	23	22	20	17	14	13	14	16	20	22	23
Rainfall mm	293	311	303	134	104	59	47	30	15	38	87	175
Raindays	16	17	17	15	13	7	7	6	5	7	9	12

CAIRNS REGION

	J	F	M	A	M	J	J	A	S	O	N	D
Maximum °C	31	31	30	29	28	26	26	27	28	29	31	31
Minimum °C	24	24	23	22	20	18	17	18	19	21	22	23
Rainfall mm	413	435	442	191	94	49	28	27	36	38	90	175
Raindays	18	19	20	17	14	10	9	8	8	8	10	13

CALENDAR OF EVENTS

JANUARY

Public holidays: New Year's Day; Australia Day. *Charters Towers:* Goldfield Ashes Cricket Carnival. *Georgetown:* Race Meeting. *Lake Awoonga (near Gladstone):* Catfish Festival. *Pittsworth:* Crimson Flash Shield (foot race). *Yeppoon:* Australia Day Celebrations.

FEBRUARY

Chinchilla: Melon Festival (odd-numbered years). *Goondiwindi:* Hell of the West Triathlon. *Killarney:* Agricultural Show. *Yeppoon:* Surf Lifesaving Championships.

MARCH

Dalby: Cotton Week. *Gin Gin:* Wild Scotchman Festival. *Stanthorpe:* Apple and Grape Harvest Festival (even-numbered years); Rodeo.

EASTER

Public holidays: Good Friday; Easter Saturday; Easter Monday. *Brisbane:* Brisbane–Gladstone Yacht Race. *Bundaberg:* Country Music Roundup. *Burketown:* World Barramundi Handline-rod Fishing Championships. *Charters Towers:* Rodeo. *Emerald:* Sunflower Festival. *Eromanga (near Quilpie):* Rodeo. *Gladstone:* Harbour Festival (includes finish of Brisbane–Gladstone Yacht Race). *Longreach:* Easter in the Outback. *Roma:* Easter in the Country. *St George:* St George's Day. *Tin Can Bay:* Easter Festival. *Warwick:* Rock Swap.

APRIL

Public holiday: Anzac Day. *Beaudesert:* Rathdowney Heritage Festival. *Charters Towers:* Towers Bonza Bash. *Hervey Bay:* Gladstone–Hervey Bay Blue Water Classic. *Julia Creek:* Dirt and Dust Triathlon. *Kilkivan (near Murgon):* Great Horse Ride. *Kingaroy:* Peanut Festival (odd-numbered years). *Laidley:* Rodeo and Heritage Day. *Mooloolaba:* Finish of Sydney–Mooloolaba Yacht Race; Triathlon. *Mount Isa:* Country Music Festival. *Quilpie:* Fishing Carnival. *Rockhampton:* Good Earth Expo. *Winton:* Waltzing Matilda Bush Poetry Festival.

MAY

Public holiday: Labour Day. *Brisbane:* Queensland Winter Racing Carnival. *Boolba (near St George):* Wool and Craft Show. *Charters Towers:* Country Music Festival. *Childers:* Agricultural Show. *Chillagoe:* Races, Concert and Rodeo. *Chinchilla:* Rotary May Day Carnival. *Eromanga (near Quilpie):* Race Day. *Gatton:* Heavy Horse Field Days. *Hervey Bay:* Yagubi Festival (multicultural festival). *Ingham:* Australian–Italian Festival. *Julia Creek:* Campdraft. *Kuranda:* Folk Festival. *Laidley:* Heavy Horse Show. *Maryborough:* Best of Brass. *Moranbah:* May Day Union Parade and Fireworks. *Mount Morgan:* Golden Mount Festival. *Port Douglas:* Village Carnivale. *Sarina:* Mud Trials. *St George:* Country Show. *Stanthorpe:* Opera at Sunset. *Strathpine:* Pine Rivers Heritage Festival. *Taroom:* Agricultural Show.

JUNE

Public holiday: Queen's Birthday. *Brisbane:* Queensland Winter Racing Carnival (contd). *Allora:* Apex Auction. *Beaudesert:* Country and Horse Festival. *Biloela:* Country and Western Muster. *Blackall:* Race Meeting. *Caboolture:* Agricultural Show; Medieval Tournament. *Cardwell:* Coral Sea Memorial. *Charters Towers:* Annual Vintage Car Restorers' Swap Meet. *Cloncurry:* Agricultural Show. *Cooktown:* Endeavour Festival. *Coolangatta:* Wintersun Festival. *Croydon:* Rodeo. *Emerald:* Wheelbarrow Derby (odd-numbered years). *Gayndah:* Orange Festival (odd-numbered years). *Gympie:* Race the Rattler. *Hamilton Island (near Shute Harbour):* Hamilton Island Cup (outrigger canoes). *Jundah:* Bronco Branding. *Landsborough:* William Landsborough Day. *Longreach:* Hall of Fame Race Meeting. *Malanda (near Yungaburra):* Agricultural Show. *Mission Beach:* Mudfest. *Monto:* Dairy Festival (even-numbered years). *Muttaburra:* Landsborough Flock Ewe Show. *Nindigully (near St George):* 5-Hour Enduro (for motorbikes). *Normanton:* Show, Rodeo and Gymkhana. *Quilpie:* Boulder Opal Expo. *Taldora Station (near Julia Creek):* Saxby Roundup. *Tin Can Bay:* Seafood and Leisure Festival. *Yungaburra:* Yuletide.

JULY

Blackall: Black Stump Camel Races. *Boulia:* Desert Sands Camel Races. *Caboolture:* St Peters and St Columbans Arts and Cultural Expo. *Cairns:* Agricultural Show. *Charleville:* Great Matilda Camel Races. *Childers:* Multicultural Food and Wine Festival. *Chinchilla:* Polocrosse Carnival. *Cooktown:* Laura-Cape York Aboriginal Dance Festival (odd-numbered years). *Emu Park (near Yeppoon):* Service of Remembrance. *Esk:* Picnic Races. *Innisfail:* Agricultural Show. *Ipswich:* Ipswich Cup. *Karumba:* Karumba Kapers. *Longreach:* Diamond Shears. *Mackay:* Festival of the Arts. *Mareeba:* Rodeo. *Nebo (near Mackay):* Rodeo. *Pomona (near Tin Can Bay):* King of the Mountain. *Rainbow Beach (near Tin Can Bay):* Fishing Classic. *Rockhampton:* Bauhinia Arts Festival; Grey Mardi Gras. *Sarina:* Visual Arts Festival. *Texas:* Agricultural Show. *Townsville:* Australian Festival of Chamber Music; Arts Festival; Show (carnival). *Yungaburra:* Jazz Festival.

AUGUST

Public holiday: Brisbane Show Day. *Brisbane:* Brisbane International Film Festival; Brisbane RiverFestival; Royal Brisbane Show ('The Ekka'). *Bowen:* Art, Craft and Orchid Expo. *Caboolture:* Air Show (odd-numbered years). *Caloundra:* Art and Craft Show. *Clermont:* Gold Festival; Rodeo. *Cloncurry:* Merry Muster Rodeo. *Emerald:* Gemfest.

Gympie: National Country Music Muster. *Hamilton Island (near Shute Harbour):* Race Week (sailing). *Hervey Bay:* Whale Festival. *Julia Creek:* Sedan Dip (car race). *Leyburn (near Clifton):* Historic Race Car Sprints. *Mission Beach:* Banana Festival. *Mount Isa:* Rodeo. *Quilpie:* Diggers Races; Kangaranga Do Street Party. *Rockhampton:* Rocky Round Up. *Sarina:* Agricultural Show. *Strathpine:* Camp Oven Bush Poets Festival. *Taroom:* Leichhardt Festival. *Yeppoon:* Ozfest (with World Cooeeing Championships).

SEPTEMBER

Brisbane: Brisbane RiverFestival (contd); Spring Hill Fair. *Airlie Beach:* Whitsunday Fun Race. *Beaudesert:* Agricultural Show. *Birdsville:* Race meeting. *Bundaberg:* Bundy in Bloom Festival. *Cunnamulla:* Opal Festival. *Emerald:* Music Spectacular. *Eulo:* World Lizard Racing Championships. *Goondiwindi:* Rodeo. *Hamilton Island (near Shute Harbour):* Beach Volleyball Pro Tour. *Kynuna:* 'Surf' Carnival. *Laidley:* Chelsea Festival. *Mackay:* Sugartime Festival. *Mareeba:* Air Show. *Maryborough:* Heritage City Festival. *Miles:* Back to the Bush (includes Wildflower Festival). *Noosa Heads:* Jazz Fest. *Quilpie:* Agricultural Show. *Sarina:* Grasstree Beach Bike Races. *Tambo:* Spring Festival. *Toowoomba:* Carnival of Flowers. *Winton:* Outback Festival (odd-numbered years). *Yeppoon:* Pineapple Festival.

OCTOBER

Brisbane: Colonial George Street Festival; Livid Festival. *Beaudesert:* Rodeo. *Biggenden:* Rose Festival (odd-numbered years). *Bowen:* Coral Coast Festival. *Bundaberg:* Arts Festival. *Cairns:* The Reef Festival. *Chinchilla:* Museum Heritage Day. *Clifton:* Rose and Iris Show. *Crows Nest:* Crows Nest Day (includes Worm Races). *Emu Park (near Yeppoon):* Octoberfest. *Gatton:* Potato Carnival. *Georgetown:* Race Meeting; Bushman's Ball. *Goondiwindi:* Spring Festival. *Gympie:* Gold Rush Festival. *Ingham:* Maraka Festival. *Innisfail:* Harvest Festival. *Ipswich:* Jacaranda Festival. *Jundah:* Race Carnival. *Mapleton (near Nambour):* Yarn Festival. *Mareeba:* Country Music Festival (even-numbered years). *Maryborough:* Masters Games. *Mission Beach:* Aquatic Festival; Sailing Regatta. *Murgon:* Fishing Carnival. *Nanango:* Pioneer Festival. *Noosa Heads:* Beach Car Classic. *Proserpine:* Harvest Festival (including World Championship Cane Cutting). *Ravenswood:* Halloween Ball. *Rockhampton:* Arts in the Park. *St George:* Regional Fishing Competition. *Stanthorpe:* Granite Belt Spring Wine Festival. *Surfers Paradise:* IndyCar Australia Race. *Toowoomba:* Festival of the Horse. *Warwick:* Rose and Rodeo City Festival. *Yandina:* Spring Flower and Ginger Festival. *Yungaburra:* Folk Festival.

NOVEMBER

Ayr: Home Hill Harvest Festival. *Bundaberg:* Coral Turtle Festival. *Caboolture:* Makin Music. *Killarney:* Rodeo. *Kynuna:* Rodeo. *Noosa Heads:* Triathlon. *Texas:* Roundup (even-numbered years).

DECEMBER

Public holidays: Christmas Day; Boxing Day. *Caboolture:* Rodeo. *Karumba:* Fishermen's Ball. *Tin Can Bay:* Robert Pryde Memorial Surf Classic. *Woodford (near Caboolture):* Folk Festival.

Note: The information given here was accurate at the time of printing. However, as the timing of events held annually is subject to change and some events may extend into the following month, it is best to check with the local tourism authority or event organisers to confirm the details. The calendar is not exhaustive. Most towns and regions throughout the State hold sporting competitions; regattas and rodeos; art, craft, and trade exhibitions; agricultural and flower shows; music festivals and other events annually. Details of these events are available from local tourism outlets.

South Molle Island

Brisbane

The city of Brisbane straddles the lazy curves of the Brisbane River, which winds its way through the suburbs to Moreton Bay. The long fingers of Moreton and Stradbroke islands create a barrier to the Pacific Ocean, providing the city with a vast body of calm water at its foreshore. Inland, a hilly subtropical terrain provides breathing space and a beautiful backdrop for the city.

The mixture of old and new, so much a feature of the Australian city, is nowhere as pronounced as it is in Brisbane. Gold-hued sandstone buildings from colonial times sit among the classic 'Queenslanders' on stilts, and the gleaming metal and glass giants of the past decade; masses of tropical foliage provide a visual link, as does the shimmering subtropical light. The streetscapes, full of odd shapes hailing from a dozen different periods, achieve a certain harmony. With a population of more than 1.6 million, this busy city offers a modern and extensive public transport system, a wide selection of restaurants, quality cultural institutions and a strong historical heritage.

EXPLORING BRISBANE

Brisbane has very little traffic congestion and has well-signed, well-maintained roads – yet it is not an easy city for the first-time visitor to negotiate. The city's phenomenal growth in recent times has resulted in a criss-crossing network of major motorways on the doorstep of the city centre and, in the city centre itself, there is a plethora of one-way streets. The river twists its way through the city and suburbs, resulting in a complex road system. An up-to-date road map, and some careful route planning at the beginning of each day, is a good idea.

Brisbane city centre is small and, with its wide streets, parks, good weather and lovely scenery, is a terrific place for strolling. The public transport system, made up of bus, rail and ferry networks, is comprehensive and efficient, with a couple of excellent bus routes designed specifically for visitors to the city. A boat trip on the Brisbane River is a must: plenty of tours are available to riverside tourist attractions, and there is an excellent commuter ferry service that stops at several points in the city and South

Pauls Breaka Beach with city skyline as backdrop

Bank area. The Moreton Bay islands are reached by car ferry from a number of spots along the coastline.

BRISBANE BY AREA

CITY CENTRE

Despite the fact that it is the commercial and retail heart of Brisbane, the city centre – with its open spaces, overhanging Moreton Bay fig trees and plenty of outdoor activity – retains the buoyant holiday spirit that pervades the entire State.

A good way to explore the city centre is to start at **Queen Street Mall** and move in a roughly clockwise direction around the city. The mall, located between Edward and George streets, is an exceptional example of the best civic planning. It is strictly pedestrian only, although a bus station is conveniently located beneath the mall. There are more than 500 shops,

including department stores, as well as buskers, cinemas, theatres, nightspots and restaurants.

Around the middle of the mall turn left into Albert Street (there is an excellent visitor information booth on the corner of Albert and Queen streets) to reach **King George Square**, the location of the impressive **Brisbane City Hall**. Erected between 1920 and 1930, the sandstone building with its classic columns, soaring clock tower and splendid interiors is fairly typical of the grand Greek Revival style that dominated public structures in Australia in the earlier years of the century. The Brisbane Tourism office is located here. Visitors can wander around the superb marbled public rooms of the ground and first floors, and take a lift up the tower for some fine city views.

A side trip from here is a visit to the **Old Windmill** in Wickham Terrace, just beyond the boundary of the city centre. Walk along Ann Street on the northern side of the Brisbane City Hall to Edward Street and turn left. Follow Edward Street until Turbot Street and then head up Jacobs Ladder, a long set of steps lying straight ahead and running up alongside **King Edward Park**. At the top, turn left along Wickham Terrace to reach the Old Windmill. Built in 1828 by convicts to grind flour and maize, the building has been used for a variety of purposes since 1861. Brisbane's oldest structure no longer has its original sails and treadmill, but the interpretive board outside the building recreates the fascinating history of the site.

Retrace your steps and turn left into Ann Street. Past Wharf Street you will find **St John's Cathedral** (consecrated 1910), a Gothic-style church with an exterior built in Brisbane porphyry stone. This cathedral is commonly described as one of the finest churches in the Southern Hemisphere. Adjacent to St John's Cathedral is the **Deanery**, built in 1850 and formerly the residence of Queensland's first governor, Sir George Bowen. From the eastern side of this cathedral complex, turn right into Adelaide Street and head south to **Anzac Square**, yet another of the generous, grassy enclaves that are so much a part of the Brisbane cityscape.

NOT TO BE MISSED

IN BRISBANE	Map Ref.
BRISBANE CITY HALL Architectural landmark of the city centre	510 D6
FORTITUDE VALLEY A lively inner-city neighbourhood encompassing Brisbane's Chinatown and Brunswick Street Mall	512 G11
LONE PINE KOALA SANCTUARY Visit the world's largest koala sanctuary	514 E4
MANLY Enjoy a day by the calm waters of Moreton Bay	513 N10
MOUNT COOT-THA FOREST PARK Take in the sensational views and wander through Mt Coot-tha Botanic Gardens	512 D13
NEWSTEAD HOUSE A classic 19th-century Australian homestead on the banks of the river	512 H10
QUEENSLAND CULTURAL CENTRE The State's top cultural institutions at South Bank	510 B7
SOUTH BANK PARKLANDS Home to over 16 hectares of parklands and inland beach	510 D10

GETTING AROUND

Airport shuttle bus
Coachtrans Airport Commuter Service
(07) 3236 1000

Motoring organisation
Royal Automobile Club of Queensland
(RACQ) 13 1905

Car rental
Avis 1800 225 533; Budget 13 2727;
Hertz 1800 550 067; Thrifty
1300 367 2277

Public transport
TransInfo (bus, ferry, rail)
13 1230

Bus tours
City Heights, City Sights and City Lights
tourist trips aboard open-air tram replicas
around the city and suburban sights
13 1230

River trips
River Ferries and CityCats 13 1230;
Club Crocodile River Queens
(07) 3221 1300; Mirimar
(07) 3221 0300

Taxis
Black & White Cabs 13 1008;
Yellow Cabs 13 1924; Brisbane Cabs
(07) 3360 0000

Walk through Anzac Square, then through **Post Office Square**, to reach the **General Post Office** on Queen Street. Built between 1871 and 1879, it stands on the site previously occupied by the Female Factory Prison and is admired for the restrained elegance of its design. Take the walkway through the Post Office to Elizabeth Street and **St Stephen's Cathedral**. The cathedral is a magnificent twin-spired Gothic Revival structure designed by the prominent colonial architect Benjamin Backhouse and completed in 1874. Next door is the more modest **Old St Stephen's Church**, a simple building in the Gothic idiom, which served as the original cathedral; it was dedicated in 1850 and stands today as Brisbane's oldest surviving church.

Continue south along Elizabeth Street to George Street, and turn left. Between Charlotte and Mary streets is the Old Government Printing Office facade, which has an interesting inscription. Immediately behind you will find **Sciencentre**, a terrific interactive science museum with around 170 hands-on displays demonstrating something of the science of having a good time – a great stop for the children. Cut down Stephens Lane to William Street where you will find the **Commissariat Stores** along to the left. This solid stone landmark, built in 1829, is an excellent example of an early colonial building constructed by convicts. Used for many purposes in the past, including a period as a migrant hostel, today it houses the offices of the Royal Historical Society of Queensland, incorporating a small museum.

Head north-west along William Street past the Conrad International Hotel, housed in the historic Executive Building, then turn right into Queen Street. In the first block lies the old Treasury Building, now **Conrad International Treasury Casino**. Built 1885–1928, it is an impressive Italian Renaissance building with concessions to the climate: a series of deep verandahs intended as cooling spaces for the rooms beyond.

CITY FORESHORE

While the south-west foreshore of central Brisbane is dominated by the Riverside Expressway, the eastern

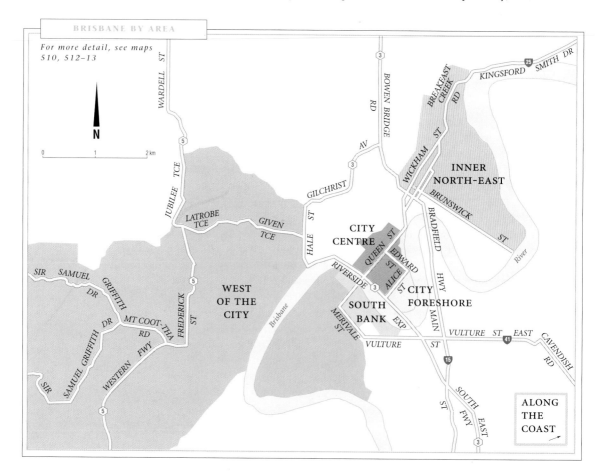

riverbank is easily accessible. In recent years this one-time wharf and warehouse precinct has been redeveloped, and is one of the city's most attractive and vibrant areas. At its northern end near the intersection of Queen and Eagle streets is **Customs House** (1889). This stately old building features an entrance of Corinthian columns and a majestic copper dome; inside there is an excellent gallery and restaurant. Look north-east from Customs House and you can't miss **Story Bridge**. This Brisbane landmark is the largest steel cantilever bridge in Australia. Just south of Customs House is the **Riverside Centre**, an office complex with restaurants and cafes fronting the river. Further south is **Eagle Street Pier**, a popular gathering spot with restaurants, bars and cafes; this is the place to be on a Friday night. On Sundays it is the site for Brisbane's liveliest street market, the **Riverside Markets**.

The **City Botanic Gardens** spread across a prime city spot, claiming absolute frontage on the south-eastern bend of this section of the Brisbane River. Ornamental plantings, lawns and glittering ponds make this one of the most pleasant places in Brisbane. Occupying 20 hectares of land, it also features a mangrove boardwalk along the bank of the river, which enables visitors to observe the fascinating marine life in the tidal mangrove reserves and the variety of resident birdlife.

Old Government House (1862), home to the National Trust of Queensland, is a graceful sandstone building on the south-western edge of the gardens. Nearby on the corner of Alice and George streets is the French-Renaissance-style **Parliament House** (1868). This is a grand public building in the best colonial traditions, fringed with beautiful mature palms. Guided tours (Monday to Friday) provide a glimpse into the world of Queensland politics.

SOUTH BANK

Across Victoria Bridge is **South Bank**, Brisbane's major leisure precinct incorporating an extensive area of parkland and the city's major cultural institutions.

The **South Bank Parklands** were developed on the World Expo '88

Brisbane City Hall clock tower

SHOPPING

*The **Queen Street Mall**, between Edward and George streets, is the heart of Brisbane and its major shopping precinct. The inner-city suburbs of **Fortitude Valley**, **Milton** and **Paddington** offer individual-style outlets selling fashion, collectibles and books.*

MARKETS

Open-air markets are a way of life in these subtropical climes, offering clothes, crafts, various new-age therapies, food and fun activities for the kids.

Map Ref.

RIVERSIDE MARKETS, CITY
Brisbane's largest open-air market at Eagle
Street Pier (Sun.)   510 F6

BRUNSWICK STREET MALL MARKET, FORTITUDE VALLEY
Open-air street market (Sat.)   510 H2

LANTERN VILLAGE MARKET, SOUTH BANK PARKLANDS
Shoppers can browse through picturesque
lantern-lit stalls (Fri.evening)   510 D10

CRAFT VILLAGE, SOUTH BANK PARKLANDS
Brightly-coloured canopies filled with arts
and handicrafts (Sat.& Sun.)   510 D10

site and cover 16 hectares of river frontage. The landscaping represents Australian environments from lagoons to beaches and rainforest, and includes **The Arbour**, a flower-covered walkway winding the full length of the precinct. It is a great place to ride bikes, walk or have a barbecue. As well, there are weekly markets, around 20 cafes and restaurants, and plenty of live entertainment, from buskers and free street entertainment to international acts in the 3000-seat **South Bank Piazza**.

Near the Victoria Bridge end of the parklands is the Rainforest Walk, where you can encounter the beautiful subtropical vegetation for which Queensland is famed. Follow the Riverside Promenade to reach **Pauls Breaka Beach**. As far as the kids are concerned, this is the draw-card of the area. Where else but in the Sunshine State would you find a palm-fringed, sandy beach, patrolled by lifesavers, slap-bang in the middle of a big city.

Just outside the south-eastern corner of the parklands is the **Queensland Maritime Museum**, offering an overview of Queensland's maritime history dating back to the Dutch landing at Cape York in 1606. In the Exhibition Hall there is an impressive collection of nautical models, re-created cabins, shipwreck relics and archives, while outside, in the old South Brisbane dry dock, the World War II frigate, HMAS *Diamantina*, can be explored from stern to bow. A vital link between the southern end of South Bank and the City Botanic Gardens will be provided by a 400-metre pedestrian and cycle bridge, currently under development and thought to be the world's longest.

There are plenty of shops and restaurants behind the parklands. Grey Street is being redeveloped as a grand, tree-lined boulevard. Here, you will find the latest entertainment addition, the **IMAX Theatre**, housing a giant cinema screen for 2- and 3-D releases. The screen has been crafted especially for this new format, which is known for its stunning image clarity. Heading north-west along Grey Street, you will

South Bank

The night lights of Story Bridge

pass the **Brisbane Convention and Exhibition Centre** on the left, a vast complex, covering 7.5 hectares, that houses the 4000-seat Great Hall, a ballroom and exhibition halls used for regular trade and retail exhibitions.

Towards the northern end of South Bank, on both sides of Melbourne Street, are the buildings of the **Queensland Cultural Centre**. The various theatres of the **Queensland Performing Arts Complex** are located on the south side. There is the intimate Cremorne Theatre (seats 350), used for works at the experimental end of the scale; the newly built 850-seat Optus Playhouse, which features the work of the Queensland Theatre Company, as well as other local and international groups; the Lyric Theatre (seats 2000) where you can expect everything from performances by Opera Queensland to the latest blockbuster musical; and the 2000-seat Concert Hall where there are regular performances by Queensland's two orchestras, as well as performances by classical and pop artists from overseas. Guided tours are available Monday to Friday.

Across Melbourne Street is the **Queensland Museum**, housed in a large modern building, the entrance of which is overseen by two giant whales. In addition to the extensive natural-history collection, including the 'endangered species' exhibit, there are excellent local social-history displays, and some hair-raising interactive displays for the kids, such as a 'virtual' trip back 220 million years. The **Queensland Art Gallery**, part of the same complex, has an internal water feature called the Water Mall and some excellent exhibition spaces. The Gallery houses important Australian and Aboriginal art collections, as well as those from the United States, Europe and Asia. The **State Library of Queensland** has been archiving and preserving books, images, prints, maps and other material charting the history and culture of Queensland since 1896. There are some excellent collections including the James Hardy Library, with its preserve of fine Australian art and rare books. The reference section is enormous and widely used for both academic and general purposes.

CITY BY NIGHT

Brisbane offers a range of night entertainment in theatres, theatre restaurants, jazz clubs, and a number of nightclubs in the city and suburbs. **Caxton Street**, crossing the suburbs of Petrie Terrace and Paddington, is full to bursting with clubs, pubs and nightspots; the **city centre** boasts a solid quota of venues; and **Kangaroo Point** has some good music venues – jazz to rock inclusive. The Brisbane Courier Mail carries an entertainment lift-out on Fridays, with a full range of what's on and where.

INNER NORTH-EAST

The suburb of **Fortitude Valley** lies on the city's north-east border. It can be easily reached on foot or by train, while drivers can make the short trip along Wickham Street. Known as the 'Valley', the area was settled in 1849 by 256 free settlers, who arrived in Moreton Bay aboard the *Fortitude*, and retains a good degree of its 19th-century heritage. Post-war it became somewhat seedy and notorious as a stomping ground for bohemians; these days it manages to hang on to an element of this despite rising property prices. It contains the best of the cheaper restaurants in Brisbane, great nightspots and the city's most eclectic shopping opportunities. The **Brunswick Street Mall** hosts a lively art, craft and anything-goes kind of market on Saturdays along with a busy cafe society. Look out for **McWhirter's Emporium Mall**, on the corner of Wickham Street and Brunswick Street Mall, a landmark dating from 1912, with an Art Deco corner facade that was added in 1930. **Chinatown** in Duncan Street was built from the ground up in the 1980s, and is the place to find Chinese cinemas, restaurants, imported goods and traditional herbalists.

Brunswick Street leads to the adjacent suburb of **New Farm**. This was the site of early farming attempts to feed the colony, before it became a residential area. Take a stroll around the streets to see some fantastic examples of domestic architecture, ranging in style from grand Victorian to Spanish Mission. The suburb has housed a significant migrant population since World War II and there are some good ethnic shops and restaurants around Brunswick Street. **New Farm Park** is nestled on the river bend at the end of Brunswick Street. Established in 1912, it offers a garden oasis filled with both tropical and traditional species. There are thousands of rose bushes in what is regarded as one of the most significant rose gardens in Australia, as well as sprawling Moreton Bay fig, poinciana and jacaranda trees.

Breakfast Creek Road, heading north, leads to **Miegunyah** (1886), in Jordan Terrace, Bowen Hills. Built in the traditional Queensland style with substantial verandahs and ironwork, the house has been refurbished in the style of its original period. It is home to the Queensland Women's Historical Association and serves as a memorial to the pioneering women of the State (open Wednesdays, weekends, or by appointment). A further half a kilometre along Breakfast Creek Road is **Newstead House** in Newstead Park. This is Brisbane's oldest house, an elegant residence overlooking the river at Breakfast Creek. Patrick Leslie, the first settler on the Darling Downs, built it in 1846. The house has been beautifully restored and, with its spacious verandahs, formal gardens and lawns down to the river, it offers an image of what the best of the quintessential Australian homestead had to offer. **Breakfast Creek Hotel**, just across the creek in Albion, is a historic pub renowned for its steak and beer.

WEST OF THE CITY

Lying just behind South Bank, the **South Brisbane/West End** area is gaining a reputation as a great place to go, be seen and enjoy the interesting range of European and Asian cafes and restaurants.

On the western city side of the river, **Red Hill**, **Paddington** and **Toowong** are among the inner suburbs that can lay claim to interesting examples of local domestic architecture. Most notable, in among the Victorian and Edwardian houses, are the Queenslanders, the traditional galvanised-iron-roofed timber houses on stumps, frequently surrounded by colourful subtropical trees and shrubbery. **Caxton Street**, at the Petrie Terrace end of Paddington, has nightclubs, interesting cafes, some good restaurants and hosts a popular wine and seafood festival each May. **Latrobe** and **Given terraces**, further west, are where many of the city's historic public buildings and sites are to be found. The **Toowong Cemetery** contains about a hundred thousand graves, some dating back to 1875; headstones tell the story of the trials, tribulations and triumphs of Queensland's early settlers.

The **Lone Pine Koala Sanctuary** at Fig Tree Pocket, some 11 kilometres south-west of the city, can be reached via the *Mirimar* cruise that leaves North Quay. This is the world's largest koala sanctuary and also houses more than 100 other species of Australian animals and birds. Visitors can cuddle a koala, feed the kangaroos, wallabies and emus, and see wombats, Tasmanian devils, possums and cockatoos in their natural environment.

Just 8 kilometres due west of the city along Milton Road is **Mount Coot-tha Forest Park**, with its extraordinary views from **Mount Coot-tha Lookout** over Greater Brisbane, Moreton Bay, and the green hills and folds of the natural landscape. There are some attractive picnic and barbecue spots within the reserve, including those at **Simpson Falls** and **J C Slaughter Falls**. The scenic Sir Samuel Griffith Drive links all the major sights. On the way, in the foothills, lies the **Mount Coot-tha Botanic Gardens**, comprised of 52 hectares of land housing some 20 000 plant species from around the world. Features include a **Tropical Dome** which hothouses a superb display of tropical plants, the supremely elegant **Japanese Garden** and the **Australian Plant Community** area, which groups plants according to ecosystems, covering everything from tropical rainforests to melaleuca wetlands. The gardens contain the largest planetarium in Australia, the **Thomas Brisbane Planetarium**, which features various public programs including projections of the night skies, and all related phenomena, on the ceiling of the domed theatre.

ALONG THE COAST

Brisbane, somewhat surprisingly for the capital of the surf and sun State, is set well back from the coast and, even when you get to the coast, you will find a glassy sheet of calm water instead of the crashing surf of the Pacific Ocean.

Redcliffe rests on the northern border of Greater Brisbane, 28 kilometres north-east of the city via Gympie Road. The Redcliffe Peninsula juts out into the bay and boasts beautiful sandy beaches. Swimming is generally safe and the fishing is excellent. From the top of the volcanic red cliffs, there are excellent

Tropical Dome, Mount Coot-tha Botanic Gardens

views of the islands across Moreton Bay. Within the town there are a number of interesting historic sites; ask at the town's information centre for a heritage trail brochure. Ferries leave from Scarborough at Redcliffe for Bulwer on Moreton Island (see Day Tours from Brisbane, p. 453).

Inland from Redcliffe, off the Bruce Highway at Kallangur, is the **Alma Park Zoo**. Set in subtropical surrounds and landscaped gardens, the zoo features exotic animals as well as hands-on contact with Australian wildlife. Visitors can hold koalas, feed kangaroos in a walk-through enclosure, and view wombats, dingoes and goannas. There is an interesting range of tropical monkeys and a walk-through deer enclosure.

(see Day Tours from Brisbane, p. 453).

TOP EVENTS

Queensland Winter Racing Carnival (May–June)
Two months of excitement on and off the racecourse

Brisbane International Film Festival (Aug.)
A showcase of Australian and international cinema

Royal Brisbane Show – 'The Ekka' (Aug.)
An ideal event for families

Brisbane RiverFestival (Aug.–Sept.)
Regattas, aquatic feats, and Dragon Boats

Spring Hill Fair (Sept.)
Two days of over 450 markets, stalls, performers and cuisine

Livid Festival (Oct.)
Australian and international bands perform; internationally renowned

Summit of Mount Coot-tha

RESTAURANTS AND CAFES
Brisbane's fantastic weather makes eating out a particularly pleasurable experience. Visitors to Brisbane should not miss the regional specialities, such as Moreton Bay bugs, tiger prawns, mudcrabs, delicious reef fish and barramundi. The revitalised wharf area at the **Story Bridge** *end of the city offers some great opportunities for riverside dining. Cafe society meets and mingles in the suburbs of* **Milton, West End, Paddington** *and* **Fortitude Valley.** *The Brisbane News publishes a critical guide to eating out called the Brisbane News Eating Out Guide; it is available in bookshops and newsagents.*

The **Wynnum–Manly** area is 15 kilometres east of the city. There are some lovely beaches here, offering good swimming and fishing, and plenty of places to unwrap a picnic. The adjoining suburbs have a history dating back to the 1860s and boast some interesting historic sights best explored on foot. Charters and hire boats are available locally for interested anglers; most of this activity is centred around Manly Boat Harbour. Tours to the island of **St Helena** depart from here. The island, now a national park, served as a penal settlement between 1867 and 1932, and prison life is recalled in the grim structures that remain.

Further south, **Cleveland** is the centre of the Redland Bay district. There is an exceptional historic house in the area: **Ormiston House** (1862), the former home of the founder of the sugar industry in Queensland (open Sunday, March to November). Cleveland is the departure point for passenger and vehicular ferries to North Stradbroke Island (see Day Tours from Brisbane, p. 453).

Continue down the coast to the peaceful holiday village of **Redland Bay**, known for its markets, gardens and annual Strawberry Festival in September. Boats can be hired right along this section of the coastline, so you can set off to do your own fishing and explore the peaceful waters of Moreton Bay.

Although Brisbane is Australia's third largest city and an international tourist destination, it has a relaxed atmosphere compared with its large southern counterparts. Its languid pace, riverside setting, subtropical vegetation and warm, sunny climate make for a welcoming environment.

DAY TOURS
from Brisbane

Brisbane is surrounded by spectacular country. Golden surf beaches spread along the coast both north and south of the city. Sparsely populated islands form a protective crescent around Moreton Bay, and offer magnificent wilderness and wild beaches right on the city's doorstep. Inland, the heavily forested hills of the D'Aguilar Ranges create a subtropical haven 20 minutes from the bustle of the city.

DAY TOURS FROM BRISBANE
For more detail, see the maps on pages 511, 512–13, 516, 517, 519, 520 & 525

MOUNT GLORIOUS

57 km to Wivenhoe Outlook via Waterworks Road 31 *and Mt Nebo Road* 31

This is a good trip for those who like to combine scenic driving with the opportunity for a leg-stretching bushwalk along the way. Mount Glorious lies to the north-west of Brisbane within the Brisbane Forest Park, a vast 28 500-hectare tract of subtropical forests and hills.

Leave Brisbane via Roma Street and get onto Waterworks Road, which becomes Mt Nebo Road. Along Mt Nebo Road, stop at the information centre for Brisbane Forest Park. Within the park is the Walk-about Creek Wildlife Centre, featuring a simulated creek environment with glass windows through which you can view a wide range of local animals including reptiles, fish and frogs. Further on, McAfee's and Jolly's lookouts offer spectacular views of the mountainous landscape. Pass through Mount Nebo, and press on to Mount Glorious, a sleepy settlement nestled within the dense forests of the mountaintop. From here it is just a kilometre to the walking tracks of the Maiala Section of D'Aguilar National Park. Ten kilometres further along is Wivenhoe Outlook, a platform with magnificent views over the massive

Lake Wivenhoe on the upper Brisbane River. Return via Mount Glorious–Samford Road, a route that is regarded as one of the most scenic in the State. Just past the township of Samford on the right is the Australian Woolshed, a sheep-farm experience with daily ram shows, sheepshearing, emus and other country delights.

THE GOLD COAST

79 km to Surfers Paradise via South East Freeway 3 *, Pacific Motorway* 1 1 *and Gold Coast Highway* 2

The Gold Coast is only an hour's drive from Brisbane and makes a terrific day trip. Take the South East Freeway, which later becomes the Pacific Motorway, out of the city and follow the well-trodden, well-signed southern route. For those planning a short trip, the main attractions are the beautiful beach frontage (some 70 kilometres in all, taking in some of the best surf beaches in the world) and the large theme parks such as Sea World, Dreamworld and Warner Bros Movie World. Spend some time soaking up the street ambience of **Surfers Paradise** with its many shops, galleries, bars and restaurants. **See also:** The Gold Coast p. 500; and individual entries in A–Z listing for towns in bold type.

GOLD COAST HINTERLAND

103 km to Binna Burra via South East Freeway ③, Pacific Motorway ① ①, Beaudesert–Nerang Road ⑨⁰, Beechmont Road and Binna Burra Road

This is the 'green behind the gold' and a real surprise: a subtropical wilderness abutting the urbanised glamour of the Gold Coast. One of the highlights is **Lamington National Park**, a spectacular environment of rainforest and bushland with prolific wildlife and more than 160 kilometres of walking trails. The two main picnic/recreation/accommodation areas are at Binna Burra (Binna Burra Lodge) and Green Mountains (O'Reilly's Rainforest Guesthouse).

To reach Binna Burra, take the South East Freeway/Pacific Motorway out of Brisbane, then take the turn-off to **Nerang**. Follow the Beaudesert–Nerang Road west out of town, then turn south onto Beechmont Road and, later, Binna Burra Road. Stop at the information centre at Binna Burra for brochures on the walks and information on the wildlife. In the area there are wonderful views down to the coast and many walking tracks through the dense rainforest.

Green Mountains is further inland. From Nerang take the Beaudesert–Nerang Road to Canungra, then take the Lamington National Park Road to the Green Mountains section of the park. The variety of birdlife is a feature of the park and the treetop walkway near O'Reilly's Rainforest Guesthouse is ideal for birdwatching.

Alternatively, **Springbrook National Park** is another great day tour in the Gold Coast Hinterland. Situated on the Springbrook Plateau, the park protects a beautiful environment of volcanic gorges,

waterfalls and dense rainforest. Follow the Pacific Highway south to Mudgeeraba, then take the Gold Coast–Springbrook Road. Stop at Wunburra Lookout, and again at Purlingbrook Falls – reputed to be the most spectacular falls in the State. Continue on to the information centre at the entrance to the Springbrook Section of the park, and explore the walks, lookouts and waterfalls in the area. **See also:** The Gold Coast p. 500; National Parks p. 460 and individual entries in A–Z listing for parks and towns in bold type.

TAMBORINE MOUNTAIN

77 km to North Tamborine via South East Freeway ③, Pacific Motorway ① ① and Tamborine–Oxenford Road ⑨⁵

Tamborine Mountain is a 552-metre plateau at the northern edge of the McPherson Range. Take the South East Freeway/Pacific Motorway out of Brisbane, then turn off at the township of Oxenford onto the Tamborine–Oxenford Road; North Tamborine is another 20 kilometres on. The area preserved within the **Tamborine National Park** is made up of 17 small sections, and offers another sensational Queensland landscape of gorges, subtropical rainforests and waterfalls. Stop at the park information centre in the township of North Tamborine to pick up brochures on the seven sections of the park that cater for visitors. There are plenty of walking tracks, most of them quite short, leading through rainforest to lookouts and waterfalls. Popular picnic spots are located at Witches Falls, Curtis Falls

and Cedar Creek Falls. Tamborine is known for the remarkable variety of its birdlife; visit early morning or late afternoon for the best birdwatching opportunities. **See also:** National Parks p. 460 for parks in bold type.

THE SUNSHINE COAST

134 km to Noosa Heads via Gympie Road ③, Bruce Highway ❶, Sunshine Motorway ⑦⁰ and David Low Way ⑥

The Sunshine Coast is a paradise of sun-drenched beaches and coastal parks, while its scenic hinterland features rainforest and rolling hills. Day trippers should head for the more southerly towns of **Caloundra**, **Mooloolaba** and **Maroochydore**, all of which have excellent tourist facilities, beautiful beaches, and opportunities for fishing and other water activities.

Leave Brisbane from its north-eastern end and get onto Gympie Road which becomes the Bruce Highway. Turn onto the Sunshine Motorway, and after crossing the Maroochy River, take David Low Way for a scenic coastal drive to **Noosa Heads**, commonly referred to as Noosa. Near the township there is access to **Noosa National Park**. The headland section of the park is particularly brilliant with its quiet coves and patches of rainforest. Noosa is a rare coastal town – it is stylish yet simple, sophisticated yet friendly, and it offers some of the best dining opportunities in the State, particularly in Hastings Street. For an extended tour through the Sunshine Coast hinterland, follow the Hinterland Escape

Lamington National Park

p. 456. **See also:** The Sunshine Coast p. 493; National Parks p. 460 and individual entries in A–Z listing for towns and parks in bold type.

BRIBIE ISLAND

67 km to Woorim via Gympie Road ③, Bruce Highway ⑪, and Caboolture–Bribie Island Road

Depart Brisbane from its north-eastern end and find your way onto Gympie Road, which becomes Bruce Highway. To reach Bribie Island, turn east along Caboolture–Bribie Island Road and cross the 1-kilometre bridge over the Pumicestone Passage

The southern end of the island has a small population, but apart from that it is mostly undeveloped. A large section of the island is a national park or conservation park. There are several settlements on the west side of the island, including Bellara (where the bridge connects), Bongaree, just to the south, and White Patch to the north, where you will find the Bribie Island Information Centre. Woorim, on the east side of the island, has a lovely low-key resort-town feel to it.

The island offers excellent fishing, boating, crabbing and bushwalking. One popular spot for day visitors is Buckleys Hole Conservation Park, at the southern end of the island, where there is a picnic spot and tracks leading to the beach. A network of sealed roads will allow you to explore the island at your leisure. Access to tracks in the pine plantations and CSIRO areas is prohibited; approval of the respective owners is required. Sand tracks through the national park are closed during wet conditions.

NORTH STRADBROKE ISLAND

Access by vehicular ferry from Cleveland

It's a fairly quick run along Old Cleveland Road to Cleveland where the vehicular ferry (bookings essential) leaves regularly for Dunwich on North Stradbroke Island. 'Straddie', as the island is popularly known, has a resident population and some development, but nature really has the upper hand on this unspoiled paradise of coastal scenery and bushland. Fishing, surfing, horseriding and canoeing are popular on the island. Dunwich offers tourist information and facilities. It was established as a quarantine station for Brisbane in the 1820s. The historic cemetery in town tells the sad story of the 28 victims of cholera who died in the 1850 epidemic. The Goompi Trail, a 1-hour tour of the town led by a local Aboriginal guide, provides an introduction to the fascinating history of the settlement and surrounding district. The 500-hectare Blue Lake National Park (accessed via Dunwich) is a sanctuary for the island's wildlife. Take a walk along the track through banksias and wallum heathland to Blue Lake, part of the island's freshwater lake system and a wetland of enormous ecological importance. Amity Point is on the far north-western tip and is the island's oldest settlement. Point Lookout at the north-eastern tip is the island's vantage point for watching the annual migration of whales beginning in June.

South Stradbroke Island has virtually no development, except for some ecologically sensitive resort activity on the eastern side. Day cruises to the island operate from Southport and Runaway Bay, on the Gold Coast. Visitors' vehicles are not permitted.

MORETON ISLAND

Access by vehicular ferry from Whyte Island near Lytton (to Tangalooma) or from Scarborough (to Bulwer)

Moreton Island is virtually all national park – the **Moreton Island National Park**. Apart from a rocky headland, the island is formed entirely of sand. The island's environment includes native scrub, banksias and freshwater lakes, which attract over 180 species of sea, wetland and forest birds.

Access around the island is four-wheel drive only; tours are available for those without a suitable vehicle. Vehicle permits can be purchased on the ferry.

The Cape Moreton Lighthouse, Queensland's oldest operating lighthouse, still guides ships into Brisbane, and is being developed as an information centre. Features of the island include the magnificent 38-kilometre beach and Mt Tempest, which, at 280 metres, is probably the highest stable sandhill in the world. At Wild Dolphin Resort, on the western side of the island at Tangalooma, wild dolphins come into shore to be hand fed. There are walking tracks behind the settlement of Bulwer and in the sand dunes area. **See also:** National Parks p. 460 for parks in bold type.

Hinterland Escape

Noosa Heads to Landsborough via the Glass House Mountains (153 km)

This journey into the Blackall Range and the Glass House Mountains is a delightful diversion from the beaches and popular resorts of Queensland's Sunshine Coast. The Blackall Range forms an impressive natural backdrop to the coast, rising almost 400 metres above the plain. From the ridge, there are expansive views over rolling hills down to the Pacific Ocean and south to the distinctive profile of the Glass House Mountains. The range features a string of charming mountain villages where you can browse through galleries, meet the local artisans and enjoy a leisurely lunch. As a grand finale, you will descend from the range and drive into the Glass House Mountains before returning to the coast. This tour can be completed in a day, but there are plenty of B & Bs and guesthouses en route if you want to make the most of your hinterland experience.

1 Noosa lifestyle

Your tour commences at **Noosa Heads**, a fashionable resort set on lovely Laguna Bay at the mouth of the Noosa River, just 140 kilometres north of Brisbane. Here you can browse through a diverse range of shops, sample the offerings of some of Australia's most innovative chefs and relax on the beautiful beaches.

The nearby headland is part of Noosa National Park, where a network of walking tracks leads through rainforest and coastal heathland to sandy beaches and dramatic cliff-top vantage points. Laguna Lookout, at the end of Viewland Drive (just off the main road into Noosa Heads) provides sweeping coastal views to the north and views of Noosa River to the west, especially beautiful at sunset. For another perspective on the waterscape, take a cruise up the Noosa River, through the inland lakes system to the reflective tannin-coloured waters of The Everglades.

Eumundi Market

Noosa Heads

2 Marvellous market

To begin your hinterland escape, drive through Noosaville and turn left onto Eumundi–Noosa Road. The road meanders inland through forest and open farmland to the historic 19th-century timber town of **Eumundi**. On Saturday mornings this is the setting for one of Australia's most colourful markets. Aim to arrive as early as possible – breakfast at the Eumundi Market is a real treat. Taste the fine locally grown produce, browse through the clothing and crafts, relax in the shade and be entertained by the buskers.

3 Ginger galore

Continue through Eumundi, travelling south for several kilometres before crossing the Bruce Highway to join Bunya Road. On reaching Yandina, turn left from the centre of town and follow the signs to **The Ginger Factory**, one of Queensland's most visited attractions. Ginger is a major local crop, and The Ginger Factory has combined its operations with a range of interesting experiences. You can see how ginger is processed, watch cooking demonstrations, purchase jams and other treats from the Ginger Shoppe, ride the historic Queensland Cane Train and visit Bunya Park, a wildlife sanctuary that is part of this complex.

The Ginger Factory
50 Pioneer Road
Yandina
Phone: (07) 5446 7096
Open: daily 9 a.m.–5 p.m.

4 Climbing the escarpment

Return to the centre of Yandina and continue south along Nambour Road, running parallel to the Bruce Highway. As you enter the outskirts of Nambour, turn right onto National Park Road which becomes Nambour–Mapleton Road.

Leaving Nambour behind, the road winds up the eastern escarpment of the Blackall Range. Just before you reach Mapleton, take time to stop at the Dulong Lookout situated at the top of the climb; to reach the lookout take the short signposted road to the left. The views are exhilarating: rolling green hills to the east and dense forest to the north.

From the centre of Mapleton, follow the Obi Obi Road to **Mapleton Falls National Park**, a pocket of remnant rainforest on the sheltered western escarpment. The falls plunge a dramatic 120 metres into the valley below. Peregrine Lookout, on the edge of the falls, is a 10-minute walk downhill from the car park.

5 Cascades

Return to Mapleton and turn right along the Montville–Mapleton Road. The road follows the ridge of the Blackall Range, providing magnificent views to the east and west as you drive along. Some of the finest views towards the coast are from Flaxton Gardens, on your left – there is a pottery workshop, winery and restaurant in the grounds.

Shortly after Flaxton, take the signposted turn-off to **Kondalilla National Park**. Here, the clear mountain waters cascade over mossy boulders and flow into a rock pool at the top of Kondalilla Falls. The park is also noted for its abundant wildlife: because of the remarkable diversity of vegetation, there are over 100 bird species in an area of only 327 hectares.

Take the Picnic Creek Circuit (1-hour return) through tall open forest to view the falls from above, or continue along the longer Kondalilla Falls Circuit through the rainforest to the base of the falls. If you take either of these walks, be warned that the uphill return is very steep.

6 Mountain village

Return to the main road and continue to **Montville**, the picturesque artistic centre of the Blackall Range. Settled by citrus growers in 1887, it has an English-style village green as its centrepiece. A signposted heritage trail starts at the Village Hall. Take time to browse through the pottery, art and craft galleries that line the streets. Montville is an ideal spot to stop for lunch – there are many cafes and restaurants to choose from.

If you prefer a picnic, turn right on Western Avenue and take the signposted road to Lake Baroon, which branches off to the left. At the foot of a very steep incline lies Baroon Pocket Dam, an attractive and accessible picnic spot: tables are set among the pine trees on the lake foreshore.

7 Unlimited vistas

Travelling south along the ridge from Montville towards Maleny, you will be treated to **12 kilometres of spectacular views** in all directions. Gerrard Lookout, situated on the left side of the road, is an absolute must. Standing here, at 375 metres above sea level, you can see the entire stretch of the Sunshine Coast – from the high-rise outline of Caloundra in the south, to the natural beauty of the coastline around Noosa Heads in the north. Balmoral Lookout, a few kilometres further on the right, offers an entirely different

perspective. Here you can see north across farmland to the nearby Lake Baroon, and westward to the forests around Kenilworth and the mountainous country beyond.

8 Looking south

When you reach the Landsborough–Maleny Road, turn right towards Maleny (as signposted). Maleny is one of the larger settlements in the Blackall Range, a service centre for the surrounding farmland and also catering for tourists. At the end of the commercial centre of town,

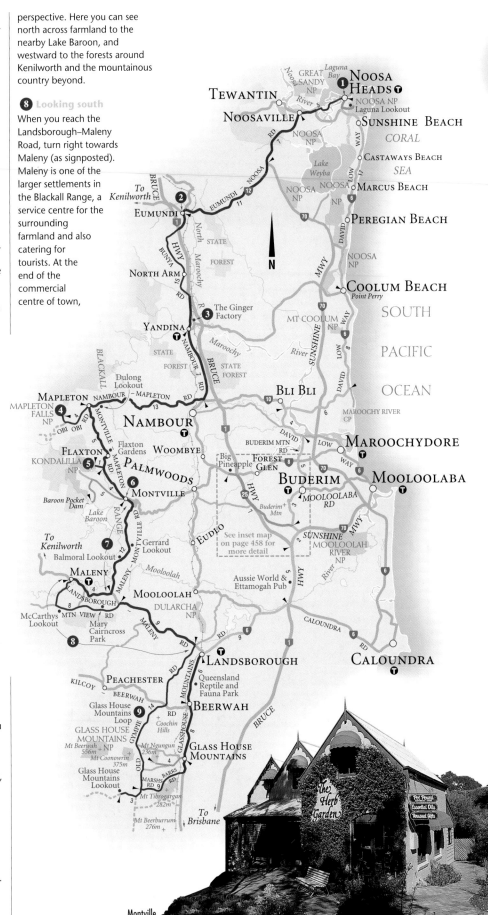

Montville

Glass House Mountains

turn left down the Maleny–Stanley River Road, then left into Mountain View Road at the T-intersection.

Almost immediately after turning onto Mountain View Road, stop at McCarthy's Lookout (on the right) for your first breathtaking **overview of the Glass House Mountains**; an illustrated sign identifies each of the 13 peaks, seven of which belong to Glass House Mountains National Park. These uncompromising formations, the eroded remnants of ancient volcanoes, rise abruptly from the plain. Captain James Cook gave the mountains their unusual name when he sailed past in 1770: viewed from the coast, they resembled the glass furnaces of his native Yorkshire.

Continue along Mountain View Road, heading east along the ridge. Mary Cairncross Park, on your left, is the legacy of 19th-century environmentalist Mary Cairncross. The park has a fascinating natural history centre that provides an introduction to the varied plant and animal life of the hinterland. There is a lookout and picnic area nearby and an easy 40-minute nature walk through the rainforest.

Mountain View Road rejoins the Landsborough–Maleny Road for the winding descent to Landsborough. Instead of continuing into the centre of town, turn right onto Old Gympie Road, immediately before the railway line, to commence your drive through the Glass House Mountains.

9 Glass House Mountains loop
Proceeding south, just after crossing Kilcoy–Beerwah Road, you are confronted with the twin peaks of Coochin Hills on the left. This is your first **close-up view of**

the Glass House Mountains. Further on, the tall and pointy shaft of rock known as Mount Coonowrin (Crook-neck), rises up on your right.

Once these peaks are behind you, watch out for a signposted turn-off to the Glass House Mountains Lookout. Here you can take in 360-degree views of the peaks, all of which are shown on a podium located at the lookout. Just to the north is Mount Beerwah, the tallest of the mountains, rising abruptly to 556 metres.

Return to the Old Gympie Road and turn left; retrace your steps for about 1 kilometre, then turn right into Marshs Road which becomes Barrs Road. The road skirts the base of Mount Tibrogargan before joining Glasshouse Mountains Road. Turn left to the township of Glass House Mountains. For more details on walks and picnic spots in the district, drop into the visitor information centre in the main street. Those seeking a challenge can inquire about the 700-metre trail to the summit of Mount Ngungun, west of town. Access to the track is via Coonowrin and Fullertons roads. If you intend to make the ascent, allow two hours (return) and be aware that the track is steep in places, often passing close to the cliff-line.

Continue along the Glasshouse Mountains Road, through Beerwah to return to Landsborough. En route you will pass the Queensland Reptile and Fauna Park, one of many great family attractions in the area.

Returning to the coast *(See map on p. 457 for return route shown in pink.)* *Continue along the Glasshouse Mountains Road until it joins the Bruce Highway. From this point, Brisbane is 82 kilometres south along the highway and Caloundra is 13 kilometres east (straight ahead) on the Caloundra Road.*

To return to Noosa Heads (50 kilometres), head north along the Bruce Highway, passing Aussie World and Ettamogah Pub on the left. At the junction of the Bruce Highway and the Sunshine Motorway follow the Tanawha–Forest Glen Tourist Drive **25** *signs to the left. After 1.5 kilometres, you have the option of turning right to Buderim or continuing along the tourist drive to visit the many family attractions in the area (see below).*

From Buderim, head north down Buderim Mountain Road to meet David Low Way on the Maroochy River. Follow this road through the outskirts of Bli Bli to the coast. The beaches of the South Pacific Ocean and the Coral Sea unfold as you travel north. Point Perry Lookout on the southern end of Coolum Beach offers expansive views extending northwards to Noosa Heads, past Peregian, Marcus, Castaways and Sunshine beaches, all easily accessible and worth a visit.

Family attractions
Superbee Honey Factory – *honey-tastings, bee-handling demonstrations, fairytale houses and tropical gardens.*
Bellingham Maze – *find your way out of Australia's largest hedge maze.*
Forest Glen Sanctuary – *deer and Australian marsupials in a bushland setting; feed the animals and pose for a photo with a furry companion.*
Big Pineapple – *one of Queensland's best-known icons; board the Sugar Cane Train for a journey through the tropical plantation; take a ride on the Nutmobile to the Macadamia Nut Factory.*
UnderWater World – *seal shows, coral displays, brilliant tropical fish and monsters of the deep; definitely worth a visit (located on the coast at Mooloolaba).*

Tanawha - Forest Glen
Tourist Drive **25**

QUEENSLAND from A to Z

Airlie Beach, on the beautiful Whitsunday coast

Airlie Beach   Pop. 3029

MAP REF. 527 K3

Airlie Beach is the centre of the thriving Whitsunday coast. Located 20 km from the Bruce Hwy at Proserpine, Airlie overlooks the Whitsunday Passage and islands, and has its own beach and marina. From Airlie and Shute Harbour passengers can travel to the outer reef and reef-fringed islands. Airlie Beach is a holiday town offering major resorts with all facilities, top-grade holiday accommodation and a range of activities and services for visitors. **In town:** Vic Hislop's Shark Show, 13 Waterson Rd. Community market each Sat. on foreshore. Aug.: Triathlon. Sept.: Whitsunday Fun Race. **In the area:** Neighbouring Shute Harbour and islands of Whitsunday Passage. Fishing trips to nearby coastal wetlands and crocodile safaris. Conway National Park, 5 km S, renowned for its natural beauty and habitat of the rock wallaby and many species of butterfly. **Visitor information:** Tourism Whitsundays, Bruce Hwy, Prosperpine; (07) 4945 3711, freecall 1800 801 252.

Allora   Pop. 998

MAP REF. 525 N10

North of Warwick just off the Toowoomba road, this picturesque town is in a prime agricultural area. **In town:** Allora Historical Museum, Drayton St (open Sun. p.m. or by appt). Feb.: Allora Show and Sunflower Festival. June: Apex Auction. **In the area:** National Trust-classified Talgai Homestead (c. 1860), 6 km W, offers meals and accommodation. Glengallan homestead (1867), 15 km N on New England Hwy, heritage-listed relic of colonial pastoral life (check times). Goomburra State Forest, 35 km E in western foothills of Great Dividing Range. **Visitor information:** 49 Albion St (New England Hwy), Warwick; (07) 4661 3122. Web site www.qldsoutherndowns.org.au

Aramac   Pop. 342

MAP REF. 526 C10, 533 Q10

This small pastoral town is 67 km N of Barcaldine. Originally called Marathon, it was renamed by explorer William Landsborough as an acronym of Sir Robert Ramsay Mackenzie (RRMac), Colonial Secretary in 1866 and Premier of Qld (1867–68). **In town:** White Bull replica, Gordon St, commemorating Captain Starlight's arrest for cattle-stealing. Tramway Museum, McWhannell St, has old rail motor and historical exhibits. May: Ballyneety Rodeo. **In the area:** Grey Rock, 35 km E, large sandstone rock with engraved names from early 1900s to present. Lake Dunn, 68 km NE, for swimming, fishing and birdwatching (follow signs to 'The Lake' rather than to adjacent Lake Dunn property). **Visitor information:** Post Office, Gordon St; (07) 4651 3147.

Atherton   Pop. 5693

MAP REF. 523 C12, 529 M7

Atherton is the agricultural hub of the Atherton Tableland. 100 km SW of Cairns on the Kennedy Hwy, the town is surrounded by a patchwork of dense rainforest that abounds in varied birdlife and tropical vegetation. The fertile basalt soil, gently undulating terrain and abundant rainfall have made the region the centre of dairy and grain-growing industries. The area between Atherton, Kairi and Tolga is particularly suited to growing tomatoes, avocados, potatoes, peanuts, maize and other grains. **In town:** Chinese Joss House and Old Post Office Gallery, Herberton Rd. Fascinating Facets and the Crystal Caves mineral museum, Main St, has a constructed underground attraction comprising tunnels and chambers, and displays of minerals and gemstones. **In the area:** Picturesque Atherton Tableland, one of oldest land masses in Australia, features rainforest-fringed volcanic crater lakes, spectacular waterfalls and fertile farmlands. Bushwalking at Halloran Hill, 1 km E; Baldy Mountain, 3 km SW; Wongabel State Forest, 8 km SE. At Tolga, 5 km N: woodworks, peanut factory and craft. At Herberton, 19 km SW: Foster's Winery; Historical Village with more than 30 restored buildings. Steam-train journeys with 1927 locomotive, from Atherton to Herberton and return, along steepest track in Qld; departs Wed. and weekends (closed Feb.) from Platypus Park, Herberton Rd. Mt Hypipamee National Park, 26 km S, includes sheer-sided explosion crater 124 m deep, and variety of wildlife. Lake Tinaroo, 15 km NE, for fishing, water-skiing and sailing; houseboat hire; Danbulla Forest Drive, 28 km scenic drive around lake. **Visitor information:** Old Post Office Gallery, Herberton Rd; (07) 4091 4222. Web site www.athertontableland.com See also: Wildlife-Watching p. 464; The Far North p. 472.

Ayr   Pop. 8697

MAP REF. 526 H1, 529 Q13

This busy town on the north side of the Burdekin delta is surrounded by intensively irrigated sugarcane fields, the most productive in Australia. The

National Parks

The diverse landscapes of Queensland's national parks lure visitors by the million each year. They are drawn not only to the endless stretches of sandy beaches and the magnificent Great Barrier Reef cays and islands off the coast, but also to the cooler mountains of the southern ranges, the inland plains and semi-arid areas, and the wilderness of Cape York.

Many parks and reserves are accessible by conventional vehicle; some require a 4WD. Their major attraction is the climate – beautiful one day, perfect the next! Daytime temperatures in the north and west can reach a searing 40°C or more in summer, and the northern wet season (November to March) brings the occasional cyclone and rainfall that can be measured in metres; but other than these extremes, the climate is ideal for activities such as bushwalking, camping and watersports.

Hinchinbrook Island, one of the world's largest national park islands

IN THE SOUTH-EAST OF THE STATE

Around Brisbane, the crescent of national parks, or Scenic Rim, includes **Main Range**, **Mount Barney**, **Lamington** and **Springbrook** national

parks, which form part of a World Heritage-listed area. These offer panoramic views, extensive walking tracks, picnic facilities and a range of recreational opportunities. Lamington attracts thousands of visitors to its cool rainforest, rich in elkhorn and staghorn ferns and over 700 other plant species, including orchids.

Tamborine National Park, in the Gold Coast hinterland, attracts many day visitors from Brisbane and the Gold Coast to its rainforests, waterfalls and scenic lookouts. **Girraween National Park**, the 'Place of Flowers', south of Stanthorpe and close to the New South Wales border, offers visitors excellent floral displays. This area is a photographer's paradise, while the park's massive granite outcrops provide a challenge for walkers.

Offshore in Moreton Bay, **Moreton Island National Park** is predominantly a wilderness area with vast tracts of sand dunes including Mt Tempest (280 m), which is probably the tallest permanent sand dune in the world. On the leeward side near the resort, wild dolphins make regular visits to be fed by visitors.

Bunya Mountains National Park, 250 kilometres north-west of Brisbane, was established to preserve the largest remaining bunya pine rainforest in the world. It was here that Aborigines gathered about every third year to feast on bunya nuts. There is camping available and excellent graded tracks for walking. Further east lie the **Glass House Mountains**, eroded volcanic plugs that rise suddenly from the landscape. First sighted by Captain Cook in 1770, seven of these mountains – Coonoorwin, Tibrogargan, Ngungun, Miketeebumulgrai, Coochin, Elimbah and Beerwah – are in the national park.

Noosa National Park, 160 kilometres north of Brisbane, offers the visitor a wide variety of coastal scenery. Walking tracks lead to lookouts from which can be seen such unusual rock formations as Hell's Gates and Boiling Pot. Located further north, off Hervey Bay, is the world's largest sand island, Fraser Island. The northern third of the island is part of **Great Sandy National Park**. This and its Cooloola section on the mainland are largely 4WD territory; the Cooloola section offers excellent boating opportunities, particularly on the Noosa River.

Launches and charter vessels from several central Queensland ports will take visitors to Heron, Masthead, North West and Lady Musgrave islands, all rich in coral and marine life and a paradise for snorkellers and scuba divers. The Southern Reef islands are outstanding rookeries of the loggerhead and green turtles, and the summer nesting-grounds for thousands of wedge-tailed shearwaters and white-capped noddies. Lady Musgrave Island section of **Capricornia Cays National Park** is a charming coral cay reached from Bundaberg and Seventeen Seventy. Around the cay's edge, exposed to wind and salt spray, grows a vegetation fringe of casuarina and pandanus, which protects the shady pisonia forest on the inner part of the island. The sheltered lagoon is popular for sailing, snorkelling and reef-viewing in glass-bottomed boats.

Coastal parks around Bundaberg include Barrum Coast National Park and Baldwin Swamp and Mon Repos conservation parks. **Burrum Coast National Park**, south of Bundaberg, covers 22 500 hectares of essential wildlife habitat; plant communities in the park include mangroves lining the Gregory and Burrum rivers, wallum heathland, eucalypt and angophora forests, tea-tree swamps and small pockets of palm forest. Roads in the park are gravel or sand, and 4WD vehicles are recommended, although at times conventional vehicle access is possible. Only 3 kilometres east of Bundaberg and covering 40 hectares is the Baldwin Wetlands, containing the **Baldwin Swamp Conservation Park**. Walking tracks and a boardwalk allow observation of the park's wildlife. **Mon Repos Conservation Park**, 14 kilometres east of Bundaberg, is eastern Australia's largest mainland turtle rookery. The turtle season is November to March. Visitors to the information centre gain some knowledge of sea turtles and acceptable human interaction with them. This ensures that a visit to the rookery is an enjoyable experience.

Eurimbula National Park is south-east of Gladstone, near the twin communities of Agnes Water and Seventeen Seventy. Over 200 years ago Captain Cook and his crew chose this picturesque stretch of coast, with its broad sandy beaches between small rocky headlands, for their first landing in what is now Queensland. Botanically this is a key coastal area, preserving a complex array of vegetation, including some plants common in southern areas and others found in northern forests. **Auburn River National Park**, south-west of Mundubbera,

Lush rainforest at Lamington National Park

protects open eucalypt forest and dry scrub. The Auburn River flows through this 390-hectare park over a jumbled mass of pink granitic boulders. Over time, water erosion has sculptured the river's rock pools and cataracts. Vegetation along the river banks includes stunted figs, and bottle trees are common. Dry rainforest species occur in some areas and small lizards can be seen sunbaking on rocks near the water. North-west of Monto, **Cania Gorge National Park** features prominent sandstone cliffs up to 70 metres high, cave formations, dry rainforest on sheltered slopes, and open eucalypt forest. This park protects a valuable scenic resource and provides an important wildlife habitat.

IN THE NORTH-EAST OF THE STATE

Queensland's central and northern coastal islands range from large, steep continental types to coral cays, many of them lying between the mainland and the outer Great Barrier Reef. Several national park islands have been developed for tourism; these include **Hinchinbrook**, one of the world's largest national park islands with 39 900 hectares of wilderness and quiet beaches. More than 90 per cent of the 100 islands in the Whitsunday Group are national parks and six also have resorts. Sail-yourself yachts are a novel way to visit some of the more isolated spots.

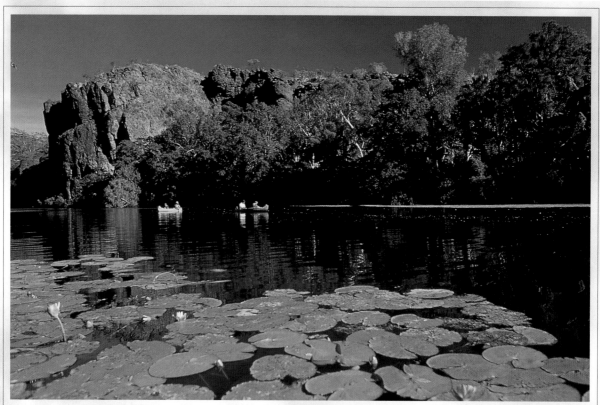

Beauty and remoteness at Lawn Hill National Park

Eungella National Park, 83 kilometres west of Mackay, is the Aboriginal 'Land of the Clouds'. It is one of Queensland's most majestic parks, and the freshness under the canopy of rainforest makes it a perfect destination for a day trip. Camping is available at Fern Flat. **Cape Hillsborough National Park**, 50 kilometres north-west of Mackay, combines the beauty of an island with the accessibility of the mainland. Wildlife includes kangaroos, wallabies, possums, echidnas and numerous bird species.

Within a several-hundred-kilometre radius of Cairns are scores of national parks catering for all tastes. About 50 kilometres from Cairns is the Atherton Tableland, on which lie several national parks. Here visitors can follow walking tracks through spectacular rainforest at **Mt Hypipamee**, or visit the 65-metre-wide **Millstream Falls**, or the famous crater lakes of Eacham and Barrine in **Crater Lakes National Park**.

A north Queensland visit would not be complete without a train trip to Kuranda via **Barron Gorge National Park** and a return gondola ride on the Skyrail Rainforest Cableway, or a visit to the **Wooroonooran**, **Lumholtz** and **Daintree** national parks. This relatively undeveloped mountainous country, with its scenic waterfalls and lush rainforest, should not be missed. **Chillagoe–Mungana Caves National Park**, three hours' drive from Cairns, is dominated by weird limestone outcrops, castle-like pinnacles that house a wonderland of colourful caves. Guided tours are conducted daily. Once Queensland's leading mineral producing area, it is still popular with fossickers.

Today Cape York Peninsula is a magnet for tourists, even though the only aim of thousands of visitors may be simply to stand at its tip. The peninsula's vast and monotonous country is interspersed with surprising pockets of forest, broad vegetation-fringed rivers and occasional waterfalls – all home to a wide variety of wildlife. **Jardine River**, **Mungkan Kandju** and **Iron Range** national parks are destinations for keen and experienced wilderness explorers. However, a growing number of visitors divert to **Lakefield**. Its fringing rainforest, paperbark woodland, open grassy plains, swamps and coastal mudflats leading to mangroves along Princess Charlotte Bay all offer a variety of attractions. Basic campsites are located along many watercourses.

CENTRAL QUEENSLAND

One of the most breathtakingly beautiful scenic reserves in Australia is **Carnarvon National Park**, 720 kilometres by road north-west of Brisbane. The Carnarvon Gorge section of this park, a dramatic, twisting chasm gouged from soft sandstone cliffs, is a popular destination for campers. Formed walking tracks lead through forests of eucalypt, she-oaks, tall cabbage palms, and relict macrozamia palms. Two major Aboriginal art sites, the Art Gallery and Cathedral Cave, contain rock stencils and engravings of great significance. Limits on campsite visitor numbers protect the ecology of the park.

IN THE NORTH-WEST OF THE STATE

In the remote north-west of Queensland, **Lawn Hill National Park** is an oasis on the edge of the Barkly Tableland. The road into the park is very rough in places, so 4WD travel is recommended, especially for caravanners. Lawn Hill Gorge has colourful cliffs rising 60 metres to the surrounding plateau. On the gorge walls are Aboriginal rock paintings, and middens also remain. Visitors can see these from the boardwalk and viewing platforms. The creek has permanent water and offers a habitat for tropical vegetation, including cabbage tree palms and Leichhardt pines. The water attracts various bird species, and reptiles including freshwater crocodiles, tortoises and water monitors. There are several walking tracks in the park. World Heritage-listed Riversleigh Fossil Field, site of unique fossil finds of previously unknown animals, is an extension of the park.

For more information about Queensland's national parks, including the requirement for camping permits, contact the Naturally Queensland Information Centre, 160 Ann St, Brisbane (PO Box 155, Brisbane Albert St 4002); (07) 3227 8185/6. Web site www.env.qld.gov.au

Burdekin River Irrigation Scheme is the largest land and water conservation scheme in the State, and allows Ayr to be the largest mango-producing area in Australia. **In town:** Ayr Nature Display, Wilmington St, fine collection of emu-egg carvings, butterflies and beetles. Burdekin Cultural Complex, Queen St, includes 530-seat theatre, library and activities centre; distinctive 'Living Lagoon' in theatre forecourt. ESA markets, Plantation Creek Park, Bruce Hwy, 3rd Sun. each month. Sept.: Water Festival. Nov.: Home Hill Harvest Festival. **In the area:** Alva Beach, 18 km N, for beach walks, birdwatching, swimming and fishing; market 1st Sun. each month. Australian Institute of Marine Science at Cape Bowling Green, 20 km N. Hutchings Lagoon, 5 km NW, for watersports and picnics. Lions Diorama, 10 km S, shows agricultural achievements of Burdekin region. At Charlie's Hill, 24 km S, WW II historic site. Good views from Mt Inkerman, 30 km S. Scenic drives in area, brochures available. **Visitor information:** 161 Queen St; (07) 4783 9897 or Tourist Hut, Plantation Creek Park, Bruce Hwy; (07) 4783 5988.

Babinda   Pop. 1228

MAP REF. 523 H13, 529 N7

A small sugar town, 57 km S of Cairns, Babinda is adjacent to Wooroonooran National Park. In the park are the State's 2 highest mountains, Mt Bartle Frere (1622 m) and Mt Bellenden Ker (1582 m), and Josephine Falls. **In town:** Deeral Cooperative, Nelson Rd, makes footwear and Aboriginal artifacts. **In the area:** The Boulders Wildland Park, 10 km W, offers excellent bushwalking along Babinda Creek below Mt Bartle Frere. Deeral, 14 km N, departure point for cruises through rainforest and the saltwater-crocodile haunts of the Mulgrave and Russell rivers. **Visitor information:** Bruce Hwy and Munro Street; (07) 4067 1008.

Barcaldine   Pop. 1592

MAP REF. 526 C11, 533 Q11

Barcaldine is a pastoral and rail town, 108 km E of Longreach. A good supply of artesian water ensures its status as Garden City of the West; all the streets are named after trees. **In town:** Mad Mick's Hoppers and Huts Funny Farm, cnr Pine and Bauhinia sts, features

8 settlers' buildings (including woolskin buyer's residence housing large doll collection, and Cobb & Co. office, now studio and art gallery), old shearing sheds with plant and press, and hand-reared wildlife. Historical Folk Museum, cnr Gidyea and Beech sts. 'Tree of Knowledge', ghost gum in Oak St, the meeting-place for 1891 shearers' strike, which resulted in the formation of the Australian Labor Party. Australian Workers' Heritage Centre, Ash St, features buildings containing tributes to Australia's workers in landscaped oasis. National Trust-classified buildings: Masonic Lodge, Beech St; Anglican Church, Elm St; Shire Hall, Ash St. Mini steam-train rides last Sun. each month (Mar.–Oct.). **In the area:** Barcaldine Outback Zoo, 1 km W: native and exotic birds, reptiles and small and large animals. Botanical walk, 9 km S, through varied bushland. Red Mountain scenic drive from Richmond Hills station, 55 km E. **Visitor information:** Oak St; (07) 4651 1724.

Beaudesert   Pop. 3734

MAP REF. 517 D11, 525 P10

Beaudesert is a major market town on the Mt Lindesay Hwy, 64 km SW of Brisbane and 60 km from the NSW border. A road west leads to the Cunningham Hwy, and the road east leads to the Gold Coast, 70 km via Tamborine. The district is noted for dairying, beef cattle, horse-breeding and fruit- and vegetable-growing. Country markets are an attraction in the area; details from information centre. **In town:** Historical Museum, Brisbane St. Apr.: Rathdowney Heritage Festival. June.: Country and Horse Festival. Sept.: Agricultural Show. Oct.: Rodeo. **In the area:** Woollahra Farmworld, 8 km N at Gleneagle. Unique flora and good views at Tamborine Mountain, 35 km E. Nearby, dig for your own thunder eggs at Cedar Creek Lodge. Bigriggen Park, 30 km SW and Darlington Park, 12 km S, both recreation areas with picnic/barbecue facilities. Lamington National Park, 40 km S, subtropical rainforest with resorts and excellent graded walking tracks. At Tamrookum, 24 km SW, fine example of a timber church; guided tours by appt. Mt Barney National Park, 55 km SW, ranger-guided tours, and camping (permit required, apply to ranger). **Visitor information:** Historical Museum, 54 Brisbane St; (07) 5541 1284.

Biggenden   Pop. 686

MAP REF. 525 N4

This agricultural centre 100 km SE of Bundaberg, is near Mt Walsh National Park and The Bluff. Oct.: Rose Festival (odd-numbered years). **In the area:** Mt Walsh National Park, 8 km S, wilderness park popular with experienced bushwalkers. Coalstoun Lakes National Park, 20 km SW, protects two volcanic crater lakes. Coongara Rock (4WD access only), 20 km S, a volcanic core surrounded by rainforest. Mt Woowoonga, 10 km NW, forestry reserve with bushwalking and picnic/barbecue facilities. Chowey Bridge (1905), 20 km NW, concrete arch railway bridge (one of two surviving in Aust.); picnic facilities nearby. Silver Bell Novelty Farm, 2 km N on Old Coach Rd, has buildings and collections; open by appt. **Visitor information:** Weekdays, Shire Council, Edward St; (07) 4127 1440, weekends and holidays, Bundaberg Regional Visitor Information Centre; (07) 4152 2333, freecall 1800 060 499.

Biloela   Pop. 5161

MAP REF. 525 K1, 527 N13

This thriving town in the fertile Callide Valley is at the crossroads of the Burnett and Dawson hwys, 142 km S of Rockhampton. The name is Aboriginal for 'white cockatoo'. Underground water provides irrigation for lucerne, cotton, sorghum, wheat and sunflower crops. **In town:** Greycliffe homestead, Gladstone Rd, open by appt. The Silo, Primary Industries Exhibition, Dawson Hwy: theme park; hi-tech farming techniques; scenes of rural life; 3 markets each year (check dates). Bus tours of town weekdays. June: Country and Western Muster. **In the area:** Callide Dam, 5 km NE, for boating, fishing and swimming. Nearby, Callide power station, tours. Lyle Semgreen Gems at Jambin, 32 km NW, open by appt. Baralaba Historical Village, 100 km NW. Mt Scoria, 14 km S, solidified volcano core. Thangool, 10 km SE, renowned for its race days. **Visitor information:** Callide St; (07) 4992 2405. **See also:** Capricorn Region p. 497.

Birdsville   Pop. 100

MAP REF. 534 E5

The historical Birdsville Track starts here on its long path into and across SA. In the 1870s the first European settlers arrived in Birdsville, nearly 2000 km by road west of

Wildlife-Watching

In keeping with the State's reputation for showmanship, there are plenty of star performers on Queensland's wildlife billing: friendly dolphins, humpback whales, turtles and tropical fish, to name a few. However, visitors who make the effort will also enjoy the thrill of a flash of blue as a Ulysses butterfly breaks into sunlight at the rainforest edge, or the anticipation of waiting for a platypus to surface in a mountain stream.

AROUND BRISBANE

Do not let the busy cityscape and bustling seaside shopping plazas fool you – there are many wildlife-watching opportunities in and around Brisbane.

Some favourite wildlife-watching destinations in the hinterland area include **Daisy Hill State Forest** and **Brisbane Forest Park**. Daisy Hill State Forest, a bushy pocket on the outskirts of Brisbane's southern suburbs, supports a variety of animals, including a colony of koalas. The Daisy Hill Koala Centre in the park provides a wealth of information on these animals and their habitats. Visitors can climb the treetop tower to scan the surrounding canopy for wild koalas. Brisbane Forest Park, which abuts the eastern suburbs of the city, features Walk-about Creek Wildlife Centre, a simulated creek environment with perspex windows. Brisbane Forest Park is also home to a colourful array of forest birdlife and nocturnal animals such as possums and gliders; inquire on (07) 3300 4855 for guided spotlight tours.

Wildlife-watching opportunities are also numerous along the coast. In particular, the waters around **Moreton Island**, only 35 km east of Brisbane, are a haven for a variety of marine mammals including dolphins, whales and dugong.

Dolphins can be seen frolicking in the warm shallow waters surrounding Moreton Island on the bay and surf sides. Tangalooma Wild Dolphin Resort has developed a wild dolphin care and hand-feeding programme. A diet chart has been developed and care is taken to feed the dolphins only one third of their daily food needs. Participants are asked not to touch or handle the dolphins in any way, although it is not uncommon for the animals to give a friendly nudge as they approach humans.

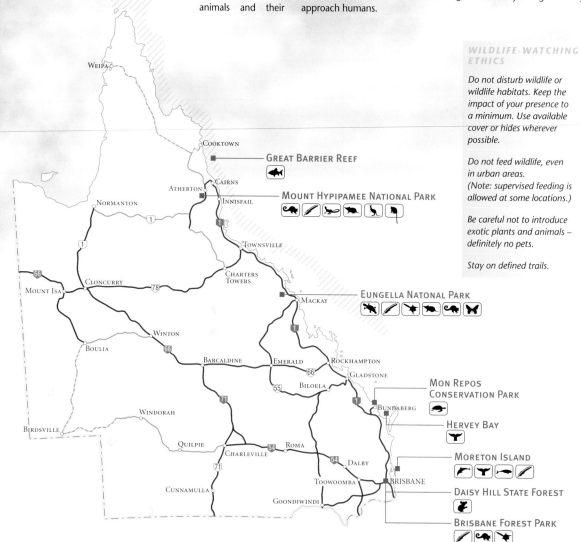

WILDLIFE-WATCHING ETHICS

Do not disturb wildlife or wildlife habitats. Keep the impact of your presence to a minimum. Use available cover or hides wherever possible.

Do not feed wildlife, even in urban areas. (Note: supervised feeding is allowed at some locations.)

Be careful not to introduce exotic plants and animals – definitely no pets.

Stay on defined trails.

The cobalt-blue Ulysses butterfly

Humpback whales can also be spotted passing the island between June and October; whale-watch cruises operate in season. There is some irony in this new attraction, given that Tangalooma was a whaling station from 1952 to 1962, when an estimated 600 whales were slaughtered per year.

Another marine mammal common to these waters is the dugong, which grazes on the seagrass beds fringing the island's western shores. These elusive creatures can sometimes be seen surfacing for air near the shores of the island.

With its variety of habitat types, ranging from inter-tidal wetlands to swamps, heathlands and open forests, Moreton Island also supports nearly one hundred species of sea and shore birds, as well as over eighty species of land birds. Prime birdwatching sites include Mirrapool and the tidal flats on the south western side of the island, where thousands of migratory birds feed and roost from September to April.

IN THE GREAT BARRIER REEF

The **Great Barrier Reef** brims with life: iridescent blue starfish; pink sponge baubles; bright green turtle weed; fragile needle coral; brain coral; mushroom coral; slender yellow trumpet fish; vivid parrot fish with beak-like jaws; schools of delicate blue pillars; butterfly fish and angel fish... This maze of coral reefs and coral cays, extending over 2000 kilometres along the Queensland coast, supports the most diverse collection of marine life to be found anywhere in the world.

The Great Barrier Reef can be viewed on one of the many day cruises operating from mainland ports, including Cairns, Port Douglas, Townsville, Airlie Beach and Mission Beach. The cruise companies offer a variety of packages and generally include expert guides and the use of snorkelling equipment. Alternatively, you might choose to base yourself on one of the islands on or near the reef. If

you go reef walking, remember to walk gently, following marked trails where available. Take care not to break the fragile coral, wear strong-soled shoes for your own protection and keep an eye on the tides. Enjoy nature's display, but refrain from collecting or disturbing the marine life.

IN THE MACKAY REGION

Eighty kilometres west of Mackay, in the enchanting rainforest setting of **Eungella National Park**, there runs a clear mountain stream which is home to one of nature's great mysteries, the platypus. This egg-laying mammal with webbed feet, a flat paddle-like tail and a duck-shaped bill is frequently spotted swimming below the special viewing platform on the banks of the Broken River.

Platypuses are generally sighted at dusk and in the early morning. It is important to keep quiet because they have sensitive hearing and are easily disturbed. Concentric rings on the water surface indicate that platypuses are active below. They feed on creatures such as insect larvae and freshwater shrimps found at the bottom of pools and creeks. The platypuses store their food in their cheeks and can be seen returning to the surface at intervals to chew and swallow.

As darkness closes in, the forest floor and treetops rustle with nocturnal life. An evening walk by torchlight will reveal a large number of busy animals, including birds such as tawny frogmouths, curlews and boobook owls, as well as gliders, bandicoots and brushtail possums.

Eungella is also known as the southernmost location of the spectacular cobalt-blue Ulysses butterfly, often sighted in the wind tunnels created by gullies and roads. The Ulysses grubs feed on the euodia trees in the park. It is not unusual to see the magical 'flashing of the blue' on a visit to Eungella, but do not expect to see these butterflies in large numbers.

A humpback whale tail-slaps as it passes the Queensland coast

ON THE FRASER COAST

Whale-watching is fast becoming a not-to-be-missed activity for visitors to Queensland's coastal destinations, from Stradbroke Island to the Whitsundays. Every year humpback whales leave the cold Antarctic waters in April and migrate along Australia's eastern shoreline, past Fraser Island and on to their breeding grounds in the Great Barrier Reef.

An estimated 400 humpback whales travel through **Hervey Bay** (between Fraser Island and the mainland) between August and October each season, making this one of the prime whale-watching spots in Queensland. The humpbacks provide great entertainment for their human audience. To see a 30–40 tonne whale exhale then arch its expansive back and roll forward, tail in air, is to bear witness to one of nature's greatest spectacles. Other antics include the 'spy hop', 'pec-slapping' and 'tail-slapping'. Numerous whale-watching cruises operate in the area. Contact the Maryborough Information Centre for information and bookings; (07) 4121 4111.

Mon Repos Conservation Park near Bundaberg features the largest mainland turtle rookery in eastern Australia. It is the hatching ground for loggerhead, green and Australian flatback turtles that nest between mid-November and February. Hatchlings emerge from January to March. A ranger is present during the turtle season to provide information and ensure visitors do not disturb the turtles. Visitor numbers are strictly limited to minimise the impact on breeding. Successful breeding here is critical to the survival of the turtles, particularly the endangered loggerhead species.

The best time of day to view nesting turtles is after dark, near high tide, whereas hatchlings are best viewed between 8 p.m. and midnight. It is recommended that you phone the Mon Repos Information Centre on (07) 4159 1652 to check times. Remember that turtles are wild marine animals, so there are occasions when they choose not to arrive.

During nesting time, visitors watch as the large female loggerheads haul themselves onto the beach and scoop a nest in the sand with their rear flippers, then fill it with eggs. Later in the season, young turtles provide another great spectacle as they emerge from the sand and scurry into the sea.

ON THE ATHERTON TABLELAND

Seven species of possum inhabit the dense rainforest surrounding an extinct volcanic crater in **Mount Hypipamee National Park**. This small pocket of dense vegetation, surrounded by farmland on the Atherton Tableland in Northern Queensland, really comes alive at night. Day visitors can expect to see the usual gang of brush turkeys scavenging for scraps around the main picnic area; honeyeaters are also commonly seen here. During daylight hours, most of the possums are asleep in their dens, but careful observation may reveal a green ringtail possum snoozing on a branch. Visitors who stay until dusk and wait quietly as the sun sets, will enjoy a more exciting wildlife-watching experience. Leaves rustle on the forest floor; geckoes, bandicoots and pademelons start to emerge. Branches crack and tree-tops shudder under the weight of heavy possums.

Most of the possum species at Mount Hypipamee can be seen by torchlight in the short distance between the main picnic area and the road leading into the park. The most common is the coppery brushtail. Other species include the green ringtail possum with green-tinged fur, and the lemuroid ringtail possum, which leaps through the air from branch to branch.

Another nocturnal mammal, the Lumholtz's tree kangaroo, is often found here and in other pockets of forest on the Atherton Tableland. These animals spend the day asleep in a crouched sitting position in the crown of a tree or on a branch. As evening approaches, they unfold their powerful limbs and display their remarkable climbing skills. Tree kangaroos are the only kangaroos that can move their hind legs independently of each other, making them able to 'walk' as well as hop.

For a good introduction to Queensland's wildlife, visit David Fleay Wildlife Park on the Gold Coast. Features include the Nocturnal House and 'Creature Feature' wildlife demonstrations. For more information on wildlife-watching in Queensland's national parks, contact the Environmental Protection Agency's Naturally Queensland Information Centre, 160 Ann St, Brisbane (PO Box 155, Brisbane Albert St 4002); (07) 3227 8185/6. Web site www.env.qld.gov.au **See also:** National Parks p. 460 and Great Barrier Reef p. 485.

Brisbane, and at the turn of the century it was a thriving settlement with 3 hotels, several stores, a customs office and a cordial factory. When the toll on cattle crossing the border near the town was abolished after Federation in 1901, prosperity declined and the population diminished. **In town:** Museum, McDonald St, features Australiana, domestic artifacts and working farm equipment. In Adelaide St: ruins of Royal Hotel (1883), reminder of Birdsville's boom days; Birdsville Hotel (1884), a hive of activity during Birdsville Races (held first Fri. and Sat. in Sept.) as population swells to about 6500. Birdsville Hotel is an important overnight stop for tourists travelling down the Track, west across the Simpson Desert (4WD country), north to Mount Isa or east to Brisbane. *Travel in this area can be hazardous, especially in the hotter months (approx. Oct.–Mar.). Supplies of food and water should always be carried, as well as at least 2 spare tyres, and petrol, oil and spare parts. Motorists are advised to ring the Northern Roads Condition Hotline on (08) 11633 for information before departing down the Track, and to advise police if heading west to the Simpson Desert National Park; motorists should also read section on Outback Motoring (p. 603). There is no hotel or fuel at Betoota, 164 km E, but fuel is available at Windorah.* The famous Flynn of the Inland founded the first Australian Inland Mission at Birdsville; there is still a well-equipped medical clinic in Adelaide St. Birdsville's water comes from a 1219-m-deep artesian bore; water emerges almost at boiling point and a cooling pond brings it to a safe temperature. Electricity is supplied by 2 diesel generators. Sept.: Race meeting (horseracing). **In the area:** Waddi trees and Dingo Cave Lookout, 14 km N. Big Red, a huge sand dune, 35 km W. **Visitor information:** Wirrarri Information Centre, Billabong Blvd; (07) 4656 3300. **See also:** Channel Country p. 469.

Blackall   Pop. 1432

MAP REF. 524 A1, 526 D13, 533 R13, 535 R1
Centre of some of the most productive sheep and cattle country in central Qld, Blackall has many sheep and cattle studs in its vicinity. In 1892 the legendary Jackie Howe set the almost unbelievable record of shearing 321 sheep with blade shears in less than 8 hours, at Alice Downs Station, 25 km N. Blackall sank the first artesian bore in Qld in 1885. **In town:** Jackie Howe statue, junction of Short and Shamrock sts. Also in

The hotel at Birdsville provides a resting place for travellers

Shamrock St: petrified tree stump, millions of years old; Major Mitchell Memorial clock. Behind the school in Thistle St is a replica of the Black Stump, a key reference point used by Thomas Frazer when he surveyed the area in 1886. Self-guide historical walk; property tours to see shearing. June: Race Meeting. July: Black Stump Camel Races. **In the area:** Steam-driven Blackall Wool Scour (1906), 4 km N on Clematis St; guided tours daily or by appt. Idalia National Park, 100 km SW, renowned as habitat of the yellow-footed rock wallaby. **Visitor information:** Short St; (07) 4657 4637.

Blackwater   Pop. 5931

MAP REF. 527 K11
This major coal-mining town is 190 km W of Rockhampton on the Capricorn Hwy. The name comes from the discolouration of the local waterholes caused by ti-trees. Coal mined in the area is railed to Gladstone. The town's population is made up of workers of many nationalities and it displays what is claimed to be the most varied collection of national flags this side of the United Nations. Cattle rearing is the traditional industry. **In town:** In town park, Capricorn Hwy: Japanese garden provided by sister town in Japan; also a Leichhardt 'Dig Tree'. **In the area:** Utah coal mine, 35 km S, tours available; bookings necessary. Expedition Range (732 m), 139 km SW near Springsure, discovered by Ludwig Leichhardt. At Comet, 30 km E, Show and Camp Draft each Sept. Rainbow Falls in Blackdown Tableland National

Park, 50 km SE, also picnic/barbecue facilities at Horseshoe Lookout and Mimosa Creek camping area. **Visitor information:** Clermont St, Emerald; (07) 4982 4142. **See also:** Capricorn Region p. 497.

Boonah   Pop. 2234

MAP REF. 517 A11, 525 P10
Eighty-six km SW of Brisbane between Warwick and Ipswich, Boonah is the main town in the Fassifern district, a highly productive agricultural and pastoral area. Its location was noted as a 'beautiful vale' by the explorer and colonial administrator Captain Logan in 1827, and by the explorer Allan Cunningham in 1828. **In town:** Art Gallery, Highbury St, leadlight and other displays. Skydiving, gliding, and ultralight tours; details from information centre. Boonah Country Markets, Springleigh Park, Sat. each fortnight. May: Country Show. **In the area:** Kalbar, 10 km N, holds Autofest in Sept. At Templin, 5 km W, Historical Village; open Sun.–Thurs. Moogerah Peaks National Park, 12 km W. Lake Moogerah, 20 km SW, for water sports. Main Range National Park, 35 km W, part of the Scenic Rim, a ring of mountains and national parks around Brisbane offering scenic drives (brochure available), bushwalking, trail-riding, rock-climbing, skydiving, water sports, picnic spots, recreation facilities, camping and accommodation; Cunninghams Gap Lookout in park has good views, with walking tracks from lookout. **Visitor information:** Boonah–Fassifern Rd; (07) 5463 2233.

View from Hummock Lookout near Bundaberg

Boulia   Pop. 243

MAP REF. 532 F9

Near the Burke River, 360 km W of Winton, 295 km S of Mt Isa and 242 km E of the NT border, Boulia is the capital of the Channel Country. **In town:** In Pituri St, town's oldest house, Stone Cottage (1880s), now a museum displaying Aboriginal artifacts and historic relics of region. In Herbert St: Min Min Centre has display on 'Min Min' light; the Red Stump, warning travellers of dangers of Simpson Desert; artificial 'Min Min' light. Tree, near Boulia State School, last known corroboree tree of Pitta Pitta community. Varied birdlife around river. Easter: Rodeo and Gymkhana. July: Desert Sands Camel Races (and festival). **In the area:** Mysterious Min Min light, first sighted near ruins of Min Min Hotel (130 km E). Cawnpore Hills, 108 km E, good views from summit. Ruins of police barracks, 19 km NE. The Burke and Wills tree, 110 km NE on the west bank of the Burke River. Diamantina National Park, 150 km SE. *Travel by road in wet season can be difficult.* **See:** Outback Motoring p. 603. **Visitor information:** Herbert St; (07) 4746 3386. **See also:** Channel Country p. 469.

Bowen   Pop. 8985

MAP REF. 527 J2

A relaxed town halfway between Mackay and Townsville, Bowen was named after the State's first Governor. The town was established in 1861 on the shores of Port Denison and was the first settlement in north Qld. It boasts an excellent climate with an average of 8 hours sunshine daily. Bowen region is famous for its tomatoes, and particularly for its mangoes (in season Nov.–Jan.). **In town:** Signposted Golden Arrow tourist drive starts at Salt Works, Don St. Twenty historical murals in central city area. Historical Museum, Gordon St. Aug.: Art, Craft and Orchid Expo. Oct. or Nov.: Coral Coast Festival. **In the area:** Excellent small bays within 7 km of town (Rose and Horseshoe bays connected by walking track) for fishing, snorkelling and swimming. Collinsville coal mines, 82 km SW. **Visitor information:** 42 Williams St; (07) 4786 4494.

Buderim   Pop. 12 458

MAP REF. 516 G4, 520 G9, 525 Q7

Buderim is a delightful town just inland from the Sunshine Coast, high on the fertile red soil of Buderim Mountain, and between Bruce Hwy and Mooloolaba on the coast. It is a popular residential and retirement area. **In town:** Several galleries in Main St. In Burnett St, Buderim Festive Markets, in Old Ginger Factory (open daily; entertainment on weekends). Pioneer timber cottage (1876), Ballinger Rd, one of Buderim's earliest houses, faithfully restored and retaining many original furnishings. Historical town walk, brochure from pioneer cottage. **In the area:** Buderim Forest Park, Quorn Close (just north of town), features waterfalls and walking tracks; wheelchair access to lower end, entry from Lindsay Rd. Rainforest walks at Foote Sanctuary, north-eastern end of town. Self-guide Forest Glen–Tanawah Tourist Drive includes: Superbee Honey Factory; Forest Glen Sanctuary (deer and native fauna); Bellingham Maze, largest hedge maze in Australia (includes aviary) and Enchanted Lair. **Visitor information:** Old Post Office, Burnett St; (07) 5477 0944. **See also:** Hinterland Escape p. 456.

Bundaberg   Pop. 41 025

MAP REF. 525 O2

Bundaberg, 368 km N of Brisbane, is the southernmost access point to the Great Barrier Reef, and an important provincial city in the centre of the fertile Burnett River plains. The district is known for its sugar (grown here since 1866), timber, beef and, in more recent years, tomatoes and avocados. Raw sugar is exported from an extensive storage and bulk facility at Port Bundaberg, 16 km NE. Industry sidelines include distilling of the world-famous Bundaberg Rum, refined sugar production, and the manufacture and export of advanced Austoft cane-harvester equipment. Bundaberg is a city of parks and botanical gardens; its wide streets lined with majestic figs, poincianas and bauhinias provide a brilliant display in spring and summer. The Burnett River flows through the city. Several notable Australians have called Bundy home: Bert Hinkler, the first man to fly solo from England to Australia in 1928; singer Gladys Moncrieff; cricketer Don Tallon; and rugby league star Mal Meninga. **In town:** Historic city walks, brochures available. Alexandra Park and Zoo on river bank, Quay St: free zoo, historic band rotunda, cactus garden and children's playground. Whaling Wall, Bourbong St, a 6-storey-high whale mural. In East Bundaberg: Bundaberg Rum Distillery, Avenue St, offers guided tours daily to see famous Aussie spirit being made;

Channel Country

The remote Channel Country is an endless horizon of plains in the far west and south-west corner of the State. It seldom rains here, but after the northern monsoons the Georgina, Hamilton and Diamantina rivers and Cooper Creek flood through hundreds of channels to reach Lake Eyre. After the 'wet without rain', enormous quantities of water vanish into waterholes, saltpans and desert sands; grass, wildflowers and bird and animal life miraculously appear, and cattle are moved in for fattening.

The region is sparsely populated except for large pastoral holdings and scattered settlements linked by essential beef-roads. The Diamantina Developmental Road runs south from Mount Isa through Dajarra and Boulia to Bedourie, then swings east across the many channels of the Diamantina River and Cooper Creek through Windorah to the railhead at Quilpie, then on to Charleville, a journey of some 1335 kilometres.

Boulia, proclaimed the capital of the Channel Country, was first settled by Europeans in 1877. It is 295 kilometres south of Mount Isa and 360 kilometres west of Winton. A friendly, relaxed town on the Burke River, its name comes from an Aboriginal word meaning 'clear water'. Burke and Wills filled their water-bags here.

Bedourie, 191 kilometres further south, is the administrative centre for the Diamantina shire, and has a school, police station, medical clinic, roadhouse, mini-mart, motel and caravan park. It has ample artesian water, without the usual pungent smell, and swimming is popular.

South of Bedourie the Diamantina Developmental Road swings east for the partly sealed drive to Windorah, 'place of large fish'. During drought the area is a dustbowl; during the monsoon it is a lake. There is a good hotel in town and sheep-raising is the only industry.

A good, narrow sealed road leads 237 kilometres east to **Quilpie** and the Channel Country. Cattle, sheep and wool are railed to the coast from here. Opals have been found here since 1880. Although the town is near Bulloo River, its water comes from a near-boiling artesian bore.

Thargomindah, 193 kilometres south of Quilpie, is a small settlement on the eastern fringe of the Channel Country, 198 kilometres from Cunnamulla. Noccundra, 122 kilometres even further west, has a tiny permanent population, but they can offer you accommodation and fuel.

The Kennedy Developmental Road from Winton to Boulia is sealed for all of its 360 kilometres. A welcome stop is the remote bush hotel at Middleton. Visitors are sure to be told about the Min Min light, an unexplained phenomenon that often appears at night near the old Min Min hotel, some 130 kilometres from Boulia, and that has been seen many times in other places in the Channel Country.

The Eyre Developmental Road starts south of Bedourie and leads to **Birdsville**, the most isolated settlement in Queensland, with the Simpson Desert to the west. It is at the top end of the Birdsville Track to Marree in South Australia. The Birdsville Developmental Road runs north-east to join the Diamantina Developmental Road and east to Windorah. *There is no hotel or fuel at Betoota, 164 kilometres east of Birdsville. Travellers heading east from Birdsville should ensure that they have sufficient fuel to reach Windorah.*

Whilst summer in the Channel Country is extremely hot, most pubs and accommodation are airconditioned and all services operate as usual. The best time to visit is between April and October. The wildflowers here usually bloom around late August, depending on rain.

For further information on the Channel Country, contact the Outback Qld Tourism Authority, Library Building, Shamrock St, Blackall; (07) 4657 4255. **See also:** individual entries in A–Z town listing for details on towns in bold type. **Map reference:** 532 F9.

The remote Channel Country around Boulia

Daintree National Park, a popular day tour destination from Cairns

Baldwin Swamp Environmental Wetlands, Steindl St, has boardwalks and pathways, waterlily lagoons, abundant birdlife and native fauna; Schmeider's Cooperage and Craft Centre, Alexandra St, has demonstrations of ancient art of barrel-making. Across the river in North Bundaberg: Botanical Gardens (Mt Perry Rd) include Hinkler House Memorial Museum (repository of aviation history), railway (steam-train rides around lakes), Bundaberg Historical Museum, and Sugar Museum in Fairymead House; Tropical Wines (unique tropical-fruit wine) and Sunny Soft Drinks also Mt Perry Rd. Shalom College Markets, Fitzgerald St, West Bundaberg, each Sun. West School Craft Markets, George St, West Bundaberg (2nd Sun. each month). Easter: Country Music Roundup. Sept.: Bundy in Bloom Festival. Oct.: Arts Festival. Nov.: Coral Turtle Festival. **In the area:** Coastal and hinterland self-drive tours, brochures available. Boat tours to see migrating humpback whales, mid-Aug.–mid-Oct. Cane fires, sugarcane harvesting season (July–Nov.). Fishing at Burnett Heads (15 km NE), Elliott Heads (18 km SE) and Moore Park (21 km NW). Popular surf beach at Bargara, 13 km NE; nearby, Neilson Park and Kelly's beaches. Hummock Lookout, 7 km NE, for excellent views over city, canefields and coast. Mon Repos Conservation Park, 15 km NE, largest and most accessible mainland loggerhead turtle rookery in Australia; giant sea turtles come ashore to lay their eggs, and babies hatch Nov.–Mar. In 1912 Bert Hinkler, engineering apprentice, flew to a height of 9 m in his home-made glider off Mon Repos Beach, marking the start of his distinguished career in aviation. Meadowvale Nature Park, 10 km W,

features rainforest and walkway to Splitters Creek. Sharon Gorge, 12 km SW, features rainforest and walkway to Burnett River. Unexplained mystery, 25 km SW: 35 intriguing craters said to be 25 million years old. Avocado Grove, 10 km S, subtropical gardens. Near Childers, 45 km S, Isis Central Sugar Mill (tours July–Nov.). Cruises to Lady Musgrave Island on MV *Lady Musgrave*, departs Bundaberg Port. Flights to Lady Elliot Island resort. **Visitor information:** cnr Mulgrave and Bourbong sts; (07) 4152 2333, freecall 1800 060 499. Web site www.sunzine. net/bundaberg **See also:** Wildlife-Watching p. 464.

Burketown   Pop. 220

MAP REF. 531 E8

The centre of rich beef country, Burketown is 229 km W of Normanton. The Gulf of Carpentaria is accessible by boat from Burketown. The town is near the Albert River and on the dividing line between the wetlands to the north and the beginning of the Gulf Savannah grass plains to the south. In Sept. and Oct. visitors can witness the unusual meteorological phenomenon locally known as Morning Glory, a tube-like cloud formation that rolls across the sky. **In town:** 100-year-old bore, which issues 68°C water. Burketown Hotel (1860s), originally customs house, oldest building in the Gulf. Burketown to Normanton telegraph line. Original post office. Easter: World Barramundi Handline-rod Fishing Championships. June: Agricultural Show. **In the area:** Original Gulf meatworks just north of town. Cemetery, 2 km N, for insights into town's historic past. Nicholson River wetlands, 17 km W,

breeding grounds for crocodiles, and variety of fish and birdlife. Escott Lodge, 17 km W, operating cattle station; camping and accommodation. Lawn Hill National Park, 205 km SW: renowned for its rare vegetation; contains World Heritage-listed Riversleigh Fossil Site; near entrance to park is Adels Grove, remains of exotic garden planted by French botanist Albert De Lestang in 1930s. Leichhardt Falls, 71 km SE: picturesque area, walks and flowing falls in rainy months. Landsborough Tree, 5 km E, blazed by explorer in 1862 when searching for Burke and Wills. **Visitor information:** Burke Shire Council, Musgrave St; (07) 4745 5100. **See also:** Gulf Savannah p. 494.

Burrum Heads   Pop. 834

MAP REF. 525 P3

This pleasant holiday resort, at the mouth of the Burrum River and on the foreshore of Hervey Bay, 45 km N of Maryborough, offers excellent fishing and beaches. **In town:** Easter: Amateur Fishing Classic. **In the area:** Fishing villages of Buxton and Walkers Point on north side of Burrum River. Magnificent ocean beach at Woodgate, 90 km N (5 km N by boat). Nearby, Burrum Coast National Park, accessible from Woodgate, features walking tracks (including boardwalk), prolific birdlife, picnic spots and camping areas. **Visitor information:** Phillips Travel, 45 Burrum St; (07) 4129 5211.

Caboolture   Pop. 17 571

MAP REF. 516 F8, 517 C1, 525 P8

Just off the Bruce Hwy, 46 km N of Brisbane, Caboolture is a developing commercial centre surrounded by

subtropical fruit farms. **In town:** Market at showground, Beerburrum Rd, each Sun. June: Agricultural Show; Medieval Tournament. July: St Peters and St Columbans Arts and Cultural Expo. Aug.: Air Show (odd-numbered years). Nov.: Makin Music (poetry and a variety of music, including local talent). Dec.: Rodeo. **In the area:** Popular fishing towns of Donnybrook and Toorbul (20 and 22 km NE), and Beachmere (13 km SE). Caboolture Historical Village, faithfully restored; 2 km N on Beerburrum Rd. Distinctive forested volcanic plugs in Glass House Mountains National Park, 22 km N. Woodford, 22 km NW, has a Folk Festival each Dec. Abbey Museum, 9 km E, just off road to Bribie Island, traces growth of Western civilisation. War Plane Museum, 2 km E, restored fighter planes. Bribie Island, 23 km E, for family day trips, picnic areas, fishing and safe swimming. **Visitor information:** 55 King St; (07) 5495 3122.

Cairns
Pop. 92 273

MAP REF. 522, 523 F8, 529 N6

This modern, colourful, coastal city is the capital of the tropical north. The cosmopolitan Esplanade traces the bay foreshore, and parks and gardens abound with tropical plants and colour. Cairns' location is superb: the Great Barrier Reef to the east, the mountain rainforests and plains of the Atherton Tableland to the west, and palm-fringed beaches to the north and south. Cairns is one of the great black-marlin fishing locations and offers easy access to the Great Barrier Reef for anglers, snorkelling enthusiasts, scuba divers and visitors wishing to see the coral from glass-bottomed boats. **In town:** National Trust-classified Regional Gallery, cnr Shields and Abbott sts. Cairns Museum, cnr Lake and Shields sts, displays of Aboriginal, gold-rush, timber and sugar-cane history. The McLeod Street Pioneer Cemetery honours local pioneers. Game-fishing boats moor at Marlin Marina, Marlin Jetty and Trinity Wharf, end of Spence St. The Reef Hotel Casino complex, Wharf St. Wetland areas including the Esplanade; opportunities for birdwatching. Flecker Botanic Gardens, Collins Ave, features plants used by Aborigines, exotic trees and shrubs, and 200 varieties of palm. Walking track links gardens to Centenary Lakes Parkland. Tanks Centre, near Botanic Gardens, multi-purpose centre in revamped WW II oil storage tanks.

Caloundra on the Sunshine Coast

Jack Barnes Bicentennial Mangrove Boardwalk, Airport Ave. Rainforest walk to top of Mt Whitfield, in park opposite airport. Royal Flying Doctor Service Visitor Centre, Junction St, Edge Hill. Rusty's Bazaar, Grafton and Sheridan sts: markets with local craft, homemade produce, plants, and new and secondhand goods (Fri. p.m., Sat. and Sun. a.m.). Bulk sugar terminal, Cook St, Portsmith, south of city centre, has guided tours during crushing season (June–Dec.). Markets at the Pier, Sat. and Sun. July: Agricultural Show. Oct.: The Reef Festival. **In the area:** Skyrail Rainforest Cableway, spectacular gondola ride with boardwalk stops through rainforest to Kuranda; departs from Caravonica Lakes Station, Smithfield, 11 km NE (return via Scenic Railway, or vice versa). Award-winning Tjapukai Aboriginal Cultural Park, adjacent to Caravonica Lakes Station, performances daily. Cairns beaches, 26 km of spectacular coastline, extend from Machans Beach (10 km N) to Ellis Beach. Holloways Beach, 11 km N, popular seaside spot. Australian Woolshed at Smithfield, 13 km N: daily ram shows, spinning, shearing, working sheepdog demonstrations. Wild World and Outback Opal Mine, 22 km NW. Freshwater Connection historical complex, 34 km NW, departure point for 100-year-old Kuranda Scenic Railway trip through Barron Gorge to rainforest village of Kuranda. Bushwalking, hiking, white-water rafting and camping in delightful rural settings of Barron and Freshwater valleys, north and south of Cairns; attractions include the Crystal Cascades, Barron Gorge hydro-electric power station and Copperlode Dam (Lake Morris). Reef and islands can be explored by private charters, daily cruises and by air (seaplane and helicopter). Longer cruises to resort islands and reef on *Coral Princess* and *Kangaroo Explorer*. Access to nearby Green Island, Fitzroy Island and the Frankland Islands on cruise vessels. Cairns also offers easy access to wilderness areas of Atherton Tableland, Daintree, Cape Tribulation, Cape York and Gulf Savannah regions. Safaris (4WD) to Cape York and Gulf Savannah. **Visitor information:** Tourism Tropical North Queensland, 51 The Esplanade; (07) 4051 3588. **See also:** The Far North p. 472; Cape York p. 507.

Caloundra
Pop. 28 329

MAP REF. 516 H6, 520 I13, 525 Q7

This popular holiday spot on the Sunshine Coast is 95 km N of Brisbane, via a turn-off from the Bruce Hwy. The main beaches are Kings, Shelly, Moffat, Dicky, Golden and Bulcock. The main shipping channel to Brisbane is just offshore. Pumicestone Channel (State Marine Park) to the south, between Bribie Island and the mainland, has sheltered waters for fishing, boating, water-skiing and sailboarding. **In town:** Queensland Air Museum at airport, Pathfinder Dr. Scenic flights available from airport. Market at Caloundra Hospital grounds, West Tce, each Sun. May: Glass House Mountains Discovery Day (family entertainment). June: William Landsborough Day (festival to commemorate explorer). Aug.: Art and Craft Show. **In the area:** Scenic drives: north along coastal strip; west to Blackall

The Far North

As you sit in a lush, tropical garden through dusk and into evening, and dine on king prawns and Queensland mud crabs, you will find it hard to believe you are at 'the end of the line' – **Port Douglas** is the most northerly of the easily accessible coastal towns of Queensland. Such a Port Douglas scene typifies the beauty of the Far North; a forest-covered hill looms over the small town and ocean beach.

Cairns, 1832 kilometres from Brisbane, is the stepping-stone to a variety of sightseeing excursions. Nestling beside Trinity Bay, this scenic city is an ideal base for visiting the surrounding tourist attractions. From Cairns you can relax on a launch cruise that takes you to see the wonders of the Great Barrier Reef or explore uninhabited islands. Visitors can enjoy snorkelling or other water sports, while anglers flock to Cairns from September to December to catch the big black marlin. Aerial tours from Cairns take you over the Great Plateau, with its lush tablelands and spectacular waterfalls.

Millaa Millaa Falls, on the Atherton Tableland

The pleasant climate in winter and early spring is one of the main attractions of this city. Delicate ferns, tropical shrubs and fragrant flowers thrive in the Flecker Botanic Gardens, where a walking track joins the Centenary Lakes Parkland, created in 1976 to mark the city's hundredth anniversary. Two lakes, one saltwater and the other freshwater, provide a haven for wildlife among native trees and shrubs. There are dozens of places around Cairns, all within easy driving distance on good roads, that will claim the traveller's attention. Port Douglas is only one of them. The 73-kilometre journey north from Cairns passes through a magnificent stretch of coastal scenery as the Cook Highway winds past white coral beaches, through tropical forest and past the islands that dot the blue northern waters.

Just north of Port Douglas is the sugar town of **Mossman**. From July to October, sugarcane farmers once created raging fires to prepare the cane for harvesting with machetes. Nowadays, however, cane is more often harvested green and cane-cutting has become automated. Sugar-growing is a major industry of the north, and the waving fields of cane wind through the mountains for hundreds of kilometres down the lush coastal plain.

Near Mossman is one of those perfect places that seem so plentiful in the north, the Mossman River Gorge. A short walk under the dense green canopy of the rainforest leads to the boulder-strewn river, which rushes in a series of cascades through the jungle-sided gorge.

There are many such places, particularly on the edge of the Atherton Tableland, where the mountains have thrown up fascinating geological oddities and where waterfalls spill. Near **Yungaburra** there are two volcanic lakes, Barrine and Eacham, where walking tracks through the rainforest give beautiful water views and a chance to see the abundant wildlife, including parrots, waterfowl, turtles, platypuses, goannas and many marsupials. On the Yungaburra–Malanda Road is the amazing and much-photographed Curtain Fig Tree, which has resulted from a strangling fig taking over its host tree and throwing down showers of roots to support its massive structure. At Malanda Falls, just west of Malanda township, water cascades over a fern-swathed precipice into a delightful swimming pool.

South-west of Malanda is **Mount Hypipamee National Park**, where visitors can walk along Dinner Creek to the falls and up to a funnel of sheer granite walls that fall away into dark and forbidding water. There are dozens of other waterfalls in this area. Near **Millaa Millaa** is The Waterfalls Circuit, where the Millaa Millaa, Zillie, Mungalli and Elinjaa waterfalls are sited amid a magnificent panorama of rainforest mountains and plains.

There are four main highways linking the tablelands with the coast; all are magnificent scenic routes. However, the most novel and popular way of getting up to the tableland is by the scenic railway to **Kuranda**, built to serve the Herberton tin mine in the 1890s. The track climbs 300 metres in 20 kilometres to traverse the Barron Gorge. The Skyrail Rainforest Cableway glides over the rainforest canopy between Smithfield, near Cairns, and Kuranda.

The Atherton and Evelyn tablelands are areas of volcanic land at altitudes between 600 and 1000 metres, mild in climate and supporting dairying and diverse crops, including maize and tea-tree (for oil). Gradually the tablelands change to dry, rough country, where tin, copper, lead and zinc were once mined. Beyond the main settlement of **Atherton** is the mining town of Herberton, with its Historical Village, museum called the Tin Pannikin and house from the boom days of the late 19th century. Ravenshoe, on the Kennedy Highway, is noted for its gemstones and fine timbers grown and milled in the area; further west is Mount Garnet, an old mining town where tourists can pan the tailings.

For further information on the Far North, contact Tourism Tropical North Queensland, 51 The Esplanade, Cairns; (07) 4051 3588. For more information on the Atherton Tableland, contact the Atherton Tableland Promotion Bureau, Herberton Rd, Atherton; (07) 4091 4222. Web site www.tnq.org.au **See also:** National Parks p. 460 and individual entries in A–Z town listing for details on parks and towns in bold type. **Map references:** 523, 529.

Range; south-west to Glass House Mountains National Park. Wreck of SS *Dicky* (1893), Dicky Beach, 3 km N. Currimundi Lake Conservation Park, 4 km N. Pt Cartwright Lookout, 15 km N. Opals Down Under and House of Herbs, Bruce Hwy, 15 km NW. Aussie World incorporating Ettamogah Pub, Bruce Hwy, 16 km NW. **Visitor information:** 7 Caloundra Rd; (07) 5491 0202. Web site www.caloundra.qld.gov.au **See also:** Day Tours from Brisbane p. 453; The Sunshine Coast p. 493.

Camooweal   Pop. 258

MAP REF. 437 R11, 532 B2

On the Barkly Hwy, 188 km NW of Mount Isa, Camooweal is the last Qld town before crossing the NT border, 13 km W. **In town:** On Barkly Hwy: Shire Hall (1922–23), The Drovers Store, Barkly Tableland Heritage Centre, and Freckleton's Store (1901); all National Trust-classified. Ellen Finlay Park, Morrison St, has shady trees ideal for picnics. **In the area:** Cemetery, 1 km E on hwy, headstones tell local history. Caves in Camooweal Caves National Park, 25 km S; challenge to experienced potholers. **Visitor information:** Post Office, Barkly Hwy; (07) 4748 2110.

Cardwell   Pop. 1421

MAP REF. 529 N10

From Cardwell, 52 km N of Ingham, there are beautiful views of Rockingham Bay and the Great Barrier Reef islands in the region. Local fishing and snorkelling is excellent. The Channel is a sheltered area for houseboats. **In town:** Museum (part of library), Victoria St. At Port Hinchinbrook, 1 km S on Bruce Hwy: departure point for cruises to nearby islands including Hinchinbrook Island (4-day walk available); houseboat and yacht hire, bookings at Visitor information. National Parks Office, Victoria St, information about local national parks and Great Barrier Reef Marine Park. Market on Cardwell Esplanade, 1st Sat. each month. June: Coral Sea Memorial. **In the area:** Scenic drives in Cardwell Forest (spectacular coastal scenery), and Kirrama Range, 9–10 km N, on Kennedy Rd. Murray Falls in State Forest Park, 42 km NW; also camping and picnic areas. Dalrymple Gap walking track (10 km), 15 km S, between Damper Creek Bridge on Bruce Hwy and Abergowrie State Forest; permission required from Cardwell or Ingham Forestry offices. Blencoe Falls, 71 km E.

Architecture of the gold boom, Charters Towers

Visitor information: Hinchinbrook Island Ferries, 131 Bruce Hwy; (07) 4066 8270. Web site www.gspeak.com.au/cardwell

Charleville   Pop. 3327

MAP REF. 524 B6

Charleville marks the terminus of the Westlander rail service and is at the centre of a rich sheep and cattle district. Charleville's river, the Warrego, was explored by Edmund Kennedy in 1847, and in 1862 William Landsborough camped nearby when searching for Burke and Wills. By the late 1890s Charleville was a frontier town with its own brewery, 10 hotels and 500 registered bullock teams. Cobb & Co. had a coach-building factory here in 1893. The last coach on Australian roads ran to Surat in 1923. A monument 19 km NW of the town marks the spot where Ross and Keith Smith landed with engine trouble on the first London–Sydney flight in 1919. Amy Johnson also landed here in 1920. Qantas started flights from Charleville in 1922. The town is the heart of Mulga Country; the mulga provide welcome shade and in times of drought are cut down for sheep fodder. **In town:** Self-guide heritage walk (brochures available), and guided tours (available most days, check with information centre). In Alfred St: Historic House Museum in restored Qld National Bank building (1880), features 5-m-long

'vortex gun' used in unsuccessful rain-making experiments in 1902; Cobb & Co. coach and craft shop. Outback Queensland Skywatch at Meteorological Bureau at airport, Sturt St, features galactic theatre and telescope garden; guided 'Tour of the Night Sky' in the evenings. National Parks and Wildlife Service Centre, Park St: captive breeding programme, rare yellow-footed rock wallabies, bilbies; open Mon.–Fri; bilby tours some nights (check times). Royal Flying Doctor Service Base and Visitors Centre, Old Cunnamulla Rd. Market, Historic House Museum, 1st Sun. each month. May: Show. July: Great Matilda Camel Races (and festival). **In the area:** Scenic and nature lovers' self-guide drives, brochures available. **Visitor information:** Graeme Andrews Parkland, Mitchell Hwy; (07) 4654 3057.

Charters Towers   Pop. 8893

MAP REF. 526 E2

Charters Towers is situated in the Burdekin basin, 132 km SW of Townsville, on both the Flinders Hwy and the rail line to Mount Isa. At the height of the gold-rush, it was Queensland's second largest city. With a population of 30 000 from all corners of the globe, it was commonly referred to as 'The World'. On 25 December 1871 an Aboriginal boy, Jupiter, made the first gold strike while

looking for horses that had bolted. He brought some gold-laden quartz back to his employer, Hugh Mosman, who rode to Ravenswood to register the claim, and the gold rush was on. Between 1872 and 1916, Charters Towers produced ore worth 25 million pounds. Today, mining and cattle-raising are the main industries in the area; several large goldmines are operating, the result of another gold boom. The town is also an important centre for education. **In town:** Much classic Australian architecture with verandahs and lacework remains, particularly facades in Mosman and Gill sts. In Mosman St: Zara Clark Museum, for local history; Stock Exchange (1887), now home to National Trust and Mining Museum; Bank of Commerce (1891) now restored as New World Theatre complex (tours daily). Guided town walks, daily from information centre. Historic homes: Ay-Ot-Lookout (1886), Hodgkinson St; Pfeiffer House (1880), Paull St. Venus Gold Battery, Millchester Rd, guided tours. Rotary Lookout, Fraser St. Showgrounds Markets, cnr Mary and Show sts, 2nd Sun. each month. National Trust Markets, Stock Exchange, 1st and 3rd Sun. each month. Jan.: Goldfield Ashes Cricket Carnival. Easter: Rodeo. Apr.–May: Towers Bonza Bash (festival including music and bush poets). May: Country Music Festival. June: Annual Vintage Car Restorers' Swap Meet. **In the area:** Guided bus tours (daily, check times). Towers Hill, 1.5 km W along Mosman St, has old mine shafts and ammunition bunkers from WW II. Mt Leyshon goldmine, 30 km S, tours Wed. Great Basalt Wall, part of the Great Basalt Wall National Park, 80 km NW, 4-million year-old solidified lava wall extending 100 km. **Visitor information:** Mosman St; (07) 4752 0314. **See also:** The Far North p. 472.

Childers

Pop. 1483

MAP REF. 525 O3

Childers is a picturesque sugar town, 53 km S of Bundaberg. Much of it was destroyed by fire in 1902; today it is a National Trust town. **In town:** Historic Childers, self-guide town walk taking in historic buildings, including Old Butcher's Shop (1896), North St, and Grand and Federal hotels, Churchill St. Also in Churchill St: Gaydon's Building (1894), now Pharmaceutical Museum, art gallery and tourist centre. Royal Hotel, Randall St. Historic Complex, Taylor St, includes school, cottage and locomotive. May:

Agricultural Show. July: Multicultural Food and Wine Festival. **In the area:** Burrum Coast National Park, 40 km E. Isis Central Sugar Mill, Cordalba, 10 km N; tours July–Nov. **Visitor information:** Pharmaceutical Museum, Churchill St; (07) 4126 1994.

Chillagoe

Pop. 250

MAP REF. 529 K7

Chillagoe, once a thriving town where copper, silver, lead, gold and wolfram were mined, is now a small outback town where the recent development of tourism, international-standard marble mines and the Red Dome goldmine have returned the town to some of its former glory. **In town:** Guided historical walking tours of town and Smelters Reserve. Local museum, Hill St: history of town, includes display of relics from old mining days. May: Races, Concert and Rodeo. **In the area:** 4WD self-guide adventure trek, mud maps and clues provided. Full- and half-day tag-along tours: Aboriginal culture, history, geology, marble quarries. Rugged limestone outcrops and magnificent caves in Chillagoe–Mungana Caves National Park, 7 km S: cave system, originally an ancient coral reef, is studied by scientists world-wide; guided tours. At Mungana, 16 km W, Aboriginal rock paintings and historic cemetery. **Visitor information:** Hill St; (07) 4094 7109. Web site www.athertontableland.com

Chinchilla

Pop. 3247

MAP REF. 525 K7

Chinchilla is a prosperous town in the western Darling Downs, 295 km NW of Brisbane on the Warrego Hwy. Ludwig Leichhardt named the area in 1844 after *jinchilla*, the local Aboriginal name for cypress pines. Grain-growing is the traditional industry, as well as cattle, sheep, pigs, timber and, more recently, grapes, cotton and watermelons. **In town:** Historical Museum, Villiers St, features working steam engines, sawmill and slab cottage (1880s). Newman's Collection of Petrified Wood, Boyd St. Market, Warrego Hwy, Easter Saturday. Feb.: Melon Festival (odd-numbered years). May: Rotary May Day Carnival. July: Polocrosse Carnival. Oct.: Museum Heritage Day. **In the area:** Fishing on Charley's Creek and Condamine River. Guided tours of surrounding area. Cactoblastis Memorial Hall, at Boonarga, 8 km E, dedicated to the insect introduced to eradicate the prickly

pear cactus. Fossicking for petrified wood, treefern and agate at 3 district properties. **Visitor information:** Warrego Hwy; (07) 4668 9564.

Clermont

Pop. 2388

MAP REF. 526 H9

Clermont is the centre of a fertile region which breeds cattle and sheep, and grows wheat, sorghum, cotton, safflower and sunflower as well as hardwood timber. The township, 274 km SW of Mackay, was established over 130 years ago after the discovery of gold. It takes its name from Clermont in France. At first the settlement was at Hoods Lagoon, but was moved to the present site on higher ground after a major flood in 1916 in which 60 people died. Remnants of the gold rushes can still be seen. **In town:** Scenic and historical drive, tape from information centre. Hoods Lagoon, Lime St on northern edge of town: Mary MacKillop Grotto; boardwalk and walking track; birdlife. Also on northern outskirts, cemetery with historic mass grave. Aug.: Gold Festival; Rodeo. **In the area:** Fossicking for gold available. Clermont and District Historical Museum, 4 km NW on road to Charters Towers. Blair Athol open-cut mine, 23 km NW, largest seam of steaming coal in the world; mine tours (Tues. and Fri.); wildlife sanctuary at mine. Copperfield Store museum, 7 km S, in original shop from coppermining era. Copperfield Chimney, 8 km SW, chimney from coppermining days. Copperfield Cemetery, 10 km SW, 19th-century graves of copper miners; monument to those who died in the district. Theresa Creek Dam, 17 km SW: water-skiing and fishing, picnic areas and bushwalks nearby. **Visitor information:** Capella St; (07) 4983 1406.

Clifton

Pop. 833

MAP REF. 525 N10

Located between Toowoomba and Warwick, Clifton is the centre of a rich grain-growing and dairying area. **In town:** Historic buildings: Club Hotel (1889), King St; Church of St James and St John (1890s), cnr Tooth St and Meara Pl. Museum in old butter factory, King St: early implements and farm life; open by appt. Alister Clark Rose Garden, Edward St, largest Qld collection of these roses. Oct.: Rose and Iris Show. **In the area:** Peanut factory, 5 km E, tours. Arthur Hoey Davis (Steele Rudd), author of *On Our Selection*, grew up at Greenmount East, 25 km N. At Nobby,

8 km N: burial site of Sister Kenny, renowned for her unorthodox method of treating poliomyelitis; Sister Kenny Memorial and Museum. Rudd's Pub (1893), where Arthur Hoey Davis used to write, has museum in dining room. Tourist drive through 'Steele Rudd country'. At Leyburn, 30 km W, Historic Race Car Sprints in Aug. **Visitor information:** Shire Offices, King St; (07) 4697 4222. Web site www.clifton.qld.gov.au

Cloncurry Pop. 2459

MAP REF. 532 G4

Cloncurry is an important mining town, 118 km E of Mount Isa in the Gulf Savannah region, with an interesting history and on the brink of another mining boom. In 1861 John McKinlay of Adelaide, leading an expedition to search for Burke and Wills, reported traces of copper in the area. Six years later, pioneer pastoralist Ernest Henry discovered the first copper lodes. A rail link to Townsville was built in 1908. During WW I, Cloncurry was the centre of a copper boom and in 1916 it was the largest source of copper in Australia, with 4 smelters operating. Copper prices slumped post-war and a burgeoning pastoral industry took its place. In 1920 a new Qantas air service linked Cloncurry to Winton. In 1928 the town became the first base for the famous Royal Flying Doctor Service (RFDS). In 1979 a rare type of pure 22-carat gold, resembling crystallised straw, was discovered and is now used for making jewellery. The region is mainly cattle country, and Cloncurry is a major railhead for transporting stock. **In town:** John Flynn Place, Daintree St, includes Fred McKay Art Gallery and RFDS Museum, cultural centre, outdoor theatre and Cloncurry Gardens. Cloncurry–Mary Kathleen Memorial Park, McIlwraith St, features 4 buildings from abandoned uranium mining town of Mary Kathleen, displaying historic items including Robert O'Hara Burke's water bottle, as well as a comprehensive rock, mineral and gem collection. Cloister of Plaques (RFDS memorial), Uhr St. In Schaeffe St: Post Office (1885); Courthouse (1898). Afghan Cemetery, Henry St. Chinese Cemetery, Flinders Hwy. In Sir Hudson Fyshe Dr.: old Qantas hangar at aerodrome; cattleholding yards. Market, at Florence Park, Scarr St, 1st Sat. each month. June: Agricultural Show. July: Camp Draft (Stockmen's Challenge, sheepdog trials, country music); Country Music and Bush Poets Festival. Aug.: Merry

Chinese shrine, Cooktown

Muster Rodeo. **In the area:** Rotary Lookout, 2 km W near Normanton Rd turn-off, Mt Isa Hwy. Burke and Wills cairn near Corella River, 43 km W. Great Australia Copper Mine, 2 km S (tours). Kuridala ghost town, 88 km S; amethyst fossicking a further 8 km, signposted. Ernest Henry Copper and Gold Mine, 29 km NE (tours, enquire at information centre). Ruins of Mount Cuthbert, gold-mining town, 10 km from Kajabbi (77 km NW). **Visitor information:** Cloncurry–Mary Kathleen Memorial Park, McIlwraith St; (07) 4742 1361. **See also:** Gulf Savannah p. 494.

Cooktown Pop. 1411

MAP REF. 529 L3

Captain James Cook beached the *Endeavour* here in 1770 for repairs after running aground on the Great Barrier Reef. Gold was discovered at Palmer River in 1873 and by 1877 Cooktown was a booming, brawling gold-rush port with 37 hotels and a transient population of some 18 000 a year, including 6000 Chinese. Cooktown today has 3 hotels and the town's main industry is tourism. Located 342 km NW of Cairns, it is the departure point for Cape York Peninsula. The district is good agriculturally and the town is also supported by prawning and fishing. **In town:** Cooktown Wharf, dates from 1880s, excellent fishing location. Historic cemetery, Boundary Rd, with grave of tutor, early immigrant and heroine Mary Watson; nearby, Chinese Shrine to the many who died on the goldfields. Grassy Hill, Hope St, offers views across the reef,

township and hinterland. James Cook Historical Museum, Helen St, has collection tracing town's two centuries of history, and an anchor from the *Endeavour*. Cooktown Museum, cnr Helen and Walker sts, features maritime history of area; also shell collection. Cooktown Botanic Gardens, Walker St. Markets at Endeavour Lions Park, every 2nd Sat. June: Cooktown Endeavour Festival (long weekend), with re-enactment of Cook's landing. July: Laura–Cape York Aboriginal Dance Festival (odd-numbered years). **In the area:** Snorkelling and diving tours to Outer Reef; fishing charters. Walking trails to Cherry Tree Bay and Finch Bay start at Botanic Gardens; brochures on other local walks available. Bicentennial National Trail (5000 km) for walkers and horse-riders, runs from Cooktown to Healesville in Vic. Endeavour River National Park, just north of town. Black Mountain, 28 km S. Spectacular white silica Elim Beach, 65 km N; Coloured Sands 400 m along beach (Aboriginal Land, permit required), check road conditions. Lakefield National Park, 146 km NW; rivers, lagoons and swamps provide habitat for a great variety of wildlife and are crucial areas for crocodile conservation. Offshore, Lizard Island, 90 km NE, offers resort, national park and secluded beaches; access by seaplane. Beautiful sandstone escarpments at Split Rock and Gu Gu Yalangi rock-art site, 12 km S of Laura (134 km W of Cooktown), perhaps the largest Aboriginal art site in Australia; guided tours of hundreds of cave paintings. **Visitor information:** Cooktown Tourism, Charlotte St; (07) 4069 6100.

Saltwater crocodile, a resident of the Daintree River

Coolangatta   Pop. 6618

MAP REF. 517 H13, 519 I11, 525 Q11
Coolangatta is the most southerly of Qld's coastal towns, with its twin town of Tweed Heads across the border in NSW. **In town:** June: Wintersun Festival. **In the area:** Scenic drive, brochure available. Coolangatta Airport, Bilinga, services Gold Coast for domestic flights, charters, joy flights and tandem skydiving. Captain Cook Memorial Lighthouse, North Head. Tom Beaston Outlook (Razorback Lookout), behind Tweed Heads, for excellent views. **Visitor information:** Shop 14B, Coolangatta Pl., cnr Griffith and Warner sts; (07) 5536 7765. **See also:** The Gold Coast p. 500.

Crows Nest   Pop. 1214

MAP REF. 525 N8
This small town, 44 km N of Toowoomba, acquired its name from Jimmy Crow, an Aborigine from the Kabi-Kabi community who once made his home in a hollow tree near what is now the police station. A memorial in Centenary Park commemorates this. **In town:** John French VC Memorial Library, William St. In Thallon St: Carbethon Folk Museum and Pioneer Village; Salts Antiques, open weekends. Oct.: Crows Nest Day (children's worm races, fun run, painting competitions). **In the area:** Walking and bike tracks to Toowoomba, map available. Crows Nest National Park, 6 km E (look for sign to Valley of Diamonds): walking tracks to falls, picnic and camping facilities. Ravensbourne National Park, 25 km SE, has red cedars and picnic areas. **Visitor**

information: Toowoomba Information Centre, cnr James and Kitchener sts, Toowoomba; (07) 4639 3797.

Croydon   Pop. 223

MAP REF. 528 F10
This Gulf town, 559 km SW of Cairns, is the eastern terminus for the Gulflander train service, which leaves each Thurs. for Normanton. In town, many original buildings (1887–97), classified by National Trust and Australian Heritage Commission, have been restored to their former splendour. **In town:** In Samwell St: Old Police Precinct includes gaol (housing Tourist and Family History Information Centre), Hospital Museum; courthouse with original furniture and historical documents; Town Hall with murals; Outdoor Museum, featuring a display of mining machinery from the age of steam; gas lamps on footpath. Hospital Ward (now a meeting place), Brown St. General Store and Museum, Sircom St. Self-guide and guided town walks. June: Rodeo. **In the area:** Working Mine Museum including battery stamper, 1 km N. Old cemetery, 1 km W, has historic graves. Lake Belmore, 5 km N, one of many sites for birdwatching. **Visitor information:** Samwell St; (07) 4745 6125 (Apr.–Sept.), and Shire Offices, Samwell St: (07) 4745 6185. **See also:** Gulf Savannah p. 494.

Cunnamulla   Pop. 1461

MAP REF. 524 A10, 535 R10
A western sheep town known for its friendliness and hospitality, Cunnamulla is near the Warrego River, 118 km N of

the NSW border. It is the biggest wool-loading station on the Qld railway network, with 2 million sheep in the area, plus beef cattle. Explorers Sir Thomas Mitchell and Edmund Kennedy were the first European visitors in 1846 and 1847 respectively, and by 1879 it had become a town with regular Cobb & Co. services. In 1880 disorganised villain Joseph Wells held up the local bank but could not find his horse to escape. Locals bailed him up in a tree (known as 'The Robber's Tree', now a landmark in Stockyard St), demanding justice and their money back. **In town:** Bicentennial Museum, John St, has Historical Society display. Yupunyah Tree planted by Princess Anne, cnr Louise and Stockyard sts. Lost Generation Arts and Crafts, Stockyard St, has local Aboriginal art. Centenary Park, Jane St, has picnic/barbecue facilities. Outback Botanic Gardens and Herbarium (in early stages of development), on Matilda Hwy on eastern outskirts of town. Apr.: Races. Sept.: Opal Festival. **In the area:** Wildflowers in spring; varied wetland birdlife, particularly black swans, brolgas, pelicans and eagles. At Noorama, 110 km SE, race meetings (horseracing) each Apr. **Visitor information:** Centenary Park; (07) 4655 2481.

Currumbin   Pop. 2696

MAP REF. 517 H12, 519 G10, 525 Q10
Situated at the mouth of the Currumbin Creek, this part of the Gold Coast has many attractions for visitors. **In town:** Currumbin Wildlife Sanctuary, 20-ha reserve owned by National Trust: free-ranging animals in open areas; lorikeet feeding (twice daily); walk-through rainforest aviary with pools and waterfalls; and rides through sanctuary on miniature railway. Opposite, World of Bees: live displays; walk with bees; honey-making; products for sale. **In the area:** Scenic drive, brochure available. David Fleay Wildlife Park (Dept of Environment), 8 km NW on West Burleigh Rd: birds and animals in natural surroundings; croc-feeding; Aboriginal culture. Olson's Bird Gardens, 9 km SW in Currumbin Valley, has large landscaped aviaries in subtropical setting. Section of Springbrook National Park, 22 km SW at end of Currumbin Creek Rd, scenic rainforest area ideal for bushwalking and picnicking. **Visitor information:** Shop 14B, Coolangatta Pl, cnr Griffith and Warner sts, Coolangatta; (07) 5536 7765. **See also:** The Gold Coast p. 500.

Daintree
Pop. 200

MAP REF. 523 A1, 529 M5

This unspoilt township, 119 km NW of Cairns, lies in the heart of the Daintree River catchment basin surrounded by the McDowall Ranges. The area has abundant native plant life, birds and tropical butterflies. Australia's prehistoric reptile, the saltwater crocodile, can be seen in the mangrove-lined creeks and tributaries of the Daintree River. **In town:** Daintree Timber Museum. Local art and craft. River cruises; vehicular ferry, one of last cable ferries in Australia. **In the area:** Wonga-Belle Orchid Gardens, 17 km SE, 3.5 ha of lush gardens. Daintree Rainforest Environmental Centre, 11 km N via ferry, has boardwalk through rainforest. Cape Tribulation, 35 km NE, where rainforest meets reef: features crystal-clear creeks; forests festooned with creepers and vines; palm trees; orchids; butterflies; cassowaries; Dubuji Boardwalk (1.2 km); Kulki Boardwalk and Lookout. Bloomfield Falls, 85 km N, via Cape Tribulation. **Visitor information:** Daintree Tourism Association; (07) 4099 4588 or Port Douglas and Cooktown Tourist Information Centre, 23 Macrossan St, Port Douglas; (07) 4099 5599.

Dalby
Pop. 9517

MAP REF. 525 M8

Dalby, 83 km NW of Toowoomba on the Darling Downs, is a pleasant, well-planned country town at the crossroads of the Warrego, Bunya and Moonie hwys. It is the centre of Australia's richest grain- and cotton-growing area. Cattle, pigs, sheep and coal add wealth to the district. **In town:** Pioneer Park Museum, Black St: historic buildings; displays of household and agricultural items; craft shop. Obelisk at crossing in Edward St marks spot where explorer Henry Dennis camped in 1841. Memorial cairn in Myall Creek picnic area, Marble St, pays homage to the cactoblastis; the Argentinian caterpillar that eradicated the dreaded prickly pear cactus in the 1920s. Cultural and Administration Centre, Drayton St, includes theatre, cinema, art gallery and restaurant. Self-guide heritage walk and self-guide drive, brochures available. Walkway along banks of Myall Creek; varied birdlife. Mar.: Cotton Week. May: Pioneer Park Field Day Weekend. **In the area:** Lake Broadwater Conservation Park, 29 km SW: boating and water-skiing on lake when full; 3-km walk; tower for birdwatching; picnic/barbecue facilities; camping. Historic Jimbour House, 29 km N, grounds open daily except in wet weather. Rimfire Vineyards and Winery, 47 km NE, tastings daily. Bunya Mountains National Park, 60 km NE, walking tracks and waterfalls. **Visitor information:** Thomas Jack Park, cnr Drayton and Condamine sts; (07) 4662 1066. **See also:** Darling Downs p. 504.

Emerald
Pop. 9345

MAP REF. 526 I11

An attractive town 270 km W of Rockhampton at the junction of the Capricorn and Gregory hwys, Emerald is the hub of the Central Highlands. The largest sapphire fields in the Southern Hemisphere are nearby. As well as the cattle industry, grain, oilseeds and soybeans, cotton and citrus fruit are important. **In town:** Shady Moreton Bay fig trees line Clermont and Egerton sts. National Trust-classified railway station (1901), Clermont St. Pioneer Cottage and Museum, Harris St. Pastoral College, Capricorn Hwy. Easter: Sunflower Festival. June: Wheelbarrow Derby (odd-numbered years). Aug.: Gemfest. Sept.: Music Spectacular. **In the area:** Day tours of local cattle stations, and farm stays. Fossicking for gems, licence required. At Rubyvale, 60 km NW: Miner's Heritage Walk-in Mine, tours of underground sapphire mine and gem-cutting displays; Bobby Dazzler Walk-in Mine, also has museum and shop; various gem outlets; 4WD tours of Tomahawk Creek gemfields and other local gemfields. At Capella, 51 km NW: Capella Pioneer Village, includes Peak Downs homestead (1869), first settlement in area; Capella Pioneer Village Arts and Crafts Fair in Apr. Lake Maraboon/Fairbairn Dam, 19 km S, for fishing and water sports. At Springsure, 66 km S: Aboriginal Yumba–Brin Crypt in Cemetery Reserve; historic schoolhouse, storehouse and slab homestead at Old Rainworth Fort. **Visitor information:** Clermont St; (07) 4982 4142. **See also:** Capricorn Region p. 497.

Esk
Pop. 953

MAP REF. 516 B10, 525 O8

Esk, in the Upper Brisbane Valley, is 99 km NW of Brisbane. The valley is renowned for its beautiful lakes and dams. **In town:** Numerous antique and local craft shops. Market, Old Hay Barn, Ipswich St, each Sat. July: Picnic Races. **In the area:** Lakes and dams: Lake Somerset (25 km NE); Lake Wivenhoe (25 km E), source of Brisbane's main water supply; Atkinson Dam (30 km S); all popular swimming, fishing and boating spots. Lake Wivenhoe is State's main centre for championship rowing. At Coominya, 22 km SE: historic Bellevue homestead; Watermelon Festival in Jan. Boss camel races in Sept. Clydesdale Bush Carnival in Oct., 44 km SE near Lowood. Further north, some of the finest grazing country in Brisbane Valley; this is deer country, where progeny of a small herd presented to the State by Queen Victoria in 1873 still roam. Caboonbah homestead (1890), 19 km NE, headquarters of Brisbane Valley Historical Society; closed Thurs. **Visitor information:** Shire Offices, 2 Redbank St; (07) 5424 1200.

Eulo
Pop. 42

MAP REF. 535 Q11

Once the centre for opal mining in the area, Eulo is on the banks of the Paroo River, 68 km W of Cunnamulla. **In town:** In Leo St: Eulo Queen Hotel, owes its name to Isobel Robinson (nee Richardson) who ran the hotel and virtually reigned over the opal fields at turn of century; WW II air-raid shelter, in grounds of General Store. Eulo Date Farm, western outskirts of town (open Aug.–Sept.). Destructo Cockroach Monument, commemorates death of a champion racing cockroach. Sept.: World Lizard Racing Championships. **In the area:** At Yowah, 87 km NW: visitors' fossicking area; tours of Fossickers' Paradise open-cut mine; spectacular panoramas from The Bluff; Craft Day in June; Opal Festival in July (includes international opal jewellery competition). Mud Springs, 7 km W, natural pressure valve to artesian basin, currently inactive. Lake Bindegolly, in Lake Bindegolly National Park, 100 km W, for birdwatching. Thargomindah, 130 km W; inquire at information centre for mud map to Burke and Wills 'Dig' Tree site. Noccundra waterhole on Wilson River, 260 km W, has good fishing. Currawinya National Park, 60 km SW, for birdwatching and fishing. **Visitor information:** Centenary Park, Cunnamulla; (07) 4655 2481.

Gatton
Pop. 5328

MAP REF. 525 O9

First settled in the 1840s, this agricultural town in the Lockyer Valley is midway between Ipswich and Toowoomba, and

Unique geological formations at Undara Volcanic National Park near Georgetown

90 km w of Brisbane via the Warrego Hwy. Small-crop farming and vegetable production are the main industries of the area. **In town:** May: Heavy Horse Field Days. Oct.: Potato Carnival. **In the area:** Agricultural College (University of Queensland), 5 km E, opened 1897. Helidon, 16 km w, noted for its sandstone, used in many Brisbane buildings, and for its spa water. Grantham, 8 km SW, known for fresh fruit and vegetables; many roadside stalls offer local produce. Tourist drive (82-km circuit) through surrounding countryside, includes visits to farms. **Visitor information:** Lake Apex Dr.; (07) 5462 3430. **See also:** Darling Downs p. 504.

Gayndah   Pop. 1781

MAP REF. 525 N4

Gayndah is one of Qld's oldest towns, founded in 1849. It is on the Burnett Hwy near the Burnett River, 147 km w of Maryborough, in a significant citrus-growing area. **In town:** Original school (1863), still in use. Several homesteads in district built around 1890s. Historical Museum, Simon St, includes Ban Ban Springs Homestead and Ideraway Homestead (both 1850s). June: Orange Festival (odd-numbered years). **In the area:** Claude Warton Weir Recreation Area, 3 km w, for fishing and picnics.

Natural springs at Ban Ban Springs, 26 km s, a popular picnic area. **Visitor information:** Historical Museum, Simon St; (07) 4161 2226.

Georgetown   Pop. 298

MAP REF. 528 I10

Georgetown is a small town on the Gulf Developmental Rd to Croydon and Normanton. It was once one of many small goldmining towns on the Etheridge Goldfield. The area is now noted for its gemstones, especially agate and gold nuggets. **In town:** Jan. and Oct.: race meetings (horseracing). June: Rodeo. Oct.: Bushman's Ball. **In the area:** From Forsayth, 40 km s, train trip on Savannahlander to Cairns, departs Friday. Cobbold Gorge, 75 km s: boat tours on river through gorge; camping. Gemfields at Agate Creek, 95 km s, and O'Briens Creek, 129 km NE. Tallaroo hot springs, 55 km E; tours of surrounding property. Undara Volcanic National Park, 129 km E: variety of birdlife; unique lava tubes, access only with guide; nearby Undara Lava Lodge is a good base, with camping/caravanning facilities and accommodation in converted railway carriages. **Visitor information:** Etheridge Shire Offices, St George St; (07) 4062 1233. **See also:** Gulf Savannah p. 494.

Gin Gin   Pop. 958

MAP REF. 525 N2

Some of Qld's oldest cattle properties are in the area around this pastoral town on the Bruce Hwy, 51 km SW of Bundaberg. The district is known as Wild Scotchman Country, after James McPherson, Qld's only authentic bushranger. **In town:** Historical Society Museum Complex, Mulgrave St: The Residence, former police sergeant's house now displaying pioneering memorabilia; 'The Bunyip', old sugarcane locomotive, part of historic railway display. March: Wild Scotchman Festival. June: Mount Perry Mountain Cup (mountain-bike race). **In the area:** Mystery Craters, 27 km NE on the Bundaberg Rd, curious formation of 35 craters, about 25 million years old. Lake Monduran, 24 km NW, held back by Fred Haigh Dam (Qld's second largest), ideal for boating and picnics. Boolboonda Tunnel, 27 km w, longest artificial non-supported tunnel in Southern Hemisphere; now part of scenic tourist drive; brochure available. Goodnight Scrub National Park, 25 km SW, has dense hoop pine forest, bottle trees, historic Kalliwa Hut, good views. **Visitor information:** Bundaberg Regional Tourist Information Centre; (07) 4152 2333, freecall 1800 060 499.

Gladstone   Pop. 26 415

MAP REF. 527 P12

Matthew Flinders discovered Port Curtis, Gladstone's impressive deep-water harbour, in 1802, but it did not develop until the 1960s. As an outlet for central Qld's mineral and agricultural wealth, Gladstone, 546 km NW of Brisbane, is now a prosperous seaboard city; its harbour is one of Australia's busiest. One reason for this growth is the opening up of the plentiful coal supplies in the hinterland. Another reason is that the world's largest single alumina refinery is at Parsons Point, where millions of tonnes of bauxite from Weipa on the Gulf of Carpentaria are processed annually into alumina, the halfway stage of aluminium. A large power station in Gladstone supplies power to the refinery and smelter and feeds into the State's electricity grid. Chemical processing is a new regional industry. Gladstone is close to the southern section of the Great Barrier Reef and Heron Island and is known for its mud crabs and prawns. **In town:** In Goondoon St: historic Kullaroo House (1911); Radar Hill Lookout. Gladstone Regional Art Gallery and Museum, cnr

Goondoon and Bramston sts. Potter's Place, Dawson Hwy, art and craft. In Glenlyon Rd: Tondoon Botanic Gardens, has only native species (tours weekends); next to gardens, Gecko Valley Vineyard (tastings and sales); Reg Tana Park, including Railway Dam. Barney Point Beach and Friend Park, Barney St. Waterfall, end Auckland St, is floodlit at night. Auckland Hill Lookout, Harbour Tce, has views of harbour and islands. Round Hill Lookout, Boles St, West Gladstone. Auckland Inlet offers anchorage alongside James Cook Park; finishing-line for annual Brisbane to Gladstone yacht race, highlight of 10-day Harbour Festival held Easter. Marina, Marina Dr., departure point for daily Barrier Reef dive and fishing trips and harbour cruises. Easter: Harbour Festival (includes finish of Brisbane–Gladstone Yacht Race). **In the area:** Tours of major industries; bookings at information centre. Curtis Island, north of town in Gladstone Harbour, is a family recreation area. Nearby towns of Boyne Island and Tannum Sands are linked by bridge. Boyne Island has beautiful foreshore parks and beaches; Boyne Aluminium Smelter on island has information centre, and guided tours on request. Tannum Sands offers long stretches of sandy beaches with year-round swimming. Various national parks in region, maps available. Spectacular views from Mt Larcom summit, 33 km W. Port Curtis Historical Village, 26 km SW at Calliope River; major art and craft markets on selected Sundays. Lake Awoonga, 30 km S, offers picnic and camping areas, water-based recreation, walking trail and varied wildlife; Catfish Festival each Jan. Many Peaks, historic town, 80 km SE. **Visitor information:** Bryan Jordan Dr.; (07) 4972 9922.

Goondiwindi   Pop. 4374

MAP REF. 116 H2, 525 K11

This country town at the junction of 6 highways is beside the picturesque MacIntyre River, which explorer Allan Cunningham reached in 1827 and which forms the State border. The Aboriginal word *goonawinna* means 'resting place of the birds'. The district's thriving economy is based on cotton, wheat, beef and wool, and a growing manufacturing sector. **In town:** Statue of famous racehorse Gunsynd, the 'Goondiwindi Grey', in Apex Park, MacIntyre St. Customs House Museum, opposite park. Historic Victoria Hotel, Marshall St. Tours of Bulk Grains depot and cotton gin (by appt, in season).

Walking track along riverbank, brochure available. Markets, in Town Park, Marshall St, 2nd Sun. each month. Feb.: Hell of the West Triathlon. Sept.: Rodeo. Oct.: Spring Festival (coincides with flowering of jacarandas and silky oaks). **In the area:** Botanic Gardens of Western Woodlands (25 ha), access from Brennans Rd, 1 km W. **Visitor information:** McLean St; (07) 4671 2653. Web site www.qldsoutherndowns.org.au **See also:** Darling Downs p. 504.

Gordonvale   Pop. 3682

MAP REF. 523 F10, 529 N7

This town is 24 km S of Cairns. **In town:** Mulgrave Sugar Mill, Gordon St, tours June–Nov. **In the area:** Gillies Hwy, with 295 bends, leads west to Atherton. Goldsborough Valley State Forest, 6 km W (15 km off Gillies Hwy), for walking, swimming, canoeing and picnicking. Wooroonooran National Park, 10 km S, spectacular views from summit of Walsh's Pyramid. Orchid Valley Nursery and Gardens, 15 km SW, tropical gardens and coffee shop; tours. **Visitor information:** Babinda Information Centre, cnr Bruce Hwy and Munro St, Babinda; (07) 4067 1008.

Gympie   Pop. 10 813

MAP REF. 525 P6

The city of Gympie started with the 'Great Australian Gold Rush' in 1867, following the discovery of gold by James Nash. The field proved extremely rich, and 4 million ounces had been found by the time the gold petered out in the 1920s. By then dairying and agriculture were well established and Gympie continued to prosper. On the banks of the Mary River and 162 km N of Brisbane via the Bruce Hwy, Gympie is the major provincial city servicing the Cooloola region. It is an attractive city with jacarandas, silky oaks, cassias, poincianas and flame trees. **In town:** Woodworks, Forestry and Timber Museum, Fraser Rd. Self-guide heritage walk. Gold-panning in Deep Creek, Counter St. Market, Gympie South State School, 2nd and 4th Sun. each month. May: Show. June: Race the Rattler (people race the steam train). Aug.: National Country Music Muster. Oct.: Gold Rush Festival. **In the area:** Historical and scenic drives, maps available. Gold Mining Museum, Brisbane Rd, 5 km S; nearby, cottage of Andrew Fisher, first Queenslander to become Prime Minister (1908).

Cooloola Rocks and Minerals, Bruce Hwy, 15 km S. Amamoor State Forest Park, 30 km S, picnics and rainforest walk. Mothar Mountain, 20 km SE, rock pools and excellent views. Imbil Forest Drive through scenic pine-forest plantations south of town. Mary Valley Scenic Way runs south between Gympie and Maleny, via Kenilworth. Mary Valley Heritage Railway operates between Gympie and Imbil. **Visitor information:** Cooloola Region Information Centre, Bruce Hwy, Kybong; (07) 5483 5554. Web site www.cooloola.org.au

Hervey Bay   Pop. 32 054

MAP REF. 525 P3

Hervey (pronounced 'Harvey') Bay is the large area of water between Maryborough and Bundaberg that is protected by Fraser Island. It is also the name of a thriving city on its shore that comprises the pleasant strip of seaside spots along its southern shore, some 34 km NE of Maryborough. An ideal climate makes the area popular, and during the winter months there is an influx of visitors from the south. Hervey Bay is actively promoted as 'Australia's family aquatic playground'. As there is no surf, swimming is safe even for children. Fishing is the main recreation; boats may be hired. **In town:** In Pialba: M. K. Model Railways, Old Maryborough Rd; Nature World Wildlife Park, Maryborough Rd, features koalas, other marsupials, lorikeets, crocodiles and other reptiles. In Scarness: Hervey Bay Historical Society Museum, Zephyr St, recalls pioneer days. In Torquay: Golf 'n' Games, Cypress St, with 18-hole mini-golf and 120-m water-slide. At Urangan: memorial at Dayman Park commemorates landing by Matthew Flinders in 1799 and the Z-Force commandos who trained there on the *Krait* in WW II; 1-km long pier, off The Esplanade, used by anglers; Neptune's Reefworld, Pulgul St, has performing seals; Vic Hislop's Shark Show, The Esplanade. Humpback whales visit Hervey Bay early Aug.–mid-Oct.; viewing cruises available. Sun. markets at Urangan and Nikenbah. Apr.: Gladstone–Hervey Bay Blue Water Classic. May: Yagubi Festival (multicultural festival). Aug.: Whale Festival. **In the area:** Day trips to Fraser Island. Hervey Bay Marine Park, 40 km N. Quiet seaside resorts at Toogoom and Burrum Heads, 15 km NW. Historic Brooklyn House at Howard, 33 km W. **Visitor information:** 10 Bideford St, Torquay; (07) 4124 9609. **See also:** Wildlife-Watching p. 464.

Hughenden
Pop. 1444

MAP REF. 526 A4, 533 O4

The first recorded Europeans to pass this spot on the Flinders River were members of the expedition led by Frederick Walker in 1861. Walker's party was searching for the lost Burke and Wills expedition. Two years later Ernest Henry visited this area to select a cattle station, and Hughenden came into existence. The town is on the Townsville–Mount Isa rail line and the Flinders Hwy, 243 km SW of Charters Towers. The major regional industries are beef cattle and merino wool. **In town:** Historic coolibah tree, Stansfield St East, on east bank of Station Creek: blazed by Walker in 1861, and again by William Landsborough in 1862 when he was also searching for the lost Burke and Wills expedition. Dinosaur Display Centre, Gray St, houses 7-m replica of *Muttaburrasaurus langdoni*. Aug.: Dinosaur Festival (even-numbered years). **In the area:** At Prairie, 44 km E on Flinders Hwy: mini-museum; historical relics at Cobb & Co. Yards. Torrens Creek, 88 km E:

Exchange Hotel, home of 'dinosaur steaks'; WW II airstrip. Porcupine Gorge National Park, 63 km N, features 'mini Grand Canyon'. Gemstone fossicking at Chudleigh Park, 138 km N. **Visitor information:** Gray St; (07) 4741 1021.

Ilfracombe
Pop. 198

MAP REF. 526 A11, 533 P11

This town, 27 km E of Longreach on the Matilda Hwy, was developed in 1891 as a transport nucleus for Wellshot Station, the largest sheep station in the world (in terms of stock numbers) at that time. The first Qld motorised mail service departed from Ilfracombe in 1910. **In town:** Langenbaker House, Mitchell St, an early settler's house. Transport Heritage Museum (several sites along highway) includes: historic Oakhampton Cottage, has local craft display; Folk Museum; Damien Curr's Back to the Bush Show (daily); extensive range of early machinery; historic Wellshot Hotel; Hilton's Bottle Display. **Visitor information:** Shire

Offices, Devon St; (07) 4658 2233. Web site ilfracombe.outbackqld.net.au

Ingham
Pop. 5012

MAP REF. 529 N11

A major sugar and sightseeing town near the waterways of the Hinchinbrook Channel, Ingham is on the Bruce Hwy, 109 km NW of Townsville. The town has a strong Italian and Spanish Basque cultural background. **In town:** Macknade Mill, Halifax Rd, oldest sugar mill still operating on original site. Victoria Sugar Mill, Forrest Beach Rd, largest in Southern Hemisphere; guided tours in crushing season (July–Nov.). Botanic Gardens, Palm Tce. Raintree market, Herbert St, 3rd Sun. each month; Conroy Hall Markets, McIlwraith St, 2nd Sat. each month. May: Australian–Italian Festival. June: Country Music Festival. Oct.: Maraka Festival. **In the area:** Cemetery, 5 km E, has interesting Italian mausoleums. Forrest Beach, 17 km SE, 16 km of sandy beach overlooking Palm Group of Islands; stinger net

Fraser Island

If you like sand, sea, fishing and plenty of peace and quiet, World Heritage-listed Fraser Island is your ideal holiday destination. Fraser is the largest sand island in the world, 123 kilometres long, and the largest island off Australia's east coast. It acts as a breakwater, protecting the coast from **Bundaberg** to well south of **Maryborough**, and forms the eastern shores of **Hervey Bay**. The sandy straits between Fraser Island and the mainland are ideal for sailing and also attract hundreds of anglers each year for the tailor season.

Fraser's remote and abundant surf beaches are particularly attractive to those with 4WD vehicles, but the island is large enough to prevent them becoming intrusive. Apart from its long stretches of beautiful beach, Fraser Island has a unique area of freshwater lakes and tangled rainforests. There are over 40 lakes on the island, all of them above sea level, and the dense forests surrounding them attract a wide range of bird and animal life.

The island is accessible by air from Brisbane or Hervey Bay, or by barge from Hervey Bay, Inskip Point (Rainbow Beach) and Mary River Heads.

Kingfisher Bay Resort and Village is at North White Cliffs, on the western side of the island opposite Mary River Heads. The following

Wreck of the *Maheno*, on Fraser Island

accommodation is on the ocean side of Fraser Island: Happy Valley, Eurong, Dilli Village and Cathedral Beach Camping Park. Korawinga Lodge at Eurong has time-share units. All these holiday centres offer family accommodation. Day tours leave daily from Hervey Bay and Rainbow Beach. Camping and vehicle permits are required. For further information on Fraser Island, contact the Queensland Parks and Wildlife Services Information Centre, Eurong; (07) 4127 9128. **See also:** individual entries in A–Z town listing for details on towns in bold type. **Map reference:** 525 Q3.

swimming enclosures installed in summer. Taylors Beach, 23 km NE, popular family seaside spot. Hinchinbrook and Orpheus resort islands offshore. Lucinda, 27 km NE on banks of Herbert River, excellent base for fishing holidays. Lumholtz National Park, 51 km NW, features 305-m Wallaman Falls, spectacular scenery, walking track, excellent camping, swimming and picnic spots. Broadwater State Forest Park, 45 km W, in the Herbert River Valley; popular camping and picnic area, includes 1.6-km circuit rainforest walk. Mt Fox, extinct volcano, 65 km SW. Jourama Falls in Paluma Range National Park, 25 km S; 1.5-km walk to lookout. Spectacular view from McClellands Lookout, 48 km S off Bruce Hwy. **Visitor information:** Bruce Hwy; (07) 4776 5211. Web site www. acecomp.com.au/hinchinbrook

Innisfail

Pop. 8987

MAP REF. 529 N8

Innisfail is a prosperous, colourful town on the banks of the North and South Johnstone rivers, 88 km SE of Cairns. Sugar has been grown here since the early 1880s and its contribution to the area is celebrated with a Harvest Festival early Oct. Besides growing sugarcane, bananas, pawpaws and other tropical and rare fruit, beef cattle are raised, and the town has a prawn and reef fishing fleet. **In town:** Local history museum, Edith St. Chinese Joss House, Owen St. Cane Cutter Monument, Fitzgerald Espl. Warrina Lakes and Botanical Gardens, Charles St. Historic town walk, brochure available. Several lovely parks with riverside picnic facilities. Market, Anzac Memorial Park, 3rd Sat. each month. July: Agricultural Show. Oct.: Harvest Festival. **In the area:** Flying Fish Point and Ella Bay, 5 km NE, swimming and camping. Johnstone River Crocodile Farm, 8 km NE. Eubenangee Swamp National Park, 29 km NE via Miriwinni, birdwatching. Bramston Beach, palm-fringed shoreline, 39 km NE. Qld's highest peak Mt Bartle Frere (1622 m), 25 km NW in Wooroonooran National Park; track to summit; Josephine Falls at base. Johnstone River Gorge, 18 km W via Palmerston Hwy, has walking tracks to several waterfalls. Crawfords Lookout, 38 km W, off the Palmerston Hwy, spectacular views of Johnstone River. Australian Sugar Museum at Mourilyan, 7 km S. Etty Bay, 15 km S, beach and picnic area. Innisfail is an excellent base for exploration of quieter lagoons and islands (including Dunk) of

Nina Peak on Hinchinbrook Island, near Ingham

Great Barrier Reef. Scenic drives, brochure available. **Visitor information:** Cassowary Coast Development Bureau, Bruce Hwy, Mourilyan; (07) 4063 2000. Web site www.gspeak.com.au/Innisfail

Ipswich

Pop. 66 048

MAP REF. 517 B7, 525 P9

In 1827 a convict settlement was established alongside the Bremer River to quarry limestone and convey it down the river to Brisbane. In 1842 the settlement, called Limestone, opened to free settlers and in 1843 it was renamed Ipswich. As well as being a major industrial centre with railways, coalmining, sawmills and foundries, Ipswich is now known for its cultural and sporting activities. Australia's largest RAAF base is in the suburb of Amberley. **In town:** Numerous heritage buildings, including Uniting Church (1858), Ellenborough St; St Paul's Anglican Church (1859), Brisbane St; St Mary's Catholic Church (1904), Elizabeth St; Claremont (1858), Milford St; Gooloowan (1864), Quarry St; Ginn Cottage, Ginn St; and Ipswich Grammar School (1863), Burnett St. Global Arts Link, cnr Limestone St and D'Arcy Doyle Pl., interactive art gallery and social history museum. Queens Park Nature Centre, Goleby Ave, native flora and fauna. Self-guide historic walk, brochure available. Showground market, Warwick Rd, each Sun. Redbank Woollen Mills markets, each Sat. and Sun. June: Winternationals Drag Racing Championship. July: Ipswich Cup.

Oct.: Jacaranda Festival. **In the area:** North-east: College's Crossing (7 km), Mt Crosby (12 km) and Lake Manchester (22 km) – all popular picnic spots (swimming at College's Crossing only). At Willowbank, 15 km W: Queensland Raceway, Champions Way, hosts V8 Supercar Series. At Rosewood, 20 km W: St Brigid's Church, largest wooden church in South Pacific (tours by appt); steam-train rides, 4 km N of Rosewood, last Sun. each month. Swanbank Power Station, 12 km SE: tours by appt; steam trains run by Qld Pioneer Steam Railway Co-op, 1st Sun. each month, bookings essential. Restored historic homestead Wolston House at Wacol, 16 km E. **Visitor information:** cnr Brisbane St and D'Arcy Doyle Pl.; (07) 3281 0555.

Isisford

Pop. 150

MAP REF. 526 A13, 533 P13, 535 O1

Established in 1877 by hawkers William and James Whitman, Isisford is 116 km S of Longreach. First called Wittown, the town was renamed in 1880 to recall the ford in the nearby Barcoo River and the proximity of Isis Downs Station homestead. **In town:** Bicentennial Museum, Centenary Dr. **In the area:** Huge (largest in Australia) semicircular prefabricated shearing shed (1913), at Isis Downs Station, 20 km E; visits by appt. Oma Waterhole, 16 km W, popular spot for fishing and water sports. **Visitor information:** Shire Offices, St Marys St; (07) 4658 8277.

The Scenic Railway between Kuranda and Cairns

Julia Creek   Pop. 519

MAP REF. 533 J4

A small cattle and rail township named after the niece of Donald McIntyre, the first European settler in the area. Located on the Flinders Hwy, Julia Creek is 134 km E of Cloncurry. A sealed road runs north to Normanton in the Gulf Savannah. The town is an important cattle-trucking and sale centre. **In town:** In Burke St: Duncan McIntyre Museum; Dunnart Craft Store, local art and craft. April: Julia Creek Dirt and Dust Triathlon. May: Campdraft (cattle drafting competition with horseriders). Aug.: Sedan Dip (car race). **In the area:** Punch Bowl, 40 km NE, waterhole picnic area. Saxby Roundup each June at Taldora Station, an isolated area 230 km N; access via Julia Creek. **Visitor information:** Shire Offices, Julia St; (07) 4746 7166. **See also:** Gulf Savannah p. 494.

Jundah   Pop. 100

MAP REF. 535 M2

Jundah (Aboriginal for 'women'), 217 km SW of Longreach, was gazetted as a town in 1880. For 20 years the area was important for opal mining, but lack of water caused the mines to close. **In town:** Barcoo Historical Museum, Perkins St. June: Bronco Branding. Oct.: Race Carnival. **In the area:** Jundah Opal Fields, 27 km NW. Welford National Park, 20 km S. **Visitor information:** Shire Offices, Dickson St; (07) 4658 6133.

Karumba   Pop. 1043

MAP REF. 528 B8, 531 H8

Karumba, 71 km NW of Normanton, is at the mouth of the Norman River and is the easiest access point for the Gulf of Carpentaria. It is the centre for the Gulf's prawning industry. A barramundi fishing industry and live-cattle industry also operate from the town. **In town:** Slipway once used by the Sydney-to-England Empire Flying Boats Service. Karumba Point, boat hire and accommodation. Barra Restocking Ponds, Riverview Dr.: barramundi display, feeding 4.45 p.m. daily. July: Karumba Kapers (fair). Dec.: Fishermen's Ball. **In the area:** Town is surrounded by flat wetlands extending 30 km inland; habitat of saltwater crocodiles and several species of birds, including brolgas and cranes. Charter vessels for fishing and exploration of the Gulf and Norman River. *The Ferryman*, cruises on Norman River. Old cemetery, 2 km NW, on road to Karumba Point, a small settlement 6 km NW. **Visitor information:** Shire Offices, Haig St, Normanton; (07) 4745 1166. **See also:** Gulf Savannah p. 494.

Kenilworth   Pop. 285

MAP REF. 525 P7

West of the Blackall Range, through the Obi Obi Valley, is Kenilworth, known for its Kenilworth Country Foods hand-crafted cheeses. This enterprise began when the local cheese factory closed and

6 employees mortgaged their homes to start the venture. **In town:** Kenilworth Museum, Alexandra St, has machinery, dairy display and audiovisuals (open Sun.). Lasting Impressions Gallery of Fine Art, Elizabeth St. **In the area:** Kenilworth Bluff, 6 km N, steep walking track to lookout point. Little Yabba Creek, 8 km S, good picnic spot where bellbirds are often heard. Lake Borumba, 32 km NW, for picnics and water sports; fishing competition each March. Nearby, Imbil Forest Drive through scenic forests and farmlands to Gympie. **Visitor information:** cnr Sixth Ave and Aerodrome Rd, Maroochydore; (07) 5479 1566.

Killarney   Pop. 832

MAP REF. 117 N1, 525 O11

This attractive small town is on the banks of the Condamine River, 33 km SE of Warwick, and very close to the NSW border. **In town:** Feb.: Agricultural Show. Nov.: Rodeo. **In the area:** Noteworthy mountain scenery. Dagg's and Brown's waterfalls, 4 km S. Cherrabah Homestead Resort, 7 km S, offers horseriding, golf, sailing and excellent bushwalking. Carrs Lookout, 33 km E. Queen Mary Falls in Main Range National Park, 15 km E; native birds fed daily at kiosk. **Visitor information:** 49 Albion St (New England Hwy), Warwick; (07) 4661 3122. Web site www.qldsoutherndowns.org.au

Kingaroy   Pop. 7013

MAP REF. 525 N6

This prosperous agricultural town is known for its peanuts and is the home of Sir Johannes (Joh) Bjelke-Petersen, the former Premier of Qld. Peanuts, maize, wheat, stonefruit and grapes, soy and navy beans are grown, and specialised agricultural equipment is manufactured. Kingaroy is 210 km NW of Brisbane, and its giant peanut silos are a distinctive landmark. Kingaroy claims the title 'Peanut Capital of Australia', and also 'Baked Bean Capital of Australia', with 75 per cent of Australia's navy beans grown in the district. **In town:** In Haly St: Kingaroy Bicentennial Heritage Museum; information centre, with videos on peanut and navy-bean industries. Apr.: Peanut Festival (odd-numbered years). **In the area:** Scenic drives, brochure available. A number of wineries open daily for sales. Mt Wooroolin scenic lookout, 3 km W. Bunya Mountains National Park, 56 km SW. **Visitor information:** Haly St (opp. silos); (07) 4162 3199.

Kuranda
Pop. 666

MAP REF. 523 E7, 529 M6

This village in the rainforest at the top of the Macalister Range is best known to tourists who have taken the 34-km trip from Cairns on the 100-year-old Scenic Railway or the more recent cableway. **In town:** Railway station with platforms adorned by lush ferns and orchids. Skyrail Rainforest Cableway, spectacular gondola ride through rainforest to Cairns; return via Scenic Railway; or vice versa. In Rod Veivers Dr.: The Incredible Birdworld, spectacular tree-lined paths and endangered birds; Australian Butterfly Sanctuary, over 2000 butterflies in forest setting; guided tours. In Coondoo St: Wildlife Noctarium, native wildlife in re-created nocturnal rainforest environment; Windmill Gallery. The Aviary, Thongon St, colourful native birds in walk-through enclosures surrounded by rainforest. River Esplanade Walk along Barron River, also Jungle Walk and Forest Walk. Markets, Rod Veivers Dr., daily. May: Folk Festival. **In the area:** River cruises depart from riverbank below railway station; also guided rainforest walks. Wrights Lookout, 7 km SE in Barron Gorge National Park, views of the Barron Falls, spectacular after heavy rain. Mini-golf, 2 km E. Rainforestation Nature Park, 35 km E: rainforest tours in amphibious army 'duck'; Pamagirri Aboriginal Dancers and Dreamtime Walk; Koala and Wildlife Park. **Visitor information:** Tourism Tropical North Queensland, 51 The Esplanade, Cairns; (07) 4051 3588. **See also:** The Far North p. 472.

Kynuna
Pop. 18

MAP REF. 533 J6

On the Matilda Hwy, 164 km NW of Winton, Kynuna was established in the 1860s and was a staging post for Cobb & Co. coaches. **In town:** Kynuna's only hotel is the famous Blue Heeler, with illuminated blue heeler statue on roof. Waltzing Matilda Exhibition, open during tourist season, in tent opposite roadhouse. Sept.: 'Surf' Carnival (inland version of Iron Man contest). Nov.: Rodeo. **In the area:** Combo Waterhole, 24 km SE on western side of old Winton–Kynuna Rd, scene of the events described in 'Waltzing Matilda', Banjo Paterson's famous song. Walkabout Creek Hotel at McKinlay, 74 km NW, location for film *Crocodile Dundee*. **Visitor information:** Roadhouse and Caravan Park, Matilda Hwy; (07) 4746 8683.

Laidley
Pop. 2329

MAP REF. 525 O9

Laidley, 87 km from Brisbane, off the Warrego Hwy, is between Ipswich and Gatton, in the Lockyer Valley. It is the principal town in an area of the Greater Brisbane Region regarded as 'Queensland's country garden'. **In town:** Das Neumann Haus (1893), William St: local history museum; information centre; art and craft; cafe. Country markets each Fri., and last Sat. each month. Apr.: Rodeo and Heritage Day. May: Heavy Horse Show. Sept.: Chelsea Festival (3 days). **In the area:** Laidley Pioneer Village, 1 km S, features original buildings from old township.

Adjacent, Narda Lagoon: flora and fauna sanctuary; suspension footbridge over lagoon; picnic/barbecue facilities. Lake Dyer, 1 km W: fishing; short-stay camping; picnic/barbecue facilities. Lake Clarendon, 17 km NW, birdwatching and picnicking. Self-guide historic and scenic walks and drives; leaflets available. **Visitor information:** Das Neumann Haus, cnr William and Patrick sts; (07) 5465 3241.

Landsborough
Pop. 1343

MAP REF. 516 G6, 520 E13, 525 P7

Landsborough is just north of the magnificent Glass House Mountains. **In town:** In Maleny St: Historical museum; De Maine Pottery. June: William Landsborough Day. **In the area:** Queensland Reptile and Fauna Park, 4 km S. Dularcha National Park, 1 km NE; *Dularcha* is the Aboriginal word for 'blackbutt country'. Big Kart Track, 5 km N, unsealed road suitable for conventional vehicles (except after heavy rain). **Visitor information:** Museum, Maleny St; (07) 5494 1755. **See also:** Hinterland Escape p. 456.

Longreach
Pop. 3766

MAP REF. 526 A11, 533 O11

Longreach has a small population, but there are 800 000 sheep and 20 000 beef cattle in the area. It is the most important and prosperous town in the central west of the State. On the Thomson River, this friendly, modern town is some 700 km by road or rail west of Rockhampton. It was here in 1870 that Harry Redford (Captain Starlight), with four mates, rounded up

Stockman's Hall of Fame and Outback Heritage Centre, Longreach

Snorkelling off Mackay

1000 cattle and drove them 2400 km into SA over wild unmapped country that 10 years before had defeated Burke and Wills. In SA Starlight sold the stolen cattle. He was arrested and brought back to Qld to be tried at Roma. Despite the evidence the jury found him not guilty, probably because his daring was admired. The events were the basis for Rolf Boldrewood's novel *Robbery Under Arms*. Although Qantas (Queensland And Northern Territory Aerial Service) started in Winton, it soon moved base to Longreach and began regular operations. The hangar used then became Australia's first aircraft factory and the first of 6 DH-50 biplanes was assembled in 1926. The world's first Flying Surgeon Service started from Longreach in 1959. **In town:** Broad streets and several historic buildings. In Galah St: Uniting Church (1892), built for Grazier's Association; courthouse (1892). Post office (1902), cnr Duck and Eagle sts. Railway station (1916), Sir Hudson Fysh Dr. Powerhouse Museum, Swan St, displays of old machinery; open Mar.–Oct. Arts and Crafts, Ibis St; open p.m. Mar.–Oct. On Matilda Hwy: Stockman's Hall of Fame and Outback Heritage Centre, featuring exhibition hall, theatre with audiovisuals, library and resource centre; nearby, Banjo's Outback Theatre and Pioneer Shearing Shed (open Mar.–Oct.); Botanical Gardens, has walking and bike trails; School of Distance

Education (tours weekdays during term); Longreach Pastoral College (tours); Qantas Founders Museum at airport. Qantas Park, Eagle St, replica of original Qantas booking office, now houses information centre. Pamela's Doll Display and Syd's Outback Collection Corner, Quail St. Cobb & Co. coach rides around town. *Yellowbelly Express* and Billabong Boat Cruises, for Thomson River cruises. Easter: Easter in the Outback. June: Hall of Fame Race Meeting. July: Diamond Shears (Australia's premier shearing competition). **In the area:** Quarter-horse stud at Longway Station, 14 km N (group tours). Oakley Station, 17 km N, sheep and cattle station (tours). Folk Museum at Ilfracombe, 27 km E. Toobrac Station, 107 km SW, 100-year-old homestead; accommodation and camping. **Visitor information:** Qantas Park, Eagle St; (07) 4658 3555. **See also:** Capricorn Region p. 497.

Mackay Pop. 44 880

MAP REF. 527 L5

Mackay, often called the sugar capital of Australia, produces one-third of the nation's sugar crop. Five mills operate in the area, and the bulk-sugar loading terminal is the world's largest. In 1866 sugar was first grown, a mill was built and Mackay became a town. It became a major port in 1939 when a breakwater

was built, making it one of Australia's largest artificial harbours. The nearby Hay Point coal-loading terminals handle the output from the central Qld coalfields. Gazetted in 1918, Mackay is now a progressive tropical city. Besides sugar and coal, the town's economy depends on beef cattle, dairying, timber, grain, seafood and the growing of tropical fruit. Tourism is a growth industry, with Brampton Island and the Great Barrier Reef accessible from Mackay. **In town:** Self-guide heritage walk of historic buildings includes: Commonwealth (1880) and National (1939) banks, town hall (1912), courthouse (1838), police station (1885), Ambassador Hotel (1937) and customs house (1902). Queens Park and Orchid House, Goldsmith St. Entertainment Centre, Gordon St. Replica of old Richmond sugar mill, Nebo Rd, houses information centre. Just north of town, lookouts at Mt Bassett Weather Station, Mt Pleasant Reservoir, Eimeo and Lamberts Beach. Numerous beaches: Harbour, Town, Blacks, Bucasia, Illawong, Lamberts and Shoal Point. Cruises, fishing charters and scenic flights. Two Sat. markets: Harbour Rd; Showgrounds, Milton St. City Heat Markets, Victoria St, Sun. July: Festival of the Arts. Sept.: Sugartime Festival. **In the area:** Discovery and eco-tours to national parks, coal mines and Whitsundays. Farleigh sugar

Great Barrier Reef

The Great Barrier Reef is a living phenomenon. Its coloured coral branches sit upon banks of limestone polyps that have been built up slowly over thousands of years from the seabed. The banks of coral are separated by channels of water, shaded from the delicate green of the shallows to the deepest blue. The reef area is over 2300 kilometres long, stretching from near the coast of western Papua New Guinea to north of Breaksea Spit, east of Bundaberg on the central Queensland coast. It is only between 15 and 20 kilometres wide in the north, but south of Cairns the reef area can extend up to 325 kilometres out to sea. The Great Barrier Reef was proclaimed a marine park in 1975 and a management programme was undertaken to balance the interests of scientists, tourists and fishing enthusiasts, and to preserve the reef for future generations. With over 700 islands scattered through the tropical sea, and the banks of reefs darkening the water, this sun-drenched, tropical paradise attracts thousands of visitors each year.

The coral presents an incredibly beautiful picture. Visitors can see it from semi-submersible vessels, which allow occupants to go underwater without getting wet, or from glass-bottomed boats; or, even better, they can swim around using snorkels or diving gear. The colours of purple, pink, yellow, white and red are intermixed and made more startling by the spectacular shapes of the coral. There are more than 400 varieties of identified coral, the most common being the staghorns, brain corals, mushroom corals, organ pipes and black corals. Spread among these are waving fields of soft coral, colourful anemones, sea urchins and sea slugs. Shellfish of all kinds, ranging from great clams to tiny cowries, cling to the reef while shoals of brightly coloured tropical fish – among them red emperors, coral trout, sweetlip, angel-fish, parrot-fish and demoiselles – glide and dart through the coral gardens. Multitudes of seabirds nest on the islands of the reef through spring and summer.

Three island resorts, Green Island, Heron Island and Lady Elliot Island, are coral cays – actually part of the reef – and at low tide it is possible to walk on the coral ledges that surround them. Other resort islands, such as Lizard Island, are continental islands; these were once part of the mainland, and are generally more wooded and mountainous.

The Great Barrier Reef is Australia's most beautiful tourist attraction, and the best way to see it is by boat. If you do not have your own yacht, and the holiday budget will not stretch to chartering one, there are many excellent cruises available through the reef and its islands. Charter boats, scuba diving and fishing trips are also available.

The resort islands off the reef and the Queensland coast offer different styles of living to suit various tastes in holidays and entertainment. The common denominator is their beautiful setting and a consistency of climate, broken only by the sudden and short-lived downpours of the monsoonal period from December to February. The period from June to November is considered the best time to visit.

For further information on the islands of the Great Barrier Reef, contact the Great Barrier Reef Visitors Bureau, PO Box 172, Milton 4064; (07) 3876 4644. Web site www.great-barrier-reef.com

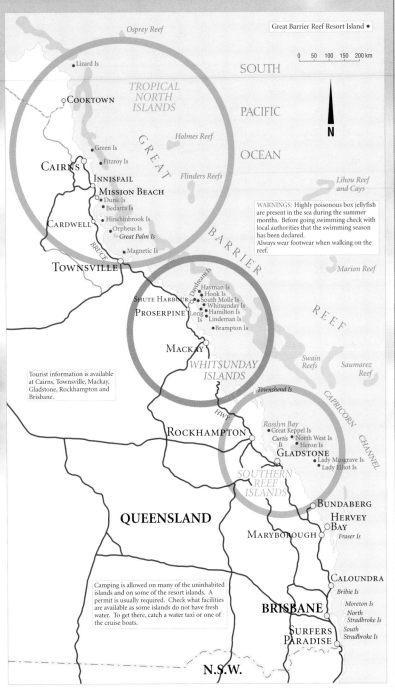

Great Barrier Reef Resort Island ●

0 50 100 150 200 km

N

WARNINGS: Highly poisonous box jellyfish are present in the sea during the summer months. Before going swimming check with local authorities that the swimming season has been declared.
Always wear footwear when walking on the reef.

Tourist information is available at Cairns, Townsville, Mackay, Gladstone, Rockhampton and Brisbane.

Camping is allowed on many of the uninhabited islands and on some of the resort islands. A permit is usually required. Check what facilities are available as some islands do not have fresh water. To get there, catch a water taxi or one of the cruise boats.

Island	Features	Activities	Access	Accommodation
SOUTHERN REEF ISLANDS The Southern Reef extends offshore from Bundaberg to Rockhampton.				
LADY ELLIOT ISLAND 80 km NE of Bundaberg	• small, sand covered coral cay • 19 major dive areas to view coral and marine life • significant bird rookeries • turtle-nesting site	Birdwatching, turtle-watching (turtles come ashore to lay eggs Nov.–Mar.; hatching can be seen late Feb.–May), humpback whale migration (late June–late Oct.), diving, snorkelling, reef walking, island walking.	From Bundaberg or Hervey Bay, by plane.	Low-key resort ranging from budget to deluxe. Max. 140 people.
LADY MUSGRAVE ISLAND 105 km NNE of Bundaberg	• superb coral cay with navigable lagoon • glass-bottomed boats • floating pontoon • semi-submersible submarine • prolific birdlife • turtle-nesting site	Birdwatching, turtle-watching (turtles come ashore to lay eggs Nov.–Mar.), snorkelling, island walking.	From Bundaberg, by seaplane, catamaran or trimaran. From Seventeen Seventy, by boat.	Camping only; permit required (contact Gladstone office of Qld Parks and Wildlife Service; (07) 4972 6055). Max. 50 people.
HERON ISLAND 72 km NE of Gladstone	• small coral cay • entire island is a national park • prolific flora and fauna • turtle-nesting site	Birdwatching, turtle-watching (turtles come ashore to lay eggs Nov.–Mar.; hatching can be seen late Dec.–May), diving, snorkelling, reef and ecology walks.	From Gladstone, by catamaran or charter helicopter.	Resort. Max. 280 people.
NORTH WEST ISLAND 75 km NE of Gladstone	• no permanent residents • second largest coral cay on reef • turtle-nesting site • breeding site of black noddy and wedge-tailed shearwater	Birdwatching, turtle-watching (turtles come ashore to lay eggs Nov.–Mar.).	From Gladstone, by charter boat.	Camping only; permit required (contact Gladstone office of Qld Parks and Wildlife Service; (07) 4972 6055). Max. 150 people.
GREAT KEPPEL ISLAND 48 km NE of Rockhampton	• 30 km of white, sandy beaches • unspoiled tropical island scenery	Tennis, water-skiing, skindiving, parasailing, coral viewing, island cruises, golf. 'Kids Klub' operates during school holidays.	From Rockhampton, by light plane. From Rosslyn Bay, by launch.	Wide range from cabins and tents to lodge or resort. Max. 650 people.
WHITSUNDAY ISLANDS There are more than 80 islands in the magnificent Whitsunday Passage; most are uninhabited.				
BRAMPTON ISLAND 32 km NE of Mackay	• national park and wildlife sanctuary • fine golden beaches • snorkelling trail	Water sports, sea-plane trips to reef, snorkelling trail (with waterproof map), bushwalking, archery.	From Mackay, by light plane or launch.	Resort. Max. 280 people.
LINDEMAN ISLAND 67 km N of Mackay	• Club Med resort • national park • prolific birds and butterflies • secluded sandy beaches • picturesque golf course • superb views from summit of Mt Oldfield	Water sports, birdwatching, butterfly-watching, tennis, golf, exercise in the gym or pool, bushwalking.	From Proserpine, by light plane. From Mackay by plane, or Hamilton Island by boat or plane.	Club Med resort. Max. 460 people.

Island	Features	Activities	Access	Accommodation
HAMILTON ISLAND 16 km SE of Shute Harbour	• most complex island resort • extensive facilities including jet airport, school, bank, post office, 24 shops and boutiques • 135-berth marina • fauna park • marina village	Wide range of activities and entertainment including windsurfing, sailing, fishing, scuba diving, parasailing, helicopter rides, tennis and squash, go-karting, catamaran cruises, reef and inter-island trips.	Direct flight from Sydney and Brisbane; connections to all major cities. From Shute Harbour by launch.	Hotel resort offering wide range of accommodation, including bungalows and beachfront units. Max. 1500 people.
LONG ISLAND 9 km from Shute Harbour	• part of Conway National Park • excellent walking tracks leading to scenic lookouts • friendly scrub turkeys • fresh oysters	Bushwalking, water sports, fishing, resort activities.	From Shute Harbour or Hamilton Island, by launch or helicopter. From Proserpine by seaplane.	3 resorts: Club Crocodile, family resort (max. 400 people); Palm Bay Hideaway for relaxation (max. 60 people); Whitsunday Wilderness Lodge for a tranquil eco-experience (max. 16 people).
SOUTH MOLLE ISLAND 8 km from Shute Harbour	• small, lightly timbered island with numerous inlets • splendid scenery and views of Whitsunday Passage from island's peaks • golf course	Bushwalking, snorkelling, scuba diving, windsurfing, golf, gym, catamaran sailing.	From Shute Harbour, by launch. From Hamilton Island, by water taxi.	Resort. Max. 520 people.
DAYDREAM ISLAND 5 km from Shute Harbour	• luxurious resort on this small island of volcanic rock and coral • dense tropical foliage	Resort activities and facilities including 'Kids Club', tennis, outdoor cinema, water sports centre, diving, trips to outer reef and other islands.	From Shute Harbour, by launch or helicopter. From Hamilton Island, by launch or helicopter.	Resort. Max. 900 people.
WHITSUNDAY ISLAND 25 km E of Shute Harbour	• uninhabited • entire island is a national park • beautiful white silica beach, Whitehaven Beach • Hill Inlet mangrove system	Bush and beach walking.	From Shute Harbour or Able Point Marina, by boat.	Camping only, permit required (contact Airlie Beach office of Qld Parks and Wildlife Service; (07) 4946 7022). Max. 40 people.
HOOK ISLAND 20 km NE of Shute Harbour	• small low-key resort • underwater observatory	Snorkelling, scuba diving, fishing, reef trips, coral submarine trips, fish-feeding.	From Shute Harbour or Able Point Marina, Airlie Beach, by launch.	Wilderness Lodge with cabins and campsites. Max. 250 people.
HAYMAN ISLAND 25 km NE of Shute Harbour	• luxury resort • prolific birdlife • northernmost island in Whitsundays; close to outer reef	Fishing, sightseeing trips, scenic flights, diving, water sports 'Kidz Club', and whale-watching excursions in season (July–early Sept.).	Direct flight to Hamilton Island from Sydney and Brisbane (connections to all major cities), then by launch to Hayman Island. From Airlie Beach, by water taxi.	Luxury resort. Max. 450 people.

Island	Features	Activities	Access	Accommodation
TROPICAL NORTH ISLANDS This group of islands is located off the north coast of Queensland between Townsville and Cooktown. Generally speaking, the reef in this section is closer to the mainland than it is further south.				
MAGNETIC ISLAND 8 km NE of Townsville	• permanent population • national park • excellent walking tracks • beautiful beaches • buses and taxis available	Horseriding, snorkelling, parasailing, swimming, fishing, sea kayaking, reef excursions, Harley tours.	From Townsville, by vehicular ferry, catamaran or water taxi.	Wide variety of hotels and accommodation from budget to deluxe.
ORPHEUS ISLAND 80 km N of Townsville	• small island surrounded by coral reefs • island is a national park • prolific birdlife	Birdwatching, water sports, coral viewing in glass-bottomed boat, island walks, fishing.	From Townsville or Cairns, by sea plane.	5-star resort (max. 74 people), or bush camping (max. 54 people). Camping permit required, contact Ingham office of Qld Parks and Wildlife Service; (07) 4066 8601.
HINCHINBROOK ISLAND 5 km E of Cardwell	• small, low-key resort • island is a national park • mountains, tropical vegetation and waterfalls • sandy beaches and secluded coves on eastern side	Snorkelling, swimming, fishing, bushwalking.	From Cardwell, by launch.	Resort Max. 45 people.
BEDARRA ISLAND 35 km NE of Cardwell	• exclusive resort • untouched tropical beauty • no day visitors or children under 15	Bushwalking, snorkelling, fishing, swimming, wind-surfing, sailing, tennis and gourmet picnics in a dinghy.	From Dunk Island, by launch.	One exclusive resort. Max. 30 people.
DUNK ISLAND 5 km SE of Mission Beach	• popular resort • island is a national park • extensive walking tracks through superb rainforest • prolific birdlife, butterflies and wild orchids	Bushwalking, birdwatching, night walks, parasailing, water-skiing, sailing, clay target shooting, horseriding.	From Cairns, by plane. From Clump Point near Mission Beach, by launch. From Wongaling Beach and South Mission Beach, by water taxi.	Resort (max. 360 people) or camping (max. 30 people).
FITZROY ISLAND 30 km SE of Cairns	• low-key resort • magnificent flora and fauna • secluded white coral beaches • 360° views from lighthouse • national park	Bushwalking, diving, snorkelling.	From Cairns, by catamaran.	Resort offering hostel-type and cabin accommodation (max. 160 people). Also camping (max. 60 people).
GREEN ISLAND 27 km NE of Cairns	• popular with day-trippers • true coral cay • thick tropical vegetation • glass-bottomed boats • underwater observatory	Reef viewing, boardwalk.	From Cairns, by catamaran, sea plane or helicopter.	Resort. Max. 90 people.
LIZARD ISLAND 93 km NE of Cooktown	• small, luxurious resort • national park • excellent reefs surround island • game-fishing offshore	Reef viewing, fishing, island walks, snorkelling, diving.	From Cairns or Cooktown, by plane or sea plane.	Bungalow-style resort (max. 80 people) or camping (max. 20 people). Camping permit required, contact Cairns office of Qld Parks and Wildlife Service; (07) 4052 3096.

mill, 15 km N; tours during crushing season (July–Oct.). That Sapphire Place, 20 km N, sapphire display and gem-cutting demonstrations. Cape Hillsborough National Park, 40 km N. Polstone Sugar Cane Farm, 15 km W; tours July–Oct. Historic Greenmount homestead, 20 km W, near Walkerston. Kinchant Dam, 20 km W of Walkerston. Stoney Creek Cottage, 32 km W, trail rides and accommodation. At Mirani, 33 km W: museum, Victoria St. Eungella National Park, 79 km W: platypuses, Ulysses butterflies, nocturnal wildlife; mangrove and Aboriginal-plant walking trails. Nebo, 93 km SW of Mackay on Peak Downs Hwy: Nebo Museum; rodeo in July. Orchidways, orchid farm on Homebush Rd, 25 km S (closed Thurs.). At Homebush, 25 km S: art and craft gallery; self-drive tour through historic area, brochure available. **Visitor information:** Mackay Tourism and Development Bureau, The Mill, 320 Nebo Rd; (07) 4952 2677. **See also:** Wildlife-Watching p. 464.

Main Beach

Pop. part of Gold Coast

MAP REF. 517 G11, 519 F5, 525 Q10
Towards the northern end of the Gold Coast strip, Main Beach is packed with attractions. **In the area:** Scenic drive, brochure available. At Main Beach on The Spit: Sea World, famous marine park; Marina Mirage and Mariner's Cove, tourist complexes with specialty shops, restaurants, outdoor cafes and weekend entertainment. **Visitor information:** Cavill Ave, Surfers Paradise; (07) 5538 4419. **See also:** The Gold Coast p. 500.

Maleny

Pop. 880

MAP REF. 516 E5, 520 B11, 525 P7
A steep road climbs from the coast west to Maleny, in the Blackall Range, 50 km SW of Maroochydore. The surrounding area is excellent dairy country. From McCarthy's Lookout, south-east of town, there is a fine view of the Glass House Mountains to the south. These 13 spectacular trachyte peaks were named by Captain Cook as he sailed up the coast in 1770, for the sun shining on the rockfaces reminded him of glasshouses in his native Yorkshire. **In town:** Art and craft galleries. **In the area:** 28-km scenic drive (one of the best in south-east Qld), north-east from Maleny through

Montville and Flaxton to Mapleton: views of Sunshine Coast, Moreton Island, Bribie Island and nearby pineapple and sugarcane fields; museums; antique shops; fruit stalls; tea rooms and tourist attractions along the way. Montville, 7 km NE: Cuckoo Clock Centre (clock museum); excellent potteries and art and craft galleries. At Flaxton, 3 km further N: miniature English village; Flower Gardens Winery has working potter and tearooms; Flaxton Winery, excellent coastal views. Flaxton Barn, 2 km further N, has model railway and tearooms. Kondalilla and Mapleton Falls national parks, between Montville and Mapleton. Howells Knob, 4 km W, lookout with 360° views. Mary Cairncross Park, 7 km SE, rainforest walks. McCarthy's Lookout, 5 km SE, spectacular views. **Visitor information:** Sunshine Coast Information, cnr Sixth Ave and Aerodrome Rd, Maroochydore; (07) 5479 1566. **See also:** Hinterland Escape p. 456; The Sunshine Coast p. 493.

Mareeba

Pop. 6874

MAP REF. 523 C9, 529 M7
Tobacco is still grown in this area, along with mango, tea-tree oil, coffee and sugarcane crops. Farms in the Mareeba–Dimbulah area are irrigated from Lake Tinaroo. Mining and cattle are also important industries. **In town:** Self-guide historical walk, brochure available. In Mason St, Bicentennial Lakes, a park with plantings to encourage wildlife. In Centenary Park, Byrnes St: Mareeba Heritage Museum, has local history exhibits including rail ambulance and old dairy shed; Mareeba Art Society Gallery; markets, 2nd Sat. each month. July: Rodeo. Sept.: Air Show. Oct.: Country Music Festival (even-numbered years). **In the area:** Horseriding at Pinevale Ranch, 10 km E. The Coffee Works, Mason St, 2 km S (tours). Aviation and Military Museum, 5 km S on Kennedy Hwy, has the Beck Collection (military hardware). Granite Gorge, 12 km SW, off Chewko Rd. Paddy's Green Plantation (North Queensland Gold coffee), 9 km W on Mareeba–Dimbulah road. Tryconnell Historic Gold Mine, 76 km W (tours). Wetlands Project, 22 km N at end of Fabis Rd, extends for 5000 ha and backs onto Hann Tablelands. **Visitor information:** Heritage Museum, Centenary Park, Byrnes St; (07) 4092 5674. **See also:** Cape York p. 507.

Maroochydore

Pop. 28 509

MAP REF. 516 H4, 520 H9, 525 Q7
A well-established and popular beach resort, Maroochydore, 106 km N of Brisbane, is the business centre of the Sunshine Coast. **In town:** Popular surfing beaches. Maroochy River, with pelicans and swans, offers safe swimming. Cotton Tree, at river mouth, popular camping area. Replica of Captain Cook's ship *Endeavour*, David Low Way. **In the area:** Cruises up Maroochy River to Dunethin Rock through sugarcane fields. Nostalgia Town, 7 km NW, emphasises humour in history. Bli Bli Castle, 10 km NW, a 'medieval' castle with dungeon torture chamber and doll museum. **Visitor information:** cnr Sixth Ave and Aerodrome Rd; (07) 5479 1566. Web site www.maroochytourism.com. **See also:** Day Tours from Brisbane p. 453; The Sunshine Coast p. 493.

Maryborough

Pop. 21 286

MAP REF. 525 P4
Maryborough is a well-planned, attractive, provincial city on the banks of the Mary River, 3 hours' drive north of Brisbane. The Maryborough region was first explored by Europeans in 1842. In 1847 a wool store was established, and a village and port soon grew to handle the wool being produced inland. The settlement was officially proclaimed a port in 1859 and a municipality in 1861. Maryborough is promoted as a Heritage City and visitors can see the excellent architecture of a bygone era. The climate is dry subtropical with warm moist summers and mild winters. **In town:** Fine examples of early Colonial architecture: St Paul's bell tower (1887), Lennox St, with one of the last sets of pealing bells in Qld; Brennan & Geraghty's Store, also in Lennox St, property of National Trust. Bond Store Museum, Wharf St, has historical displays. Croydon Foundry Office Museum, Ferry St. Pioneer gravesites and original township site in Alice St, Baddow; historic time gun outside city hall, Kent St. Several parks: in Sussex St, Queen's Park, unusual domed fernery and waterfall; in Kent St, Elizabeth Park, rose gardens; on cnr Cheapside and Alice sts, Anzac Park; Ululah Lagoon, off Lions Dr., a scenic waterbird sanctuary where black swans, wild geese, ducks and waterhens may be hand-fed. Maryborough Heritage Walk

Step back in time at Brennan & Geraghty's Store, Maryborough

and Drive, brochure available. Heritage City Market, Adelaide and Ellena sts, each Thurs. May: Best of Brass. Sept.: Heritage City Festival. Oct.: Maryborough Masters Games. **In the area:** Pioneer museum at Brooweena, 49 km W on Biggenden Rd. Teddington Weir, 15 km S. Tuan Forest, 24 km SE. **Visitor information:** 30 Ferry St; (07) 4121 4111.

Miles   Pop. 1187

MAP REF. 525 K7
Ludwig Leichhardt passed through the Miles district (337 km NW of Brisbane) on 3 separate expeditions. He named the place Dogwood Crossing, after the shrub that grows on the creek banks. In 1878 the western railway line reached Dogwood Crossing, and Cobb & Co. continued the journey to Roma. The town was renamed Miles after a local member of parliament. The area has always been good sheep country, but today the emphasis is on cattle (mainly Herefords), and wheat; tall silos dominate the surrounding plains. After the spring rains the wildflowers are magnificent. **In town:** Historical village, Warrego Hwy: 'pioneer settlement' with all types of early buildings, a war museum, and vehicles and implements

on display. Sept.: Back to the Bush (includes Wildflower Festival). **In the area:** Myall Park Botanical Gardens at Glenmorgan, 134 km SW. Wildflower drive in Sept., brochure available. **Visitor information:** Historical village, Warrego Hwy; (07) 4627 1492.

Millaa Millaa   Pop. 324

MAP REF. 529 M8
Located 73 km inland from Innisfail, Millaa Millaa is central to many spectacular waterfalls in the area, and other Atherton Tableland attractions. The town's main industry is dairying. **In town:** Eacham Historical Society Museum, Main St. **In the area:** Millaa Millaa Falls, Zillie Falls and Ellinjaa Falls – all seen from 15-km Waterfalls Circuit road (mostly sealed) that leaves and rejoins Palmerston Hwy east of town; also nearby, Souita, Papina and Mungalli falls. World Heritage-listed Wooroonooran National park, 20 km SE: rainforest walks; Nandroya, Walicher and Tchupala Falls; Crawfords Lookout. Millstream Falls, 40 km SW. Millaa Millaa Lookout to west of town for excellent 360° views of district. At Ravenshoe, 26 km SW, heritage steam-train ride to nearby Tumoulin and return; departure times from

information centre. **Visitor information:** The Falls Holiday Park, Malanda Rd; (07) 4097 2290. Web site www.eachamshire.qld.gov.au **See also:** The Far North p. 472

Millmerran   Pop. 1054

MAP REF. 525 M10
This town on the Condamine River produces eggs, cotton, grain, vegetables, cattle and wool. **In town:** Historical Society Museum, Charlotte St. Oct.: Camp Oven Festival. **In the area:** Ned's Corner, 27 km N, offers camp-oven meals, Australiana, yarns and poetry (open by appt). **Visitor information:** Toowoomba Information Centre, 476 Ruthven St, Toowoomba; (07) 4638 7555.

Miriam Vale   Pop. 421

MAP REF. 525 M1, 527 Q13
Situated on the Bruce Hwy, 150 km N of Bundaberg, this town is renowned for its mud-crab sandwiches. Watch for the Giant Crab. The hinterland is ideal for bushwalking, four-wheel driving and horseriding. **In the area:** Twin towns of Agnes Water, 57 km NE (the most northerly surfing beach in Qld), and Seventeen Seventy, 63 km NE. Captain Cook, while on his voyage of discovery in Australian waters, made his first landing in Qld at the town of Seventeen Seventy; commemorative Festival held each May in honour of this. Estuary and beaches provide ideal spots to get away from it all; fishing is excellent. Nearby, Eurimbula and Deepwater national parks; 4WD necessary. **Visitor information:** Discovery Coast Information Centre, Bruce Hwy; (07) 4974 5428.

Mission Beach   Pop. 1013

MAP REF. 529 N9
This quiet 14-km-long beach with magnificent golden sand, close to Tully, is fringed by coconut palms and World Heritage-listed wet tropical rainforest. The Great Barrier Reef is closest to shore here. Day cruises and sailing trips to Beaver Cay and Dunk and surrounding islands can be taken from the jetty at Clump Point. A cairn at South Mission Beach Esplanade commemorates the ill-fated 1848 Cape York expedition of Edmund Kennedy. Many artists, potters, sculptors, jewellers, tapestry artists and cane weavers have settled in the area, attracted by the beautiful

rainforest and relaxed lifestyle. **In town:** Next to information centre, Porters Promenade, woodcarving exhibition and rainforest arboretum. Markets: Porters Promenade, 1st Sat., 3rd Sun. each month; Monster Markets, Recreation Centre, Cassowary Dr., last Sun. each month (Easter–Nov.). June: Mudfest (3-day music and cultural festival). Aug.: Banana Festival. Oct.: Aquatic Festival; Sailing Regatta. **In the area:** Art and craft galleries. Boat, catamaran and jetski hire, tandem parachuting, game and island reef fishing. Water taxi to Dunk Island, departs Wongaling Beach. Spectacular walking trails to Bicton Hill and Cuttens Lookout, from base of Bicton Hill, off Mission Beach, to Bingil Bay Rd. Guided and self-guide rainforest walks; scenic drives; calm-water, guided, canoe and kayak trips; game-fishing; croc-spotting tours on Hull River. **Visitor information:** Porters Promenade; (07) 4068 7099. Web site www.gspeak.com. au/missionb

Mitchell Pop. 967

MAP REF. 524 F6

Mitchell on the banks of the Maranoa River and 600 km W of Brisbane, lies on the Warrego Hwy between Roma and Charleville. The town was named after Sir Thomas Mitchell, explorer and Surveyor-General of NSW, who visited the region in 1846. **In town:** Kenniff Courthouse and Visitor Information Centre, Cambridge St, features bushranger exhibition, art and craft, and video of local points of interest; landscaped courthouse grounds incorporate community mosaic, operating artesian windmill and small billabong. Also in Cambridge St: Great Artesian Spa, opportunity to relax in artesian waters of ideal temperature, in garden surroundings; Nalingu Aboriginal Corporation for guided tours of local area. **In the area:** *Read section on Outback Motoring (p. 603).* This region was stronghold of turn-of-century bushrangers, the Kenniff brothers; monument and statues erected 7 km S at the site of their last stand. Day trips to Mt Moffatt National Park, 256 km N: camping; walking tracks; 2 major Aboriginal art sites; views of impressive sandstone rock formations. Bird sanctuary and picnic/barbecue facilities near Neil Turner Weir, 3.5 km NW. Maranoa River Nature Walk (1.8-km circuit) commences at Fishermans Rest, 1.7 km W. **Visitor information:** Cambridge St; (07) 4623 1133. Web site www.maranoa.org.au

Monto Pop. 1339

MAP REF. 525 M2

Monto, on the Burnett Hwy, 250 km inland from Bundaberg, is the centre of a rich dairying, beef cattle and agricultural district. **In town:** Monto History Centre, cnr Kelvin and Lister sts, local history displays and videos. June: Dairy Festival (even-numbered years). **In the area:** Cania Gorge National Park, 25 km NW. The Bonnie View Collection, 2 km S, includes over 1000 dolls. Wuruma Dam, 50 km S: swimming, sailing, waterskiing. Wattle Dale Ostrich Farm, 28 km SW. **Visitor information:** Three Moon Motel, 4 Flinders St; (07) 4166 1777.

Mooloolaba Pop. part of Maroochydore

MAP REF. 516 H4, 520 H9, 525 Q7

Because of its excellent beach and variety of restaurants and nightlife, Mooloolaba is popular for both family and young people's holidays. The Mooloolaba Esplanade, offering beachside resort shopping, rises to the bluff at Alexandra Headland. From the headland there are sweeping views up the beach to the Maroochy River and Mudjimba Island, with Mt Coolum creating an impressive backdrop. Alexandra Headland beach is popular for surfing. One of the safest anchorages on the eastern coast is at Mooloolaba Harbour. **In town:** UnderWater World complex, includes 80-m transparent tunnel for viewing three separate marine environments; the Wharf, and many restaurants and specialty shops. Harbour, finishing point for the annual Sydney-to-Mooloolaba Yacht Race in Apr., and base for Sunshine Coast's main prawning and fishing fleet. Yachting and game-fishing trips to nearby offshore reefs. Paraflying off Mooloolaba Beach. Apr.: Triathlon. **Visitor information:** Sunshine Coast Information, cnr Aerodrome Rd and Sixth Ave, Maroochydore; (07) 5479 1566. Web site www.maroochytourism.com **See also:** Day Tours from Brisbane p. 453.

Moranbah Pop. 6508

MAP REF. 526 I7

Just off the Peak Downs Hwy, 182 km SW of Mackay, this modern mining town established in 1971 services the huge open-cut coal mines of the expanding Bowen Coal Basin. Coking coal is railed to the Hay Point export terminal just south of Mackay. **In town:** Tours to BHP's Peak Downs Mine leave Town Square each Thurs. 10 a.m. (bookings through information centre). May: May Day Union Parade and Fireworks. Sept.: Country Music Festival. **Visitor information:** Library, Town Square; (07) 4941 7221.

Mossman Pop. 1917

MAP REF. 523 B3, 529 M5

Mossman, the sugar town of the north and 82 km NW of Cairns on the Captain Cook Hwy, is surrounded by green mountains and fields of sugarcane. **In town:** Markets, Front St, each Sat. **In the area:** Mt Demi (1159 m) towers over town. Popular beaches: Cooya Beach, Newell and Wonga. Mossman Gorge, 9 km W: short walk through rainforest to picturesque cascades; regular guided walks by Kuku Yulanji people whose ancestors were original inhabitants. Hartleys Creek Wildlife Reserve, 35 km S, features crocodiles and other native fauna. Daintree National Park, 64 km NE, largest tract of tropical rainforest in Australia. Karnak Rainforest Sanctuary, 9 km N. Tropical fruit and restaurant in rainforest setting at High Falls Farm, Miallo, 15 km N. **Visitor information:** Port Douglas and Cooktown Visitor Information Centre, 23 Macrossan St, Port Douglas; (07) 4099 5599. **See also:** The Far North p. 472.

Mount Isa Pop. 21 751

MAP REF. 532 E4

In 1923, John Campbell Miles discovered a rich silver-lead deposit on the western edge of the Cloncurry field. Today the city of Mount Isa is the most important industrial, commercial and administrative centre in north-west Qld, an oasis of civilisation in the vast expanse of outback spinifex and cattle country. Mount Isa Mines operates one of the largest silver-lead mines in the world; copper and zinc are also mined and processed. Ore trains run 900 km E to Townsville for shipment. Mount Isa hosts the third-largest rodeo in the world, attracting rough-riders from all over Qld and almost doubling the town's population. **In town:** Surface and underground mine tours, advance bookings essential. Lead smelter stack, Australia's tallest free-standing structure (265 m). Riversleigh Fossils Museum and Tourist Information Centre, Centenary Park, Marian St, features displays of fossil discoveries from the Riversleigh area, and of early Aboriginal occupation. John Middlin Mining Display and Visitors Centre, Church St. Frank Aston Underground Museum, Shackleton St. National Trust Tent House, Fourth Ave. In Marian St: Kalkadoon Tribal Centre and Cultural Keeping Place; clock tower with ashes of John Campbell Miles, discoverer of silver-lead ore in this area. Mount Isa Potters Gallery, Alma St. Royal Flying Doctor Service Base and Visitors Centre, Barkly Hwy. School of Distance Education, Kalkadoon High School, Abel Smith Pde; open schooldays, tours a.m. City Lookout, Hilary St. Donaldson Memorial Lookout and walking track, off Marian St. Sat. market, West St; Sun. market, Camooweal St. Apr.: Country Music Festival. Aug.: Rodeo. **In the area:** Tours of World Heritage-listed Riversleigh Fossil Site, 267 km NW, an extension of Lawn Hill National Park, 332 km NW. Artificial Lake Moondarra, 20 km N, a wildlife sanctuary offering swimming, water sports and picnic/barbecue facilities. Gunpowder Resort, 127 km N, offers activities ranging from bull-catching to water-skiing. West Leichhardt Station, 30 km NE, 113 400-ha cattle property; inquire at information centre for day or overnight visits. Lake Julius and surrounds, 99 km NE, features Aboriginal cave paintings, fishing, water-skiing, nature trails and abandoned goldmine. Air-charter companies provide flights to excellent barramundi fishing grounds near Birri Fishing Lodge at Birri Beach on Mornington Island and Sweers Island in Gulf of Carpentaria. Mount Frosty, 53 km E, old limestone mine and swimming-hole (not recommended for children as hole is some 9 m deep with no shallow areas); popular area for fossickers; Burke and Wills memorial cairn near Corella River, 74 km E. Malbon Vale Station, 43 km S, 172 000-ha cattle property; inquire at information centre for day or overnight visits. **Visitor information:** Riversleigh Fossils Centre, Centenary Park, Marian St; (07) 4749 1555. **See also:** Gulf Savannah p. 494.

Mount Morgan   Pop. 2487

MAP REF. 527 N11
Located 38 km SW of Rockhampton, the crater of the Mount Morgan open-cut gold, silver and copper mine is the largest excavation in the Southern Hemisphere, measuring some 800 m across and 185 m deep. In the golden heyday of the mine, around 1910, the town had 14 000 people.

In town: Historical Museum, Morgan St. Courthouse and other historic buildings have National Trust classifications. At Railway Station, Burnett Hwy: tearooms and rail museum; restored 1904 steam engine operates Sun.; fettler's trolley-rides along 4-km track operate Mon.–Fri. May: Golden Mount Festival. **In the area:** The Big Dam, 2.7 km N via William St, for good boating and fishing. At Wowan, 40 km SW, Scrub Turkey Museum in old butter factory. **Visitor information:** Railway Station, Burnett Hwy; (07) 4938 2312. **See also:** Capricorn Region p. 497.

Mourilyan   Pop. 484

MAP REF. 529 N8
Mourilyan, located 8 km S of Innisfail, is the bulk-sugar outlet for sugar produced in the Innisfail area. **In town:** Australian Sugar Museum, Bruce Hwy. **In the area:** South-west on Old Bruce Hwy: tours of South Johnstone Sugar Mill (8 km) in season (July–Oct.); National Trust-classified Paronella Park (14 km), ruins of Spanish-style castle set in rainforest; suspension bridge, waterfall, and picnic and camping areas nearby. Etty Bay, 9 km E: quiet tropical beach, caravan and camping facilities. **Visitor information:** Cassowary Coast Development Bureau, Bruce Hwy; (07) 4063 2000.

Mundubbera   Pop. 1238

MAP REF. 525 M4
Mundubbera, 2 km off the Burnett Hwy and 398 km NW of Brisbane, is the main citrus-growing area for the State but also has dairies, piggeries, broad-acre farming and a timber mill. **In town:** Jones Weir, Bauer St. **In the area:** Golden Mile Orchard, 5 km S, open Apr.–Sept. (tours of packing sheds). Auburn River National Park, 40 km SW. Peanut, maize and bean crops on Gurgeena and Binjour plateaus, to north-east. Rare *Neoceratodus* (lungfish) found in Burnett River. **Visitor information:** Big Mandarin Information Centre, Mundubbera–Durong Rd; (07) 4165 4549.

Murgon   Pop. 2088

MAP REF. 525 N6
Murgon, known as the beef capital of the Burnett, is one of the most attractive towns in southern Qld. Settlement dates back to 1853 and the name comes from an Aboriginal word meaning 'lily pond'. Beef, dairying, pigs and mixed crops are the main industries. A local wine industry is

being established. The town is 96 km inland from Gympie and 46 km N of Kingaroy. **In town:** Queensland Dairy Museum, Gayndah Rd. Adjacent, relocated Trinity homestead, one of district's original buildings. Oct.: Fishing Carnival (water levels permitting, at Bjelke-Petersen Dam). **In the area:** Wineries immediately outside town: Barambah Ridge, Rodericks, Bridgeman Downs, Burnett Valley; tastings and sales. Cherbourg Emu Farm at Cherbourg Aboriginal Community, 5 km SW, has walk-through enclosures, educational displays, and sales of emu products and Aboriginal artifacts. Bjelke-Petersen Dam, 15 km SE, for water sports and fishing. Scenic drives, brochures available. Nature walk and views in Jack Smith Scrub Conservation Park, 15 km NE; self-guide walks in Boat Mountain Conservation Park, adjacent. Goomeri, 19 km NE, known as 'clock town': unique memorial clock in town centre. Part of Bicentennial National Trail (5000-km trail for walkers and horse-riders) runs through Kilkivan, 44 km NE. Also at Kilkivan, Great Horse Ride in April. **Visitor information:** 118 Lamb St; (07) 4168 1984.

Muttaburra   Pop. 92

MAP REF. 526 A9, 533 P9
Muttaburra, 119 km N of Longreach, was developed as a town in the late 1870s, the name being derived from an Aboriginal word meaning 'meeting of the waters'. **In town:** Dr Arratta Memorial Museum, in old hospital, Sword St; tours by appt. Behind museum, site of 1891 Shearers' Strike. Replica of dinosaur, Bruford St. June: Landsborough Flock Ewe Show. **In the area:** The area has many fossil remains as it was formerly part of an inland sea. The name *Muttaburrasaurus* was given to a previously unknown dinosaur, the fossilised bones of which were discovered in a creek close to Thomson River in 1963. Fishing and water-skiing in Thomson River, 6 km S, bush camping on riverbanks. Agate fossicking, 5 km W. **Visitor information:** Post Office, Sword St; (07) 4658 7147.

Nambour   Pop. 12 205

MAP REF. 516 F4, 520 E8, 525 P7
Nambour is a busy provincial town, 106 km N of Brisbane, just off the Bruce Hwy. Development began in the 1860s, mainly by disappointed miners from the Gympie goldfields, and sugar has been the main crop since the 1890s. Small

The Sunshine Coast

A chain of sundrenched beaches bathed by the cobalt-blue Pacific stretches from Rainbow Beach southward to the tip of Bribie Island to form Queensland's Sunshine Coast. This scenic coastal region, with its average winter temperature of 25°C, its leisurely pace and its wide variety of natural attractions and sporting facilities, offers an attractive alternative to the more commercialised Gold Coast.

While huge waves thunder onto white sand beaches to provide year-round surfing, the calmer waters of protected beaches ensure safe swimming, boating and water-skiing. Rivers and streams are alive with fish to lure the angler, and the foreshores of forest-fringed lakes become perfect picnic spots for the family.

The Sunshine Coast is blessed with many natural wonders. The coloured sands of Teewah in the Cooloola section of **Great Sandy National Park**, between Tewantin and Rainbow Beach, rise in multi-coloured cliffs to over 200 metres. Geologists consider that these sandcliffs are over 40 000 years old and claim the main colouring is either the result of oxidisation or the dye of vegetation decay. However, an Aboriginal legend relates that the colours come from a rainbow serpent killed by a boomerang when it came to the rescue of a young woman. Another marvel of nature, the Glass House Mountains, were formed by giant cores of long-extinct volcanoes.

The Big Pineapple complex, south of Nambour

The Noosa area, at the northern end of the region, has facilities for fishing, boating and golf. Poised on the edge of Laguna Bay is the resort area of **Noosa Heads**, next to the Noosa Heads section of the 2280-hectare **Noosa National Park**. This coastal park contains a network of walking tracks, some winding through rainforests, others giving spectacular ocean views of such unusual rock formations as Hell's Gates, Paradise Caves, Lion's Rock, Devil's Kitchen and Witches' Cauldron.

The southernmost town of the Sunshine Coast is **Caloundra**, meaning 'the beautiful place', where Aborigines once came down from the hills to feast on seafood.

The hinterland of the Sunshine Coast is like a huge cultivated garden, covered with pineapples, sugarcane, ginger and citrus; dotted with dairy farms and enclosing within its folds cascading waterfalls, lush rainforests and bubbling streams. Looming majestically behind the coast is the Blackall Range, a world apart, with art and craft galleries, Devonshire-tea places, comfortable hotels and a feeling of 'olde England'. The scenic drive through the towns of Mapleton, Flaxton, Montville and Maleny is one of the best in south-east Queensland. The **Kondalilla National Park** is a must for nature lovers. The park includes the 80-metre Kondalilla Falls which drop into a valley of rainforest. The Mapleton Hotel offers authentic country-pub hospitality and panoramas from the traditional Queensland verandah.

Visit the miniature English village at Flaxton with its castles, churches, thatched cottages and inns. A number of art and craft cottages surround Montville's Village Green. Take in the view from the picture window at the De'Lisle Gallery while being surrounded by works of art from the Sunshine Coast's best artists. McCarthy's Lookout, at the southern end of the range, gives breathtaking views of the coast and the Glass House Mountains. **Nambour** is conveniently located, just off the Bruce Highway, for trips to the mountains of the Blackall Range or to the beach.

Just 7 kilometres south of Nambour is the Big Pineapple complex, a working plantation of pineapples and macadamia nuts, and home of the Big Pineapple.

The Sunshine Coast has accommodation to suit all tastes and budgets, from beachfront caravan parks through to luxury 5-star international hotels; and if you enjoy dining out, there are dozens of fine restaurants in the area.

For more information on the Sunshine Coast, contact Sunshine Coast Information, cnr Sixth Ave and Aerodrome Rd, Maroochydore; (07) 5479 1566. Web site www.sunshinecoast.org **See also:** Day Tours from Brisbane p. 453 and Hinterland Escape p. 456. For details on parks and towns in bold type, see National Parks p. 460 and individual entries in A–Z town listing. **Map references:** 516 H4, 520, 525 Q7.

Gulf Savannah

The Gulf Savannah is a vast, remote, thinly populated region stretching east to the Undara Volcanic National Park, north from **Mount Isa** and **Cloncurry** to the mangrove-covered shores of the Gulf of Carpentaria, and west to the Queensland-Northern Territory border. The explorer Leichhardt and the unfortunate Burke and Wills travelled through the region, although the waters of the Gulf itself were first charted by Dutch navigators almost 400 years ago. The country is flat and open, and has more rivers than roads. April to October is the recommended time to see the Gulf country. During the wet season, generally November to March, rain may close the dirt roads. However, bird-migration patterns make this the best time for observing the spectacular birdlife. This is not 'Sunday driving' country – although main roads have been upgraded – and motorists should plan accordingly. An alternative way to travel is to fly in from Cairns, Mount Isa or Karumba. The Gulf Savannah is ideal for getting away from it all.

Lawn Hill National Park, in the west of the State

The wide expanses of the Gulf Savannah region divide themselves into separate areas. The Eastern Savannah is easily reached via the Savannah Way (Gulf Developmental Road), which winds up the eastern face of the Dividing Range, passing above Cairns. As an alternative route to Georgetown, or for travellers with only limited time to explore the outback, the Undara Loop is a leisurely three to five day round trip from Cairns through The Lynd, Einasleigh and Forsayth to Georgetown.

Georgetown, 411 kilometres from Cairns, is the centre of the Etheridge Goldfield, where nuggets can still be found. Completing the loop back to Cairns takes the traveller to the mineral-charged thermal springs at Tallaroo Hot Springs, to Mount Surprise and to Undara Volcanic National Park, where you can see the lava tubes, a geological phenomenon. The *Savannahlander* train operates twice weekly between Cairns and Forsayth, taking passengers to Mount Surprise for an overnight stay on the return trip.

From Georgetown the traveller can head west 150 kilometres to **Croydon**, terminus of the railway from Normanton, a historic link established to service Croydon, last century a rich goldmining town. The railway between the two towns is not connected to any other system. It is used once a week by the tourist train *Gulflander*, which leaves Normanton every Wednesday and arrives in Croydon at midday for an overnight stop. Many of Croydon's buildings have been classified by the National Trust and the Australian Heritage Commission.

Normanton is the central town of the whole Gulf Savannah, with a population of 1328, although in the gold days of 1891 it had a population of about 3000 people.

Karumba, 71 kilometres north-west of Normanton on the mouth of the Norman River, is the centre of the Gulf prawning industry and home to the barramundi fishing industry. Keen anglers from all over Australia come to Karumba to try their skills.

The Western Savannah has endless flat grassed plains stretching as far as the eye can see, while the wetlands around Karumba stretch across the top of the Western Savannah above Burketown and beyond to the border. Here rivers some 8 kilometres apart overflow their banks during the monsoons and form an unbroken sheet of water.

The town of **Burketown**, close to the Gulf, can be isolated for long periods during the wet. Explorer John Stokes termed the surrounding area the 'Plains of Promise', and today, like most of the Gulf region, it is cattle country. Barramundi fishing and birdwatching attract adventurers; a well-equipped 4WD vehicle is advisable in some areas, but is not essential for a visit to the majority of locations.

Lawn Hill National Park includes the World Heritage-listed Riversleigh Fossil Field Site. The park is west of the hotel at Gregory, a welcome watering-hole for the traveller. In the park, 60-metre sheer sandstone walls form Lawn Hill Gorge, with emerald-green water at their base. The National Parks Service has established 20 kilometres of walking tracks to enable visitors to see this beautiful country safely.

The Gulf Savannah is a new frontier in Australia that is opening up to those in search of interesting but authentic travel and adventure experiences. To assist visitors, an organisation of Savannah Guides has been formed. These guides are professional interpreters who have lived in the Gulf Savannah for many years and are able to offer a wide range of knowledge concerning the wilderness environment. There are guide stations at Hells Gate, Undara Volcanic National Park, Lawn Hill National Park (at Adels Grove), and Cobbold Gorge.

For further information on the area, including road reports and free birdwatching guidebooks, contact Gulf Savannah Tourist Organisation, 55 McLeod St, Cairns; (07) 4051 4658. Web site www.internetnorth.com.au/gulf/ **See also:** National Parks p. 460 and individual entries in A–Z town listing for details on parks and towns in bold type. **Map references:** 528 C12, 531 H12.

locomotives pulling trucks of sugar-cane trundle across the main street to Moreton Central Mill during the crushing season (July–Oct.). Pineapples and other tropical fruit are grown extensively. *Nambour* is the Aboriginal name for the red-flowering tea-tree that grows locally. **In the area:** Spectacular Glass House Mountains to south, and scenic Blackall Range to west. The Big Pineapple complex and Macadamia Nut Factory, 7 km S. Forest Glen Sanctuary (deer and native wildlife)and Superbee Honey Factory, 10 km further S on Forest Glen–Tanawah Tourist Dr. Mapleton, 13 km W, has a Yarn Festival (storytelling) in Oct. **Visitor information:** cnr Aerodrome Rd and Sixth Ave, Maroochydore; (07) 5479 1566. **See also:** The Sunshine Coast p. 493.

Nanango　　Pop. 2711

MAP REF. 525 N7

Gold was mined here from 1850 to 1900, but the area, 24 km SE of Kingaroy, now produces beef cattle, beans and grain, while grape-growing is expanding. The 1400-megawatt Tarong Power Station and Meandu Coal Mine, 16 km SW, are also of economic importance to the area. **In town:** Ringsfield Museum (1908), originally a house, became a maternity hospital 1912; restored 1993, now a local history museum (check times, also by appt). Market, 1st Sat. each month. Oct.: Pioneer Festival. **In the area:** Forest drives, permit and maps from Forestry Dept, Yarraman. Berlin's Gem and Historical Museum, 17 km SW. Coomba Falls, near Maidenwell, 28 km SW. Bunya Mountains National Park, 70 km SW. Seven Mile Diggings, 11 km SE, gold- and gem-fossicking area. Tipperary Flat, 2 km E: park with replica of old goldmining camp, picnic facilities. **Visitor information:** Shire Offices, 48 Drayton St; (07) 4163 1307.

Nerang　　Pop. 14 467

MAP REF. 517 G11, 519 C5, 525 Q10

This town in the Gold Coast hinterland is 10 km W of Southport. **In the area:** Scenic drive, brochure available. At Carrara, 5 km SE, weekend Hinterland country market. Hinze Dam on Advancetown Lake, 8 km SW, good for sailing and bass-fishing. Spectacular scenery in Numinbah Valley area, 15 km SW near Beechmont. Towards Springbrook, 42 km SW: Wunburra Lookout on Springbrook Plateau; Best of All View, off Repeater Station Rd;

Purlingbrook Falls in Springbrook National Park. Natural Bridge section of Springbrook National Park, 38 km SW: popular picnic spot, walking tracks through scenic rainforest, lookout nearby, glow-worms in cave under bridge. Paradise Country, 2 km W, small working farm. Historic River Mill (1910), 10 km W, arrowroot mill. Lookout near Mt Tamborine village, 20 km NE, offers spectacular views to Gold Coast and north to South Stradbroke Island. **Visitor information:** Cavill Ave, Surfers Paradise; (07) 5538 4419. **See also:** Day Tours from Brisbane p. 453.

Noosa Heads　　Pop. 17 776

MAP REF. 516 H1, 520 H1, 525 Q6

Noosa Heads (commonly known as Noosa) is a coastal resort set on Laguna Bay on the Sunshine Coast. The relaxed lifestyle, the Queensland weather and the opportunity for safe year-round swimming make this a popular holiday destination. All development here is low-rise and the beautiful natural setting is one of the great attractions. Only walking distance from the cosmopolitan Hastings Street is the magnificent headland area of Noosa National Park, 477 hectares of protected coves, surfing beaches and seascapes. **In town:** In Hastings St: numerous restaurants, shops and galleries. Noosa Main Beach for safe family swimming. Sept.: Jazz Fest. Oct.: Beach Car Classic. Nov.: Triathlon. **In the area:** In Noosa National Park, 1 km E: Cook's Monument; Hell's Gates, coastal rock formation; Devils Kitchen, blowhole; and walks through rainforest and heathland. Sunshine Beach, 3 km SE, popular for surfing. Laguna Lookout, on Noosa Hill, for views of Noosa River and lakes. Noosaville, 5 km N, family-style resort with Noosa River as focal point; departure point for river cruises. At Tewantin, 7 km N: Noosa Regional Gallery, Big Shell and House of Bottles. Cooloola section of Great Sandy National Park, 14 km N, separated from Sunshine Coast by Noosa River (accessible via ferry from Tewantin): bushwalking, camel riding, horseriding, surfing; Coloured Sands, multicoloured sand cliffs; shipwrecked freighter *Cherry Venture* (accessible via 4WD or inland by conventional vehicle); beach access to departure point of Fraser Island ferry. Lakes Cooroibah and Cootharaba, 27 km N, ideal for boating, sailing and windsurfing (accessible by car or boat from Noosaville). At Lake

Cootharaba: sleepy lakeside town of Boreen Point; 2-km walk from Teewah Landing to North Shore beaches; Kinaba Information Centre; boardwalks into surrounding wetlands. Noosa River extends over 40 km north into Great Sandy National Park: cruises to Everglades, waters known for their reflections; Harry's Hut, relic of timber-cutting days. Eumundi, 24 km SW, known for market held each Sat. a.m. Volcanic gems at Thunder Egg Farm, 29 km SW. **Visitor information:** Hastings St roundabout, Noosa Heads; (07) 5447 4988, freecall 1800 448 833. Web site www.tourismnoosa.com.au **See also:** Day Tours from Brisbane p. 453; Hinterland Escape p. 456; The Sunshine Coast p. 493.

Normanton　　Pop. 1328

MAP REF. 528 C8, 531 I8

Normanton, 153 km W of Croydon, is the central town of the Gulf Savannah and is on a high, gravel ridge on the edge of the savannah grasslands extending west and wetlands extending north. The town is also the terminus of the historic Normanton-to-Croydon railway, and the Normanton railway station is the home of the award-winning *Gulflander* tourist train. **In town:** Penitentiary, Haig St. Restored Bank of NSW building, Little Brown St. Disused town well, Landsborough St. In Shire Office Gardens, Haig St: life-size replica of Krys the Savannah King, 8.6-metre saltwater crocodile. Self-guide scenic walk and drive, brochure available. Giant barramundi, outside Gulfland Motel in Landsborough St. June: Show, Rodeo and Gymkhana. **In the area:** Fishing and camping at Walkers Creek, 32 km NW, and Norman River at Glenore Crossing, 25 km SE. Lakes on outskirts of Normanton attract jabirus, brolgas, herons and other birds. Shady Lagoon, 18 km E, for bush camping, birdwatching and wildlife. Dorunda Station, 197 km NE, cattle station offering barramundi and saratoga fishing in lake and rivers, and accommodation. Kowanyama Aboriginal Community, 359 km NE: excellent barramundi fishing, guest house, camping; Aboriginal Land, permit to visit required from Kowanyama Community Council. Burke and Wills Cairn, 40 km SW. Bang Bang Jump Up rock formation, 106 km SW: a solitary hill on the surrounding flat plains, road goes over top, excellent views. **Visitor information:** Shire Offices, Haig St; (07) 4745 1166. **See also:** Gulf Savannah p. 494; Cape York p. 507.

Four Mile Beach, Port Douglas

Oakey   Pop. 3396

MAP REF. 525 N9
On the Warrego Hwy, 29 km NW of
Toowoomba, Oakey is the base for
Australian Army Aviation. The town is
surrounded by beautiful rolling hills
and dark soil plains. **In town:** Bronze
statue of racehorse Bernborough in front of
Community Centre, Campbell St. Oakey
Historical Museum, Warrego Hwy. Flypast
Museum of Australian Army Flying, at
army base via Kelvinaugh Rd, has large
collection of original and replica aircraft
(some in flying condition), and aviation
memorabilia. **In the area:** Acland Coal
Mine Museum, 18 km N; open Mar.–Jan.,
Sat.–Wed. or by appt. Jondaryan Woolshed
(1859), off Warrego Hwy, 22 km NW:
memorial to pioneers of wool industry;
includes huge woolshed and other buildings, shearing demonstrations, sheep dogs,
billy tea and damper, and sales of goods at
wool store; Australian heritage festival, at
Woolshed in Aug. **Visitor information:**
Library, 64 Campbell St; (07) 4691 2306.

Palm Cove   Pop. 2800

MAP REF. 523 E7, 529 M6
Serene Palm Cove, 27 km NW of Cairns,
offers visitors an inviting selection of
accommodation with splendid boutiques,
art galleries and souvenir shops – all set on
a tropical beach. Dive and tour bookings
to the Great Barrier Reef are available,
as are pick-up services for day tours to
the Atherton Tableland and surrounding
areas. There is also convenient access to
Mossman and Port Douglas. **In the area:**
On Captain Cook Hwy at Clifton Beach,
3 km S: Wild World, features exotic range
of flora and fauna; Outback Opal Mine,
simulated mine with displays of Australia's
most famous stone. Bungee tower in rainforest, McGregor Rd, Smithfield, 14 km S.
Hartley's Crocodile Farm, 15 km N: hundreds of crocodiles, including 'Charlie',
there since 1934; native fauna; snake
shows and pat-the-animal. Rex Lookout,
17 km N, for stunning coastal views.
Visitor information: Tourism Tropical
North Queensland, 51 The Esplanade,
Cairns; (07) 4051 3588.

Pittsworth   Pop. 2323

MAP REF. 525 N9
Pittsworth is a typical Darling Downs
town, situated 46 km SW of Toowoomba
on the road to Millmerran. It is the
centre of a rich grain and dairying district
and cotton is grown with the help of irrigation. The jacarandas and silky oaks in
and around the town are a spectacular
sight in late spring. **In town:** Some buildings listed by National Trust: Folk
Museum; Pioneer Way, includes pioneer
cottage; blacksmith's shop; early school.
Private gardens open at certain times
(check with information centre). Jan.
(Australia Day): Crimson Flash Shield (foot
race). **Visitor information:** Sunkist Cafe,
Yandilla St; (07) 4693 1246.

Pomona   Pop. 967

MAP REF. 516 E1, 520 B1, 525 P6
This small farming centre is in the northern hinterland of the Sunshine Coast,
33 km S of Gympie. Mt Cooroora (439 m)
dominates the town. **In town:** Majestic
Theatre, cinema museum and location
for annual film festival. July: King of
the Mountain (race attracting mountain
runners world-wide). Sept: Country Show.
In the area: Water sports at Lake
Cootharaba, 19 km NE, a large, shallow
saltwater lake on Noosa River near
where Mrs Eliza Fraser spent time
with Aborigines after wreck of *Stirling
Castle* on Fraser Island in 1836. **Visitor
information:** Noosa Information Centre,
Hastings St roundabout, Noosa Heads;
(07) 5447 4988, freecall 1800 448 833.

Port Douglas   Pop. 3641

MAP REF. 523 C4, 529 M5
Just 73 km NW of Cairns, along one of the
most scenic coastal drives in Australia,
Port Douglas offers the contrast of
cosmopolitanism in a tropical mountain
setting beside the Coral Sea. Once a small
village, Port Douglas has become an
international tourist destination. The
town, off the main highway, is surrounded by lush vegetation and pristine
rainforests. This setting, along with its
proximity to the Great Barrier Reef, makes
it an ideal holiday destination. **In town:**
Ben Cropp's Shipwreck Museum and
Courthouse Museum, Anzac Park,
Macrossan St. Rainforest Habitat, Port
Douglas Rd; wildlife sanctuary with treetop walk, flora and fauna in natural
setting. Flagstaff Hill, end Murphy St,
commands excellent views of Four Mile
Beach and Low Isles. Tours available from
town include: horse trail-riding; rainforest
tours; 4WD safaris; coach tours to
Mossman Gorge, Daintree National Park,
Cape Tribulation, Kuranda and Cooktown;
reef tours to Outer Barrier Reef and Low
Isles; *Lady Douglas* paddlewheel cruise.
Market, Anzac Park, each Sun. May:
Village Carnivale. **Visitor information:**
Port Douglas and Cooktown Information
Centre, 23 Macrossan St; (07) 4099 5599.
See also: The Far North p. 472.

Capricorn Region

This rich and varied slice of Queensland stretches inland from Rockhampton and the Capricorn Coast out to Jericho, and straddles the Tropic of Capricorn. The area includes the Capricorn Coast, Rockhampton city and surrounds, the central highlands and the rural hinterlands, and is drained by the Fitzroy, Mackenzie, Comet, Nogoa and Dawson rivers. The district was opened up by gold- and copper-mining around **Emerald** in the 1860s, and the discovery of sapphires around Anakie. Professional and amateur fossickers still find gems in the region. The original owners of the land have left superb and mysterious rock paintings on the stone walls of the Carnarvon Ranges to the south. Cattle have been the economic mainstay of the region since European settlement, but vast tracts of brigalow scrub were cleared after World War II to grow wheat, maize, sorghum and safflower. These days coal is dominant, with mainly American companies mining enormous deposits for local and Japanese markets.

For a pleasurable tour of the region, drive west from **Rockhampton**, the commercial and manufacturing capital, along the Capricorn Highway. Detour to Blackdown Tableland National Park where there are waterfalls, rock pools and camping areas; the turn-off is between Dingo and Blackwater. To camp in the park, you will need a permit – available on arrival, except during busy holiday periods when you must obtain a permit from the regional office of the Queensland Parks and Wildlife Service; (07) 4986 1964. At Emerald turn south to Springsure, then east to **Biloela** on the Dawson Highway. Continue north on the Burnett Highway via **Mount Morgan** to Rockhampton.

Mount Hay Gemstone Tourist Park, 41 kilometres west of Rockhampton, allows visitors to fossick for thunder eggs and rhyolite, which may be cut and polished at the factory in the park. Utah's Blackwater coal mine produces 4 million tonnes of coking coal and almost 3 million tonnes of steaming coal annually. Tours can be arranged.

Emerald is the main town in the Central Highlands region, with the central–western railway continuing west to **Longreach** and the Channel Country. Clermont and the Blair Athol coalfields are 106 kilometres to the north-west. The gemfields of Anakie, Rubyvale, Sapphire, Willows Gemfields and Tomahawk Creek, west of Emerald, are popular for those seeking a different holiday. (A fossicker's licence is necessary.)

Springsure, 66 kilometres south of Emerald, is one of Queensland's oldest towns, surveyed in 1854. It produces beef and grain. In Springsure Cemetery Reserve is the Yumba–Burin Crypt, which holds the remains of aboriginal people of the Mansion Downs area. The remains had been kept in the Queensland Museum for 70 years before being released for burial in 1998. Nearby is the Old Rainworth Fort at Burnside, where early farm equipment and wool presses form a fascinating display. The fort was built in 1853 from local stone.

Rolleston, 70 kilometres to the south-east, is the turn-off to the magnificent **Carnarvon National Park**, 103 kilometres further south. The park covers 298 000 hectares of rugged mountains, forests, rock overhangs and deep gorges, some of which are Australia's earliest art galleries. There are countless Aboriginal paintings and engravings, which in places extend in a colourful frieze for more than 50 metres.

The Callide open-cut mine is near Biloela, the principal town in the Callide Valley. The nearby Callide Power Station supplies the Rockhampton, Moura and Blackwater districts as well as Biloela.

'The Snowy Mounts', in the Fitzroy River delta between Bajool and Port Alma, are actually huge piles of salt. Underground salty water is pumped to the surface and the salt is harvested after solar evaporation.

For further information on the Capricorn Region, contact the Capricorn Information Centre, The Spire, Gladstone Rd, Rockhampton; (07) 4927 2055. **See also:** National Parks p. 460 and individual entries in A–Z town listing for details on parks and towns in bold type. **Map reference:** 526–9.

Farm field at Capella, west of Rockhampton

Proserpine
Pop. 3247

MAP REF. 527 J3

A sugar town, Proserpine is close to Airlie Beach, Shute Harbour and the islands of Whitsunday Passage. **In town:** Proserpine Historical Museum, Main St (check opening times). Oct.: Harvest Festival (includes World Championship Cane Cutting). **In the area:** Conway National Park, 10 km SE, views across islands of Whitsunday Passage from vantage points within park. Lake Proserpine at Peter Faust Dam, 20 km W, offers boat hire, water-skiing, fishing and swimming; nearby, Cedar Creek Falls. **Visitor information:** Bruce Hwy; (07) 4945 3711, freecall 1800 801 252. Web site www.whitsundayinformation.com.au.

Quilpie
Pop. 730

MAP REF. 535 O7

Quilpie, 200 km W of Charleville, was established as a rail centre for the large sheep and cattle properties in the area, but is better known as a boulder opal town. It takes its name from the Aboriginal word *quilpeta*, meaning 'stone curlew'. *Travellers heading west to Birdsville should note that there is no hotel or fuel at Betoota – extra fuel should therefore be carried from Windorah.* **In town:** Museum and gallery at information centre, Brolga St; historical and modern exhibitions. Sales of opals at various outlets in town. Altar, font and lectern of St Finbarr's Catholic Church, Buln Buln St, made from opal-bearing rock. Apr.: Fishing Carnival. June: Boulder Opal Expo. June and Aug.: Diggers Races. Late Aug.–early Sept.: Kangaranga Do Street Party. Sept.: Agricultural Show. **In the area:** Opal workings just outside town. Lake Houdraman, 6 km NE on river road to Adavale, popular recreation area. Baldy Top, large geological formation 3 km S, allowing spectacular views. At Toompine Road-house, 76 km S, historic hotel and cemetery; designated opal-fossicking areas nearby. Guided tours of opal fields, 75 km W (no general access). Eromanga, 103 km W, reputedly the furthest town from the sea in Australia: Royal Hotel, once Cobb & Co. staging post; Easter Rodeo; Race Day in May. **Visitor information:** Brolga St; (07) 4656 2166. **See also:** Channel Country p. 469.

Ravenswood
Pop. 300

MAP REF. 526 G2

Ravenswood, friendly and 'not quite a ghost town', is 85 km E of Charters Towers via Mingela. One hundred years ago it was the classic gold-rush town. Visitors will find interesting old workings and perhaps a little gold along with the nostalgia. **In town:** Several restored historic buildings in town, including Courthouse Museum and Craft Shop, Imperial Railway Hotel, other shops and current ambulance centre. Thrice-weekly gold-panning (check times). May: Back to Ravenswood Festival. Oct.: Halloween Ball. **In the area:** Burdekin Falls Dam, 80 km SE, popular recreational area. Rodeo each May at Mingela, 38 km NW. **Visitor information:** Tourist Information Centre, Mosman St, Charters Towers; (07) 4752 0314.

Richmond
Pop. 733

MAP REF. 533 M4

This small town on the Flinders River, 500 km SW of Townsville, serves the surrounding sheep and cattle properties. The town's main street is lined with beautiful bougainvilleas. **In town:** In Goldring St: restored Cobb & Co. coach; Richmond Hotel, known as Mud Hut Hotel, historic flagstone and adobe building; Gidgee Wheel Arts and Craft. Kronosaurus Korner, cnr Goldring St and Flinders Hwy, exhibits of excellent vertebrae fossils, all found in Richmond Shire. St Johns Church, Crawford St, has silky-oak fittings and leadlight windows. Sandalwood Mill, Simpson St. Pioneer Cemetery, Flinders Hwy, on western edge of town. **In the area:** The area is rich in fossils. **Visitor information:** cnr Goldring St and Flinders Hwy; (07) 4741 3429.

Rockhampton
Pop. 57 770

MAP REF. 527 N11

Rockhampton is called the beef capital of Australia, with some 2.5 million cattle in the region. Gold was discovered at Canoona, 60 km NW of Rockhampton, in 1858; however, cattle became the major industry, with Herefords the main breed. In recent years cross-breeding with more exotic breeds has produced disease-resistant herds. Rockhampton straddles the Tropic of Capricorn. It is a prosperous city on the banks of the Fitzroy River and has considerable architectural charm. Many of the original stone buildings and churches remain, set off by flowering bauhinia and brilliant bougainvilleas. **In town:** In Quay St, Australia's longest National Trust-classified street, with over 20 classified buildings: ANZ Bank (1864) and Customs House (1901). Cruises on Fitzroy River, departing Quay St wharf, cover history of river and district. Heritage walk around city centre. Scattered around city are old Queensland houses carefully preserved. Botanic Gardens on Athelstane Range, via Spencer St, has fine tropical displays, orchid and fern house, a Japanese-style garden, monkeys, koala park and walk-in aviary. Kershaw Gardens, Bruce Hwy, features Australian native flora Braille Trail. Fitzroy River Barrage, Savage St: separates tidal saltwater from upstream freshwater; opportunities for barramundi fishing. Capricorn Spire (14 m) at Curtis Park, Gladstone Rd, marks the line of Tropic of Capricorn. Rockhampton City Art Gallery, Victoria Pde: changing exhibitions, chamber music recital 2nd Sun. each month. Rocky markets, Denison St, Sat. and Sun. Apr.: Good Earth Expo. July: Bauhinia Arts Festival; Grey Mardi Gras. Aug.: Rocky Round Up. Oct.: Arts in the Park. **In the area:** Natural events: bent-wing bats exodus, late Nov.–late Jan; summer solstice light spectacular, early Dec.–mid-Jan. Capricorn Scenic Loop tourist drive, brochure available. Old Glenmore historic homestead, 8 km N, has displays and historic buildings. Dreamtime Cultural Centre, 7 km N on Bruce Hwy, features culture of the Darumbal language group. St Christopher's Chapel, 20 km N, on Emu Park Rd, built by American servicemen. Rockhampton Heritage Village, Parkhurst, 9 km N: heritage buildings with hall of clocks and pioneering tools, also steam engine; open daily, working displays weekends only. Olsen's Capricorn Caverns and Cammoo Caves, both limestone cave systems, 23 km N; tours daily; Carols in the Caverns, in Olsen's Capricorn Caverns, each Dec. Mt Hay Gemstone Tourist Park, 40 km W on Capricorn Hwy, thunder-egg fossicking. Pleasant drive to lookout at top of Mt Archer, 6 km E. **Visitor information:** The Spire, Gladstone Rd; (07) 4927 2055. **See also:** Capricorn Region p. 497.

Roma
Pop. 5744

MAP REF. 524 H6

Roma is 267 km W of Dalby at the junction of the Warrego and the Carnarvon

Carnarvon Gorge in Carnarvon National Park near Roma

hwys. It was named after the wife of Sir George Bowen, Qld's first Governor, and was first surveyed in 1862. The Mt Abundance cattle station was established in 1847, and sheep and cattle have been the area's economic mainstay ever since. The historic trial of Harry Redford, alias Captain Starlight, was held in Roma in 1872. In 1863 Samuel Symons Bassett brought vine cuttings to Roma and Qld's first wine-making enterprise began. Australia's first natural gas strike was made at Hospital Hill in 1900 (tourist drive, brochure available), and this gas was used, in 1906, to light the town. Further deposits were found, and 'oil' (actually gas and condensate) caused excitement in the area in the late 1920s. Roma has supplied Brisbane with gas via a 450-km pipeline since 1969, but a major pipeline now brings gas from far western Qld to supplement the Roma area's depleting reserves. **In town:** Oil rig, named Big Rig by locals, at eastern entrance to town on Warrego Hwy; adjacent, Big Rig Research Centre records early oil exploration in area. Romavilla Winery, Injune Rd. Roma–Bungil Cultural Centre, cnr Bungil and Injune rds, includes three-dimensional mural by local artists. Roma Bottle Trees, in Heroes'

Ave, planted to commemorate local soldiers who died in WW I; adjacent park has picnic facilities. Markets at Big Rig site, 2nd and 4th Sun. each month. Easter: Easter in the Country. **In the area:** Largest inland cattle market in Australia, 4 km E on Warrego Hwy. Meadowbank Museum, 15 km W on Warrego Hwy. Carnarvon National Park, 244 km NW: Carnarvon Gorge, Aboriginal cave paintings, varied scenery and walks; guided tours; accommodation. **Visitor information:** Big Rig site, Lower McDowall St; (07) 4622 4355. Web site www.maranoa.org.au

St George   Pop. 2463

MAP REF. 524 G10

Situated at a major road junction, St George is in the centre of a rich grape, peanut and cotton-growing district. It is on the Balonne River, 118 km NW of Mungindi on the Carnarvon Hwy, and 289 km SW of Dalby on the Moonie Hwy. It is often referred to as the inland fishing capital of Qld as there are many fishing spots yielding Murray cod and yellow-belly, particularly in the Balonne River. As St George has a rainfall of only 500 mm a year, extensive irrigation is carried out by

means of a dam and 3 weirs. Cotton-growing and harvesting is completely mechanised; planting Oct. to Nov., harvesting Apr. to June. Wheat, barley, oats and sunflowers are also irrigated, and sheep and cattle are raised. **In town:** Riversands Vineyards, Whytes Rd. Carved, illuminated emu eggs displayed at Balonne Sports store, Victoria St. Easter: St George's Day. May: Country Show. Oct.: Regional Fishing Competition. **In the area:** Boolba Wool and Craft Show, variety of events, held in May at Boolba, 50 km W. Rosehill Aviaries, 64 km W, one of Australia's largest private collections of Australian parrots. At Bollon, 112 km W: large koala population in trees along Wallan Creek; Heritage and craft centre, George St, local history exhibits. Pastoral township, Dirranbandi, 97 km SW near the NSW border: Railway Park, Railway St; Cubbie Station, 33 km further west, largest privately owned cotton property in State, tours available. Culgoa Floodplain National Park, 130 km SW of Dirranbandi: floodplain and mulga country; birdlife; 4WD access only; campers must be self-sufficent. Cotton Ginnery, 20 km S; open by appt Mar.–July. Historic hotel (1863) at Nindigully, 44 km SE,

The Gold Coast

Sunshine, sand and surf on the Gold Coast

The Gold Coast, Australia's premier holiday destination, consists of 70 kilometres of coastline, and boasts 42 kilometres of golden beaches stretching from South Stradbroke Island in the north to Cabarita Beach in New South Wales. The Gold Coast hinterland forms a lush subtropical backdrop – the 'green behind the gold'.

Only one hour's drive south of Brisbane, this international resort city offers a multitude of constructed and natural attractions, and, of course, superb surfing beaches – 35 patrolled beaches, including Main Beach, Surfers Paradise, Broadbeach, Mermaid Beach, Miami, Burleigh Heads, Tallebudgera, Palm Beach, Currumbin, Tugun, Kirra and Coolangatta.

With almost 300 days of sunshine each year – an average winter maximum of 21°C and an average summer maximum of 28°C – the Gold Coast region is the country's holiday playground, attracting almost 4 million visitors annually.

Accommodation caters for all budgets, ranging from international five-star-plus hotels and resorts to hotels, motels, apartments, guest houses, caravan parks, camping grounds and backpackers' hostels. It is estimated there are more than 50 000 rooms with more than 80 000 beds available on the Gold Coast. A variety of theme parks, sporting facilities, restaurants, markets, shops, nightlife and entertainment guarantee to satisfy all tastes. The Gold Coast is said to have the largest number of restaurants per square kilometre in Australia.

With its towering skyline and beachfront esplanade, Surfers Paradise is the hub of the central Gold Coast region, while the Gold Coast hinterland is a subtropical hideaway with numerous national parks and reserves complete with massive trees, spectacular views, cascading waterfalls and bush walks only 30 minutes from the hustle and bustle of the city.

Moving west from the coastline into the hinterland, the terrain climbs steadily to 1000 metres and breathtaking scenery in the Numinbah Valley and at Springbrook. Highlights here include Canyon Lookout, the 190-metre Purlingbrook Falls, Wunburra Lookout and the Hinze Dam.

In the Numinbah Valley is the Natural Bridge, a spectacular waterfall which plummets through a stone archway into a rock pool below. This picturesque area is excellent for picnics, barbecues and bush walks.

At Oxenford: Warner Bros Movie World, based on the famous Hollywood movie set, is a theme park and part of a fully operational movie set. Close by is Wet 'n' Wild Water World, Australia's largest aquatic fun park.

At Coomera: To the north is Dreamworld, a theme park with 'themed worlds' including Tiger Island, the Tower of Terror and the Giant Drop. Nearby is the exclusive Sanctuary Cove resort, which incorporates the

Hyatt Regency Sanctuary Cove, two golf courses and a marina. Just south is Cable Ski World and Pine Ridge Conservation Park at Coombabah.

At **Main Beach**: Sea World, on The Spit, is the largest marine park in the Southern Hemisphere. Its world-class attractions include performing dolphins, a monorail, a skyway, water-ski ballet, helicopter rides, a replica of the *Endeavour*, the Old Fort, an exciting corkscrew rollercoaster, and for a journey into the unknown, a 'lifeboat' voyage to the Bermuda Triangle. It adjoins the Sea World Nara Resort. Mariner's Cove is also along the Broadwater with its indoor climbing and thrill rides, marina, shopping and restaurants, and Marina Mirage, an upmarket shopping and boating complex. Visitors can enjoy a wide variety of water sports on the Broadwater.

At **Surfers Paradise**: Attractions include Ripleys Believe It or Not Museum, family entertainment centres, resort shopping, restaurants, many international hotels, numerous nightclubs and the sport of people-watching. The Gold Coast Arts Centre is near Surfers Paradise at Bundall.

At Broadbeach: Pacific Fair shopping resort is on the Nerang River. Conrad Jupiters Hotel and Casino are linked by monorail to the Oasis Shopping Resort and the Grand Mercure Hotel Broadbeach. Cascade Park and Gardens on the Nerang River is ideal for picnicking. View the area by an open-cockpit flight in a Tiger Moth plane.

At Mermaid Beach: A huge cinema complex is located near family restaurants and a variety of other restaurants.

At Burleigh Heads: Burleigh Knoll Conservation Park, Burleigh Head National Park, and David Fleay's Wildlife Park, which also has indoor climbing, are all worth a visit.

Inland at Mudgeeraba are the Gold Coast War Museum with indoor and outdoor displays of army memorabilia and skirmish, and Balloon Down Under for balloon rides over the Gold Coast.

At Robina: Robina Town Centre, one of Queensland's largest shopping complexes.

At **Currumbin**: Feed the thousands of lorikeets that flock to the Currumbin Wildlife Sanctuary daily. World of Bees is opposite. Visit Olson's Bird Gardens, the Currumbin Rock Pool, and the Mount Cougal section of Springbrook National Park. On the way, visit Schusters Lookout and further south-west Arthur Freeman Lookout – both offer superb views over Currumbin Valley.

At **Coolangatta**: Beach House Plaza links the main street with the beachfront; and the lighthouse and Captain Cook Memorial at Point Danger.

At Tweed Heads: Across the border from Coolangatta, visit the Minjungbal Aboriginal Culture Centre. It is also home to some of Australia's largest sports and entertainment clubs.

For further information contact the Gold Coast Tourism Bureau, 64 Ferny Ave, Surfers Paradise; (07) 5592 2699. There are information centres at Cavill Ave, Surfers Paradise; (07) 5538 4419, and Shop 14B, Coolangatta Pl., cnr Griffith and Warner sts, Coolangatta; (07) 5536 7765. Web site www.goldcoasttourism. com.au **See also:** Day Tours from Brisbane p. 453. For details on towns in bold type, see individual entries in A–Z town listing. **Map references:** 517 G11, 519, 525 R10.

Cavill Avenue, the heart of Surfers Paradise

Shute Harbour at sunset

motorbike riders arrive each June for Nindigully 5-hour Enduro. Thallon, 76 km SE: swimming and fishing at Barney's Beach on Moonie River; nearby historic Bullamon homestead (1860), mentioned in Steele Rudd's 'Memoirs of Corporal Keeley', has original shingle roof and canvas ceilings, tours by appt. Further 3 km, restored vintage tractor collection, open by appt. Ancient rock well, 37 km E, hand hewn by Aborigines possibly thousands of years ago. E. J. Beardmore Dam, 21 km N, for fishing and water sports; scenic picnic spots in surrounding parklands. **Visitor information:** Shire Offices, Victoria St; (07) 4625 3222 and Kamarooka Caravan Park, 56 Victoria St; (07) 4625 3120.

Sarina   Pop. 3201

MAP REF. 527 L6

In the sugar belt, Sarina lies 36 km S of Mackay on the Bruce Hwy. The area has many fine beaches, including Sarina Beach, Campwin Beach, Grasstree, Salonika, Half Tide, and, to the south, Armstrong Beach. Sarina produces molasses and ethyl alcohol as by-products of the sugar industry. Sarina is also the location for the CSR Plane Creek Central Sugar Mill and Distillery, Bruce Hwy, which produces fertiliser for local sugarcane crops. **In town:** In Broad St: rose gardens; Sarina Surprise pictorial

quilt at library, 3.5 m x 2.5 m depiction of town's buildings, landmarks, industries and lifestyle. In Railway Sq.: palm and rose gardens; old courthouse (1901), houses Sarina Tourist Art and Craft Centre, with local arts and craft and local industry information. Flea market, Broad St, last Thurs. each month. Beach markets, last Sun. each month. May: Mud Trials (buggy-racing on a mud track). June: Fishing Classic. July: Visual Arts Festival. Aug.: Agricultural Show. Sept.: Grasstree Beach Bike Races. **In the area:** Cape Palmerston National Park, 78 km SE, 4WD access only. Viewing gallery at Hay Point and Dalrymple Bay coal terminal complex, 12 km N. **Visitor information:** Railway Sq.; (07) 4956 2251.

Shute Harbour   Pop. 200

MAP REF. 527 K3

Shute Harbour, 36 km NE of Proserpine, has one of the largest marine passenger terminals in Australia, second only to Sydney's Circular Quay. **In town:** Jetty at Shute Harbour, best place to start exploring the 74 tropical islands in the beautiful Whitsunday waters, including well-known Hayman, Daydream, South Molle, Hamilton and Lindeman islands; variety of cruise boats depart daily; booking offices, souvenir and food outlets on main jetty. Boom-net riding daily. Seaplane ride to Hardy's Lagoon on the

outer Great Barrier Reef for snorkelling among the coral. Day trips to the pontoon at Hardy Reef for swimming, scuba diving and snorkelling. Sail and power vessels, varying sizes and classes, for hire. Lions Lookout, Whitsunday Dr., for spectacular views. June: Hamilton Island Cup (outrigger canoes). Aug.: Hamilton Island Race Week (sailing). Sept.: Hamilton Island Beach Volleyball Pro Tour. **In the area:** Conway National Park, 15 km S. Great Barrier Reef and Whitsunday islands. **Visitor information:** Tourism Whitsundays, Bruce Hwy, Proserpine; (07) 4945 3711, freecall 1800 801 252.

Stanthorpe   Pop. 4154

MAP REF. 117 M2, 525 N12

The main town in the Granite Belt and in the mountain ranges along the border between Qld and NSW, Stanthorpe, 221 km SW of Brisbane, came into being after the discovery of tin at Quartpot Creek in 1872. Silver and lead were discovered in 1880 but the minerals boom did not last. The area has produced excellent wool for more than a century but is best known for its large-scale growing of apples, pears, plums, peaches and grapes. Stanthorpe is 915 m above sea level and is often the coolest part of the State. Spring is particularly beautiful with fruit trees and wattles in bloom. There are 90 varieties of wild orchids found in the area. **In town:** Museum, High St. Art Gallery and Library Complex, Weeroona Park, Marsh St. Market in the Mountains, cnr Marsh and Lock sts, 2nd Sun. each month. Mar.: Apple and Grape Harvest Festival (even-numbered years); Rodeo. May: Opera at Sunset. Oct.: Granite Belt Spring Wine Festival. **In the area:** Heritage trail, towns in area, brochure available. Granite Belt wineries, most open for tastings and cellar-door sales: Old Caves, just north of town; Stanthorpe Wine Centre, 9 km N; Castle Glen at The Summit, 10 km N; Heritage Wines at Cottonvale, 12 km N; Inigo Wines, Stone Ridge, Felsberg, Mountview, Kominos and the Bramble Patch berry gardens and winery, near Glen Aplin, 11 km SW; Rumbalara at Fletcher, 14 km SW; Ballandean Estate, Golden Grove, Winewood, Bungawarra and Robinson's Family Winery, near Ballandean, 21 km SW; Bald Mountain at Wallangarra, 30 km S. Girraween National Park, 32 km S, for camping, bushwalking, rock climbing and spectacular wildflowers in spring. Sundown Observatory at Ballandean, 21 km SW, astronomy displays; open nightly, check with information centre. Sundown National Park, 79 km SW: wilderness area; camping on Severn River in south-west of park. Mt Marlay, 2 km E, for excellent views. Storm King Dam, 26 km SE, for canoeing and water-skiing. Falls in Boonoo Boonoo National Park (NSW), 60 km SE. **Visitor information:** 26 Leslie Pde; (07) 4681 2057. Web site www. qldsoutherndowns.org.au

Strathpine   Pop. 10 108

MAP REF. 512 D3, 516 F11, 517 D3
Strathpine is located north of Brisbane in the Pine Rivers region, a peaceful rural district that includes the forested areas and national parks closest to Brisbane. Taking advantage of this rural setting so close to the city are a number of art and craft industries. **In town:** May: Pine Rivers Heritage Festival. Aug.: Camp Oven Bush Poets Festival. **In the area:** Self-guide scenic mountain walks, brochures available. Alma Park Zoo at Dakabin, 14 km N, features native and exotic animals, and a

Friendship Farm for children. Lakeside Racing Circuit, 14 km N, venue for major events. Osprey House, environmental centre, Dohles Rocks Rd, 18 km N. Sun. market at North Pine Country Park, 6 km NW, local art and craft, food and buskers. Australian Woolshed at Ferny Hills, 16 km SW: demonstrations of shearing, spinning and sheepdogs working; bush dances with bush band. Brisbane Forest Park, via Ferny Hills. **Visitor information:** Shire Offices, cnr Gympie and Southpine rds; (07) 3205 4793. Web site www. maxlink.com.au

Surfers Paradise
Pop. part of Gold Coast

MAP REF. 517 G11, 519 F5, 525 Q10
In terms of visitor numbers, Surfers Paradise is Australia's most popular holiday destination. With world-famous surf beaches, international standard accommodation and exciting attractions, Surfers Paradise appeals to a wide range of holiday-makers. During the

winter months, the sunny subtropical climate and festive atmosphere make Surfers Paradise particularly attractive to southerners. **In town:** Attractions include: mall at Cavill Ave, regular free entertainment, Hard Rock Cafe, Ripleys Believe It or Not Museum; Orchid Avenue, just off Cavill Ave, European designer fashions and outdoor cafes; beach volleyball area near Cavill Ave; beachfront art and craft markets, each Friday evening; KP Go Karting, Ferny Ave; Flycoaster and Bungee Rocket thrill rides, Cypress Ave; Gold Coast City Art Gallery and Arts Centre, and riverside Evandale sculpture walk, Bundall Rd. Oct.: IndyCar Australia Race. **Visitor information:** Cavill Ave; (07) 5538 4419. **See also:** Day Tours from Brisbane p. 453; The Gold Coast p. 500.

Tambo   Pop. 378

MAP REF. 524 B2
Tambo, 101 km SE of Blackall on the Matilda Hwy, was established

Fishing in Queensland

Bream fishing on the Sunshine Coast

The tropical climate, breathtaking scenery and variety of fishing combine to make the State a wonderful destination for the angler. The coast is the chief attraction, with Cairns being world famous as a location for black marlin and other game-fishing. The Great Barrier Reef is closest to the coast north of Cairns and is easily fished on day trips either in your own boat or from a charter boat. Coral trout, red emperor and nannygai are here and, for those with an inclination for sportfishing, Spanish mackerel, giant trevally and marlin. Cairns is a major centre for charter boats going out to the Great Barrier Reef and deepwater game-fishing. Further north, the remote regions of Cape York provide a frontier experience for those seeking barramundi, queenfish and giant trevally.

Around Brisbane, the warm tropical currents provide a mix of temperate fish, such as bream, whiting and flathead and tropical fish species including snapper, sweetlips and reef cod. Estuary, beach, reef and offshore fishing are possible. Further north, the tailor at Hervey Bay are legendary, and the nearby Great Sandy Strait has a large variety of estuary species in the mangrove channels. Around Townsville the mangrove estuaries on the coastline are renowned for barramundi and mangrove jack. Further down the coast are the wonders of the Whitsundays surrounded by waters teeming with mackerel, queenfish, trevally and other species.

Inland fishing areas, particularly in the north, are considerable distances from major population centres. In the south-east the stocking of impoundments has improved inland fishing; anglers can now fish for golden and silver perch and Murray cod.

For information on fishing regulations and licence requirements, contact Queensland Fisheries Management Authority, 40 Tank St, Brisbane; (07) 3225 1773. Web site www.qfma.qld.gov.au

in the mid-1860s and is the oldest town in Qld's Central West. From a point where the town now stands, explorer Thomas Mitchell first saw the Barcoo River in 1846. **In town:** Self-guide heritage walk; Coolibah Walk, nature walk along Barcoo River; brochures available. Arthur St: In Shire Hall, Tambo Teddies Workshop, produces all-wool teddy bears; courthouse (1888), now library. Apr.: Stockshow. Sept.: Spring Festival. **In the area:** Wilderness Way 320-km self-guide drive, includes historic sites, Aboriginal rock art, and Salvator Rosa section of Carnarvon National Park, 130 km E (camping permitted). Park area named by Major Mitchell, who was reminded of 17th-century artist's landscapes. Contact information centre for drive brochures and information about road conditions. **Visitor information:** Shire Hall, Arthur St; (07) 4654 6133.

Taroom
Pop. 662

MAP REF. 525 J4

Taroom is on the banks of the Dawson River almost 300 km W of Maryborough. Cattle-raising is the main industry. **Of interest:** Coolibah tree in main street, marked 'L. L.' by explorer Ludwig Leichhardt on his 1844 trip from Jimbour House near Dalby to Port Essington (north of Darwin). Museum, Kelman St, features old telephone-exchange equipment, farm machinery and items of local history, by appt only. May: Agricultural Show. Aug.: Leichhardt Festival. **In the area:** Scenic and historic tourist drives, brochure available. Rare Livistona palms near Leichhardt Hwy, 15 km N. Lake Murphy, 30 km N, pristine lake with birdlife, picnics, camping. Glebe Weir, 40 km N, off Leichhardt Hwy, water-skiing and fishing. **Visitor information:** Shire Offices, Yaldwyn St; (07) 4627 3211.

Texas
Pop. 772

MAP REF. 117 K3, 525 M12

Texas lies alongside the Dumaresq River and the Qld–NSW border, 55 km S of Inglewood. **In town:** Historical Museum in old police station (1893), Fleming St, open Sat. or by appt. Old Texas, on river off Schwenke St, remains of original town. July: Agricultural Show. Nov.: Roundup (even-numbered years). **In the area:** Beacon Lookout, 3 km SE, on Stanthorpe Rd. Good fishing along the river and in Glenlyon Dam, 45 km SE. Whyalla Feedlot, eastern side of Texas–Yelarbon Rd, largest cattle feedlot in Australia. Cunningham Weir, 31 km W off Texas–Yelarbon Rd, site where Allan Cunningham crossed the Dumaresq River in 1827. Coolmunda Reservoir, 75 km N: boating, pelicans and swans. **Visitor information:** Ridgways, 40 High St; (07) 4653 1245. Web site www.southerndowns.org.au

Darling Downs

The 72 500 square kilometres of black volcanic soil on the Darling Downs produce 90 per cent of the State's wheat, 50 per cent of its maize, 90 per cent of its oilseeds, two-thirds of its fruit and one-third of its tobacco, as well as oats, sorghum, millet, cotton, soybeans and navy beans. It is a major sheep, cattle and dairying area and the home of several famous bloodstock studs.

Allan Cunningham was the first European to ride across these fertile plains in 1827. The Darling Downs is rural Australia at its best, with a touch of England in the oaks, elms, plane trees and poplars of **Toowoomba's** parks, and the rose gardens of **Warwick** in the south. The climate is cooler and more bracing than in the rest of the State. The Downs with its neat strips of grainfields, lush pastures, patches of forest and national parks, and well-established homesteads, give the visitor a lasting impression of beauty and quiet prosperity.

The Warrego Highway leads north-west from Toowoomba to the wheatfields and silos of **Dalby**. The New England Highway, the main Sydney to Brisbane inland route, turns into the Cunningham Highway at Warwick and descends to the coast through Cunninghams Gap. Main Range National Park has lovely rainforest, palms and native wildlife. An alternative Brisbane–Melbourne inland route is the Newell Highway,

Toowoomba countryside

running west from Warwick to **Goondiwindi** and south into New South Wales. A less used but scenic route is the Heifer Creek Way through the Lockyer Valley from near Greenmount East to **Gatton**.

For further information on the Darling Downs, contact the Southern Downs Tourist Association, 49 Albion St (New England Hwy), Warwick; (07) 4661 3122. Web site www.qldsoutherndowns.org.au **See also:** individual entries in A–Z town listing for details on towns in bold type. **Map reference:** 525 M9.

Theodore
Pop. 508

MAP REF. 525 J2

Grain and cotton are the main crops on the irrigated land around this town on the Leichhardt Hwy, 220 km N of Miles. Timber-milling and cattle-grazing are also significant and you can see the huge draglines operating at the coal mines. Theodore was named after Edward Theodore, Qld Premier 1919–25, and designed by Walter Burley Griffin. **In town:** Theodore Hotel, The Boulevard, only cooperative hotel in Qld. Dawson Folk Museum, Second Ave, open by appt. **In the area:** Irrigation area: bird-watching, cotton-picking (Mar.–May). Fishing on Theodore Weir, southern outskirts of town. Isla Gorge National Park, 35 km SW. Cracow, 49 km SE, where gold was produced from famous Golden Plateau mine 1932–76. **Visitor information:** Theodore Hotel, The Boulevard; (07) 4993 1244.

Tin Can Bay
Pop. 1779

MAP REF. 525 P5

Half an hour's drive north-east of Gympie takes travellers to Tin Can Bay and nearby Rainbow Beach. These two hamlets are popular fishing, prawning and crabbing areas; the quiet waters of Tin Can Bay are ideal for boating and fishing, while Rainbow Beach has good surfing. **In town:** Boat and yacht hire. Market, Gympie Rd, 3rd Sat. each month. Easter: Festival. June: Seafood and Leisure Festival. Dec.: Robert Pryde Memorial Surf Classic. **In the area:** Fishing Classic at Rainbow Beach, 41 km E, each July. Road south from Rainbow Beach (4WD) leads to coloured sands and beaches of Cooloola section of Great Sandy National Park. At Inskip Point, 53 km NE: camping access along Point; ferry to Fraser Island. At Carlo Point, 3 km E: cruising, fishing, swimming, houseboats and yachts for hire. **Visitor information:** 4 Gympie Rd; (07) 5486 4333.

Toowoomba
Pop. 83 350

MAP REF. 525 N9

This garden city has a distinctive charm and graciousness in its wide, tree-lined streets, colonial architecture and many fine parks and gardens. Toowoomba is 127 km W of Brisbane, on the rim of the Great Dividing Range. It began in 1849 as a village near an important staging post for teamsters and travellers, and was known as The Swamp. Aborigines pronounced the name 'T'wamp-bah'; this became 'Toowoomba'. Today it is the commercial centre for the fertile Darling Downs, with butter and cheese factories, sawmills, flour mills, tanneries, engineering and railway workshops, a modern iron foundry, clothing and shoe factories. It has an active cultural and artistic life. **In town:** Self-guide Russell St heritage walk, brochure available. Cobb & Co. Museum, Lindsay St, traces history of horse-drawn vehicles. St Patrick's Cathedral (1880s), James St. St Luke's Anglican Church (1897), cnr Herries and Ruthven sts. Parks include: Lake Annand, MacKenzie St, for bird-lovers; Laurel Bank, scented gardens; Botanic Gardens and adjacent Queens Park, Lindsay St; Waterbird Habitat, MacKenzie St. Royal Bull's Head Inn (1847), Brisbane St, fully restored by National Trust. Toowoomba Art Gallery in Ruthven St, brochure available. Antique and craft shops. Tourist drive with floral markers, brochure available. Markets: Eat Street Market, Margaret St, 1st Sun. each month; Queens Park, Margaret St, 3rd Sun. each month. Sept.: Carnival of Flowers. Oct.: Festival of the Horse. **In the area:** Walking and bike tracks, 'Fitch's Feats' brochure available. Self-guide scenic drives of varying lengths, brochure available: 48-km circuit to Spring Bluff (old railway station at Spring Bluff, approx. 16 km N of city, has superb gardens) and Murphys Creek, approx. 25 km N; 100-km circuit to Heifer Creek, known as Valley of the Sun, provides spectacular scenery; 255-km circuit takes in Bernborough Centre, Jondaryan Woolshed, Cecil Plains Cotton Ginnery, Millmerran Museum and Pittsworth Folk Museum. Picnic Point, 5 km E, offers mountain views and waterfall. At Highfields, 12 km N: Orchid Park, Danish Flower Art, Pioneer Village. At Cabarlah, 19 km N: Black Forest Hill Cuckoo Clock Centre, Country Markets last Sun. each month. **Visitor information:** 476 Ruthven St; (07) 4638 7555. Web site www.toowoomba.qld.gov.au **See also:** Darling Downs p. 504.

Townsville
Pop. 75 990

MAP REF. 521, 529 P12

In 1864 sea captain Robert Towns commissioned James Melton Black to build a wharf and establish a settlement on Cleveland Bay to service the new inland cattle industry. Townsville was gazetted in 1865 and declared a city in 1903. Today, including its twin city of Thuringowa it is Australia's largest tropical city. There are many handsome historic buildings, particularly in the waterfront park area around Cleveland Bay. The city's busy port handles minerals from Mount Isa and Cloncurry; beef and wool from the western plains; sugar and timber from the rich coastal region; and its own manufacturing and processing industries. Townsville is the administrative, commercial, education and manufacturing capital of northern Qld. It is becoming a renowned centre for research into marine life and is the headquarters for the Great Barrier Reef Marine Park Authority. **In town:** The Strand has tropical parks, waterfall and overhanging bougainvillea gardens. At the end of The Strand: rockpool for year-round swimming; Jezzine Military Museum. Jupiters Townsville Hotel and Casino, Sir Leslie Thiess Dr. Flinders St East: historic buildings; Reef HQ, features aquarium with touch-tank and walk-through transparent underwater viewing-tunnel, Omnimax Theatre and Museum of Tropical Queensland; ferry terminal for Magnetic Island and day cruises to the Great Barrier Reef. Billabong Sanctuary, Bruce Hwy, features koala feeding and crocodile shows. Perc Tucker Regional Art Gallery, Flinders Mall. Queen's Gardens, cnr Paxton and Gregory sts. Botanic Gardens, Anderson Park, Kings Rd. Castle Hill Lookout, off Stanley St. Town Common and Environmental Park, Pallarenda Rd, a coastline park with prolific birdlife. Maritime Museum, Palmer St, South Townsville. Cotters Market in Flinders Mall each Sun. July: Australian Festival of Chamber Music; Arts Festival; Show (carnival). **In the area:** Cruises to Cairns via resort islands and reef on luxury catamaran *Coral Princess*; reef day-trips and dive cruises; day sailing around Magnetic Island; daily connections to Magnetic, Orpheus, Hinchinbrook, Bedarra and Dunk resort islands; day outback tours, rainforest and whitewater rafting tours. Bowling Green Bay National Park, 25 km S, off Bruce Hwy. Pangola Park, 32 km S. Near Giru, 50 km SE: waterfalls, bushwalks, swimming, and picnic and camping facilities. Australian Institute of Marine Science, 30 km E at Cape Ferguson, tours

Townsville harbour

(bookings required). Offshore, Magnetic Island, resident population of more than 2000; two-thirds of island is national park featuring beaches, walks and wildlife. **Visitor information:** Flinders Mall; (07) 4721 3660. Web site www.tel.com.au **See also:** The Far North p. 472.

Tully   Pop. 2509

MAP REF. 529 N9
Situated at the foot of Mt Tyson, Tully receives one of the highest annual rainfalls in Australia, averaging around 4200 mm annually. Major industries are sugarcane, bananas, tropical fruit, cattle and timber. **In town:** Tully Sugar Mill tours (June–Nov.), bookings essential. Market, 2nd Sat. each month. July: Show. Nov.: Rodeo. **In the area:** Reef and island cruising. Whitewater rafting and kayaking on Tully River, beginning at Tully Gorge; also superb scenery and swimming in the top reaches of the river. Fishing and beautiful Googorra Beach at Tully Heads, 22 km SE. Alligators Nest, 10 km S; beautiful rainforest, swimming in stream. Spectacular rainforests at Murray Falls (40 km SW) and Tully River Gorge (44 km W). **Visitor information:** Bruce Hwy; (07) 4068 2288.

Warwick   Pop. 10 947

MAP REF. 117 M1, 525 N11
An attractive city in the Southern Downs, Warwick is 158 km SW of Brisbane on the Cunningham Hwy and 86 km S of Toowoomba on the New England Hwy. The area was explored by Allan Cunningham in 1827; in 1840 the Leslie brothers arrived from the south and established a sheep station at Canning Downs; other pastoralists followed. The NSW government asked Patrick Leslie to select a town site, and in 1849 Warwick was surveyed and established. It was the first free settlement, after Brisbane, in what became Qld. The railway from Ipswich was opened in 1871 and Warwick became a city in 1936. In what seemed to be a minor incident in 1917, Prime Minister Billy Hughes was hit by an egg while addressing a crowd on the controversial conscription issue of the day. He asked a local policeman to arrest the man responsible but the policeman refused. The result was the formation of the Federal Police Force. Warwick is alongside the willow-shaded Condamine River, 458 m above sea level, and calls itself 'the Rose and Rodeo City'. The surrounding rich pastures support famous

horse and cattle studs, and produce some of Australia's finest wool and grain. Fruit, vegetables and timber grow well, and the area is noted for its dairy products and bacon. **In town:** Self-guide walk around historic buildings, map available. Pringle Cottage (1870), Dragon St, houses large historic photo collection, vehicles and machinery. Jubilee Gardens, cnr Alice and Helene sts, features displays of roses. Warwick Regional Art Gallery, Albion St. Easter: Rock Swap. May: Bush Week. Oct.: Rose and Rodeo City Festival. **In the area:** Heritage and cultural 80-km drive, brochure available. Leslie Dam, 15 km W, for water sports. Sheep and emu farm at Mirambeena, 15 km E, along Yangan Rd and right at Wiedmans Rd. **Visitor information:** 49 Albion St (New England Hwy); (07) 4661 3122. Web site www.qldsouthemdowns.org.au **See also:** Darling Downs p. 504.

Weipa   Pop. 2200

MAP REF. 530 B7
Located on the west coast of Cape York, the township of Weipa is the home of the world's largest bauxite mine. This small mining town provides a comprehensive range of services and facilities

Cape York

The Cape York Peninsula is a vast area as large as Victoria. There are more than 10 000 people living on the Cape; about half live in Weipa, and the rest in Aboriginal and Islander communities, isolated townships and on scattered pastoral stations. Many of these are along the telegraph line that runs to the northern tip.

The first European exploration of Cape York was in the 1840s and the 1860s by the Jardine brothers, John Bradford, Robert Jack, and the ill-fated Edmund Kennedy and his famous Aboriginal guide Jacky Jacky. Vegetation varies from gums and anthills in the south to swamps and rainforests in the north. Many areas of the Cape are traditional Aboriginal lands, national parks and a sanctuary for much of Australia's unique flora and fauna.

There are two distinct seasons: the wet and the dry. During the wet virtually all road transport stops as there are almost no sealed roads or bridges in the area. Movement during this season is limited to regular flights with Flight West, Sunstate and Trans Pacific airlines; all run scheduled daily flights to Cape York Airport. There is also sea access (year round) on the *Kangaroo Explorer* departing weekly from Cairns. Some 50 kilometres further along, a dirt track leads to the northernmost area of Cape York. The local Aboriginal place name for this area is Pajinka. Situated 400 metres from the very tip of the peninsula, on traditional Aboriginal land, is the comfortable Pajinka Wilderness Lodge providing cabin-style rooms with private amenities. Adjacent to the lodge is the Pajinka camping ground. Both are owned and operated by the Injinoo Aboriginal Community. Permits are required to enter the Injinoo area north of the Dulhunty River; these can be obtained on board the Jardine River ferry, or by contacting the Injinoo Community Council on (07) 4069 3252.

All Aboriginal and Islander communities are self-sufficient and may be visited, but *it is essential that a permit be obtained in writing beforehand.* The main communities are Lockhart River on the east coast; Injinoo and Pajinka at the tip; and Edward River, the town of Weipa South, and Aurukun on the Gulf. The Ang-Gnarra Aboriginal Corporations at Laura offer a guide and ranger service to visitors; details at the caravan park.

The Cape is the ideal place to go exploring. A reliable and well-equipped 4WD vehicle, preferably with a winch, is essential for this area. It is possible to drive north from Cairns or Mareeba to Bamaga through Laura and Coen. The Royal Automobile Club of Queensland provides an excellent map and information sheet, both of which are essential reading before an expedition north is planned. *Conditions on the track are often unpredictable and the RACQ or police at Cairns should be contacted before heading north.*

June to November are the recommended travel months. At the peak of the season over one hundred vehicles travel northern Cape roads daily. The narrow, rough and blind roads are difficult, and a motorist travelling fast has no chance of avoiding an oncoming car. There are many accidents in this area each year. Drivers are advised to travel slowly and exercise particular care. The Laura, Kennedy, Stewart, Archer, Wenlock and Dulhunty rivers must be forded. The Jardine River provides the main source of water for the local communities. In order to maintain this natural asset, it is requested that motorists do not attempt to cross the river at any point other than the ferry crossing. During good, dry conditions it is possible to take a conventional car, with care, north to Coen and west to Weipa.

Weipa, on the Gulf of Carpentaria, has the world's largest deposits of bauxite. Comalco offers conducted tours of the bauxite mining operation. Direct access to Weipa is by regular Ansett flights from Cairns.

Further information on the national parks in the area and permits for camping may be obtained from the Department of Environment, McLeod St, Cairns; (07) 4052 3096.

For further information on Cape York, contact Tourism Tropical North Queensland, 51 The Esplanade, Cairns; (07) 4051 3588. Web site www.tnq.org.au **See also:** individual entries in A–Z town listing for details on towns in bold type. **Map references:** 528 G2, 530.

Cape York, the northernmost region in Queensland, is largely a wilderness area for travellers. **In town:** Guided tours of bauxite mine provide excellent coverage of whole mining process at Weipa. **In the area:** Number of fishing and camping areas near the town, developed for the well-equipped visitor. **Visitor information:** 51 The Esplanade, Cairns; (07) 4051 3588. **See also:** Cape York p. 507.

Winton   Pop. 1142

MAP REF. 533 M8

Banjo Paterson wrote Australia's most famous song, 'Waltzing Matilda', on Dagworth Station near Winton in 1895. Combo Waterhole was then part of Dagworth, and the ballad had its first public airing in Winton on 6 April, 1895. The town is 177 km NW of Longreach on the Matilda Hwy. A major sheep area, Winton is also a large trucking centre for the giant road trains bringing cattle from the Channel Country to the railhead. In 1920 the first office of a company called Qantas was registered in Winton. The town's water supply comes out of deep artesian bores at a temperature of 83°C. **In town:** In Elderslie St: Historic Royal Theatre, open-air movie theatre and museum, one of the oldest still operating in Australia; swagman statue near swimming pool; Gift and Gem Shop with 'Opal Walk' set up inside. Also in Elderslie St, Waltzing Matilda Centre: interactive and interpretive displays based on the famous song; Qantilda Museum, highlights Winton's role in the birth of the airline and displays a 9000-item heritage collection; opal mining display; outback art gallery. Arno's Wall, Vindex St, opposite Shire Offices, ongoing concrete-wall creation containing 'every item imaginable'. Apr.: Waltzing Matilda Bush Poetry Festival. Sept.: Outback Festival (odd-numbered years). **In the area:** Bladensburg National Park, 2 km S, self-drive tour of park. Skull Hole, 40 km S, has Aboriginal paintings and bora ceremonial grounds. Opalton, 115 km S, remains of historic town; working gemfields nearby. Carisbrooke Station, 85 km SW, a working sheep station; Aboriginal cave paintings and scenic drives in surrounds; day tours and accommodation. Lark Quarry Conservation Park, 110 km SW, features preserved tracks of dinosaur 'stampede'. Combo Waterhole Conservation Park, 150 km NW via Matilda Hwy.

Visitor information: Waltzing Matilda Centre, Elderslie St; (07) 4657 1466. Web site www.matildacentre.com.au

Yandina   Pop. 931

MAP REF. 520 E6

Yandina lies 9 km N of Nambour and is the home of The Ginger Factory, the largest such factory in the world, located in Pioneer Rd. Visitors can wander through Gingertown, watch ginger cooking demonstrations, see ginger being processed and take a ride on the historic Queensland Cane Train which operates through the landscaped gardens. Bunya Park, a wildlife sanctuary, is in the grounds of The Ginger Factory. **In town:** Opposite Ginger Factory, Nutworks Macadamia Factory and tourist Complex: see processing of macadamia nuts; tastings. Carinya, historic homestead on Bruce Hwy at northern edge of town. Oct.: Spring Flower and Ginger Festival. **In the area:** Wappa Dam, just west of town. At Eumundi, 10 km N: Country Fair selling fresh produce each Wed.; widely known markets each Sat. a.m., selling goods ranging from locally grown fruit and vegetables to art and craft; old and impressive Imperial Hotel near markets. **Visitor information:** Sunshine Coast Information, cnr Aerodrome Rd and Sixth Ave, Maroochydore; (07) 5479 1566. **See also:** Hinterland Escape p. 456.

Yeppoon   Pop. 8810

MAP REF. 527 O10

This popular coastal resort, 40 km NE of Rockhampton, lies on the shores of Keppel Bay. Yeppoon and the strip of beaches to its south – Cooee Bay, Rosslyn Bay, Causeway Lake, Emu Park and Keppel Sands – are known as the Capricorn Coast. Great Keppel Island Resort is 13 km offshore. Market, 1st Sun. each month. Fig Tree Markets, next to information centre, 3rd Sun. each month. Jan.: Australia Day Celebrations. Feb.: Surf Lifesaving Championships. Aug.: Ozfest, with World Cooeeing Competition. Sept.: Pineapple Festival. **In the area:** Scenic drives and adventure tours. Wetland Tour at Capricorn International Resort, 9 km N. Cooberrie Park, 15 km N, a noted flora and fauna reserve. Further 17 km N, Byfield State Forest, home of extremely rare Byfield fern, boardwalk

along Waterpark Creek; rainforest cabins nearby. Keppel Bay Marina at Rosslyn Bay Harbour, 7 km S, bareboat and fishing charters. Blow Hole at Double Head, 7 km S. At Emu Park, 19 km S: unusual 'singing ship' memorial to Captain Cook (sea breezes cause hidden organ pipes to make sounds); Service of Remembrance (memorial to American troops) each July; Octoberfest each Oct. Koorana Crocodile Reserve, 38 km SW, off Emu Park–Rockhampton Rd. Catamaran service daily to Great Keppel Island and nearby underwater observatory. **Visitor information:** Capricorn Coast Tourist Information Centre, Ross Creek Roundabout; (07) 4939 4888.

Yungaburra   Pop. 985

MAP REF. 523 D12, 529 M7

On the edge of the Atherton Tableland, 13 km E of Atherton, the town is known for its National Trust Historic Precinct listing. **In town:** Self-guide Historic Precinct Buildings Walk. Lake Eacham Hotel, Cedar St. Platypus-viewing platform at Peterson Creek, on Gillies Hwy, best times sunrise and sunset. The Chalet Rainforest Gallery, Gillies Hwy: murals, timber art and Rainforest Folk (dolls). Artists Galleries, cnr Gillies Hwy and Cedar St. Various gem and craft shops. Widely known produce and craft markets, on Gillies Hwy, 4th Sat. each month. June: Yuletide. July: Jazz Festival. Oct.: Folk Festival. **In the area:** Curtain Fig Tree, 2.5 km SW, spectacular example of strangler fig, with aerial roots in curtain-like formation. The Seven Sisters, seven rolling hills, 2 km N. Tinaburra, 3 km N on the shores of Lake Tinaroo. Views of lake from Tinaroo Falls dam outlet, 23 km N. Spectacular views over Gillies Range from Heales Outlook Lookout, 16 km NE. In Crater Lakes National Park, 2 volcanic lakes: Lake Eacham (5 km E) has circuit track through rainforest; Lake Barrine (10 km NE), has cruises. At Malanda, 20 km S: 19th-century Majestic Theatre; market, 3rd Sat. each month; Agricultural Show in June. Malanda Falls Conservation Park, on the edge of town, signposted rainforest walks and the Jungle Interpretive Centre. McHugh Road Lookout, 20 km S of Malanda. **Visitor information:** Nick's Swiss–Italian Restaurant, Gillies Hwy; (07) 4095 3330. Web site www.eachamshire.qld.gov.au

Queensland

LOCATION MAP

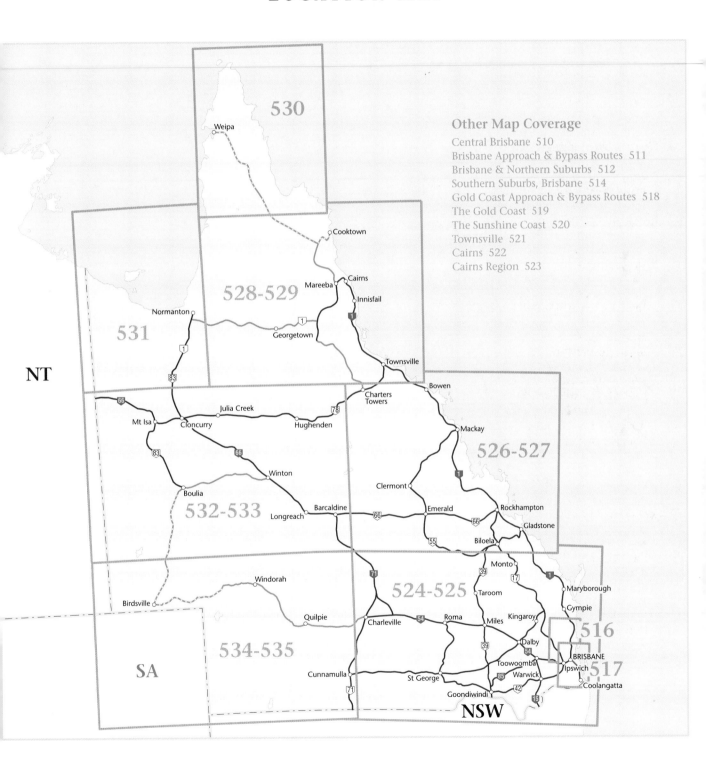

Other Map Coverage

Central Brisbane 510
Brisbane Approach & Bypass Routes 511
Brisbane & Northern Suburbs 512
Southern Suburbs, Brisbane 514
Gold Coast Approach & Bypass Routes 518
The Gold Coast 519
The Sunshine Coast 520
Townsville 521
Cairns 522
Cairns Region 523

NT

SA

NSW

530

528-529

531

526-527

532-533

524-525

534-535

516

517

Weipa
Cooktown
Mareeba
Cairns
Innisfail
Normanton
Georgetown
Townsville
Bowen
Charters Towers
Mt Isa
Cloncurry
Julia Creek
Hughenden
Mackay
Winton
Clermont
Boulia
Barcaldine
Emerald
Rockhampton
Longreach
Gladstone
Biloela
Monto
Windorah
Maryborough
Taroom
Gympie
Birdsville
Quilpie
Charleville
Roma
Miles
Kingaroy
Dalby
BRISBANE
Cunnamulla
Toowoomba
Warwick
Ipswich
St George
Coolangatta
Goondiwindi

510 Central Brisbane

0   0.25   0.5   0.75   1 km

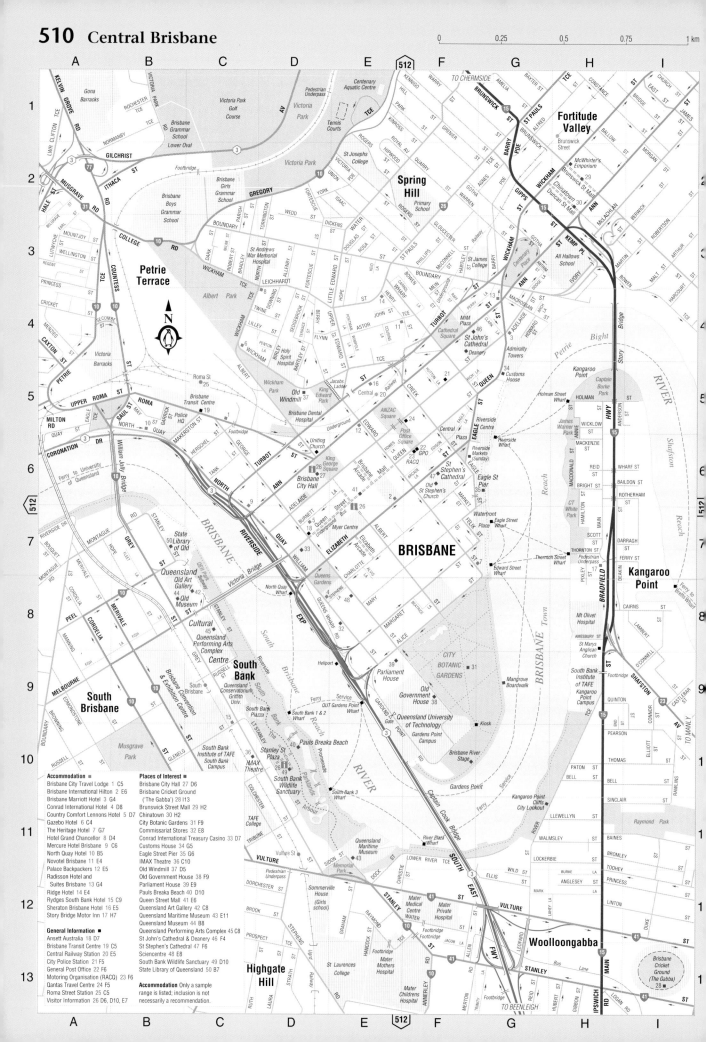

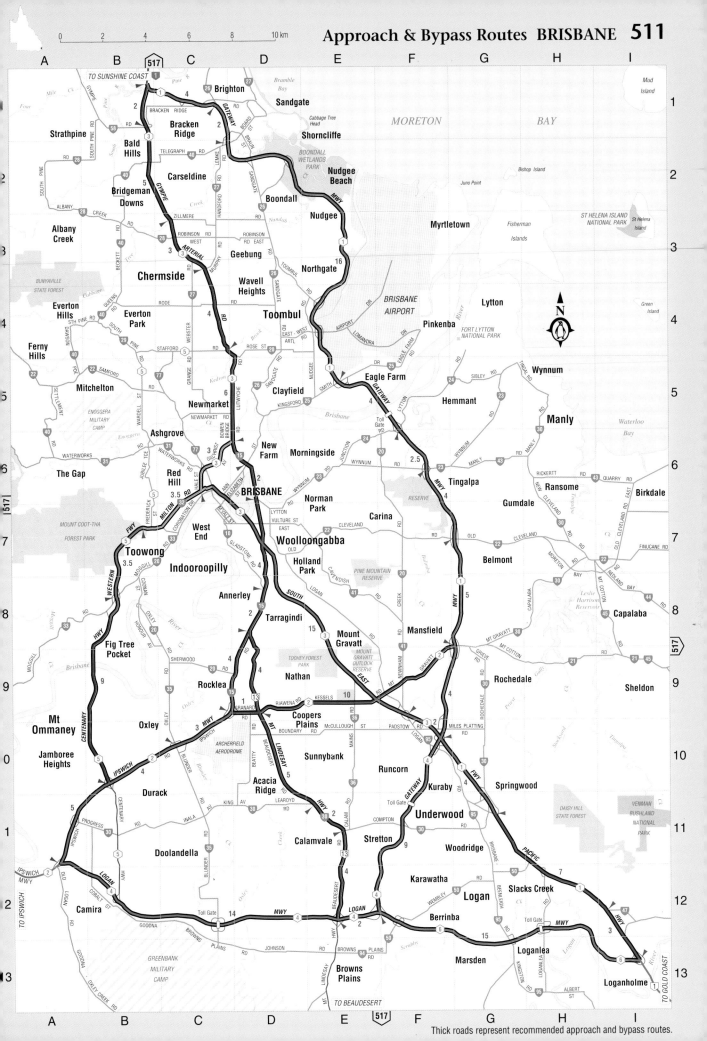

Thick roads represent recommended approach and bypass routes.

N

J K L M N O P Q R

MORETON

BAY

MUD ISLAND

For more detail on Central
Brisbane see page 510

ST HELENA ISLAND

ST HELENA
ISLAND
NATIONAL
PARK

Juno Point

CHANNEL

Port of
Brisbane

Luggage
Point

FISHERMAN
ISLANDS

Green
Island

BRISBANE
AIRPORT

Domestic
Terminal

International
Terminal

Myrtletown

Oil Refinery

Boat
Passage

Whyte
Island

Bulwer Island

FORT LYTTON
NATIONAL PARK

Lytton

Oil Refinery

Pinkenba

Meeandah

Eagle Farm

Royal
Queensland
Golf Club

Gateway
Bridge

Toll
Gate

Queensport

Murarrie

Murarrie
Recreation
Reserve

Cannon
Hill

en Hills

Carina

Carindale

Belmont
Hospital

Camp Hill

PRITCHARD

Wynnum
North

Elanora
Park

Oyster Point

Sibley

Lindum

Crawfords

New
Lindum

Preston

Hemmant

Hemmant
Park

Doboy

Wynnum Golf Course

Memorial
Park

Wynnum
West

Wynnum

Darling Point

Manly
Boat Harbour

Manly

Manly
West

Lota

King Island

CONSERVATION
PARK

Wellington Point

Erobin

Waterloo
Bay

Fig Tree Point

Mooroondu Point

Geoff Skinner
Reserve

Wakerley

Ransome

Rickertt

Thorneside

Quarry

Birkdale

Wellington
Point

Birkdale

Ormiston House

Tingalpa

Villanova
College
Sports
Ground

Cemetery

Howeston
Golf Course

Tingalpa
Creek
Reserve

Gumdale

Meadowlands
Picnic
Ground

Clem Jones
Centre

Meadowlands

Belmont
Rifle Range

Cannon
Hill
Rifle Range

Chandler
(Sleeman)
Sports
Complex

Chandler

John Frederick
Park

Finucane

Ormiston

Sturgeon

J K L M N O P Q R

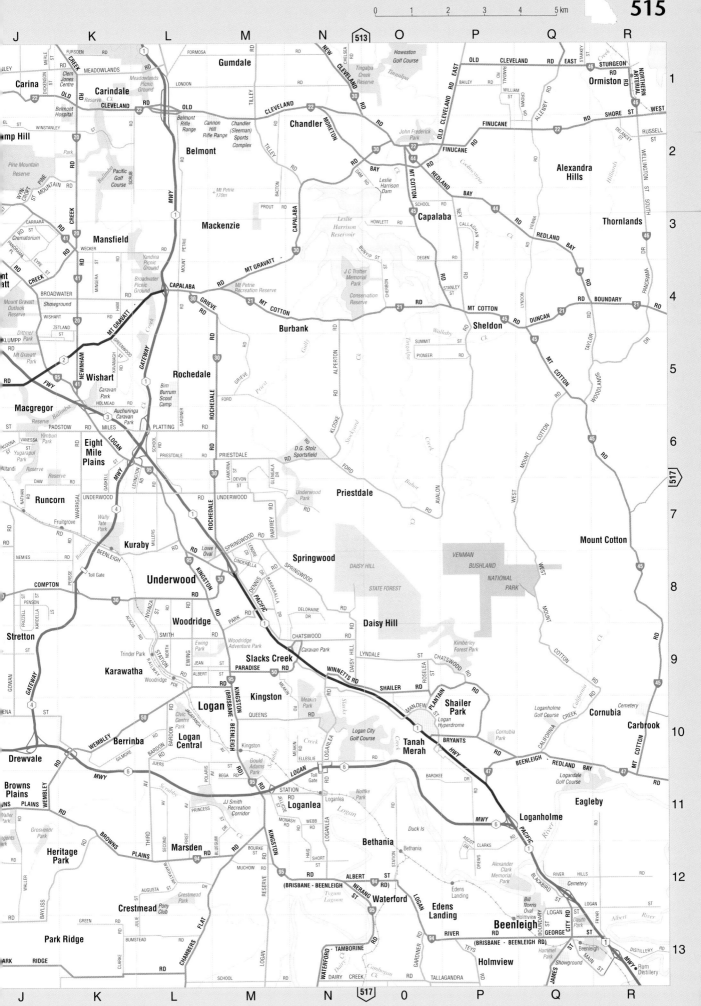

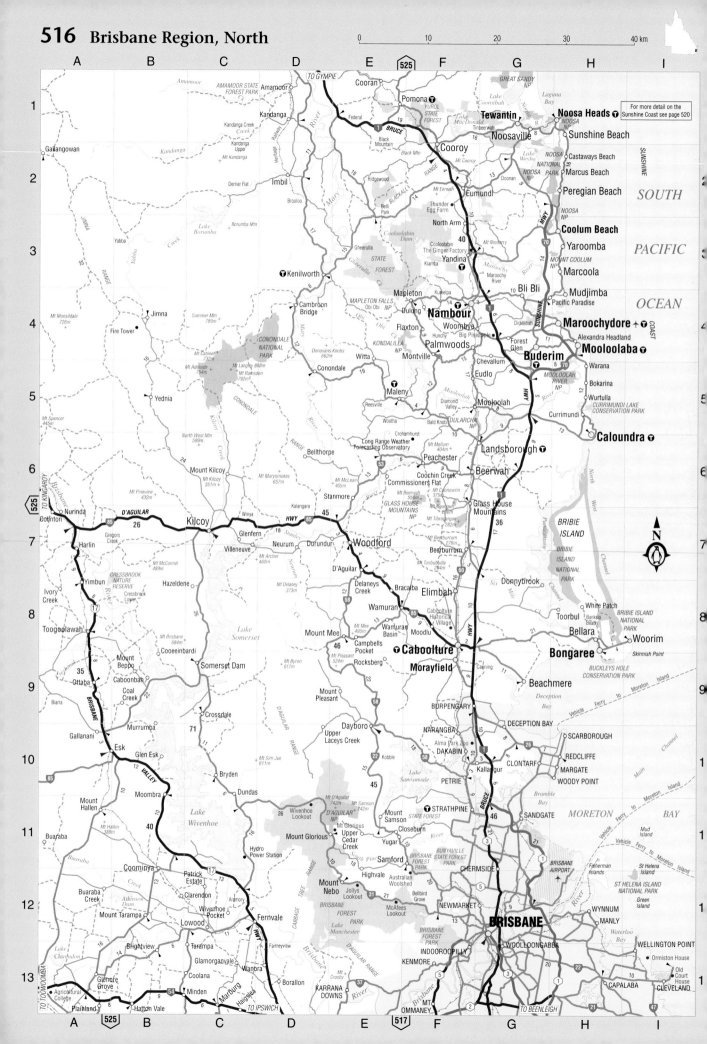

0   10   20   30   40 km

A   B   C   D   E   F   G   H   I

SOUTH

PACIFIC

OCEAN

TO WOODFORD
516
TO NAMBOUR

Wamuran
Caboolture Historical Village
Mt Mee +495m
Mount Mee
Campbells Pocket
Wamuran Basin
Moodlu
Rocksberg
Mt Pleasant 524m
Caboolture
Morayfield
Canning

White Patch
Toorbul
BRIBIE ISLAND NP
Bellara
Banksia Beach
BRIBIE ISLAND
Bongaree
Woorim
Skirmish Point

North Point
Cape Moreton
MORETON ISLAND

Mount Pleasant
Dayboro
Upper Laceys Creek
NARANGBA
BURPENGARY
DECEPTION BAY
Beachmere
Deception Bay
Bulwer
MORETON ISLAND NATIONAL PARK
Mt Tempest 280m

Mt Byron +617m
Kobble
Alma Park Zoo
DAKABIN
SCARBOROUGH
Cowan Cowan Point

Mt Sim Jue 611m
45
Upper Cedar Creek
Closeburn
Yugar
Mount Samson
Kallangur
PETRIE
CLONTARF
REDCLIFFE
MARGATE
WOODY POINT

Tangalooma
Moreton Island Tourist Resort

Wivenhoe Lookout
D'AGUILAR NP
Mt O'Aguilar 742m
Mt Samson 742m
STRATHPINE
Bramble Bay
SANDGATE
MORETON BAY

Hydro Power Station
Mt Glorious
Samford
CHERMSIDE
Mud Island
St Helena Island

Mt Nebo
Highvale
NEWMARKET
BRISBANE AIRPORT
Fisherman Islands
St Helena Island NATIONAL PARK
Green Island

For more detail on Brisbane Suburbs see pages 512 - 515

Fernvale
BRISBANE
WOOLLOONGABBA
WYNNUM
MANLY
Waterloo Bay
Amity Point
Captain Cook Memorial
Rocky Point
Point Lookout

Wanora
Borallon
INDOOROOPILLY
KENMORE
WELLINGTON POINT
Ormiston House
Peel Island
NORTH STRADBROKE ISLAND

KARRANA DOWNS
MT OMMANEY
CAPALABA
Old Court House
GLEVELAND
Dunwich
Historical Cemetery
Mt Hardcore 219m
BLUE LAKE

Walloon
RIVERVIEW
INALA
SUNNYBANK
VICTORIA POINT
MacLeay Island
Blue Lake NATIONAL PARK

IPSWICH
Amberley
WOODRIDGE
LOGAN
REDLAND BAY
Ibis Lagoon

REDBANK PLAINS
GREENBANK MILITARY CAMP
BROWNS PLAINS
POINT TALBURPIN
Russell Island
Native Companion Lagoon

Loamside
Ripley
Purga
LOGANHOLME
Alberton
Rum Distillery
Cabbage Tree Point

Mutdapilly
Flinders
Peak Crossing
BEENLEIGH
YATALA
Woongoolba
Steiglitz

Harrisville
Limestone Ridge
North Maclean
Wolfdene
Ormeau
Jacobs Well
SOUTH STRADBROKE ISLAND

Roadvale
Munbilla
Milbong
Jimboomba
Kagaru
Cedar Grove
Couran
SOUTH STRADBROKE ISLAND CONSERVATION PARK

Templin
Woodhill
Veresdale
Tamborine
Upper Coomera
Dreamworld
Coomera
Sanctuary Cove
Currigee

Boonah
Milford
Gleneagle
North Tamborine
Eagle Heights
Movie World
Oxenford
HELENSVALE

For more detail on the Gold Coast see page 519

Kooralbyn
Bromelton
Beaudesert
Boys Town
Mount Tamborine
Maudsland
Nerang
SOUTHPORT
Sea World
MAIN BEACH
SURFERS PARADISE

Josephville
Canungra
Worongary
Gilston
BROADBEACH
Conrad Jupiters Casino

Laravale
Advancetown
Mudgeeraba
BURLEIGH HEADS
BURLEIGH HEAD NP

Tamrookum
Tabooba
Kerry
Beechmont
Gold Coast War Museum & Skirmish
CURRUMBIN
COOLANGATTA

Maroon
Rathdowney
QUEENSLAND
SPRINGBROOK NP
Springbrook
Purlingbrook Falls
Currumbin Rock Pool
BILINGA
Captain Cook Memorial & Lighthouse
North Head
TWEED HEADS

MOUNT BARNEY NATIONAL PARK
LAMINGTON NATIONAL PARK
Binna Burra Lodge
Natural Bridge
Canyon Lookout
NSW
Banora Point
Terranora
Piggabeen
Cobaki
Bilambil
Chinderah
Fingal

TO WOODENBONG
525
TO MURWILLUMBAH

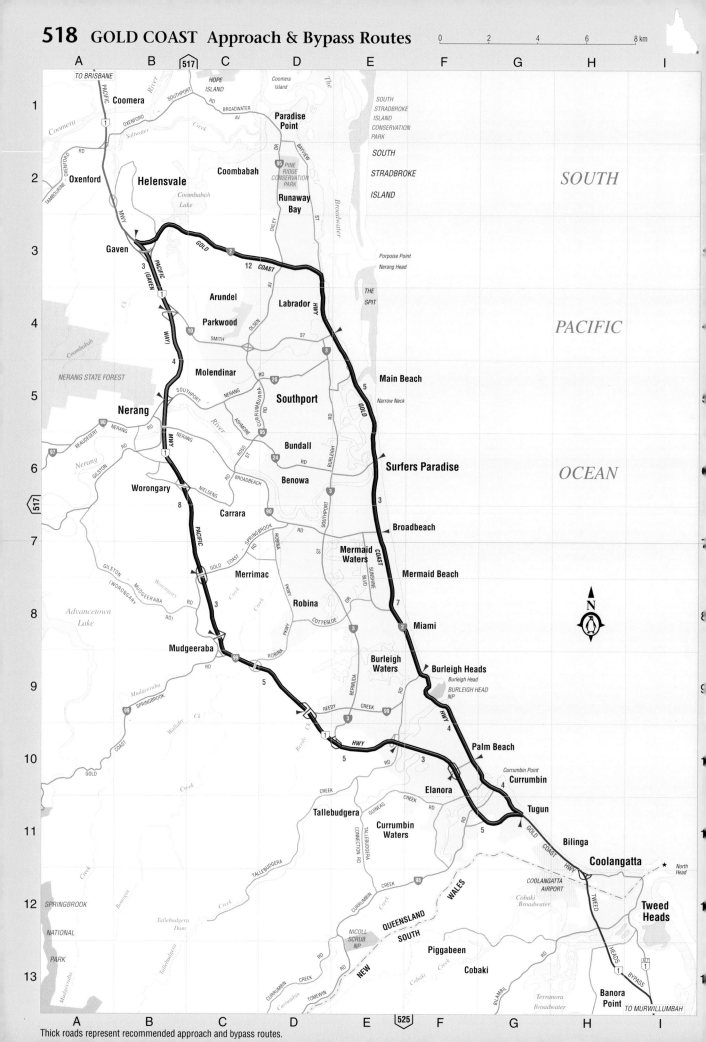

518 GOLD COAST Approach & Bypass Routes

0 2 4 6 8 10 km

DREAMWORLD: A family-oriented entertainment complex set amid landscaped gardens & natural bushland. It features various exciting rides, a computerised animated koala theatre, a water playground, specialty shops and restaurants.

SANCTUARY COVE: Exclusive residential resort with waterfront shopping village, marina, golf courses, tennis complex and Hyatt Regency Hotel.

WARNER BROS MOVIE WORLD: Based on the world-famous Hollywood movie set, it is a theme park as part of a fully operational movie studio.

WET 'N' WILD WATER WORLD: An amazing variety of waterslides and pools set in a landscaped barbecue and picnic area.

SOUTH STRADBROKE ISLAND: Cruises leave from Southport for this largely uninhabited island.

SEA WORLD: A popular family-oriented theme park featuring dolphin and sea-lion performances, shark-feeding demonstrations, a walk-through aquarium, water-ski shows and many exciting rides.

VISITOR INFORMATION:
Coolangatta (cnr Griffith and Warner sts)
Surfers Paradise (Cavill Ave)

ADVANCETOWN LAKE: Sailing (no power boats), picnic and barbecue facilities, scenic drives and the Hinze Dam.

DAVID FLEAY WILDLIFE PARK: Wildlife park run by the Queensland Parks & Wildlife Service to display and breed many of Queensland's rarer animals. Visit the nocturnal house to see the bilbies.

WAR MUSEUM: Indoor and outdoor displays of army memorabilia, military equipment and games.

CURRUMBIN WILDLIFE SANCTUARY: Australian fauna, including waterbirds, koalas and kangaroos. Visitors can feed the brightly coloured lorikeets twice daily.

PURLINGBROOK FALLS: One of the most spectacular falls in the hinterland. Resorts such as Binna Burra and O'Reillys are in nearby Lamington National Park.

OLSON'S BIRD GARDENS: Exotic pheasants, colourful parrots and tiny finches in huge walk-through landscaped aviaries.

SOUTH

PACIFIC

OCEAN

SOUTH STRADBROKE ISLAND CONSERVATION PARK

SOUTH STRADBROKE ISLAND

QUEENSLAND

NEW SOUTH WALES

SPRINGBROOK NATIONAL PARK

McPHERSON RANGE

TO BRISBANE
TO MURWILLUMBAH

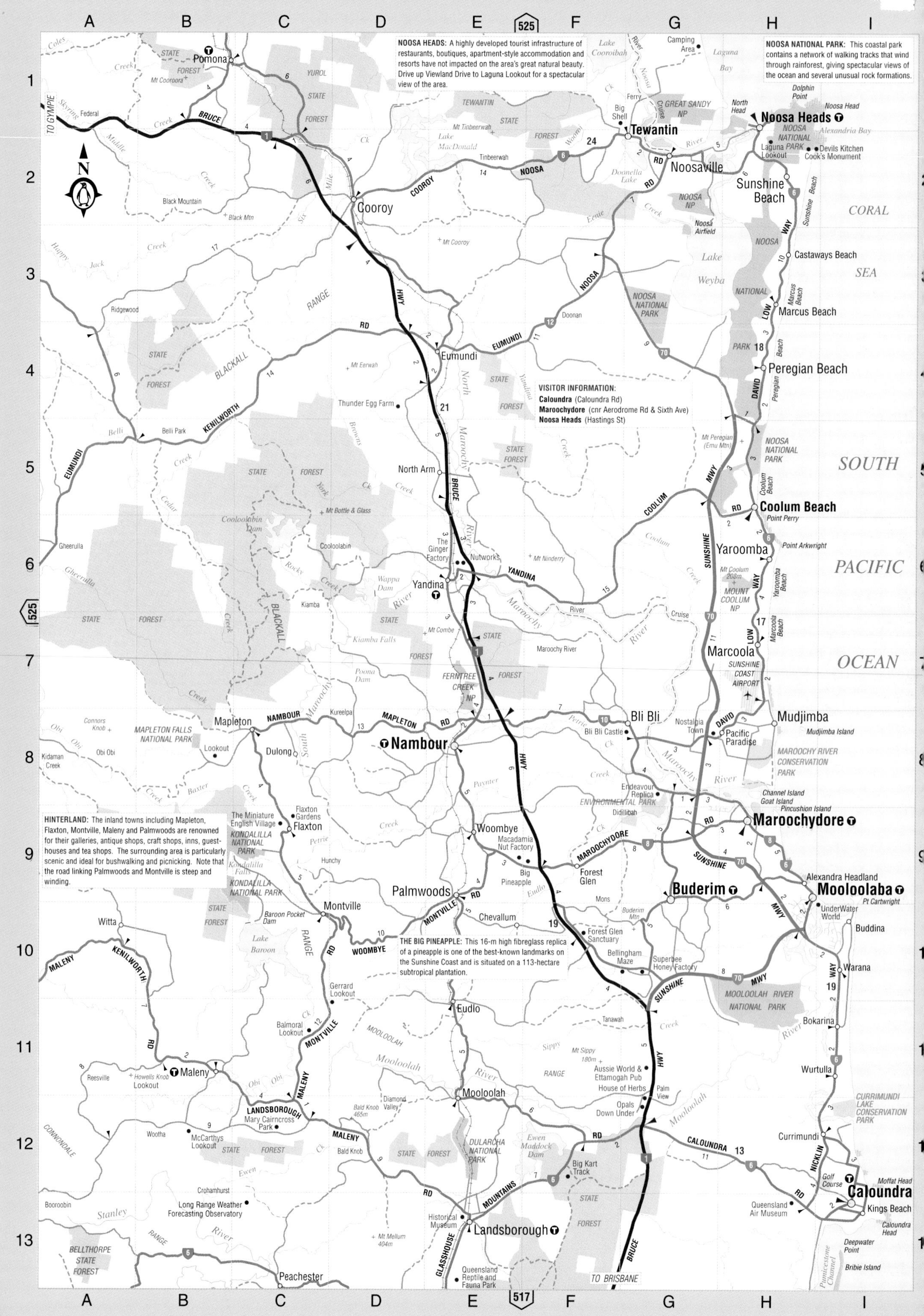

0 2 4 6 8 10 km
NOOSA HEADS: A highly developed tourist infrastructure of restaurants, boutiques, apartment-style accommodation and resorts have not impacted on the area's great natural beauty. Drive up Viewland Drive to Laguna Lookout for a spectacular view of the area.
NOOSA NATIONAL PARK: This coastal park contains a network of walking tracks that wind through rainforest, giving spectacular views of the ocean and several unusual rock formations.
VISITOR INFORMATION:
Caloundra (Caloundra Rd)
Maroochydore (cnr Aerodrome Rd & Sixth Ave)
Noosa Heads (Hastings St)
HINTERLAND: The inland towns including Mapleton, Flaxton, Montville, Maleny and Palmwoods are renowned for their galleries, antique shops, craft shops, inns, guest-houses and tea shops. The surrounding area is particularly scenic and ideal for bushwalking and picnicking. Note that the road linking Palmwoods and Montville is steep and winding.
THE BIG PINEAPPLE: This 16-m high fibreglass replica of a pineapple is one of the best-known landmarks on the Sunshine Coast and is situated on a 113-hectare subtropical plantation.
TO GYMPIE
TO BRISBANE
525
517
Pomona
Cooroy
Tewantin
Noosa Heads
Noosaville
Sunshine Beach
Castaways Beach
Marcus Beach
Peregian Beach
Coolum Beach
Yaroomba
Marcoola
Mudjimba
Pacific Paradise
Bli Bli
Maroochydore
Mooloolaba
Buderim
Eumundi
North Arm
Yandina
Nambour
Mapleton
Flaxton
Montville
Woombye
Palmwoods
Eudlo
Mooloolah
Maleny
Landsborough
Caloundra
Kings Beach
Currimundi
Wurtulla
Bokarina
Warana
Buddina
Alexandra Headland
Peachester
Witta
Ridgewood
Belli Park
Gheerulla
Kiamba
Doonan
Tinbeerwah
Federal
Black Mountain
Dulong
Kureelpa
Hunchy
Chevallum
Forest Glen
Mons
Wootha
Reesville
Booroobin
Crohamhurst
Bald Knob
Tanawah
CORAL SEA
SOUTH PACIFIC OCEAN
NOOSA NATIONAL PARK
MAPLETON FALLS NATIONAL PARK
KONDALILLA NATIONAL PARK
MOOLOOLAH RIVER NATIONAL PARK
DULARCHA NATIONAL PARK
FERNTREE CREEK NP
MOUNT COOLUM NP
GREAT SANDY NP
MAROOCHY RIVER CONSERVATION PARK
CURRIMUNDI LAKE CONSERVATION PARK
BELLTHORPE STATE FOREST
SUNSHINE COAST AIRPORT
BRUCE HWY
SUNSHINE MWY
DAVID LOW WAY
NICKLIN WAY
Lake Weyba
Lake Cooroibah
Lake Baroon
Baroon Pocket Dam
Cooloolabin Dam
Wappa Dam
Poona Dam
Ewen Maddock Dam
The Ginger Factory
Big Pineapple
Macadamia Nut Factory
Aussie World & Ettamogah Pub
House of Herbs
Opals Down Under
Big Kart Track
Superbee Honey Factory
Bellingham Maze
Forest Glen Sanctuary
UnderWater World
Queensland Air Museum
Queensland Reptile and Fauna Park
Historical Museum
Long Range Weather Forecasting Observatory
McCarthys Lookout
Mary Cairncross Park
Gerrard Lookout
Balmoral Lookout
The Miniature English Village
Flaxton Gardens
Thunder Egg Farm
Bli Bli Castle
Endeavour Replica
Nostalgia Town
Camping Area
Noosa Airfield
Laguna Lookout
Devils Kitchen
Cook's Monument
Dolphin Point
Noosa Head
Alexandria Bay
North Head
Point Perry
Point Arkwright
Mudjimba Island
Channel Island
Goat Island
Pincushion Island
Pt Cartwright
Moffat Head
Caloundra Head
Deepwater Point
Bribie Island
Pumicestone Channel

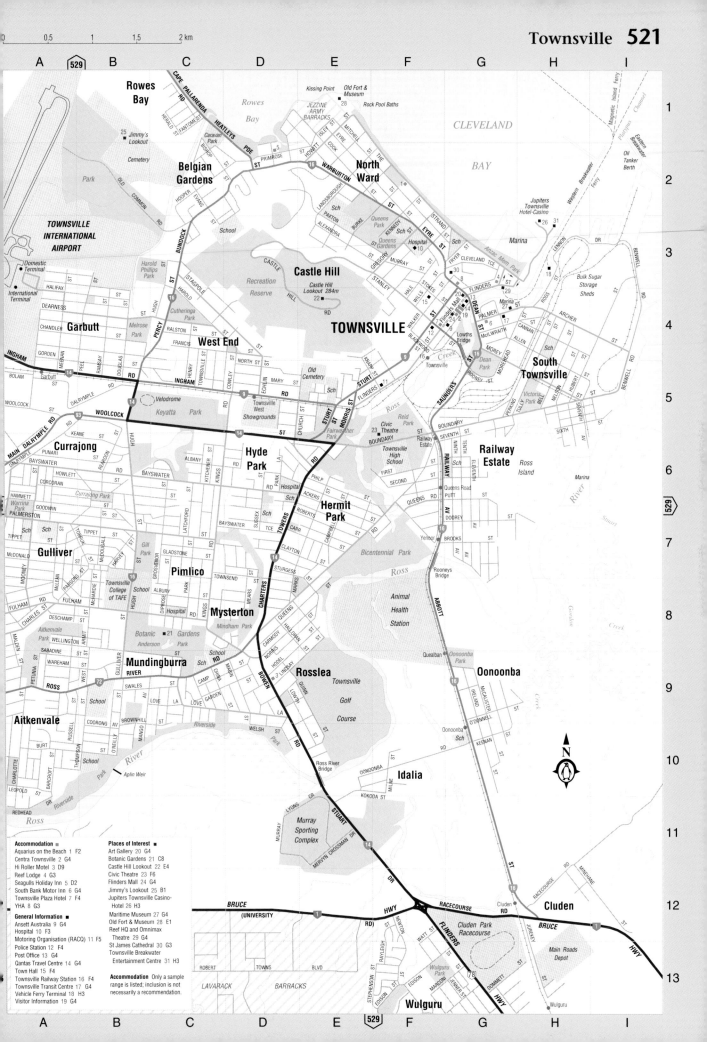

Scale: 0 0.5 1 1.5 2 km

A529

Places / Labels

Rowes Bay
Belgian Gardens
North Ward
Castle Hill
TOWNSVILLE
Garbutt
West End
South Townsville
Currajong
Hyde Park
Hermit Park
Railway Estate
Gulliver
Pimlico
Mysterton
Mundingburra
Rosslea
Oonoonba
Aitkenvale
Idalia
Cluden
Wulguru

CLEVELAND BAY

TOWNSVILLE INTERNATIONAL AIRPORT

Ross River
Ross Island

Townsville Golf Course

Cluden Park Racecourse

Legend

Accommodation
Aquarius on the Beach 1 F2
Centra Townsville 2 G4
Hi Roller Motel 3 D9
Reef Lodge 4 G3
Seagulls Holiday Inn 5 D2
South Bank Motor Inn 6 G4
Townsville Plaza Hotel 7 F4
YHA 8 G3

General Information
Ansett Australia 9 G4
Hospital 10 F3
Motoring Organisation (RACQ) 11 F5
Police Station 12 F4
Post Office 13 G4
Qantas Travel Centre 14 G4
Town Hall 15 F4
Townsville Railway Station 16 F4
Townsville Transit Centre 17 G4
Vehicle Ferry Terminal 18 H3
Visitor Information 19 G4

Places of Interest
Art Gallery 20 G4
Botanic Gardens 21 C8
Castle Hill Lookout 22 E4
Civic Theatre 23 F6
Flinders Mall 24 G4
Jimmy's Lookout 25 B1
Jupiters Townsville Casino-
  Hotel 26 H3
Maritime Museum 27 G4
Old Fort & Museum 28 E1
Reef HQ and Omnimax
  Theatre 29 G4
St James Cathedral 30 G3
Townsville Breakwater
  Entertainment Centre 31 H3

Accommodation Only a sample
range is listed; inclusion is not
necessarily a recommendation.

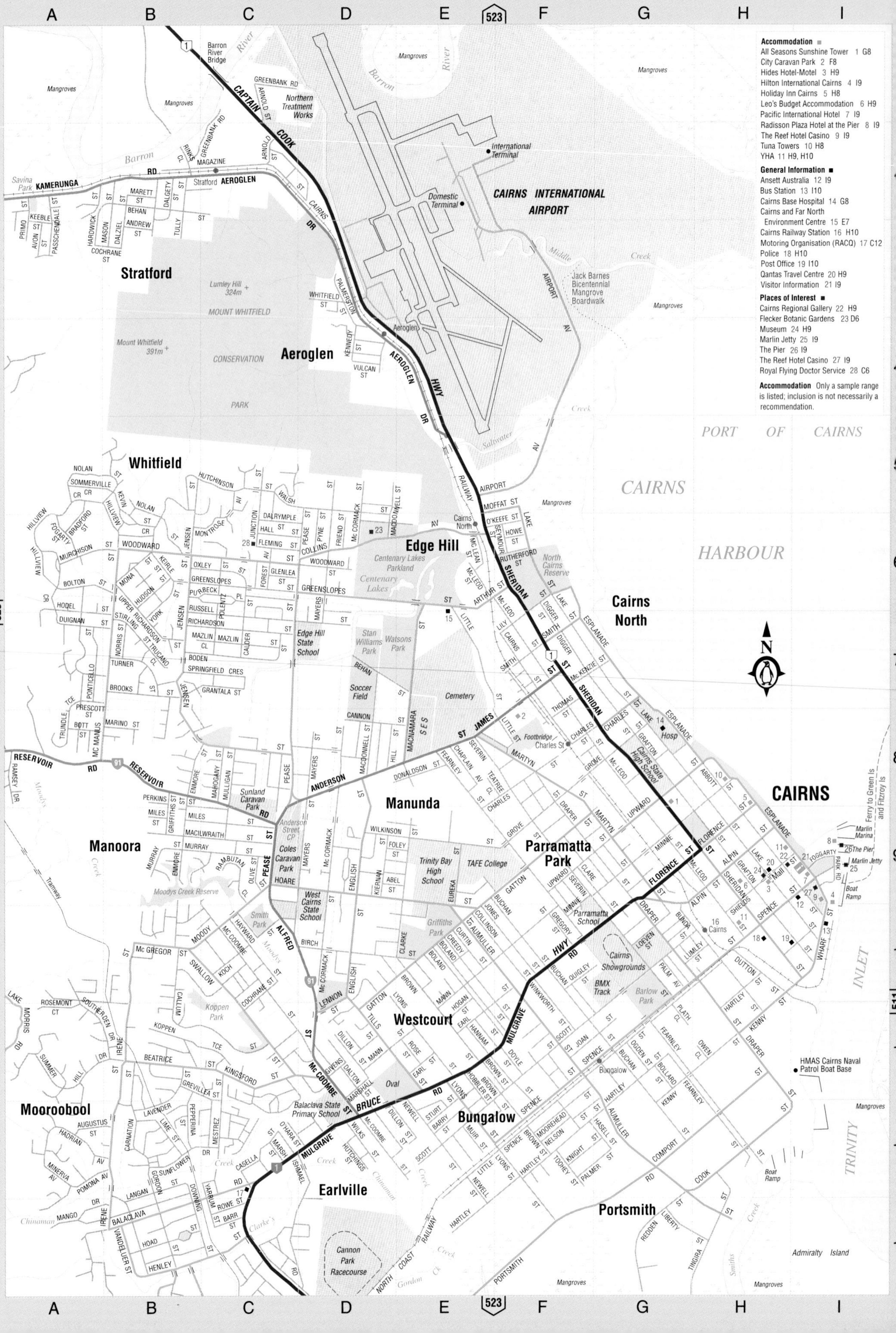

0   0.5   1   1.5   2 km

Accommodation ■
All Seasons Sunshine Tower 1 G8
City Caravan Park 2 F8
Hides Hotel-Motel 3 H9
Hilton International Cairns 4 I9
Holiday Inn Cairns 5 H8
Leo's Budget Accommodation 6 H9
Pacific International Hotel 7 I9
Radisson Plaza Hotel at the Pier 8 I9
The Reef Hotel Casino 9 I9
Tuna Towers 10 H8
YHA 11 H9, H10

General Information ■
Ansett Australia 12 I9
Bus Station 13 I10
Cairns Base Hospital 14 G8
Cairns and Far North
  Environment Centre 15 E7
Cairns Railway Station 16 H10
Motoring Organisation (RACQ) 17 C12
Police 18 H10
Post Office 19 I10
Qantas Travel Centre 20 H9
Visitor Information 21 I9

Places of Interest ■
Cairns Regional Gallery 22 H9
Flecker Botanic Gardens 23 D6
Museum 24 H9
Marlin Jetty 25 I9
The Pier 26 I9
The Reef Hotel Casino 27 I9
Royal Flying Doctor Service 28 C6

Accommodation Only a sample range
is listed; inclusion is not necessarily a
recommendation.

PORT   OF   CAIRNS

CAIRNS

HARBOUR

CAIRNS INTERNATIONAL
AIRPORT

International
Terminal

Domestic
Terminal

Jack Barnes
Bicentennial
Mangrove
Boardwalk

Stratford

Aeroglen

Whitfield

Mount Whitfield
391m

Mount Whitfield
CONSERVATION
PARK

Lumley Hill
324m

MOUNT WHITFIELD

Edge Hill

Cairns
North

Manoora

Manunda

Parramatta
Park

Westcourt

Bungalow

Mooroobool

Earlville

Portsmith

Admiralty Island

TRINITY

INLET

HMAS Cairns Naval
Patrol Boat Base

Cannon
Park
Racecourse

Balaclava State
Primary School

Barron River
Bridge

Northern
Treatment
Works

Stratford

Kamerunga

Savina
Park

Centenary Lakes
Parkland

Centenary
Lakes

Stan
Williams
Park

Watsons
Park

Edge Hill
State
School

Soccer
Field

Cemetery

Trinity Bay
High
School

TAFE College

West
Cairns
State
School

Griffiths
Park

Cairns State
High School

Parramatta
School

Cairns
Showgrounds

BMX
Track

Barlow
Park

Koppen
Park

Smith
Park

Sunland
Caravan
Park

Coles
Caravan
Park

Anderson
Street
CP

Footbridge
Charles St

Hosp

Marlin Marina

The Pier

Marlin Jetty

Boat
Ramp

Boat
Ramp

Ferry to Green Is
and Fitzroy Is

Mall

Cairns

Mangroves

Penguin

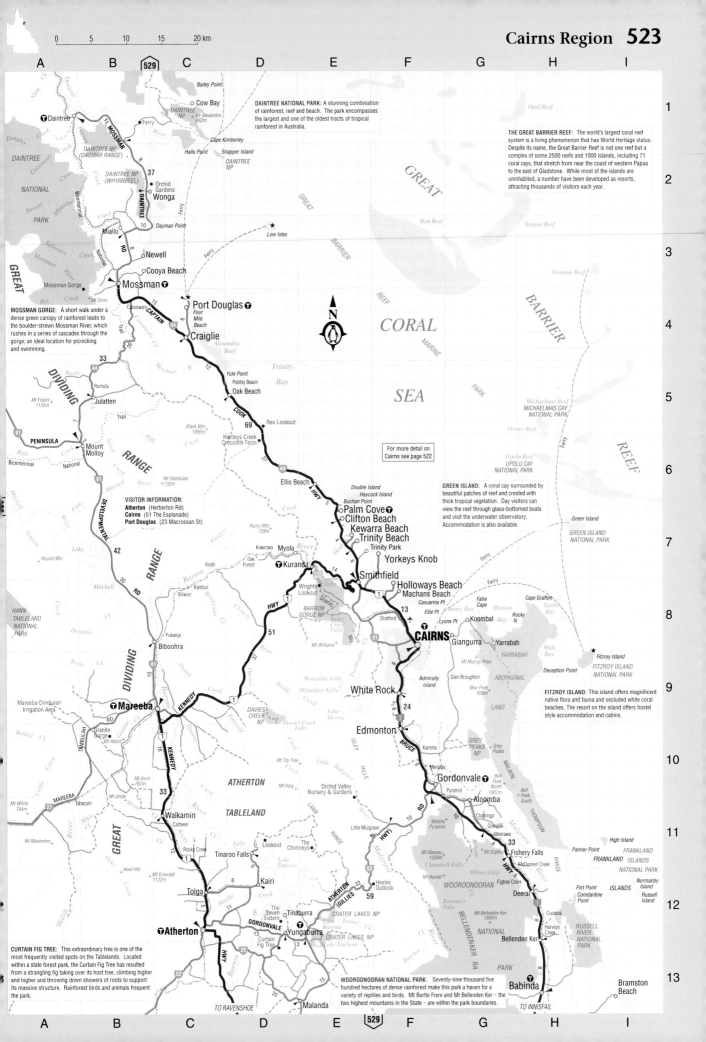

0   5   10   15   20 km

For more detail on Cairns see page 522

DAINTREE NATIONAL PARK: A stunning combination of rainforest, reef and beach. The park encompasses the largest and one of the oldest tracts of tropical rainforest in Australia.

THE GREAT BARRIER REEF: The world's largest coral reef system is a living phenomenon that has World Heritage status. Despite its name, the Great Barrier Reef is not one reef but a complex of some 2500 reefs and 1000 islands, including 71 coral cays, that stretch from near the coast of western Papua to the east of Gladstone. While most of the islands are uninhabited, a number have been developed as resorts, attracting thousands of visitors each year.

MOSSMAN GORGE: A short walk under a dense green canopy of rainforest leads to the boulder-strewn Mossman River, which rushes in a series of cascades through the gorge; an ideal location for picnicking and swimming.

GREEN ISLAND: A coral cay surrounded by beautiful patches of reef and crested with thick tropical vegetation. Day visitors can view the reef through glass-bottomed boats and visit the underwater observatory. Accommodation is also available.

VISITOR INFORMATION:
Atherton (Herberton Rd)
Cairns (51 The Esplanade)
Port Douglas (23 Macrossan St)

FITZROY ISLAND: This island offers magnificent native flora and fauna and secluded white coral beaches. The resort on the island offers hostel style accommodation and cabins.

CURTAIN FIG TREE: This extraordinary tree is one of the most frequently visited spots on the Tablelands. Located within a state forest park, the Curtain Fig Tree has resulted from a strangling fig taking over its host tree, climbing higher and higher and throwing down showers of roots to support its massive structure. Rainforest birds and animals frequent the park.

WOOROONOORAN NATIONAL PARK: Seventy-nine thousand five hundred hectares of dense rainforest make this park a haven for a variety of reptiles and birds. Mt Bartle Frere and Mt Bellenden Ker – the two highest mountains in the State – are within the park boundaries.

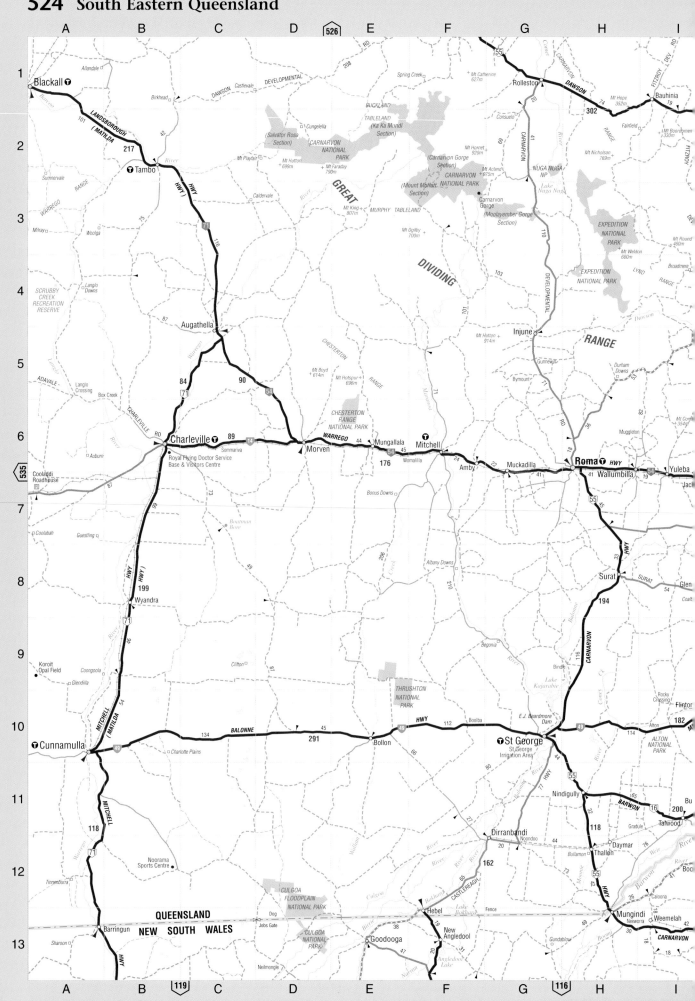

0 25 50 75 100 km

SOUTH

PACIFIC

OCEAN

HERVEY BAY

GREAT SANDY NATIONAL PARK

FRASER ISLAND

Sandy Cape
Rooney Point
Platypus Bay
Orchid Beach
Double Island Point

N

QUEENSLAND

NEW SOUTH WALES

Bundaberg
Hervey Bay
Maryborough
Gympie
Noosa Heads
Sunshine Beach
Peregian Beach
Coolum Beach
Maroochydore
Mooloolaba
Nambour
Buderim
Caloundra
Bongaree
Caboolture
Brisbane
Toowoomba
Gatton
Ipswich
Nerang
Beaudesert
Surfers Paradise
Burleigh Heads
Coolangatta
Tweed Heads
Banora Point
Kingscliff
Murwillumbah
Mullumbimby
Brunswick Heads
Byron Bay
Suffolk Park
Lennox Head
Ballina
Lismore
Casino
Evans Head
Biloela
Monto
Theodore
Mundubbera
Gayndah
Murgon
Wondai
Kingaroy
Nanango
Dalby
Chinchilla
Miles
Moonie
Millmerran
Warwick
Stanthorpe
Goondiwindi
Tenterfield

Childers
Gin Gin
Burnett Heads
Bargara
Moore Park
Woodgate
Burrum Heads
Toogoom
Howard
Torbanlea
Tiaro
Tin Can Bay
Rainbow Beach
Bauple
Gundiah
Kilkivan
Goomeri
Cooroy
Tewantin
Pomona
Eumundi
Kenilworth
Yandina
Bli Bli
Maleny
Landsborough
Beerwah
Glass House Mountains
Woodford
Wamuran
Elimbah
Burpengary
Deception Bay
Redcliffe
Strathpine
Samford
Cleveland
Dunwich
Victoria Point
Redland Bay
Logan
Beenleigh
Jacobs Well
Helensvale
Main Beach
Tamborine
Jimboomba
Boonah
Mudgeeraba
Currumbin
Springbrook
Chinderah
Bogangar
Hastings Point
Pottsville
Ocean Shores
Kyogle
Nimbin
Bangalow
Clunes
Coraki
Woodburn
Broadwater
Wardell

J K L M N O P Q R
1 2 3 4 5 6 7 8 9 10 11 12 13

For more detail on Brisbane Region see pages 516 & 517

For more detailed coverage of localities in New South Wales see page 117

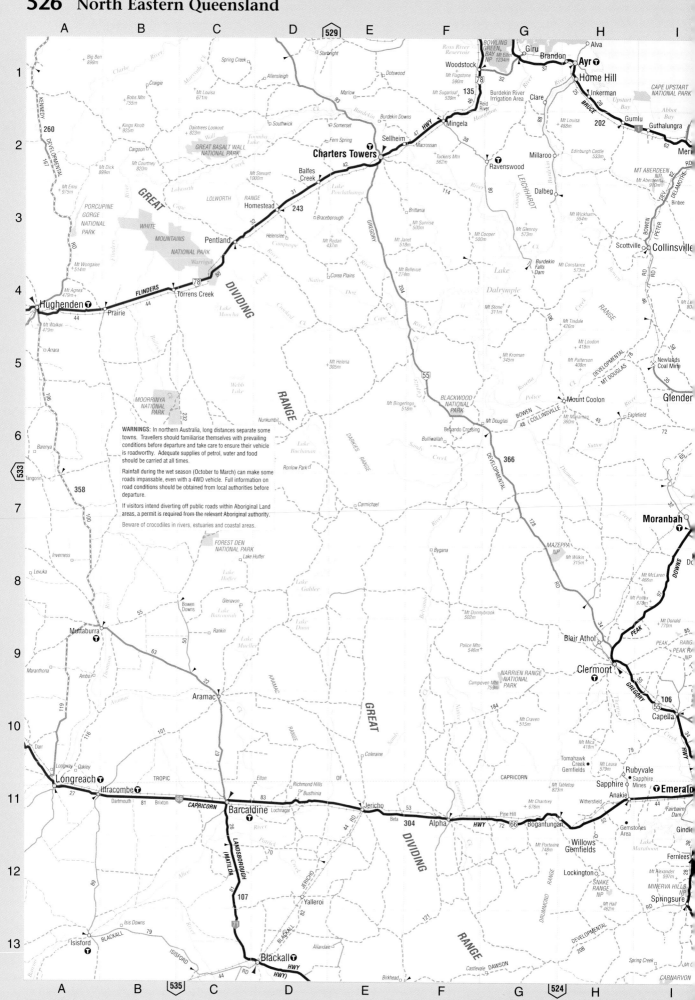

529

535

524

WARNINGS: In northern Australia, long distances separate some towns. Travellers should familiarise themselves with prevailing conditions before departure and take care to ensure their vehicle is roadworthy. Adequate supplies of petrol, water and food should be carried at all times.

Rainfall during the wet season (October to March) can make some roads impassable, even with a 4WD vehicle. Full information on road conditions should be obtained from local authorities before departure.

If visitors intend diverting off public roads within Aboriginal Land areas, a permit is required from the relevant Aboriginal authority.

Beware of crocodiles in rivers, estuaries and coastal areas.

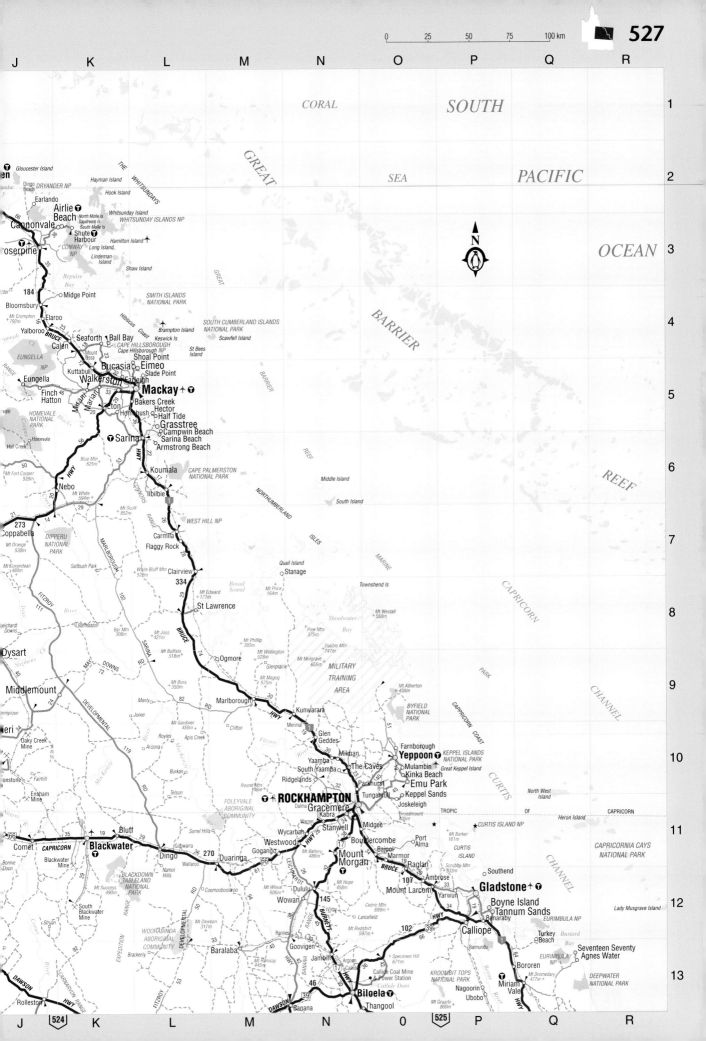

SOUTH

PACIFIC

OCEAN

CORAL

GREAT

SEA

BARRIER

REEF

N

Gloucester Island
en
DRYANDER NP
Dingo Beach
Hayman Island
THE WHITSUNDAYS
Earlando
Airlie Beach
Hook Island
Cannonvale
North Molle Is
Daydream Is
South Molle Is
Whitsunday Island
WHITSUNDAY ISLANDS NP
oserpine
Shute Harbour
Hamilton Island
Long Island
CONWAY NP
Lindeman Island
Shaw Island

GREAT

Repulse Bay
184
Midge Point
SMITH ISLANDS NATIONAL PARK
Bloomsbury
Mt Crompton 792m
Elaroo
SOUTH CUMBERLAND ISLANDS NATIONAL PARK
Brampton Island
Scawfell Island
Yalboroo
BRUCE
23
Calen
Seaforth
Ball Bay
Keswick Is
St Bees Island
CAPE HILLSBOROUGH
Cape Hillsborough NP
Mount Jessa
EUNGELLA NP
Kuttabul
Shoal Point
Bucasia
Eimeo
Slade Point
Eungella
Walkerston
Farleigh
Mackay
Finch Hatton
Marian
Eton
Bakers Creek
Hector
HOMEVALE NATIONAL PARK
Homevale
Half Tide
Grasstree
Campwin Beach
Sarina
Sarina Beach
Armstrong Beach

HWY

REEF

Blue Mtn 625m
Koumala
CAPE PALMERSTON NATIONAL PARK
Mt Fort Cooper 528m
Nebo
Ilbilbie
Middle Island
Mt White 594m
South Island
29
Mt Scott 852m
Carmilla
WEST HILL NP
21
273
Coppabella
Flaggy Rock
DIPPERU NATIONAL PARK
Mt Orange 530m
White Bluff Mtn 572m
Clairview
MARLBOROUGH
Quail Island
Saltbush Park
334
Stanage
102
Mt Edward 171m
Mt Price 164m
Townshend Is
FITZROY
111
Bat Mtn 308m
St Lawrence
Pine Mtn 375m
Double Mtn 747m
Dysart
Mt Joss 421m
BRUCE
Mt Buffalo 518m
74
Ogmore
Mt Phillip 393m
Mt Westall 550m
Middlemount
Mt Bora 350m
Mt Wellington 528m
Mt Mulgrave 655m
Shoalwater Bay
82
Manly
Mt Magog 575m
MILITARY TRAINING AREA
Mt Atherton 438m
24
Junee
Mt Gardiner 450m
Clifton
Marlborough
30
Kunwarara
HWY
BYFIELD NATIONAL PARK
Oaky Creek Mine
Arizona
Merimal
51
Farnborough
KEPPEL ISLANDS NATIONAL PARK
eri
Burkan
Glen Geddes
Yeppoon
Great Keppel Island
Ensham Mine
Telson
Yaamba
Milman
Mulambin
Kinka Beach
South Yaamba
The Caves
onstone
Faithill
Round Mtn
Ridgelands
Parkhurst
Emu Park
Keppel Sands
ROCKHAMPTON
Tungamull
Joskeleigh
Dalma
Gracemere
Kabra
FOLEYVALE ABORIGINAL COMMUNITY
NORTH WEST ISLAND
TROPIC
OF
CAPRICORN
Heron Island
66
Bluff
Sorrel Hills
Midgee
CURTIS ISLAND NP
Comet
CAPRICORN
Blackwater
Dingo
Duaringa
270
Wycarbah
Westwood
Stanwell
Bouldercombe
Bajool
Port Alma
CURTIS ISLAND
CAPRICORNIA CAYS NATIONAL PARK
Blackwater Mine
66
Gogango
Wallaroo
61
Marmor
Raglan
Southend
BLACKDOWN TABLELAND NATIONAL PARK
Namoi Hills
107
Ambrose
Mount Morgan
Mt Battery 486m
Mt Hope 458m
BRUCE
Mount Larcom
Gladstone
South Blackwater Mine
Mt Success 490m
Dululu
Warwun
Boyne Island
Tannum Sands
WOORABINDA ABORIGINAL COMMUNITY
Wowan
145
Mt Dawson 317m
Cedric Mtn 699m
Benaraby
EURIMBULA NP
Lady Musgrave Island
Baralaba
Ranees
Goovigen
102
Calliope
Turkey Beach
Bustard Bay
Mt Ramsay 445m
39
Specimen Hill 671m
Mt Redshirt 597m
Seventeen Seventy
Agnes Water
Jambin
Argoon
Bororen
DEEPWATER NATIONAL PARK
DAWSON
46
KROOMBIT TOPS NATIONAL PARK
Mt Dromedary 477m
Miriam Vale
Rollestan
HWY
Banana
Biloela
Thangool
Nagoorin
Ubobo

GULF

OF

CARPENTARIA

CAPE

YORK

PENINSULA

GREAT

DIVIDING

Musgrave Roadhouse

PENINSULA 63

310

Hann River Roadhouse

Mary Va

New Dixie

Killarney

Kimba

Pinnacles

King P

King Junction

34

Strathleven

90

PORMPURAAW / EDWARD RIVER ABORIGINAL LAND

Edward

River

New Strathgordon

227

Strathmay

Strathaven

Coleman

Creek

Pormpuraaw

Wallaby Island

Mitchell

Motte

Alice

KOWANYAMA ABORIGINAL LAND

Kowanyama

MITCHELL - ALICE RIVERS NATIONAL PARK

Sefton

Oriners

Crosbie

Alice

River

Magnificent

Creek

105

RUTLAND PLAINS

Koolatah

Nassau

River

Dunbar

BURKE

Mitchell

Drumduff

Windermere Lagoon

48

Purumu Lagoon

Kingfish Lagoon

Mosquito Lagoon

Twelve Mile Lagoon

Rosser

Inkerman

Geddes

Creek

Clark

Creek

River

DEVELOPMENTAL

STAATEN RIVER NATIONAL PARK

Highbury Lagoon

Longreach Lagoon

171

Dinner Camp Lagoon

Wa

86

Staaten

Waaba

Dorunda

RD

River

Back

Pandanus

Staaten

Bulimba

Waukanaka Lagoon

Middle

Creek

Byrnes

Creek

River

Point Burrowes

Delta Downs

Smithburne

Gilbert

River

DEVELOPMENTAL

176

Vanrook

Creek

Pelican

Creek

Sandy

Ponds

Red

Creek

Torwo

Fitzmaurice Point

Snake Ck

Fitzmaurice

Creek

River

Walker

Miranda Downs

Creek

BULLE NATION.

Karumba Point

Karumba

Barge Service Karumba to Weipa

41

30

BURKE

Wills

Creek

Fish

Creek

Hole

Fourteen Mile

Creek

Eimixleigh

Jungoon

Abingdon Downs

Middle Point

Bynoe

Flinders

River

Normanton

Shady Lagoon

Mutton Hole

Rocky

Creek

Etheridge

Mt Campbell 366m +

Vanlee

Rocky Lake

Manrika Lake

Burke & Wills Cairn

Magowra

25

Twelve Mile Lagoon

Glenore

68

GULF

Carron

Clarina

Creek

Strathmore

69

River

51

95

Dagworth

Huonfels

Tallaroo Ho

Inverleigh

83

195

Creek

The Lakes

Belmore

(SAVANNAH

60

DEVELOPMENTAL

WAY)

Croydon

Chadshunt

Gilbert River

Mt Turner + 457m

Kutchera

73

GULF

NEWCASTLE

Gamboola

Macalister

RD

132

Jumble

Hole

Coralie

Creek

Alehvale

Inorunie

449

75

RD

Little

River

Georgetown

Delaney R.

Spear

60

Bang Bang Jump Up Rock Formation

141

River

142

Templeton

GREGORY

Forsayth

67

531

Neumayer Valley

1

Bang Bang

Wondoola

Racecourse Lagoon

Clara

Yappar

Mittagong

114

Lunsdon

Gilbert

Goldsmiths

Donors Hill

61

Iffley

Muggera Lagoon

Claraville

162

River

Esmeralda

Glenora

Malacura

RANGE

Cobbold Gorge

Robin Ho

Macura

BURKE

DEVELOPMENTAL

72

RD

Flinders

Chinaway

River

Sandy

Forrest

River

Momba

Nara

Robertson

River

Agate Creek Gemfields

Baird's Table Mountain 914m

Burke & Wills Roadhouse

DEVELOPMENTAL

95

RD

Victoria Vale

Perry Vale

BURKE

(MATILDA

WILLS

Dismal

River

Boomarra

Canobie

Lyrian Waterhole

Taldora

Twelve

Mile

Ck

Boorabin

Creek

Pelham

Gorge Ca

Gorge Cr

GULF

SAVANNAH

531

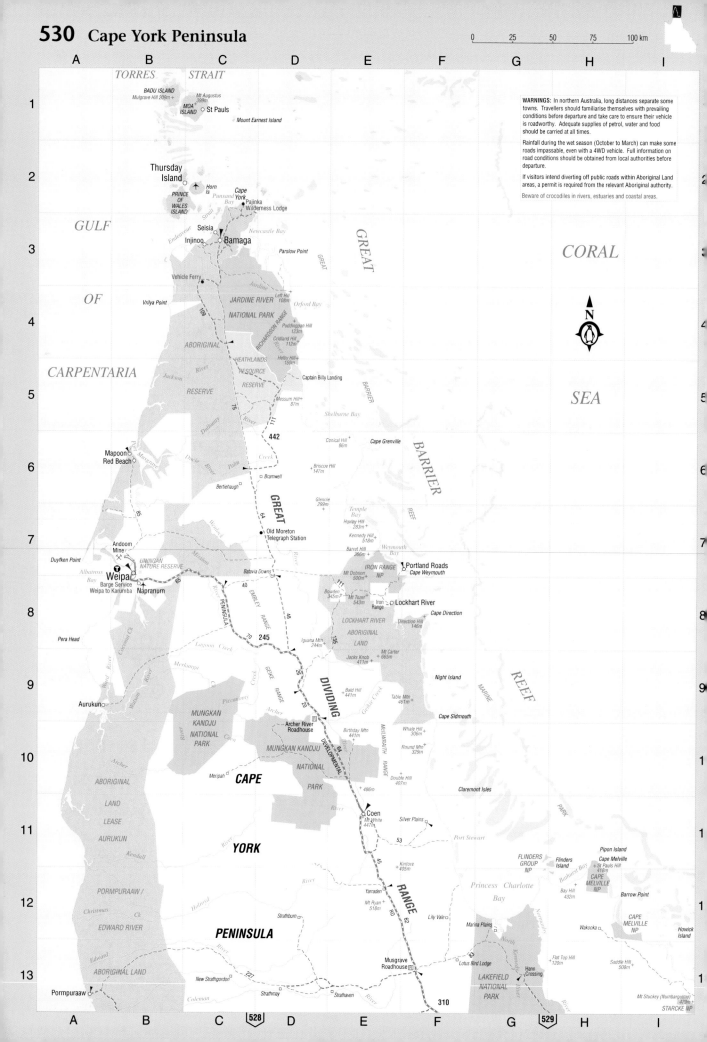

0 25 50 75 100 km

A   B   C   D   E   F   G   H   I

TORRES   STRAIT

BADU ISLAND
Mulgrave Hill 209m +
Mt Augustus 399m
MOA ISLAND ○ St Pauls

Mount Earnest Island

GULF

Thursday Island
Horn Is
PRINCE OF WALES ISLAND
Cape York Pajinka
Wilderness Lodge
Punsand Bay
Seisia
Endeavour Strait Injinoo Bamaga
Newcastle Bay

OF

CORAL

Parslow Point

GREAT

Vehicle Ferry
JARDINE RIVER
Jardine *Left Hill 108m* *Orford Bay*
Vrilya Point *NATIONAL PARK*
RICHARDSON RANGE
Puddingpan Hill 123m +
CARPENTARIA *ABORIGINAL* *Cridland Hill 112m +*
HEATHLANDS *Helby Hill 150m +*
RESOURCE
RESERVE *RESERVE* *Captain Billy Landing*
Messum Hill 87m + *Shelburne Bay*
Dulhunty *River*

SEA

BARRIER

442
Conical Hill 86m + *Cape Grenville*

Mapoon
Red Beach *Briscoe Hill 147m +*

BARRIER
Bramwell
Bertiehaugh *GREAT*
Glennie 299m +
64 *Temple Bay*
Huxley Hill 283m + *REEF*
● Old Moreton Telegraph Station
Kennedy Hill 518m +
Weymouth Bay
Andoom Mine *Barret Hill 366m +*
Duyfken Point *UNINGAN NATURE RESERVE* Batavia Downs *IRON RANGE* Portland Roads
Albatross Bay Weipa *Cape Weymouth*
Barge Service 65 40 *Mt Dobson 500m +*
Weipa to Karumba Napranum 48 111
Bowden 345m +
Mt Tozer 543m + Iron ○ Lockhart River
Range
Pera Head *PENINSULA* 70 245 *LOCKHART RIVER* *Cape Direction*
Lagoon Creek *Iguana Mtn 244m +* *ABORIGINAL* *Direction Hill 146m +*
Cococnut Ck *EMBLEY RANGE* 135 *LAND*
Merkunga 26 *Jacks Knob 411m +* *Mt Carter 665m +*
Aurukun 20 *Bald Hill 441m +* *Night Island* *MARINE*
GEIKE RANGE *DIVIDING* *Geikie Creek* *Cape Sidmouth* *REEF*
Piccaninny *Archer* *Table Mtn 461m +*
MUNGKAN KANDJU NATIONAL PARK Archer River Roadhouse *Birthday Mtn 441m +* *Whale Hill 306m +*
DEVELOPMENTAL *Claremont Isles*
Caen *MUNGKAN KANDJU* *Round Mtn 329m +*
Meripah *NATIONAL* 64 *Double Hill 407m +*
CAPE *PARK* *+ 486m* *PARK*
Archer River
Coen Silver Plains *FLINDERS GROUP NP* *Pipon Island*
Kendall *YORK* Mt White 447m 53 *Port Stewart* Flinders Island Cape Melville + St Pauls Hill 418m
Bathurst Bay *CAPE MELVILLE NP*
Kintore 405m + 45 *Bay Hill 432m +* Barrow Point
PORMPURAAW / *RANGE* Yarraden *Princess Charlotte Bay*
Christmas Ck Mt Ryan 518m *Lily Vale* *CAPE MELVILLE NP*
EDWARD RIVER 63 Marina Plains Wakooka *Howick Island*
PENINSULA Strathburn *North Kennedy River*
New Strathgordon 227 Musgrave Roadhouse Lotus Bird Lodge Hann Crossing *Saddle Hill 508m +*
ABORIGINAL LAND *LAKEFIELD NATIONAL PARK* *Flat Top Hill 120m +*
Pormpuraaw *Coleman* Strathmay Strathaven 310 *Mt Stuckey (Numbargulpie) 479m +*
STARCKE NP

528 529

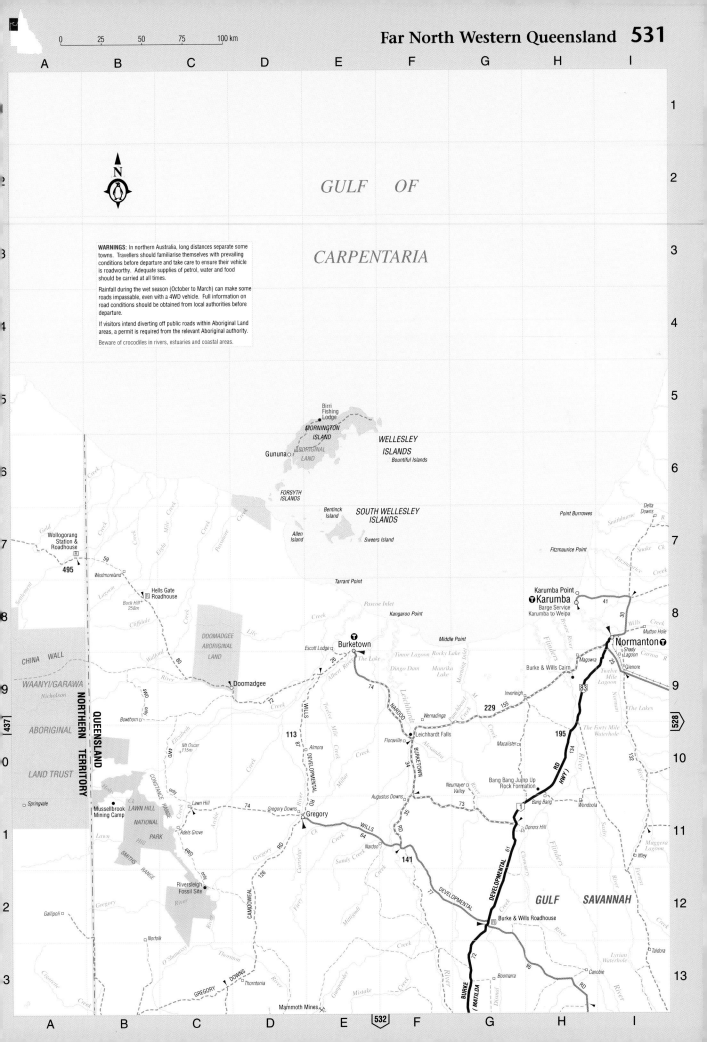

0   25   50   75   100 km

A   B   C   D   E   F   G   H   I

GULF OF

CARPENTARIA

WARNINGS: In northern Australia, long distances separate some towns. Travellers should familiarise themselves with prevailing conditions before departure and take care to ensure their vehicle is roadworthy. Adequate supplies of petrol, water and food should be carried at all times.

Rainfall during the wet season (October to March) can make some roads impassable, even with a 4WD vehicle. Full information on road conditions should be obtained from local authorities before departure.

If visitors intend diverting off public roads within Aboriginal Land areas, a permit is required from the relevant Aboriginal authority.

Beware of crocodiles in rivers, estuaries and coastal areas.

Birri Fishing Lodge

MORNINGTON ISLAND

WELLESLEY ISLANDS

Gununa   *ABORIGINAL LAND*

Bountiful Islands

FORSYTH ISLANDS

Bentinck Island   *SOUTH WELLESLEY ISLANDS*

Allen Island   Sweers Island

Point Burrowes   Smithburne   Delta Downs

Fitzmaurice Point   Snake Ck

Tarrant Point

Pascoe Inlet   Karumba Point   Karumba   Barge Service Karumba to Weipa   41   Wills   Ck   Mutton Hole

Kangaroo Point   30   Normanton   Shady Lagoon

Gold   Wollogorang Station & Roadhouse   **495**   59   Westmoreland   Hells Gate Roadhouse   Buck Hill 258m   *DOOMADGEE ABORIGINAL LAND*   Lily   Timor Lagoon   Rocky Lake   Middle Point   Burke & Wills Cairn   Magowra   Glenore

CHINA WALL   80   Escott Lodge   26   Burketown   The Lake   Dingo Dam   Manrika Lake   Mornington Inlet   Inverleigh   83   Twelve Mile Lagoon

WAANYI/GARAWA   Nicholson   Doomadgee   72   74   Floraville   Leichhardt Falls   229   155   The Lakes

ABORIGINAL   Bowthorn   113   Almora   Wernadinga   Macalister   195   The Forty Mile Waterhole   132

LAND TRUST   Springvale   Mt Oscar 115m   Lawn Hill   74   Gregory Downs   Gregory   Augustus Downs   73   Neumayer Valley   Bang Bang Jump Up Rock Formation   134   Bang Bang   Wondoola

Mussellbrook Mining Camp   *LAWN HILL NATIONAL PARK*   Adels Grove   Wills   64   Nardoo   141   Donors Hill   Iffley   Muggera Lagoon

Gallipoli   Riversleigh Fossil Site   126   Gregory   Cloncurry   GULF   SAVANNAH

Norfolk   CAMOOWEAL   77   DEVELOPMENTAL   61   Burke & Wills Roadhouse   Taldora

Cloncurry   Boomarra   95   Canobie   Lyrian Waterhole

BURKE (MATILDA)   Dismal   Mammoth Mines

532

A   B   C   D   E   F   G   H   I

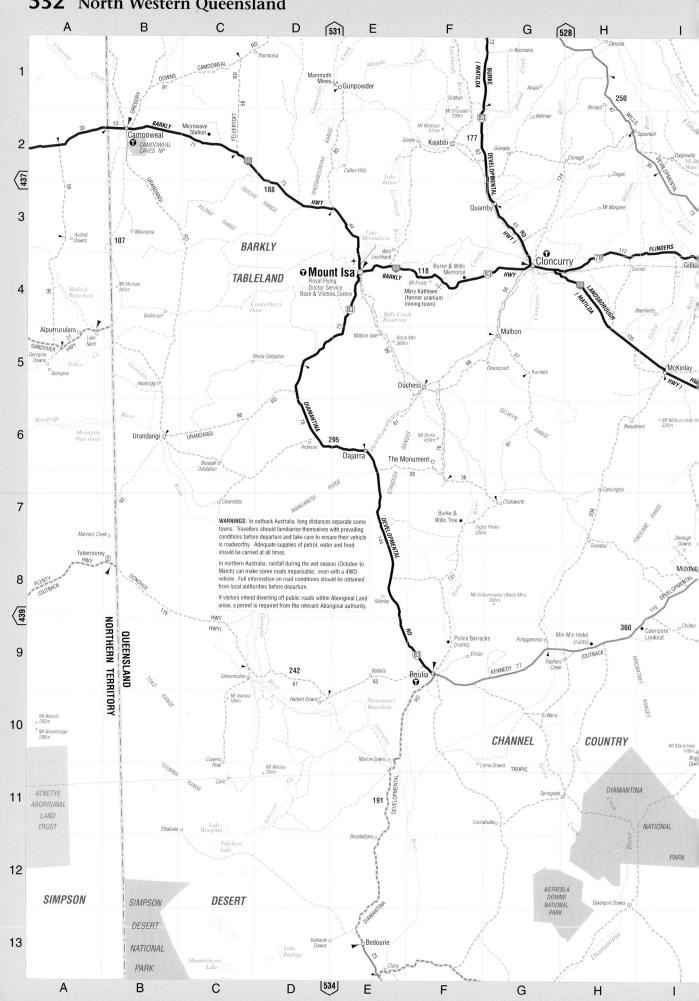

WARNINGS: In outback Australia, long distances separate some towns. Travellers should familiarise themselves with prevailing conditions before departure and take care to ensure their vehicle is roadworthy. Adequate supplies of petrol, water and food should be carried at all times.

In northern Australia, rainfall during the wet season (October to March) can make some roads impassable, even with a 4WD vehicle. Full information on road conditions should be obtained from local authorities before departure.

If visitors intend diverting off public roads within Aboriginal Land areas, a permit is required from the relevant Aboriginal authority.

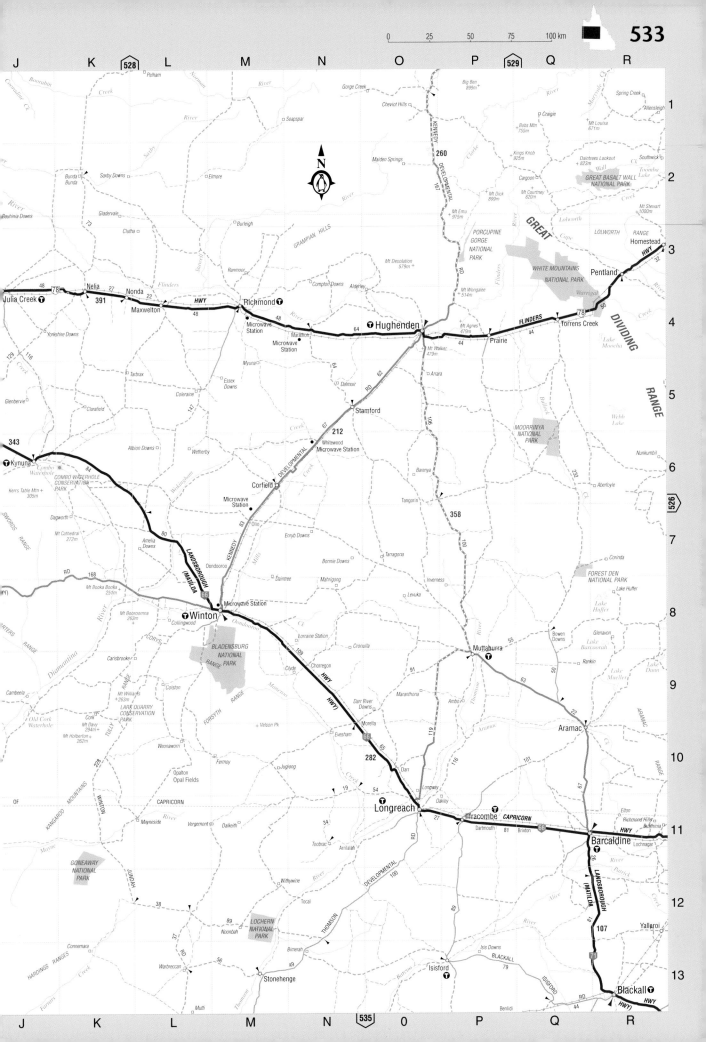

0   25   50   75   100 km

J   K   528   L   M   N   529   O   P   Q   R

Coorabone Ck
Booraban
Creek
Pelham

Norman
Norman
River
River
Creek
River

Gorge Creek

Big Ben
899m+

River
Spring Creek

Cheviot Hills

Allensleigh

Craigie
Mt Louisa
671m+
Southwick
Toomba
Lake

1

Bunda
Bunda
Saxby Downs
Elmore

Soapspar

Maiden Springs

260

Bobs Mtn
755m
Mt Dick
899m

Cargoon
Kings Knob
925m+
Mt Courtney
820m

Daintrees Lookout
+823m

GREAT BASALT WALL
NATIONAL PARK

Mt Stewart
+1000m

2

River
River
Gladervale
Clutha
Burleigh
GRAMPIAN HILLS
Stawell
Ranmoor

PORCUPINE
GORGE
NATIONAL
PARK

WHITE MOUNTAINS
NATIONAL PARK

GREAT
LOLWORTH
Cape
LOLWORTH
RANGE

Homestead
HWY
32

3

73
River

Mt Desolation
579m +

Mt Emu
975m

Mt Wongalee
+514m

Pentland

DIVIDING

Julia Creek ●
48
78
Nelia
27
Nonda
HWY
Richmond ●
Maxwelton
22
48
48
River
Microwave
Station
Marathon
Microwave
Station
64
Hughenden ●
Mt Agnes
479m
Prairie
44
FLINDERS
78
Torrens Creek
44
50
Warrigal
Lake
Moocha

4

129
116
Creek
Yorkshire Downs

391

Myuna

Dalmuir
62
RD
Arara
Mt Walkez
479m
106

Webb
Lake

RANGE

5

343
Glenbervie
Clarafield
Coleraine
147
Essex Downs
Tarbrax

Stamford
67
212
Whitewood
Microwave Station
Barenya

MOORRINYA
NATIONAL
PARK

Bullock
Creek

Nunkumbil

526

6

Kynuna ●
Combo
Waterhole
Albion Downs
Wetherby
DEVELOPMENTAL
Corfield
Tangorin
Aberfoyle

Kerrs Table Mtn +
305m

COMBO WATERHOLE
CONSERVATION
PARK

Microwave
Station
232

7

SWORDS
RANGE
Dagworth
Mt Cathedral
272m+

84
Wokingham
80
Amelia
Downs
KENNEDY
83
Olio
Oondooroo
Enryb Downs
Bonnie Downs
Tarragona

358
100
Inverness

Corinda

FOREST DEN
NATIONAL
PARK

Lake Huffer

8

RD
168
Mt Booka Booka
251m
(HWY)
LANDSBOROUGH
(MATILDA)
66
Microwave Station
Mills
Daintree
Mahrigong
Levuka

Lake
Huffer

Bowen
Downs
55
Glenavon
Lake
Barcoorah
Lake
Dann

9

Diamantina
Cambeela
Old Cork
Waterhole
Carisbrooke
Mt Williams
+263m
CORYS
Collingwood
Winton ●
BLADENSBURG
NATIONAL
PARK
RANGE
Lorraine Station
Cronulla
Clyde
Chorregon
109
91
Maranthona
Muttaburra ●
Ambo
63
50
Rankin
Lake
Mueller

10

Mt Booroomna
263m +
LARK QUARRY
CONSERVATION
PARK
Mt Davy 294m +
Mt Holberton +
262m
FORSYTH
RANGE
Manuroo
Colston
Weonaworn
Fermoy
Opalton
Opal Fields
228
Maneroo Ck
Jugiong
Evesham
66
65
Morella
282
Darr River
Downs
119
116
Aramac
22
ARAMAC
RANGE

Cork

Mayne
TULLY RANGE
WINTON
Darr
19
54
Longway
Dakley
101
97

11

Mayneside
Vergemont
Dalkeith
Creek
34
Toobrac
Arrilalah
RD
Longreach ●
27
Ifracombe ●
Dartmouth
81
Broxton
CAPRICORN
66
HWY
Barcaldine ●
Lochnagar
Elton
Richmond Hills
Bushbinha

CAPRICORN

River
Patrick Creek
26
Alice
LANDSBOROUGH
(MATILDA)

12

GONEAWAY
NATIONAL
PARK
JUNDAH
38
Withywine
THOMSON RIVER
Tocal
Creek
100
DEVELOPMENTAL

81
107
Yalleroi

KANGAROO MOUNTAINS
HARDINGS RANGES
Connemara
37
89
Noonbah
LOCHERN
NATIONAL
PARK
Bimerah
Withywine
Isis Downs
89
BLACKALL
ISISFORD
RD

71

13

Coolah Ferrars
Creek
Multi
Warbreccan
56
Stonehenge
49
Barcoo
River
Isisford ●
79
Benlidi
44
Blackall ●
HWY

J   K   L   M   535   N   O   P   Q   R

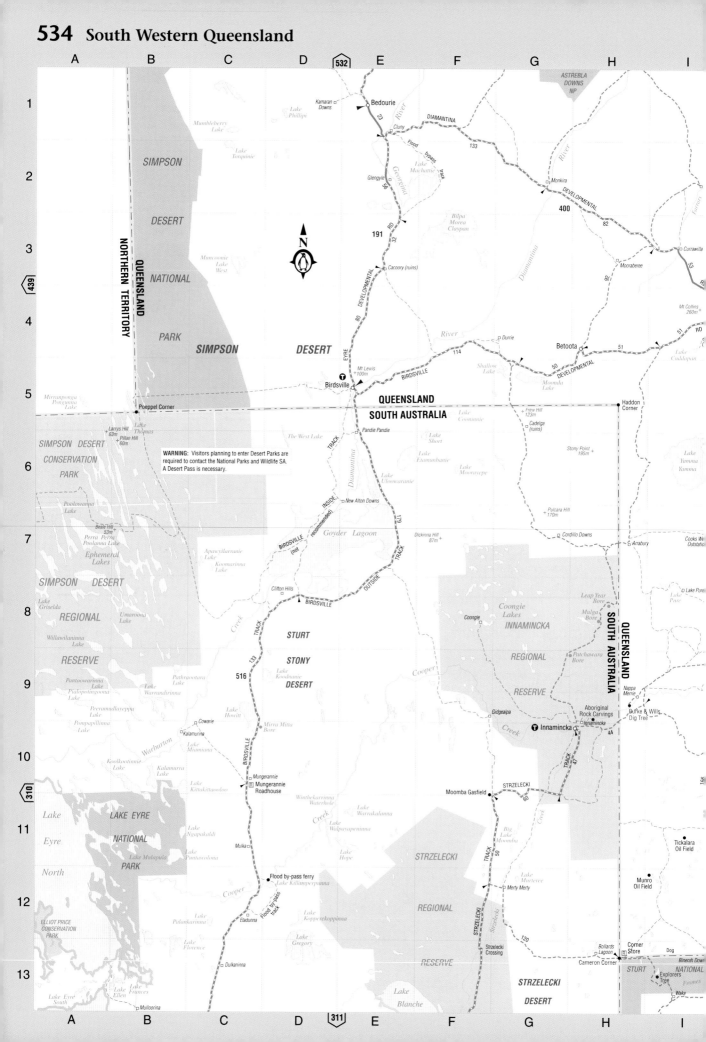

A B C D 532 E F G H I

1

SIMPSON

2

DESERT

NORTHERN TERRITORY

Queensland

3 439

NATIONAL

4

PARK

SIMPSON   DESERT

Lake Phillipi

Mumbleberry Lake

Lake Torquinie

Lake West

Muncoonie

Kamaran Downs

Bedourie

23

Cluny

Flood   bypass

Glengyle   56

191   32

RD   Cacoory (ruins)

EYRE

DEVELOPMENTAL

80

114

Mt Lewis
+100m

Birdsville

BIRDSVILLE

DIAMANTINA

133

Lake Machattie

Bilpa
Morea
Claypan

track

River

Monkira

DEVELOPMENTAL

400

82

Mooraberee

Durrie

Shallow
Lake

Betoota

50   51

Moonda
Lake

DEVELOPMENTAL

Mt Collins
260m

53

Currawilla

51   RD

Lake
Cuddapan

5

Birdsville

QUEENSLAND

SOUTH AUSTRALIA

Haddon
Corner

Mirranponga
Pongunna
Lake

Poeppel Corner

Larrys Hill
63m   Pillan Hill
+60m

Lake
Thomas

The West Lake

Pandie Pandie

Lake
Coonunie

Frew Hill
+123m

Cadelga
(ruins)

Stony Point
195m

Lake
Yamma
Yamma

6

SIMPSON DESERT

CONSERVATION

PARK

WARNING: Visitors planning to enter Desert Parks are
required to contact the National Parks and Wildlife SA.
A Desert Pass is necessary.

Poolowanna
Lake

TRACK

Diamantina

INSIDE

New Alton Downs

Lake
Short

Lake
Etamunbanie

Lake
Mooravepe

Lake
Uloowaranie

Pulcara Hill
+170m

7

Betlie Hill
53m

Perra Perra
Poolanna Lake

Ephemeral

Lakes

SIMPSON   DESERT

BIRDSVILLE

(not

recommended)

Apuwilaranie
Lake

Koomarinnia
Lake

Goyder Lagoon

179

TRACK

Dickinna Hill
87m

Cordillo Downs

Arrabury

Cooks Well
Outstatio

Lake
Purel

8

Lake
Griselda

REGIONAL

Umaroona
Lake

Willawilaninna
Lake

Clifton Hills

BIRDSVILLE

OUTSIDE

Creek

TRACK

STURT

STONY

DESERT

Coonie

Coongie
Lakes

INNAMINCKA

REGIONAL

Coongie

Leap Year
Bore

Mulga
Bore

Patchawara
Bore

QUEENSLAND   SOUTH AUSTRALIA

9

RESERVE

Pantoowarinna Lake

Pialepitngoona
Lake

Peeramudlaseppa
Lake

Pompapillinna
Lake

Pathraootara
Lake

Lake
Warrandirinna

Cowarie

Kalamurina

133

516

Lake
Koodnanie

Lake
Howitt

Mirra Mitta
Bore

RESERVE

Cooper

Gidgealpa

Innamincka

Aboriginal
Rock Carvings

Innamincka

4A

Nappa
Merrie

Burke & Wills
Dig Tree

10 310

Koolkootinnie
Lake

Lake
Miamana

Kalamurra
Lake

Lake
Kittakittaooloo

Warburton

BIRDSVILLE

Mungerannie

Mungerannie
Roadhouse

Winbekarrinna
Waterhole

Creek

TRACK   41

STRZELECKI

Moomba Gasfield

80

11

Lake
Eyre

LAKE EYRE

NATIONAL

Lake Malapula

Lake
Ngapakaldi

Mulka

Lake
Punacalona

Lake
Walpuyapenimma

Lake
Warrakalanna

STRZELECKI

REGIONAL

Big
Lake
Moomba

Lake
Marteree

TRACK   50

Creek

Tickalara
Oil Field

12

North

ELLIOT PRICE
CONSERVATION
PARK

PARK

Lake
Palankarinna

Etadunna

Cooper

Flood by-pass ferry

Flood by-pass   track

Lake Killamperpunna

Lake
Hope

Lake
Kopperekoppinna

RESERVE

Merty Merty

STRZELECKI

120

Bollards
Lagoon

Strzelecki
Crossing

Munro
Oil Field

Dog

Corner
Store

Binerah Down

13

Lake Eyre
South

Lake
Ellen

Lake
Frances

Mulloorina

Dulkaninna

Lake
Florence

Lake
Gregory

Lake
Blanche

STRZELECKI

DESERT

Cameron Corner

STURT   NATIONAL

Explorers
Tree

Waka

Fyones

A B C D 311 E F G H I

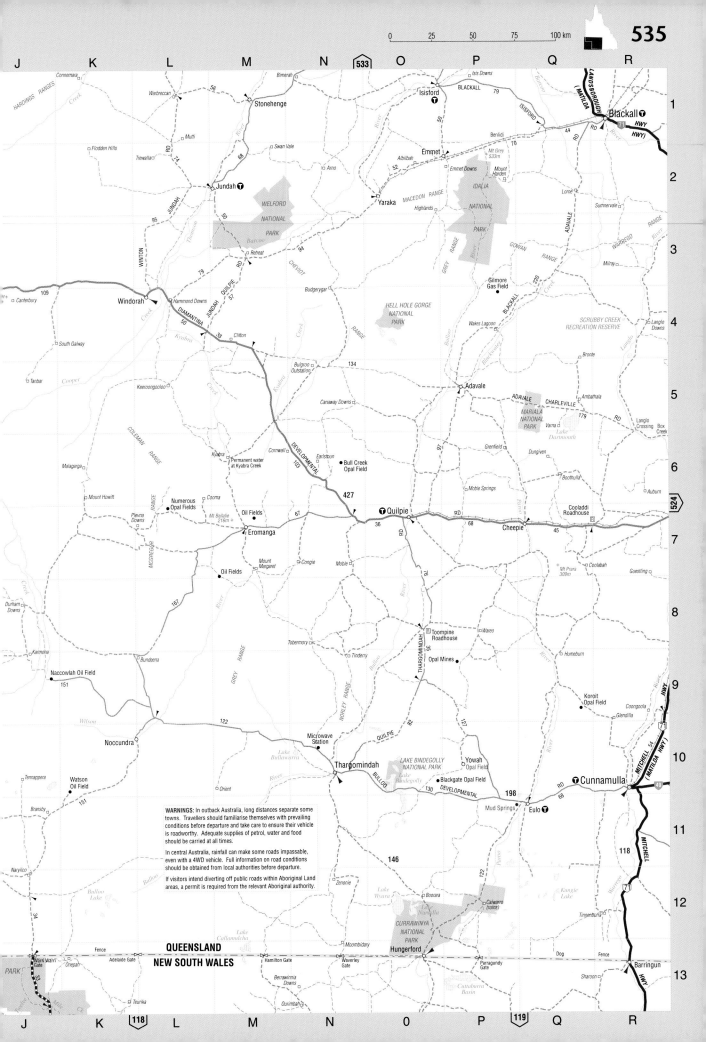

TASMANIA

Lavender farm, northern Tasmania

T asmania has certainly won many more hearts than it can claim square kilometres. It has only 68 000 of the latter, but it crams into them its rugged west, a central plateau broken by steep mountains and narrow river valleys, and an eastern coastal region offering a more gentle pastoral beauty.

The physical beauty of the island State, its landscapes more often resembling Britain than Australia, contribute much to its distinct character and the tourism so important to its economy. Tasmania has been a popular tourist attraction for visitors, particularly Australians from 'the mainland,' for many years.

This dramatically beautiful island, however, has a far from beautiful early history. The first European to sight the island was Abel Tasman in 1642; it was later claimed by Captain Cook for the English and the British settlement dates from 1803. For the next fifty years it was maintained primarily as a penal colony, although prosperous settlements developed around Hobart and New Norfolk. The convicts did the hard labour and lived in brutal conditions at Port Arthur. The Tasmanian Aborigines, who resisted the takeover of their land, were treated even more harshly than the convicts.

Political separation from New South Wales was granted in 1825 and transportation of convicts ceased in 1853. Today the ruins of Port Arthur have taken on a mellow charm and Tasmania is an infinitely more hospitable place.

Tasmania's economy is basically agricultural with the major growth area being in quality specialised food products. The Tasmanian hydro-electric system has a greater output than that of the Snowy Mountains Scheme; Tasmania's high rainfall helps this. The climate offers mild summers and cool winters, with much of the mountain regions receiving heavy winter snowfall. Mid-December to late February is very popular with tourists; late spring or autumn are also pleasant. Even the winter months offer good touring.

When planning a trip to Tasmania in the peak season, note the heavy booking for the *Spirit of Tasmania* passenger/ vehicle ferry service between Melbourne and Devonport. Alternatively, take the *Devil Cat Ferry* to Georgetown (Dec.–Apr.), or consider a fly/drive holiday, which can be a relaxing and economic alternative. Tasmania's roads are well suited to relaxed meandering, many of them being winding and narrow. In a fortnight you can happily complete what is virtually a round tour of the island.

Hobart, the capital of Tasmania, is built on both sides of the Derwent River, and is dominated by Mount Wellington. The

NOT TO BE MISSED

IN TASMANIA	Map Ref.
BICHENO Old sealing and whaling town, now home port for crayfishing boats	583 Q2
CATARACT GORGE Launceston's own piece of wilderness	581 N10
CLARENDON One of the finest Georgian homes in the country	581 P13
CRADLE MOUNTAIN–LAKE ST CLAIR NATIONAL PARK For excellent bushwalking in this famous mountain wilderness	582 F1
DON RIVER RAILWAY A scenic train trip along the banks of the river	580 D5
FREYCINET PENINSULA Features a magnificent rocky coastline	583 Q5
GORDON RIVER Enjoy its beauty from a cruise boat	582 E5
PORT ARTHUR One of Australia's most significant heritage sites	579 N10
RICHMOND Delightful, well-preserved Georgian village	583 M7
STANLEY Quiet historic township nestled under The Nut	584 D3
STRAHAN VISITORS CENTRE For fascinating history in a unique hands-on museum	582 D3

city's many historic buildings and rich colonial heritage draw visitors from around Australia. Within easy reach are Port Arthur, Richmond with its beautiful bridge (the oldest in Australia), and the settlements of Bothwell and New Norfolk.

South of Hobart is the Huon Valley, known for its berry farms and apple orchards. To the west are the picturesque hop fields of the Derwent Valley. Further west is Lake Pedder; the flooding of this area was a source of great controversy when it was made part of the hydro-electric scheme. The surrounding country makes up the Southwest National Park. The Lyell Highway leads to Cradle Mountain–Lake St Clair National Park. Queenstown is the largest settlement in this wild, forested region. Nearby coastal Strahan, once a mining boom-town is now the departure point for the Gordon River cruises and scenic flights over the Franklin–Gordon Wild Rivers National Park.

The north coast is yet another area of contrasts. Burnie is one of the larger towns and Stanley is a National Trust-classified town situated beneath The Nut, an unusual peninsula. East of Burnie, the Bass Highway hugs the coast as far as Devonport. Inland is Launceston, Tasmania's second largest city, situated on the Tamar River. Only minutes from the city centre is the beautiful Cataract Gorge. The nearby colonial villages of Evandale, Westbury, Carrick, Perth and Longford are well worth a visit.

A mild climate, good surfing beaches and sheltered seaside towns add to the attraction of the east-coast region. St Helens is the principal resort town. Try not to miss Bicheno, a picturesque old port and one-time whaling town. Further south, The Hazards, a red granite mountain range, towers up behind Coles Bay, in Freycinet National Park.

Many visitors to Tasmania choose to stay in colonial accommodation. There is a wide variety of beautiful 19th-century buildings offering modern facilities; this is a great way to experience the historic charm of the island.

VISITOR INFORMATION
Tasmanian Travel & Information Centre
20 Davey Street, Hobart
(03) 6230 8233
www.tourism.tas.gov.au

CLIMATE GUIDE

HOBART

	J	F	M	A	M	J	J	A	S	O	N	D
Maximum °C	22	22	21	18	15	13	12	13	15	17	19	20
Minimum °C	12	12	11	9	6	5	4	5	6	7	9	11
Rainfall mm	37	38	40	49	41	29	49	49	42	48	48	59
Raindays	9	8	10	11	13	11	13	15	14	13	14	13

LAUNCESTON REGION

	J	F	M	A	M	J	J	A	S	O	N	D
Maximum °C	23	23	21	17	14	11	11	12	14	16	19	21
Minimum °C	10	10	9	7	5	3	2	3	4	6	7	9
Rainfall mm	40	43	43	58	63	61	81	80	65	63	51	53
Raindays	8	7	9	11	13	13	16	16	13	13	11	10

CRADLE MOUNTAIN REGION

	J	F	M	A	M	J	J	A	S	O	N	D
Maximum °C	17	18	14	11	8	5	5	5	7	10	12	14
Minimum °C	6	7	6	4	2	0	0	-1	2	3	4
Rainfall mm	147	131	158	228	288	276	329	309	277	249	216	192
Raindays	16	14	18	20	21	21	24	23	22	21	19	19

BICHENO REGION

	J	F	M	A	M	J	J	A	S	O	N	D
Maximum °C	21	21	20	19	16	14	14	14	16	18	18	19
Minimum °C	12	13	12	10	9	7	6	6	8	8	10	11
Rainfall mm	47	61	60	63	63	66	54	51	43	56	55	70
Raindays	7	7	7	9	9	9	9	9	7	9	9	9

Historic Richmond

Coles Bay, near Freycinet National Park

CALENDAR OF EVENTS

JANUARY
Public holidays: New Year's Day; Australia Day. *Hobart:* Hobart Cup Carnival; Antique Fair. *Burnie:* Athletic Club New Year's Day Carnival. *Cygnet:* Huon Valley Folk and Music Festival. *George Town:* Folk Festival. *Latrobe:* Australia Day Carnival; Henley-on-the-Mersey. *Latrobe–Port Sorell:* Summer Festival. *Longford:* Longford Cup. *Strahan:* Mt Lyell Picnic.

FEBRUARY
Hobart: Royal Hobart Regatta. *Bruny Island:* Barnes Bay Regatta. *Devonport:* Food and Wine Festival. *Evandale:* Village Fair and National Penny Farthing Championships. *Launceston:* Country Music Festival; Launceston Cup (State's biggest race day). *Oatlands:* Rodeo. *Richmond:* St Andrews Pipe Band Competition. *Ulverstone:* Twilight Rodeo. *Waratah:* Axemen's Carnival.

MARCH
Public holiday: Eight Hours Day. *Bothwell:* International Highland Spin-In (wool-spinning competition). *Campbell Town:* Highland Games. *Devonport:* Regatta. *Fingal:* Fingal Valley Festival. *George Town:* Pipers Brook Concert. *Launceston:* A Night in the Gorge; Festivale. *Longford:* Blessing of the Harvest Festival; Brickendon and Woolmers Hunt. *New Norfolk:* Hop Harvest Festival. *Penguin:* Splash of Colour Festival. *St Helens:* Tasmanian Game-Fishing Classic. *Sheffield:* Steam Fest. *Strahan:* Piners' Festival. *Westbury:* St Patrick's Day Festival.

EASTER
Public holidays: Good Friday; Easter Monday; Easter Tuesday. *Beauty Point:* Three Peaks Yacht Race (to Hobart). *Deloraine:* Grand National Steeplechase.

APRIL
Public holiday: Anzac Day. *George Town:* The Prologue (5-day car rally).

MAY
Carrick (near Hadspen): Agfest. *Sheffield:* Mt Roland Folk Festival.

JUNE
Public holiday: Queen's Birthday. *Campbell Town:* Agricultural Show (oldest in Australia). *St Helens:* Suncoast Jazz Festival. *Scottsdale:* Arts and Crafts Exhibition.

JULY
Hobart: Working Craft Fair.

AUGUST
New Norfolk: Winter Challenge (canoeing and cycling competition). *Ulverstone:* Doll, Toy and Miniature Fair.

SEPTEMBER
Hobart: Tasmanian Football League Grand Final (sometimes Oct.); Tulip Festival of Tasmania. *Launceston:* Garden Festival. *Sheffield:* Daffodil Festival.

OCTOBER
Public holidays: Hobart Show Day (southern Tas. only); Launceston Show Day (northern Tas. only); Flinders Island Show Day (Flinders Island only); Burnie Show Day (Burnie only). *Hobart:* Royal Hobart Agricultural Show. *Bruny Island:* Flower Festival. *Burnie:* Rhododendron Festival. *Derby:* Derby River Derby. *Devonport:* Classic Challenge Motorsport Event. *Kingston:* Olie Bollen (Dutch community) Festival. *Launceston:* Royal National Show; Tasmanian Poetry Festival. *New Norfolk:* Spring in the Valley (including open gardens). *Queenstown:* Robert Sticht Festival. *Richmond:* Village Fair. *Ulverstone:* Show; North-West Woodcraft Guild Exhibition. *Wynyard:* Tulip Festival.

NOVEMBER
Public holiday: Recreation Day (northern Tas. only). *Hobart:* Point to Pinnacle Road Run and Walk; Australian Wooden Boat Festival (even-numbered years). *Beaconsfield:* Gold Festival. *Burnie:* Food Festival. *Deloraine:* Tasmanian Craft Fair. *Evandale:* Railex (model-train exhibition). *Huonville:* Huon Agricultural Show (biggest one-day agricultural show in State). *Longford:* Village Green Garden Festival. *Scottsdale:* Agricultural Show. *Sorell:* Bushranger Festival. *Stanley:* Tasmania Day. *Westbury:* Steam Spectacular.

DECEMBER
Public holidays: Christmas Day; Boxing Day. *Hobart:* Sydney to Hobart/Melbourne to Hobart Yacht Race; Taste of Tasmania. *Devonport:* Melbourne–Devonport Yacht Race. *Latrobe:* Bicycle Race Club Christmas Carnival (includes Wheel Race and Gift). *Port Arthur:* Boxing Day Woodchop. *Stanley:* Agricultural Show. *Ulverstone:* Christmas Mardi Gras.

Note: The information given here was accurate at the time of printing. However, as the timing of events held annually is subject to change and some events may extend into the following month, it is best to check with the local tourism authority or event organisers to confirm the details. The calendar is not exhaustive. Most towns and regions hold sporting competitions, art, craft, and trade exhibitions, agricultural and flower shows, music festivals and other events annually. Details of these events are available from local tourism outlets.

Hobart

Hobart, Australia's second oldest and most southerly city, is situated on the broad estuary of the River Derwent under the spell of majestic Mount Wellington. A strong maritime flavour and sense of the past give Hobart an almost European air.

VISITOR INFORMATION
Tasmanian Travel & Information Centre
20 Davey Street, Hobart
(03) 6230 8233
www.tourism.tas.gov.au

GETTING AROUND
Airport shuttle bus
Tasmanian Redline Coaches
(03) 6231 3233
Motoring organisation
Royal Automobile Club of Tasmania (RACT)
13 2722
Car rental
Avis 1800 225 533; Budget 13 2727;
Hertz 13 3039; Thrifty 1800 030 730
Public transport
Metropolitan Transport Trust 13 2201
Taxis
City Cabs 13 1008;
Taxi Combined 13 2227
River cruises
The Cruise Company (03) 6234 9294
Captain Fells Ferries (03) 6223 5893

This feeling is heightened in winter when Mount Wellington is often snow-capped and daytime temperatures drop to a crisp average maximum of 12°C. However, it is also very much an Australian city, surrounded as it is by bushland and boasting prime examples of distinctive colonial architecture.

Hobart's population of approximately 195 000 spreads on both sides of the graceful Tasman Bridge and extends into the foothills of Mount Wellington. The city centre is probably the most historically intact in Australia. Whole areas appear today as they would have when Hobart was a seafaring town in the 19th century. Houses, churches and warehouses were built with social and commercial urgency rather than with forethought. The result is a small, compact city without the usual distinction between residential, business and retail precincts. It is a short stroll from the cottages of Battery Point to the grandeur of Parliament House, from the vibrant seafront to the bustle of the city centre.

EXPLORING HOBART

Motorists will discover that the traffic flows freely throughout Hobart. Be warned though, many of the city streets are one-way. Metered street parking is readily available and the Hobart City Council operates several multi-storey car parks at modest rates. Alternatively, there is public transport. Metro Tasmania operates a bus service that runs frequently during business hours, with a limited evening/weekend timetable. Much of Hobart's city centre can be covered on foot – for those who are not put off by the undulating streets. Walking is certainly the best way to appreciate the rich historical experience of the waterfront and Battery Point.

Victoria Dock

River cruises offer an opportunity to extend your acquaintance with this waterside city. Ferries and cruise boats leave regularly from Franklin Wharf and Brooke Street Pier at Sullivans Cove. The Cruise Company's *Derwent Explorer* cruise to the Cadbury Schweppes Chocolate Factory is a year-round favourite. During summer, ketches run charter tours as far afield as Port Arthur and Bruny Island. There are also a number of coach tours, including a daily tour of the city and suburbs.

HOBART BY AREA

QUEENS DOMAIN

The parklands of Queens Domain, on the western side of the Tasman Bridge, form a gentle interlude between the river and the city centre. To visit the **Royal Tasmanian Botanical Gardens**, turn off the Tasman Highway, near the Gothic-style **Government House**. The beautifully landscaped botanical gardens, contained within convict-built walls, are set on the side of a hill overlooking the river and include the Botanical Discovery Centre, which has an Interpretation Gallery, a new Plant House and a restaurant. Beyond the rather English confines of the gardens, the **Queens Domain** features tracts of remnant bushland, sports fields and the **Tattersall's Hobart Aquatic Centre** which has an Olympic-size swimming pool and excellent facilities for children. The fields in front of Government House give the Domain a friendly rural feel, unusual for an area so close to the central business district – it is not uncommon to see cows grazing here. On the other side of the highway, open lawns extend up to the **Cenotaph** and down towards the shipyard area. From here, a cycle path follows the old railway line to Hobart's northern suburbs. Bicycles and rollerblades are available for hire on weekends and public holidays.

INNER CITY – NORTH

Just off the Tasman Highway near the main waterfront precinct is the **Gasworks Shopping Village**, home to Australia's only commercial whisky distillery (open daily for tours). To explore Hobart's historic inner-city buildings, continue along Davey Street past Constitution Dock and turn right into Argyle Street. The sandstone building on the corner is the **Tasmanian Museum and Art Gallery**, notable for its magnificent collection of colonial landscape paintings. Within the museum complex is the Bond Store, central Hobart's oldest building, completed in 1808. Near the intersection of Argyle and Macquarie streets, facing the Italianate columns of the **Town Hall**, is **Ingle Hall**. This fine Georgian-style 1814 building is the oldest residential building still standing in the city centre. Turn right at the intersection into Macquarie Street and continue to Market Place. On the corner you will see the **Hope and Anchor Tavern**, reputedly Australia's oldest licensed hotel (1807).

Return to Ingle Hall. From there continue along Argyle Street and turn right into Brisbane Street. The convict-built

HISTORY

Hobart, Australia's second oldest city, was established in 1803 in response to fears held by the Governor of New South Wales of possible French colonisation. Convicts formed the majority of the European settlers in the early 19th century and their forced labour built many of the beautiful old buildings that can be seen today. The small colony flourished and Hobart's deepwater harbour soon became a thriving seaport, particularly as a base for the whaling and sealing ships operating in the Southern Ocean. Hobart retains more of its historic heritage than any other Australian capital, as it has not developed as rapidly this century as the mainland capitals. This, combined with the care taken to preserve historic buildings, has resulted in the survival of a wealth of colonial Georgian buildings and precincts.

HOBART ON FOOT
Battery Point
National Trust guided walk; leaves Franklin Square each Sat. morning; bookings essential

Battery Point & Sullivans Cove
Self-guide walk; brochure available

Battery Point Lamplight Walking Tours
Historical walk; bookings essential

Hobart Rivulet Tour
Underground walk; bookings essential

'In Her Stride'
Women's history walk; bookings essential

For further information and bookings, contact the **Tasmanian Travel & Information Centre**

Penitentiary Chapel and Criminal Courts are located on the corner of Brisbane and Campbell streets. Visitors can view the tunnels, courtrooms and solitary confinement cells inside these buildings; ghost tours operate most evenings. Returning to the waterfront via Campbell Street, look out for the tiny **Theatre Royal** (1837) on the left, opposite the Royal Hobart Hospital. The theatre's charming Georgian interior is still in use, making it Australia's oldest operating venue. Adjacent to the theatre is the one-time red-light district of **Wapping**, which is being redeveloped as a tourist and residential precinct.

ALONG THE WATERFRONT

Hobart's waterfront retains much of its early character and it is easy to imagine the early whaling days when this was a brawling seaport known to sailors around the world. **The Maritime Museum of Tasmania** on the corner of Davey and Argyle streets, has relics and documents from this period, as well as various displays relating to shipbuilding and early exploration. Today, foreign ships tie up almost in the centre of town and battered whalers are now replaced by trawlers and pleasure boats moored at the docks along Franklin Wharf. At **Victoria Dock** and **Constitution Dock**, you can buy fresh seafood from the moored punts that line the dock, or dine at the renowned Mures Fish Centre, a two-storey restaurant and cafe complex. Shortly after Christmas every year, Constitution Dock is the setting for one of Australia's greatest parties, when the crews from the boats competing in the Sydney to Hobart Yacht Race celebrate the end of their long and challenging haul. The **Elizabeth Street Pier** has been developed as apartment accommodation and a restaurant complex. **Franklin Wharf** and **Brooke Street Pier** are the main departure points for ferries and cruise boats.

Salamanca Place, situated at the southern end of the waterfront, displays the finest row of early merchant warehouses in Australia. Built between 1835 and 1840, the warehouses are now home to quality art and craft galleries, as well as an increasing number of cafes and restaurants. On Saturdays, a bustling market attracts shoppers and buskers, and the politically active voice their concerns amid the general cacophony.

Salamanca Square, just off Salamanca Place, is a residential and tourist development built in a disused quarry. It features **Antarctic Adventure**, an interpretative centre celebrating Australia's relationship with the great southern continent. The centre's hands-on exhibits range from the rather gimmicky Blizzard simulator ride, to evocative accounts of researchers based in the inhospitable Antarctic environment. **Time Warp House**, also in the square, is a complex that includes activities for children, as well as rooms depicting five eras of daily life since 1900.

BATTERY POINT

The steep **Kellys Steps**, wedged between two old warehouses in Salamanca Place,

HOBART BY AREA

For more detail, see maps 575 & 576–7

RIVER

DOMAIN HWY

B36

BROOKER

TASMAN HWY
A3

NORTHERN SUBURBS AND BEYOND

QUEENS DOMAIN

EAST OF THE DERWENT

A3

AV

DERWENT

INNER CITY – NORTH

CENTRAL SHOPPING AREA

ST

ALONG THE WATERFRONT

ST

Sullivans Cove

INNER CITY – SOUTH

A6

SANDY

MACQUARIE

DAVEY

BATTERY POINT

ST

A6

BAY

DAVEY

SOUTHERN OUTLET

B64

B68

SOUTHERN SUBURBS AND BEYOND

RD

N

0   0.5   1 km

lead to the heart of Battery Point. This delightful part of Hobart was once a lively mariners' village with fishermen's cottages, shops, churches, a village green and a riot of pubs. Today, Battery Point has many inviting restaurants and tea-rooms, and several antique shops to explore, but it is still mainly a residential area. Most of the houses are tiny dormer-windowed fishermen's cottages, with a few grander houses such as **Narryna** and **Lenna**. Narryna now houses the **Van Diemen's Land Folk Museum**, with its interesting collection of colonial relics, and the lavish Italianate Lenna is a boutique hotel.

A stroll around the narrow, hilly streets of Battery Point reveals enchanting glimpses of the harbour, yachts and mountains at every turn. On top of the hill in De Witt Street (off Hampden Road) is **St George's Anglican Church**, built in the 1830s and 1840s. The church's octagonal tower, based on the Temple of Winds in Athens, is floodlit each night until 10.30 p.m. One of the highlights of Battery Point is **Arthurs Circus**, where fifteen immaculately preserved Georgian cottages are built around the former village green. Pubs such as Knopwood's Retreat and the Shipright's Arms add to the feeling that time has stood still.

Battery Point got its name from a battery of guns set up on the hill in front of a small guardhouse in 1818. This soon became a **signalling station** and is now the oldest building in Battery Point. To see this building, return to Salamanca Place via Princes Park, where there is a fascinating interpretive board explaining the history of the site.

INNER CITY – SOUTH

Towards the city end of Salamanca Place, behind a square of old European trees, is Tasmania's **Parliament House**. Originally used as a customs house, the building was designed by the colonial architect John Lee Archer and constructed by convicts between 1835 and 1840. Visitors may ask to see the Legislative Council Chamber; the ceiling has been painstakingly repainted in its original ornate pastel patterns and the benches refurbished in plush red velvet.

Shot Tower near Taroona

TOP EVENTS

Antique Fair (New Year period)
The State's largest antique fair, held over 5 days at City Hall

Hobart Cup Carnival (Jan.)
Tasmania's premier racing carnival

People in the Parks (Jan.–Mar.)
Enjoy a variety of activities from jazz to kite-flying

Royal Hobart Regatta (Feb.)
Family regatta and fireworks display

Working Craft Fair (July)
Over a hundred exhibitors display their craft at the Derwent Entertainment Centre

Tulip Festival of Tasmania (Sept.)
Hobart welcomes spring

Point to Pinnacle Road Run and Walk (Nov.)
A 22-km journey to the summit of Mount Wellington

Australian Wooden Boat Festival (Nov., even-numbered years)
Hobart's waterfront at its colourful best

Sydney to Hobart/Melbourne to Hobart Yacht Race (Dec.)
Party time at Constitution Dock

Taste of Tasmania (Dec.)
The very best of Tasmanian food and wine

For further details visit the web site www.tas.gov.au/tasevents

---

SHOPPING

	Map Ref.
BATTERY POINT An antique shop around every corner	575 G9
CENTRAL SHOPPING AREA Department stores and specialty shops	575 F7
SALAMANCA MARKET (Sat.) Local art, craft and food produce	575 G8
SALAMANCA PLACE Quality art and craft in historic warehouses	575 G8

Salamanca Market

St David's Park, on the corner of Salamanca Place and Davey Street, is an ideal place to rest. One side of this park was Hobart's first colonial burial ground – the pioneer gravestones, which date from 1804, make fascinating reading. Opposite the park in Davey Street is the **Royal Tennis Court**, built in 1875. The unusual walled court still operates as a venue for the ancient game of Royal Tennis; there is a small display on the outside wall and visitors are welcome to go inside and watch Royal Tennis being played.

Hobart has a wealth of beautiful Georgian buildings, mostly concentrated around Macquarie and Davey streets. More than ninety of them have a National Trust classification. Built around 1846, the **Anglesea Barracks**, off Davey Street, is the oldest military establishment in Australia still used by the army. The buildings are remarkable for their simple Georgian elegance; guided tours are available on Tuesday mornings.

Those with an interest in rare books and antiques will want to visit the **State Library/Allport Library and Museum of Fine Arts** on the corner of Murray and Bathurst streets. Also in Murray Street is **St David's Cathedral**, Hobart's first purpose-built church, consecrated in 1824.

CENTRAL SHOPPING AREA

The main shopping area of Hobart is centred around the **Elizabeth Street Mall**, between Collins and Liverpool streets. This is where you will find Myer and Harris Scarfe, Hobart's main department stores, as well as bookshops, bushwalking stores and other specialty shops. The **Cat and Fiddle Arcade**, an under-cover shopping area located between the mall and Murray Street, is named after the charmingly kitsch animated mural that performs on the hour. Out in the mall, shoppers and city workers relax and enjoy the lunchtime street entertainment.

SOUTHERN SUBURBS & BEYOND

Just south of the city centre, under the towering bluff of Battery Point, is the suburb of **Sandy Bay**. Sailing is one of Tasmania's most popular sports and the prestigious Royal Yacht Club of Tasmania has its headquarters here. Nearby is the distinctive tower of **Wrest Point Hotel-Casino**, Australia's first casino. For inspiring views of the Derwent estuary, head for the **Mount Nelson Signal Station Lookout** or the convict-built **Shot Tower** just past Taroona. Lower Sandy Bay is also home to the unusual **Tudor Court Model Village**.

A visit to Hobart would not be complete without a drive to the summit of **Mount Wellington**, which rises 1270 metres above the city. The enclosed lookout point commands panoramic views of the D'Entrecasteaux Channel to the south and the Derwent Valley to the north. The summit itself has the qualities of an alpine wilderness, remarkable for a location that is just 20 kilometres from the city centre. Be prepared for gusty winds and a considerable drop in temperature, even in summer.

Cascade Brewery, in the foothills of Mount Wellington, makes an interesting return stop. Over 150 years old, the brewery offers tours on weekdays. The ruins of the historic **Female Factory** – a workhouse prison for female convicts where they made soap, took in Hobart's washing, spun wool and made blankets –

are nearby in Degraves Street at the base of the Cascade Gardens. One of the five prison yards is now occupied by Island Produce Confectionery. The confectionery factory is open weekdays and Saturdays; inquire about guided tours of the factory and historic site. Bookings are essential for the confectionery and brewery tours, and closed footwear must be worn.

NORTHERN SUBURBS & BEYOND

North Hobart, only a few minutes from the centre of the city, is the gourmand's suburb. A concentration of excellent restaurants and delicatessens have proliferated here to the delight of both residents and visitors. Slightly further north, in the suburb of New Town, is **Runnymede**, a Georgian-style National Trust homestead. Beautifully restored and set in a lovely garden, it commands views over New Town Bay and Risdon Cove, where Hobart's first European settlement began.

The **Tasmanian Transport Museum**, built around the relocated New Town railway station, is just off the Brooker Highway in the suburb of Glenorchy. The museum, which is open on weekend and public holiday afternoons, has a wide range of rolling stock in various stages of restoration. It is also the departure point for Classic Rail Tours (bookings through the RACT).

Moorilla Estate Winery is located at Berriedale in a scenic riverside setting. The Vineyard Restaurant is open Tuesday to Sunday; tours and cellar-door sales are available daily. From here it is only a five-minute drive to one of Hobart's premier attractions, the **Cadbury Schweppes Chocolate Factory** at Claremont. Tours operate on weekdays, except on public holidays and during some school holidays; book early to avoid disappointment and remember to wear closed footwear. The aroma of chocolate and toffee inside the factory is truly memorable. Free samples are offered during the tour and participants are able to purchase chocolate at bargain prices in the factory shop. If all that chocolate leads to thoughts of Switzerland, Claremont is also home to **Alpenrail**, an indoor Swiss model village and railway.

EAST OF THE DERWENT

Across the Tasman Bridge in Bellerive are the ruins of the **fort at Bellerive Bluff**, built to guard Hobart against a feared Russian invasion late last century. Bellerive is also the home of Tasmanian cricket; the seaside cricket ground features regularly on televised test matches. To reach some of Hobart's best beaches, take the South Arm Highway to the western shores of Frederick Henry Bay. **Seven Mile Beach**, **Lauderdale** and **Cremorne** are popular for swimming and beachside strolls, and the wild ocean beach at **Clifton** is ideal for surfing.

Four kilometres north-west of Lauderdale is **Rokeby** (1809), which produced the first wheat grown in Tasmania and the first export apples. Rokeby's historic cemetery contains graves of many First Fleeters. St Matthew's Church (1843) contains some chancel chairs that were carved from wood from a ship in Nelson's fleet; the church's organ, brought from England in 1825, is still in use.

Hobart offers the visitor an impressive State capital, rich in history and with a wide variety of natural attractions only minutes away.

RESTAURANTS AND CAFES

*Eating out is an integral part of experiencing Hobart. Increasingly this city and its surrounding countryside are attracting gourmet travellers keen to sample the innovative menus, fine seasonal produce and distinctive local wines. The local seafood is hard to beat – whether it is masterfully presented in one of the many waterfront restaurants or unwrapped and eaten with gusto on the edge of a pier. **Battery Point** and the suburb of **North Hobart** are home to some of Hobart's most highly praised restaurants and cafes. For more information, refer to* A Guide to Tasmania's Restaurants, *a free publication produced by the Restaurant and Caterers Association of Tasmania, available from the Tasmanian Travel & Information Centre.*

Battery Point

DAY TOURS
from Hobart

Some of Tasmania's most beautiful scenery is located within an easy day's drive of Hobart. A tour of the coastal roads of southern Tasmania – around the jagged Tasman Peninsula or along the shores of the D'Entrecasteaux Channel – is an unforgettable experience, especially on a fine day. Other popular destinations include historic Richmond, the picturesque Huon Valley, and Mount Field National Park via the Derwent Valley.

DAY TOURS FROM HOBART

For more detail, see maps 578–9

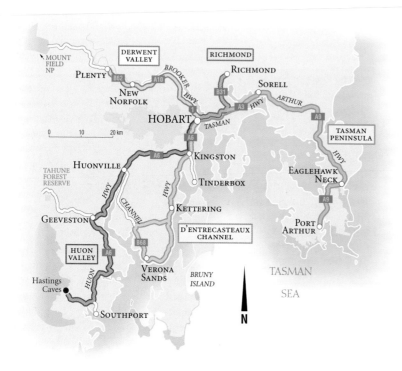

RICHMOND

26 km to Richmond via Tasman Highway A3 *, Cambridge Road* B31 *and Colebrook Road* B31

A short drive north-east of Hobart brings the visitor to **Richmond**, a beautifully preserved Georgian village and one of Tasmania's most popular tourist attractions. The much-photographed Richmond Bridge is the oldest surviving bridge in Australia, and the gaol, which pre-dates Port Arthur, once served as a staging post for convicts. Also of note is St John's Catholic Church, the oldest Catholic Church still in use in Australia. Galleries and cafes are housed in historic buildings throughout the village, and a scenic drive north takes in the surrounding vineyards.

TASMAN PENINSULA

100 km to Port Arthur via Tasman Highway A3 *and Arthur Highway* A9

Most visitors to the Tasman Peninsula explore the historic ruins of **Port Arthur**. They are often surprised that this former penal settlement, which symbolises the harsh convict era, has a beautiful setting. Along the way, see the spectacular rock formations around **Eaglehawk Neck** – the Tessellated Pavement, Tasman Blowhole, Tasmans Arch and Devils Kitchen – and the museum in the Officers' Quarters. For an extended visit to the peninsula, taking in the southern shores, follow the Peninsula Trail on page 548.

DERWENT VALLEY

50 km to Plenty via Brooker Highway 1 *, Lyell Highway* A10 *and Glenora Road* B62

The productive countryside of the Derwent Valley has a distinctly ordered

Derwent Valley

appearance. Characteristic of the area are extensive hop fields, which provide a main ingredient of Hobart's famous Cascade beers. The River Derwent narrows at **New Norfolk**, where visitors can see the Oast House and the hop museum and art gallery. For the more energetic, exhilarating jet boat rides on the Derwent rapids leave from near New Norfolk's Bush Inn Hotel.

Salmon Ponds, located a further 13 kilometres upstream at Plenty, is the oldest trout hatchery in the Southern Hemisphere. Since 1864, trout have been raised here for release into Tasmania's waters. Visitors can feed the various species of trout and salmon in six large display ponds and wander through the Museum of Trout Fishing which illustrates the history of trout fishing on the island.

For a longer day tour, New Norfolk and Salmon Ponds are en route to **Mount Field National Park**, one of Tasmania's oldest and most loved national parks. Easy family walks take visitors past thundering cascades and into a lush green world of tree ferns and myrtles. Signs along the Tall Trees Walk tell how these 85-metre giants came to thrive here. A summer option is the 13-kilometre drive through the rainforest to Lake Dobson and the high country beyond. **See also:** National Parks p. 554 and individual entries in A–Z listing for parks and towns in bold type.

D'ENTRECASTEAUX CHANNEL

68 km to Verona Sands via Southern Outlet A6 *and Channel Highway* B68
A leisurely drive along the shores of the D'Entrecasteaux Channel offers fine coastal vistas. There are magical glimpses

of water around almost every bend; if the weather is fine, divert from the highway at **Kingston** and follow the coastal road to Tinderbox for a spectacular view through the entrance of the channel out to Storm Bay.

At **Kettering** you have the option of the car ferry to **Bruny Island** (check times; (03) 6267 4753) or following the coastline to Verona Sands. On a clear day, Dennes Point, at the northern end of Bruny Island, provides yet another perspective, offering views across the mouth of the channel to Hobart's suburbs. Most visitors to Bruny Island head straight across the isthmus to South Bruny Island, where Cookville, the historic landing place for Captains Cook, Bligh and Furneaux, is one of the highlights. The inlet of Cloudy Bay is a dramatic sight, especially on a blustery day, and on the towering cliffs at Cape Bruny is Australia's second oldest lighthouse.

Those who follow the coastline to Verona Sands and beyond will enjoy views of the entrance to the Huon River, the south-west mountain range forming a dramatic backdrop. Thirteen kilometres past Verona Sands is a road leading via Gardners Bay to Woodbridge. Rejoin the Channel Highway here or continue on the Channel Highway and meander back to Hobart via Huonville. Either way it is a superb round trip. **See also:** individual entries in A–Z listing for towns in bold type.

HUON VALLEY

112 km to Hastings Caves via Southern Outlet A6 *and Huon Highway* A6
The Huon Valley, just south-west of Hobart, is the centre of the island's

famous apple-growing district. The route from Hobart, which forms part of the extensive Huon Trail, winds along the valley, providing views of mountain peaks, often dusted with snow in winter. After about 15 kilometres, the valley opens out and the first apple orchards appear. Around **Huonville**, the landscape is divided up with rows of gracefully espaliered apple trees. In November, the valley is coloured with soft pastel blossom, while April and May are the best months to sample the wonderful variety of fresh apples. Remarkably, many of the roadside fruit stalls still operate on an honesty basis. Attractions include the Apple and Heritage Museum just out of Grove, and Huon River jet boat rides over rapids to Glen Huon.

Continuing further south, the fast-flowing Huon River broadens and orchards reach almost the river's edge. At **Geeveston**, the Forest and Heritage Centre features an interpretive 'forest room', wood-turning demonstrations and a gallery. From Geeveston you can take the tourist drive west to the tall trees of Tahune Forest Reserve and some of the grandeur of the southern forests.

Otherwise, continue through Geeveston, past **Dover** to the dolomite cave at **Hastings**. Visitors can tour the vast, richly adorned chambers and swim in the warm thermal springs nearby. For a longer day trip, return to the Huon Highway and continue south to Southport. At Southport, turn left along the beach road for breathtaking views across to the cliffs and lighthouse of South Bruny Island. **See also:** individual entries in A–Z listing for towns in bold type.

CLASSIC TOUR

Peninsula Trail

Hobart to Coal Mines Historic Site via Port Arthur (143 km)

This two to three-day tour to the Forestier and Tasman peninsulas is an ideal introduction to Tasmania's fascinating past and extraordinary natural heritage. The ruins of Port Arthur convict settlement are undoubtedly the highlight, but the sombre beauty of the coastline is just as evocative. While it is possible to visit Port Arthur as a day trip from Hobart, this tour offers a much richer experience – from the quiet eccentricity of Copping and Doo Town, to the grandeur of the eastern cliffs and the isolation of the western dunes.

❶ Another time

The tour commences in Hobart. Follow the Tasman Highway (A3) past the airport and along the narrow causeway that extends for kilometres across the shallows of Pitt Water to Sorell. On a windy day, waves break at the roadside and the air is filled with seaspray.

At Sorell take the Arthur Highway (A9) which winds through open farmland to the tiny settlement of **Copping**, home to a truly eccentric museum, the Copping Colonial and Convict Collection. The collection is a marvellously overcrowded jumble of artifacts and features rather eerie-looking figures, cleverly positioned throughout the display, which come to life at the push of a button – lights flicker, wheels turn and bellows fill with air.

Copping Colonial and Convict Collection
Arthur Hwy
Copping
Phone: (03) 6253 5373
Open: 9 a.m.–5 p.m. daily (summer);
9 a.m.–1 p.m. daily (winter)

❷ Prepare to slow down

From Copping, continue to **Dunalley**, a quiet fishing village situated on a narrow isthmus which marks the start of the Forestier Peninsula. Early this century, bullock teams and a small locomotive engine were used to build a canal through the isthmus. This shortcut for fishing vessels travelling between Hobart and the east coast of Tasmania is still in use. You may have to stop at the swing bridge while a boat chugs through the entrance.

❸ Nature's mosaic

Follow the highway until you reach the signposted turn-off to Pirates Bay Drive. After 700 metres, pull in at Pirates Bay

Pirates Bay

Lookout. On a fine day you can expect to see across the bay, past the eastern side of Eaglehawk Neck to the massive coastal cliffs of the Tasman Peninsula. This vantage point offers a scenic overview of the next section of the tour, where the interplay between land and sea is at its most dramatic.

Pirates Bay Drive descends through eucalypt forest to the Art Deco-style Lufra Hotel. Below the hotel is one of the most interesting rock formations on this section of the coast, the **Tessellated Pavement**, a mudstone platform on the edge of the sea. A gentle, 300-metre walking track leads down to this seemingly man-made mosaic of square rock 'tiles', reminiscent of the ruins of a forgotten civilisation. The tiled appearance, known as jointing, is the product of fluctuating moisture levels and the smoothing action of the sea. The best time to

view the pavement is at low tide, when the surface is exposed.

❹ The Neck

Pirates Bay Drive rejoins the highway just before **Eaglehawk Neck**, a narrow strip of land less than 100 metres wide, which connects the Forestier and Tasman peninsulas.

For the convicts at nearby Port Arthur penal settlement, Eaglehawk Neck was a formidable natural barrier between servitude and freedom. Those daring or desperate enough to make the dash for freedom had to evade military guards and ferocious dogs spread in a line across this narrow strip of land. To discourage sea escapes, dogs were also kept on pontoons in the bay. This, combined with a rumour that the surrounding waters were shark-infested, ensured that few convicts tried their luck as 'bolters'. Even fewer

were successful. At Eaglehawk Neck Historic Site, the Dogline, reached by walking track from the Officers' Quarters, is marked by a bronze dog sculpture.

The Officers' Quarters is the only building left from the period of military occupation. Believed to be the oldest wooden military building in Australia, it is well worth a visit. The historical display inside provides vivid accounts of the relationship between this wild landscape and the people who lived there. One of the most interesting stories is the connection between the site and the Pydairrerme Aborigines, a band of the East Coast Oyster Bay tribe.

Officers' Quarters
Eaglehawk Neck Historic Site
Off Arthur Hwy
Eaglehawk Neck
Phone: (03) 6250 3635
Open: daily (inquire at Officers' Mess)

❺ Confronting the elements

Just south of Eaglehawk Neck, a signposted turn-off leads to tiny Doo Town, where all the house names incorporate the name 'Doo'. Here, the road branches off to three dramatic rock features: the **Tasman Blowhole, Tasmans Arch** and **Devils Kitchen**. Constantly pounding wave action has caused the cliff-line to collapse and erode in places, resulting in a series of impressive formations. The confrontation between land and sea is a dynamic spectacle as water blasts through fissures in the cliff-face, floods rock pools and creates random spray patterns.

If you are seeking a more contemplative experience away from the inevitable summer crowds, follow the walking track from Devils Kitchen to Waterfall Bay (2 hours return). This cliff-side track passes through banksia forest and heathland and offers

marvellous views of the coastline.
Take care, as some of the lookout
points are unfenced. For those
interested in bushwalking there
are many other wonderful
opportunities on the peninsula,
including the strenuous but truly
spectacular overnight hikes to
Cape Pillar and Cape Raoul.

6 Devils and snakes

Return to Eaglehawk Neck and
continue south along the highway
as it skirts the gentle western
shores of the peninsula. Just after
the township of Taranna is the
**Tasmanian Devil Park Wildlife
Rescue Centre**, where injured
and orphaned native animals are
nursed. Tasmanian devils are
permanent residents here and are
best seen at feeding times:
10 a.m. and 11 a.m daily. Other
guests may include quolls, rare
golden possums, eagles and owls.
Another feature of the centre is
the Tasman Bird Trail, which
winds for 1.5 kilometres, past a
lovely natural brook and through
open shrubland to the shore of
nearby Norfolk Bay. This is a great
place to spot eagles, falcons,
honeyeaters and a range of
seabirds. Binoculars and bird
identification notes are available
for hire at the centre.

The **World Tiger Snake
Centre**, the world's only tiger
snake farm, is located here as well.
This is a unique medical research
facility which, in conjunction with
a number of Australian
universities, conducts medical
research into new anti-venoms
and anti-inflammatory drugs.
During breeding season in
summer, there are nearly 1000
snakes housed here. Visitors at this
time might be lucky enough to
see tiger snakes being born. From
June to September, visitors can
view the smaller indoor display
which is open while most of the
outdoor snakes are hibernating.

*Tasmanian Devil Park Wildlife
Rescue Centre*
Arthur Hwy
Taranna
Phone: (03) 6250 3230
Open: 9 a.m.–5 p.m. daily

World Tiger Snake Centre
Arthur Hwy
Taranna
Phone: (03) 6250 3230
Open: 9 a.m.–5 p.m. daily

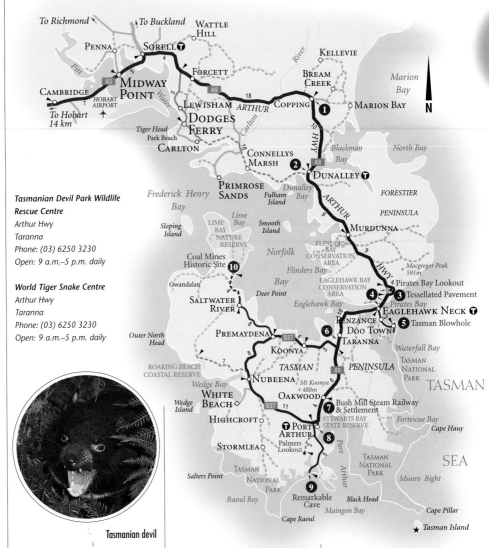

Tasmanian devil

7 Life at the mill

Continue along the highway and,
a short distance after the township
of Oakwood, you will find the
boldly signposted **Bush Mill
Steam Railway and Settlement**.
The Bush Mill depicts the life of
the timber cutters on the
peninsula in the late 1800s.

Buildings on the reconstructed
mill site include a rough slab hut,
bark shelters, mill manager's
cottage and general store. A
steam-powered sawmill,
imaginative sound and light
displays and a working blacksmith
bring this era back to life. A
miniature K-class Garratt

locomotive, built in the mill's own
workshops, takes visitors on a
4-kilometre narrow-gauge railway
through scenic bushland.

*Bush Mill Steam Railway
and Settlement*
Arthur Hwy
Port Arthur
Phone: (03) 6250 2221
*Open: 9 a.m.–4 p.m. daily;
until 5 p.m. in summer*

8 Convict heritage

Further along the highway is the
entrance to the **Port Arthur
Historic Site**, the most poignant
symbol of Tasmania's days as a
penal colony. Its sandstone walls
once resounded with the blows of
the convict chisel; they now stand
testament to the incredible
hardships and human tragedy of
early convict life. It is still possible,
particularly in bleak weather, for
the ruins to impart some of the

Bush Mill Steam Railway

atmosphere of hopelessness and misery that existed here about 160 years ago. The prison settlement was established in 1830, and was home to around 12 000 convicts before the cell doors closed for the last time in 1877.

Today the historic site encompasses 40 hectares, including the separate prison with its cell blocks and chapel, the asylum, the commandant's house and the port area. Hourly guided walks are conducted on a daily basis. In summer, visitors can take a harbour cruise to the Isle of the Dead, where hundreds of convicts, civilians and military personnel are buried. Scenic flights operate when weather permits. Your entry ticket entitles you to two days at Port Arthur. As there is a range of accommodation near the site, and given the concentration of attractions nearby, this would make an ideal overnight stop. The lamplight ghost tours of the historic site are an added bonus for those who decide to break their journey here, and the self-guide nature trail to Stewarts Bay would make a pleasant early-morning walk.

The Visitor Centre
Port Arthur Historic Site
Off Arthur Hwy
Port Arthur
Phone: (03) 6250 2539,
freecall 1800 659 101
Open: 8.30 a.m.–dusk, daily

Port Arthur sunset

❾ Remarkable places
Just 400 metres along the highway after the Port Arthur Historic Site is a signposted turn-off to Palmers Lookout and Remarkable Cave. To visit Palmers Lookout, take the turn-off and then the unsealed road almost immediately to the right. Carefully tended flower beds and a collection of gnomes mark the entrance to this charming picnic spot. The view from the lookout is superb – from here you can see the point at which the sheltered waters of Port Arthur enter the open sea.

Palmers Lookout

Return to the sealed road to continue to **Remarkable Cave**, a majestic rock formation. After parking at the car park, you will need to descend a long, steep set of steps to reach the viewing platform. Remarkable Cave is located in a deep gully, the base of which is lined with perfectly tumbled rocks. Between the gully and the ocean is a cliff about 30 metres thick. Ocean water thunders through a tunnel in the cliff and rushes over the rocks at irregular intervals.

❿ The beauty and the terror
Return to the Arthur Highway and continue to the coastal settlement of Nubeena. The road passes through forest, open farmland and a very pretty valley, before reaching the sea at Wedge Bay. There is an interesting diversion just after Nubeena: take a left turn and drive along a windy, unsealed road past the Atlantic salmon ponds to the wild, grassy sand dunes of Roaring Beach Coastal Reserve. If you venture down this road after rain, take special care at the bends. From Nubeena, the road rises through the hills to the centre of the peninsula. During winter and spring, the rolling pasture is emerald green and the blue sea in the distance makes a brilliant backdrop. At Premaydena, turn left and continue past farmland to Saltwater River. A further 4 kilometres along a largely unsealed road is the **Coal Mines Historic Site**. Tasmania's first mine was established here following the discovery of coal in 1833. By 1839 there were 150 convicts working the site, along with 29 officers.

Repeat offenders 'of the worst class' from Port Arthur were sent to the mines. Conditions underground were appalling. Bathed in dirt and perspiration, convicts toiled relentlessly in damp, dark and stifling tunnels. The most intractable of the inmates were denied the light of day, housed underground in punishment cells. In 1848 the coal mines were closed, for both moral and financial reasons.

Ruins of the settlement have been stabilised, and a walking trail joins the various buildings. The remains of the convict barracks, chapel and officers' quarters are still evident, along with the commissariat store and main shaft. On a sunny day it is hard to imagine the hardship that was life for some in this once-isolated settlement.

Returning to Hobart

From the Coal Mines Historic Site return to Premaydena and turn left to go through Koonya and on to the Arthur Highway to return to Hobart. If you are reluctant to leave the coast at Dunalley, take the coastal route back via Dodges Ferry. It will not take much longer and you will be rewarded with lingering views of turquoise seas and beaches fringed with she-oaks.

TASMANIA from A to Z

Seaside tranquillity in the former whaling town of Bicheno

Beaconsfield   Pop. 1014

MAP REF. 581 J5, 585 K7

Several impressive brick ruins with Romanesque arches dominate this quiet town on the West Tamar Hwy, 46 km NW of Launceston. Formerly a thriving gold township (called Cabbage Tree Hill), the ruins are of buildings erected at the Tasmanian Gold Mine pithead in 1904. When the mine closed 10 years later after water seepage, 6 million dollars' worth of ore had been won from the reef. Now the mine shaft of the recently reopened Beaconsfield Gold Mine towers over the town. **In town:** Grubb Shaft Gold and Heritage Museum in old mine building, West St, features working models, relics and interactive displays. Restored miner's cottage and original Flowery Gully School opposite museum. Van Diemen's Gallery, Weld St, art and craft. Nov.: Gold Festival. **In the area:** York Town monument at site of first European settlement in northern Tasmania, 9 km N on Kelso–Greens Beach Rd. At Rowella, 15 km E, Holm Oak Vineyards. Auld Kirk (1843), historic convict-built church at Sidmouth, 13 km SE; nearby, Batman Bridge, its A-frame reaching 100 m above Tamar River. **Visitor information:** Tamar Visitor Centre, Main Rd, Exeter; (03) 6394 4454, freecall 1800 637 989.

Beauty Point   Pop. 1194

MAP REF. 581 K5, 585 K6

This popular fishing and yachting centre on the West Tamar Hwy, 48 km NW of Launceston, is the oldest deepwater port in the area. Originally constructed to serve the Beaconsfield goldmine, the port facilities today serve the Australian Maritime College. Commercial cargo is loaded at Bell Bay across the river. **In town:** Seahorse Australia, a seahorse aquaculture farm, guided tours; (03) 6383 4811. Nearby Sandy Beach for safe swimming. Easter: Three Peaks Yacht Race (to Hobart). **In the area:** Holiday towns: Kelso, 15 km NW, dates back to early York Town settlement; Greens Beach, 20 km NW, at mouth of Tamar River. Asbestos Range National Park, 25 km NW, coastline views, walks ranging from 10 minutes to the 5-hour trail from Badger Head to Bakers Beach. Marion's Vineyard on Foreshore Dr., Deviot, 21 km SE. **Visitor information:** Tamar Visitor Centre, Main Rd, Exeter; (03) 6394 4454.

Bicheno   Pop. 700

MAP REF. 583 Q2, 585 Q12

A sealing and whaling town from about 1803, and later a coal-mining port (1854), Bicheno's main industry today is crayfishing. Situated 195 km NE of Hobart, this small fishing port on the east coast is a popular holiday destination. Visitors are attracted by the town's mild climate, nearby sandy beaches and picturesque setting. There are opportunities for fishing in the surf, off rocks, offshore and in the estuary. Licensed seafood restaurants and a range of accommodation add to Bicheno's appeal. **In town:** Dive Centre, Tasman Hwy, offers diving instruction and charters. Foreshore walkway, from Redbill Point north of town, south to Blowhole. Lookouts at top of twin hills: Whalers Lookout, off Foster St, and National Park Lookout, off Morrison St; rock orchids, unique to east coast, spectacular in Oct. and Nov. Grave of Aboriginal heroine Waubedebar, in Lions Park, Burgess St. Mountain-bike hire from information centre. Historic tours. Seafood outlets with crayfish in season. **In the area:** Fishing and scuba diving charters, and glass-bottomed boat rides to see underwater life in Governor Island Marine Reserve. Little (fairy) penguin colony, 6 km N; nightly guided tours in season. East Coast Birdlife and Animal Park, 8 km N, exhibits Tasmanian devils and other native fauna. Adjacent is Denison River Trail Rides, for beach and forest horserides. Douglas Apsley Vineyard, 11 km N. Lookout in Douglas–Apsley National Park, 14 km NW. Wardlaw's Cray Store, 27 km N (Nov.–May). Freycinet Vineyard and the adjacent Springbrook Vineyard, 18 km SW on Tasman Hwy; Jazz in the Vineyard festival at Freycinet Vineyard, Easter Sun. Scenic flights from Belarine Aviation, Coles Bay Rd, 20 km S. Freycinet National Park, 40 km S, for coastal scenery and wildlife-watching. **Visitor information:** Bicheno Penguin Adventure Tours, Tasman Hwy; (03) 6375 1333. **See also:** Touring Tasmania p. 552.

Boat Harbour   Pop. 109

MAP REF. 584 F5

The clear water and rocky points of this attractive village make it ideal for diving and spear-fishing. Situated on the north-west coast, 31 km W of Burnie, it adjoins one of the State's richest agricultural areas. **In town:** Shannondoah Cottage, Bass Hwy, for local craft, lunches, Devonshire teas. **In the area:** Boat Harbour Beach, 3 km N, offers safe swimming, marine life in pools at low tide, fishing, water-skiing and bushwalking. Mallavale Farm, 3 km NW, local art and craft, tearooms and coastal views. Sisters Beach, 8 km NW, good fishing and swimming. Nearby, Birdland Native Gardens. Aboriginal caves and coastal walks in Rocky Cape National Park, 19 km NW; brochures at Wynyard information centre. **Visitor information:** Seaside Garden Motel, The Esplanade; (03) 6445 1111.

Touring Tasmania

Tasmania is small, but its sights are grand. Nurtured by the temperate climate, the trees are taller here than on the mainland (Tasmania has the world's tallest hardwood trees, some exceeding 90 metres); mountains vault to the skies from wild forest land. The great inland lakes in the mountains feed boisterous rivers, some of which are harnessed for the State's hydro-electric schemes. The hills and valleys are harshly carved by the weather and become gentle only in the rolling pastoral lands of the Midlands and the north.

In this romantic landscape, more reminiscent of Scotland than Australia, are the remnants of a rich history of convict and colonial life – the prisons, churches, cottages and court-houses, the barracks, mansions and homesteads from the earliest days of European settlement.

Historic bridge at Campbell Town

Most travellers start their Tasmanian holiday in the north, where they have either taken their car off the ferry or have hired a car or mobile home for the journey south. The Scenic Circle Route is a popular tour that covers some of the State's best scenic and historical attractions. A shorter route, the Heritage Highway, links Launceston and Hobart. Travellers can choose between these two routes or combine sections of each to suit their interests.

SCENIC CIRCLE ROUTE

This magnificent touring route will take you through some of the most fascinating country that Australia has to offer: the incomparable wilderness of the west coast, the lavish orchard country around Launceston and the Huon Valley, and the snug beaches, bays and villages of the east coast.

From **Devonport** the coast road to the west runs with the northern railway along the sea's edge. Along this road are the thriving towns of **Ulverstone** and **Burnie**. **Wynyard**, **Stanley** and the striking headlands of Table Cape, Rocky Cape and The Nut are worth a special trip, as is a detour down the side road from **Penguin** to the peaceful mountain farmland of Gunns Plains and the Gunns Plains caves. The road from Forth into the vast wilderness areas of the magnificent **Cradle Mountain–Lake St Clair National Park** is also well worth a visit, but the turn-off to follow the Scenic Circle Route is at Somerset. From there you head south down the Murchison Highway towards the increasingly mountainous country of the west coast. An interesting diversion leads to Corinna, once a thriving town but now virtually abandoned, on the beautiful Pieman River, not far from its mouth. A launch trip from Corinna travels through deeply-cut river gorges.

Back on the main road, the mountain scenery is unique and quite spectacular. The towns here developed as a result of their mineral wealth. **Zeehan** now has only a small population, but at the turn

of the century there were more than 10 000 inhabitants when silver, lead and zinc mining was at its height. Many buildings from those early days still stand. The larger town of **Queenstown** has grown up around the Mount Lyell copper mine, in a valley beneath bare, bleached hills, streaked and stained with the hues of minerals – chrome, purple, grey and pink. Nearby is **Strahan** on Macquarie Harbour, the only coastal town in the west. The harbour can be reached only by shallow-draught vessels through the notorious passage called Hell's Gates. Cruises are available through wilderness country along the Gordon River, past the ruins of the remote convict settlement on Sarah Island; or take a sea-plane flight over the **Franklin–Gordon Wild Rivers National Park**.

The road turns inland from these towns, avoiding the almost inaccessible south-west, and travels through the Franklin–Gordon Wild Rivers National Park, across the central highlands past Lake St Clair and down the Derwent Valley through the town of **New Norfolk**, centre of the Tasmanian hop-growing industry. This valley, beautiful in spring and brilliantly coloured with foliage in autumn, is of both scenic and historic interest. It was settled by Europeans in 1808, the site having been chosen by Governor Macquarie.

A detour from the Hobart road leads to the old town of **Richmond**, probably the best example of a Tasmanian historic town, with its old Georgian houses and cottages clustered together and its convict-built bridge, the oldest freestone bridge still in use in Australia. The gaol pre-dates Port Arthur as a penal settlement; two churches, a courthouse, a schoolhouse, a rectory, the hotel granary, a general store and a flour mill were all built in the 1820s and 1830s.

Hobart, Australia's second oldest and most southerly city, is attractively sited on the River Derwent, with Mount Wellington looming behind. The port area at Salamanca Place, where the old bond stores and warehouses are located, is a reminder of the days when the whaling fleet and the timber ships tied up at the wharf and sailors went out on the town. Battery Point with its barracks, workers' cottages and Arthurs Circus – Georgian-style houses built around a circular green – is part of Hobart's beginnings.

The grim but beautiful penal settlement of **Port Arthur** is on the Tasman Peninsula, south-east of Hobart. Here, within the forbidding walls, visitors will sense the hopelessness felt by the thousands of convicts who passed through this settlement during its 47 years of existence.

South of Hobart is the scenic Huon Valley, particularly spectacular when the apple trees are in blossom. At the southern end of the route is Cockle Creek on Recherche Bay, where the South Coast walking track begins.

North on the Scenic Circle Route from Hobart, the Tasman Highway traverses the east coast, a region enjoying a generally mild and equable climate. Many attractive seaside towns are set on sheltered inlets but within easy reach of surf beaches and fishing grounds: towns like **Triabunna**, **Swansea**, **Bicheno**, Scamander and **St Helens**.

Off the Tasman Highway near Bicheno is **Freycinet National Park** on the Freycinet Peninsula. There are many walking tracks through this park which is dominated by The Hazards, a red-granite mountain range.

The road cuts across the less developed farming country of the north and goes west to **Launceston**, the northern capital of Tasmania, 64 kilometres from the north coast. Located at the junction of the North Esk, South Esk and Tamar rivers, it is a smaller, more provincial city than Hobart. Set in hilly countryside, it makes an excellent base from which to explore the rich coastal plain of the Tamar Valley and the mountain country to the north. Cataract Gorge is a popular natural attraction, while historic Franklin House and Entally House are within easy reach of Launceston.

THE HERITAGE HIGHWAY

The first Europeans to travel between Launceston and Hobart made the journey by foot in 1807, after which a regular stagecoach service was established. Today visitors can take a similar route along the Midland Highway through the gentle pastoral landscape of the Midlands, stopping at some of the most beautiful and historic towns in Australia. Colonial bed and breakfast accommodation abounds, as does a wonderful variety of antique shops and galleries housed in historic buildings.

Just south of Launceston are the finely preserved Georgian-period townships of **Evandale** and **Longford**. Christ Church (1839) at Longford has an outstanding stained-glass window and pioneer grave-yard. A little further on from the town is Brumbys Creek at Cressy, one of the State's premier fly-fishing locations. February is a good time to visit Evandale for the annual Village Fair and National Penny Farthing Championships, while garden-lovers will enjoy the extensive formal gardens at nearby Clarendon mansion.

Further south, short detours lead to the former garrison towns of **Ross** and **Campbell Town**. Ross is set amongst some of Australia's finest merino wool country, and the Tasmanian Wool Centre's Heritage and Wool Museum in town highlights its rural history. At Ross is one of Australia's finest historical bridges — its arches contain 186 stones depicting Celtic symbols, interspersed with images of notable personalities and animals. So fine was the stonework that the two convict stonemasons who worked on the bridge received pardons for their efforts.

Several other historic towns feature along the Heritage Highway, including **Oatlands** and **Pontville**. A side trip south of Oatlands leads to peaceful **Bothwell** on the Clyde River, with over 50 National Trust-classified buildings and the oldest golf club in Australia. Quarries near Pontville provided quality stone for many of the State's oldest buildings.

For further information, contact the Tasmanian Travel and Information Centre, 20 Davey St, Hobart; (03) 6230 8233. Web site www.tourism. tas.gov.au **See also:** Day Tours from Hobart p. 546 and Peninsula Trail p. 548. For details on parks and towns in bold type, see National Parks p. 554, and individual entries in A–Z town listing.

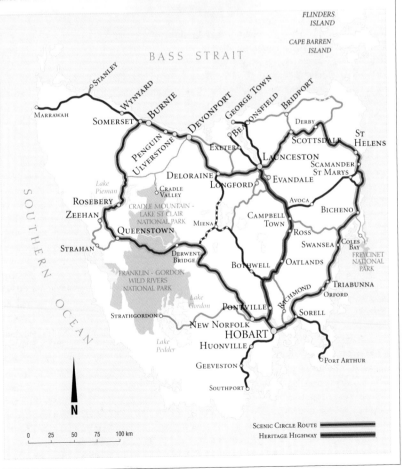

National Parks

Tasmania packs an incredible variety into a compact area. Even in a few days you can experience a surprising cross-section of the natural and cultural heritage that helps to make Tasmania unique. But the best of the island State, from wild rivers and deep forests to grand mountains and ancient cave shelters, is to be found in its national parks. The island's landscape is shaped by ice as much as by isolation. In the national parks you can find mountains, tarns and lakes carved out during the Ice Ages, and unique flora and fauna from ancient times.

The Parks and Wildlife Service of Tasmania manages the State's 18 national parks and the many State reserves. There are Aboriginal sites, natural features and European historic sites that date back to 1803, when Europeans first arrived in Tasmania.

All parks are accessible year-round. An entry fee applies in all national parks. Some tourists believe the highland parks are best in summer and autumn, when the weather is more reliable, the wildflowers bloom in profusion and flowering trees and shrubs attract birdlife. Bushwalking in the parks is popular; however in the highland parks there can be sudden storms and snowfalls, even in summer. Be prepared for unexpected changes in the weather.

Russell Falls in Mount Field National Park

NEAR HOBART

Mount Field National Park, 80 kilometres north-west of Hobart, offers a diversity of activities ranging from picnicking to overnight bushwalking. It also has the only developed skiing area in southern Tasmania. There are several waterfalls in the park, the best-known being Russell Falls, first seen by Europeans in 1856. Here water plunges in two stages into a forested valley where tree ferns filter sunlight and create a mosaic effect. The forest includes large myrtles, giant 250-year-old gum trees, sassafras, huge tree ferns, the unique horizontal scrub and a variety of mosses, ferns, lichens and fungi. The drive to Lake Dobson enables visitors to enjoy the high country with its snow gums, alpine moorlands and glacial lakes. There are many walks, including the Tall Trees Walk and a gentle circuit walk that takes in Russell, Horseshoe and Lady Barron falls.

A one-and-a-half-hour drive from Hobart, through Geeveston to the south-west, brings visitors to the popular bushwalking area of **Hartz Mountains National Park**. Most of the area is over 600 metres in altitude, while Hartz Peak is 1255 metres. There are basic facilities for the day visitor and no camping facilities, although camping is permitted.

South Bruny National Park, on South Bruny Island, is one of Tasmania's newer parks. It takes in spectacular and varied coastal scenery, including the rugged cliffs of Fluted Cape and Tasman Head. Sea birds and marine mammals can be seen, including little (fairy) penguins, albatrosses, Australian fur seals and dolphins.

Proclaimed in 1999 is **Tasman National Park**, which covers 9346 hectares south-east of Hobart on the Forestier and Tasman peninsulas. This new park offers magnificent coastal scenery including unusual dolerite rock formations. Day trippers can visit Eaglehawk Neck and nearby Tasman Blowhole, Tasmans Arch, Waterfall Bay and Remarkable Cave. The park also contains rare plants (including three rare species of *Euphrasia*) and provides opportunities to see raptors, seals, penguins, dolphins and whales. Camping is available at Fortescue Bay.

IN THE SOUTH-WEST OF THE STATE

Tasmania's largest national park is **Southwest National Park**, which has 618 010 hectares of mainly remote wilderness country. Here there are dolerite- and quartzite-capped mountains, sharp ridges and steep glacial valleys. The dense forests are made up of eucalypts, myrtles, sassafras and leatherwood, often covered with mosses, ferns and lichens, and tangled with pink-flowered climbing heath and bauera. The Creepy Crawly Nature Trail is an ideal introduction to the temperate rainforest environment. Climbers will find a challenge in Federation Peak, Mount Anne and Precipitous Bluff; anglers can fish for trout at lakes Pedder and Gordon. A specially built bird hide at Melaleuca can be used in summer to observe the rare and endangered orange-bellied parrot.

The 446 000-hectare **Franklin–Gordon Wild Rivers National Park** forms the central portion of Tasmania's World Heritage Area. The Franklin River attracts wilderness adventurers world-wide to test its challenging rapids. Along the slightly more placid lower Gordon River are stands of 2000-year-old Huon pine. The Lyell Highway, the road link between Hobart and the west coast, runs through the park. Excellent short walks lead off the highway to rainforests, waterfalls and spectacular lookouts. For experienced bushwalkers, the 4 to 5 day Frenchmans Cap track offers majestic scenery.

IN THE CENTRAL NORTH OF THE STATE

Covering some of Tasmania's highest country is **Cradle Mountain–Lake St Clair National Park**. There is a visitor centre and accommodation near the northern park entrance at Cradle Mountain, and a nature walk into the nearby rainforest. Cradle Mountain has a variety of bushwalks and is the starting point for one of Australia's best-known walking routes, the 85-kilometre Overland Track, through forests of deciduous beech, Tasmanian 'myrtle', pandanus, King Billy pine and a wealth of wildflowers. On the shores of Lake St Clair at the southern end of the park, there is a visitor centre with displays on the history of the area. The tranquil Lake St Clair, with a depth of over 200 metres, occupies a basin gouged out by glaciers more than 20 000 years ago. Cruises operate daily. A five to eight day trek traverses the park, taking in Mt Ossa (Tasmania's highest mountain) and a range of highland lakes and waterfalls. At Lake St Clair there are several campsites and cabins, and luxury accommodation nearby.

Steep, jagged mountains create a natural amphitheatre at the **Walls of Jerusalem National Park** (51 800 hectares) and ancient forests of pencil pines ring tiny glacially-formed lakes, making the park very popular with bushwalkers. The park is not accessible for day trips.

IN THE NORTH OF THE STATE

The central north coastal strip of **Asbestos Range National Park** is a refuge for a wide variety of birds, as well as wombats, kangaroos and wallabies. Its islands off Port Sorell provide an important breeding area for little (fairy) penguins, and the tidal and mud flats are ideal feeding grounds for migratory seabirds. On the unspoiled beaches, white sands come to life with thousands of soldier crabs.

Further west, **Rocky Cape National Park** (3064 hectares) encompasses rugged coastline with small sheltered beaches backed by heath-covered hills. It is known for its rock shelters used for over 8000 years by Tasmanian Aborigines.

In the north central region, **Mole Creek Karst National Park** is located in the forested hills below the impressive Western Tiers. Underground streams have made caves with splendid calcite formations. Guided tours of King Solomons and Marakoopa caves are available.

IN THE EAST OF THE STATE

Many of Tasmania's national parks are important wildlife reserves. The 18 439-hectare **Mount William National Park**, is a sanctuary for native creatures, including the Forester kangaroo (Tasmania's only kangaroo), pademelon, Tasmanian devil and the Australian grayling in Ansons River. At Lookout Point, thousands of colourful rock orchids cover the granite rocks, and wildflowers carpet the park in spring. The rush lily (vanilla plant) and smoke-bush, both rare, have their habitat here. Sheltered bays and beaches complete this little-known but beautiful park.

Fifty kilometres south-east of Launceston is **Ben Lomond National Park**, one of Tasmania's two main ski fields offering downhill and cross-country skiing, with an alpine village, ski-tows, ski hire, tavern with accommodation, and a public shelter.

A short distance north of Freycinet National Park is **Douglas–Apsley National Park** (16 080 hectares). Proclaimed in 1990, this park contains the State's last large dry sclerophyll forest and can be traversed along a 3-day north–south walking track. Lightly forested ridges contrast with patches of rainforest and river gorges, while waterfalls and spectacular coastal views add to the grandeur of the area.

Freycinet National Park offers wide stretches of white sand, rocky headlands, granite peaks, quiet beaches and small coves, and an excellent choice of short and long walking tracks. Freycinet National Park also includes Schouten Island, separated from the Freycinet Peninsula by a kilometre-wide passage, and reached only by boat. Near the park is Coles Bay, a fishing and swimming destination with delightful coastal scenery and a range of accommodation.

Maria Island, off the east coast, is well worth a visit. You can get there by light aircraft or passenger ferry from Louisville. On arrival you step into another world, for no tourist vehicles are permitted. This island national park embraces magnificently coloured sandstone cliffs and is a refuge for over 80 species of birds. Forester kangaroos and Cape Barren geese roam freely in this unspoiled landscape. Its intriguing history and historic buildings date back to the convict era which began in 1825.

For further information on Tasmania's national parks, contact the Parks and Wildlife Service, 134 Macquarie Street, Hobart (GPO Box 44A, Hobart 7001); (03) 6233 6191. Web site www.parks.tas.gov.au

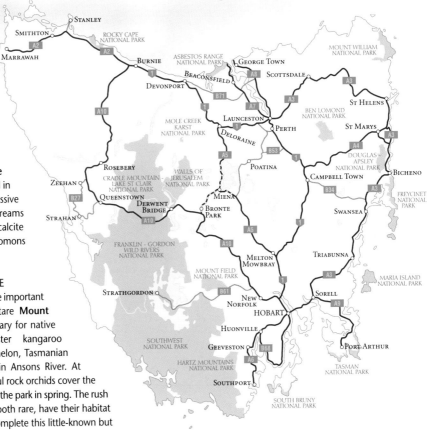

Bothwell   Pop. 356

MAP REF. 583 K5

This peaceful place in the beautiful Clyde River valley, 74 km NW of Hobart, has been proclaimed a historic village. It has 52 buildings classified or registered by the National Trust. Surveyed 1824 and named by Lieutenant-Governor Arthur after the Scottish town, it is now the centre of sheep and cattle country. It is claimed that golf was first played in Australia at the nearby homestead of Ratho in the 1830s. This course is open to visitors with golf-club membership elsewhere. **In town:** Bothwell Grange (c. 1836), Alexander St, guesthouse with tearooms and art gallery. Australasian Golf Museum, Market Pl. On Patrick St: Expressions of Interest Art Gallery features leading Tasmanian artists; Lamont Weaving Studio, home of Tasmanian tartan, has demonstrations and sales. St Luke's Church (1830), Dennistoun Rd. In High St: Georgian brick Slate Cottage (1836), restored and furnished heritage-style; Old Bootmaker's Shop, tours by appt. Self-guide walking trail, brochure available. Mar.: International Highland Spin-In (wool spinning competition). **Visitor information:** Australasian Golf Museum, Market Pl.; (03) 6259 4033.

Bridgewater   Pop. 4250

MAP REF. 578 H4, 583 L7

This town, 19 km N of Hobart, is situated at the main northern crossing of the River Derwent. The 1830s causeway was built by 200 convicts, who barrowed 2 million tonnes of stone and clay from a nearby quarry. The original bridge was opened in 1849; the present one dates from 1946. **In the area:** At Granton, 1 km S across bridge: Old Watch House (1838), now a petrol station, was built by convicts to guard the causeway and has the smallest cell in Australia (50 cm square, 2 m high); Black Snake Inn (1833), also convict-built. Risdon Cove Historic Site, 15 km SE, site of original Hobart town settlement. **Visitor information:** Council Offices, Tivoli Rd, Gagebrook; (03) 6263 0333.

Bridport   Pop. 1234

MAP REF. 581 R2, 585 N6

Bridport is a popular holiday and fishing town on the north-east coast, 85 km NE of Launceston. **In town:** Fine beaches,

excellent fishing in rivers, lakes and sea. Wildflower Reserve on western outskirts, best months Sept.–Oct. Scenic walking path, brochure available. **In the area:** Bowood homestead (1838), 8 km W; gardens open by appt. Views from Waterhouse Point and Ranson's Beach. Winegrowing at Piper's Brook, 18 km SW. **Visitor information:** '2000 Plus' Information Shop, Main St, 10 a.m.–4 p.m.; (08) 6356 0280. Web site www.bridport.tco.asn.au

Bruny Island   Pop. 581

MAP REF. 578 H12, 583 M11

Almost two islands, separated by a narrow isthmus, Bruny was named after the French Admiral Bruni D'Entrecasteaux, who surveyed the channel between the island and the mainland in 1792; the Aboriginal name for the island was Lunawannaaloona. Abel Tasman saw the island in 1642 but did not land. Other 18th-century European visitors included Furneaux (1773), James Cook (1777) and William Bligh (1788, 1792). The first apple trees in Tasmania are said to have been planted here by a Bligh expedition botanist. **In the area:** Bruny Island ferry departs from mainland Kettering 10 times daily. Nature tours of the island, including wildlife and temperate rainforest. Cape Queen Elizabeth Walk, 3 hrs return. Morella Island Retreat, hothouse, cafe, gumtree maze. On the isthmus between North and South Bruny: memorial to Truganini, Tasmania's last full-blood Aborigine (died 1876); lookout with coastal views; boardwalk; little (fairy) penguins and short-tailed shearwaters (muttonbirds). On South Bruny: Bligh Museum, exhibits island's recorded history; Captain Cook's Landing Place, has model of Cook's ship; Mavista Falls, in scenic reserve; lookouts at Adventure and Cloudy bays; lighthouse (1836) at Cape Bruny, second oldest in Australia; walking tracks to Mt Mangana and Mt Bruny. Boat tours from Adventure Bay. On North Bruny: Dennes Point beach, D'Entrecasteaux Channel, has picnic/barbecue facilities; at Variety Bay, remains of convict-built church on private property near airstrip, conducted tours; at Barnes Bay, vault of early settler William Lawrence. Fishing, camel tours. Feb.: Barnes Bay Regatta. Oct.: Flower Festival. **Visitor information:** Bruny D'Entrecasteaux Visitor Centre, Ferry Rd, Kettering; (03) 6267 4494. Web site www.tasmaniaholiday.com **See also:** Day Tours from Hobart p. 546.

Buckland   Pop. 228

MAP REF. 579 M2, 583 N7

A stained-glass window depicting the life of John the Baptist and dating back to the 14th century is in the church in this tiny township, 64 km NE of Hobart. History links the window with England's Battle Abbey. Oliver Cromwell sacked the abbey in the 17th century, but the window was hidden for safety; two centuries later the Marquis of Salisbury gave it to Rev. T. H. Fox, Buckland's first rector. It is now in the east wall of the Church of St John the Baptist (1846), on the Tasman Hwy. The original figure-work is intact. Also of interest is Ye Olde Buckland Inn, Kent St, 19th-century tavern and restaurant. **Visitor information:** Ye Olde Buckland Inn, Kent St; (03) 6257 5114.

Burnie   Pop. 16 007

MAP REF. 584 G6

The rapid expansion of Burnie, now Tasmania's fourth largest city, is based on one of the State's largest enterprises, Australian Paper. Situated on the banks of Emu Bay, 148 km NW of Launceston, Burnie has a deepwater port, which serves the west coast mining centres. Other industries include the production of mining equipment, and dried milk, chocolate products and cheese. **In town:** Lactos Cheese Tasting and Sales Centre, Old Surrey Rd. Free guided tours of Amcor paper mill, (Mon.–Fri.), Marine Tce (book at information centre). Pioneer Village Museum, at information centre, includes reconstruction of small shops (c. 1900). Burnie Inn, town's oldest building, re-erected as a cafe in Burnie Park. Glen Osborne, Aileen Cres., historic building, now B&B. Market, Spring St (opp. railway), 1st and 3rd Sat. each month. Scenic and heritage walk through Burnie, brochure available. Jan: Athletic Club New Year's Day Carnival. Oct.: Rhododendron Festival; Show. Nov.: Food Festival. **In the area:** Views from Round Hill, 5 km E. Fern Glade, off Old Surrey Rd, 5 km W, for riverside walks and picnics. Emu Valley Rhododendron Gardens, off Cascade Rd, 6 km S. Annsleigh Gardens, 9 km S on Mount Rd, closed in winter. Guide Falls near Ridgley, 17 km S; Guide Falls Alpaca Farm, 1 km further on. Upper Natone Forest Reserve, 20 km S, for picnics. Scenic drive north-west via Somerset, then inland through Elliott to Yolla. **Visitor information:** Tasmanian Travel

Picturesque farmland near Deloraine

and Information Centre, Civic Centre Precinct, Little Alexander St; (03) 6434 6111. **See also:** Touring Tasmania p. 552.

Campbell Town   Pop. 816

MAP REF. 583 M2, 585 N12

Campbell Town, 66 km SE of Launceston on the Midland Hwy, has strong links with the wool industry; Saxon merinos were introduced to the Macquarie Valley, west of the town in the early 1820s. Timber and stud beef are also important primary industries. The town and the Elizabeth River were named by Governor Macquarie for his wife, the former Elizabeth Campbell. **In town:** Self-guide heritage walks, brochure available. National Trust-classified buildings in King St are Wesleyan Chapel (1846), no longer operational, and St Michael's Church (1857); in Bridge St is Balmoral Cottage (1840s); in High St are Fox Hunters Return (1830s), now colonial accommodation, St Luke's Church (1839), The Grange (1847), Campbell Town Inn (1840), convict-built Red Bridge (1837) and Kean's Brewery (1840), now an antique emporium. Also in High St: memorial to Harold Gatty, first round-the-world flight navigator; displays at Heritage Highway Museum; market at Town Hall, 4th Sun. each month. Mar.: Highland Games. June: Agricultural Show (oldest in Australia). **In the area:** Trout fishing, particularly in Lake Leake, 30 km SE. Evansville Game Park, 30 km E. **Visitor information:** Heritage Highway Museum and Visitor Centre, Campbell Town Courthouse, 103 High St; (03) 6381 1353. **See also:** Touring Tasmania p. 552.

Coles Bay   Pop. 120

MAP REF. 583 Q4, 585 Q13

This beautiful unspoiled bay, 42 km S of Bicheno on the Freycinet Peninsula, is a good base for visits to Freycinet National Park. **In the area:** At Freycinet National Park: pleasant beaches, clear waters and heathland; ideal for swimming, game-fishing and bushwalking (including scenic walk to Wineglass Bay); abundant birdlife; wildflowers, including 60 varieties of ground orchid; rock-climbing on The Hazards, spectacular granite peaks rising to 620 m, and nearby cliffs; water-skiing, scuba-diving, canoeing, sailing; charter boat trips to Schouten Island. Freycinet Marine Farm, 9 km N, oysters (5 p.m.–6 p.m.) and tours; (03) 6257 0140. **Visitor information:** Park Ranger; (03) 6257 0107. **See also:** National Parks p. 554.

Cygnet   Pop. 851

MAP REF. 578 F10, 583 K10

The centre of a fruit-growing district 52 km SW of Hobart, the town was originally named Port de Cygne Noir (Black Swan Port) by the French Admiral Bruni D'Entrecasteaux because of the number of swans in the bay. **In town:** Art and craft shops. Cygnet Guest House, Mary St, has woodcraft, art gallery, Devonshire tea and B&B. Jan.: Huon Valley Folk and Music Festival. **In the area:** Boating, fishing, bushwalking, gem-fossicking, wineries, small berry-fruit farms. Magnificent wattle, apple and pear blossom Sept.–Oct. Nine Pin Point Marine Nature Reserve, 18 km S, near Verona Sands. Good beaches and boat-launching facilities at Randalls Bay, 14 km S, nearby

Verona Sands, and Egg and Bacon Bay, 15 km S. Panorama Vineyard, 9 km N. Unique Lymington lace agate sometimes found at Drip Beach, Lymington, 7.5 km SW. Lymington Geological (car) Trail; brochure available. Pelverata Falls 20 km N on Sandfly Rd. The Deepings, woodturners' workshop and sales, 10 km E at Nicholls Rivulet. Talune Wildlife Park and Koala Gardens, 6 km SE at Gardners Bay: good picnic/barbecue facilities, sells own cider and fruit wine. Hartzview Wine Centre, 10 km SE. **Visitor information:** Talune Wildlife Park, Gardners Bay; (03) 6295 1775. Web site www.southcom.com.au/~wombat

Deloraine   Pop. 2168

MAP REF. 580 I11, 585 J9

With Bass Strait to the north and the Great Western Tiers to the south, Deloraine is an ideal base for exploring northern Tasmania. The surrounding countryside is used mainly for dairying and mixed farming. **In town:** Deloraine Folk Museum, 98 Emu Bay Road. Gallery 9, West Barrack St. 'Yarns', large multi-panelled artwork in silk, Community Complex, Alveston Dr., open Mon.–Wed. or by appt. Walk along riverbank, through parkland. Markets at showgrounds, Lake Hwy, 1st Sat. each month. Easter: Grand National Steeplechase. Nov.: Tasmanian Craft Fair. **In the area:** Elizabeth Town, 10 km NW: Ashgrove Farm, English-style cheese; Christmas Hills Raspberry Farm. Lobster Falls, 15 km W, 2-hr return walk from roadside; Westmoreland Falls, further 10 km SW at Caveside. Trowunna Wildlife Park, 18 km W on Mole Creek Rd, has nocturnal enclosure. Montana Falls, 9 km SW, small but pretty; 5–10 min. walk. Meander Falls in Meander Forest Reserve, 22 km SW, 5-hr return walk from carpark (not accessible after heavy snow); other walking tracks in reserve. Quamby Bluff, 20 km S, solitary mountain behind town; walking track to summit (6-hr return, medium difficulty) starts near Lake Hwy. Liffey Falls, 29 km S, 45-min. return walk from carpark. Brochures available for all walks. Scenic drive south to Central Highlands, through Golden Valley, to Great Lake, one of the largest high-water lakes in Australia; check road conditions, (03) 6259 8163. Dry's Bluff, 40 km SE, part of Great Western Tiers. Excellent trout fishing on lake and in Mersey and Meander rivers. **Visitor information:** Deloraine Folk Museum, 98 Emu Bay Rd; (03) 6362 3471. Web site www.deloraine.tasonline.org

Wildlife-Watching

Tasmania's isolation from the Australian mainland ensures some truly unique wildlife-watching experiences. Pademelons, spotted-tailed quolls and eastern quolls are now rare or extinct on the mainland, but are still plentiful in Tasmania. This is largely due to the absence of both foxes and dingoes in this scenic island State. Tasmania is also a haven for a wide variety of birdlife including little (fairy) penguins. Its coastline is home to many of the popular marine mammals.

IN AND AROUND HOBART

Hobart is one of the most accessible places in Australia to view wild peregrine falcons. Visitors who venture down to the Tasman Bridge at dusk in winter might be lucky enough to see these birds of prey in action. Peregrines swoop down on the flocks of starlings returning to roost under the bridge. Keep your binoculars ready to see the peregrines catch their prey in mid-air.

For a more tranquil bird-watching experience, visit Orielton Lagoon at **Sorell**, north-east of Hobart. This wetland area is protected by the international Ramsar Convention because of its significance as a habitat for migratory birds. Birds seen wading here at low tide have travelled many thousands of kilometres along the East Asian–Australasian Flyway from as far afield as Siberia. Waders, such as plovers and oystercatchers, feed on the mud flats as the tide is falling and when the tide is almost high they seek a safe roosting place. Tide times are published in the

THE THYLACINE (TASMANIAN TIGER)

Along with its smaller relative the Tasmanian devil, the thylacine (Tasmanian tiger) would have to be one the State's best-known native animals. This is despite the fact that the last recorded thylacine was captured in 1933 and died in 1936. Like a mythical beast, the thylacine has lived on in the popular imagination, sustained by well-publicised but unsubstantiated sightings.

Referred to as the Tasmanian tiger because of the stripes on its back and rump, this lean-bodied marsupial with a large head and short legs is more like a dog in overall appearance.

In recent years, most reported sightings of the thylacine have occurred in the north of the State. However, if you are keen to come face-to-face with this mysterious creature, your best opportunity is to visit the life-size hologram at Lake St Clair Park Centre in Cradle Mountain–Lake St Clair National Park.

Mercury newspaper; Sorell's low tide is 2.5 hours later than Hobart's. There are a number of access points to the lagoon: from the Sorell Causeway, from Henry Street on the east side of the lagoon and from Shark Point Road. You will need patience, a good field guide, binoculars and, after rain, a pair of gumboots.

ON THE EAST COAST

Maria Island National Park, a short ferry ride from Louisville on the east coast, is a natural showcase for Tasmania's unique bird species. It is the only national park where all of the State's 11 endemic species can be spotted. These include the yellow wattlebird, Tasmanian thornbill, yellow-throated honeyeater and the dusky robin. This range of birdlife is the result of incredibly diverse habitats on this small

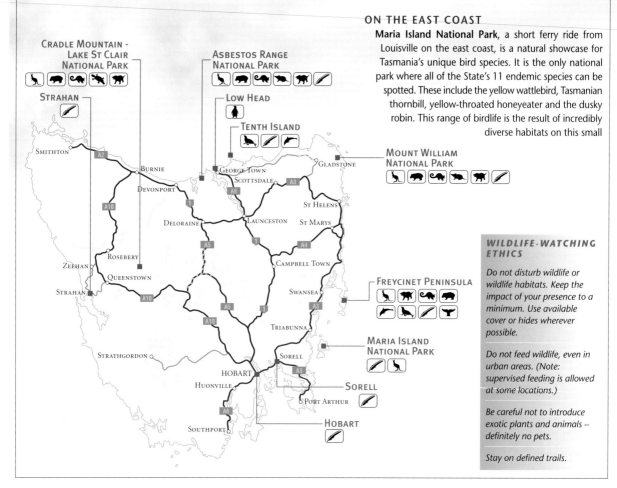

WILDLIFE-WATCHING ETHICS

Do not disturb wildlife or wildlife habitats. Keep the impact of your presence to a minimum. Use available cover or hides wherever possible.

Do not feed wildlife, even in urban areas. (Note: supervised feeding is allowed at some locations.)

Be careful not to introduce exotic plants and animals – definitely no pets.

Stay on defined trails.

island, ranging from ocean, wetland, cleared-grazing and dry sclerophyll forest, to moist gully environments.

The grasslands of Darlington at the northern end of the island are active with wildlife throughout the day. Bennett's wallabies and pademelons (also a type of wallaby) graze here, as does Tasmania's only kangaroo, the Forester kangaroo. Flocks of Cape Barren geese regularly graze and breed in this area; they pair off to mate in autumn and lay eggs in grassland tussocks. The fluffy goslings develop rapidly in winter and are ready to fly by late spring.

Freycinet Peninsula, roughly midway between Hobart and Launceston, offers a range of wildlife-watching opportunities. Bennett's wallabies and pademelons tend to congregate in the Freycinet National Park carpark throughout the day and in the grassland by the beaches at dusk. Nocturnal mammals include Tasmanian devils, brushtail possums and common wombats.

Freycinet Sea Charters operate regular wildlife cruises featuring seasonal sightings of bottlenose and common dolphins, Australian fur seals, white-bellied sea-eagles and southern right and humpback whales.

Moulting Lagoon Game Reserve, located at the beginning of Freycinet Peninsula, is another wetland of international significance protected by the Ramsar Convention. Birds commonly seen here include the migratory waders, as well as black swans, wild ducks, egrets, cormorants, pelicans and birds of prey.

Bennett's wallabies can be seen at many locations across the State

IN THE NORTH-EAST OF THE STATE

Mount William National Park was originally established as a national park in order to protect its substantial Forester kangaroo population. Forester Kangaroo Drive passes through the pasture area in the northern section of the park, where Bennett's wallabies can also be seen, especially at dawn or dusk. As darkness falls, a whole cast of nocturnal wildlife appears. Common wombats, possums, pademelons and eastern quolls are just some of the characters you might expect to see.

Asbestos Range National Park, which has the advantage of being slightly closer to the main ports of Devonport and Launceston, has a similar array of wildlife. These parks are probably the best places in the State to view the icon of Tasmanian wildlife, the Tasmanian devil. This squat little meat-eater, renowned for its spine-chilling screeches, is active after dark, when it roams in search of carcasses.

Birdwatching is a popular activity in these two north-eastern parks. Gulls, oystercatchers, terns, dotterels, pelicans and albatrosses can all be sighted along the coastline. Musselroe Point and Campsite 4 in Mount William National Park and the bird hide behind Bakers Beach in Asbestos Range National Park are prime birdwatching locations.

Also in the north-east is George Town, the jumping-off point for cruises to see the Australian fur seal colony at **Tenth Island**. These seals, with their endearing whiskered faces, can be seen year-round. As the boat approaches, the playful pups swim towards it and dive underneath, while the large bull seals look on from the rocks about 100 metres away. Pelicans, black swans and dolphins are a common sight en route to Tenth Island.

At **Low Head** near George Town, little (fairy) penguins can be viewed at dusk during the breeding period (July to April). Access is by tour only; inquire at the George Town information centre for cruise and tour details; (03) 6382 1700.

IN THE WEST OF THE STATE

Cradle Mountain–Lake St Clair National Park is one of the State's best-known wildlife-watching destinations. Visitors are guaranteed to see a range of nocturnal marsupials such as Bennett's wallabies, pademelons, wombats and possums around the camping and accommodation areas, especially in the evenings. Platypuses live in the lakes and streams but are far more elusive. Tasmanian devils are generally spotted at night on the edges of roadways, ripping apart the carcasses of animals killed by cars.

Strahan is probably best-known as the jumping-off point for cruises along the Gordon River. Many visitors, however, have discovered another more low-key attraction during the summer months. Every year in late September, the first of thousands of short-tailed shearwaters (muttonbirds) reach their rookeries on Ocean Beach, having travelled 15 000 kilometres from the Arctic region. Throughout summer, the sky fills with shearwaters every evening as they return with food for their young.

For more information on wildlife-watching in Tasmania's national parks, contact the Parks and Wildlife Service, 134 Macquarie Street, Hobart (GPO Box 44A, Hobart 7001); (03) 6233 6191. Web site www.parks.tas.gov.au

Derby

Pop. 200

MAP REF. 585 O7

Derby is a former mining town on the Tasman Hwy, 34 km E of Scottsdale in the north-east. Although tin is still worked in the area, there has been a gradual swing to rural production. **In town:** In Main St: Derby Tin Mine Museum, in old school (1897), has history displays, gemstones, minerals and tin panning; reconstructed Shanty Town has a number of original shop and office buildings from the area and two cells from old Derby gaol; woodcraft at Classic Crafts and The Gallery; Bank House Antiques and Craft, in old bank. Oct.: Derby River Derby. **In the area:** At Moorina, 8 km NE: gemstone fossicking park on Tasman Hwy; cemetery has graves of Chinese miners. At former tin-mining town of Branxholm, 12 km SW, Y. Woodcrafts (wood-turning). Near Ringarooma, 24 km SW, Ralph Falls; lookouts at Mathinna Hill and Mt Victoria; scenic drives. Ringarooma Agricultural Show in Oct. **Visitor information:** Derby Tin Mine Museum, Main St; (03) 6354 2262.

Devonport

Pop. 22 299

MAP REF. 580 E5, 584 I6

Devonport is a busy port for agricultural and industrial exports and terminal for the vehicular ferry *Spirit of Tasmania* which crosses Bass Strait from Melbourne. The town also has its own airport, and is an ideal base for seeing northern Tasmania. **In town:** Tiagarra, Tasmanian Aboriginal Culture and Art Centre, Bluff Rd, Mersey Bluff; 1-km circuit walk to Tasmanian Aboriginal rock engravings. Devonport Gallery and Arts Centre in historic church, Stewart St. Devonport Maritime Museum and Historical Society, Victoria Pde; model ships and history room. National Trust-classified Home Hill, Middle Rd, home of former Prime Minister Joseph Lyons and Dame Enid Lyons (check opening times). Scenic flights. Feb.: Food and Wine Festival. Mar.: Regatta. Oct.: Classic Challenge Motorsport Event. Dec.: Melbourne–Devonport Yacht Race. **In the area:** Walking and cycling track from town to Don, 7 km W, via Mersey Bluff lighthouse, for excellent coastal views. At Don: Don River Railway and Museum; vintage trains run Mon–Sat., steam trains Sun. and public holidays.

Braddon's Lookout, 9 km W near Forth, has panoramic view of coastline. Tasmanian Aboretum (45 ha), 10 km S at Eugenana; also picnic area and walking tracks. **Visitor information:** Tasmanian Travel and Information, Devonport Showcase, 5 Best St; (03) 6424 4466. Web site www.devonport. tco.asn.au **See also:** Touring Tasmania p. 552; Stately Homes p. 572.

Dover

Pop. 481

MAP REF. 578 E12, 583 K11

This attractive fishing port, south-west of Hobart, was once a convict station. The Commandant's Office still stands but the underground cells, near the wharf, can no longer be seen. From late 1850s several large sawmills produced first-class timber. The main industries today are fruit-growing, fishing and Atlantic salmon fish-farming. Quaint cottages and English trees give the town an old-world atmosphere. The three bay islands are called Faith, Hope and Charity. **In town:** Charter fishing trips, Atlantic salmon cruises, and twilight and adventure cruises on *Olive May*, depart end Jetty Rd. **In the area:** Attractive scenery and unspoiled beaches, ideal for bushwalking

The Bass Strait Islands

King Island and Flinders Island, Tasmania's two main Bass Strait islands, are ideal holiday spots for the adventurous. You can fish, swim, go bushwalking or scuba-dive among the wrecks of the many ships that foundered off the islands' shores last century. Birdwatching is also popular and each spring millions of short-tailed shearwaters (muttonbirds) make a spectacular sight as they fly in to nest in coastal rookeries on the islands.

King Island, at the western end of the strait, is accessible only by air. It is a picturesque, rugged island with an unspoiled coastline of beautiful sandy beaches on the east and north coasts, contrasting with the forbidding cliffs of Seal Rocks and the lonely coast to the south. The lighthouse at Cape Wickham is the largest in Australia, and there is a penguin colony on the breakwater at Grassy which can be visited at dusk. The island's main industries today are dairy and beef products, kelp harvesting, fishing and sheep farming. King Island dairy and beef products have earned a reputation for their high quality; the King Island Dairy, on North Rd, is open Sunday to Friday. In the north is Penny's Lagoon, a tranquil freshwater suspended lake, similar to those on Fraser Island in Queensland. South is Cataraqui Point, site of Australia's worst peacetime maritime disaster. The main town is Currie, which has a kelp factory. At the King Island Museum in Currie, visitors can see shipwreck relics and learn about the island's history. Accommodation includes a hotel, two motels, numerous holiday cottages and a caravan park.

Flinders Island is renowned for its excellent fishing, its magnificent granite mountains and its gemstone, the Killiecrankie 'diamond' (actually a kind of topaz). The island produces fine woollen products, handmade chocolates and gourmet fare. Strzelecki National Park, near the town of Whitemark, provides challenging rock-climbing. From Whitemark, 4WD tours are available to remote beaches. The island is also popular with scuba-divers, naturalists and photographers. Accommodation on the island includes two hotels, several host farms and holiday cottages, and a cabin park. Flinders is one of more than 50 islands in the Furneaux Group that were once part of the land bridge that linked Tasmania with the mainland.

In the 1830s the few surviving Tasmanian Aborigines were settled near Emita on Flinders Island. All that remains of the settlement today is the graveyard and Wybalenna Chapel, which has been restored by the National Trust. Nearby, there are historic displays relating to the Furneaux Islands in the Museum (open 1 p.m.–5 p.m. weekends).

Fishing is the main industry of the tiny community of Lady Barron to the south, a port village overlooking Franklin Sound and Cape Barren Island.

For general information and holiday bookings, contact the Tasmanian Travel and Information Centre, 20 Davey St, Hobart; (03) 6230 8233.

and swimming. Tasmanian Trail: 477-km Dover–Devonport trail for walkers, mountain-bikers and horseriders; booklet available. Several old graves on Faith Island. **Visitor information:** Forest and Heritage Centre, Church St, Geeveston; (03) 6297 1836.

Dunalley
Pop. 286

MAP REF. 579 M6, 583 N9
This small fishing village borders the narrow isthmus connecting the Forestier Peninsula to the rest of Tasmania. The Denison Canal, spanned by a swing bridge, provides access to the east coast for small vessels. **In town:** Tasman Memorial, Imlay St, marks first landing by Europeans in 1642; actual landing occurred to the north-east, near Cape Paul Lamanon. **In the area:** Just east, tours of Bangor Farm on Arthur Hwy, a conservation and sheep and cattle farm, once home of Oyster Bay Aborigines, also site of Abel Tasman's landing; bookings essential; (03) 6253 5233. Memorabilia at Copping Colonial and Convict Collection, 11 km N. **Visitor information:** Dunalley Hotel, 210 Arthur Hwy; (03) 6253 5101. **See also:** Peninsula Trail p. 548.

Eaglehawk Neck
Pop. 209

MAP REF. 579 N8, 583 O9
In convict days this narrow isthmus, which separates the Tasman and Forestier peninsulas, was guarded by a line of ferocious, tethered dogs. Soldiers and police also stood guard to ensure that no convicts escaped from the notorious convict settlement at Port Arthur. The only prisoners to escape did so by sea. The town today is a pleasant fishing destination. A charter tuna-fishing fleet operates from Pirates Bay. **In town:** Museum in restored historic Officers' Quarters, off Arthur Hwy, features story of Port Arthur escapee Martin Cash. Dogline marked by bronze dog sculpture; access by short walking track. **In the area:** Tessellated Pavement, 1 km N and Pirates Bay Lookout, 1.5 km N; halfway between is Eaglehawk Dive Centre, lessons and charters. Unusual features in Tasman National Park, 4 km E, off Arthur Hwy: Tasmans Arch, Devils Kitchen and Tasman Blowhole. Tasmanian Devil Park Wildlife Rescue Centre and World Tiger Snake Centre, 12 km S. South along coast from Waterfall Bay to Munro Bight: water sports; picnics in Tasman National Park; coastal walking track from Waterfall Bay to Fortescue Bay. Good sailing in Eaglehawk Bay. Port Arthur Historic Site, 21 km SW.

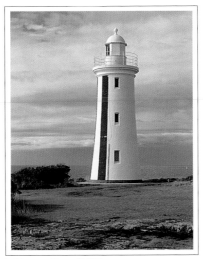
Lighthouse on Mersey Bluff, Devonport

Visitor information: Officers' Mess, off Arthur Hwy; (03) 6250 3635. **See also:** Day Tours from Hobart p. 546; Peninsula Trail p. 548; National Parks p. 554.

Evandale
Pop. 1033

MAP REF. 581 P12, 585 M9
This little township, 20 km from Launceston and 4 km from the airport, has been proclaimed a historic village. Founded 1829, some of its buildings date from 1809. Originally Morven, it was renamed in 1836 in honour of Tasmania's first Surveyor-General, G. W. Evans. Streetscapes remain unspoiled and there are many buildings of historical and architectural significance. **In town:** Numerous antique and craft outlets. Self-guide heritage walk from Tourism and History Centre, High St; brochure available. Also in High St: Solomon House (1836), now cafe and accommodation; St Andrew's Anglican (1871) and Uniting (1839) churches; Blenheim (1840s), now workshop (antiques and sales of stained glass). Clarendon Arms Hotel, Russell St, has mural depicting local history. Cornwall Cottage, Scone St, unusual bicycles for hire. Market, each Sun. a.m. at Falls Park, Russell St. Feb.: Village Fair and National Penny Farthing Championships. Nov.: Railex (model-train exhibition). **In the area:** Clarendon (1838), 8 km S near Nile, grand Georgian mansion in extensive formal gardens. Symmons Plains Raceway, 10 km S, venue for national and State Touring Car Championships (usually in Mar.), track open for public use; (03) 6249 4683. At Deddington, 24 km SE, chapel (1840) on private land, designed by artist John Glover; Glover's grave beside chapel.

Trout fishing in South Esk and North Esk rivers. **Visitor information:** Tourism and History Centre, 18 High St; (03) 6391 8128. **See also:** Touring Tasmania p. 552; Stately Homes p. 572.

Exeter
Pop. 382

MAP REF. 581 L7, 585 L7
Exeter, once a busy shipyard town 24 km NW of Launceston, now serves a large fruit-growing and wine-producing area. **In town:** In Main St: outdoor go-kart track, Tatana Karts; historic Exeter Bakery, wood-fired oven; Kerrisons Orchard, fruit sales. **In the area:** Four wineries with cellar-door sales in West Tamar area; Wine Centre in Tamar Court Brasserie, Main Rd, tastings and sales of local wines; Tasmanian Wine Route, brochure available. Mini golf at Crazy Putt Golf, 5 km E at Gravelly Beach. Walking track (5 km return) from Paper Beach, 9 km E, to Supply River. Near mouth of Supply River, 10 km N off Gravelly Beach Rd, ruins of first water-driven flour mill in Tasmania, built 1825. At Robigana, 10 km N, Artisan Gallery. Notley Fern Gorge at Notley Hills, 11 km SW, 10-ha rainforest reserve with picnic/barbecue areas. On Rosevears Dr., just south of Exeter: historic Rosevears Hotel, first licensed 1831; Waterbird Haven, wetlands habitat with treetop hide; Clever Hands Crafts; monument to John Batman's locally built ship *Rebecca*, in which he crossed Bass Strait to Yarra River; St Matthias Vineyard; Strathlynn Wine Centre. 5 km SE in State reserve, Brady's Lookout, a rocky outcrop used by notorious bushranger Matthew Brady. Grindelwald Swiss Village, 10 km SE, a resort in Swiss-architectural style. **Visitor information:** Tamar Visitor Centre, Main Rd; (03) 6394 4454.

Fingal
Pop. 379

MAP REF. 583 P1, 585 P10
In the Esk Valley, 21 km inland from St Marys on the South Esk River, Fingal is the headquarters of the State's coal industry. The first payable gold in Tasmania was found in 1852 at The Nook, near Fingal. **In town:** Historic buildings: St Joseph's Church, Grey St; Masonic Lodge, Brown St. In Talbot St: St Peter's Church; Holder Bros. General Store (1859); Fingal Hotel (licensed 1844); Fingal History Room, by appt only. On eastern outskirts, view coal-washing process at Cornwell Coal Company washery. Mar.: Fingal Valley Festival (incorporating World Coal

Shovelling Championships and Roof Bolting Championships). **In the area:** In Evercreech Forest Reserve, 30 km N on road to Mathinna, large white gums, including 89-m specimen; also picnic/barbecue area and walking tracks. Mathinna Falls, 36 km N near Mathinna; picnic/barbecue area nearby. At Avoca, 27 km SW, historic buildings; town in foothills of Ben Lomond. **Visitor information:** Old Tasmanian Hotel Community Centre, Main Rd; (03) 6374 2344. **See also:** Stately Homes p. 572.

Geeveston
Pop. 778

MAP REF. 578 D10, 583 J10
This timber town is the gateway to Tasmania's south-west World Heritage Area. **In town:** In Church St: Forest and Heritage Centre, complex featuring interpretive 'forest room' and Hartz Gallery (quality woodcrafts and exhibitions); The Bears Went Over the Mountain, shop selling traditional teddy bears. **In the area:** Apple blossom late Sept.–early Oct. Scenic drives and walks through Arve Valley, west of town, include Arve Road Forest Dr.: Arve River Picnic Area (10 km W); Big Tree Lookout (15 km W), world's tallest flowering plant, *Eucalyptus regnans* – Tasmanian Swamp Gum, 87 m; Keoghs Creek Walk (15 km W); West Creek Lookout (20 km W) over fern gully, leatherwood and swamp gums; Tahune Forest Reserve (27 km W), camping, fishing, rafting, short walks among Huon pines. Hartz Mountains National Park, 23 km SW off Arve Rd: birdwatching; waratah and other wildflowers spring and summer; short walks to waterfalls, glacial tarns, Waratah Lookout; self-guide brochure available. At Port Huon, 4 km NE, river cruises visit salmon farms. **Visitor information:** Forest and Heritage Centre, Church St; (03) 6297 1836.

George Town
Pop. 4522

MAP REF. 581 K4, 585 K6
Situated at the mouth of the Tamar River, George Town (Australia's third settled town, after Sydney and Hobart) was settled by Europeans in 1811 and named for King George III. Today it is a commercial centre, mainly for the Comalco plant at Bell Bay and other industrial developments, and the terminal for the *Devil Cat Ferry* (George Town to Melbourne Dec.–Apr.), bookings essential; 13 2010. **In town:** Self-guide Discovery Trail of region, brochure available. Monument on Esplanade commemorates landing in 1804

Entally House, near Hadspen

when Lieut.-Col. William Paterson and his crew in HMS *Buffalo* ran aground during a storm. The Grove (c. 1838), cnr Elizabeth and Cimitiere sts, Devonshire teas and lunches. Market at Community Hall, Macquarie St, 2nd Sat. each month. Jan.: Folk Festival. Mar.: Pipers Brook Concert. Apr.: The Prologue (5-day car rally). **In the area:** At Bell Bay, 6 km S: Comalco and BHP Temco plants; tours available. At Hillwood, 24 km SE, apple orchards and Hillwood Strawberry Farm, Fruit Wine and Cheese Centre. Lookout from Mt George, 1 km E. Lefroy, 10 km E, former goldmining settlement with ruins, old diggings, cemetery. Wineries in Pipers Brook region to the east; tastings, cellar-door sales. Tasmanian Wine Route brochure available. Historic maritime village Low Head, 5 km N, has surf and river beaches; Maritime Museum in Australia's oldest continuously used pilot station, opened 1803; nearby, lighthouse and little (fairy) penguin colony, guided tours at dusk. Cruises to fur seal colony at mouth of Tamar River. **Visitor information:** Main Rd; (03) 6382 1700. **See also:** Stately Homes p. 572.

Gladstone
Pop. 200

MAP REF. 585 P6
Gladstone is a small service centre for surrounding dairy, sheep and cattle farms. The district was once a thriving tin and goldmining area, with a colourful early history. Now many of the once substantial townships nearby are ghost towns or nearly so. **In town:** Chinese graves at Gladstone Cemetery, eastern outskirts of town. **In the area:** Geological formations south-west in

area between Gladstone and South Mount Cameron. At South Mount Cameron, 8 km S, Blue Lake, a disused tin mine filled with brilliant blue water coloured by pyrites. At Mt William National Park, 25 km E: prolific flora and fauna, excellent beaches, historic lighthouse at Eddystone Point (35 km E). **Visitor information:** Gladstone Hotel, Chaffey St; (03) 6357 2143.

Hadspen
Pop. 1730

MAP REF. 581 N11, 585 L9
The township of Hadspen, first settled in the early 1820s, has many historic buildings, some of which offer accommodation and/or meals. **In town:** Row of Georgian buildings, Main Rd: Red Feather Inn (c. 1844); old coaching station; Hadspen Gaol (c. 1840); Church of the Good Shepherd – construction began 1858, funded by Thomas Reibey, who withdrew his support after a dispute with the bishop; completed 1961, almost 50 years after Reibey's death. **In the area:** Entally House (1819), 1 km W on banks of South Esk River, one of Tasmania's most famous historic homes; Regency furniture and fine silverware. Carrick, 10 km SW, Georgian and Victorian buildings; Agfest held May. **Visitor information:** Gateway Tasmanian Travel Centre, cnr St John and Paterson sts, Launceston; (03) 6336 3133. **See also:** Stately Homes p. 572.

Hamilton
Pop. 150

MAP REF. 578 D1, 583 J6
A National Trust-classified historic town in a rural setting, Hamilton has retained

many of its colonial buildings. **In town:** Old School House (1858), Lyell Hwy; B&B accommodation and antique shop in grounds. Glen Clyde House (c. 1840), Grace St, tearooms and craft gallery with works of over 100 craftspeople. Jackson's Emporium (1856), local products, wines. **In the area:** Guided tours of farming and industry. Meadowbank Lake, 10 km NW, a popular venue for picnics, boating, water-skiing and trout fishing. **Visitor information:** Council Offices, Tarleton St; (03) 6286 3202.

Hastings   Pop. 20

MAP REF. 578 D13, 583 J12

This tiny town, about 100 km SW of Hobart on the Huon Hwy, attracts many tourists to its dolomite caves, local gemstones and nearby scenic railway. **In the area:** Hastings Forest Tour, self-drive, cassette guide available, begins off Hastings Rd and leads north-west to Esperance River. Hastings Caves, 13 km NW: tours of illuminated Newdegate Cave, swimming in thermal pool, streamside walks, picnic/barbecue facilities. Lune River, 2 km S, haven for gem collectors. Beyond river, 2 km further S, Ida Bay Scenic Railway, originally built to carry dolomite, now carries passengers 7 km to Deep Hole and back; picnic facilities at both ends of track. Cockle Creek, 41 km S, in Southwest National Park at the start of extended South Coast walking track, offers fishing, boating, bushwalking. Southport, 6 km SE, a fishing port in the days of sealers and whalers, offers good fishing, swimming, surfing, bush-walking. **Visitor information:** Forest and Heritage Centre, Church St, Geeveston; (03) 6297 1836. **See also:** Day Tours from Hobart p. 546.

Huonville   Pop. 1718

MAP REF. 578 F8, 583 K9

Huonville is the centre of the apple-producing district and is the largest township in the region. As well as apples, which can be bought year-round, the Huon Valley grows cherries, blueber-ries, strawberries, and raspberries, which in season can be purchased from roadside stalls and at pick-your-own farms. The prized Huon pine was discovered in this district. **In town:** Fishing for trout and salmon is popular in the Huon River and tributaries; fish punt on foreshore. Horseback Wilderness Tours, Sale St. Pedal boat and aqua-bike hire, Esplanade. Nov.:

Huon Agricultural Show (biggest one-day agricultural show in State). **In the area:** Huon River jet boat rides over rapids to Glen Huon. Scenic drives, brochures avail-able. Doran's Jam Factory and the Apple and Heritage Museum at Grove, 6 km NE. Antique Motor Museum near Ranelagh, 5 km NW. Snowy Range Trout Fishery, Little Dennison River, 25 km NW. Appleheads and Model Village at Glen Huon, 8 km W, features apples carved to resemble heads. At wooden-boatbuilding town of Franklin, 8 km SW: Franklin Tea Gardens beside river has cottage gardens, crafts and curios; Franklin Lodge, one of the State's most established colonial accommodation. River cruises to salmon farms at Plenty depart Port Huon, 18 km SW. **Visitor information:** Huon River Jet Boats, Esplanade; (03) 6264 1838. **See also:** Day Tours from Hobart p. 546.

Kettering   Pop. 314

MAP REF. 578 H9, 583 L10

This town on the Channel Hwy south of Hobart serves a large fruit-growing district. **In town:** Bruny Island ferry, leaves 10 times daily from Ferry Rd terminal; extra services during holidays. Oyster Cove Inn and marina, Ferry Rd. Variety of boats for hire; skippered cruises and fishing charters available. Roaring 40s Ocean Kayaking, Ferry Rd, for sea-kayak lessons, rentals and tours. **In the area:** Bruny Island. Channel Historical and Folk Museum, 5 km N, open Nov.–Apr. Nearby, Coningham, 6 km N, for good swimming and boating. At Snug, 8 km N: Mother's Favourites, for seafood; holiday cottages; pleasant walks in Snug Falls Track area. Woodbridge Hill Hand-weaving Studio, 4 km S on Woodbridge Hill Rd. Monument to French explorer Admiral Bruni D'Entrecasteaux, 21 km S at Gordon. **Visitor information:** Bruny D'Entrecasteaux Visitor Centre, Ferry Rd; (03) 6267 4494. **See also:** Day Tours from Hobart p. 546.

Kingston   Pop. 5588

MAP REF. 578 H7, 583 L9

Kingston, 12 km S of Hobart, is the admin-istrative centre for the D'Entrecasteaux Channel and Bruny Island districts. **In town:** Foyer display in Federal Government's Antarctic research head-quarters, southern outskirts on Channel Hwy; open Mon.–Fri. Market every Sun., Coles carpark. Oct.: Olie Bollen (Dutch community) Festival . **In the area:** Boronia Hill Flora Trail (2 km) follows ridgeline

between Kingston and Blackmans Bay through remnant bush. Scenic drives south through Blackmans Bay, Tinderbox and Howden; magnificent views of Droughty Point, South Arm Peninsula, Storm Bay and Bruny Island from Piersons Point. At Margate, 3 km S, 1950s passenger train (non-operational); tearooms in buffet car; adjacent antique sales and Sun. market. Small blowhole at Blackmans Bay, 7 km S at reserve on Blowhole Rd; spectacular in stormy weather. At Tinderbox, 11 km S, underwater snorkel trail in Tinderbox Marine Reserve. Shot Tower, 7 km NE near Taroona; wonderful views of Derwent River estuary from top. **Visitor information:** Tasmanian Travel and Information Centre, 20 Davey St, Hobart; (03) 6230 8233. **See also:** Day Tours from Hobart p. 546.

Latrobe   Pop. 2765

MAP REF. 580 E6, 584 I7

This historic township (gazetted 1851) is situated on the Mersey River, 9 km SE of Devonport. Once a busy shipyard town, today it is the site of one of the biggest cycling carnivals in Australia. **In town:** Buildings and shopfronts dating from 1840s, some National Trust-classified; self-guide walk, leaflet available. Court House Museum, Gilbert St, for local history, including prints and artefacts; open Fri. and Sun. Bells Parade Reserve, off Gilbert St along riverbank, has sculpture and picnic areas. Also on Bells Pde, Sherwood Hall is a historic timber structure. Sheean Memorial Walk, Gilbert St, 3-km return walk commemorates local soldiers and WW II hero. Mount Roland Cheese, Speedway Dr. (weekdays). Markets, every Sun. at Gilbert and James sts. Jan.: Latrobe–Port Sorell Summer Festival; Australia Day Carnival; Henley-on-the-Mersey. Dec.: Bicycle Race Club Christmas Carnival (includes Wheel Race and Gift). **In the area:** Myrtle Hole, 3 km S, for picnics and water sports. Henry Somerset Orchard Reserve, 7 km S, has platypus, native orchids and other rare flora. **Visitor information:** Shop 1, 70 Gilbert St; (03) 6426 2693.

Launceston   Pop. 67 701

MAP REF. 580 O10, 585 L8

Although Tasmania's second-largest city and a busy tourist centre, Launceston retains a relaxed, friendly atmosphere. Nestled in hilly country where the Tamar, North Esk and South Esk rivers meet, Launceston is also at the junction of three

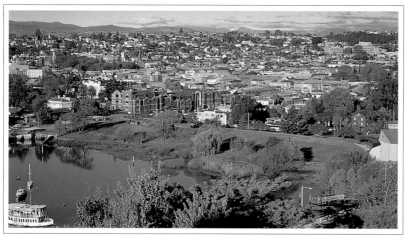

Launceston, Tasmania's second-largest city

main highways and has direct air links with Melbourne and Hobart. It is sometimes known as the Garden City because of its parks and gardens. **In town:** Yorktown Square, The Avenue, Quadrant Mall, Civic Square, and Prince's Square with its magnificent baroque-style fountain and fine surrounding buildings. Main shopping area is around the Mall. Old Umbrella Shop, George St, unique 1860s shop preserved by National Trust. Penny Royal World, Paterson St, collection of buildings originally near Cressy, and moved stone by stone to Launceston; includes tavern, museum, working water-mill, corn mill, windmill, Mole Hill Fantasy (popular mole diorama), accommodation, restaurants; linked by restored tramway to Penny Royal Gunpowder Mill at old Cataract quarry site; boat trips on artificial lake, paddlesteamer cruise on *Lady Stelfox* along the Tamar River and nearby Cataract Gorge. This spectacular gorge is one of Launceston's outstanding natural attractions. Historic Kings Bridge (1867) spans the Tamar River at the gorge entrance. Cataract Cliff Grounds Reserve, on north side of gorge, a formal park with lawns, European trees, peacocks and restaurant. Area linked to swimming pool and kiosk on south side by chairlift and suspension bridge. Walks on both sides of gorge. Ritchies Mill Arts Centre, Paterson St; art and craft. National Automobile Museum, Cimitiere St. Parks include 5-ha City Park with Monkey Island and conservatory (nearby Design Centre of Tasmania displays contemporary art and craft), end of Cameron St; Royal Park, formal civic park on South Esk River; Zig Zag Reserve, leading to Cataract Gorge area. At Queen Victoria Museum and Art Gallery, in Royal Park off Wellington St, displays of: Aboriginal and convict relics;

Tasmania's mineral wealth; flora and fauna; early china and glassware; colonial and modern art. Boags Brewery, William St, guided tours or self-guide tours, brochures available. Feb.: Country Music Festival; Launceston Cup (State's biggest race day). Mar.: A Night in the Gorge; Festivale (food and wine). Sept.: Garden Festival. Oct.: Royal National Show; Tasmanian Poetry Festival. **In the area:** Trevallyn Dam, 6 km w, good picnic spot. Nearby, Australia's only cable hang-gliding simulator. Launceston Lakes Trout Fishery, 17 km w, has fly-fishing lessons. Punchbowl Reserve and Rhododendron Gardens, 5 km sw, has native and European fauna in natural surroundings. Alpine Village in Ben Lomond National Park, 60 km se; open during ski season. Launceston Federal Country Club Casino, 7 km sw. Waverley Woollen Mills, 5 km e, offers tours that include historic collection of plant machinery used to create the industry for which Launceston earned its national reputation. St Matthias' Church, Windermere, 15 km n. Tasmanian Wine Route, Pipers Brook and Tamar Valley regions, north of the city; brochure available. Three National Trust historic houses: Entally House, 18 km sw at Hadspen; Franklin House, 6 km s; Clarendon 28 km se, near Nile. **Visitor information:** Gateway Tasmania Travel Centre, cnr St John and Paterson sts; (03) 6336 3133. **See also:** Touring Tasmania p. 552; Angler's Paradise p. 565; Stately Homes p. 572.

Lilydale   Pop. 343

MAP REF. 581 P6, 585 M7

Situated at the foot of Mt Arthur, 27 km from Launceston, the town of Lilydale has many bush tracks and picnic spots.

In the area: Tasmanian Wine Route, brochure available. Lilydale Falls Reserve, 3 km n, has two oak trees grown from Windsor Great Park acorns, planted on coronation day of British King George IV in 1937. Clover Hill Vineyards, 12 km n. Brook Eden Vineyard, 15 km n. At Lalla, 4 km w, Walker Rhododendron Reserve; Appleshed Tea House, for local art and craft; Providence Vineyards. Ash tree plantation at Hollybank Forest Reserve, Underwood, 5 km s; picnic/barbecue areas. Scenic walks to top of Mt Arthur (1187 m), 20 km se. **Visitor information:** Gateway Tasmania Travel Centre, cnr St John and Paterson sts, Launceston; (03) 6336 3133.

Longford   Pop. 2829

MAP REF. 581 N13, 585 L9

Longford, 22 km s of Launceston, was established 1813 when former settlers of Norfolk Island were given land grants in the area. It has had two name changes; its previous names were Norfolk Plains and Latour. Now classified as a historic town, it serves a rich agricultural district. Australian artist Tom Roberts spent his last few years here and was buried in the area. **In town:** Historic buildings, including some convict-built and many now converted to self-contained colonial cottage and B&B accommodation. In Wellington St: Christ Church (1839), has outstanding stained-glass window and pioneer gravestones; 'Car in window' and Grand Prix memorabilia at Country Club Hotel. Tom Roberts Gallery in Marlborough St, has old prints, books and information. Walking track along South Esk River; Heritage and Headstones Tour. The Village Green, cnr Wellington and Archer sts, originally the town market, now a picnic/barbecue spot. Jan.: Longford Cup. Mar.: Blessing of the Harvest Festival; Brickendon and Woolmers Hunt. Nov.: Village Green Garden Festival. **In the area:** Brickendon, 2 km s, a homestead built by William Archer (1824) and still owned by descendants; now a working farm and historic farm village. Cressy, 10 km s, renowned for its fly-fishing at Brumbys Creek, especially in Nov. when mayflies hatch. Woolmers Estate (c. 1816), 5 km se, colonial cottages, tea rooms and guided tours of main house and gardens. At Perth, 5 km ne, historic buildings: Eskleigh, Jolly Farmer Inn, Old Crown Inn and Leather Bottell Inn. Perth Market, every Sun. a.m., in Old School. Bowthorpe Farm and Gardens, 11 km n, pastoral estate set on South Esk River;

features Georgian farmhouse, cottage garden and tearooms. **Visitor information:** 3 Marlborough St; (03) 6391 1181. **See also:** Touring Tasmania p. 552; Stately Homes p. 572.

Miena
Pop. 46

MAP REF. 583 J2, 585 J12

This small settlement, on the shores of Great Lake in Tasmania's Central Plateau, has been popular with anglers since brown trout were first released into the lake in 1870. The surrounding region, also known as the Lake Country, is an important supplier of hydro-electric power. Be prepared when travelling in this relatively remote region – snow and freezing weather are a possibility, even in summer; road closures may occur. **In the area:** Excellent trout fishing at many lakes, including Great Lake (one of Australia's largest freshwater lakes), Little Pine Lagoon (9 km SW) and Arthurs Lake (23 km E). At Liawenee, 10 km N, Inland Fisheries Commission hosts annual stripping of ova from spawning trout in May. West of Liawenee, hundreds of isolated lakes and tarns for fly-fishing (4WD recommended for several lakes; some only accessible to experienced bushwalkers). Walls of Jerusalem National Park, access via Liawenee or Bass Highway in the north, for experienced bushwalkers only (no day trippers). At Steppes, 27 km SE: old Steppes homestead, by appt; Circle of Life bronze sculptures by Steven Walker, each representing an aspect of region's history and character; rodeo each May. At Waddamana: 33 km S, Power Museum includes history of hydro-electricity in Tasmania and display of early electrical appliances. Boat service from Cynthia Bay on Lake St Clair, 63 km W, provides access to north of lake and to famous 85-km Overland Track, which passes through the spectacular Cradle Mountain–Lake St Clair National Park. **Visitor information:** Great Lake Hotel, Great Lake Hwy; (03) 6259 8163. **See also:** National Parks p. 554; Angler's Paradise p. 565.

Mole Creek
Pop. 256

MAP REF. 580 E12, 584 I9

This town, 74 km S of Devonport, and nestled at the foot of the Great Western Tiers, serves an important farming and forestry district. It was named after the creek which 'burrows' underground. The unique honey from the leatherwood tree, which grows only in the west-coast rainforests of Tasmania, is processed here. Each summer, apiarists transport hives to the nearby leatherwood forests. **In town:** Stephen's Honey Factory, Pioneer Dr., for extraction and processing of honey; open Mon.–Fri. **In the area:** Guided tours of fine limestone caves in Mole Creek Karst National Park: Marakoopa Cave, 8 km W, has glow-worm display; smaller but still spectacular King Solomons Cave 16 km W. Wild Cave Tours, full- or half-day tours of underdeveloped caves. Walls of Jerusalem National Park, 45 km SW, treks for experienced bushwalkers only (no day trippers). Devils Gullet, 40 km SE, a natural lookout overlooking Fisher River Valley, in World Heritage area; reached by 30-min return walking track. Trowunna Wildlife Park, 4 km E. Spectacular Alum Cliffs Gorge, 3 km NE, 30 min return. **Visitor information:** Mole Creek Guest House, Pioneer Dr.; (03) 6363 1399. Web site www.deloraine.tasonline.org/tourism/molecrk.htm

Angler's Paradise

Fish are biting all year round in Tasmania, which is why it is an angler's paradise by any standards. Tasmania is famous for three species of fish: trout in fresh water, bream in the estuaries, and tuna on the east coast.

One area alone contains hundreds of lakes and lagoons stocked with trout of world-class size; this is the undeveloped region of the Central Plateau known as the Western Lakes. There is, however, a huge range of more accessible areas brimming with trout in the central highlands region, reputed to offer some of the best trout fishing in Australia. Top spots include Great Lake, Bronte Lagoon and Arthurs Lake. Lowland waterways, such as Brumbys Creek and Macquarie River, also offer good sport.

Tasmania is well known world-wide for its 'sighted' fishing, that is fly-fishing to individual fish. Early in the season in particular, when lake levels are high, brown trout move into shallow water in the weedy lake margins, providing exciting fly-fishing at close range. In summer, it is possible for the angler wearing polarised glasses to spot individual fish in bright light conditions and present flies to them.

Around March, game fish begin to move down the mild east coast and anglers start hauling in the big ones: bluefin tuna, yellowfin tuna and marlin. Then, as the bluefin leave in the midwinter months, large schools of Australian salmon return to the estuaries and along the shoreline.

In spring, one of the great sport fish of Tasmania, the tasty black bream, arrives in the river estuaries. Anglers regard this as one of the best fighting fish of its size.

January and February are peak months for inland trout fishing, and from February to March schools of Australian salmon swim close to the

Trout fishing in the central highlands

shoreline of Tasmania's many river estuaries, providing exciting fishing for the angler from the beach or rocks. Flathead are plentiful, and provide good summer sport across the island.

For further information on licence requirements, fees, bag limits, seasons and regulations for freshwater fishing, contact the Inland Fisheries Commission, 6B Lampten Ave, Derwent Park 7009; (03) 6233 4140. For more information on sea-fishing, contact the Department of Primary Industries and Fisheries, Marine Resources Division, 1 Franklin Wharf, Hobart 7000; (03) 6233 7042. Web site www.dpif.tas.gov.au

New Norfolk   Pop. 5286

MAP REF. 578 F4, 583 K8

Colonial buildings among English trees and oast houses in hop fields give this National Trust-classified historic town a look that has often been compared to that of Kent in England. Located on the River Derwent, 33 km NW of Hobart, the town was called New Norfolk because European settlers from the abandoned Norfolk Island settlement were granted land here. Although the district produces most of the hops used by Australian breweries, the chief industry today is paper manufacture. **In town:** River walk from Esplanade to Tynwald Park Wetlands Conservation Area. At Historical Centre in Council Chambers, Circle St: genealogical and other records; also self-guide historic walk leaflets. Scenic lookouts: Peppermint Hill, off Blair St; Pulpit Rock and Four Winds Display Gardens, off Rocks Rd. Old Colony Inn (1835), Montague St, now museum with large antique dolls' house and original kitchen. On Lyell Hwy: Oast House, Tynwald Park, with hop museum, Hop House Cafe, and art gallery; Bush Inn Hotel (1815), has one of the oldest licences in Commonwealth. Jet boat rides on Derwent River rapids leave from near Bush Inn Hotel. St Matthew's Church (1823), Bathurst St, reputedly oldest church in Tasmania; craft centre in adjoining close. Sat. market, Stephen St. Mar.: Hop Harvest Festival. Aug.: Winter Challenge (canoeing and cycling competition). Oct.: Spring in the Valley (including open gardens). **In the area:** Tours of Australian Newsprint Mill, 5 km E at Boyer; 24 hrs notice required. Salmon Ponds, 11 km NW at Plenty, first brown and rainbow trout in Southern Hemisphere bred here in 1864; restaurant, Museum of Trout Fishing. Meadowbank Vineyard, 20 km NW. Mt Field National Park, 40 km NW, features impressive Russell Falls. Trout fishing in Lake Peddar, 96 km NW. Tour of Gordon Power Station from Gordon Dam, 156 km NW, bookings essential; (03) 6280 1166. **Visitor information:** Oast House, Tynwald Park (Wed.–Sun.); (03) 6261 1030 or Council Offices, Circle St; (03) 6261 0700. **See also:** Day Tours from Hobart p. 546; Touring Tasmania p. 552; Stately Homes p. 572.

Oatlands   Pop. 539

MAP REF. 583 M5

This National Trust-classified historic town on the shores of Lake Dulverton, 84 km N of Hobart, attracts both anglers and lovers of history. It was designated as a garrison town by Governor Macquarie in 1821 and surveyed in 1832. Many of the town's unique sandstone buildings were constructed in the 1830s and most residents live in historic houses. **In town:** Convict-built courthouse (1829), Campbell St. St Peter's Church (c. 1838), William St, contains wide range of tapestries; viewing by arrangement with information centre. Callington Flour Mill (1836), Mill La. Lake Dulverton Wildlife Sanctuary, Esplanade. Historic self-guide walks around town and on lake foreshore; brochures available. Fielding's Ghost Tours. Feb.: Rodeo. **In the area:** Convict-built mud walls, 13 km S on Jericho Rd. Trout fishing in Lake Sorell, 29 km NW, and adjoining Lake Crescent. Guided garden tours in spring, brochures available, bookings essential; (03) 6230 8233. **Visitor information:** Central Tasmanian Tourism Centre, 77 High St; (03) 6254 1212. **See also:** Touring Tasmania p. 552.

Penguin   Pop. 3030

MAP REF. 580 A4, 584 H6

The Dial Range rises over this quiet town, named after the nearby colonies of little (fairy) penguins. **In town:** In Main St: St Stephen's Church and Uniting Church, both National Trust-classified; Percy Studio, glass engravers and artists; much-photographed Big Penguin. Hiscutt Park, off Crescent St, has Dutch windmill and tulips in season. Miniature Railway on foreshore, 2nd and 4th Sun. each month. Penguin colony on eastern outskirts, tours by appt (Sept.–Apr.). Penguin Roadside Gardens, on Old Coast Rd to Ulverstone, tended by community volunteers. Old School Market, King Edward St, 2nd and 4th Sun. each month. Mar.: Splash of Colour Festival. **In the area:** Mt Montgomery, 5 km S, magnificent view from summit. Mason's Fuchsia Fantasy, 20 km E on Lillico Rd, 1200 varieties; open Mon.–Fri. p.m. and Sat. Ferndene Gorge Nature Reserve, 6 km S, has scenic picnic spot and good walking tracks. Pioneer Park, 10 km SW at Riana, with gardens, walks and picnic facilities. Pindari Deer Farm, 15 km SW, has wildlife park, restaurant and accomodation; check opening times; (03) 6437 6171. Scenic drive south-east to Ulverstone via Coast Road. **Visitor information:** Main St; (03) 6437 1421. **See also:** Touring Tasmania p. 552.

Pontville   Pop. 1424

MAP REF. 578 H3, 583 L7

Much of the freestone used in Tasmania's old buildings was quarried near this National Trust-classified historic town. On the Midland Hwy, 27 km N of Hobart, Pontville was founded in 1830 and many early buildings remain. **In town:** Historic buildings on or adjacent to Midland Hwy include: St Mark's Church (1841); The Sheiling (built 1819, restored 1953), behind church; old post office; Crown Inn; and 'The Row', thought to have been built in 1824 as soldiers' quarters, now restored. **In the area:** Towns nearby with historic buildings: Bagdad, 8 km N; Kempton, 11 km further N; Broadmarsh, 10 km W; Tea Tree, 7 km E. Brighton, 3 km S, an important military post; Agricultural Show held Nov. Bonorong Park Wildlife Centre, 5 km S. **Visitor information:** Council Offices, Tivoli Rd, Gagebrook; (03) 6263 0333. **See also:** Touring Tasmania p. 552.

Port Arthur   Pop. 190

MAP REF. 579 N10, 583 N10

This historic settlement on the scenic Tasman Peninsula was one of Australia's most infamous penal settlements from the 1830s to the 1870s. Today it is still possible to sense the incredible hardship endured by the convict population. In 1996 Port Arthur was the site of a tragic massacre; a Huon pine cross and plaque on the waterfront commemorate the victims. **In town:** Port Arthur Historic Site: stabilised and restored ruins of the convict settlement, period houses, museum; self-guide and guided walks available; scenic flights. The Visitor Centre: interpretation gallery, giftshop, cafe, restaurant, ghost tour bookings. Dec.: Boxing Day Woodchop. **In the area:** Daily cruises on harbour and to Isle of the Dead (1100 convict, military and civil graves). Historic and nature walk to nearby Stewarts Bay, brochure available. Steam-train rides at Bush Mill Steam Railway and Settlement, 1km N. Coal Mines Historic Site, 30 km NW, Tasmania's first operational mine. Palmers Lookout, 3 km S, views of harbour and coastline. Remarkable Cave, 6 km S on coast in Tasman National Park. Sea-kayaking tours. **Visitor information:** The Visitor Centre, Historic Site, Arthur Hwy; (03) 6250 2539, freecall 1800 659 101. **See also:** Day Tours from Hobart p. 546; Peninsula Trail p. 548; Touring Tasmania p. 552; National Parks p. 554.

Port Sorell

Pop. 1818

MAP REF. 580 G5, 585 J6

Sheltered by hills, this holiday town on the Rubicon River estuary, 18 km E of Devonport, enjoys a mild climate. Named after Governor Sorell and established in 1822, it is the oldest township on the north-west coast. Unfortunately many of its oldest buildings were destroyed by bushfires early this century. **In town:** River and sea-fishing, swimming, boating and bushwalking. Views from Watch House Hill, off Meredith St, once site of old gaol, now a bowling green. Asbestos Range National Park across estuary, with numerous isolated beaches, sand dunes and grasslands covered in wildflowers. Jan.–Feb.: Latrobe–Port Sorell Summer Festival. **In the area:** Walking track from Port Sorell (beach end of Rice St) to Hawley Beach (6 km return); excellent views of Asbestos Range National Park and coastline. At Hawley Beach: safe swimming, good fishing; historic Hawley House (1878) offers meals and accommodation. **Visitor information:** Shop 1, 70 Gilbert St, Latrobe; (03) 6426 2693. **See also:** National Parks p. 554.

Queenstown

Pop. 2631

MAP REF. 582 E3, 584 E12

The discovery of gold and mineral resources in the Mt Lyell field in the 1880s led to the almost overnight emergence of Queenstown, a town carved out of the mountains that tower starkly around it. Mining was continuous in Queenstown from 1893 to 1994, and the field produced more than 670 000 tonnes of copper, 510 000 kg of silver and 20 000 kg of gold. Copper Mines of Tasmania resumed mining for copper, silver and gold at the end of 1995; tours of the mine are available. The

The Gourmet Island

Mount Roland Cheese

Tasmania has a growing reputation for fresh produce and wine, and there is a wide variety of gourmet options for the traveller. For an overview of gourmet Tasmania, visit the Taste of Tasmania festival in Hobart, held at Princes Wharf each Dec.–Jan. The best of the island's produce is on show, from specialty cheeses and chargrilled seafood to delicious relishes, smoked quail, pink-eye potatoes, leatherwood honey, apple drinks, ginger beer and regional wines.

Try to be in Hobart on a Saturday to explore the famous Salamanca Market, where you will find some of Tasmania's most innovative food producers. The Wursthaus Kitchen, in Montpellier Retreat just off Salamanca Place, is open daily and offers a wonderful range of Tasmanian delicatessen products.

Cascade Premium Lager, with its distinctive Tasmanian tiger label, has become a highly prized beer in recent years. Tours of the historic brewery in South Hobart are held on weekdays.

The Huon Valley is one of Tasmania's apple- and cherry-growing centres. During the summer months roadside stalls and pick-your-own orchards offer a variety of stone fruits to passing travellers. Fresh apricots are a particular favourite.

Central Tasmania is famous for its trout fishing; there are many lakes that provide anglers with the chance to catch fresh trout. For the less dedicated there are a number of outlets in Tasmania that sell smoked trout. Apart from trout, Atlantic salmon is also one of Tasmania's finest fish. A significant salmon-farming industry has developed on the south coast; salmon and salmon roe can be purchased across the State. Boat tours of the Huon River salmon farms leave daily from Port Huon.

Between Launceston and Hobart are a number of small food producers, including Butlers Butchery in Campbell Town, which specialises in large 'stag snags' (venison sausages).

An unusual place to sample Tasmanian beers is the Pub in the Paddock at Pyengana, near St Helens. It is precisely that: a hotel in the middle of a large empty paddock, where drinkers can share their Premium Lagers with the resident pig.

In the north of the island, travel the Tasmanian Wine Route from Launceston across the Tamar River to Bridport, returning via Lilydale. The highlight of this drive is the Pipers Brook wine region, noted for its good rieslings, chardonnays and pinot noirs. In less than three decades it has become the State's premier wine region, and is now responsible for half Tasmania's wine production. Most of the wineries in this region encourage cellar-door sales. Strathlynn, a wine centre and cafe at Rosevears on the west bank of the Tamar, is a pleasant lunch or tea stop. Lake Barrington Estate Vineyard, 10 kilometres west of Sheffield, is one of the most picturesque vineyards in the State.

West and south of Launceston is some of the finest dairy country in Australia. Visitors can taste and buy at Heidi Farm Cheese, near Westbury, and at Mount Roland Cheese in Latrobe. Lactos cheese-tasting and sales centre in Old Surrey Rd, Burnie, has a wide range of cheeses, including washed-rind and blue cheeses. At Railton, south-east of Burnie, visitors can taste and buy Belgian-style chocolates at Anvers Confectionery, which also has an outlet in Devonport.

Off the north-west coast is King Island, known for its crayfish, smoked meats, pure cream and double brie. Visitors can taste excellent cheeses at the King Island Dairy.

Vineyards and fresh food producers are dotted across Tasmania. Take a basket, and stop at roadside stalls and farms to buy the best food and wine that the island has to offer.

The West Coast

Strahan, a popular holiday town on Macquarie Harbour

The beautiful but inhospitable west coast, with its wild mountain ranges, lakes, rivers, eerie valleys and dense rainforests, is one of Tasmania's most fascinating regions. The majestic, untamed beauty of this coast is in complete contrast to the State's pretty pastures. The area's vast mineral wealth and colourful mining history is reflected in its towns. The discovery of tin and copper in 1871 and 1883 started a rush to the west coast, booming at the turn of the century. **Queenstown**, the largest town, as well as other main towns – **Zeehan** and **Strahan** – largely owe their existence to mining.

It was not until 1932 that a rough road was pushed through the mountainous country between Queenstown and Hobart. Fortunately, modern road-making techniques have improved the situation and today west coast towns are linked by the Murchison, Zeehan and Waratah highways, and the Lyell Highway (the original road to Hobart) has been brought up to modern standards. In fact, the flooding of Lake Burbury has resulted in the re-routing of the highway, which now takes motorists across the lake itself, enhancing the spectacular entry to Queenstown. Driving around the west coast road circuit and seeing the scenery and towns of the area is an unforgettable experience. The only drawback is that the area is subject to heavy rainfall, even in summer and autumn, as well as snow in winter.

The little township of Zeehan, north-west of Queenstown, typifies the changing fortunes of mining towns. Following the rich silver-lead ore discoveries in 1882, its population swelled to 10 000 and the town boasted 26 hotels and the Gaiety Theatre, with seating for over 10 000, where Dame Nellie Melba sang. Many of these fine buildings from the boom period can still be seen, including the Gaiety Theatre at the Grand Hotel. Zeehan's West Coast Pioneers' Memorial Museum, housed in the former School of Mines, is a popular tourist attraction.

One of the most spectacular views on any highway in Australia can be seen as you drive into Queenstown. As the narrow road winds down the steep slopes of Mt Owen, you can see the amazingly bare hills – tinged with pale pinks, purples, golds and greys – that surround the town. At the turn of the century, bushfires, combined with logging of trees to fuel copper smelters, denuded the hills. Pollution from the smelters prevented the vegetation from recovering and the high rainfall eroded the remaining topsoil, revealing the strangely hued rocks beneath. The copper smelters closed in 1969, and today the hills are slowly recovering.

The first European settlement on the west coast was established in 1821, when the most unruly convicts from Hobart were dispatched to establish a penitentiary on Sarah Island (Settlement Island) in Macquarie Harbour and to work the valuable Huon pine forests around the Gordon and King rivers. Sarah Island soon became a notorious prison and many of the unfortunate convicts who managed to escape died in the magnificent but unyielding surrounding bush. The horrors of that time are echoed in the name of the entrance to the harbour – Hells Gates. Today the port of Strahan on Macquarie Harbour has thousands of visitors each year, many attracted to the spectacular Gordon River, one of Tasmania's largest and most remote wild rivers. Cruise boats make regular trips to Heritage Landing, 12 kilometres upriver. On the return trip they stop along the way to allow visitors to see the old convict ruins on Sarah Island. Scenic flights departing from Strahan enable visitors to take in the beauty of more inaccessible areas. Another interesting trip from Strahan is to Ocean Beach, 6 kilometres from the town. This long, lonely stretch of beach, lashed by spectacular breakers, somehow typifies the beautiful wild west coast.

The magnificent scenic wilderness in Tasmania's remote south-west can be reached only by plane or boat. Flights leave Cambridge Airport near Hobart daily. Good fishing, hiking and sailing are offered in this incredibly rugged area of Tasmania; also, sightings of the rare and endangered orange-bellied parrot are becoming more frequent.

See also: individual entries in A–Z town listing for details on towns in bold type.

town has modern facilities, but its wide streets, remaining historic buildings and unique setting give it an old mining-town flavour. In certain lights, multi-coloured boulders on the bare hillsides surrounding the town reflect the sun's rays and turn to amazing shades of pink and gold. **In town:** Spion Kop Lookout, off Bowes St in town centre. Famous gravel football oval, Bachelor St. Penghana, former mine manager's residence (c. 1898), off Preston St. Guided tours of Mt Lyell Mine depart from information centre; surface tours by minibus (1 hr 15 min) and underground mine tours (3 hrs 30 min). Galley Museum, cnr Sticht and Driffield sts, displays history of west coast, photographs and memorabilia. Chairlift, from Penghana Rd to old silica and limestone quarries; magnificent views, particularly at sunset. Oct.: Robert Sticht Festival (celebration of history of Queenstown, triathlon, slag-shovelling, home-brew beer-tastings). **In the area:** Spectacular views from Lyell Hwy as it climbs steeply out of town. Original Iron Blow goldmine (1883), off Lyell Hwy at Gormanston, 6 km E. Ghost town of Linda, 9 km E. Mt Jukes Rd lookout, 7 km S; road leads past old mining settlement of Lynchford, and Crotty Dam. Lake Burbury, offers excellent brown and rainbow trout fishing. Lake Margaret, 12 km N. Lyell Tours, offers 4WD day or half-day tours south to Bird River rainforest area and Mt McCall. **Visitor information:** Mt Lyell Mine Tour Office, Driffield St; (03) 6471 2388 or Strahan Visitor Centre; (03) 6471 7622. **See also:** Touring Tasmania p. 552.

Richmond   Pop. 768

MAP REF. 579 J4, 583 M7

Richmond, 26 km from Hobart, is the most important historic town in Tasmania. The much-photographed Richmond Bridge is the oldest surviving freestone bridge in Australia (1823–25), and many of the town's buildings were constructed in the 1830s or earlier. The bridge and some of these structures were built by convicts under appalling conditions. Legend has it that the ghost of an overseer who was murdered by convicts still haunts the bridge. **In town:** Self-guide leaflet of town and area available. Old Richmond Gaol (1825), Bathurst St, one of Australia's best-preserved convict prisons; guided tours. St John's (1837), St John's Circle, oldest Catholic church in Australia still in use. St Luke's Church (1834–36), Torrens St, has fine timber ceiling. General store and former post office (1832), Bridge St, oldest

postal building in Australia. Also in Bridge St: galleries featuring local art and craft, including Saddler's Court (c. 1848) and Peppercorn Gallery (c. 1850); restored Bridge Inn, one of town's oldest buildings, housing complex of shops including courtyard Bakery Cafe; Richmond Arms Hotel (1888); Old Hobart Town, a model of Hobart in early 1800s; Toy Museum; The Maze; Village Store (1836), one of oldest general stores still operating in Tasmania. Prospect House (1830s), Georgian mansion, off Hobart Rd, supposedly haunted by ghost of Mrs Buscombe; offers meals and colonial accommodation. Feb.: Country Music Festival; St Andrews Pipe Band Competition. Oct.: Village Fair. **In the area:** Scenic drive north through Campania (8 km) and Colebrook (19 km). Stoney Vineyard, 6 km N, on Colebrook Rd. Crosswinds Vineyard, 10 km NW. **Visitor information:** Saddler's Court Gallery, 48 Bridge St; (03) 6260 2132. Web site www.richmondvillage.com.au **See also:** Day Tours from Hobart p. 546; Touring Tasmania p. 552; Stately Homes p. 572.

Ross   Pop. 275

MAP REF. 583 M3, 585 N12

One of the oldest and most beautiful bridges in Australia spans the Macquarie River at this National Trust-classified historic township. The bridge, completed 1836, was designed by colonial architect John Lee Archer and built by convicts. The convict stonemason Daniel Herbert received a free pardon (along with a second convict stonemason) in recognition of his 186 fine bridge carvings. Herbert's grave is in the old burial ground in Park St. Ross was established in 1812 as a military post for the protection of travellers who stopped there to change coaches. Today it is still an important stopping-place on the Midland Hwy between Launceston and Hobart and has a range of accommodation including self-contained colonial cottages. The district is famous for its superfine wool. **In town:** Self-guide and guided walks; brochures available. Off Bond St: Female Factory Historic Site, the most archaeologically intact female convict site in Australia; Overseer's Cottage has historical display and model of Female Factory, a prison workhouse 1847–54. In Church St: Heritage and Wool Museum at information centre, highlights area's links with wool industry; avenue of English elms complements historic sandstone buildings, including Scotch Thistle Inn

and Coach House, former coaching stop; old Ross General Store and Tea Room, now selling Tasmanian crafts and Devonshire teas; Uniting Church (1885), prominent on hill overlooking town; Orderly Rooms, original headquarters of 50th Ordinance Corps in early 1830s, moved two doors south in 1836 to present Memorial Library, Billiard and Recreation Room. In Bridge St, old barracks building, restored by local National Trust; street leads to Ross Bridge (floodlit at night). The four corners of the intersection of Church and Bridge sts at the centre of town are said to represent temptation (hotel), recreation (Town Hall), salvation (church) and damnation (gaol, now a residence). **In the area:** World-class fly-fishing for brown trout in Macquarie River. Some of the State's best trout-fishing lakes – Sorell, Crescent, Tooms and Leake – are within an hour's drive of town. **Visitor information:** Tasmanian Wool Centre, Church St; (03) 6381 5466. Web site www.taswoolcentre.com.au **See also:** Touring Tasmania p. 552.

St Helens   Pop. 1280

MAP REF. 585 Q8

This popular resort on the shores of Georges Bay is renowned for its crayfish and scalefish. Three fish-processing plants handle the catch of the fishing fleet based in its harbour. **In town:** St Helens History Rooms, Cecilia St: mining history, information for rainforest walks and 4WD tours; (03) 6376 1744. Bay beaches ideal for swimming, coastal beaches for surfing. Charter boats for deep-sea fishing and dinghy hire for bay fishing, Tasman Hwy. Excellent fishing for bream and trout on Scamander River. Many local restaurants specialise in fish dishes. Mar.: Tasmanian Game-Fishing Classic. June: Suncoast Jazz Festival. **In the area:** Bushwalks and tours (20 min to 5 hours) to view birdlife and wildflowers. Binalong Bay, 11 km NE, has good surf- and rock-fishing. Beaumaris, 12 km S, good beaches and lagoons. Scamander, holiday town 17 km S, offers sea and river fishing, good swimming, walks and drives in forest plantations south of town. 10 km W of Scamander, Trout Creek Reserve has fishing landing stage and picnic/barbecue facilities. At Pyengana, 28 km W: St Columba Falls; Healey's Cheese Factory; the 'Pub in the Paddock', hotel in middle of empty paddock. Several coastal reserves in Bay of Fires district offer camping and good beach fishing. **Visitor information:** St Helens Secretariat, 20 Cecilia St; (03) 6376 1329.

The Nut, Stanley

St Marys   Pop. 588

MAP REF. 585 Q10

The chief town of the Break O'Day Plains, St Marys is situated in the Eastern highlands at the head of the Fingal Valley. Access to the town is through picturesque passes or the valley. **In town:** Rivulet Park: platypus, Tasmanian native hens and picnic/barbecue facilities. Public golf course. **In the area:** Convict-built St Marys Pass (1842–5), 1.5 km N; Grey Mare's Trail to St Marys Waterfall at top, 10 min return. St Patricks ('Paddys') Head, 1.5 km E, named by Capt. Furneaux in 1773: challenging walk (1 hr 40 min return) to top for excellent coastal views. South Sister, 3 km NW, spectacular views of Fingal Valley from hilltop; more views to south through Elephant Pass, 4 km S, sole habitat of blind velvet worm. Small coastal township of Falmouth, 14 km NE, historic early settlement, with several convict-built structures, fine beaches, rocky headlands and good fishing. **Visitor information:** Library, 31 Main St (Mon., Wed., Fri.); (03) 6372 2114, and St Marys Coach House Restaurant, 34 Main St; (03) 6372 2529. **See also:** Touring Tasmania p. 552.

Scottsdale   Pop. 1922

MAP REF. 585 N7

Scottsdale, the major town in Tasmania's north-east, serves some of the richest agricultural and forestry country on the island. The town's main industries are food, specialising in the deep-freezing of locally grown potatoes, and timber. **In town:** Settlers Museum and Gift Shop, King St, which operated as a theatre 1924–72, has photos and an old tools collection. Materials Research Laboratory (MRL), George St, makes dried food; tours on request. June: Arts and Crafts Exhibition. Nov.: Agricultural Show. **In the area:** Cuckoo Falls at Tonganah, 8 km SE. Bridestowe Lavender Farm near Nabowla, 13 km W, for sales of lavender products; tours in flowering season, Dec.–Jan. Views of township and surrounding countryside from Sideling Lookout, 16 km W. Golconda, 20 km W, holds Tasmanian Circus Festival each Feb. South Springfield Forest Park, 20 km S. Mt Maurice Forest Reserve, 30 km S. **Visitor information:** Lyric Snack Bar, 27 King St; (03) 6352 3235.

Sheffield   Pop. 1016

MAP REF. 580 D9, 584 I8

Sheffield, 30 km S of Devonport, is located in the foothills of Mt Roland, in one of the most scenic areas of the State. The town's economy is based on farming. **In town:** 36 murals on various buildings depict area's history; video explanation of murals at Diversity, Main St. Kentish Museum, Main St, has exhibits on local history and hydro-electricity. Mural House, High St, unusual interior murals. Red Water Creek Steam and Heritage Society runs steam train 1st weekend of month (departs cnr Spring and Main sts) and daily around New Year. Claude Road Hall markets, 3rd weekend in Mar., June, Sept. and Dec. Feb.: Tasmazia Lavender Harvest Festival. Mar.: Steam Fest. May: Mt Roland Folk Festival. Sept.: Daffodil Festival. **In the area:** Lakes and dams of Mersey-Forth Power Development Scheme, 10 km W. Lake Barrington, part of the scheme, a major recreation area and international rowing venue, 14 km SW. At entrance to rowing venue is Tasmazia, world's largest maze complex: lavender farm, model village, Honey Boutique, restaurant and Pancake Parlour. Lake Barrington Estate Vineyard, 10 km W, for tastings and cellar-door sales. Devil's Gate Dam, 13 km NW, with semi-circular dam wall; spectacular scenery from viewing areas. Stoodley Forest Reserve, 7 km NE, between Sheffield and Railton; walking tracks and picnic/barbecue areas. Cradle Mountain–Lake St Clair National Park, 61 km SW for bushwalking, spectacular rainforest and mountain scenery, and flora and fauna. **Visitor information:** 5 Pioneer Cres.; (03) 6491 1036. **See also:** National Parks p. 554.

Smithton   Pop. 3313

MAP REF. 584 C4

This substantial township is the administrative centre of Circular Head, which is renowned for its unique blackwood swamp forests and was the first European settlement in the far north-west. Smithton serves the most productive dairying and vegetable-growing area in the State, and is also the centre of one of Tasmania's most significant forestry areas, with several large sawmills. Fishing is another major industry. **In town:** Lookout tower, Tier Hill, end of Massey St. Western Esplanade Community Park, centre of town overlooking the mouth of Duck River; fishing, walking and picnic spot. **In the area:** Forestry Tasmania reserves throughout the district offer a wide range of recreational activities. Duck River and Duck Bay, 2 km N, for fishing and boating. Lacrum Tasmanian Dairy Farm, 6 km W at Mella, has milking demonstrations during summer, afternoon teas, cheese-tastings and sales. Nearby, Wombat Tarn has picnic/barbecue area, lookout, bushwalks and playground. At Marrawah, 51 km SW, excellent surfing and wave-sailing; Rip Curl West Coast Classic each Feb.–Mar. Sumac Lookout, 4 km S on Sumac Rd, for views over Arthur River and surrounding eucalypt forest. Allendale Gardens, 13 km S at Edith Creek, offers rainforest walks and Devonshire teas. At Arthur River, 70 km SW, river cruises (Aug.–mid-June); nearby at Gardiner Point is The Edge of the World landmark. **Visitor information:** Council Offices, Goldie St; (03) 6452 1265.

Sorell   Pop. 3199

MAP REF. 579 K5, 583 M8

Named after Governor Sorell, this town is 23 km NE of Hobart. Founded in 1821, it played an important part in early colonial history by providing most of the grain for the State from 1816–60. It also supplied grain to the colony of NSW for more than 20 years. The area is still an important agricultural district, specialising in sheep-farming and forestry. **In town:** In Somerville St is the historic Blue Bell Inn. Pioneer Park, Parsonage Pl., has picnic/barbecue facilities. Orielton Lagoon, internationally significant bird sanctuary, on western shore of town. Market at Memorial Hall, Cole St, 2nd and 4th Sun. each month, Mon. if long weekend. Nov.: Bushranger Festival. **In the area:** Orani Vineyard, 3 km E. Bream Creek Vineyard, 22 km E. Sorell Fruit Farm, 2 km E, off Arthur Highway. Popular beach areas around Dodges Ferry and Carlton, 18 km S. **Visitor information:** Council Offices, 12 Somerville St; (03) 6265 2201. **See also:** Peninsula Trail p. 548.

Stanley   Pop. 543

MAP REF. 584 D3

This quaint village, steeped in history, nestles under an ancient outcrop called The Nut, which rises to 152 m sheer on three sides. Stanley was the site for the headquarters of the Van Diemen's Land (VDL) Company, set up in 1825 to establish a high quality merino wool industry. Its wharf then handled whalers and sailing ships; today these are replaced by a strong fleet of cray and other fishing boats, but little else has changed. The birthplace of Australia's only Tasmanian prime minister, the Hon. J. A. (Joe) Lyons, Stanley has been declared a historic town. **In town:** Historic buildings in wharf area: bluestone bond store, Wharf Rd; former VDL Co. store, in Marine Park, designed by colonial architect John Lee Archer, who lived in township. Archer's own home, now Poet's Cottage, Alexander Tce, at base of The Nut; not open to public. Also in Alexander Tce, Lyons Cottage, birthplace of J. A. Lyons. In Church St: still-licensed Union Hotel (1849), with cellars and narrow stairways; Commercial Hotel (1842), now private residence; Stanley Craft Centre with fine Tasmanian craft; Discovery Centre Folk Museum. Touchwood, quality craft and woodwork, in Main St. Chairlift, from Browns Rd to top of The Nut (152 m). Graves in burial ground on Browns Rd, dating from 1828, include those of John Lee Archer and explorer Henry Hellyer. Small colonies of little (fairy) penguins near wharf and cemetery, and on Scenic Dr. Nov.: Tasmania Day. Dec.: Agricultural Show. **In the area:** Highfield Historic Site (1835), headquarters of VDL Co., 2 km N on Scenic Dr.: homestead, chapel, schoolhouse, barn, stables, workers' cottages and remains of barracks nearby; two arched gates remain of former deer park. Dip Falls,

40 km SE off hwy, via Mawbanna; nearby, Big Tree (giant eucalypt) and picnic area. Pelletising plant of Savage River Mines, Port Latta, 20 km SE, where ore is moved by conveyor to jetty for loading onto bulk-ore ships. **Visitor information:** The Nut Chairlift, Browns Rd; (03) 6458 1286. **See also:** Touring Tasmania p. 552.

Strahan   Pop. 701

MAP REF. 582 D3, 584 D12

This pretty little port on Macquarie Harbour, on Tasmania's forbidding west coast, is best known as the departure point for cruises to the Franklin-Gordon Wild Rivers National Park. Originally a Huon pine timber-milling town, its growth was boosted by the copper boom at the Mt Lyell Mine. When the Strahan–Zeehan railway opened in 1892 it became a busy port. Today it is a popular holiday town with a variety of accommodation, including holiday units and cabins. It is also used as a base by crayfish, abalone and shark-fishing operators, but the harbour is limited by the formidable bar at Hells Gates, its mouth. **In town:** At Strahan Visitors Centre: excellent historical display of Tasmania's south-west, from Aboriginal times to present, including the fight to save the Franklin River; audio-visual slide show; nightly performance of 'The Ship That Never Was' in amphitheatre. Adjacent: Morrison's Mill, one of four remaining Huon pine saw-mills in Tasmania; woodturning, art and craft at Strahan Woodworks. Tuts Whittle Wonders, Reid St, features carvings from forest wood. Ormiston House, The Esplanade, one of Strahan's first houses, for morning or afternoon tea in luxurious setting. Excellent views of township and harbour from Water Tower Hill. Mineral and gemstone display, Innes St. Jan.: Mt Lyell Picnic. Mar.: Piners' Festival. **In the area:** Ocean Beach, 6 km W, Tasmania's longest beach (36 km), offers area for horseriding and beach fishing; also has short-tailed shearwater (muttonbird) rookeries (Oct.–Mar.). King River Forest Dr. passes through Teepookana Forest Reserve, 16 km SE, brochure available. At the reserve: Huon pines, walking tracks, historic iron bridge and 10-m viewing platform for bird's-eye view of forest. At Henty Dunes, 12 km N on Strahan–Zeehan Hwy, spectacular vast sand dunes, lagoon and picnic/barbecue areas. Contact information centre for details of and bookings for: cruises upstream along the Gordon River to Heritage Landing and Sarah Island (Settlement Island), and across Macquarie

Harbour to Hells Gates; guided tours of convict settlement ruins on Sarah Island; helicopter flights around Strahan; seaplane flights over Gordon River and Frenchmans Cap, landing at Sir John's Falls; jet boat rides; yacht charters overnight to Gordon River and evening or fishing cruises; hovercraft for joyrides and charter; 4WD tours, including fishing tour; Huon pine forestry tour; Henty Dunes tour; horse trail-rides; sea kayaks, canoes, motorbikes and bicycles for hire. **Visitor information:** The Esplanade; (03) 6471 7622. **See also:** Touring Tasmania p. 552; The West Coast p. 568.

Swansea   Pop. 495

MAP REF. 583 P4, 585 P13

Swansea is a small town of historic interest on scenic Great Oyster Bay, in the centre of Tasmania's east coast. **In town:** Self-guide leaflet on town and area available. Original council chambers (c. 1860), Noyes St, still in use. At information centre: The Swansea Bark Mill and Yesteryear Museum (c. 1885); restored wattlebark mill machinery; Wine and Wool Centre, outlet for Tasmanian wines; tearooms. In Franklin St: Morris' General Store (1838), run by Morris family for over 100 years; Community Centre (c. 1860), has museum with unusually large slate billiard table made for 1880 World Exhibition. Many colonial accommodation places (some self-contained cottages, some B&B) in and around town. Waterloo Point, at edge of golf course near town centre, has 1-km walking track for short-tailed shearwater (muttonbird) viewing at dusk, Aboriginal middens and views across bay to Freycinet Peninsula. Coswell Beach, 1 km S along coast from Waterloo Point, for little (fairy) penguin viewing at dusk. **In the area:** Guided garden tours in spring, bookings essential; (03) 6230 8233. Kate's Berry Farm, 2 km S: fresh berries, ice-cream and fruit wines. Splendid views from Duncombes Lookout, 3 km S. Spikey Beach, 7 km S, with picnic area and excellent rock-fishing. Kabuki, Japanese restaurant on clifftop, 12 km S. Mayfield Beach, 14 km S, for safe swimming, fishing and walking (track from camping area to Three Arch Bridge). Meetus and Lost falls, 50 km NW. At Cranbrook, 15 km N: Craft Fair, 1st Sun. in Dec.; Springvale, Coombend, Freycinet and Craigie Knowe vineyards for cellar-door sales (weekends and holidays). **Visitor information:** The Swansea Bark Mill, 96 Tasman Hwy; (03) 6257 8382. **See also:** Touring Tasmania p. 552.

Triabunna
Pop. 766

MAP REF. 579 O1, 583 O6

When Maria Island was a penal settlement, Triabunna, 86 km NE of Hobart, was a garrison town and whaling base. Today it is a centre for the scallop and abalone industries, with a major export wood-chipping mill just south of the town. **In town:** On Esplanade: Tasmanian Seafarers' Memorial, commemorating all seafarers lost in Tasmanian waters; Bicentennial Park, with picnic/barbecue areas; National Trust-run Pioneer Park, featuring machinery exhibits. Girraween Gardens and Tearooms, Henry St. **In the area:** Daily ferry from Eastcoaster Resort at Louisville Point, 7 km S, to Maria Island. On Maria Island: Painted Cliffs, extensive fossil deposits. Historic penal settlement of Darlington in Maria Island National Park; buildings include Coffee Palace (1888), housing old photographs and newspapers, mess room (1845) and chapel (1847); dormitory-style accommodation and camping; walking trails across island (good map essential, check weather conditions, no food available on island). At Orford, 7 km SW of Triabunna, walk along Old Convict Rd following Prosser River. Thumbs Lookout, 9 km SW, overlooks Maria Island. Local beaches for swimming, water-skiing and fishing. **Visitor information:** cnr Charles St and Esplanade West; (03) 6257 4090. **See also:** Touring Tasmania p. 552; National Parks p. 554.

Ulverstone
Pop. 9792

MAP REF. 580 B5, 584 H6

Situated 19 km W of Devonport, near the mouth of the Leven River, Ulverstone is a well-equipped tourist centre that was established as a town in 1852. Dairying, furniture-making and poultry- and vegetable-farming are the main industries of the area. **In town:** Shrine of Remembrance Clock Tower (1953), Reibey St. History Museum, Main St. On Beach Rd: Riverside Anzac Park, with playground and picnic/barbecue areas; Fairway Park, a wildfowl reserve, with giant water slide. Footpath, inscribed with excerpts of 75-year history of Royal Australian Navy, leads from town centre to HMAS *Shropshire* Naval Memorial Park in Dial St. Numerous antique and art and craft shops. Legion Park, on Esplanade in West Ulverstone, has magnificent coastal position. Boer War Memorial in Tobruk Park, Hobbs Pde; Queens Gardens in Kings Pde. Weeda Copper, Eastland Dr., for handmade local copperware. Lookout at eastern end of Upper Maud St. Apex House Market, Grove St, 1st and 3rd Sun. each month. Feb.: Twilight Rodeo. Aug.: Doll, Toy and Miniature Fair. Oct.: Show; North-West Woodcraft Guild Exhibition. Dec.: Christmas Mardi Gras. **In the area:** Extensive beaches east and west of town, safe swimming for children. Good beach, river and estuary fishing. Miniature railway, 2 km E; check opening times. At Leith, 12 km E, little (fairy) penguins at

Stately Homes

One of Tasmania's attractions is its wealth of beautiful stately homes with a distinctly English air. You can dine in style in some, such as **Prospect House** in the historic town of Richmond, and stay in others.

Several mansions, including **Malahide** and **Killymoon**, both on the Esk Highway near Fingal, are privately owned and cannot be inspected, but many are open daily to the public.

Clarendon, via Evandale, 27 kilometres from Launceston, is probably Australia's grandest Georgian mansion. Completed in 1838 for woolgrower James Cox and given to the National Trust in 1962, it has been meticulously restored.

Four other stately homesteads within reach of Launceston are Franklin House, 6 kilometres south; Entally House at Hadspen, 18 kilometres south-west; and Brickendon and Woolmers Estate, both at Longford, 22 kilometres south.

Franklin House, an elegant Georgian mansion now owned by the National Trust, was built in 1838 for Mr Britton Jones, a Launceston brewer and innkeeper. In 1842 it became the W.K. Hawkes School for Boys.

Charming **Entally House**, the most historic of the Trust houses, was built in 1819. Set in superb grounds, Entally has a greenhouse, chapel and coach-house. It was opened to the public in 1950.

Two-storeyed, shuttered **Brickendon**, built in 1824 by William Archer, is still owned by his descendants. The architecture looks French, but stretches of hawthorn hedge and old chestnuts, oaks, ash and junipers make it seem part of an English landscape.

Woolmers Estate was built by Thomas Archer in 1816. Described as a 'time capsule of Australian colonial history', it is open daily.

The Grove in George Town, north of Launceston, is privately owned and open to visitors. Built in the 1820s, it has been restored by the owners, who serve lunch and teas in period costume.

Home Hill in Middle Road, Devonport, once the home of former Prime Minister Joseph Lyons and Dame Enid Lyons, was built by them in 1916.

Runnymede, one of several National Trust properties

Now open to the public, the house and grounds are owned by the City of Devonport. The contents of the house are owned by the National Trust.

Hobart has two houses open for inspection: Runnymede in New Town and Narryna in Battery Point. Graceful **Runnymede**, built c. 1836, has been restored by the National Trust. **Narryna**, a Georgian sandstone and brick townhouse with a walled courtyard, is set in a shady old-world garden. Also known as the Van Diemen's Land Memorial Folk Museum, it houses a significant collection of colonial artifacts and is owned and operated by the State government.

The misleadingly named **Old Colony Inn** (1835) in New Norfolk was never used as an inn. It serves light lunches and Devonshire teas. Three rooms are set aside for antique objects. This beautiful old building, set in delightful grounds, is one of Tasmania's most photographed attractions.

For further information on National Trust properties, contact the National Trust of Australia (Tasmania), PO Box 711, Launceston 7250; (03) 6344 6233. Web site www.austnattrust.com.au

dusk. Goat Island Sanctuary, 5 km W; walking access to island at low tide only. At Gunns Plains, 24 km SW: Gallery 321, Raymond Rd, for art, craft, light refreshments. Near Gunns Plains: Gunns Plains Hop Farm, basket-weaving workshop in Mar.; limestone caves featuring underground river and glow-worms (guided tours). Scenic views at Preston Falls, 19 km S. Castra Falls, 30 km S. Walking tracks to viewing platform with spectacular views at Leven Canyon, 41 km S; beyond, south-west of South Nietta, Winterbrook Walk and Falls in rainforest. **Visitor information:** Car Park La., (behind post office); (03) 6425 2839. **See also:** Touring Tasmania p. 552.

Waratah
Pop. 230

MAP REF. 584 E8

This picturesque little settlement, set in mountain heathland 100 km N of Queenstown, was the site of the first mining boom in Tasmania. In 1900 it had a population of 2000 and Mount Bischoff was the richest tin mine in the world. The deposits were discovered in 1871 by James 'Philosopher' Smith, a colourful local character, and the mine closed in 1947, with dividends totalling 200 pounds for every one pound of original investment. **In town:** Self-drive tour of town, brochure available. In Smith St: Waratah Waterfall in heart of town; Waratah Museum and Gift Shop, for early photographs and artifacts; adjacent, Philosopher Smith's Hut, replica of miner's hut; Atheneum Hall (c. 1887), has portrait of Smith; St James' Anglican Church (1880), first church in Tasmania to be lit by hydropower. Near Lake Waratah, Rhododendron Garden offers picnic/barbecue areas and camping. Feb.: Axemen's Carnival. **In the area:** Walks and drive to old mining sites, brochure available. Trout fishing in rivers and lakes. At the fascinating former goldmining town of Corinna, 66 km SW, cruises on Pieman River, bookings essential; (03) 6446 1170. **Visitor information:** Fossey River Information Bay, 8 km S on Murchison Hwy; or Council Offices, Smith St; (03) 6439 1231. **See also:** The West Coast p. 572.

Westbury
Pop. 1280

MAP REF. 581 K11, 585 K9

A village green, said to be unique in Australia, gives this town a decidedly English air. Situated on the Bass Hwy, 35 km SW of Launceston, Westbury was surveyed in 1823 and laid out in 1828; it has several fine old colonial buildings. **In town:** Self-guide leaflet on town and area available. On the Village Green, King St: White House (c. 1841), comprising extensive colonial museum (featuring superb antique dolls' house), house, bakery, coach-house, courtyard and stable complex (open Tues.–Sun., Sept.–June); former police barracks (c. 1832), now an RSL Club; St Andrews Church; antique shop and colonial accommodation. On Bass Hwy: Hedge maze, open Oct.–June; Pearn's Steam World, a large collection of working steam traction engines. Tractor Shed, Veterans Row, a museum of old tractors and farm machinery; also scale-model tractor exhibition. Culzean in William St, .5 km N, an open garden Sept.–May. Market, 2nd Sun. each month at St Andrews Church. Mar.: St Patrick's Day Festival. Nov.: Steam Spectacular. **In the area:** At Hagley, 5 km E, St Mary's Anglican Church, fine east window donated by Lady Dry, wife of Sir Richard Dry, first Tasmanian-born premier. Heidi Farm Cheese, 7 km W, tastings and sales. Trout fishing at Brushy Lagoon, 15 km NW, and Four Springs Creek, 15 km NE. **Visitor information:** Clarke's Antiques and Gingerbread Cottages, 52 William St; (03) 6393 1140.

Wynyard
Pop. 4509

MAP REF. 584 F5

This small centre at the mouth of the Inglis River, west of Burnie, has become a well-developed tourist centre, offering a range of accommodation and easy access to many attractions and activities. There are daily flights between nearby Burnie–Wynyard airport, King Island and Melbourne. The Waratah–Wynyard region is a prosperous dairying and mixed-farming district and the town has a large, modern dairy factory. **In town:** Gutteridge Gardens, riverside gardens in heart of town. Tasmanian Tiger (Thylacine) interpretive sculpture, at information centre. Table Cape Tulip Farm, open in season. Oct.: Tulip Festival. **In the area:** Scenic walks and drives in Wynyard and surrounding districts, brochures available; network of nature walks, including boardwalk along Inglis River. Scenic flights over coast and wilderness. Excellent sea-fishing and fly-fishing for trout. Oldest marsupial fossil in Australia found at Fossil Bluff, 3 km N; displayed at the Tasmanian Museum and Art Gallery in Hobart. Table Cape Lookout, 5 km N, for coastal and inland views.

Renowned Lapoinya Rhododendron Gardens, 20 km W, Australia's largest collection of rhododendrons and exotic shrubs, in bushland setting. **Visitor information:** cnr Hogg and Goldie sts; (03) 6442 4143. **See also:** Touring Tasmania p. 552; National Parks p. 554.

Zeehan
Pop. 1116

MAP REF. 582 D1, 584 D11

Named after one of Abel Tasman's ships, this former mining town, 36 km NW of Queenstown, is now a National Trust-classified historic town. Silver-lead deposits were discovered here in 1882. By 1901, Zeehan had 26 hotels and a population of 11 000, making it Tasmania's third largest town. Just 7 years later mining began to decline and Zeehan became almost a ghost town. In the boom period between 1893 and 1908, 8 million dollars' worth of ore had been recovered. Now the town is again on an upward swing with the reopening of the Renison Bell tin mine. **In town:** Self-guide scenic drives in town and surrounding area, brochures available. Many 'boom' buildings in Main St, including Gaiety Theatre at Grand Hotel; ANZ Bank; St Luke's Church; post office and courthouse. Four old miners' cottages in Main St available as accommodation. West Coast Pioneers' Memorial Museum, in School of Mines building (1894), Main St, has mineral, historical, geological and biological collections. Beside museum, display of steam locomotives and rail carriages used on west coast. Frank Long Memorial Park, Dodd St; Long discovered silver-lead deposit here. Pioneer cemetery, on southern outskirts of town. **In the area:** Old mine workings at Dundas, 13 km E. Montezuma Falls, highest waterfall in State, 17 km NE; accessible by 4WD or walking track. Surface tours of zinc mine, 22 km NE at Rosebery. Picturesque lake near Tullah, further 12 km NE. Nearby, historical Wee Georgie Wood Railway; check operating times. Corinna, 48 km NW, once a bustling goldmining town, now a base for gold-panning, trout fishing, bushwalking; *Fatman* car ferry crosses Pieman River to link the Western Explorer road. Fishing and boating on Lake Pieman, 50 km NW. Trial Harbour, 20 km W, popular fishing area. Unsealed roads to both areas often in poor condition; check before departure. Trout fishing on Henty River, 25 km S. **Visitor information:** West Coast Pioneers' Memorial Museum, Main St; (03) 6471 6225. **See also:** The West Coast p. 568.

Tasmania

LOCATION MAP

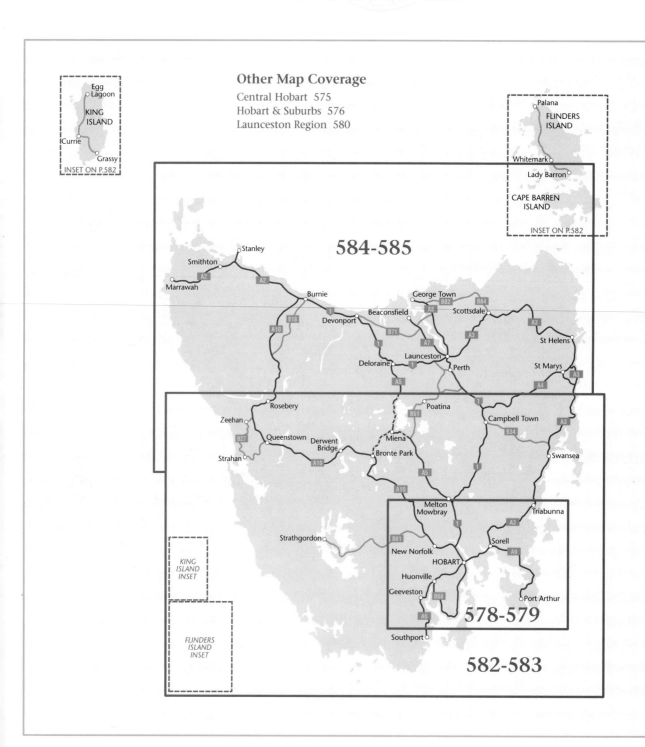

Egg Lagoon
KING ISLAND
Currie
Grassy
INSET ON P.582

Other Map Coverage
Central Hobart 575
Hobart & Suburbs 576
Launceston Region 580

Palana
FLINDERS ISLAND
Whitemark
Lady Barron
CAPE BARREN ISLAND
INSET ON P.582

584-585

Stanley
Smithton
Marrawah
A2
A2
Burnie
George Town
B52
B84
Devonport
Beaconsfield
A9
Scottsdale
B18
B71
A3
A3
A10
1
Deloraine
Launceston
St Helens
A7
Perth
St Marys
A5
A4
A3
Rosebery
Poatina
Zeehan
B51
Campbell Town
Queenstown
Derwent Bridge
Miena
B34
A3
B27
Bronte Park
Swansea
Strahan
A10
A5
1
A10
Melton Mowbray
Triabunna
Strathgordon
B61
1
A3
New Norfolk
Sorell
HOBART
A9
Huonville
Geeveston
B68
Port Arthur
A6
578-579
Southport
582-583

KING ISLAND INSET

FLINDERS ISLAND INSET

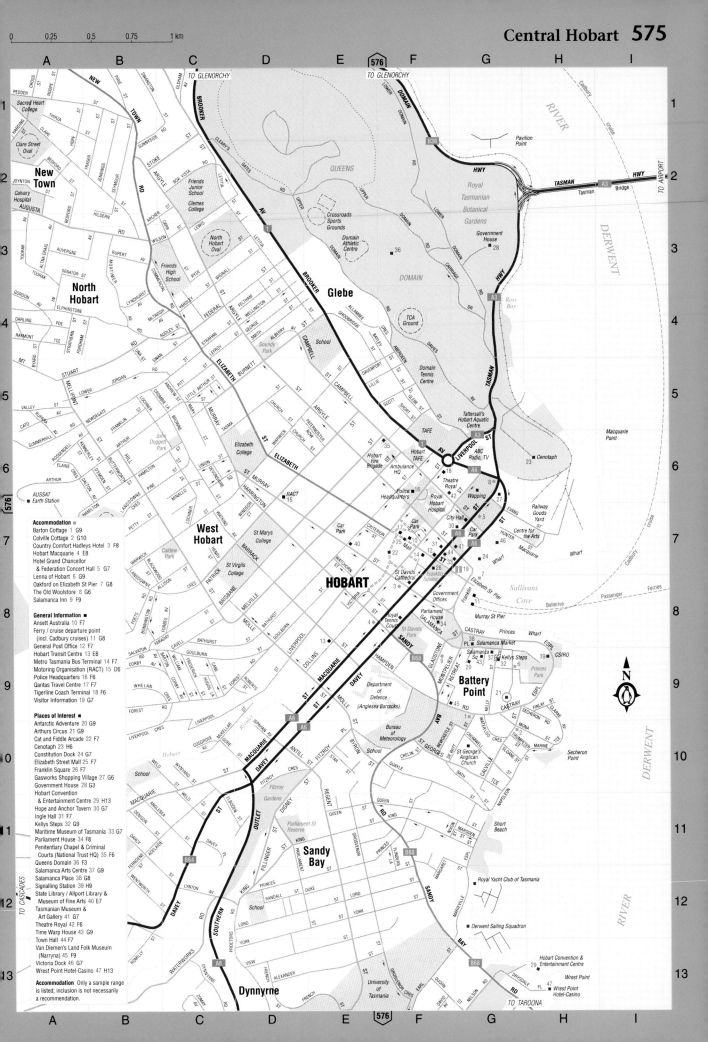

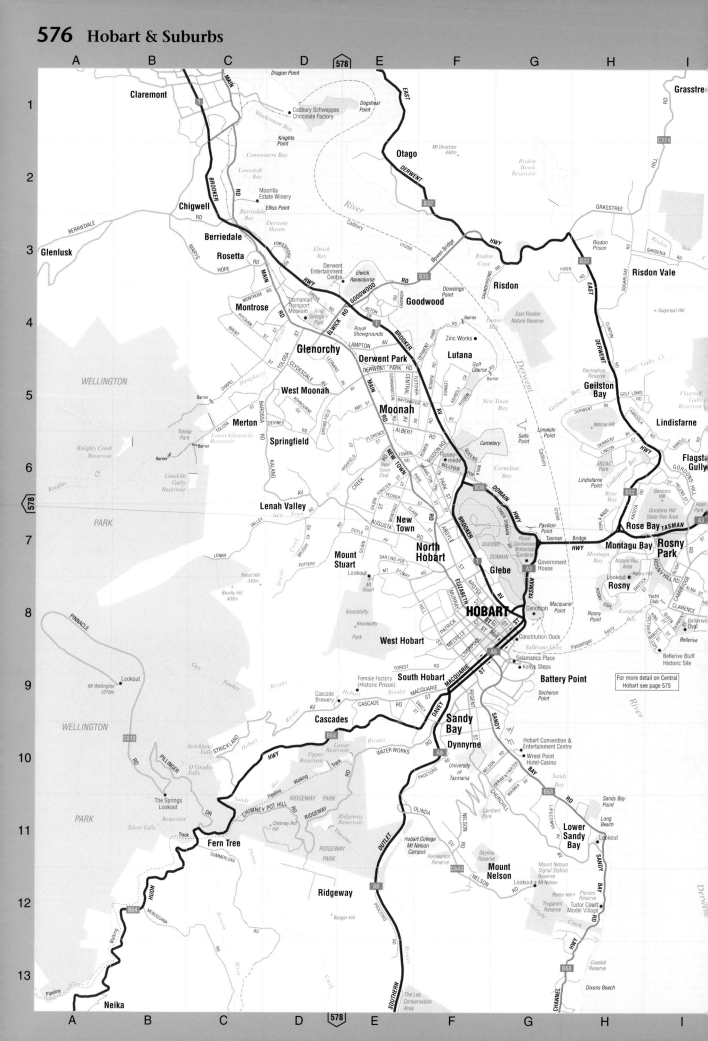

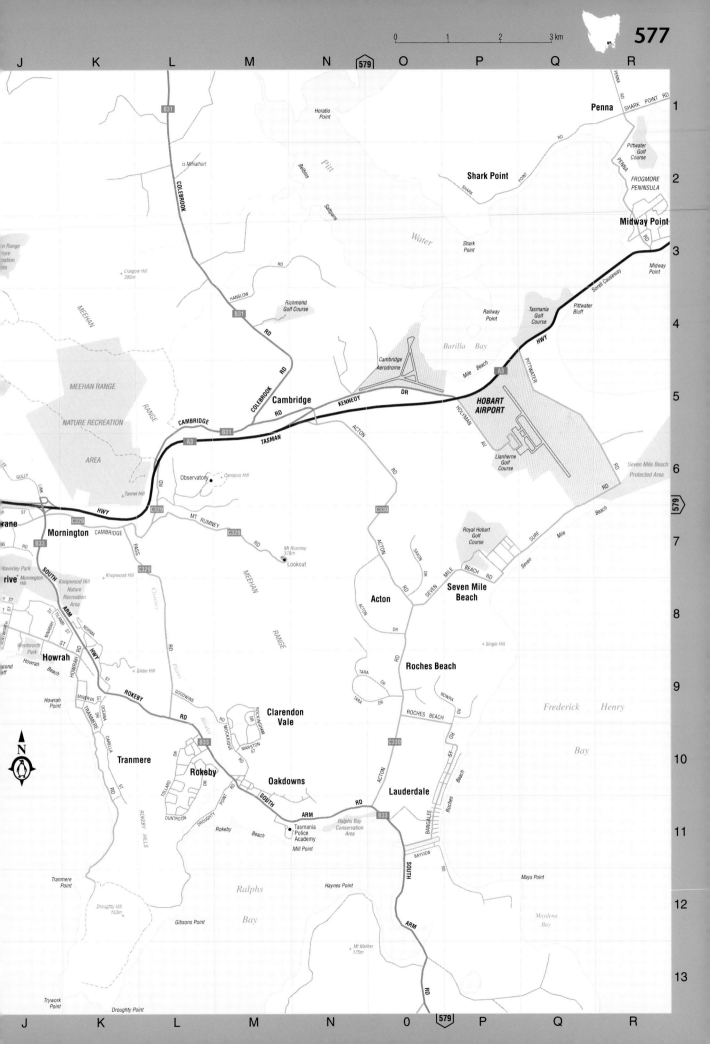

J K L M N 579 O P Q R

0 1 2 3 km

1

Penna

PENNA RD

SHARK POINT RD

□ Minalhort

COLEBROOK

Horatio Point

Pitt

Balbins

Saltpans

Pittwater
Golf
Course

Shark Point

FROGMORE
PENINSULA

2

PENNA RD

Midway Point

Water

SHARK POINT RD

Shark
Point

Midway
Point

3

Sorell Causeway

HWY

+ Craigow Hill
395m

RD

HANSLOW

B31

Richmond
Golf Course

RD

Railway
Point

Tasmania Golf
Course

Pittwater
Bluff

PITTWATER

4

Barilla Bay

Mile Beach

HWY

A3

MEEHAN

RD

COLEBROOK

Cambridge

KENNEDY

Cambridge
Aerodrome

DR

**HOBART
AIRPORT**

HOLYMAN

AV

Beach

5

MEEHAN RANGE

RANGE

CAMBRIDGE

RD

TASMAN

ACTON

Seven Mile Beach
Protected Area

6

NATURE RECREATION

n Range
ature
reation
ea

A3

Observatory ●

Canopus Hill

MT RUMNEY

ACTON

Llanherne
Golf Course

RD

579

AREA

RD

C329

Royal Hobart
Golf Course

SURF

Mile

Beach

7

GULLY

+ Tunnel Hills

C328

RD

RD

Mt Rumney
378m

ACTON

SAXON DR

SEVEN MILE

BEACH RD

Seven

LINK

HWY

Mornington

C329

CAMBRIDGE

PASS

Lookout ●

RANGE

Seven Mile
Beach

RD

ST

ane

Waverley Park

RD

B33

SOUTH

Knopwood Hill
Nature Recreation
Area

+ Knopwood Hill

C329

MEEHAN

ACTON

Acton

SEVEN

RD

8

rive

Mornington
Hill

ARM

HWY

Charence

RD

DR

+ Single Hill

ST

ST

Howrah
Beach

NORMA

Howrah

Plains

+ Glebe Hill

GOODWINS

DR

TARA

Roches Beach

NOWRA

Frederick   Henry

9

Wentworth
Park

HOWRAH RD

ST

ROKEBY

RD

ST

TARA DR

ROCHES BEACH

RD

Howrah
Point

MINERVA ST

RD

**Clarendon
Vale**

C330

ST

Bay

10

N

CARELLA

OCEANA DR

TRANMERE

Rivulet

ROCKINGHAM DR

MARSTON ST

MOCKRIDGE

POINT RD

Oakdowns

ACTON

Lauderdale

Roches Beach

Tranmere

RD

B33

SOUTH

RD

BANGALEE

11

ROKERY HILLS

TOLLARD DR

DUNTROON

Rokeby

Beach

ARM

Tasmania
Police
Academy ●

Mill Point

*Ralphs Bay
Conservation
Area*

B33

BAYVIEW

RD

Mays Point

Tranmere
Point

Droughty Hill
153m +

Gibsons Point

Ralphs

Haynes Point

SOUTH

RD

*Maydena
Bay*

12

Bay

+ Mt Mather
175m

ARM

13

Trywork
Point

Droughty Point

RD

J K L M N O 579 P Q R

TASMANIAN TRAIL: This 477-km trail is accessible to bushwalkers, horseriders and mountain-bike riders. Winding from Dover in the south to Devonport in the north, the trail passes through a variety of landscapes including farmlands, forests and highland plateaus.

MOUNT FIELD NATIONAL PARK

SOUTHWEST NATIONAL PARK

Part of World Heritage Area

HARTZ MOUNTAINS NATIONAL PARK

WELLINGTON RANGE

WELLINGTON PARK

NORTH BRUNY ISLAND

SOUTH BRUNY ISLAND

BRUNY ISLAND

TO QUEENSTOWN
TO LAUNCESTON
TO LAKE PEDDER
TO SOUTHPORT

Hamilton · Glen Clyde House · Ellendale · Fentonbury · Westerway · National Park · Tyenna · Fitzgerald · Maydena · Karanja · Glenora · Bushy Park · Macquarie Plains · Plenty · Hayes · Magra · New Norfolk · Gretna · Rosegarland · Uxbridge · Moogara · Feilton · Glenfern · Mount Lloyd · Lachlan · Lonnavale · Crabtree · Judbury · Lucaston · Ranelagh · Glen Huon · Huonville · Franklin · Castle Forbes Bay · Port Huon · Geeveston · Cairns Bay · Waterloo · Surges Bay · Glendevie · Police Point · Hideaway Bay · Surveyors Bay · Francistown · Raminea · Stramblane · Dover · Hastings · Hastings Caves · Thermal Springs Pool

Cradoc · Glaziers Bay · Wattle Grove · Cygnet · Petcheys Bay · Lymington · Garden Island Creek · Verona Sands · Gordon · Woodstock · Upper Woodstock

Pelham · Elderslie · Broadmarsh · Black Hills · Dromedary · Bridgewater · Granton · Boyer · Australian Newsprint Mill · Malbina · Molesworth · Berriedale · Claremont · Glenorchy · Moonah · North Hobart · HOBART · Battery Point · Sandy Bay · Fern Tree · Ridgeway · Neika · Longley · Leslie Vale · Grove · Sandfly · Kaoota · Allens Rivulet · Nierinna · Kingston · Kingston Beach · Blackmans Bay · Margate · Electrona · Snug · Coningham · Howden · Tinderbox

Kempton · Bagdad · Mangalore · Pontville · Brighton · Gagebrook · Old Beach · Otago · Risdor Vale

Oyster Cove · Kettering · Nicholls Rivulet · Woodbridge · Gardners Bay · Birchs Bay · Flowerpot · Middleton · Killora · Barnes Bay · Dennes Point · Alonnah · Lunawanna · Adventure Bay · Cookville

Mount Wellington
SOUTHWEST NATIONAL PARK

Part of World Heritage Area

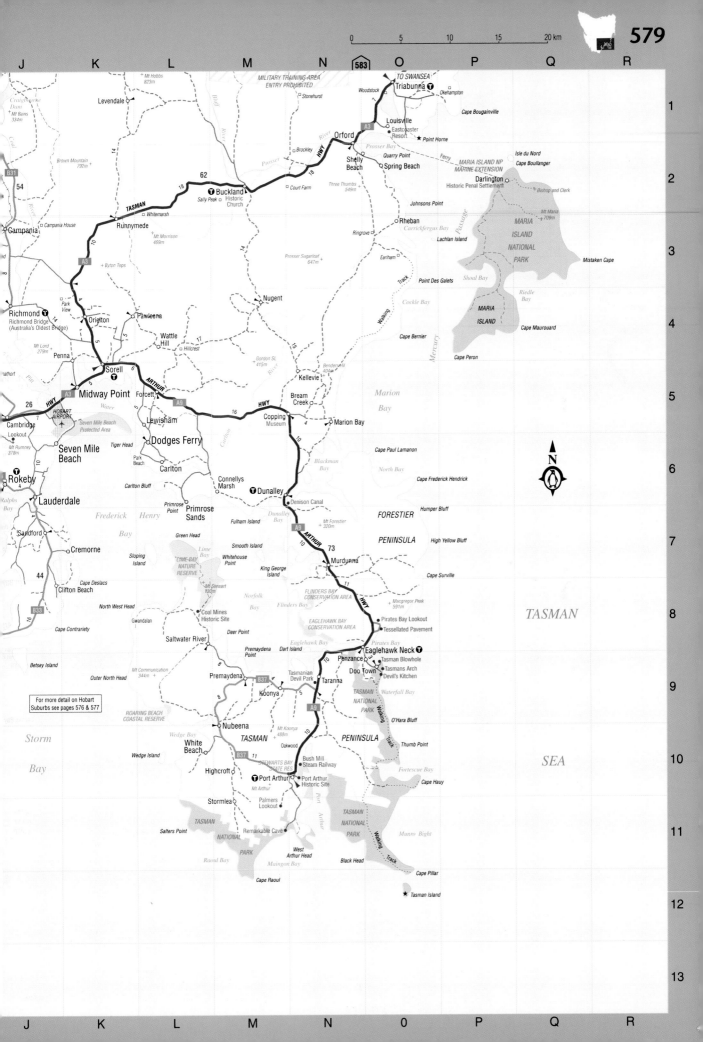

A B C D E F G H I

1 2 3 4 5 6 7 8 9 10 11 12 13

N (compass)

BASS *STRAIT*

SPIRIT OF TASMANIA: Ferries passengers and cars across Bass Strait between Melbourne and Devonport. This powerful sea voyager offers all the facilities of an ocean cruise-liner, accommodating passengers seeking luxury to the budget-conscious backpacker.

Spirit of Tasmania Ferry Devonport to Melbourne

ASBESTOS RANGE NATIONAL PARK: Lying between Greens Beach and Port Sorell, this scenic northern coastal park has numerous isolated beaches, sand dunes and grasslands covered in wildflowers. Mineral asbestos was mined nearby during the last century.

West Head

Badger Head

Sulphur Creek
TO BURNIE
Penguin
B17
Mt Montgomery
Ferndene
Leven
Ulverstone
Turners Beach
Leith
10
Braeside
Gawler
B15
North Motton
B17
Abbotsham
B16
C124
C145
Spalford
Kindred
B16
Melrose
C125
Sprent
Paloona
C145
Warringa
Preston
Central Castra
B14
Caves
Gunns Plains
Paloona Power Station
C132
Lower Barrington
C150
Upper Castra
B15
Lake Paloona
Barrington
Lower Wilmot
Nook
C133
Devils Gate Dam & Power Station
C143
Nietta
Wilmot
West Kentish
Sheffield
B14
C156
Narrawa
South Nietta
Lake Barrington
Roland
Stoodley
Sunnyside
Leven Canyon
Lake Barrington Nature Reserve
Tasmazia (Maze Complex)
Rowing
Winterbrook Falls Rainforest Walk
C132
Erriba
Staverton
C140
C136
Claude Road
Paradise
Beulah
Moina
Wilmot Power Station
Cethana Power Station
Gowrie Park
Mt Roland 1234m
Lower Beulah
Weegena
C137
Dunorlan
C132
GOG RANGE
Lorinna
C138
Liena
King Solomons Cave
B12
Mayberry
Mole Creek
Chudleigh
Daisy Dell
C139
Lemonthyme Power Station
Marakoopa Cave
MOLE CREEK KARST NATIONAL PARK
C171
CENTRAL PLATEAU CONSERVATION AREA
CRADLE MOUNTAIN- LAKE ST CLAIR NATIONAL PARK

Forth
B19
Don
Don River Railway Museum
Devonport
Quoiba
Spreyton
Eugenana
Tasmanian Trail Devonport to Dover
Searoad Terminal
DEVONPORT AIRPORT
Latrobe
BASS
Sassafras East
Sassafras
Robin Hood
B13
Railton
Mersey River
Merseylea
C150
STOODLEY FOREST RESERVE
Murals
B153
C160
Kimberley
Moltema
B13
Elizabeth Town
C159
C161
Trowunna Wildlife Park
B12
24
Needles
C168
Caveside
C169
Montana
C166
Mountleigh

Port Sorell
Hawley Beach
Shearwater
Point Sorell
Port Sorell
Bakers Beach
ASBESTOS RANGE NATIONAL PARK
Rubicon Estate
Northdown
Wesley Vale
B74
B71
Moriarty
Thirlstane
C704
Harford
C740
Squeaking Point
FRANKFORD
65
19
B871
Rosslyn
West Frankfort
HWY
BASS
51
22
Parkham
C711
C710
Reedy Marsh
Weetah
Wattle Bank
HWY
Lemana
Red Hills
Deloraine
LAKE
C163
C164
A5
Quamby Brook
C503
C504
Go Va
HWY
TO HOBART

584

584

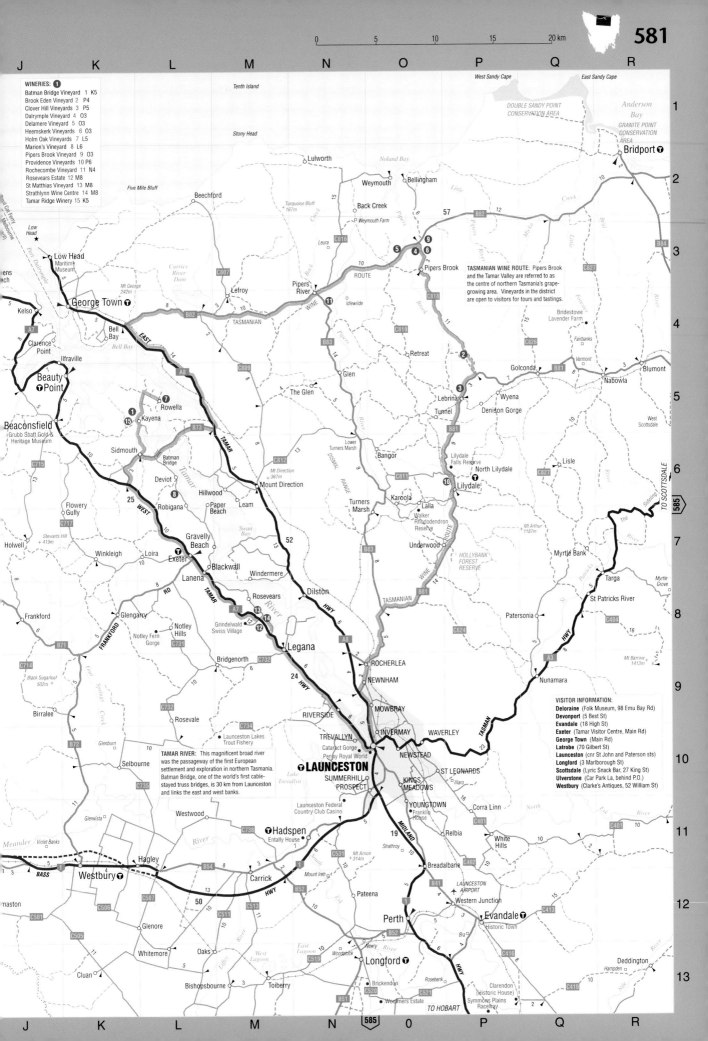

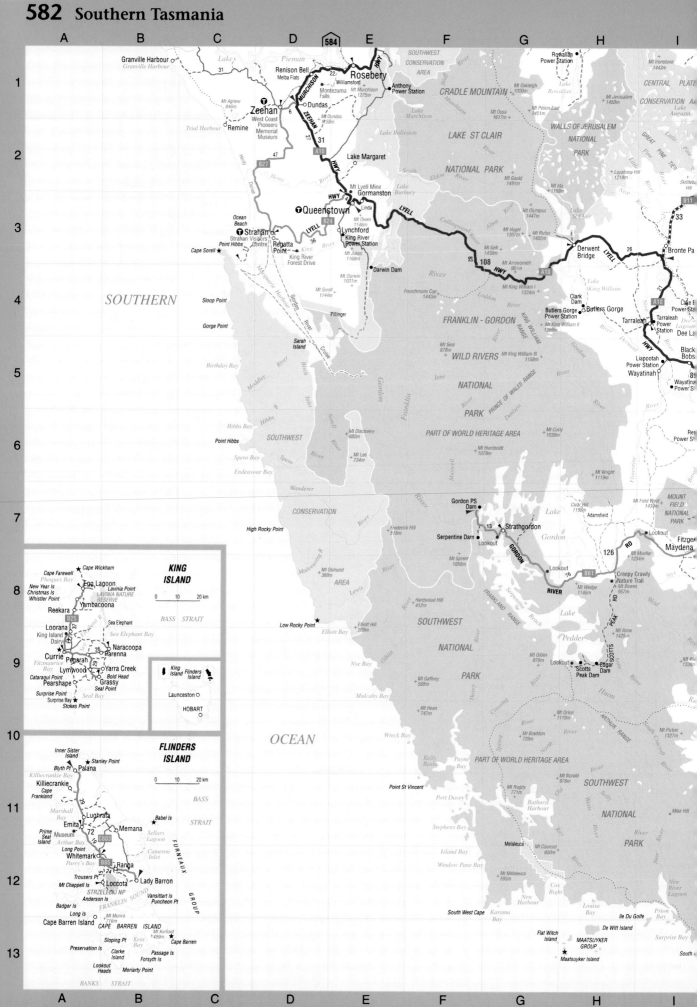

KING ISLAND

Cape Farewell
Cape Wickham
Phoques Bay
New Year Is
Christmas Is
Whistler Point
Egg Lagoon
Lavinia Point
LAVINIA NATURE
RESERVE
Yambacoona
Reekara
Loorana
King Island
Dairy
Currie
Pegarah
Lymwood
Cataraqui Point
Fitzmaurice
Bay
Pearshape
Surprise Point
Surprise Bay
Stokes Point
Naracoopa
Parenna
Yarra Creek
Bold Head
Grassy
Seal Point
Seal Bay

Sea Elephant
Sea Elephant Bay

BASS STRAIT

0   10   20 km

King
Island   Flinders
Island

Launceston

HOBART

FLINDERS
ISLAND

Inner Sister
Island
Stanley Point
Blyth Pt
Palana
Killiecrankie Bay
Killiecrankie
Cape
Frankland
Marshall
Bay
Lughrata
Emita
Museum
Prime
Seal
Island
Arthur Bay
Long Point
Whitemark
Parry's Bay
Trousers Pt
Mt Chappell Is
Loccota
Badger Is
Long Is
Mt Munro
216m
Cape Barren Island
Preservation Is
Sloping Pt
Clarke Is
Lookout
Heads
Moriarty Point
BANKS   STRAIT

Memana
Babel Is
Sellars
Lagoon
Cameron
Inlet
Ranga
Lady Barron
STRZELECKI NP
Vansittart Is
Puncheon Pt
FRANKLIN SOUND
FURNEAUX
GROUP
CAPE   BARREN   ISLAND
Mt Kerford
499m
Cape Barren
Kent
Bay
Passage Is
Forsyth Is

0   10   20 km

BASS

STRAIT

SOUTHERN

OCEAN

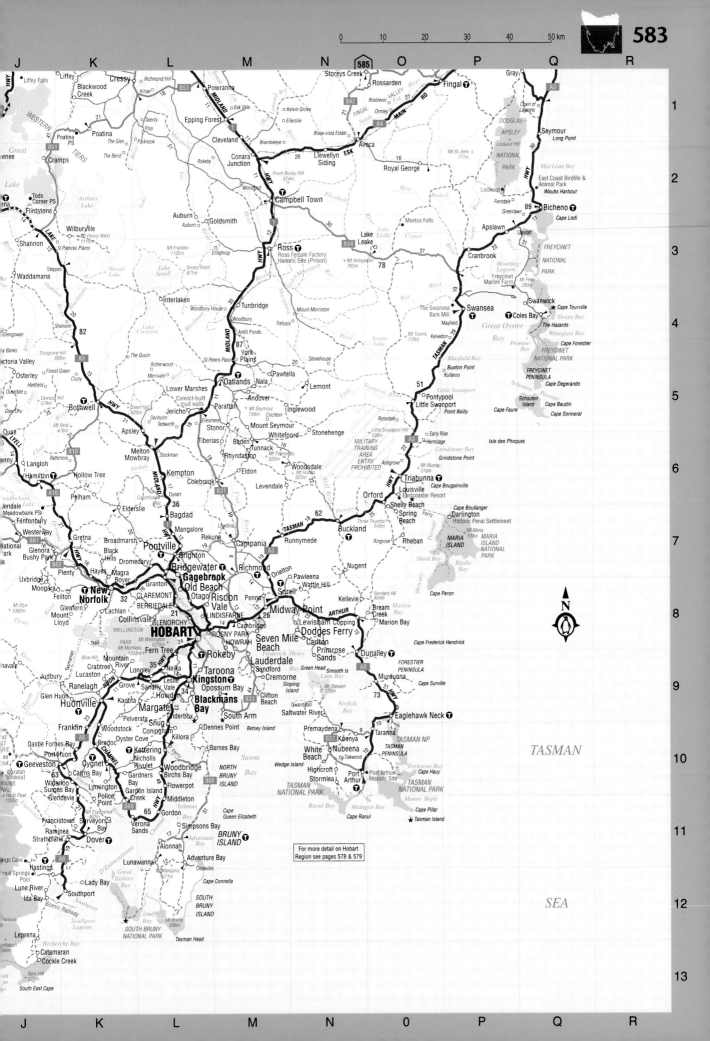

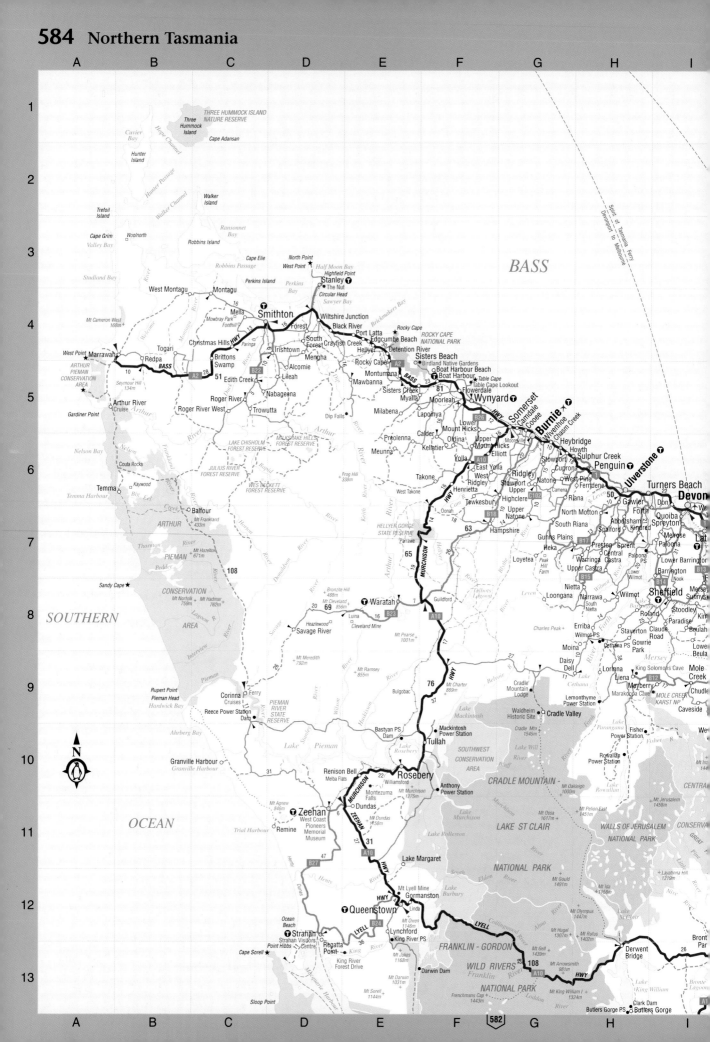

BASS

SOUTHERN

OCEAN

0 10 20 30 40 50 km

J K L M N O P Q R

STRAIT

FLINDERS ISLAND

Ranga B85
Loccota
Lady Barron

Trousers Pt
Mt Chappell Is
STRZELECKI NATIONAL PARK
Great Dog Is

Adelaide Bay

Anderson Is
Vansittart Is
Puncheon Pt

Badger Is
Long Is
FRANKLIN
SOUND

Cape Barren Island
+ Mt Munro 716m
CAPE BARREN ISLAND

Lesley Cove

Mt Kerford 499m
Kent Bay

Sloping Pt
Preservation Is

Clarke Island
Forsyth Is
Passage Is

Lookout Heads
Moriarty Point

BANKS STRAIT

Cape Portland
Vinegar Hill 52m
Swan Island
Lyme Regis

Waterhouse Island
Waterhouse Point
Petal Point
Cape Portland

Great Musselroe Bay

Ninth Island
Ringarooma Bay
Musselroe Bay
Cape Naturaliste

West Sandy Cape
Rushy Lagoon
River

Croppies Point
WATERHOUSE CONSERVATION AREA
East Sandy Cape
Icena

Mt William + 216m
MOUNT WILLIAM NATIONAL PARK

Anderson Bay
Waterhouse

Stony Head
Lulworth
Noland Bay
Bellingham
Bridport
26
Mt Cameron 551m
Gladstone B82
Eddystone Point
★ Eddystone Point

Five Mile Bluff
Low Head
Beechford
Weymouth
Back Creek
Waterhouse
37
Ansons Bay

West Head
Greens Beach
Low Head
Leura
George Town
Pipers River
Pipers Brook
B84
Forester
23
South Mount Cameron
B82
Ansons Bay

Badger Head
Kelso
Clarence Point
EAST TAMAR
Lefroy
Jetsonville
North Scottsdale
Winnaleah
Herrick
Moorina
99
Bay of Fires

Port Sorell
Bell Bay
Beauty Point
Rowella
Kayena
The Glen
Glen
Lebrina
Golconda
Scottsdale
Warrentinna
Telita
Kamona
Derby
Branxholm
TASMAN HWY
Weldborough
The Gardens

Beaconsfield
Sidmouth
Beaconsfield
Beviot
Robigana
Turners Marsh
North Lilydale
Nabowla
Lietinna
West Scottsdale
Tonganah
Talendeena
Legerwood
Lottah
Goulds Country

Sassafras East
Holwell
Flowery Gully
Winkleigh
Stewarts Hill 419m
Mount Direction
Turners
Lilydale
Lisle
Springfield
Cuckoo
Cuckoo Hill 732m
Ringarooma
Goshen
Priory
Mt Pearson 373m
Grants Point
Binalong Bay

Glengarry
Exeter
Lanena
Rosevears
Windermere
Beach
Dilston
Karoola
Lalla
Myrtle Bank
SOUTH SPRINGFIELD FOREST PARK
Mt Maurice + 1120m
Pyengana
26
St Helens Point
Akaroa
Stieglitz

Frankford
Notley Hills
Legana
ROCHERLEA
MOWBRAY
Patersonia
70
Targa
St Patricks River
Diddleum Plains
Talawa
Alberton
St Columba Falls
10
St Helens
Parkside
St Helens Island
Dianas Basin

Parkham
Birralee
Rosevale
Bridgenorth
RIVERSIDE
TREVALLYN
LAUNCESTON
Corra Linn
Nunamara
Mt Barrow 1413m
Tayene
Trenah
Mt Victoria 1208m
Mt Young 903m
Beaumaris

Reedy Marsh
Selbourne
Westwood
Hagley
Hadspen
White Hills
Breadalbane
Burns Creek
Musselboro
Upper Blessington
ROSES TIER
Roses Tier
16
Mt Saddleback
Upper Esk
Scamander

Elizabeth Town
Weetah
Deloraine
BASS HWY
Exton
Westbury
B54
Pateena
Perth
Relbia
Blessington
Carr Villa
Alpine Village
Ben Lomond 1572m
Mt Nicholas 869m
Cornwall
37
Falmouth

Red Hills
Osmaston
Whitemore
Glenore
Oaks
Longford
Evandale
English Town
BEN LOMOND NATIONAL PARK
Tower Hill
St Marys
Gray
Four Mile Creek
A3

Montana
Quamby Brook
Cluan
Bishopsbourne
Toiberry
Kilrae
Nile
Deddington
Hampden
Mangana
B42
Rossarden
Storeys Creek
15
Fingal
74
MAIN RD
TASMAN

Golden Valley
Jackeys Marsh
Cressy
Richmond Hill
B53
Powranna
Symmons Plains Raceway
Rokeby
Talenty
Pisa
Parknook
Kelvin Grove
Ellersley
Rostrevor
Ormley
FINGAL VALLEY
Avoca
Seymour
Long Point

GREAT
LAKE
66
Breona
WESTERN TIERS
Poatina PS
Poatina
The Glen
The Bend
Epping Forest
Cleveland
Brambletye
Bona-vista Estate
ESK HWY
Avoca
APSLEY
Lookout Hill 777m
NATIONAL PARK

Liawenee
Cramps
Conara Junction
Llewellyn Siding
Royal George
Mt St John 777m
Lookout
Chain of Lagoons
MacLean Bay

Tods Corner PS
Flintstone
Miena
Arthurs Lake
Front Rocky Hill 574m
Woodpod
East Coast Birdlife & Animal Park
Waubs Harbour

Wilburville
Mt Penny West 1115m
St Patricks Plains
Auburn
Goldsmith
Campbell Town
Lake Leake
B34
Mt Hobgoblin 763m
Ferndale
89
Bicheno
Cape Lodi

Shannon
Waddamana
Lake Echo
Lake Sorell
Ross
Ross Female Factory Historic Site (Prison)
78
Llandaff
Apslawn
FREYCINET NATIONAL PARK

Steppes
Woods Lake
Snobs Point 971m
Cranbrook
A3
Freycinet Marine Farm

Interlaken
Lake Crescent
Tunbridge
Mount Morriston
TASMAN HWY
Mt Peter 280m
Swanwick
Cape Tourville

Glengowan
Shannon
Antill Ponds
Woodbury House
Trefusis
The Swansea Bark Mill
Mayfield
Swansea
Coles Bay
Sleepy Bay
The Hazards
Great Oyster Bay

SEA

TASMAN

583

MAKING THE MOST OF YOUR TRIP

The road to Uluru (Ayers Rock)

Planning Ahead

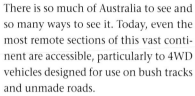

There is so much of Australia to see and so many ways to see it. Today, even the most remote sections of this vast continent are accessible, particularly to 4WD vehicles designed for use on bush tracks and unmade roads.

For some, exploring Australia will mean touring the sealed highways and staying in motels, B & B and farm-stays. Others will tow their accommodation behind them in the form of a caravan or camper trailer, and probably, as a result, stay mainly on made roads. Still others will opt for a mobile home with sleeping and cooking facilities, and yet another group, perhaps the true adventurers, will load a tent into the back of a 4WD and go bush. In all cases, some careful planning will enhance the journey immeasurably.

ADVANCE INFORMATION

Try to gather as much information as possible as far ahead of your planned departure as you can. Remember, the planning is half the fun. Research will confirm, or perhaps deny, your original choice of destination; it also will reveal ways and means, and problems where they exist. Always bear in mind that although information sources are extensive, there is nothing like local 'on-the-spot' knowledge.

The first places to obtain information are: State tourist bureaus and motoring organisations (**see:** Useful Information p. 589). They are excellent sources for travel brochures, regional maps and accommodation guides, and they usually have up-to-date knowledge of local conditions. For details of specific areas, they can put you in touch with the appropriate tourist authority.

Travel agencies, airline travel centres and the main railway booking offices in each State can help if you are planning a fly/drive holiday, or intend to combine rail and motor travel.

HOW FAR AHEAD TO START

It can be a major disappointment to decide on a certain destination and then discover that motels, caravan parks and camping grounds in the area are booked out. In some regions at certain times of the year – Christmas, Easter, and school holiday periods – accommodation can be booked out a year in advance. When booking accommodation, always remember to allow enough time to travel comfortably to your destination. Your trip will lose a great deal of its charm if you have to rush from one point to the next (**see:** Itineraries p. 591).

While all popular destinations are likely to be busy at holiday peak times, some will be booked out around the time of special events: Melbourne at Melbourne Cup time, for example (**see:** Calendar of Events in the introduction to each State).

If you wish to go to a favourite hotel or try a special type of accommodation – a farmstay, a houseboat or B & B – book well ahead. And remember, a number of national parks require advance notice for camping permits.

WHEN TO GO

With a few exceptions you can travel Australia at any time of the year. The exceptions include parts of the Far North between October and May, that is, in the 'wet' or tropical monsoon season (this applies particularly if you plan to use bush tracks and unmade roads, many of which are impassable for months). Tropical cyclones are random summer hazards between November and March. In the New South Wales and Victorian high country, from about May to August, many roads will be snowbound. The Red Centre is not especially inviting in midsummer, when daytime temperatures can reach 45°C.

Otherwise, remember the holiday peaks. If you can avoid travelling during major holiday periods, do so.

WHICH WAY TO GO

If you flinch at the thought of driving seemingly endless kilometres, you should consider an alternative: both fly/drive packages and motor-rail facilities eliminate time-consuming travel and allow for concentration on areas of interest. Cost

A network of sealed roads ensures pleasant touring

them out against the expenses involved in using your own car for the entire trip.

Fly/drive. Contact a travel agent or airline travel centre for advice and information on fly/drive packages.

Motor-rail. For information on this easy way of covering long distances, contact the railway companies (see below). Inquire about discount fares; a reduction in rail fare is available on some interstate services if travel is booked and paid for in advance.

Great Southern Railway
Indian Pacific
Perth–Sydney–Perth
Crosses the continent from ocean to ocean; over the Blue Mountains and across the Nullarbor Plain. Two services a week each way: leaves Sydney Mon. and Thurs., leaves Perth Fri. and Mon.; 68 hours.
Perth–Adelaide–Perth
Two services a week each way: leaves Adelaide Tues. and Fri., leaves Perth Mon. and Fri.; 38 hours. This service connects with *The Overland* to Melbourne.
The Overland
Melbourne–Adelaide–Melbourne
Daily, except Wed. & Sat., each way (overnight); 11 hours.
The Ghan
Sydney–Alice Springs–Sydney
Melbourne–Alice Springs–Melbourne
Adelaide–Alice Springs–Adelaide
A classic and adventurous journey. Travel in luxury across the outback, one service a week from Melbourne and Sydney, twice weekly from Adelaide in

both directions; 45 hours, 36 hours and 20 hours respectively.
For all bookings and inquiries:
Great Southern Railway
Keswick Rail Passenger Terminal
(Marleston Business Centre,
PO Box 445, SA 5033)
13 2147

Queensland Rail
The Queenslander
Brisbane–Townsville–Cairns–
Townsville–Brisbane
Operates March–December, one service a week each way: leaves Brisbane Sun., leaves Cairns Tues.; 31 hours.
Spirit of the Outback
Brisbane–Longreach–Brisbane
Two services a week each way: leaves Brisbane Tues. and Fri., leaves Longreach Thurs. and Sun.
For all bookings and inquiries:
Queensland Rail
305 Edward St, Brisbane 4000
(07) 3235 2222

Heritage Train Company
Great South Pacific Express
Sydney–Brisbane–Cairns/Kuranda–
Brisbane–Sydney
Travels Australia's eastern coast, includes side-trip to Great Barrier Reef and Kuranda Skyrail. Two services fortnightly each way: leaves Sydney Sun. & Tues., leaves Kuranda Tues. & Thurs.; 89 hours.
Sydney–Brisbane–Sydney
One service a week each way: leaves Sydney Sat.; leaves Brisbane Fri.; 22 hours.

Brisbane–Cairns/Kuranda–Brisbane
Two services a week each way: leaves Brisbane Sun. & Tues., leaves Kuranda Tues. & Thurs.; 48 hours.
For all bookings and inquiries:
Heritage Train Company
33 Park Rd, Milton 4064
(07) 3247 6595; freecall 1800 000 395

For information on passenger services contact the following State railway offices:
New South Wales
Countrylink Travel Centre
11–31 York St, Sydney 2000
13 2232
Victoria
V/Line Reservations and Information
Level 2, Transport House
589 Collins St, Melbourne 3000
13 6196
Western Australia
Westrail Centre
West Pde, East Perth 6000
(08) 9326 2222, 13 1053 (WA only)

OTHER TOURING POSSIBILITIES
Ferries to Tasmania. The *Spirit of Tasmania* passenger and car ferry makes at least three return voyages weekly (more in peak season) across Bass Strait between Melbourne and Devonport, northern Tasmania. The *Devil Cat Ferry* service runs between Melbourne and George Town eight times weekly (summer only, more in peak season). Bookings can be made through the TT Line Tasmania, on 13 2010, or through your local Tasmanian Travel and Information Centre or travel agent.

Campervan rental. Available in all States and most cities and major towns, the campervans are fully equipped and vary in size and level of luxury. Costs vary accordingly, depending also on the season. There are often restrictions on where you can take a campervan; so check first.

Escorted group trips. If you are interested in a full-on adventure tour, but are intimidated by the thought of doing it alone, motoring organisations and many private tour operators provide escorted group trips into more remote areas such as Cape York. These tag-along tours save you the worry of navigation

Useful Information

MOTORING ORGANISATIONS

New South Wales
National Roads & Motorists' Association (NRMA)
388 George St, Sydney 2000
13 2132

Australian Capital Territory
National Roads & Motorists' Association (NRMA)
92 Northbourne Ave, Canberra 2601
13 2132

Victoria
Royal Automobile Club of Victoria (RACV)
360 Bourke St, Melbourne 3000
13 1955

South Australia
Royal Automobile Association of SA (RAA)
41 Hindmarsh Sq., Adelaide 5000
(08) 8202 4600

Western Australia
Royal Automobile Club of WA (RAC)
228 Adelaide Tce, Perth 6000
13 1111 (WA only)

Northern Territory
Automobile Association of NT (AANT)
AANT Building
79–81 Smith St, Darwin 0800
(08) 8981 3837

Queensland
Royal Automobile Club of Queensland (RACQ)
300 St Pauls Tce, Fortitude Valley 4006
13 1905

Tasmania
Royal Automobile Club of Tasmania (RACT)
cnr Patrick and Murray sts, Hobart 7000
(03) 6232 6300, 13 2722 (Tasmania only)

For Motorcyclists
Motorcycle Riders' Association of Australia
380 Elizabeth St, Melbourne 3000
(03) 9699 1811; Fax (03) 9699 1833

VEHICLE STANDARDS AUTHORITIES

New South Wales
Vehicle Registration Branch
Roads and Traffic Authority
Centennial Plaza, 260 Elizabeth St,
Surry Hills 2010
13 2213 (NSW only), 1800 624 384
www.rta.nsw.gov.au

Australian Capital Territory
Road User Services
Department of Urban Services
13–15 Challis St, Dickson 2602
(02) 6207 7000

Victoria
Road Safety Department, VicRoads
60 Denmark St, Kew 3101
(03) 9854 2666
www.vicroads.vic.gov.au

South Australia
Vehicles Unit
Transport SA
Kateena St, Regency Park 5942
(08) 8348 9599
www.transport.sa.gov.au

Western Australia
Department of Transport
441 Murray St, Perth 6000
(08) 9320 9320
www.transport.wa.gov.au

Northern Territory
Motor Vehicle Registry
Department of Transport and Works
Goyder Rd, Darwin 0801
(08) 8999 3124

Queensland
Queensland Transport
GPO Box 673, Fortitude Valley 4006
13 2380 (Qld only), (07) 3253 4010
www.transport.qld.gov.au

Tasmania
Vehicle Operations Branch
Department of Infrastructure, Energy and
Resources
7th Floor, 10 Murray St, Hobart 7000
(03) 6233 5347
www.transport.tas.gov.au

TOURIST BUREAUS

New South Wales
New South Wales Visitor Information Line
13 2077
www.tourism.nsw.gov.au

Australian Capital Territory
Canberra Visitors Centre
Northbourne Ave, Dickson 2602
(02) 6205 0044
1800 100 660 (accommodation/activities)
www.canberratourism.com.au

Victoria
Melbourne Visitor Information Centre
Melbourne Town Hall
cnr Swanston and Little Collins sts,
Melbourne 3000
13 2842
www.tourism.vic.gov.au

South Australia
South Australian Travel Centre
1 King William St, Adelaide 5000
(08) 8303 2033, 1300 655 276
www.visit-southaustralia.com.au

Western Australia
Western Australian Tourist Centre
cnr Forrest Pl. and Wellington St, Perth 6000
(08) 9483 1111, 1300 361 351
www.westernaustralia.net

Northern Territory
Northern Territory Tourist Commission
1800 621 336
www.nttc.com.au

Darwin Region Tourism Association
cnr Mitchell and Knuckey sts,
Darwin 0800
(08) 8981 4300

Central Australian Tourism Industry Association
cnr Gregory Tce and Todd St, Alice Springs 0870
(08) 8952 5800
www.catia.asn.au/catia

Queensland
Tourism Queensland
Level 36, Riverside Centre, 123 Eagle St,
Brisbane 4000
(07) 3406 5400

Tasmania
Tasmanian Travel and Information Centre
20 Davey St, Hobart 7000
(03) 6230 8233
www.tourism.tas.gov.au

ACCOMMODATION

Bed and Breakfast Australia
PO Box 727, Newport Beach 2106
(02) 9999 0366; Fax (02) 9999 0377

Farmstays

Australia-wide/New South Wales
Australian Farm Host Holidays Pty Ltd
PO Box 41, Walla Walla 2659
(02) 6029 8621; Fax (02) 6029 8770

Victoria
Farm & Country Tourism Victoria
6th Floor, 230 Collins St, Melbourne 3000
(03) 9650 2922; Fax (03) 9650 9434

South Australia
SA Farm and Country Holidays Inc.
Ryans Deer Farm, Burra 5417
(08) 8892 2617

Western Australia
Farm and Country Holidays WA
PO Box 594, Joondalup 6919
(08) 9304 9100

Queensland
Australian Holidays
130 Bundall Rd, Bundall 4217
1800 351 572; Fax (07) 5574 1533

Tasmania
Homehost and Heritage Tasmania
PO Box 780, Sandy Bay 7005
(03) 6224 1612; Fax (03) 6233 5510

YHA Australia
PO Box 314, Camperdown 1450
(02) 9565 1699; Fax (02) 9565 1325

EMERGENCY (for all States)
Police, ambulance and fire-brigade, dial 000

Spirit of Tasmania, a car and passenger ferry between Melbourne and Devonport

and planning (except for your vehicle) and also provide expert help and backup in case of a mechanical breakdown.

Other ideas. You could leave your vehicle behind and tour in a 4WD coach, take a camel trek or try a canoe adventure – or travel almost any way you choose. Check with your travel agent or tourist bureau (**see:** Useful Information p. 589).

WHERE TO STAY

State motoring organisations, tourist bureaus and booksellers all have accommodation guides; some include information on camping and caravan parks. Travel agents and airline travel centres can also provide information.

Resorts, hotels and motels. Contact the relevant State tourist bureau, motoring organisation (**see:** Useful Information p. 589), your travel agent or airline travel centre for details and bookings. Major motel chains, such as Best Western, Budget Motel Chain, Golden Chain and Flag Choice Hotels, cover most of the country. Brochures detailing accommodation are available from the central booking offices.

Self-contained holiday units, cottages and apartments. If you are planning a stay in a city or at any holiday destination for a length of time, this provides a sensible family alternative to motel or hotel accommodation. The relevant tourist bureau (**see:** Useful

Information p. 589) will provide you with the details.

House swapping. This is yet another possibility for a lengthy stay. This can be arranged through home exchange organisations (see *Yellow Pages* telephone book). In addition, advertisements for those seeking a house-swapping holiday often appear in the classified sections of the newspapers. Make sure you are totally satisfied with the arrangements made concerning your commitments and that you are happy with the people with whom you are dealing. Also check that your householder's insurance covers you in such circumstances (**see:** Insurance p. 591).

Farmstays. Such accommodation varies from spartan to luxurious and, in some cases, guests are invited to take part in farm life. Associations in each State (**see:** Useful Information p. 589) or tourist authorities will provide details.

Bed and breakfast accommodation. Contact Bed & Breakfast Australia (**see:** Useful Information p. 589) for information on B & B accommodation in homestay or farmstay environments throughout Australia.

Guesthouses. This form of accommodation is currently making something of a comeback. Standards vary greatly – some guesthouses are magnificently renovated with modern amenities and excellent restaurants, while others are

budget-style with shared bathrooms but plenty of charm.

Backpacker accommodation. This type of accommodation is provided at budget rates in a communal environment and is becoming very popular, particularly amongst younger travellers. Note, however, that the accommodation offered is not always suitable for children. To obtain information on the range of accommodation available, contact VIP Backpackers Resorts of Australia (**see:** Useful Information p. 589). There are also over 100 youth hostels throughout Australia open to members and (for an additional fee) non-members. YHA accommodation is used by all age groups and rooms range from large dormitories to private rooms. For information, contact YHA Australia (**see:** Useful Information p. 589).

Floating accommodation. If you are into staying afloat, consider hiring a houseboat on the Hawkesbury River or Eildon Weir, taking a paddle wheeler cruise on the Murray, or even chartering a yacht to cruise in the Whitsundays. Obtain details from your travel agent or the relevent State tourist bureau (**see:** Useful Information p. 589).

DIVIDING UP THE DOLLARS

Very few people can afford the 'money-no-object' approach to holidays, no matter what the length of stay. You will need principally to consider accommodation, food, fuel and entertainment, although emergency funds should not be forgotten. Travel insurance is a wise precaution (**see:** Insurance p. 591).

Accommodation. Accommodation costs can be estimated when you book, but you might simply average the figure. If you do, estimate high rather than low.

Food. This is a matter of personal choice: you may eat out every night or prepare all or some of your meals yourself. Allow for the unexpected, and for the higher cost of food and meals in popular holiday destinations or in remote areas. Remember to budget for snacks and treats, especially if you are travelling with children.

Fuel. Once you know your vehicle's fuel consumption you can work out your fuel costs in advance. The usual method is based on litres per 100 kilometres. If your vehicle uses 16 litres per 100 kilometres and your journey distance works out at 5000 kilometres, you will use 50 times 16 litres of fuel, or 800 litres. Allow for rises in the cost of petrol and remember that fuel is more expensive in remote areas.

Entertainment and other costs.
When budgeting, allow for such 'budget biters' as admission charges, postcards, camera film, chemist's items, bridge/ferry tolls and car repairs. Remember also that accommodation, travel and rental charges rise during peak periods.

Carrying large amounts of cash with you is not a good idea, hence credit cards, EFTPOS and Automatic Teller Machines are a good alternative (except in some remote areas). It is advisable to carry more than one card in case a card is 'eaten' by an ATM or damaged during use.

CAR MAINTENANCE COURSES

If you plan to tour in remote areas, you should acquire basic mechanical knowledge and skills. In general you should have a broad understanding of the technology of your vehicle and know how much roadside repair is possible in the event of a breakdown (**see:** Breakdowns p. 606). You should also have some specific knowledge; for example how to change a tyre on the vehicle you will be using; and whether you can use jumper leads to start your car and if so, how it is done. Car care and basic car-maintenance courses are run by Adult Education centres, TAFE Colleges and motoring organisations in all States. Test your knowledge by reading through the Trouble Shooting flow-charts and the Tools and Spare Parts list (**see:** Breakdowns p. 606).

INSURANCE

The benefits of a comprehensive insurance policy on your vehicle, caravan or trailer are obvious. As well as cover against loss or damage due to accident, theft and vandalism, your personal effects are covered against loss or damage when they are in the insured vehicle. Additional policies will cover such eventualities as, for example, the cost of temporary accommodation should your caravan become uninhabitable. Short-term travel insurance is available from several companies to cover loss of luggage or cancellation of accommodation bookings, etc. Information and advice can be obtained from the various motoring organisations (**see:** Useful Information p. 589), insurance companies and travel agents.

ITINERARIES

Some people make itineraries and stick to them; others do not. At the very least, a rough schedule to ensure a good mixture of travel and sightseeing time is essential. Build some flexibility into your plans. You never know what might detain you: the weather (frequent rest breaks are necessary in extreme heat), or children, who have a low tolerance for long periods without a break (**see:** Child's Play p. 610).

CLOTHING

Be strict with yourself and the family when you are packing and travel as lightly as you can. It is better to spend an hour at a laundromat than overburden your vehicle with clothing you probably will not wear.

Essentials are a jumper or jacket, even in summer; sensible comfortable shoes; and a wide-brimmed hat to protect yourself from the sun at all times. Carry items like swimwear, towels, spare socks and jumpers in a bag that can be kept within easy reach. Gumboots are a handy item also.

FIRST-AID KIT

A first-aid kit is essential. Include band-aids, bandages, headache tablets, extra blockout, insect repellent and a soothing lotion for bites. Eye drops are a good idea, as is a thermometer and a pressure bandage. Kits are available from various suppliers including St John Ambulance Australia, which also conducts basic courses in first aid. As car sickness is often a problem on long journeys, particularly with young children, include medication to counter this. Your chemist or a doctor will advise you.

USEFUL EXTRAS

Depending on the length and nature of your tour, some items are valuable, some essential (**see:** Tools and Spare Parts p. 607). Carry picnic and barbecue equipment, tissues, toilet paper and a container or plastic bag for rubbish (if there are no bins take it with you rather than leaving it behind). Rugs or blankets are a necessary extra, as is a large sheet of plastic, which can be used as an emergency windscreen. Having a mobile phone may be useful if you are travelling within signal range; check the coverage before departure. If you are going to the outback, a necessary item is some type of shade cover, such as a tarpaulin, in case of an emergency stop (**see:** Outback Motoring p. 603).

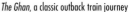
The Ghan, a classic outback train journey

Other Information

PETS

Leaving them behind

- Pet care services (see *Yellow Pages* telephone book): provide care of pets in their own environment. They will also care for plants and property, etc.
- Dog boarding kennels and catteries (see *Yellow Pages*): provide care and accommodation. Some have pickup and delivery services.
- Animal welfare organisations and veterinary surgeons (see *Yellow Pages*): for advice and information.

Taking them with you

- Make sure, in advance, that the accommodation or mode of travel permits animals. Many caravan parks and most national parks do not admit animals.
- During the trip, carry additional water and stop at regular intervals for toileting and exercise.
- Do not leave an animal unattended in a vehicle for any length of time; always provide fresh air.
- Allow sufficient room in the vehicle to comfortably accommodate the animal.
- Do not transport an animal in a moving caravan.
- Consider purchasing a dog harness for your vehicle to protect yourself and the animal in case of sudden braking.
- See *Holidaying with Dogs*, published by Life. Be In It, for more suggestions.

BEFORE DEPARTURE

- Cancel newspapers, mail deliveries.
- Make arrangements for the garden to be watered and lawns mowed. Board out your indoor plants or place them in the sink, surround with damp peat and water thoroughly. Encasing each pot in a sealed polythene bag also helps retain moisture.
- If you have a pet, arrange for its safekeeping well in advance.
- Arrange for a neighbour to keep an eye on the house. Alternatively, consult a professional home security service (see *Yellow Pages*).
- Valuable items, such as jewellery, are best left for safekeeping at your bank.
- Turn the electricity off at the mains and leave the fridge door open. If you have equipment that must operate in your absence, for example a stocked freezer, leave power on and remove plugs from all other power points. Make sure that everything else that should be turned off is off.
- Check that all windows and doors are locked; then check again.
- Always leave a contact address with a friend or neighbour.

Camping by the Pentecost River, Western Australia

CARRYING A CAMERA

You probably will want to preserve the highlights of your trip on film. Check the following points:

- If you have recently bought a camera, take at least one test film before departure so that you know how the equipment reacts to different light conditions.
- As weather conditions may vary, it is a good idea to carry film with a range of speeds. If you are not an expert, talk to your local dealer about the varieties of film available.
- Before you leave, have a good supply of film, fresh batteries and a lens brush. Other useful accessories are a close-up lens, lens hood, filters and a tripod.
- Keep your equipment in a plastic bag inside a camera bag to protect it from water, heat, sand and dust. It can get very hot in a closed car, so always keep the camera in the shade. The best place is on the floor, on the side opposite the exhaust pipe. Make sure, however, that the bag cannot rattle around.
- High temperatures and humidity can damage colour film. Store your film in the coolest spot available and do not break the watertight vapour seal until just before use. Once the film is used, remove it from the camera, mark it with an E for 'exposed'.
- When using the camera in bright conditions, even with automatic exposure, it may be necessary to allow one stop or half of a stop down to compensate for the brilliance of the light. If in doubt, consult the instruction sheet included with the film.
- Check that your personal property insurance covers the loss of cameras and photographic equipment while travelling (**see:** Insurance p. 591).

TIME ZONES

Australia has 4 time zones:

- Eastern Standard Time (EST), in Queensland, Australian Capital Territory, New South Wales, Victoria and Tasmania. (Note: Broken Hill, in central western New South Wales, operates on CST, half an hour behind the rest of New South Wales.)
- Central Standard Time (CST is half an hour behind EST), in South Australia and Northern Territory.
- Western Standard Time (WST is 2 hours behind EST), in Western Australia.
- Central Western Time (CWT is 45 minutes ahead of WST), a local time zone operating from 3 km east of Caiguna in Western Australia to the South Australian border.

Daylight saving is adopted by some States in summer. In New South Wales, Victoria, Tasmania, Australian Capital Territory and South Australia, clocks are put forward 1 hour at the begining of summer (the last Sunday in October, except in Tasmania, where the clocks are adjusted on the first Sunday in October). In 2000, daylight saving will commence on the 27th August in New South Wales, Victoria and Tasmania. Northern Territory, Western Australia and Queensland do not have daylight saving.

QUARANTINE REGULATIONS

Throughout Australia, State quarantine regulations prohibit the transport by travellers of certain plants and foods, and even soil, across State borders. Further information is available from offices of agricultural departments in all States.

Inter-city Route Maps

The following inter-city route maps will help you plan your route between major cities. As well, you can use the maps during your journey, since they provide information on distances between towns along the route, roadside rest areas, road conditions and which towns are described in the A–Z listings. The map below provides an overview of the routes mapped.

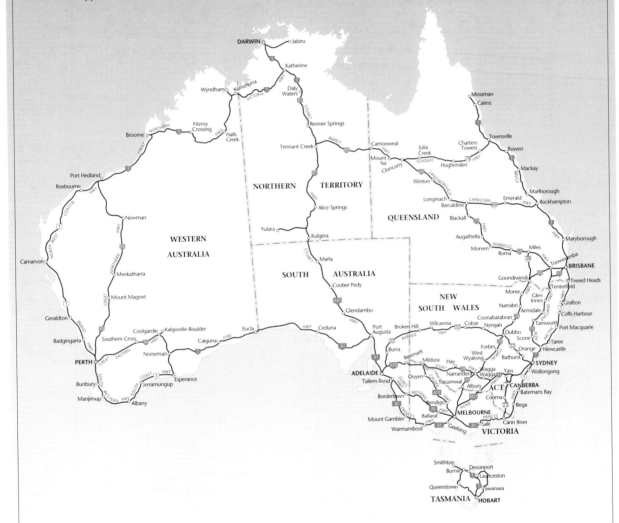

PAGE	ROUTE	DISTANCE	TRAVELLING TIME
594	Sydney–Melbourne via Hume Hwy/Fwy	873 km	12 hrs
	Sydney–Melbourne via Princes Hwy	1040 km	15 hrs
	Sydney–Brisbane via New England Hwy	1001 km	14 hrs
	Melbourne–Adelaide via Western & Dukes hwys	732 km	8 hrs
	Melbourne–Adelaide via Princes Hwy	906 km	11 hrs
595	Melbourne–Brisbane via Newell Hwy	1671 km	20 hrs
	Adelaide–Darwin via Stuart Hwy	3051 km	31 hrs
	Adelaide–Perth via Eyre & Great Eastern hwys	2716 km	32 hrs
	Adelaide–Sydney via Sturt & Hume hwys	1415 km	19 hrs
	Perth–Darwin via Great Northern Hwy	4049 km	46 hrs
596	Sydney–Brisbane via Pacific Hwy	984 km	14 hrs
	Brisbane–Darwin via Warrego Hwy	3429 km	39 hrs
	Brisbane–Cairns via Bruce Hwy	1699 km	20 hrs
	Hobart–Launceston via Midland Hwy	200 km	3 hrs
	Hobart–Devonport via Midland & Bass hwys	282 km	4 hrs

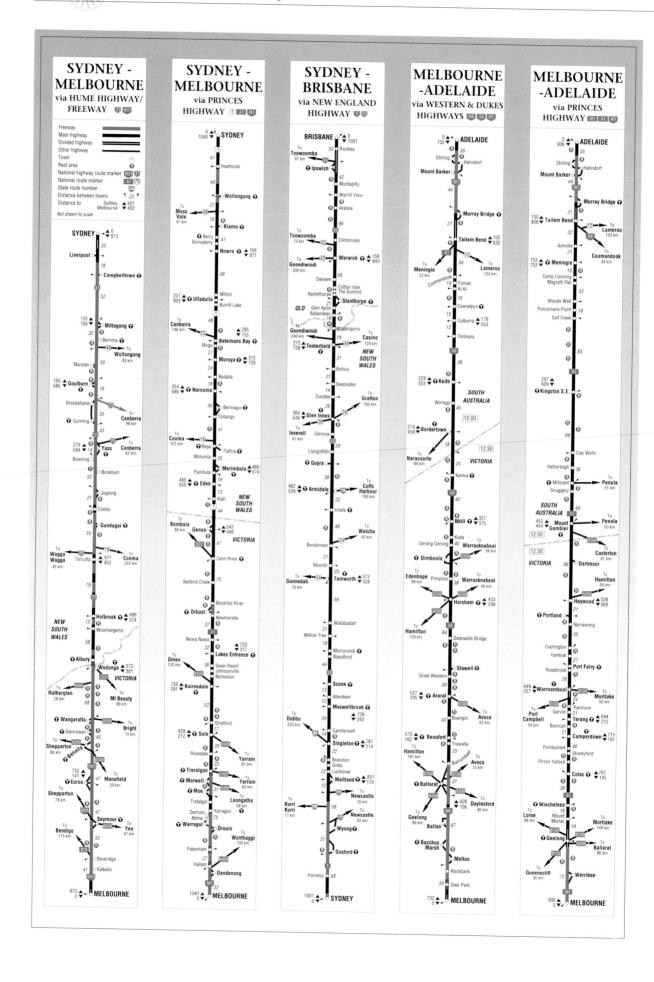

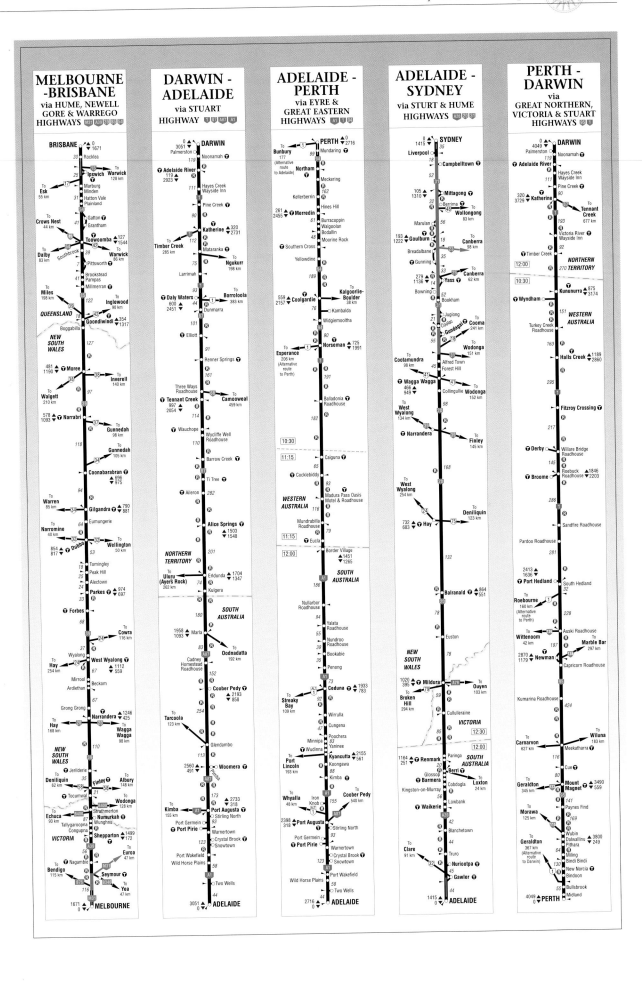

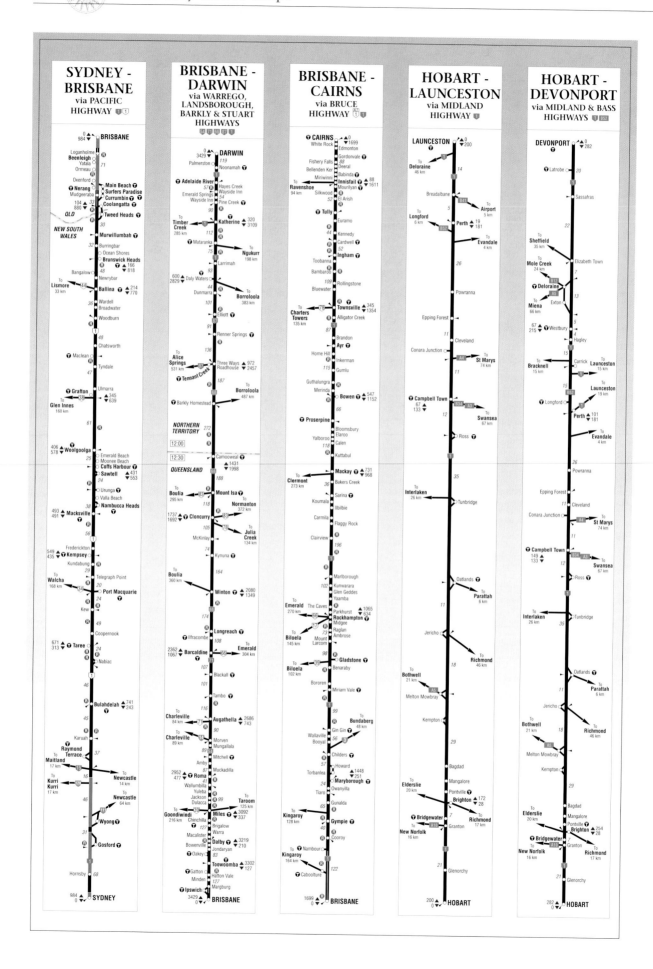

Have a Good Trip

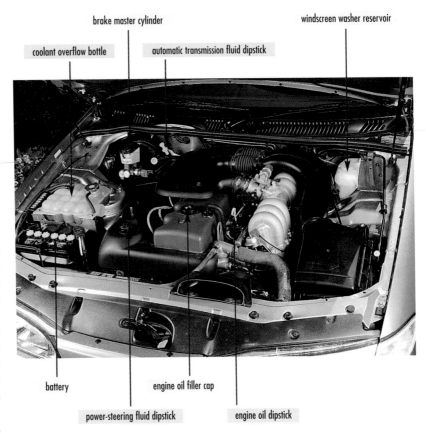

brake master cylinder

coolant overflow bottle

automatic transmission fluid dipstick

windscreen washer reservoir

battery

power-steering fluid dipstick

engine oil filler cap

engine oil dipstick

CHECKING THE CAR

All the care that you devote to your own comfort can be for nothing if you do not make sure that the car checks out too.

For a one-, two- or three-day tour, you could simply fuel up, check the tyre pressures, clean all the windows and head off; if you maintain your vehicle at all times in reasonable condition – as indeed you should – probably little further preparation is required. However, a vacation of a week or more, or journey involving long-distance driving, will need more thorough preparation. If you plan to travel through remote areas, for example, you should first check that your vehicle is able to handle off-road conditions. The service department of your State motoring organisations (**see:** Useful Information p. 589) will give advice and will make a preliminary inspection of your vehicle.

Regardless of the length of your tour, you should check the wheelbrace, jack and under-vehicle jacking points, in case you have to change a tyre.

Unless you are able to service your vehicle yourself, this preparation should be left to your mechanic. To avoid breakdowns and to confirm the reliability of safety-related items, ask the mechanic to include a check of the fuel supply, electrics, brakes, tyres and certain ancillary equipment, as follows.

Fuel supply. Check fuel pump for flow. Check carburettor for wear and potential blockages or check condition of electronic or mechanical fuel injection. When the tank is almost empty, remove the drain plug and drain the tank to check that the remaining fuel is perfectly clean. Check fuel-supply lines for cracks and poor connections, and make sure no fuel line is exposed to damage by rocks or low-clearance projections.

Electrics. Check battery output and condition (including terminals), alternator/generator output and condition, spark plugs, condenser, coil, distributor and all terminals and cables. If the vehicle is fitted with electronic ignition it should be carefully checked in the prescribed manner.

Lights. Check all lights, not just to see that they work, but to make sure that they are aligned correctly and are likely to continue working. It can be extremely dark at night in outback Australia.

Brakes. Check wear of pads and/or linings, check discs for runout and drums for scoring. Brake dust should be cleaned off. Check brake lines and hoses for cracks and wear. Make sure brake lines are not liable to be damaged by rocks or low projections. Check parking brake for adjustment and cable stretch.

Tyres. Check for uneven or excessive wear. Check walls for cracks and stone or kerb fractures. Check pressures. Include spare (or spares) in all checks. Make sure that the spare wheel matches those on the car, and uses the same kind of wheel nuts.

Windscreen-wiper blades. Check for wear and proper contact, and check washers for direction and effectiveness. Include rear wiper and washer, where fitted.

Windscreen glass. Check for cracks and replace if necessary.

Seat mountings and adjustments. Check.

Lubricant levels. Check (including brake and clutch fluid) and either top up or drain and refill.

Wheel bearings. Check for play and adjust or replace.

Universal and constant velocity joints. Check and replace if necessary.

Dust and water sealing. A pre-run test in appropriate conditions will reveal any problems. What you do not need is dust, exhaust fumes or water inside the vehicle.

Roof rack. Check mounts and welds for weaknesses and cracks.

Seat belts. Check for tears or sun-hardening. Replace if necessary. Also check inertia reels.

Radiator water level and condition. Check; drain and flush if necessary. Check radiator for leaks and radiator pressure cap for pressure release accuracy. Check water-pump operation. Check radiator and heater hoses for cracks and general condition, and replace if necessary. Check hose clamps.

Fan belt. Check for tension and fraying.

Hazards

FLOOD

In some remote areas, floods can occur without warning. Do not camp in dry river beds or close to the edges of creeks or streams. Always exercise extreme caution when approaching flooded roads or bridges.

If you are caught in a flash flood there is a good chance you will lose some possessions – and perhaps the car. However, your life is more important than both, so get out of the car and onto high ground and worry about the car and possessions later. If the car is washed away, it is not likely to travel far before being stopped by a tree or rock or stranded in shallow water.

If you cannot keep your feet after leaving the car, swim or float *with* fast-running water, not against it, and look out for a projecting embankment or overhanging limb to help you climb to higher ground.

When the flood has passed you may be able to retrieve the vehicle, dry it out on higher ground and continue.

Exercise extreme caution when crossing water

BUSHFIRE

If you have to travel on days of critical fire danger (that is, total fire ban days), make sure you carry some woollen blankets and a filled water container. If you are trapped as a bushfire approaches:
- Do not panic.
- Stop the car in the nearest cleared area.
- Wind up all the windows.
- Turn on the hazard lights to warn any other traffic.
- DO NOT GET OUT OF YOUR CAR. The temperature may become unbearably hot, but it is still safer to stay in the car.
- Lie on the car floor, below window level, to avoid radiant heat.
- Cover yourself and your passengers with blankets.

The car will not explode or catch fire, and a fast-moving wildfire will pass quickly overhead.

ANIMALS

Although some species of Australia's unique wildlife are immensely appealing, some species are extremely dangerous.

Marine life
- **Box jellyfish (or marine stingers).** These are found in the coastal waters of Queensland and northern Australia in the summer months (from October–May). A sting from their many long tentacles can be lethal, and for that reason swimming on coastal beaches north of Rockhampton is prohibited at this time. Walking or paddling in a few centimetres of water is just as dangerous as swimming.
- **Stonefish.** Among Australia's several species of poisonous stinging fish, the stonefish, found all around the northern coastline, is particularly dangerous. Walking gently in the water, wearing sandshoes and not turning over coral and rocks will reduce the likelihood of a sting.
- **Blue-ringed octopuses.** Common in rock pools in all Australian States, their bite can paralyse in 15 minutes resulting in death. Do not handle in any circumstances and warn children of the potential hazard. Unless provoked, the distinctive blue rings of this dangerous octopus may not be evident.
- **Sharks.** Sharks are common in Australian waters. Do not swim where sharks have been seen or are known to congregate. Do not swim near dogs or other domestic pets. Do not swim at dusk or after dark, or at locations where water becomes abruptly deeper. Avoid areas of low visibility and turbid water.
- **Freshwater and saltwater crocodiles.** These are found throughout northern Australia. The saltwater crocodile is particularly dangerous and may be found in both salt water (including the sea) and fresh water. The freshwater crocodile will also bite, thus caution is necessary for both species. Neither species is easy to see in the water. Heed local warning signs and do not swim or paddle in fresh or salt water or allow children or animals near the water's edge. People standing in or near water while feeding or cleaning fish are particularly vulnerable, as are shore-based anglers and small-boat operators.

Snakes
As a rule, snakes are timid and generally do not attack unless threatened. However, several species are highly venomous.

Spiders
Funnel-web spiders and **red-back spiders**. The bite from both species can be deadly. The funnel-web is found in southern and eastern States. The red-back is found in all of the Australian States.

Insects
Wasps, bees, ants (particularly **bull-ants**), **scorpions, centipedes** and **mosquitoes**. These insects are found throughout Australia. Their sting or bite normally is not harmful, except to those people who are allergy-prone, but it may cause pain and discomfort. Mosquitoes are of more serious concern in areas affected by Ross River virus. **Ticks** are a serious health threat, especially for children. When located, a tick should be removed promptly with tweezers, keeping the body intact. Do not compress the body.

Study Australia's wildlife and learn to identify dangerous species. Remember that some plant species are also poisonous. When visiting a new area, check with local authorities to ascertain which dangerous species, if any, are found there.

All this should be done as near as practicable to your departure date. Allow time for unexpected work or part replacement, and for a return to the garage if a particular problem persists. *Note: Nothing should be overlooked – lives may be at stake.*

PACKING THE CAR

First and most important, you should limit the items carried in the passenger compartment to include only the necessities. In a sedan this is not difficult. You have a boot, and that is where most items should be carried; but in a station wagon it is much more difficult and some planning is required. Loose items in the passenger compartment get under your feet (especially hazardous for the driver), interfere with your comfort and become dangerous projectiles if you have a collision. So for your station wagon, buy or rig up a safety net, which can be fitted behind the rear seat to separate you from the objects that could otherwise harm you.

This rule applies also to food and drink. Empty bottles and cartons should be stowed out of the way in a rubbish bag, until you are able to dispose of them properly.

In order to provide extra space, many drivers fix a roof rack to their vehicle. This is not recommended. Laden roof racks upset the balance of the vehicle by changing its centre of gravity, making it top-heavy. They disturb the air flow, which can destabilise the vehicle, and they certainly increase fuel consumption by interfering with the aerodynamics. In some circumstances they can snag on overhanging limbs of trees.

If you must use a roof rack, carry as little on it as possible and keep the maximum loading height as low as you can. Protect the load by wrapping it in a tarpaulin or groundsheet and, if possible, create a sharp (aerofoil) leading edge on the load to improve air flow.

A good alternative to a roof rack is a small, strong, lightweight trailer, but there are times when towing will be a disadvantage, so you need to consider the terrain.

If you are towing a caravan, some items can be carried inside the van on

An early start at Bright, Victoria

the floor, preferably strapped down (anything loose will be flung about) and located over the axle (or axles). In some States, caravans must be fitted with a fire extinguisher. And remember, no people or animals are to be transported in a towed caravan.

Once your vehicle is loaded, and preferably with the passengers aboard, check the tyre pressures (yes, even as you leave home on day one). The additional load will mean higher pressures are needed. The tyre placard or owner's handbook can be used as a guideline. The tyre will bag if it is under-inflated and destabilise the car. It also will offer a baggy sidewall to rocks and stones, encouraging wall fractures and potential blowouts. Laden-tyre pressure requirements vary with tyre size and design, but the pressure is important. If in any doubt contact the tyre manufacturer.

WHEN TO SET OFF

There is evidence to suggest that people drive best during the hours in which they are accustomed to being awake, and probably at work. As drowsiness is deadly in drivers, this is worth noting. Leaving home, for example at 1 a.m., might avoid the heat of the day and beat the traffic to a large extent, but somewhere between 3 and 5 a.m. you are likely to find yourself wanting to doze off again.

Plan to share long-distance driving as much as possible. Depart around or just before sunrise and stop no later than sundown. Allow regular stops, not just to stretch your legs but to take nourishment as well. Food helps keep the energy levels up. You might care to leave later if you are travelling east, to avoid the rising sun shining in your eyes, and finish earlier if you are travelling west, for the converse reason.

LEAVING HOME

Everyone knows the feeling that usually comes when you are a good distance from home: did I lock all the windows, turn off the electricity at the meter, cancel the newspaper and mail delivery? Usually all is well, but it is reassuring to double-check everything before you leave (**see:** Before Departure p. 592).

Better Driving

In skilful driving, the two most important ingredients are concentration and smoothness.

Concentration. Find a comfortable position and stay comfortable; discomfort destroys concentration. Lack of concentration is the biggest single cause of road accidents.

Wear the right clothes: loose-fitting, cool or warm as appropriate, but capable of being changed (not while you are driving!) as temperatures change. Lightweight shoes are better than boots. Wear good quality antiglare sunglasses. Sit comfortably: neither too close to the steering wheel and cramped, nor too far back and stretching; and be sure you can reach the foot controls through the entire length of their movement. Drive with both hands all the time. No one can control a car properly with one

Take extra care on icy roads

hand. Driving gloves are recommended. Make all seat, belt and rear-view mirror adjustments before you drive off (particularly if you share the driving with someone who is not your size).

Concentration means *no distractions*. It is probably unrealistic to suggest that no conversation takes place while you are driving, but do not allow conversations to interfere with your concentration. Aim to keep the children quiet and amused (**see:** Child's Play p. 610). If an important issue needs to be resolved, first stop the car and then sort it out.

Smoothness. Smoothness is vital for the vehicle's safe, effective operation, but unfortunately many people are not smooth drivers. A vehicle in motion is a tonne or so of iron, steel and plastic sitting atop a set of springs. It is inherently unstable and prone to influences such as pitch and roll. This is difficult enough to control in normal motion, but worse when the driver exaggerates these instabilities by stabbing at the brakes, jerking the steering wheel and crashing the gears. Two things derive from being a smooth driver. The first is passenger comfort; on a long trip, everyone will arrive much fresher and more relaxed if the driver has provided a smooth and therefore pleasant journey. The second is increased safety; the vehicle will react better to smooth driving than it will to hamfisted driving. Smooth driving brings even further benefits: less wear and tear and lower fuel consumption.

However, to define better driving as a combination of concentration and smoothness only would not be wholly accurate. There are other factors:

Know your vehicle. Understand its breaking capacities, especially in emergencies – some cars move around a lot, or become directionally unstable under harsh braking. Be aware of its usable power and its limitations. And drive well within the cornering and road-holding limits of the vehicle's suspension and tyre combination.

Drive defensively. It is worth assuming that a proportion of road users are inattentive or devoid of skill. It is remarkable how your driving awareness

is increased by such an attitude.

Do not be impatient. Advance planning should have provided you with ample time for the day's journey.

Do not drive with an incapacitating illness or injury. Something as simple as a bruised elbow might restrict rapid arm movement when you most need it.

DRIVING EMERGENCIES

Of course, the best way to handle emergencies is to avoid them. However, to suggest one problem or another will never occur is unrealistic. A course in defensive driving is an advantage; contact your local motoring organisation to obtain more information (**see:** Useful Information p. 589).

Skidding. The possibility of skidding worries most drivers, as well it should. There are a number of causes of a skid, some of them composite. Essentially, skidding occurs when the tyres lose their grip on the road.

The most common form is a front-wheel (or sometimes all-wheel) skid caused by over-braking. When the wheels stop rolling, the vehicle will no longer react to steering input. If you avoid jumping on the brake pedal (that is, drive smoothly) you will avoid this type of skid. However if you do skid, quickly ease just sufficient pressure off the brake pedal to allow the wheels to roll again. The steering will come back, which at least will allow you to take avoiding action as well as to slow down.

A rear-wheel skid also may occur as a result of harsh braking, usually while turning at the same time (for example if corner entry speed is too high, or braking too harsh). In slippery conditions the tail of the car may also fishtail because you have entered a corner too fast or, in rear-wheel drive vehicles, because too much power has been applied too soon, causing the rear tyres to break traction. A rear-wheel skid of any kind requires some reverse steering, often only briefly. It is not enough to advise turning the steering in the direction of the skid: the question is, by how much? Turn the steering wheels to point them in the direction you wish to travel and, at the same time, try to recognise what you did to cause the skid in the first place. If it was because of excessive acceleration, back off a little and re-apply the accelerator more gently. If it was because you entered the corner too fast or because of your braking (or both at the same time), ease the brakes and let your corrective steering realign the car and then, smoothly, increase the power again by gently applying the accelerator.

Skids can be complex and difficult to control. Over-correction is common, with the result that the vehicle swings into another skid in the opposite direction. It is important not to panic, and to be smooth in your reaction. Easy to say – not so easy to do!

Aquaplaning. This is a form of skidding where the tyres roll a layer of water up in front of the vehicle and then ride on to it, breaking contact with the road surface. What you sense is a sudden loss of driving 'feel'. Slow down, very smoothly, until the tyres come off the layer of water and then proceed more carefully. Watch out for deep puddles: they are the danger.

Driving in snow, ice and mud also produces adhesion problems. Once again, smooth, steady progress, while 'feeling' the vehicle and staying on top of its movements, is the only answer.

Icy roads. For a visit to the snow, your vehicle should be fitted with chains. If it is not and the car's back wheels begin to spin wildly on packed and rutted snow or ice:
- Stop the car.
- Look for and remove any obstructions under the car.
- Pack loose gravel, sticks or vegetation under the driving wheels.
- Remember that on a level surface a gentle push sometimes will get the car moving again.

Because it cannot be seen, ice can be more dangerous than snow.

Foggy conditions. When driving in fog:
- Switch on dipped headlights, or fog-lights if your car is fitted with them.
- Use front and back demisters.
- If visibility is reduced to such an extent that driving becomes an ordeal, pull as far off the road as you can, switch on your emergency lights and wait until the fog lifts and you feel able to continue.

The advice in this section applies equally to driving in the cities and in the outback. The techniques are the same; only the conditions vary (**see:** Outback Motoring p. 603, for more detail on driving in the outback).

Safe Driving

BASIC TRAFFIC LAWS

In December 1999, Australia's State and Territory governments introduced uniform national road rules. This has necessitated a number of changes to existing legislation in each State and Territory and all of these amendments are scheduled to be implemented by March 2000. A number of rules which involve linemarking, signage and other physical changes will be phased in over several years as part of regular maintenance work.

It is important to note that some rules will still be different to suit local conditions. One example is the undefined speed limit outside town areas in the Northern Territory. Another is the unique hook turn in the centre of Melbourne, necessitated by the concentration of trams – at specified intersections a vehicle making a righthand turn must move to the far left of the intersection and wait until the traffic clears and the traffic lights change to green on the road that the vehicle is entering before completing the turn. Overtaking on the right of a tram is forbidden and no vehicle may pass a stationary tram at a recognised tram stop.

For more information on road rules and State/Territory differences, contact your local motoring organisation (**see:** Useful Information p. 589) or access the National Road Transport Commission website, www.nrtc.gov.au.

IN CASE OF ACCIDENT

In all States of Australia, any accident in which someone is injured or killed must be reported to police at once, or within 24 hours. In Western Australia, all car accidents must be reported if damage exceeds $1000, if drugs or alcohol are involved, or if there is any dispute.

It is highly advisable to report to the nearest police station any accident that involves substantial property damage, especially if you are unable to report to the property owner. Police may or may not decide to attend the scene, but they at least will have your report on record, which may well be useful should there be legal proceedings or insurance claims.

When involved in an accident, you *must* produce your driver's licence to police upon request. If you do not have it with you, you may be liable for an on-the-spot fine.

It is advisable to obtain the insurance details of the other parties involved in the accident. You should also exchange names, addresses, and vehicle registration details. *Do not volunteer any other information.* In particular, do not discuss the accident. Should court action result, you may find something said in the stress of the aftermath of the accident used against you. Above all, *do not admit you are at fault in any way.*

You are not obliged to make a statement to police. If you are disturbed and upset, wait until you can think clearly.

An accident that involves damage to persons or property should be reported to your insurance company as soon as possible.

POSITIONING

Positioning is vital on any road.
- Try to stagger the position of your car in the line of traffic so that you can see well ahead.

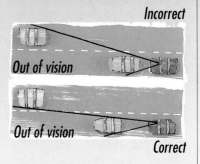

Incorrect

Out of vision

Out of vision

Correct

- When turning right on a two-lane highway, do not angle the car; keep it square to the other traffic so that cars can pass on the left.

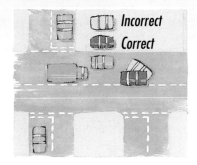

Incorrect

Correct

Towing

Towing your accommodation behind you will provide the advantage of low-budget touring and flexibility with stopovers. It can be a disadvantage also, in that it may restrict access to some areas. You can, however, use the caravan for most sections of your journey and park it in a safe place while you go off in the car and explore the more difficult tracks.

Obtain advice. If you are new to towing, the first thing you must do is contact the local vehicle standards authority (**see:** Useful Information p. 589) for advice on your towing hitch and information on towing regulations. It is very important that the rig (that is, car and caravan, boat or trailer) is balanced and the weight over the tow ball is not excessive. An adjustable height hitch with spring bars is best.

Learn to reverse. Once you have decided on the hitch and you have learned how to hook up and unhook, you must learn to reverse the rig. Find a wide open area, an empty car park for example, and practise. Get the feel of the rig and aim to be proficient at reversing before you depart.

Allow for added length. On the road, remember to make allowances for the added overall length and give yourself extra space for turning and extra distance for overtaking. The added weight will obviously affect the towing vehicle's performance with regard to acceleration and braking.

Know the speed limit. High-speed towing of vans and trailers can cause major difficulties, magnifying driving problems substantially. Contact the local vehicle standards authority for information on speed limits (**see:** Useful Information p. 589).

Avoid trailer sway. Cross-winds can be a problem when towing a caravan; the van's slab sides act like sails. The combination of high speed and cross-winds can cause trailer sway, a dangerous characteristic that dramatically destabilises both towing vehicle and caravan. You probably will feel it happening before you see it, but checking in the rear-view mirrors will confirm it. Should the trailer begin to move about, ease back on your speed, braking if necessary, but very gently. Harsh or sudden braking will compound the problem. When the caravan stabilises, resume speed, perhaps very gradually if you are continuing in a cross-wind area.

Fit good-quality towing mirrors on your vehicle. It is very important that your rear view down both sides of the trailer or caravan is not obscured.

Be courteous. If, because of the relative slowness of your progress, you observe in the rear-view mirror a line of vehicles banking up behind you, be courteous and pull over when and where you can, to allow vehicles to overtake.

Locate load correctly. The carrying of goods and equipment in a caravan has been mentioned, but it is worth repeating that such items should be located as much as possible over and just to the front of the caravan axle (or axles); never behind, as this will lift the front of the caravan and the tow ball.

Check the rig. Before setting off and every day of the trip, whatever the vehicle, always check and double-check that the hitch is secure, that the safety chains are correctly fitted, and that the electrical connections are working so that indicator lights function at the rear of the towed vehicle.

Allow extra time. Remember to allow extra time for each day's travel, and remain alert.

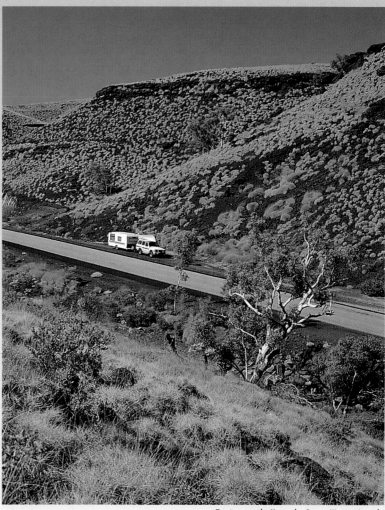
Touring near the Hamersley Range, Western Australia

CHECKLIST
When towing anything:
- Contact the local vehicle standards authority (**see:** Useful Information p. 589) for advice and details on national towing regulations.
- Check the hitch for security. The law in most States demands that tow bars are fitted with safety chains.
- Check that the tail and stop lights, marker lights and signal lights are working.
- Remember to check the air pressure in the caravan or trailer tyres.
- If towing a boat, check the lashings.
- Check that caravan doors, windows and roof vents are closed before departure.
- If the caravan or trailer is fitted with separate brakes, check these as soon as you start to move.

Outback Motoring

Australia's size and remoteness deter many people from exploring it. However, properly set up and equipped, and armed with common sense and a little background knowledge, every intending traveller can explore the country's huge open spaces.

If you intend travelling in the outback, planning ahead is vital, for it is possible to travel in some sections of the Australian outback and not see another vehicle or person for several days. The Canning Stock Route is a good example.

It is possible to travel in some areas of the outback in a 2WD vehicle, but it is safer and much more practical to use a 4WD vehicle suited to off-road conditions. Remember that if you rent a vehicle, there may be restrictions on insurance if you drive on unclassified roads; seek advice from the car rental company before you make any plans.

Your vehicle should be fitted with air conditioning to counteract high inland daytime temperatures and to allow you to drive with all the windows closed through dusty areas. You should be able to carry out small running repairs and must carry an owner's manual for the vehicle, tools and spare parts (**see:** Tools and Spare Parts p. 607).

Track in Purnululu National Park, Western Australia

DRIVING CONDITIONS

Outback driving conditions vary greatly. The deserts are usually dry; conditions change after rain. Many parts of the tropics are accessible only in the 'dry' season, and even then there are streams to ford and washaways to contend with.

Pre-reading road conditions is vital. Always be on the alert. Recognising that a patch of different colour may represent a change in surface is an example. Sand can give way to rock; rock may lead to mud; hard surfaces become bulldust with little warning.

Soft sand, bulldust and mud. These are best negotiated at the highest reasonable speed and in the highest possible gear and in 4WD. However, examine the road surface first. Never enter deep mud or mud covered with water without first establishing the depth of either or both.

Deep sand. Requires low tyre pressures. Carry a tyre pressure gauge and drop pressures to about 10 psi. Reinflate when on gravel or bitumen roads again, because the soft tyres will perform very badly and may blow out as a result of stone fractures on hard surfaces.

Crossing a creek or stream. Stop to check the track across for clear passage and water depth. If the water is deep but fordable, cover the front of the vehicle with a tarpaulin and remove the fan belt to stop water being sprayed over the engine electrics. Drive through in low range second gear or high range first gear, and clear the opposite embankment before stopping again. If it has rained, beware of flash flooding.

Dips. Dips are common on outback roads and can break suspension components if you enter too fast. To cross a dip, brake on entry to drop the vehicle's nose, and hold the brake on until just before the bottom of the depression. Then accelerate again to lift the nose

and therefore the suspension, as you exit. This will prevent the springs from bottoming out and will also give maximum clearance.

Cattle grids. Also a potential hazard, as they are often neglected, with broken approaches and exits. If a grid appears to be in disrepair, stop and check first, before attempting to cross.

Road trains. These multi-trailered, long trucks are difficult and often dangerous to overtake, particularly on dusty roads. Wait for a chance to get the front of your vehicle out to a position where the road-train driver can see you in the rear-view mirror, but even then do not try to overtake until the driver has signalled acknowledgement that you are there. Sometimes it is prudent to stop and take a break, rather than try to overtake a road train. If you meet an oncoming road train, pull over and stop until it has passed.

Animals. There are vast areas of unfenced property in the outback where stock roam free. A bullock or a large kangaroo can seriously damage your vehicle. Be especially wary around sunrise and sunset when animals are more active. A bull-bar or roo-bar provides limited protection at low speeds only, especially against larger animals. Driver concentration should be at as high a level as in city peak hours.

SURVIVING IN THE OUTBACK
You might be stranded in a remote area with a major mechanical breakdown, or if your vehicle becomes bogged. For this eventuality you should be equipped to wait at that spot until you are found. Always carry a week's supply of spare water, a minimum of 21 litres per head. Keep it for an emergency. Emergency supplies of dry biscuits and canned food will keep hunger at bay, but body evaporation and thirst is the vital factor. Do not drink radiator coolant. Often it is not water but a chemical compound, and even if it is water, usually it has been treated with chemicals.

Do not try to walk out of a remote area. You are going to survive only if you wait by the car. Before entering a remote area, check with police or a local authority, and tell them where and when you are going, and when you expect to arrive. When you reach your destination, telephone and advise of your arrival. This is important as failure to do so causes unneccessary and expensive searches.

If stranded, set up some type of shelter and, in the heat of the day, remain in its shade as motionless as possible. Movement accelerates fluid loss.

Direction Finding

Clever electronic hand-held navigation devices, using the Global Positioning System (GPS), are now available from bushwalking shops, boating stores and outdoor centres. These can be used with or without a map and are much more sophisticated and accurate than a magnetic compass.

If you cannot read a map or use a compass – or if you have no navigational device with you – it is vital to have some means of orientating yourself if you are lost.

A simple method of finding north is to use a conventional wristwatch.

Place the 12 on the watch in line with the sun and bisect the angle between it and the hour hand. This will give a fairly accurate indication of north.

At night, the Southern Cross can be used to determine south.

When exploring a side track off the main road, be sure to make a rough sketch of the route you are following, noting all turnoffs and distances between them (using the speedometer), together with any prominent landmarks. When you return, reconcile your return route with the sketch, point by point.

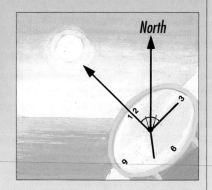

How to Obtain Water

Less than 24 hours without water can be fatal in outback heat.
- It is essential to conserve body moisture. Take advantage of any shade that can be found.
- **DO NOT LEAVE your vehicle**. It may be the only effective shade available.
- Ration your drinking water. Do not drink your car's radiator coolant.

Although a river or creek bed may be dry, there is often an underground water source. A hole dug about a metre deep may produce a useful soak.

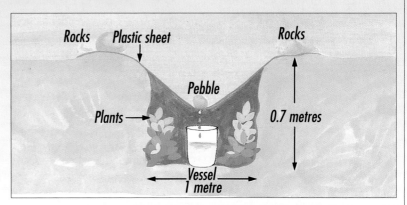

Making an Arizona Still
Where there is vegetation, it is possible to extract water from it using an Arizona still.
- Before the heat of the day, dig a hole about one metre across and a little more than half a metre deep.
- Put a vessel of some kind in the hole's centre to collect the water.
- Surround the vessel with cut vegetation. (Fleshy plants hold more moisture than drier saltbush.)

- Cover the hole with a plastic sheet held down by closely packed rocks, so that the hole is sealed off.
- Put a small stone in the centre of the sheet, directly above the collection vessel.

The sun's heat will evaporate moisture from the plants. This moisture will condense on the inside of the plastic, run down the cone formed by the weight of the stone and drip off into the vessel. In uninterrupted sunlight, with suitable plants, about one litre of water should be collected about every six hours. The Arizona still takes about three hours to start producing and it will become less efficient as the ground moisture dries out. A new hole will need to be dug at intervals.

Outback Advice

CRITICAL RULES FOR OUTBACK MOTORING

- Check intended routes carefully.
- Check the best time of year to travel.
- Check that your vehicle is suited to outback conditions.
- Keep your load to a minimum.
- Check ahead for local road conditions, weather forecasts and fuel availability.
- Advise someone of your route, destination and arrival time.
- Ensure that you have essential supplies: water, food, fuel, spare parts.
- Carry detailed maps.
- Carry an extra supply of food and water in case of emergency; four to five litres of water per person per day in hot areas.
- Always remain with your vehicle if it breaks down.

Warning

When driving on desert roads, remember:
- There is no water, except after rains.
- Unmade roads can be extremely hazardous, especially when wet.
- Traffic is almost non-existent, except on main roads.

OUTBACK ADVICE SERVICE

The Royal Flying Doctor Service of Australia (RFDS) provides emergency outback assistance. RFDS bases provide advice on outback safety, communications and emergency procedures. The base at Broken Hill (NSW) also hires out HF radio transceiver sets with a fixed emergency call button in case of accident or sickness; Charleville (Qld) and Jandakot (WA) bases can obtain sets from Broken Hill if advance notice is given. Some bases that do not hire out sets can suggest local outlets for them. Note that mobile phones are ineffective in many areas; they cannot be relied upon for communication in remote parts of Australia.

New South Wales
Broken Hill: Broken Hill Airport 2880
(08) 8080 1777 (base)
(08) 8088 1188 (emergency assistance)

South Australia
Port Augusta: 4 Vincent St 5700
(08) 8642 2044

Western Australia
Emergency assistance for all of WA:
1800 625800
Derby: Clarendon St 6728
(08) 9191 1211
Jandakot: 3 Eagle Dr., Jandakot Airport 6164
(08) 9417 6300
Kalgoorlie: Kalgoorlie-Boulder Airport 6430
(08) 9093 1500

Sign beside the Eyre Highway in South Australia

Northern Territory
Alice Springs: Stuart Tce 0870
(08) 8952 1033 (base)
(08) 8952 1033 (emergency assistance)
(08) 8952 5733 (after hours emergency assistance)

Queensland
Brisbane: Casuarina St, Eagle Farm 4007
(07) 3860 5388 (base)
(07) 3364 1311 (emergency assistance)
Cairns: 1 Junction St 4870
(07) 4053 1952 (base)
(07) 4053 5419 (emergency assistance)
Charleville: Old Cunnamulla Rd 4470
(07) 4654 1233 (base)
(07) 4654 1443 (emergency assistance)
Mount Isa: Barkly Highway 4825
(07) 4743 2800 (base)
(07) 4743 2802 (emergency assistance)
Rockhampton: Cannonna Rd 4700
(07) 4921 2221 (base)
(07) 4931 7198 (after hours)
Townsville: Airport 4810
(07) 4775 3111 (base)
(07) 4727 4870 (after hours)

For general information on the Royal Flying Doctor Service, contact: The Australian Council of the Royal Flying Doctor Service of Australia, Level 5, 15–17 Young St, Sydney 2000; (02) 9241 2411. Web site www.flyingdoctor.net

SHARING THE OUTBACK

As you travel through the outback, remember you are sharing the land with its traditional Aboriginal owners, pastoralists, other tourists – and even nature itself. In order to protect and preserve the outback for future visitors:
- Respect Aboriginal sacred and cultural sites, and heritage buildings and pioneer relics.
- Protect native flora and fauna; take photographs not specimens.
- Follow restrictions on the use of firearms. These restrictions protect wildlife and stock.
- Carry your own fuel source (for example a portable gas stove), to avoid lighting fires in fire-sensitive areas.
- When lighting a campfire (if you must), keep it small and use any fallen wood sparingly. Never leave a fire unattended; extinguish completely before you move on.
- Do not drive off-road.
- Do not camp immediately adjacent to water sources (for example on riverbanks or by dams). Allow access for stock and native animals.
- Do not bury your rubbish; carry out everything you take in.
- Dispose of faecal waste by burial.
- Leave gates as you find them: open or shut.
- Do not ignore signs warning of dangers or entry restrictions. These are there for your protection.

Breakdowns

There are many causes of motor vehicle breakdown, but fortunately modern vehicle technology has vastly reduced the possibility of being stuck by the roadside. Breakdowns that do occur can sometimes be cured with a roadside 'fix'; but this is often less possible with today's computer-driven vehicles. Inexpert or makeshift repairs may lead to further complications and a bigger repair bill.

Proper vehicle preparation and maintenance should at least reduce the possibility of roadside breakdowns and, on long journeys, the regular vehicle-service schedule should be maintained.

In areas where you have access to service through a motoring organisation, it is better to leave even slightly complicated repairs to the specialist. Remember to carry your membership card, which entitles you to assistance in other States (**see:** Useful Information p. 589). If you are driving a rental car, most rental companies list their recognised repair organisations in the manual supplied. Before you drive the car, you should check that these details are provided. If your rental vehicle cannot be repaired immediately, you should request an exchange vehicle.

If you plan to journey into remote areas, it is a good idea to first take a basic course in vehicle maintenance (**see:** Car Maintenance Courses p. 591). As well, you should carry a range of tools and spare parts (**see:** Tools and Spare Parts p. 607).

MODERN VEHICLES

Most modern vehicles are fitted with electronic engine-management systems, or with electronic ignition and fuel injection. Generally these are more reliable than older systems and usually, in case of partial failure of the system, they have a 'limp home' mode, which enables travelling a limited distance at limited speed. However, total failure of such a system is difficult or impossible to remedy at the roadside without expert knowledge and equipment. This means that travel into remote areas is

Roadside repairs in northern Queensland

rendered much safer by travelling with at least one other vehicle, and by installing or hiring an appropriate long-range radio transmitter, receiver and aerial (**see:** Outback Advice p. 605).

EARLIER-MODEL VEHICLES

For those who drive earlier-model vehicles with less complex electrical and fuel systems, the trouble-shooting flow-charts are designed to be of assistance (**see:** Trouble Shooting p. 608). But first, always remember to:

Watch warning gauges. These have been installed to warn that things may be going wrong. A flickering battery warning light will suggest all is not well with the generator/alternator charge rate and should be attended to promptly. A fluctuating temperature gauge *may* suggest the onset of a problem with the cooling system. Act on the warning at the earliest opportunity.

Make a daily check of fluid levels. Check fuel, water and oil (including spare supplies); also tyre pressures, and fan-belt tension and condition.

Make a regular check of brake-fluid and battery-acid levels, and pressure of spare tyre.

If the vehicle develops an unexplained sound, move to the side of the road as soon as possible. Park on flat ground if you can. You may have to spend some time under the bonnet, so look for shade or shelter. Try to locate the source of the sound. If it is coming from the engine, do nothing and seek help.

WHEN THE ENGINE STOPS

When the engine either splutters to a stop, constantly misfires or stops suddenly but was otherwise running smoothly, the problem is probably in one of two areas: fuel supply or electrics. Use the Trouble Shooting flow-charts (p. 608) to establish where the problem lies. If the problem is within the drive-train – the gearbox, drive-shaft or differential – once again, seek help.

Tools and Spare Parts

Remote-area travelling requires a sound knowledge of the basics of breakdown repairs (**see:** Breakdowns p. 606). This means carrying emergency tools, spare parts and spare fuel, and the *vehicle owner's manual*. The following is a guide to what may be appropriate for your vehicle:

TOOLS

- Set of screwdrivers (blade and Phillips head)
- Small set of socket spanners
- Set of open-end/ring combination spanners
- Small and medium adjustable wrenches
- Small ball pein (engineer's) hammer
- Pliers and wire-cutters
- Hand drill and bits
- Workshop scissors
- Aerosol puncture repair can
- Tyre pump
- Puncture repair kit
- Tyre-pressure gauge
- Wheel brace
- Jack with supplementary wide base for sand or mud (block of wood, approximately the size of an A4 sheet of paper and 3 cm thick)
- Jumper leads (capacitor-type if for EFL engine)
- Hydrometer
- Small spade
- Vice grips
- Good quality tow-rope
- Heavy duty torch, spare batteries and globe
- Pocket knife
- Fire extinguisher(s)

SPARE PARTS

- Epoxy resin bonding 'goo' (for repair of punctured fuel tank)
- Plastic insulating tape
- Spare radiator and heater hoses
- Engine accessory belts (fan, alternator, power steering, etc.)
- Roll of cloth adhesive tape
- 1 metre fuel line (reinforced plastic)
- Insulated electric wire
- Spare electrical connections (range)
- Spare hose-clips (range)
- Distributor cap
- Set of high tension leads
- Condenser (where appropriate)
- Rotor
- Set of spark plugs
- Can of dewatering spray
- Set of points
- Spare fuel, air and oil filters
- Fuel pump kit, water pump kit
- Small-diameter plastic tubing
- Range of spare light globes and fuses
- Nuts, bolts, washers, split pins
- Lubricants: automatic transmission and power steering fluid
- Radiator sealant
- Tube of hand cleaner, clean rags

FUEL

- Spare fuel (40 litres minimum) in steel jerry cans. Do not use non-approved plastic containers; some plastics react with fuel. Also check fuel range, and the distance between refuelling points.
- At least one spare wheel (slightly over-inflated to allow for some air loss). If travelling in remote areas, consider additional tyres/tubes.

Be prepared when travelling in remote areas

Trouble Shooting (for earlier-model vehicles)

ENGINE WILL NOT TURN OVER

1 Check battery for charge.

2 If battery is flat...
recharge or replace, or tow-start (if manual transmission vehicle) until next service opportunity. If automatic, check handbook. Most autos cannot be tow- or clutch-started.

3 If battery is OK...
check if battery terminals and straps are loose, broken or dirty. If so, clean, repair or replace.

4 If terminals are OK...
check for jammed starter motor. For manual vehicle, put in top gear and rock back and forth to try to free pinion. An indication that starter may be jammed is an audible click when you try to start the engine and it will not turn over. With an automatic vehicle, try to turn engine back and forth with a spanner on crankshaft pulley to free pinion. Put gearbox into 'N' first.

5 If starter motor is free...
it is possible a solenoid has failed. Unless you are an auto electrician and carry a spare, seek help.

STARTER MOTOR WHIRRS BUT WILL NOT TURN ENGINE

Very likely, you have stripped a starter ring-gear, which means major repair work. But check to see that the starter motor is fully bolted to its mounting bracket, and tighten if not.

King Leopold Range in the Kimberley, Western Australia

ENGINE TURNS OVER BUT WILL NOT FIRE, OR FIRES BUT WILL NOT RUN CLEANLY, OR MISFIRES REGULARLY, OR RUNS AND STOPS

Problem may be electrics or fuel supply. If unsure, begin with electrics.

Electrics
1 Check that spark is getting to spark plugs. Remove high tension (HT) lead from No. 1 plug and remove No. 1 plug. Reattach HT lead to plug and hold plug body with pliers 1 mm from cylinder-head bolt or similar and turn engine over. Spark plug should produce strong blue spark at regular intervals.

2 If there is a problem with the electrics...
the simplest and fastest way to deal with an electrical problem is to replace parts, either at once or progressively, with spares (**see:** Tools and Spare Parts p. 607). Replace coil and all HT leads and try engine. If problem persists, remove distributor cap and replace condenser and points. Re-set points and fit new rotor and distributor cap. Engine should start and run cleanly.

3 If you carry no spare parts...
you can still confirm electrics as the problem by a process of elimination. If there is no spark at the spark plugs, the problem has to be between battery and plug. Check that low tension lead at side of distributor is connected properly and tightly mounted. If so, remove distributor cap and check for cracks. If there is a crack, repair with an epoxy glue/filler until it can be replaced. Check that condenser is tightly mounted and its LT wire is connected.

Check that points open and close properly by turning engine over by hand slowly and watching for a spark between points. Points may be burned or deeply pitted. If so, remove points and use nail-file to clean up faces, then replace and re-set. If, however, you have established an electrical problem and you have no spares, seek assistance.

4 If you have a spark at the plugs...
most likely you have a fuel-supply problem.

Fuel supply
1 Check fuel tank for fuel. Despite gauge reading, it is possible that the gauge is faulty.

2 If fuel is OK...
check accelerator cable connection and for free operation, and check choke cable and

operation. For vehicle with automatic choke, remove air-cleaner carrier and element, and look down choke tube. If choke butterfly is not fully open, open it and check to see if it stays open. If it closes again, engine is flooding, and may not run for that reason. A faulty auto choke cannot be repaired at the roadside.

3 If accelerator and choke cables are operating correctly...
do not replace air cleaner; remove fuel line to carburettor and turn engine over. Fuel should flow freely. If so, check it is not contaminated by pumping small amount into clear glass or plastic container and examine for water and/or dirt.

4 If water or dirt are apparent...
check and replace fuel filter and remove and check fuel pump. Examine glass for contamination. If none or very little, replace fuel line to carburettor and try engine again.

5 If there is substantial contamination...
it may be coming from fuel tank. Tank will need to be drained and perhaps flushed.

Drained fuel should be saved and strained back. If you are travelling a long way before next fuel stop, be careful not to waste fuel.

6 If there is no fuel at fuel line and no apparent blockage...
fuel pump has failed for some reason. If you are carrying a spare, replace pump. If not, seek mechanical assistance.

7 If fuel is clean and running freely...
blockage may be inside carburettor. Carefully remove top and then main jet and float. Clear main jet and clean out float bowl. Be careful not to interfere with float level. Replace parts and try engine again.

OVERHEATING IN A WATER-COOLED ENGINE

Occurs when coolant level falls or circulation is interrupted. Dash gauge gives warning, but vehicle also will lose power.

1 Stop vehicle. Do not remove radiator cap. Check hoses and hose connections for signs of leakage, or steam if system is boiling. Any identified leak can be cured temporarily with spare hoses or binding with cloth tape.

2 If there is no sign of leakage...
after about 10 minutes and holding radiator cap with a thick cloth, slowly remove cap, letting out steam under pressure at same time. Top up radiator while engine is running and car's heater is on hot setting. Do not add cold water until engine is running.

3 Check again for leaks.

4 If there is a slow drip from radiator core...
fix with an internal chemical sealant or externally with an epoxy filler or adhesive.

5 If no leak is apparent...
check fanbelt for tension. It may be slipping and not driving water pump. If so, tighten by releasing bolts on generator/alternator and increasing tension and re-tightening.

6 If you cannot account for overheating by any of the preceding...
you may have a failed water-pump, a blocked system, a failed pressure cap or a combination of all three. Seek help as soon as possible, but you may drive on if you can continue topping up.

The Great Ocean Road, Victoria

Child's Play

Everyone in the family looks forward to a holiday, but most parents dread a long car trip when children travelling in the back seat can become bored and irritable passengers.

Most children are good travellers, but there are some car journeys that are inappropriate for small children (say, under the age of 10). Usually children will consider every trip an adventure and start looking forward to it for weeks ahead. A little thought and planning by parents will avoid the boredom of a long drive and ease the strain on all concerned, particularly the driver, who needs total concentration.

DOS AND DON'TS

Several days before setting out, make a list of 'dos' and 'don'ts' for the children and explain, seriously, why their cooperation is necessary. Make it quite clear that you expect them to observe the rules because they are safety measures, and reinforce this message at the time of departure. For example:

DO NOT fight or yell while the car is in motion. This distracts the driver and can cause a collision or a serious mishap, which might bring the holiday to an abrupt end.

DO NOT play with door handles or locks. (Set the child-proof locks on rear doors before departure.)

DO keep head, arms and hands inside the car.

DO NOT lean out of the windows.

DO NOT unbuckle seat belts or restraints while the car is in motion.

HANDY HINTS

- Any long car trip, even with frequent stops, can be tiring. Make sure the children are as cool and comfortable as possible. Curtains (or substitutes, for example a towel) or sun screens on rear windows are advisable. Babies and pre-school children may need their security blankets or favourite soft toys. These items can save the day if the children are upset or sleepy.

- Pack a small bag – a cosmetic bag is ideal – along with packets of moist towelettes or a damp face cloth.

- Make sure your first-aid kit contains some junior paracetamol and supplies of any other medication taken by the children. It is important to carry some insect repellent and sunblock, since children tend to get bitten easily, and their skin must be protected from the sun. Also bring a mosquito net to cover your baby's bassinette when you are outdoors.

- Make up a 'busy box' for the children to take on the trip. Use a small box – a shoe box is best – and keep it on the back seat where the children can reach it easily. Fill the box with small note-pads, crayons or felt-tipped pens (pencils break and need to be sharpened) and activity books. Choose activity books for each child's age group. Do not forget to include your children's favourite storybooks.

- Include some tapes of stories for entertainment, and children's songs for 'quiet times'. Music soothes and lulls children to sleep.

- Although your primary concern will be to keep the children happy and occupied during the car trip, it is also important to take along some games, such as Snakes and Ladders, pocket-sized video games or a pack of cards, to keep them amused in the evenings and on rainy days. Also encourage older children to keep a diary. A rubber ball and skipping rope will be welcomed by young children who enjoy playing outdoors.

- If you have room, breakfast trays can be used as book supports for drawing or colouring-in. If not, a clipboard will serve as well.

- When travelling with young children, make sure that you stop the car every hour or so, so that they can stretch their legs and let off steam. Try to stop at a park or an area with some play equipment. If it is raining, stop at a newsagent or bookshop where the children can browse and perhaps buy something to read.

- If children complain of feeling sick, stop the car as soon as possible and let them out for some fresh air. Sit with them for a while and persuade them to take a sip of water before returning to the car and continuing the trip.

- When approaching a rest area, a garage or a small town, offer the children a toilet stop. Do not delay until they get desperate and cannot wait.

- Even though you plan to stop for meals and snacks on your journey, you should still pack some food and drink. Children become very hungry and thirsty when travelling and it is important that they eat little but often. Pack small snacks in their own lunch boxes. Avoid chocolate, which is messy and can make children feel sick, and potato chips which are almost as messy and encourage thirst. Avoid greasy foods. Sultanas, nuts (for older children only), bananas, grapes, cheese cubes, celery and carrot sticks, and boiled sweets are good for snacks. For lunches, pack easy-to-eat meals like chicken drumsticks or bite-size rolled-up pieces of cold meat with crackers on the side. Children can find large sandwiches difficult to handle, so remember to cut their sandwiches small. Sandwich fillings require some thought, avoid anything moist or runny.

- Avoid spills and breakages by buying milk or fruit juice in small cartons and making sure you have a good supply of drinking straws. If you carry drinks in a flask, take training cups for younger children. For older children use paper or styrofoam cups with tight-fitting lids and with straws, and recycle as much as possible.

- Have plastic bags for waste paper and empty drink cartons in the cars.

- When eating out, choose places that have fast service – or have meals sent to your room.

CHILD RESTRAINTS

Note that the law in each State and Territory is very specific when it comes to child restraints in cars. As the law differs from State to State, it is important to check with the State motoring organisation (**see:** Useful Information p. 589) when travelling with children. Under certain ages and weights, children in passenger cars are required to be seated in the rear seat, and in an approved child restraint.

GAMES

To while away the long hours you will spend in the car with your children, here are some games for them to play.

For younger children

Colour contest: Each child selects one colour, then tries to spot cars of that colour. The first with ten cars wins.

Spot the mistake in the story: Either you or an older child tells a story with obvious mistakes. For example, 'Once upon a time, there was a little boy called Goldilocks, and he visited the house of the seven dwarfs.'

Scavenger: Make a list of 10 things you are likely to come across during your trip. For example: farmhouse, bus stop, cow, lamb, chemist shop, woman with a hat. Ask the children to spot them, one at a time. Older children cross the objects off the list as they are seen.

Alphabet game: Select a letter and ask the children to spot as many things as possible beginning with that particular letter of the alphabet.

For older children

Rhyme stories: One child starts a story, and the next has to take up the story with a line that rhymes. The second child also continues the story with a line of new rhyme. For example:
1st child: 'I know a man called Sam.'
2nd child: 'He loves to eat ham.
The more he eats the more he wants.'

Cliff-hangers: One child begins a story and stops at the most exciting part, leaving the next child to continue.

I packed my bag...A good memory game in which each player has to name one object she or he puts into a bag. As each child takes a turn, she or he lists all the objects in order and adds a new item to the list. For example:
1st child: 'I packed my bag and put an apple in it.'
2nd child: 'I packed my bag and put an apple and a comb in it.'
3rd child: 'I packed my bag and put an apple, a comb and a key in it.'
4th child: 'I packed my bag and put an apple, a comb, a key and a ball in it.'

What am I? This is an old favourite. One player thinks of an object or an animal and keeps it secret. The others take turns to ask questions, which must be answered only by 'Yes' or 'No', for clues to the identity of the object or animal.

Number-plate messages: Note the letters of the number plate on a nearby car and ask the children to make up a message or conversation from them. For example:
WFL: 'What's for lunch?'

Navigation: All you need is a spare road-map covering the route you are taking. The children can follow your progress with a coloured marker.

Word scramble: Prepare a list of words with jumbled letters and get the children to unscramble them.

Crossword: Draw crossword squares on several note-pads. During the trip, play the crossword game by calling out letters at random. The children write the letters in any square they wish and try to make up words.

Safety

SAFE SWIMMING, SURFING

- Swim or surf only at those beaches patrolled by lifesavers.
- Never swim alone.
- Read and obey all warning signs.
- Swim or surf within the area indicated by the red and yellow flags. (An amber flag indicates that the surf is dangerous. A red flag and sign 'Danger – closed to bathing' indicates the beach is unsafe; do not swim or surf in this area.)
- Do not enter the water directly after a meal or under the influence of alcohol or drugs.
- If you are caught in a rip or strong current and you are a strong swimmer, swim across it to safer waters. Otherwise, float and raise one arm as a distress signal until help arrives; **do not panic**.
- If seized with a cramp, keep the affected part perfectly still, float and raise one arm until help arrives.
- Don't run and dive in the water, even if you have checked for hazards earlier – conditions can change.

SAFE BOATING

- Tell someone where you are going.
- Check the weather forecast.

- Carry adequate equipment.
- Carry adequate clothing (including sunscreen, long sleeved clothing, hat and sunglasses).
- Carry effective life jackets.
- Carry enough fuel and water.
- Ensure engine reliability.
- Guard against fire.
- Do not overload the craft.
- Know the boating rules and local regulations; also distress signals.
- Watch the weather.
- Do not drink alcohol while boating.

SAFE SKIING

Skiing is fun, but like any sport, there is the risk of injury. It is also strenuous. If possible, train beforehand, and avoid overdoing it on the slopes. All ski resorts have instructors if you need to take lessons.

- Choose slopes that suit your ability.
- Wear clothing suited to the conditions.
- Check equipment before setting out.
- Avoid skiing alone; if you must, then tell someone where you are going.
- If lost, stay where you are; only retrace your tracks if they are very clear.

For safety, swim in a patrolled area

Cross-country skiing requires careful planning:
- Tell someone in authority of your intended route.
- Travel in a group.
- Take plenty of food and adequate equipment for your survival.
- Protect yourself against sunburn.
- Watch the weather.
- Be alert for signs of exposure (hypothermia): tiredness, reluctance to carry on, clumsiness, loss of judgement and collapse.

INDEX OF PLACE NAMES

This index includes all towns, localities, roadhouses and national parks shown on the maps and mentioned in the text. In addition, it includes major places of interest, landforms and water features.

Place names are followed by a map page number and grid reference, and/or the text page number on which that place name occurs. A page number set in bold type indicates the main text entry for that place name. For example:

Bairnsdale Vic. 231 P4, 240 F13, **166**, 186
Bairnsdale – Place name
Vic. – State
231 P4, 240 F13 – Bairnsdale appears on these map pages

166 – Main entry for Bairnsdale
186 – Bairnsdale is also mentioned on this page

The alphabetical order followed in the index is that of 'word-by-word', where all entries under one word are grouped together. Where a place name consists of more than one word, the order is governed by the first and then the second word. For example:
Green River
Greenbank
Greens Beach
Greenwood Forest
Greg Greg
Gregafell

Names beginning with Mc are indexed as Mac and those beginning with St, as Saint.

The following abbreviations and contractions are used in the index:
ACT – Australian Capital Territory
JBT – Jervis Bay Territory
NSW – New South Wales
NT – Northern Territory
Qld – Queensland
SA – South Australia
St – Saint
Tas. – Tasmania
Vic. – Victoria
WA – Western Australia

Moorleah Tas. 584 F5
Moormbool Vic. 238 F8
Moorngag Vic. 228 B5, 239 L8
Mooroobool Qld 522 A12
Moorooduc Vic. 217 K10, 219 L4
Moorook SA 307 P7
Moorooka Qld 514 G4
Moorookyle Vic. 216 D2
Mooroolbark Vic. 214 E7
Mooroopna Vic. 238 H6, 200
Moorooroo SA 304 E7
Moorowie SA 306 H10
Moorrinya National Park Qld 526 B6,
533 Q5
Moorumbine WA 386 G5, 365
Moppin NSW 116 G4, 525 J13
Moranbah Qld 526 I7, 491
Morangarell NSW 113 A1, 114 C9
Morawa WA 388 C4, 359
Morayfield Qld 516 F9, 517 C1
Morchard SA 307 K1, 309 K12
Mordialloc Vic. 215 C6, 217 K8
Morea Vic. 234 C10
Moree NSW 116 G5, 71
Moree Vic. 232 D2, 234 D13
Morella Qld 533 N10
Moreton Island Qld 525 Q8
Moreton Island National Park Qld
517 H1, 525 Q8, 455, 460, 464, 465
Morgan SA 307 N6, 280
Morgans Crossing NSW 111 D7, 113 F10,
241 P6
Moriac Vic. 216 E10, 223 C8, 233 Q8,
182, 202
Moriarty Tas. 580 F6, 585 J7
Morisset NSW 99 Q1, 106 F12, 115 M5
Morkalla Vic. 120 B7, 236 B4, 307 R7
Morley WA 377 K9
Morningside Qld 512 I11
Mornington Tas. 577 J7
Mornington Vic. 217 K10, 219 J3, 230 D7,
157, 192, 207
Mornington Island Qld 531 E5, 492
Mornington Peninsula Vic. 217 J12,
218 G10, 230 C8, 141, 157, 207
Mornington Peninsula National Park
Vic. 216 H11, 217 J12, 218 H10,
223 H10, 230 B8, 157, 163, 200
Morongla NSW 113 D1, 114 F8
Morpeth NSW 106 D6, 115 N4, 71
Morphett Vale SA 300 A12, 301 F3,
302 D4
Morphettville SA 296 E10, 251
Morri Morri Vic. 226 B3, 235 K10
Morrisons Vic. 216 E6, 223 C1
Mortat Vic. 234 C9
Mortchup Vic. 216 A5, 226 G12, 233 M4
Mortdale NSW 96 I6
Mortlake NSW 92 H8
Mortlake Vic. 233 J7
Morton National Park NSW 110 A11,
113 H4, 115 J11, 139 O1, 35, 37, 44, 52,
76, 78, 84
Morton Plains Vic. 235 K5
Morundah NSW 121 O9
Moruya NSW 113 H7, 139 M8, 72
Moruya Heads NSW 113 H7, 139 N8
Morven NSW 121 Q12, 239 Q1
Morven Qld 524 D6

Morwell Vic. 231 J7, 193
Morwell National Park Vic. 231 J8, 193
Mosman NSW 93 O8, 99 O8, 28
Mosman Park WA 374 B7, 323
Mosquito Creek NSW 116 I5
Mosquito Flat SA 301 H6
Moss Vale NSW 110 B7, 113 I3, 115 J10,
36, 72
Mossgiel NSW 121 J3
Mossiface Vic. 231 Q4, 240 G13
Mossman Qld 523 B3, 529 M5, 472, 491
Mossy Point NSW 113 H7, 139 N8
Moulamein NSW 120 I10, 237 P9, 72
Moulyinning WA 386 H7
Mount Aberdeen National Park Qld
526 H2
Mount Adrah NSW 113 B5, 114 C12
Mount Alford Qld 525 P10
Mount Alfred Vic. 113 A8, 240 F1
Mount Arapiles Vic. 234 E9, 194
Mount Augustus National Park WA
387 F7, 350, 359
Mount Barker SA 300 E11, 301 I2,
305 C2, 307 L10
Mount Barker WA 383 M9, 386 H12,
388 E12, 335, 359
Mount Barnett Roadhouse WA 384 H6,
393 M6
Mount Barney National Park Qld
117 O1, 517 A13, 525 P11, 460, 463
Mount Bartle Frere Qld 529 N8, 463, 481
Mount Bauple National Park Qld 525 O5
Mount Baw Baw Vic. 217 R7, 231 J4,
165, 190, 192
Mount Beauty Vic. 229 N5, 239 Q8,
240 D6, 193, 202
Mount Beckworth Vic. 216 B2, 227 J8, 175
Mount Bellenden Ker Qld 523 G12, 463
Mount Benson SA 305 F9
Mount Beppo Qld 516 B9
Mount Best Vic. 231 J9
Mount Blue Cow NSW 112 D11, 44, 66,
81, 82
Mount Bogong Vic. 229 P5, 240 D6, 164,
193
Mount Bruce SA 305 G10
Mount Bruce WA 387 I4, 390 B5, 337, 366
Mount Bryan SA 307 L4
Mount Bryan East SA 307 M4
Mount Buffalo Chalet Vic. 229 K5,
239 P8, 240 B6
Mount Buffalo National Park Vic. 229 J4,
239 O7, 240 B5, 164, 168, 173, 174, 190
Mount Buller Vic. 228 G11, 239 N11,
189, 190
Mount Burr SA 305 G11, 279
Mount Bute Vic. 216 A7, 221 E1, 233 M5
Mount Camel Vic. 238 E8
Mount Carbine Qld 529 L5
Mount Christie SA 315 M4
Mount Claremont WA 374 C3, 322
Mount Clear Vic. 227 K12
Mount Colah NSW 94 F7
Mount Cole Vic. 226 E8
Mount Compass SA 301 G5, 305 B3,
307 K10, 290
Mount Cook National Park Qld 529 L3
Mount Coolon Qld 526 H5

Mount Coolum National Park Qld
516 G3, 520 H6
Mount Cooper SA 306 A3, 315 Q13
Mount Coot-tha Qld 512 D13, 514 D2
Mount Coot-tha Forest Park Qld
512 D13, 514 D1, 445, 451
Mount Cotton Qld 515 Q7
Mount Cottrell Vic. 216 H6, 223 H2
Mount Damper SA 306 B3, 308 A13,
315 R13
Mount Dandenong Vic. 214 F10
Mount Darrah NSW 111 C8
Mount David NSW 98 C8, 114 H7
Mount Direction Tas. 581 M6, 585 L7
Mount Donna Buang Vic. 217 O5,
230 G3, 190, 203
Mount Doran Vic. 216 D5, 233 P4
Mount Druitt NSW 99 L8
Mount Drysdale NSW 119 N9, 55
Mount Duneed Vic. 216 F10, 223 E8
Mount Ebenezer Roadhouse NT 432 I12,
438 H11
Mount Eccles Vic. 217 P12, 230 H8, 183
Mount Eccles National Park Vic. 232 F7,
165, 197
Mount Egerton Vic. 216 E5, 227 N12,
233 Q4
Mount Eliza Vic. 219 K2
Mount Emu Vic. 216 A5, 226 G12, 233 M4
Mount Evelyn Vic. 214 G7, 220 B9
Mount Fairy NSW 139 K1
Mount Feathertop Vic. 229 N8, 240 D7,
164, 183
Mount Field National Park Tas. 578 A2,
582 I7, 547, 554, 566
Mount Frankland National Park WA
382 F9, 386 F12, 388 D12, 369
Mount Franklin Vic. 216 E2, 227 N8, 177
Mount Gambier SA 305 H12, 243, 277,
281
Mount Garnet Qld 529 L8, 472
Mount George NSW 115 O1, 117 N13
Mount Glorious Qld 516 E11, 517 B4, 453
Mount Gravatt Qld 515 J4
Mount Hallen Qld 516 A11
Mount Hawthorn WA 376 G12
Mount Helen Vic. 216 C4, 227 K12,
233 O4
Mount Helena WA 378 E4, 386 D3, 360
Mount Hope NSW 121 N2
Mount Hope SA 306 C6, 267
Mount Horeb NSW 113 B5, 114 D12
Mount Hotham Vic. 229 N9, 239 Q10,
240 D8, 164, 186, 190
Mount Hunter NSW 99 K10, 110 E1
Mount Hypipamee National Park Qld
529 M8, 459, 462, 466, 472
Mount Imlay National Park NSW
111 E12, 113 F12, 241 P9
Mount Irvine NSW 98 I4
Mount Isa Qld 532 E4, 441, 442, 469,
491, 494
Mount Kaputar National Park NSW
116 H7, 44, 46, 74
Mount Keira NSW 108 A10, 87
Mount Keith WA 388 H1, 390 F12
Mount Kembla NSW 110 G6, 87
Mount Kilcoy Qld 516 C6

Mount Kosciuszko NSW 112 C12,
113 B10, 138 A13, 240 I4, 56, 66, 81,
82, 132
Mount Kuring-gai NSW 94 G6
Mount Lambie NSW 98 E4
Mount Larcom Qld 527 O12
Mount Lawley WA 375 J1, 377 J12
Mount Lewis NSW 92 E13, 96 G3
Mount Liebig NT 432 C2, 438 E7
Mount Lloyd Tas. 578 E5, 583 K8
Mount Lofty SA 297 O9, 300 C10, 255,
262, 269
Mount Lonarch Vic. 226 G8, 233 M1,
235 M13, 166
Mount Macedon Vic. 216 H3, 227 R10,
230 B1, 238 E12, 158, 206
Mount McIntyre SA 305 H11
Mount Magnet WA 388 E2, 360
Mount Martha Vic. 217 J10, 219 J5,
230 D7, 157, 193, 207
Mount Mary SA 307 N6
Mount Mee Qld 516 E8, 517 B1
Mount Meharry WA 387 I5, 390 C5, 367
Mount Mercer Vic. 216 C6, 233 O5
Mount Molloy Qld 523 B6, 529 M6
Mount Morgan Qld 527 N11, 492, 497
Mount Moriac Vic. 216 E10, 223 C8,
233 Q8
Mount Muirhead SA 305 G11
Mount Mulligan Qld 529 L6
Mount Nebo Qld 516 E12, 517 B4, 453
Mount Nelson Tas. 576 F12
Mount Olive NSW 115 L3
Mount Ommaney Qld 514 C6, 516 F13,
517 C6
Mount Osmond SA 297 M8
Mount Ossa Qld 527 K4, 582 G1, 584 G11
Mount Ossa Tas. 582 G1, 584 G11, 555
Mount Ousley NSW 108 C6, 110 H6
Mount Perry Qld 525 N3
Mount Pleasant NSW 108 A6
Mount Pleasant Qld 516 E9, 517 B2
Mount Pleasant SA 300 G8, 305 D1,
307 M9
Mount Pleasant Vic. 225 E10
Mount Pleasant WA 374 G8
Mount Pritchard NSW 96 A2
Mount Rat SA 306 I8
Mount Remarkable National Park SA
307 J1, 308 I12, 263, 269, 279, 285, 291
Mount Richmond Vic. 232 C8
Mount Richmond National Park Vic.
232 C8, 197
Mount Roland Tas. 580 D10
Mount Rowan Vic. 216 C3, 227 K10
Mount St Gwinear Vic. 231 J4, 190
Mount St Thomas NSW 108 B13
Mount Samson Qld 516 E11, 517 B4
Mount Schank SA 305 H12, 281, 286
Mount Seaview NSW 117 M12
Mount Selwyn NSW 112 D4, 113 C7,
138 C8, 41, 44, 81
Mount Seymour Tas. 583 M5
Mount Slide Vic. 217 M4, 220 C3
Mount Stirling Vic. 228 G11, 239 N11,
240 A9, 189, 190
Mount Stuart Tas. 576 D7
Mount Surprise Qld 529 J10, 494

Viking
A division of Penguin Books Australia Ltd
487 Maroondah Highway, PO Box 257
  Ringwood, Victoria 3134, Australia
Penguin Books Ltd
Harmondsworth, Middlesex, England
Penguin Putnam Inc.
375 Hudson Street, New York, New York
  10014, USA
Penguin Books Canada Limited
10 Alcorn Avenue, Toronto, Ontario,
  Canada M4V 3B2
Penguin Books (N.Z.) Ltd
Cnr Rosedale and Airborne Roads,
  Albany, Auckland, New Zealand
Penguin Books (South Africa) (Pty) Ltd
5 Watkins Street, Denver Ext 4, 2094,
  South Africa
Penguin Books India (P) Ltd
11, Community Centre, Panchsheel Park
  New Delhi 110 017, India

This nineteenth edition published by
Penguin Books Australia Ltd, 2000
First published by George Philip &
  O'Neil Pty Ltd, 1980
Second edition 1981
Third edition 1983
Reprinted 1984
Fourth edition 1985
Fifth edition 1986
Sixth edition published by Penguin Books
  Australia Ltd 1987
Seventh edition 1988
Eighth edition 1989
Ninth edition 1990
Tenth edition 1991
Eleventh edition 1992
Twelfth edition 1993
Thirteenth edition 1994
Fourteenth edition 1995
Fifteen edition 1996
Sixteenth edition 1997
Seventeenth edition 1998
Eighteenth edition 1999

Copyright © Penguin Books Australia Ltd,
2000

ISBN 0 670 88972 5

Printed in China by Midas Printing (Asia) Ltd

Publisher's Note: Every effort has been
made to ensure that the information in
this book is accurate at the time of going
to press. The publisher welcomes
information and suggestions for
corrections or improvement. email:
cartog@penguin.com.au
A Suggestion Form is provided on
page 655.

Disclaimers: The publisher cannot accept
responsibility for any errors or omissions.
The representation on the maps of any
road or track is not necessarily evidence
of public right of way.

ACKNOWLEDGEMENTS

GENERAL EDITOR
Astrid Browne

COVER DESIGN
Cathy Larsen, Penguin Design Studio

TEXT DESIGN
Penguin Design Studio

DESKTOP PUBLISHING
P.A.G.E. Pty Ltd

CARTOGRAPHY
Penguin Cartographic: Michael Archer,
Colin Critchell, Paul de Leur, Damien
Demaj, Bruce McGurty, Julie Sheridan

COPY EDITING
Jenny Lang, Susan McLeish,
Heidi Marfurt, Katrina Webb

MAP AND TEXT RESEARCH
Michael Archer, Damien Demaj,
Simon Hrabe, Bruce McGurty,
Susan McLeish, Heidi Marfurt,
Julie Sheridan, Katrina Webb

PICTURE RESEARCH
Heidi Marfurt, Katrina Webb

ASSISTANCE WITH RESEARCH
This edition was produced with
assistance of local visitor information
centres throughout Australia and the
following organisations and individuals:
Australian Bureau of Statistics (for
  assistance with population figures)
Bureau of Meteorology (for climate
  information)
National Road Transport Commission
  (for information on road rules)
St John Ambulance Australia (for Accident
  Action photographs and information)
Surf Life Saving Victoria (for information
  on water safety)
New South Wales
Geographical Names Board
National Parks and Wildlife Service
Sydney Visitors Centre
Tamara Clark (Leighton Contractors)
Australian Capital Territory
Canberra Tourism and Events
  Corporation
Environment ACT
Victoria
Geographic Names Victoria
Parks Victoria
Tourism Victoria
South Australia
Adelaide Convention and Tourism
  Authority
Department of Environment, Heritage
  and Aboriginal Affairs
Geographical Names Advisory
  Committee
South Australian Tourism Commission
Western Australia
Department of Conservation and Land
  Management
Geographic Names Committee of
  Western Australia
Western Australian Tourism Commission
Northern Territory
Central Australian Tourism Industry
  Association
Darwin Region Tourism Association
Northern and Central land councils
Northern Territory Tourist Commission
Parks and Wildlife Commission of the
  Northern Territory
Parks Australia
Place Names Committee

Queensland
Brisbane Tourism
David Gibson (Newstead House)
Department of Natural Resources
Great Barrier Reef Marine Park Authority
Queensland Parks and Wildlife Service
Tourism Queensland
Tasmania
Martyn Cove
Nomenclature Board of Tasmania
Parks and Wildlife Service, Tasmania
Tourism Tasmania

The publisher also wishes to
acknowledge local government offices
and the following State road authorities
for their assistance with map research:
Commonwealth Department of
Transport and Regional Development;
Roads and Traffic Authority New South
Wales; Vicroads, Victoria; Department of
Transport, Urban Planning and the Arts,
South Australia; Main Roads Western
Australia; Department of Transport and
Works, Northern Territory; Department of
Main Roads, Queensland; Department
of Transport, Tasmania.

The following individuals also assisted with
map research and/or cartography: Michael
Cove, Tahir Demaj and Michael Vella.

PHOTO CREDITS
Half-title page Errinundra National Park,
Vic., *John Meier;* **Title page** Little Sandy
Desert, WA, *AUSCAPE (Tim Acker);*
p. iv Rippled sand, Sturt Stony Desert,
SA, *Ted Mead;* Lotus lilies, Kakadu
National Park, NT, *Stock Photos
(Otto Rogge);* The Twelve Apostles, Vic.,
AUSCAPE (Jean-Paul Ferrero); Jagged
peaks, Cradle Mountain–Lake St Clair
National Park, Tas., *Ted Mead;* Kings
Canyon, NT, *Ted Mead;* Lake Gairdner
National Park, SA, *AUSCAPE (Jean-Paul
Ferrero);* **p. v** Shark Bay, WA, *AUSCAPE
(Jean-Paul Ferrero);* Sand dunes, Shark
Bay, WA, *AUSCAPE (Jean-Paul Ferrero);*
Minnamurra Falls near Nowra, NSW,
John Meier; **p. vi** Red lechenaultia,
Lochman Transparencies (Jiri Lochman);
Grevillea, *Lochman Transparencies
(Jiri Lochman);* Bitter pea, *Lochman
Transparencies (Jiri Lochman);*
p. vii Thorny devil, *Australian Picture
Library (Derek Roff);* Red lacewing,
*Lochman Transparencies (Hans & Judy
Beste);* Woma python, *Stock Photos
(Stewart Roper);* **p. viii** Francois Peron
National Park, WA, *Andrew Gregory;*
p. 2 St George Falls, Angahook–Lorne
State Park, Vic., *John Meier;* Budawang
National Park, NSW, *John Meier;*
p. 3 Green tree frog, *Lochman
Transparencies (Jiri Lochman);* Green tree
snake, *Australian Picture Library
(Gary Lewis);* **p. 4** Waterlilies, Kakadu
National Park, NT, *Australian Picture
Library (Lightstorm);* **p. 5** Great egrets,
Australian Picture Library (John Carnemolla);
Jabiru, *AUSCAPE (Jean-Paul Ferrero);*
p. 6 Humpback whale tail, *Darren Jew;*
Whitehaven Beach, Whitsunday Island,
Qld., *Australian Picture Library (La Motte
Editions);* Cox Bight, Southwest National
Park, Tas., *AUSCAPE (Dennis Harding);*
p. 8 Hardy Reef and Hook Reef, Great
Barrier Reef, Qld., *AUSCAPE
(Jean-Paul Ferrero);* Blue sea star, *Lochman
Transparencies (Clay Bryce);* **p. 9** Orange
basslets, *Australian Picture Library
(Gary Bell);* Biscuit star fish, *Lochman
Transparencies (Eva Boogaard);* **p. 10** Red
kangaroo, *Australian Picture Library
(Fritz Prenzel);* Frill-necked lizard, *AUSCAPE*

(Jean-Paul Ferrero); **p. 11** Koala, *Lochman
Transparencies (Jiri Lochman);* Kookaburra,
Australian Picture Library (Leo Meier);
p. 12 Uluru, NT, *Ted Mead;* Grevillea,
Australian Picture Library (Gerry Whitmont);
Sturt's desert pea, *Lochman Transparencies
(Bill Belson);* **p. 13** Native rock fig,
Steve Strike; **p. 14** Aboriginal rock art, NT,
Ted Mead; **p. 16** *Andrew Gregory;*
p. 22 *Stock Photos (Robert Della-Piana);*
p. 122 *Penguin Books Australia (J.P. & E.S.
Baker)* **p. 124** *The Photo Library
(Claver Carroll);* **p. 140** *John Meier;*
p. 144 *Stock Photos (Bill Bachman);*
p. 242 *Australian Picture Library
(Nick Rains);* **p. 246** *Australian Picture
Library (J.P. & E.S. Baker);*
p. 316 *Andrew Gregory;* **p. 320** *Austral
(Jocelyn Burt);* **p. 394** *Ted Mead;*
p. 398 *Steve Strike;* **p. 440** *John Meier;*
p. 444 *Tourism Queensland;* **p. 536** *Stock
Photos (Images Colour Library);*
p. 540 *Geoff Murray;* **p. 586** *Richard I'Anson*

OTHER PHOTOGRAPHS COURTESY OF:
All Saints Estate; Allsport (Rob Cianflone);
AMP Tower Centrepoint; Michael Archer;
Australian Picture Library (J.P. & E.S. Baker);
Canberra Tourism and Events Corporation;
Andrew Chapman; Cloudehill Gardens;
Douglas Coughran; Fremantle Tourism;
Great Southern Railway; Andrew Gregory;
Richard I'Anson; Alex Julius; Lochman
Transparencies (Brian Downs, Nick Gales,
Dennis Sarson); Ted Mead; John Meier;
Percy Munchenberg; Geoff Murray;
Pajinka Wilderness Lodge; Penguin Books
Australia (J.P. & E.S. Baker, Chris Groenhout,
Graeme and Margaret Herald,
Leon Kowalski, Gary Lewis, Heidi Marfurt,
Nick Rains, Julie Sheridan, Don Skirrow,
Ken Stepnell); Nick Rains; Don Skirrow;
Robin Smith; South Australian Tourism
Commission; Sovereign Hill, Ballarat;
Ken Stepnell; Stock Photos (Kelvin Aitken,
Bill Bachman, Diana Calder, John Carr,
Chris Clark, Roger Du Buisson,
Jeff Fitzpatrick, Robert Fox, Andy Game,
Ted Grambeau, Great Western Images,
Owen Hughes, Noeline Kelly, Gary Lewis,
Pauline Madden, Nadish Naoroji,
Lance Nelson, Otto Rogge, David Scaletti,
David Simmonds, Don Skirrow, Paul Steel,
Ken Stepnell, Stocktake, Ken Straiton,
Tim Vanderlaan, Michael Wennrich);
Steve Strike; Surf Life Saving Victoria
(Stephen Harman); The Photo Library
(Rob Jung); Tourism New South Wales
(Nick Rains); Tourism Queensland;
Tourism Tasmania (Richard Eastwood,
John de la Roche, James Pozarik)

SUGGESTION FORM

This 19th edition of *Explore Australia* is updated from information supplied by consultants, tourist organisations and the general public. We would welcome suggestions from you.

SUGGESTED AMENDMENT OR ADDITION

Text

Page no.	Amendment/Addition

Maps

Page no.	Grid	Amendment/Addition

GENERAL COMMENTS

OPTIONAL

Name:

Address:

Phone no.: _____ email address:

Place of purchase (shop name and suburb):

Date of purchase:

Age group:
20 and under ☐   20–29 ☐   30–39 ☐   40–49 ☐   50–59 ☐   60 and over ☐

I would like to receive information on new and updated guides, maps and atlases in the Explore Australia range: YES/NO (please indicate).

Please cut out and send to: Managing Editor, Penguin Cartographic
PO Box 257, Ringwood Vic. 3134. Alternatively, email your comments to cartog@penguin.com.au

ACCIDENT ACTION

Simple first aid can save a life.

When you approach the scene of an accident, remember to follow the DRABC action plan:

D DANGER
R RESPONSE
A AIRWAY
B BREATHING
C CIRCULATION

1. Check for DANGER –
to yourself and others.

- Do not touch occupants or vehicle if live wires are in contact with car.

- Turn off ignition of crashed car.

- If power lines are causing sparks nearby but not touching car, remove people quickly in case spilt petrol is set alight.

- Ensure no one is smoking.

- Station people to warn oncoming cars and people of the danger ahead.

- At night, light up area and use flashing indicators on vehicles as additional warning.

- Where possible, people, vehicles and debris should be cleared from roadway.

- Only move victim when in danger (for example, from fire, traffic or burns from hot roadway) or when victim's position makes it impossible to carry out essential treatment (such as stopping bleeding).

- If you do have to move victim, get three or four people to help if possible. Avoid bending or twisting neck or back – keep them straight. Support any injured limbs.

REMEMBER: Most casualties will be suffering some degree of shock. One of the best ways of treating this is by reassuring them – but never give alcohol. Keep casualties calm and protect them from uncomfortable weather conditions, particularly hot sun.

2. Check for RESPONSE –
see if the casualty is conscious.

- Gently shake and ask 'Can you hear me?'.

- If conscious, check for bleeding (see Stopping Bleeding on opposite page).

3. Check and clear AIRWAY –
if unconscious, ensure airway is not blocked.

- Remove any obstructions, such as blood, vomit, loose teeth or broken dentures and teeth.

- Lie victim on side and tilt head back to clear airway.

- Quickly clear mouth, using fingers if necessary. If breathing, leave on side.

- If victim is trapped in car, tilt head back and support jaw to clear airway.

4. Check BREATHING –
see if casualty is breathing.

- Look, listen and feel for breathing.

- If breathing, leave on side and check for other injuries.

- If not breathing, turn on to back and commence Expired Air Resuscitation (see opposite page).

5. Check CIRCULATION –
check for pulse.

- Feel for pulse by placing end of your finger in groove behind the Adam's apple, on either side of neck.

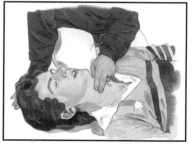

- If no pulse, perform cardiopulmonary resuscitation, if you have been taught this procedure (15 compressions to 2 breaths in 15 seconds).

LEARN BASIC FIRST AID

There are several organisations including St John Ambulance Australia that teach cardiopulmonary resuscitation and how to handle emergencies.